D1681620

In course of Publication, handsomely printed in 8vo,

A SERIES OF THE

GREEK AND LATIN AUTHORS,

UNDER THE GENERAL TITLE OF

BIBLIOTHECA CLASSICA,

EDITED BY VARIOUS HANDS, UNDER THE DIRECTION OF

GEORGE LONG, M.A.

FORMERLY FELLOW OF TRINITY COLLEGE, CAMBRIDGE; CLASSICAL LECTURER OF BRIGHTON COLLEGE;

AND THE LATE REV.

ARTHUR JOHN MACLEANE, M.A.

TRINITY COLLEGE, CAMBRIDGE; AND HEAD MASTER OF KING EDWARD'S SCHOOL, BATH.

The attention of Scholars is requested to the following editions of the Classics. They are already in use in the leading Public and Private Schools throughout the kingdom, and are admitted to be the best editions for Educational purposes that have hitherto been published. They will be found also, on comparison, cheaper than any other editions, English or Foreign, which may stand in the same rank with respect to scholarship.

THE AENEID OF VIRGIL,

WITH AN ENGLISH COMMENTARY, &c. &c.
By JOHN CONINGTON, M.A.
PROFESSOR OF LATIN, AND FELLOW OF CORPUS CHRISTI COLLEGE, OXFORD.

The First Six Books,
forming the Second Volume of the "Works of Virgil."
Price 14s. cloth.

Vol. I.   Containing the Eclogues and Georgics.   Price 12s. cloth.

THE EPICS OF HESIOD,

WITH AN ENGLISH COMMENTARY, &c. &c.
By F. A. PALEY, M.A.
EDITOR OF AESCHYLUS, EURIPIDES, &c. &c.

Price 10s. 6d. cloth.

THE TRAGEDIES OF SOPHOCLES,

WITH AN ENGLISH COMMENTARY, &c. &c.
By THE REV. F. H. M. BLAYDES, M.A.
VICAR OF HARRINGWORTH, NORTHAMPTONSHIRE; LATE STUDENT OF CHRIST CHURCH, OXFORD.

Vol. I.   Containing Oedipus Rex, Oedipus Coloneus, and Antigone.
Price 18s. cloth.

DEMOSTHENES. VOL. I.

WITH AN ENGLISH COMMENTARY, &c. &c.
By THE REV. R. WHISTON, M.A.
HEAD MASTER OF ROCHESTER GRAMMAR SCHOOL.

Price 16s. cloth.

THE COMEDIES OF TERENCE,

WITH AN ENGLISH COMMENTARY, &c. &c.
By THE REV. E. ST. JOHN PARRY, M.A.
PRINCIPAL OF LEAMINGTON COLLEGE, LATE OF BALLIOL COLLEGE, OXFORD.

Price 18s. cloth.

BIBLIOTHECA CLASSICA (*continued*).

THE TRAGEDIES OF EURIPIDES,
WITH AN ENGLISH COMMENTARY, &c. &c.
BY F. A. PALEY, M.A.
EDITOR OF AESCHYLUS, OVID'S FASTI, &c. &c.
In 3 Volumes. Each Volume, price 16s. cloth.

JUVENAL AND PERSIUS,
WITH AN ENGLISH COMMENTARY, &c. &c.
BY THE LATE REV. ARTHUR JOHN MACLEANE, M.A.
EDITOR OF HORACE, &c.
Price 14s. cloth.

THE TRAGEDIES OF AESCHYLUS,
RE-EDITED, WITH AN ENGLISH COMMENTARY.
BY F. A. PALEY, M.A.
EDITOR OF EURIPIDES, OVID'S FASTI, &c.
Price 18s. cloth.

HERODOTUS,
WITH AN ENGLISH COMMENTARY.
BY THE REV. JOSEPH WILLIAMS BLAKESLEY, B.D.
LATE FELLOW AND TUTOR OF TRINITY COLLEGE, CAMBRIDGE.
2 vols. Price 32s. cloth.

THE WORKS OF HORACE,
WITH AN ENGLISH COMMENTARY, &c. &c.
BY THE LATE REV. ARTHUR JOHN MACLEANE, M.A.
TRINITY COLLEGE, CAMBRIDGE; AND HEAD MASTER OF KING EDWARD'S SCHOOL, BATH.
Price 18s. cloth.

CICERO'S ORATIONS,
WITH AN ENGLISH COMMENTARY, &c. &c.
BY GEORGE LONG, M.A.
FORMERLY FELLOW OF TRINITY COLLEGE, CAMBRIDGE.

Vol. I. Price 16s. cloth.
Vol. II. Price 14s. cloth.
Vol. III. Price 16s. cloth.
Vol. IV. Price 18s. cloth.
Completing "THE ORATIONS."

The undermentioned volumes are in progress.

PLATO.
Vol. I. Containing the Gorgias, Phaedrus, and Symposium.
BY THE REV. W. HEPWORTH THOMPSON, M.A.
FELLOW OF TRINITY COLLEGE, CAMBRIDGE,
AND REGIUS PROFESSOR OF GREEK IN THE UNIVERSITY OF CAMBRIDGE.

VIRGIL.
Vol. III.
BY JOHN CONINGTON, M.A.
PROFESSOR OF LATIN, AND FELLOW OF CORPUS CHRISTI COLLEGE, OXFORD.

SOPHOCLES.
Vol. II. Completing the Work.
BY THE REV. F. H. M. BLAYDES, M.A.
VICAR OF HARRINGWORTH, NORTHAMPTONSHIRE.

In course of Publication, uniformly printed in foolscap 8vo, at a moderate price,

GRAMMAR SCHOOL CLASSICS,

A SERIES OF GREEK AND ROMAN AUTHORS, NEWLY EDITED, WITH ENGLISH NOTES.

C. SALLUSTI CRISPI CATILINA ET JUGURTHA,
WITH ENGLISH NOTES.
By GEORGE LONG, M.A.
Price 5s. cloth.

THE CYROPAEDIA OF XENOPHON,
WITH ENGLISH NOTES, &c.
By the Rev. G. M. GORHAM, M.A.
LATE FELLOW OF TRINITY COLLEGE, CAMBRIDGE.
Price 6s. cloth.

THE ANABASIS OF XENOPHON:
BASED UPON THE TEXT OF BORNEMANN,
With Introduction, Geographical and other Notes (chiefly English), Itinerary, and Three Maps compiled from recent Surveys, and other authentic Documents.
By the Rev. J. F. MACMICHAEL, B.A.
TRINITY COLLEGE, CAMBRIDGE; HEAD MASTER OF THE GRAMMAR SCHOOL, RIPON.
New Edition, revised, price 5s. cloth.

M. TULLII CICERONIS
CATO MAJOR SIVE DE SENECTUTE, LAELIUS SIVE DE AMICITIA, ET EPISTOLAE SELECTAE.
With English Notes and an Index,
By GEORGE LONG, M.A.
New Edition. Price 4s. 6d. cloth.

J. CAESARIS COMMENTARII
DE BELLO GALLICO.
With Notes, Preface, Introduction, &c.
By GEORGE LONG, M.A.
New Edition. Price 5s. 6d. cloth.

J. CAESARIS COMMENTARII DE BELLO GALLICO.
Books I. to III.
With English Notes for Junior Classes, and Four Plans,
By GEORGE LONG, M.A.
Price 2s. 6d. cloth.

P. OVIDII NASONIS FASTORUM LIBRI SEX.
With English Notes,
By F. A. PALEY, M.A.
EDITOR OF AESCHYLUS, EURIPIDES, &c.
New Edition. Price 5s. cloth.

GRAMMAR SCHOOL CLASSICS (*continued*).

QUINTI HORATII FLACCI OPERA OMNIA.

With English Notes,
By the Rev. A. J. MACLEANE, M.A.
LATE HEAD MASTER OF KING EDWARD'S SCHOOL, BATH.

Price 6s. 6d. cloth.

MR. LONG'S NEW CLASSICAL ATLASES.

AN ATLAS OF CLASSICAL GEOGRAPHY,

Containing Twenty-four Maps, constructed by W. HUGHES, F.R.G.S.,
AND EDITED BY GEORGE LONG, M.A.

WITH AN INDEX OF PLACES.
Second Edition, revised, with coloured Outlines.
In 8vo. Price 12s. 6d. half-bound.

"Certainly the best Atlas of Ancient Geography that we possess in this country."
Literary Gazette.

A GRAMMAR SCHOOL ATLAS OF CLASSICAL GEOGRAPHY.

Containing Ten Maps selected from the larger Atlas,
CONSTRUCTED BY W. HUGHES, AND EDITED BY GEORGE LONG.
Second Edition, revised, with coloured Outlines.
In 8vo. Price 5s. cloth.

THE NEW TESTAMENT IN GREEK:

BASED ON THE TEXT OF SCHOLZ,
With English Notes and Prefaces; a Synopsis of the Four Gospels; and Chronological Tables, illustrating the Gospel Narrative.
EDITED BY THE REV. J. F. MACMICHAEL, B.A.
Uniform with the "Grammar School Classics." 730 pages. Price 7s. 6d. cloth.

In 12mo, price 4s. 6d. cloth, with an improved Set of Figures and Exercises,

THE ELEMENTS OF EUCLID,

BOOKS I—VI.; XI. (1—12); XII. (1, 2.)
A NEW TEXT, BASED ON THAT OF SIMSON.
EDITED BY HENRY J. HOSE, B.A.
LATE SCHOLAR OF TRINITY COLLEGE, CAMBRIDGE, AND MATHEMATICAL MASTER OF WESTMINSTER SCHOOL.

"Mr. Hose has supplied all that was wanting in Simson's valuable work to render the propositions complete in every part—enunciation, construction, demonstration, and corollary. All possible hypotheses are taken into account, every thing requiring proof is rigorously demonstrated, a full explanation is given of each step, and the corollaries, instead of being barely stated, are carefully worked out. Other good points about this edition are strict accuracy of expression, and distinctness of arrangement—the several parts of each proposition being clearly marked so as to facilitate the comprehension and recollection of the whole."—*Athenæum.*

WHITTAKER AND CO., AVE MARIA LANE;
GEORGE BELL, 186, FLEET STREET.

BIBLIOTHECA CLASSICA.

EDITED BY

GEORGE LONG, M.A.

FORMERLY FELLOW OF TRINITY COLLEGE, CAMBRIDGE,

AND THE

REV. A. J. MACLEANE, M.A.

TRINITY COLLEGE, CAMBRIDGE.

EURIPIDES,

WITH AN ENGLISH COMMENTARY,

BY

F. A. PALEY.

VOL. II.

LONDON:
WHITTAKER AND CO. AVE MARIA LANE;
GEORGE BELL, FLEET STREET.
1858.

882.3
Eu7p

LONDON:
GILBERT AND RIVINGTON, PRINTERS,
ST. JOHN'S SQUARE.

EURIPIDES.

WITH AN ENGLISH COMMENTARY

BY

F. A. PALEY,

EDITOR OF AESCHYLUS, ETC.

IN THREE VOLUMES.

VOL. II.

LONDON.
WHITTAKER AND CO. AVE MARIA LANE;
GEORGE BELL, FLEET STREET.
1858.

PREFACE.

Time necessary for carefully editing Euripides.—Explanatory more generally useful than diffuse learned notes.—A work done *quickly* need not be done *hastily*.—Want of practical English editions.—MSS. of Euripides.—Character of the plays contained in this volume.—Merit of Euripides as a poet.—Mistaken idea that his plays are easy.—His versatile genius.—Hermann's comparative sketch of the three tragic writers.—Choral odes of Euripides.—The decline of an art not always to be distinguished from its development.—Choral parts secondary to dialogue and narration.—Characteristics of the later plays.—Metrical licences.—Length of later plays.—Free use of rhetorical terms.—Repetition of words.—Later Atticisms.—The poet's fondness for disputations.—Exact numerical equality in the speeches of two disputants.—Examples from Aeschylus.—Examples from Euripides.—Passages with more intricate antithetical arrangement.—Interpolation of the Greek plays.—Probable causes of it suggested.—Controversial parts essential to Euripides' plays.—Narrations of messengers.—Epic element of tragedy.—Sophocles' monologues of heroes.—Why messengers are essential to Greek tragedy.—Plays treating of the Trojan affairs.—Adapted from the Cyclic poems.—Why never borrowed from Homer himself.—Pisistratus' edition of Homer.—Loss of the Cyclus.—Materials of Attic tragedy derived from other sources.—Classification of the subjects.—Extant plays of Euripides on the Trojan affairs chronologically arranged.—Story of Orestes why peculiarly popular.—The Electra of Euripides.

IT is probable that while many will freely blame the haste, few will care to praise the industry, of an editor who brings out a second volume, containing a large portion of the works of a really difficult author, within a year after the publication of the first, and, indeed, without allowing himself even the briefest interval of rest. It will naturally be objected, that a work of this kind, which no one will pretend to call a light one, cannot be done well, if it has also been done quickly. Sophocles truly said [1],

φιλεῖ γὰρ ὀκνεῖν πρᾶγμ' ἀνὴρ πράσσων μέγα,

and the words well enough represent the hesitation with which this edition was commenced, though such a feeling may perhaps appear to be scarcely consistent with the rather rapid progress that has already been made in it [2]. To edit and annotate upon the whole of EURIPIDES carefully, thoughtfully, and with a strict view to practical utility, is certainly a formidable undertaking; and it is one that, under any circumstances, must require at least some years of nearly exclusive attention. The mere labour of consulting so many editions, and the constant intellectual effort of deciding between the conflicting opinions of critics and interpreters, is a very heavy task in itself. There is no doubt, that to do the fullest justice to such an author as Euripides, even after all that has already been done by others, the labour of half a life would not be too much. But where is the man now to be found who would consent to spend half a life on so thankless a task? Would the present age appreciate his labours, or in any way reward such heroic devotion to Greek literature? Posterity might indeed honour him; but the present age would more probably regard him, perhaps not altogether unjustly, as a martyr to a mere whim, and as wasting years that might have been far more profitably employed to the benefit of mankind. The fact is, when a demand arises, in consequence of any changes introduced into our scholastic systems, such a demand must be supplied without unreasonable delay. A work like the present must be done, not indeed *hastily*, (for that is altogether inexcusable,) but *quickly*, because it is wanted. Twenty years ago, it would have been looked upon as little short of insanity to predict, that Monk's, Elmsley's, Porson's, or Blomfield's commentaries would some day be found insufficient for

---

[1] Electra 320.

[2] It is perhaps fair to state here, that the Editor's sole and exclusive pains have been given to this work since its commencement in 1855, and that it has not been done at intervals snatched from any other occupation.

the use of general students. It was thought, and rightly thought, that the learning of these great scholars was not likely ever to be surpassed, and that little could remain to be done after their extensive and varied literary labours. Experience however has shown, that what are commonly called *learned* notes are not necessarily the most useful, nor in any sense the best for educational purposes. The primary object of notes on any given text is *to explain the meaning of the author*. Now it happens that this is just the last thing that the editors above mentioned thought of effecting, at least in the way of direct interpretation. They were rather in the habit of converting their notes into disquisitions on particular words, or critical and grammatical essays, or repertories of conjectural emendations on other writings. Some notes are much better adapted to set forth the editor's fund of classical learning than the author's mind and aim. Accordingly as either of these ideas is uppermost in an editor's mind, so his notes will unavoidably receive this or that impress. The egotistic writer will show that he was ever thinking chiefly of his own cleverness, and the sincere admirer and cautious interpreter of his author will likewise show that on *him* before every thing else his real interest is centered. Generally, whatever distracts the reader's attention from the author to his commentator, i.e. whatever makes the subjectivity of the latter the more conspicuous, is to be regarded as ill-judged and misplaced. It may be added, that classical notes may be, and too often are, written with so little of poetical feeling, or of genial appreciation of the author's real position as a representative of times and opinions very different from our own, that both their dulness and their inadequate conception of ancient character displease rather than assist an inquiring reader, who would often gladly exchange a great deal of mere learning for a very small proportion of intelligent and honest explanation.

Although all the ancient classical writers do undoubtedly afford ample scope for deep thought and patient research, it is a mistake to suppose that an editor, who commences his work with a fair knowledge, derived, as it can only be, from the long study of his author, must needs make twice as good a book by taking twice the time in its preparation. There are some considerable advantages in that energy which prompts us to write while the interest is freshly and keenly excited, and which expends itself upon a work while memories are recent and admiration is ardent; while the mind seems to be teeming and labouring with the author's conceptions, and his very words are constantly sounding in our ears. In truth, if a man really understands his author, he ought to be able to explain his writings clearly to others. If he does not, all the learning in the world will not conceal his ignorance on the main point.

It is not intended however, by these remarks, to justify any hurried or slovenly performance in classical literature. Such a proceeding is a fraud on the public and a just discredit to all who are concerned in committing it. Certainly the remembrance of those great scholars of past times, who wrote for posterity rather than for present praise, and with the consciousness and intention of doing so, should restrain a haste which might be called unseemly compared with their patient labours. All the great and standard editions of the classics were doubtless elaborated with infinite pains; and for this reason they have maintained, and will still maintain, their ground, if not for the critical revision of the texts, at least as the sources of abundant information and illustration to all succeeding scholars [3]. Of course, the actual labour of editing at the present day is less, in proportion to the learning and research of previous editors. But, with reference to Euripides in particular, it may be doubted if the text of this author is in so

---

[3] The editions of Euripides by Barnes and Musgrave, though, of course, they were not exempt from serious metrical and grammatical errors at a time when the philological niceties of the language had not been fully investigated, are remarkable monuments of the learning which, as classical antiquaries, they could bring to bear upon the illustration of their author. If they owed much to their predecessors, they also contributed much from their own resources. Modern *scholarship*, based on the canons of Porson, Hermann, and others, has formed, as it were, the supplement to the somewhat ponderous and not always well-digested or pointedly-applied *learning* of the older editors.

satisfactory a state, and if his meaning is always so fully understood, as is commonly supposed. It is not perhaps to be expected that much further addition will be made to our present knowledge of Greek tragedy. The corruptions, interpolations, and various readings of the text are constant obstacles; and thus, although shrewdness and sagacity may recover something occasionally, it seldom happens that we can get much beyond guessing. Almost all that scholarship can do, in the most general sense of the word, the labours of preceding critics have already done. What *we* are now trying to effect, in a series of English editions, is the application of common sense and practical classical knowledge, because that seems now to be wanted rather than extensive and varied research. Little or nothing more is likely to be gleaned from the known MSS. and the ancient editions. They have been collated over and over again, and the results are set forth with the minutest accuracy in editions accessible to all who care more for the critical department than for the sense of the author. In respect of this last, which we have ventured to regard as really the most important part of an editor's duty, it is indeed surprising how very little aid is generally to be obtained even from the most approved editions. One is often left in doubt whether the editor was unconscious of a difficulty, or, perceiving it, purposely evaded it, or lastly, whether the feeling in his mind was, that if we can only recover the exact and genuine *words* of the writer, his *meaning* is a fair subject for speculation and dispute between those who care to investigate it minutely. The notes to this volume have been compiled with a full consciousness of this fact; and the explanations have been somewhat more fully given than in the preceding volume, because the plays herein commented upon are much less generally read by ordinary scholars, and the editions available for their use are much more scanty than those of many of the other plays. It was the intention of the editor, as announced in the former volume, to have prefixed to the present one some account of the MSS. of Euripides. But this has been, for several reasons, postponed to the third and concluding volume. A tolerably complete catalogue might indeed easily be compiled from the notes and prefaces of Matthiae, W. Dindorf, Hermann, Elmsley, and many other editors of separate plays; but this would probably be altogether uninteresting and unprofitable to English readers in general. Some notice however of the MSS. preserved and accessible in the English libraries may hereafter be given, should an opportunity of inspecting them occur, which hitherto circumstances have prevented. It is needless to add, that a new collation of them, or even of any one of them, would have added immensely to the labour, but probably little or absolutely nothing to the critical recension of the present edition. Moreover, it was simply impossible to give anything like a complete account of the various readings, without an enormous addition to the bulk of the notes, which would have defeated the very end for which these volumes were compiled.

This volume contains six of the plays which, though not perhaps the most generally popular, have strong claims to be considered as equal to any in merit and general interest. Of these the *Ion* and the *Helena* have somewhat involved plots and difficult dialogues, and altogether are among the more abstruse of the poet's extant works; others, as the *Andromache* and the *Hecuba*, are comparatively easy, and are justly regarded as finished specimens of the poet's simpler style. It is greatly to be regretted that the *Electra* should be, by a sort of common consent, proscribed as almost unworthy of a student's close attention,—in other words, should be pointed to by some modern critics as a proof how badly Euripides could write, rather than as an illustration (which it more truly is) of his human sympathies, and his knowledge of the more minute traits of character in both the sexes. The present editor can aver with the utmost sincerity, that his admiration for Euripides only increases with a closer intimacy, and with a more full consideration of the charges so commonly and so unsparingly brought against him as a poet, a moralist, a citizen,

UNJUSTLY ESTIMATED. xi

and a man[4]. It has been said, that every editor, as a matter of course, likes his own author the best. Doubtless the very fact of bestowing pains upon a particular writer, in tracing the bent of his mind and observing its development in his various characters, tends to make him a favourite in some degree. It is a friendship contracted with the mighty dead through the same medium, reciprocity of sentiment, which actuates us in our intercourse with the living. It is well that it is so, so long as partiality does not degenerate into an unreasoning admiration for what may be really faulty as well as for what is undoubtedly excellent. For, as living friends are the most trusty guardians and the most faithful representatives of each other's feelings and sentiments, so that commentator who can warmly enter into the mind and character of his author, is the most likely person to do justice to his writings. With regard to Euripides, it is hardly an exaggeration to say, that many are induced to read his plays with the principal object in view of establishing their inferiority to those of Aeschylus and Sophocles. With such motives, who is likely to do justice to this poet? At least, it would be more fair to suspend judgment on this point till we are certain that we can fully understand, not only Euripides himself, but the real laws and scope of the Attic Drama. It is not easy to fathom the depths of a great mind. Aeschylus and Sophocles are difficult at the first sight, and there is no mistaking the fact, that a great amount of study must be expended upon them. But there is a certain *apparent* facility in the style of Euripides, which is very deceptive; and the reader has already been warned[5] against too great confidence in his powers of readily understanding this author. Because some parts, such as the long narratives of messengers,

---

[4] It is amusing enough to observe with what timidity an editor here and there ventures to express an opinion, that Euripides is not so bad a poet after all! Thus Professor Scholefield, in his edition of the four Porsonian plays, says (Preface, p. vii), "Non sum ego ex illorum numero, qui nihil in eo pulchrum, nihil grande, nihil cothurno dignum inveniant" (!) What are young students to think, when they read such statements?

[5] Preface to vol. i. p. vii.

a 2

are generally intelligible to a tolerably advanced student, it is assumed that all the parts are much alike, and so the real force and meaning of the dialogue, and of the many argumentative and rhetorically involved speeches, are apt to be very imperfectly apprehended. It is not too much to say, that they are often construed without any regard to the logical coherence of one verse with another. Many are struck with the fine versification and the sounding words of the two elder tragic poets, who are unable to see that, in his peculiar way, Euripides challenges our admiration, and demands our most thoughtful attention too, for his deep insight into human nature. Euripides was an independent thinker and reasoner, unfettered by traditional opinions; and his remarks often contain truths at once striking and profound. In a word, he is the most *natural* of all the Greek poets, excepting Homer. Moreover, he is one of the most versatile; he can describe foibles the most varied and opposite with equal truthfulness and power. Parental affection, military valour, self-devoting patriotism, passionate love, sisterly gentleness, the pride of birth, the humble merit of the cottager, the absolute authority of the chieftain, the fidelity of the despised slave, the folly of youth and the sober wisdom of age,—all these and many more traits of human character are well delineated in his dramas. There is a passage in one of Hermann's writings [6], at once so elegantly and so happily expressed, and so well setting forth the respective claims of the three great tragic poets, that we shall be pardoned for quoting it here at length:—" Stupent omnes Aeschyli vim et magnitudinem et grandiloquentiam, aliquando illam subtumidam; cujus Martius incessus animis legentium robur, violenti impetus metum et horrorem inspirant. Admiramur decoram gravitatem Sophoclis, suavi aequabilitate temperatam, quae neque exuberat aut effraenata ruit, neque remittit aut desiderari nervos patitur, sed ubique nitida est, elegans, polita.——Euripidis versatile et diversissimis argumentis aptum ingenium

---

[6] Preface to *Hecuba*, p. xiv, ed. 1831.

memini ante multos annos Goethium in sermone quodam, quum ego Aeschylum et Sophoclem anteferrem, multa cum laude praedicare. Manebit merito haec laus Euripidi, etiam si non ejus sit solius propria. Certe, ut Sophocleae quas habemus fabulae inter se similiores sint, at in totidem Aeschyleis admirabilis est inventionis, morum, animi affectionum tum in diverbiis tum in canticis varietas et dissimilitudo. Euripidi, quamvis eximia praedito indole, tamen a natura neque Sophoclis illa moderata gravitas, neque Aeschyli insita erat divina vis atque elatio. Itaque in molliores sensus quam in vehementes animi motus proclivior, mores hominum, ut Aristotelis verbis utar, magis quales sunt, quam quales esse debent, imitando expressit; isque etiam orationis color est." He goes on to say, that the fondness of Euripides for dialectic subtleties unsuited him for composing the lyric parts of his dramas; but this is an opinion from which the present editor, for one, ventures to dissent. In judging of the choral odes of Euripides, we should remember, first, that this part of the Attic drama is at once the least like our own, and the least capable of being fully understood at the present day; secondly, that it is very difficult indeed, in criticising art, to distinguish that which is really *decline* from that which is *legitimate development*. We might instance the well-known case of Gothic architecture, in which some will insist that the perpendicular lines and the excessive ornamentation of surfaces prevalent during the fifteenth century are a debasement from the rich and shadowy profiles and recessed arcades of the thirteenth century. But here also there are different opinions. It is presumptuous to lay our finger upon one particular period of antiquity (and especially of a very remote antiquity), and to say, This is the standard of excellence, by which all that went before and all that followed after must be tested. That the dialogue in the Attic drama (and still more, as we shall have to notice below, the *descriptive* or epic element), gradually superseded the lyric, or, to speak quite plainly, that talking and narrating was found to be a more effective mimetic aid than dancing and singing, seems clear from a comparison of the long Aeschylean *stasima* with the generally shorter odes of Euripides, especially as the wider scope of the subjects in the latter, so often alleged as a fault, may be regarded rather as an effort to separate the true action, conducted by the dialogue, from the merely accessory choral parts which mark the intervals of that action. It would not be difficult to show, that in this respect Euripides really followed the soundest principles of art.

The plays in the present volume (the *Bacchae* excepted) belong to a style and a class intermediate between the severer dramas of the earlier date (the *Medea, Hippolytus, Alcestis, Heraclidae*), and the latest developments of Euripides' Muse, as displayed in the florid laxity and bold metrical innovations which are so conspicuous in the *Phoenissae*, the *Iphigenia at Aulis*, the *Bacchae*, and particularly in the *Orestes*. As these two classes of plays have quite distinct characteristics, it may be well here to point out some of the principal differences to the reader who has not yet made himself master of the nineteen extant dramas of our author.

The earlier plays are marked by a regular and stately flow of iambic verse, not inferior to the style of either Aeschylus or Sophocles in a metrical point of view. But in his latest plays Euripides seems really to have tried how far metrical licence could be carried, so long as the verse retained the legitimate scansion of the tragic senarius. Here, undoubtedly, we recognize a real decadence in rhythmical laws, for our ears painfully feel the lameness of the looser sort of verse. In the earlier compositions there are very few instances of that inharmonious foot, the anapaest in the beginning of the verse; and even dactyls and tribrachs are rather sparingly employed. All these are very freely admitted in the later versification, and even the tribrach in the fifth foot was by no means unfrequent, as in *Iph. Taur.* 985,

ὡς τἄμ' ὄλωλε πάντα καὶ τὰ Πελοπιδῶν,
οὐράνιον εἰ μὴ ληψόμεσθα θεᾶς βρέτας.

OF THE LATER PLAYS. XV

There is the widest difference between the rhythm of these two kinds of verses,

> ὦ δώματ' Ἀδμήτει', ἐν οἷς ἔτλην ἐγὼ
> θῆσσαν τράπεζαν αἰνέσαι θεός περ ὤν [7],

and the halting irregular step of the following [8],

> ἀμφότερον, ἀπολειφθὲν γὰρ οὐδὲν θάτερον.—
> καὶ γὰρ πατήρ σε· τόδ' ἴσον ὑπὲρ ἀμφοῖν λέγεις.—
> φιλοτιμίᾳ μὲν ἐνέχεται, δεινῷ κακῷ.—
> εἰ τὰ καλὰ πᾶσι φανερὰ καὶ τὰ μὴ καλά,
> τούτου τίς ἀνδρῶν ἐγένετ' ἀσυνετώτερος ;—
> καλεῖ σ' Ὀρέστης παῖς σὸς ἐπίκουρον μολεῖν
> τοῖς δεομένοισι. διὰ σὲ γὰρ πάσχω τάλας
> ἀδίκως, προδέδομαι δ' ὑπὸ κασιγνήτου σέθεν.

Of this latter sort, not only single verses are frequent in the later plays, but whole passages are composed in similar style, as if resolved feet were purposely preferred, for mere novelty's sake, to the more monotonous, but much more pleasing and impressive beat of the regular senarius. Take the following as rather striking examples.

> ΚΛ. τί δῆτ' ἂν εἴη ; σὺ πάλιν αὖ λόγους ἐμοὺς
> θαυμάζ'. ἐμοὶ γὰρ θαύματ' ἐστὶ τὰ παρὰ σοῦ.
> ΑΧ. εἴκαζε· κοινόν ἐστιν εἰκάζειν τάδε·
> ἄμφω γὰρ οὖν ψευδόμεθα τοῖς λόγοις ἴσως.—
> ἀλλ' ἀμελίᾳ δὸς αὐτὰ καὶ φαύλως φέρε.
> ΚΛ. χαῖρ'· οὐ γὰρ ὀρθοῖς ὄμμασίν σ' ἔτ' εἰσορῶ,
> ψευδὴς γενομένη καὶ παθοῦσ' ἀνάξια [9].

Again in the *Orestes* [1],

> ΟΡ. πῶς εἶπας ; ἥκει φῶς ἐμοῖς καὶ σοῖς κακοῖς,
> ἀνὴρ ὁμογενὴς καὶ χάριτας ἔχων πατρός ;
> ΗΛ. ἥκει· τὸ πιστὸν τόδε λόγων ἐμῶν δέχου,
> Ἑλένην ἀγόμενος Τρωϊκῶν ἐκ τειχέων.
> ΟΡ. εἰ μόνος ἐσώθη, μᾶλλον ἂν ζηλωτὸς ἦν·
> εἰ δ' ἄλοχον ἄγεται, κακὸν ἔχων ἥκει μέγα.
> ΗΛ. ἐπίσημον ἔτεκε Τυνδάρεως ἐς τὸν ψόγον
> γένος θυγατέρων δυσκλεές τ' ἀν' Ἑλλάδα.

The marked difference which had hitherto existed between the tragic and the comic iambic verse, though it was not wholly broken down, was nevertheless sensibly diminished by Euri-

---

[7] Alcest. 1, 2.
[8] Phoen. 747. Iph. A. 641. 527. Orest. 492—3. 1226—8.
[9] Iph. A. 843—52.   [1] v. 243—50.

pides, who latterly wrote verses much more approaching to the Aristophanic than to the Aeschylean senarius[2]. In his choral metres too Euripides latterly fell into some considerable laxity. His favourite metre, the glyconean, a naturally soft and effeminate measure, was, if we may use the expression, so far trifled with, that not only were numerous varieties of it introduced, which were all so many innovations on the old rhythm (as employed by Sophocles, and more rarely by Aeschylus), but the antistrophic correspondence of syllable with syllable became less and less accurate, by the resolution of the feet, and even by one sort of glyconean being made antithetical to another. The use too of iambic and trochaic short metres, which always form a large portion of the earlier choral verses, was gradually less and less adopted, or, at least, they were more and more disguised by the use of resolved syllables. One marked feature of the later as compared with the earlier plays is the excessive length to which the former were spun out. Thus the *Helena* and the *Orestes* have very nearly 1700, and the *Phoenissae* nearly 1800 verses[3]. A third characteristic of the later plays is the habit of repeating words in the choral parts,—a propensity which has been ridiculed by Aristophanes in the *Frogs*[4]. Instances are sufficiently numerous; the following may be cited as examples:—

περὶ δὲ γόνυ χέρας ἱκεσίους
ἔβαλον ἔβαλον Ἑλένας ἄμφω.
ἀνὰ δὲ δρομάδες ἔθορον ἔθορον
ἀμφίπολοι Φρύγες.—
ΦΡ. Φρυγίοις ἔτυχον Φρυγίοισι νόμοις

---

[2] Both Aeschylus and Sophocles studiously avoid anapaests and dactyls in the beginning, and generally tribrachs in any part of the iambic verse. They both admit them as *licences*, rather than employ them, as Euripides did, quite indifferently.

[3] It is worthy of remark, that the latest play of Sophocles, the *Oedipus at Colonus*, has nearly 1800 lines. The *Agamemnon* is the only play of Aeschylus that much exceeds 1000 verses.

[4] See the note on Hel. 191. It might be added, as a mark of the earlier plays (if we except the *Rhesus*), that Euripides does not employ the trochaic metre nor the *deus ex machina*. He at first used trochaics in short and energetic narratives or speeches (Troades, Herc. Furens), afterwards in long dialogues (Phoenissae, Orestes, Iphigenia at Aulis, Ion). Yet the trochaic is really the older metre (Müller, Hist. Gr. Lit. p. 293).

παρὰ βόστρυχον αὔραν αὔραν
Ἑλένας Ἑλένας εὐπᾶγι κύκλῳ
πτερίνῳ πρὸ παρηΐδος ἄσσων [5].

Similarly in the *Phoenissae* [6];

ἔφερες ἔφερες ἄχεα πατρίδι
φόνια· φόνιος ἐκ θεῶν
ὃς τάδ᾽ ἦν ὁ πράξας.
ἰάλεμοι δὲ ματέρων,
ἰάλεμοι δὲ παρθένων
ἐστέναζον οἴκοις·
ἰήιον βοὰν βοὰν
ἰήιον μέλος μέλος
ἄλλος ἄλλ᾽ ἐπωτότυζε
διαδοχαῖς ἀνὰ πτόλιν.

And again in the same play [7];—

δάκρυα δάκρυα γοερὰ γοερὰ
φανερὰ πᾶσι τιθεμένα,
τέκεσι μαστὸν ἔφερεν ἔφερεν
ἱκέτις ἱκέταν ὁρομένα.

Euripides, in his later plays especially, made use of some words not employed by the earlier tragic writers, nor apparently even by himself at first, but which approximate to the later Attic dialect. He wished, probably, to enlarge the tragic vocabulary which had been hitherto in use (and by that very use had become somewhat hackneyed), by the free admission of forms and words derived from the ordinary conversation of the people; and it is clear that, to treat naturally of men, a great artist must make them speak naturally. The same propensity is observable in some of the most popular poets of our own time. They do not scruple to sanction the use of new and even common-place words whenever they have occasion for them; and so in a sense it may be said of them that they

Communi feriunt carmen triviale moneta.

Thus, Euripides employs the rare active perfects τέθεικε and παρεῖκε [8], the aorist προσηκάμην [9], and very frequently the plural of first aorists in -αν, as παρέδωκαν, ἔθηκαν, ἀνῆκαν, &c., from verbs in μι, the more legitimate Attic forms of which, in

---

[5] Orest. 1414—29. [6] v. 1030 seqq. [7] v. 1567 seqq.
[8] El. 7. Hel. 1059. [9] El. 622.

VOL. II.

the older dialect, are παρέδοσαν, ἔθεσαν, ἀνεῖσαν &c. But a more serious deterioration in the diction of the later plays consists in the large number of *rhetorical* terms, that is, of words more suited to prose composition, to the speeches and arguments of orators and sophists, in a word, to the assembly of the people and the law-courts, than to the Attic stage. Such words are (to give a few specimens out of many), ἐπίδειγμα, παραμυθεῖσθαι, ἐπιμελεῖσθαι, ἐπίπροσθεν, ἐνίοτε, παράλογον, ἀξιόχρεως, λόγιος, λελογισμένος, ἐλογισάμην, δυσάρεστος, ἀμαθέστερος, ἀκόλαστος, ἀσυνετώτερος, καταδουλοῦσθαι, μεταβουλεύεσθαι, ὑπολείπεσθαι, ὁμόσε χωρεῖν, οὐδὲν ὑγιές, ἐπίτηδες, ἀφροσύνη, πλεονεξία, φιλοτιμία, ἀφασία, ἀμελία, &c., to which might be added several terms and phrases more befitting the familiar and bantering language of comedy. It is clear that a vocabulary of this kind is neither poetical in itself, nor adapted in the form of the words to tragic metre, especially the senarius. Such a vocabulary was, as it were, forced into the service, though at variance with the steady and majestic beat of the magnificent Aeschylean iambic. We cannot indeed conceive Aeschylus employing either such phraseology or such terms (to say nothing of such metre), as Euripides latterly allowed himself to indulge in. He was not only thinking of the Pnyx, but of its language too, in describing a man as

> ὀλιγάκις ἄστυ κἀγορᾶς χραίνων κύκλον,
> αὐτουργὸς, οἵπερ καὶ μόνοι σώζουσι γῆν,
> ξυνετὸς δὲ χωρεῖν ὁμόσε τοῖς λόγοις θέλων,
> ἀκέραιος, ἀνεπίληπτον ἠσκηκὼς βίον [1].

It is by contrasting passages of this kind with the same number of verses taken almost at random from Aeschylus, that the difference between the early and the late tragedy is most strongly felt. Euripides had a habit of assimilating the speeches of his characters to the oratory of the bema and the pleadings of the law courts, because he was a poet of every-day life, and he took advantage of the people's fondness for these political exhibitions, to introduce a similar element into the composition of his

---

[1] Orest. 917.

tragedies². This, indeed, is too well known to require further discussion. But there is one interesting peculiarity connected with this practice, which, so far as we are aware, has never yet been sufficiently noticed, if it has been noticed at all.

When Euripides represents two persons arguing or pleading against each other, he appears in many instances *designedly* to assign to each speaker exactly the same number of verses. We say *designedly*, because it is not improbable that he had in view the favourite Greek maxim ἴσα λέγειν, ἴσα ἀντακούειν.

Let us however begin by seeking a precedent for this usage from Aeschylus. And it happens that more examples can be adduced from the extant tragedies than the paucity of them would have led us to suppose.

Of shorter speeches exactly answering to each other in length, the *Choephori* and the *Eumenides* offer several clear instances. Thus, the reply of Electra (Cho. 227) consists of *eleven* lines, corresponding numerically to that of her brother immediately preceding (one having been lost, as critics had detected independently of this fact). So again Electra speaks *nine* verses at v. 247, in answer to the nine of Orestes. In Eumen. 748—774, the whole passage is distinctly antistrophic to 775—800, each speech of Athena containing *thirteen* senarii, one (v. 768) having been rightly ejected by Hermann as a manifest and ungrammatical interpolation. A much more curious, because more extensive and systematic, correspondence in the length of several consecutive speeches in the *Seven against Thebes* has been pointed out by the present editor in the recent reprint of the text of Aeschylus³. In the *Choephori*, there is a similar agreement between the speech of Electra (twenty-nine lines) at v. 116 of the same play, and her second speech of exactly the same length at v. 175; so that here the question arises whether, after all, Hermann is right in dividing this latter speech at v. 193 by giving four of the verses to the chorus. Once more, in the *Agamemnon* the address of Aga-

---

² Compare the λόγος ἐπιτάφιος, Suppl. 857 seqq.
³ Praef ad ed. Cant. 1858, p. vi.

memnon to Clytemnestra (v. 887) answers exactly to her reply at v. 931, each ῥῆσις containing *seventeen* verses.

Now it may naturally enough be said, by those who have not looked into this question, that among so great a number of tragic ῥήσεις it would be strange indeed if some few pairs could not be found, the number of verses in which did not more or less closely coincide. Allowing some weight to the objection, and allowing also that there are a great many more speeches, even those which are distinctly addresses and answers, but which do *not* numerically coincide, we nevertheless think that a case can be made out, and also that, if it can be established, it is one of the highest critical value, for reasons shortly to be stated. If we turn to Sophocles, we shall find little ground to suppose that he attended to this usage, if such it be. In the *Antigone* indeed [4], Haemon replies (v. 683) in *forty-one* verses to the attack of Creon (v. 639) in *forty-two;* and it might be alleged, with no very faint degree of probability, that a line has been lost after v. 690, so that a now obscure passage may have originally stood thus:—

τὸ γὰρ σὸν ὄμμα δεινὸν ἀνδρὶ δημότῃ
[παρρησίᾳ λέγοντι, καὶ κεχρημένῳ]
λόγοις τοιούτοις, οἷς σὺ μὴ τέρψει κλύων.

But there are at least *ten* instances in the remaining plays of Euripides, where an exact agreement in the number of verses between two disputants seems undeniable. And there are several others where the same agreement is more than probable, though apparent interpolations have rendered the matter uncertain. In shorter passages of from five to ten lines, the correspondence is even frequent.

[4] Without attributing even the least weight to the fact that in the prologue of the *Antigone* Ismene replies in *seven* lines to her sister's address in *ten*, we think there is every reason to regard the three very difficult (not to say, in every sense bad) verses that succeed the first three, as a mere interpolation. No attempt to emend οὔτ' ἄτης ἄτερ in the second of these lines can be called successful; the repetition of ὁποῖον οὐ from v. 3, and κακῶν from v. 2, besides the unparalleled and all but ungrammatical accumulation of negatives, and lastly, the tame and pointless climax οὔτ' ἀλγεινὸν οὔτ' αἰσχρὸν οὔτ' ἄτιμον, seem evidences that Sophocles could never have penned such verses.—This is mentioned by the way, and as an independent opinion. Others perhaps may have anticipated this piece of criticism.

EQUALITY IN SPEECHES.

I. In the *Medea*, the speech of Jason in reply to the accusations of his wife (v. 465—575), has *fifty-four* to her *fifty-five* verses; but here v. 468 has long ago been ejected, as interpolated from v. 1324.

II. In the *Helena*, Menelaus and Helen in their address to Theonöe (v. 894—995), speak *forty-nine* verses apiece. One verse (v. 905) is here also clearly spurious,

ἐατέος δ' ὁ πλοῦτος ἄδικός τις ὤν.

III. In the *Electra*, Clytemnestra and her daughter speak each *forty* verses in mutual recrimination (v. 1011—1099).

IV. In the *Hecuba*, Polymestor and Hecuba both speak exactly *fifty-one* in accusation and defence (v. 1132—1237).

V. In the *Heraclidae* (134—231), the herald Copreus and Iolaus argue the question of giving up the Suppliants in *forty-five* verses. This example is not less interesting from the interpolation of two verses (at v. 221) in Iolaus' speech, that had already occurred at v. 97—8, and of four others (220—5), partly unmetrical, partly patched up from another play, the rejection of which restores the exact balance of numbers with all but absolute certainty.

VI. In the *Phoenissae*, Polynices and Eteocles maintain their respective claims before their mother Jocasta, in *twenty-seven* verses apiece. Here also one spurious verse (476) requires to be omitted, on the ground that it destroys the grammatical construction of the passage.

VII. In the *Orestes* (1131—1176) Pylades and Orestes discourse in *twenty-two* verses.

VIII. In the *Phoenissae* again (865—1018) Teiresias speaks *thirty-one* and afterwards *thirty* verses, with the interval of a dialogue of *thirty-four*. Creon next has *fifteen* (half of thirty) verses, and then the ῥῆσις of Menoeceus concludes the scene with *thirty-four*. Now, in the first speech of Teiresias we should clearly omit v. 869. Barnes, who perceived the absurdity of the vulgate, proposed τέκνωσε for τεκνώθη in the preceding line.

IX. In the *Mad Hercules*, (v. 1255—1393,) Theseus speaks *twenty-eight* verses, while the speech of Hercules both before and after it has *fifty-six*, or exactly double that number, if we mark the loss of one after v. 1361. Who will say that this is mere accident? It is true again that Theseus in fact is made to speak *twenty-nine* in the old copies; but one line has been lost at the beginning, as W. Dindorf rightly perceived; and for the last two verses, it may be said that they are so obviously spurious, that the present editor had marked them so many years ago, before he had the least idea of a numerical law of this kind. Nevertheless, the discovery of such a law is surely an interesting confirmation of a suspicion entertained on wholly different grounds.

X. In the *Orestes* (491—604) Tyndareus speaks *fifty* lines, and Orestes *sixty-one* in reply. In this latter speech there are several verses very suspicious in their composition. W. Dindorf has already ejected 588—90; and the concluding five, together with v. 596, will hardly stand the test of a critical examination. It is very probable therefore that these were exactly equal. It is remarkable that Stobaeus (Flor. 69, 13) quotes v. 602—4, without citing the name of the play.

There are not a few other speeches of the like controversial character, as between Hector and Rhesus, Theseus and Hippolytus, Admetus and Pheres, Hecuba and Helen in the *Troades*, Peleus and Menelaus in the *Andromache*, where we might have looked for the same exact correspondence in the number of verses. But in all these instances, though the number is *nearly* equal in each pair of speeches, there is no ground for suspecting either interpolation or omission such as might, as in other cases, plausibly account for a slight inequality in each pair of speeches. These may fairly be regarded as instances where the law has been rather laxly carried out, and therefore they in fact confirm rather than invalidate the principle contended for. It will be said, that nothing is easier than to invent a theory, and then to force refractory passages to suit it. With a full consciousness of this, we venture to think there is some reality in the present theory: and the following considerations will be allowed still further to confirm it.

There are two passages at least which seem to present a more elaborate and complex antithetical arrangement. One of these occurs in the *Electra*[5], and the observation of it has led to a rather important critical result, in the transposition of two verses which had hitherto occupied a wrong place. Another is in the *Orestes*[6], where Orestes speaks *five*, then *three times five*, then *twice five* verses; and he is answered by Pylades in *fifteen*, after which, (with the interval of a monostich dialogue between them of *thirty one*[7],) Orestes and Pylades again speak in *twenty-two* lines each. Beyond this[8], Electra and Orestes converse in *fourteen* alternate lines or couplets, and then Electra delivers a speech of *thirteen*, answered by Orestes in *fifteen* as before, and then (v. 1231—45) there is another dialogue of *fifteen* verses preceding a system of dochmiacs.—In all this a general, if not a particular and exact, coincidence is observable, which argues design and intention on the part of the poet, but which is very unlike mere accident. Now, the investigation of the rule, if such it be, is by no means without both utility and interest in a critical point of view. It affords a test of interpolations and omissions, we do not say, certain in itself, but at least of considerable value as confirmatory of suspicions reasonably conceived on independent grounds. There is no part of a critic's duty which requires more shrewdness than the detection of interpolated lines. That the Attic tragedies have been rather extensively tampered with in this respect, is the growing conviction of the present editor. Of course, it is to be expected that difference of opinion will exist on such delicate points of scholarship. W. Dindorf appears to be sometimes rash in condemning verses; while not a few others, which have been marked as spurious for the first time in this edition[9], have

[5] It has been pointed out in the note on v. 544. Two other passages of the like kind deserve consideration; Iph. T. 1284—1326, and Cycl. 179—346.

[6] v. 1047 to 1176.

[7] Or *twice fifteen;* where the exact number *thirty* was impossible, as will be seen by referring to the passage.

[8] V. 1177—90; where again, the exact number *fifteen* was inadmissible.

[9] It may here be mentioned, that the following passage (Heracl. 525—34) contains some verses of questionable genuineness:—

escaped his suspicion. There is a *prima facie* probability that the
early Alexandrine critics, in their recensions of and comments
on the Greek poets, occasionally took liberties with the existing
texts. Euripides especially, who was a great favourite with
the Greek Christians, seems to have been liable to these interpolations from several causes. In some cases the real or apparent coincidence of doctrine may have led to quotations from
Christian poets; in others, the learning or caprice of grammarians may have led them to amplify some of the sentiments,
or to compare passages from other plays; or the reproduction
of the more popular dramas upon the stage at an early period
may have induced actors and stage poets to enlarge some, to
curtail or omit other passages. This latter indeed is one of the
most probable causes of the alteration of the original writings;
and we occasionally meet with a direct testimony to the fact[1].
Doubtless, it is neither agreeable nor satisfactory to have our
faith in the genuineness of the ancient writings shaken by these
unwelcome surmises. They are mentioned only as probabilities;
but we need not shut our eyes to them even as such, because
whatever tends, in the study of the classics, to promote close
observation and inductive reasoning, is so much in their favour,
and deserves to be encouraged rather than repressed, even
though absolute certainty is unattainable. That some con-

οὐκοῦν θανεῖν ἄμεινον ἢ τούτων τυχεῖν
[ἀναξίαν· ἄλλῃ δὲ καὶ πρέπει τινὶ
μᾶλλον τάδ', ἥτις μὴ 'πίσημος ὡς ἐγώ.]
ἡγεῖσθ' ὅπου δεῖ σῶμα κατθανεῖν τόδε,
[καὶ στεμματοῦτε, καὶ κατάρχεσθ', εἰ δοκεῖ·]
νικᾶτε δ' ἐχθρούς· ἥδε γὰρ ψυχὴ πάρα
ἑκοῦσα κοὐκ ἄκουσα· κἀξαγγέλλομαι
θνήσκειν ἀδελφῶν τῶνδε κἀμαυτῆς ὕπερ.
[εὕρημα γάρτοι μὴ φιλοψυχοῦσ' ἐγὼ
κάλλιστον ηὕρηκ', εὐκλεῶς λιπεῖν βίον.]

It is doubtful if μὴ φιλοψυχοῦσα can be defended by examples of such a use of μὴ in
the old Attic dialect. On the other hand, writers like Lucian and Plutarch very
commonly put μὴ for οὐ. The verb στεμματοῦν is not less suspicious, as ἅπαξ
λεγόμενον.

[1] See, for instance, the Greek Argument to the *Rhesus*; the Scholiast on Med.
228.

siderable losses have been sustained by single lines or whole passages having dropped out, is more easily proved; and this evidently furnishes some analogy for believing that there are in a corresponding degree spurious interpolations. The practice of collecting γνῶμαι from the tragic writers, and of arranging them under different heads (as in the Extracts of Stobaeus) led naturally to the observation of parallelisms, and so to the wrong appropriation of some verses, as we actually find to be sometimes the case in Stobaeus. It is manifest that this alone would account for even genuine lines and passages of an author being disarranged or foisted into the wrong plays[2].

So fond was Euripides of bringing two actors on the stage in controversy with each other, that this is with him a part of the drama not less essential to its completeness than is the long narrative of some messenger. Indeed, his plays, which are otherwise sufficiently diversified and distinct in style and treatment, must be allowed to have a remarkable sameness in both these respects. There is scarcely one of all his extant tragedies that does not comprise both of these features. There must be two characters to argue a question of right and wrong, and there must be a messenger to relate what has just occurred out of sight of the acting parties. That the audience were pleased with such rhetorical discussions we must of course conclude; and the fact that they were so has been already explained on the known fondness of the Athenians for the business of the law-courts. But it is curious to remark, that in his later plays Euripides somewhat relaxed and curtailed the controversial scenes, and compensated for it by giving either *double* narratives of messengers, almost equally long and graphic in their cha-

---

[2] Thus, for instance, in the *Florilegium* of Stobaeus, xlix, 4, two verses are quoted as from the *Electra* of Euripides, which do not occur there. In lxxix, 2, a distich is wrongly given as from the *Heraclidae*. In xci, 23, eight lines are attributed to the *Hecuba* which no where occur in that play. In xciv, 5, a distich from the *Electra* (v. 943—4) is quoted as from the *Phoenissae*. In xcviii, 41, three verses from the *Ion* (381—3) are assigned to the *Iphigenia*. And so in lxxv, 10, two verses in the *Orestes* (542—3) are cited as from Dicaeogenes. In fact, the dramatic writers were often quoted from memory; and hence it is that various readings occur, to which it is dangerous to attach any high degree of critical importance.

VOL. II. c

racter (as in the *Bacchae,* the *Iphigenia at Tauri,* the *Phoenissae,*) or introducing, as in the *Helena* and the *Hecuba,* the personal narrative of the adventures or the sufferings of one of the characters. The *Rhesus,* though believed to be one of the earliest of his plays, affords a good instance of this; for we there have both the arrival of Rhesus described by a messenger, and also the account of the charioteer's injury related by himself. But here also we have the usual Euripidean controversy between Aeneas and Hector, and Rhesus and Hector. The *Troades* stands alone in the plays of this author in having no report of a messenger; but the herald Talthybius to a certain extent supplies the place. Sophocles has a messenger in all his plays but the *Philoctetes:* Aeschylus only in the *Persae,* the *Agamemnon,* and the *Seven against Thebes.* The inference seems inevitable, that descriptive narration was an element that was held more essential, and was more fully developed, in the later period of the Attic stage. There is nothing surprising in this. It was merely a reaction from the dithyrambic element of tragedy in favour of the epic. Euripides in every instance takes his messengers from the common people; a herdsman, an attendant, a captive slave, a sailor, a common soldier. This indeed is not unnatural, from the very notion of a messenger; yet Sophocles varies the character, for in the *Trachiniae* it is Hyllus who brings an account of his father, and in the *Ajax* the narrative of Tecmessa takes precedence, in point of importance, over the brief speech of the real messenger. Sophocles indeed shows a very marked preference to the display of personal heroism and endurance under suffering, as we see in his characters of Hercules, Ajax, Oedipus, Deianira, Antigone, Philoctetes,— where in each instance his or her monologue forms the longest or at least the most prominent part of the respective plays.

These considerations are not unimportant. They show one of the radical differences between the treatment of a play in the hands of these two great masters of the tragic art.

Sophocles, in fact, laboured to bring out the character ($\mathring{\eta}\theta o\varsigma$) of his heroes rather by letting them speak for themselves, and describe their own feelings under trying conjunctures. But Euripides, who makes his actors rather the slaves of circumstances than as rising superior to them, is fond of representing *events*, such as involved pathetic catastrophes. Now no event is so pathetic as the sudden outburst of an unexpected calamity affecting us in our nearest domestic relations. It is this very suddenness which almost demands a messenger as the medium of communication. It must be described in detail, in order that the spectators may be worked up to a pitch of excitement; and therefore it is most proper that an eye-witness or one who has taken a part in the affair should relate it to others. The events themselves are in all cases *narrated*, never *represented*. The ear, but not the eye, was the chosen vehicle of pathos to the Greeks; and this is one of the great distinctive characteristics of ancient and modern tragedy. Every one of the plays in this volume amply bear out this view, which is not here urged as any thing new [3], but that the reader may more clearly comprehend what is the real essence of Greek tragedy. It is by the narrative of a servant that the chorus (identified with the cause of Creusa) learn the attempt of a mother to murder her son; that Theoclymenus is informed of the loss of the bride whom he had just got within his grasp; that Peleus is apprised of his grandson's barbarous murder; that Electra hears of Aegisthus' death; Cadmus, that his daughter has torn to pieces her own son; Hecuba, that her daughter has been sacrificed at the tomb of Achilles.

The *Persians* of Aeschylus, among its many excellencies, realizes the idea of a messenger under circumstances the most

---

[3] See Müller, Hist. Gr. Lit. p. 307;—" It is never the outward act with which the interest of ancient tragedy is most intimately bound up. The action which forms the basis of every tragedy of those times is internal and spiritual; the reflections, resolutions, feelings, the mental or moral phenomena, which can be expressed in speech, are developed on the stage. For outward action, which is generally mute, or, at all events, cannot be adequately represented by words, the epic form, narration, is the only appropriate vehicle. Battles, single combats, murders, sacrifices, funerals, and the like, whatever in mythology is accomplished by strength of hand, passes behind the scenes; even when it might, without any considerable difficulty, be performed in front of them."

favourable for tragic effect. This, and the account of Orestes' death at the chariot race in the *Electra* of Sophocles, are the nearest in resemblance to the part which Euripides seems to have made the most prominent in each of his plays.

Of the extant dramas of Euripides, not less than half treat of the Trojan affairs. Of these only one (the *Rhesus*) is taken directly from the Iliad. The rest were adapted from the Cyclic poems, as were also very many of the plays, of which little more than the titles is known to us, of Aeschylus and Sophocles. This fact is certainly remarkable. The celebrity of these epics must have been very great in the fifth century before the Christian era. Founded mainly, but not exclusively, on the Homeric poems, they would seem to have enjoyed a popularity, through the recitations of the rhapsodists, little, if indeed at all, inferior to that of Homer himself. It appears[4] that both the date and the authorship of the Cyclus were early forgotten, and that they were commonly regarded as of equal merit and equal antiquity with the Iliad and the Odyssey. Indeed, we venture to think that this is the view which the tragic poets themselves must have taken. They did not, as we now do, and as the later Greeks undoubtedly did, regard Homer himself as transcendantly superior to so many minor imitators, but they regarded the Greek epos collectively as the great and sacred national repository of poetry and religion. Probably it was this very fact which induced Pisistratus to undertake (about B.C. 550) the task of collecting and arranging the genuine Homeric poems. He would hardly have done this, if those poems had not then been in danger of being no longer orally perpetuated in their true form. Another century would probably have found them undistinguishable from the amplifications and interpolations of the rhapsodists. Is it not highly probable also, that the total loss of the Cyclus,—a circumstance which may well seem surprising when we consider its great and wide celebrity,— must be accounted for on the ground that it never received any

---

[4] Proclus, quoted by Müller, Hist. Gr. Lit. p. 64.

such formal recension, that no ἔκδοσις of it was ever sanctioned by state authority?

It is worthy of remark, that under Pisistratus tragedy itself took its rise, or at least, began to assume a definite and important shape. It is scarcely hazardous to conclude, that the sole material for it in its early development was embodied in the epos. No effort was made to devise any new themes; the epos was now first *acted*, where before it had been only *recited*. Now, there must be some reason why such a very large number of plays were taken from the Cyclus, and none at all, it might almost be said[5], from the Iliad and the Odyssey. We think the reason was this: the Cyclus continued to be a more popular subject with the rhapsodists, and therefore more familiar to the people generally, when the separation of the Homeric poems from the rest of the epos had invested them with a peculiar sanctity and reserve, and caused them to be regarded as a literary possession and an inviolable deposit of national character and traditions[6], rather than as a theme which would allow of arbitrary variations and additions under dramatic treatment. The subject which, next to the Trojan war, was most frequently treated of in Attic tragedy, the war of the Argives against Thebes, was also derived from the same fertile source; for the *Thebais* was one of the poems of the Cyclus. But there were evidently other subjects,—perhaps forming parts of the national epos, or perhaps preserved in ballads or local legends,—unconnected with either Troy or Thebes (except, perhaps, incidentally), which fell within the province of the tragic writers, and furnished them with appropriate themes for the highest display of their art.

It seems probable that *all* the Greek tragedies, so far as we know them by their titles or by the fragments preserved, may be classed under ten principal subjects[7]. Now, if two or three

---

[5] The *Rhesus* and the *Cyclops* are the only exceptions that we know of.

[6] The Aeneid of Virgil owes more to the epic Cyclus than to the Odyssey. Ovid, Propertius, Statius, and other Roman poets were largely indebted to the former source.

[7] Of course, the rare exceptions of the historic dramas, such as the *Capture of*

hundred plays, and perhaps many more, could be composed from such limited materials, and if not only the very same subjects, but occasionally even the very same titles, were chosen by the rival dramatic writers, these facts conclusively show, that no tragic poet ever thought of *inventing a story*. Some real existing myth, scarcely, if at all, distinguished in the mind of the people from actual historic truth, was selected as a framework, upon which to hang the sentiments and the philosophy of the poet. The treatment might vary under different hands; but the subjects themselves were immutably the same, simply because they were *established* subjects. Assuming this view to be at least highly probable, we may enumerate the following as the current literature of Hellas in the fifth and sixth centuries before Christ[8]:—

i. Legends of Troy.
ii. Of Thebes.
iii. Of Argos.
iv. Of Corinth.
v. Of Hercules.
vi. Of Dionysus.
vii. Of the early Attic kings.
viii. Of the Argonauts.
ix. Of Crete.
x. Of Thrace.

Aeschylus, perhaps, took a somewhat wider range in the selection of themes. Still there are very few of the titles of his lost plays that may not easily be traced to some one or other of the above heads. Of his extant plays, the *Suppliants* manifestly falls under the third, the *Prometheus* under the fifth.

Miletus and *Phoenissae* of Phrynichus, and the *Persae* of Aeschylus, are not taken into account.

[8] It would take a considerable space to illustrate, by quotations of the titles of plays, the theory here advanced. Suffice it to say, it has been founded on a careful consideration of those now known to us. Not a few of the plays presuppose a *Perseid*, or Adventures of Perseus. But this will fall under the head *Legends of Argos*.

Besides the nine extant tragedies of Euripides relating to the Trojan war and the events following it, we have fragments of at least seven others on the same subject; and these too were in all probability taken wholly from the Cyclic poems[9]. These were, the *Alexandrus*, the *Palamedes*, the *Protesilaus*, the *Scyriae*, the *Telephus*, the *Philoctetes*, and the *Phoenix;* to which may be added the *Epeus*, though the name alone of this play is preserved. In the historical order, or chronological sequence of the events, the extant plays of Euripides on the Trojan war are to be arranged as follows:—

1. *Iphigenia at Aulis.* This belongs to the period of the expedition of the Argives from Greece. The subject seems to have been taken from the *Cypria* of Stasinus.

2. *Rhesus.* The war is now in progress. The events are those described in the tenth book of the Iliad. It is rather remarkable that this book was by some ancient authorities believed not to be really Homer's work[1], or at least, not a part of the original Iliad.

3. *Hecuba.* Troy has been taken, and the army are about to return to Argos, but are detained by the angry shade of Achilles, who demands the sacrifice of a Trojan captive. Polyxena is accordingly immolated on his tomb at Sigeum.

4. *The Trojan Captives.* This play relates to nearly the same period; but in v. 40 the death of Polyxena is spoken of as having already occurred. The distribution of the captives among the conquerors, the murder of Astyanax, and the final demolition of the city, are the subjects of this play, which was undoubtedly adapted from the *Little Iliad* of Lesches.

5. *Helena.* Menelaus returns home after eight years wandering on unknown seas. He recovers his wife Helen, who has

---

[9] Not less than thirty of the lost plays of Sophocles, and about ten of Aeschylus appear to have been derived from the same source, while not one of them seems to have been borrowed from Homer himself.

[1] Müller, Hist. Gr. Lit. p. 53. Assuming this to be true, we should have the remarkable fact, that at least sixty known plays were derived from a kind of poetical appendix to Homer, not one from Homer himself (the Satyric Cyclops is hardly worthy of being taken into account).

been detained in Egypt, while a mere semblance or airy likeness of her was present at Troy. In this play the author was indebted to Stesichorus and to the *Nosti* of Agias.

6. *Electra.* It is not quite clear whether the poet himself regarded the action of this play as anterior or subsequent to that of the last[2]. Orestes on returning to Argos discovers his sister living in seclusion, and nominally married to a countryman. Together they plot to slay both Aegisthus and Clytemnestra, who had murdered Agamemnon on his return from Troy eight years previously.

7. *Orestes.* Here the return of Menelaus is spoken of as past (v. 53), whereas in the *Helena* he has but just left Pharos for Nauplia. Orestes, pursued by the Furies, is seized with madness, and is condemned to die by the Argives, but escapes, and is directed by Apollo to fly to Athens, where he shall be tried by the court of the Areopagus. (Between this and the next play the *Eumenides* of Aeschylus intervenes, and fills a void left in the plays of Euripides.)

8. *Iphigenia at Tauri.* Orestes, driven from land to land by the Furies, has at length been acquitted by the Areopagus. He is however still pursued by those Furies who desired his condemnation (v. 970), till he comes to Tauri on the Euxine, where he recognises his sister Iphigenia in the priestess of the temple, and succeeds by stratagem in carrying away her, together with the sacred image of Artemis, back to Argos.

9. *Andromache.* The events of this play belong to a still later period than the return of the Greeks. Neoptolemus, the son of Achilles, who in the *Orestes* (v. 1655) was forewarned of his death at Delphi, is in the present play described as having married Hermione the daughter of Menelaus, after cohabiting

---

[2] It is evident from Electr. 1280, that the murder of Aegisthus followed close on the return of Menelaus. But in Orest. 472, the latter event is spoken of as having just occurred, though the murder of Clytemnestra and her paramour has been accomplished some time ago. Homer (Od. iii. 311) represents Menelaus as returning to Argos on the very same day that Orestes buried Aegisthus; and he says that this was eight years after Agamemnon's death. Consequently, as Menelaus wandered for eight years after the capture of Troy, Agamemnon must have returned at once. Compare El. 1152.

with the captive Andromache. While absent at Delphi, he is beset by the Delphians, instigated by his enemy Orestes, and murdered on suspicion of being a thief having designs on the wealth of the Delphian temple.

10. The satyric *Cyclops* describes the adventure of Ulysses with Polyphemus, at some indefinite period of his long wanderings after the capture of Troy. The subject is from the ninth book of the Odyssey. The speech of Cassandra in the *Troades* (v. 424 seqq.) also enumerates the principal circumstances in the return of Ulysses, as described in the Odyssey.

It is evident that of all the subjects of Greek tragedy connected with Troy, the murder of Agamemnon and the revenge afterwards taken by Orestes, was by no means the least famous. Not less than seven of the extant plays of the three tragic authors treat of this single event, if, as we clearly should do, we include the *Iphigenia at Tauri* among the number. Though Homer had mentioned the event in the third, the fourth, and the eleventh books of the Odyssey, it is probable that the poem of Agias, known as the *Nosti*, or *Return of the Atridae*, contributed its share to the details as they were worked out in these plays. So strong a hold upon the minds of an intellectual people had the doctrine, whether derived from reason, or observation, or from that instinctive perception of God's eternal justice which seems to be implanted in man,—that crime must be overtaken by punishment, and that neither wealth, nor greatness, nor power, can long keep the demon Retribution away from the guilty hearth. Moreover, such a theme suited the natural disposition of the Greeks, who held revenge to be a most sacred duty. The point of the story,—that which gave its harrowing interest to a Greek audience,—was the strong conflict not only between natural *feelings*, but between *principles*. The legal and the illegal were at issue,—the virtue of avenging a father, with the crime of slaying a mother. Faith in the commands of a god came in to turn the scale; obedience to those commands, however incomprehensible to the reasonings of a dutiful son, is rewarded by the final triumph of his cause, after long sufferings and occasional misgivings of conscience (Electra, v. 971—9).

Such a story suited the different genius of each of the three great tragic writers; and though the manner in which Euripides has treated it in the *Electra* has met with little approval from modern critics, who have generally included the *Orestes* in their condemnation, it may be doubted if, after all, the fault does not rather lie with them than with the poet. We know that custom and the authority of learned writers have great influence; but we know also that customs change; and perhaps the time may come when Euripides will once more occupy the tragic προεδρία from which neither Aristophanes nor the German critics will be able again to dethrone him.

Postscript. The *Helena* had been printed to about 750 verses before the notes of Mr. W. G. Clark on this play, published in the Journal of Philology, were received. Of course therefore they came too late to obtain that full consideration throughout which the Author's name entitles him to expect; for the whole of the copy was at the time in the printer's hands, and hence it happens that they are but casually referred to in the latter part.

Mr. Clark's reading of v. 122 seems to be better than any yet proposed;—

αὐτὸς γὰρ ὄσσοις εἶδον, εἰ καὶ νῦν σ' ὁρῶ.

In v. 297, an ingenious emendation communicated to Mr. Clark is καὶ τὸ βρῶμ' ἐστὶν πικρὸν, (for καὶ τὸ σῶμ',) where the mention of *food* certainly well suits the πλουσία τράπεζα. On the whole however, τὸ σῶν, the conjecture of Seidler, seems safer.

In v. 442, ἄνες χόλον (or χόλου) is a plausible suggestion for ἄνες λόγον. Mr. Clark compares τῆς ὀργῆς ἀνέντες in Ran. v. 700.

In v. 613 Mr. Clark is perhaps right in reading πάλιν ἐς οὐρανὸν ἄπειμι, for πατέρ' ἐς οὐρανόν.

In v. 1653, it is probable that, as Bothe and others suggest, a colon should be placed after οὐκέτι, and then the following verse will better stand thus;—

νῦν τοῖσιν αὐτοῖς δεῖ νιν ἐζεῦχθαι γάμοις,

where the old copies give ἐν τοῖσιν αὐτοῖς κτλ.

The present occasion may be taken for suggesting a better metrical arrangement than has yet been given in Hippol. 1268 seqq.

σὺ τὰν θεῶν ἄκαμπτον φρένα καὶ βροτῶν ἄγεις, *ὦ Κύπρι.
σὺν δ' ὁ ποικιλόπτερος ἀμφιβαλὼν
ὠκυτάτῳ πτερῷ.
ποτᾶται δὲ γᾶν εὐάχητον ἁλμυρόν θ' ἐπὶ πόντον.
θέλγει δ' Ἔρως, ᾧ μαινομένᾳ κραδίᾳ
πτανὸς ἐφορμάσῃ χρυσοφαὴς, φύσιν
ὀρεσκόων σκυλάκων
πελαγίων θ' ὅσα τε γᾶ τρέφει,
τὰν *θεὸς αἰθομέναν δέρκεται,
ἄνδρας τ'· *ἐν δὲ πάντων βασιληῖδα τιμὰν,
*ὦ Κύπρι, τῶνδε μόνα κρατύνεις.

The verses thus arranged and occasionally corrected are, (1) dochmiac trimeter. (2) troch. dipod. + dactylic dimeter. (3) dochmius. (4) dochmiac trimeter (the τε being transposed from the preceding word, and γᾶν put for γαῖαν). (5) iambelegus. (6) dochmiac dimeter. (7) glyconeus cum anacrusi. (8) resolved cretic + dochmius. (9) dochmius + cretic. The common reading Ἅλιος is here unmetrical. (10) dochmiac dimeter hypercatalectic. Here the old reading is again quite unmetrical,

ἄνδρας τε· συμπάντων δὲ βασιληῖδα τιμάν.

(11) Logaoedic. Here, as in the first verse, the ὦ seems to have dropped out before Κύπρι. But the two last verses may be arranged as one, in which case the superfluous syllable in τιμὰν will combine to form a dactyl with Κύπρι.

CONTENTS OF VOL. II.

	PAGE
PREFACE	v
ION	1
HELENA	109
ANDROMACHE	221
ELECTRA	301
BACCHAE	389
HECUBA	481
INDEX I.—OF WORDS AND PROPER NAMES	563
INDEX II.—GRAMMATICAL, PHILOLOGICAL, &c.	576

ΕΥΡΙΠΙΔΟΥ ΙΩΝ.

ΥΠΟΘΕΣΙΣ.

Κρέουσαν τὴν Ἐρεχθέως Ἀπόλλων φθείρας ἔγκυον ἐποίησεν ἐν Ἀθήναις· ἡ δὲ τὸ γεννηθὲν ὑπὸ τὴν ἀκρόπολιν ἐξέθηκε, τὸν αὐτὸν τόπον καὶ τοῦ ἀδικήματος καὶ τῆς λοχείας μάρτυρα λαβοῦσα. τὸ μὲν οὖν βρέφος Ἑρμῆς ἀνελόμενος εἰς Δελφοὺς ἤνεγκεν· εὑροῦσα δ' ἡ προφῆτις ἀνέθρεψε· τὴν Κρέουσαν δὲ Ξοῦθος ἔγημε· συμμαχήσας γὰρ Ἀθηναίοις τὴν βασιλείαν καὶ τὸν τῆς προειρημένης γάμον ἔλαβε δῶρον. τούτῳ μὲν οὖν ἄλλος παῖς οὐκ ἐγένετο· τὸν δ' ἐκτραφέντα ὑπὸ τῆς προφήτιδος οἱ Δελφοὶ νεωκόρον ἐποίησαν. ὁ δ' ἀγνοῶν ἐδούλευσε τῷ πατρί.

Ἡ σκηνὴ τοῦ δράματος ὑπόκειται ἐν Δελφοῖς.

ION.

Though the *Ion* may safely be pronounced one of the most perfect and beautiful of the Greek Tragedies, it does not appear to have been regarded with any particular favour by the ancient schoolmen. We have no scholia upon the text, and but few references to or quotations from the play in the grammatical Treatises and Lexicons of the early Christian ages. Yet very few of the extant dramas are more artistic in the plot, or more happy in the delineation of the passions. If to excite the combined emotions of *fear* and *pity* be the chief end of a Greek Tragedy, then the *Ion* must be judged eminently to fulfil these primary conditions. It may be added, that none of his plays so clearly show the fine mind of Euripides, or impress us with a more favourable idea of his virtuous and humane character. Not even is the date of the *Ion*, nor the trilogy to which it belonged, nor are the circumstances under which it was brought out, known to us. It can only be inferred, from the style of the versification, that it was intermediate between the earlier and severer compositions, and the licentious and florid elegancies of his latest plays. Accordingly W. Dindorf places it between Ol. 88 and Ol. 91, and Hermann[1] considers, from internal evidences, that it was written "nec post Olymp. lxxxix., nec multo prius." The general composition of the play may be described rather as pleasing than as powerful. It was designed to extol the pure blood of the Athenians, and to show that the Ionian stock from which they claimed descent was not, as represented in ordinary legends, that derived from the Hellenic stranger Xuthus, but had originated from Apollo himself. Creusa, who is represented as the principal character, is the daughter of the old autochthonic King Erechtheus. In early life she had been seduced by Apollo, and given birth at home to a son, whom from fear of her parents she exposed in a grotto under the Acropolis. Apollo however is not forgetful of his child. Hermes is desired by him to convey the infant to Delphi, and there to leave him before the

[1] *Præfatio*, p. xxxii.

temple, if perchance some Delphian maid may take pity on the foundling and rear it as her own. In the course of years the boy Ion is appointed to an honourable service in the temple of his patron god. He knows not his origin; a stranger and an orphan, he lives an ascetic life, serving with pious zeal the god at whose altars he is maintained, and cheerfully conversing with the visitors to the renowned Delphic shrine.

Meanwhile Creusa, the mother, has married Xuthus, who, though a foreigner, has been deemed by the Athenians worthy the hand of an Erechtheid, as a return for the services he had rendered them in a war with the Euboeans. Though long married, they are childless, and have resolved on an expedition to Delphi to consult the god on the chance of their having a family.

It so happens on their arrival at that famed temple, that Creusa first meets with her own son Ion; and in a very touching and well devised dialogue, each is made acquainted with the anxieties of the other,—Ion finding that Creusa sighs for a son, Creusa that Ion,—he of the noble mien and obliging and courteous temper,—knows not who are his parents. All this is so artistically contrived, that the spectators are kept in a state of suspense how the ἀναγνώρισις is to be effected between two persons whom a mutual liking seems already to have mysteriously united. Creusa, ashamed of her frailty in early youth, pretends that she has come to Delphi on behalf of a friend who had been the victim of an amour with the god, and who wishes to hear of her child. This gives occasion to the poet to express, under the character of the artless and ingenuous Ion, some fine reflections on the injustice and immoralities of those beings whom men are taught to look up to for examples of every virtue.

Xuthus, the husband, now returns from the neighbouring oracle of Trophonius, where he has been told that the first person he meets on going forth shall be his son. This proves to be Ion, whose surprise at being greeted under the strange appellation of *My son*, is well and naturally depicted. His faith in oracles however is such, that he is easily convinced. Xuthus informs him of a scheme for introducing him to Athens as a stranger at first, in order to avoid the jealousy of Creusa, should she have reason to believe that the childlessness is on her part alone. And he then departs with the intention of making a thank-offering to the gods, and charges Ion to superintend the preparations for entertaining all the Delphians at a grand banquet in honour of the event.

The chorus, who are handmaids of Creusa, have heard the intentions of Xuthus, and are enjoined by him under penalty of death not to reveal them to their mistress. This warning however they disregard; Creusa is made acquainted with all that has occurred. Her jealousy is fomented by the wicked counsels of an old man, who had once been the attendant on Erechtheus. He represents to her that the adoption of Ion is a slight upon the house to which he has long been attached. A stranger will henceforth sit on the throne of the Erechtheids. She is moved by his arguments, not only as an injured wife, but as a daughter proud of her pure autochthony. They conspire to murder Ion. The old man is to put some drops of a subtle poison in his cup while he is preparing a libation after the banquet which is about to be given by Xuthus. The scheme is however frustrated by an accident, brought about by the interposition of Apollo. A flock of pigeons enters the banquetting room; and one of them, which has tasted the poisoned wine that had, from a slight informality in the ceremony, been poured upon the ground, dies in convulsions. The old man is arrested on the spot by Ion himself, and confesses that he is the accomplice of Creusa. Both are immediately condemned by the Delphians to die. Ion, as the party to whom a sacrilegious wrong had been offered, and full of zeal for the cause of the god, comes forward as the resolute opponent of one whom he little supposes to be his own mother, but regards only as an impious invader of the sanctity of the Delphian precincts. He charges her face to face with her wickedness, and avows that she shall die, even though she has taken refuge at the altars.

But now the old prophetess, who many years ago had preserved the life of the infant foundling, and had secretly kept the crib in which he was laid, and in it the clothes and ornaments which he then wore, comes forward, and presents to him these tokens, in case he should obtain any clue to his mother either at Athens or elsewhere. Ion opens the box, which had remained intact for so many years, and exposes to the view of Creusa, who is present in the scene, the very ornaments which she had herself attached to the child at his birth. Thus the recognition is effected. Creusa publickly acknowledges that Phoebus was the father. Ion's doubts on this last point are quickly removed by the appearance of Athena, who is sent by Phoebus to confirm her story, and to order that Ion should be placed on the throne of Athens, her own city. From him shall descend the four Ionic tribes, *Teleontes*, *Hopletes*, *Ergades* or *Argades*, and *Aegicores;* and these shall colonize the coast of Asia Minor and the intermediate Aegean isles, to be called *Ionia* from the name of Ion.

Xuthus does not take a prominent part in the play. He is introduced as the husband of Creusa according to the current Athenian legends; but the assigning to him Ion as his son is a mere stratagem to account for the youth's succeeding to the throne of Athens with his concurrence. The terms indeed on which Apollo presented Ion to him as a *gift* would have roused the suspicions of a more sagacious man :—

> πεφυκέναι μὲν οὐχὶ, δωρεῖται δέ σε
> αὐτοῦ γεγῶτα· καὶ γὰρ ἂν φίλος φίλῳ
> δοίη τὸν αὑτοῦ παῖδα δεσπότην δόμων,

is the account of the affair given to Ion by Creusa in explanation (v. 1534). But the plot is so contrived, that Xuthus is at once content to believe Ion to be his own child, and is anxious to conceal his own fruitfulness from the very wife who was really the parent. The very fact that Apollo gives him to Xuthus as a son, is, as Hermann observes, a recognition that such was really believed to be the human parentage, till the vanity of the Athenians led them to look for a divine origin of their race.

The scene throughout is laid at Delphi. There are three actors in the piece, as is clear from the scene where Creusa is present at the conversation between Ion and the prophetess, v. 1395, &c., and from the concluding dialogue between Ion, Creusa, and Athena.

ΤΑ ΤΟΥ ΔΡΑΜΑΤΟΣ ΠΡΟΣΩΠΑ.

ΕΡΜΗΣ.
ΙΩΝ.
ΧΟΡΟΣ ΘΕΡΑΠΑΙΝΙΔΩΝ ΚΡΕΟΥΣΗΣ.
ΚΡΕΟΥΣΑ.
ΞΟΥΘΟΣ.
ΠΡΕΣΒΥΤΗΣ ἢ ΠΑΙΔΑΓΩΓΟΣ.
ΘΕΡΑΠΩΝ ΚΡΕΟΥΣΗΣ.
ΠΥΘΙΑ ἤτοι ΠΡΟΦΗΤΙΣ.
ΑΘΗΝΑ.

ΕΥΡΙΠΙΔΟΥ ΙΩΝ.

ΕΡΜΗΣ.

Ἄτλας, ὁ χαλκέοισι νώτοις οὐρανὸν,
θεῶν παλαιὸν οἶκον, ἐκτρίβων, θεῶν

1—81. The Prologue. Perhaps no play better illustrates Euripides' way of explaining the whole plot at the outset, than the *Ion*. It is well known that the practice has been alleged as a fault against the poet,—perhaps from no better reason than that Aristophanes in the *Frogs* has made some jokes about it. But Euripides had the sense to know that the merit of a good play is to affect the audience not so much by surprise, as by the way in which the story is told, and the manner in which it is represented. He is not afraid of telling his hearers beforehand *what* is going to be acted, but on the contrary, he regards this as an important aid to the right understanding of the characters. The *drama* is essentially *action;* and it is just for this reason that we are never tired of seeing a good play well acted, even long after we have become familiar with every one of the incidents.

In the present play, Hermes announces that he has come to Delphi to witness the restoration of the foundling Ion to his true mother Creusa, and his reputed father Xuthus, the son of Aeolus, and her husband. To Delphi the god had formerly gone at the express request of his brother Apollo, who was the real father of Ion, in order that he might bring the new-born infant from a grotto under the Acropolis of Athens, where it was then exposed, to the Temple of the Pythian god, and so secure its preservation under the fostering care of his priestess. And in order that the recognition of his mother at some future time (which time has now arrived) might be without difficulty brought to pass, he had conveyed the infant in its cradle with all the swathing bands and little ornaments attached to it by its parent at the time of the secret birth.

1. The metre of this verse, which directly violates the well-known canon of Porson (quoted on Alcest. 671), has given rise to several conjectures. Bothe, following him and Elmsley, transposes thus, Ἄτλας, ὁ νώτοις χαλκέοισιν οὐρανὸν κτλ., which is undeniably weaker than the common order. Hermann thinks that the line is purposely constructed so as to represent, in the recitation, the weight and the labour that is described. Dr. Badham supposes οὐρανὸν to be a gloss that has crept into the text in place of the original νώτοισιν πόλον. He might have added that this is the very word used by Aeschylus in speaking of the very same person, Prom. 436, Ἄτλανθ᾽, ὃς αἰὲν | ὑπέροχον σθένος κραταιὸν | οὐράνιόν τε πόλον | νώτοις ὑποστενάζει. We may be, perhaps, content with the vulgate, whatever may have been the poet's reason for departing from a law which he usually, but not invariably, observes. In Oed. Col. 664 there is an equally plain violation of the ordinary iambic rhythm, θαρσεῖν μὲν οὖν ἔγωγε κἄνευ τῆς ἐμῆς | γνώμης ἐπαινῶ, and it is needless to cite other instances, well known to scholars, and sufficiently numerous to show that Porson's so-called canon is only

μιᾶς ἔφυσε Μαῖαν, ᾗ 'μ' ἐγείνατο
Ἑρμῆν μεγίστῳ Ζηνὶ, δαιμόνων λάτριν.
ἥκω δὲ Δελφῶν τήνδε γῆν, ἵν' ὀμφαλὸν 5
μέσον καθίζων Φοῖβος ὑμνῳδεῖ βροτοῖς,
τά τ' ὄντα καὶ μέλλοντα θεσπίζων ἀεί.
ἔστιν γὰρ οὐκ ἄσημος Ἑλλήνων πόλις,
τῆς χρυσολόγχου Παλλάδος κεκλημένη,
οὗ παῖδ' Ἐρεχθέως Φοῖβος ἔζευξεν γάμοις 10
βίᾳ Κρέουσαν, ἔνθα προσβόρρους πέτρας
Παλλάδος ὑπ' ὄχθῳ τῆς Ἀθηναίων χθονὸς

a generally observed arrangement, resulting from the fine ear for harmony which the Greeks undoubtedly possessed.—ἐκτρίβων is a highly poetical word for ἀνέχων. But it requires some explanation, as it may be understood in two ways. A person might be said τρίβειν or ἐκτρίβειν ὤμους, to gall or wear out his shoulders by a burden, and so by a sort of metonymy, τρίβειν οὐρανὸν ὤμοις, because the friction is exerted on one of two bodies as much as on the other. But ἐκτρίβειν may also bear the sense which Hermann assigns to it, of gradually performing a long and unremitting toil, ἐκτρίβων ἄχθος οὐρανοῦ,—wearing it out, that is, by persevering endeavours, though it is destined never to come to an end. He compares Oed. Col. 248, ἄμορον ἐκτρῖψαι βίον, and in a similar sense we have τρίβειν βίον Heracl. 84.

3. ᾗ 'μ', for the unemphatic ᾗ μ', is the reading of L. Dindorf, approved by Hermann and others. In the next verse Dr. Badham is clearly right in transposing the comma usually placed after Ἑρμῆν, by which the meaning was, 'messenger to Zeus the chief of all the gods.' The mention of the father adds weight to the passage, while that of the supremacy of Zeus is here quite needless. With δαιμόνων λάτριν compare θεῶν ὑπηρέτον, said of Hermes, Prom. 975.—θεῶν μιᾶς, Pleïone. Apollodor. i. 3. 10. Ovid, Fast. v. 81,

" Duxerat Oceanus quondam Titanida Tethyn,
Qui terram liquidis, qua patet, ambit aquis.
Hinc sata Pleïone cum caelifero Atlante
Jungitur, ut fama est, Pleïadasque parit.

Quarum Maia suas forma superasse sorores
Traditur, et summo concubuisse Jovi.
Haec enixa jugo cupressiferae Cyllenes
Aetherium volucri qui pede carpit iter."

6. ὑμνῳδεῖ. There is an allusion to the metrical form in which oracles were delivered. So ἔχρησας ὑμνῳδίαν inf. 681. ἀνύμνησας δίκαν El. 1190.

7. τὰ ὄντα καὶ (τὰ) μέλλοντα is an instance of a poetical licence similar to Ag. 315, τῶν ἁλόντων καὶ κρατησάντων. Helen. 923, τά τ' ὄντα καὶ μή, and ibid. v. 14, where the same words as here occur. Androm. 405, πρὸς τὰς παρούσας ἢ παρελθούσας τύχας.

8. ἔστιν γάρ. ('And I am come to Delphi for this reason'):—there is a city sacred to Pallas, where Creusa brought forth a child to Apollo, and from which I formerly brought it to this place,' &c.—οὐκ ἄσημος, i. e. κλεινοτάτη. The epithet χρυσολόγχου refers to the great bronze statue of Pallas Πρόμαχος on the Acropolis.

11. ἔνθα κτλ. In the *Paneum*, or grotto hollowed out in the base of the Acropolis at its N.W. angle, and dedicated in common to Apollo and Pan. The whole north side of the Acropolis probably obtained the name of Μακραὶ on account of its being much longer in that direction than at the two ends to the east and west. The cave of Pan still remains, and was explored by Dr. C. Wordsworth; see *Athens and Attica*, chap. xii.

12. τῆς Ἀθ. χθονὸς is added for the sake of clearness, and is to be construed with Π. ὄχθῳ, not, as Bothe contends, with ἔνθα.—ἄνακτες, the lords, that is, the inhabitants generally, of the Attic soil.

Μακρὰς καλοῦσι γῆς ἄνακτες Ἀτθίδος.
ἀγνὼς δὲ πατρὶ, τῷ θεῷ γὰρ ἦν φίλον,
γαστρὸς διήνεγκ᾽ ὄγκον· ὡς δ᾽ ἦλθεν χρόνος,   15
τεκοῦσ᾽ ἐν οἴκοις παῖδ᾽ ἀπήνεγκεν βρέφος
ἐς ταυτὸν ἄντρον οὗπερ ηὐνάσθη θεῷ
Κρέουσα, κἀκτίθησιν ὡς θανούμενον
κοίλης ἐν ἀντίπηγος εὐτρόχῳ κύκλῳ,
προγόνων νόμον σώζουσα τοῦ τε γηγενοῦς   20
Ἐριχθονίου· κείνῳ γὰρ ἡ Διὸς κόρη
φρουρὼ παραζεύξασα φύλακε σώματος
δισσὼ δράκοντε, παρθένοις Ἀγραυλίσι

So Δελφῶν ἄνακτες inf. 1222. By ὄχθος the Acropolis of course is meant, as in Troad. 798, ὄχθοις ἱεροῖς ἵν᾽ ἐλαίας πρῶτον ἔδειξε κλάδον γλαυκᾶς Ἀθάνα.
17. ταυτὸν ἄντρον. See on v. 1400, and on v. 949.
19. ἀντίπηξ. The derivation from ἀντὶ and πηγνύναι, implying something fixed in front of another, seems to indicate an original usage of which we know nothing, unless it meant ' fastened in front,' by a lock or other contrivance. Hesychius explains it to mean 'a chest,' or box; but the epithet πλεκτὸν shows that it was of wicker work, and εὔτροχος indicates its round shape. Inf. v. 1391, ἰδοὺ περίπτυγμ᾽ ἀντίπηγος εὐκύκλου Ὡς οὐ γεγήρακ᾽ ἔκ τινὸς θεηλάτου, Εὑρώς τ᾽ ἄπεστι πλέγματων. We may conceive therefore that it was a sort of hamper.
22. φύλακε. So Porson by an obvious correction for φύλακας. The meaning is, that Creusa deposited the infant in the basket, after attaching to it (viz. round the neck, δέραια φέρειν, v. 1431) a golden ornament fashioned in the device of two snakes intertwined, such being the ancient custom of her family, which she did not neglect to observe even in a time of alarm and anxiety. Whether the snakes affixed by Hera to Erichthonius were real ones, or merely ornaments, called φρουρὼ in the sense of *charms*, is a question determined by the authority of Apollodorus (quoted on v. 270). See Ovid, Met. ii. 553,

" Pallas Erichthonium, prolem sine matre creatam,
Clauserat Actaeo texta de vimine cista,
Virginibusque tribus, gemino de Cecrope natis,

Hanc legem dederat, sua ne secreta viderent.
——— at intus
Infantemque vident apporrectumque draconem."

Hence the use of the ἀντίπηξ as well as of the snakes was part of the ancestral custom observed by Creusa. Hence, too, when the basket is opened, and its contents are examined, in v. 1427, Creusa finds therein δράκοντε μαρμαίροντε παγχρύσῳ γένυι. Similar ornaments have been discovered, as bracelets, at Pompeii. (See Lucian, Ἔρωτες, p. 442.) Cecrops himself, the representative of the indigenous inhabitants, was τὰ πρὸς ποδῶν δρακοντίδης, Ar. Vesp. 438; in fact he has been ingeniously identified with the τέττιξ (worn by the old Athenians in their hair, Thuc. i. 6), his daughters, according to the legend, viz. Agraulos, Pandrosus, and Herse, (Apollodorus, iii. 14, 2,) being merely epithets indicative of the field-piping and dew-drinking propensities of that insect. The curling up of the tail or body of this κέκροψ or κέρκωψ (κερκώπη), is expressed by the very derivation of the word from κερκός. And hence the statues of Cecrops were made with serpent-like folds in place of legs and feet. See Pausan. Attic. cap. xviii. § 2. Inf. 1163, κατ᾽ εἰσόδους δὲ Κέκροπα θυγατέρων πέλας, Σπείραις συνειλίσσοντα.
23. παρθένοις Ἀγραυλίσι, the daughters of Cecrops. The name of the eldest is spelt both Ἄγραυλος and Ἄγλαυρος, but for the reason given above, the former appears the true orthography. The wife of Cecrops was also called Ἄγραυλος. Cf. v. 496.

ΕΥΡΙΠΙΔΟΥ

δίδωσι σώζειν. ὅθεν Ἐρεχθείδαις ἐκεῖ
νόμος τίς ἐστιν ὄφεσιν ἐν χρυσηλάτοις 25
τρέφειν τέκν'. ἀλλ' ἦν εἶχε παρθένος χλιδὴν
τέκνῳ προσάψασ' ἔλιπεν, ὡς θανουμένῳ.
καί μ' ὢν ἀδελφὸς Φοῖβος αἰτεῖται τάδε·
Ὦ σύγγον', ἐλθὼν λαὸν εἰς αὐτόχθονα
κλεινῶν Ἀθηνῶν, οἶσθα γὰρ θεᾶς πόλιν, 30
λαβὼν βρέφος νεογνὸν ἐκ κοίλης πέτρας
αὐτῷ σὺν ἄγγει σπαργάνοισί θ' οἷς ἔχει
ἔνεγκε Δελφῶν τἀμὰ πρὸς χρηστήρια,
καὶ θὲς πρὸς αὐταῖς εἰσόδοις δόμων ἐμῶν.
τὰ δ' ἄλλ', ἐμὸς γάρ ἐστιν, ὡς εἰδῇς, ὁ παῖς, 35
ἡμῖν μελήσει. Λοξίᾳ δ' ἐγὼ χάριν
πράσσων ἀδελφῷ πλεκτὸν ἐξάρας κύτος
ἤνεγκα, καὶ τὸν παῖδα κρηπίδων ἔπι
τίθημι ναοῦ τοῦδ', ἀναπτύξας κύτος
ἑλικτὸν ἀντίπηγος, ὡς ὁρῷθ' ὁ παῖς. 40
κυρεῖ δ' ἅμ' ἱππεύοντος ἡλίου κύκλῳ
προφῆτις εἰσβαίνουσα μαντεῖον θεοῦ·
ὄψιν δὲ προσβαλοῦσα παιδὶ νηπίῳ
ἐθαύμασ' εἴ τις Δελφίδων τλαίη κόρη
λαθραῖον ὠδῖν' ἐς θεοῦ ῥῖψαι δόμον, 45

24. ἐκεῖ. 'There at Athens,' (i. e. not here at Delphi,) as Homer uses ὑπ' Ἴλιον αὐτοῦ &c. The conjectures proposed Ἐρεχθείδαισι καὶ (Bothe), Ἐρ. ἀεὶ (Elmsley), Ἐρ. ἔτι (Barnes), do not seem to be any improvement.—ἐν ὄφεσιν, i. e. ὄφεις or ὀφέων εἰκόνας ἐξάπτοντας.
26. ἀλλά. But, as I was saying, &c., i. e. to return from this digression.— χλιδὴν, the piece of embroidered peplus described below, v. 1417 seqq. That it was the custom to affix some kind of κόσμος to those about to be consigned to the tomb, will appear from Alcest. 160. 618. Brodaeus is therefore wrong in explaining χλιδὴν by crepundia.
30. οἶσθα γάρ. Added as a eulogy on Athens, οὐκ ἄσημος Ἑλλήνων πόλις, v. 8.
33. Δελφῶν. The correction of Reiske and Musgrave for ἀδελφῷ, and rightly approved by Herm. Dind. Bothe and Matthiae. Hermann well says, "inutilis hic fratris, necessaria loci mentio est in pluribus quae Apollo habuit oraculis."
36. χάριν πράσσων, 'doing a favour,' as we say by a precisely similar idiom. Cf. inf. 895. Electr. 1133.
38. κρηπίδων. Properly, the raised platform or basement of squared stones on which Greek temples always stood. Here perhaps for βάθρων, the steps. The child was laid on one of the front steps, that the priestess might not fail to see it on first entering the shrine. And hence, apparently, the poet adds ὑπὲρ θυμέλας διορίσαι, v. 46, to cast it without and beyond the flight of steps; for θυμέλαι are strictly the steps of an altar.—διορίσαι. Helen. 394. 828.
40. ὀρῷθ' (ὁράοιτο) Scaliger for ὁρᾶθ' or ὁρᾶσθ'.

ΙΩΝ.

ὑπὲρ δὲ θυμέλας διορίσαι πρόθυμος ἦν·
οἴκτῳ δ' ἀφῆκεν ὠμότητα, καὶ θεὸς
συνεργὸς ἦν τῷ παιδὶ μὴ 'κπεσεῖν δόμων.
τρέφει δέ νιν λαβοῦσα· τὸν σπείραντα δὲ
οὐκ οἶδε Φοῖβον, οὐδὲ μητέρ' ἧς ἔφυ, 50
ὁ παῖς τε τοὺς τεκόντας οὐκ ἐπίσταται.
νέος μὲν οὖν ὢν ἀμφὶ βωμίους τροφὰς
ἠλᾶτ' ἀθύρων· ὡς δ' ἀπηνδρώθη δέμας,
Δελφοί σφ' ἔθεντο χρυσοφύλακα τοῦ θεοῦ
ταμίαν τε πάντων πιστὸν, ἐν δ' ἀνακτόροις 55
θεοῦ καταζῇ δεῦρ' ἀεὶ σεμνὸν βίον.
Κρέουσα δ' ἡ τεκοῦσα τὸν νεανίαν
Ξούθῳ γαμεῖται συμφορᾶς τοιᾶσδ' ὕπο·
ἦν ταῖς Ἀθήναις τοῖς τε Χαλκωδοντίδαις,
οἳ γῆν ἔχουσ' Εὐβοῖδα, πολέμιος κλύδων· 60
ὃν συμπονήσας καὶ ξυνεξελὼν δορὶ
γάμων Κρεούσης ἀξίωμ' ἐδέξατο,
οὐκ ἐγγενὴς ὢν, Αἰόλου δὲ τοῦ Διὸς
γεγὼς Ἀχαιός· χρόνια δὲ σπείρας λέχη,

49. τὸν σπείραντα. For οὐκ οἶδε Φοῖβον πατέρα ὄντα. Of course the sense is not, 'she knows not Phoebus *who* begot him,' but ὁ σπείρων is for πατήρ, as ἡ τεκοῦσα so often stands for μήτηρ, sometimes even with a genitive after it.— οἶδε, sc. ἡ προφῆτις.
52. νέος κτλ. 'Whilst then he was yet young, he used to ramble in boyish sport round the altars that fed him; but when he had come to man's stature, the Delphians appointed him gold-keeper of the god,' &c. Some difficulty seems to have been felt about the first of these lines, which Dr. Badham renders, "he wandered round the food of the altars, coaxing (for some)." Hermann too seems to have missed the sense, in translating ἠλᾶτο *exulabat*, and reading ἀμφιβωμίους, "quasi dicas ἠλᾶτο ἔχων ἀμφιβωμίους τροφάς." In his Preface however (p. v,) he gives the right sense from Seidler. The truth is, τροφαὶ here stands, (by an Attic idiom illustrated on Med. 68, πεσσοὺς προσελθών,) for τόπος ὅπου ἐτρέφετο, and βώμιοι is added to specify the source and nature of his maintenance,

the offerings at the altars, or the victims sacrificed thereon. Cf. v. 323, βωμοὶ μ' ἔφερβον, οὑπιών τ' ἀεὶ ξένος.—ἀθύρων, 'playing,' 'sporting.' Frag. 272, τίς δ' οὐχὶ χαίρει νηπίοις ἀθύρμασιν; The picture is prettily drawn by Euripides, who tenderly loved little children.
59. Chalcodon was an ancient king of Euboea, said to have been slain by Amphitryo, and to have given his name to the inhabitants of that island. Cf. v. 294—7. Barnes, after Brodaeus, cites Il. ii. 541, Χαλκωδοντιάδης, μεγαθύμων ἀρχὸς Ἀβάντων, where Eustathius has this comment, ὅτι δὲ οὕτω ἐπίσημος ὁ Χαλκώδων, ὡς ἀπ' αὐτοῦ καὶ Χαλκωδοντιάδας λέγεσθαι τοὺς Εὐβοεῖς, δηλοῖ Εὐριπίδης Ἴωνι, εἰπὼν, τοῖς Ἀθηναίοις τοῖς τε Χαλκωδοντιάδαις, οἳ γῆν ἔχουσιν Εὐβοΐδα.
62. The meaning is, ἠξιώθη γάμων, he was deemed worthy of receiving a reward in the marriage with Creusa. For ἀξίωμα is the honour, dignity &c., as in Orest. 9.
64. Ἀχαιός. Ἡ, the Aeolus (frag. 15,) the poet made Hellen the son of Zeus, and Aeolus the son of Hellen. Among

14 ΕΥΡΙΠΙΔΟΥ

ἄτεκνός ἐστι, καὶ Κρέουσ'· ὧν οὕνεκα 65
ἥκουσι πρὸς μαντεῖ' Ἀπόλλωνος τάδε
ἔρωτι παίδων. Λοξίας δὲ τὴν τύχην
ἐς τοῦτ' ἐλαύνει, κοὐ λέληθεν, ὡς δοκεῖ.
δώσει γὰρ εἰσελθόντι μαντεῖον τόδε
Ξούθῳ τὸν αὑτοῦ παῖδα, καὶ πεφυκέναι 70
κείνου σφε φήσει, μητρὸς ὡς ἐλθὼν δόμους
γνωσθῇ Κρεούσῃ, καὶ γάμοι τε Λοξίου
κρυπτοὶ γένωνται παῖς τ' ἔχῃ τὰ πρόσφορα·
Ἴωνα δ' αὐτὸν, κτίστορ' Ἀσιάδος χθονὸς,
ὄνομα κεκλῆσθαι θήσεται καθ' Ἑλλάδα. 75
ἀλλ' ἐς δαφνώδη γύαλα βήσομαι τάδε,
τὸ κρανθὲν ὡς ἂν ἐκμάθω παιδὸς πέρι.
ὁρῶ γὰρ ἐκβαίνοντα Λοξίου γόνον
τόνδ', ὡς πρὸ ναοῦ λαμπρὰ θῇ πυλώματα
δάφνης κλάδοισιν. ὄνομα δ', οὗ μέλλει τυχεῖν, 80
Ἴων' ἐγώ σφε πρῶτος ὀνομάζω θεῶν.

ΙΩΝ.

ἅρματα μὲν τάδε λαμπρὰ τεθρίππων

the sons of Aeolus he makes no mention of Xuthus. As Hellen was king of Phthia in Thessaly, *Achaean* here means, as it often does, *Phthian*, and has nothing to do with the Achaea in the Peloponnese, as Bothe imagined. See Rhes. 237. Heracl. 193.

68. ἐλαύνει. Apollo has merely postponed or held in abeyance the fortunes of his son Ion, and has not really forgotten him, as he seems to have done.

71. ὡς γνωσθῇ. If Ion had not been believed to be the son of Xuthus, the latter would not have taken him to Athens and introduced him to his house as his heir, inf. v. 655. The ἀναγνώρισις or recognition by Creusa in fact took place at Delphi; cf. v. 1395 seqq.

74. κτίστορα. He means that after Ion the colonies of Ionia in Asia Minor, or the twelve confederate Ionic cities in Caria and Lydia, were to take their name.

77. τὸ κρανθέν, κτλ. That he may hear the oracle which is to be delivered to Xuthus and Creusa.—γύαλα, any hollow, valley, or recess, especially applied to the site of Delphi. Cf. Androm. 1093, χρυσοῦ γέμοντα γύαλα.

79. πυλώματα. *Vestibulum*, the space in front of the door, which it was the duty of Ion to keep clean and bright (it being paved, perhaps, with polished marble,) by a brush or besom of bay-twigs, inf. 113. 145. Bothe understands this of affixing twigs of bay to the front of the temple, as on a festive occasion (v. 91). In the former case, which is supported by v. 103, 115, 121, &c., Ion must be supposed to be approaching with the necessary implements; in the latter case, bearing green twigs in his hand. The epithet λαμπρὰ is equally suited to either interpretation. Hermann inclines to Wakefield's reading προνάου, ' of the pronaos' or προνηΐον, Herod. i. 51. But cf. 129. A similar substantive προβώμιον occurs Heracl. 79.

81. σφε. This word was added by L. Dindorf. The MSS. have ἐγὼ πρῶτος, but one or two give ἔγωγε. Scaliger supplied νιν, and one or the other can hardly fail to be right, unless we read μέλλεις and ἐγώ σε κτλ., in which there is considerable probability.

82. Ion, a comely youth, now appears on the stage. He is habited as a servant,

ἥλιος ἤδη κάμπτει κατὰ γῆν,
ἄστρα δὲ φεύγει πῦρ τόδ' ἀπ' αἰθέρος
ἐς νύχθ' ἱερὰν, 85
Παρνησιάδες δ' ἄβατοι κορυφαὶ
καταλαμπόμεναι τὴν ἡμερίαν
ἀψῖδα βροτοῖσι δέχονται.
σμύρνης δ' ἀνύδρου καπνὸς εἰς ὀρόφους
Φοίβου πέτεται, 90
θάσσει δὲ γυνὴ τρίποδα ζάθεον

but not a humble one, of the august temple which is represented on the proscenium. He carries a bow and arrow, the usual accoutrement of Apollo (Alcest. 40), his patron-god. In a monody of remarkable beauty, and full of pure-minded and devout sentiments, he describes with enthusiasm the pleasure he takes in the service of the deity. It is morning; the peaks of Parnassus are just gilded with the first rays; it is a sacred day, for already the priestess has taken her seat on the prophetic tripod, and the incense fills the shrine with its fragrance. The Delphic people are warned to use good words, and to perform the prescribed rite of ablution in the spring of Castaly. For himself, he will sprinkle the pavement and sweep it with the tender and fragrant shoots of the bay. See! birds are already flying from Parnassus towards the temple. He bids them go; for the temple and its offerings may not be defiled.—The metre at first consists of pure and very elegant anapaestics. It then passes into varieties of the glyconic, and afterwards into irregular or spondaic anapaests (v. 144—183).

83. The old reading was λάμπει, 'lights up.' So Hel. 1131, δόλιον ἀστέρα λάμψας. Electr. 586, κατέλαμψας, ἔδειξας ἐμφανῆ πόλει πυρσόν. Compare Med. 1194, where the passive is used, as in καταλαμπόμενος inf. 87. Tro. 1070. Dr. Badham has edited κάμπτει, which is certainly ingenious and probable; 'Lo! here is the bright car of four yoked steeds, which now the sun is turning for their career over Earth; and the stars are retiring before this his blaze, from the ether into sacred night.' The objections to the vulgate are, first, that καταλαμπόμεναι occurs just below, and secondly, that λάμπει λαμπρὰ is very inharmonious; while κάμπτει is perfectly applicable to the turn round the stadium of the sun's celestial career upon the earth, the other limb of the δίαυλος representing his hidden path by night.

84. The common reading is πυρὶ τῷδ'. The oldest MS. (the Palatine) has πῦρ τόδ', whence Dr. Badham gives ἄστρα δὲ φεύγει πῦρ τόδ' ἀπ' αἰθέρος κτλ., which is certainly an improvement to both sense and metre.

86. ἄβατοι. Not 'inaccessible' from any difficulty of climbing them, but 'untrodden' because sacred to Bacchus and Apollo. Cf. Bacch. 10, αἰνῶ δὲ Κάδμον, ἄβατον ὃς πέδον τόδε τίθησι.

87. ἡμερίαν ἀψῖδα, diurnum currum, μεθημερινήν. The MSS. give ἡμέραν, emended by Canter. One has the gloss τὴν πραεῖαν, which Matthiae injudiciously admits with the addition of the useless particle γε. This gloss obviously refers to the corrupt reading ἡμέραν, as from ἥμερος.—βροτοῖσι is the dative used acquisitively, as grammarians call it; for the use of mortals, for their benefit and pleasure &c. – ἀψὶς, properly 'the wheel,' Hippol. 1233.

89. ἀνύδρου, the product of waterless deserts.—πέτεται Musgrave for πέταται. Hermann defends the vulgate, thinking πέταμαι connected rather with πετάννυμι than with πέτομαι. The root of the word, as shown on Med. 1, is πτε or πετ, and it is likely that πέταμαι was a form introduced by the grammarians, in their attempts to explain the irregular aorist ἐπτάμην. The idea of smoke or dust flying aloft on wings is defended by Tro. 1320. Aesch. Suppl. 761. "Tenendum est, diem, quo haec acta finguntur, ex maxime sanctis fuisse, caeremoniasque adeo hic enarrari non quotidianas, sed praecipui quiddam, quod talis diei solemnitas celebritasque exigebat." Bothe.

16   ΕΥΡΙΠΙΔΟΥ

Δελφὶς, ἀείδουσ᾽ Ἕλλησι βοὰς,
ἃς ἂν Ἀπόλλων κελαδήσῃ.
ἀλλ᾽, ὦ Φοίβου Δελφοὶ θέραπες,
τὰς Κασταλίας ἀργυροειδεῖς   95
βαίνετε δίνας, καθαραῖς δὲ δρόσοις
ἀφυδρανάμενοι στείχετε ναούς·
στόμα τ᾽ εὔφημον φρουρεῖτ᾽ ἀγαθὸν,
φήμας τ᾽ ἀγαθὰς τοῖς ἐθέλουσιν
μαντεύεσθαι   100
γλώσσης ἰδίας ἀποφαίνειν.
ἡμεῖς δὲ, πόνους οὓς ἐκ παιδὸς
μοχθοῦμεν ἀεὶ, πτόρθοισι δάφνης
στέφεσίν θ᾽ ἱεροῖς ἐσόδους Φοίβου
καθαρὰς θήσομεν ὑγραῖς τε πέδον   105
ῥανίσιν νοτερὸν, πτηνῶν τ᾽ ἀγέλας,
αἳ βλάπτουσιν

93. κελαδήσῃ. Properly, κελαδεῖν is 'to ring in one's ears,' and the idea is, that the priestess merely utters such sounds as Apollo may miraculously dictate. Compare Eum. 33, μαντεύομαι γὰρ ὡς ἂν ἡγῆται θεός. On the particular days appointed for giving oracles, which occurred once only in every month, see the note on Eum. 31. Inf. 420, βούλομαι δ᾽ ἐν ἡμέρᾳ τῇδ᾽, αἰσία γὰρ, θεοῦ λαβεῖν μαντεύματα.

94. θέραπες. All the Delphian people are probably meant. Some refer this to the ἐξηγηταὶ or ὑποφῆται, who made it their business and their profit to interpret the oracles to the applicants, ὡς τοὺς ἀκούοντας ἄλλου δεομένους Πυθίου πρὸς τὴν ἐξήγησιν τῶν χρησμῶν, Lucian, Vol. ii. p. 674, and who, by putting their own construction on the words of the god, as conveyed through the priestess, might be said to use τὴν ἰδίαν γλῶσσαν in contrast with the divine voice. Here nothing more seems to be meant, than a caution to use good words in the temple of the god of joy and brightness. The attendant ministers are desired to say nothing δύσφημον to the applicants for oracles on this day of peculiar sanctity; each is to keep guard over his own tongue, for it would have been thought unlucky to seek an oracular response just after one had heard some βλασφημία from any of the attendants. See inf. 1189.

98. For φρουρεῖτ᾽ L. Dindorf reads φρουρεῖν, sc. ἀγαθόν ἐστι, and for εὔφημον Dr. Badham proposes εὐφημεῖν, both of which rest on the supposition that ἀγαθὸν is superfluous after εὔφημον. The latter regards both εὐφημεῖν and ἀποφαίνειν as governed by φρουρεῖτ᾽, as Suppl. 900, ἐφρούρει μηδὲν ἐξαμαρτάνειν. There is however little difficulty in taking ἀποφαίνειν for ἀποφαίνετε, by a slight change of construction; and it is quite consistent with Greek usage to combine several epithets without any connecting particle. Bothe and Hermann read φρουρεῖτ᾽ ἀγαθῶν, the former omitting φήμας ἀγαθὰς as a gloss, the latter connecting ἀγαθῶν φήμας, bona bonorum omina.

105. Dr. Badham says that the metre of this verse and of v. 109, and the repetition of θήσομεν, indicate the patchwork of grammarians. There is certainly no law which forbids a dactyl following an anapaest, though the sort of rhythm it produces appears to have been thought less pleasing. It would be easy in the latter passage to read φυγάδας θήσω· τὼς γὰρ ἀμήτωρ κτλ. (for θήσω is better suited to ἐμοῖς, though τὼς is rather an Aeschylean word); but in this the preceding ἡμεῖς makes θήσομεν necessary.

σέμν' ἀναθήματα, τόξοισιν ἐμοῖς
φυγάδας θήσομεν· ὡς γὰρ ἀμήτωρ
ἀπάτωρ τε γεγὼς τοὺς θρέψαντας   110
Φοίβου ναοὺς θεραπεύω.
ἄγ' ὦ νεηθαλὲς ὦ   στρ.
καλλίστας προπόλευμα δάφνας,
ἃ τὰν Φοίβου θυμέλαν
σαίρεις ὑπὸ ναοῖς   115
κήπων ἐξ ἀθανάτων,
ἵνα δρόσοι τέγγουσ' ἱεραὶ
†τὰν ἀέναον παγὰν
ἐκπροϊεῖσαι
μυρσίνας ἱερὰν φόβαν,   120
ᾇ σαίρω δάπεδον θεοῦ
παναμέριος ἅμ' ἀελίου πτέρυγι θοᾷ
λατρεύων τὸ κατ' ἦμαρ.
ὦ Παιὰν ὦ Παιάν,
εὐαίων εὐαίων   125

112. Those who are fond of disparaging Euripides, and who see only a ludicrous or at least an unseemly image in the boy's address to his broom, should notice how a common-place idea can be rendered uncommon and even highly elegant by being invested with poetical language.—κάλλιστον, the reading of Dobree for καλλίστας, is adopted by Dr. Badham; but it does not seem more than probable.—προπόλευμα, 'sacred ministry,' from πρόπολος, the attendant on a god.

118. The old reading, τὰν ἀένναον παγὰν, is corrupt, not only on account of the form of the epithet (a slight matter, corrected by Hermann), but because something is wanting, certainly to the metre, and probably also to the sense. Dr. Badham is perhaps right in supposing τὰν an insertion of the transcribers. Either for ἵνα we should read ἃν, sc. ἣν δάφνην, or some accusative should be supplied as the lost word, if Dr. Badham rightly suggests μυρσίνας θ' ἱερὰν φόβαν in v. 120. And this is probable for two reasons:—it is not the usual custom of Euripides to separate the accusative from its verb by a parenthetical clause; and it is scarcely good sense to say, 'O bay tree,

from the garden of Phoebus, where fountains bedew the *myrtle* which I use.' But he might well say, 'O bay tree &c., where fountains bedew thee, *and* the myrtle which I use.' Comparing Hipp. 124, παγὰν προϊεῖσα κρημνῶν, and observing that the addition of ἐκ to the participle here seems to require some genitive, we might with some probability read thus;

ἃν δρόσοι τέγγουσ' ἱεραὶ
κρημνῶν ἀέναον παγὰν
ἐκπροϊεῖσαι,
μυρσίνας θ' ἱερὰν φόβαν, κτλ.

122. ἀελίου W. Dindorf for ἠελίου. He regards the α as short, making the verse a senarius of resolved feet, after Matthiae. The metre is rather doubtful; Hermann scans it as two glyconic verses, Bothe as an asynartete.—τὸ κατ' ἦμαρ, 'daily.' The meaning is, 'all day long and day by day.' The article is added as in the phrase τὸ μεσημβρινὸν, 'at midday,' Theocr. i. 15. Compare Electr. 145, γόους, οἷς ἀεὶ τὸ κατ' ἦμαρ διέπομαι.

125. εὐαίων εἴης. This appears rather a singular wish addressed to a god, 'mayst thou be happy,' especially as εὐαίων is

VOL. II.   D

εἴης, ὦ Λατοῦς παῖ.
καλόν γε τὸν πόνον, ὦ   ἀντ.
Φοῖβε, σοὶ πρὸ δόμων λατρεύω,
τιμῶν μαντεῖον ἕδραν·   130
κλεινὸς δ' ὁ πόνος μοι,
θεοῖσιν δούλαν χέρ' ἔχειν,
οὐ θνατοῖς, ἀλλ' ἀθανάτοις·
εὐφάμοις δὲ πόνοις μοχθεῖν
οὐκ ἀποκάμνω.   135
Φοῖβός μοι γενέτωρ πατήρ·
τὸν βόσκοντα γὰρ εὐλογῶ.
τὸ δ' ὠφέλιμον ἐμοὶ πατέρος ὄνομα λέγω
Φοίβου τοῦ κατὰ ναόν.
ὦ Παιὰν ὦ Παιάν,   140
εὐαίων εὐαίων
εἴης, ὦ Λατοῦς παῖ.
ἀλλ' ἐκπαύσω γὰρ μόχθους
δάφνας ὁλκοῖς·

peculiarly applied to the secure and tranquil life of the celestials, as Pers. 707, βίοτον εὐαίωνα, Πέρσαις ὡς θεὸς, διήγαγες. Bacch. 424, μισεῖ δ' (ὁ Διόνυσος) ᾧ μὴ ταῦτα μέλει, κατὰ φάος νύκτας τε φίλας εὐαίωνα διαζῆν. Trach. 81, βίοτον εὐαίων' ἔχειν, said of the destiny of Hercules. Probably here it is a formula of praise and worship addressed to the patron god, who was specially the god of joy and happiness.

133. Hermann places the colon after οὐ θνατοῖς, and reads εὐφάμοισι. But δὲ, which was before wanting, and was supplied by L. Dindorf on conjecture, has since been recovered from the Palatine MS. Porson would read εὐφήμους πόνους, but the dative seems as legitimate as the cognate accusative. The sense is, ' At labours that are holy I am never weary of toiling.'

137. εὐλογῶ, scil. ὡς πατέρα, καίπερ οὐκ ὄντα.

138. τὸ δ' ὠφέλιμον κτλ. The old reading τὸν δ' ὠφ. was corrected by Musgrave. It was not so much the *name*, according to Hermann's view, as the god himself who was ὠφέλιμος. He considers the meaning to be, Φοῖβον—πατέρα λέγω, ὠφέλιμον ἐμοὶ ὄντα, but we need not press this, if we translate simply,

' And the name of *father* which is serviceable to me, that of Phoebus the god of this temple, I repeat.' It was the name or repute of Phoebus, as the oracular god, that brought visitors to his shrine, and, consequently, maintenance to his servant: and it was as necessary to Ion as to any one else, on other considerations, to be accounted γνήσιος. To construe, as Dr. Badham does, ' I call the usefulness of Phoebus to me by the name of father,' is totally to overlook the order of the words.

143. Here follows a system of those irregular spondaic anapaests, the principles of which have been pointed out on Tro. 99. See inf. 881 seqq. There appears to be nothing more exceptional in vv. 148—50, than is occasionally to be met with in such verses, where resolved feet are allowed a place. Thus, if ⏑⏑⏑⏑ be taken as isochronous with ‒ ‒, the four verses may be scanned as monometer hypercatalectic anapaestics. See Hec. 62. 76. 1072. Hermann and Dind. prefer to call ἂν—δῖναι dochmiac. The form ἀποχεύονται, i. e. ἀποχέϜονται, is deserving of notice. The digamma appears also in χεύσω and ἔχευα. Cf. Hes. Opp. 580, ἠχέτα τέττιξ δένδρῳ ἐφεζόμενος λιγυρὴν ἐπιχεύετ' ἀοιδήν.

ΙΩΝ.

χρυσέων δ' ἐκ τευχέων ῥίψω 145
γαίας παγὰν,
ἂν ἀποχεύονται
Κασταλίας δῖναι,
νοτερὸν ὕδωρ βάλλων,
ὅσιος ἀπ' εὐνᾶς ὤν. 150
εἴθ' οὕτως ἀεὶ Φοίβῳ
λατρεύων μὴ παυσαίμαν, ἢ
παυσαίμαν ἀγαθᾷ μοίρᾳ.
ἔα ἔα.
φοιτῶσ' ἤδη λείπουσίν τε
πτανοὶ Παρνασοῦ κοίτας· 155
αὐδῶ μὴ χρίμπτειν θριγκοῖς
μηδ' ἐς χρυσήρεις οἴκους.
μάρψω σ' αὖ τόξοις, ὦ Ζηνὸς
κῆρυξ, ὀρνίθων γαμφηλαῖς
ἰσχὺν νικῶν· 160
ὅδε πρὸς θυμέλας ἄλλος ἐρέσσει
κύκνος· οὐκ ἄλλᾳ
φοινικοφαῆ πόδα κινήσεις ;
οὐδέν σ' ἁ φόρμιγξ ἁ Φοίβου
σύμμολπος τόξων ῥύσαιτ' ἄν· 165
πάραγε πτέρυγας·
λίμνας ἐπίβα τᾶς Δηλιάδος·
αἱμάξεις, εἰ μὴ πείσει,
τὰς καλλιφθόγγους ᾠδάς.

150. ὅσιος ἀπ' εὐνᾶς. "Alioqui lustratione ei opus fuisset ante faciendam rem sacram." *Bothe.*
151. ἀεὶ Elmsley for ἀρὰ or ἀρεί.—ἀγαθᾷ μοίρᾳ, εὐτυχῶς, a wish having reference to the great fortunes which really await him.
157. οἴκους. Dr. Badham's conjecture, τοίχους, on account of the better apposition to θριγκοῖς, is elegant.
158. Ζηνὸς κῆρυξ, the eagle, which is supposed to be flying overhead.—αὖ, a second time, implying that his skill with the bow had been proved on a former occasion. Bothe absurdly gives μάρψω σ'

ἄν.—ὀρνίθων ἰσχὺν, i. e. the strongest birds that you attack.
161. ἄλλος κύκνος. Not 'another swan,' but 'another bird, and that a swan.' So Aeschylus, in describing, after the diminutive Tydeus (μικρὸς δέμας, Il. v. 801), the huge Capaneus, says γίγας ὅδ' ἄλλος, Theb. 419.
164. οὐδὲν κτλ. The sense is, 'the fact of your being musical in common with Phoebus, will not protect you from this bow, if you profane his shrine.'
169. ᾠδάς. Poetically used for τὴν καλλίφθογγον δέρην.

ἔα ἔα. 170
τίς ὅδ᾽ ὀρνίθων καινὸς προσέβα ;
μῶν ὑπὸ θριγκοὺς εὐναίας
καρφηρὰς θήσων τέκνοις ;
ψαλμοί σ᾽ εἴρξουσιν τόξων.
οὐ πείσει ; χωρῶν ἐν δίναις
ταῖς Ἀλφειοῦ παιδούργει, 175
ἢ νάπος Ἴσθμιον,
ὡς ἀναθήματα μὴ βλάπτηται
ναοί θ᾽ οἱ Φοίβου.
κτείνειν δ᾽ ὑμᾶς αἰδοῦμαι
τοὺς θεῶν ἀγγέλλοντας φάμας 180
θνατοῖς· οἷς δ᾽ ἔγκειμαι μόχθοις,
Φοίβῳ δουλεύσω, κοὐ λήξω
τοὺς βόσκοντας θεραπεύων.

ΧΟΡΟΣ.

ΧΟ. α΄. οὐκ ἐν ταῖς ζαθέαις Ἀθά- στρ. α΄.

173. καρφηρὰς, properly an adjective, is explained by Hesychius, from this passage, αἱ ἐκ τῶν ξηρῶν ξύλων γινόμεναι κοῖται. But he erroneously writes it καρφυλαί, whence Musgrave proposed καρφηλὰς, a substantive formed like θυηλὴ, γαμφηλὴ, &c. But Hermann observes that the order of the letters in Hesychius shows that he wrote καρφυραί. The word is formed from κάρφος, a bit of dry stick ; and it is a question whether we should not read καρφήρεις rather than καρφηράς. See on v. 1123. Bacch. 107. In either case, εὐναία seems to have been used for εὐνὴ, like the plural οὐραῖα in v. 1154.—ψαλμοὶ, the *twang*, or sharp pulling of the string. Bacch. 784, πέλτας θ᾽ ὅσοι πάλλουσι, καὶ τόξων χερὶ ψάλλουσι νευράς. Herc. F. 1064, τοξήρει ψαλμῷ τοξεύσας.
177. βλάπτηται. The allusion is to the dirt of birds, to which, especially on the statues of the gods, the Greeks had a superstitious objection. See the note on ἐπ᾽ ὀρόφων μιαίνοντα, Aesch. Suppl. 637.
178. The metre is the same as 148—50 and 908—9. W. Dindorf very needlessly marks the loss of one or more words.

179. κτείνειν. I warn you to depart, for I have a reluctance to slay the interpreters of the god's will to mankind. In all the actions and the language of Ion a ceremonial piety is observable ; cf. v. 1191.
184. Ion has now retired into the temple to perform such duties as required his presence there. The chorus, advancing in front of the temple, amuse themselves by commenting on the sculptures and statues exhibited on the façade of the proscenium and hyposcenia. It was a common practice for strangers to do this : the party of Neoptolemus spent three days in sight-seeing at Delphi, Androm. 1086. The metre now passes to glyconic. According to Hermann, the first speech in each strophe and antistrophe is spoken by the Leader of the chorus, the rest being the remarks of the individual choreutae (fourteen in number, exclusive of the Hegemon,) to her and to each other. We have already seen an instance of this division of an ode into fifteen distinct speeches, in Hippol. 1102 seqq. Dindorf divides στρ. α΄, ἀντ. α΄, and στρ. β΄, between the hemichoria, while ἀντ. β΄, (which, the student will carefully observe, is interpolated with anapaestic verses of

ναις εὐκίονες ἦσαν αὐ- 185
λαὶ θεῶν μόνον, οὐδ' ἀγυιάτιδες θεραπεῖαι·
ἀλλὰ καὶ παρὰ Λοξίᾳ
τῷ Λατοῦς διδύμων προσώ-
πων <u>καλλιβλέφαρον</u> φῶς.
ΧΟ. β'. ἰδοὺ τάνδ' ἄθρησον, 190
Λερναῖον ὕδραν ἐναίρει
χρυσέαις ἅρπαις ὁ Διὸς παῖς·
φίλα, πρόσιδ' ὄσσοις.
ΧΟ. α'. ὁρῶ. καὶ πέλας ἄλλος αὐ-   ἀντ. α'.
τοῦ πανὸν πυρίφλεκτον αἴ- 195
ρει· τίς ; ἆρ' ὃς ἐμαῖσι μυ-

Ion's, not included in the antithetical arrangement,) is given by him to the Chorus, meaning probably, distinct persons of the Chorus. The present editor has followed Hermann; in the old copies there is, as usual, much confusion and inaccuracy respecting the persons.
186. The chorus, consisting of Athenian handmaidens, the attendants on Creusa, remark that there were other temples beside those in their native city which contained fair sculptures.—ἀγυιάτιδες, the service of Apollo ἀγυιεύς. See Phoen. 631. Aesch. Agam. 1048. Hesychius, quoted by Hermann, ἀγυιάτιδες, αἱ πρὸ τῶν θυρῶν θεραπεῖαι. The present passage is so evidently referred to, that we may safely read ἀγυιάτιδες θεραπεῖαι· αἱ πρὸ τῶν θυρῶν. The altar of this god was regularly placed on the stage near the central or main entrance of the proscenium.— ἀλλὰ Hermann for ἀλλά γε.
189 καλλιβλέφαρον. So Brodaeus for καλλίφαρον. In long words, especially in compounds, a syllable was occasionally overlooked by the scribes, as in Aesch. Suppl. 3, the MSS. give λεπτομαθῶν for λεπτοψαμάθων, and ibid. v. 355, γεραφρονῶν for γεραροφρονῶν. Perhaps this in some measure supports the correction proposed inf. 390, ἐξερευνᾶν for ἐᾶν. A curious example occurs in Troad. 444, where ἐξακοντίζω has been corrupted first into ἐξαντίζω, then into ἐξανθίζω. So perhaps inf. 1396, πολεμία has successively become πολία and πολλά. And in Electr. 181, Porson has successfully restored χορεύω for χεύω. The sun and the moon, symbols of Apollo and Latona, appear to be indicated. This is at least probable from the word φῶς. Hermann thinks statues are meant. A similar instance of a symbolical painting, the sun represented under the figure of a cock, occurs in Aesch. Suppl. 208. The commentators differ as to which is intended by the following description, painting or statuary. The argument of Musgrave is in favour of the former is ingenious, that the *golden* sickle, the *blazing* torch, the *fire-breathing* chimaera, are subjects requiring colour for their full effect. Dindorf sees in v. 206 an allusion to the Gigantomachia embroidered on the peplus of Pallas. The question is by no means important; in either case a magnificent stage effect must have been produced. Musgrave further supposes, (and as Hermann thinks, with probability,) that the poet is describing the new portico which the Athenians had just before dedicated at Delphi. Pausan. x. 11, 5, ᾠκοδόμησαν δὲ καὶ Ἀθηναῖοι στοὰν ἀπὸ χρημάτων, ἃ ἐν τῷ πολέμῳ σφίσιν ἐγένετο ἀπό τε Πελοποννησίων, καὶ ὅσοι Πελοποννησίοις ἦσαν τοῦ Ἑλληνικοῦ σύμμαχοι. ἀνάκειται δὲ καὶ πλοίων τὰ ἄκρα κοσμήματα καὶ ἀσπίδες χαλκαῖ.—τὸ ἐπίγραμμα ἐς Φορμίωνα τὸν Ἀσωπίχου ἐστὶ ἐς τοῦ Φορμίωνος τὰ ἔργα. The victory of Phormio over the Lacedaemonians at Rhium took place in Ol. 87. 4, and the date of this play is placed somewhere between Ol. 88 and Ol. 91.

θεύεται παρὰ πήναις
ἀσπιστὰς Ἰόλαος, ὃς
κοινοὺς αἰρόμενος πόνους
Δίῳ παιδὶ συναντλεῖ; 200
ΧΟ. γ'. καὶ μὰν τόνδ' ἄθρησον
πτεροῦντος ἔφεδρον ἵππου·
τὰν πυρπνέουσαν ἐναίρει
τρισώματον ἀλκάν.
ΧΟ. α'. παντᾷ τοι βλέφαρον διώκω. στρ. β'. 205
σκέψαι κλόνον ἐν †τείχεσι
λαΐνοισι Γιγάντων.
ΧΟ. δ'. ὧδε δερκόμεθ', ὦ φίλαι, * *
ΧΟ. ε'. λεύσσεις οὖν ἐπ' Ἐγκελάδῳ
γοργωπὸν πάλλουσαν ἴτυν; 210
ΧΟ. ϛ'. λεύσσω Παλλάδ' ἐμὰν θεόν.
ΧΟ. ζ'. τί γάρ; κεραυνὸν
ἀμφίπυρον ὄβριμον ἐν Διὸς
ἑκηβόλοισι χερσίν;
ΧΟ. η'. ὁρῶ, τὸν δάϊον Μίμαντα
πυρὶ καταιθαλοῖ. 215

196. μυθεύεται. 'Is it not he, whose legend is related to me as I sit at my weaving?' i. e. described by another who superintends the working of the story in embroidered patterns. Cf. 506. Virg. Georg. iv. 334, 345.

201. τόνδε, Bellerophon, who rode on the winged Pegasus to slay the Chimaera. —τρισώματος, made up of three forms, a lion in front, a snake behind, and a goat in the middle. An ancient Terra-cotta of this monster is engraved on the title-page of Sir Charles Fellows' Travels in Lycia. He remarks on it (p. 348), "The Lion is seen everywhere throughout the valley of the Xanthus: every bas-relief, tomb, seat or coin, shows the figure or limbs of this animal. Lions still live in its mountains, the goat is found at the top, while the serpent infests the base of the Cragus, illustrating the imaginary monster of its early fables." The epithet πυρπνέουσαν is readily explained by referring it to a volcanic mountain, probably the *Yanah Dah*, on the east coast of Lycia, where a jet of inflammable gas is constantly burning. Cf. Electr. 474, πύρπνοος ἔσπευδε δρόμῳ λέαινα χαλαῖς.

206. τείχεσι. This word is corrupt. Hermann gives τύκαισι, (i. e. τυκίσμασι, Herc. 1096,) Musgrave πτυχαῖσι, from Hesych. πτυχαί, στοαί, περιβολαί. The latter has been admitted by Dr. Badham, and is highly plausible.

208. A word is lost at the end of this line. Dr. Badham supplies γυναῖκες. In v. 223 πυθοίμεθ' is a likely reading.

209—10. Neither of these verses appears exactly to suit the antistrophe. But the difference in fact consists merely in the change of place of the choriambus, a legitimate variation. As they now stand, each verse is *glyconeus polyschematistus*.

211. ἐμὰν θεόν. 'I see,' replies the other, 'the same goddess whom I worship at Athens.'—θεὸν is to be scanned as a monosyllable.

215. For the device (in embroidery) of Zeus slaying the Giants, see Hec. 470.

ΧΟ. θ'. καὶ Βρόμιος ἄλλον
ἀπολέμοις κισσίνοισι βάκτροις
ἐναίρει Γᾶς τέκνων ὁ Βακχεύς.
ΧΟ. α'. σέ τοι τὸν παρὰ ναὸν αὐδῶ,   ἀντ. β'.
θέμις γυάλων ὑπερβῆ-   220
ναι λευκῷ ποδί γ' * *.
ΙΩ. οὐ θέμις, ὦ ξέναι.
ΧΟ. ί. οὐδ' ἂν ἐκ σέθεν ἂν πυθοίμαν αὐδάν;
ΙΩ. τίνα δῆτα θέλεις;
ΧΟ. ια'. ἆρ' ὄντως μέσον ὀμφαλὸν
γᾶς Φοίβου κατέχει δόμος;
ΙΩ. στέμμασί γ' ἐνδυτὸν, ἀμφὶ δὲ Γοργόνες.
ΧΟ. ιβ'. οὕτω καὶ φάτις αὐδᾷ.   225
ΙΩ. εἰ μὲν ἐθύσατε πέλανον πρὸ δόμων

218. τέκνων Hermann and Elmsley for τέκνον. By ἄλλον Γᾶς τέκνων Alcyoneus is said to be meant, one of the giants slain by Bacchus, for which Hermann quotes the authority of Nonnus, lib. xxv. 90. But why not Rhoetus? Of whom Horace writes, Od. ii. 19, 21, 'Tu cum parentis regna per ardua Cohors Gigantum scanderet impia, Rhoetum retorsisti leonis Unguibus, horribilique mala.' Bacchus had slain him by the ivied wand, and not with the pointed thyrsus. On the distinction between these, see Bacch. 704. For ὁ Βακχεὺς, see ibid. 145.

219. Ion here re-appears from within the shrine. He is asked whether he will permit the strangers to pass beyond the inclosure. On his informing them that it is not lawful, they inquire into the truth of the rumour they have heard, that Delphi stands in the very centre of the earth. After ποδὶ some word is lost. Possibly the γ' is the first letter of it. Hermann supplies βηλὸν (βαλὸν Dind.), but it is uncertain what is meant by γυάλων. One would almost fancy some kind of intervening τάφρος or moat was had in view. Perhaps it was a general term, properly meaning the valley, the site of the temple, and thence the temple itself, as it appears to do in Androm. 1093, χρυσοῦ γέμοντα γύαλα, θησαυροὺς βροτῶν. —λευκῷ ποδὶ, which some understand of the naked foot, is rather, perhaps, an epitheton ornans. Cf. Cycl. 72.

224. ἐνδυτὸν for —ὸς Musgrave. It was not the temple, but the altar known as the ὀμφαλὸς (Eum. 40) that was so adorned. Hermann quotes Strabo, lib. ix. p. 420, δείκνυνται δὲ καὶ ὀμφαλὸς ἐν τῷ ναῷ τεταινιωμένος, καὶ ἐπ' αὐτῷ αἱ δύο εἰκόνες τοῦ μύθου. These latter he thinks our poet calls Gorgons; but the geographer seems rather to speak of the two eagles whom Zeus sent from the two ends of the earth, and which were fabled to have met at Delphi. Hence μεσόμφαλόν θ' ἵδρυμα, Λοξίου πέδον, Aesch. Cho. 1025. We may perhaps understand those ancient sculptures which Aeschylus calls Γοργεῖοι τύποι, Eum. 49, on which see Müller's Dissertation, p. 188.

226. ἐθύσατε πέλανον. On the rare licence of an anapaest following a dactyl, see Tro. 177. So in Hec. 99, πέμψατε, δαίμονες, ἱκετεύω. It is however questionable whether the singular ought not to be restored in this passage, which would then be read thus, (see above, v. 105, 109,)

εἰ μὲν ἔθυσας πέλανον πρὸ δόμων
καί τι πυθέσθαι χρῄζεις Φοίβου,
πάριθ' ἐς θυμέλας· ἐπὶ δ' ἀσφάκτοις
μήλοισι δόμων μὴ πάριθ' ἐς μυχόν.

There are two conditions upon which Ion is willing, notwithstanding his former prohibition, to admit the women; they must offer a salt cake, or lesser sacrifice, as an earnest of their devotion, and they must have the intention of obtaining an

καί τι πυθέσθαι χρήζετε Φοίβου,
πάριτ' ἐς θυμέλας· ἐπὶ δ' ἀσφάκτοις
μήλοισι δόμων μὴ πάριτ' ἐς μυχόν.
ΧΟ. ιγ'. ἔχω μαθοῦσα· 230
θεοῦ δὲ νόμον οὐ παραβαίνομεν·
ἃ δ' ἐκτὸς, ὄμμα τέρψει.
ΙΩ. πάντα θεᾶσθ', ὅ τι καὶ θέμις, ὄμμασι.
ΧΟ. ιδ'. μεθεῖσαν δεσπόται θεοῦ με
γύαλα τάδ' εἰσιδεῖν.
ΙΩ. δμωαὶ δὲ τίνων κλῄζεσθε δόμων;
ΧΟ. ιε'. Παλλάδος ἔνοικα 235
τρόφιμα μέλαθρα τῶν ἐμῶν τυράννων.
παρούσας δ' ἀμφὶ τᾶσδ' ἐρωτᾷς.
ΙΩ. γενναιότης σοι, καὶ τρόπων τεκμήριον

oracular response. But to be admitted into the actual adytum, δόμων μυχὸν, could not be allowed without the sacrifice of living victims. To the latter indeed it appears doubtful if women were ever admitted, as Musgrave shows from Plutarch, Op. Mor. p. 685. Dr. Badham contends that both θυμέλαι and μυχὸς must mean the actual χρηστήρια, because the poet would not otherwise have added καί τι πυθέσθαι &c. The explanation given above makes this clear, and some distinction between πέλανος and μῆλα seems evidently intended.—ἐπὶ ἀσφάκτοις μήλοις is literally, ' with sheep unslaughtered.' So Antig. 556, ἀλλ' οὐκ ἐπ' ἀρρήτοις γε τοῖς ἐμοῖς λόγοις, ' at all events not with my words unsaid.'

231. θεοῦ is again a monosyllable, as in v. 211.—οὐ παραβαίνομεν, we are not for transgressing, we are content to stay here.

233. μεθεῖσαν, have let me go, have given me the liberty &c. This verse is antispastic, and the next a dochmiac. Hermann transposes the two last words, and makes με θεοῦ γύαλα τάδ' εἰσιδεῖν one verse, in which he is followed by W. Dindorf, θεοῦ being one syllable.

235. To the question, ' Of what house are ye the handmaids?' the reply is, 'The temple dwelt in by Pallas is the home of my masters,' i. e. of Creusa and Xuthus. As Ion himself was nurtured in and by the temple of Apollo, so the Chorus represent their masters as the servants of the goddess at Athens. Dr. Badham can make nothing of the passage, without reading Παλλάδος σύνοικα κτλ., ' the house in which my masters were bred and born is in the neighbourhood of the Temple of Pallas.' But this alteration is against the metre, which is iambic, the next being apparently antispastic, and identical with v. 214, ὁρῶ τὸν δάϊον Μίμαντα, except that the first long syllable is resolved into two short. The common reading perhaps requires to be corrected by the omission of τῶν before ἐμῶν. Hermann and Dindorf give ἀπολέμοισι after Musgrave, in v. 217.

237. παρούσας, i. e. παρούσης. ' But you are asking about one who is present here before you,' viz. Creusa, whom they call δέσποινα in v. 567. She has been seen approaching, and is now at hand to receive the greeting of Ion.

238. γενναιότητος τῶν τρόπων is Boissonade's conjecture, admitted by Dr. Badham. But the change is surely needless, and indeed the use of the article with τρόπων, when it is omitted with the former noun, is not very common. The sense is the same as γενναία τις εἶ, and with τρόπων it is self-evident that γενναίων or some such word must be mentally supplied. 'You are well born,' he says, ' and your demeanour is a proof of it.' We are in the habit of saying a person looks like a lady or gentleman, judging merely by that nameless something which is implied in σχῆμα.

τὸ σχῆμ' ἔχεις τόδ', ἥτις εἶ ποτ', ὦ γύναι.
γνοίη δ' ἂν ὡς τὰ πολλά γ' ἀνθρώπου πέρι
τὸ σχῆμ' ἰδών τις εἰ πέφυκεν εὐγενής. 240
ἔα·
ἀλλ' ἐξέπληξάς μ' ὄμμα συγκλῄσασα σὸν
δακρύοις θ' ὑγράνασ' εὐγενῆ παρηίδα,
ὡς εἶδες ἁγνὰ Λοξίου χρηστήρια.
τί ποτε μερίμνης ἐς τόδ' ἦλθες, ὦ γύναι;
οὗ πάντες ἄλλοι γύαλα λεύσσοντες θεοῦ 245
χαίρουσιν, ἐνταῦθ' ὄμμα σὸν δακρυρροεῖ.

ΚΡΕΟΥΣΑ.

ὦ ξένε, τὸ μὲν σὸν οὐκ ἀπαιδεύτως ἔχει
ἐς θαύματ' ἐλθεῖν δακρύων ἐμῶν πέρι·
ἐγὼ δ' ἰδοῦσα τούσδ' Ἀπόλλωνος δόμους
μνήμην παλαιὰν ἀνεμετρησάμην τινά, 250
οἴκοι δὲ τὸν νοῦν ἔσχον ἐνθάδ' οὖσά που.
ὦ τλήμονες γυναῖκες· ὦ τολμήματα
θεῶν. τί δῆτα; ποῖ δίκην ἀνοίσομεν,

246. χαίρουσι. Here is a clear allusion to that superstition of the Greeks which made them dislike to combine in any way, even in narration, the joyful with the sorrowful. And the doctrine is a key to the right understanding of many passages. Thus *inf.* 1017, κακῷ γὰρ ἐσθλὸν οὐ συμμίγνυται. Aesch. Ag. 619, εὔφημον ἦμαρ οὐ πρέπει κακαγγέλῳ γλώσσῃ μιαίνειν· χωρὶς ἡ τιμὴ θεῶν. Compare Phoen. 1215—17. Inf. 639, ὑπηρετῶν χαίρουσιν, οὐ γοωμένοις. Suppl. 289, μὴ δακρυρροέι, σεμναῖσι Δηοῦς ἐσχάραις παρημένη. See the note *ibid.* v. 38, and on Hippol. 792. Especially did they think it wrong to appear before Phoebus, the god of joy and brightness, with a sorrowful face. Hence Ag. 1041, τί ταῦτ' ἀνωτότυξας ἀμφὶ Λοξίου; Οὐ γὰρ τοιοῦτος ὥστε θρηνητοῦ τυχεῖν.

247. οὐκ ἀπαιδεύτως ἔχει. It is very polite in you, it shows your good breeding, to express surprise at, and to inquire the cause of, my tears.—ἐγὼ δὲ κτλ., 'The fact is, that I,' &c.

251. ἔσχον. This, though only a conjecture of H. Stephens, appears the true reading. The MSS. give ἔχομεν or ἔσχο-

μεν. The plural is retained by Hermann and Dindorf, and it might indeed be defended, construed with a participle in the singular, as *inf.* 1251, διωκόμεσθα—κρατηθεῖσα. But the aorist seems required by the sense: 'I *had* my thoughts at home, though bodily present here.' Dobree and Hermann give περ for που. Mr. Burges, on Troad. 662, proposes ἐκεῖ for οἴκοι, by which a good antithesis is gained with ἐνθάδε.

253. ποῖ; ἐς τίνα; 'to whom shall we refer the attribute of *Just*, or in whose hands is justice placed, if the gods our superiors are themselves unjust to us?' So Bacch. 29, ἐς Ζῆν' ἀναφέρειν τὴν ἁμαρτίαν λέχους. The old reading ἀνήσομεν was corrected by Musgrave, and ὀλοίμεθα by Matthiae. The former is however retained by Bothe, in the sense 'to whom shall we commit the exercise of justice?' But οι and η are very often confused, e. g. *inf.* v. 1351, 1396. The sentiment is quite in accordance with the feeling elsewhere shown by Euripides about the charges of immorality which the common legends brought against the gods. See Androm. 1161, *inf.* 436 seqq.

VOL. II. E

ΕΥΡΙΠΙΔΟΥ

εἰ τῶν κρατούντων ἀδικίαις ὀλούμεθα;
ΙΩ. τί χρῆμα δ' ἀνερεύνητα δυσθυμεῖ, γύναι; 255
ΚΡ. οὐδέν, μεθῆκα τόξα· τἀπὶ τῷδε δὲ
ἐγώ τε σιγῶ καὶ σὺ μὴ φρόντιζ' ἔτι.
ΙΩ. τίς δ' εἶ; πόθεν γῆς ἦλθες; ἐκ ποίου πατρὸς
πέφυκας; ὄνομα τί σε καλεῖν ἡμᾶς χρεών;
ΚΡ. Κρέουσα μέν μοι τοὔνομ', ἐκ δ' Ἐρεχθέως 260
πέφυκα, πατρὶς γῆ δ' Ἀθηναίων πόλις.
ΙΩ. ὦ κλεινὸν οἰκοῦσ' ἄστυ, γενναίων τ' ἄπο
τραφεῖσα πατέρων, ὥς σε θαυμάζω, γύναι.
ΚΡ. τοσαῦτα κεὐτυχοῦμεν, ὦ ξέν', οὐ πέρα.
ΙΩ. πρὸς θεῶν ἀληθῶς, ὡς μεμύθευται βροτοῖς, 265
ΚΡ. τί χρῆμ' ἐρωτᾷς, ὦ ξέν', ἐκμαθεῖν θέλω.
ΙΩ. ἐκ γῆς πατρός σου πρόγονος ἔβλαστεν πατήρ;
ΚΡ. Ἐριχθόνιός γε· τὸ δὲ γένος μ' οὐκ ὠφελεῖ.
ΙΩ. ἦ καί σφ' Ἀθάνα γῆθεν ἐξανείλετο;
ΚΡ. ἐς παρθένους γε χεῖρας, οὐ τεκοῦσά νιν. 270

255. ἀνερεύνητα. 'About matters not to be inquired into by me.' He says this, because she had given no direct reply to his question at v. 244, τί ποτε μερίμνης ἐς τόδ' ἦλθες, ὦ γύναι; The accusative is used after δυσθυμεῖσθαι (Med. 91), according to the usual syntax of verbs expressing mental emotion, as χαίρειν, δυσχεραίνειν τι &c.
256. Hermann construes οὐδὲν μεθῆκα τόξα temere haec dicta jeci, and he compares ξίφος μεθιέναι ἔς τινα, Orest. 1133. But how can οὐδὲν stand for εἰκῆ or μάτην? The old way, of putting a stop at οὐδέν, seems much better : ' 'Tis nothing ; I relax (or drop) my bow ;' i. e. I say not a word further. So οὐδέν is used in v. 288. For τοξεύειν = λέγειν cf. Hec. 603, καὶ ταῦτα μὲν δὴ νοῦς ἐτόξευσεν μάτην. Eum. 646, ἡμῖν μὲν ἤδη πᾶν τετόξευται βέλος. Androm. 365, καί σου τὸ σῶφρον ἐξετόξευσεν φρενός, 'has expended its arrows,' 'has said all it could say.'
258. ποίου πατρός. Dr. Badham and G. Dindorf adopt this correction of L. Dindorf and Bothe for ποίας πάτρας. To the three questions as to country, parents, and name, Creusa replies in inverted order, name, parents, and country. This is a strong argument that πατρὸς is right. But Hermann says, "sine libris non praeferam in poeta patriae commemorandae studioso."
266. θέλω. Dr. Badham reads θέλων, i. e. τί χρῆμα ἐκμαθεῖν θέλεις ἐρωτῶν; He calls θέλω 'a languid addition ;' but such additions are in fact common in a στιχομυθία, where the filling up a single verse was sometimes a matter of some little difficulty. Creusa shows her willingness to listen at v. 276.
267. πρόγονος. The pedigree was, Erichthonius, Pandion, Erechtheus, Creusa.
270. ἐς π. χεῖρας. 'Into her own virgin hands, not being his mother.' He was born from Hephaestus in consequence of attempted violence to Pallas ; but the poet means, that though a son was born, and even acknowledged in a manner by the goddess, she still retained her virginity. Apollodor. iii. 14, 6, φευγούσης δὲ αὐτῆς, καὶ τῆς γονῆς εἰς γῆν πεσούσης, Ἐριχθόνιος γίνεται. Τοῦτον Ἀθηνᾶ κρύφα τῶν ἄλλων θεῶν ἔτρεφεν, ἀθάνατον θέλουσα ποιῆσαι· καὶ καταθεῖσα αὐτὸν εἰς κίστην, Πανδρόσῳ τῇ Κέκροπος παρακατέθετο, ἀπειποῦσα τὴν κίστην ἀνοίγειν. Αἱ δὲ ἀδελφαὶ τῆς Πανδρόσου ἀνοίγουσιν ὑπὸ περιεργίας, καὶ θεῶνται τῷ βρέφει παρεσπειραμένον (cf. παραζεύξασα, above, v. 22), δράκοντα· καὶ ὡς μὲν ἔνιοι

ΙΩΝ.   27

ΙΩ.   δίδωσι δ', ὥσπερ ἐν γραφῇ νομίζεται ;
ΚΡ.   Κέκροπός γε σώζειν παισὶν οὐχ ὁρώμενον.
ΙΩ.   ἤκουσα λῦσαι παρθένους τεῦχος θεᾶς.
ΚΡ.   τοιγὰρ θανοῦσαι σκόπελον ἤμαξαν πέτρας.
ΙΩ.   εἶεν·
       τί δαὶ τόδ' ; ἆρ' ἀληθὲς ἢ μάτην λόγος ;   275
ΚΡ.   τί χρῆμ' ἐρωτᾷς ; καὶ γὰρ οὐ κάμνω σχολῇ.
ΙΩ.   πατὴρ Ἐρεχθεὺς σὰς ἔθυσε συγγόνους ;
ΚΡ.   ἔτλη πρὸ γαίας σφάγια παρθένους κτανεῖν.
ΙΩ.   σὺ δ' ἐξεσώθης πῶς κασιγνήτων μόνη ;
ΚΡ.   βρέφος νεογνὸν μητρὸς ἦν ἐν ἀγκάλαις.   280
ΙΩ.   πατέρα δ' ἀληθῶς χάσμα σὸν κρύπτει χθονός ;
ΚΡ.   πληγαὶ τριαίνης ποντίου σφ' ἀπώλεσαν.
ΙΩ.   Μακραὶ δὲ χῶρός ἐστ' ἐκεῖ κεκλημένος ;
ΚΡ.   τί δ' ἱστορεῖς τόδ' ; ὥς μ' ἀνέμνησάς τινος.
ΙΩ.   τιμᾷ σφε Πύθιος ἀστραπαί τε Πύθιαι ;   285

λέγουσιν, ὑπ' αὐτοῦ διεφθάρησαν τοῦ δράκοντος, ὡς δὲ ἔνιοι, δι' ὀργὴν Ἀθηνᾶς ἐμμανεῖς γενόμεναι, κατὰ τῆς ἀκροπόλεως αὑτὰς ἔρριψαν.
271. ἐν γραφῇ, as is commonly represented in paintings. The point of the question is, whether the infant was really adorned with golden snakes round its neck; cf. v. 22. The conversation, the student will observe, is ingeniously framed so as to remind Creusa of the exact circumstances of Ion's birth. Cf. 1428-9.
276. οὐ κάμνω σχολῇ, 'I am not pressed for time ;' 'I am not badly off in respect of leisure.' Cf. Prom. 835, σχολὴ δὲ πλείων ἢ θέλω πάρεστί μοι.
280. ἦν. For this form of the first person see Troad. 474. Hipp. 1012. The legend is thus related by Apollodorus, iii. 15, 4, καὶ πολέμου ἐνστάντος πρὸς Ἀθηναίους τοῖς Ἐλευσινίοις,—Ἐρεχθεῖ ὑπὲρ Ἀθηναίων νίκης χρωμένῳ ἔχρησεν ὁ θεὸς κατορθώσειν τὸν πόλεμον, ἐὰν μίαν τῶν θυγατέρων σφάξῃ. Καὶ σφάξαντος αὐτοῦ τὴν νεωτάτην, καὶ αἱ λοιπαὶ ἑαυτὰς κατέσφαξαν· ἐπεποίηντο γὰρ, ὡς ἔφασάν τινες, συνωμοσίαν ἀλλήλαις συναπολέσθαι. Γενομένης δὲ μετὰ σφαγὴν τῆς μάχης, Ἐρεχθεὺς μὲν ἀνεῖλεν Εὔμολπον. Ποσειδῶνος δὲ καὶ τὸν Ἐρεχθέα καὶ τὴν οἰκίαν αὐτοῦ καταλύσαντος, Κέκροψ ὁ πρεσβύτατος τῶν Ἐρεχθέως παίδων ἐβασίλευσεν.

This is the subject of that splendid ῥῆσις of Praxithea, the mother of the maid, preserved by the Orator Lycurgus (Eur. frag. 353, Dind.). Of the vengeance taken by Poseidon against Erechtheus, two visible marks were shown in the Acropolis ; the impression of a trident, alluded to in Aesch. Suppl. 214, and the spring or tank of brackish water known by the name of θάλασσα.
285. Πύθιος. The reading is rather doubtful, but not certainly corrupt, because examples of a similar synizesis are not wanting, e. g. αἰφνίδιος μόρος Prom. 698, μυριόνταρχον Pers. 975, and perhaps inf. 602, τῶν δ' αὖ λογίων τε. See Hipp. 821. Electr. 314. Hermann gives Πυθώ τ', suggesting also Πυθεὺς, for which he quotes Stephanus of Byzantium in v. Πυθώ. Matthiae thinks the true reading is Φοῖβος. The explanation of the passage can hardly be given in fewer words than Hermann's note : "Mos erat ex oraculi praecepto Athenis, teste Strabone ix. p. 404, ut Pythiastae tribus trium mensium diebus et noctibus ab ara Jovis Fulguratoris, quae erat inter Pythium et Olympieum, ad locum qui Harma dicebatur prospectantes fulgura observarent : quod si fulgurasset, mittebatur Delphos pompa." Apollodor. i. 9, 26, Ἀπόλλων δὲ στὰς ἐπὶ τὰς Μελαντίους δειρὰς, τοξεύ-

E 2

ΕΥΡΙΠΙΔΟΥ

ΚΡ. τιμᾷ. τί τιμᾷ; μήποτ' ὤφελόν σφ' ἰδεῖν.
ΙΩ. τί δέ; στυγεῖς σὺ τοῦ θεοῦ τὰ φίλτατα;
ΚΡ. οὐδέν· ξύνοιδ' ἄντροισιν αἰσχύνην τινά.
ΙΩ. πόσις δὲ τίς σ' ἔγημ' Ἀθηναίων, γύναι;
ΚΡ. οὐκ ἀστὸς, ἀλλ' ἐπακτὸς ἐξ ἄλλης χθονός. 290
ΙΩ. τίς; εὐγενῆ νιν δεῖ πεφυκέναι τινά.
ΚΡ. Ξοῦθος, πεφυκὼς Αἰόλου Διός τ' ἄπο.
ΙΩ. καὶ πῶς ξένος σ' ὢν ἔσχεν οὖσαν ἐγγενῆ;
ΚΡ. Εὐβοῖ' Ἀθήναις ἔστι τις γείτων πόλις·
ΙΩ. ὅροις ὑγροῖσιν, ὡς λέγουσ', ὡρισμένη. 295
ΚΡ. ταύτην ἔπερσε Κεκροπίδαις κοινῷ δορί.
ΙΩ. ἐπίκουρος ἐλθὼν, κᾆτα σὸν γαμεῖ λέχος;
ΚΡ. φερνάς γε πολέμου καὶ δορὸς λαβὼν γέρας.
ΙΩ. σὺν ἀνδρὶ δ' ἥκεις ἢ μόνη χρηστήρια;
ΚΡ. σὺν ἀνδρί. σηκοὺς δ' ἐνστρέφει Τροφωνίου· 300
ΙΩ. πότερα θεατὴς, ἢ χάριν μαντευμάτων;
ΚΡ. κείνου τε Φοίβου θ' ἓν θέλων μαθεῖν ἔπος.

σας τῷ βέλει εἰς τὴν θάλασσαν κατῄστραψεν.—ἰδρυσάμενοι δὲ βωμὸν Ἀπόλλωνος Αἰγλήτου, καὶ θυσιάσαντες ἐπ' εὐωχίαν ἐτράπησαν [οἱ Ἀργοναῦται]. To this attribute of Apollo, which manifestly arose from the flashing of the rays of sun-light, Musgrave ingeniously refers the epithet 'fulgente decorus arcu,' Hor. Carm. Saec. 61, and perhaps also it will serve to explain that grand passage on the battle of Actium, Aen. viii. 704,

"Actius haec cernens arcum intendebat
  Apollo
Desuper: omnis eo terrore Aegyptus
  et Indi,
Omnis Arabs, omnes vertebant terga
  Sabaei."

They saw a strange and sudden light in the sky, and fled. Suidas says, Πύθιον ἱερὸν Ἀπόλλωνος Ἀθήνῃσι. Now we have only to suppose this temple was situated near the rocks called Μακραὶ, and that it was dedicated to Apollo the god of lightning, and the meaning of the verse is perfectly clear.
286. τιμᾷ. 'He does honour the place (i. e. by his presence there). Honour it, indeed! I would I had never seen him (there).' The reading in the text is Hermann's; the old copies giving τιμᾷ τιμᾷ.

Hermann however places the interrogation after the first τιμᾷ. Bothe reads τιμᾷ γ' ἄτιμ', G. Burges on Troad. 122, τιμᾷ γ' ἀτίμως, Schaefer ἄτιμα τιμᾷ, Matthiae, from an anonymous conjecture (and one of the best), τιμᾷ; τί μήν; 'Honour it? Of course he does.' But Hermann's emendation most satisfactorily accounts for the corruption of the MSS., while the sense is thus most easily restored. So Alcest. 807, τί ζῶσιν; οὐ κάτοισθα τὰν δόμοις κακά. Iph. A. 460, τὴν δ' αὖ τάλαιναν παρθένον, τί παρθένον; Phoen. 1725, ἰὼ ἰὼ, δεινὰ δείν' ἐγὼ τλάς. AN. τί τλάς; τί τλάς; Dr. Badham suggests τιμᾷ σφε, τιμᾷ. μήποτ' ὤφελόν σφ' ἰδεῖν. We might compare the accidental omission of σφε in v. 81.
287. τί δέ; 'What! do you hate what the god regards as very dear?' The reader will notice the emphatic σύ.
288. ξύνοιδ' is the elegant correction of Tyrwhitt for οὐδέν, ξέν'. οἶδ' &c.
295. ὅροις. Aesch. Suppl. 254, συντέμνει δ' ὅρος ὑγρᾶς θαλάσσης. For the account of Creusa's marriage see v. 59.
302. κείνου τε κτλ. 'Wishing to obtain both from Trophonius and from Phoebus one common declaration,' i. e. to confirm the response of the one by the independent oracle of the other.

ΙΩ. καρποῦ δ' ὑπὲρ γῆς ἥκετ', ἢ παίδων πέρι;
ΚΡ. ἄπαιδές ἐσμεν, χρόνι' ἔχοντ' εὐνήματα.
ΙΩ. οὐδ' ἔτεκες οὐδὲν πώποτ', ἀλλ' ἄτεκνος εἶ;   305
ΚΡ. ὁ Φοῖβος οἶδε τὴν ἐμὴν ἀπαιδίαν.
ΙΩ. ὦ τλῆμον, ὡς τἄλλ' εὐτυχοῦσ' οὐκ εὐτυχεῖς.
ΚΡ. σὺ δ' εἶ τίς; ὥς σου τὴν τεκοῦσαν ὤλβισα.
ΙΩ. τοῦ θεοῦ καλοῦμαι δοῦλος εἰμί τ', ὦ γύναι.
ΚΡ. ἀνάθημα πόλεως, ἤ τινος πραθεὶς ὕπο;   310
ΙΩ. οὐκ οἶδα, πλὴν ἕν, Λοξίου κεκλήμεθα.
ΚΡ. ἡμεῖς σ' ἆρ' αὖθις, ὦ ξέν', ἀντοικτείρομεν.
ΙΩ. ὡς μὴ εἰδόθ' ἥτις μ' ἔτεκεν ἐξ ὅτου τ' ἔφυν.
ΚΡ. ναοῖσι δ' οἰκεῖς τοισίδ', ἢ κατὰ στέγας;
ΙΩ. ἅπαν θεοῦ μοι δῶμ', ἵν' ἂν λάβῃ μ' ὕπνος.   315
ΚΡ. παῖς δ' ὢν ἀφίκου ναὸν, ἢ νεανίας;
ΙΩ. βρέφος λέγουσιν οἱ δοκοῦντες εἰδέναι.
ΚΡ. καὶ τίς γάλακτί σ' ἐξέθρεψε Δελφίδων;
ΙΩ. οὐπώποτ' ἔγνων μαστόν. ἡ δ' ἔθρεψέ με
ΚΡ. τίς, ὦ ταλαίπωρ; ὡς νοσοῦσ' ηὗρον νόσους.   320
ΙΩ. Φοίβου προφῆτις, μητέρ' ὡς νομίζομεν.
ΚΡ. ἐς δ' ἄνδρ' ἀφίκου τίνα τροφὴν κεκτημένος;
ΙΩ. βωμοί μ' ἔφερβον οὐπιῶν τ' ἀεὶ ξένος.
ΚΡ. τάλαιν' ἆρ' ἡ τεκοῦσά σ', ἥτις ἦν ποτε.
ΙΩ. ἀδίκημά του γυναικὸς ἐγενόμην ἴσως.   325
ΚΡ. ἔχεις δὲ βίοτον; εὖ γὰρ ἤσκησαι πέπλοις.
ΙΩ. τοῖς τοῦ θεοῦ κοσμούμεθ', ᾧ δουλεύομεν.

305. οὐδὲν πώποτε. Ion means, to her husband Xuthus; but *she* refers it to the time before her marriage, and ambiguously replies, 'Phoebus knows whether I am childless or not.'
307. οὐκ εὐτυχεῖς. This means ἄπαις εἶ. See Androm. 420.
308. ὤλβισα, μακαρίζω, θαυμάζω, εὐδαιμονίζω.
314. κατὰ στέγας, in a house, κατ' οἶκον. Seidler (ap. Herm. Praef. p. ix,) interprets *in habitaculis ad templum pertinentibus*. In the next verse we may either repeat δῶμα, with Matthiae, or supply δέδοται or ἀνεῖταί μοι. 'The whole temple of the god is my home, wherever sleep may overtake me.'

321. Φοίβου προφῆτις. Dr. Badham thinks it is impossible to construe μητέρ' ὡς νομίζομεν unless we read προφῆτιν. But it is very easy to supply ταύτην, as Hermann proposes, or to suppose the poet intended to say τὴν δὲ θρέψασάν με μητέρα νομίζω, but on account of the interposed τίς was induced to write the nominative προφῆτις in reply; after giving which he resumes the former construction.
324. τάλαιν' ἆρ' κτλ. The reading of Dobree for τάλαινά σ' ἡ τεκοῦσ', ἥτις ποτ' ἦν ἄρα.
325. ἀδίκημα, the fruit of an ἀδικία or wrong done to the mother.

ΕΥΡΙΠΙΔΟΥ

ΚΡ. οὐδ' ἧξας εἰς ἔρευναν ἐξευρεῖν γονάς;
ΙΩ. ἔχω γὰρ οὐδέν, ὦ γύναι, τεκμήριον.
ΚΡ. φεῦ.
πέπονθέ τις σῇ μητρὶ ταῦτ' ἄλλη γυνή. 330
ΙΩ. τίς; εἰ πόνου μοι ξυλλάβοι, χαίροιμεν ἄν.
ΚΡ. ἧς οὕνεκ' ἦλθον δεῦρο πρὶν πόσιν μολεῖν.
ΙΩ. ποῖόν τι χρῄζουσ'; ὡς ὑπουργήσω, γύναι.
ΚΡ. μάντευμα κρυπτὸν δεομένη Φοίβου μαθεῖν.
ΙΩ. λέγοις ἄν· ἡμεῖς τἄλλα προξενήσομεν. 335
ΚΡ. ἄκουε δὴ τὸν μῦθον. ἀλλ' αἰδούμεθα.
ΙΩ. οὔ τἄρα πράξεις οὐδέν· ἀργὸς ἡ θεός.
ΚΡ. Φοίβῳ μιγῆναί φησί τις φίλων ἐμῶν.
ΙΩ. Φοίβῳ γυνὴ γεγῶσα; μὴ λέγ', ὦ ξένη.
ΚΡ. καὶ παῖδά γ' ἔτεκε τῷ θεῷ λάθρα πατρός. 340
ΙΩ. οὐκ ἔστιν· ἀνδρὸς ἀδικίαν αἰσχύνεται.
ΚΡ. οὔ φησιν αὐτή· καὶ πέπονθεν ἄθλια.
ΙΩ. τί χρῆμα δράσασ', εἰ θεῷ συνεζύγη;
ΚΡ. τὸν παῖδ' ὃν ἔτεκεν ἐξέθηκε δωμάτων.
ΙΩ. ὁ δ' ἐκτεθεὶς παῖς ποῦ 'στιν; εἰσορᾷ φάος; 345
ΚΡ. οὐκ οἶδεν οὐδείς. ταῦτα καὶ μαντεύομαι.
ΙΩ. εἰ δ' οὐκέτ' ἔστι, τίνι τρόπῳ διεφθάρη;
ΚΡ. θῆράς σφε τὸν δύστηνον ἐλπίζει κτανεῖν.
ΙΩ. ποίῳ τόδ' ἔγνω χρωμένη τεκμηρίῳ;
ΚΡ. ἐλθοῦσ' ἵν' αὐτὸν ἐξέθηκ' οὐχ ηὗρ' ἔτι. 350

331. εἰ πόνου μοι ξυλλάβοι, 'if she would undertake (a part) of the labour with me, I should be glad.' The old reading τίς; εἶπον εἰ &c. was corrected by Hermann and before him by a pupil of Seidler's, as he tells us in his note. There cannot be a doubt but that they are right.—Of course, Creusa is speaking of her own case under pretence of being concerned for a friend of her's, φίλων τις, v. 338.
335. προξενήσομεν. See on Helen. 146.
337. ἡ θεός. The goddess αἰδὼς is ἄεργος, because shame prevents those who entertain that feeling from acting.
341. ἀνδρός. There is no direct antithesis with θεὸς, (for that would have required ἀνθρώπου,) but the meaning is, that the parentage of the child is referred to Phoebus, because the mother is ashamed to avow her seduction by a man. So Bacch. 28, Σεμέλην δὲ νυμφευθεῖσαν ἐκ θνητοῦ τινος 'Ες Ζῆν' ἀναφέρειν τὴν ἁμαρτίαν λέχους.
342. οὔ φησιν Herm. and Dobree for ὅ φησιν. Bothe explains ὅ φησιν thus, 'What she says she has suffered, she has really suffered,'—her woes are not merely λόγοι, but ἔργα δεινά. Of course he edits ἀθλία, not ἄθλια, but the latter is necessary on account of the following verse.
343. The sense is, 'If she really married a god, which was a glorious fortune in itself, what did she do to make her wretched?'

ΙΩ. ἦν δὲ σταλαγμὸς ἐν στίβῳ τις αἵματος;
ΚΡ. οὔ φησι· καίτοι πόλλ' ἐπεστράφη πέδον.
ΙΩ. χρόνος δὲ τίς τῷ παιδὶ διαπεπραγμένῳ;
ΚΡ. σοὶ ταυτὸν ἥβης, εἴπερ ἦν, εἶχ' ἂν μέτρον.
ΙΩ. οὔκουν ἔτ' ἄλλον ὕστερον τίκτει γόνον; 355
ΚΡ. ἀδικεῖ νιν ὁ θεός· οὐ τεκοῦσα δ' ἀθλία.
ΙΩ. τί δ', εἰ λάθρα νιν Φοῖβος ἐκτρέφει λαβών;
ΚΡ. τὰ κοινὰ χαίρων οὐ δίκαια δρᾷ μόνος.
ΙΩ. οἴμοι· προσῳδὸς ἡ τύχη τὠμῷ πάθει.
ΚΡ. καὶ σ', ὦ ξέν', οἶμαι μητέρ' ἀθλίαν ποθεῖν. 360
ΙΩ. καὶ μή γ' ἐπ' οἰκτόν μ' ἔξαγ' οὗ λελήσμεθα.
ΚΡ. σιγῶ· πέραινε δ' ὧν σ' ἀνιστορῶ πέρι.
ΙΩ. οἶσθ' οὖν ὃ κάμνει τοῦ λόγου μάλιστά σοι;

354. εἶχ' ἄν. This is one of the very few passages where the elision of the ε of the third person before ἄν seems to have been admitted. It appears to have been regarded by the Tragic writers in the same light as the elision of ι in the dative, viz. as a thing to be avoided if possible. Hermann thinks the verse undoubtedly corrupt, and he would read ἔχων, agreeing with χρόνος. Even εἶχεν without ἄν might be defended; see on Hec. 1113, Tro. 398, Πάρις δ' ἔγημε τὴν Διὸς, γήμας δὲ μὴ Σιγώμενον τὸ κῆδος εἶχεν ἐν δόμοις. Or we might correct, as Elmsley suggests, σοὶ ταῦτ' ἂν ἥβης, εἴπερ ἦν, εἶχεν μέτρα. The conditional way of putting it seems to have been preferred, because Creusa implies, in her despair, ἀλλ' οὐκ ἔστι. Otherwise she might have said, εἴπερ ἔστ', ἔχει μέτρον.

355. The transposition of this and the next verse, and the reading οὐ τεκοῦσα for ἡ τεκοῦσα, is due to Hermann. Creusa having hinted that the child is probably dead, Ion asks, if the mother has not another child, as a consolation for her loss? And Creusa, speaking as before of herself, replies, 'The god wronged her, (i. e. seduced her, but did not continue his visits to her,) and in not having any other son, she is unhappy.' So Creusa had said in v. 304, ἄπαιδές ἐσμεν, χρόνι' ἔχοντ' εὐνήματα. The common order of the lines, as Dindorf gives them, might mean, 'The god wrongs him, and the mother too is to be pitied.'—'At least, she had no other son after that,' i. e. which makes her the more to be pitied.

358. Dr. Badham remarks with truth that the sense of this verse has been grievously mistaken by those commentators who have attempted to explain it. He himself translates it thus: "He who does open wrong with impunity, does not do justice in secret." Even this is not exactly the poet's meaning. He opposes μόνος, *individually*, to κοινὸς, *in a public capacity*; and the full sentence would be, τὰ κοινὰ δίκαια χαίρων δρῶν, μόνος οὐ δρᾷ δίκαια, scil. οὐκ ἐκτρέφων τὸν αὑτοῦ παῖδα. 'Though he rejoices in doing justice publicly, (viz. by his oracles, cf. v. 366,) he does it not in his private actions.' For Apollo was reputed not only for his veracity but also for his justice, as ὁ τῶν δικαίων πᾶσιν ἀνθρώποις κρίτης, Androm. 1162. Thus Orestes addresses him in Eum. 85, ἄναξ Ἄπολλον, οἶσθα μὲν τὸ μὴ ἀδικεῖν. Hence the peculiar force of ἀδικεῖ νιν ὁ θεὸς just above.

361. Dobree's proposed reading οὗ 'λελήσμεθα, 'which we *had* forgotten,' seems rather fanciful; but it is approved by Dindorf and Dr. Badham.

362. πέραινε. Perform for me (as πρόξενος, v. 335,) what I am asking about; assist me in procuring an oracle respecting my childlessness. To which Ion replies, 'Are you aware of the weak point in your application? The god will never reveal in the oracle secrets against himself.' — 'He must do so,' rejoins Creusa, 'if he prefers public utility to private interest.'

32 ΕΥΡΙΠΙΔΟΥ

ΚΡ. τί δ' οὐκ ἐκείνῃ τῇ ταλαιπώρῳ νοσεῖ;
ΙΩ. πῶς ὁ θεὸς ὃ λαθεῖν βούλεται μαντεύσεται; 365
ΚΡ. εἴπερ καθίζει τρίποδα κοινὸν Ἑλλάδος.
ΙΩ. αἰσχύνεται τὸ πρᾶγμα· μὴ 'ξέλεγχέ νιν.
ΚΡ. ἀλγύνεται δέ γ' ἡ παθοῦσα τῇ τύχῃ.
ΙΩ. οὐκ ἔστιν ὅστις σοι προφητεύσει τάδε.
ἐν τοῖς γὰρ αὐτοῦ δώμασιν κακὸς φανεὶς 370
Φοῖβος δικαίως τὸν θεμιστεύοντά σοι
δράσειεν ἄν τι πῆμ'· ἀπαλλάσσου, γύναι·
τῷ γὰρ θεῷ τἀναντί' οὐ μαντευτέον.
ἐς γὰρ τοσοῦτον ἀμαθίας ἔλθοιμεν ἄν,
εἰ τοὺς θεοὺς ἄκοντας ἐκπονήσομεν 375
φράζειν ἃ μὴ θέλουσιν ἢ προβωμίοις
σφαγαῖσι μήλων ἢ δι' οἰωνῶν πτεροῖς.
ἂν γὰρ βίᾳ σπεύδωμεν ἀκόντων θεῶν,
οὐκ ὄντα κεκτήμεσθα τἀγάθ', ὦ γύναι·
ἃ δ' ἂν διδῶσ' ἑκόντες, ὠφελούμεθα. 380
ΧΟ. πολλαί γε πολλοῖς εἰσι συμφοραὶ βροτῶν,
μορφαὶ δὲ διαφέρουσιν. ἓν δ' ἂν εὐτυχὲς
μόλις ποτ' ἐξεύροι τις ἀνθρώπων βίῳ.
ΚΡ. ὦ Φοῖβε, κἀκεῖ κἀνθάδ' οὐ δίκαιος εἶ

---

367. ἐξέλεγχε, 'do not question him.' The same inharmonious collision of αἰσχύνομαι and ἀλγύνομαι occurs in Heracl. 541—2. The force of the γε is, 'Aye, and if he will persist in silence through shame, she will persist in her inquiry through grief.'

369—371. θεμιστεύειν and προφητεύειν are here used (as is clear from v. 413) of the priest or minister who acts as the medium between the applicant and the oracular god. Such an inquiry, Ion objects, could not be sustained by any minister of the temple; he would fear to be struck dead on the spot, and justly so. Properly, θεμιστεύειν is said of the god himself. Photius, θεμιστεύειν, χρησμῳδεῖν, Λυσίας· γέγονε δὲ τὸ ὄνομα ἀπὸ τοῦ Θέμιν ἐσχηκέναι ποτὲ τὸ μαντεῖον πρὸ τοῦ Ἀπόλλωνος (Eum. 2).—ἀπαλλάσσου, desist, give up the idea.

374. ἐς τοσοῦτον ἀμαθίας, sc. ὥστε πείθειν αὐτοὺς τὰ σφισὶν αὐτοῖς ἐναντία μαντεύεσθαι.—ἐκπονήσομεν, ἀναγκάσομεν. See the note on Hel. 752.

377. δι' οἰωνῶν πτεροῖς is, 'by omens obtained through birds.' So Oed. Col. 97, οὐκ ἔσθ' ὅπως οὐ πιστὸν ἐξ ὑμῶν πτερὸν εἰσήγαγ' ἐς τόδ' ἄλσος. For the omission of the article (τοῖς δι' οἰωνῶν) compare Hippol. 952, δι' ἀψύχου βορᾶς σίτοις, inf. 508, θεόθεν τέκνα θνατοῖς, and the note on Med. 1260. There is no reason why Dr. Badham should call these words untranslateable. Bothe's version, aut avibus per auguria, should have been aut auguriis per aves.

379. οὐκ ὄντα is here the predicate, 'unreal,' 'unsubstantial.' See on Rhes. 163. This is the emendation of Wakefield and Matthiae for ἄκοντα, but the next verse rather suggests ἀνόνητα.

382. ἐν εὐτυχὲς, one unvarying course of prosperity. Dr. Badham says, "one single piece of unmixed good fortune."

ΙΩΝ. 33

ἐς τὴν ἀποῦσαν, ἧς πάρεισιν οἱ λόγοι. 385
σύ τ' οὐκ ἔσωσας τὸν σὸν, ὃν σῶσαί σ' ἐχρῆν,
οὔθ' ἱστορούσῃ μητρὶ μάντις ὢν ἐρεῖς,
ὡς, εἰ μὲν οὐκέτ' ἔστιν, ὀγκωθῇ τάφῳ,
εἰ δ' ἔστιν, ἔλθῃ μητρὸς εἰς ὄψιν ποτέ.
ἀλλ' *ἐξερευνᾶν χρὴ τάδ', εἰ πρὸς τοῦ θεοῦ 390
κωλυόμεσθα μὴ μαθεῖν ἃ βούλομαι.
ἀλλ', ὦ ξέν', εἰσορῶ γὰρ εὐγενῆ πόσιν
Ξοῦθον πέλας δὴ τόνδε τὰς Τροφωνίου
λιπόντα θαλάμας, τοὺς λελεγμένους λόγους
σίγα πρὸς ἄνδρα, μή τιν' αἰσχύνην λάβω 395
διακονοῦσα κρυπτά, καὶ προβῇ λόγος
οὐχ ᾗπερ ἡμεῖς αὐτὸν ἐξειλίσσομεν.
τὰ γὰρ γυναικῶν δυσχερῆ πρὸς ἄρσενας,
κἂν ταῖς κακαῖσιν ἀγαθαὶ μεμιγμέναι
μισούμεθ'· οὕτω δυστυχεῖς πεφύκαμεν. 400

ΞΟΥΘΟΣ.

πρῶτον μὲν ὁ θεὸς τῶν ἐμῶν προσφθεγμάτων
λαβὼν ἀπαρχὰς χαιρέτω, σύ τ', ὦ γύναι.
μῶν χρόνιος ἐλθών σ' ἐξέπληξ' ὀρρωδίᾳ;

385. ἧς πάρεισιν κτλ. Creusa continues to speak equivocally of herself, as if she were merely conveying the request of some friend. By καὶ ἐκεῖ καὶ ἐνθάδε she means, both on the occasion of her seduction and now in refusing an oracle. The words τὴν ἀποῦσαν are intended to mislead. Applied to herself, they have no intelligible relation either to past or to present circumstances. She might have said, εἰς τὴν λόγῳ μὲν ἀποῦσαν ἔργῳ δὲ παροῦσαν. But she speaks of herself as the messenger or mouth-piece of her absent friend, τῆς ἀπούσης.

386. σύ τ' for σύ γ' was corrected by L. Dindorf and Dobree. The latter would prefer ὅς γ', and so perhaps should we, if only Euripides had written it. Hermann ὃς οὔτ' ἔσωσας.

390. The old reading ἀλλ' ἐὰν χρὴ τάδ' is not easily restored by conjecture. Wakefield's ἀλλ' οὖν ἐάν γε, approved by Hermann and Dindorf, seems mere patchwork. Dr. Badham is perhaps right in thinking ἐᾶν is a gloss, and that the poet wrote something like ἀλλ' αἰνέσαι με χρὴ τάδ'. Barnes gives ἀλλ' ὡς ἐᾶν χρὴ ταῦτά γ'. The general sense would seem to indicate that Euripides wrote, but the transcribers contrived to clip and curtail, ἀλλ' ἐ[ξερευν]ᾶν χρὴ τάδ', 'well, I must look into this matter for myself, if the god will not help me.' See the note on v. 189, and compare v. 328, οὐδ' ἧξας εἰς ἔρευναν ἐξευρεῖν γονάς;

396. προβῇ, προχωρῇ, lest the matter should take a different turn from the way in which we are now unravelling it; that is, lest it should appear that some intrigues are being plotted by me. Others explain προβῇ, 'should go forth,' 'should be promulgated,' viz. the report that some man, and not the god, as she hopes in the end to show, was her seducer. This sense of προβῆναι however appears doubtful.—τὰ γὰρ κτλ., 'for the position of women is difficult in its relation to males,' i. e. is apt to be jealously regarded.

401. On πρῶτον μέν—τε, see Med. 125.

VOL. II. F

402. χαιρέτω usually used in reference to a mortal. ἵληκοι in reference to a god: ex.
Ἀλλ', ἄγεθ', ἵληκοι μὲν Ἀπόλλων Ἀρτέμιδι ξὺν
χαίρετε δ' ὑμεῖς πᾶσαι. Thuc. III. 104.

ΕΥΡΙΠΙΔΟΥ

ΚΡ. οὐδέν γ'· ἀφίκου δ' ἐς μέριμναν. ἀλλά μοι
λέξον τί θέσπισμ' ἐκ Τροφωνίου φέρεις, 405
παίδων ὅπως νῷν σπέρμα συγκραθήσεται.
ΞΟ. οὐκ ἠξίωσε τοῦ θεοῦ προλαμβάνειν
μαντεύμαθ'· ἓν δ' οὖν εἶπεν, οὐκ ἄπαιδά με
πρὸς οἶκον ἥξειν οὐδὲ σ' ἐκ χρηστηρίων.
ΚΡ. ὦ πότνια Φοίβου μῆτερ, εἰ γὰρ αἰσίως 410
ἔλθοιμεν, ἅ τε νῷν συμβόλαια πρόσθεν ἦν
ἐς παῖδα τὸν σὸν, μεταπέσοι βελτίονα.
ΞΟ. ἔσται τάδ'· ἀλλὰ τίς προφητεύει θεοῦ ;
ΙΩ. ἡμεῖς τά γ' ἔξω, τῶν ἔσω δ' ἄλλοις μέλει,
οἳ πλησίον θάσσουσι τρίποδος, ὦ ξένε, 415
Δελφῶν ἀριστῆς, οὓς ἐκλήρωσεν πάλος.

404. οὐδέν γε. Compare v. 256, and Iph. Taur. 564, οὐδείς γε. The meaning of ἀφίκου δ' ἐς μέριμναν has been overlooked, though Hippol. 792 is a good comment on the words. It was thought ill-omined to receive any one who had just returned from an oracle, with an anxious look or any expression of grief. Creusa means therefore to say, 'I am sorry that I cannot welcome you as joyfully as I ought, for you have come at a time of grief and distress.'
406. συγκραθήσεται Wakefield for συγκαθήσεται. The physical doctrine is alluded to, that childlessness was caused by some such defect as is implied by the context ; ὅταν μὴ ἐξ ἀμφοῖν ὡς δεῖ συναρμοσθῇ, &c. Aristot. H. A. x. 6. 15.
407. προλαμβάνειν. As an inferior power, and only a δαίμων, he did not think fit to anticipate the oracle of Phoebus. Perhaps this sort of excuse was often made to those who, like Xuthus, (v. 302,) had resolved on trying whether they could get the same response from two distinct shrines. Such a supposition however is on the assumption that oracular powers were invariably impostures, which is a point on which conflicting opinions have ever existed.
408. ἐν δ' οὖν Herm. and Dind., for ἐν γοῦν. The latter would mean 'one thing, at all events,' which is much the same sense as δ' οὖν, but that the latter supplies the adversative particle. See on Rhes. 336.
411. νῷν. Creusa secretly means the compacts or relations between herself and Apollo ; Photius, συμβόλαια, τὰ συναλλάγματα. But Xuthus is to take νῷν for himself and his wife, in which sense συμβόλαια are the sacrifices (literally, the votive offerings, bargains or agreements,) which they two had formerly made to Apollo for children. No explanation can be better than Hermann's, Quod nobis prius cum filio tuo commercii intercessit, melius cadat. Ita Xutho videbitur orare, ut quae nunc sacra facturi sint, magis propitia mente accipiat Apollo, quam quae ei antehac fuerint oblata : ipsa autem optat, ut quae sibi olim infelix fuit cum Apolline consuetudo, quippe cujus praemium orbitatem habet, ea ut in melius convertatur, ereptumque sibi filium inveniat."—μεταπέσοι is a metaphor from dice. So μεταπίπτοντος δαίμονος in Alcest. 912.
413. προφητεύει. Cf. v. 364. It is a mistake to suppose that the word prophet properly implies the power of predicting : προφήτης was one who was the mouthpiece of another, and spoke in his place, as Apollo was the προφήτης of Ζεὺς, and Glaucus of Nereus, Orest. 364.
416. ἀριστῆς. Herm. has ἀρίστοις, but the old reading appears to be ἀριστεῖς. The office of προφήτης seems to have been to communicate between the applicant and the god. The ὁ ἔξω προφήτης is mentioned in v. 335 ; but it was confided to a few of the best-born Delphians (hence called Φοίβου θέραπες in v. 94,) to attend at the adytum and receive the answer of the god.

ΞΟ. καλῶς· ἔχω δὴ πάνθ᾽ ὅσων ἐχρῄζομεν.
στείχοιμ᾽ ἂν εἴσω· καὶ γὰρ, ὡς ἐγὼ κλύω,
χρηστήριον πέπτωκε τοῖς ἐπήλυσι
κοινὸν πρὸ ναοῦ· βούλομαι δ᾽ ἐν ἡμέρᾳ   420
τῇδ᾽, αἰσία γὰρ, θεοῦ λαβεῖν μαντεύματα.
σὺ δ᾽ ἀμφὶ βωμοὺς, ὦ γύναι, δαφνηφόρους
λαβοῦσα κλῶνας εὐτέκνους εὔχου θεοῖς
χρησμούς μ᾽ ἐνεγκεῖν ἐξ Ἀπόλλωνος δόμων.
ΚΡ. ἔσται τάδ᾽ ἔσται. Λοξίας δ᾽ ἐὰν θέλῃ   425
νῦν ἀλλὰ τὰς πρὶν ἀναλαβεῖν ἁμαρτίας,
ἅπας μὲν οὐ γένοιτ᾽ ἂν εἰς ἡμᾶς φίλος,
ὅσον δὲ χρῄζει, θεὸς γάρ ἐστι, δέξομαι.
ΙΩ. τί ποτε λόγοισιν ἡ ξένη πρὸς τὸν θεὸν
κρυπτοῖσιν ἀεὶ λοιδοροῦσ᾽ αἰνίσσεται   430
ἤτοι φιλοῦσά γ᾽ ἧς ὕπερ μαντεύεται,
ἢ καί τι σιγῶσ᾽ ὧν σιωπᾶσθαι χρεών;
ἀτὰρ θυγατρὸς τῆς Ἐρεχθέως τί μοι
μέλει; προσήκει γ᾽ οὐδέν. ἀλλὰ χρυσέαις

419. πέπτωκε. Hermann's explanation is probably right, that this means 'a public victim (viz. one in behalf of all the θεωροί present on the occasion) has been slain in front of the temple.' In this sense we have πεσεῖν χρηστήρια θεοῖσι πολλοῖς πολλά in Aesch. Suppl. 445. It appears from Plutarch, (De Oraculi Defectu p. 435, B., quoted by Hermann) that an oracle was not delivered unless certain favourable omens had been derived from the death of the victim. This having now been done, the day is called αἰσία, one suitable for obtaining an answer. Older commentators explain, *per sortem cecidit advenis oraculum*.

422. Here also a curious custom appears to be described. The altars being decorated with the sacred bay of Apollo on these holidays, the friends of the admitted applicants seem to have sat down by the said altars, and taken in their hands twigs to be used in the manner of suppliant boughs, as described in Suppl. 32. Heracl. 124.

426. ἀναλαβεῖν, to retract, to make amends for. Both Xuthus and Creusa here leave the stage. The former enters the temple, at v. 424, the other the house (by the side door) at v. 428, whence she re-appears at v. 725 to inquire what response has been given. Left alone on the stage, Ion ponders on the mysterious words and obscure hints of the stranger lady, and doubts if she be not really interested for herself rather than for her friend. He concludes his soliloquy with some very fine reflections on the bad example set by the gods to mankind, if the tales about their amours are true.

431. Musgrave first gave γ᾽ ἧς for γῆς. This is a better correction than τῆς, the article for the relative, because ἤτοι—γε is a proper combination, as in Rhes. 817.

433. τῆς Ἐρεχθέως. He had learnt this at v. 260.—προσήκει γ᾽ οὐδέν Reiske and Herm. for προσήκει τ᾽ οὐδάς. Justin Martyr, who quotes this ῥῆσις from 433 to the end, has προσήκει μ᾽ οὐθέν. Of other conjectures, that of Wakefield, προσῆκον οὐδέν, 'there being no relationship,' (the accusative absolute, like ἧκον in Alcest. 291,) seems better than Elmsley's and Matthiae's προσήκοντ᾽ οὐδέν, which W. Dindorf has edited. So probably in Suppl. 471, we should read μηδ᾽ ἀναιρεῖσθαι νεκροὺς βίᾳ, προσήκει οὐδὲν Ἀργείων πόλει, for ἀναιρεῖσθαι—προσήκοντ᾽. Translate, 'Truly, she is no relation of mine.'

πρόχοισιν ἐλθὼν εἰς ἀπορραντήρια 435
δρόσον καθήσω. νουθετητέος δέ μοι
Φοῖβος, τί πάσχει· παρθένους βίᾳ γαμῶν
προδίδωσι· παῖδας ἐκτεκνούμενος λάθρα
θνήσκοντας ἀμελεῖ. μὴ σύ γ'· ἀλλ' ἐπεὶ κρατεῖς,
ἀρετὰς δίωκε. καὶ γὰρ ὅστις ἂν βροτῶν 440
κακὸς πεφύκῃ, ζημιοῦσιν οἱ θεοί.
πῶς οὖν δίκαιον τοὺς νόμους ὑμᾶς βροτοῖς
γράψαντας αὐτοὺς ἀνομίαν ὀφλισκάνειν;
εἰ δ', οὐ γὰρ ἔσται, τῷ λόγῳ δὲ χρήσομαι,
δίκας βιαίων δώσετ' ἀνθρώποις γάμων, 445
σὺ καὶ Ποσειδῶν Ζεύς θ' ὃς οὐρανοῦ κρατεῖ,
ναοὺς τίνοντες ἀδικίας κενώσετε.
τὰς ἡδονὰς γὰρ τῆς προμηθίας πάρος
σπεύδοντες ἀδικεῖτ'· οὐκέτ' ἀνθρώπους κακοὺς
λέγειν δίκαιον, εἰ τὰ τῶν θεῶν κακὰ 450
μιμούμεθ', ἀλλὰ τοὺς διδάσκοντας τάδε.
ΧΟ.   σὲ τὰν ὠδίνων λοχιᾶν   στρ.

435. πρόχοισιν for προχόοισιν, like Ἀλκάθου for -όου in Heracl. 278. Antig. 430, εὐκροτήτου χαλκέας πρόχου. Translate, 'But I must go, and with my golden pitcher put water into the vessels for sprinkling; and I must say a friendly word to Phoebus, to ask what he means by his conduct; here he is marrying girls against their will, and then deserting them; having children secretly born to him, and leaving them to die by his neglect. Act not thus, O Apollo; but, since thou art a god, pursue the paths of Virtue!'
437. τί πάσχων Canter and Dind. for τί πάσχει. The former is the common Attic idiom, as τί πάσχων ταῦτα ποιεῖς; 'What is coming over you now, that you are acting thus?'—οὐκ οἶδ' ὅτι μαθὼν ταῦτα ποιεῖς, 'I know not who taught you to do this,' &c. However, the alteration here is quite unjustifiable, especially as Justin Martyr has τί παρέχει.
439. ἐπεὶ κρατεῖς. Since you are εἷς τῶν κρατούντων, one of the supreme gods, who were often called οἱ κρατοῦντες and οἱ κρείσσονες.
443. ἀνομίαν, 'a charge of lawlessness.' Both Justin Martyr and Clement of Alexandria quote ἀδικίας ὀφλισκάνειν,

—perhaps from ἀδικίας below.
447. ναοὺς κτλ. You will empty your temples of their wealth in paying fines for your acts of injustice.
448. πέρα, the correction of Prof. Conington for πάρος, has been admitted by Dr. Badham. It is confirmed by the reading of Justin, πέρας. The sense will then be, 'pursuing your pleasures beyond the bounds of caution,' not 'in preference to caution,' or discretion. But the true meaning appears to be, that the care of the gods for the welfare of man is made secondary to their own pleasures. This passage is in every way a remarkable one; the theology of it is discussed in the preface to Vol. i. p. xxvi.
452 seqq. An invocation to Pallas to leave Athens and fly to Delphi in company with her virgin sister Artemis, in order that they may intercede with their brother Apollo in favour of the ancient royal house of Erechtheus. To possess children in one's family is a permanent source of happiness; they supply a hope of succession, a support in trouble, a delight in prosperity, a protection in time of war. Moderate wealth and the blessing of children is all that one need desire.—

ἀνειλείθυιαν, ἐμὰν
'Αθάναν ἱκετεύω,
Προμηθεῖ Τιτᾶνι λοχευ- 455
θεῖσαν κατ' ἀκροτάτας
κορυφᾶς Διός· ὦ πότνα Νίκα,
μόλε Πύθιον οἶκον,
'Ολύμπου χρυσέων θαλάμων
πταμένα πρὸς ἀγυιὰς, 460
Φοιβήιος ἔνθα γᾶς
μεσόμφαλος ἑστία
παρὰ χορευομένῳ τρίποδι
μαντεύματα κραίνει,
σὺ καὶ παῖς ἁ Λατογενὴς, 465
δύο θεαὶ δύο παρθένοι,
κασίγνηται σεμναὶ τοῦ Φοίβου.
ἱκετεύσατε δ', ὦ κόραι,
τὸ παλαιὸν 'Ερεχθέως
γένος εὐτεκνίας χρονίου καθαροῖς 470

The metre is glyconic, many of the verses being of the variety called *polyschematistic*, viz. ∪ _́ _ _ ∪ _́ ∪ ∪ _.

453. Hesych. ἀνειλείθυιαν, ἄτοκον, whence this passage was restored, the old reading being εἰλείθυιάν τε. Of the preternatural birth of Pallas Aeschylus speaks, Eum. 634, where there is reason to think a verse has been lost describing this very event;

πατὴρ μὲν ἂν γένοιτ' ἄνευ μητρός· πέλας
μάρτυς πάρεστι παῖς 'Ολυμπίου Διὸς
[πατρὸς λοχευθεῖσ' ἐξ ἄκρου κρατός ποτε,]
οὐδ' ἐν σκότοισι νηδύος τεθραμμένη.

455. Τιτᾶνι. For this dative of the agent compare Bacch. 3.
460. πταμένα. "The Temple of Victory stood a little to the west of the southern wing of the Propylaea" (that is, on the side of the acropolis which is the furthest from the theatre). "The statue of Victory in this temple was sculptured wingless. Such a representation of Victory was conformable to the more ancient, but not to the then received method of exhibiting that Goddess." *Athens and Attica*, p. 107. Either to this goddess, or to Παλλὰς Πρόμαχος on the acropolis,

Aristophanes alludes, Av. 574, αὐτίκα Νίκη πέτεται πτερυγοῖν χρυσαῖν.—'Ολύμπου, supply ἀπό. We might read Οὐλύμπου on account of the metre, as in Herc. F. 872, but it is not necessary; compare 453 with 473.

463. χορευομένῳ. 'Danced round,' as a central object, according to the custom in reciting dithyrambs; for the worship of Dionysus and of Apollo had very intimate relations. Hence it is that Cassandra in Tro. 451, calls the ensigns of prophecy derived from Apollo, ἀγάλματ' εὔϊα, and *ib.* 500 she is σύμβακχος θεοῖς.
—κραίνει, *perfecta reddit*, J. Barnes. Cf. Oed. Col. 453, συννοῶν τε τἀξ ἐμοῦ παλαίφαθ', ἁμοὶ Φοῖβος ἤνυσέν ποτε. *Infra*, v. 570.

467. τοῦ Φοίβου. The article is rather unusual; perhaps it is justified by the similar example of τὰν Κύπριν in Med. 836, ὁ Βακχεὺς sup. v. 218. Hermann gives θεοῦ Φοίβου, " quod referendum ad δύο θεαί." It is remarkable that the τοῦ is wanting in the Palatine MS.; but the antistrophic v. 487 seems to admit of no alteration.

470. καθαροῖς, σαφέσιν, ἀκριβέσι, *non obscuris aut ambiguis*, Bothe.

μαντεύμασι κῦρσαι.
ὑπερβαλλούσας γὰρ ἔχει ἀντ.
θνατοῖς εὐδαιμονίας
ἀκίνητον ἀφορμὰν,
τέκνων οἷς ἂν †καρποτρόφοι 475
λάμπωσιν ἐν θαλάμοις
πατρίοισι νεάνιδες ἧβαι,
διαδέκτορα πλοῦτον
ὡς ἕξοντές ἐκ πατέρων
ἑτέροις ἐπὶ τέκνοις· 480
ἀλκά τε γὰρ ἐν κακοῖς,
σύν τ' εὐτυχίαις φίλον,
δορί τε γᾷ πατρίᾳ φέρει
σωτήριον ἀλκάν.
ἐμοὶ μὲν πλούτου τε πάρος 485
βασιλικῶν θαλάμων τ' εἶεν
τροφαὶ κήδειοι κεδνῶν τέκνων.
τὸν ἄπαιδα δ' ἀποστυγῶ
βίον, ᾧ τε δοκεῖ, ψέγω·
μετὰ δὲ κτεάνων μετρίων βιοτᾶς 490

474. ἀφορμὴ, a source, fund, or supply of happiness. It is called ἀκίνητος from being, as it were, stored up in reserve, whereas a man is said κινεῖν χρήματα who constantly draws on his banker's account.
475. The old reading καρποτρόφοι is retained by Hermann and Bothe. Dindorf gives κουροτρόφοι with Musgrave, Dr. Badham καρποτρόφοις. Hermann remarks, apparently with truth, that καρπὸς is never used of children,—though indeed we find ἄλλης γυναικὸς παῖδας ἐκκαρπούμενος inf. v. 815, and Δίοισι καρποῖς in v. 922. There is no difficulty in κουρότροφοι (accented thus) as an epithet to ἥβαι, the sense being ἥβαι κούρων τραφέντων. But perhaps καρποφόροι, 'bringing their reward,' is the simplest and most probable reading.
479. ὡς ἕξοντες, 'with the prospect of inheriting from their fathers a wealth that shall have owners in succession, with other children after them,' i. e. which will be handed down from generation to generation. The masculine participle refers to παῖδες implied in ἥβαι. The γ' which followed ἕξοντες was omitted by Hermann, and Dindorf says it is not found in the Palatine MS.—ἑτέροις ἐπὶ τέκνοις, with other children yet in reserve. Wealth itself is here called διαδέκτωρ, i. e. διαδεξόμενος ἄλλους δεσπότας, whereas usually it is the δεσπότης who is said διαδέχεσθαι πλοῦτον. Barnes paraphrases thus, τὸν ἐκ διαδοχῆς προ(πρὸς?)γινόμενον. But δέκτωρ is active in Aesch. Eum. 195; and it is not uncommon to personify Wealth, as in Agam. 1303 seqq.
487. κήδειοι τροφαὶ, 'the careful nurture.' The doctrine here laid down is opposed to the sentiment expressed in other places by the poet, that an unmarried life is that most free from care. See Med. 1091. Alcest. 882. There is a very beautiful passage in the Danae (frag. 327) in which the blessing of offspring to the childless is described. See also Androm. 419.
490. ἔχεσθαι βιοτᾶς is to adhere to it, not to resign it in favour of any other estate.

εὔπαιδος ἐχοίμαν.
ὦ Πανὸς θακήματα καὶ
παραυλίζουσα πέτρα
μυχώδεσι Μακραῖς,
ἵνα χοροὺς στείβουσι ποδοῖν   495
Ἀγραύλου κόραι τρίγονοι
στάδια χλοερὰ πρὸ Παλλάδος
ναῶν, συρίγγων
ὑπ' αἰόλας ἰαχᾶς
ὕμνων, ὅταν αὐλίοις   500
συρίζῃς, ὦ Πάν,
τοῖσι σοῖς ἐν ἄντροις,
ἵνα τεκοῦσά τις παρθένος, ὦ μελέα,

493. πέτρα. For this grotto of Pan and the shrine of Agraulos or Aglauros, in the Acropolis, see Wordsworth's *Athens and Attica*, chap. xii. (p. 85—88). " At the distance of sixty yards to the east of the cave of Pan, there is an excavation at the base of the rock of the acropolis, which is here very abrupt : and forty yards further to the east there is another grotto near the summit of the rock, and immediately under the wall of the citadel. One of these two is certainly the cave of Agraulos.—The expression μυχώδεις μακραὶ (*hollowed steep*) applied by Euripides to the cave of Agraulos, denoting both a secret cavity and a steep ascent, together with his indication of its proximity to the cave of Pan, corresponds to this (the former) cave better than to any other." The learned writer appears however to be wrong in referring μακραῖς here to the subterranean way which exists between the grotto and the acropolis above. The meaning merely is 'close to the Μακραὶ (or northern cliff of the acropolis) full of μυχοὶ, or artificial caves,' at least three of which existed, for so many still remain. It will be observed that the Paneum and the grotto of Agraulos are here spoken of as quite distinct. See on v. 1400.—μυχώδεσι for μυχοὶ δαισὶ is Tyrwhitt's good, though sufficiently obvious emendation. Matthiae gives μυχάταισι Μακραῖς.

495. χοροὺς στείβουσι. 'Tread the ring,' χορὸς bearing its primary and Homeric sense of 'dancing-place.' Hence εὐρύχοροι ἀγυιαὶ are 'streets wide enough to dance in.' The analogy with χῶρος and εὐρύχωρος is manifest. Hermann refers the reader to Herod. vi. 105. viii. 53, and Pausan. i. 28, 2 and 4, for an account of the sacred caverns or rather subterranean chapels here described. He adds, " Has puellas credebant cum Pane, noctu opinor, choreas ducere, nympharum eas instar habentes."—Ἀγραύλου κόραι, see on v. 23.

497. στάδια χλοερά. In apposition to χορούς. As if these maidens ascended by night from their cave, and danced on the olive-planted terraces before the Erechtheum and the Parthenon. What follows may be rendered, 'to the varied sound of hymns (sung to) the pipe.' Pan is conceived as seated beneath in his cave, and playing music to the dancers above. The faery scene is described with all the romantic imagination of a Greek poet. We see that Euripides could sometimes forget his sophistry, and throw himself into the regions of the supernatural.

503—8. The metres have passed from glyconic to rhythms introductory of the trochaics which follow. Both dochmiac and trochaic verses express excitement and the hurry of passion ; hence vv. 503, 505, 508, are of the former metre. V. 504 is rather irregular, and has an antispastic rather than a baccheo-molossic beat. Dindorf compares it with v. 467. As for 506 and 507, it is best to scan them as irregular anapaestics, in which, as usual, the pause of regular systems is neglected.

βρέφος Φοίβῳ πτανοῖς ἐξώριζεν θοίναν
θηρσί τε φοινίαν δαῖτα, πικρῶν γάμων 505
ὕβριν. οὔτ' ἐπὶ κερκίσιν οὔτε λόγοις
φάτιν ἄιον εὐτυχίας μετέχειν
θεόθεν τέκνα θνατοῖς.

ΙΩ. πρόσπολοι γυναῖκες, αἳ τῶνδ' ἀμφὶ κρηπῖδας δόμων 510
θυοδόκων φρούρημ' ἔχουσαι δεσπότην φυλάσσετε,
ἐκλέλοιπ' ἤδη τὸν ἱρὸν τρίποδα καὶ χρηστήριον
Ξοῦθος, ἢ μίμνει κατ' οἶκον ἱστορῶν ἀπαιδίαν;

ΧΟ. ἐν δόμοις ἔστ', ὦ ξέν'· οὔπω δῶμ' ὑπερβαίνει τόδε.
ὡς δ' ἐπ' ἐξόδοισιν ὄντος τῶνδ' ἀκούομεν πυλῶν
δοῦπον, ἐξιόντα τ' ἤδη δεσπότην ὁρᾶν πάρα. 516

ΞΟ. ὦ τέκνον, χαῖρ'· ἡ γὰρ ἀρχὴ τοῦ λόγου πρέπουσά
μοι.

ΙΩ. χαίρομεν· σὺ δ' εὖ φρόνει γε, καὶ δύ' ὄντ' εὖ πράξομεν.

505. πικρῶν γάμων ὕβριν, the fruit of a forced union full of sorrow to herself. The child itself is called ὕβρις, like ἀδίκημα in v. 325.

506. ἐπὶ κερκίσιν ἄιον, I have never learnt while seated at the web, nor yet in stories. Cf. v. 196. The heroes and demigods were often represented in embroidery as performing some stupendous labour, like Atlas, Hercules, Theseus, &c.—θεόθεν τέκνα, τὰ ἐκ θεῶν γεννηθέντα. See on v. 377.

510. Ion, now deeply interested in the fortunes of Creusa, wishes to see Xuthus, and inquires of the chorus (the servants of Creusa) whether or not he has left the temple. While yet speaking, he is surprised by Xuthus, who with hurried step and joyous countenance rushes into his embrace. The god has declared that the first person he shall have met on leaving the shrine will be his (Xuthus') son. Full of faith in the veracity of his patron god, the young man easily allows himself to be persuaded that he has found his father. A few questions as to the circumstances of his birth tend to remove all difficulties; he has nothing now left, but to sigh for the discovery of his mother (v. 564).

Ibid. κρηπῖδας, the altars, properly, the steps. See Hel. 547.—ἔχουσαι for ἔχοντα is the correction of H. Stephens, who, as usual, pretended MSS. authority for it. It is necessary to the sense, since the next lines show that Xuthus was not waiting ἀμφὶ βωμοὺς, but had retired into the interior.

517. Dr. Badham reads ἥδε γ' ἀρχὴ, which he says the sense imperatively requires. This may be doubted; but even if we grant that the demonstrative is wanted, there are not a few passages where the article has a meaning nearest to our 'this,' or 'those,' or 'that' &c. And so Bothe observes, "ἡ pro αὕτη," though perhaps he wrongly took it for the Homeric use of the article.

518. εὖ φρόνει. A question arises, whether this rare meaning, 'rejoice,' εὐφραίνου, should not be distinguished from the other, which we have below, v. 520, 'to be in one's right senses,' by being written εὐφρόνει, on the analogy of εὖ σέβειν and εὐσεβεῖν. And in fact the early editions of Hervagius and Brubach, as Hermann noticed, so print the word. The meaning, at all events, would be determined by the context, were no other example to be found; ἐγὼ χαίρω, καὶ σὺ χαῖρε, καὶ ἄμφω εὖ πράξομεν. But in Aesch. Cho. 761, ἀλλ' ἦ φρονεῖς εὖ τοῖσι νῦν ἠγγελμένοις; 'Can it be that you are at heart glad at the death of Orestes,

ΙΩΝ.   41

ΞΟ. δὸς χερὸς φίλημά μοι σῆς σώματός τ' ἀμφιπτυχάς.
ΙΩ. εὖ φρονεῖς μέν, ἤ σ' ἔμηνε θεοῦ τις, ὦ ξένε, βλάβη;
ΞΟ. σωφρονῶ, τὰ φίλταθ' εὑρὼν εἰ φιλεῖν ἐφίεμαι.   521
ΙΩ. παῦε, μὴ ψαύσας τὰ τοῦ θεοῦ στέμματα ῥήξῃς χερί.
ΞΟ. ἅψομαι κοὐ ῥυσιάζω, τἀμὰ δ' εὑρίσκω φίλα.
ΙΩ. οὐκ ἀπαλλάξει, πρὶν εἴσω τόξα πνευμόνων λαβεῖν;
ΞΟ. ὡς τί δὴ φεύγεις με, σαυτοῦ γνωρίσας τὰ φίλτατα;
ΙΩ. οὐ φιλῶ φρενοῦν ἀμούσους καὶ μεμηνότας ξένους.
ΞΟ. κτεῖνε καὶ πίμπρη· πατρὸς γάρ, ἢν κτάνῃς, ἔσει
    φονεύς.   527
ΙΩ. ποῦ δέ μοι πατὴρ σύ; ταῦτ' οὖν οὐ γέλως κλύειν
    ἐμοί;
ΞΟ. οὔ· τρέχων ὁ μῦθος ἄν σοι τἀμὰ σημήνειεν ἄν.
ΙΩ. καὶ τί μοι λέξεις;   530
ΞΟ.   πατὴρ σός εἰμι καὶ σὺ παῖς ἐμός.
ΙΩ. τίς λέγει τάδ'; ΞΟ. ὅς σ' ἔθρεψεν ὄντα Λοξίας ἐμόν.

when you ought rather to mourn?' and also in Agam. 262, εὖ γὰρ φρονοῦντος ὄμμα σοῦ κατηγορεῖ, which is the answer to χαρά μ' ὑφέρπει, δάκρυον ἐκκαλουμένη, —in both these passages εὖ φρονεῖν is certainly a synonym of εὐφραίνεσθαι. In the former, the Schol. explains it by χαίρεις.
520. εὖ φρονεῖς μέν; 'Are you sure you are in your senses?' The μέν interrogatively used implies a faint degree of doubt, because, in fact, the particle asserts, while the question again invalidates the position; 'You are in your senses, of course; are you not?' See Med. 1129. Alcest. 147.
521. σωφρονῶ. 'I am in my senses,' i. e. there is nothing in my conduct to prove I am not, 'if having found one who is dearest to me I am desirous to show my affection for him.' Hermann and Dindorf adopt the reading of Jacobs, οὐ φρονῶ, with a question at the end of the verse. This is probable, but it is certainly not necessary. See Helen. 97. So of the Mad Hercules, ἀμπνοάς τ' οὐ σωφρονίζει, Herc. 869, and of the inspired Cassandra Hecuba says, οὐδὲ σαὶ τύχαι, τέκνον, σεσωφρόνηκας', Tro. 350. The adjective commonly used was not σώφρων, but ἔμφρων, inf. v. 553, Iph. Taur. 315. There is another reading φυγεῖν, which

has resulted from understanding the verse interrogatively; 'Am I wise if I wish to shun my own son?'
523. ἅψομαι κτλ. 'I shall lay hands on you, and (in doing so) I am not forcibly seizing what is not my own, but only recovering my dearest rights.' The meaning of this verb ῥυσιάζειν has been fully explained on Aesch. Suppl. 406. It is commonly combined with ἅπτεσθαι or ἐφάπτεσθαι, as in that passage, and ib. 708. Oed. Col. 858. The proper meaning is 'to distrain.' Inf. 1406, ῥυσιάζομαι λόγῳ. Aesch. Suppl. 417, μηδ' ἴδῃς μ' ἐξ ἑδρᾶν πολυθέων ῥυσιασθεῖσαν.
524. τόξα, here for οἰστόν. He was armed with a bow, v. 108, 165, not only to keep away the birds, but because Apollo himself was the god of the bow, and his servant thought to do him honour by assuming the same attire.
525. γνωρίσας. Improperly used for εὑρών, ἐντυχών. Hermann reads γνώρισον, because Ion "repperit quidem patrem, sed non agnovit."—For ὡς τί δὴ see Herc. F. 1407.
528. ποῦ κτλ. The real meaning is, 'You are not my father.' See on Heracl. 369. " Cum indignatione negat," as Elmsley rightly explains this usage.
530. On καὶ τί, expressing incredulity, see Hel. 583.

VOL. II.   G

ΙΩ. μαρτυρεῖς σαυτῷ.
ΞΟ. τὰ τοῦ θεοῦ γ' ἐκμαθὼν χρηστήρια.
ΙΩ. ἐσφάλης αἴνιγμ' ἀκούσας.
ΞΟ. οὐκ ἄρ' ὀρθ' ἀκούομεν.
ΙΩ. ὁ δὲ λόγος τίς ἐστὶ Φοίβου;
ΞΟ. τὸν συναντήσαντά μοι
ΙΩ. τίνα συνάντησιν; ΞΟ. δόμων τῶνδ' ἐξιόντι τοῦ θεοῦ
ΙΩ. συμφορᾶς τίνος κυρῆσαι; ΞΟ. παῖδ' ἐμὸν πεφυκέναι.
ΙΩ. σὸν γεγῶτ', ἢ δῶρον ἄλλων; 537
ΞΟ. δῶρον, ὄντα δ' ἐξ ἐμοῦ.
ΙΩ. πρῶτα δῆτ' ἐμοὶ ξυνάπτεις πόδα σόν;
ΞΟ. οὐκ ἄλλῳ, τέκνον.
ΙΩ. ἡ τύχη πόθεν ποθ' ἥκει; ΞΟ. δύο μίαν θαυμάζομεν.
ΙΩ. ἔα· τίνος δέ σοι πέφυκα μητρός; 540
ΞΟ. οὐκ ἔχω φράσαι.
ΙΩ. οὐδὲ Φοῖβος εἶπε;
ΞΟ. τερφθεὶς τοῦτο, κεῖν' οὐκ ἠρόμην.
ΙΩ. γῆς ἄρ' ἐκπέφυκα μητρός. ΞΟ. οὐ πέδον τίκτει τέκνα.
ΙΩ. πῶς ἂν οὖν εἴην σός;
ΞΟ. οὐκ οἶδ', ἀναφέρω δ' ἐς τὸν θεόν.
ΙΩ. φέρε λόγων ἀψώμεθ' ἄλλων.
ΞΟ. ταῦτ' ἄμεινον, ὦ τέκνον.
ΙΩ. ἦλθες ἐς νόθον τι λέκτρον; ΞΟ. μωρίᾳ γε τοῦ νέου.

537. ἄλλων. So Dobree for ἄλλως, which Matthiae explains *nil nisi donum*. Musgrave had corrected ὄντα σ' ἐξ ἐμοῦ to ὄντα δ'. The answer is, δῶρον μὲν, οὐκ ἐξ ἄλλων δὲ, ἀλλ' ἐξ ἐμοῦ πεφυκότα. For Apollo had told him this for the reasons assigned v. 70. The words are a sort of quibble, for δῶρον implies, what was really the case, that a son was given to a childless man merely in the way of a foster-child; but Xuthus, instead of selecting one of the two alternatives suggested by Ion, combines them both, according to the response he had received. He believed Ion to be truly his son, but he regarded him as a δῶρον, because he was the property of Apollo, as being a minister of his temple.
542. γῆς ἄρ'. Dr. Badham thinks it the height of absurdity to make Ion say this as if he believed it; and he puts a question at μητρός. Generally the words of Ion in this dialogue are questions, and those of Xuthus only replies; for which reason the question commonly placed at the end of v. 533 has been omitted. There is however no other difficulty here than the slight irony, which indeed is obvious enough. 'I suppose then I am a son of earth;' and Xuthus, in an equally playful way, denies that there is any reality in a traditional and proverbial phrase. (The origin of it may be found in the Homeric and Hesiodic expression for autochthony, ἀπὸ δρυὸς καὶ πέτρης. See Müller's History of Greek Literature, p. 82, note.)
545. μωρίᾳ γε τοῦ νέου, διὰ τὴν τῆς νεό-

ΙΩ. πρὶν κόρην λαβεῖν Ἐρεχθέως;   546
ΞΟ.   οὐ γὰρ ὕστερόν γέ πω.
ΙΩ. ἆρα δῆτ' ἐκεῖ μ' ἔφυσας;
ΞΟ.   τῷ χρόνῳ γε συντρέχει.
ΙΩ. κᾆτα πῶς ἀφικόμεσθα δεῦρο; ΞΟ. ταῦτ' ἀμηχανῶ.
ΙΩ. διὰ μακρᾶς ἐλθὼν κελεύθου;
ΞΟ.   τοῦτο κἄμ' ἀπαιολᾷ.
ΙΩ. Πυθίαν δ' ἦλθες πέτραν πρίν; 550
ΞΟ.   ἐς φανάς γε Βακχίου.
ΙΩ. προξένων δ' ἔν του κατέσχες;
ΞΟ.   ὅς με Δελφίσιν κόραις
ΙΩ. ἐθιάσευσ', ἢ πῶς τάδ' αὐδᾷς;
ΞΟ.   Μαινάσιν γε Βακχίου.
ΙΩ. ἔμφρον', ἢ κάτοινον ὄντα; ΞΟ. Βακχίου πρὸς ἡδοναῖς.
ΙΩ. τοῦτ' ἐκεῖν' ἵν' ἐσπάρημεν.
ΞΟ.   ὁ πότμος ἐξηῦρεν, τέκνον.
ΙΩ. πῶς δ' ἀφικόμεσθα ναούς; ΞΟ. ἔκβολον κόρης ἴσως.
ΙΩ. ἐκπεφεύγαμεν τὸ δοῦλον.   556

τητος ἀκράτειαν. See Hippol. 966. Tro. 988. Helen. 1018.
547. ἐκεῖ, viz. ἐν νόθῳ λέκτρῳ, at Athens, or perhaps in Phthiotis, v. 64.
549. ἐλθών. Used after ἀφικόμεσθα as inf. 1251. Ion here suggests a difficulty as to his having been born from an Athenian or Euboean mother, and accordingly asks if he may not have been the fruit of some former amour at Delphi.—The old reading ἀπαιολεῖ is retained by Hermann. Dindorf follows Musgrave in restoring the only form known to us from the grammarians. Hesych. ἀπαιολᾶν, παραλογίζεσθαι. See Hel. 1056.
550. φανάς, the orgies, mystic rites, τελετάς. Rhes. 943, μυστηρίων τε τῶν ἀπορρήτων φανὰς ἔδειξεν Ὀρφεύς. Hermann accents the word φάνας. Photius, φανὰς, τὰς ἐκλάμψεις.
551. ἔν του W. Dind. for ἐν τῷ, and so Dr. Badham. ἔν τῳ L. Dind. Herm.—κατασχεῖν or καταλύειν ἔν τινὸς is the usual phrase for 'to lodge in a person's house.' The former verb is a metaphor from putting a ship ashore. Cf. Heracl. 83, πέραθεν ἁλίῳ πλάτᾳ κατέχετε;

552. ἐθιάσευσε, 'introduced you to the company of' &c. See on Hel. 541. Bacch. 75. 378.—In what follows γε for τε is Musgrave's, who also corrected the corrupt ἐθίασέ σ'. Similarly in Bacch. 377, one MS. has θιεύσειν for θιασεύειν.
554. τοῦτ' ἐκεῖν' ἵν' κτλ. 'That was the very occasion whereon I was begotten.' The clever emendation of Elmsley for τοῦτ' ἐκεῖ νῦν. Cf. Med. 98, τόδ' ἐκεῖνο, φίλοι παῖδες· μάτηρ κινεῖ κραδίαν. Hel. 622, τοῦτ' ἔστ' ἐκεῖνο. Dr. Badham says, "ἵνα could in no case be a relative to ἐκεῖνο." But in saying it he does not give the Greek language due credit for the pliancy it possesses. No doubt ἵνα means 'where,' and ἐκεῖνο includes place, time, and the general circumstances of the birth. In retaining ὁ πότμος σ' ἐξεῦρεν (which violates the metre, and which was corrected by Hermann and before him by Heath), Dr. Badham gives his readers an evidence that he has dealt hastily with the passage.
555. ἔκβολον, an outcast. This substantive occurs Hel. 422.
556. τὸ δοῦλον. 'Then I am not the

ΞΟ.   πατέρα νυν δέχου, τέκνον.
ΙΩ.   τῷ θεῷ γοῦν οὐκ ἀπιστεῖν εἰκός.
ΞΟ.   εὖ φρονεῖς ἄρα.
ΙΩ.   καὶ τί βουλόμεσθά γ' ἄλλο·
ΞΟ.   νῦν ὁρᾷς ἃ χρή σ' ὁρᾶν.
ΙΩ.   ἦ Διὸς παιδὸς γενέσθαι παῖς;
ΞΟ.   ὃ σοί γε γίγνεται.
ΙΩ.   ἦ θίγω δῆθ' οἵ μ' ἔφυσαν;   560
ΞΟ.   πιθόμενός γε τῷ θεῷ.
ΙΩ.   χαῖρέ μοι, πάτερ,
ΞΟ.   φίλον γε φθέγμ' ἐδεξάμην τόδε.
ΙΩ.   ἡμέρα θ' ἡ νῦν παροῦσα.
ΞΟ.   μακάριόν γ' ἔθηκέ με.
ΙΩ.   ὦ φίλη μῆτερ, πότ' ἆρα καὶ σὸν ὄψομαι δέμας;
      νῦν ποθῶ σε μᾶλλον ἢ πρὶν, ἥτις εἶ ποτ', εἰσιδεῖν.
      ἀλλ' ἴσως τέθνηκας, ἡμεῖς δ' οὐδὲν ἂν δυναίμεθα.
ΧΟ.   κοιναὶ μὲν ἡμῖν δωμάτων εὐπραξίαι·   566
      ὅμως δὲ καὶ δέσποιναν ἐς τέκν' εὐτυχεῖν
      ἐβουλόμην ἂν τούς τ' Ἐρεχθέως δόμους.
ΞΟ.   ὦ τέκνον, ἐς μὲν σὴν ἀνεύρεσιν θεὸς
      ὀρθῶς ἔκρανε, καὶ συνῆψ' ἐμοί τε σὲ,   570
      σύ τ' αὖ τὰ φίλταθ' ηὗρες, οὐκ εἰδὼς πάρος.
      ὃ δ' ἧξας ὀρθῶς, τοῦτο κἄμ' ἔχει πόθος,

supposititious child of some female slave.'
Cf. Alcest. 638, δουλίου δ' ἀφ' αἵματος
Μαστῷ γυναικὸς σῆς ὑπεβλήθην λάθρα.
559. Διὸς παιδὸς παῖς. Ion knew that
Xuthus was a descendant of Zeus, sup.
v. 292. But the words are so framed, as
Barnes well observes, that they may also
signify, what was in fact the case, that
the youth was the son of Apollo, who
was παῖς Διός.—ὃ for ᾗ Scaliger.
563. πότ' ἆρα, for ἆρά ποτε. Rhes.
360, ἆρά ποτ' αὖθις ἁ παλαιὰ Τροία τοὺς
προπότας παναμερεύσει θιάσους; Bacch.
862, ἆρ' ἐν παννυχίοις χοροῖς θήσω ποτὲ
λευκὸν πόδ' ἀναβακχεύουσα; It is not
here to be regarded as a transposition
(for the enclitic ποτε would then stand
first,) but as a mixture of two questions,
'Shall I ever see it?' and 'When shall I
see it?' Compare τίς ἆρα, Iph. T. 472.
565. οὐδὲν δύνασθαι is used absolutely

for 'to be helpless,' viz. to be unable to
find the looked-for object by any efforts
that might be employed.
566. κοιναὶ ἡμῖν. Whether on the part
of Xuthus, or on that of Creusa, the
royal family of Athens has met with good
fortune, it is alike shared in by us. Still,
if we had a choice, we should have preferred that our mistress, who is of the
direct line of Erechtheus, had found a
son, rather than Xuthus, who is an
alien.
570. Dr. Badham finds difficulty in
ὀρθῶς, which merely means that the god
has given a true oracle as the result has
shown, viz. in saying that the first person
Xuthus met would be his son. We have
μαντεύματα κραίνει in v. 464. Suppl.
139, τί δ' εἴπ' Ἀπόλλων, παρθένοις κραίνων
γάμον;
572. ὃ ἧξας. With regard to the point

ὅπως σύ τ', ὦ παῖ, μητέρ' εὑρήσεις σέθεν,
ἐγώ θ' ὁποίας μοι γυναικὸς ἐξέφυς.
χρόνῳ δὲ δόντες ταῦτ' ἴσως εὕροιμεν ἄν.   575
ἀλλ' ἐκλιπὼν θεοῦ δάπεδ' ἀλητείαν τε σὴν
ἐς τὰς Ἀθήνας στεῖχε κοινόφρων πατρὶ,
οὗ σ' ὄλβιον μὲν σκῆπτρον ἀναμένει πατρὸς,
πολὺς δὲ πλοῦτος· οὐδὲ θάτερον νοσῶν
δυοῖν κεκλήσει δυσγενὴς πένης θ' ἅμα,   580
ἀλλ' εὐγενής τε καὶ πολυκτήμων βίου.
σιγᾷς; τί πρὸς γῆν ὄμμα σὸν βαλὼν ἔχεις;
ἐς φροντίδας δ' ἀπῆλθες, ἐκ δὲ χαρμονῆς
πάλιν μεταστὰς δεῖμα προσβάλλεις πατρί.

ΙΩ. οὐ ταυτὸν εἶδος φαίνεται τῶν πραγμάτων   585

which you rightly mooted, or, in pursuit of which you started, ὃ μετῆλθες, ἐφ' ὃ ὥρμησας. Cf. v. 328, οὐδ' ἦξας εἰς ἔρευναν ἐξευρεῖν γονάς;—κἄμ' ἔχει φόβος is for κἀγὼ φοβοῦμαι, and therefore takes an accusative. Pflugk on Heracl. 739 compares τοῦτο γὰρ φόβος, and Bacch. 1289, λέγ', ὡς τὸ μέλλον καρδία πήδημ' ἔχει.

574. μοι. The dative is used as in v. 4.

576. ἀλητείαν σήν. The Greek idea of ἀλήτης was rather an absentee from home, than one who actually wandered about. Hence the word applies well enough to Ion. Matthiae well quotes Hel. 934, τὴν ἐνθάδ' ἐκλιποῦσ' ἀλητείαν πικράν.

577. ἐς τὰς Ἀθήνας. The article is occasionally added, as inf. 1021, Heracl. 69, ὦ τὰς Ἀθήνας δαρὸν οἰκοῦντες χρόνον.

579. θάτερον δυοῖν. Though badly off in respect of one of two things, viz. not knowing your mother. But for the next line, where Xuthus says he shall be called both well-born and wealthy, τὸ ἕτερον might have meant πενία, 'though poor, you shall not be called also base-born.' Poverty however was not one of the evils of which Ion had complained. Cf v. 326, εὖ γὰρ ἤσκησαι πέπλοις.

583. φροντίδας τ' Dindorf, who, with other editors, place the interrogation at the end of v. 584.

585. The speech of Ion is full of political import,—in fact it is an encomium on the constitution of Athens. The first part of it is evidently directed against the ambition of meddling μέτοικοι, who would intrude themselves into office in a state naturally jealous of foreign influences. See on Suppl. 892.—He begins by remarking that men view things differently from a distance and from close at hand. At first sight he was overjoyed at finding his father; but there are difficulties which he foresees will present an obstacle to his removal to Athens. That people are proud of their indigenous descent. The man who is at once an alien and born out of wedlock will meet with nothing but taunts. Thus, if powerless, he will remain in obscurity; if he attains to office in the state, he will be envied by those of inferior ability. The good and wise, but retiring citizens, will condemn and deride his ambition; the influential statesmen will oppose him in all his public measures. Again, in a domestic point of view, nothing but unhappiness will accrue from his introduction to Creusa's family. Before, she shared the reproach of childlessness with her lord; now she will have to bear it alone. The wife will be jealous, and the husband will have to choose his side between a wife and a son. Who can calculate on the schemes that a jealous woman may plot against the life of her husband! Besides, he feels pity for the hopeless barrenness she will then have to bewail in her latter years. Against these evils he will not weigh the charms of overpraised sovereignty. It is fair in aspect, but full of troubles within. Who can be really happy who lives in constant fear? He had rather dwell in security as a pri-

ΕΥΡΙΠΙΔΟΥ

πρόσωθεν ὄντων ἐγγύθεν θ᾽ ὁρωμένων.
ἐγὼ δὲ τὴν μὲν συμφορὰν ἀσπάζομαι,
πατέρα σ᾽ ἀνευρών· ὧν δὲ γιγνώσκω πέρι
ἄκουσον. εἶναί φασι τὰς αὐτόχθονας
κλεινὰς Ἀθήνας οὐκ ἐπείσακτον γένος,   590
ἵν᾽ εἰσπεσοῦμαι δύο νόσω κεκτημένος,
πατρός τ᾽ ἐπακτοῦ καὐτὸς ὢν νοθαγενής.
καὶ τοῦτ᾽ ἔχων τοὔνειδος, ἀσθενὴς μὲν ὤν,
— * * *   μηδὲν κοὐδένων κεκλήσομαι·
ἦν δ᾽ ἐς τὸ πρῶτον πόλεος ὁρμηθεὶς ζυγὸν   595
ζητῶ τις εἶναι, τῶν μὲν ἀδυνάτων ὕπο
μισησόμεσθα· λυπρὰ γὰρ τὰ κρείσσονα·
ὅσοι δὲ χρηστοὶ δυνάμενοί τ᾽ εἶναι σοφοὶ

vate citizen, than as a tyrant who fears the good, and is compelled to attach to himself the bad. Wealth has no counterbalance for these anxieties; a sufficiency without cares is a happier lot. In his present position he enjoyed many blessings. He had leisure, and he commanded the respect of all. The service of the gods and the conversation of men, the absence of sorrowful faces, the continual succession of strangers, and lastly, the disposition to be just, are delights which he prizes above the splendid misery of a proffered throne.

588. γιγνώσκω, what I am thinking about, what I am entertaining an opinion upon.—τὰς αὐτόχθονας, i. e. καλουμένας, as Hermann maintains, in order to avoid a tautology, 'they say that the indigenous Athenians are not an imported race.' This however is merely another way of saying, 'They tell us that the Athenians are indigenous, and not an imported race.'

594. The old reading was μηδὲν καὶ οὐδὲν ὢν κεκλήσομαι. Hermann and Dr. Badham rightly object to ὤν, the one because it is repeated after ἀσθενὴς μὲν ὤν, the other because καλεῖσθαι ὤν is not the usual idiom. Dindorf gives Scaliger's correction as improved by Valckenaer, ὁ (Scaliger τὸ) μηδὲν ὢν κἀξ οὐδένων κεκλήσομαι. Hermann reads as given in the text, with the marks of a lacuna. So also Dr. Badham, who supplies αὐτὸς τὸ μηδὲν κτλ., which gives a good antithesis between Ion's own personal worthlessness and that of his parents. One might also conjecture ἀσθενὴς μὲν ὢν ἀνὴρ, τὸ μηδὲν κοὐδένων κεκλήσομαι.

595. ζυγόν. A metaphor from the first bench of rowers in a trireme. The second rowers were indeed called ζυγῖται, but the epithet πρῶτον here distinguishes the principal seat. See the note on Agam. 1595, σὺ ταῦτα φωνεῖς νερτέρα προσήμενος κώπῃ, κρατούντων τῶν ἐπὶ ζυγῷ δορός; and Phoen. 74, ἐπεὶ δ᾽ ἐπὶ ζυγοῖς καθέζετ᾽ ἀρχῆς.

596. ἀδυνάτων, those who have attained no influence in the state. See on Bacch. 270. Such persons will envy him, because superiority in a rival is ever odious. Cf. Med. 301, τῶν δ᾽ αὖ δοκούντων εἰδέναι τι ποικίλον κρείσσων νομισθεὶς λυπρὸς ἐν πόλει φανεῖ.

598. δυνάμενοι εἶναι σοφοί. Those who could, if they pleased, attain the reputation of clever statesmen, but who, being naturally ἀπράγμονες and ἡσυχαῖοι, ridicule others who are more energetic, as being foolish to take so much trouble in a city which is sure to disparage them. Dr. Donaldson (New Cratylus, p. 406,) considers that the poet is here describing the καλοὶ κἀγαθοὶ, and that the expression in the text implies that facility of acquiring knowledge and accomplishments, by the attainment of which the nobles became καλοί.—ψόγου for φόβου is the correction of Musgrave. It seems required by the context; yet Hermann and Dindorf retain the vulgate. Stephens' ψόφον, for which he pretended the authority of MSS., is inapplicable, for ψόφος is not used like θόρυβος, for popular clamour.

σιγῶσι κοὐ σπεύδουσιν ἐς τὰ πράγματα,
γέλωτ' ἐν αὐτοῖς μωρίαν τε λήψομαι 600
οὐχ ἡσυχάζων ἐν πόλει ψόγου πλέᾳ.
τῶν δ' αὖ λογίων τε χρωμένων τε τῇ πόλει
εἰς ἀξίωμα βὰς, πλέον φρουρήσομαι
ψήφοισιν. οὕτω γὰρ τάδ', ὦ πάτερ, φιλεῖ·
οἳ τὰς πόλεις ἔχουσι κἀξιώματα, 605
τοῖς ἀνθαμίλλοις εἰσὶ πολεμιώτατοι.
ἐλθὼν δ' ἐς οἶκον ἀλλότριον ἔπηλυς ὢν,
γυναῖκά θ' ὡς ἄτεκνον, ἣ κοινουμένη
τὰς συμφοράς σοι πρόσθεν, ἀπολαχοῦσα νῦν
αὐτὴ καθ' αὑτὴν τὴν τύχην οἴσει πικρῶς, 610
πῶς δ' οὐχ ὑπ' αὐτῆς εἰκότως μισήσομαι,
ὅταν παραστῶ σοὶ μὲν ἐγγύθεν ποδὸς,
ἡ δ' οὖσ' ἄτεκνος τὰ σὰ φίλ' εἰσορᾷ πικρῶς,
κᾆτ' ἢ προδοὺς σύ μ' ἐς δάμαρτα σὴν βλέπῃς,
ἢ τἀμὰ τιμῶν δῶμα συγχέας ἔχῃς; 615
ὅσας σφαγὰς δὴ φαρμάκων τε θανασίμων

602. λογίων τε. Most editors have regarded these words as corrupt; see however on v. 285. Virgil and the other Roman poets must have been familiar with this pronunciation, because they make *fluviorum, ariete,* &c. long in the first syllable to adapt them to hexameter verse. Matthiae doubts the meaning which is here required, viz. 'men of repute,' as not used except by historic writers; and he reads τῶν δ' ἐν λόγῳ τε, which Hermann and Dindorf adopt. Dr. Badham thinks it possible that λογίων was a gloss on σοφῶν used in a rather uncommon sense for 'eloquent.' Heath proposed τῶν δ' αὖτε λογίων. None of these conjectures carry much weight with them. The present editor is inclined to think the reading given above is the genuine one. The αὖ contrasts the ἀδύνατοι with the λόγιοι, and shows that the sense is 'clever,' 'well educated in the arts of statesmen,' including, of course, eloquence. Translate: ' But if on the other hand I shall have aspired to the dignity of those who are called able men, and who manage the affairs of the state, I shall be more guardedly kept in check by their votes (i. e. at the ἀρχαιρεσίαι, or annual election to office, unless, as Schaefer and Hermann think, there is an allusion to ostracism,) for such, my father, is wont to be the case in cities; those who hold in their hands the governments and the dignities of office, are ever most hostile to their opponents.'

605. Stobaeus, who quotes this and the next verse, xlv. 4, has οἱ τὰς πόλεις ἔχοντες ἀξιώματά τε, which Dindorf adopts. Dr. Badham, in reading ἀξιώματος and construing it with ἀνθαμίλλοις, has not sufficiently attended to the order of the words. Hermann thus sums up the general sense from v. 595; "Si re publica gerenda aliquid laudis consequi studebo, apud vulgus in odium incurram; a sapientibus, qui privatae vitae tranquillitatem praeferunt, ridebor; a potentibus in civitate, quo plus auctoritatis adeptus ero, eo majore petar invidia."

609. ἀπολαχοῦσα, having a separate lot, viz. bearing all the discredit of childlessness in her own person.

611. πῶς δ'. The δὲ, omitted by Dindorf after Canter, is defended by Herm. and Matth., as marking the apodosis, *quomodo, inquam,* &c.

616. ὅσας, 'how many!' See on Helen. 461. The τε was added by Tyrwhitt. The conjecture mentioned by Dr. Bad-

γυναῖκες ηὗρον ἀνδράσιν διαφθοράς.
ἄλλως τε τὴν σὴν ἄλοχον οἰκτείρω, πάτερ,
ἄπαιδα γηράσκουσαν· οὐ γὰρ ἀξία
πατέρων ἀπ' ἐσθλῶν οὖσ' ἀπαιδίᾳ νοσεῖν. 620
τυραννίδος δὲ τῆς μάτην αἰνουμένης
τὸ μὲν πρόσωπον ἡδύ, τἀν δόμοισι δὲ
λυπηρά· τίς γὰρ μακάριος, τίς εὐτυχὴς,
ὅστις δεδοικὼς καὶ παραβλέπων βίαν
αἰῶνα τείνει; δημότης δ' ἂν εὐτυχὴς 625
ζῆν ἂν θέλοιμι μᾶλλον ἢ τύραννος ὤν,
ᾧ τοὺς πονηροὺς ἡδονὴ φίλους ἔχειν,
ἐσθλοὺς δὲ μισεῖ κατθανεῖν φοβούμενος.
εἴποις ἂν ὡς ὁ χρυσὸς ἐκνικᾷ τάδε,
πλουτεῖν τε τερπνόν· οὐ φιλῶ ψόγους κλύειν 630
ἐν χερσὶ σώζων ὄλβον οὐδ' ἔχειν πόνους.
εἴη δ' ἐμοὶ μὲν μέτρια μὴ λυπουμένῳ.

ham, θυμοφθόρων, is wrong in point of sense, for θυμοφθόρα φάρμακα are drugs which cause stupor, and destroy the intellect rather than the life. Besides, some particle is necessary to connect σφαγὰς with διαφθορὰς, because σφαγὴ refers to death by the sword, while διαφθείρειν φαρμάκοις is elsewhere used, e. g. in Hipp. 389. Compare *inf.* 844—5. Dindorf has a fancy that these two verses are interpolated. The connexion however is quite obvious; 'many a wife before now has poisoned her husband; beware of provoking Creusa to a similar deed.' Cf. Frag. Cress. 467, γαμεῖτε, νῦν γαμεῖτε, κᾆτα θνήσκετε ἢ φαρμάκοισιν ἐκ γυναικὸς ἢ δόλοις. Med. 384, κράτιστα τὴν εὐθεῖαν, ᾗ πεφύκαμεν σοφαὶ μάλιστα, φαρμάκοις αὐτοὺς ἑλεῖν.
618. ἄλλως τε. Cf. Suppl. 417.
620. ἀπαιδίᾳ Hermann and others for —αν. It is one thing to say νόσον νοσεῖν, another to say ἀπαιδίαν νοσεῖν, which is not a cognate accusative.
621. Stobaeus, who quotes this and the following lines to v. 628, has τῆς μάτην θρυλλουμένης, Vol. ii. p. 284, ed. Teubner (xlviii. 2).
624. παραβλέπων βίαν, 'looking aside for violence,' watching lest an attack should be made on him on the right or the left. Stobaeus has περιβλέπων, and both he and the MSS. of Euripides give βίον, which was corrected by Stephens. The compound with παρὰ presents a much more forcible picture. The tyrant walks along with head erect and stately mien, unwilling to show the least fear of his subjects. But if you mark his eye, you will see it is nervously cast on each side of him in quick succession; for every doubtful face suggests a concealed dagger.
625. δημότης δ' εὐτυχής. Hippol. 1016,
ἐγὼ δ' ἀγῶνας μὲν κρατεῖν Ἑλληνικοὺς
πρῶτος θέλοιμ' ἄν· ἐν πόλει δὲ δεύτερος
σὺν τοῖς ἀρίστοις εὐτυχεῖν ἀεὶ φίλοις.
πράσσειν γὰρ εὖ πάρεστι, κίνδυνός τ' ἀπὼν
κρείσσω δίδωσι τῆς τυραννίδος χάριν.

The δὲ is omitted by Dindorf, after Stobaeus. But the connexion of sentences by some particle or other is a matter in which a little observation will show that the tragic writers were extremely careful.
630. ψόγους Brodaeus for ψόφους.
632. ἐμοὶ μὲν Herm. with ed. Brubach., the others having ἐμοί. Some antithesis is implied, as ἄλλοις δὲ ἄλλα ἀρέσκει. Aesch. Ag. 896, ἐν ποικίλοις δὲ θνητὸν ὄντα κάλλεσιν βαίνειν, ἐμοὶ μὲν οὐδαμῶς ἄνευ φθόνου. See on Androm. 147. Dind. gives ἔμοιγε after Lenting. With μέτρια understand χρήματα, implied in ὄλβον preceding.

ἃ δ' ἐνθάδ' εἶχον ἀγάθ' ἄκουσόν μου, πάτερ·
τὴν φιλτάτην μὲν πρῶτον ἀνθρώποις σχολὴν
ὄχλον τε μέτριον· οὐδέ μ' ἐξέπληξ' ὁδοῦ   635
πονηρὸς οὐδείς· κεῖνο δ' οὐκ ἀνασχετὸν,
εἴκειν ὁδοῦ χαλῶντα τοῖς κακίοσιν.
θεῶν δ' ἐν εὐχαῖς ἢ λόγοισιν ἢ βροτῶν,
ὑπηρετῶν χαίρουσιν, οὐ γοωμένοις.
καὶ τοὺς μὲν ἐξέπεμπον, οἱ δ' ἧκον ξένοι,   640
ὥσθ' ἡδὺς ἀεὶ καινὸς ὢν καινοῖσιν ἦν.
ὃ δ' εὐκτὸν ἀνθρώποισι, κἂν ἄκουσιν ᾖ,
δίκαιον εἶναί μ' ὁ νόμος ἡ φύσις θ' ἅμα
παρεῖχε τῷ θεῷ. ταῦτα συννοούμενος
κρείσσω νομίζω τἀνθάδ' ἢ τἀκεῖ, πάτερ.   645
ἔα δ' ἐμαυτῷ ζῆν· ἴση γὰρ ἡ χάρις,

634. ἀνθρώποις Dobree for ἀνθρώπων. Dr. Badham says ἀνθρώπῳ would be a gentler change, which is true, though that is not always the point which a critic attends to. If ἀνθρώπων were a mere slip of the pen, we should certainly say ἀνθρώπῳ was right. But if a mistaken construction, viz. making the genitive depend either on σχολὴν or on φιλτάτην, was the cause of the error, we must then decide what Euripides was most likely to have written. Compare Hippol. 383, εἰσὶ δ' ἡδοναὶ πολλαὶ βίου, μακραί τε λέσχαι καὶ σχολὴ, τερπνὸν κακόν.
635. ὄχλον μέτριον, ' the common people well-disposed and respectful to me.' What follows shows that this is the meaning, rather than ' little annoyance.'
637. χαλῶντα, like our vulgar phrase, ' giving elbow room.' —εἴκειν ὁδοῦ is the regular construction, as εἴκειν προθύρου Od. xviii. 10, εἶκε θυμοῦ Antig. 718, and sometimes παραχωρεῖν ὁδοῦ. On the equal rights of slaves and free-men in the matter of ὕβρις, see Hec. 291.
638. ἢ λόγοισιν ἢ. So Musgrave for ἢ γόοισιν ἢ κτλ. He confirms the correction, with his usual learning, from a passage of Heliodorus (ii. 27, p. 108), who evidently had these verses in view, and who paraphrases ἢ φιλοσοφοῦσι διελεγόμην. Barnes gives a conjecture of Hugo Grotius, θεῶν δ' ἐν εὐχαῖς ἤγουν αἰών' ἢ βροτῶν. For the phrase ἐν λόγοις εἶναι compare Hippol. 452, αὐτοὶ δ' εἰσὶν ἐν μούσαις ἀεί. As for the form of the first person in ἢ (contracted from the Homeric ἔα), although Euripides elsewhere uses ἦν from the necessity of the metre, (see Hippol. 1012,) which is, according to strict analogy, the third person (compare ᾔδη with ᾔδειν) there seems no reason to assume that he would have preferred ἦν to ἢ in a passage where the metre allows of either. Cf. Troad. 474, ἢ μὲν τύραννος κεῖς τύρανν' ἐγημάμην. Hermann however gives ἦν as the more Attic form. On the allusion in χαίρουσιν οὐ γοωμένοις see above, v. 246.
642. κἂν ἄκουσιν ᾖ. The doctrine of involuntary or compulsory virtue, as the result of education and of philosophy, where men are by nature averse from that which they yet feel to be desirable, is treated of in three passages at least of the tragic writers, Hippol. 79, Bacch. 315, and Aesch. Eum. 520, ἑκὼν δ' ἀνάγκας ἄτερ δίκαιος ὢν οὐκ ἄνολβος ἔσται. Here Ion says that both natural disposition and also the law, viz. the fear of punishment and disgrace, made him serve the god uprightly. Or he may mean by νόμος the law imposed by Apollo, who was himself the god of justice; cf. 442.
646. ζῆν. Dindorf gives ζῆν μ', Hermann ἔα δέ μ' αὑτῷ ζῆν. The wish may seem rather selfish; but the character of Ion, as a devotee of Phoebus, and one who holds his own aggrandisement to be undesirable for the reasons he has alleged, makes his choice by no means an unnatural one, as Dr. Badham objects. He could

50   ΕΥΡΙΠΙΔΟΥ

μεγάλοισι χαίρειν σμικρά θ' ἡδέως ἔχειν.
ΧΟ. καλῶς ἔλεξας, εἴπερ οὓς ἐγὼ φιλῶ
ἐν τοῖσι σοῖσιν εὐτυχήσουσιν λόγοις.
ΞΟ. παῦσαι λόγων τῶνδ', εὐτυχεῖν δ' ἐπίστασο·   650
θέλω γὰρ οὗπέρ σ' ηὗρον ἄρξασθαι, τέκνον,
κοινῆς τραπέζης δαῖτα πρὸς κοινὴν πεσών,
θῦσαί θ' ἅ σου πρὶν γενέθλι' οὐκ ἐθύσαμεν.
καὶ νῦν μὲν ὡς δὴ ξένον ἄγων σ' ἐφέστιον
δείπνοισι τέρψω· τῆς δ' Ἀθηναίων χθονὸς   655
ἄξω θεατὴν δῆθεν, ὡς οὐκ ὄντ' ἐμόν.
καὶ γὰρ γυναῖκα τὴν ἐμὴν οὐ βούλομαι
λυπεῖν ἄτεκνον οὖσαν αὐτὸς εὐτυχῶν.
χρόνῳ δὲ καιρὸν λαμβάνων προσάξομαι
δάμαρτ' ἐᾶν σε σκῆπτρα τἄμ' ἔχειν χθονός.   660
Ἴωνα δ' ὀνομάζω σε, τῇ τύχῃ πρέπον,
ὁθούνεκ' ἀδύτων ἐξιόντι μοι θεοῦ
ἴχνος συνῆψας πρῶτος. ἀλλὰ τῶν φίλων
πλήρωμ' ἀθροίσας βουθύτῳ σὺν ἡδονῇ

not be suddenly inspired with an ardent affection for a parent whom he had but just seen; he wished to spare the feelings of Creusa, and he was contented and happy in his present position. The chorus do not dissent from his choice, provided Creusa (for to her they allude in the words οὓς ἐγὼ φιλῶ) is satisfied with his decision.
647. σμικρὰ κτλ. It is not the greatness of things that constitutes superior happiness. Whether in humble or in high life, so long as a man is equally pleased with his lot, the one is as gratifying as the other. Of course, χαίρειν is a stronger word than ἡδέως ἔχειν, i.e. στέργειν, ἀγαπᾶν. But placid and secure contentment is put on a level with the exultation attending great fortunes.
650. εὐτυχεῖν. This appears to refer to εὐτυχήσουσιν, and therefore to be said of Creusa. 'Be assured that she is fortunate,' and therefore express no anxiety about her. Barnes gives felix esse disce; and in this sense we might compare Aesch. Suppl. 894, ξένος μὲν εἶναι πρῶτον οὐκ ἐπίστασαι. Rather, however, we should have thus expected εὐτυχῶν, be assured of your own happiness in having found a father. But the next γὰρ refers to παῦσαι, 'cease, I say, for I wish to make a commencement' (i.e. to enter on my new fortune with an appropriate acknowledgment) 'on the very spot where I have found you, my son, by joining in the common banquet of a common table.' Hermann thinks ἄρξασθαι cannot mean 'auspicium facere,' and proposes εὔξασθαι. Bothe construes ἄρξασθαι πεσὼν, incipere epulari. But in fact the following θῦσαί τε is exegetical of ἄρξασθαι. In πεσὼν there is an allusion perhaps to the reclining attitude of banqueters. We have no idiom exactly like it, unless it be the vulgar phrase 'to fall to.' Cf. v. 673.
653. By θύειν γενέθλια he means the thank-offering which was usually made on the feast of the ἀμφιδρόμια, or eighth day after the birth of a child, when a banquet, among other ceremonies, was given to the friends. Lucian, Ὄνειρος, p. 715, θυγατρὸς τήμερον ἑστιῶ γενέθλια καὶ παρεκάλεσα τῶν φίλων μάλα πολλούς. As Xuthus had not kept this festival before in honour of his supposed son, he thought it better to do so now than to omit it altogether. Inf. 1130, θύσας δὲ γενέταις θεοῖσιν ἦν μακρὸν χρόνον μένω.

πρόσειπε, μέλλων Δελφίδ' ἐκλιπεῖν πόλιν. 665
ὑμῖν δὲ σιγᾶν, δμωίδες, λέγω τάδε,
ἢ θάνατον εἰπούσαισι πρὸς δάμαρτ' ἐμήν.

ΙΩ. στείχοιμ' ἄν· ἓν δὲ τῆς τύχης ἄπεστί μοι·
εἰ μὴ γὰρ ἥτις μ' ἔτεκεν εὑρήσω, πάτερ,
ἀβίωτον ἡμῖν· εἰ δ' ἐπεύξασθαι χρεὼν, 670
ἐκ τῶν Ἀθηνῶν μ' ἡ τεκοῦσ' εἴη γυνὴ,
ὥς μοι γένηται μητρόθεν παρρησία.
καθαρὰν γὰρ ἤν τις ἐς πόλιν πέσῃ ξένος,
κἂν τοῖς λόγοισιν ἀστὸς ᾖ, τό γε στόμα
δοῦλον πέπαται κοὐκ ἔχει παρρησίαν. 675

ΧΟ. ὁρῶ δάκρυα *δάκρυα καὶ πενθίμους στρ.

665. πρόσειπε. Bid them farewell, say χαῖρε &c. The same word is used of Alcestis' parting address, Alc. 195, and of the attendants accompanying the corpse, ib. v. 610. For τῶν Hermann proposes σῶν φίλων, but the article conveys the same sense.

667. εἰπούσαισι, 'if you tell it' &c. Thus the chorus (though unsuccessfully, v. 760,) is enlisted in the cause of deceit; for Creusa is not to know that Ion is more than a stranger introduced by her husband. Müller's remark (Hist. of Grecian Literature, p. 364,) on the use to which Euripides turns the chorus in many of his plays, is a good one; "The chorus fulfils its proper office when it comes forward to mediate between, to advise, and to tranquillize opposing parties.— Euripides likes to make his chorus the confidant and accomplice of the person whom he represents as under the influence of passion: the chorus receives his wicked proposals, and even lets itself be bound by an oath not to betray them, so that, however much it may wish to hinder the bad consequences resulting from them, it is no longer capable of doing so."

674. λόγοισιν. Dr. Badham gives νόμοισιν after Prof. Conington. The correction is rather plausible, but it fails to carry with it conviction of its truth. It is easier to assert than to prove that "the article would be inadmissible" with λόγοισιν. The poet appears to vary the more common expression, λόγῳ μὲν ἀστός ἐστι, ἔργῳ δὲ δοῦλος. Compare Frag. Erechth. 353, v. 11,

ὅστις δ' ἀπ' ἄλλης πόλεος οἰκίζει πόλιν,
ἁρμὸς πονηρὸς ὥσπερ ἐν ξύλῳ παγεὶς,
λόγῳ πολίτης ἐστὶ, τοῖς δ' ἔργοισιν οὔ.

No one would here assert that τοῖς ἔργοισιν differs materially from ἔργῳ. The meaning of τοῖς λόγοισιν &c. is, 'Though he should be a citizen *in words*,' viz. in *the* words which men say respecting him. That Euripides was no friend to the admixture of ξένοι and μέτοικοι in the administration of the state, has been elsewhere observed.

676. The chorus predicts the distress of Creusa on discovering her own childlessness, and that her husband has a son. They have doubts about the oracle delivered respecting the youth, whether it be not a deceitful one; and they hesitate whether or not they shall declare the whole matter to Creusa. They imprecate destruction on the head of him who has deceived their mistress, and beg the gods not to accept his sacrifices.

Ibid. There are serious corruptions, which have much perplexed the critics, in the common reading of the first two lines, ὁρῶ δάκρυα μὲν, καὶ πενθίμους ἄλλας γε στεναγμῶν εἰσβολάς. Except Musgrave's στεναγμάτων, which is at once obvious, none of the corrections proposed are satisfactory. Hermann first saw that μὲν should be omitted, and his view has been confirmed by the excellent Palatine MS. Then all agree that ἄλλας γε is the result of some attempted patchwork. Dr. Badham's ἐσομένας will, indeed, suit the old reading of the antistrophe, τάδε τορῶς

[ἄλλας γε] στεναγμάτων εἰσβολὰς,
ὅταν ἐμὰ τύραννος εὐπαιδίαν
πόσιν ἔχοντ᾽ ἴδῃ,
αὐτὴ δ᾽ ἄπαις ᾖ καὶ λελειμμένη τέκνων.   680
τίν᾽, ὦ παῖ πρόμαντι Λατοῦς, ἔχρησας ὑμνῳδίαν;
πόθεν ὁ παῖς ὅδ᾽ ἀμφὶ ναοὺς σέθεν
τρόφιμος ἐξέβα, γυναικῶν τίνος;
οὐ γάρ με σαίνει θέσφατα,   685
μή τιν᾽ ἔχῃ δόλον.
δειμαίνω συμφορὰν
ἐφ᾽ ὅ ποτε βάσεται.
ἄτοπος ἄτοπα γὰρ παραδίδωσί μοι,   690
†τῳδί ποτ᾽ εὔφημα.
ἔχει δόλον τύχαν θ᾽ ὁ παῖς
ἄλλων τραφεὶς ἐξ αἱμάτων.

ἐς οὓς γεγωνήσομεν, and will make a good dochmiac verse; but where is the probability of such an alteration? The present editor has ventured to repeat δάκρυα, (cf. 776. 791,) and in the antistrophe to inclose ἐς οὓς as a gloss on τορῶς. Thus the first verse is a double dochmiac, the second an iambic dipodia with a cretic.
684. ἐξέβα, ἐκπέφηνε, εὑρέθη. The incredulity of the chorus rests on the circumstance, that the father of the child alone has been declared; but a suspicious mystery respecting the mother yet remains to be solved.
685. σαίνει. See Rhes. 55. 'The oracles delivered about him do not please me, lest they should have some trick.' The μή, it is scarcely necessary to remark, depends on the implied sense of δέδοικα. See on Hec. 344.
689. This verse may be scanned as a dochmiac, and in the antistrophe (706) πέλανον ἐπὶ may be regarded as isochronous with βάσεται. Nevertheless, either ἐφ᾽ ὅτι ποτὲ βάσεται or ἐφ᾽ ὅ ποτε προβάσεται is likely to be right. Alcest. 785, τὸ τῆς τύχης γὰρ ἀφανὲς οἷ προβήσεται.
691. The words here are corrupt, and the loss of the antistrophic verse deprives us of the surest guide in restoring this. The MSS. vary in τὸ δήποτε, τὸ δί ποτ᾽, τὸ δέ ποτ᾽. Seidler ingeniously elicited δεσπό-

του from δε ποτ ευ, and Dr. Badham improves on this by editing ἁ δεσπότου φάμα, which is much more probable than Hermann's τάδ᾽ ὁπότ᾽ εὔφημα. 'The story of my master by its strangeness (ἄτοπος οὖσα) gives me strange surmises.' Bothe is perhaps right in supposing the verse to be an interpolation: for clumsy attempts were occasionally made to accommodate passages to the mutilated and corrupt antistrophic clause.
692. δόλον τύχαν τε. Either with Matthiae we must take this for δόλιον τύχην, or with Hermann make τύχαν refer to what follows, for τύχην τοῦ τραφῆναι, or τύχην ἀλλογενῆ, as he paraphrases it. Tyrwhitt proposed δόμον for δόλον, i. e. domum et fortunam Erechthidarum, and Bothe approves this. But ἔχει δόλον seems here purposely repeated from v. 686. The chorus think Ion has been affiliated on Xuthus by fraud, and that the boy, born in fact from some other race, is a child of luck or chance, in happening to be thus allotted to Xuthus.—τίς οὐ κτλ., quisnam in his non conveniet nobiscum? Hermann. Cf. Aesch. Suppl. 239, μόνον τόδ᾽ Ἑλλὰς χθὼν ξυνοίσεται στόχῳ.—Every one, says the chorus, will agree that there is some mystery, some deception, in this young man's alleged origin.

ΙΩΝ. 53

τίς οὐ τάδε ξυνοίσεται;
φίλαι, πότερ' ἐμᾷ δεσποίνᾳ τάδε   ἀντ. 695
τορῶς [ἐς οὖς] γεγωνήσομεν
πόσιν, ἐν ᾧ τὰ πάντ' ἔχουσ' ἐλπίδων
μέτοχος ἦν τλάμων;
νῦν δ' ἡ μὲν ἔρρει συμφοραῖς, ὁ δ' εὐτυχεῖ,
πολιὸν εἰσπεσοῦσα γῆρας, πόσις δ' ἀτίετος φίλων.
μέλεος, ὃς θυραῖος ἐλθὼν δόμους   701
μέγαν ἐς ὄλβον οὐκ ἔσωσεν τύχας.
ὄλοιτ' ὄλοιθ' ὁ πότνιαν
ἐξαπαφὼν ἐμάν·
καὶ θεοῖσιν μὴ τύχοι   705
καλλίφλογα πέλανον ἐπὶ
πυρὶ καθαγνίσας· τὸ δ' ἐμὸν εἴσεται
   *   *   *
                                                710
*   *   τυραννίδος φίλα.
ἤδη πέλας δείπνων κυρεῖ

696. The words ἐς οὖς, as observed on v. 676, are likely to have been a gloss, for the strophic verse bears evident marks of interpolation in order to make up for the lengthening of this. The word τορῶς, in its Aeschylean sense of a clear, piercing, or penetrating sound, is sufficient to convey the idea, especially when combined with γεγωνεῖν, ' to speak audibly ' (El. 809). The syntax τάδε γεγωνεῖν πόσιν, ' to tell this about her husband,' viz. his not being ἄπαις, is the same as the common κακὸν λέγειν τινὰ &c.—τὰ πάντα κτλ., cf. Med. 228, ἐν ᾧ γὰρ ἦν μοι πάντα, γιγνώσκεις καλῶς, κάκιστος ἀνδρῶν ἐκβέβηχ' οὑμὸς πόσις.
699. εὐτυχεῖ, is not childless. See inf. 772—5. Androm. 418. Hec. 989.
700. εἰσπεσοῦσα. Hermann translates quum consenuerit, and calls attention to a rare use of the aorist. In v. 619 Creusa was described as ἄπαιδα γηράσκουσαν. By γῆρας, applied to a woman, the Greeks only meant the age when she ceased to bear children, which was doubtless much earlier in life than in our climate. So Helen speaks of her daughter Hermione as ' growing hoary in virginity,' πολιὰ παρθενεύεται, Hel. 283, though Helen herself is represented as not only yet beautiful (v. 263), but as eagerly sought in marriage by Theoclymenus. Similarly Electra is spoken of as growing old, though she was afterwards married to Pylades.— ἀτίετος φίλων, contemptor uxoris, Herm.
702. οὐκ ἔσωσεν τύχας, has not acted consistently with his fortune, i.e. has proved base, though he received the honour of a foreign alliance as a reward for virtue or valour, v. 62. Compare Hel. 613, τὸ μόρσιμον σώσασα. Dr. Badham thinks we have no choice but to read φρένας.
705—7. μὴ τύχοι καθαγνίσας is, ' may he not obtain his wishes (or the favour of the gods, θεῶν μὴ τύχοι,) when he offers on the fire a well-burning cake,' viz. a cake which sends forth a clear and bright flame.
711. In the early edd. τυραννίδος is repeated, but it is found only once in the Palatine and Florence MSS. It is difficult to supply the lacuna by conjecture. Hermann thinks it may have stood thus, τὸ δ' ἐμὸν εἴσεται τᾶς χθονὸς ἀρχαίας (or τᾶς ἀπ' Ἐρεχθέως) ὅσον τυραννίδος φίλα, ' he shall find out my attachment to the ancient dynasty of the Erechtheids.'
712. πέλας for πελάσας Seidler, ἤδη for ἦ δὴ Reiske.

παῖς καὶ πατὴρ νέος νέων.
ἰὼ δειράδες Παρνασοῦ πέτρας   ἐπῳδ.
ἔχουσαι σκόπελον οὐράνιόν θ' ἕδραν,   715
ἵνα Βάκχιος ἀμφιπύρους ἀνέχων πεύκας
λαιψηρὰ πηδᾷ νυκτιπόλοις ἅμα σὺν Βάκχαις.
μή τί ποτ' εἰς ἐμὰν πόλιν ἵκοιθ' ὁ παῖς,
νέαν δ' ἀμέραν ἀπολιπὼν θάνοι.   720
στενομένα γὰρ ἂν πόλις ἔχοι σκῆψιν
ξενικὸν εἰσβολάν.
ἅλις δ' ἅλις ὁ πάρος ἀρχαγὸς ὢν
Ἐρεχθεὺς ἄναξ.
ΚΡ. ὦ πρέσβυ παιδαγώγ' Ἐρεχθέως πατρὸς   725
τοὐμοῦ ποτ' ὄντος, ἡνίκ' ἦν ἔτ' ἐν φάει,

714. Dr. Badham's correction of ἰὼ for ἵνα is deserving of much praise. There is hardly a doubt of its truth. The continuation of the antistrophe, in respect of syntax, into the epodus, is a rare and objectionable licence (see Rhes. 351, Hipp. 131), and the custom of Euripides to apostrophize the scenery is here quite borne out by the spirit and tenour of the whole passage. The unmetrical ἵνα seems to have been erroneously written for ἰὼ in consequence of the ἵνα in the next verse but one.—πέτρας σκόπελον is here to be joined, as in v. 274, τοιγὰρ θανοῦσαι σκόπελον ᾕμαξαν πέτρας.
719. μή τί ποτε. So Aesch. Suppl. 386, μή τί ποτ' οὖν γενοίμαν ὑποχείριος κράτεσιν ἀρσένων.
721. στενομένα. Dr. Badham follows Matthiae in taking this in the Homeric sense of στεινόμενος, 'embarrassed,' and explains it very well, "when a city is inconsiderable in point of strength or numbers, it may have a pretext for admitting foreign intruders." He thinks however that something has been lost, in which the verb (participle?) of admitting was added. If some infinitive is wanting, e.g. ξενικὸν εἰσβολὰν ἀπωθεῖν (or ἐλαύνειν) βίᾳ, not only would the double dochmiac be completed, but a sense would be gained well suited to the context, 'For the city, being disappointed in the result, might find a plea for forcibly ejecting the stranger who has been thrust upon it.' Bothe's version is on the whole the best, nam gemens advenarum (Xuthi atque Ionis) irruptionem causam (gemendi) habuerit civitas. Hermann reads πενομένα, si indigeret urbs, haberet praetextum, quo peregrinum admitteret. Aeschylus twice uses the deponent στένομαι, Theb. 866 and Pers. 62, and perhaps here it is sufficient to understand 'when in a time of grief.'
723. ἅλις δ' Hermann for ἀλίσας. Scaliger ἅλις ἅλις, which will make up a dochmiac if we insert δ'. The sense appears to be complete, 'we are content with our ancient king Erechtheus, without your new-comers.' Dindorf gives the improbable and un-Attic form ἅλιας, on the authority of the Etymol. M. p. 63, 18, and an obscure grammarian who says that Hipponax used it. The as of the corrupt ἀλίσας seems to be the first and last letter of the second ἅλις.
725. Creusa advances alone upon the stage, and calls her aged attendant to come from the orchestra, by the stairs leading up to the λογεῖον, in order that he may hear, in company with herself, the response that has been given. The old man appears to invite her to descend from the stage and assist him up the steps (v. 738). At all events, she reaches out her hand to help him. These steps represented the ascent in front of, or perhaps on all the sides of (περιφερῆ, v. 743) the temple. The same arrangement is observable in the Electra, where the old man ascends the πρόσβασις ὀρθία (v. 489) to the cottage of the husbandman.—πατρὸς κτλ., i.e. τοῦ ὄντος ποτὲ ἐμοῦ πατρός.

ἔπαιρε σαυτὸν πρὸς θεοῦ χρηστήρια,
ὥς μοι συνησθῇς, εἴ τι Λοξίας ἄναξ
θέσπισμα παίδων ἐς γονὰς ἐφθέγξατο·
σὺν τοῖς φίλοις γὰρ ἡδὺ μὲν πράσσειν καλῶς,   730
ὃ μὴ γένοιτο δ', εἴ τι τυγχάνοι κακόν,
εἰς ὄμματ' εὔνου φωτὸς ἐμβλέψαι γλυκύ.
ἐγὼ δέ σ', ὥσπερ καὶ σὺ πατέρ' ἐμόν ποτε,
δέσποιν' ὅμως οὖσ' ἀντικηδεύω πατρός.

ΠΑΙΔΑΓΩΓΟΣ.

ὦ θύγατερ, ἄξι' ἀξίων γεννητόρων   735
ἤθη φυλάσσεις κοὐ καταισχύνασ' ἔχεις
τοὺς σοὺς παλαιοὺς ἐκγόνους αὐτόχθονας.
ἕλχ' ἕλκε πρὸς μέλαθρα καὶ κόμιζέ με.
αἰπεινά τοι μαντεῖα· τοῦ γήρως δέ μοι
συνεκπονοῦσα κῶλον ἰατρὸς γενοῦ.   740
ΚΡ. ἕπου νυν· ἴχνος δ' ἐκφύλασσ' ὅπου τίθης.
ΠΑ. ἰδού.
τὸ τοῦ ποδὸς μὲν βραδὺ, τὸ τοῦ δὲ νοῦ ταχύ.
ΚΡ. βάκτρῳ δ' ἐρείδου περιφερῆ στίβον χθονός.

734. ἀντικηδεύω. Hermann reads ἀντὶ κηδεύω. In Suppl. 361, τοῖς τεκοῦσι γὰρ δύστηνος ὅστις μὴ ἀντιδουλεύει τέκνων, the genitive depends on ὅστις, 'woe to the son who does not stand in the place of a slave to his parents.' We observe here that kindly feeling towards slaves which in many other passages shows the naturally humane disposition of the poet.
735. Eumen. 413, πῶς δ' οὔ; σέβουσαί γ' ἀξίαν κἀπ' ἀξίων. Eur. Suppl. 813, σφαγέντα τ' οὐκ ἄξι' οὐδ' ὑπ' ἀξίων.
737. τοῦ σοῦ—ἐκ γένους is the emendation of Bothe, approved by Hermann, Dindorf, and Dr. Badham, for τοὺς σοὺς—ἐκγόνους. The latter word should rather have been προγόνους. Hermann has edited ἐκγόνοις, 'you do not disgrace your ancestors by their descendants.' But neither is οἱ σοὶ παλαιοὶ αὐτόχθονες a correct expression, nor is the order of the words adapted to the above sense. Barnes considers the sense to be τοὺς πάλαι ἐξ αὐτῆς τῆς χθονὸς γεγεννημένους, viz. Erichthonius. Cf. v. 267. It is possible that this is what the poet meant, though the expression is rather a harsh one. He should rather have written τοὺς γῆς παλαιοὺς ἐκγόνους αὐτόχθονας. Seidler (Herm. Praef. p. xiv,) has advocated the same view; but Hermann calls it "durum et nimis insolens."
739. τοι Valckenaer for δέ μοι. Hermann gives μοι. If τοι is right (and it is preferred by Dindorf,) one might suspect that δέ μοι had accidentally been copied twice in the verse. Perhaps αἰπεινὰ γὰρ κτλ.
741. ἐκφύλασσε seems to mean ἔκλεγε φυλάσσων. Compare with this dialogue that between Iolaus and the attendant in Heracl. 729 seqq.
743. περιφερῆ στίβον. See on v. 725. Seidler's explanation, "solum quod circa te est," is unsatisfactory, though Hermann so far approves it as to modify it slightly to explora solum scipione circa te. Some contrivance for representing these pathways up a declivity probably existed. Such a device appears in Suppl. 989. The accusative is that of motion over a place (Hel. 598). More fully, βάκτρῳ ἐρείδου (cf. Tro. 150. Hec. 66), στίβον πορευόμενος. There is no need of

ΕΥΡΙΠΙΔΟΥ

ΠΑ. καὶ τοῦτο τυφλὸν, ὅταν ἐγὼ βλέπω βραχύ.
ΚΡ. ὀρθῶς ἔλεξας· ἀλλὰ μὴ παρῇς κόπῳ. 745
ΠΑ. οὔκουν ἑκών γε, τοῦ δ' ἀπόντος οὐ κρατῶ.
ΚΡ. γυναῖκες, ἱστῶν τῶν ἐμῶν καὶ κερκίδος
δούλευμα πιστὸν, τίνα τύχην λαβὼν πόσις
βέβηκε παίδων ὦνπερ οὕνεχ' ἥκομεν
σημήνατ'· εἰ γὰρ ἀγαθά μοι μηνύσετε, 750
οὐκ εἰς ἀπίστους δεσπότας βαλεῖς χαράν.
ΧΟ. ἰὼ δαῖμον.
ΠΑ. τὸ φροίμιον μὲν τῶν λόγων οὐκ εὐτυχές.
ΧΟ. ἰὼ τλᾶμον.
ΠΑ. ἀλλ' ἦ τι θεσφάτοισι δεσποτῶν νοσῶ ; 755
ΧΟ. εἶεν· τί δρῶμεν θάνατος ὧν κεῖται πέρι ;
ΚΡ. τίς ἥδε μοῦσα, χὼ φόβος τίνων πέρι ;

Dr. Badham's conjecture, περιφερῆ στεί- βων χθόνα. The real difficulty is rather in the epithet περιφερῆ than in the grammatical construction.
744. καὶ τοῦτο. Even a stick is a blind guide when one has no eyes to see where to set it. Cf. σκήπτρῳ προδεικνὺς Oed. Tyr. 456.
Ibid. The ἐγὼ in this verse is emphatic, as in fact it nearly always is. The sense is, καὶ τοῦτο τὸ βάκτρον τυφλόν ἐστιν, ὅταν ἐγὼ τυφλὸς ὦ, 'the stick will have no eyes, when my own fail,' i. e. it is guidance rather than support that I require.
745. μὴ παρῇς. The old reading was μὴ 'παρεσκέπω. Herm. gives μὴ 'πάρεσκέ πω (i. e. ἀπάρεσκε), Tyrwhitt μὴ πάρες κόπῳ, which, according to the usual idiom, should be μὴ παρῇς, viz. σεαυτόν. Cf. Bacch. 634, κόπου δ' ὑπὸ—παρεῖται.—τοῦ ἀπόντος, i. e. σθένους. So Reiske for ἄκοντος.
747. Creusa and the old attendant now stand on the stage. The chorus seem to have assumed some new position while the old man was clambering up the stairs; for they are now addressed as if they had returned either from Xuthus or from within the temple. They had been forbidden on pain of death (v. 667) to tell Creusa the real declaration of the oracle. It will be observed that Xuthus had left the stage with that injunction, to prepare for the banquet, (cf. 804, 1125,) and he does not again appear in the play. Hence Creusa here says βέβηκε. Both the chorus and the old man are devoted to Creusa, and to the house of Erechtheus. They consequently regard Xuthus with little favour, and by no means approve of his scheme for introducing a foreigner as successor to the throne. The chorus therefore are ready to give the forbidden information, and the old man is not only willing but forward to plot against the life of the youth. In all this we see the usual Athenian dislike of ξένοι. The attempted murder of Ion, and the assent of Creusa to it, would probably strike the spectators with the less horror, as they would regard with leniency any scheme to preserve untainted their cherished autochthony.
748. τίνα τύχην παίδων, what luck concerning children.
751. ἀπίστους. As you are πιστοὶ to us (v. 748), so we will keep our word of honour with you, and reward you punctually and faithfully for your good tidings. But βάλλειν χαρὰν εἴς τινα is an unusual phrase; Elmsley proposed χάριν, which would be like θέσθαι χάριν, ' to store up a favour.'
752. Hermann points out the fact, that the dialogue commencing at this verse, as far as v. 800, is antistrophic, mostly in short systems of from two to four verses. Thus ἰὼ δαῖμον with the following senarius corresponds to ἰὼ τλᾶμον &c., then the single verses of the chorus and Creusa to the next pair, the three following of the chorus forming an *epodus*.

ΙΩΝ. 57

XO. εἴπωμεν ἢ σιγῶμεν ἢ τί δράσομεν;
KP. εἴφ'· ὡς ἔχεις γε συμφοράν τιν' εἰς ἐμέ.
XO. εἰρήσεταί τοι, κεἰ θανεῖν μέλλω διπλῆ. 760
ουκ ἔστι σοι, δέσποιν', ἐπ' ἀγκάλαις λαβεῖν
τέκν', οὐδὲ μαστῷ σῷ προσαρμόσαι ποτέ.
KP. ὤμοι θάνοιμι.
ΠΑ. θύγατερ. KP. ὦ τάλαιν' ἐγὼ συμφορᾶς.
ἔλαβον, ἔπαθον ἄχος ἄβιον, ὦ φίλαι.
ΠΑ. διοιχόμεσθα, 765
τέκνον. KP. αἰαῖ αἰαῖ, διανταῖος ἔτυ-
πεν ὀδύνα με πνευμόνων τῶνδ' ἔσω.
ΠΑ. μήπω στενάξῃς, KP. ἀλλὰ πάρεισι γόοι.
ΠΑ. πρὶν ἂν μάθωμεν, KP. ἀγγελίαν τίνα μοι; 770
ΠΑ. εἰ ταὐτὰ πράσσων δεσπότης τῆς συμφορᾶς
κοινωνός ἐστιν, ἢ μόνη σὺ δυστυχεῖς.
XO. κείνῳ μὲν, ὦ γεραιὲ, παῖδα Λοξίας
ἔδωκεν, ἰδίᾳ δ' εὐτυχεῖ ταύτης δίχα. 775
KP. τόδ' ἐπὶ τῷδε κακὸν ἄκρον ἔλακες *ἔλακες ἄχος ἐμοὶ
στένειν.
ΠΑ. πότερα δὲ φῦναι δεῖ γυναικὸς ἔκ τινος
τὸν παῖδ' ὃν εἶπας, ἢ γεγῶτ' ἐθέσπισεν;
XO. ἤδη πεφυκότ' ἐκτελῆ νεανίαν 780
δίδωσιν αὐτῷ Λοξίας· παρῆν δ' ἐγώ.
KP. πῶς φῄς; ἄφατον ἄφατον ἀναύδητον λόγον ἐμοὶ
θροεῖς.

758. On the future indicative following the deliberative aorist subjunctive, see on Aesch. Cho. 80, πῶς εὔφρον' εἴπω, πῶς κατεύξομαι πατρί;
759. ἔχεις, κεύθεις, ἐπίστασαι.
762. ποτὲ for τάδε is Wakefield's correction.
764. ἄβιον Herm. for βίοτον, quoting Bekker's Anecdota p. 323, ὁ μέντοι Εὐριπίδης ἐπὶ τοῦ δυσβίου ἐχρήσατο τῇ λέξει.
767. The active form ἔτυπεν is doubtful, for the reason given on Helen. 448. We have however the passive τυπεὶς in Androm. 1150, Prom. 369, Agam. 131.— ἔσω, see Helen. 356. This couple of verses, with that preceding, are dochmiacs, as Dr. Badham perceived, the pen-

themimeris ὤμοι θάνοιμι corresponding to διοιχόμεσθα. The two next verses are iambelegi, as in Androm. 766—8.
771. ταὐτὰ Canter for ταῦτα. Again δυστυχεῖν and εὐτυχεῖν signify the having no family, and the contrary.
776. ἔλακες was repeated by Seidler on account of the metre.
780. ἐκτελῆ, grown up. In this sense ἐντελὴς (if the reading be right) is used by Aeschylus, Cho. 242, of the young eagle.
783. This dochmiac verse is deficient in the usual caesura, being divided thus, πῶς φῄς; ἄφατον ἄ|φατον ἀναύδητον | λόγον ἐμοὶ θροεῖς. But perhaps ὡς should be inserted before λόγον, so that πῶς φῄς; ἄφατον ἄφατον would form a doch-

VOL. II. I

ΕΥΡΙΠΙΔΟΥ

ΠΑ. κἄμοιγε. πῶς δ' ὁ χρησμὸς ἐκπεραίνεται 785
σαφέστερόν μοι φράζε, χὤστις ἔσθ' ὁ παῖς.
ΧΟ. ὅτῳ ξυναντήσειεν ἐκ θεοῦ συθεὶς
πρώτῳ πόσις σὸς, παῖδ' ἔδωκ' αὐτῷ θεός.
ΚΡ. ὀτοτοτοῖ, τὸ δ' ἐμὸν
ἄτεκνον ἄτεκνον ἔλαβεν *ἔλαβεν ἄρα βίοτον, ἐν
ἐρημίᾳ δ' 790
ὀρφανοὺς δόμους οἰκήσω.
ΠΑ. τίς οὖν ἐχρήσθη; τῷ συνῆψ' ἴχνος ποδὸς
πόσις ταλαίνης; πῶς δὲ ποῦ νιν εἰσιδών;
ΧΟ. οἶσθ', ὦ φίλη δέσποινα, τὸν νεανίαν
ὃς τόνδ' ἔσαιρε ναόν; οὗτός ἐσθ' ὁ παῖς. 795
ΚΡ. ἀν' ὑγρὸν ἀμπταίην
αἰθέρα πόρσω γαίας Ἑλλανίας, ἀστέρας ἑσπέρους,
οἷον οἷον ἄλγος ἔπαθον, φίλαι.
ΠΑ. ὄνομα δὲ ποῖον αὐτὸν ὀνομάζει πατὴρ 800
οἶσθ', ἢ σιωπῇ τοῦτ' ἀκύρωτον μένει;
ΧΟ. Ἴων', ἐπείπερ πρῶτος ἤντησεν πατρί.
ΠΑ. μητρὸς δὲ ποίας ἐστίν;
ΧΟ. οὐκ ἔχω φράσαι.
φροῦδος δ', ἵν' εἰδῇς πάντα τἀπ' ἐμοῦ, γέρον,
παιδὸς προθύσων ξένια καὶ γενέθλια 805
σκηνὰς ἐς ἱρὰς τῆσδε λαθραίως πόσις,
κοινῇ ξυνάψων δαῖτα παιδὶ τῷ νέῳ.
ΠΑ. δέσποινα, προδεδόμεσθα, σὺν γάρ σοι νοσῶ,
τοῦ σοῦ πρὸς ἀνδρὸς, καὶ μεμηχανημένως
ὑβριζόμεσθα, δωμάτων τ' Ἐρεχθέως 810

---

mius of resolved spondees. A similar verse however occurs *inf.* 790. Hermann here reads ἄφατον, ἄφατόν τιν', with Seidler.
790. ἔλαβεν was repeated by Hermann. The sense is, ἐγὼ ἔλαβον ἄρα ἄτεκνον βίοτον. After οἰκήσω it is probable that πατρὸς has been dropped. In the antistrophic v. 799, φίλαι has been recovered from the Palatine MS. Hermann had conjectured τλάμων to supply the lacuna.
797. ἑσπέρους Seidler for ἑσπερίους. Cf. Prom. 356, ὃς πρὸς ἑσπέρους τόπους ἕστηκε.

802. ἐπείπερ κτλ. Cf. v. 831.
805. παιδὸς προθύσων ξένια. In Suppl. 28, τυγχάνω δ' ὑπὲρ χθονὸς ἀρότου προθύουσ', the genitive undoubtedly depends on the preposition. Here the sense seems rather to be, 'to offer in the first place a thanksgiving for having found a son in a stranger (ξένια παιδὸς), and a birth-day sacrifice.'
809. μεμηχανημένως, 'designedly.' Compare σεσωφρονισμένως Aesch. Suppl.
704. λελογισμένως Iph. A. 1021.

ἐκβαλλόμεσθα. καὶ σὸν οὐ στυγῶν πόσιν
λέγω, σὲ μέντοι μᾶλλον ἢ κεῖνον φιλῶν,
ὅστις σε γήμας ξένος ἐπεισελθὼν πόλιν
καὶ δῶμα, καὶ σὴν παραλαβὼν παγκληρίαν,
ἄλλης γυναικὸς παῖδας ἐκκαρπούμενος   815
λάθρα πέφηνεν· ὡς λάθρα δ᾽, ἐγὼ φράσω·
ἐπεί σ᾽ ἄτεκνον ᾔσθετ᾽, οὐκ ἔστεργέ σοι
ὅμοιος εἶναι τῆς τύχης τ᾽ ἴσον φέρειν,
λαβὼν δὲ δοῦλα λέκτρα νυμφεύσας λάθρα
τὸν παῖδ᾽ ἔφυσεν, ἐξενωμένον δέ τῳ   820
Δελφῶν δίδωσιν ἐκτρέφειν· ὁ δ᾽ ἐν θεοῦ
δόμοισιν ἄφετος, ὡς λάθοι, παιδεύεται.
νεανίαν δ᾽ ὡς ᾔσθετ᾽ ἐκτεθραμμένον,
ἐλθεῖν σ᾽ ἔπεισε δεῦρ᾽ ἀπαιδίας χάριν.
κᾆθ᾽ ὁ θεὸς οὐκ ἐψεύσαθ᾽, ὅδε δ᾽ ἐψεύσατο   825
πάλαι τρέφων τὸν παῖδα, κἄπλεκεν πλοκὰς
τοιάσδ᾽· ἁλοὺς μὲν ἀνέφερ᾽ ἐς τὸν δαίμονα,

---

815. ἐκκαρπούμενος. Poetically for ἐκτεκνούμενος, v. 438. See the note on v. 475.
820. ἐξενωμένον, sent out of the country, as the young Orestes was sent to Strophius, and Polydorus to the Thracian Polymestor. So Trach. 65, πατρὸς οὕτω δαρὸν ἐξενωμένου.
822. ἄφετος, free and unconfined. *Sup.* v. 52, ἀμφὶ βωμίους τροφὰς ἠλᾶτ᾽ ἀθύρων. Consecrated animals were allowed to wander freely over their pasture grounds, as Io was sent from home ἄφετον ἀλᾶσθαι, Prom. 684. Hence in Iph. T. 469, the chains are removed from the Greek strangers who are about to be sacrificed, ὡς ὄντες ἱροὶ μηκέτ᾽ ὦσι δέσμιοι.
825. κᾆθ᾽. 'So then it was not the god who spoke falsely, but this husband of yours who deceived you.' Apollo had used the words δῶρον and διδόναι (v. 537, 775, 788,) thus leaving it ambiguous whether the boy was the son of Xuthus or his own son. In the former case, which the old man conceives to be the true one, Apollo did not speak falsely in saying δίδωμί σοι τὸν παῖδα, 'I surrender to you your own.' We should rather perhaps have expected ἔσθ᾽. Hermann gives καί σ᾽ ὁ θεὸς κτλ.
827. ἀνέφερε, *referebat*, he had made up his mind to lay the blame on the god,
who had chosen to say Ion was his son. For this sense of ἀναφέρειν see Bacch. 29. Or. 76. Electr. 1296. In the next verse Musgrave proposed λαθὼν, while Matthiae, after Canter, gives ἐλὼν, *sin causam vicisset*, as the natural antithesis to ἁλούς. The argument of the old man, in a few words, is this:—Xuthus secretly begot a son from a slave, when he found Creusa was childless, and had him educated at Delphi, in order that, if the affair came to the knowledge of his wife, he might declare the youth was given to him by Apollo; but otherwise, when the chance of detection had diminished by the lapse of time, he might invest him, as an adopted son, with the sovereignty of Athens. Dr. Badham gives up the passage in despair; but he proposes καινοῖ in the next verse, in place of supplying ἐστὶ with πεπλασμένον. Hermann says, "Dici vix potest, quantum hic versus negotii viris doctis creaverit." Seidler's reading τὸν φθόνον gives a good sense, 'wishing to repel from himself the odium,' i. e. of appointing a stranger as his successor, by asserting that it was Apollo's will. So ἐξαμύνασθαι θεὰς, 'to ward off the Furies,' Orest. 269. Possibly the poet may mean, 'having returned to Athens, and wishing to take advantage of the time.' Thus ἐλθὼν is for ἀνελθὼν, as in Hel. 846.

60   ΕΥΡΙΠΙΔΟΥ

ἐλθὼν δὲ καὶ τὸν χρόνον ἀμύνεσθαι θέλων,
τυραννίδ' αὐτῷ περιβαλεῖν ἔμελλε γῆς.
καινὸν δὲ τοὔνομ' ἀνὰ χρόνον πεπλασμένον,   830
Ἴων, ἰόντι δῆθεν ὅτι συνήντετο.
ΧΟ. οἴμοι, κακούργους ἄνδρας ὡς ἀεὶ στυγῶ,
οἳ συντιθέντες τἄδικ' εἶτα μηχαναῖς
κοσμοῦσι. φαῦλον χρηστὸν ἂν λαβεῖν φίλον
θέλοιμι μᾶλλον ἢ κακὸν σοφώτερον.   835
ΠΑ. καὶ τῶνδ' ἁπάντων ἔσχατον πείσει κακὸν,
ἀμήτορ', ἀναρίθμητον, ἐκ δούλης τινὸς
γυναικὸς, ἐς σὸν δῶμα δεσπότην ἄγειν.
ἁπλοῦν ἂν ἦν γὰρ τὸ κακὸν, εἰ παρ' εὐγενοῦς
μητρὸς, πιθών σε, σὴν λέγων ἀπαιδίαν,   840
εἰσῴκισ' οἴκους· εἰ δὲ σοὶ τόδ' ἦν πικρὸν,
τῶν Αἰόλου νιν χρῆν ὀρεχθῆναι γάμων.
ἐκ τῶνδε δεῖ σε δὴ γυναικεῖόν τι δρᾶν·

929. Bothe's explanation is, ἐλθὼν δὲ Δελφοὺς, καὶ ἔμελλε κτλ., "profectus Delphos, non recipere modo voluit filium, sed etiam regnum ei comparare," and he understands τὸν χρόνον κτλ. thus, ' wishing to make up for the time he (Ion) had spent in retirement, by giving him the sovereignty.'
830. ἀνὰ χρόνον. This seems to mean, ' according to the circumstances of the time,' i.e. the name was an after-thought, suggested by the occurrence. Hermann suspects ἀνὰ λόγον to be the right reading. Translate, ' But as for the name, that was newly devised in the course of time, Ion, because forsooth he met him going forth.' Hermann takes ὄνομα as the accusative after περιβαλεῖν, and gives Ἴων' in the next verse.
832—5. These lines were first assigned to the chorus by Hermann.—μηχαναῖς Steph. for -άς.
836 κτλ. ' Besides, you will have to suffer that which is the crowning evil of all these,—his bringing into your house, as its future lord, one who is of no descent by his mother, a mere cypher, and the son of some slave.' Here ἄγειν is for τὸ ἄγειν ἐκεῖνον, i.e. ὅτι ἐκεῖνος εἰσάξει. Why Hermann should condemn this, and read ἄγει, in which he is followed by Dindorf, is by no means clear. The infinitive is often used without the article, in an exegetical sense. There is a good example of this in Suppl. 792, νῦν δ' ὁρῶ σαφέστατον κακὸν, τέκνων φιλτάτων στερεῖσθαι, where Hermann and others needlessly give στερεῖσα. Compare also Alcest. 879. sup. v. 636.—ἀναρίθμητος, one who is held in no count, not worthy of being regarded as an individual. But οὐκ ἀριθμὸς, ' no mere cypher,' Heracl. 997. Tro. 476. See this more fully explained on Hel. 1679.
839. εὐγενοῦς. It would have been bad enough to have introduced the son of a well-born lady; but it is a double evil to have brought the son of a slave. It would have been bad, even had he obtained your consent, on the plea of your childlessness; but now he has insulted you by not deigning so much as to inform you of his intention.
841. εἰ δὲ σοὶ κτλ. ' But if even this was painful to you (as it was sure to have been,) why then he ought not to have aspired to the hand of one descended from Erechtheus, but to have sought a wife among his own clan, the family of Aeolus' (sup. v. 63). "Magna cum acerbitate dictum." Herm.
843. ἐκ τῶνδε, in consequence of all this. For the same phrase see Electr. 31. Aesch. Ag. 850. 1194. 1581.—γυναικεῖόν τι. Med. 384, κράτιστα τὴν εὐθεῖαν, ἧ πεφύκαμεν Σοφαὶ μάλιστα, φαρμάκοις αὐτοὺς ἑλεῖν.

ἢ γὰρ ξίφος λαβοῦσαν ἢ δόλῳ τινὶ
ἢ φαρμάκοισι σὸν κατακτεῖναι πόσιν   845
καὶ παῖδα, πρὶν σοὶ θάνατον ἐκ κείνων μολεῖν·
εἰ γὰρ σὺ φείσει τοῦδ', ἀπαλλάξει βίου·
δυοῖν γὰρ ἐχθροῖν εἰς ἓν ἐλθόντοιν στέγος,
ἢ θάτερον δεῖ δυστυχεῖν ἢ θάτερον.
ἐγὼ μὲν οὖν σοι καὶ συνεκπονεῖν θέλω,   850
καὶ συμφονεύειν παῖδ' ἐπεισελθὼν δόμοις
οὗ δαῖθ' ὁπλίζει, καὶ τροφεῖα δεσπόταις
ἀποδοὺς θανεῖν τε ζῶν τε φέγγος εἰσορᾶν.
ἓν γάρ τι τοῖς δούλοισιν αἰσχύνην φέρει,
τοὔνομα· τὰ δ' ἄλλα πάντα τῶν ἐλευθέρων   855
οὐδεὶς κακίων δοῦλος, ὅστις ἐσθλὸς ᾖ.
ΧΟ. κἀγώ, φίλη δέσποινα, συμφορὰν θέλω
κοινουμένη τήνδ' ἢ θανεῖν ἢ ζῆν καλῶς.
ΚΡ. ὦ ψυχά, πῶς σιγάσω ;

847. εἰ γὰρ σὺ φείσει τοῦδ' is Dr. Badham's clever emendation for εἰ γάρ γ' ὑφήσεις, τοῦδ' &c. Hermann gives δεῖ σ'· εἰ δ' ὑφήσεις, &c., and W. Dindorf, who in his last edition adopted this, in his notes condemns the whole verse. Without doubt, κατακτεῖναι may depend on the preceding δεῖ (843); but there is one point, which, if it were not capable of a plausible explanation, would have been fatal to Dr. Badham's reading. It has been stated on Rhes. 17, that the nominative of the personal pronoun is not used unless where emphasis is intended. The only exception to this rule appears to be found in a few phrases which were metrically convenient, as in σάφ' οἶδ' ἐγώ. Here, the σὺ was inadmissible, except that the sense may, by a sort of hyperbaton, be explained thus ; εἰ γὰρ ὅδε μὴ θανεῖται, σὺ αὐτὴ θανεῖ. The improper use of σὺ is a strong evidence against the genuineness of v. 1396 inf.

848. δυοῖν ἐχθροῖν. 'When two hostile things come together under one roof, either the one or the other is sure to come off badly.' The proverb is stated generally of things, though the application of it is to persons ; viz. of two enemies in the same house, one is sure to kill the other. Dr. Badham condemns these two verses ; but his reasons are not cogent.

850. ἐγώ. The reading of the two Florence MSS., ἀγὼ (i.e. ἁγώ, ἃ ἐγώ,) is to be rejected on account of μὲν οὖν, for which Hermann supposes there may have been a reading πρόφρων, 'in all which matters I am ready to assist you.'

852. τροφεῖα ἀποδούς. See Suppl. 364. Aesch. Theb. 472, where other examples are given of ἀποδοῦναι τροφεῖα, 'to pay back the price of one's nurture.' The sense is, 'so long as I repay my mistress, I am willing to die, if it should be needful, or to live and look at the light' (i. e. without being ashamed, καλῶς v. 858).

855. τῶν ἐλευθέρων. See Preface to Vol. i. p. xiii, and for ὅστις ᾖ, Med. 516. The sense is, modo sit bonus, which is obviously different from ὅστις ἂν ᾖ. So in Oed. Col. 395, γέροντα δ' ὀρθοῦν φλαῦρον, ὃς νέος πέσῃ, the true meaning is, ' if he shall have fallen in his youth.' The uncertainty of the event is not in the indefiniteness of the person, (as in ὅστις ἂν &c.) but in the circumstances attaching to his case.

859. Creusa, in a very beautiful monody, whereof the former part (862 to 880) is a regular system, the latter composed of irregular anapaests, (see on v. 144,) deliberates first on the question, whether she should any longer hesitate, for the sake of a husband whom she believes unfaithful, to remove from herself

62   ΕΥΡΙΠΙΔΟΥ

πῶς δὲ σκοτίας ἀναφήνω   860
εὐνὰς, αἰδοῦς δ' ἀπολειφθῶ ;
τί γὰρ ἐμπόδιον κώλυμ' ἔτι μοι ;
πρὸς τίν' ἀγῶνας τιθέμεσθ' ἀρετῆς ;
οὐ πόσις ἡμῶν προδότης γέγονεν ;
στέρομαι δ' οἴκων, στέρομαι παίδων,   865
φροῦδαι δ' ἐλπίδες, ἃς διαθέσθαι
χρῄζουσα καλῶς οὐκ ἐδυνήθην,
σιγῶσα γάμους,
σιγῶσα τόκους πολυκλαύτους.
ἀλλ' οὐ τὸ Διὸς πολύαστρον ἕδος   870
καὶ τὴν ἐπ' ἐμοῖς σκοπέλοισι θεὰν
λίμνης τ' ἐνύδρου Τριτωνιάδος
πότνιαν ἀκτὰν,
οὐκέτι κρύψω λέχος, ὡς στέρνων
ἀπονησαμένη ῥᾴων ἔσομαι.   875
στάζουσι κόραι δακρύοισιν ἐμαί,

the reproach of childlessness by avowing her amour with Apollo; and then, having decided that she will relieve her mind by revealing the long-cherished secret, she relates the circumstances of her seduction by the god. Few choral passages in Euripides are more remarkable at once for poetry and for pathos than that which here follows. Dr. Badham remarks, "Nothing could be more effective than this complaint of Creusa, in which the sense of grievous and heartless wrong triumphs over her shame, and moves her publicly to upbraid the god before his own temple with the recital of his perfidy. Nothing also could be better timed, as making the transition from a scene of suspicion and indignation to the plottings of revenge."

859—61. These opening verses belong to the irregular system after v. 880. On σκότιος in the sense of νόθος see Alcest. 990.

862. '(And yet, why should I not?) For what hindrance is yet left to prevent me? With whom do we now engage in contests of virtue?' That is, there is now no one left to whom I should care to represent myself more virtuous than other women, or, whom I should strive to outstrip in virtue.—ἀγῶνας is Musgrave's reading for ἀγῶνα. Dr. Badham supposes the transcribers introduced the latter to agree with τινα, but he also thinks ἀγῶνα may have been a gloss on ἅμιλλαν. W. Dindorf and Hermann approve L. Dindorf's reading πρὸς τίν' ἀγῶν' ἂν θείμεσθ' ἀρετῆς. The elision ἀγῶν' ἂν does not quite please the ear. For ἀγὼν πρός τινα see Orest. 491. Dr. Badham adopts οὗ, Dobree's conjecture for οὐ, in the next verse.

866. By διαθέσθαι ἐλπίδας she means, ἃς εἶχον ἐλπίδας τὰ πράγματα εὖ διαθέσθαι. 'Gone are the hopes which I had entertained that I should arrange matters well by keeping the secret of my marriage, but now I have been unable to do this.'

870. ἀλλ' οὐ κτλ. The ellipse of μὰ (which is added in the Florence MSS.) is justified by Rhes. 825, οὐ τὰς Σιμοεντιάδας πηγὰς, which is required by the metre for οὐ μὰ τὰς Σ. π. So also Theocr. iv. 17, οὐ δᾶν, 'no, by earth!' Ibid. iv. 29, οὐ τήνα γ', οὐ Νύμφας, and v. 14, οὐ μὰν, οὐ τὸν Πᾶνα τὸν ἄκτιον.—ἐδυνήθην Elmsley for ἐδυνάσθην.

875. ἀπονησαμένη, 'having removed the load from my breast.' Hesych. ἀποσωρεύουσα. Homer has νηῆσαι (νηέω), and νῆσαι from νέω occurs Ar. Lysist. 269, and Herc. F. 243. Barnes has ἀποσεισαμένη, MSS. ἀπονισαμένη.—ὡς here means 'since.'

ψυχὰ δ' ἀλγεῖ, κακοβουλευθεῖσ'
ἔκ τ' ἀνθρώπων ἔκ τ' ἀθανάτων,
οὓς ἀποδείξω
λέκτρων προδότας ἀχαρίστους. 880
ὦ τᾶς ἑπταφθόγγου μέλπων
κιθάρας ἐνοπὰν, ἅτ' ἀγραύλοις
†κέρασιν ἐν ἀψύχοις ἀχεῖ
μουσᾶν ὕμνους εὐαχήτους,
σοὶ μομφὰν, ὦ Λατοῦς παῖ, 885
πρὸς τάνδ' αὐγὰν αὐδάσω.
ἦλθές μοι χρυσῷ χαίταν
μαρμαίρων, εὖτ' ἐς κόλπους
κρόκεα πέταλα φάρεσιν ἔδρεπον
ἀνθίζοντα χρυσαυγῆ· 890

877. κακοβουλευθεῖσ'. Hermann, after Barnes, proposes κακοβουληθεῖσ', on the ground that the verb representing κακόβουλός εἰμι is κακοβουλέω, not -εύω. But Hermann at the same time doubts whether the poet did not purposely avoid the form in -έω, on the ground that κακόβουλος rather means 'foolish.' He also suggests, with Barnes, and Dindorf approves, κακὰ βουλευθεῖσ', in which case the participle must stand for ἐπιβουλευθεῖσα. The question is a difficult one, because Euripides used great licence in compounding verbs. The following are all exceptional in their formation: πυραίθειν Rhes. 41, δυσθνήσκειν ib. 791, ἐξαμηχανεῖν Heracl. 495, ἐπιβωμιοστατεῖν ib. 44, σταδιοδραμοῦμαι Herc. F. 863. Dr. Donaldson gives the following as the law of compound verbs (New Cratylus, p. 520); "All compound nouns, whether made up of prepositions, or of nouns, or of ἀ—, δυσ, or εὖ, and verbal roots, are actually melted down into individual words incapable of divulsion (tmesis), and it is from these compound nouns that the verbs in question are formed; therefore they are derivative verbs, and the length of the word would generally induce a necessity for the shortest kind of derivation which is in έω."

881—911. This part of the monody Hermann divides into στρ. α' (881—890), ἀντ. α' (891—901), στρ. β' (902—906), and ἀντ. β' (907—911), the conclusion being the ἐπῳδός. Although there are appearances of antithetical arrangement, this is hardly more than would inevitably occur from the monotonous beat of spondaic catalectic dimeter anapaestics; and it requires some credulity to believe that the verses 894—5 were intentionally exempted from antistrophic correspondence in order to express Creusa's mental excitement.

883. Though metrically ⏑ ⏑ ⏑ ⏑ might answer to — — in this irregular system, as inf. 889, Troad. 124, 136, and in many other places, yet it is doubtful if the α in κέρασιν is ever legitimately short. See Bacch. 921. Hence there is a suspicion of some corruption.—ἐν means 'on' the horn, which (it appears from Cic. De Nat. D. ii. 59, quoted by Musgrave,) was used as a sounding-board to the heptachord lute.

886. πρὸς τάνδ' αὐγάν. This is said, not only because the Greeks were fond of disburdening their griefs to the early morning light, (as Electr. 59, γόους τ' ἀφείην αἰθέρ' ἐς μέγαν πατρί,) but because the sun was Apollo himself, who was thus directly impeached.

888. ἐς κόλπους φάρεσιν, into the lap for my dress to hold (or, for decorating my dress). So Proserpina and her companions gather the flowers from the meads of Enna, in the beautiful description of Ovid, Fast. iv. 436, 'haec gremium, laxos degravat illa sinus.'

890. Dr. Badham not without reason suspects the old reading ἀνθίζειν χρυσανταυγῇ to be corrupt; for χρυσανταυγής,

λευκοῖς δ' ἐμφὺς καρποῖς χειρῶν
εἰς ἄντρου κοίτας κραυγὰν
ὦ μᾶτερ *μᾶτέρ μ' αὐδῶσαν
θεὸς ὁμευνέτας ἆγες ἀναιδείᾳ
Κύπριδι χάριν πράσσων. 895
τίκτω δ' ἁ δύστανός σοι
κοῦρον, τὸν φρίκᾳ ματρὸς
εἰς εὐνὰν βάλλω τὰν σὰν,
ἵνα μ' ἐν λέχεσιν μελέαν μελέοις 900
ἐζεύξω τὰν δύστανον·
οἴμοι μοι· καὶ νῦν ἔρρει
πτανοῖς ἁρπασθεὶς θοίνα
παῖς μοι σὸς τλάμων, σὺ δὲ κιθάρᾳ 905
κλάζεις παιᾶνας μέλπων.
ὠὴ, τὸν Λατοῦς αὐδῶ,
ὅς γ' ὀμφὰν κληροῖς,
πρὸς χρυσέους θάκους

'golden when held against the light,' is a strange compound, and ἀνθίζειν is difficult to construe. Probably the simple verb means 'to blossom,' as distinct from ἀνθεῖν, 'to flourish,' a more general word. Bothe interprets, *ut me* (floribus) *ornarent;* and in Soph. El. 43, ἠνθισμένον shows at least the existence of an active and transitive ἀνθίζειν. We may compare καρπίζειν, 'to make fruit.' The compounds ἐπανθίζειν and ἀπανθίζειν are found in an active sense, Aesch. Ag. 1434 and 1640. Here we venture to read ἀνθίζοντα χρυσαυγῆ. We have χρυσαυγὴς κρόκος in Oed. Col. 685. The οντα written in the margin as a correction of ἀνθίζειν was by some mistake added after the first syllable of χρυσαυγῆ.

891. ἐμφὺς Reiske and others for ἐμφύσας. It is obviously the Homeric ἐν δ' ἄρα οἱ φῦ χειρί &c. Cf. Oed. Col. 1113, ἐρείσατ', ὦ παῖ, πλευρὸν ἀμφιδέξιον, ἐμφύντε τῷ φύσαντι. Theocritus xiii. 47, ταὶ δ' ἐν χερὶ πᾶσαι ἔφυσαν.

893. μᾶτερ was doubled by Hermann. —ἀναιδείᾳ, ἀναιδῶς, without regard to my feelings of virgin modesty.—χάριν πράσσων, v. 36. These two verses are dochmiac.

898. φρίκᾳ ματρὸς, through fear of my mother. See v. 16.—εὐνὰν τὰν σὰν, the grotto which was the scene of my seduction.

900. μ' ἐν λέχεσιν for με λέχεσι Heath. The verse is thus a regular anapaestic, whereas by the old reading it was difficult to reduce it either to a dochmiac or to any form of resolved anapaestics. Hermann, followed by Dindorf, gives μέλεα μέλεος. There is no difficulty in τὰν δύστανον after μελέαν. The sense is, 'me, I repeat, the unhappy one.' The meaning would almost justify a comma after ἐζεύξω.

904. This verse is anapaestic, with the final spondees resolved. The καὶ is rightly omitted before σὸς by Matth. Herm. and Dind. If καὶ were right, it must have παῖς ἐμὸς καὶ σός. Cf. 916. But the dative without καὶ is to be compared with Δῖος πόρτις βοὸς Aesch. Suppl. 308, ὁ Στρυμόνιος πῶλος ἀοιδοῦ Rhes. 387.—σὺ δὲ κτλ., but you meanwhile play on the lyre songs of joy, as if nothing had happened to distress you. After κιθάρᾳ in one of the Florence MSS. is the note of something lost (λείπει). The sense however is complete as the text stands.

908. There is certainly irony in the γε, which is omitted in the Palatine MS. 'To

καὶ γαίας μεσσήρεις ἕδρας 910
εἰς οὓς αὐδὰν καρύξω·
ἰώ,
κακὸς εὐνάτωρ,
ὃς τῷ μὲν ἐμῷ νυμφεύτᾳ
χάριν οὐ προλαβὼν
παῖδ' εἰς οἴκους οἰκίζεις· 915
ὁ δ' ἐμὸς γενέτας καὶ σός γ' ἀμαθὴς
οἰωνοῖς ἔρρει συλαθεὶς,
σπάργανα ματέρος ἐξαλλάξας.
μισεῖ σ' ἁ Δᾶλος καὶ δάφνας
ἔρνεα φοίνικα παρ' ἀβροκόμαν, 920
ἔνθα λοχεύματα σέμν' ἐλοχεύσατο
Λατὼ Δίοισί σε καρποῖς.

you who, forsooth, profess to give oracles to all who consult you, in the order assigned them by lot, to you, I say, I will utter my complaint in your ear, at your very shrine.' For the metre see v. 178. The following crimination, κακὸς εὐνάτωρ &c., she regards as too reproachful to be publicly made, and therefore she adds εἰς οὓς. By κληροῦν ὀμφὰν she means διδόναι ὀμφὰν τοῖς κληρουμένοις. So Aesch. Eum. 32, ἵτων πάλῳ λαχόντες, ὡς νομίζεται. Cf. 416, Δελφῶν ἀριστῆς, οὓς ἐκλήρωσεν πάλος. Dr. Badham rather carelessly renders it, 'who possessest the oracle.' For κληροῦν is properly 'to assign some thing or person by lot;' the middle is 'to have it assigned to yourself,' κληρώσασθαι, or 'to endeavour to obtain it,' i. e. 'to draw lots for it,' κληροῦσθαι. So Theb. 55, κληρουμένους ἔλειπον, 'I left them drawing lots.' Tro. 29, δεσπότας κληρουμένων.—πρὸς θάκους, scil. κηρύξω.
912. Probably this should be a dimeter verse, ἰὼ ἰὼ, κακὸς εὐνάτωρ.
913. νυμφεύτᾳ, πόσει, viz. Xuthus. 'Base seducer that thou art,' she exclaims, 'who, without having received any favour from him, (which thou mightest repay,) art settling a son in the house of my husband!'
916. γενέτας. Hesych. ἔκγονος. So in Oed. Tyr. 470, ὁ Διὸς γενέτας for Apollo.—ἀμαθὴς, for ἀγνώς. The same passive sense is found in δυσμαθὴς, 're-

cognised with difficulty,' Med. 1196. Or it may mean, as Bothe thinks, 'unconscious of its woes.'—συλαθεὶς, ἁρπασθεὶς, ἑλκυσθείς. After this word the old copies add οἰκεῖα, which Hermann, Dindorf, and Dr. Badham agree in rejecting as spurious. It is opposed to the metre rather than to the sense; and this objection might also be removed by reading τᾶς οἰκείας | σπάργανα ματέρος ἐξαλλάξας, 'having exchanged (for others) the swathing bands of his own mother.' For Creusa had exposed the child wrapped in her shawl, ἡμεῖς ἐν ὄρφνῃ σπαργανώσαντες πέπλοις, inf. 955.
920. φοίνικα is the obvious correction of Brodaeus for φοίνια. The connexion of the date-palm and the bay tree with the birth of Apollo is frequently mentioned by the poets. Compare Iph. T. 1100, Hec. 458.—λοχεύματα, in apposition to σε, as Hippolytus is ἁγνοῦ Πιτθέως παιδεύματα, Hipp. 11, or rather, a cognate accusative, 'delivered herself of thee by a supernatural delivery.' Matthiae thinks Artemis as well as Apollo is meant, but this is a needless supposition.—Δίοισι καρποῖς, for Διὸς ἐκκαρπουμένη, as Hermann explains, comparing v. 815. See on v. 475. The dative appears the same as in v. 4, but it may also be regarded as that of the mode, as if ὑπὸ Διὸς, or τῇ Διὸς συνουσίᾳ. Dr. Badham translates, 'Where Latona being made fruitful by Jove bare thee, a divine offspring.'

VOL. II. K

ΧΟ. οἴμοι, μέγας θησαυρὸς ὡς ἀνοίγνυται
κακῶν, ἐφ᾽ οἷσι πᾶς ἂν ἐκβάλοι δάκρυ.
ΠΑ. ὦ θύγατερ, οὔτοι σὸν βλέπων ἐμπίμπλαμαι   925
πρόσωπον, ἔξω δ᾽ ἐγενόμην γνώμης ἐμῆς.
κακῶν γὰρ ἄρτι κῦμ᾽ ὑπεξαντλῶν φρενί,
πρύμνηθεν αἴρει μ᾽ ἄλλο σῶν λόγων ὕπο,
οὓς ἐκβαλοῦσα τῶν παρεστώτων κακῶν
μετῆλθες ἄλλων πημάτων κακὰς ὁδούς.   930
τί φῄς ; τίνα λόγον Λοξίου κατηγορεῖς ;
ποῖον τεκεῖν φῂς παῖδα ; ποῦ θεῖναι πόλεως
θηρσὶν φίλον τύμβευμ᾽ ; ἀνελθέ μοι πάλιν.
ΚΡ. αἰσχύνομαι μέν σ᾽, ὦ γέρον, λέξω δ᾽ ὅμως.
ΠΑ. ὡς συστενάζειν γ᾽ οἶδα γενναίως φίλοις.   935
ΚΡ. ἄκουε τοίνυν· οἶσθα Κεκροπίας πέτρας
πρόσβορρον ἄντρον, ἃς Μακρὰς κικλήσκομεν ;

923. μέγας θ. ὡς for ὡς μέγας θ. κτλ., 'how great a treasure-house of evils is being opened, at which any one might shed a tear!' Hermann's ὅδε γ᾽ for ὡς is a groundless suspicion.
925. ἐμπίμπλαμαι Barnes for ἐμπίπλ. Compare Hipp. 664, μισῶν οὔποτ᾽ ἐμπλησθήσομαι γυναῖκας.
927. κακῶν κῦμα, see Suppl. 824. The construction in the next verse is changed from αἴρομαι ὑπὸ ἄλλου κύματος to ἄλλο κῦμα αἴρει με. 'I was just now getting rid of a wave of troubles in my mind, and now another wave at the stern (i. e. which was yet behind) heaves me up in consequence of your words, which you had no sooner uttered concerning the grievances immediately before you, than you pursued an evil course of other woes.' Few passages have been more strangely misinterpreted than this, and solely from a misapprehension of a common idiom, λόγοι τινὸς, 'talk about a person or subject.' The old man says, that he knows not what to think about the matter now; for his mistress, having touched on her present troubles, (οὐ πόσις ἡμῶν προδότης γέγονεν &c., v. 864,) has gone on to describe a totally new and still more perplexing matter, her amour with Apollo. He calls this 'pursuing a bad path,'—unless Musgrave's plausible reading καινὰς ὁδοὺς be right,— because it was one which involved a god in a serious accusation, and her language respecting that god was any thing but σεμνὸν, εὔφημον, εὐσεβές. Compare Hippol. 858, τέκνων ἐπιστολὰς, 'injunctions about her children.' Ajac. 998, ὀξεῖα σοῦ βάξις, 'a quickly-spread report about you.' Oed. Col. 355, μαντεῖα—ἃ τοῦδ᾽ ἐχρήσθη σώματος. Eur. El. 228, ἥκω φέρων σοι σοῦ κασιγνήτου λόγους. Ibid. 347, Ὀρέστου κήρυκες λόγων, 'bringing tidings about Orestes.' The usage is the same in πένθος τινὸς, 'mourning for a person' &c.
931. τίνα λόγον. Dr. Badham proposes τίνα δόλον. And δόλος and λόχος are confused in Rhes. 16. 92. But in either case the verse is very inharmonious. It is likely that λόγον is a gloss on αὐδὰν, used in the sense of ὄνειδος, as in v. 911.
932. ποῖον κτλ. 'What do you mean, in saying that you gave birth to a son?' Cf. v. 896—903.
934. αἰσχύνομαί σε, 'I feel abashed before you.' But Dobree is perhaps right in omitting the σ᾽.
937. This verse has been condemned by some critics, rather as interfering with the order of the στιχομυθία than as containing any fault in itself, though Dr. Badham thinks he finds arguments on the latter score which are "conclusive against its genuineness." The sense is, 'Do you know the grotto on the north side of the Acropolis, (in that part of the cliff) which we call The Long rocks?'

ΠΑ. οἶδ᾽, ἔνθα Πανὸς ἄδυτα καὶ βωμοὶ πέλας.
ΚΡ. ἐνταῦθ᾽ ἀγῶνα δεινὸν ἠγωνίσμεθα.
ΠΑ. τίν᾽ ; ὡς ἀπαντᾷ δάκρυά μοι τοῖς σοῖς λόγοις. 940
ΚΡ. Φοίβῳ ξυνῆψ᾽ ἄκουσα δύστηνον γάμον.
ΠΑ. ὦ θύγατερ, ἆρ᾽ ἦν ταῦθ᾽ ἅ γ᾽ ᾐσθόμην ἐγώ ;
ΚΡ. οὐκ οἶδ᾽· ἀληθῆ δ᾽ εἰ λέγεις φαίημεν ἄν.
ΠΑ. νόσον κρυφαίαν ἡνίκ᾽ ἔστενες λάθρα ;
ΚΡ. τότ᾽ ἦν ἃ νῦν σοι φανερὰ σημαίνω κακά. 945
ΠΑ. κᾆτ᾽ ἐξέκλεψας πῶς Ἀπόλλωνος γάμους ;
ΚΡ. ἔτεκον ἀνάσχου ταῦτ᾽ ἐμοῦ κλύων, γέρον.
ΠΑ. ποῦ τίς λοχεύει σ᾽ ; ἢ μόνη μοχθεῖς τάδε ;
ΚΡ. μόνη κατ᾽ ἄντρον οὗπερ ἐζεύχθην γάμοις.
ΠΑ. ὁ παῖς δὲ ποῦ 'στιν ; ἵνα σὺ μηκέτ᾽ ᾖς ἄπαις. 950
ΚΡ. τέθνηκεν, ὦ γεραιέ, θηρσὶν ἐκτεθείς.
ΠΑ. τέθνηκ᾽ ; Ἀπόλλων δ᾽ ὁ κακὸς οὐδὲν ἤρκεσεν ;
ΚΡ. οὐκ ἤρκεσ᾽, Ἅιδου δ᾽ ἐν δόμοις παιδεύεται.
ΠΑ. τίς γάρ νιν ἐξέθηκεν ; οὐ γὰρ δὴ σύ γε.
ΚΡ. ἡμεῖς, ἐν ὄρφνῃ σπαργανώσαντες πέπλοις. 955
ΠΑ. οὐδὲ ξυνῄδει σοί τις ἔκθεσιν τέκνου ;
ΚΡ. αἱ ξυμφοραί γε καὶ τὸ λανθάνειν μόνον.

Cf. v. 13. 283. 1400, which latter verse, in the phrase Μακρὰς πετρηρεφεῖς, contains a reply to Dr. Badham's objection, that the ἄντρον and the Μακραὶ are distinct. That they were so in truth cannot for a moment be questioned; the former is but a part of the latter; yet there is no reason why a particular cave should not have been called after the whole rock in which it was situated. However, the ἃs agreeing with Μακρὰς, rather than ἣν πέτραν, is quite consistent with the genius of the language. If v. 937 be really spurious, πέτρας will be the genitive by aposiopesis.
942. ἅ γ᾽ ᾐσθόμην. He had heard some vague story, veiled under the term νόσος κρυφαία, from other sources besides her own recent confession, at which he certainly was present; cf. v. 931 ; or he remembers her indisposition ἐν οἴκοις, v. 16. He wishes to know, whether the two accounts relate to one and the same event; and the affirmative answer is given in the next verse. Dr. Badham's ἃ κ᾽ ᾐσθόμην is not satisfactory. He should have adduced actual examples of a crasis so unusual.
947. ἀνάσχου. At the word ἔτεκον the old man must be supposed to have visibly started.—ποῦ τίς κτλ., see Hel. 873, 1543, πῶς ἐκ τίνος νεώς ποτε ;
949. μόνη κατ᾽ ἄντρον. This does not seem to agree with the account in v. 16, τεκοῦσ᾽ ἐν οἴκοις παῖδ᾽ ἀπήνεγκεν βρέφος Ἐς ταυτὸν ἄντρον οὗπερ ηὐνάσθη θεῷ.
950. ἵνα σὺ κτλ. The meaning is either, 'The boy must be found, in order that,' &c., or, ('which I ask, not from idle curiosity, but) with a view to your being no longer reproached with childlessness,' i. e. any more than Xuthus.
952. Ἀπόλλων ὁ κακὸς, that naughty Apollo, i. e. ὁ μάτην δίκαιος καλούμενος.
953. As ὀρφανεύεσθαι and παρθενεύεσθαι are 'to pass an orphan life,' &c., Alc. 535, Hel. 283, so παιδεύεσθαι here has the rather unusual sense of 'is spending the time of his boyhood,' viz. what would have been so on earth.
957. Dr. Badham translates, 'Calamity and concealment were my only witnesses.' This omits both the article and the γε.

68   ΕΥΡΙΠΙΔΟΥ

ΠΑ. καὶ πῶς ἐν ἄντρῳ παῖδα σὸν λιπεῖν ἔτλης ;
ΚΡ. πῶς δ' ; οἰκτρὰ πολλὰ στόματος ἐκβαλοῦσ' ἔπη.
ΠΑ. φεῦ·
    τλήμων σὺ τόλμης, ὁ δὲ θεὸς μᾶλλον σέθεν.   960
ΚΡ. εἰ παῖδά γ' εἶδες χεῖρας ἐκτείνοντά μοι.
ΠΑ. μαστὸν διώκοντ' ἢ πρὸς ἀγκάλαις πεσεῖν ;
ΚΡ. ἐνταῦθ' ἵν' οὐκ ὢν ἄδικ' ἔπασχεν ἐξ ἐμοῦ.
ΠΑ. σοὶ δ' ἐς τί δόξης ἦλθεν ἐκβαλεῖν τέκνον ;
ΚΡ. ὡς τὸν θεὸν σώσοντα τόν γ' αὑτοῦ γόνον.   965
ΠΑ. οἴμοι, δόμων σῶν ὄλβος ὡς χειμάζεται.
ΚΡ. τί κρᾶτα κρύψας, ὦ γέρον, δακρυρροεῖς ;
ΠΑ. σὲ καὶ πατέρα σὸν δυστυχοῦντας εἰσορῶν.
ΚΡ. τὰ θνητὰ τοιαῦτ'· οὐδὲν ἐν ταὐτῷ μένει.
ΠΑ. μή νυν ἔτ' οἴκτων, θύγατερ, ἀντεχώμεθα.   970
ΚΡ. τί γάρ με χρὴ δρᾶν ; ἀπορία τὸ δυστυχεῖν.
ΠΑ. τὸν πρῶτον ἀδικήσαντά σ' ἀποτίνου θεόν.
ΚΡ. καὶ πῶς τὰ κρείσσω θνητὸς οὖσ' ὑπερδράμω ;
ΠΑ. πίμπρη τὰ σεμνὰ Λοξίου χρηστήρια.
ΚΡ. δέδοικα· καὶ νῦν πημάτων ἄδην ἔχω.   975
ΠΑ. τὰ δυνατά νυν τόλμησον, ἄνδρα σὸν κτανεῖν.

'Was no one an accomplice with you in the exposure of your child?'—'Yes; my woes, and the secrecy of the place; and these alone.'
959. πῶς δ'; 'How indeed?' The well known πῶς taken up by ὅπως in Aristophanes, is the counterpart of this rather uncommon tragic expression. Hermann says the δὲ represents the fuller question, σὺ δὲ λέγεις, Πῶς; Compare Aesch. Cho. 753, ΧΟ. πῶς οὖν κελεύει νιν μολεῖν ἐσταλμένον; ΤΡ. ᾖ πῶς;
963. ἐνταῦθα, πρὸς στέρνῳ, scil. πεσεῖν. 'To lie there, where not being he was wronged by me,' who deprived him of the mother's breast. Hermann objects, (though without making allowance for a poetical passage, or for the poet's constant effort after *pathos*,) that the question of the old man which elicited this reply, is altogether absurd (*terque quaterque ineptum*). For newly born infants do not seek for the breast. On the contrary, it is sometimes difficult to make them take it. But it is very pardonable in a poet not to be curiously accurate in such matters.

964. ἐς τί δόξης ἦλθέ σοι for σὺ δὲ πῶς ἐς δόξαν ἦλθες. Hermann gives σοὶ δ' ἐς τί δόξ' εἰσῆλθεν. With the following ὡς supply ἐξέβαλον ὡς νομίζουσα &c. See Rhes. 145. The old reading σώζοντα was corrected by several critics.
968. If πατέρα σὸν is right, the allusion is to δόμων σῶν ὄλβος, for the woes of the daughter might be said to make the father unhappy even in Hades. Dr. Badham rather confidently proposes πάτραν σήν, but, as a question of probabilities, we should much prefer σὲ καὶ πόσιν σόν. Thus δυστυχοῦντας would mean ἄπαιδας (v. 772). It is rare to find a senarius, the second foot of which is a tribrach of one word. See Bacch. 18.
972. τὸν πρῶτον ἀδικήσαντα for τὸν ἀδικίας ὑπάρχοντα. According to the Greek idea of wrong, the question *who began it* was all in all.
973. ὑπερδράμω. This refers to the difficulty of escaping punishment if she should offend the god; and καὶ πῶς as usual implies that an objection is made.

ΚΡ. αἰδούμεθ' εὐνὰς τὰς τόθ' ἡνίκ' ἐσθλὸς ἦν.
ΠΑ. σὺ δ' ἀλλὰ παῖδα τὸν ἐπὶ σοὶ πεφηνότα.
ΚΡ. πῶς ; εἰ γὰρ εἴη δυνατόν. ὡς θέλοιμί γ' ἄν.
ΠΑ. ξιφηφόρους σοὺς ὁπλίσασ' ὀπάονας. 980
ΚΡ. στείχοιμ' ἄν· ἀλλὰ ποῦ γενήσεται τόδε ;
ΠΑ. ἱραῖσιν ἐν σκηναῖσιν, οὗ θοινᾷ φίλους.
ΚΡ. ἐπίσημον ὁ φόνος, καὶ τὸ δοῦλον ἀσθενές.
ΠΑ. οἴμοι, κακίζει. φέρε, σύ νυν βούλευέ τι.
ΚΡ. καὶ μὴν ἔχω γε δόλια καὶ δραστήρια. 985
ΠΑ. ἀμφοῖν ἂν εἴην τοῖνδ' ὑπηρέτης ἐγώ.
ΚΡ. ἄκουε τοίνυν· οἶσθα γηγενῆ μάχην ;
ΠΑ. οἶδ', ἣν Φλέγρᾳ Γίγαντες ἔστησαν θεοῖς.
ΚΡ. ἐνταῦθα Γοργόν' ἔτεκε Γῆ, δεινὸν τέρας.
ΠΑ. ἦ παισὶν αὐτῆς σύμμαχον, θεῶν πόνον ; 990

978. σὺ δ' ἀλλά Herm. for νῦν δ' ἀλλά. 'Do you *then* slay the youth who has appeared as a usurper over you,' i.e. over your house.

982. θοινᾷ φίλους. Though ἑστιᾶν τινα (Alc. 765) is used, and this phrase is like our's, 'to feast one's friends,' the active θοινᾶν is rare. The middle is a favourite word with Euripides, for ἐσθίειν.

984. κακίζει, 'you are turning coward.' After just now saying, ὡς θέλοιμί γ' ἄν, (v. 979,) the very first plan proposed you reject on the ground that it is too daring. Accordingly, he gives up his own plan, and adds, 'come then, propose something yourself.' Dr. Badham is here wrong in every particular. The οἴμοι conveys regret that what appears to him the best scheme must be given up through her faint-heartedness. So far from its being "quite ridiculous in the old man to charge Creusa with cowardice," it is obviously most natural; for her answer was a cowardly one,—' We are not strong enough : Murder is sure to be found out,' &c. As for the emphatic σύ, it is equally plain that the antithesis is, 'if you reject *my* advice, let me hear *yours*.' There is nothing in v. 1022 to justify Dr. Badham's alteration of the text, τοὐμὸν κακίζεις. The old man says καὶ σὺ γὰρ τοὐμὸν ψέγεις because Creusa had here objected to the plan τοῦ ὁπλίζειν ὀπάονας. Hermann puts an interrogation at κακίζει, which is certainly no improvement.

986. ἀμφοῖν τοῖνδε, viz. τοῦ τε δόλου καὶ τοῦ δρᾶν. But there is a double sense in δραστήρια, which means 'effective,' 1185.

990. θεῶν πόνον, i.e. θεοῖς ἀνταγωνιστήν, θεοῖς πόνους ποιοῦσαν. Hermann gets into needless intricacies by following the Aldine in placing no stop at σύμμαχον, as if it were συμμαχήσουσαν θεῶν μάχην. Euripides makes a statement contrary to all the legends we possess, in representing the Gorgons born in the Phlegraean fields (Φλεγραίαν πλάκα, Aesch. Eum. 285), i.e. the volcanic district of Campania, on the occasion of the Gigantomachia. Hermann observes, "Haec quoque quaestio, ut plures quae deinceps sequuntur, indoctae multitudinis causa ab Euripide inventa est." The passage which follows may be regarded as a *locus classicus* on the aegis of Pallas. The fringed goat-skin represented on her statues as wrapped round the chest, and clasped or brooched in the centre with a Gorgon's head, is here regarded as the skin of the monster itself. The Gorgons were δρακοντόμαλλοι, Aesch. Prom. 818. But Euripides supposes the snaky θώραξ, worn by the Gorgon in the conflict; to have been attached to the skin of the dead monster, by way of a fringe or border to the aegis. The story arose from an ancient method of cutting the edges of a hide into slits, and twisting and knotting each in rude imitation of a serpent.

70   ΕΥΡΙΠΙΔΟΥ

ΚΡ. ναί· καί νιν ἔκτειν' ἡ Διὸς Παλλὰς θεά.
ΠΑ. ποῖόν τι μορφῆς σχῆμ' ἔχουσαν ἀγρίας;
ΚΡ. θώρακ' ἐχίδνης περιβόλοις ὡπλισμένον.
ΠΑ. ἆρ' οὗτός ἐσθ' ὁ μῦθος ὃν κλύω πάλαι;
ΚΡ. ταύτης Ἀθάναν δέρος ἐπὶ στέρνοις ἔχειν.   995
ΠΑ. ἦν αἰγίδ' ὀνομάζουσι, Παλλάδος στολήν;
ΚΡ. τόδ' ἔσχεν ὄνομα θεῶν ὅτ' ἦλθεν ἐς δόρυ.
ΠΑ. τί δῆτα, θύγατερ, τοῦτο σοῖς ἐχθροῖς βλάβος;
ΚΡ. Ἐριχθόνιον οἶσθ', ἢ οὔ; τί δ' οὐ μέλλεις, γέρον;
ΠΑ. ὃν πρῶτον ὑμῶν πρόγονον ἐξανῆκε γῆ;   1000
ΚΡ. τούτῳ δίδωσι Παλλὰς ὄντι νεογόνῳ
ΠΑ. τί χρῆμα; μέλλον γάρ τι προσφέρεις ἔπος.
ΚΡ. δισσοὺς σταλαγμοὺς αἵματος Γοργοῦς ἄπο.
ΠΑ. ἰσχὺν ἔχοι δ' ἂν τίνα πρὸς ἀνθρώπου φύσιν;
ΚΡ. τὸν μὲν θανάσιμον, τὸν δ' ἀκεσφόρον νόσων.   1005
ΠΑ. ἐν τῷ καθάψασ' ἀμφὶ παιδὶ σώματος;
ΚΡ. χρυσοῖσι δεσμοῖς· ὁ δὲ δίδωσ' ἐμῷ πατρί.
ΠΑ. κείνου δὲ κατθανόντος ἐς σ' ἀφίκετο;
ΚΡ. ναί· κἀπὶ καρπῷ γ' αὖτ' ἐγὼ χερὸς φέρω.
ΠΑ. πῶς οὖν κέκρανται δίπτυχον δῶρον θεᾶς;   1010

997. He probably means, that the aegis now first obtained its name from ἀΐσσειν, not from αἴξ.—ἦλθεν, scil. Παλλάς.
999. ἢ οὔ is Dr. Badham's correction; 'Do you know Erichthonius, or not? But of course you do.' The old reading was ἢ τί δ' οὐ μέλλεις, for which Hermann gives ἢ τί γ' οὐ μέλλεις (γ' being written above δ' in two MSS.) and W. Dindorf ventures on such a verse as no man of taste would willingly attribute to Euripides, Ἐριχθόνιον οἶσθας, τί δ' οὐ μέλλεις, γέρον;
1002. μέλλον τι ἔπος. 'A reluctant saying,' Dr. Badham. Cunctanter eloqueris, Matthiae and Hermann. And so Barnes, μόγις λαλεῖς καὶ βραδέως προσφέρεις εἰς τὸ μέσον. If we suppose a short pause at νεογόνῳ, this will doubtless be the meaning. But the sense might also be, 'I expect to hear something,' or, 'there is something in what you are going to say;'—μέλλον, expectatione plenum.
1004. ἔχοντας Herm. and Dobree for ἔχοιτ' ἂν or ἔχοι θ' ἄν. A more probable reading is ἰσχὺν ἔχοι δ' ἂν τίνα κτλ., like τλήμων ἂν εἴης Hel. 91. The nominative would then be τὸ αἷμα, and in the next verse the construction is continued from δίδωσι, unless τὴν μὲν—τὴν δὲ be read.
1006. ἐν τῷ κτλ. 'By what means (or, in what inclosure,) attaching it to the boy from his body?' Bothe is quite wrong in explaining it ἀμφὶ σώματος παιδί. The genitive is used exactly as if he had said ἐξάψασα. Cf. Bacch. 24, νεβρίδ' ἐξάψας χροός. By δεσμοῖς a bracelet appears to be meant, whence αὐτὰ in v. 1009, rather than αὐτὸ, agreeing with δῶρον implied. The ἐγὼ in this verse is slightly emphatic; 'I myself, and none other, now wear it on my wrist;' and so is the σὲ just above.
1010. πῶς κέκρανται, how is it carried into effect, i. e. what is to be done with these two drops to make them produce the results described? There is not very much meaning in Dr. Badham's version, 'How is the double gift ordained?' In v. 1012, it is clear that χρῆσθαι depends

ΙΩΝ. 71

ΚΡ. κοίλης μὲν ὅστις φλεβὸς ἀπέσταξεν φόνου
ΠΑ. τί τῷδε χρῆσθαι; δύνασιν ἐκφέρει τίνα;
ΚΡ. νόσους ἀπείργει καὶ τροφὰς ἔχει βίου.
ΠΑ. ὁ δεύτερος δ' ἀριθμὸς ὃν λέγεις τί δρᾷ;
ΚΡ. κτείνει, δρακόντων ἰὸς ὢν τῶν Γοργόνος. 1015
ΠΑ. εἰς ἓν δὲ κραθέντ' αὐτὸν ἢ χωρὶς φορεῖς;
ΚΡ. χωρίς· κακῷ γὰρ ἐσθλὸν οὐ συμμίγνυται.
ΠΑ. ὦ φιλτάτη παῖ, πάντ' ἔχεις ὅσων σε δεῖ.
ΚΡ. τούτῳ θανεῖται παῖς· σὺ δ' ὁ κτείνων ἔσει.
ΠΑ. ποῦ καὶ τί δράσας; σὸν λέγειν, τολμᾶν δ' ἐμόν. 1020
ΚΡ. ἐν ταῖς Ἀθήναις, δῶμ' ὅταν τοὐμὸν μόλῃ.
ΠΑ. οὐκ εὖ τόδ' εἶπας· καὶ σὺ γὰρ τοὐμὸν ψέγεις.
ΚΡ. πῶς; ἆρ' ὑπείδου τοῦθ' ὃ κἄμ' εἰσέρχεται;
ΠΑ. σὺ παῖδα δόξεις διολέσαι, κεἰ μὴ κτενεῖς.
ΚΡ. ὀρθῶς· φθονεῖν γάρ φασι μητρυιὰς τέκνοις. 1025
ΠΑ. αὐτοῦ νυν αὐτὸν κτεῖν', ἵν' ἀρνήσῃ φόνους.
ΚΡ. προλάζυμαι γοῦν τῷ χρόνῳ τῆς ἡδονῆς.
ΠΑ. καὶ σόν γε λήσεις πόσιν ἅ σε σπεύδει λαθεῖν.

on κέκρανται, so that the full sense would be πῶς or τί ἂν πράσσοντες κραίνοιμεν δ. δ. θεᾶς; Hermann rightly says, "Latine dicas, *quomodo constitutum est*. Nam habet in mente χρῆσθαι αὐτῷ." There is no authority for δῶρον beyond the conjecture of Stephens. The old copies give θέρος or δέρος. Perhaps, δίπτυχον μέρος, the two-fold choice or alternative.

1011. ὅστις κτλ. 'That which dropped from the gore of the hollow vein' (i.e. the jugular, when the head was cut off, though others understand the *Vena cava* on the right side of the chest). See v. 1053, Γοργοῦς λαιμοτόμων ἀπὸ σταλαγμῶν. Canter proposed φόνος, which Dr. Badham pronounces undoubtedly right. There is more difficulty in ὅστις, sc. σταλαγμὸς, in the unusual sense, 'of the two, that which' &c. But Hermann's conjecture has little to commend it, κοίλης μὲν ὃς πρὸς φλεβὸς ἀπέσταξεν φόνου. If the vulgate text be right, this is one of the very few passages where ὅστις is a synonym of ὅς.

1015. τῶν Γοργόνος is Dobree's restoration. The old reading τῶν Γοργόνων is a curious instance of the *assimilation* of cases. In the next verse Musgrave records the emendation of Snape for κραθὲν ταὐτὸν ἰχὼρ' εἰσφορεῖς.

1017. οὐ συμμίγνυται, i.e. διχοστατεῖ, like the oil and vinegar in Agam. 314. They will not blend, or keep company together, for the one would destroy or neutralise the other. But besides the physical notion, there is an allusion to the doctrine that good things and bad things, joy and grief, &c., are to be kept separate, χωρὶς ἡ τιμὴ θεῶν, Agam. 620. See above, v. 246.

1021. ταῖς Ἀθήναις. For the article see v. 577.

1022. ψέγεις, disparage, think lightly of. He means the schemes proposed to her in v. 974 and 978.

1027. τῆς ἡδονῆς, scil. μέρος τι. 'If I have not already slain him, at least I have a foretaste of the pleasure by the time,' that is, I can put out of my thoughts the time that must elapse before the act, and realize it as already done. For the genitive compare Hel. 700.

1028. λήσεις. 'Your husband will never know that you are acquainted with those very circumstances which he wishes you not to know,' viz. that Ion is his son. "Eo tutius Ioni parabis interitum, quod

ΕΥΡΙΠΙΔΟΥ

ΚΡ. οἶσθ' οὖν ὃ δρᾶσον; χειρὸς ἐξ ἐμῆς λαβὼν
χρύσωμ' Ἀθάνας τόδε, παλαιὸν ὄργανον, 1030
ἐλθὼν ἵν' ἡμῖν βουθυτεῖ λάθρα πόσις,
δείπνων ὅταν λήγωσι καὶ σπονδὰς θεοῖς
μέλλωσι λείβειν, ἐν πέπλοις ἔχων τόδε,
κάθες βαλὼν ἐς πῶμα τῷ νεανίᾳ
[ἰδίᾳ δὲ, μή τι πᾶσι, χωρίσας ποτὸν] 1035
τῷ τῶν ἐμῶν μέλλοντι δεσπόζειν δόμων.
κἄνπερ διέλθῃ λαιμὸν, οὔποθ' ἵξεται
κλεινὰς Ἀθήνας, κατθανὼν δ' αὐτοῦ μενεῖ.
ΠΑ. σὺ μέν νυν εἴσω προξένων μέθες πόδα·
ἡμεῖς δ' ἐφ' ᾧ τετάγμεθ' ἐκπονήσομεν. 1040
ἄγ,' ὦ γεραιὲ πούς, νεανίας γενοῦ
ἔργοισι, κεἰ μὴ τῷ χρόνῳ πάρεστί σοι.
ἐχθρὸν δ' ἐπ' ἄνδρα στεῖχε δεσποτῶν μέτα,
καὶ συμφόνευε καὶ συνεξαίρει δόμων.
τὴν δ' εὐσέβειαν εὐτυχοῦσι μὲν καλὸν 1045
τιμᾶν, ὅταν δὲ πολεμίους δρᾶσαι κακῶς
θέλῃ τις, οὐδεὶς ἐμποδὼν κεῖται νόμος.

nullam tibi ejus perdendi caussam fuisse putabit." *Hermann.*

1030. χρύσωμα τόδε, the bracelet or small casket described in v. 1007—9.— Ἀθάνας, see v. 1001.

1034. κάθες, discharge the contents (viz. the separate portion of it that is deadly) into the young man's cup.' Cf. δρόσον καθήσω v. 436. Hel. 1061, δοῦναι κελεύσω πορθμίδ', ᾗ καθήσομεν κόσμον τάφῳ σῷ πελαγίας ἐς ἀγκάλας.—In the next line τι was added by Wakefield.
Dindorf gives μὴ ^{'ν ἃ} πᾶσι as the reading of the Palatine MS., and adds that this may be a corruption for μή γ' ἄπασι. It is much more likely that it was the attempt of a grammarian to fill up the deficiency of a spurious verse. L. Dindorf compares Trach. 383, ὄλοιντο μή τι πάντες οἱ κακοί. Cf. *sup.* v. 719. But the line is suspicious in other respects; first, on account of δὲ, used for μέντοι, without a finite verb; secondly, because the clauses are rather involved, ἰδίᾳ χωρίσας ποτὸν, μή τι πᾶσι δούς. And thirdly, because the answer of the old man contains *nine* verses, corresponding to the speech of Creusa, if this one be ejected.

1039. εἴσω προξένων, into the house of the public entertainers, whose duty it was to find a lodging for strangers at Delphi. Without doubt the Athenian θεωροὶ were regularly provided for by an officer appointed at the public cost.

1043. δεσποτῶν μέτα, with the concurrence of Creusa. He says this to remove the odium which would fall on himself exclusively; and he uses the plural, instead of δεσποίνης, for the same reason, not to implicate her alone in the charge of being an accomplice. Hence also the σὺν in the next verse. Cf. Tro. 24, "Ἥρας Ἀθάνας θ', αἳ ξυνεξεῖλον Φρύγας. Hippol. 18, κυσὶν ταχείαις θῆρας ἐξαιρεῖ χθονός.

1045—7. This is a passage which might, though unjustly, be adduced as evidence against the moral principles of Euripides. At first sight, it is a startling sentiment enough, 'It is all very well for the prosperous to hold righteousness in honour; there is no law to prevent us doing harm to our enemies.' Euripides however consistently puts this doctrine into the mouth of a bad man. He does not

ΧΟ. Εἰνοδία, θύγατερ Δάματρος, ἃ τῶν   στρ. α'.
νυκτιπόλων ἐφόδων ἀνάσσεις,
καὶ μεθαμερίων ὅδωσον δυσθανάτων   1050
κρατήρων πληρώματ᾽, ἐφ᾽ οἷσι πέμπει
πότνια πότνι᾽ ἐμὰ χθονίας
Γοργοῦς λαιμοτόμων ἀπὸ σταλαγμῶν   1055
τῷ τῶν Ἐρεχθεϊδᾶν
δόμων ἐφαπτομένῳ·
μηδέ ποτ᾽ ἄλλος ἄλλων ἀπ᾽ οἴκων πόλεως ἀνάσσοι
πλὴν τῶν εὐγενετᾶν Ἐρεχθειδᾶν.   1060

mean that it is a *right* doctrine, albeit it was unquestionably that which was commonly held by the Greeks in his time. His own views we are justified in assuming to be the converse of all this, at least as to εὐσέβεια, which, as elsewhere remarked, means the upright and honourable dealing of one man towards another. See on Hel. 901. "Certe hoc," says Barnes, "neque Christianis, neque hominibus philosophis, prudentibusque et piis fuit usquequaque comprobatum ; quicquid poetae nobiles, qui Naturam imitantur, nonnullis personis pro characteris illorum ratione aliquando affigere placuerunt." See on this subject the remarks in the Preface to Vol. i. p. xxxv and xli.

1048. Hecate is invoked, as the goddess presiding over drugs and baleful poisons, to direct to a favourable issue this stealthy attempt on Ion's life. The chorus wish this, because, as the handmaids of Creusa, they are alike interested in resisting the intrusion of a stranger into the family of the Erechtheidae. If, they say, Creusa should fail in her design, she will certainly commit suicide, for she will never endure to see a stranger lord of her house. They are ashamed for the far-famed gods, Bacchus and Demeter, if the son of a slave shall be admitted, as ruler of Athens, to witness the sacred mysteries. Let poets henceforth cease to sing of the wickedness of women. After this daring act of Xuthus, let men be rather the subject of their reproaches. He has been faithless to his wife in that he has raised up a son to succeed him begotten from another woman.

Ibid. Hecate is called daughter of Demeter because she was identified with Cora, just as by the Romans Diana, Proserpina, and Trivia, were either connected or confused with each other. See on Med. 396. To Hecate was attributed the power of sending apparitions ; hence Hel. 570, οὐ νυκτίφαντον πρόπολον Εἰνοδίας μ᾽ ὁρᾷς. By ἔφοδοι all such sudden and alarming visions appear to be meant. So of the Furies, in Aesch. Eum. 353, ἁμετέραις ἐφόδοις μελανείμοσιν. And Hecate is said ἀνάσσειν ἐφόδων in the same sense as will be noticed on Hel. 1040.

1050. καὶ μεθαμερίων. As you command apparitions by night, so in this instance direct the filling of a fatal cup for a deed to be done in the light of day. Hermann construes νυκτιπόλων ἐφόδων καὶ μεθαμερίων, but this does not afford the antithesis which seems to be intended. —ἐφ᾽ οἷσι πέμπει is variously, but not satisfactorily interpreted. Hermann understands, ὅδωσον κρατῆρας πληρωθέντας οἴνῳ ἐπὶ τούτοις τοῖς φαρμάκοις ἃ πέμπει ἡ δέσποινα τῷ Ἴωνι. But in his Preface, p. xvii, he says, " verissime Seidlerus, ἐφ᾽ οἷσι pro ἐπὶ τούτοις, ἐφ᾽ οἷς, i. e. ἐπὶ θανάτῳ." Dr. Badham translates, "for the purposes for which," but inclines to read ἐφ᾽ ᾧ σφε πέμπει. Matthiae appears to understand, ' for which (cup-filling) Creusa is sending the old man,' but he adds another, which Dindorf approves, and which is adopted by Dr. Badham. In the judgment of the present editor, the poet's meaning is this, ὅδωσον πληρώματα κρατήρων ἐπὶ ἐκείνοις, ἐφ᾽ οἷς πέμπει πότνι᾽ ἐμὰ, (τουτέστι) τῷ τῶν κτλ., ' direct the filling of the fatal bowl against those, for whom my mistress is sending it (viz. the drug, implied in πληρώματα), taken from the drops trickling from the wounded throat of the earth-born Gorgon, namely, for him who is aspiring to the house of the Erechtheidae.'

ΕΥΡΙΠΙΔΟΥ

εἰ δ' ἀτελὴς θάνατος σπουδαί τε δεσποί-   ἀντ. α'.
νας, ὅ τε καιρὸς ἄπεισι τόλμας,
ᾇ τε νῦν φέρετ' ἐλπὶς, ἢ θηκτὸν ξίφος ἢ
λαιμῶν ἐξάψει βρόχον ἀμφὶ δειρὴν,   1065
πάθεσι πάθεα δ' ἐξανύτουσ'
εἰς ἄλλας βιότου κάτεισι μορφάς.
οὐ γὰρ δόμων γ' ἑτέρους
ἄρχοντας ἀλλοδαποὺς   1070
ζῶσά ποτ' ὀμμάτων ἐν φαενναῖς ἀνέχοιτ' ἂν αὐγαῖς
ἁ τῶν εὐπατριδᾶν γεγῶσ' οἴκων.
αἰσχύνομαι τὸν πολύυμνον   στρ. β.

1061. εἰ δ' ἀτελὴς κτλ. 'But if his death should fail to be accomplished, and the eager schemes of our mistress, and the opportunity for the daring deed shall pass away, and the hope (should be vain, ἀτελὴς) by which she is now sustained; then she will either (take) a sharpened sword, or will tie a noose fast to her throat around her neck; and so finishing one suffering by another, she will descend to another kind of life' (viz. that in Hades). Here there is little to detain the reader. The crasis, or rather, the elision, of φέρεται may be defended by Trach. 216, ἀείρομ' οὐδ' ἀπώσομαι τὸν αὐλόν. Prom. 854, ἡ Διὸς κλεινὴ δάμαρ μέλλουσ' ἔσεσθαι, εἰ τῶνδε προσσαίνει σέ τι. Iph. T. 679, δόξω—προδούς σε σώζεσθαι αὐτὸς εἰς οἴκους μόνος. For φέρεσθαι ἐλπίδι see on Rhes. 15, τί φέρει θορύβῳ; Hel. 1642, ἐπίσχες ὀργὰς, αἷσιν οὐκ ὀρθῶς φέρει. This confirms Hermann's correction ᾇτε for ἄτε. Dr. Badham, who has misunderstood not only the meaning of the author but the meaning of Matthiae's note, proposes ᾧ νυν (meaning perhaps νῦν, the enclitic being here a solecism) ἔλπις (ἐλπὶς) ἐφαίνετ', ἢ θηκτὸν κτλ. Bothe too wrongly understands ἅ τε νῦν ἐφέρετο ἐλπὶς, quaeque modo spes afferebatur.—With ξίφος we may supply λήψεται, just as in Soph. El. 435, ἢ πνοαῖσιν (μέθες) ἢ βαθυσκαφεῖ κόνει κρύψον νιν.

1067. ἄλλας μορφάς. Another form or phase of life, viz. that in Hades. Compare Med. 1039, ἐς ἄλλο σχῆμ' ἀποστάντες βίου.

1074. τὸν π. θεόν. Bacchus, who was escorted with a solemn torch-procession from Athens to Eleusis on the twentieth day of the month Boedromion. He was worshipped there together with Demeter, these two, Liber et alma Ceres, as Virgil calls them conjointly, being, according to one form of mythology, the sun and the moon, whence also the λαμπάδες and the παννυχίδες in their honour. See Ar. Ran. 340 seqq., and the schol. Barnes has a long and learned note on this passage, in which he proves from Plutarch and others that the εἰκάδες was a name given to the nine days' festival of the τὰ μεγάλα μυστήρια. For Callichorus, a spring near Eleusis, see Suppl. 392. It was so called from the cyclic dances there first instituted in honour of Demeter.—ὄψεται, i. e. if Ion shall be allowed to see the mysteries on that sacred day, and to take a part in the vigils. As the supposed son of a slave, and not a γνήσιος πολίτης, the chorus apprehends that Ion would bring a disgrace on the god if allowed to join in his worship. Bothe thinks the nominative to be supplied is not Ion, but Bacchus, as if we should say, 'I am ashamed for him, if he shall dare to show his face,' &c. But Hermann appears more correctly to judge, "apertum est Ionem hic intelligi etiam nullo nomine appellatum;" and he sums up the purport of a long note thus, "Itaque hoc pudendum dicit chorus, si adolescens ex serva natus et semibarbarus ad sanctissima sacra admittatur." There seems no necessity to read, with Hermann, ἐννύχιος ὄψετ' ἄυπνος ὤν, which he calls an iambic verse. The α in ἀθεμίτων, v. 1093, appears to be made long by an epic licence, as in ἀπαράμυθον Prom. 192. The verse however is of a very anomalous scansion, and to use Hermann's words, "omni numero caret."

θεὸν, εἰ περὶ Καλλιχόροισι παγαῖς 1075
λαμπάδα θεωρὸν εἰκάδων
ὄψεται ἐννύχιος ἄϋπνος ὤν,
ὅτε καὶ Διὸς ἀστερωπὸς
ἀνεχόρευσεν αἰθὴρ,
χορεύει δὲ Σελάνα 1080
καὶ πεντήκοντα κόραι
Νηρέος, αἱ κατὰ πόντον
ἀενάων τε ποταμῶν
δίνας χορευόμεναι,
τὰν χρυσοστέφανον κόραν 1085
καὶ ματέρα σεμνάν·
ἵν' ἐλπίζει βασιλεύσειν,
ἄλλων πόνον εἰσπεσὼν,
ὁ Φοίβειος ἀλάτας.
ὁρᾶθ' ὅσοι δυσκελάδοισιν   ἀντ. β'. 1090

1078. ὅτε καὶ κτλ. When the starry ether of Zeus, the Moon and the sea, join in the worship of the dread deities. The awfulness of their power is finely expressed by the idea, that the very elements unite with mortals in the service of Demeter and Cora. The construction appears to be, ὅτε χορεύει Σελάνα τὰν χρ. Κόραν. But some irregularities of the strophic metres give grounds for suspicions as to the integrity of the text. Hermann's alteration is rather bold, Νηρέος ὅσαι τε πόντον | κατ' ἀενάων τε ποταμῶν | δίνας, χορευομέναν | κτλ. Thus χορεύειν actively and χορεύεσθαι passively agree pretty well with the use in v. 463, παρὰ χορευομένῳ τρίποδι. " Significatur nymphas illas choreis celebrare Cererem et Proserpinam eodem tempore, quo iisdem deabus a populo Atheniensi choreae instituantur." W. Dindorf's conjecture, that the true reading εἱλισσόμεναι has given place to a gloss χορευόμεναι, derives some support from Tro. 2, ἔνθα Νηρῄδων χοροὶ Κάλλιστον ἴχνος ἐξελίσσουσιν ποδός.
1087. ἵνα. This refers back to Καλλιχόροισι παγαῖς, 'for there,' viz. at Athens, 'this homeless foster-child of Phoebus hopes to reign, having intruded himself into the property of others.' The old reading ἄλλον πόνον τ' εἰσπεσεῖν was corrected by Heath and others. For the use of πόνος in the sense of τὸ ἐκπονηθὲν, compare Aesch. Cho. 130, ἐν τοῖσι σοῖς πόνοισι χλίουσιν μέγα. Xen. Anab. vii. 6, 9, ὁ δὲ τοὺς ἡμετέρους πόνους ἔχει, 'the fruits of our labours.' Barnes correctly explains it, " quasi nihil agendo incidere in haereditatem, quam aliorum labores auxerunt in immensum."
1090. ὁρᾶθ' ὅσοι κτλ. 'See, ye who, pursuing the course of song, celebrate with ill-sounding strains the marriage-beds of us women, and the unlawful unholy alliances brought about by Cypris, how much we surpass in moral rectitude the unrighteous race of men.' What they are told to see, is the supposed flagitiousness of Xuthus. Difficulty has been found in κατὰ μοῦσαν ἰόντες, which Hermann and others alter to ἰέντες, 'letting down the Muse to unworthy subjects,'—a very forced sense of καθιέναι. Matthiae avows that he cannot adduce another instance of the phrase. It is, however, the same as in Tro. 103, πλεῖ κατὰ πορθμὸν, πλεῖ κατὰ δαίμονα, where other examples are given in the note. Bothe rightly explains, illi, qui cantionem seu carmen venantur. Cf. Plat. Phaedr. p. 253, β., οἱ δὲ Ἀπόλλωνός τε καὶ ἑκάστου τῶν θεῶν οὕτω κατὰ τὸν θεὸν ἰόντες ζητοῦσι τὸν σφέτερον παῖδα πεφυκέναι.

L 2

κατὰ μοῦσαν ἰόντες ἀείδεθ' ὕμνοις
ἀμέτερα λέχεα καὶ γάμους
Κύπριδος ἀθεμίτους ἀνοσίους
ὅσον εὐσεβίᾳ κρατοῦμεν
ἄδικον ἄροτον ἀνδρῶν.   1095
παλίμφαμος ἀοιδὰ
καὶ μοῦσ' εἰς ἄνδρας ἴτω
δυσκέλαδος ἀμφὶ λέκτρων.
δείκνυσι γὰρ ὁ Διὸς ἐκ
παίδων ἀμνημοσύναν,   1100
οὐ κοινὰν τεκέων τύχαν
οἴκοισι φυτεύσας
δεσποίνᾳ· πρὸς δ' Ἀφροδίταν
ἄλλαν θέμενος χάριν
νόθου παιδὸς ἔκυρσεν.   1105

ΘΕΡΑΠΩΝ.

ξέναι γυναῖκες, ποῦ κόρην Ἐρεχθέως
δέσποιναν εὕρω ; πανταχῇ γὰρ ἄστεως
ζητῶν νιν ἐξέπλησα, κοὐκ ἔχω λαβεῖν.

1093. ἀθεμίτους is the reading of the Palatine MS. for ἀθέμιτας. — ἄροτον, a race, for ἄροτρον, is due to Barnes. The word occurs in this sense in Med. 1281.
1096. παλίμφαμος, a synonym of δύσφημος. So in Aesch. Theb. 247, παλινστομεῖς is rightly explained by the Schol. δυσφημεῖς. Most commentators take πάλιν here to have its ordinary sense, ' a song, the converse of what it was before.' The old reading παλίμφαος was corrected by Brodaeus. Photius has παλίμφημα· δύσφημα· κακά· ἐναντία. It appears therefore that either of the above interpretations is justifiable. For ἀμφὶ we should perhaps read περὶ, to suit the metre of v. 1082. For the sentiment compare Med. 417, ἔρχεται τιμὰ γυναικείῳ γένει· οὐκέτι δυσκέλαδος φάμα γυναῖκας ἕξει.
1099. ὁ Διὸς ἐκ παίδων, namely, Xuthus, who was Αἰόλου τοῦ Διὸς γεγὼς Ἀχαιὸς, v. 63. The metre of this verse does not suit with v. 1083. Hermann reads δείκνυσι γὰρ οὖν, Dr. Badham δείκνυσιν γὰρ ὁ Διὸς, omitting ἐκ. But the preposition could not possibly be omitted unless the sense were δείκνυσι παίδων ἀμνημοσύναν, whereas the meaning is ἀμνημοσύναν δεσποίνας.
1101. οὐ κοινὰν κτλ. is a mere periphrasis for χωρὶς ἀλόχου φυτεύσας παῖδα. —θέμενος χάριν is ' making himself agreeable,' literally, ' laying in store for himself an obligation,' πρὸς ἄλλαν Ἀφρ., i.e. γυναῖκα, or ἄλλαν χάριν, for ἄλλης γυναικὸς, πρὸς Ἀφρ. Cf. Iph. T. 602.
1106. ξέναι. The MSS. and old edd. agree in the strange reading κλειναί. This is of course inapplicable to slaves, of which the chorus was composed ; and there appears to be no example of such a ὑποκόρισμα in the known colloquy of σύνδουλοι. Elmsley suggests φίλαι, Dobree ξέναι, which is adopted by Dr. Badham and W. Dindorf. The reading ξεῖναι might possibly have passed into κλειναί. Hermann and Bothe follow Reiske, κλεινὴν, γυναῖκες, ποῦ κόρην κτλ., but this is very unlike the style of Euripides.
1108. ἐξέπλησα, ' I have gone over

ΙΩΝ. 77

ΧΟ. τί δ' ἔστιν, ὦ ξύνδουλε; τίς προθυμία
ποδῶν ἔχει σε, καὶ λόγους τίνας φέρεις; 1110
ΘΕ. θηρώμεθ'· ἀρχαὶ δ' ἀπιχώριοι χθονὸς
ζητοῦσιν αὐτήν, ὡς θάνῃ πετρουμένη.
ΧΟ. οἴμοι, τί λέξεις; οὔ τί που λελήμμεθα
κρυφαῖον ἐς παῖδ' ἐκπορίζουσαι φόνον;
ΘΕ. ἔγνως· μεθέξεις δ' οὐκ ἐν ὑστάτοις κακοῦ. 1115
ΧΟ. ὤφθη δὲ πῶς τὰ κρυπτὰ μηχανήματα;
ΘΕ. τὸ μὴ δίκαιον τῆς δίκης ἡσσώμενον
ἐξηῦρεν ὁ θεός, οὐ μιανθῆναι θέλων.
ΧΟ. πῶς; ἀντιάζω σ' ἱκέτις ἐξειπεῖν τάδε.
πεπυσμέναι γὰρ εἰ θανεῖν ἡμᾶς χρεών, 1120
ἥδιον ἂν θάνοιμεν, εἴθ' ὁρᾶν φάος.
ΘΕ. ἐπεὶ θεοῦ μαντεῖον ᾤχετ' ἐκλιπὼν
πόσις Κρεούσης, παῖδα τὸν καινὸν λαβών,
πρὸς δεῖπνα θυσίας θ' ἃς θεοῖς ὡπλίζετο,
Ξοῦθος μὲν ᾤχετ' ἔνθα πῦρ πηδᾷ θεοῦ 1125
βακχεῖον, ὡς σφαγαῖσι Διονύσου πέτρας

every part of it,' τὸ ἄστυ. As remarked on Rhes. 987, the proper sense is not so much 'to fill,' as 'to occupy vacancy,' i.e. the notion of *repletion* does not necessarily attach to πληροῦν, πιμπλάναι &c. See Orest. 54, λιμένα δὲ Ναυπλίειον ἐκπληρῶν πλάτῃ, and Porson's note. Hel. 1570, πλήσασα κλιμακτῆρας εὐσφύρου ποδός, 'treading all the rounds of the ladder in succession.'

1113. λελήμμεθα. For this Ionic form see Rhes. 74.

1115. μεθέξεις δ'. The δ' was added by Hermann. The restoration of the verse was made by Porson, who perceived that a mere misconception of the letters gave rise to the reading in the MSS., ἐγνώσμεθ' ἐξ ἴσου, κἂν ὑστάτοις κακοῖς. The conjecture, in itself certain, is confirmed by the reading of the Palatine MS. κὲν for κἂν. Compare a similar corruption in v. 1016.

1117. τὸ μὴ δίκαιον κτλ. 'The god, not choosing to be defiled (by murder committed on his sacred ground), discovered the unrighteous act, which was defeated by justice,' i.e. by the arrest of the guilty party. The discovery is attributed to Apollo, because it was made in a kind of miraculous manner by the doves that built their nests in his temple, v. 1197.

1121. ἥδιον, because the torture and anxiety of uncertainty would at least be wanting.

1122—1228. The servant gives a graphic account of the preparations made by Xuthus for the banquet in honour of his newly-found son; of the plot against Ion's life, its failure, the arrest of the guilty accomplice, and his confession. This is one of the finest and most elaborate of the narrations in Euripides; and he generally exerts his best powers on that important part of an Attic tragedy.

1124. θυσίας, see v. 653.

1125. πῦρ πηδᾷ. The two peaks of Parnassus were sacred to Bacchus and Apollo respectively. On one of them lights were seen, either really or in fancy, which were attributed to the torch-light dances of Bacchus with the nymphs. See Bacch. 306, ἔτ' αὐτὸν ὄψει κἀπὶ Δελφίσιν πέτραις πηδῶντα σὺν πεύκαισι δικόρυφον πλάκα, where Elmsley refers also to Phoen. 226. Antig. 1126. See above, v. 716.

δεύσειε δισσὰς παιδὸς ἀντ' ὀπτηρίων,
λέξας, σὺ μέν νυν, τέκνον, ἀμφήρεις μένων
σκηνὰς ἀνίστη τεκτόνων μοχθήμασιν.
θύσας δὲ γενέταις θεοῖσιν ἦν μακρὸν χρόνον   1130
μένω, παροῦσι δαῖτες ἔστωσαν φίλοις.
λαβὼν δὲ μόσχους ᾤχεθ'. ὁ δὲ νεανίας
σεμνῶς ἀτοίχους περιβολὰς σκηνωμάτων

1127. ἀντ' ὀπτηρίων. As the ὀπτήρια (which appear to have included both thanksgivings to the gods and presents to the friends on showing them the child on the eighth or ninth day after birth) had not been celebrated in the case of the infant Ion, the present sacrifice was intended by the father as an equivalent for it.

1128. ἀμφήρης may be compared with ἀμφιλαφὴς, used of spreading trees, and with κατήρης, Suppl. 110, where see the note. The root is, perhaps, ἀρ to fit (ἄρω), but the principal force lies in ἀμφὶ, which implies something doublesided, and therefore, by implication, spatious. So ἀντήρης Phoen. 754, διήρης ibid. 90. But in Cycl. 15, ἀμφῆρες δόρυ points rather to ἐρέσσειν. Possibly ἤρης is only an adjectival termination, as in ξιφήρης, τυμβήρης, &c. to be compared with ηρὸς in οἰνηρὸς &c., though the latter termination is generally confined to words implying the use to which things are put. Hermann compares ἀμφήρη ξύλα in Herc. F. 243, which merely means wood piled up or fitted on every side of an altar.—γενέταις θεοῖς, the gods who preside over birth. See Aesch. Suppl. 73. Apollo is here principally meant; but Bacchus is doubtless included, whose phallic worship indicates that he presided over the generative powers of Nature. Besides, the δισσαὶ πέτραι were to receive the sprinkling of the victims' blood, v. 1126, where especial mention is made of Dionysus.

1133. σεμνῶς, rite, in due form, with all prescribed ceremonies. It is more singular that Dobree's correct judgment should have thought σεμνῶν an improvement, than that Dindorf should have admitted it into the text. Certain prayers and libations were probably offered, after the practice which is still continued on laying the first stone of any important building. Compare Hel. 866, θεῖον δὲ σεμνὸν θεσμὸν αἰθέρος μυχόν.—ὀρθοστάταις, 'with uprights,' i.e. poles, or props, which at once marked the limits and formed the skeleton frame of the tent. See Hel. 547. The middle ἱδρύετο has reference to the τέκτονες in v. 1129, for the actual work, τὸ ἱδρύειν, was theirs.

1133—5. Several rather bold alterations have been introduced into this passage, φλόγα (Bothe), θεοῦ for βίον (Hermann), and lastly, the transposition of θεοῦ and βολὰς (Dindorf), so that the text in the last named edition stands thus,

ἡλίου φλόγα
καλῶς φυλάξας, οὔτε πρὸς μέσας θεοῦ
ἀκτῖνας οὔτ' αὖ πρὸς τελευτώσας βολάς.

This, of course, is all very well, if we could feel any degree of confidence that Euripides so wrote it. But no change in the text is imperatively called for. The evening rays of the sun may be said τελευτᾶν βίον just as, by a converse figure of speech, one about to die is said to have his sun setting, Theocr. i. 102, Agam. 1092. The construction is, καλῶς φυλάξας, ὥστε ἱδρύεσθαι οὔτε πρὸς μέσας βολὰς ἡλίου φλογὸς, οὔτ' αὖ πρὸς ἀκτῖνας κτλ. For βίον τελευτᾶν cf. Agam. 902. It has been supposed that the poet had in view the usual position of Theatres, viz. so that the square described from the lines of the proscenium stands intermediate between the cardinal points, thus

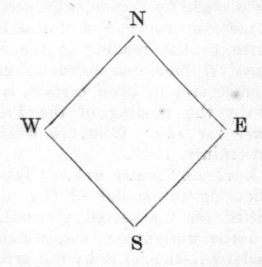

```
        N
      ◇
  W       E
      ◇
        S
```

The stage of the theatre at Athens in fact faced NN.W. The supposed reference to

ΙΩΝ. 79

ὀρθοστάταις ἱδρύεθ᾽, ἡλίου φλογὸς
καλῶς φυλάξας οὔτε πρὸς μέσας βολὰς,   1135
ἀκτῖνας οὔτ᾽ αὖ πρὸς τελευτώσας βίον,
πλέθρου σταθμήσας μῆκος εἰς εὐγώνιον,
[μέτρημ᾽ ἔχουσαν τοὐν μέσῳ γε μυρίων
ποδῶν ἀριθμὸν, ὡς λέγουσιν οἱ σοφοὶ,]
ὡς πάντα Δελφῶν λαὸν ἐς θοίνην καλῶν.   1140
λαβὼν δ᾽ ὑφάσμαθ᾽ ἱρὰ θησαυρῶν πάρα
κατεσκίαζε, θαύματ᾽ ἀνθρώποις ὁρᾶν.
πρῶτον μὲν ὀρόφῳ πτέρυγα περιβάλλει πέπλων,
ἀνάθημα Δίου παιδὸς, οὓς Ἡρακλέης
Ἀμαζόνων σκυλεύματ᾽ ἤνεγκεν θεῷ.   1145
ἐνῆν δ᾽ ὑφανταὶ γράμμασιν τοιαίδ᾽ ὑφαί·

the *proportions* of the Parthenon has been shown by Hermann to be erroneous. But Dr. Wordsworth, *Athens and Attica*, p. 121, draws a probable inference from v. 1141, that the cella of the Parthenon was *hypaethral*, or unroofed, but protected by an extended awning or *velarium*, worked with embroidery. The ancient custom of painting church ceilings and vaults with stars, fantastic animals, and quaint patterns intermixed, perhaps took its origin from these *velaria*.

1137. σταθμήσας, having measured the ground, εἰς εὐγώνιον μῆκος πλέθρου, to a rectangle of 100 feet, which of course includes an area of 10,000 square feet. It is quite needless to read εὐγωνίαν with Elmsley, in order to supply a substantive with which ἔχουσαν in the next verse may agree. Nor is Hermann's ἐχούσας any better, which he appears to refer back to περιβολὰς in v. 1133. These two verses are undoubtedly spurious. The γε is alone a sufficient proof of this. The Athenians were not so ignorant of arithmetic as to require to be told that 100 × 100 = 10,000, and Euripides was not the man to call those who could perform that feat in multiplication οἱ σοφοί. Besides, ἔχουσαν has simply no construction at all. The distich was added by some genius who had more concern for sums than for syntax.

1141. παρὰ θησαυρῶν, for ἐκ or ἀπὸ, is rare. There is an example in Rhes. 366, Ἀτρειδᾶν οἰχομένων Ἰλιάδος παρ᾽ ἀκτᾶς. The epithet ἱρὰ of course implies that these embroidered cloths were borrowed from the sacred stores of the temple, over which Ion himself presided as ταμίας πάντων πιστὸς, v. 55.—κατεσκίαζε, scil. τὸ οἴκημα. So συσκιάζειν is used in Bacch. 1052.

1143. πτέρυγα, a fold or tuck of pepli, —" ducta metaphora," says Barnes, " ab avibus foetus suos alis et plumis operientibus." An awning laid across the ridge and falling upon the slanting roof on either side, would appropriately be called πτέρυξ, as resembling the drooping pinions of a bird. Hermann thinks that in the following account the poet is describing some of the eastern vestments consecrated at Delphi from the victory over the Persians. And the allusion to the battle of Salamis in v. 1160 seems very clear.—Ἀμαζόνων, see Herc. F. 408. *Ibid.* 415, ζωστῆρος ὀλεθρίους ἄγρας, i. e. the belt of Hippolyte, queen of the Amazons. It was on this occasion that Hercules slew many of the Amazons, and carried off their fine Indian shawls as spoils to be consecrated at Delphi.

1146. ἐνῆν. This usage, where a verb, placed before a substantive in the plural masculine or feminine, is itself in the singular number, is rare in Attic Greek. Compare Pers. 49, στεῦται δ᾽ ἱεροῦ Τμώλου πελάται Ζυγὸν ἀμφιβαλεῖν δούλιον Ἑλλάδι. Soph. Trach. 520, ἦν δ᾽ ἀμφίπλεκτοι κλίμακες, ἦν δὲ μετώπων ὀλόεντα πλήγματα. Lucian, Ἔρωτες, p. 410, ἦν δ᾽ ὑπὸ ταῖς ἄγαν παλινσκίοις ὕλαις ἱλαραὶ κλισίαι τοῖς ἐνεστιᾶσθαι θέλουσιν. Bacch. 1350, αἰαῖ, δέδοκται, πρέσβυ, τλήμονες φυγαί. Hel. 1358, μέγα τοι δύναται

ΕΥΡΙΠΙΔΟΥ

Οὐρανὸς ἀθροίζων ἄστρ' ἐν αἰθέρος κύκλῳ·
ἵππους μὲν ἤλαυν' ἐς τελευταίαν φλόγα
Ἥλιος, ἐφέλκων λαμπρὸν Ἑσπέρου φάος.
μελάμπεπλος δὲ Νὺξ ἀσείρωτον ζυγοῖς   1150
ὄχημ' ἔπαλλεν· ἄστρα δ' ὠμάρτει θεᾷ.
Πλειὰς μὲν ᾔει μεσοπόρου δι' αἰθέρος,
ὅ τε ξιφήρης Ὠρίων· ὕπερθε δὲ
Ἄρκτος στρέφουσ' οὐραῖα χρυσήρει πόλῳ.
κύκλος δὲ πανσέληνος ἠκόντιζ' ἄνω   1155
μηνὸς διχήρης, Ὑάδες τε ναυτίλοις
σαφέστατον σημεῖον, ἥ τε φωσφόρος
Ἕως διώκουσ' ἄστρα. τοίχοισιν δ' ἔπι

νεβρῶν πάμποίκιλοι στολίδες.—γράμμασιν, for γραφαῖς, in pictured forms. The device appears to have been as follows. The circle of heaven (πόλος) had enthroned in some conspicuous position a symbolical figure (Οὐρανὸς) marshalling the stars around him. The sun was seen retiring from the margin of the circle, and bringing on in its train (cf. Androm. 200) the evening star (Φωσφόρος or Ἕσπερος, the planet Venus). At the opposite point, Night, attended by a train of stars, was driving her car upon the area which the sun had left. The constellations distinguished either by their position or their symbolical form were the Pleiads, nearest the centre of the circle (μεσόπορος), Orion, the great Bear turning round its tail-stars on the inclosing circle or πόλος, the full Moon shooting upwards, the Hyades, and lastly, perhaps just seen on another part of or without the circle, Aurora chasing away the stars of night. This astronomical device accords with the known studies of the Chaldaean and Babylonian people by whom such embroideries were especially made (Martial calls them *Babylonica* and *Semiramia quae variantur acu*, lib. viii. 28). At the same time the poet indulges his fondness for this science by expatiating somewhat largely on the subject.—As usual in narratives of this kind, the imperfect tense is used with remarkable care and regularity where the duration of any action is expressed; but in the latter half of the ῥῆσις, where the sudden acts of the old man and of Ion are described, the aorist occurs with nearly equal uniformity.

1150. ἀσείρωτον. Without side (or trace) horses, but driving only two horses under the yoke (ζυγοῖς πάλλουσα). For so the car of night was commonly represented, while that of the sun was τέθριππον.

1152. μεσοπόρου. The compound (in which μέσος alone gives an important sense) is to be compared with ἑπτάποροι Πλειάδες Iph. A. 7, Rhes. 529, and with similar examples there quoted in the note. —The ι in Ὠρίων is made short also in Cycl. 213.

1154. στρέφουσ' οὐραῖα. Whatever may be the exact meaning of this rather obscure phrase, it is certain that it cannot mean, as Dr. Badham supposes, 'turning tailwise to the golden pole.' For στρέφειν is always to twist or spin round on an axis, which axis seems here to be called πόλος, and thus the dative is either that of the instrument by which it was turned, or that of place, as in Hel. 375. 1201. With οὐραῖα it is best to supply ἄστρα, though it may stand for οὐρὰν, as εὐκταῖα for εὐχαὶ in Aesch. Suppl. 625, εὐναία for εὐνὴ sup. 172.

1156. μηνὸς διχήρης, dividing the month. The full moon of course fell on the middle of a lunar month. The adjective διχήρης may be compared with ἀμφήρης, which see on v. 1128.

1158. τοίχοισιν. Properly speaking, the building was without walls, ἄτοιχος, v. 1133. But the placing of the embroideries on the open framework, so as of themselves to form a wall, is meant; though we need not, with Bothe, render it *eo consilio ut ista vela essent pro lateribus*.—ἤμπισχεν, for περιβαλὼν ἐτίθει. More properly, ἤμπισχεν τοίχους ὑφάσ-

ἤμπισχεν ἄλλα βαρβάρων ὑφάσματα,
εὐηρέτμους ναῦς ἀντίας Ἑλληνίσιν,　　　　　　1160
καὶ μιξόθηρας φῶτας ἱππείας τ' ἄγρας,
ἐλάφων λεόντων τ' ἀγρίων θηράματα,
κατ' εἰσόδους δὲ Κέκροπα θυγατέρων πέλας
σπείραις συνειλίσσοντ', Ἀθηναίων τινὸς
ἀνάθημα· χρυσέους τ' ἐν μέσῳ συσσιτίῳ　　　　1165
κρατῆρας ἔστησ'· ἐν δ' ἄκροισι βὰς ποσὶ
κῆρυξ ἀνεῖπε τὸν θέλοντ' ἐγχωρίων
ἐς δαῖτα χωρεῖν. ὡς δ' ἐπληρώθη στέγη,
στεφάνοισι κοσμηθέντες εὐόχθου βορᾶς
ψυχὴν ἐπλήρουν. ὡς δ' ἀνεῖσαν ἡδονὴν,　　　　1170
* *　παρελθὼν πρέσβυς ἐς μέσον πέδον
ἔστη, γέλων δ' ἔθηκε συνδείπνοις πολὺν
πρόθυμα πράσσων· ἔκ τε γὰρ κρωσσῶν ὕδωρ
χεροῖν ἔπεμπε νίπτρα, κἀξεθυμία
σμύρνης ἱδρῶτα, χρυσέων τ' ἐκπωμάτων　　　　1175

μασιν. Cf. v. 1522, περικαλύψαι τοῖσι πράγμασι σκότον. There is no reason why βαρβάρων ὑφάσματα should be taken to mean "textae imagines barbarorum" (Dind. after Bothe), rather than ὑφάσματα, ἔργα βαρβάρων. Of course, there is a portentous anachronism in the allusion to the battle of Salamis; but this is quite in the fashion of the Tragic writers; see Suppl. 406.

1161. ἱππείας ἄγρας. Probably the steeds of the Thracian Diomed, Alcest. 483 seqq. For it is clear that the Centaurs, the Nemean lion, and the brazen-hoofed stag, other labours of Hercules, are here described.

1164. σπείραις. This has been explained on v. 22. As this monster-hero was peculiarly Athenian, the embroidered picture of it is appropriately attributed to a donor belonging to that state, and not less appropriately it is set up over the entrance, rather than on the roof; where it would be less conspicuously seen. Hermann, followed by Dindorf, reads σπείραισιν εἰλίσσοντ'. The change is small; but it does not appear that συνειλίσσειν is an inappropriate word for the doubling and coiling of a serpent's tail, as Bothe also appears to think.

1169. εὐόχθου is explained 'abundant,'

or 'joyful.' It is an obscure word, perhaps connected with the root of ὀχθεῖν and ἄχθος. Hesiod has a similar participle, Opp. 475, εὐοχθέων δ' ἵξεαι πολιὸν ἔαρ, οὐδὲ πρὸς ἄλλους αὐγάσεαι. Photius, εὐόχοον, πλήρη· ἀπὸ τῶν ποταμῶν μετῆκται. It is clear that Θ must here be written for the penultimate O. He supposed the word to come from ὄχθη, 'a bank,' and hence explained it as a metaphor from rivers.—ἀνεῖσαν ἡδονὴν, from the Homeric ἐπεὶ πόσιος καὶ ἐδητύος ἐξ ἔρον ἕντο. The word lost at the beginning of the next verse has been variously supplied by conjecture. Perhaps εὐθὺς is more probable than any that has been proposed.

1173. ἐκ κρωσσῶν. This illustrates the 'water-pots' which Christ is recorded to have miraculously changed to wine at the marriage feast at Cana, John ii. 6.

1175. ἐκπωμάτων ἦρχ'. Undertook the management of the vessels from which the libations were made. So this word is applied in Thuc. vi. 32, where the army on embarking for Sicily is described as κρατῆράς τε κεράσαντες παρ' ἅπαν τὸ στράτευμα καὶ ἐκπώμασι χρυσοῖς τε καὶ ἀργυροῖς οἵ τε ἐπιβάται καὶ οἱ ἄρχοντες σπένδοντες. Similar instances of officiousness in serving at banquets are men-

82   ΕΥΡΙΠΙΔΟΥ

ἦρχ᾽, αὐτὸς αὑτῷ τόνδε προστάξας πόνον.
ἐπεὶ δ᾽ ἐς αὐλοὺς ἧκον ἐς κρατῆρά τε
κοινὸν, γέρων ἔλεξ᾽, ἀφαρπάζειν χρεὼν
οἰνηρὰ τεύχη σμικρὰ, μεγάλα δ᾽ εἰσφέρειν,
ὡς θᾶσσον ἔλθωσ᾽ οἵδ᾽ ἐς ἡδονὰς φρενῶν.   1180
ἢν δὴ φερόντων μόχθος ἀργυρηλάτους
χρυσέας τε φιάλας· ὁ δὲ λαβὼν ἐξαίρετον,
ὡς τῷ νέῳ δὴ δεσπότῃ χάριν φέρων,
"δωκε πλῆρες τεῦχος, εἰς οἶνον βαλὼν
ὅ φασι δοῦναι φάρμακον δραστήριον   1185
δέσποιναν, ὡς παῖς ὁ νέος ἐκλίποι φάος·
κοὐδεὶς τάδ᾽ ᾔδειν· ἐν χεροῖν ἔχοντι δὲ
σπονδὰς μετ᾽ ἄλλων παιδὶ τῷ πεφηνότι
βλασφημίαν τις οἰκετῶν ἐφθέγξατο·
ὁ δ᾽, ὡς ἐν ἱρῷ μάντεσίν τ᾽ ἐσθλοῖς τραφείς,   1190
οἰωνὸν ἔθετο, κἀκέλευσ᾽ ἄλλον νέον

tioned by Theophrastus, in his characteristics of περιεργία. Καὶ πλείω δὲ ἐπαναγκάσαι τὸν παῖδα κεράσαι ἢ ὅσα δύνανται οἱ παρόντες ἐκπιεῖν, &c.

1177. ἐς αὐλοὺς, viz. to the introduction of the flute-players and female singers, Aesch. Ag. 235, when after the banquet the paean was to be sung and the triple-libation poured out. The κοινὸς κρατήρ is the bowl used for mixing the wine and water for the company generally; but from v. 1195 it appears that the libation was taken out of a different bowl, κρατὴρ ἱερός. The σμικρὰ τεύχη appear to be the smaller wine-cups used during the consumption of the viands. The bringing in of larger goblets was a common expedient at feasts: see Plat. Symp. 213, E., where Alcibiades exclaims, ἀλλὰ φερέτω Ἀγάθων, εἴ τι ἔστιν ἔκπωμα μέγα· μᾶλλον δὲ οὐδὲν δεῖ, ἀλλὰ φέρε, παῖ, φάναι, τὸν ψυκτῆρα ἐκεῖνον, ἰδόντα αὐτὸν πλέον ἢ ὀκτὼ κοτύλας χωροῦντα.

1178. The old reading καινὸν was corrected by Musgrave, and in the next verse σκεύη by Porson.—οἵδε, 'the company here,' for the messenger quotes the very words which the old man had used.

1182. ἐξαίρετον agrees with τεῦχος, but he means, apparently, a choice and precious φιάλη (circular flat vessel used for libations,) by way of paying a compliment to Ion. It appears that the parties who made the libation also tasted of the same wine. This is clearly implied in the context. The whole contents of the first κρατήρ, or mixer, were thrown away (v. 1192) from the accident of an evil omen. That in the hands of Ion proved fatal to the doves which tasted it on the ground; and it would seem that, though the φιάλη was altogether distinct from the drinking cup, each party sipped of the contents either before or after pouring the λοιβή.

1187. ᾔδειν. For this third person see Suppl. 650. The metre is of course in this passage conclusive; but the grammarians thought ᾔδειν (not ᾔδη) was properly the first person; and hence the MSS. here give ᾔδει. Photius, ᾔδη, ἀντὶ τοῦ ᾔδειν.

1189. βλασφημίαν. 'An unlucky word;' for it can hardly mean 'an evil wish,' ἀρά. The etymology of this compound is rather obscure; it has been derived from βλαψ- or βλαψί-φημος, like βλαψί-φρων. It was to avoid the chance of any such unlucky expressions, and the troublesome consequences which they involved, that the people were bid εὔφημα φωνεῖν at a sacrifice or other religious ceremony. See v. 98.

1191. ἔθετο, 'esteemed it,' 'reckoned it an omen.' So τίθεσθαι Eur. frag. 319 &c. Musgrave infers, from the words

κρατῆρα πληροῦν· τὰς δὲ πρὶν σπονδὰς θεοῦ
δίδωσι γαίᾳ, πᾶσί τ' ἐκσπένδειν λέγει.
σιγὴ δ' ὑπῆλθεν. ἐκ δ' ἐπίμπλαμεν δρόσου
κρατῆρας ἱροὺς Βυβλίνου τε πώματος. 1195
κἂν τῷδε μόχθῳ πτηνὸς εἰσπίπτει δόμοις
κῶμος πελειῶν· Λοξίου γὰρ ἐν δόμοις
ἄτρεστα ναίουσ'. ὡς δ' ἀπέσπεισαν μέθυ,
εἰς αὐτὸ χείλη πώματος κεχρημέναι
καθῆκαν, εἷλκον δ' εὐπτέρους εἰς αὐχένας. 1200
καὶ ταῖς μὲν ἄλλαις ἄνοσος ἦν λοιβὴ θεοῦ·
ᾗ δ' ἕζετ' ἔνθ' ὁ καινὸς ἔσπεισεν γόνος,
ποτοῦ τ' ἐγεύσατ', εὐθὺς εὔπτερον δέμας
ἔσεισε, κἀβάκχευσεν, ἐκ δ' ἔκλαγξ' ὄπα
ἀξύνετον αἰάζουσα· θάμβησεν δὲ πᾶς 1205
θοινατόρων ὅμιλος ὄρνιθος πόνους·
θνήσκει δ' ἀπασπαίρουσα, φοινικοσκελεῖς
χηλὰς παρεῖσα. γυμνὰ δ' ἐκ πέπλων μέλη

δίδωσι γαίᾳ, that libations were regularly and properly poured on the table. And Bothe appositely quotes Aen. i. 736, 'Dixit, et *in mensam* laticum libavit honorem.' Perhaps however no such contrast is here meant, but simply that the guests threw their intended libations away.

1195. Βυβλίνου. On this Thracian wine see Blomf. Gloss. ad Prom. 836. Theocr. xiv. 15, ἀνῷξα δὲ Βύβλινον αὐτοῖς, εὐώδη, τετόρων ἐτέων σχεδόν, ὡς ἀπὸ λανῶ. Hesiod, Opp. 589, εἴη πετραίη τε σκιὴ καὶ Βύβλινος οἶνος. There is considerable doubt as to the place from which this famous wine came. Probably after the custom of the poets, a particular sort is put for the thing generally.

1197. κῶμος. A metaphor from a company of revellers; see Aesch. Agam. 1160. Hipp. 55.

1199. The difficulty which existed in this passage is entirely removed by the reading of the Palatine MS. εἰς αὐτὸ for κεῖς αὐτά. 'When they (the guests) had poured away the wine, (then) they (the doves), wanting drink, dipped their beaks into it, and drew it into their feathered throats.' The form καθῆκαν, more commonly used in the second aorist, καθεῖσαν, may be compared with παρέδωκαν Med.

630, ἔθηκαν Herc. F. 590, Bacch. 129, ἀνῆκαν Bacch. 448. Neither Aeschylus nor Sophocles use this form.

1205. θάμβησεν. The augment is occasionally omitted in the ῥήσεις of messengers, (e. g. Oed. R. 1249. Oed. Col. 1624. Bacch. 767, 1084, 1134,) so that we need not follow Heath in reading ἐθάμβησεν with the elision of the preceding α.—ἀξύνετον, strange, unintelligible; a bad omen in itself. So Antig. 1001, ἀγνῶτ' ἀκούω φθόγγον ὀρνίθων.

1208. παρεῖσα, relaxing in death. Alcest. 204, παρειμένη χειρὸς ἄθλιον βάρος. —γυμνὰ ἐκ πέπλων, with his garment (properly his ἱμάτιον) thrown back so as to leave his arms uncovered. There is nothing in the words themselves to prevent us from understanding that Ion leaped upon or over the table to arrest the murderer; but the action would be undignified. Hermann, after Matthiae, compares Iph. T. 1404, γυμνὰς ἐκβαλόντες ὠλένας, and for ἱέναι used of the hands or arms, Electr. 799, πρὸς ἔργον πάντες ἵεσαν χέρας. Bothe has an absurd idea that Ion threw himself prostrate on the table, and he adds, "Dicit haec (βοᾷ δὲ κτλ.) postquam paulisper acquievit, respiravitque, jam relevans e mensa corpus, et inter medios convivas consis-

ΕΥΡΙΠΙΔΟΥ

ὑπὲρ τραπέζης ᾖχ' ὁ μαντευτὸς γόνος,
βοᾷ δὲ, τίς μ' ἔμελλεν ἀνθρώπων κτανεῖν; 1210
σήμαινε, πρέσβυ· σὴ γὰρ ἡ προθυμία,
καὶ πῶμα χειρὸς σῆς ἐδεξάμην πάρα.
εὐθὺς δ' ἐρευνᾷ γραῖαν ὠλένην λαβών,
ἐπ' αὐτοφώρῳ πρέσβυν ὡς ἔχονθ' ἕλοι.
ὤφθη δὲ καὶ κατεῖπ' ἀναγκασθεὶς μόγις 1215
τόλμας Κρεούσης πώματός τε μηχανάς.
θεῖ δ' εὐθὺς ἔξω συλλαβὼν θοινάτορας
ὁ πυθόχρηστος Λοξίου νεανίας,
κἀν κοιράνοισι Πυθικοῖς σταθεὶς λέγει,
ὦ γαῖα σεμνή, τῆς Ἐρεχθέως ὕπο 1220
ξένης γυναικὸς φαρμάκοισι θνήσκομεν.
Δελφῶν δ' ἄνακτες ὥρισαν πετρορριφῆ
θανεῖν ἐμὴν δέσποιναν οὐ ψήφῳ μιᾷ,
τὸν ἱρὸν ὡς κτείνουσαν ἔν τ' ἀνακτόροις
φόνον τιθεῖσαν. πᾶσα δὲ ζητεῖ πόλις 1225
τὴν ἀθλίως σπεύσασαν ἀθλίαν ὁδόν·
παίδων γὰρ ἐλθοῦσ' εἰς ἔρον Φοίβου πάρα
τὸ σῶμα κοινῇ τοῖς τέκνοις ἀπώλεσεν.
ΧΟ. οὐκ ἔστ' οὐκ ἔστιν θανάτου

tens." It is quite evident that βοᾷ δὲ &c. is meant to describe his energetic conduct on the first impulse of the moment; and he seems to have extended his arms in order to point to the old man.
1213. ἐρευνᾷ, he searches him, to find the poison actually in his possession (ἔχοντα τὸ φάρμακον).
1215. ὤφθη, *manifestus fit*, cf. 1116. —κατεῖπε, see Hel. 898.
1222. Δελφῶν ἄνακτες. The same, perhaps, as the Δελφῶν ἀριστῆς in v. 416. They appear to have constituted a tribunal of justice in case of violence or disputes arising between the visitors to the shrine.—πετρορριφῆ, by being hurled from a rock; cf. 1268. From v. 1236, it might seem that being stoned to death is meant. But the chorus appear to use the latter term in an improper sense to imply the former. As Hermann observes on the latter verse, "πέτρωμα est, sive quis obruitur lapidibus, sive de rupe in saxa praecipitatur."—For οὐ ψήφῳ μιᾷ he might

have said μιᾷ ψήφῳ, by an unanimous vote. So Aesch. Suppl. 919, τοιάδε δημόπρακτος ἐκ πόλεως μία ψῆφος κέκρανται. The negative implies, 'not merely by one vote, but by many.'
1226. ἀθλίαν ὁδὸν, the route from Athens to Delphi.
1227. Φοίβου Matthiae for Φοίβον. It was to ask children *from* Phoebus that she came, rather than *to* Phoebus εἰς ἔρον παίδων, which should have been δι' ἔρωτα.
1228. κοινῇ. The meaning is rather, ἅμα τῷ σώματι, sc. τῷ βίῳ, ἀπώλεσεν ἐλπίδα τέκνων.
1229. The preceding narration has filled the chorus with alarm. They see no way of escape either for themselves or their mistress. To sink below the earth, to soar aloft on wings, to fly by sea or on a chariot,—all is vain, unless the god will lend his aid to conceal them. They fear that the stern law of requital, δράσαντι παθεῖν, has now to take its course against them.

παρατροπὰ μελέᾳ μοι· 1230
φανερὰ γὰρ φανερὰ τάδ᾽ ἤδη
σπονδᾶς ἐκ Διονύσου βοτρύων θοαῖς
ἐχίδνας σταγόσιν μιγνυμένας φόνῳ,
φανερὰ θύματα νερτέρων,
συμφοραὶ μὲν ἐμῷ βίῳ, 1235
λεύσιμοι δὲ καταφθοραὶ δεσποίνᾳ.
τίνα φυγὰν πτερόεσσαν ἢ
χθονὸς ὑπὸ σκοτίων μυχῶν πορευθῶ
θανάτου λεύσιμον ἄταν ἀποφεύγουσα, τεθρίππων
ὠκίσταν χαλᾶν ἐπιβᾶσ᾽, 1241
ἢ πρύμνας ἐπὶ ναῶν;
οὐκ ἔστι λαθεῖν, ὅτε μὴ χρῄζων
θεὸς ἐκκλέπτει.
τί ποτ᾽, ὦ μελέα δέσποινα, μένει 1245
ψυχῇ σε παθεῖν; ἆρα θέλουσαι
δρᾶσαί τι κακὸν τοὺς πέλας αὐταὶ
πεισόμεθ᾽, ὥσπερ τὸ δίκαιον;
ΚΡ. πρόσπολοι, διωκόμεσθα θανασίμους ἐπὶ σφαγὰς,
Πυθίᾳ ψήφῳ κρατηθεῖσ᾽, ἔκδοτος δὲ γίγνομαι. 1251

1232. σπονδᾶς Herm. and Dobree for σπονδάς. The construction is, φανερὰ φόνῳ σπονδᾶς—μιγνυμένας σταγόσιν ἐχίδνας. 'All these schemes of ours have been detected by the deadly effect of the libation made from the Bacchic grape and mixed with the speedy venom-drops of the viper' (of the Gorgon, v. 1015).—θοαῖς is Dobree's reading for θοάς.
1234. θύματα νερτέρων, the victim offered to the gods below,—the attempted murder of Ion.
1236. This verse is choriambic dochmiac. The next two are forms of glyconean verses. Then follows a line which it is best to scan as Ionic a minore. Hermann arranges 1237—40 as choriambics, like vv. 1232—3.
1237. On this favourite alternative of escape, by flying above or sinking below the earth, see Med. 1296. The more common construction, when *motion under* is expressed, would be ὑπὸ χθονίους μυχούς. Still it is needless to take φυγὴν χθονὸς for χθονίαν, with Hermann; for φυγὴν ὑπὸ χθονὸς μυχῶν means a flight by which one may be concealed beneath the earth.
1243. λαθεῖν Stephens for λαβεῖν.— ὅτε μὴ κτλ., a general proposition; 'a man cannot escape unless when the god, desiring it, gets him out of harm's way.'— μένει Portus for μέλει.
1248. ὥσπερ τὸ δίκαιον, as is the established law of justice or retribution, as above, v. 1229.
1250. Creusa rushes in wild consternation upon the stage. The trochaic metre expresses the hurry and alarm of the guilty parties. She has just escaped with her life from the pursuit of justice. Scarcely has she time to take refuge at the altar, when Ion, followed by a band of armed Delphians, comes on, probably from the opposite side of the stage, to drag her to condign punishment. On the plural verb followed by the singular participle, see v. 251, 549.

86   ΕΥΡΙΠΙΔΟΥ

ΧΟ. ἴσμεν, ὦ τάλαινα, τὰς σὰς συμφοράς, ἵν᾽ εἶ τύχης.
ΚΡ. ποῖ φύγω δῆτ᾽; ἐκ γὰρ οἴκων προὔλαβον μόγις
    πόδα
    μὴ θανεῖν· κλοπῇ δ᾽ ἀφῖγμαι διαφυγοῦσα πολεμίους.
ΧΟ. ποῖ δ᾽ ἂν ἄλλοσ᾽ ἢ 'πὶ βωμόν;   1255
ΚΡ.   καὶ τί μοι πλέον τόδε;
ΧΟ. ἱκέτιν οὐ θέμις φονεύειν.
ΚΡ.   τῷ νόμῳ δέ γ᾽ ὄλλυμαι.
ΧΟ. χειρία γ᾽ ἁλοῦσα.
ΚΡ.   καὶ μὴν οἵδ᾽ ἀγωνισταὶ πικροὶ
    δεῦρ᾽ ἐπείγονται ξιφήρεις.
ΧΟ.   ἷζε νῦν πυρᾶς ἔπι.
    κἂν θάνῃς γὰρ ἐνθάδ᾽ οὖσα, τοῖς ἀποκτείνασί σε
    προστρόπαιον αἷμα θήσεις· οἰστέον δὲ τὴν τύχην.
ΙΩ. ὦ ταυρόμορφον ὄμμα Κηφισοῦ πατρός,   1261
    οἵαν ἔχιδναν τήνδ᾽ ἔφυσας, ἢ πυρὸς
    δράκοντ᾽ ἀναβλέποντα φοινίαν φλόγα,
    ᾗ τόλμα πᾶσ᾽ ἔνεστιν, οὐδ᾽ ἥσσων ἔφυ
    Γοργοῦς σταλαγμῶν, οἷς ἔμελλέ με κτανεῖν.   1265
    λάζυσθ᾽, ἵν᾽ αὐτῆς τοὺς ἀκηράτους πλόκους

1252. ἵν᾽ εἶ τύχης is Scaliger's ingenious emendation for ἵν᾽ εὐτυχῆς or εὐτυχεῖς. Hermann gives ἵν᾽ εὐτύχεις, 'where you were before fortunate,' i. e. we know the sad reverse which you have experienced. But this is by no means so satisfactory as the slight alteration of εὖ into εἶ.
1253. προὔλαβον, viz. ἔφθασα πόδα ὑπεξάγουσα, ὥστε μὴ θανεῖν.—κλοπῇ κτλ., 'tis only by stealth that I have come here at all, namely, by eluding my enemies.
1257. χειρία γε. 'Yes, provided they get you into their power, but not otherwise.' Cf. Androm. 411. 628.
1260. προστρόπαιον, that calls for vengeance; that entails a curse on the perpetrator. Those deceased persons seem to have been called προστρόπαιοι, who appealed in Hades to their friends on earth to avenge them. They were said προστρέπεσθαι, to supplicate. Hence προστρόπαιον αἷμα meant ἄγος or μίασμα, as Photius explains it. The notions of ἀλάστωρ and μιάστωρ were closely connected with this; see Med. 1371. Indeed, Photius has προστρόπαιος, δαίμων τις ἐπὶ τῶν ἐναγῶν, though he wrongly derives it from τρόπαιον. Cf. Herc. F. 1161. 1259. See on Heracl. 1015.
1261. Arrived upon the stage, Ion finds himself disappointed of his victim, who has already taken refuge at the altar. He assures her that even this shall not save her, and congratulates himself on his narrow escape from falling into the hands of such a woman.—Κηφισοῦ πατρός, of Cephisus the father (i. e. ancestor) of Creusa. Apollodor. iii. 15, 1, γήμας δὲ Ἐρεχθεὺς Πραξιθέαν τὴν Φρασίμου καὶ Διογενείας τῆς Κηφισοῦ, ἔσχε παῖδας Κέκροπα, Πάνδωρον, Μητίονα· θυγατέρας δὲ, Πρόκριν, Κρέουσαν, Χθονίαν, Ὠρείθυιαν, ἣν ἥρπασε Βορέας. The custom of representing river-gods as tauriform is well known from Soph. Trach. 11, Hor. Carm. iv. 14. 25, and other passages. So the Alpheus is σῆμα ταυρόπουν ὁρᾶν, Iph. A. 276.
1266. τοὺς ἀκ. πλόκους, 'those unsullied locks of hers,'— meaning thereby, 'which shall soon be disfigured by her

κόμης καταξήνωσι Παρνασοῦ πλάκες,
ὅθεν πετραῖον ἅλμα δισκευθήσεται.
ἐσθλοῦ δ' ἔκυρσα δαίμονος, πρὶν ἐς πόλιν
μολεῖν Ἀθηνῶν χὑπὸ μητρυιὰν πεσεῖν.   1270
ἐν συμμάχοις γὰρ ἀνεμετρησάμην φρένας
τὰς σάς, ὅσον μοι πῆμα δυσμενής τ' ἔφυς·
εἴσω γὰρ ἄν με περιβαλοῦσα δωμάτων
ἄρδην ἂν ἐξέπεμψας εἰς Ἅιδου δόμους.
ἀλλ' οὔτε βωμὸς οὔτ' Ἀπόλλωνος δόμος   1275
σώσει σ', ὁ δ' οἶκτος ὁ σὸς ἐμοὶ κρείσσων πάρα
καὶ μητρὶ τἠμῇ· καὶ γὰρ εἰ τὸ σῶμά μοι
ἄπεστιν αὐτῆς, τοὔνομ' οὐκ ἄπεστί πω.
ἴδεσθε τὴν πανοῦργον, ἐκ τέχνης τέχνην

fatal fall.'—δισκευθήσεται, cf. Tro. 1121, where Astyanax is called πύργων δίσκημα πικρόν.

1269. ἐσθλοῦ κτλ. 'Truly, 'twas a good fortune that I met with before I went to the city of Athens and fell into the hands of a step-mother; for among those who have befriended me I reckon your feelings towards me, so far as you were a bane to me and evilly-disposed; for if once you had gotten me within the inclosure of your house, you would have sent me entirely out of sight to the abodes of Hades.' He seems to mean, 'I thank you for your hostility, for it has been the means of saving me.' Dr. Badham gives the sense thus, 'I counted as much on your friendship as I have discovered your malice;' and so Hermann appears to understand the passage, for he explains συμμάχοις, "inter eos qui mihi opem laturi erant." But the γὰρ seems directly to connect ξυμμάχοις with ἐσθλοῦ δαίμονος, of which words it is an epexegesis.—πεσεῖν ὑπό, as Heracl. 230, ἅπαντα γὰρ ταῦτ' ἐστὶ κρείσσω πλὴν ὑπ' Ἀργείοις πεσεῖν.

1273. δωμάτων. Dobree needlessly proposed δικτύων. The word περιβαλεῖν is constantly used in metaphors from hunting, where there is no express mention of the net. Cf. Suppl. 500, of the chariot of Amphiaraus, οὐδ' ἥρπασεν Χάρυβδις οἰωνοσκόπον, τέθριππον ἅρμα περιβαλοῦσα χάσματι.

1276. οἶκτος ὁ σός. 'The feeling of pity for you is stronger for myself and my mother,' i. e. my sense of justice prevails over my compassion. Cf. Prom. 396, μὴ γάρ σε θρῆνος οὑμὸς εἰς ἔχθραν βάλῃ. He adds καὶ μητρὶ τῇ ἐμῇ, because the object foremost in his mind was the discovery of his mother, who had so nearly been deprived of a son, and because the spectators are thus led forcibly to contemplate the unconscious matricide that he is now intending. Dr. Badham's change of καί into τῇ appears unwarrantable in itself, and to be no improvement on the sense. Ion says that pity for himself is present in his mind, not as a selfish sentiment, but because he was conscious that his position as a newly-found son was such as called for more than ordinary sympathy. Bothe takes οἶκτος ὁ σός to mean, 'all this lamentation about yourself is stronger with me and my mother.'

1278. οὐκ ἄπεστί πω. "Adhuc eam appellare possum, ut qui nondum abs te sim interemptus." Bothe. Perhaps he merely means, that he has not yet forgotten his mother.

1279. ἐκ τέχνης τέχνην. The first trick was the attempt to kill him, the second, the attempt to evade justice. Before βωμὸν the MSS. add οὐ, which Hermann and Elmsley rightly omit. Dobree, followed by Dr. Badham and W. Dindorf, gives ἢ βωμὸν &c. But οὐ is a word that is often both added and omitted according to the grammarians' misapprehension of the meaning. Examples of its intrusion are, Aesch. Theb. 468, 1041; of its omission, Med. 708, Rhes. 115, Tro. 982. Thus, here they supposed the meaning to be, that Creusa was not re-

οἵαν ἔπλεξε· βωμὸν ἔπτηξεν θεοῦ, 1280
ὡς οὐ δίκην δώσουσα τῶν εἰργασμένων.
ΚΡ. ἀπεννέπω σε μὴ κατακτείνειν ἐμὲ
ὑπέρ τ' ἐμαυτῆς τοῦ θεοῦ θ', ἵν' ἕσταμεν.
ΙΩ. τί δ' ἐστὶ Φοίβῳ σοί τε κοινὸν ἐν μέσῳ;
ΚΡ. ἱρὸν τὸ σῶμα τῷ θεῷ δίδωμ' ἔχειν. 1285
ΙΩ. κἄπειτ' ἔκαινες φαρμάκοις τὸν τοῦ θεοῦ;
ΚΡ. ἀλλ' οὐκέτ' ἦσθα Λοξίου, πατρὸς δὲ σοῦ.
ΙΩ. ἀλλ' ἐγενόμεσθα, πατρὸς ἀπουσίαν λέγω.
ΚΡ. οὐκοῦν τότ' ἦσθα· νῦν δ' ἐγώ, σὺ δ' οὐκέτ' εἶ.
ΙΩ. οὐκ εὐσεβής γε, τἀμὰ δ' εὐσεβῆ τότ' ἦν. 1290
ΚΡ. ἔκτεινα δ' ὄντα πολέμιον δόμοις ἐμοῖς.
ΙΩ. οὔτοι σὺν ὅπλοις ἦλθον ἐς τὴν σὴν χθόνα.
ΚΡ. μάλιστα· κἀπίμπρας γ' Ἐρεχθέως δόμους.
ΙΩ. ποίοισι πανοῖς ἢ πυρὸς ποίᾳ φλογί;
ΚΡ. ἔμελλες οἰκεῖν τἄμ', ἐμοῦ βίᾳ λαβών. 1295
ΙΩ. πατρός γε γῆν διδόντος ἣν ἐκτήσατο.

strained by fear of the sacredness of the place from attempting to commit murder. As a mere corruption, it is very unlikely that ἢ should accidentally have been written οὐ. The accusative is unusual, but ἔπτηξεν implies φυγεῖν ἐς βωμὸν or λαβεῖν βωμόν. We may compare δυσοίζειν θάμνον in Agam. 1286.

1282. The interest of the play has now reached its crisis. A son is standing ready to drag to a cruel death his own mother, not only ignorant that she is such, but believing that he is about to perform a just and even a religious act. Such however is the sanctity of the altar where she has taken refuge, that he fears to act. The delay has saved her life; for the intervention of the aged priestess of the temple gives a new turn to the scene.

1286. ἔκαινες. So Heath for ἔκτεινας or ἔκτανες. Dindorf gives the bolder alteration proposed by Musgrave, κᾆτ' ἔκτανές με φαρμάκοις κτλ. But the imperfect is more suited to express the attempt. The verb itself occurs in Cho. 872, τὸν ζῶντα καίνειν τοὺς τεθνηκότας λέγω. Compare however *inf.* v. 1291.

1288. πατρὸς ἀπουσίαν Seidler for πατρὸς δ' οὐσίαν. The Δ perhaps represents the first letter Α, and thus π only remains to be supplied. The sense is, 'But I was Apollo's, I mean, in the absence of my real father.' Creusa's reply is, 'Certainly you were so (i. e. Apollo's) *then;* but now I am his, (viz. his suppliant,) and you no longer belong to him.' Thus she artfully turns his own argument against himself, that one sacred to the god cannot be lawfully slain.—Dobree would read οὐκέτι.

1290. εὐσεβὴς for -εῖς L. Dindorf. 'If you are under the protection of the god as a suppliant, you are one who has acted impiously towards him, whereas my conduct then was dutiful,'—which, he implies, makes all the difference between our respective positions.

1291. ἔκτεινα δ'. 'And therefore (as being no longer Apollo's) I killed you, because you were an enemy,' &c. Hermann seems rightly to reject Wakefield's ἔκτεινά σ'. The sense is continued from v. 1287, ἔκτεινα μέν σε οὐκέτι ὄντα Λοξίου, ἔκτεινα δὲ ὄντα πολέμιον ἐμοῖς δόμοις.

1293. ἐπίμπρας, a rather unusual imperfect. 'Yes, and you tried to set the house of Erechtheus in a blaze,' i. e. to embroil it by domestic jealousies. Aeschylus uses the same figure, Choeph. 618, τίῳ δ' ἀθέρμαντον ἐστίαν δόμων. Compare the phrase διὰ πυρὸς ἐλθεῖν τινί.

ΚΡ. τοῖς Αἰόλου δὲ πῶς μετῆν τῆς Παλλάδος ;
ΙΩ. ὅπλοισιν αὐτὴν οὐ λόγοις ἐρρύσατο.
ΚΡ. ἐπίκουρος οἰκήτωρ γ᾽ ἂν οὐκ εἴη χθονός.
ΙΩ. κἄπειτα τοῦ μέλλειν μ᾽ ἀπέκτεινες φόβῳ ; 1300
ΚΡ. ὡς μὴ θάνοιμί γ᾽, εἰ σὺ μὴ μέλλων τύχοις.
ΙΩ. φθονεῖς, ἄπαις οὖσ᾽, εἰ πατὴρ ἐξηῦρέ με ;
ΚΡ. σὺ τῶν ἀτέκνων δῆτ᾽ ἀναρπάσεις δόμους ;
ΙΩ. ἡμῖν δέ γ᾽ ἀλλὰ πατρικῆς οὐκ ἦν μέρος ;
ΚΡ. ὅσ᾽ ἀσπὶς ἔγχος θ᾽· ἥδε σοι παμπησία. 1305
ΙΩ. ἔκλειπε βωμὸν καὶ θεηλάτους ἕδρας.
ΚΡ. τὴν σὴν ὅπου σοι μητέρ᾽ ἐστὶ νουθέτει.
ΙΩ. σὺ δ᾽ οὐχ ὑφέξεις ζημίαν, κτείνουσ᾽ ἐμέ ;
ΚΡ. ἤν γ᾽ ἐντὸς ἀδύτων τῶνδέ με σφάξαι θέλῃς.
ΙΩ. τίς ἡδονή σοι θεοῦ θανεῖν ἐν στέμμασι ; 1310
ΚΡ. λυπήσομέν τιν᾽ ὧν λελυπήμεσθ᾽ ὕπο.

1298. οὐ λόγοις, not by mere promises and professions. This looks like a political allusion to some events of the time. Hermann thinks Cleon may be meant; but Cleon died as early as B.C. 422.

1299. οἰκήτωρ. An original settler or occupant of the land. So λαὸς οἰκήτωρ θεοῦ of the Delphians, Andr. 1089.

1300. τοῦ μέλλειν. In reference to v. 1295.

1301. There are several ways of explaining this rather obscure verse. Hermann, Matthiae, Dindorf, and Bothe, take it thus:—'That I might escape death, if you were not destined to inhabit my house.' Dr. Badham, who says Matthiae has "perfectly misunderstood" the latter clause, thinks there is a play on μέλλειν, 'Aye, lest I should die if you happened not to tarry.' But the interpreters too often fail to notice the necessary emphasis on the nominative of the personal pronoun. The third and old way of explaining the verse appears to be the only correct one, 'yes, that I might not die, if *you* were not destined to die first,'—ἵνα μὴ θάνοιμι, ὃ ἐγένετο ἄν, εἰ μὴ σὺ ἔθανες. We might read, εἰ σὺ μή μ᾽ ἐλὼν τύχοις, 'if *you* did not succeed in killing me.' Cf. 1291.

1304. ἀλλὰ πατρικῆς. At least of my father's land, if not of yours. Either γῆς or οὐσίας may be supplied. She regards Ion simply as an invader of her home; but he reminds her that Xuthus had some possessions in his own right.

1306. θεηλάτους, here simply for θείας, for Ion was not likely to mean εἰς ἃς θεία τύχη ἤγαγέ σε. Matthiae explains 'divinely built,' because Apollo himself chose Delphi for his shrine. This seems one of those numerous words, where the second part of the compound is almost *otiose*.

1307. νουθέτει. This is ambiguously said. The spectators, who know that Creusa is really the mother, are to understand, 'Bid your own mother to leave the altar, and so be her murderess.' But Creusa herself throws a taunt on Ion's parentage, by saying, 'go and give your advice to your mother, wherever she is,' i.e. alive or dead, who knows? So ὅπου πέρ ἐστι is used of one in Hades, Alcest. 1092. Heracl. 946. The hyperbaton of μητέρα is remarkable. It is to be explained on the principle noticed on Rhes. 719, that the two clauses are considered as one integral proposition. Mr. Shilleto (on Dem. de Fals. Leg. p. 404,) cites this passage as if the poet had said τὴν σὴν ὅπου σοι μήτηρ ἐστί, which is a very different idiom.

1310. στέμμασι. See v. 224, 422. Probably she had grasped the sacred wreaths which decked the altar, as if they had been suppliant boughs; see on Suppl. 32.

1311. ὧν. She means Phoebus in particular; but, as Ion yet knows nothing of

ΙΩ. φεῦ.
δεινόν γε, θνητοῖς τοὺς νόμους ὡς οὐ καλῶς
ἔθηκεν ὁ θεὸς οὐδ' ἀπὸ γνώμης σοφῆς·
τοὺς μὲν γὰρ ἀδίκους βωμὸν οὐχ ἵζειν ἐχρῆν,
ἀλλ' ἐξελαύνειν· οὐδὲ γὰρ ψαύειν καλὸν   1315
θεῶν πονηρὰν χεῖρα, τοῖσι δ' ἐνδίκοις
ἱερὰ καθίζειν, ὅστις ἠδικεῖτ', ἐχρῆν,
καὶ μὴ 'πὶ ταὐτὸ τοῦτ' ἰόντ' ἔχειν ἴσον
τόν τ' ἐσθλὸν ὄντα τόν τε μὴ θεῶν πάρα.

ΠΥΘΙΑ.

ἐπίσχες, ὦ παῖ· τρίποδα γὰρ χρηστήριον   1320
λιποῦσα θριγκοῦ τοῦδ' ὑπερβάλλω ποδὶ
Φοίβου προφῆτις, τρίποδος ἀρχαῖον νόμον
σώζουσα, πασῶν Δελφίδων ἐξαίρετος.
ΙΩ. χαῖρ', ὦ φίλη μοι μῆτερ, οὐ τεκοῦσά περ.

her seduction by the god, she uses the plural, as Hermann observes, with an intentional ambiguity, to include both Ion and Xuthus.

1314. οὐχ ἵζειν ἐχρῆν. See on Hippol. 507.

1317. ὅστις ἠδικεῖτο. Not ὁ ἀδικῶν, he says, but ὁ ἀδικούμενος, ought to be allowed to take refuge in a sanctuary. Euripides appears to have regarded these asylums, as indeed they have ever been found to be, as great abuses. Compare Heracl. 259, δεῦρ', ὡς ἔοικε, τοῖς κακοῖσι φευκτέον. Frag. 871, ed. Dind.,

ἐγὼ γάρ, ὅστις μὴ δίκαιος ὢν ἀνὴρ
βωμὸν προσίζει, τὸν νόμον χαίρειν ἐῶν
πρὸς τὴν δίκην ἄγοιμ' ἂν οὐ τρέσας θεούς.
κακὸν γὰρ ἄνδρα χρὴ κακῶς πράσσειν ἀεί.

For τοῖσι δ' ἐνδίκοις Dobree would read τοὺς δέ γ' ἐνδίκους. It is not easy to defend the construction of χρὴ with a dative. A passage of the Eumenides, v. 680, where it occurred, seems rightly to have been altered to the accusative. Antig. 736, ἄλλῳ γὰρ ἢ 'μοὶ χρή γε τῆσδ' ἄρχειν χθονός; where Dindorf edits χρή με.

1321. θριγκοῦ τοῦδε. According to Hermann, who construes τρίποδα θριγκοῦ τοῦδε λιποῦσα ὑπερβάλλω αὐτόν, the word is used in the singular for a low wall or stone ledge which protected the adytum of the temple. And this indeed is recognised by Photius, who has θριγκὸς, τὸ περίφραγμα, στεφάνη, μικρὸν τειχίον, περίβολον. From within this adytum, where the tripod stood, the priestess now appears, stepping over the inclosure. If this be true, Dobree's conjecture θριγκοὺς τούσδε, would have quite a different meaning; compare Tro. 489, and Iph. T. 47 with 129. The poet, of course, might have written θριγκὸν τόνδε, as in Alcest. 795, τάσδ' ὑπερβαλὼν πύλας. Of course also he might have written πόδα, as Dr. Badham gives in his text. Both these alterations are very uncertain; they are mere vague probabilities. Matthiae compares v. 220, θέμις γυάλων ὑπερβῆναι λευκῷ ποδί, but there some word is wanting on which γυάλων perhaps depended. The genitive here may be governed by the sense of ἐξελθοῦσα.

1323. ἐξαίρετος. Chosen out of all the Delphian women according to the ancient custom of the tripod. Seidler seems wrong in saying, "referendum fortasse est ad ipsum praegressum Φοίβου προφῆτις," as if it were αἱρεθεῖσα προφῆτις. Hermann, in a learned note, gives grounds for supposing that the Pythoness "non gentem aut natales, sed integritatem vitae praedicat, quum se πασῶν Δελφίδων ἐξαίρετον dicit."

ΙΩΝ. 91

ΠΥ. ἀλλ' οὖν ἐλεγόμεθ'· ἡ φάτις δ' οὔ μοι πικρά. 1325
ΙΩ. ἤκουσας ὡς μ' ἔκτεινεν ἥδε μηχαναῖς;
ΠΥ. ἤκουσα· καὶ σύ γ' ὠμὸς ὢν ἁμαρτάνεις.
ΙΩ. οὐ χρή με τοὺς κτείνοντας ἀνταπολλύναι;
ΠΥ. προγόνοις δάμαρτες δυσμενεῖς ἀεί ποτε.
ΙΩ. ἡμεῖς δὲ μητρυιαῖς γε πάσχοντες κακῶς. 1330
ΠΥ. μὴ ταῦτα· λείπων ἱρὰ καὶ στείχων πάτραν
ΙΩ. τί δή με δρᾶσαι νουθετούμενον χρεών;
ΠΥ. καθαρῶς Ἀθήνας ἔλθ' ὑπ' οἰωνῶν καλῶν.
ΙΩ. καθαρὸς ἅπας τοι πολεμίους ὃς ἂν κτάνῃ.
ΠΥ. μὴ σύ γε· παρ' ἡμῶν δ' ἔκλαβ' οὓς ἔχω λόγους. 1335
ΙΩ. λέγοις ἄν· εὔνους δ' οὔσ' ἐρεῖς ὅσ' ἂν λέγῃς.
ΠΥ. ὁρᾷς τόδ' ἄγγος χερὸς ὑπαγκάλισμ' ἐμῆς;
ΙΩ. ὁρῶ παλαιὰν ἀντίπηγ' ἐν στέμμασιν.
ΠΥ. ἐν τῇδέ σ' ἔλαβον νεόγονον βρέφος ποτέ.
ΙΩ. τί φῄς; ὁ μῦθος εἰσενήνεκται νέος. 1340
ΠΥ. σιγῇ γὰρ εἶχον αὐτά, νῦν δὲ δείκνυμεν.
ΙΩ. πῶς οὖν ἔκρυπτες τότε λαβοῦσ' ἡμᾶς πάλαι;
ΠΥ. ὁ θεός σ' ἐβούλετ' ἐν δόμοις ἔχειν λάτριν.
ΙΩ. νῦν δ' οὐχὶ χρῄζει; τῷ τόδε γνῶναί με χρή;
ΠΥ. πατέρα κατειπὼν τῆσδέ σ' ἐκπέμπει χθονός. 1345
ΙΩ. σὺ δ' ἐκ κελευσμῶν, ἢ πόθεν, σώζεις τάδε;

1325. ἐλεγόμεθ' Dr. Badham. Elmsley λεγόμεθά γ'. The old reading was λεγόμεσθ'. See v. 49.
1329. προγόνοις, to those born before, viz. to step-sons. Lucian, Ἀποκηρυττόμενος, Vol. ii. p. 185, ὁρᾷς ὡς οἴονται πάντες εἶναί τι μῖσος πρὸς τοὺς προγόνους πάσαις μητρυιαῖς, κἂν ὦσι χρησταί.
1333. καθαρῶς. καθαρὸς Porson; but the sense is surely the same, 'without the pollution of blood.'—ὑπ' οἰωνῶν, 'attended by good omens.' See on Hipp. 1299. The reply to this shows, as has been elsewhere remarked, that the Greeks thought revenge, even to the shedding of blood, a positive duty, and wholly free from guilt.
1337. ὑπαγκάλισμ' ἐμῆς, the conjecture of Elmsley for ὑπ' ἀγκάλαις ἐμαῖς, though rejected by Hermann, Matthiae, and Dindorf, appears to be rightly admitted by Dr. Badham. For it is one thing to say 'the embrace of my hand,' another to use the very incorrect expression, 'the arms of my hand.'
1338. ἀντίπηγα, a box or basket; see v. 40.—ἐν στέμμασιν, dressed with chaplets, or fillets, probably of wool or some equally durable material.
1340. ὁ μῦθος κτλ. For νέος ἐστὶν ὁ μῦθος ὃς εἰσενήνεκται, i.e. οὐπώποτε ταὐτά σου ἤκουσα.
1342. τότε Hermann for τόδε. The order is, πῶς πάλαι ἔκρυπτες ἡμᾶς, τότε λαβοῦσα (αὐτήν); see v. 1307. Perhaps however the poet wrote πῶς οὖν ἔκρυπτες τόδε, λαθοῦσ' ἡμᾶς πάλαι; 'how was it that you so long escaped my notice in concealing this?'
1343. θεὸς may be a monosyllable, as Dindorf suggests; for initial anapaests should be of one word; but perhaps we should read ὁ θεὸς ἐβούλετ' ἐν δόμοις σ' ἔχειν λάτριν, or even omit the unnecessary σε.

ΠΥ. ἐνθύμιόν μοι τότε τίθησι Λοξίας
ΙΩ. τί χρῆμα δράσειν; λέγε, πέραινε σοὺς λόγους.
ΠΥ. σῶσαι τόδ' εὕρημ' ἐς τὸν ὄντα νῦν χρόνον.
ΙΩ. ἔχει δέ μοι τί κέρδος ἢ τίνα βλάβην; 1350
ΠΥ. ἐνθάδε κέκρυπται σπάργαν' οἷς ἐνῆσθα σύ.
ΙΩ. μητρὸς τάδ' ἡμῖν ἐκφέρεις ζητήματα.
ΠΥ. ἐπεί γ' ὁ δαίμων βούλεται, πάροιθε δ' οὔ.
ΙΩ. ὦ μακαρίων μοι φασμάτων ἥδ' ἡμέρα.
ΠΥ. λαβὼν νυν αὐτὰ τὴν τεκοῦσαν ἐκπόνει. 1355
πᾶσαν δ' ἐπελθὼν Ἀσιάδ' Εὐρώπης θ' ὅρους
γνώσει τάδ' αὐτός. τοῦ θεοῦ δ' ἕκατί σε
ἔθρεψά τ', ὦ παῖ, καὶ τάδ' ἀποδίδωμί σοι,
ἃ κεῖνος ἀκέλευστόν μ' ἐβουλήθη λαβεῖν
σῶσαί θ'· ὅτου δ' ἐβούλετ' οὐκ ἔχω λέγειν. 1360
ᾔδει δὲ θνητῶν οὔτις ἀνθρώπων τάδε
ἔχοντας ἡμᾶς, οὐδ' ἵν' ἦν κεκρυμμένα.

1347. ἐνθύμιον, i.e. he put it into my mind as a suggestion. Bothe cites Herod. vii. 54, εἴτε καὶ ἐνθύμιον οἱ ἐγένετο ἐμπρήσαντι τὸ ἱρόν.
1348. δράσειν. Dindorf and Elmsley adopt Musgrave's reading δρᾶσαι. Hermann, who supplies from v. 1346, ἐνθύμιόν σοι τίθησι σώζειν τάδε, supposes the future to bear this sense, 'to do what with it at some future time?' and the answer to be, 'to keep it safe till now,' so that ἐς τὸν ὄντα νῦν χρόνον contains an allusion to the then future. The aorist σῶσαι is thus correctly used, because it has reference to a former intention now realised and completed.
1351. οἷς ἐνῆσθα is Reiske's emendation for σπαργάνοισιν οἶσθα σύ. The confusion of η and οι is familiar to all who have paid attention to various readings. See on v. 253.
1352. ἐκφέρεις, you reveal, disclose, tokens which will be of avail in the search for my mother. For hitherto she had kept the matter secret, v. 1361. For this use of ἐκφέρειν, see Hippol. 649. The contents of the box are called σπάργανα generally; but it is clear from 1413 seqq. that it included such ornaments as Creusa had been able to affix to the child, with a view to its recognition if it should chance to be saved. See v. 955 seqq.

1354. μακαρίων. Hermann remarks that μακαρία would give a more usual construction; and it is very probable that such is the true reading.
1356. ἐπελθών, visiting, i.e. in the search after your mother. The allusion is to the Ionian colonies of Asia Minor. By γνώσει τάδ' αὐτὸς, which Dr. Badham is unable to explain, she means, 'you shall personally make yourself acquainted with the matter now before you,' viz. not by mere vicarious inquiry, but by going about the continent yourself, and bearing with you these credentials, you shall find out who is your mother.
1357. τοῦ θεοῦ δ' κτλ. 'As I brought you up on account of the god, (i.e. by his providential interposition in your behalf,) so now I restore to you these tokens, which he willed that I should take and keep, though he did not command me to do it.'
1360. ὅτου δ' ἄρ' οὕνεκ' is the conjecture of Mr. Shilleto on Dem. de Fals. Leg. p. 443. Aldus gives ὅτου δ' ἐβούλεθ' οὕνεκ' but the MSS. omit the last word. It is a question whether οὕνεκα or ἐβούλετο was a marginal gloss. The reading may have been ὅτου δ' ἐβούλεθ' οὕνεκ' οὐ λέγω. The objection to Mr. Shilleto's emendation is the useless ἄρα. For the genitive see Alc. 5.

ΙΩΝ.

καὶ χαῖρ'· ἴσον γάρ σ' ὡς τεκοῦσ' ἀσπάζομαι.
ἄρξαι δ' ὅθεν σὴν μητέρα ζητεῖν σε χρή·
πρῶτον μὲν εἴ τις Δελφίδων τεκοῦσά σε   1365
ἐς τούσδε ναοὺς ἐξέθηκε παρθένος,
ἔπειτα δ' εἴ τις Ἑλλάς. ἐξ ἡμῶν δ' ἔχεις
ἅπαντα Φοίβου θ', ὃς μετέσχε τῆς τύχης.

ΙΩ. φεῦ φεῦ· κατ' ὄσσων ὡς ὑγρὸν βάλλω δάκρυ,
ἐκεῖσε τὸν νοῦν δοὺς ὅθ' ἡ τεκοῦσά με   1370
κρυφαῖα νυμφευθεῖσ' ἀπημπόλα λάθρα,
καὶ μαστὸν οὐχ ὑπέσχεν· ἀλλ' ἀνώνυμος
ἐν θεοῦ μελάθροις εἶχον οἰκέτην βίον.
τὰ τοῦ θεοῦ μὲν χρηστά, τοῦ δὲ δαίμονος
βαρέα· χρόνον γὰρ ὅν μ' ἐχρῆν ἐν ἀγκάλαις   1375
μητρὸς τρυφῆσαι καί τι τερφθῆναι βίου,
ἀπεστερήθην φιλτάτης μητρὸς τροφῆς.
τλήμων δὲ χἠ τεκοῦσά μ', ὡς ταυτὸν πάθος
πέπονθε, παιδὸς ἀπολέσασα χαρμονάς.
καὶ νῦν λαβὼν τήνδ' ἀντίπηγ' οἴσω θεῷ   1380
ἀνάθημ', ἵν' εὕρω μηδὲν ὧν οὐ βούλομαι.
εἰ γάρ με δούλη τυγχάνει τεκοῦσά τις,
εὑρεῖν κάκιον μητέρ' ἢ σιγῶντ' ἐᾶν.

1364. ἄρξαι ὅθεν is an instance of attraction for ἄρξαι ἐκεῖθεν, οὗ κτλ. For the Greeks regularly say ἐκ τινὸς ἄρχεσθαι. Compare a very similar passage, Hippol. 991, πρῶτα δ' ἄρξομαι λέγειν Ὅθεν μ' ὑπῆλθες πρῶτον. The sense is, 'Begin on the spot where you ought to commence the inquiry,' viz. at Delphi itself. Hermann seems to be wrong in supposing the poet should have used ἐξευρεῖν for ζητεῖν. The sense is, ἄρξαι ζητεῖν ὅθεν (or οὗ) χρή σε ἄρχεσθαι ζητεῖν. Bothe, in making ὅθεν ask a question, forgets that this would be πόθεν. See on Hel. 461.

1367. The construction Ἑλλὰς παρθένος need not cause surprise. The word is always an adjective, though γῆ is commonly left to be supplied. The same may be said of οἰκέτης βίος, v. 1373.—μετέσχε, cf. v. 47, καὶ θεὸς Συνεργὸς ἦν τῷ παιδὶ μὴ 'κπεσεῖν δόμων.

1371. ἀπημπόλα, 'sold me away,' i. e. got rid of me, (Phoen. 1228, Iph. T. 1360,) a common metaphor, derived from dealing in the offspring of slaves, whose infants were occasionally purchased as supposititious children, Alcest. 639. Cf. Choeph. 125, πεπραμένοι γὰρ νῦν γέ πως ἀλώμεθα πρὸς τῆς τεκούσης. Ar. Thesm. 502, ἑτέραν δ' ἐγᾦδ' ἣ 'φάσκεν ὠδίνειν γυνὴ δέχ' ἡμέρας, ἕως ἐπρίατο παιδίον.—For ὑπέσχεν Dobree proposes ἐπέσχεν. The preposition ὑπὸ is used rather of putting the child to the breast, than of giving the breast to the child. Cf. Suppl. 1160, φέρ' ἀμφὶ μαστὸν ὑποβάλω σποδὸν τέκνου.

1374. The antithesis between θεὸς and δαίμων, Luck, and also the aorist τρυφῆσαι used of duration of time, are deserving of attention.

1381. ἵν' εὕρω μηδὲν, for ἵνα μὴ εὕρω τι τῶν τοιούτων ἃ οὐ βούλομαι, viz. that he may not discover that he is the son of some slave.

1383. εὑρεῖν κάκιον κτλ. A Greek way of saying, ἄμεινον σιγᾶν ἢ εὑρεῖν. Compare Phoen. 731, ἅπαν κάκιον τοῦ φυλάσσεσθαι καλῶς, 'Nothing so good as to be

ὦ Φοῖβε, ναοῖς ἀνατίθημι τήνδε σοῖς.
καίτοι τί πάσχω ; τοῦ θεοῦ προθυμίᾳ   1385
πολεμῶ, τὰ μητρὸς σύμβολ' ὃς σέσωκέ μοι.
ἀνοικτέον τάδ' ἐστὶ καὶ τολμητέον.
τὰ γὰρ πεπρωμέν' οὐδ' ὑπερβαίην ποτ' ἄν.
ὦ στέμμαθ' ἱρά, τί ποτέ μοι κεκεύθατε,
καὶ σύνδεθ', οἷσι τἄμ' ἐφρουρήθη φίλα ;   1390
ἰδοὺ περίπτυγμ' ἀντίπηγος εὐκύκλου
ὡς οὐ γεγήρακ' ἔκ τινος θεηλάτου,
εὐρώς τ' ἄπεστι πλεγμάτων· ὁ δ' ἐν μέσῳ
χρόνος πολὺς δὴ τοῖσδε θησαυρίσμασιν.
ΚΡ. τί δῆτα φάσμα τῶν ἀνελπίστων ὁρῶ ;   1395
ΙΩ. σίγα· πολεμία καὶ πάροιθεν ἦσθά μοι.
ΚΡ. οὐκ ἐν σιωπῇ τἀμά· μή με νουθέτει.
ὁρῶ γὰρ ἄγγος οὗ 'ξέθηκ' ἐγώ ποτε

well guarded.' Androm. 726, μηδενὸς βελτίονες for ἁπάντων χείρους.

1386. σέσωκε Dobree for ἔσωσε. Others read ὅς γ' after Stephens. We might also read ὡς ἔσωσε, 'the good will of the god in my behalf, (shewn by the fact) that he preserved,' &c.—ἀνοικτέον κτλ., 'I must open this casket, and make the venture,' (i. e. even though it should lead to the discovery which I dread ;) 'for what is fated I am not likely ever to escape from.' The metaphor is from a hunting net, which the animal inclosed was sometimes able to leap over, ὑπερτελέσαι. The old reading ὑπερβαίη was corrected by Barnes, but W. Dindorf believes the MSS. give ὑπερβαίην. It is best to regard οὐδέ—ποτε as separated by *tmesis*.

1390. σύνδετα, the tie or fastening of the chest.—τἀμὰ φίλα, the clothes, ornaments, playthings &c., dear to him in infancy. For στέμματα see v. 1338. The box or casket was enwrapped in some outer envelope, on opening which he exclaims ἰδοὺ κτλ.

1396. This verse was first given to Ion instead of the chorus by Heath. The common reading is undoubtedly corrupt, σιγᾶν σὺ πολλὰ καὶ πάροιθεν οἶσθά μοι. Bothe, who retains the person of the chorus, interprets it *multa tu et antea tacere scisti*, which he calls "perspicua et apta Chori personae sententia." Both Hermann and L. Dindorf read σίγα for σιγᾶν, but this scarcely satisfies the sense, especially as the σὺ is redundant where no emphasis is conveyed. That the verse belongs to Ion is clear from the reply of Creusa, that she will not be silenced. Besides, the chorus takes no part whatever through the whole of this scene. Hermann thinks the latter part of the verse genuine, and explains πολλὰ οἶσθα of Creusa's crafty attempt to defend her murderous intent, v. 1287 seqq. This explanation however fails to remove the main difficulty, the present οἶσθα with the adverb of past time, πάροιθεν. We have indeed in Bacch. 2, Διόνυσος ὃν τίκτει ποθ' ἡ Κάδμου κόρη, where the *praesens historicum* is rather harsh with the specific adjunct ποτέ. W. Dindorf proposes to read σίγα σύ· πολλὰ καὶ πάροιθ' ᾔδησθά μοι, and accepts Hermann's somewhat forced interpretation. Dr. Badham acquiesces in σίγα σύ, but can make nothing of the rest. The present editor has ventured to restore

σίγα· πολεμία καὶ πάροιθεν ἦσθά μοι.

When πολεμία had been corrupted to πολλά, (by the loss of the middle syllable, as remarked on v. 189,) the offending σὺ was added as a metrical makeshift. For the change of ᾔσθα into οἶσθα see v. 1351. It is true that ἐχθρὰ is a more correct word than πολεμία for Creusa's hostile attempt on his life ; still the latter may

ΙΩΝ. 95

σέ γ' ὦ τέκνον μοι βρέφος ἔτ' ὄντα νήπιον
[Κέκροπος ἐς ἄντρα καὶ Μακρὰς πετρηρεφεῖς].   1400
λείψω δὲ βωμὸν τόνδε, κεἰ θανεῖν με χρή.

ΙΩ. λάζυσθε τήνδε· θεομανὴς γὰρ ἥλατο
βωμοῦ λιποῦσα ξόανα· δεῦτε δ' ὠλένας.

ΚΡ. σφάζοντες οὐ λήγοιτ' ἄν· ὡς ἀνθέξομαι
καὶ τῆσδε καὶ σοῦ τῶν τ' ἔσω κεκρυμμένων.   1405

ΙΩ. τάδ' οὐχὶ δεινά; ῥυσιάζομαι λόγῳ.

ΚΡ. οὐκ, ἀλλὰ σοῖς φίλοισιν εὑρίσκει φίλος.

ΙΩ. ἐγὼ φίλος σός; κᾆτά μ' ἔκτεινες λάθρα;

ΚΡ. παῖς γ', εἰ τόδ' ἐστὶ τοῖς τεκοῦσι φίλτατον.

ΙΩ. παῦσαι πλέκουσα· λήψομαί σ' ἐγὼ καλῶς.   1410

ΚΡ. ἐς τοῦθ' ἱκοίμην, τοῦδε τοξεύω, τέκνον.

ΙΩ. κενὸν τόδ' ἄγγος, ἢ στέγει πλήρωμά τι;

ΚΡ. σά γ' ἐνδύθ', οἷσί σ' ἐξέθηκ' ἐγώ ποτε.

---

have been used by a kind of *catachresis.* Cf. v. 1291. El. 833. *inf.* 1553, οὐ γὰρ πολεμίαν με φεύγετε. Hec. 741, δούλην πολεμίαν θ' ἡγούμενος.

1399. σέ γ' ὦ τέκνον. She addresses Ion, whom she now first knows to be her son, and identical with the infant whom she supposed that she had lost.—οὗ, 'where,' i. e. in which. So Lenting and Dobree for οὐξέθηκ'.

1400. Κέκροπος ἄντρα. This can only mean the cave of Aglauros, daughter of Cecrops; see on v. 492. The two grottos were quite distinct, the *Paneum* being some sixty yards to the west of the former. How to reconcile this with v. 17, where Creusa is said to have exposed the infant in the same cave where she was seduced by the god, and with v. 938, where that cave is distinctly specified as the *Paneum,* is by no means clear. Probably this is a spurious verse. It is quite unnecessary to the context.

1404. οὐ λήγοιτ' ἄν, 'you need not cease killing me,' i. e. go on to kill me if you will: οὐκ ἂν φθάνοιτε σφάζοντες. Virtually, οὐ λήγοιτ' ἄν is equivalent to μὴ λήγετε. Hermann, and Dindorf after Boissonade, read οὖν for οὐ, 'then you shall end the matter by killing me.' But the old reading is apparently right, for the following words show that she dares them to violate those pledges which her excited feelings cause her to regard as not less sacred than the altar itself.

1405. τῶν τ' ἔσω Tyrwhitt for τῶν τε σῶν, which Hermann does not successfully defend, "si sic loqueretur, arcam potissimum videretur in mente habere. At filius est, quo invento gaudet." — καὶ τῆσδε, scil. ἀντίπηγος.

1406. ῥυσιάζομαι, I am being dragged off on a mere pretext. See on v. 523. *Ficta vindicatione corripior,* Hermann. —εὑρίσκειν is a word used in contrast with βίᾳ ἄγειν, the τὸ δικαίως with the τὸ ἀδίκως. So Aesch. Suppl. 895, τἀπολωλόθ' εὑρίσκων ἐγὼ—ἄγοιμ' ἄν, εἴ τις τάσδε μὴ 'ξαιρήσεται.

1410. σ' for δ' Tyrwhitt. Ion still thinks the whole affair is a plot (λόγῳ, 1406,) and bids her to cease her pretended claims, for he shall convict her effectually of falsehood and fraud, by questioning her about the contents of the box. She, pretending not to understand his meaning, replies, 'That is the very point I am aiming at,' viz. τὸ ληφθῆναι ὑπὸ σοῦ, the being taken and accepted by you as your true mother. In the other sense, there is a metaphor from the wrestling school, where καλῶς λαβέσθαι meant to get a good grasp of the antagonist. The verse has been wrongly explained to mean, that Creusa is anxious to get possession of the chest and its contents.—For the genitive after τοξεύειν see Bacch. 1099. Soph. Aj. 154, μεγάλων ψυχῶν ἱείς.

ΙΩ. καὶ τοὔνομ' αὐτῶν ἐξερεῖς, πρὶν εἰσιδεῖν ;
ΚΡ. κἂν μὴ φράσω γε, κατθανεῖν ὑφίσταμαι.   1415
ΙΩ. λέγ'. ὡς ἔχει τι δεινὸν ἤ γε τόλμα σου.
ΚΡ. σκέψασθ' ὃ παῖς ποτ' οὖσ' ὕφασμ' ὕφην' ἐγώ.
ΙΩ. ποῖόν τι ; πολλὰ παρθένων ὑφάσματα.
ΚΡ. οὐ τέλεον, οἷον δ' ἐκδίδαγμα κερκίδος.
ΙΩ. μορφὴν ἔχον τίν' ; ὡς με μὴ ταύτῃ λάβῃς.   1420
ΚΡ. Γοργὼ μὲν ἐν μέσοισιν ἠτρίοις πέπλων.
ΙΩ. ὦ Ζεῦ, τίς ἡμᾶς ἐκκυνηγετεῖ πότμος ;
ΚΡ. κεκρασπέδωται δ' ὄφεσιν αἰγίδος τρόπον.
ΙΩ. ἰδού.
τόδ' ἔσθ' ὕφασμα· θέσφαθ' ὡς εὑρίσκομεν.
ΚΡ. ὦ χρόνιον ἱστὸν παρθενευμάτων ἐμῶν.   1425
ΙΩ. ἔστιν τι πρὸς τῷδ', ἢ μόνῳ τῷδ' εὐτυχεῖς ;
ΚΡ. †δράκοντες ἀρχαῖόν τι παγχρύσῳ γένυι.

1416. ἤ γε τόλμα σου Herm. for ἡ τόλμα γέ σου. L. Dindorf and Dr. Badham read ἤδε τόλμα σου, W. Dindorf ἡ τόλμῃ γέ σου, quoting Phrynichus in Bekk. Anecd. i. p. 66, τόλμῃ καὶ τόλμα, πρύμνῃ καὶ πρύμνα, to which might be added, δίψῃ καὶ δίψα (Aesch. Cho. 743). The γε however, in which Dr. Badham can see no force, has no merely imaginary emphasis. Ion is astonished and perplexed by the unexpected assertion, that she is willing to be slain if she is mistaken in the contents of the box, which he is still holding out of her reach. He relents a little at this, and replies, 'speak then, for certainly there is something serious in so bold a challenge as that.'
1417. σκέψασθε, 'look for,' as if she had added, εἰ ἐνταῦθα ἔνεστι &c.
1419. οὐ τέλεον κτλ., 'Not finished, but such as one might call a first lesson at weaving.'—οἷον, scil. ἂν εἴη. Dindorf proposes οἷον, 'only,' but this is hardly a tragic word. She describes much such a piece of work as children now call "a sampler" (exemplar).
1420. λάβῃς. See v. 1410. 'That you may not catch me in this' means, 'that you may not deceive me by a successful guess,' i. e. where a guess might easily be made.
1421. ἠτρίοις Musgrave for ἠτρίων. Properly, ἤτριον is the warp in a web of cloth; whence it seems to have meant any fine texture not densely interlaced with the woof. Photius, ἤτριον, ἔνδυμα ὑμενῶδες. Theocr. xviii. 33, οὔτ' ἐνὶ δαιδαλέῳ πυκινώτερον ἄτριον ἱστῷ Κερκίδι συμπλέξασα μακρῶν ἔταμ' ἐκ κελεόντων.
1423. αἰγίδος. See v. 990 seqq.
1424. The stop formerly placed after θέσφαθ', was transposed by Hermann, who explains, "nam invenimus significata ab oraculo," i. e. we are beginning to discover the meaning of Apollo's oracle, which told me I was the son of Xuthus, but did not mention my mother. It is better to acquiesce in this, than with Dindorf and others to read δεσμά θ', after Musgrave, who quotes from Hesychius σπάργανα· δεσμά. (So also Photius explains σπαργανώματα by δεσμοί.) But Hermann truly observes that ὡς εὑρίσκομεν is a frigid addition in this case. We should rather have looked for ὡς ἔλεξας.
1425. The old reading, ὦ χρόνιον ἱστῶν παρθένευμα τῶν ἐμῶν was corrected by Dr. Badham, except that he gives ὦ χρόνιος ἱστός. The accusative, while it is much nearer to the MSS., is equally good, though more common as a Latin usage.
1426. εὐτυχεῖς; are you lucky in your guess? Pierson's εὐστοχεῖς is but another word for expressing exactly the same thing. Cf. ἐπεικάσας τύχω Choeph. 12.
1427. δράκοντε μαρμαίροντε, Porson's emendation for δράκοντες ἀρχαῖόν τι, is far from being certain. It is rejected by

ΙΩ. δώρημ' Ἀθάνας, ἢ τέκν' ἐντρέφειν λέγει;
ΚΡ. Ἐριχθονίου γε τοῦ πάλαι μιμήματα.
ΙΩ. τί δρᾶν, τί χρῆσθαι, φράζε μοι, χρυσώματι. 1430
ΚΡ. δέραια παιδὶ νεογόνῳ φέρειν, τέκνον.
ΙΩ. ἔνεισιν οἵδε· τὸ δὲ τρίτον ποθῶ μαθεῖν.
ΚΡ. στέφανον ἐλαίας ἀμφέθηκά σοι τότε,
ἣν πρῶτ' Ἀθάνα σκόπελον εἰσηνέγκατο·
ὃς, εἴπερ ἔστιν, οὔποτ' ἐκλείπει χλόην, 1435
θάλλει δ' ἐλαίας ἐξ ἀκηράτου γεγώς.
ΙΩ. ὦ φιλτάτη μοι μῆτερ, ἄσμενός σ' ἰδὼν
πρὸς ἀσμένας πέπτωκα σὰς παρηίδας.
ΚΡ. ὦ τέκνον, ὦ φῶς μητρὶ κρεῖσσον ἡλίου,

Hermann, who gives δράκοντες, ἀρχαῖόν τι, πάγχρυσοι γένυν, after Toup. This however is hardly satisfactory. Dr. Badham's correction σαρκάζοντε is ingenious, but fails to carry conviction with it. The word itself is by no means tragic; it is used in Ar. Pac. 482, of the grimaces of the half-starved Megarians, γλισχρότατα σαρκάζοντες ὥσπερ κυνίδια. Photius, σαρκάζων, μετὰ πικρίας καὶ θυμοῦ γελῶν. The appropriateness of such a word in this place may well be questioned. On the other hand, ἀρχαῖόν τι is certainly very proper in itself, were the construction a natural one. Possibly we should read ἀρχαῖόν τι πάγχρυσον γάνος. So Aeschylus uses ἀρχαῖον γάνος of bright armour, Agam. 562.

1428. The old reading, ἢ τέκν' ἐντρέφειν λέγει, has been retained by Hermann. Aldus has ἢ κτλ. The sense is, 'do you mean a gift of Athena's, who enjoined (Athenian) children to be reared with these ornaments upon them?' And her answer is, 'Yes, in imitation of what she did to Erichthonius of old.' In saying this, Ion has regard to the narrative of Creusa in v. 269 seqq. One might suggest, with some probability, ἢν—λόγος for λέγει. Dobree's reading is approved by Dr. Badham, ἢ τέκν' ἐντρέφειν; λέγε. Whatever may be the true reading, it is evident that the poet dwells particularly on the fact, because it pleased the vanity of the Athenians.

1430. χρυσώματι Hermann, χρυσώμασι L. Dindorf, for χρυσώμια. This is another proof that this part of the play had been very carelessly or very illegibly written in the archetypus MS.

1433. ἐλαίας. Hence, as it would seem, and not, (as Wordsworth thinks, *Athens and Attica*, p. 138,) from its general propagation, the olive is called παιδοτρόφος in Oed. Col. 701. It was probably a custom of the Athenians to place an olive wreath on the head of newly-born children, because this would supply a motive to the poet for attributing it to their remote ancestor Ion.

1434. Ἀθάνα for ·as is Matthiae's correction, approved by Hermann. Dr. Badham prefers the reading of Stephens and Scaliger, Ἀθάνας σκόπελος ἐξηνέγκατο, because Pallas did not, according to one legend, bring or introduce it from without to her acropolis, but made it grow spontaneously therefrom. Euripides however is fond of varying the ancient accounts both of persons and events. The acropolis is called ἐλαιοφόρος ὄχθος in Herc. F. 1178. *Inf.* 1480, τὸν ἐλαιοφυῆ πάγον.

1436. ἀκηράτου, the pure and original tree, not from a stock subsequently reared. Dr. Badham gives ἀγηράτου, which is, (as he says,) obvious as a conjecture; but it is not so obviously an improvement on the old reading. For the unfading quality of the leaves is here supposed to be a miraculous proof of its having been taken from the very tree which Pallas planted; or rather, perhaps, it is called ἀκήρατος because, like all the Morian olives, it was sacred, and not touched with the knife. So a sacred meadow is ἀκήρατος λειμών in Hipp. 73, where neither flocks had been fed nor the scythe had been used.

98 ΕΥΡΙΠΙΔΟΥ

συγγνώσεται γὰρ ὁ θεὸς, ἐν χεροῖν σ' ἔχω,　　1440
ἄελπτον εὕρημ', ὃν κατὰ γᾶς ἐνέρων
χθόνιον μετὰ Περσεφόνας τ' ἐδόκουν ναίειν.

ΙΩ. ἀλλ', ὦ φίλη μοι μῆτερ, ἐν χεροῖν σέθεν
ὁ κατθανών τε κοὐ θανὼν φαντάζομαι.

ΚΡ. ἰὼ ἰὼ λαμπρᾶς αἰθέρος ἀμπτυχαὶ,　　1445
τίν' αὐδὰν ἀΰσω, βοάσω; πόθεν μοι
συνέκυρσ' ἀδόκητος ἀδονά; πόθεν
ἐλάβομεν χαράν;

ΙΩ. ἐμοὶ γενέσθαι πάντα μᾶλλον ἄν ποτε,
μῆτερ, παρέστη τῶνδ' ὅπως σός εἰμ' ἐγώ.　　1450

ΚΡ. ἔτι φόβῳ τρέμω.

1440. ὁ θεός, the sun will pardon the presumptuous comparison. Dr. Badham and Bothe explain ὁ θεὸς of Apollo. The identity of these two divinities is not very clearly to be made out, though to a certain extent it without doubt existed, in the earlier ages of the Attic religion.

1441. ἐνέρων. This depends on the μετὰ following. Perhaps ὃν—ναίειν should be scanned as a single dactylic verse terminated by a dochmius. The dialogue of two actors, one or both of whom use the choric metres, (technically called τὰ ἀπὸ σκηνῆς,) is usually indicative of feelings too excited for expression by the staid and deliberate tragic senarius. Hermann's note here is so good, that a translation of it is given at length:—" This lyric passage is composed with singular art, and is excellently adapted to express the varied emotions of Creusa's mind. She had come to Delphi for the purpose of seeking the son whom she supposed to be lost. She had imagined that her hopes had been frustrated by a wicked design. She had been in danger of her life in consequence of the plot she had engaged in against Ion; and now, finding that no other than the very person she had attempted to destroy is her long-lost son, she is suddenly raised to the highest pitch of delight; but this emotion is as suddenly checked by the sense of shame at being forced to confess the frailty of her early life, and by grief at the illegitimate birth of her son. Taking however consolation from the reflexion that a god is his father, she next turns her thoughts to the fate of her child, formerly exposed by her to perish, and now again all but slain by a wicked design upon his life. She thinks of these strange vicissitudes, and perceives a glimmering of hope that henceforth all will be well. The mind of Ion is very differently affected. So contented had he been with his lot, that he did not care to change it, even when he might have done so, for a better. He is of course rejoiced to find that she whom he had wished to put to death is his own mother; yet, since one who had never known a mother could not regret the loss of one, he is much less moved than Creusa, besides that the mind of a man has more firmness and self-control than that of a woman. Hence it is that the poet has so arranged the dialogue, that Ion always uses the staid iambic verse, while Creusa gives vent to her feelings principally in the dochmiac measure, with other energetic metres occasionally interposed." Hermann should have compared the precisely similar composition of a passage in the *Helena*, v. 646 seqq., and also in Andom. 825 seqq.

1446. βοάσω. Not the future, which is βοήσομαι, but the deliberative conjunctive, as in Pers. 640 (according to the reading of the old copies). This verse is bacchiac. The intransitive use of συνέκυρσε for συνέβη in the next is deserving of notice. So Sophocles uses κύρω for κυρῶ in Oed. Col. 1159, and Homer ἐπικύρσας for ἐντυχών. The metre of this verse, which can only be called asynartete, may be compared with v. 1466.

1449. ἐμοὶ κτλ. 'To me indeed anything in the world would have occurred rather than this, that I am your son, my mother.'

ΙΩΝ.

ΙΩ. μῶν οὐκ ἔχειν μ' ἔχουσα;
ΚΡ. τὰς γὰρ ἐλπίδας
ἀπέβαλον πρόσω.
ἰὼ γύναι, πόθεν πόθεν ἔλαβες ἐμὸν
βρέφος ἐς ἀγκάλας;
τίν' ἀνὰ χέρα δόμους ἔβα Λοξίου; 1455
ΙΩ. θεῖον τόδ'· ἀλλὰ τἀπίλοιπα τῆς τύχης
εὐδαιμονοῖμεν, ὡς τὰ πρόσθε δυστυχῆ.
ΚΡ. οὐκ ἀδάκρυτος ἐκλοχεύει, τέκνον,
γόοις δὲ ματρὸς ἐκ χερῶν ὁρίζει·
νῦν δὲ γενειάσιν παρὰ σέθεν πνέω, 1460
μακαριωτάτας τυχοῦσ' ἁδονᾶς.
ΙΩ. τοὐμὸν λέγουσα καὶ τὸ σὸν κοινῶς λέγεις.
ΚΡ. ἄπαιδες οὐκέτ' ἐσμὲν οὐδ' ἄτεκνοι·
δῶμ' ἑστιοῦται, γᾶ δ' ἔχει τυράννους·
ἀνηβᾷ δ' Ἐρεχθεύς, 1465
ὅ τε γηγενέτας δόμος οὐκέτι νύκτα δέρκεται,
ἀελίου δ' ἀναβλέπει λαμπάσιν.
ΙΩ. μῆτερ, παρών μοι καὶ πατὴρ μετασχέτω
τῆς ἡδονῆς τῆσδ' ἧς ἔδωχ' ὑμῖν ἐγώ. 1469
ΚΡ. ὦ τέκνον, *τέκνον, τί φής; οἷον οἷον ἀνελέγχομαι.

1453. ἀπέβαλον, ' I had cast away my hopes far from me;' *omnem spem abjeceram*. It was ἀδόκητος ἡδονή, v. 1447, for she had despaired of her own life, and therefore, of ever seeing her son.—γύναι, κτλ. she appeals to the priestess (who however is not present on the stage) to know from whom she had received the infant, thus strangely transported from Athens to Delphi (v. 31—3).
1457. δυστυχῆ. Bothe reads ἐδυστύχει.
1458. By transposing τέκνον from the beginning to the end of this line, a dochmiac is given for a wholly unmetrical verse, the second a of ἀδάκρυτος being short.
1462. τοὐμὸν κτλ. In describing my case, sorrow at first and then happiness, you describe your own;—what is true of one is true of the other.
1464. γᾶ δ' Reiske for τάδε δ'. When γᾶ δὲ was written (as was sometimes done) without the elision, the next transcriber mistook Γ for Τ, and added δ' on account of the hiatus.—ἑστιοῦται, ἑστίαν ἔχει, for a house without an heir is regarded as a deserted mansion. Similarly a person is said δωματοῦσθαι, to be housed, or to have a house built for him, in Aesch. Suppl. 935.
1466. γηγενέτας. See v. 269.—ἀναβλέπει, 'looks *up* with (or *to*) the light of the sun.' An exactly parallel simile occurs in Aesch. Cho. 794, εὖ δὸς ἀνιδεῖν δόμον ἀνδρὸς | φιλίοις ὄμμασι λαμπρῶς | ἐκ δνοφερᾶς καλύπτρας. This latter verse is a good dochmiac: the preceding should probably be read thus: ὁ δέ γε γηγενέτας οὐκέτι νῦν δόμος νύχια δέρκεται. As it stands, it is anapaestic + iamb. dipodia, as v. 1482 &c., or they may be regarded as a form of hypercatalectic glyconean. See on v. 1496.
1470. τέκνον was doubled by Hermann, by which a trimeter dochmiac is made up.

ΕΥΡΙΠΙΔΟΥ

ΙΩ. πῶς εἶπας;
ΚΡ.   ἄλλοθεν σὺ γέγονας, ἄλλοθεν.
ΙΩ. ὤμοι· νόθον με παρθένευμ' ἔτικτε σόν;
ΚΡ. οὐχ ὑπὸ λαμπάδων οὐδὲ χορευμάτων
     ὑμέναιος ἐμὸς,   1475
     τέκνον, ἔτικτε σὸν κάρα.
ΙΩ. αἰαῖ· πέφυκα δυσγενής, μῆτερ, ποθέν;
ΚΡ. ἴστω Γοργοφόνα,
ΙΩ. τί τοῦτ' ἔλεξας;
ΚΡ. ἃ σκοπέλοις ἐπ' ἐμοῖς
     τὸν ἐλαιοφυῆ πάγον θάσσει.   1480
ΙΩ. λέγεις *λέγεις μοι δόλια κοὐ σαφῆ τάδε.
ΚΡ. παρ' ἀηδόνιον πέτραν Φοίβῳ
ΙΩ. τί Φοῖβον αὐδᾷς;
ΚΡ. κρυπτόμενον λέχος ηὐνάσθην.
ΙΩ. λέγ'· ὡς ἐρεῖς τι κεδνὸν εὐτυχές τέ μοι.   1485
ΚΡ. δεκάτῳ δέ σε μηνὸς ἐν κύκλῳ
     κρύφιον ὠδῖν' ἔτεκον Φοίβῳ.
ΙΩ. ὦ φίλτατ' εἰποῦσ', εἰ λέγεις ἐτήτυμα.
ΚΡ. παρθένια δὲ σᾶς ματέρος

1477. ποθέν; Commonly, πόθεν; But the sense seems to be, 'Am I the son of some slave?'
1478. Γοργοφόνα. 'I call to witness Pallas, the slayer of the Gorgon, who has her seat on the olive-bearing hill, the acropolis of my city.' See v. 1436.
1481. λέγεις was doubled by Bothe. This is better than Hermann's arrangement, of making θάσσει from the preceding verse commence the senarius.—δόλια κοὐ σαφῆ, this, which you say, is some trick, and not sure, not certainly to be relied on.
1482. ἀηδόνιον, frequented by nightingales. Whether this peculiarity of the northern side of the acropolis (v. 937) is elsewhere mentioned, the commentators say not.
1489. The common reading is δ' ἐμᾶς, which should apparently be altered either to δ' ἐμοῦ or to δὲ σᾶς. The former was suggested by Barnes. Hermann explains, *virgineum velamen a matre mea*, viz. which Creusa, when a girl, had received from her mother for the purpose of embroidering it. But, comparing v. 1425, ᾧ χρόνιον ἱστὸν παρθενευμάτων ἐμῶν, we may be sure the sense intended was no other than this, 'You had for your swathing bands the handywork of your mother, made when she was a virgin.' Hence παρθένια ματέρος σπάργανα must stand for σπάργανα, παρθένου ἔργα, ἢ μήτηρ σου ἐγένετο. Hermann omits σπάργανα as a gloss, and to complete the dochmiac gives ἀπ' ἐμᾶς κτλ. Perhaps the true reading is παρθενίου δὲ σᾶς ματέρος ἀμφίβολα | σοὶ τάδ' ἀνῆψα, κερκίδος ἐμᾶς πλάνους. That something is wrong is clear from the faulty metre of the vulgate. W. Dindorf, with very bad judgment, reads ἀνῆψα, i. e. ἃ ἐνῆψα, the MSS., with one exception, having ἐνῆψα. The usual verb however is ἀνάπτειν.—πλάνους, the *blunders* of my shuttle; for it was only ἐκδίδαγμα κερκίδος, v. 1419. So Musgrave understands it; but Hermann may be right in taking it simply for πόνους.

ΙΩΝ. 101

†σπάργαν' ἀμφίβολά σοι τάδ' ἀν- 1490
ῆψα, κερκίδος ἐμᾶς πλάνους.
γάλακτι δ' οὐκ ἐπέσχον, οὐδὲ μαστῷ
τροφεῖα ματρὸς, οὐδὲ λουτρὰ χειροῖν,
ἀνὰ δ' ἄντρον ἔρημον οἰωνῶν
γαμφηλαῖς φόνευμα θοίναμά τ' εἰς 1495
Ἅιδαν ἐκβάλλει.
ΙΩ. ὦ δεινὰ τλᾶσα μῆτερ.
ΚΡ. φόβῳ καταδεθεῖσα *τὰν σὰν ψυχὰν
ἀπέβαλον, τέκνον·
ἔκτεινά σ' ἄκουσ'. 1500
ΙΩ. ἐξ ἐμοῦ τ' οὐχ ὅσι' ἔθνησκες.
ΚΡ. ἰὼ ἰὼ δειναὶ μὲν αἱ τότε τύχαι,
δεινὰ δὲ καὶ τάδ'· ἑλισσόμεσθ' ἐκεῖθεν
ἐνθάδε δυστυχίαισιν 1505
εὐτυχίαις τε πάλιν,
μεθίσταται δὲ πνεύματα.
μενέτω· τὰ πάροιθεν ἅλις κακά· νῦν δ'

1493. τροφεῖα, here for τροφήν. 'Neither with milk nor at the breast did I offer a mother's nurture.' Cf. Oed. Col. 341, τἄξω βίου τροφεῖα πορσύνουσ' ἀεί.
1496. ἐκβάλλει for ἐξεβάλλου, you were exposed, cast out, in a desert cave, a prey to the talons of birds. This verse may be scanned like 1466, 1480—2, 1486.
1498. The old reading again was wholly unmetrical, ἐν φόβῳ καταδεθεῖσα σὰν | ψυχὰν ἀπέβαλον, τέκνον. The double dochmiac is easily restored by omitting the worse than superfluous ἐν, and adding τὰν before σάν. An equally satisfactory result is obtained in v. 1503 by repeating ἰώ. ''Twas under the influence of fear (i. e. the obligation of it, cf. v. 898,) that I cast away thy life, my child; 'twas against my better feelings that I slew thee.' The confession is followed by a similar one on the part of Ion, that the attempt to kill her was an unholy one. The student should here observe, that even an *attempt* is sometimes expressed by an aorist, instead of an imperfect, where that attempt in itself constitutes an act which was complete, (for even one that has failed of its end may be complete in so far as it was carried into effect,) and not extending in point of time beyond the moment of its execution. Thus Soph. Aj. 1126, δίκαια γὰρ τόνδ' εὐτυχεῖν, κτείναντά με;
1504. δεινὰ Barnes for δειλία. Scaliger proposed δείλαια, but Barnes rightly remarks that the preceding δειναὶ μὲν clearly requires δεινὰ δὲ here. The metre now passes from dochmiac to dactylic. Probably this verse should be read thus: δεινὰ δὲ καὶ τάδ'· ἑλισσόμεθ' αὖθις ἐκεῖθεν. The sense is, 'We are tossed to and fro, hither and thither, by a succession of events, first unhappy, then fortunate.'— πνεύματα, the gales of Fortune,—a common metaphor.
1508. μενέτω, 'let them now remain constant; the past evils have been enough; but now a breeze has sprung up to waft us out of our troubles, my son.' A similar passage is Aesch. Theb. 703, as emended by Prof. Conington; δαίμων | λήματος αὖ τροπαίᾳ χρονίᾳ μετάλ|λακτὸς ἴσως ἂν ἔλθοι θελεμωτέρῳ | πνεύματι· νῦν δ' ἔτι ζεῖ. The metre of the last verse is defective. Perhaps, ἐγένετ' οὖρος ἐκ κακῶν τις, τέκνον.

102   ΕΥΡΙΠΙΔΟΥ

   ἐγένετό τις οὖρος ἐκ κακῶν, ὦ παῖ.
XO. μηδεὶς δοκείτω μηδὲν ἀνθρώπων ποτὲ   1510
   ἄελπτον εἶναι πρὸς τὰ τυγχάνοντα νῦν.
ΙΩ. ὦ μεταβαλοῦσα μυρίους ἤδη βροτῶν
   καὶ δυστυχῆσαι καὖθις αὖ πρᾶξαι καλῶς,
   Τύχη, παρ' οἴαν ἤλθομεν στάθμην βίου,
   μητέρα φονεῦσαι καὶ παθεῖν ἀνάξια.   1515
   φεῦ·
   ἆρ' ἐν φαενναῖς ἡλίου περιπτυχαῖς
   ἔνεστι πάντα τάδε καθ' ἡμέραν μαθεῖν;
   φίλον μὲν οὖν σ' εὕρημα, μῆτερ, ηὕρομεν,
   καὶ τὸ γένος οὐδὲν μεμπτὸν ὡς ἡμῖν τόδε·
   τὰ δ' ἄλλα πρὸς σὲ βούλομαι μόνην φράσαι. 1520
   δεῦρ' ἔλθ'· ἐς οὓς γὰρ τοὺς λόγους εἰπεῖν θέλω,
   καὶ περικαλύψαι τοῖσι πράγμασι σκότον.
   ὅρα σὺ, μῆτερ, μὴ σφαλεῖσ' ἃ παρθένοις

1510. ἀνθρώπων. W. Dindorf admits the unnecessary alteration of Dobree, ἀνθρώποις.—πρὸς κτλ., scil. βλέπων.

1513. αὖ for εὖ Pierson. Hermann however retains the old reading.

1514. There are two senses of the phrase παρὰ στάθμην, 'beside (deviating from) the plumb-line,' and 'by (or true to) it.' In the former we have Agam. 1012, where upstart masters are called ᾡμοί τε δούλοις πάντα καὶ παρὰ στάθμην. In the latter, Soph. frag. 421, ὥστε τέκτονος | παρὰ στάθμην ἰόντος ὀρθοῦται κανών. Photius, στάθμη· τὸ σπαρτίον (the plumb-line). In the present passage a third sense is perceptible, derived either from the phrase παρ' ὀλίγον ἀποφυγεῖν &c., 'to have a narrow escape,' or from the γραμμή in a stadium, 'to what a stage in life's career have we arrived in so nearly having killed a mother.'

1516. ἆρα κτλ. 'Is it not in the power of the sun's bright rays (or course) to become acquainted with all these freaks of fortune day by day?' i.e. do not such things commonly occur? By περιπτυχαὶ (Phoen. 1357) he seems to mean the circular orb; cf. v. 1445, αἰθέρος ἀμπτυχαί. Bothe, after Matthiae, explains, 'Nonne hoc videre licet quotidie?' And περιπτυχαῖς is taken by Barnes and Musgrave for 'revolutions,' περιειλιγμοῖς. (See however the Preface to Vol. i. p. xxix.) True it is, we should have expected ἔξεστι rather than ἔνεστι, and something like τὰ τοιαῦτα, if the mere caprices of Fortune had been meant.

1519. ὡς ἡμῖν, 'in our judgment.' Soph. Antig. 1161, Κρέων γὰρ ἦν ζηλωτὸς, ὡς ἐμοὶ, ποτέ.

1523—5. μὴ—προστίθης. 'Consider whether you are not laying the blame on the god.' Vereor ne Phoebum culpes. This use of μὴ with an indicative, past or present, is not very uncommon. Hel. 119, σκοπεῖτε μὴ δόκησιν εἴχετ' ἐκ θεοῦ. Orest. 208, ὅρα—μὴ κατθανών σε σύγγονος λέληθ' ὅδε. Troad. 179. Theocr. 12, 36, χρυσὸν ὁποίη πεύθονται, μὴ φαῦλος, ἐτήτυμον ἀργυραμοιβοί, i.e. μὴ φαῦλος ἐστί. Phoen. 92. Heracl. 482, &c. —σφαλεῖσ' ἃ παρθένοις is Musgrave's correction for σφαλεῖσα παρθένος. For this peculiar sense of σφαλῆναι, a sort of euphemism for yielding to the passion of love, see Hippol. 6. Frag. 508,

ἄλγιστον ἐστι θῆλυ μισηθὲν γένος·
αἱ γὰρ σφαλεῖσαι ταῖσιν οὐκ ἐσφαλμέναις
αἴσχος γυναιξὶ, καὶ κεκοίνωνται ψόγον.

On the same principle νόσος is often used as a synonym of ἔρως. 'Perhaps,' Ion suggests to his mother, 'you yielded to those feelings which are natural to girls

ΙΩΝ.

ἐγγίγνεται νοσήματ' ἐς κρυπτοὺς γάμους,
ἔπειτα τῷ θεῷ προστίθης τὴν αἰτίαν, 1525
καὶ τοὐμὸν αἰσχρὸν ἀποφυγεῖν πειρωμένη
Φοίβῳ τεκεῖν με φῇς, τεκοῦσ' οὐκ ἐκ θεοῦ.
ΚΡ. μὰ τὴν παρασπίζουσαν ἅρμασίν ποτε
Νίκην Ἀθάναν Ζηνὶ γηγενεῖς ἔπι,
οὐκ ἔστιν ὅστις σοι πατὴρ θνητῶν, τέκνον, 1530
ἀλλ' ὅσπερ ἐξέθρεψε Λοξίας ἄναξ.
ΙΩ. πῶς οὖν τὸν αὑτοῦ παῖδ' ἔδωκ' ἄλλῳ πατρὶ,
Ξούθου τέ φησι παῖδά μ' ἐκπεφυκέναι;
ΚΡ. πεφυκέναι μὲν οὐχὶ, δωρεῖται δέ σε
αὑτοῦ γεγῶτα· καὶ γὰρ ἂν φίλος φίλῳ 1535
δοίη τὸν αὑτοῦ παῖδα δεσπότην δόμων.
ΙΩ. ὁ θεὸς ἀληθὴς, ἢ μάτην μαντεύεται,
ἐμοῦ ταράσσει, μῆτερ, εἰκότως φρένα.
ΚΡ. ἄκουε δή νυν ἅμ' ἐσῆλθεν, ὦ τέκνον·
εὐεργετῶν σε Λοξίας εἰς εὐγενῆ 1540
δόμον καθίζει· τοῦ θεοῦ δὲ λεγόμενος
οὐκ ἔσχες ἄν ποτ' οὔτε παγκλήρους δόμους
οὔτ' ὄνομα πατρός. πῶς γὰρ, οὗ γ' ἐγὼ γάμους

in their secret attachments, and then wish to lay the blame of it on Apollo,' as your seducer. Cf. Bacch. 28.

1526. τοὐμὸν αἰσχρὸν, the discredit that would attach to me. Ion thinks she has invented a story which would save him from the reputation of being νόθος or δυσγενὴς,—her motives not being selfish, but arising from affection to her son. In fact, her own case is considered in vv. 1523—5, her son's in 1526—7.

1529. Νίκην Ἀθάναν. See *sup.* 457. Heracl. 352. Herc. F. 1002. Wordsworth, *Athens and Attica*, chap. xvi. The derivation of Νίκη here given, from the assistance rendered to Zeus in the Gigantomachia, is perhaps an invention of the poet's. In allusion to that event Aeschylus (Eum. 285) makes Orestes summon her from the Phlegraean plains, the scene of the conflict.

1531. ὅσπερ ἐξ., the very same god who brought you up and maintained you in his temple.

1535. αὑτοῦ Herm. with the old editions. αὐτοῦ, Dindorf, Bothe, and others.

The antithesis is between Apollo and Xuthus, so that the reflexive pronoun is not here required. " Si ipse loqueretur Apollo, diceret δωροῦμαί σε ἐμοῦ γεγῶτα, non ἐμαυτοῦ." *Herm.*

1538. ταράσσει. The nominative is not θεὸς, as Matthiae suggests, but the meaning is, εἴτε ἀληθής ἐστιν ὁ θεὸς, ἢ μάτην μ., τοῦτο ταράσσει με.—ἐμοῦ (if the true reading is not rather ἐμοὶ), appears to be somewhat more emphatic than ἐμήν.

1543. ὄνομα πατρός. Without this, an Athenian citizen could not secure any political rights; for by the name of his father, and that of the deme or parish, he was enrolled in the ληξιαρχικὸν γραμματεῖον, and it was by this process only that he became entitled to enter upon an inheritance. Of course, the name of some putative father at least was required for enrolment; and this is the point of v. 1545.—πῶς γὰρ κτλ. 'For how could you have held the name of that father, my marriage with whom I myself wished to conceal, and was for secretly killing you? It was to benefit you that he

ΕΥΡΙΠΙΔΟΥ

ἔκρυπτον αὐτὴ καί σ' ἀπέκτεινον λάθρα;
ὁ δ' ὠφελῶν σε προστίθησ' ἄλλῳ πατρί. 1545

ΙΩ. οὐχ ὧδε φαύλως αὔτ' ἐγὼ μετέρχομαι
ἀλλ' ἱστορήσω Φοῖβον εἰσελθὼν δόμους
εἴτ' εἰμὶ θνητοῦ πατρὸς εἴτε Λοξίου.
ἔα· τίς οἴκων θυοδόκων ὑπερτελὴς
ἀντήλιον πρόσωπον ἐκφαίνει θεῶν; 1550
φεύγωμεν, ὦ τεκοῦσα, μὴ τὰ δαιμόνων
ὁρῶμεν, εἰ μὴ καιρός ἐσθ' ἡμᾶς ὁρᾶν.

ΑΘΗΝΑ.

μὴ φεύγετ'· οὐ γὰρ πολεμίαν με φεύγετε,
ἀλλ' ἔν τ' Ἀθήναις κἀνθάδ' οὖσαν εὐμενῆ.
ἐπώνυμος δὲ σῆς ἀφικόμην χθονός, 1555
Παλλάς, δρόμῳ σπεύσασ' Ἀπόλλωνος πάρα,
ὃς ἐς μὲν ὄψιν σφῷν μολεῖν οὐκ ἠξίου,
μὴ τῶν πάροιθε μέμψις ἐς μέσον μόλῃ,
ἡμᾶς δὲ πέμπει τοὺς λόγους ὑμῖν φράσαι,
ὡς ἥδε τίκτει σ' ἐξ Ἀπόλλωνος πατρός, 1560
δίδωσι δ' οἷς ἔδωκεν, οὐ φύσασί σε,
ἀλλ' ὡς κομίζῃ σ' οἶκον εὐγενέστατον.
ἐπεὶ δ' ἀνεῴχθη πρᾶγμα μηνυθὲν τόδε,
θανεῖν σε δείσας μητρὸς ἐκ βουλευμάτων
καὶ τήνδε πρὸς σοῦ, μηχαναῖς ἐρρύσατο. 1565
ἔμελλε δ' αὐτὰ διασιωπήσας ἄναξ

affiliated you to another father.' He could not have had πάγκληροι δόμοι for both reasons, viz. because he had no known father, and because she would have put him to death but for Apollo's interposition in his behalf.

1546. φαύλως, indifferently, εὐχερῶς. So Pers. 522, of a dream, ὑμεῖς δὲ φαύλως αὔτ' ἄγαν ἐκρίνατε.

1549. θυοδόκων Pierson for θεοδότων. —ὑπερτελής, (ὑπερτέλλειν, Orest. 6,) Agam. 277.—ἀντήλιον Blomf. on Agam. 502 for ἀνθήλιον. It is one of those words which retained the Ionic form, to the rejection of the aspirate. The meaning here, as in δαίμονες ἀντήλιοι in the *Agamemnon*, is, that the transverse rays of the rising sun (the Attic stage facing NN.W.) imparted brightness to the countenances of the statues or persons of the gods, as seen by the audience in the theatre.

1555. σῆς χθονός. She addresses Creusa,—Ἀθάνα ἐπώνυμος τῶν Ἀθηνῶν.

1561. οὐ φύσασί σε H. Stephens for οὗ φασί σε.—κομίζῃ σ' Lenting and Hermann, for νομίζεις or -ῃς. It is singular that these verbs are so often confounded in MSS. The nominative to κομίζῃ seems to be Xuthus, for Apollo would be said κομίζεσθαι rather than κομίζειν, to *have* him conveyed.

1566. ἔμελλε δ' κτλ. 'But it *was* the intention of the god to have kept silence on the subject, and to have made Creusa

ἐν ταῖς Ἀθήναις γνωριεῖν ταύτην τε σὴν
σέ θ', ὡς πέφυκας τῆσδε καὶ Φοίβου πατρός.
ἀλλ' ὡς περαίνω πρᾶγμα καὶ χρησμοὺς θεῷ,
ἐφ' οἷσιν ἔζευξ' ἅρματ', εἰσακούσατον. 1570
λαβοῦσα τόνδε παῖδα Κεκροπίαν χθόνα
χώρει, Κρέουσα, κεἰς θρόνους τυραννικοὺς
ἵδρυσον· ἐκ γὰρ τῶν Ἐρεχθέως γεγὼς
δίκαιος ἄρχειν τῆς γ' ἐμῆς ὅδε χθονός.
ἔσται δ' ἂν Ἑλλάδ' εὐκλεής· οἱ τοῦδε γὰρ 1575
παῖδες γενόμενοι τέσσαρες ῥίζης μιᾶς,
ἐπώνυμοι γῆς κἀπιφυλίου χθονὸς
λαῶν ἔσονται, σκόπελον οἳ ναίουσ' ἐμόν.
Τελέων μὲν ἔσται πρῶτος· εἶτα δεύτερον
Ὅπλητες Ἀργαδῆς τ', ἐμῆς τ' ἀπ' αἰγίδος 1580
ἓν φῦλον ἕξουσ' Αἰγικορῆς. οἱ τῶνδε δ' αὖ
παῖδες γενόμενοι σὺν χρόνῳ πεπρωμένῳ
Κυκλάδας ἐποικήσουσι νησαίας πόλεις

known at Athens (and not at Delphi) as your mother, and your birth from her and from Phoebus your father.' Lest Phoebus should seem to have been led by unexpected circumstances unwillingly to make a declaration against himself, Athena assures the spectators that he would have revealed all the circumstances at the proper time and place.

1570. ἐφ' οἷσιν ἔζευξ' Scaliger for ἐφ' οἷς ἐζεύξασθ' or -αθ'. Thus Pallas in Eum. 383 appears, πώλοις ἀκμαίοις τόνδ' ἐπιζεύξασ' ὄχον, where Hermann edits κώλοις limbs, the present passage being strongly in favour of the MSS. reading.

1574. δίκαιος, he is a fit person. See on Heracl. 142.

1577. ἐπώνυμοι ἔσονται, shall give names to the land and to the people of the country arranged in tribes. The four primitive tribes of Attica, Τελέοντες (the tax-payers), Ὅπλητες (the fighting-men), Ἐργαδεῖς (the agriculturists), and Αἰγικορεῖς (the goat-feeders), are here alluded to, though fanciful derivations are given to the names. Pallas seems to mean, that Ion's four sons shall respectively be called Τελέων, Ὅπλης, Ἀργάδης, and Αἰγικορεὺς, the last παρὰ τὴν τῆς Κόρης Αἰγίδα, from the aegis of the virgin goddess. In progress of time, these ancient titles, the true meaning of which had been wholly lost, became more or less corrupted; thus Ἐργαδεῖς was written Ἀργαδεῖς, and Τελέοντες was sometimes spelt Γελέοντες, which has been interpreted to mean 'the illustrious,' i.e. the nobles. See the dissertation of Schoemann on the Attic tribes, at the end of his 'Assemblies of the Athenians.' Hermann indeed (Praef. p. xxvi) considers the orthography Γελέοντες so clearly established on the authority of inscriptions, that little reliance is to be placed on the other. The reader who wishes to enter at length upon a much disputed and intricate question may refer, besides the modern writers quoted in Hermann's preface to this play, to Herod. v. 66. Strab. viii. p. 383. Plut. Vit. Solon. § 23.

1579. δεύτερον, i.e. φῦλον ἕξουσι, as Hermann has pointed out, correcting ἓν φῦλον for ἔμφυλον.

1583. ἐποικήσουσι, shall become the ἔποικοι or colonists of. The Cyclades, with the islands of Samos and Chios, were included in the original Ionian settlements in Asia Minor. The χέρσοι πάραλοι are the western shores of Asia Minor, especially the twelve cities which constituted the Ionian confederacy. These are said σθένος διδόναι as contributing to

χέρσους τε παράλους, ὃ σθένος τῇμῇ χθονὶ
δίδωσιν· ἀντίπορθμα δ' ἠπείροιν δυοῖν   1585
πεδία κατοικήσουσιν, Ἀσιάδος τε γῆς
Εὐρωπίας τε· τοῦδε δ' ὀνόματος χάριν
Ἴωνες ὀνομασθέντες ἕξουσιν κλέος.
Ξούθῳ δὲ καὶ σοὶ γίγνεται κοινὸν γένος,
Δῶρος μέν, ἔνθεν Δωρὶς ὑμνηθήσεται   1590
πόλις· κατ' αἶαν Πελοπίαν δ' ὁ δεύτερος
Ἀχαιός, ὃς γῆς παραλίας Ῥίου πέλας
τύραννος ἔσται, κἀπισημανθήσεται
κείνου κεκλῆσθαι λαὸς ὄνομ' ἐπώνυμος.
καλῶς δ' Ἀπόλλων πάντ' ἔπραξε· πρῶτα μὲν   1595
ἄνοσον λοχεύει σ', ὥστε μὴ γνῶναι φίλους·
ἐπεὶ δ' ἔτικτες τόνδε παῖδα κἀπέθου
ἐν σπαργάνοισιν, ἁρπάσαντ' εἰς ἀγκάλας
Ἑρμῆν κελεύει δεῦρο πορθμεῦσαι βρέφος,
ἔθρεψέ τ' οὐδ' εἴασεν ἐκπνεῦσαι βίον.   1600
νῦν οὖν σιώπα παῖς ὅδ' ὡς πέφυκε σός,
ἵν' ἡ δόκησις Ξοῦθον ἡδέως ἔχῃ,
σύ τ' αὖ τὰ σαυτῆς ἀγάθ' ἔχουσ' ἴῃς, γύναι.
καὶ χαίρετ'· ἐκ γὰρ τῆσδ' ἀναψυχῆς πόνων

the revenues of the mother country, besides the aid which they were bound to afford as allies, and in gratitude for their deliverance by the Athenians from the Persian yoke.

1585. ἀντίπορθμα πεδία. The lands lying opposite to each other on the ford between Asia and Europe, i.e. on the Hellespont. "Nam in utraque ora coloniae consederunt Ionum, quae Elaeuntem, Lampsacum, aliasque urbes condiderunt." *Herm.*

1590. Δωρὶς πόλις. The state or district adjoining Locris and Phocis in upper Greece, and the country of the Dorian race properly so called.

1592. Ῥίου πέλας. The mention of Rhium, as descriptive of the coast line along the gulf of Corinth, (Rhium being only a promontory at the entrance of it,) has been supposed to allude to the victory of Phormio over the Peloponnesian fleet B.C. 429. (Thucyd. ii. 84.) That event however happened, in all probability, several years before the exhibition of the *Ion.* At all events, no inference can be drawn from it as to the date of the play.

1593. ἐπισημανθήσεται, 'the people (of Achaea) shall be distinguished as being called after his name.' The construction appears to be, ἐπώνυμος κεκλῆσθαι κείνου ὄνομα. At least there is nothing in the verb ἐπισημαίνεσθαι to govern an infinitive. Bothe understands ὡς κεκλῆσθαι, "insignietur eo, quod ab Achaeo appellabitur." Or should we read λαὸν—ἐπώνυμον? "He (Achaeus) shall be distinguished by the people being called after his name."

1597. ἀπέθου, ἐξέθηκας, put away, exposed the child.

1603. ἴῃς Wakefield for εἴη or εἴης. It is hardly likely that the poet would have used ἔχων εἶναι for ἔχειν, when the verse might so easily have been turned in another way.

εὐδαίμον' ὑμῖν πότμον ἐξαγγέλλομαι. 1605
ΙΩ. ὦ Διὸς Παλλὰς μεγίστου θύγατερ, οὐκ ἀπιστίᾳ
σοὺς λόγους ἐνδεξόμεσθα· πείθομαι δ' εἶναι πατρὸς
Λοξίου καὶ τῆσδε· καὶ πρὶν τοῦτο δ' οὐκ ἄπιστον ἦν.
ΚΡ. τἀμά νυν ἄκουσον· αἰνῶ Φοῖβον οὐκ αἰνοῦσα πρίν,
οὕνεχ' οὗ ποτ' ἠμέλησε παιδὸς ἀποδίδωσί μοι. 1610
αἵδε δ' εὐωποὶ πύλαι μοι καὶ θεοῦ χρηστήρια,
δυσμενῆ πάροιθεν ὄντα. νῦν δὲ καὶ ῥόπτρων χέρας
ἡδέως ἐκκρημνάμεσθα καὶ προσεννέπω πύλας.
ΑΘ. ᾔνεσ' οὕνεκ' εὐλογεῖς θεὸν μεταβαλοῦσ'· ἀεί ποτε
χρόνια μὲν τὰ τῶν θεῶν πως, ἐς τέλος δ' οὐκ
ἀσθενῆ. 1615
ΚΡ. ὦ τέκνον, στείχωμεν οἴκους.
ΑΘ. στείχεθ', ἕψομαι δ' ἐγώ.
ΙΩ. ἀξία γ' ἡμῶν ὁδουρός.
ΚΡ. καὶ φιλοῦσά γε πτόλιν.
ΑΘ. ἐς θρόνους δ' ἵζου παλαιούς.
ΙΩ. ἄξιον τὸ κτῆμά μοι. 1620

1605. ἐξαγγέλλομαι, 'I promise.' See Heracl. 531.
1607. ἐνδεξόμεσθα, cum approbatione accipiemus, Hermann, who compares Androm. 1238. Suppl. 976. Heracl. 549.
1608. τοῦτο δ'. Although καὶ—δὲ appears to be not wholly unused by the tragic writers, yet here τοῦτό γ' is at once more natural, and more consistent with the slight irony of the passage. As Ion had never known any father but Apollo whom he served, he says, that *that* always appeared to him credible enough, viz. that he was actually the son of Apollo. There seems little probability either in Hermann's reading, καὶ πρὶν γοῦν τόδ' οὐκ ἄπιστον ἦν, or in Dobree's κεἰ πρὶν τοῦτ' ἄπιστον ἦν ἐμοί.
1612. καὶ ῥόπτρων κτλ. 'I even hang from the ring by my hands,' ἀντέχομαι τῆς θύρας. The word ῥόπτρον is explained by Photius, from Lysias, τὸν τῆς θύρας κρίκον. Some take it for 'the knocker;' but perhaps one and the same appendage served for both purposes (as was often the case in buildings of the middle ages). Harpocration agrees with Photius, and cites the *Amphiaraus* of Aristophanes for an example of its use. Sir Charles Fel-

lows found a Greek tomb at Pinara in Lycia, with the door "highly finished, representing frame and nails, and on the panels handsome *ring-knockers*, all cut in the marble rock." (p. 323.)—προσεννέπω πύλας, Aesch. Ag. 1262.
1614. ποτε for που L. Dindorf. Perhaps ἀεί γέ που, as Grotius proposed. So ἀεί γε δὴ in Prom. 42.
1616. It is clear that the company move off the stage in solemn procession, escorted by Pallas, who is thus made to conduct Ion in person to occupy the throne of her own ancient city. The spectacle certainly was well adapted to the taste of an Athenian audience.
1618. ἵζου. This is said, of course, to Ion, who, in language complimentary to the Athenians, is made to say 'the possession is worth the having.' The persons of the dialogue were rightly restored by Hermann, v. 1617 having formerly been wholly given to Creusa, as well as the latter half of the next. The name of Ion was probably struck out by some one who fancied there were but two actors in the play.
1619—22. Besides this play, the *Oedipus Rex* is the only one that con-

P 2

XO. ὦ Διὸς Λητοῦς τ' Ἄπολλον, χαῖρ'· ὅτῳ δ' ἐλαύνεται
συμφοραῖς οἶκος, σέβοντα δαίμονας θαρσεῖν χρεών·
ἐς τέλος γὰρ οἱ μὲν ἐσθλοὶ τυγχάνουσιν ἀξίων,
οἱ κακοὶ δ', ὥσπερ πεφύκασ', οὔποτ' εὖ πράξειαν ἄν.

cludes with trochaics spoken by the chorus. The Agamemnon and the Phoenissae (if the three last lines appended to the latter be really spurious) end with trochaics from one of the actors. It is not often that this metre is made the vehicle of sententious reflexions, as here and in the *Oedipus*. The encouragement here given by the poet implies a just perception of the dealings of Providence with man, and more faith in the ultimate justice of the deity than his speculative mind was always willing to express. 'Sooner or later,' he says, 'even in this life, the good are proved to be really good, and receive their deserts as such.' Of course, the observation is only generally true.— ὥσπερ πεφύκασ', i.e. ὥσπερ κακοί εἰσι τὴν φύσιν, οὕτω καὶ κακῶς ἀεὶ πράξουσι. On the final ι of the perfect elided, see on Troad. 350.

ΕΥΡΙΠΙΔΟΥ ΕΛΕΝΗ.

ΥΠΟΘΕΣΙΣ.

Ἡρόδοτος ἱστορεῖ περὶ Ἑλένης καί φησιν ἐλθεῖν μὲν αὐτὴν εἰς Αἴγυπτον, καὶ τοῦτο φάσκειν καὶ τὸν Ὅμηρον, ποιοῦντα τὴν Ἑλένην παρέχειν τῷ Τηλεμάχῳ ἐν Ὀδυσσείᾳ τὸ ληθικηδὲς φάρμακον, τό οἱ πόρε Πολυδάμνα Θόωνος παράκοιτις, οὐ μὴν δὲ οὕτως, ὡς Εὐριπίδης φησίν. οἱ μὲν γὰρ πλανωμένην φασὶν αὐτὴν μετὰ τοῦ Μενελάου μετὰ τὴν τῆς Ἰλίου πόρθησιν καὶ εἰς Αἴγυπτον παραγενέσθαι, κἀκεῖθεν πεπορίσθαι τὰ φάρμακα· ὁ δὲ τὴν μὲν ἀληθῶς Ἑλένην φησὶ μηδ' ὁπωσοῦν ἐλθεῖν εἰς Τροίαν, τὸ εἴδωλον δὲ αὐτῆς. κλέψας γὰρ αὐτὴν ὁ Ἑρμῆς Ἥρας βουλῇ Πρωτεῖ τῷ βασιλεῖ τῆς Αἰγύπτου φυλάττειν παρέδωκε. τούτου δὲ θανόντος ὁ υἱὸς αὐτοῦ Θεοκλύμενος ἐπειρᾶτο γαμεῖν αὐτήν. ἡ δὲ ἱκέτις παρεκάθητο τῷ τοῦ Πρωτέως μνημείῳ, ὅθεν αὐτῇ ἐπιφαίνεται Μενέλεως, τὰς μὲν ναῦς ἐν τῇ θαλάσσῃ ἀπολέσας, ὀλίγους δέ τινας τῶν ἑταίρων ἐν ἄντρῳ καθειργμένους σώζων. εἰς λόγους δὲ ἐλθόντες καὶ μηχανορραφήσαντες ἀπατῶσι μὲν τὸν Θεοκλύμενον, αὐτοὶ δὲ νηῒ ἐμβάντες, ὡς δὴ τῷ Μενέλεῳ θανόντι κατὰ θάλατταν θύσοντες, εἰς τὴν ἰδίαν διασώζονται.

HELENA.

The subject of this romantic and eventful play was suggested by the famous *Palinodia* of Stesichorus. The story was (see Plat. Phaedr. p. 243), that this poet having been struck with blindness, as he conceived, for having spoken evil of Helen, afterwards recanted, and pretended that it was not really Helen, but only her semblance or *wraith* that had gone to Troy. Euripides, however, though the plot of the play turns mainly on this extravagant fiction, has followed other writers,—probably Herodotus[1],—in laying the scene of the action in Egypt. The historian had heard a story about Helen, as having been carried by adverse winds to the coast of Egypt, while on her course from Sparta to Troy in company with Paris, and there being received at the court of King Proteus, who, being a just man, and indignant at the treachery of Paris, detained her until her lawful husband could reclaim her. The righteous character of Proteus, and the idea of making his tomb an asylum from the offered violence of his son, are clearly adapted from Herodotus, who states that the attendants of Paris left him on reaching Egypt, and took sanctuary in a temple of Hercules on the shore. That Homer had already spoken of the visit of Helen to Egypt[2] is noticed by Herodotus himself; though in fact Menelaus is described in the Odyssey as having touched there on his return from Troy, as he is made to do, with the εἴδωλον of Helen, in the present play. What Stesichorus did with the true Helen, i.e. whether she remained in Greece, as Müller[3] supposes, or, as Hermann[4] thinks, was transported to the island Leuce in the Euxine (Pausan. iii. 19, 11,) is uncertain, and it imports little to the subject to inquire. Euripides appears to have added to the current legends this further invention of his own, that while the Greeks were fighting for the εἴδωλον of Helen at Troy, the true Helen had been conveyed by Hermes through the air, first to a small islet close to the Attic shore, (Pausan. i. 35, 1,) afterwards to

---

[1] Lib. ii. 113.   [2] Od. iv.
[3] Hist. Gr. Lit. p. 201.   [4] Praef. p. ix.

the land of Egypt. From the Cyclic poem of the Νόστοι he has derived several of the accessory facts, as the account of Menelaus' return from Troy and the loss of the Grecian fleet off Euboea. On the whole, the materials at his disposal have been worked up into a good play, not perhaps great as a tragedy, but very full of incident, and one in which the interest never flags, long as is the drama, from the artless prologue of Helena to the exciting narrative of the escape by sea at the end[5]. There is much of that sort of irony which rejoices in clever equivocations, and several passages partaking of rather a comic tone, especially in the character of the old portress in the palace of Proteus, and the speech of Menelaus, where he first appears in the masquerade of a shipwrecked mariner. For these reasons the Helena has as good a claim perhaps to the title of a tragi-comedy as the *Orestes* has. Mistaken identity, and the ludicrous perplexities resulting therefrom, was an essentially comic subject, as more than one of Plautus' plays will serve to show. The affection of Helen, the dignified mien and humane character of Theonöe, are very pleasingly drawn; but Helen is too prompt in the arts of deception to suit our ideas of a thoroughly sincere woman, and her grief for the supposed death of her husband is not unmixed with something of selfish commiseration for her own lot.

The outline of the play is briefly as follows. Helen, who is importunately sought in marriage by Theoclymenus, the son and successor of Proteus, king of Egypt, and who is herself fully conscious that Menelaus has been fighting at Troy for her mere εἴδωλον, has taken sanctuary at the tomb of Proteus (represented on the stage, vv. 797, 961), that she may preserve her virtue inviolate for her lawful husband, whose safe return from Troy she is constantly expecting. Teucer, who is on his voyage to Cyprus, having been expelled from Salamis by his father, visits Egypt in order to consult Theonöe, the prophetic daughter of Proteus; and meeting with Helen, whom he recognises at once by her likeness to the εἴδωλον, informs her of the result of the Trojan war, and the reported death of Menelaus by a storm on his return. She does not however make herself known; and Teucer departs with the belief that he has merely seen a stranger bearing a striking likeness to Helen. The chorus and Helen then, in a long *commos*, bewail the fate of Menelaus. The chorus however, entertaining some doubts as to the truth of Teucer's information, advise Helen to consult Theonöe whether her lord is yet alive

---

[5] "Haud sane optima haec tragoedia est, non quod non habet tristem exitum: nam in exitu nec vis tragoediae nec virtus posita est : sed quod nec gravis metus in ea, nec magna miseratio invenitur." Hermann, Praef. p. xiv.

VOL. II.   Q

or really dead. While she is absent for this purpose, Menelaus himself suddenly appears. He has been shipwrecked, and has barely escaped with his supposed Helen (i. e. the εἴδωλον) and a few of his companions to the coast of Egypt. Leaving these in a cavern, he seeks admittance at the palace of Theoclymenus, but is denied entrance by the portress, who, to his utter amazement, informs him that Helen is within, and advises him to fly for his life, since her master is hostile to the Greeks. Convinced however that there must be some mistake, he resolves to seek for aid from Theoclymenus, and to throw himself upon his compassion. Helen, having now learnt from Theonöe that her lord is yet alive, and is sailing about in unknown seas, again betakes herself to the tomb of Proteus; and here she is met by Menelaus. She recognises him and claims him as her husband; but he, naturally enough, remains incredulous, knowing that he has just left his wife in the custody of his companions by the sea-shore. At this juncture a messenger arrives, to inform him that this very wife, who has been recovered with so much toil, has suddenly disappeared and melted into air: but, seeing the true Helen at the tomb, he thinks she has suddenly come thither. Thus the recognition between husband and wife is at length effected. After mutual endearments they deliberate on the best means of escape to Sparta. Theonöe now steps on the stage attended by torch-bearers, and with the solemn pomp due to her sacred character, and informs the perplexed lovers that on her depends their common safety: that Cypris and Hera are at variance on the subject, the former desiring the destruction, the latter the preservation of Menelaus. If she informs her brother of Menelaus' arrival, they are undone. Helen then, and in turn Menelaus, supplicate Theonöe, in touching appeals to her compassion, not to betray them. She consents to aid them so far, that she will be silent respecting them to her brother. The plan then agreed upon at the suggestion of Helen is, that she should ask from Theoclymenus a ship with the necessary crew, and supplies under the name of offerings, in order to perform certain pretended funeral rites to her husband who has perished at sea. On his return from the chase Theoclymenus is surprised to find Helen dressed in the garb of deep mourning. On learning her bereavement, so welcome to himself, as removing the only obstacle to his union with her, he readily consents to lend the ship for her use; and Menelaus, who is pointed to as the messenger who has just brought the sad tidings, is to be the conductor of the ceremony. The pair take leave of Theoclymenus and of the chorus, with the promise, on their return to Greece, to effect the liberation of the latter. Content with this, the chorus sing an ode in which a prosperous voyage is invoked on the adventurers. A messenger then arrives and informs the king of their escape. Menelaus, by a preconcerted plan, had met his own crew on the shore, under the guise of strangers who wished to take a part in the intended rites, and all had embarked together. When out at sea, the Greeks had risen and massacred the Egyptians. He alone has escaped by swimming to announce the issue of the pretended funeral ceremonies. Enraged at the loss of his bride, Theoclymenus threatens to kill his sister for having withheld from him the truth. But the Dioscuri, the brothers of Helen, intercede, and inform him of the counsels of the gods respecting Menelaus and Helen; whereupon he at once forgives his sister and acquiesces in their unmolested return to Greece.

The date of the play is determined by that of the *Andromeda*, which the Scholiast on the *Thesmophoriazusae*, v. 1012, tells us was brought out together with the *Helena*. Now that comedy, in which Aristophanes parodies the present play as τὴν καινὴν Ἑλένην, appeared the year after, Ol. xcii. 1. The Scholiast on the *Ranae*, which was acted Ol. xciii. 3, states (v. 53) that the *Andromeda* had come out eight years before. Consequently the *Helena* was brought out Ol. xci. 4, B.C. 413, the very year of the disastrous termination of the Sicilian expedition. (Müller however, Hist. Gr. Lit. p. 375, makes it B.C. 412, in which case Euripides must have written it with a full knowledge of the circumstances; see v. 1151 seqq.) By a singular misinterpretation of the words τὴν καινὴν Ἑλένην, Barnes came to the conclusion that the poet " edidit et aliam *Helenam* novam, quam alii *Helenae* repetitionem vocant, ex qua Aristophanes in *Thesmophoriazusis* multa per Parodiam transcripsit." The Ἑλένης ἀπαίτησις is known to have been a play of Sophocles.

The chorus is composed of captive Spartan maidens. The scene is laid entirely in the island of Pharos, at the palace of Theoclymenus, king of Egypt. There are three actors in the piece, as appears from the dialogue between Helena, Menelaus, and Theoclymenus, v. 1193 seqq. It is to be regretted that the *Helena* is one of the most corrupt and difficult of the plays of Euripides. It is to this circumstance that we must attribute the fact of so admirable a drama being comparatively little read in the schools. There are no extant scholia upon it. Hermann's excellent edition has done much in restoring and rightly interpreting many of the most difficult passages, upon which his immediate predecessor Pflugk could throw but a faint and uncertain light.

ΤΑ ΤΟΥ ΔΡΑΜΑΤΟΣ ΠΡΟΣΩΠΑ.

ΕΛΕΝΗ.
ΤΕΥΚΡΟΣ.
ΧΟΡΟΣ.
ΜΕΝΕΛΑΟΣ.
ΓΡΑΥΣ.
ΑΓΓΕΛΟΣ.
ΘΕΟΝΟΗ.
ΘΕΟΚΛΥΜΕΝΟΣ.
[ΕΤΕΡΟΣ ΑΓΓΕΛΟΣ.]*
ΔΙΟΣΚΟΡΟΙ.

* " Haec persona in edd. vett. omissa." *Herm.*

ΕΥΡΙΠΙΔΟΥ ΕΛΕΝΗ.

ΕΛΕΝΗ.

Νείλου μὲν αἴδε καλλιπάρθενοι ῥοαί,
ὃς ἀντὶ δίας ψακάδος Αἰγύπτου πέδον
λευκῆς τακείσης χιόνος ὑγραίνει γύας.

1—67. In the prologue Helen explains the cause of her presence in the land of Egypt. Her supposed marriage with Paris was frustrated by the jealousy of Hera, who had been defeated in the contest of beauty, of which he was the umpire. The Helen for whom the Greeks fought at Troy was but an unsubstantial shade, fashioned to deceive, after the likeness of herself, the true and living Helen. Transported by Hermes through the air to Egypt, she had been deposited in the palace of King Proteus, a discreet and god-fearing man. But Proteus being now dead, his son Theoclymenus is eager to obtain her for his wife. She, however, resolved on preserving her marriage vows inviolate, persists in refusing his request; and to avoid his importunity she has taken refuge at the tomb of Proteus, determined that if her name is wrongly detested in Hellas, her person shall at least be subjected to no indignities in a barbaric land.

1. καλλιπάρθενοι. The commentators generally understand καθαραί, but Hermann says, " non videtur dubitandum esse, quin aquas Nili nullius cum alius fluvii aquis commixtas, sed ex solis nivibus prognatas significare voluerit Euripides." Others, as J. Barnes, suppose the nymphs of the river are alluded to. The compound is formed as καλλίπαις in Agam. 737, and we may compare παρθένος πηγὴ in Pers. 615, εὐπάρθενε Δίρκα Bacch. 520. Translate therefore, ' Of Nile indeed these are the beauteous virgin streams.' It is sometimes difficult to determine the exact force which poetical compounds of this nature were designed to have. Perhaps this falls under the class of epithets pointed out on Alcest. 428, the intended sense being merely καλὴν ὄψιν ἔχουσαι. So καλλιπάρθενος δέρη in Iph. A. 1574. It is said that Euripides derived his opinion about the overflow of the Nile from Anaxagoras; and in Frag. 227 are several verses on this subject which are assigned to his *Archelaus*. They cannot however have come from the pen of our poet. He would not have used the form μελαμβρότοιο in a senarius, still less the ευ in τεθριππευόντός as a short syllable. Aristophanes, Thesm. 855—7, quotes the two first lines of the present play as from ' the new Helena,' but facetiously travesties the third thus, λευκῆς νοτίζει μελανοσυρμαῖον λεών, in allusion to the συρμαίη of Herodotus, ii. 125.—The form ψακάδος for ψεκάδος has been restored from Aristophanes and others. Cf. Agam. 1361, βάλλει μ' ἐρεμνῇ ψακάδι φοινίας δρόσου. Ibid. v. 1512, the MSS. wrongly give ψεκὰς δὲ λήγει, this being a post-Attic form.

3. γύας. " Negligentius adjectum quasi non praecessisset πέδον. Sic πόλιν Herc. F. v. 946 post τὰ Κυκλώπων βάθρα v. 944." *Dind.* " Explicari talia possunt

Πρωτεὺς δ᾽, ὅτ᾽ ἔζη, τῆσδε γῆς τύραννος ἦν,
Φάρον μὲν οἰκῶν νῆσον, Αἰγύπτου δ᾽ ἄναξ, 5
ὃς τῶν κατ᾽ οἶδμα παρθένων μίαν γαμεῖ
Ψαμάθην, ἐπειδὴ λέκτρ᾽ ἀφῆκεν Αἰακοῦ.
τίκτει δὲ τέκνα δισσὰ τοῖσδε δώμασι,
Θεοκλύμενον μὲν ἄρσεν᾽, ὃς θεοὺς σέβων
βίον διήνεγκ᾽, εὐγενῆ τε παρθένον 10
Εἰδώ, τὸ μητρὸς ἀγλάϊσμ᾽, ὅτ᾽ ἦν βρέφος,
ἐπεὶ δ᾽ ἐς ἥβην ἦλθεν ὡραίων γάμων,
καλοῦσιν αὐτὴν Θεονόην· τὰ θεῖα γὰρ
τά τ᾽ ὄντα καὶ μέλλοντα πάντ᾽ ἠπίστατο,
προγόνου λαβοῦσα Νηρέως τιμὰς πάρα. 15

repetito verbo, quasi dicat Αἴγυπτον ὑγραίνων ὑγραίνει γύας." Herm. For ὁ γύης see Heracl. 839.

5. Φάρον μὲν κτλ. 'Who, if he dwelt in the small island of Pharos, was still king of all Egypt.' This island is mentioned in Od. iv. 354, as distant a whole day's voyage from the coast. But it was much closer in Strabo's time (p. 30, 37), and indeed was united by a mole to the coast, under Alexander.

7. Αἰακοῦ is Musgrave's correction for Αἰόλου, from Apollodor. iii. 12, 6, μίγνυται δὲ αὖθις Αἰακὸς Ψαμάθῃ τῇ Νηρέως εἰς φώκην ἠλλαγμένῃ διὰ τὸ μὴ βούλεσθαι συνελθεῖν, καὶ τεκνοῖ παῖδα Φῶκον. Hesiod, Theog. 1002,

αὐτὰρ Νηρῆος κοῦραι ἁλίοιο γέροντος
ἤτοι Φῶκον μὲν Ψαμάθη τέκε δῖα θεάων,
Αἰακοῦ ἐν φιλότητι.

The mention of Proteus and the island Pharos was suggested to the poet by the fourth book of the Odyssey, v. 354. 385; and from the prophetic powers there attributed to Proteus, his daughter Theonoë is here alleged to derive the same faculty (v. 14).

9. The common reading of this verse is Θεοκλύμενον ἄρσεν᾽, ὅτι δὴ θεοὺς σέβων. The correction, which is so obvious that it must immediately occur to any one moderately versed in criticism, was made by Scaliger, and also by Hermann; while W. Dindorf retains the vulgate, with Pflugk, and Bothe gives the not more metrical verse Θεοκλύμενον μὲν ἄρσεν᾽, ὅτι δὴ θεοὺς σέβων. There is not a doubt that the prosaic ὅτι δὴ resulted from a clumsy attempt to make the verse scan,

after μὲν had dropped out, or had been omitted in ignorance that it may rightly be followed by τε.

11. Εἰδώ. This is the admirable emendation of Matthiae for εἶδος, which Pflugk alone retains. It is clear, by the mention of her after-name Theonöe, that the poet ought to have recorded that given to her in infancy. Besides, τὸ μητρὸς ἀγλάϊσμ᾽ is added as a reason why she was called 'Beauty,' just as ὃς θεοὺς σέβων &c. illustrates the name of Theoclymenus. Were there any doubt about the true reading, it would be removed by Od. iv. 365, Πρωτέος ἰφθίμου θυγάτηρ, ἁλίοιο γέροντος, Εἰδοθέη. Not that Εἰδώ is a *diminutive* of the latter name, but a variant of it, formed on the analogy of εἰκώ, Γοργώ, ἀηδώ &c.

12. ὡραίων. Hermann seems rightly to retain this against Musgrave's alteration ὡραίαν, adopted by W. Dindorf. Similarly in Choeph. 562, for βαλὼν ἕρκειον πυλῶν Stanley proposes ἑρκείων. In phrases of this kind it matters little with which substantive the epithet grammatically agrees. In Hippol. 1140, νυμφιδία δ᾽ ἀπόλωλε φυγᾷ σᾷ λέκτρων ἅμιλλα κούραις, some editors would read νυμφιδίων.

14. τὰ ὄντα καὶ μέλλοντα, for καὶ τὰ μέλλοντα. See *inf.* 923. Ion 7.

15. προγόνου Νηρέως. "Others supposed that Proteus, the marine demigod skilled in metamorphoses, went to the island of Pharos, and there formed a false Helen with which he deceived Paris; a version of the story which even the ancient scholiasts have confounded with that of Stesichorus. As this Proteus was con-

ἡμῖν δὲ γῆ μὲν πατρὶς οὐκ ἀνώνυμος
Σπάρτη, πατὴρ δὲ Τυνδάρεως· ἔστιν δὲ δὴ
λόγος τις ὡς Ζεὺς μητέρ' ἔπτατ' εἰς ἐμὴν
Λήδαν, κύκνου μορφώματ' ὄρνιθος λαβὼν,
ὃς δόλιον εὐνὴν ἐξέπραξ' ὑπ' αἰετοῦ   20
δίωγμα φεύγων, εἰ σαφὴς οὗτος λόγος.
Ἑλένη δ' ἐκλήθην· ἃ δὲ πεπόνθαμεν κακὰ
λέγοιμ' ἄν. ἦλθον τρεῖς θεαὶ κάλλους πέρι
Ἰδαῖον ἐς κευθμῶν' Ἀλέξανδρον πάρα,
Ἥρα Κύπρις τε Διογενής τε παρθένος,   25
μορφῆς θέλουσαι διαπεράνασθαι κρίσιν.
τοὐμὸν δὲ κάλλος, εἰ καλὸν τὸ δυστυχὲς,
Κύπρις προτείνασ' ὡς Ἀλέξανδρος γαμεῖ,
νικᾷ· λιπὼν δὲ βούσταθμ' Ἰδαῖος Πάρις
Σπάρτην ἀφίκεθ', ὡς ἐμὸν σχήσων λέχος.   30
Ἥρα δὲ μεμφθεῖσ' οὕνεκ' οὐ νικᾷ θεὰς
ἐξηνέμωσε τἄμ' Ἀλεξάνδρῳ λέχη,
δίδωσι δ' οὐκ ἔμ', ἀλλ' ὁμοιώσασ' ἐμοὶ

verted by the Egyptian interpreters into a king of Egypt, this king was said to have taken Helen from Paris, and to have kept her for Menelaus." In the treatment of the subject by Euripides, "Proteus completely loses the character which he bears in the ancient Greek mythus; but the events tend to situations which suited the pathetic tragedy" of the poet. (Müller, Hist. Gr. Lit. p. 201.)

17. ἔστιν δὲ δὴ, 'and there *is* a story (though I do not put any faith in it;) that' &c. The tone of the clause is sufficiently defined by δὴ and τις.

19. κύκνου—ὄρνιθος. These words are not to be joined like substantive and epithet. " Sententia est ὀρνίθεια μορφώματα κύκνου." *Herm.* An exactly similar passage is Oed. Col. 109, οἰκτείρατ' ἀνδρὸς Οἰδίπου τόδ' ἄθλιον εἴδωλον, 'this form of Oedipus, which is but the semblance of a man.'

21. σαφής, 'true.' See v. 309. Both Herm. and Bothe construe ὑπὸ with φεύγων. The obvious sense is, διωκόμενος ὑπ' ἀετοῦ. The device of the pursuit was adopted that the god might take refuge in the arms of Leda.

23. It is clearly correct to join ἦλθον περὶ κάλλους, not διαπ. κρίσιν περὶ κάλλους μορφῆς, which is quite contrary to the order of the words. They came to Paris about the disputed question of beauty, wishing to *have* the decision respecting their personal charms finally made,—such being the force of the middle aorist. On θέλειν see Alc. 281.

27. εἰ καλὸν κτλ. " Si modo recte pulcrum dicitur, quod potius miserum dicendum est." Pflugk. After γαμεῖ it is best to supply ἐμέ.—προτείνειν is 'to hold out as a bribe,' generally with the notion of a mere lure or bait which is not to be realised; as in this case Paris obtained only the κενὴ δόκησις or shadow of Helen.

31. μεμφθεῖσα, 'being dissatisfied.' With a genitive of the cause, Hipp. 1402, τιμῆς ἐμέμφθη. Compare Virg. Aen. i. 26, 'manet alta mente repostum Judicium Paridis, spretaeque injuria formae.' —ἐξηνέμωσε, made void, or in the literal sense, 'turned into empty air.' In Androm. 938, ἐξηνεμώθην μωρίᾳ is, 'I was puffed up with foolish jealousy.' For the physical sense of this word see Aristot. H. A. x. 3.

120 ΕΥΡΙΠΙΔΟΥ

εἴδωλον ἔμπνουν οὐρανοῦ ξυνθεῖσ' ἄπο,
Πριάμου τυράννῳ παιδί· καὶ δοκεῖ μ' ἔχειν, 35
κενὴν δόκησιν, οὐκ ἔχων. τὰ δ' αὖ Διὸς
βουλεύματ' ἄλλα τοῖσδε συμβαίνει κακοῖς·
πόλεμον γὰρ εἰσήνεγκεν Ἑλλήνων χθονὶ
καὶ Φρυξὶ δυστήνοισιν, ὡς ὄχλου βροτῶν
πλήθους τε κουφίσειε μητέρα χθόνα, 40
γνωτόν τε θείη τὸν κράτιστον Ἑλλάδος.
Φρυγῶν δ' ἐς ἀλκὴν προὐτέθην, ἐγὼ μὲν οὔ,
τὸ δ' ὄνομα τοὐμόν, ἆθλον Ἕλλησιν δορός.
λαβὼν δέ μ' Ἑρμῆς ἐν πτυχαῖσιν αἰθέρος
νεφέλῃ καλύψας, οὐ γὰρ ἠμέλησέ μου 45
Ζεύς, τόνδ' ἐς οἶκον Πρωτέως ἱδρύσατο,
πάντων προκρίνας σωφρονέστατον βροτῶν,

34. ἄπο. So Herm. Dind. Bothe after Reiske, for ὕπο, which Pflugk retains without remark. The latter preposition could only mean, 'having put together a living likeness of me, through the aid (or agency) of upper air.' The dative might have meant, '*in* the sky.' According to the Anaxagorean doctrine, the Ether, or bright etherial fluid above our atmosphere, was the source of life to all organic forms. Hence in v. 583, when Menelaus, alluding to this pseudo-Helen, asks καὶ τίς βλέποντα σῶμα' ἐξεργάζεται; Helen replies, αἰθήρ, ὅθεν σὺ θεοπόνητ' ἔχεις λέχια. Compare Bacch. 292. In this sense, ὕπο is certainly defensible. However, the change to ἄπο is easy, and the meaning seems clearer, 'taking a portion of the sky to form it into a likeness.' Cf. Electr. 1282, Ζεὺς δ' ὡς ἔρις γένοιτο καὶ φόνος βροτῶν, εἴδωλον Ἑλένης ἐξέπεμψ' εἰς Ἴλιον.

35. τυράννῳ Herm. for τυράννου, which is both weak and superfluous, whereas the *royal* son of Priam implies that he was more than a mere herdsman. Cf. Alcest. 1150, Σθενέλου τυράννῳ παιδί.

37. Though τὰ Διὸς βουλεύματα ἄλλα is by no means usual Greek (on account of the article) for ἄλλα τῶν Δ. βουλευμάτων, it does not seem possible to take ἄλλα for a predicate, for the poet would unquestionably have written ἄλλως unless he had meant something else. Barnes translates, "Jovis porro consilia alia accesserunt ad haec mala." The verse is by no means easy, though the commentators are silent upon it, being intent on illustrating from Orest. 1642 and the Schol. on Il. i. 5, the motives of the god in bringing the Trojan war, and from Rhes. 281 and elsewhere, the sufficiently obvious genitive after κουφίζειν. Helen appears to mean, that together with her own private troubles other designs of Zeus were carried into effect, viz. to relieve mother earth from the pressure of an overgrown population, and to glorify Achilles. The former idea is said to be borrowed from a verse in the Cyclic Κύπρια ἔπη, quoted by the Schol. on Il. i. 5, Ζεὺς—σύνθετο κουφίσαι ἀνθρώπων παμβώτορα γαῖαν.

42. προὐτέθην. So Musgrave for προὐθέμην, which is incapable of a passive sense.

45. οὐ γὰρ ἠμέλησέ μου. It was the common opinion that the children of gods were not lost sight of, though a certain amount of trouble had to be borne by them, and though their divine parents appeared for a time to withdraw their countenance and protection. Cf. v. 18. So with respect to the youthful Ion, v. 67, Λοξίας δὲ τὴν τύχην ἐς τοῦτ' ἐλαύνει, κοὐ λέληθεν, ὡς δοκεῖ.

47. προκρίνας. The meaning is, πάντων βροτῶν προκρίνας αὐτόν, ὡς σωφρονέστατον ὄντα, though the genitive appears to depend on the superlative at least as much as on the preposition.—

ἀκέραιον ὡς σώσαιμι Μενέλεῳ λέχος.
κἀγὼ μὲν ἐνθάδ' εἴμ', ὁ δ' ἄθλιος πόσις
στράτευμ' ἀθροίσας τὰς ἐμὰς ἀναρπαγὰς 50
θηρᾷ πορευθεὶς Ἰλίου πυργώματα.
ψυχαὶ δὲ πολλαὶ δι' ἔμ' ἐπὶ Σκαμανδρίοις
ῥοαῖσιν ἔθανον· ἡ δὲ πάντα τλᾶσ' ἐγὼ
κατάρατός εἰμι, καὶ δοκῶ προδοῦσ' ἐμὸν
πόσιν συνάψαι πόλεμον Ἕλλησιν μέγαν. 55
τί δῆτ' ἔτι ζῶ; θεοῦ τόδ' εἰσήκουσ' ἔπος
Ἑρμοῦ, τὸ κλεινὸν ἔτι κατοικήσειν πέδον
Σπάρτης σὺν ἀνδρί, γνόντος ὡς ἐς Ἴλιον
οὐκ ἦλθον, ἵνα μὴ λέκτρ' ὑποστρώσω τινί.
ἕως μὲν οὖν φῶς ἡλίου τόδ' ἔβλεπε 60
Πρωτεύς, ἄσυλος ἦν γάμων· ἐπεὶ δὲ γῆς
σκότῳ κέκρυπται, παῖς ὁ τοῦ τεθνηκότος
θηρᾷ γαμεῖν με. τὸν πάλαι δ' ἐμὸν πόσιν
τιμῶσα Πρωτέως μνῆμα προσπίτνω τόδε
ἱκέτις, ἵν' ἀνδρὶ τἀμὰ διασώσῃ λέχη, 65

Μενελέῳ Dind. Herm. and others for Μενελέω.
49. This verse and 52—3, ψυχαὶ—ἔθανον, are quoted by Aristoph., Thesm. 864—6, but in inverted order.
50. ἀναρπαγάς. A mixed expression, implying both ἐμὲ τὴν ἁρπασθεῖσαν θηρᾷ, and τὰς ἐμὰς (i.e. ἐμοῦ) ἀναρπαγὰς τίσασθαι θέλει. Cf. Rhes. 121, οὐδ' ὧδ' Ἀχαιοὺς ὡς δοκεῖς ἀναρπάσαι.
53. ἡ πάντα τλᾶσα, for ἡ πάντολμος λεγομένη, the sense being ἀδίκως, μάτην κατάρατος.
56. τί δῆτ' ἔτι ζῶ; These words also are quoted Thesm. 868. Helen anticipates an objection that may be raised against her conduct, in still living when she might have ended her troubles by suicide (which the Greeks thought noble under such circumstances,) by alleging the promise of Hermes, made to her at the time of her removal, that she should some day be restored to her country and her husband. In the next verse Hermann, followed by Dindorf, reads τὸ κλεινόν μ' ἔτι κτλ., but the μ' seems by no means necessary. See on v. 802.
58. γνόντος. Why γνόντος αὐτοῦ, i. e. τοῦ ἀνδρὸς, should be understood, rather

than Ἑρμοῦ, does not seem at all clear. Hermes made the promise, because he very well knew that the Helen at Troy was not the real Helen; and he made it too, with this object and intent, that Helen might not marry another, but might reserve herself intact for Menelaus. The whole passage might be thus paraphrased; τί δῆτ' ἔτι ζῶ; διὰ τήνδε τὴν αἰτίαν· ἔφη γὰρ ὁ θεὸς, ἵνα μὴ γημαίμην ἄλλῳ, ἔτι με κατοικήσειν Σπάρτην· ἔγνω γὰρ ὅτι ἐκεῖσε οὐκ ἦλθον, ἀλλ' ἐν τῇ Αἰγύπτῳ καθιδρύθην. But she uses the subjunctive ὑποστρώσω in reference to the present tense ἔτι ζῶ, "traducta cogitatione ab eo, quod efficere voluisset Mercurius, ad id, quod dei monitu faciendum sibi ducebat," as Pflugk explains it. —" ὑποστρώσω dicit, quia hoc ipso tempore in eo discrimine est, ut Theoclymeno nubere cogatur." Matth.
61. " Helena se dicit ἄσυλον γάμων fuisse, quod sibi salvum manserit Menelai connubium, neque ab eo fuerit avulsa." Herm.
65. διασώσῃ, viz. Proteus, by his influence as a δαίμων over the conduct of his son, the suitor. Homer, Od. iv. 385, calls him ἀθάνατος Πρωτεὺς Αἰγύπτιος.

ὡς, εἰ καθ' Ἑλλάδ' ὄνομα δυσκλεὲς φέρω,
μή μοι τὸ σῶμά γ' ἐνθάδ' αἰσχύνην ὄφλῃ.

ΤΕΥΚΡΟΣ.

τίς τῶνδ' ἐρυμνῶν δωμάτων ἔχει κράτος;
Πλούτου γὰρ οἶκος ἄξιος προσεικάσαι,
βασίλειά τ' ἀμφιβλήματ' εὔθριγκοί θ' ἕδραι.   70
ἔα.
ὦ θεοί, τίν' εἶδον ὄψιν; ἐχθίστην ὁρῶ
γυναικὸς εἰκὼ φόνιον, ἥ μ' ἀπώλεσε
πάντας τ' Ἀχαιούς. θεοί σ', ὅσον μίμημ' ἔχεις
Ἑλένης, ἀποπτύσαιεν. εἰ δὲ μὴ 'ν ξένῃ   75
γαίᾳ πόδ' εἶχον, τῷδ' ἂν εὐστόχῳ πτερῷ
ἀπόλαυσιν εἰκοῦς ἔθανες ἂν Διὸς κόρης.

ΕΛ. τί δ', ὦ ταλαίπωρ', ὅστις ὢν μ' ἀπεστράφης,
καὶ ταῖς ἐκείνης συμφοραῖς ἐμὲ στυγεῖς;

ΤΕ. ἥμαρτον· ὀργῇ δ' εἶξα μᾶλλον ἤ μ' ἐχρῆν·   80
μισεῖ γὰρ Ἑλλὰς πᾶσα τὴν Διὸς κόρην.

Without attributing to him immortality, Euripides seems to have regarded him as φύσιν θειότερος.

68. Teucer, the son of Telamon, on his way to the new colony which he was destined to found in Cyprus (see Hor. Carm. i. 7,) happens to visit Egypt, in order to consult the omniscient Theonöe (v. 145), and informs Helen of the events which have occurred at Troy, of the supposed death of Menelaus, and of the fate of the other members of her family. He is warned by her to depart with speed, lest the son of Proteus should kill him; and he leaves her with all good wishes for her welfare in return for this service.

69. Πλούτου, scil. οἴκῳ or εἶναι. So with a dative in Aesch. Cho. 10, ποίᾳ ξυμφορᾷ προσεικάσω;

73. εἰκώ. For this form see Med. 1162.

75. ξένῃ. Because it was a sort of motto with the Greeks, ξένον προσχωρεῖν πόλει, Med. 222.—πόδ' for ποτ' is the correction of Faber.

76. πτερῷ, i.e. οἰστῷ. Teucer appears on the stage armed with his bow. As an archer he is represented in the Ajax, in the well-known passage ὁ τοξότης ἔοικεν οὐ σμικρὸν φρονεῖν, κτλ., v. 1120. The old reading, corrected by Elmsley, was πέτρῳ. These words are confused in Aesch. Theb. 673, where the true reading seems to be πέτρων, not πτερῶν. In the present passage the epithet εὔστοχον determines the meaning, which πτερὸν alone could scarcely bear. The proper term for the feathering of an arrow was πτέρωμα, Aesch. frag. 123, whence the whole weapon is poetically called πτερόν.

77. ἀπόλαυσιν εἰκοῦς. 'As a return (benefit) for your resemblance.' The accusative in apposition to the sentence, exactly as Aeschylus has τίνος ἀμπλακίας ποινὰς ὀλέκει; Prom. 575. Cf. Tro. 878, κᾆτ' ἐκεῖ δοῦναι κτανεῖν, ποινὰς ὅσοι τεθνᾶσι. Herc. F. 58—60. Alcest. 7. Hippol. 757. The old reading was ἀπώλλυσ' or ἀπώλεσ' ἵν' εἰκοῦς, emended by Reiske.

78. ὅστις ὤν. For ὅστις εἶ ὃς ἀπεστράφης με.—τί, scil. τί καὶ ἐμὲ στυγεῖς διὰ τὰς ἐκείνης συμφοράς; Examples of the causal dative are given on Heracl. 675. See also Electr. 149. 376, and for ἀποστρέφεσθαί τινα, Iph. T. 801.

81. μισεῖ γάρ. ('However, there was some excuse for my conduct,) for' &c. In the next verse both ἡμῖν and λελεγμένοις seem to be governed by σύγγνωθι, though τὰ λελεγμένα ἡμῖν is also good

ΕΛΕΝΗ. 123

σύγγνωθι δ' ἡμῖν τοῖς λελεγμένοις, γύναι.
ΕΛ. τίς δ' εἶ, πόθεν γῆς τῆσδ' ἐπεστράφης πέδον;
ΤΕ. εἷς τῶν Ἀχαιῶν, ὦ γύναι, τῶν ἀθλίων.
ΕΛ. οὔ τἄρα σ' Ἑλένην εἰ στυγεῖς θαυμαστέον. 85
ἀτὰρ τίς εἶ; πόθεν; τίν' ἐξαυδᾶν σε χρή;
ΤΕ. ὄνομα μὲν ἡμῖν Τεῦκρος, ὁ δὲ φύσας πατὴρ
Τελαμών, Σαλαμὶς δὲ πατρὶς ἡ θρέψασά με.
ΕΛ. τί δῆτα Νείλου τούσδ' ἐπιστρέφει γύας;
ΤΕ. φυγὰς πατρῴας ἐξελήλαμαι χθονός. 90
ΕΛ. τλήμων ἂν εἴης· τίς δέ σ' ἐκβάλλει πάτρας;
ΤΕ. Τελαμὼν ὁ φύσας. τίν' ἂν ἔχοις μᾶλλον φίλον;
ΕΛ. ἐκ τοῦ; τὸ γάρ τοι πρᾶγμα συμφορὰν ἔχει.
ΤΕ. Αἴας μ' ἀδελφὸς ὤλεσ' ἐν Τροίᾳ θανών.
ΕΛ. πῶς; οὔ τί που σῷ φασγάνῳ βίον στερείς; 95
ΤΕ. οἰκεῖον αὐτὸν ὤλεσ' ἅλμ' ἐπὶ ξίφος.
ΕΛ. μανέντ'; ἐπεὶ τίς σωφρονῶν τλαίη τάδ' ἄν;
ΤΕ. τὸν Πηλέως τιν' οἶσθ' Ἀχιλλέα γόνον;
ΕΛ. μνηστήρ ποθ' Ἑλένης ἦλθεν, ὡς ἀκούομεν.
ΤΕ. θανὼν ὅδ' ὅπλων ἔριν ἔθηκε συμμάχοις. 100
ΕΛ. καὶ δὴ τί τοῦτ' Αἴαντι γίγνεται κακόν;
ΤΕ. ἄλλου λαβόντος ὅπλ' ἀπηλλάχθη βίου.

Greek. Compare Heracl. 474, ξένοι, θράσος μοι μηδὲν ἐξόδοις ἐμαῖς προσθῆτε.

84. τῶν Ἀχαιῶν τῶν ἀθλίων. 'One of *those* wretched Argives,' i. e. just mentioned in v. 74. Such is the force of the article, as Hermann has pointed out.

85. οὐ χρὴ θαυμάζειν σε, εἰ στυγεῖς κτλ., is according to the usual idiom, οἶδά σε ὃς εἶ &c. But θαυμάζειν τινὰ is more commonly 'to pay respect to a person,' θαυμάζειν τινὸς 'to be surprised at him.'

86. τίν'. So Herm. and Pflugk for τίνος; ἐξαυδᾶν σε χρή. The verse has been variously emended. Dindorf gives ἀτὰρ τίς εἶ, πόθεν, τίνος σ' αὐδᾶν χρεών; A better reading would have been ἀτὰρ τίς εἶ ποτ', ἢ τίνος σ' αὐδᾶν χρεών; However, such violent alterations carry with them but little probability.

88. Σαλαμίς. The final ἰς is long, as in κηλίς, κόνις, ὄρνις &c., which prevented the poet from writing πατρὶς δὲ Σαλαμὶς ἡ θρέψασά με.

92. τίν' ἂν ἔχοις κτλ. The sense is,

ὑπὸ τῶν φιλτάτων ἐκβέβλημαι, τουτέστι, τοῦ ἐμαυτοῦ πατρός.

93. ἐκ τοῦ; 'From what cause?' *Inf.* 1270, τί δὴ τόδ' Ἑλλὰς νόμιμον ἐκ τίνος σέβει; So ἐκ τῶνδε, 'on this account,' Ion 843. Electr. 31. The reply is, 'It was the death of my brother Ajax at Troy that was my ruin,' because he had not avenged his death as, in the opinion of Telamon, he ought to have done. — τὸ πρᾶγμα κτλ., certainly the banishment of a son by a father involves or implies some serious mishap.

95. βίον is used, where we might have expected βίου, as in Soph. El. 960, πλούτου πατρῴου κτῆσιν ἐστερημένη, and as a man is said ἀφαιρεθῆναί τι.

97. σωφρονῶν. Hermann reads at a venture εὖ φρονῶν. But σώφρων is opposed to μανεὶς in Herc. F. 869, ἀμπνοὰς τ' οὐ σωφρονίζει. See Ion 521. Troad. 350.

100. ὅδ' for δ' is the correction of Portus, also made by Barnes.

R 2

124   ΕΥΡΙΠΙΔΟΥ

ΕΛ. σὺ τοῖς ἐκείνου δῆτα πήμασιν νοσεῖς ;
ΤΕ. ὁθούνεκ' αὐτῷ γ' οὐ ξυνωλόμην ὁμοῦ.
ΕΛ. ἦλθες γὰρ, ὦ ξέν', Ἰλίου κλεινὴν πόλιν ;   105
ΤΕ. καὶ ξύν γε πέρσας αὐτὸς ἀνταπωλόμην.
ΕΛ. ἤδη γὰρ ἧπται καὶ κατείργασται πυρί ;
ΤΕ. ὥστ' οὐδ' ἴχνος γε τειχέων εἶναι σαφές.
ΕΛ. ὦ τλῆμον Ἑλένη, διὰ σ' ἀπόλλυνται Φρύγες.
ΤΕ. καὶ πρός γ' Ἀχαιοί· μεγάλα δ' εἴργασται κακά.   110
ΕΛ. πόσον χρόνον γὰρ διαπεπόρθηται πόλις ;
ΤΕ. ἑπτὰ σχεδόν τι καρπίμους ἐτῶν κύκλους.
ΕΛ. χρόνον δ' ἐμείνατ' ἄλλον ἐν Τροίᾳ πόσον ;
ΤΕ. πολλὰς σελήνας, δέκα διελθούσας ἔτη.
ΕΛ. ἦ καὶ γυναῖκα Σπαρτιᾶτιν εἵλετε ;   115
ΤΕ. Μενέλαος αὐτὴν ἦγ' ἐπισπάσας κόμης.
ΕΛ. εἶδες σὺ τὴν δύστηνον ; ἦ κλύων λέγεις ;
ΤΕ. ὥσπερ σέ γ', οὐδὲν ἧσσον, ὀφθαλμοῖς ὁρῶ.
ΕΛ. σκοπεῖτε μὴ δόκησιν εἴχετ' ἐκ θεῶν.

104. ὁθούνεκ' κτλ. This reply is somewhat παρ' ὑπόνοιαν. The expected answer was to the effect that the death of his brother had been the cause of his own banishment. The sense is, οὕτω νοσῶ, ὥσθ' ἡδέως ἂν ξὺν αὐτῷ ἀπέθανον. A more obvious rejoinder would have been, ὁθούνεκ' αὐτοῦ γ' οὐκ ἐτισάμην φόνου.

107. Agam. 509, Τροίαν κατασκάψαντα τοῦ δικηφόρου Διὸς μακέλλῃ, τῇ κατείργασται πέδον, where however the primary sense of tilling, or upturning with the spade, is preserved. In the next line ὥστ' οὐδὲ is to be noticed for ὥστε μηδέ. Compare Phoen. 1357, οὐ μακρὰν γὰρ τειχέων περιπτυχαί, ὥστ' οὐχ ἅπαντά σ' εἰδέναι τὰ δρώμενα, where, on account of the preceding οὐ, we should perhaps read ὡς μὴ οὐχ ἅπαντα &c. Soph. El. 780, ὥστ' οὔτε νυκτὸς ὕπνον οὔτ' ἐξ ἡμέρας ἐμὲ στεγάζειν ἡδύν. Here Dr. Donaldson, (in No. viii. p. 207, of the Journal of Classical and Sacred Philology,) would read ὕπνος—ἐμ' ἐστέγαζεν ἡδύς. See Shilleto on Dem. De Fals. Leg., Appendix B, p. 204.

111. This verse and v. 773, compared with Ag. 269, ποίου χρόνου δὲ καὶ πεπόρθηται πόλις, well illustrate the difference between 'how long ago,' and 'at what time.' The reply to this is, ἑπτὰ ἔτη, that to the other, τῆς νῦν τεκούσης φῶς τόδ' εὐφρόνης λέγω, 'last night.' Euripides makes the interval seven years, as Hermann observes, because Homer represented Menelaus as having returned to Sparta on the eighth year, Od. iv. 82. His visit to Egypt being prior to that event, the computation is thus accurately kept. See below, v. 775.

117. σύ. Emphatic, as usual, but rather unusually put for σὺ αὐτός. See inf. 850.

118. ὁρῶ. Perhaps ὁρῶν, as Hermann has edited.

119. μὴ εἴχετε. Helen, aware of the unreality of the Trojan Helen, as she had explained in the prologue, exclaims, 'Look to it, whether ye had an imaginary Helen imposed on you by the gods.' See on Ion 1523. Heracl. 481. Plat. Symp. p. 219, A., ἄμεινον σκόπει, μή σε λανθάνω οὐδὲν ὤν. Teucer replies, that he is so certain of it that he cannot bear to hear another word on the subject. 'Do you then,' asks Helen, 'think this opinion of yours so infallibly true ?'—'Why, I saw her myself as clearly as I now see you,' is Teucer's answer. Few will hesitate to accept Hermann's emendation of v. 122, καὶ νῦν σ' ὁρῶ for καὶ νοῦς ὁρᾷ. Dobree proposed ὡς νῦν σ' ὁρῶ, but αὔτως = ὁμοίως (for the

ΕΛΕΝΗ. 125

ΤΕ. ἄλλου λόγου μέμνησο, μὴ κείνης ἔτι. 120
ΕΛ. οὕτω δοκεῖτε τὴν δόκησιν ἀσφαλῆ;
ΤΕ. αὔτως γὰρ ὅσσοις εἰδόμην καὶ νῦν σ' ὁρῶ.
ΕΛ. ἤδη δ' ἐν οἴκοις σὺν δάμαρτι Μενέλεως;
ΤΕ. οὔκουν ἐν Ἄργει γ', οὐδ' ἐπ' Εὐρώτα ῥοαῖς.
ΕΛ. αἰαῖ. κακὸν τόδ' εἶπας οἷς κακὸν λέγεις. 125
ΤΕ. ὡς κεῖνος ἀφανὴς σὺν δάμαρτι κλῄζεται.
ΕΛ. οὐ πᾶσι πορθμὸς αὐτὸς Ἀργείοισιν ἦν;
ΤΕ. ἦν, ἀλλὰ χειμὼν ἄλλοσ' ἄλλον ὤρισεν.
ΕΛ. ποίοισιν ἐν νώτοισι ποντίας ἁλός;
ΤΕ. μέσον περῶσι πέλαγος Αἰγαίου πόρου. 130
ΕΛ. κἀκ τοῦδε Μενέλεων οὔτις οἶδ' ἀφιγμένον;
ΤΕ. οὐδείς· θανὼν δὲ κλῄζεται καθ' Ἑλλάδα.
ΕΛ. ἀπωλόμεσθα· Θεστιὰς δ' ἔστιν κόρη;
ΤΕ. Λήδαν ἔλεξας; οἴχεται θανοῦσα δή.
ΕΛ. οὔ πού νιν Ἑλένης αἰσχρὸν ὤλεσεν κλέος; 135
ΤΕ. φασίν, βρόχῳ γ' ἅψασαν εὐγενῆ δέρην.
ΕΛ. οἱ Τυνδάρειοι δ' εἰσὶν ἢ οὐκ εἰσὶν κόροι;

---

vulg. αὐτοῖς) is necessary to the context, for ὁμοίως καὶ is the usual idiom for 'equally as.' The adverb αὔτως or αὕτως occurs in Med. 319. Soph. Trach. 1040.

124. The γ', added by Musgrave, is as essential to the sense as to the metre; for οὖν—γε is sometimes equivalent to γοῦν. The meaning is, 'Certainly he is not at Argos nor at Sparta' (wherever else he may be). Argos is mentioned as the seat of Agamemnon, and so in a certain sense the οἶκος of Menelaus also.

125. οἷς κακὸν λέγεις. This is a common equivocation when any one wishes to conceal a relationship with another. Helen means, that to Menelaus it is perhaps no such great evil after all, since he may yet touch at Egypt and recover his true wife. Dindorf and Pflugk contend that Helen means herself, who is unknown to Teucer as being the real sufferer by Menelaus' wanderings. But Hermann truly objects, that so far from this being an evil to her, it was much less so than if Menelaus had been safe at Sparta, living in unconscious security with his εἴδωλον.

126. ἀφανής. 'Drowned' A curious euphemism. See on Iph. T. 757. So in describing the same storm Aeschylus says the damaged ships ᾤχοντ' ἄφαντοι, Ag. 640, where see the note. Ibid. v. 607, ἀνὴρ ἄφαντος ἐξ Ἀχαιϊκοῦ στρατοῦ.—κλῄζεται, ibid. v. 614. inf. 132.

128. ἄλλοσ' ἄλλον, sc. πορθμόν. 'A storm marked out one course for some, another for others,' i. e. dispersed them over the sea. That this is the true sense seems probable, because, as Hermann observes, he would have said περῶντας in v. 130, if ἄλλον had meant ναύτην. (The dative might however refer to v. 127.)

131. Μενέλεων is Barnes' reading for Μενέλαον. However, the former word scarcely occurs as a trisyllable, and hence Hermann gives Μενέλαόν τις οἶδ' ἀφιγμένον; Perhaps Μενέλαν (Rhes. 253. Tro. 212) should be restored, though it seems rather a lyric licence than a form for dialogue or narrative.

135. οὔ που Seidler and Dobree for οὔπω. Musgrave read ἦπου. Of the former combination, more commonly οὔτι πω, Dindorf gives many examples. See Electr. 235. 630.

ΕΥΡΙΠΙΔΟΥ

ΤΕ. τεθνᾶσι κοὐ τεθνᾶσι· δύο δ' ἐστὸν λόγω.
ΕΛ. πότερος ὁ κρείσσων ; ὦ τάλαιν' ἐγὼ κακῶν.
ΤΕ. ἄστροις σφ' ὁμοιωθέντε φάσ' εἶναι θεώ. 140
ΕΛ. καλῶς ἔλεξας τοῦτο· θάτερον δὲ τί ;
ΤΕ. σφαγαῖς ἀδελφῆς οὕνεκ' ἐκπνεῦσαι βίον.
ἅλις δὲ μύθων· οὐ διπλᾶ χρῄζω στένειν.
ὧν δ' οὕνεκ' ἦλθον τούσδε βασιλείους δόμους,
τὴν θεσπιῳδὸν Θεονόην χρῄζων ἰδεῖν, 145
σὺ προξένησον, ὡς τύχω μαντευμάτων
ὅπῃ νεὼς στείλαιμ' ἂν οὔριον πτερὸν
ἐς γῆν ἐναλίαν Κύπρον, οὗ μ' ἐθέσπισεν
οἰκεῖν Ἀπόλλων, ὄνομα νησιωτικὸν
Σαλαμῖνα θέμενον τῆς ἐκεῖ χάριν πάτρας. 150
ΕΛ. πλοῦς, ὦ ξέν', αὐτὸς σημανεῖ· σὺ δ' ἐκλιπὼν
γῆν τήνδε φεῦγε, πρίν σε παῖδα Πρωτέως
ἰδεῖν, ὃς ἄρχει τῆσδε γῆς· ἄπεστι δὲ

138. τεθνᾶσι κοὐ τεθνᾶσι. For similar instances of this form of speech, a very favourite one with Euripides, see Preface to Vol. i. p. xxx.
141. θάτερον, scil. τὸ τεθνᾶσι.
142. σφαγαῖς, by suicide. See on Alcest. 772, and compare *inf.* v. 301. This legend is not elsewhere recorded, according to Musgrave.—διπλᾶ, viz. both at the suffering and again at the relation. Compare Hec. 518.
146. The old reading συμπροξένησον, corrected by Jacobs, is wrong, not so much from the form of the compound, though that is rather unusual, but because προξενεῖν is properly applied to those who as it were introduce an applicant to the prophet whom he is visiting, and so guarantee his sincerity of intent,— a precaution very necessary on account of the prodigious treasures stored up in the more celebrated shrines. Compare Oed. Col. 465, ὦ φίλταθ', ὡς νῦν πᾶν τελοῦντι προξένει, 'be my instructor as to what I am to do.' This meaning is especially clear from Androm. 1103, where the messenger, one of a party suspected of sacrilegious designs, comes to sacrifice at the altar σὺν προξένοισι, and one of these asks, ὦ νεανία, τί σοὶ θεῷ κατευξώμεσθα ; They seem, in fact, vicarious applicants to the god, and doubtless not without receiving a gratuity. Ion 333 :—

ΙΩΝ. ποῖόν τι χρῄζουσ' ; ὡς ὑπουργήσω, γύναι.
ΚΡ. μάντευμα κρυπτὸν δεομένῃ Φοίβου μαθεῖν.
ΙΩΝ. λέγοις ἄν· ἡμεῖς τἄλλα προξενήσομεν.

147. ὅπῃ κτλ. 'In what direction (having gone) to a land lying somewhere in these seas, by name Cyprus, I am to furl my sail sped by favouring gales.' Hermann on Hec. 1052 (1080 Dind.), commenting on the similar words λινόκροκον φᾶρος στέλλων, contends that this is the true meaning of the words here and elsewhere. The passage in Aesch. Suppl. 703 is very decisive, αὐτὴ δ' ἡγεμὼν ὑπὸ χθόνα στείλασα λαῖφος παγκρότως ἐρέσσεται. But στέλλειν, when used of a ship generally, (as it perhaps is here,) means 'to equip,' 'to set out on its voyage.' Alcest. 112, ἀλλ' οὐδὲ ναυκληρίαν ἔσθ' ὅποι τις αἶας στείλας, κτλ.—On the use of πτερὰ for *sails* see Med. 1.
150. Σαλαμῖνα. The Salamis in Cyprus was named after Teucer's native island. Hor. i. 7 fin. *Certus enim promisit Apollo Ambiguam tellure nova Salamina futuram.*
151. αὐτὸς σημανεῖ. The meaning is, the way is so clear and easy to find that it does not require to be pointed out. So the Greeks often say αὐτὸ δείξει &c.

ΕΛΕΝΗ. 127

κυσὶν πεποιθὼς ἐν φοναῖς θηροκτόνοις·
κτείνει γὰρ Ἕλλην᾽ ὅντιν᾽ ἂν λάβῃ ξένον.   155
ὅτου δ᾽ ἕκατι, μήτε σὺ ζήτει μαθεῖν
ἐγώ τε σιγῶ· τί γὰρ ἂν ὠφελοῖμί σε;
ΤΕ. καλῶς ἔλεξας, ὦ γύναι. θεοὶ δέ σοι
ἐσθλῶν ἀμοιβὰς ἀντιδωρησαίατο.
Ἑλένῃ δ᾽ ὅμοιον σῶμ᾽ ἔχουσ᾽ οὐ τὰς φρένας 160
ἔχεις ὁμοίας, ἀλλὰ διαφόρους πολύ.
κακῶς δ᾽ ὄλοιτο, μηδ᾽ ἐπ᾽ Εὐρώτα ῥοὰς
ἔλθοι. σὺ δ᾽ εἴης εὐτυχὴς ἀεί, γύναι.
ΕΛ. ὦ μεγάλων ἀχέων καταβαλλομένα μέγαν οἶκτον,
ποῖον ἀμιλλαθῶ γόον; ἢ τίνα μοῦσαν ἐπέλθω,   165

156. ὅτου ἕκατι. The reason, which she could not explain without revealing herself, was, that no one coming from Hellas should attempt to entice away his intended bride.
159. ἐσθλῶν ἀμοιβὰς, 'a return of good,' i. e. consisting in good things. This is one of the formulas of courtesy at parting, Teucer finally leaving the stage at v. 163. His meeting with Helen prepares the spectators to look for the arrival of Menelaus, which occurs at 386. In all other respects it is an episode unconnected with the plot.—For the Ionic termination -ατο for -ντο see Pers. 362. 453. Aj. 842.
164. The monody which follows, answered as it is by the chorus of Spartan captives, belongs to that class of strains which are called *commatic*. There is a similar instance in El. 112. Helen informs her friends of the news she has just heard; the destruction of Troy, the death of her husband. They sympathize with her as one whose fate from the first has been most unfortunate, and enumerate the accumulation of evils which have now been crowned, as it were, by this last and greatest blow, the loss of all her long cherished hopes.
Ibid. καταβαλλομένα. This word, which is rendered 'laying the foundations of,' 'commencing a lamentation for griefs,' is not easily defended by examples from tragic usage, though a few instances are cited by Pflugk and others from later writers. Hermann has no hesitation in admitting Musgrave's reading μεταβαλλομένα, 'taking a great sorrow (viz. the death of Menelaus) in exchange for other grievous woes,' namely, the forced marriage with Theoclymenus. A more probable emendation would be ἀναβαλλομένα, a word technically used of the prelude or air of a song. So Theocr. x. 22, καί τι κόρας φιλικὸν μέλος ἀμβαλεῦ. However, we find in Lucian (Ἔρωτες, p. 458,) οὐκ ἀνέξομαί σου ἄλλην ἀρχὴν καταβαλλομένου τρίτων λόγων. In Diodorus Siculus, (iii. § 62,) μυθογράφων καὶ ποιητῶν τερατώδεις λόγους καταβεβλημένων,—passages which illustrate the very same use of καταβάλλεσθαι which Euripides appears to have adopted.
165. ἀμιλλαθῶ. It is difficult to translate this word, which represents ποίαν γόων ἄμιλλαν ἀμιλληθῶ (cf. v. 387,) or πῶς ἀγωνίζωμαι γόοις; 'what sort of lamentation must I painfully engage in, or what strain must I commence?' The datives which follow are intended to specify the kinds of μοῦσα or dirge which she proposes to adopt. Pflugk translates, *quam naeniam inveniam, quae satis habeat lacrimarum aut lamentorum aut maeroris;* but this cannot be really correct. Rather the sense seems to be, 'Shall it be that expressed by tears alone, or that by dirges, or that by mourning for the dead?' If we inquire the difference between θρῆνοι and πένθη, (both of which are properly used of lamentation for a death,) we must probably conclude, that the former implies the accompaniment of doleful music and beating of the breast, while the latter means exclamations of woe, as αἰαῖ &c.

ΕΥΡΙΠΙΔΟΥ

δάκρυσιν, ἢ θρήνοις, ἢ πένθεσιν;
ἒ ἔ.
πτεροφόροι νεάνιδες,　　　　　　　　　　　στρ. α΄.
παρθένοι Χθονὸς κόραι,
Σειρῆνες, εἴθ᾽ ἐμοῖς γόοις
μόλοιτ᾽ ἔχουσαι Λίβυν　　　　　　　　　　　170
λωτὸν ἢ σύριγγας, αἴλιν᾽ ὃς κακοῖς
τοῖς ἐμοῖσι σύνοχα δάκρυα,
πάθεσι πάθεα, μέλεσι μέλεα,
†μουσεῖά τε θρηνήμασι ξυνῳδὰ
πέμψειε Φερσεφάσσᾳ　　　　　　　　　　　175

167. Helen, struck with consternation at the news she has just heard, of the loss of Menelaus and the suicide of her relations through shame and grief at her supposed ill-conduct, now invokes the aid of the Sirens in singing a sweet and touching strain. There appears to be no further point in the address to these goddesses, if such they were, than because they were traditionally the mistresses of witching song. Compare Androm. 936, κλύουσα τούσδε Σειρήνων λόγους, σοφῶν, πανούργων, ποικίλων λαλημάτων. In like manner the aid of the nightingale is frequently implored by those about to sing doleful lamentations.

170. The old reading was τὸν Λίβυν, and in v. 182, αὐγαῖσιν ἐν ταῖς χρυσέαις. Every well-practised ear will feel the improvement introduced by Hermann, who omits the article in both places. There was no commoner interpolation of grammarians than this. As a general rule it may be stated, that the article is used with *distinctive*, but not with *otiose* or purely poetical epithets, and not at all with mere substantives, unless some degree of emphasis on the particular thing is intended.—αἴλιν᾽ ὃς is Hermann's slight alteration for αἰλίνοις. The ὃς refers to λωτόν, the words ἢ σύριγγας being added without breaking the intended syntax. To Hermann also the dative Φερσεφάσσᾳ is due in place of the nominative. Translate, 'Ye winged maidens, virgin daughters of Earth, would that ye could come to my griefs, bringing with you the Libyan flute or the pan-pipes, which (flute) might convey to Proserpine songs of woe, tears suited to my misfortunes, sufferings upon sufferings, strains upon strains, and melodies consonant with dirges,—melodies of death (φόνια), in order that she (Proserpine) may receive as a favour from me, with my tears, paeans to the departed dead in her gloomy palace below.' Helen means, that she wishes she could convey to her relations in Hades, (i. e. those who have died by suicide, to whom the epithet φόνια alludes,) a song or dirge of the dead, which she calls a *paean* by a common euphemism; see on Aesch. Theb. 862, Ἅιδᾳ ἐχθρὸν παιᾶν᾽ ἐπιμέλπειν. Troad. 1230, νεκρῶν Ἴακχον. Such dirges were considered acceptable to those below; and hence they are called χάριτες to Proserpine. Compare Aesch. Cho. 313, χάριτες δ᾽ ὁμοίως κέκληνται γόος εὐκλεὴς προσθοδόμοις Ἀτρείδαις, where the Schol. remarks, χάριτας δὲ νεκρῶν πάντες φασὶ τὸν γόον.—ἐπὶ δάκρυσι, σὺν δάκρυσι or διὰ δακρύων. The same expression occurs in Troad. 316.

174. μουσεῖα. This word is marked as corrupt, for it means 'a place of song' inf. 1108, and in those elegant lines, πολὺς δ᾽ ἀνεῖρπε κισσός, εὐφυὴς κλάδος, χελιδόνων μουσεῖα, frag. Alcmen. 91. Hermann ingeniously reads Μύσι᾽, ἅτ᾽ ἒ ἒ | θρηνήμασι ξυνῳδά, quoting Aesch. Pers. 1033, καὶ στέρν᾽ ἄρασσε, καὶ βόα τὸ Μύσιον, i. e. in the tone of Mysian mourners. He might have added, what is equally to the purpose, ἔκοψα κομμὸν Ἄριον, 'I strike my breast like an Arian mourner,' Choeph. 415. Matthiae's explanation, re-echoed by his follower Pflugk, 'may Proserpine send a company of mourners,' i. e. the same Sirens, must yield in probability to Hermann's emendation.

ΕΛΕΝΗ.

φόνια, φόνια, χάριτας ἵν' ἐπὶ
δάκρυσι παρ' ἐμέθεν ὑπὸ μέλαθρα
νύχια παιᾶνας
νέκυσιν ὀλομένοις λάβῃ.

ΧΟΡΟΣ.

κυανοειδὲς ἀμφ' ὕδωρ   ἀντ. α'.
ἔτυχον ἕλικά τ' ἀνὰ χλόαν   180
φοίνικας ἁλίῳ πέπλους
αὐγαῖσιν ἐν χρυσέαις
ἀμφιθάλπουσ' ἔν τε δόνακος ἔρνεσιν·
ἔνθεν οἰκτρὸν ἀνεβόασεν,
ὅμαδον †ἔκλυον, ἄλυρον ἔλεγον,   185
ὅ τι ποτ' ἔλακεν αἰάγμασι στένουσα,
Νύμφα τις οἷα Ναῒς
ὄρεσι φυγάδα νόμον ἰεῖσα

---

178. Dindorf and Pflugk wrongly omit the word παιᾶνας, the force and meaning of which have been already explained.
179. The wish of Helen, that the Sirens might come to aid her in singing, is in a manner realised by the approach of the chorus, who respond antithetically to her monody. They were engaged (like the informant of the chorus in Hippol. 122 seqq.) in the washing and drying of the clothes belonging to the palace, when the noise of woe reached them like the echo from some mountain nymph in distress at being pursued by the amorous Pan. There is great beauty in this antistrophe, which may be rendered as follows: —' By the dark water and over the twining herbage I happened at the time to be drying (literally, 'warming on both sides') purple garments in the sun under his golden rays; and upon the young shoots of the reeds, where (literally 'whence,' but the Greek ideas of *at a place* and *from a place* are often curiously interchanged,) some one shrieked a piteous lament, a joyless strain, whatever it was that she uttered, groaning with exclamations of grief, like some Naiad nymph on the mountains sending forth a woeful song in her flight, and the deep rocky valleys re-echo to her cries the violence offered by Pan.'—κυανοειδὲς is explained by Pflugk *sea-water*. But the mention of reeds, which are fresh-water plants, and the poet's care in particularizing sweet spring water for washing purple clothes in Hippol. 123, seem to show that the latter is meant.

181. ἁλίῳ. So Herm. for ἁλίῳ or ἁλίου. See above on v. 170.—Musgrave shows, from Pollux 1. 49, that the chemical effect of the sunlight on garments dyed with the sea-purple is to refresh and heighten the hues. Hippol. 125, ὅθι μοί τις ἦν φίλα | φάρεα πορφύρεα | ποταμίᾳ δρόσῳ | τέγγουσα, θερμᾶς δ' ἐπὶ νῶτα πέτρας | εὐαλίου κατέβαλλε. From this property of the sea-purple Aeschylus calls it κηκὶς παγκαίνιστος, Agam. 933, capable of being entirely renewed when faded.

185. ἔκλυον. This word is clearly corrupt. Some epithet to ὅμαδον is lost. Hermann edits ὅμαδον ὀλοόν, and perhaps no more probable word could be suggested. Matthiae's idea, that this verse is a parenthesis, is deserving of little credit, though Pflugk as usual accepts it. The old editions put a full stop after ἀνεβόασεν.

188. νόμον. So Musgrave for γάμον. In the next verse μύχατα is Canter's correction for μύχαλα. Dindorf omits the word as a gloss, but it is necessary even for the metre.—κλαγγαῖσιν is Hermann's reading for κλαγγάς. This word is only found in one Florentine MS., and has been overlooked or disregarded by the

VOL. II.   S

ΕΥΡΙΠΙΔΟΥ

γοερὸν, ὑπὸ δὲ πέτρινα μύχατα
γύαλα κλαγγαῖσιν
Πανὸς ἀναβοᾷ γάμους. 190
ΕΛ. ἰὼ ἰώ. στρ. β'.
θήραμα βαρβάρου πλάτας,
Ἑλλανίδες κόραι,
ναύτας Ἀχαιῶν τις ἔμολεν ἔμολε,
δάκρυα δάκρυσί μοι φέρων, 195
Ἰλίου κατασκαφὰν
πυρὶ μέλουσαν δαΐῳ
δι' ἐμὲ τὰν πολυκτόνον,
δι' ἐμὸν ὄνομα πολύπονον.
Λήδα δ' ἐν ἀγχόναις 200
θάνατον ἔλαβεν
αἰσχύνας ἐμᾶς ὑπ' ἀλγέων.
ὁ δ' ἐμὸς ἐν ἁλὶ πολυπλανὴς
πόσις ὀλόμενος οἴχεται,
Κάστορός τε συγγόνου τε 205

editors in general. By its restoration both the sense and the metre of the strophic verse are satisfactorily recovered.

191. Helen replies to their inquiry (for such it virtually is) about the cause of her grief. 'Ye maidens of Hellas, captives of a foreign crew, a sailor of the Argive army hath come bringing me tearful tidings in addition to my present griefs, that the destruction of Troy hath been effected by hostile fire, all through me, the author of many deaths, and through my name, the cause of so much toil.' We may notice in this passage, as *inf.* 640, 650, 1117, Phoen. 1030—7, that repetition of words which Aristophanes ridicules in Ran. 1352, ὁ δ' ἀνέπτατ' ἀνέπτατ' ἐς αἰθέρα | κουφοτάταις πτερύγων ἀκμαῖς· | ἐμοὶ δ' ἄχε· ἄχεα κατέλιπε, | δάκρυα δάκρυα δ' ἀπ' ὀμμάτων | ἔβαλον ἔβαλον ἁ τλάμων. It is one of the indications of the later style of the poet, and though occasionally it conveys a becoming emphasis, it becomes tiresome when too commonly introduced.

197. μέλουσαν. Troy has been left to the mercy of fire; it is a *care to fire* to complete its destruction. Hermann transposes Ἰλίου and δαΐῳ, on account of the metre; but the ν in κύκνου (v. 216) may be scanned as a long syllable, and the old reading is commended by a more natural order of the words. Perhaps indeed, as the narrative in v. 200 and 203 is *direct*, i. e. not depending on φέρων, we should here also adopt the same construction, Ἰλίου κατασκαφὰ πυρὶ μέλουσα δαΐῳ, for μέλουσά ἐστι.

202. ἄλγος αἰσχύνας, 'grief at my shame,' is the same idiom as πένθος τινὸς, 'mourning for a person,' on which see Alc. 336, στοναχὰς τεκέων Androm. 1037, &c. Teucer had said (v. 135) that the cause of Leda's death was αἰσχρὸν Ἑλένης κλέος.

205. Κάστορός τε κτλ. 'And the twin ornaments of their country, Castor and his brother, disappearing have left the steed-trampled plains and the exercising-grounds of the reedy Eurotas, the toil of their youth.' So Hippolytus is lamented as no longer destined to practise his horses in their wonted course, Hipp. 1131.—νεανίαν, here for an adjective; see on νεανίας λόγους Alc. 679. Pflugk quotes Propert. iii. 12, 17, 'Qualis et Eurotae Pollux et Castor arenis, Hic victor pugnis, ille futurus equis.'

ΕΛΕΝΗ. 131

διδυμογενὲς ἄγαλμα πατρίδος
ἀφανὲς ἀφανὲς ἱππόκροτα λέλοιπε δάπεδα
γυμνάσιά τε δονακόεντος
Εὐρώτα, νεανίαν πόνον.
ΧΟ. αἰαῖ αἰαῖ. ἀντ. β'. 210
ὦ δαίμονος πολυστόνου
μοίρας τε σᾶς, γύναι.
αἰὼν δυσαίων τις ἔλαχεν ἔλαχεν,
ὅτε σε τέκετο ματρόθεν
Ζεὺς πρέπων δι' αἰθέρος 215
χιονόχρως κύκνου πτερῷ·
τί γὰρ ἄπεστί σοι κακῶν;
τίνα δὲ βίοτον οὐκ ἔτλας;
μάτηρ μὲν οἴχεται,
δίδυμά τε Διὸς 220
οὐκ εὐδαιμονεῖ τέκεα φίλα,
χθόνα δὲ πάτριον οὐχ ὁρᾷς,
διὰ δὲ πόλεας ἔρχεται
βάξις, ἅ σε βαρβάροισι
λέχεσι, πότνια, παραδίδωσιν, 225
ὁ δὲ σὸς ἐν ἁλὶ κύμασί τε λέλοιπε βίοτον,
οὐδέ ποτ' ἔτι πάτρια μέλαθρα
καὶ τὰν Χαλκίοικον ὀλβιεῖς.
ΕΛ. φεῦ, τίς ἦν Φρυγῶν, τίς ἦν, στρ. γ'.

214. ὅτε κτλ., from the first hour of your birth.—τέκετο. The middle voice sometimes means 'to beget,' because the male 'has a child born to him.' So of the poison from the wounds of the Centaur Nessus, inflicted by an arrow dipped in the Hydra's venom, Soph. Trach. 834, ὃν τέκετο Θάνατος ἔτεκε δ' αἰόλος δράκων. For the legend alluded to see inf. v. 258.
221. οὐκ εὐδαιμονεῖ for ἀθλίως τεθνᾶσι. See v. 142.
224. βαρβάροισι λέχεσι is the same as βαρβάρῳ πόσει, viz. Paris; and hence ὁ σὸς in the next verse naturally means, by contrast, 'your own husband Menelaus.'
228. Χαλκίοικον. The goddess Athena of the Brazen Temple at Sparta. Thucyd.

i. 134. Pausan. iii. 17, 3, ἐνταῦθα (viz. on the low acropolis) Ἀθηνᾶς ἱερὸν πεποίηται, Πολιούχου καλουμένης καὶ Χαλκιοίκου τῆς αὐτῆς. τοῦ δὲ ἱεροῦ τῆς κατασκευῆς Τυνδάρεως, καθὰ λέγουσιν, ἤρξατο.—Λακεδαιμόνιοι πολλοῖς ἔτεσιν ὕστερον τόν τε ναὸν ὁμοίως καὶ ἄγαλμα ἐποιήσαντο Ἀθηνᾶς χαλκοῦν. Either from this statue, or from the joints of the squared stones externally being inlaid with brass, (after the manner described by Sir Charles Fellows, in p. 84 of his Travels in Asia Minor,) the title of Chalcioecus may have been derived. See however Troad. 1112, where she is χαλκόπυλος θεά, as if from the bronze gates of her temple.
229 seqq. The concluding part of this ode is commonly called the epodus, a term

s 2

τὰν δακρυόεσσαν Ἰλίῳ τε πεύκαν 230
*ὃς ἔτεμε τοῖς θ' Ἑλλανίας ἀπὸ χθονός;
ἔνθεν ὀλόμενον σκάφος
ὁ Πριαμίδας συναρμόσας
ἔπλευσε βαρβάρῳ πλάτᾳ
τὰν ἐμὰν ἐφ' ἑστίαν, 235
ἐπὶ τὸ δυστυχές *τε κάλλος
ὡς γάμον ἐμὸν, ἅ τε δόλιος
ἁ πολυκτόνος Κύπρις
Δαναΐδαις θάνατον ἄγουσα Πριαμίδαις τε.
ὦ τάλαινα συμφορᾶς. 240

which is too often conveniently applied to verses which critics cannot reduce to any regular antithetical method of scanning. Hermann pronounces it "apertissime antistrophica," and thinks the corruptions that occur in it have arisen from the archetypus MS. being in this place difficult to decypher, so that some licence was left to the transcriber's conjecture. To Mr. Burges, in his Appendix to the Troades, p. 151, is due the credit of first perceiving that these verses were antistrophic; but his attempts at emendation are less successful than Hermann's. The readings of the latter critic are accordingly given in the text, as none of his corrections are so violent as to exceed a high degree of probability.

229. The old reading, destitute alike of sense and metre, was φεῦ. φεῦ. τίς ἦν Φρυγῶν; ἦ τίς Ἑλλανίας ἀπὸ χθονὸς, ἔτεμε τὰν δακρυόεσσαν Ἰλίῳ πεύκαν. Not to say that the construction should have been τίς ἦν Φρυγῶν ὁ τεμὼν or ὃς ἔτεμε, (as W. Dindorf observes, himself proposing τίς ἢ Φρυγῶν,) it was an absurdity to ask who of the Trojans or *who of the Greeks* built Paris' ships. Dindorf would explain this, "*quis tandem mortalium.* Nam duo genera hominum distinguere Græci solent, Græcos et barbaros." But the man's name was recorded by Homer, Il. v. 59 seqq.

Μηριόνης δὲ Φέρεκλον ἐνήρατο, τέκτονος υἱόν
Ἁρμονίδεω, ὃς χερσὶν ἐπίστατο δαίδαλα πάντα,—
ὃς καὶ Ἀλεξάνδρῳ τεκτήνατο νῆας ἐΐσας ἀρχεκάκους, αἳ πᾶσι κακὸν Τρώεσσι γένοντο.

Now, that Euripides had this passage in view is probable, because τὰν δακρυόεσσαν Ἰλίῳ contains the same sentiment as the last verse. At all events the passage must have been familiar to him; and if so, he was hardly likely to have put such a question in the mouth of Helen, who might indeed have been ignorant of the name of the Trojan, but could hardly have been so of one of her own countrymen. The insertion of ὃς, which is necessary to the sense, and the change of τίς into τοῖς θ', are but slight alterations.

233. The present editor is responsible for transposing the words συναρμόσας ὁ Πριαμίδας, on account of the antistrophic verse.

236. Hermann has added τε before κάλλος, and in the next verse omitted ἕλοι before γάμον. He regards the verb as having been added by some one who failed to perceive that ὡς γάμον meant ὡς ἐς γάμον. It may also have been a mere mistake arising from ἐμὸν, Λ and Μ, and the final Ι and Ν, being often confused. W. Dindorf here suggests a sweeping measure of reform, "delenda haec verba, quae manifestum, si quod aliud, additamentum interpretis sunt, compositum fortasse ex versibus prologi 27—30."— ἅ τε δόλιος Matth. and Herm. for ἁ δὲ δόλιος. Supply ἔπλευσε, and compare Tro. 940, where Paris is said to have come οὐχὶ μικρὰν θεὸν ἔχων αὐτοῦ μέτα, and Agam. 675, where ἔπλευσαν is understood in precisely a similar sentence. See also on v. 1309 *inf.*

239. θάνατον ἄγουσα Herm. for ἄγουσα θάνατον.

ΕΛΕΝΗ. 133

ἁ δὲ χρυσέοις θρόνοις   ἀντ. γ΄.
*ἁ Διὸς ὑπαγκάλισμα σεμνὸν Ἥρα
τὸν ὠκύπουν ἔπεμψε Μαιάδος γόνον,
ὅς με χλοερὰ δρεπομέναν
ῥόδεά τε πέταλ᾽ ἔσω πέπλων
τὰν Χαλκίοικον ὡς μόλοιμ᾽,   245
ἁρπάσας δι᾽ αἰθέρος
τάνδε γαῖαν εἰς ἄνολβον
ἔριν ἔριν τάλαιναν ἔθετο
Πριαμίδαισιν Ἑλλάδος.
τὸ δ᾽ ἐμὸν ὄνομα παρὰ Σιμουντίοις ῥοαῖσι   250
μαψίδιον ἔχει φάτιν.
ΧΟ. ἔχεις μὲν ἀλγείν᾽, οἶδα· σύμφορον δέ τοι
ὡς ῥᾷστα τἀναγκαῖα τοῦ βίου φέρειν.
ΕΛ. φίλαι γυναῖκες, τίνι πότμῳ συνεζύγην;   255
ἆρ᾽ ἡ τεκοῦσά μ᾽ ἔτεκεν ἀνθρώποις τέρας;
γυνὴ γὰρ οὔθ᾽ Ἑλληνὶς οὔτε βάρβαρος
τεῦχος νεοσσῶν λευκὸν ἐκλοχεύεται,
ἐν ᾧ με Λήδαν φασὶν ἐκ Διὸς τεκεῖν.
τέρας γὰρ ὁ βίος καὶ τὰ πράγματ᾽ ἐστί μοι,   260
τὰ μὲν δι᾽ Ἥραν, τὰ δὲ τὸ κάλλος αἴτιον.

242. Hermann adds ἁ in this verse, and reads ἐν δὲ for ἡ δὲ in 241. The epithet applied by Homer to Hera is χρυσόθρονος.
245. ὡς μόλοιμ᾽. She was gathering flowers into her lap that she might go with an offering to the temple of Athena. Cf. Hipp. 73. Ion 889. Before the verb the gloss Ἀθάναν is found in the old copies. It is rightly omitted by Hermann; compare v. 228. Dindorf again grows impatient, and proposes to strike out as a gloss χαλκίοικον ὡς Ἀθάναν μόλοιμ᾽, which he contends will neither scan nor make sense. —In the next verse Herm. gives ἁρπάσας for ἀναρπάσας. The meaning is, 'having hurried me through the air to this unblest land of Egypt, he caused an unhappy quarrel (or, made me the unhappy one a cause of quarrel) between Hellas and the sons of Priam,' i. e. he left the εἴδωλον of Helen to be an object of contention. Pflugk, "de qua Graecia cum Priamidis certaret: cf. v. 1134, ἔριν Δαναῶν νεφέλαν."

251. μαψίδιον, because in fact she had never been at Troy at all.
252. τοι, the usual particle in sententious remarks, is L. Dindorf's reading for σοι. If we retain the latter, that which ought to be a general reflection becomes a tame truism in a limited and particular application.
256. τέρας. The argument is, the origin of her life in being born from an egg, and her subsequent strange adventures, seem to show that she was destined to be regarded as something portentous by mankind.—τεῦχος νεοσσῶν, a happy expression for ᾠόν. Zeus had visited Leda in the form of a swan, sup. v. 216. Apollodor. iii. 10, 7. This wonderful egg was shown in the time of Pausanias at Sparta, in the temple of Hιλάιρα and Phoebe, iii. 16, 2, ἐνταῦθα ἀνήρτηται ᾠὸν τοῦ ὀρόφου κατειλημένον ταινίαις. εἶναι δέ φασιν ᾠὸν ἐκεῖνο, ὃ τεκεῖν Λήδαν ἔχει λόγος.
261. δι᾽ Ἥραν. See v. 31.

εἴθ' ἐξαλειφθεῖσ', ὡς ἄγαλμ', αὖθις πάλιν
αἴσχιον εἶδος ἀντὶ τοῦ καλοῦ λάβοιν,
καὶ τὰς τύχας μὲν τὰς κακὰς, ἃς νῦν ἔχω,
Ἕλληνες ἐπελάθοντο, τὰς δὲ μὴ κακὰς   265
ἔσωζον ὥσπερ τὰς κακὰς σώζουσί μου.
ὅστις μὲν οὖν ἐς μίαν ἀποβλέπων τύχην
πρὸς θεῶν κακοῦται, βαρὺ μὲν, οἰστέον δ' ὅμως·
ἡμεῖς δὲ πολλαῖς συμφοραῖς ἐγκείμεθα.
πρῶτον μὲν, οὐκ οὖσ' ἄδικος, εἰμὶ δυσκλεής.   270
καὶ τοῦτο μεῖζον τῆς ἀληθείας κακὸν,
ὅστις τὰ μὴ προσόντα κέκτηται κακά.
ἔπειτα πατρίδος θεοί μ' ἀφιδρύσαντο γῆς
ἐς βάρβαρ' ἤθη, καὶ φίλων τητωμένη
δούλη καθέστηκ', οὖσ' ἐλευθέρων ἄπο·   275
τὰ βαρβάρων γὰρ δοῦλα πάντα πλὴν ἑνός.
ἄγκυρα δ' ἥ μου τὰς τύχας ὤχει μόνη,

262. ἐξαλειφθεῖσα, wiped out, obliterated, like a portrait, ἄγαλμα. The verb was technically used in this sense, as the present editor has shown on Aesch. Ag. 1299.—λάβοιν, for λάβοιμι, is Hermann's correction of λάβω or λαβεῖν, both of which are false Greek. The form is acknowledged as Euripidean by the Etym. M. in v. τρέφοιν (Eur. frag. 1045,) ἄφρων ἂν εἴην, εἰ τρέφοιν τὰ τῶν πέλας. So also frag. Erechth. 353, v. 6, πρῶτα μὲν πόλιν Οὐκ ἄν τιν' ἄλλην τῆσδε βελτίω λάβοιν. See on Troad. 226. Dindorf gives ἀντὶ τοῦ καλοῦ 'λαβον, after Porson, because the following indicatives ἐπελάθοντο and ἔσωζον suit the aorist better. But a correct translation makes the meaning clear enough: 'Would that being expunged like a painting, I could take again (as if by a second sketch) a plainer appearance instead of this comely one, and that the Greeks had forgot the evil incidents, which at present I am forced to bear, and were now remembering such as have been not amiss, (viz. her fidelity to Menelaus,) in the same degree as they do remember the bad.' She would be content, that is, to lose her far-famed beauty, if only the Greeks could do justice to her much-maligned character. Of course, she speaks of the εἴδωλον as having incurred the blame which they remember, but of herself as having all along been virtuous.

267. ἀποβλέπων. Having his whole thoughts centered on one fortune; for on that he will consider his happiness to depend, and yet if he fails in it, he has further hope. Compare Med. 247, ἡμῖν δ' ἀνάγκη πρὸς μίαν ψυχὴν βλέπειν. It is clear that μίαν and πολλαῖς are opposed. — οἰστέον, tolerabile rather than tolerandum, as Pflugk has pointed out.

272. κέκτηται, possesses the reputation of &c. So Med. 218, δύσκλειαν ἐκτήσαντο καὶ ῥαθυμίαν. By μεῖζον τῆς ἀληθείας she means, μεῖζον τοῦ ἀληθῶς προσόντα κεκτῆσθαι. It is harder, she thinks, to bear an unjust charge, than one which we are conscious of deserving. The one provokes a virtuous indignation; to the latter the really guilty are tolerably indifferent.

276. πλὴν ἑνός. One is the βασιλεὺς or τύραννος, all the rest are not only his subjects, but his slaves.

277. The old reading, ἄγκυρα δή μου τὰς τύχας ὀχεῖ μόνη, is retained by Pflugk and Matthiae; but this leaves an awkward asyndeton in the sentence. Hermann and Dindorf rightly admit the corrections of Scaliger and Musgrave. For the phrase ἐπ' ἐλπίδος ὀχεῖσθαι see Equit. 1241, Hec. 80, and for the anchor as the symbol of hope, Agam. 488. 'The hope that alone sustained my for-

πόσιν ποθ' ἥξειν καί μ' ἀπαλλάξειν κακῶν,
οὗτος τέθνηκεν, οὗτος οὐκέτ' ἔστι δή.
μήτηρ δ' ὄλωλε, καὶ φονεὺς αὐτῆς ἐγὼ 280
ἀδίκως μέν, ἀλλὰ τἄδικον τοῦτ' ἔστ' ἐμόν·
ἣ δ' ἀγλάϊσμα δωμάτων ἐμοῦ τ' ἔφυ,
θυγάτηρ ἄνανδρος πολιὰ παρθενεύεται·
τὼ τοῦ Διὸς δὲ λεγομένω Διοσκόρω
οὐκ ἐστόν. ἀλλὰ πάντ' ἔχουσα δυστυχῆ 285
τοῖς πράγμασιν τέθνηκα, τοῖς δ' ἔργοισιν οὔ.
τὸ δ' ἔσχατον τοῦτ', εἰ μόλοιμεν ἐς πάτραν,
κλήθροις ἂν εἰργοίμεσθα, τὴν ὑπ' Ἰλίῳ
δοκοῦντες Ἑλένην Μενέλεώ μ' ἐλθεῖν μέτα.
εἰ μὲν γὰρ ἔζη πόσις, ἀνεγνώσθημεν ἂν 290
ἐς ξύμβολ' ἐλθόνθ', ἃ φανέρ' ἂν μόνοις ἂν ἦν.

tunes,' says Helen, 'that my husband would return some day and rid me of my troubles,—this husband is dead; he is no longer existing, it seems.' Hermann's correction, εἴπερ τέθνηκεν οὗτος, 'if he is really dead,' is highly ingenious and probable, for these reasons; (1) it saves a tautology; (2) it gives a verb to ἄγκυρα, instead of assuming another nominative οὗτος, (3) it avoids a repetion of the pronoun which is weak and unmeaning.— There is a reading ἀπαλλάξαι, good in itself, and preferred by Pflugk. Its force would be, ' to rid me at once and for ever from my troubles,' as Aesch. Eum. 83, ὥστ' ἐς τὸ πᾶν σε τῶνδ' ἀπαλλάξαι πόνων.

281. ἀδίκως. As this Helen is assumed not to have been the cause of all the evils, but only her εἴδωλον, it follows that νομίζομαι is to be understood with φονεύς. Compare v. 53.—τἄδικον τοῦτο, this unjust charge has to be borne by me; ἐμόν ἐστι, καίπερ ἀληθῶς ἀλλότριον ὄν.

283. πολιά. Hermann, in a good philological note, denies that πολιά can here stand for πολιῶς, and accordingly he reads πολιὰ παρθενεύματα. He lays it down as a law, that " adverbia non rerum, sed actionum praedicata sunt: quare quod in actionem non cadit, id neque adverbio nec vocabulo potestatem habente adverbii significari potest. Hinc colorum appellationes carent adverbiis, nisi quum non proprio significatu usurpantur, ut ab Latinis candide. Nec juvenem quisquam μελάνως ἡβᾶν, nec senem λευκῶς γηράσκειν dixit." These remarks appear to be true. But in fact πολιά is an adjective agreeing with a cognate accusative understood, πολιὰ παρθενεύματα παρθενεύεται, which simply means, that Hermione is growing old in her virginity,— i. e. according to the Greek notions of old as applied to marriageable women. See on Ion v. 700.

285. ἀλλὰ κτλ. ' (So I have none left to live for,) but, being altogether unfortunate, I am dead in my affairs, though not through my own deeds.' Here πράγμασιν appears to stand for τοῖς πάθεσι, or rather, perhaps, for τοῖς πεπραγμένοις generally, contrasted with τοῖς ὑπ' ἐμοῦ εἰργασμένοις specifically. Dindorf compares τὰ πράγματα in v. 260. So in Bacch. 369 and Suppl. 747, quoted by Pflugk.

289. δοκοῦντες. As if she had said, εἴργοιέν με for εἰργοίμεσθα. Similarly Heracl. 39, δυοῖν γερόντοιν δὲ στρατηγεῖται φυγή· ἐγὼ μὲν ἀμφὶ τοῖσδε καλχαίνων τέκνοις κτλ. The sense is, ' Thinking that if I were the Helen at Troy, I should have returned with my husband.' As she supposes she cannot now do this, she fears that if she should return alone to Sparta, she would be imprisoned as an impostor.

291. ἐς ξύμβολ' ἐλθόνθ'. ' Having recourse to tokens, which would have been known to us alone.' Med. 613, ξένοις τε πέμπειν ξύμβολ', οἳ δράσουσί σ' εὖ, where see the note. Barnes very appositely

νῦν δ' οὔτε τοῦτ' ἔστ' οὔτε μὴ σωθῇ ποτέ.
τί δῆτ' ἔτι ζῶ ; τίν' ὑπολείπομαι τύχην ;
γάμους ἑλομένη τῶν κακῶν ὑπαλλαγὰς,
μετ' ἀνδρὸς οἰκεῖν βαρβάρου, πρὸς πλουσίαν   295
τράπεζαν ἵζουσ' ; ἀλλ' ὅταν πόσις πικρὸς
ξυνῇ γυναικὶ, καὶ τὸ σῶν ἐστὶν πικρόν.
θανεῖν κράτιστον· πῶς θάνοιμ' ἂν οὖν καλῶς ;
ἀσχήμονες μὲν ἀγχόναι μετάρσιοι,
κἂν τοῖσι δούλοις δυσπρεπὲς νομίζεται,   300
σφαγαὶ δ' ἔχουσιν εὐγενές τι καὶ καλὸν,
σμικρὸν δ' ὁ καιρὸς σάρκ' ἀπαλλάξαι βίου.
ἐς γὰρ τοσοῦτον ἤλθομεν βάθος κακῶν·

quotes Od. xxiii. 109, where Penelope says of herself and her husband, ἦ μάλα νῶι Γνωσόμεθ' ἀλλήλων καὶ λώιον, ἔστι γὰρ ἡμῖν Σήμαθ', ἃ δὴ καὶ νῶι κεκρυμμένα ἴδμεν ἀπ' ἄλλων. The old reading was εἰς ξύμβολ' ἐλθόντες ἃ κτλ., the unrhythmical sound of which condemns it as corrupt. The only objection to that in the text, which is Porson's (on Orest. 51) is the somewhat unusual repetition of ἂν with an imperfect tense.—ἐλθόντ' seems best taken for ἐλθόντε, viz. the husband and wife, who would have attested each other's identity, sooner or later, if called in question by the Spartans. Hermann seems to take it for ἐλθόντες, by an irregular construction like that in the preceding distich, for he immediately adds, " nam ἀνεγνώσθημεν de sola Helena a Spartanis agnoscenda dictum." It would have been simpler, he says, to write εἰς ξύμβολ' ἐλθοῦσ' οἷς φανερὰ μόνοις ἂν ἦν. If however ἐλθόντε is the dual, it does not seem possible to refer it to any but Helen and her husband. The accusative ἐλθόντα, even if grammatically defensible, could only have referred to Menelaus, which is contrary to the sense of the passage.

292. οὐ μὴ σωθῇ. See the note on Heracl. 384. The sense, as usual, is ' nor is there a chance of his safe return some future day.'

293. ὑπολείπομαι, *mihi relictam habeo*. In the next verse Hermann defends ὑπαλλαγὰς against the alteration of Matthiae, ἀπαλλαγὰς, admitted by Pflugk and W. Dindorf. Translate, ' Is it in reserve for me, having chosen marriage as an alternative (properly, an exchange) of misfortunes, to live with a foreign husband, taking my seat at a rich table ?' i. e. with an Egyptian, who is also a king.

297. καὶ τὸ σῶν Seidler for καὶ τὸ σῶμ'. 'When a husband who is the object of her dislike cohabits with a wife, even security itself is embittered.' In attempting a translation, we must sacrifice the repetition of πικρὸς, the meaning of which is, that the πικρότης of the man imparts πικρότης to an otherwise happy lot in life.

301. σφαγαὶ, stabbing by the sword. See v. 142, Heracl. 583, and on Hippol. 772. In the next verse the old copies give ἄρτ'. Boissonade κάρτ', followed by Dindorf. An emendation of C. Keil's, recorded by Hermann, is ἄρθρ'. Hermann himself gives σάρκ', and the same correction occurred independently to the present editor. Pflugk retains the evidently corrupt ἄρτ' without a word of critical comment. The poet probably used σάρκα in place of πνεῦμα, because he had in mind the flesh-wounds implied by σφαγαί. *Inf.* 356, αὐτοσίδαρον ἔσω πελάσω διὰ σαρκὸς ἄμιλλαν.—σμικρὸν, scil. χρῆμα ἐστὶν, ' the moment of separating the body from life is a trifling matter;' not a thing to be weighed against the endurance of ill. The Greeks highly applauded that sort of firmness and resolution which could deal the fatal blow, but did not generally estimate that much greater courage which makes men dare to live on in apparently hopeless misery. Euripides has a fine sentiment on this subject in Frag. 895.

ΕΛΕΝΗ.

αἱ μὲν γὰρ ἄλλαι διὰ τὸ κάλλος εὐτυχεῖς
γυναῖκες, ἡμᾶς δ' αὐτὸ τοῦτ' ἀπώλεσεν.   305
ΧΟ. Ἑλένη, τὸν ἐλθόνθ', ὅστις ἐστὶν ὁ ξένος,
μὴ πάντ' ἀληθῆ δοξάσῃς εἰρηκέναι.
ΕΛ. καὶ μὴν σαφῶς γ' ἔλεξ' ὀλωλέναι πόσιν.
ΧΟ. πόλλ' ἂν γένοιτο καὶ διὰ ψευδῶν σαφῆ.
ΕΛ. καὶ τἄμπαλίν γε τῶνδ' ἀληθείας ἔπη.   310
ΧΟ. ἐς ξυμφορὰν γὰρ ἀντὶ τἀγαθοῦ φέρει.
ΕΛ. φόβος γὰρ ἐς τὸ δεῖμα περιβαλών μ' ἄγει.
ΧΟ. πῶς δ' εὐμενείας τοισίδ' ἐν δόμοις ἔχεις;
ΕΛ. πάντες φίλοι μοι πλὴν ὁ θηρεύων γάμους.
ΧΟ. οἶσθ' οὖν ὃ δρᾶσον; μνήματος λιποῦσ' ἕδραν,   315
ΕΛ. ἐς ποῖον ἕρπεις μῦθον ἢ παραίνεσιν;
ΧΟ. ἐλθοῦσ' ἐς οἴκους, ᾗ τὰ πάντ' ἐπίσταται,
τῆς ποντίας Νηρῇδος ἐκγόνου κόρης,
πυθοῦ πόσιν σὸν Θεονόης εἴτ' ἔστ' ἔτι
εἴτ' ἐκλέλοιπε φέγγος· ἐκμαθοῦσα δ' εὖ,   320
πρὸς τὰς τύχας τὸ χάρμα τοὺς γόους τ' ἔχε.
πρὶν δ' οὐδὲν ὀρθῶς εἰδέναι, τί σοι πλέον

309—10. These verses are obscure. Hermann has made them somewhat easier by transposing the final words ἔπη and σαφῆ. Says the Chorus, insisting that Helen has been deceived, 'Many things may be *clear and certain* (σαφῶς εἰρημένα, v. 308) by falsehood,' and not in reality, as for example, Menelaus *may* return, though he is reported certainly dead. To which she replies, 'Yes, and even lies may turn out truths, and so, though the report may be in fact false at the present time, it may prove true in the event;' that is, even if Menelaus is alive now, he may never return. Helen's answer in fact amounts to this, καὶ πολλὰ ἔπη ἀληθείας γένοιτο ἂν, τὰ ἔμπαλιν τῶν ψευδέων, i. e. contrary to the falsehoods which you suspect. For τὰ ἔμπαλιν τῶνδε Hermann compares Pers. 223, τἄμπαλιν δὲ τῶνδε γαίας κάτοχ' ἀμαυροῦσθαι σκότῳ. But he does not seem to improve the sense by reading χἂ διὰ ψευδῶν σαφῆ, *etiam quae per mendacium certa sunt*. W. Dindorf's explanation of the vulgate reading, καὶ τἄμπαλίν γε τῶνδ' ἀληθείας σαφῆ, is to supply διὰ from the preceding διὰ ψευδῶν, and Pflugk is so well satisfied with this, that he has hardly a word to say on the meaning of the passage, beyond the expression of a hope that no one will presume to tamper with the vulgate text. But this, as Hermann objects, gives an absurd sentiment, that 'even the contrary to falsehood,' i. e. truth itself, 'may be true.' By reading ἀληθείᾳ, the old order of the words might perhaps stand:—'A good deal may be affirmed, that is false.'—'Aye, and on the other hand, it may be true too' (plain in truth).

311. γάρ. 'You take this gloomy view,' says the chorus, 'because you are inclined to calamity rather than to the good.'

312. περιβαλών, surrounding me and as it were taking me captive.

313 πῶς εὐμενείας; As we say in familiar language, 'how are you off for good feeling towards you?' 'how do you stand with respect to good will in this family?' Cf. 1253, ὡς ἂν παρούσης οὐσίας ἕκαστος ᾖ, and the note on El. 238.

322. πρὶν—εἰδέναι. Confused between πρὶν πάντα εἰδέναι, and ἐπεὶ οὐδὲν οἶσθα.

λυπουμένη γένοιτ' ἄν ; ἀλλ' ἐμοὶ πιθοῦ·
τάφον λιποῦσα τόνδε σύμμιξον κόρῃ,
ὅθενπερ εἴσει πάντα, τἀληθῆ φράσαι.   325
ἔχουσ' ἐν οἴκοις τοῖσδε, τί βλέπεις πρόσω ;
θέλω δὲ κἀγὼ σοὶ συνεισελθεῖν δόμους,
καὶ συμπυθέσθαι παρθένου θεσπίσματα·
γυναῖκα γὰρ δὴ συμπονεῖν γυναικὶ χρή.

ΕΛ. φίλαι, λόγους ἐδεξάμαν.   στρ. 330
βᾶτε βᾶτε δ' ἐς δόμους,
ἀγῶνας ἐντὸς δόμων
ὡς πύθησθε τοὺς ἐμούς.

ΧΟ. θέλουσαν οὐ μόλις καλεῖς.

ΕΛ. ἰὼ μέλεος *ἅδ' ἁμέρα.   335
τίν' ἄρα τάλαινα τίνα λόγον
δακρυόεντ' ἀκούσομαι ;

ΧΟ. μὴ πρόμαντις ἀλγέων
προλάμβαν', ὦ φίλα, γόους.

ΕΛ. τί μοι πόσις μέλεος ἔτλα ;   ἀντ. 340
πότερα δέρκεται φάος

325. τἀληθῆ φράσαι, i. e. ὥστε ἐκείνην. 'Have an interview with the maiden, that she may tell you the truth.'—ἔχουσα, sc. αὐτήν, 'since you have one at home who is competent to inform you, why look further ?' Dindorf and Pflugk, after Musgrave, put a full stop at πάντα, and take the following clause thus, 'having one here in the house to tell you the truth,' &c. Hermann gives the obvious and right interpretation of the passage.

330—347. That these verses are antistrophic there can hardly be a doubt, and so Hermann has edited them. The only difficulty is to conceive a loss of two verses between 343 and 344, when the construction with πότερα—ἢ seems so complete. Nevertheless, it is extremely common in dialogues to find the chorus interrupting the speaker on the stage, who afterwards continues the tale without noticing or replying to them, or, if at all, doing so in a single verse having reference solely to such interruption. Of this last there is a clear instance in Agam. 1064, where Cassandra says μαρτυρίοισι γὰρ τοῖσδ' ἐπιπείθομαι in reply to the chorus, and then immediately resumes the strain broken off at 1060. Here, then, it requires no great stretch of imagination to conceive that the lost verses may have run thus :—

ΧΟ. ἥξει, τάλαινα, σὸς πόσις.
ΕΛ. ἀλλ' οὐ γὰρ οἶδ' εἴτ' ἔστ' ἔτι,
ἢ νέκυς κτλ.

In the first clause of this dialogue, Helen accepts the proposal of the Chorus to consult Theonoë, and begs them to enter the house with her. Consequently, as they assent to her request, at v. 385, where Menelaus first appears on the stage, there is a short pause in the action, during which both stage and orchestra are vacant.

334. θέλουσαν οὐ μόλις. Non parum cupidam. Hermann. Ingeniously, but needlessly, Elmsley proposed οὔ με δὶς καλεῖς.

335. ἅδ' is the insertion of Seidler. This and the next verse are iambic dimeter, and the whole of the strophe alternates with similar trochaic lines, except the third verse, which ends with a cretic.

ΕΛΕΝΗ.

τέθριππά τ' εἰς ἁλίου
ἐς κέλευθά τ' ἀστέρων;
ΧΟ. * * * *
ΕΛ. * * * *
ἢ * νέκυσι κατὰ χθονὸς
τὰν χθόνιον ἔχει τύχαν; 345
ΧΟ. ἐς τὸ φέρτερον τίθει
τὸ μέλλον, ὅ τι γενήσεται.
ΕΛ. σὲ γὰρ ἐκάλεσα, σὲ δὲ κατόμοσα,
τὸν ὑδρόεντι δόνακι χλωρὸν
Εὐρώταν, θανόντος ἀνδρὸς εἰ 350
βάξις ἔτυμος ἅδε μοι.
ΧΟ. τί τάδ' ἀσύνετα;
ΕΛ. φόνιον αἰώρημα

342. εἰς ἁλίου Herm. for ἀελίου. Compare Cho. 223, ἰδοῦ δ' ὕφασμα τοῦτο, σῆς ἔργον χερὸς, σπάθης τε πληγὰς, εἰς δὲ θήρειον γραφήν,—unless, as there is some reason to fear, a line following has been lost, in which some participle like βλέπουσα occurred.
344. ἢ νέκυσι. Lenting and Matthiae, followed by Herm. Dind. Pflugk, but not by Bothe, give ἢ 'ν νέκυσι, to which Hermann adds δὴ for the sake of the metre. Perhaps ἢ μετὰ νέκυσι, equivalent to a diiambus.—τύχαν, i. e. τιμήν, as kings in Hades were considered to have especial honour with the gods below. Cf. Aesch. Choeph. 350.
348. κατόμοσα Elmsley for κατώμοσα. Hermann doubts the omission of the augment even in choral trochaics, and supposes some word has been lost which admitted the elision κατώμοσ', but he can suggest nothing more probable than ἆ 'να, or ἁγνὲ, or εἰπέ. The article is so commonly used in these addresses, σὲ τὸν, σὲ τὴν &c., (cf. v. 546,) that we should feel some hesitation in reading the passage thus,

σὲ γὰρ ἐκάλεσα, σὲ δὲ κατώμοσ',
ὑδρόεντι δόνακι χλωρὸν
Εὐρώταν, θανόντος ἀνδρὸς
εἰ βάξις ἔτυμος ἅδε μοι.

Where the first three lines are trochaic, the last iambic, dimeter acatalectic.—ὑδρόεντι for —α is Reiske's probable correction.
350. ἀνδρὸς was restored to its natural and proper place by Hermann. In the old copies it followed ἔτυμος.
352. Whether these words belong to the Chorus or to Helen, is very uncertain, and the old copies do not agree on the matter. Both Hermann and Dindorf think that something is lost after φόνιον αἰώρημα, and there is no doubt that διὰ δέρης is very inaptly used of tying a noose round the throat. It is easy enough to supply either τί λέγω or τί λέγεις to τάδ' ἀσύνετα, 'these ravings,' 'these incoherent words.' But the preceding invocation of the Eurotas, if somewhat wild, was not ἀσύνετος. Besides, the metre is hardly satisfied by this single verse, which may be called trochaic monometer, and which leaves the next also very inharmonious. If the obnoxious word διὰ were omitted, the lines would run smoothly and easily as follows:—

τί τάδ' ἀσύνετα; φόνιον αἰώ-
ρημ' ὀρέξομαι δέρης, κτλ.

Hermann thinks Helen meant to say τί τάδ' ἀσύνετα, εἰ φόνιον αἰώρημα ὀρέξομαι; and Pflugk takes them for the words of the chorus, virtually saying to Helen, 'What is the use of all this vain and uncertain speculation about your husband's death?' The present editor confesses his inability to decide. Hermann thinks the true reading may have been διὰ βρόχων δέρης ὀρέξομαι, in which case αἰώρημα would be a sort of cognate accusative.

ΕΥΡΙΠΙΔΟΥ

διὰ δέρης ὀρέξομαι,
ἢ ξιφοκτόνον δίωγμα
λαιμορύτου σφαγᾶς   355
αὐτοσίδαρον ἔσω πελάσω διὰ σαρκὸς ἅμιλλαν,
θῦμα τριζύγοις θεαῖσι
τῷ τε συρίγγων ἀοιδὰν σεβίζοντι Πριαμίδᾳ ποτ' ἀμφὶ βουστάθμους.

ΧΟ. ἄλλοσ' ἀποτροπὰ κακῶν   360
     γένοιτο, τὸ δὲ σὸν εὐτυχές.

ΕΛ. ἰὼ τάλαινα Τροία
     δι' ἔργ' ἄνεργ' ὄλλυσαι, μέλεά τ' ἔτλας·
     τὰ δ' ἐμὰ δῶρα Κύπριδος ἔτεκε
     πολὺ μὲν αἷμα, πολὺ δὲ δάκρυον
     ἀχεά τ' ἄχεσι, δάκρυα δάκρυσιν.   365
     †ἔλαβε πάθεα   *   *

354—6. This is just one of those idiomatic passages which, easy enough to understand, it is impossible to translate in a manner wholly satisfactory. By διώκειν ξίφος the thrusting or *following up* of a sword is meant; cf. Ion 205, πάντα τοι βλέφαρον διώκω. For the syntax, Hermann says the meaning is, ξίφος ἔσω σφαγῆς διὰ σαρκὸς πελάσω αὐτοσιδήρῳ ἁμίλλᾳ. It amounts to precisely the same if we consider the accusative δίωγμα to fall under the same head as αἰώρημα just mentioned, and the direct or proximate object to πελάσω to be αὐτ. ἅμιλλαν. With this phrase, nearly equivalent to ἅμιλλαν σιδήρου, we may compare ἅμιλλαν πολύτεκνον in Med. 557, and understand by it 'an effort with the sword made by myself.'—ἔσω σφαγᾶς λαιμορύτου is ἔσω λαιμοῦ σφαγέντος, αἵματι ῥέοντος. Similarly Electr. 1222, ματέρος ἔσω δέρας μεθεὶς, sc. φάσγανον. Rhes. 750, οἵα μ' ὀδύνη τείρει φονίου τραύματος εἴσω. Ion 767, διανταῖος ἔτυπεν ὀδύνα με πνευμόνων τῶνδ' ἔσω. Agam. 1314, πέπληγμαι καιρίαν πληγὴν ἔσω.

357. θῦμα. As a sacrifice pleasing to the three goddesses and to Paris who gave judgment upon them. The concluding words are very corrupt in the old copies, τῷ τε (τόν τε) σύραγγ' ἀοιδαὶ σέβιζον Πριαμίδας. Canter first restored σύριγγ'. Hermann gives ἀοιδὰν and with Elmsley συρίγγων. Matthiae, followed by Pflugk and Dindorf, ἂν' Ἴδᾳ.—σεβίζοντι is much the same as νομίζοντι, practising, habitually using, preferring the music of the pipe. See Med. 641.

361. εὐτυχὲς, scil. γένοιτο.

362. τάλαινα Τροία Herm. for Τροία τάλαινα. W. Dindorf would repeat ἰὼ ἰὼ &c.—"ἔργ' ἄνεργα dicit propter raptum sui, qui quidem videbatur esse verus, revera autem erat impostura et fucus Deorum." *J. Barnes.* In what follows, Κύπριδος was restored by L. Dindorf for Κύπρις. The meaning is, 'the gifts of Cypris to me,' viz. personal charms, 'have given birth to much slaughter and many a tear.'

366. The words ἔλαβε πάθεα are probably corrupt. It is not very difficult to restore what is the regular Euripidean mode of expression, πάθεα πάθεσι, but then some words appear to have been lost, as Hermann has pointed out, wherein mention was made of wives bewailing their slain husbands, and mothers their children. For ὤλεσαν seems clearly a grammarian's interpolation to make some sort of sense. Something like the following would probably give an outline of the original:

ἄχε' ἐπ' ἄχεσι, δάκρυα δάκρυσιν,
πάθεα πάθεσιν ἔλαχε μελέα,

ΕΛΕΝΗ.

* * *

μᾰτέρες τε παῖδας [ὤλεσαν].
ἀπὸ δὲ παρθένοι κόμας
ἔθεντο σύγγονοι νεκρῶν Σκαμάνδριον
ἀμφὶ Φρύγιον οἶδμα.
βοὰν βοὰν δ' Ἑλλὰς *αἶα   370
ἐκελάδησ', ἀνωτότυξεν,
ἐπὶ δὲ κρατὶ χέρας ἔθηκεν,
ὄνυχι δ' ἁπαλόχροα γένυν
ἔδευσε φονίαισι πλαγαῖς.
ὦ μάκαρ Ἀρκαδίᾳ ποτὲ παρθένε   375
Καλλιστοῖ, Διὸς ἃ λεχέων ἐπέβας τετραβάμοσι
  γυίοις,
ὡς πολὺ ματρὸς ἐμᾶς ἔλαχες πλέον,
ἃ μορφᾶς θηρῶν λαχνογυίων
ὄμματι λάβρῳ σχῆμα διαίνεις
ἐξαλλάξασ' ἄχθεα λύπης·   380
ἄν τέ ποτ' Ἄρτεμις ἐξεχορεύσατο,

ἄνδρα δ' ἄλοχος ἐστέναξε
ματέρες τε παῖδας.

Such guesses are indeed of little avail, except so far as they serve to show the corruption of the present text, and to give a better idea of the poet's train of thought than the ordinary readings. Pflugk, placing a colon at δάκρυσιν, understands ἔλαβε πάθεα σὲ τὴν Τροίαν. Hermann thinks the lost accusative may have been πόσιν ὀλόμενον.

370. αἶα. This word has been inserted by the present editor, as the metre not only naturally suggests, but appears even to require it.—ἐκελάδησε Herm. for κελάδησε, who also gives κἀνωτότυξεν for κἀνοτότυξεν. See on v. 348. But the trochaic rhythm of the passage can only be restored by omitting the καὶ, as given above.

375. Ἀρκαδίᾳ. The dative of place, as Ἄργει in Heracl. 339. Inf. v. 1210, ποῦ βαρβάροισι πελάγεσιν ναυσθλούμενον; The story is told by Apollodorus, iii. 8. 2. Ovid, Fast. ii. 153 seqq. Propertius, iii. 20, 23, ' Callisto Arcadios erraverat ursa per agros : Nunc nocturna suo sidere vela regit.'

377. ἔλαχες πλέον. How much better

you are off than my mother Leda ; for you, having lost your human shape, have only to lament the change, but are freed from a constant succession of human ills. The metre from v. 375 passes into dactylic, the last (385) being ithyphallic. On the feminine form μάκαρ see Bacch. 565.

379. διαίνεις. Dindorf has done well in adopting this clever emendation of Hermann's for λεαίνης. Callisto was changed into a bear, not into a lioness; and the verb is wanted to govern σχῆμα. Translate, ' who with gushing eye dost ever bewail the appearance of a shaggy bear's shape, having changed the burden of your grief.' The lesser corruptions in the vulgate text, ἃ μορφᾷ θηρᾶν λάχνα γυίων, and ἄχεα, were also successfully removed by Hermann, who adds, " σχῆμα μορφῆς dixit in Ione v. 992, ποῖόν τι μορφῆς σχῆμ' ἔχουσαν ἀγρίας ; Διαίνειν πῆμα dixit Aeschylus in Persis v. 1043." (v. 1017, δίαινε, δίαινε πῆμα, πρὸς δόμους δ' ἴθι.) Callisto is said to have changed her grief, because she has got a new one for a former one,—the form of a bear for the loss of virginity.

381. ἄν τε, i. e. καὶ ἐκείνη πλέον ἔλαχε κτλ., v. 377. Of the legend of the

χρυσοκέρατ' ἔλαφον, Μέροπος Τιτανίδα κούραν
καλλοσύνας ἕνεκεν· τὸ δ' ἐμὸν δέμας
ὤλεσεν ὤλεσε Πέργαμα Δαρδανίας
ὀλομένους τ' Ἀχαιούς. 385

ΜΕΝΕΛΑΟΣ.

ὦ τὰς τεθρίππους Οἰνομάῳ Πῖσαν κάτα
Πέλοψ ἁμίλλας ἐξαμιλληθείς ποτε,
εἴθ' ὤφελες τόθ', ἡνίκ' ἔρανον ἐς θεοὺς

daughter of Merops being turned into a stag, no account has been preserved. Translate, ' She too, whom Artemis once thrust forth from the dance, (changed into) a stag with gilt horns, the Titan (earth-born) daughter of Merops, on account of her beauty' (beautifulness). Musgrave (after Barnes) quotes Stephanus of Byzantium in v. Κῶς, who states that Merops was γηγενής. Of the verb ἐξεχορεύσατο Pflugk says, without much reason, " est omnino obscura vocabuli hujus potestas propter fabulae ignorantiam." Hermann compares what Ovid says of Callisto, *deque suo jussit secedere coetu*. A similar form is ἐκβακχεύσασθαι in Suppl. 1001.

383. τὸ δ' ἐμὸν δέμας κτλ. *You* were both unfortunate on account of your beauty; but you did not, like me, cause the destruction of cities and men, but only suffered in your own persons.

386. Menelaus, in the garb of a shipwrecked mariner (v. 422), comes upon the vacant stage, and narrates his adventures since the capture of Troy. He wishes that his ancestor Pelops had never survived the banquet wherein he was offered by his father to the gods, but restored to life by Zeus; then would he never have been born to conduct with his brother the unhappy expedition to Troy. Of the army, some are dead, some have reached home in safety; but to himself return seems denied by the gods: for he no sooner approaches his native land than he is storm-tossed and driven from its shore. He has at last been cast up from the wreck of his vessel on this unknown coast, in company with his Helen. He is ashamed to appear before the people, without clothes, without food; but he is compelled by hard necessity, and has come to the door of the first wealthy abode he has found, to beg assistance for himself and his companions, whom he has left to guard Helen in a cave on the shore.

Ibid. τὰς τεθρίππους ἁμίλλας, that far-famed contest with the chariot, wherein Pelops won Hippodamia the daughter of Oenomaus, (cf. Iph. Taur. 825,)—shortly put for τεθρίππων ἁρμάτων ἅμιλλαν. Cf. v. 356. The force of the ἐξ in composition (see *inf*. 1471) seems here to be that of completion or success.

388—9. There is evidently something wrong in this passage. Canter and the subsequent editors, deceived by Stephens, who pretended that he had found πρισθεὶς for πεισθεὶς in a MS., have unsuspectingly adopted the reading; but Hermann thinks that more is required for the full meaning of the poet. His own conjectural restoration is very ingenious ;—

εἴθ' ὤφελες τόθ', ἡνίκ' ἔρανον εἰς θεῶν
σφαγέντα καινὸν Ζεὺς πάλιν Δηοῦς λιταῖς
πεισθεὶς ἐποίει σ', εὐθέως λιπεῖν βίον,

though we might perhaps criticise the Greek ποιεῖν τινὰ καινὸν for ἀνανεῶσαι, ἀποκαταστῆσαι. A participle that would tolerably well complete the meaning, as the passage now stands, would be δαισθεὶς, 'when, divided as food among the gods (δαισθεὶς εἰς θεοὺς), you were making a banquet for them.' But though Homer uses δάσασθαι and δέδασμαι exactly in this sense, to apportion shares of food, and ἔδαισέ νιν occurs Orest. 15, and ζῶν με δαίσεις, Eum. 295, there appears to be no authority for δαισθεὶς, though δαισθεὶς from δαίω *to burn* occurs in Heracl. 914. Or should we read ἐν θεοῖς τυθεὶς (Choeph. 234)? The word ἔρανος is used by Pindar in describing this banquet, Ol. i. 38, but it properly means a feast to which each one brings his contribution of provisions.

ΕΛΕΝΗ.

†πεισθεὶς ἐποίεις, ἐν θεοῖς λιπεῖν βίον,
πρὶν τὸν ἐμὸν Ἀτρέα πατέρα γεννῆσαί ποτε,   390
ὃς ἐξέφυσεν Ἀερόπης λέκτρων ἄπο
Ἀγαμέμνον' ἐμέ τε Μενέλεων, κλεινὸν ζυγόν·
πλεῖστον γὰρ οἶμαι, καὶ τόδ' οὐ κόμπῳ λέγω,
στράτευμα κώπῃ διορίσαι Τροίαν ἔπι
τύραννος, οὐδὲν πρὸς βίαν στρατηλατῶν,   395
ἑκοῦσι δ' ἄρξας Ἑλλάδος νεανίαις.
καὶ τοὺς μὲν οὐκέτ' ὄντας ἀριθμῆσαι πάρα,
τοὺς δ' ἐκ θαλάσσης ἀσμένως πεφευγότας,
νεκρῶν φέροντας ὀνόματ' εἰς οἴκους πάλιν.
ἐγὼ δ' ἐπ' οἶδμα πόντιον γλαυκῆς ἁλὸς   400
τλήμων ἀλῶμαι χρόνον ὅσονπερ Ἰλίου
πύργους ἔπερσα, κεἰς πάτραν χρῄζων μολεῖν
οὐκ ἀξιοῦμαι τοῦδε πρὸς θεῶν τυχεῖν,
Λιβύης δ' ἐρήμους ἀξένους τ' ἐπιδρομὰς
πέπλευκα πάσας· χὤταν ἐγγὺς ὦ πάτρας,   405

390. Ἀτρέα is probably a dissyllable, though Euripides sometimes makes the final α, as in φονέα, short. See Hec. 882. Ajac. 1293—5. Orest. 18. 1009.

394. κώπῃ διορίσαι, to have separated from their native shores by ships; for πορθμεῦσαι, διαπεραιῶσαι. Cf. v. 828, ἐκ γῆς διορίσαιμεν ἂν πόδα. Ion 46, ὑπὲρ δὲ θυμέλας διορίσαι πρόθυμος ἦν, scil. αὐτόν. Thucydides, i. 9 and 10, in discussing the Trojan war, agrees in this view, that we should consider this expedition μεγίστην μὲν γενέσθαι τῶν πρὸ αὑτῆς, λειπομένην δὲ τῶν νῦν, but he does not agree that the service of the Greeks was voluntarily rendered, for he contends that Agamemnon τὴν στρατείαν οὐ χάριτι τὸ πλεῖον ἢ φόβῳ ξυναγαγὼν ποιήσασθαι. Aeschylus plainly represents it as a forced obedience, Ag. 436 seqq.

397. ἀριθμῆσαι. Aeschylus calls this τοὺς ἀναλωθέντας ἐν ψήφῳ λέγειν, Ag. 553. He means, 'It is known who are dead and who are returned,' i. e. there is no uncertainty about *their* fate to their friends, as there is about mine.

399. ὀνόματα. Their *names*, not their ashes in urns, Agam. 426. It would be easy to read σώματ', as we have νεκύων σώματα in Suppl. 62, though the Attics, unlike Homer, generally use σῶμα of the living. However it clearly means 'a corpse' in Heracl. 1024. Probably the poet used φέρειν ὀνόματα in reference to those who, dispersed and shipwrecked on their return, could bring with them nothing beyond verbal report to their friends.

401. χρόνον ὅσονπερ. He appears to mean χρόνον ἐξ οὗ, not 'for the same time that it took me to capture Troy,' viz. ten years; for he returned to Sparta on the eighth year, according to Homer. See v. 112.—ἀξιοῦμαι, used passively, which appears to be somewhat uncommon.

404. Λιβύης δ' Herm. for —τ', since the preceding sentence with οὐκ implies opposition.—The ι is made long before δρ as ē in ὀλεθρίαν, Suppl. 116, ō in γηροτρόφος Alcest. 663, and many similar examples. Euripides indeed seems to have freely used what the other two tragic writers regarded as a licence. Aeschylus has θεōπρόπους Prom. 677, and μηλōτρόφος Pers. 759. The word here means 'landing-places.' Hermann's ἀξένους τ' ἂν ἐπιδρομὰς is quite needless. The accusative is as inf. v. 532. 598.—For the voyage to Libya see Od. iv. 85.

πάλιν μ' ἀπωθεῖ πνεῦμα, κοὔποτ' οὔριον
εἰσῆλθε λαῖφος, ὥστε μ' ἐς πάτραν μολεῖν.
καὶ νῦν τάλας ναυαγὸς, ἀπολέσας φίλους,
ἐξέπεσον ἐς γῆν τήνδε· ναῦς δὲ πρὸς πέτρας
πολλοὺς ἀριθμοὺς ἄγνυται ναυαγίων.   410
τρόπις δ' ἐλείφθη ποικίλων ἁρμοσμάτων,
ἐφ' ἧς ἐσώθην μόλις ἀνελπίστῳ τύχῃ
Ἑλένη τε, Τροίας ἣν ἀποσπάσας ἔχω.
ὄνομα δὲ χώρας, ἥτις ἥδε καὶ λεώς,
οὐκ οἶδ'· ὄχλον γὰρ εἰσπεσεῖν ᾐσχυνόμην,   415
ὥσθ' ἱστορῆσαι τὰς ἐμὰς δυσχλαινίας,
κρύπτων ὑπ' αἰδοῦς τὰς τύχας. ὅταν δ' ἀνὴρ
πράξῃ κακῶς ὑψηλὸς, εἰς ἀηθίαν
πίπτει κακίω τοῦ πάλαι δυσδαίμονος.
χρεία δὲ τείρει μ'· οὔτε γὰρ σῖτος πάρα   420
οὔτ' ἀμφὶ χρῶτ' ἐσθῆτες· αὐτὰ δ' εἰκάσαι
πάρεστι ναὸς ἐκβόλοις ἀμπίσχομαι.
πέπλους δὲ τοὺς πρὶν λαμπρά τ' ἀμφιβλήματα
χλιδάς τε πόντος ἥρπασ'· ἐν δ' ἄντρου μυχοῖς
κρύψας γυναῖκα τὴν κακῶν πάντων ἐμοὶ   425
ἄρξασαν ἥκω, τούς τε περιλελειμμένους

406. οὔριον εἰσῆλθε, favourably enters or fills the sail.
410. ἀριθμούς. As the Attics say πέντε τέμνειν, 'to cut *into* five,' &c., so the result of the fracture is here expressed by the accusative without the preposition. —ἐλείφθη, 'started from its intricate fastenings,' became detached from the ribs. It was by the same means that Ulysses floated ashore, Od. xix. 278, as Pflugk reminds us. The MSS., by a constant error, give ἐλήφθη, corrected by Stephens.—ἐσώθην μόλις, 'I got in safe at last.' Virg. Aen. vi. 356, '*vix lumine quarto Prospexi Italiam.*'
416. ὥσθ' ἱστορῆσαι κτλ. So that they should make inquiries respecting (literally, 'inform themselves about,') my tattered garments. The subject of the infinitive is changed, as in v. 324, σύμμιξον κόρῃ— (ὥστε αὐτὴν) φράσαι.
418. He means by ἀηθίαν, that a man feels his reverses the more from being unused to adversity. 'He falls into a state in which suffering is strange to him, and therefore worse than it is to one who has been long wretched.' Compare Troad. 634, ὁ δ' εὐτυχήσας ἐς τὸ δυστυχὲς πεσὼν ψυχὴν ἀλᾶται τῆς πάροιθ' εὐπραξίας, and see Alcest. 926.
421. W. Dindorf tacitly gives αὐτὰ δ' εἰκάσαι πάρεστι ναὸς ἔκβολ', οἷς ἀμπίσχομαι. But it may be doubted if this is any improvement. The meaning is, 'The thing itself is before you to guess at (i. e. the fact that I am destitute); I am clad in rags cast on shore from the ship.' The substantive ἔκβολον occurs also in Ion 555. Bacch. 91.
426. Hermann is undoubtedly right in reading τούς τε for τούς γε, where the γε would be quite intolerable. If it had any meaning at all, it would have this, a sufficiently absurd one,—'the *survivors* at least, for I cannot compel those who are dead.' But the syntax is simpler thus, κρύψας γυναῖκα ἀναγκάσας τε φίλους φυλάσσειν αὐτήν, than the construction

ΕΛΕΝΗ. 145

φίλων φυλάσσειν τἄμ' ἀναγκάσας λέχη.
μόνος δὲ νοστῶ, τοῖς ἐκεῖ ζητῶν φίλοις
τὰ πρόσφορ' ἤν πως ἐξερευνήσας λάβω.
ἰδὼν δὲ δῶμα περιφερὲς θριγκοῖς τόδε 430
πύλας τε σεμνὰς ἀνδρὸς ὀλβίου τινός,
προσῆλθον· ἐλπὶς δ' ἔκ γε πλουσίων δόμων
λαβεῖν τι ναύταις, ἐκ δὲ μὴ 'χόντων βίον,
οὐδ' εἰ θέλοιεν, ὠφελεῖν ἔχοιεν ἄν.
ὠή· τίς ἂν πυλωρὸς ἐκ δόμων μόλοι, 435
ὅστις διαγγείλειε τἄμ' εἴσω κακά;

ΓΡΑΥΣ.

τίς πρὸς πύλαισιν; οὐκ ἀπαλλάξει δόμων
καὶ μὴ πρὸς αὐλείοισιν ἑστηκὼς πύλαις
ὄχλον παρέξεις δεσπόταις; ἢ κατθανεῖ
Ἕλλην πεφυκώς, οἷσιν οὐκ ἐπιστροφαί. 440

ΜΕ. ὦ γραῖα, ταῦτα πάντ' ἔπη καλῶς λέγεις.
ἔξεστι· πείσομαι γάρ· ἀλλ' ἄνες μόνον.

ΓΡ. ἄπελθ'· ἐμοὶ γὰρ τοῦτο πρόσκειται, ξένε,
μηδένα πελάζειν τοισίδ' Ἑλλήνων δόμοις.

---

pointed out by him, κρύψας γυναῖκα φίλους τε, ἀναγκάσας αὐτοὺς φυλάσσειν αὐτήν. Either way is a great improvement on the old reading. Conversely ἔκ γε for ἔκ τε Musgrave in v. 432.

431. πύλαι σεμναί, are what we call 'fine doors.' See on Hippol. 957. That this is the same palace as was before described by Teucer, i.e. that the scene has not been changed, is clear from v. 69, 70.

434. ἔχοιεν ἄν. A confused construction between ἔχοις ἂν ὠφελεῖσθαι, and οἱ δὲ μὴ ἔχοντες βίον.

436. διαγγείλειε. The optative by attraction. Cf. v. 175. Bacch. 1253, εἴθε παῖς ἐμὸς εὔθηρος εἴη,—ὅτε θηρῶν ὀριγνῷτ'. Troad. 700, and the note there.

438. καὶ μή, i.e. καὶ οὐ μή, from the preceding. Cf. Hippol. 498, οὐχὶ συγκλήσεις στόμα, καὶ μὴ μεθήσεις αὖθις αἰσχίστους λόγους; Ajac. 75, οὐ σῖγ' ἀνέξει μηδὲ δειλίαν ἀρεῖς;

440. ἐπιστροφαί, converse, admission to hospitality. So Theb. 645, πατρῴων δωμάτων ἐπιστροφάς. Eum. 517, ξενοτίμους ἐπιστροφὰς δωμάτων. This scene has much of a comic character about it, like several others in Euripides. See Preface to Vol. i. p. xxxiv, and on Heracl. 630.—The plural οἷσιν is used, because Ἕλλην represents one of a class. Pflugk well compares Orest. 920, αὐτουργός, οἵπερ καὶ μόνοι σάζουσι γῆν. So *inf.* 449, ξένος, ἀσύλητον γένος. Suppl. 868, φίλος τ' ἀληθὴς ἦν,—ὧν ἀριθμὸς οὐ πολύς.

442. ἔξεστι is a formula of acquiescence, 'certainly,' 'by all means,' 'if you please,' &c. See Bacch. 844.—μόνον for λόγον is Hermann's highly ingenious correction. He compares Bacch. 448, κλῇδές τ' ἀνῆκαν θύρετρ' ἄνευ θνητῆς χερός. The old portress is closing the door in his face, when he makes a last effort to gain admission by assenting to what she says, 'It is all right,—only loosen the bar.' Matthiae's interpretation, 'don't speak so harshly' (in saying ἀπαλλάσσου δόμων), 'be gentle in your expressions,' is tame, and besides that, very un-Greek as to the sentiment.

443. πρόσκειται, προστέτακται.

ΜΕ. ἆ, μὴ προσείλει χεῖρα, μηδ' ὤθει βίᾳ. 445
ΓΡ. πείθει γὰρ οὐδὲν ὧν λέγω· σὺ δ' αἴτιος.
ΜΕ. ἄγγειλον εἴσω δεσπόταισι τοῖσι σοῖς.
ΓΡ. πικρῶς ἂν οἶμαί γ' ἀγγελεῖν τοὺς σοὺς λόγους.
ΜΕ. ναυαγὸς ἥκω, ξένος, ἀσύλητον γένος.
ΓΡ. οἶκον πρὸς ἄλλον νῦν τιν' ἀντὶ τοῦδ' ἴθι. 450
ΜΕ. οὔκ, ἀλλ' ἔσω πάρειμι· καὶ σύ μοι πιθοῦ.
ΓΡ. ὀχληρὸς ἴσθ' ὤν· καὶ τάχ' ὠσθήσει βίᾳ.
ΜΕ. αἰαῖ· τὰ κλεινὰ ποῦ 'στί μοι στρατεύματα;
ΓΡ. οὔκουν ἐκεῖ που σεμνὸς ἦσθ', οὐκ ἐνθάδε.
ΜΕ. ὦ δαῖμον, ὡς ἀνάξι' ἠτιμώμεθα. 455
ΓΡ. τί βλέφαρα τέγγεις δάκρυσι; πρὸς τί δ' οἰκτρὸς εἶ;
ΜΕ. πρὸς τὰς πάροιθε συμφορὰς εὐδαίμονας.
ΓΡ. οὔκουν ἀπελθὼν δάκρυα σοῖς δώσεις φίλοις;
ΜΕ. τίς δ' ἥδε χώρα; τοῦ δὲ βασίλειοι δόμοι;
ΓΡ. Πρωτεὺς τάδ' οἰκεῖ δώματ', Αἴγυπτος δὲ γῆ. 460
ΜΕ. Αἴγυπτος; ὦ δύστηνος, οἷ πέπλευκ' ἄρα.

445. προσείλει. So the MSS., but Aldus has προσείλα. Matthiae's reading πρόσειε has little probability, (see Bacch. 930, Herc. F. 1218,) though his follower Pflugk does not hesitate to adopt it. Bothe, Dind., and Herm. retain προσείλει, but the sense which Bothe gives, 'do not repel my suppliant hand,' cannot be defended. He compares, as does Hermann, Il. x. 347, where πρὸς νῆας προσειλεῖν is 'to hem into a narrow space towards the ships.' The best comment on the word is what we cannot now obtain, the action of the portress on the stage. Hermann translates, *ne admove manum, ut me arceas*. One might suspect that he wrote χειρί, 'do not push me into a corner (i. e. against the door-post) with your hand.' This slight alteration removes so much obscurity, that it would not perhaps be too bold to restore it.

448. τοὺς σοὺς λόγους. '*Your* words,' of all men in the world, as being a Greek, to whom access is forbidden.—πικρῶς, 'to my cost.' This verse is suspicious from the position of γε, and still more on account of the ἂν with a future. Though some few instances of this use have been collected by grammarians, it is equally difficult to defend on principle and by passages of undoubted integrity. What Hermann says we might read, ἀγγελοῖμι or even ἀγγελοῖν (see v. 263,) seems nothing less than a plain solecism. But he must have written this note ἐκεῖσε τὸν νοῦν ἔχων, or he never would have attributed such a verse as this to Euripides,

πικρῶς ἂν οἶμαι 'γὼ 'γγελεῖν τοὺς σοὺς λόγους.

Though the received text of Herodotus has the second aorist ἀπήγγελον in lib. iv. 153, it is more than probable that he wrote ἀπήγγελλον, since there are scarcely three regular verbs in the Greek language which have both transitive aorists in use, like ἔκτανον and ἔκτεινα.

451. ἔσω πάρειμι. See on παρελθεῖν δόμους, Med. 1137. Suppl. 468.

456. πρὸς τί δ' for πρὸς τίν' Matthiae. Pflugk defends the latter, supplying ἀποβλέπων with πρὸς in the next verse; but Hermann rightly points out that the answer of Menelaus requires πρὸς τί.—οἰκτίζεσθαι πρός τινα, *inf.* v. 1054.

461. ὦ δύστηνος. *Me miserum!* See on Med. 61, ὦ μῶρος.—οἷ, the exclamation, to be distinguished from ποῖ the question, though good scholars have sometimes confused them. Thus in Ion 614, ὅσας—διαφθοράς by Matthiae and others has been construed as if it were πόσας. But in Suppl. 769, οἴμοι· πόσῳ σφιν συν-

ΕΛΕΝΗ.

ΓΡ. τί δὴ τὸ Νείλου μεμπτόν ἐστί σοι γένος ;
ΜΕ. οὐ τοῦτ' ἐμέμφθην· τὰς ἐμὰς στένω τύχας.
ΓΡ. πολλοὶ κακῶς πράσσουσιν, οὐ σὺ δὴ μόνος.
ΜΕ. ἔστ' οὖν ἐν οἴκοις ὄντιν' ὀνομάζεις ἄναξ ; 465
ΓΡ. τόδ' ἔστιν αὐτοῦ μνῆμα, παῖς δ' ἄρχει χθονός.
ΜΕ. ποῦ δῆτ' ἂν εἴη ; πότερον ἐκτὸς ἢ 'ν δόμοις ;
ΓΡ. οὐκ ἔνδον· Ἕλλησιν δὲ πολεμιώτατος.
ΜΕ. τίν' αἰτίαν σχὼν ἧς ἐπηυρόμην ἐγώ ;
ΓΡ. Ἑλένη κατ' οἴκους ἐστὶ τοῦσδ' ἡ τοῦ Διός. 470
ΜΕ. πῶς φῄς ; τίν' εἶπας μῦθον ; αὖθίς μοι φράσον.
ΓΡ. ἡ Τυνδαρὶς παῖς, ἣ κατὰ Σπάρτην ποτ' ἦν.
ΜΕ. πόθεν μολοῦσα ; τίνα τὸ πρᾶγμ' ἔχει λόγον ;
ΓΡ. Λακεδαίμονος γῆς δεῦρο νοστήσασ' ἄπο.
ΜΕ. πότ' ; οὔ τί που λελήσμεθ' ἐξ ἄντρων λέχος ; 475
ΓΡ. πρὶν τοὺς Ἀχαιοὺς, ὦ ξέν', ἐς Τροίαν μολεῖν.
     ἀλλ' ἕρπ' ἀπ' οἴκων· ἔστι γάρ τις ἐν δόμοις
     τύχῃ, τύραννος ᾗ ταράσσεται δόμος.
     καιρὸν γὰρ οὐδέν' ἦλθες· ἢν δὲ δεσπότης

θανεῖν ἂν ἤθελον, it seems that πόσῳ is improperly used for ὅσῳ. See Elmsley on Bacch. 662, who does not know what to make of Od. i. 173, τίς πόθεν εἶς ἀνδρῶν; πόθι τοι πόλις ἠδὲ τοκῆες; ὁπποίης δ' ἐπὶ νηὸς ἀφίκεο; But here ὁπποίης is really an *indirect* question, εἰπὲ ὁπποίης κτλ. The interjectional use is rather infrequent. Cf. Ar. Vesp. 188, ὦ μιαρώτατος, ἵν' ὑποδέδυκεν. This verse is parodied in Ar. Thesm. 878,

MN. Αἴγυπτον. ΕΥΡ. ὦ δύστηνος, οἷ πεπλώκαμεν.

And *inf.* v. 532, the old copies agree in πεπλωκότα, so that πέπλωκα is here a probable correction.

462. γάνος, the reading of Victorius, is adopted by Herm. and Dind., for γένος. The Nile water was famed for its excellence, and the old portress thinks that as a matter of course he ought rather to praise than to disparage the country in consequence. See on Aesch. Suppl. 555. 836.

465. ὄντινα. As the Attic writers never use ὅστις in place of ὅς, the sense of these words is, ὅστις ἐστὶν ὃν ὀνομάζεις, 'whoever this person is whom you call Proteus.' So in Aesch. Cho. 902, ποῦ δῆθ' ὁ τῖμος, ὄντιν' ἀντεδεξάμην; for ὅστις

ποτ' ἦν, ὃν κτλ. Aj. 1044, τίς δ' ἐστὶν ὄντιν' ἄνδρα προσλεύσσεις στρατοῦ; The woman had said that Proteus lived in the βασίλειοι δόμοι, v. 459—60, and therefore he was ἄναξ.

467. ποῦ δῆτ' ἂν εἴη; 'Where then may he be?' In prose, ποῦ ἄπεστι; So in v. 91, τλήμων ἂν εἴης for —εἶ. Soph. El. 1450, ποῦ δῆτ' ἂν εἶεν οἱ ξένοι;

469. σχὼν κτλ. "*Quae ei caussa extitit, cujus ego fructum perciperem?*" Hermann. But why not rather *perceperim?* 'What reason had he which *I* suffered for?' i.e. which I have just experienced, or felt the bad effects of, in being repelled from his door.

475. οὔ τι που κτλ. 'Surely I have not been robbed of my wife out of the cave?' (cf. v. 424.) This, as Barnes and Hermann remark, is said aside. The old readings λελήσμεθ' and λέχους were corrected by Brodaeus and Heath.

478. τύχη. See v. 788. The intended marriage with Helen is meant.

479. καιρὸν οὐδένα, 'in no fit time.' So in Ajac. 34, καιρὸν δ' ἐφήκεις. See on Med. 127. This is really the accusative denoting the *point* (not the duration) of time. See on Bacch. 723, αἱ δὲ τὴν τεταγμένην ὥραν ἐκίνουν θύρσον εἰς βακ-

U 2

ΕΥΡΙΠΙΔΟΥ

λάβῃ σε, θάνατος ξένιά σοι γενήσεται. 480
εὔνους γὰρ εἰμ᾽ Ἕλλησιν, οὐχ ὅσον πικροὺς
λόγους ἔδωκα δεσπότην φοβουμένη.
ΜΕ. τί φῶ ; τί λέξω ; συμφορὰς γὰρ ἀθλίας
ἐκ τῶν πάροιθε τὰς παρεστώσας κλύω,
εἰ τὴν μὲν αἱρεθεῖσαν ἐκ Τροίας ἄγων 485
ἥκω δάμαρτα καὶ κατ᾽ ἄντρα σώζεται,
ὄνομα δὲ ταυτὸν τῆς ἐμῆς ἔχουσά τις
δάμαρτος ἄλλη τοισίδ᾽ ἐνναίει δόμοις.
Διὸς δ᾽ ἔλεξε παῖδά νιν πεφυκέναι.
ἀλλ᾽ ἦ τίς ἐστι Ζηνὸς ὄνομ᾽ ἔχων ἀνὴρ 490
Νείλου παρ᾽ ὄχθας ; εἷς γὰρ ὅ γε κατ᾽ οὐρανόν.
Σπάρτη δὲ ποῦ γῆς ἐστι πλὴν ἵνα ῥοαὶ
τοῦ καλλιδόνακός εἰσιν Εὐρώτα μόνον ;
ἁπλοῦν δὲ Τυνδάρειον ὄνομα κλήζεται.
Λακεδαίμονος δὲ γαῖά τις ξυνώνυμος 495
Τροίας τ᾽ ; ἐγὼ μὲν οὐκ ἔχω τί χρὴ λέγειν.
πολλοὶ γάρ, ὡς εἴξασιν, ἐν πολλῇ χθονὶ
ὀνόματα ταῦτ᾽ ἔχουσι, καὶ πόλις πόλει
γυνὴ γυναικί τ᾽· οὐδὲν οὖν θαυμαστέον.
οὐδ᾽ αὖ τὸ δεινὸν προσπόλου φευξούμεθα. 500
ἀνὴρ γὰρ οὐδεὶς ὧδε βάρβαρος φρένας,
ὃς ὄνομ᾽ ἀκούσας τοὐμὸν οὐ δώσει βοράν.
κλεινὸν τὸ Τροίας πῦρ ἐγώ θ᾽, ὃς ἧψά νιν,
Μενέλαος, οὐκ ἄγνωστος ἐν πάσῃ χθονί.
*　　　*　　　*　　　*

δόμων ἄνακτα προσμένων· ἔχει δέ μοι 505

χεύματα.—οὐδέν᾽ for οὐδὲν is Musgrave's correction.
481. οὐχ ὅσον. Compare οὐχ ὡς Bacch. 929. μήδ᾽ ὥσπερ Alcest. 167. Pflugk rightly explains it, οὐ τοσοῦτον πικρὰ ὅσον πικροὺς λόγους ἔδωκα.
484. τὰς παρεστώσας. As if he had said ἐν γὰρ τοῖς παρεστῶσι πράγμασιν ἄλλας συμφορὰς κλύω πρὸς τοῖς π.
489. Διὸς κτλ. See v. 470. The comic tone of this ῥῆσις will hardly escape the reader.
494. ἁπλοῦν κτλ. There is only one Tyndareus whose name is talked of. Cf. 132.

497. ὡς εἴξασιν. For ὡς ἔοικε, by a well-known idiom, as Med. 337, ὄχλον παρέξεις, ὡς ἔοικας, ὦ γύναι.
500. τὸ δεινὸν προσπόλου, the fear suggested by the portress, that I should be put to death as a Greek, v. 440.
501. βάρβαρος. Here, as in Troad. 759, ὦ βάρβαρ᾽ ἐξευρόντες Ἕλληνες κακά, the transition to our meaning of the word is clearly marked. Hec. 1129, ἐκβαλὼν καρδίας τὸ βάρβαρον. Cf. Orest. 485.
505. προσμένων. The old reading was προσμενῶ, after which δ᾽ was inserted by

ΕΛΕΝΗ.

δισσὰς φυλάξεις· ἢν μὲν ὠμόφρων τις ᾖ,
κρύψας ἐμαυτὸν εἶμι πρὸς ναυάγια,
ἢν δ' ἐνδιδῷ τι μαλθακὸν, τὰ πρόσφορα
τῆς νῦν παρούσης συμφορᾶς αἰτήσομαι.
κακῶν μὲν ἡμῖν ἔσχατον τοῖς ἀθλίοις,   510
ἄλλους τυράννους αὐτὸν ὄντα βασιλέα
βίον προσαιτεῖν· ἀλλ' ἀναγκαίως ἔχει.
λόγος γάρ ἐστιν οὐκ ἐμὸς, σοφῶν δ' ἔπος,
δεινῆς ἀνάγκης οὐδὲν ἰσχύειν πλέον.
ΧΟ.   ἤκουσα τᾶς θεσπιῳδοῦ κόρας,   515
ἃ χρήζουσ' ἐφάνη τυράννοις

Hermann. Pflugk has προσμενῶ γ' with Barnes, where γε is wholly inadmissible; Dindorf transposes δισσὰς δέ μοι ἔχει φυλάξεις, after Musgrave. With much more probability he suspects a verse to have been lost. At all events some connecting particle is required. We seem to expect a continuation of the narrative to this effect;

ὡς καρτερήσω πρόσθεν αὐλείων πυλῶν
δόμων ἄνακτα προσμένων.

—ἔχει here is for παρέχει, as in the phrase μέμψιν ἔχει. Pflugk takes the nominative to ἔχει to be τὸ προσμένειν. And so Barnes had explained it, τοῦτο τὸ ἐπιχείρημα ἐν τῷ προσμένειν Θεοκλύμενον.
508. πρόσφορα. Hermann, objecting to the genitive in this singular idiom, does not seem to have remembered Aesch. Cho. 697, ἀλλ' ἔσθ' ὁ καιρὸς ἡμερεύοντας ξένους μακρᾶς κελεύθου τυγχάνειν τὰ πρόσφορα. These last two verses however are rather obscure, since ἡμερεύειν κελεύθου may possibly mean πανήμερον πορεύεσθαι, and we do not see why the poet did not write ἡμερεύσαντας, as their journey was now done. Hermann suggests that the construction may be τῆς νῦν συμφορᾶς παρούσης, the genitive absolute. But this is scarcely plausible, as the words so much more naturally mean συμφορᾶς τῆς νῦν παρούσης. A not improbable correction is that proposed by Reiske, ταῖς νῦν παρούσαις συμφοραῖς, for Elmsley (Med. 34) remarks on the frequent interchange in MSS. between the cases of the singular and the plural of this noun.
510. κακῶν μέν. The old reading was κακῶν δέ θ'. Hermann κακῶν δέ γ', Porson and Blomfield κακῶν δ' ἔθ'. But none of these is in the least appropriate. The μέν is so certainly and obviously required (the antithesis being ἀλλ' ἀναγκαίως ἔχει), that the present editor has felt no hesitation in restoring it. The μέν and the δέ were by some accident exchanged, and then the θ' was thrust in as a stop-gap. For the sentiment compare the apology of Adrastus to Theseus, in Suppl. 164, ἐν μὲν αἰσχύναις ἔχω πίτνων πρὸς οὐδας γόνυ σὸν ἀμπίσχειν χερὶ, πολιὸς ἀνὴρ τύραννος εὐδαίμων πάρος.
513. σοφῶν ἔπος. "Respicit, ut opinor, Simonideum illud, ἀνάγκῃ δ' οὐδὲ θεοὶ μάχονται." Pflugk. Compare Alcest. 965, κρεῖσσον οὐδὲν ἀνάγκας ηὗρον. Hermann's correction σοφὸν δ' ἔπος δεινῶς, ἀνάγκης κτλ., does not seem in good taste. The two Paris MSS. indeed give σοφὸν for σοφῶν. But the antithesis required is this, οὐκ ἐγὼ, ἀλλ' οἱ σοφοὶ ἔλεξαν.
515. The chorus, who at v. 319 had invited Helen to approach the prophetic maid, and had in turn been invited to accompany her within to hear the response, now return to the orchestra and announce that Menelaus is declared to be still alive, but wandering far from home on his return from Troy. The general character of the metre is glyconic, except that the first verse is iamb. dipodia + cretic dipodia, and v. 526 appears to be glyconeus polyschematistus.
516. χρήζουσ' ἐφάνη. For ἔχρησε, says Pflugk, who takes τυράννοις δόμοις for Helen and Menelaus. By ἐφάνη the result of the oracle, as now known, is implied. Hermann reads ἔφηνε, and for metrical reasons, which however do not appear to be cogent, makes a further change by placing ὡς after Μενέλαος.—

150   ΕΥΡΙΠΙΔΟΥ

δόμοις, ὡς Μενέλαος οὔπω
μελαμφαὲς οἴχεται
δι᾿ ἔρεβος, χθονὶ κρυφθείς,
ἀλλ᾿ ἔτι κατ᾿ οἶδμ᾿ ἅλιον   520
τρυχόμενος οὔπω λιμένων
ψαύσειεν πατρίας γᾶς,
ἀλατείᾳ βιότου
ταλαίφρων, ἄφιλος φίλων,
παντοδαπᾶς ἐπὶ γᾶς   525
πόδα χριμπτόμενος εἰναλίῳ
κώπᾳ Τρῳάδος ἐκ γᾶς.

ΕΛ. ἥδ᾿ αὖ τάφου τοῦδ᾿ εἰς ἕδρας ἐγὼ πάλιν
στείχω, μαθοῦσα Θεονόης φίλους λόγους,
ἣ πάντ᾿ ἀληθῶς οἶδε· φησὶ δ᾿ ἐν φάει   530
πόσιν τὸν ἀμὸν ζῶντα φέγγος εἰσορᾶν,
πορθμοὺς δ᾿ ἀλᾶσθαι μυρίους πεπλωκότα
ἐκεῖσε κἀκεῖσ᾿, οὐδ᾿ ἀγύμναστον πλάνοις
ἥξειν, ὅταν δὴ πημάτων λάβῃ τέλος.
ἓν δ᾿ οὐκ ἔλεξεν, εἰ μολὼν σωθήσεται.   535
ἐγὼ δ᾿ ἀπέστην τοῦτ᾿ ἐρωτῆσαι σαφῶς,

χρήξειν, as distinct from χρῄζειν, is a traditional form = χρᾶν. See Etym. M. in v. Schol. ad Aesch. Cho. 340. Hermann with good reason doubts if they are really distinct words. And the old copies appear to give χρήζουσ᾿.

522. ψαύσειεν. As if she had said, in the past tense, ἔλεξεν ὅτι ἔτι ζώῃ καὶ &c. Our own idiom is nearly identical; 'Theonöe said that Menelaus is not dead, but that in his wanderings he had not yet touched the harbours of his native land.'

526. The sense is, καίπερ ἀεὶ χριμπτόμενος πόδα γῇ πατρίᾳ, 'Though ever approaching his home in a ship in his return from Troy.' The preceding words are equivalent to τάλας ἀλώμενος παντοδαπᾶς ἐπὶ γᾶς.

528. ἥδ᾿ αὖ κτλ. Convinced that her husband yet survives, Helen redoubles her efforts to resist the marriage with Theoclymenus, and for this end again throws herself upon the protection of the tomb of Proteus, as in v. 64.

530. ἐν φάει—φέγγος. We notice here the same carelessness of expression as in Rhes. 970, where it is said that Rhesus shall be hidden in a subterranean cave βλέπων φάος. The notion of *light* was so far lost in that of *vitality*, that it scarcely occurred to the poet's mind either here as a tautology or there as a contradiction.

531. ἀμὸν Herm. and others with the old copies. Dindorf gives ἀμὸν, the former being for ἡμέτερον, the latter for ἐμόν. He also, with Matthiae, here reads πεπλευκότα, and so Pflugk, but not Hermann, who considers the Ionic form to have been intentionally ridiculed by Aristophanes. See v. 461. The accusative may depend either on the participle or on ἀλᾶσθαι. Theocr. xiii. 66, ἀλώμενος ὅσσ᾿ ἐμόγησεν ὤρεα καὶ δρυμώς. *Inf.* v. 598. Oed. Col. 1685, πῶς γὰρ ἤ τιν᾿ ἀπίαν γᾶν | ἢ πόντιον κλύδων᾿ ἀλώμεναι βίου | δύσοιστον ἕξομεν τροφάν;

535. σωθήσεται, 'he will return alive.' She does not mean, whether the man or merely his corpse will come, (though the words would signify this,) but, whether, having got as far as Egypt, he is destined to get back to Sparta.

ΕΛΕΝΗ.

ἡσθεῖσ᾽, ἐπεί νιν εἶπέ μοι σεσωσμένον·
ἐγγὺς δέ νύν που τῆσδ᾽ ἔφασκ᾽ εἶναι χθονὸς,
ναυαγὸν ἐκπεσόντα σὺν παύροις φίλοις,
ὅς μοι πόθ᾽ ἥξεις ; ὡς ποθεινὸς ἂν μόλοις.   540
ἔα, τίς οὗτος ; οὔ τί που κρυπτεύομαι
Πρωτέως ἀσέπτου παιδὸς ἐκ βουλευμάτων ;
οὐχ ὡς δρομαία πῶλος ἢ βάκχη θεοῦ
τάφῳ ξυνάψω κῶλον ; ἄγριος δέ τις
μορφὴν ὅδ᾽ ἐστὶν, ὅς με θηρᾶται λαβεῖν.   545
ΜΕ. σὲ τὴν ὄρεγμα δεινὸν ἡμιλλημένην
τύμβου 'πὶ κρηπῖδ᾽ ἐμπύρους τ᾽ ὀρθοστάτας,
μεῖνον· τί φεύγεις ; ὡς δέμας δείξασα σὸν

540. ὃς for ὥς is Seidler's correction, which W. Dindorf and Hermann adopt. Pflugk is for explaining ὡς "*quemadmodum quando aderis?* i. e. vel sic tamen quando venies?" Perhaps ὤμοι (οἴμοι Musgrave) is the true reading.—κρυπτεύομαι, Hesych. ἐνεδρεύομαι, probably from this place. The active κρυπτεύειν occurs Bacch. 888, and the analogous form διορθεύειν in Suppl. 417. These verbs represent the adjectives κρυπτὸς, ὀρθὸς, with εἰμί, properly, 'to be in concealment,' 'to be in the right.' On the passive use of such neuter words see the editor's note on Aesch. Theb. 58. We have both θιασεύειν and θιασεύεσθαι in Ion 552 and Bacch. 75. παρθενεύειν παῖδας Suppl. 452, and παρθενεύεσθαι *sup.* v. 283, σαλεύειν and σαλεύεσθαι, &c. παῖδας ὀρφανεύειν in Alc. 297, and ὠρφανεύετο *ib.* 535. Compare καλλιστεύεται in Med. 967.—Seeing the rough and ill-clad form of Menelaus, Helen supposes him to be some ruffian sent by Theoclymenus to drag her from the altar. Menelaus is now seen lurking in the hiding-place he had taken at v. 505.— ἀσέπτου, ἀσεβοῦς. He is so called, because she feared Theoclymenus in his passion would violate the sanctity of the altar-tomb. But in v. 9 he is said to have lived a pious life, θεοὺς σέβων, in allusion to his name.

546. σὲ τὴν κτλ. We must supply λέγω or καλῶ, unless indeed either of these words has been supplanted by μεῖνον. But Pflugk well compares Antig. 441, where the same ellipse occurs.— ὄρεγμα, Hesych. ὅρμημα. So χερῶν ὀρέγματα Agam. 1080. Cho. 418. βημάτων ὄρεγμα Cho. 785.—By κρηπὶς she means the plinth or base of the tomb,— the θυμέλη, regarding it as an altar. Photius, κρηπὶς, θεμέλιος—ὑποβάθρα. See on Ion 38. By ὀρθοστάτας the pillars supporting the tomb are meant. So ὀρθοστάται are the *uprights* forming the frame of the tent in Ion 1133. Cf. Herc. F. 980. Sir Charles Fellows has given drawings of many such tombs, of an earlier date than Euripides, discovered by him in Lycia. Some of them are quite altar-shaped, and there is not a doubt that victims were slain, and perhaps afterwards burnt on them as an offering to the daemon. Hence the epithet ἐμπύρους. See Alcest. 845, and the note. Heracl. 1040, ἀλλὰ μήτε μοι χοὰς μήθ᾽ αἷμ᾽ ἐάσῃς εἰς ἐμὸν στάξαι τάφον. Sir Charles also records the curious fact, (without knowing which we cannot fully understand all these expressions, e. g. Aesch. Cho. 157, ἔχει μὲν ἤδη γαπότους χοὰς πατήρ,) that the blood or the libations offered were actually poured down through a pipe or hole into the interior θήκη or chamber of the dead. With the above facts before him, the reader will hardly place much reliance on the explanation which, after Musgrave, the commentators give of ὀρθοστάτας, *placentas in ignem conjectas*. For so Pollux and Hesychius interpret the word. That Proteus was worshipped as a hero by the Egyptians appears from Herod. ii. 112, quoted by Bothe.

548. μεῖνον. He here seizes her, as is clear from v. 551.

ἔκπληξιν ἡμῖν ἀφασίαν τε προστίθης.
ΕΛ. ἀδικούμεθ', ὦ γυναῖκες· εἰργόμεσθα γὰρ 550
τάφου πρὸς ἀνδρὸς τοῦδε, καί μ' ἑλὼν θέλει
δοῦναι τυράννοις, ὧν ἐφεύγομεν γάμους.
ΜΕ. οὐ κλῶπές ἐσμεν, οὐχ, ὑπηρέται κακῶν.
ΕΛ. καὶ μὴν στολήν γ' ἄμορφον ἀμφὶ σῶμ' ἔχεις.
ΜΕ. στῆσον, φόβου μεθεῖσα, λαιψηρὸν πόδα. 555
ΕΛ. ἵστημ', ἐπεί γε τοῦδ' ἐφάπτομαι τόπου.
ΜΕ. τίς εἶ; τίν' ὄψιν σὴν, γύναι, προσδέρκομαι;
ΕΛ. σὺ δ' εἶ τίς; αὐτὸς γὰρ σὲ κἄμ' ἔχει λόγος.
ΜΕ. οὐπώποτ' εἶδον προσφερέστερον δέμας.
ΕΛ. ὦ θεοί. θεὸς γὰρ καὶ τὸ γιγνώσκειν φίλους. 560
ΜΕ. Ἑλληνὶς εἶ τις ἢ 'πιχωρία γυνή;
ΕΛ. Ἑλληνίς· ἀλλὰ καὶ τὸ σὸν θέλω μαθεῖν.
ΜΕ. Ἑλένῃ σ' ὁμοίαν δὴ μάλιστ' εἶδον, γύναι.
ΕΛ. ἐγὼ δὲ Μενέλεῳ γέ σ'· οὐδ' ἔχω τί φῶ.
ΜΕ. ἔγνως γὰρ ὀρθῶς ἄνδρα δυστυχέστατον. 565
ΕΛ. ὦ χρόνιος ἐλθὼν σῆς δάμαρτος ἐς χέρας.
ΜΕ. ποίας δάμαρτος; μὴ θίγῃς ἐμῶν πέπλων.
ΕΛ. ἣν σοι δίδωσι Τυνδάρεως, ἐμὸς πατήρ.
ΜΕ. ὦ φωσφόρ' Ἑκάτη, πέμπε φάσματ' εὐμενῆ.
ΕΛ. οὐ νυκτίφαντον πρόπολον Ἐνοδίας μ' ὁρᾷς. 570
ΜΕ. οὐ μὴν γυναικῶν γ' εἰς δυοῖν ἔφυν πόσις.
ΕΛ. ποίων δὲ λέκτρων δεσπότης ἄλλων ἔφυς;

553. οὐχ, 'no indeed.' Hermann, who well compares Agam. 1270, οὐκ ἔστ' ἄλυξις, οὔ, ξένοι, χρόνον πλέω, (though ὦ ξένοι is of course a likely reading,) rightly puts a comma after οὐχ. W. Dindorf, in his dogmatic way, says "scribendum οὐδ'," as accordingly he edits.

555. φόβου. Hermann, followed by Dindorf, gives φόβους, though he admits that the plural is hardly used by the tragic writers. Perhaps he forgot φόβοισι in Ajax 531. The genitive however is capable of being explained in three ways; (1) by supplying μέρος τι. (2) by construing μεθεῖσα πόδα ἐκ φόβου. (3) by making μεθιέναι τινὸς follow the analogy of ἀνιέναι τινὸς, which occurs in Med. 456.

560. θεὸς γὰρ κτλ. A similar passage is Choeph. 50, τὸ δ' εὐτυχεῖν, τόδ' ἐν βροτοῖς θεός τε καὶ θεοῦ πλέον.

561. This verse, accidentally omitted in the MSS. and early editions, on account of the same word commencing the next verse, was restored by Markland from Ar. Thesm. 907, where this passage is quoted as far as 566, though the conclusion of 564 is travestied. Aristophanes also uses v. 558.

570. πρόπολον. Spectres were regarded as the ministers or infernal attendants of Hecate, in the same manner that δαίμονες of superior dignity on earth were the πρόπολοι of Persephone. See Hes. Opp. 141. Aesch. Cho. 350. Ion 1048. Alcest. 746. As commonly appearing in the night, they were νυκτίφαντα or νυκτίφοιτα, for both readings are found in Aesch. Prom. 675.

ΕΛΕΝΗ.

ΜΕ. ἣν ἄντρα κεύθει κἀκ Φρυγῶν κομίζομαι.
ΕΛ. οὐκ ἔστιν ἄλλη σή τις ἀντ' ἐμοῦ γυνή.
ΜΕ. οὔ που φρονῶ μὲν εὖ, τὸ δ' ὄμμα μου νοσεῖ; 575
ΕΛ. οὐ γάρ με λεύσσων σὴν δάμαρθ' ὁρᾶν δοκεῖς;
ΜΕ. τὸ σῶμ' ὅμοιον, τὸ δὲ σαφές μ' ἀποστερεῖ.
ΕΛ. σκέψαι· τί σοι δεῖ τοῦδε; τίς σαφέστερος;
ΜΕ. ἔοικας· οὔτοι τοῦτό γ' ἐξαρνήσομαι.
ΕΛ. τίς οὖν διδάξει σ' ἄλλος ἢ σά γ' ὄμματα; 580
ΜΕ. ἐκεῖ νοσοῦμεν, ὅτι δάμαρτ' ἄλλην ἔχω.
ΕΛ. οὐκ ἦλθον ἐς γῆν Τρῳάδ', ἀλλ' εἴδωλον ἦν.
ΜΕ. καὶ τίς βλέποντα σώματ' ἐξεργάζεται;
ΕΛ. αἰθήρ, ὅθεν σὺ θεοπόνητ' ἔχεις λέχη.
ΜΕ. τίνος πλάσαντος θεῶν; ἄελπτα γὰρ λέγεις. 585
ΕΛ. Ἥρας, διάλλαγμ', ὡς Πάρις με μὴ λάβοι.
ΜΕ. πῶς οὖν ἂν ἐνθάδ' ἦσθά τ' ἐν Τροίᾳ θ' ἅμα;
ΕΛ. τοὔνομα γένοιτ' ἂν πολλαχοῦ, τὸ σῶμα δ' οὔ.

577. τὸ σαφὲς, the certain fact, viz. that I have just left my own wife concealed in a cave, deprives me of you, makes it impossible that I should acknowledge you. So Hermann, who rightly disapproves of taking τὸ σῶμα as the subject, τὸ σαφὲς as the object. Perhaps however we should read ἀποστερεῖς, viz. you make it impossible for me to be sure, by being, as it were, the double of my present wife; or τὸ δὲ σαφές γ' ἀποστατεῖ, 'there is a *likeness*, but the absence of *certainty*.'

578. This verse is unfortunately corrupt, σκέψαι τί σου δεῖ· τίς ἐστί σου σοφώτερος; Dindorf and Matthiae, and (as usual) also Pflugk, adopt a not very probable emendation of Wyttenbach, σκέψαι· τὸ δ' οὐδείς ἐστί σου σοφώτερος ; Hermann admits with praise the equally unsatisfactory reading of Seidler, σκέψαι τί σοὐνδεῖ; πίστις οὐ σαφεστέρα, except that he chooses to retain the masculine, σαφέστερος. A more probable correction seems to be that given above; 'Why do you wait for *that*?' viz. absolute certainty, τὸ σαφές. 'Who can possibly be more evident than I am to you?' To which Menelaus replies, 'Why, certainly you are like; *that* I cannot deny.'

580. σά γ' ὄμματα Hermann for τὰ σά γ' ὄμματα. So also Dobree proposed. Dindorf prefers Matthiae's reading ἢ τὰ σ' ὄμματα. See Tro. 918. The sense is, σά γε ὄμματα διδάξει, εἰ μή τις ἄλλος.

583. καὶ τίς (like καὶ πῶς &c.) expresses incredulity. 'You don't mean to say that any one can make living bodies!' So in Troad. 1280, ἰὼ θεοί. καὶ τί τοὺς θεοὺς καλῶ; Καὶ πρὶν γὰρ οὐκ ἤκουσαν ἀνακαλούμενοι. Ion 530, καὶ τί μοι λέξεις; 'Truly, I should like to hear what you will have to say.' Aesch. Cho. 208, καὶ τίνα σύνοισθά μοι καλουμένῃ βροτῶν;

586. Ἥρας, sc. πλασάσης. See v. 31—4.—διάλλαγμα, an exchange, a substitute; agreeing with, or in apposition to, εἴδωλον. Pflugk construes Ἥρας διάλλαγμα very differently, as if referring to λέχη. 'You have a substitute of Juno's making,' &c.

587. ἦσθά τ'. The τε was added by Barnes. Hermann repeats ἂν, ἦσθ' ἂν κτλ., and explains, 'How could you have been here and at Troy at the same time?' And so Pflugk, to whom indeed the right interpretation of the passage is due. Dindorf adopts the not improbable correction of an anonymous critic, πῶς οὖν ἂμ' ἐνθάδ' κτλ. But this use of ἂν with an imperfect, expressing a condition which has been fulfilled, is well illustrated by Agam. 1223, ἦ κάρτ' ἄρ' ἂν παρεσκόπεις χρησμῶν ἐμῶν, 'You must have strangely misunderstood the meaning of my warnings;' where see the editor's note.

VOL. II.

ΜΕ. μέθες με, λύπης ἅλις ἔχων ἐλήλυθα.
ΕΛ. λείψεις γὰρ ἡμᾶς, τὰ δὲ κέν' ἐξάξεις λέχη ; 590
ΜΕ. καὶ χαῖρέ γ' Ἑλένη προσφερὴς ὀθούνεκ' εἶ.
ΕΛ. ἀπωλόμην· λαβοῦσά σ' οὐχ ἕξω πόσιν.
ΜΕ. τοὐκεῖ με μέγεθος τῶν πόνων πείθει, σὺ δ' οὔ.
ΕΛ. οἳ 'γώ· τίς ἡμῶν ἐγένετ' ἀθλιωτέρα ;
οἱ φίλτατοι λείπουσιν· οὐδ' ἀφίξομαι 595
Ἕλληνας οὐδὲ πατρίδα τὴν ἐμήν ποτε.

ΑΓΓΕΛΟΣ.

Μενέλαε, μαστεύων σε κιγχάνω μόλις,
πᾶσαν πλανηθεὶς τήνδε βάρβαρον χθόνα,
πεμφθεὶς ἑταίρων τῶν λελειμμένων ὕπο.
ΜΕ. τί δ' ἔστιν ; οὔ που βαρβάρων συλᾶσθ' ὕπο ; 600
ΑΓ. θαυμάστ', ἔλασσον τοὔνομ' ἢ τὸ πρᾶγμ' ἔχον.
ΜΕ. λέγ', ὡς φέρεις τι τῇδε τῇ σπουδῇ νέον.
ΑΓ. λέγω πόνους σε μυρίους τλῆναι μάτην.
ΜΕ. παλαιὰ θρηνεῖς πήματ'· ἀγγέλλεις δὲ τί ;
ΑΓ. βέβηκεν ἄλοχος σὴ πρὸς αἰθέρος πτυχὰς 605
ἀρθεῖσ' ἄφαντος· οὐρανῷ δὲ κρύπτεται,
λιποῦσα σεμνὸν ἄντρον οὗ σφ' ἐσώζομεν,
τοσόνδε λέξασ', Ὦ ταλαίπωροι Φρύγες
πάντες τ' Ἀχαιοί, δι' ἔμ' ἐπὶ Σκαμανδρίοις

589. λύπας vulg., and so Pflugk, who compares Med. 1107, καὶ δὴ γὰρ ἅλις βίοτόν θ' ηὗρον. Others read λύπης with Elmsley on Heracl. 471. Both constructions are used; but ἅλις in the adverbial sense means, according to Hermann, 'to one's heart's content.'
593. σὺ δ' οὔ. I am more convinced by the troubles I have endured at Troy, than by your pretensions. At this verse Menelaus leaves the tomb for a little distance, when he is met by the messenger.
595. λείπουσί μ' Musgrave for λείπουσιν. And so Hermann and W. Dindorf. It is however very easy to supply ἡμᾶς. See above on v. 57.
598. πλανηθεὶς χθόνα. See v. 532. Bacch. 873, θρώσκειν πεδίον παραποτάμιον. The expression is of course hyperbolical for μόλις εὑρών σε.
601. ἔχον Barnes and Musgrave for ἔχων. Hermann explains, " duo respondet ad τί δ' ἔστιν ; primo θαυμαστὰ, deinde per singularem." Pflugk, retaining ἔχων, and putting no stop in the verse, regards the construction as continued from κιγχάνω, " mira non tam dictu quam re nuntians." Where either will do, it is not always easy to choose. It is however the more regular practice in monostich dialogue to reply to the question immediately preceding. Scaliger's θαῦμ' ἔστ', adopted by Dindorf, is less satisfactory.
605. πτυχὰς Hermann after Elmsley for πτύχας, i. e. as from πτυχή, not from πτύξ.
607. σεμνὸν ἄντρον. It was doubtless consecrated to some of the nymphs or gods of Ocean.
609. πάντες. Hermann thinks the poet must have been ineptus atque in-

ΕΛΕΝΗ. 155

ἀκταῖσιν Ἥρας μηχαναῖς ἐθνήσκετε, 610
δοκοῦντες Ἑλένην οὐκ ἔχοντ᾽ ἔχειν Πάριν.
ἐγὼ δ᾽ ἐπειδὴ χρόνον ἔμειν᾽ ὅσον μ᾽ ἐχρῆν,
τὸ μόρσιμον σώσασα, πατέρ᾽ ἐς οὐρανὸν
ἄπειμι· φήμας δ᾽ ἡ τάλαινα Τυνδαρὶς
ἄλλως κακὰς ἤκουσεν οὐδὲν αἰτία. 615
ὦ χαῖρε, Λήδας θύγατερ, ἐνθάδ᾽ ἦσθ᾽ ἄρα;
ἐγὼ δέ σ᾽ ἄστρων ὡς βεβηκυῖαν μυχοὺς
ἤγγελλον, εἰδὼς οὐδὲν ὡς ὑπόπτερον
δέμας φοροίης. οὐκ ἐῶ σε κερτομεῖν
ἡμᾶς τόδ᾽ αὖθις, ὡς μάτην ἐν Ἰλίῳ 620
πόνους παρεῖχες σῷ πόσει καὶ συμμάχοις.

ΜΕ. τοῦτ᾽ ἔστ᾽ ἐκεῖνο· ξυμβεβᾶσιν οἱ λόγοι
οἱ τῆσδ᾽ ἀληθεῖς· ὦ ποθεινὸς ἡμέρα,
ὥς σ᾽ εἰς ἐμὰς ἔδωκεν ὠλένας λαβεῖν.

ΕΛ. ὦ φίλτατ᾽ ἀνδρῶν Μενέλεως, ὁ μὲν χρόνος 625
παλαιός, ἡ δὲ τέρψις ἀρτίως πάρα.
ἔλαβον ἀσμένα πόσιν ἐμὸν, φίλαι,
περιπετάσασα χέρα

sanus to have written πάντες with δι᾽ ἐμὲ ἐθνήσκετε. And accordingly he reads τάλανές τ᾽, which, to say the least, sounds badly after ταλαίπωροι. Of course, the poet merely meant, what the imperfect properly expresses, that they *were dying*, day by day, for all that long time, to no purpose, but for a mere εἴδωλον. Cf. Hec. 35, πάντες τ᾽ Ἀχαιοὶ ναῦς ἔχοντες ἥσυχοι θάσσουσι.

613. σώσασα, having kept, having observed, the allotted time of my presence on earth.—πατέρα may agree with οὐρανὸν, as αἰθὴρ was regarded as her parent in v. 584. Pflugk takes it for the accusative after ἄπειμι, i. e. πρὸς πατέρα Ζῆνα.

616. ὦ χαῖρε. Helen had left the tomb on hearing the words of the messenger, and is now recognised by him as the same Helen who had been wafted to the sky. Here again, we seem to feel that a touch of comedy prevails in the scene.

620—1. μάτην and σῷ are the corrections of Barnes and Milton for ἄδην and ᾧ. The messenger alludes to v. 603. Matthiae defends ἄδην, as does Vater in p. cxviii of his Preface to the *Rhesus*; "ὡς dictum pro ἐπεὶ, et hoc vult nun-

tius: *non sinam te rursus nos fallere, siquidem satis in Troja negotia exhibere solebas marito et sociis.*" But in this version he overlooks τόδε, which closely belongs to ὡς, ' this fact, namely that' &c. As for κερτομεῖν, though it means ' to deceive,' (see the note on Alcest. 1125,) it also more commonly signifies ' to reproach,' *exprobrare aliquid*, as in Suppl. 321. ' You have done this once by your escape,' he says, ' but you shall not do it again.'

623. ὦ ποθεινός. *O laetum diem*, not *O laeta dies*, as Pflugk without distinction of idioms would construe it. See above, v. 461. Med. 61. In the next line ὥς σ᾽ for ὡς is Hermann's. Dindorf and Pflugk give ἤ σ᾽, after Canter. But ὡς is the exclamation, for ὡς εὐτυχῶς.

625. ὁ μὲν χρόνος. The opposition of παλαιὸς with ἀρτίως shews the sense to be, ' the time of rejoicing has been long coming, but at last it has arrived, and at the present moment.' Hermann, *diu quidem est ex quo non sum gavisa: modo autem paratum est gaudium.*

628. Hermann makes a dochmiac of this verse, περί τ᾽ ἐπέτασα χέρα.

x 2

156   ΕΥΡΙΠΙΔΟΥ

φίλιον ἐν μακρᾷ φλογὶ φαεσφόρῳ.
ΜΕ. κἀγὼ σέ· πολλοὺς δ' ἐν μέσῳ λόγους ἔχων   630
οὐκ οἶδ' ὁποίου πρῶτον ἄρξωμαι τὰ νῦν.
ΕΛ. γέγηθα, κρατὶ δ' ὀρθίους ἐθείρας
ἀνεπτέρωκα, καὶ δάκρυ σταλάσσω,
περὶ δὲ γυῖα χεῖρας ἔβαλον
ἡδονὰν ὡς λάβω, ὦ πόσις.*   635
ΜΕ. ὦ φιλτάτη πρόσοψις, οὐκ ἐμέμφθην·
ἔχω τὰ τῆς Διός τε λέκτρα Λήδας θ',
ἃν ὑπὸ λαμπάδων κόροι λεύκιπποι
*σοὶ ξυνομαίμονες ὤλβισαν ὤλβισαν   640
τὸ πρόσθεν, ἐκ δόμων δ' ἐνόσφισαν θεοί.

631. οὐκ οἶδα κτλ. Compare Med. 376—7, πολλὰς δ' ἔχουσα θανασίμους αὐτοῖς ὁδούς, οὐκ οἶδ' ὁποίᾳ πρῶτον ἐγχειρῶ, φίλαι. The λόγοι ἐν μέσῳ are the matters she has to talk about since she last saw him.—ἄρξωμαι is Hermann's reading for ἄρξομαι, the deliberative subjunctive being usual in such idioms as οὐκ οἶδα τί ποιῶ, οὐκ ἔχω ὅτι λέγω &c. He remarks on the ensuing conversation (between two of the actors, in lyric measures, but without the chorus, called τὰ ἀπὸ σκηνῆς,) that Menelaus, as a man of dignity, and having no other cause of joy than the having got his true wife in place of an εἴδωλον, is less profuse in his expressions of satisfaction than Helen, to whom the return of Menelaus was all in all, especially at the present conjuncture. Accordingly, Menelaus uses for the most part the stately and sedate iambic measure, while Helen speaks in hurried dochmiacs. Compare Ion 1445 seqq. There is no division of strophe and antistrophe, unless Hermann be right in making (by the aid of rather violent alterations) vv. 632—635 correspond with 636—640, including in Menelaus' answer the words ὦ φιλτάτη πρόσοψις, as Reisig and Elmsley had proposed. In the latter point they are clearly right, for it is incredible that Menelaus should give utterance in such a scene to the frigid words οὐκ ἐμέμφθην without the addition of some term of endearment.

633. ἀνεπτέρωκα. Here in a very unusual sense, 'I ruffle up as feathers.' Pflugk compares Ajac. 692, ἔφριξ' ἔρωτι, περιχαρὴς δ' ἀνεπτόμαν. The same active perfect, in the sense of 'to scare,' 'to flutter,' occurs Orest. 876.

634. Something is lost here. The dochmiac might be restored thus,

περὶ δὲ γυῖα χεῖρ' ἔβαλον, ἡδονὰν
ὡς λάβω, ὦ πόσις,

where the ω short might be defended by the frequent use of ἰὼ ἰὼ at the beginning of a dochmiac, though the transposition of the words is easy, ὦ πόσις, ὡς λάβω. Hermann edits the passage thus;

περὶ δὲ γυῖα χέρας ἔβαλον ἔβαλον ἡ-
δονὰν ὡς λάβω, ὦ πόσις, ὦ πόσις.

638. τὰ τῆς Διός τε Elmsley on Med. 581 for τὰ τοῦ Διός. In the former phrase ἔχω λέκτρα means 'I hold in marriage the daughter of Zeus and Leda;' but τὰ Διὸς λέκτρα is 'the wife of Zeus.'

640. Hermann restores the double dochmiac by adding σοὶ before ξυνομαίμονες. Perhaps γε (nempe) should follow it.

641. After ἐνόσφισαν the old copies add σ' ὁμοῦ, which later editors have altered to σ' ἐμοῦ. The latter, which is probably an earlier reading than σ' ὁμοῦ, would seem to have been added by some one who did not observe that the accusative ἃν depended on both verbs alike. Elmsley would read, ἐκ δόμων δὲ νοσφίσας ἐμοῦ, | πρὸς ἄλλαν κτλ., and Hermann agrees in commencing the next speech of Helen with τὸ κακὸν κτλ. It is impossible to place much reliance on any one of the severally plausible conjectures that have been made on this passage. The next verse is bacchiac. Hermann converts it into a senarius by an ingenious

ΕΛΕΝΗ. 157

πρὸς ἄλλαν δ' ἐλαύνει θεὸς συμφορὰν τᾶσδε κρείσσω·
ΕΛ. τὸ κακὸν δ' ἀγαθὸν σέ τε κἀμὲ συνάγαγεν, πόσι,
χρόνιον, ἀλλ' ὅμως ὀναίμαν τύχας. 645
ΜΕ. ὄναιο δῆτα. ταὐτὰ δὴ ξυνεύχομαι·
δυοῖν γὰρ ὄντοιν οὐχ ὁ μὲν τλήμων, ὁ δ' οὔ.
ΕΛ. φίλαι φίλαι, τὰ πάρος οὐκέτι
στένομεν, οὐδ' ἀλγῶ.
πόσιν ἐμὸν *ἐμὸν ἔχομεν ἔχομεν, ὃν ἔμενον 650
ἔμενον ἐκ Τροίας πολυετῆ μολεῖν.
ΜΕ. ἔχεις μ' ἔχω τέ σ'· ἡλίους δὲ μυρίους
μόγις διελθὼν ᾐσθόμην τὰ τῆς θεοῦ.
ἐμὰ δὲ δάκρυα χαρμονᾷ πλέον ἔχει
χάριτος ἢ λύπας. 655
ΕΛ. τί φῶ; τίς ἂν τάδ' ἤλπισεν βροτῶν ποτέ;
ἀδόκητον ἔχω σε πρὸς στέρνοις.
ΜΕ. κἀγὼ σὲ τὴν δοκοῦσαν Ἰδαίαν πόλιν
μολεῖν Ἰλίου τε μελέους πύργους.
ΕΛ. ἐὴ ἐὴ, πικρὰς ἐς ἀρχὰς βαίνεις· 660
ΜΕ. πρὸς θεῶν, δόμων πῶς τῶν ἐμῶν ἀπεστάλης;
ΕΛ. ἐὴ ἐὴ, πικρὰν δ' ἐρευνᾷς φάτιν.
ΜΕ. λέγ', ὡς ἀκουστά· πάντα δῶρα δαιμόνων.

process, ὁμοῦ δ' ἐλαύνει, ξυμφορὰν ἄλλην, θεός. He regards τᾶσδε κρείσσω as a gloss on ἄλλην. The meaning is, 'though the gods separated us for a long time, heaven is bringing us to a different fortune, and one better than this which we have hitherto had.'

644. τὸ κακὸν δ' ἀγαθὸν, sc. ἀγαθὸν ὄν, "periculosus Menelai adventus in Aegyptum," Bothe. 'What we thought our misfortune has turned to our good, and has united you and me, my husband; after a long time indeed, but still I say, May I be blest in my good luck.'—πόσι is Hermann's reading for πόσιν. Dindorf ὦ πόσι. The accusative arose from this and the next verse being wrongly assigned to Menelaus, which involved the further error of giving 646—7 to Helen.

647. Pers. 798, συμβαίνει γὰρ οὐ τὰ μέν, τὰ δ' οὔ.

650. ἐμὸν was repeated by Seidler. Hermann improves the resolved double dochmiac by transposing the words, πό-σιν ἔχομεν ἔχομεν ἐμὸν ἐμὸν ὃν ἔμενον.

653. τὰ τῆς θεοῦ. The trick put upon me by Hera, in making an εἴδωλον so long take the place of my true wife.

654. χαρμονᾷ is Hermann's slight correction for —ὰν or —ά, by which the meaning is made clear and simple, 'My tears through joy have more of pleasure in them than of grief.' Cf. Agam. 261, χαρά μ' ὑφέρπει δάκρυον ἐκκαλουμένη.

661. This verse was transposed by Hermann, who rightly observes that the question πρὸς θεῶν &c. is too abrupt unless introduced and suggested by some remark of Helen's. The natural and regular order of the dialogue is undoubtedly that given above. The old arrangement made Helen reply the two verses beginning with ἐὴ ἐὴ (MSS. ἒ ἒ) to the iambic πρὸς θεῶν &c.

663. ὡς ἀκουστά. 'Since (however disagreeable) it must be heard. All things that befal us are sent by heaven.' Cf. Androm. 1084. Hermann first put a

158 ΕΥΡΙΠΙΔΟΥ

ΕΛ. ἀπέπτυσα μὲν λόγον, οἷον οἷον ἐσοίσομαι.
ΜΕ. ὅμως δὲ λέξον· ἡδύ τοι μόχθων κλύειν. 665
ΕΛ. οὐκ ἐπὶ λέκτρα βαρβάρου νεανία,
πετομένας κώπας,
πετομένου δ' ἔρωτος ἀδίκων γάμων.
ΜΕ. τίς *γάρ σε δαίμων ἢ πότμος συλᾷ πάτρας;
ΕΛ. ὁ Διὸς ὁ Διὸς, ὦ πόσι, με παῖς *Ἑρμᾶς 670
ἐπέλασεν Νείλῳ.
ΜΕ. θαυμαστά· τοῦ πέμψαντος; ὦ δεινοὶ λόγοι.
ΕΛ. κατεδάκρυσα καὶ βλέφαρον ὑγραίνω
δάκρυσιν· ἁ Διός μ' ἄλοχος ὤλεσεν.
ΜΕ. Ἥρα; τί νῷν χρῄζουσα προσθεῖναι κακόν; 675
ΕΛ. ὤμοι ἐμῶν δεινῶν, λουτρῶν καὶ κρηνῶν,
ἵνα θεαὶ μορφὰν
ἐφαίδρυναν ἔνθεν ἔμολεν κρίσις.

colon at ἀκουστὰ, and the context shows he is right. For Helen's reluctance to comply, even after his encouraging words, is expressed in the next verse. That reluctance seems to arise from a dislike to tell Menelaus that he has been cohabiting with an εἴδωλον, for, according to her account of the matter, no discredit attaches to herself.

665. μόχθων, i. e. τῶν οἰχομένων. Cf. Frag. Andromed. 145, ἀλλ' ἡδύ τοι σωθέντα μεμνῆσθαι πόνων.

666. οὐκ ἐπὶ λέκτρα, scil. ἀπεστάλην, v. 661. 'I was not fetched away as the bride of the Trojan youth' (as men say). The old reading λέκτρου was corrected by Hermann and L. Dindorf.—νεανία is to be read as a cretic.

668. πετομένου. As Eros was represented as winged (Hippol. 1275), there is an ingenious play on the preceding πετομένας (cf. Med. 1), as if the god flew along with the ship across the Aegean sea to Troy. Moreover, πέτεσθαι 'to be flighty' was aptly said of persons who were themselves in love. Pflugk compares Herod. ii. 115, ἀναπτερώσας αὐτὴν οἴχεαι ἔχων ἐκκλέψας, said of Paris having seduced Helen. But Ἔρως is not in fact personified, for the poet puts instead of the god 'the desire of an unrighteous marriage.'

669. τίς γὰρ Barnes for τίς.

670. με παῖς Ἑρμᾶς is Hermann's correction, adopted by W. Dindorf, for παῖς μ'. The metre is faulty in the vulgate. Less weight is perhaps to be attributed to Hermann's argument, that Zeus had so many sons that without specifying which of them was meant the narration would be vague. The same consideration however induced Elmsley to propose Μαίας με παῖς.

675. τί νῷν is the elegant correction of Hermann for τίνων, which Matthiae and Pflugk vainly attempt to explain by the convenient doctrine of confused constructions. To Hermann also is due the interrogative Ἥρα given to Menelaus, the old copies continuing it to Helen.—κακὸν for κακῶν is W. Dindorf's. The Greeks say τίς φίλων &c. in preference to τίς φίλος, but τί κακὸν much more commonly than τί κακῶν, unless in specifying one of several evils.

678. Before appearing to Paris in all their radiant beauty, the rival goddesses had bathed in a secluded spring. Cf. Androm. 284, ταὶ δ' ἐπεὶ ὑλόκομον νάπος ἤλυθον | οὐρειᾶν πιδάκων | νίψαν αἰγλᾶντα σώματ' ἐν ῥοαῖς. The same romantic tale is most poetically told in Iph. A. 1291 seqq.—φαιδρύνειν was peculiarly applied to the clear glossy hue imparted to the skin by the use of the bath. Hesiod, Opp. 751, μηδὲ γυναικείῳ λουτρῷ χρόα φαιδρύνεσθαι ἀνέρα. Aesch. Ag. 1077, τὸν ὁμοδέμνιον πόσιν λουτροῖσι φαιδρύ-

ΕΛΕΝΗ. 159

ΜΕ. τί δ' ἐς κρίσιν σοι τήνδ' ἐφῆχ' Ἥρα κακόν;
ΕΛ. Κύπριν ὡς ἀφέλοιτο ΜΕ. πῶς, αὔδα. 680
ΕΛ. Πάριν, ᾧ μ' ἐπένευσεν, ΜΕ. ὦ τλᾶμον
ΕΛ. τλάμονα τλάμον' ὧδ' ἐπέλασ' Αἰγύπτῳ.
ΜΕ. εἶτ' ἀντέδωκ' εἴδωλον, ὡς σέθεν κλύω.
ΕΛ. τά τε σὰ κατὰ μέλαθρα πάθεα πάθεα, μᾶ-
τερ, οἲ 'γώ. ΜΕ. τί φῄς; 685
ΕΛ. οὐκ ἔστιν μάτηρ· ἀγχόνιον βρόχον
δι' ἐμὲ κατεδήσατο, δύσγαμον αἰσχύναν.
ΜΕ. ὤμοι· θυγατρὸς δ' Ἑρμιόνης ἔστιν βίος;
ΕΛ. ἄγαμος, ἄτεκνος, ὦ πόσι, καταστένει
γάμον ἄγαμον ἐμόν. 690
ΜΕ. ὦ πᾶν κατ' ἄκρας δῶμ' ἐμὸν πέρσας Πάρις,
τάδε καὶ σὲ διώλεσε μυριάδας τε
χαλκεόπλων Δαναῶν.
ΕΛ. ἐμὲ δὲ πατρίδος ἄπο κακόποτμον ἀραίαν

νασα.—ἔνθεν κτλ., 'from which spot proceeded the decision' of their rival charms.

679. This is a very difficult verse. The old reading was, τάδ' εἰς κρίσιν σοι τῶνδ' ἔθηχ' Ἥρα κακῶν; which is evidently without meaning. If we look to the context, we shall see that the required sense is, 'What harm did Hera do to you by this trial?' And the reply is, 'She sent me to Egypt in order that she might take me from Paris,' (and consequently, from her rival Cypris, who had offered him the marriage of Helen as a bribe, Tro. 930.) Hence we can hardly avoid introducing τί in some part of the verse, whether for τάδ', with Musgrave, or for σοι, with Hermann. The latter reads thus, τὰ δ' εἰς κρίσιν τί τῶνδ' ἔθηχ' Ἥρα κακῶν; 'Into which of your troubles did Hera convert the affair of the trial?' W. Dindorf, after Musgrave and Seidler, τί δ' ἐς κρίσιν σοι τήνδ' ἐφῆχ' Ἥρα κακόν; 'What harm did Hera send on you in respect of this trial?' But neither of these is altogether satisfactory. Hermann's τὰ εἰς κρίσιν is better Greek than εἰς κρίσιν in the sense of διὰ τὴν κρίσιν.

681. Πάριν. The same accusative after ἀφέλοιτο as Κύπριν, and exegetical of it. For in taking Helen from Paris, Hera took her out of the hands of Cypris.—In the next verse Hermann has restored τλάμονα τλάμον' for τλάμων τλάμων, on metrical considerations.

684. τά τε σὰ Hermann for τὰ δέ. "Accusativi pendent ab ἀντέδωκε." Dind. So also Hermann. Rather she appears to continue an incoherent soliloquy from v. 674. It is possible that πάθεα μέλεα was the old reading, ἦν being supplied. Pflugk may be right in supposing an aposiopesis, and that she would have said πῶς φράσω or οἷα ἐγένετο.

687. Helen calls herself δύσγαμος αἰσχύνα, a reproach on account of her unhappy marriage with Paris, as in Troad. 1114 she is described as δύσγαμον αἶσχος. The old reading was δύσγαμος, corrected by Canter. Hermann also gives αἰσχύνᾳ, 'she hanged herself through shame,' δι' ἐμὲ τὴν δύσγαμον. This is a very plausible reading and one that is confirmed by v. 200, Λήδα τ' ἐν ἀγχόναις θάνατον ἔλαβεν αἰσχύνας ἐμᾶς ὑπ' ἀλγέων.

690. L. Dindorf, followed by Hermann and W. Dindorf, reads ἐμὸν in place of αἰσχύνᾳ, which violates the metre, and appears to have been interpolated from 687.

692. τάδε. ''Twas this that caused thy death too, and countless numbers of Argives.' Younger students will notice that καὶ—τε can never be construed as τε—καί. By τάδε he means, the mere εἴδωλον of Helen.—μυριάδας, cf. Rhes. 914.

ΕΥΡΙΠΙΔΟΥ

ἔβαλε θεὸς ἀπό τε πόλεος ἀπό τε σέθεν, 695
ὅτι μέλαθρα λέχεά τ' ἔλιπον οὐ λιποῦσ'
ἐπ' αἰσχροῖς γάμοις.

ΧΟ. εἰ καὶ τὰ λοιπὰ τῆς τύχης εὐδαίμονος
τύχοιτε, πρὸς τὰ πρόσθεν ἀρκέσειεν ἄν.

ΑΓ. Μενέλαε, κἀμοὶ †πρόσδοτέ τι τῆς ἡδονῆς, 700
ἣν μανθάνω μὲν καὐτὸς, οὐ σαφῶς δ' ἔχω.

ΜΕ. ἀλλ', ὦ γεραιὲ, καὶ σὺ κοινώνει λόγων.

ΑΓ. οὐχ ἥδε μόχθων τῶν ἐν Ἰλίῳ βραβεύς;

ΜΕ. οὐχ ἥδε, πρὸς θεῶν δ' ἦμεν ἠπατημένοι,
νεφέλης ἄγαλμ' ἔχοντες ἐν χεροῖν λυγρόν. 705

ΑΓ. τί φῄς;
νεφέλης ἄρ' ἄλλως εἴχομεν πόνους πέρι;

ΜΕ. Ἥρας τάδ' ἔργα καὶ θεῶν τρισσῶν ἔρις.

ΑΓ. ἡ δ' οὖσ' ἀληθῶς ἐστὶν ἥδε σὴ δάμαρ;

ΜΕ. αὕτη· λόγοις δ' ἐμοῖσι πίστευσον τάδε. 710

ΑΓ. ὦ θύγατερ, ὁ θεὸς ὡς ἔφυ τι ποικίλον
καὶ δυστέκμαρτον. εὖ δέ πως ἀναστρέφει,

---

696. ὅτι. 'Fortune has made me an outcast from my city (i. e. they will not receive me at Sparta) and from my husband, because I left my home, though I did not really leave it, for an adulterous marriage.'

698. It would be easy to read εὐδαίμονες, i. e. ὄντες, and so construe τὰ λοιπὰ τῆς τύχης. But τυχεῖν τῆς τύχης τὰ λοιπὰ εὐδαίμονος is correct, in point of grammar, in the sense 'to meet with fortune favourable for the future also, as it has been on the present occasion.' This, says the chorus, will suffice, will compensate, for the former miseries. Hermann rejects Pflugk's interpretation of τὰ λοιπὰ, *ceteris in rebus*, and compares Soph. El. 1226, ΗΛ. ἔχω σε χερσίν; ΟΡ. ὡς τὰ λοίπ' ἔχοις ἀεί.

700. The common reading, πρόσδοτέ τι τῆς ἡδονῆς, is intolerable on account of the metre. Hermann gives τῆσδε πρόσδοθ' ἡδονῆς. Why not προσδότω, i. e. Ἑλένη? For the genitive cf. Suppl. 350, τοῦ λόγου προσδούς. The messenger, who has stood by during the preceding interview, and seen and heard the expressions of joy from both, (as v. 632, 654,) would as naturally request that Helen should explain the cause of their happiness as that Menelaus should do so himself. In fact, as remarked on v. 631, the ἡδονὴ was more on the side of Helen than of Menelaus; hence the correction proposed would rather improve the sense. The alteration may easily have been made by some one who thought the insertion of τι necessary.

703. βραβεύς. She was properly the prize or object of contention; but he calls her the *umpire*, because on her will depended the continuance of the war. In the same sense Cypris is said ῥαβδονομεῖν in the contest between Hercules and Achelous for the possession of Deianira, Trach. 516.

705. λυγρὸν, *misellum*, φαῦλον, ἄθλιον. Valckenaer's conjecture ὑγρὸν is rightly rejected by Hermann, as worse than useless.

712. ἀναστρέφει. Suppl. 331, ὁ γὰρ θεὸς πάντ' ἀναστρέφει πάλιν. She means, that the god has a certain clever or cunning way of changing men's circumstances, and bringing successes and reverses first to this man and then to that. For εὖ πως see Phoen. 1126, εὖ πως στρόφιγξιν ἔνδοθεν κυκλούμεναι πόρπαχ' ὑπ' αὐτόν. The

ΕΛΕΝΗ.

ἐκεῖσε κἀκεῖσ' ἀναφέρων· ὁ μὲν πονεῖ,
ὁ δ' οὐ πονήσας αὖθις ὄλλυται κακῶς,
βέβαιον οὐδὲν τῆς ἀεὶ τύχης ἔχων. 715
σὺ γὰρ πόσις τε σὸς πόνων μετέσχετε,
σὺ μὲν λόγοισιν, ὁ δὲ δορὸς προθυμίᾳ.
σπεύδων δ', ὅτ' ἔσπευδ', οὐδὲν εἶχε· νῦν δ' ἔχει
αὐτόματα πράξας τἀγάθ' εὐτυχέστατα.
οὐκ ἄρα γέροντα πατέρα καὶ Διοσκόρω 720
ᾔσχυνας, οὐδ' ἔδρασας οἷα κλῄζεται.
νῦν ἀνανεοῦμαι τὸν σὸν ὑμέναιον πάλιν,
καὶ λαμπάδων μεμνήμεθ', ἃς τετραόροις
ἵπποις τροχάζων παρέφερον· σὺ δ' ἐν δίφροις
σὺν τῷδε νύμφη δῶμ' ἔλειπες ὄλβιον. 725
κακὸς γὰρ ὅστις μὴ σέβει τὰ δεσποτῶν
καὶ ξυγγέγηθε καὶ ξυνωδίνει κακοῖς.
ἐγὼ μὲν εἴην, κεἰ πέφυχ' ὅμως λάτρις,
ἐν τοῖσι γενναίοισιν ἠριθμημένος
δούλοισι, τοὔνομ' οὐκ ἔχων ἐλεύθερον, 730
τὸν νοῦν δέ. κρεῖσσον γὰρ τόδ' ἢ δυοῖν κακοῖν
ἕν' ὄντα χρῆσθαι, τὰς φρένας τ' ἔχειν κακὰς
ἄλλων τ' ἀκούειν δοῦλον ὄντα τῶν πέλας.
ΜΕ. ἄγ', ὦ γεραιέ, πολλὰ μὲν παρ' ἀσπίδα
μοχθήματ' ἐξέπλησας ἐκπονῶν ἐμοί, 735
καὶ νῦν μετασχὼν τῆς ἐμῆς εὐπραξίας
ἄγγειλον ἐλθὼν τοῖς λελειμμένοις φίλοις
τάδ' ὡς ἔχονθ' ηὕρηκας οἷ τ' ἐσμὲν τύχης,
μένειν τ' ἐπ' ἀκταῖς τούς τ' ἐμοὺς καραδοκεῖν

---

sentiment is illustrated, first generally; 'Thus, one man suffers present trouble, (but at length is released) while he who has hitherto been exempt from trouble afterwards perishes miserably;' then specially, by the case of Helen and her husband, who have suffered much both in reputation and in the fatigues of war, but now (her character is vindicated, and) he, though he gained little or nothing at the time by his exertions, has the blessings he is enjoying spontaneously poured upon him, having fared most prosperously. The order of the last words seems to be a little broken by the necessity of the metre, for ἔχει τὰ ἀγαθὰ αὐτόματα, πράξας εὐτυχέστατα. Pflugk explains πράξας by διαπραξάμενος, εὑρόμενος. And so Aeschylus has πράξασ' ἀρωγὴν, Suppl. 754.

728. For the humane view which Euripides delights to take of the condition of slaves, see Preface to Vol. i. p. xiii.

732. χρῆσθαι. So Med. 347, συμφορᾷ κεχρημένους.

735. ἐκπονῶν ἐμοὶ Barnes for ἐκ πόνων ἐμῶν.

738. οἷ ἐσμὲν, for εἰς οἵαν τύχην καθεστήκαμεν. Tyrwhitt would read οὗ.

ἀγῶνας, εἰ μένουσί μ', οὓς ἐλπίζομεν, 740
κεἰ τήνδε πως δυναίμεθ' ἐκκλέψαι χθονὸς,
φρουρεῖν ὅπως ἂν εἰς ἓν ἐλθόντες τύχης
ἐκ βαρβάρων σωθῶμεν, ἢν δυνώμεθα.
ΑΓ. ἔσται τάδ', ὦναξ. ἀλλά τοι τὰ μάντεων
ἐσεῖδον ὡς φαῦλ' ἐστὶ καὶ ψευδῶν πλέα· 745
οὐδ' ἦν ἄρ' ὑγιὲς οὐδὲν ἐμπύρου φλογὸς
οὔτε πτερωτῶν φθέγματ'· εὔηθες δέ τοι
τὸ καὶ δοκεῖν ὄρνιθας ὠφελεῖν βροτούς.
Κάλχας γὰρ οὐκ εἶπ' οὐδ' ἐσήμηνε στρατῷ,
νεφέλης ὕπερ θνήσκοντας εἰσορῶν φίλους, 750
οὐδ' Ἕλενος, ἀλλὰ πόλις ἀνηρπάσθη μάτην.
εἴποις ἂν, οὕνεχ' ὁ θεὸς οὐκ ἠβούλετο·
τί δῆτα μαντευόμεθα; τοῖς θεοῖσι χρὴ
θύοντας αἰτεῖν ἀγαθὰ, μαντείας δ' ἐᾶν·
βίου γὰρ ἄλλως δέλεαρ ηὑρέθη τόδε, 755
κοὐδεὶς ἐπλούτησ' ἐμπύροισιν, ἀργὸς ὤν.
γνώμη δ' ἀρίστη μάντις ἥ τ' εὐβουλία.

740. εἰ Herm for οἵ. The sense is, εἰ ἐκεῖνοι ἀγῶνες, οὓς ἐλπίζομεν, &c., namely, the danger and difficulty of getting Helen out of the hands of Theoclymenus.
741. κεἰ for καὶ L. Dindorf, and ἐκκλέψαι for ἐκπλεῦσαι Matthiae, two MSS. giving ἐκπλέξαι. Translate, 'And, if we should by some means or other chance to succeed in removing her stealthily out of the country, to be on the watch, in order that, being all united in the same good fortune, we may get safely away from these barbarians, if we can.'
747. πτερωτῶν, for ὀρνίθων. Aesch. Suppl. 504, οὔτοι πτερωτῶν ἁρπαγῇ σ' ἐκδώσομεν. Bacch. 257, σκοπεῖν πτερωτοὺς κἀμπύρων μισθοὺς ἔχειν. On the contempt of Euripides for the μάντεις, see Preface to vol. i. p. xxi. There is little doubt that, like Aristophanes, he regarded them as mischievous tools in the hands of the war party.—οὐχ ὑγιὲς οὐδὲν, see Bacch. 262.—τὸ καὶ δοκεῖν, 'the very notion that,' &c. So Med. 1052, τὸ καὶ προέσθαι μαλθακοὺς λόγους φρενός.
751. οὐδ' Ἕλενος for οὐδέν γε is one of Porson's acute and certain emendations.
752. οὐκ ἠβούλετο, scil. φράζειν. Without doubt this was the common excuse of seers when they were reproached for not having seen a coming event. It is alluded to in Ion 375,

εἰ τοὺς θεοὺς ἄκοντας ἐκπονήσομεν
φράζειν & μὴ θέλουσιν ἢ προβωμίοις
σφαγαῖσι μήλων ἢ δι' οἰωνῶν πτεροῖς.

754. μαντείας ἐᾶν. Electr. 400, βροτῶν δὲ μαντικὴν χαίρειν ἐῶ.
756. οὐδεὶς ἐπλούτησε. The seers themselves were regarded as fond of money. Even Sophocles, who always speaks of them with singular respect, alludes to this frailty, Antig. 1055, where Creon says to Teiresias, τὸ μαντικὸν γὰρ πᾶν φιλάργυρον γένος. Euripides however, who was not likely to deny the charge, (see on Bacch. 255,) is not here speaking of the seers, but of their victims, who thought to find fortune by trusting to divination. Müller thinks (Hist. of Lit. p. 375, note,) that these invectives against the soothsayers are here especially made in reference to the recent failure of the Sicilian expedition, which this worthless class of idlers had especially urged the people to undertake.
757. γνώμη, common sense, sound judgment. Aeschylus has θυμόμαντις,

ΕΛΕΝΗ. 163

ΧΟ. ἐς ταὐτὸ κἀμοὶ δόξα μάντεων πέρι
χωρεῖ γέροντι· τοὺς θεοὺς ἔχων τις ἂν
φίλους ἀρίστην μαντικὴν ἔχοι δόμοις. 760
ΕΛ. εἶεν· τὰ μὲν δὴ δεῦρ' ἀεὶ καλῶς ἔχει.
ὅπως δ' ἐσώθης, ὦ τάλας, Τροίας ἄπο,
κέρδος μὲν οὐδὲν εἰδέναι, πόθος δέ τις
τὰ τῶν φίλων φίλοισιν αἰσθέσθαι κακά.
ΜΕ. ἦ πόλλ' ἀνήρου μ' ἑνὶ λόγῳ μιᾷ θ' ὁδῷ. 765
τί σοι λέγοιμ' ἂν τὰς ἐν Αἰγαίῳ φθορὰς,
τὰ Ναυπλίου τ' Εὐβοικὰ πυρπολήματα,
Κρήτην τε Λιβύης θ' ἃς ἐπεστράφην πόλεις,
σκοπιάς τε Περσέως; οὐ γὰρ ἐμπλήσαιμί σε
μύθῳ, λέγων τ' ἄν σοι κάκ' ἀλγοίην ἔτι, 770
πάσχων τ' ἔκαμνον· δὶς δὲ λυπηθεῖμεν ἄν.
ΕΛ. κάλλιον εἶπας ἤ σ' ἀνηρόμην ἐγώ.
ἐν δ' εἰπὲ πάντα παραλιπὼν, πόσον χρόνον
πόντου 'πὶ νώτοις ἅλιον ἐφθείρου πλάνον.

Pers. 226. Theocr. xxi. 32, ὃς γὰρ ἂν εἰκάξῃ κατὰ τὸν νόον, οὗτος ἄριστος 'Εστὶν ὀνειροκρίτας. Eur. Frag. 944, μάντις δ' ἄριστος ὅστις εἰκάζει καλῶς.—At this verse the messenger leaves the stage.
761. δεῦρ' ἀεὶ, Ion 56. Med. 670. Suppl. 787.
765. ἑνὶ λόγῳ Pierson for ἐν ὀλίγῳ.
766. φθορὰς, wanderings. A person who had lost his way was said φθείρεσθαι. Cf. *inf.* 774. Hence shipwrecked mariners are ναυτίλοι ἐφθαρμένοι, Iph. T. 276. El. 234, οὐχ ἕνα νομίζων φθείρεται πόλεως νόμον. The incidents here alluded to are borrowed from the Νόστοι of Agias, one of the Cyclic poets. Nauplius, to avenge the death of his son Palamedes, lighted up a fire on the southern promontory of Euboea, by which the Greeks were deceived, and suffered a great loss of their ships. See *inf.* 1127. Schol. ad Orest. 432, Ναύπλιος δὲ ἀκούσας [scil. τὸν Παλαμήδους φόνον] ἦλθεν εἰς "Ιλιον, δικάσαι τὸν φόνον τοῦ παιδός. τῶν δὲ Ἑλλήνων κατολιγωρούντων αὐτοῦ, πρὸς τὸ κεχαρισμένον τοῖς βασιλεῦσιν ἀποπλεύσας εἰς τὴν πατρίδα καὶ πυθόμενος ἀποπλεῖν τοὺς Ἕλληνας, ἧκεν εἰς Εὔβοιαν, καὶ χειμῶνα φυλάξας, φρυκτωρίας ἧψε περὶ τὰς ἀκτὰς τῆς Εὐβοίας· οἱ δὲ εὐεπίβατον νομίσαντες τὸν τόπον, προσορμίζονταί τε καὶ ἐν ταῖς πέτραις ἀπόλλυνται πάμπολλοι.
768. Λιβύης Reiske for Λιβύην. The promontory in Egypt called Περσέως σκοπιαὶ, because Perseus there watched for the Gorgons, is mentioned by Herodotus, ii. 15, as the western boundary of the Delta of Egypt.
770. μύθῳ Hermann for μύθων. The dative, which the context evidently requires, is ' I should satisfy you *by* the narration,' as Hipp. 664, μισῶν οὔποτ' ἐμπλησθήσομαι γυναῖκας, Ion 925, οὗτοι σὸν βλέπων ἐμπίμπλαμαι πρόσωπον, but the other means 'I should fill you *with* words.' Hermann also defends the old reading οὐ γὰρ ἐμπλήσαιμί σε against L. Dindorf's οὔτ' ἂν κτλ., on the ground that the ἂν in v. 766 is continued in sense to the latter optative. Rather, perhaps, ἐμπλήσαιμι depends on the following ἂν, as Theocr. xxix. 38—40, νῦν μὲν κἠπὶ τὰ χρύσεα μᾶλ' ἕνεκεν σέθεν βαίην,—τόκα δ' οὐδὲ καλεῦντος ἐπ' αὐλείαις θύραις προμόλοιμί κε. (Compare *inf.* 834. 913. Agam. 1016, πείθοι' ἄν, εἰ πείθοι', ἀπειθοίης δ' ἴσως, and the similar instances quoted in the note there.) On the sentiment δὶς λυπεῖσθαι see Hec. 518. Oed. Col. 363.
772. κάλλιον, σοφώτερον. Your reply is wiser than was my question.

ΕΥΡΙΠΙΔΟΥ

ΜΕ. ἐνιαυσίων πρὸς τοῖσιν ἐν Τροίᾳ δέκα 775
ἔτεσι διῆλθον ἑπτὰ περιδρομὰς ἐτῶν.
ΕΛ. φεῦ φεῦ· μακρόν γ' ἔλεξας, ὦ τάλας, χρόνον.
σωθεὶς δ' ἐκεῖθεν ἐνθάδ' ἦλθες ἐς σφαγάς.
ΜΕ. πῶς φῄς; τί λέξεις; ὥς μ' ἀπώλεσας, γύναι.
ΕΛ. [φεῦγ' ὡς τάχιστα τῆσδ' ἀπαλλαχθεὶς χθονός.]
θανεῖ πρὸς ἀνδρὸς οὗ τάδ' ἐστὶ δώματα. 781
ΜΕ. τί χρῆμα δράσας ἄξιον τῆς συμφορᾶς;
ΕΛ. ἥκεις ἄελπτος ἐμποδών τ' ἐμοῖς γάμοις.
ΜΕ. ἦ γὰρ γαμεῖν τις τἄμ' ἐβουλήθη λέχη;
ΕΛ. ὕβριν θ' ὑβρίζειν εἰς ἔμ' ἣν ἔτλην ἐγώ. 785
ΜΕ. ἰδίᾳ σθένων τις ἢ τυραννεύων χθονός;
ΕΛ. ὃς γῆς ἀνάσσει τῆσδε Πρωτέως γόνος.
ΜΕ. τόδ' ἔστ' ἐκεῖν' αἴνιγμ' ὃ προσπόλου κλύω.
ΕΛ. ποίοις ἐπιστὰς βαρβάροις πυλώμασιν;
ΜΕ. τοῖσδ', ἔνθεν ὥσπερ πτωχὸς ἐξηλαυνόμην. 790
ΕΛ. οὔ που προσῄτεις βίοτον; ὦ τάλαιν' ἐγώ.
ΜΕ. τοὔργον μὲν ἦν τοῦτ', ὄνομα δ' οὐκ εἶχον τόδε.

775. ἐνιαυσίων Herm. after Heath, for ἐνιαύσιον. He compares Ran. 347, χρονίους ἐτῶν παλαιῶν ἐνιαυτούς, and for the return of Menelaus from Troy on the eighth year, refers to Od. iii. 305. iv. 82. See above, v. 112. Orest. 473. Pflugk, retaining the vulgate, thinks χρόνος ἐνιαύσιος is "nove dictum" for a term made up of several years; whereas it is clear that it could only signify 'the space of one year,' like ἐνιαυσίαν φυγήν, Hippol. 37. W. Dindorf edits ἐνιαυσίους. Mr. W. G. Clark proposes ἐναίσιον, 'the time-fated.' The old copies have διῆλθον δ'.
780. Hermann, Pflugk, and Dindorf, after Valckenaer, condemn this verse, as interpolated from Phoen. 972. The chief reason against its genuineness here is, that the στιχομυθία is violated, unless we suppose a verse to have been lost from the preceding question of Menelaus.
785. ὕβριν ὑβρίζειν. Hermann thinks this verse means, that Theoclymenus will take advantage of Helen's position as a slave to obtain possession of her person, if she persists in refusing marriage. This explanation seems very doubtful. The verse he quotes as showing she was a slave, (275,) δούλη καθέστηκ', οὐδ' ἐλευθέρων ἄπο, loses its point unless taken in connexion with the following, τὰ βαρβάρων γὰρ δοῦλα πάντα πλὴν ἑνός. Where the γὰρ shows that she was not *really* a slave, but only in that modified sense wherein all the subjects of a tyrant are his slaves. Besides, if she had been his slave, he never would have made so much difficulty about winning her in marriage. It is only necessary to suppose that Theoclymenus had attempted some violence, to avoid which she had fled to the tomb of Proteus, v. 64. The sense therefore simply is, 'Aye, and to offer the insults to me which I have had to endure.'
788. αἴνιγμα. See v. 477, where the old portress had told him, ἔστι γάρ τις ἐν δόμοις τύχη.
791. προσαιτεῖν was properly said of beggars, because they asked for alms *at* the various houses. Plat. Symp. p. 203, B., ἐπειδὴ δὲ ἐδείπνησαν, προσαιτήσουσα οἷον δὴ εὐωχίας οὔσης ἀφίκετο ἡ Πενία, καὶ ἦν περὶ τὰς θύρας. So Acharn. 428, κἀκεῖνος μὲν ἦν χωλὸς, προσαιτῶν, στωμύλος. Rhes. 715, βίον ἐπαιτῶν.
792. οὐκ εἶχον. I did not call myself a beggar, i. e. the matter was not quite so bad as that.—οὐκ ἔοικας, cf. Med. 337. Heracl. 427. sup. v. 497.

ΕΛΕΝΗ. 165

ΕΛ. πάντ' οἶσθ' ἄρ', ὡς ἔοικας, ἀμφ' ἐμῶν γάμων.
ΜΕ. οἶδ'· εἰ δὲ λέκτρα διέφυγες τάδ' οὐκ ἔχω.
ΕΛ. ἄθικτον εὐνὴν ἴσθι σοι σεσωσμένην. 795
ΜΕ. τίς τοῦδε πειθώ; φίλα γάρ, εἰ σαφῆ, λέγεις.
ΕΛ. ὁρᾷς τάφου τοῦδ' ἀθλίους ἕδρας ἐμάς;
ΜΕ. ὁρῶ, τάλαινα, στιβάδας, ὧν τί σοὶ μέτα;
ΕΛ. ἐνταῦθα λέκτρων ἱκετεύομεν φυγάς.
ΜΕ. βωμοῦ σπανίζουσ', ἢ νόμοισι βαρβάροις; 800
ΕΛ. ἐρρύεθ' ἡμᾶς τοῦτ' ἴσον ναοῖς θεῶν.
ΜΕ. οὐδ' ἄρα πρὸς οἴκους ναυστολεῖν ἔξεστί μοι;
ΕΛ. ξίφος μένει σε μᾶλλον ἢ τοὐμὸν λέχος.
ΜΕ. οὕτως ἂν εἴην ἀθλιώτατος βροτῶν.
ΕΛ. μή νυν καταιδοῦ· φεῦγε δ' ἐκ τῆσδε χθονός. 805
ΜΕ. λιπών σε; Τροίαν ἐξέπερσα σὴν χάριν.
ΕΛ. κρεῖσσον γὰρ ἤ σε τἄμ' ἀποκτεῖναι λέχη.
ΜΕ. ἄνανδρ' ἄρ' εἶπας Ἰλίου τ' οὐκ ἄξια.
ΕΛ. οὐκ ἂν κτάνοις τύραννον, ὃ σπεύδεις ἴσως.
ΜΕ. οὕτω σιδήρῳ τρωτὸν οὐκ ἔχει δέμας; 810
ΕΛ. εἴσει. τὸ τολμᾶν δ' ἀδύνατ' ἀνδρὸς οὐ σοφοῦ.
ΜΕ. σιγῇ παράσχω δῆτ' ἐμὰς δῆσαι χέρας;
ΕΛ. εἰς ἄπορον ἥκεις· δεῖ δὲ μηχανῆς τινός.
ΜΕ. δρῶντας γὰρ ἢ μὴ δρῶντας ἥδιον θανεῖν.
ΕΛ. μί' ἐστὶν ἐλπίς, ᾗ μόνῃ σωθεῖμεν ἄν. 815
ΜΕ. ὠνητὸς ἢ τολμητὸς ἢ λόγων ὕπο;

800. σπανίζουσα. For the singular participle with the plural verb, see Ion 549. 1250. El. 613.
802. ναυστολεῖν. Musgrave, Hermann, Pflugk, and Dindorf, add σ', and critics seem as fond of inserting σ' or μ' wherever the metre will admit it, as the ancient writers appear to have been indifferent about it. See above, v. 57. *inf.* 817. 1053. In this place it is easy to supply σὺν σοί.
805. καταιδοῦ. The meaning evidently is, ' do not lose time in pitying yourself,' i. e. in saying you will be ἀθλιώτατος, ' but fly at once.' The κατὰ has the same force in Prom. 36, εἶεν, τί μέλλεις καὶ κατοικτίζει μάτην;
807. 'That were better than for my marriage to be the cause of your death.'

Cf. v. 783.
808. ἄρ'. This particle is hardly required; perhaps he wrote ἄνανδρά τ' εἶπας, ' what you say (about my flying) is both unmanly and unworthy of my deeds at Troy.'
809. ὃ for ὃν Seidler, and so Herm. Dind., though we might without much difficulty supply ὃν σπεύδεις κτανεῖν. In the next verse Hermann remarks on the unusual expression τρωτὸν οὐκ ἔχει for ἄτρωτον ἔχει.
811. εἴσει. 'You will find out to your cost, if you try.' See Heracl. 269, πειρώμενος δὴ τοῦτό γ' αὐτίκ' εἴσομαι, and *ibid.* 65.—ἀδύνατ' Scaliger for ἀδύνατον.
816. ὠνητὸς κτλ. 'A hope depending on bribes, or on daring, or on persuasion?' In the next verse Schaefer added

ΕΥΡΙΠΙΔΟΥ

ΕΛ. εἰ μὴ τύραννος ἐκπύθοιτ' ἀφιγμένον.
ΜΕ. ἐρεῖ δὲ τίς μ'; οὐ γνώσεταί γ' ὅς εἰμ' ἐγώ.
ΕΛ. ἔστ' ἔνδον αὐτῷ ξύμμαχος θεοῖς ἴση.
ΜΕ. φήμη τις οἴκων ἐν μυχοῖς ἱδρυμένη; 820
ΕΛ. οὔκ, ἀλλ' ἀδελφή· Θεονόην καλοῦσί νιν.
ΜΕ. χρηστήριον μὲν τοὔνομ'· ὅ τι δὲ δρᾷ φράσον.
ΕΛ. πάντ' οἶδ', ἐρεῖ τε συγγόνῳ παρόντα σέ.
ΜΕ. θνήσκοιμεν ἄν· λαθεῖν γὰρ οὐχ οἷόν τέ μοι.
ΕΛ. εἴ πως ἂν ἀναπείσαιμεν ἱκετεύοντέ νιν. 825
ΜΕ. τί χρῆμα δρᾶσαι; τίν' ὑπάγεις μ' εἰς ἐλπίδα;
ΕΛ. παρόντα γαίᾳ μὴ φράσαι σε συγγόνῳ.
ΜΕ. πείσαντε δ' ἐκ γῆς διορίσαιμεν ἂν πόδα;
ΕΛ. κοινῇ γ' ἐκείνῃ ῥᾳδίως, λάθρα δ' ἂν οὔ.
ΜΕ. σὸν ἔργον, ὡς γυναικὶ πρόσφορον γυνή. 830
ΕΛ. ὡς οὐκ ἄχρωστα γόνατ' ἐμῶν ἕξει χερῶν.
ΜΕ. φέρ', ἢν δὲ δὴ νῷν μὴ ἀποδέξηται λόγους;
ΕΛ. θανεῖ· γαμοῦμαι δ' ἡ τάλαιν' ἐγὼ βίᾳ.
ΜΕ. προδότις ἂν εἴης· τὴν βίαν σκήψασ' ἔχεις.

σ' after τύραννος, and he is followed by the recent editors. See above, v. 802.

818. οὐ γνώσεται. Theoclymenus surely will not know who *I* am, unless some one tells him; and there is no one to tell him. Hermann explains, "*Certe non noscet qui sim:* quare nominare non poterit."

820. φήμη, a prophetic voice. The Greeks put great faith in those casual and unexpected sounds or voices which they fancied they heard among woods or rocks or in wildernesses. These are the κληδόνες δύσκριτοι of Aeschylus, Prom. 494. φήμη of Od. xx. 100. Aelian, Var. Hist. iv. 7, says Pythagoras taught that ὁ πολλάκις ἐμπίπτων τοῖς ὠσὶν ἦχος was the φωνὴ τῶν κρειττόνων. But the mention in this place of an echo or supernatural voice in the palace, which could be consulted as an oracle, is perhaps to be referred rather to the custom of keeping domestic shrines; see on Med. 396, Ἑκάτην, μυχοῖς ναίουσαν ἐστίας ἐμῆς. *Inf.* 1191, φάτιν τιν' οἴκοθεν ἔχουσα.

825. Though εἰ ἄν with an optative is an unusual construction (see the note on Agam. 903,) it becomes scarcely worthy of remark where εἴπως is equivalent to ἴσως.

828. διορίσαιμεν, cf. v. 394. Translate, 'And when we *have* persuaded her, can we get our feet clear away out of the land?'

829. λάθρα δ' ἂν οὔ is the excellent emendation of L. Dindorf for λάθρ' οὐδαμοῦ.

830. γυνὴ for γύναι Brodaeus, who compares a similar verse, παῖς παιδί, καὶ γυναικὶ πρόσφορον γυνὴ, in Plutarch De Adul. p. 51, E.

831. ὡς, ἴσθι ὡς, Med. 609.—ἄχρωστα, compare Med. 497. Heracl. 915.

834. προδότις κτλ. 'You want to betray me; it is this pretended compulsion (βία, 833,) that you have been making your excuse.' Compare τλήμων ἂν εἴης in v. 91. Hermann gives προδότης ἂν εἴην, σὺ δὲ βίαν σκήψασ' ἔχοις, 'In that case I should be a (base) betrayer of you, while *you* would be able to plead compulsion,' and therefore the fault would be wholly mine. Cf. v. 850. The common reading, he objects, makes Menelaus to charge his wife with the deliberate intention of marrying another, just when he has

ΕΛ. ἀλλ' ἁγνὸν ὅρκον σὸν κάρα κατώμοσα. 835
ΜΕ. τί φής; θανεῖσθαι κοὔποτ' ἀλλάξειν λέχη;
ΕΛ. ταὐτῷ ξίφει γε· κείσομαι δὲ σοῦ πέλας.
ΜΕ. ἐπὶ τοῖσδε τοίνυν δεξιᾶς ἐμῆς θίγε.
ΕΛ. ψαύω, θανόντος σοῦ τόδ' ἐκλείψειν φάος.
ΜΕ. κἀγὼ στερηθεὶς σοῦ τελευτήσω βίον. 840
ΕΛ. πῶς οὖν θανούμεθ' ὥστε καὶ δόξαν λαβεῖν;
ΜΕ. τύμβου 'πὶ νώτῳ σὲ κτανὼν ἐμὲ κτενῶ.
πρῶτον δ' ἀγῶνα μέγαν ἀγωνιούμεθα
λέκτρων ὑπὲρ σῶν· ὁ δὲ θέλων ἴτω πέλας·
τὸ Τρωικὸν γὰρ οὐ καταισχυνῶ κλέος, 845
οὐδ' Ἑλλάδ' ἐλθὼν λήψομαι πολὺν ψόγον,
ὅστις Θέτιν μὲν ἐστέρησ' Ἀχιλλέως,
Τελαμωνίου δ' Αἴαντος εἰσεῖδον σφαγὰς,
τὸν Νηλέως τ' ἄπαιδα· διὰ δὲ τὴν ἐμὴν

learnt all that she has undergone to preserve herself intact for him. And certainly the absence of a copulative particle with τὴν βίαν is suspicious. It was to avoid such a fault that the grammarians introduced a still worse one in τήνδε, i. e. τὴν δὲ βίαν. The reading προδότις appears only to be given as a variant in one MS. —The phrase σκήπτειν βίαν for σκῆψιν ποιεῖσθαι, is worthy of notice. It is more common in the middle voice. Photius, σκήπτεται, προφασίζεται.
835. ἁγνὸν, sanctum, 'a holy oath,' viz. one which in a peculiar manner would bind a faithful wife. In the next verse Hermann reads θανεῖσθαι; κοὔποτ' ἀλλάξεις λέχη; which is good enough in itself, but then it is not so easy to prove οὐ (for μὴ) ἀλλάξειν to be really a solecism. A precisely similar instance in Theocr. xx. 59, ὤμοσα δ' οὐκέτι λοιπὸν ὑπὲρ πελάγους πόδα θεῖναι, he gets over by altering the text, μηκέτι δ' ὤμοσα λοιπὸν, or λοιπὸν δ' ὤμοσα μηκέθ' κτλ. The truth perhaps is, that as οὐ φημὶ, οὐ δοκῶ, οὐ θέλω, οὐ χρὴ, οὐκ ἀξιῶ &c. are sometimes constructed where φημὶ μὴ &c. is so obviously the meaning, that οὐ is placed directly before the infinitive (like χρὴ μὲν οὔ σ' ἁμαρτάνειν in Hipp. 507, ὀφείλω οὐκ ἀεὶ πράσσειν κακῶς, inf. v. 1448,) and as μὴ ὤφελον ἰδεῖν may be regarded as a similar hyperbaton for ὤφελον μὴ, so ὄμνυμι οὐ ποιήσειν originally represented οὐ φημὶ ποιήσειν, ὅρκῳ κατειλημμένος, 'I assert with an oath that I will not do it.' Hermann supports his emendation by the fact that one MS. has ἀλλάξειν σὸν λέχη, which he ingeniously explains as arising from a superscribed variant, ἀλλάξειν.
838. ἐπὶ τοῖσδε. See inf. 1234. Alcest. 375, ἐπὶ τοῖσδε παῖδας χειρὸς ἐξ ἐμῆς δέχου. Ran. 589, δέχομαι τὸν ὅρκον, κἀπὶ τούτοις λαμβάνω.—τοίνυν Canter for τοῖς νῦν.
840. τελευτήσειν Hermann after Fritzsch; a probable correction.
842. κτενῶ Heath and others for κτανεῖ. On ἐμὲ for ἐμαυτὸν see Hipp. 1409. Androm. 256, ἀλλ' οὐδ' ἐγὼ μὴν πρόσθεν ἐκδώσω με σοί.
843. πρῶτον, before I am driven to that last resource. At the words ὁ δὲ θέλων he draws his sword to show his readiness for the fight.—ἐλθὼν for ἀνελθὼν, inf. 929. Ion 828.
849. τὸν Νηλέως τ' ἄπαιδα. The old reading τὸν Θησέως τε παῖδα was so corrected, the proper name by Musgrave, the substantive by Bothe. Hermann and Dindorf rightly adopt these unquestionable emendations. The death of Antilochus, the son of Nestor, who was the son of Neleus, is clearly meant. Her-

οὐκ ἀξιώσω κατθανεῖν δάμαρτ' ἐγώ;   850
μάλιστά γ'· εἰ γάρ εἰσιν οἱ θεοὶ σοφοί,
εὔψυχον ἄνδρα πολεμίων θανόνθ' ὕπο
κούφῃ καταμπίσχουσιν ἐν τύμβῳ χθονί,
κακοὺς δ' ἐφ' ἕρμα στερεὸν ἐκβάλλουσι γῆς.

ΧΟ.   ὦ θεοί, γενέσθω δήποτ' εὐτυχὲς γένος   855
τὸ Ταντάλειον καὶ μεταστήτω κακῶν.

ΕΛ.   οἲ 'γὼ τάλαινα. τῆς τύχης γὰρ ὧδ' ἔχω·
Μενέλαε, διαπεπράγμεθ'· ἐκβαίνει δόμων
ἡ θεσπιῳδὸς Θεονόη. κτυπεῖ δόμος
κλῄθρων λυθέντων· φεῦγ'· ἀτὰρ τί φευκτέον;   860
ἀποῦσα γάρ σε καὶ παροῦσ' ἀφιγμένον
δεῦρ' οἶδεν· ὦ δύστηνος, ὡς ἀπωλόμην.
Τροίας δὲ σωθεὶς κἀπὸ βαρβάρου χθονὸς
ἐς βάρβαρ' ἐλθὼν φάσγαν' αὖθις ἐμπεσεῖ.

ΘΕΟΝ.

ἡγοῦ σύ μοι φέρουσα λαμπτήρων σέλας,   865

mann considers Euripides here to have followed Homer, Od. iii. 109, where Nestor says to Telemachus

ἔνθα μὲν Αἴας κεῖται ἀρήϊος, ἔνθα δ' Ἀχιλλεύς,
ἔνθα δὲ Πάτροκλος, θεόφιν μήστωρ ἀτάλαντος,
ἔνθα δ' ἐμὸς φίλος υἱός.

But by ἐστέρησα Menelaus only means that he was the *cause* of death to all these heroes, as being the author of the war. According to the Cyclic poems, it was Paris who killed Achilles the son of Thetis.

850. ἐγώ. Here apparently for αὐτός. Compare the note on σὺ in Ion 847. *sup.* 117.

853. The compound ἐπαμπίσχειν occurs in Tro. 1148, of throwing earth over an unburied corpse.—ἐφ' ἕρμα, for which Pflugk and Bothe give the false reading ὑφ' ἕρμα after Stephens, is rightly explained by Hermann, "ignavos projici ab diis duro in solo dicit, ubi insepulti jaceant : quod putabatur esse tristissimum." On such a naked rock no earth would be found to throw on the body, even if any one should wish to perform that pious rite. By ὑφ' ἕρμα a very different sense would be conveyed, the contrary to that pious wish κούφα σοι χθὼν ἐπάνωθε πέσοι, γύναι, Alcest. 463. But thus the antithetical word to κούφῃ should have been βαρὺ rather than στερεόν.—γῆς seems to belong to ἕρμα, not to ἐκβάλλουσι.

855. δήποτε, *tandem.* Hipp. 1181. These two lines were first assigned to the chorus by Musgrave, instead of being continued to Menelaus.

857. ὧδε τῆς τύχης, like πῶς εὐμενείας in v. 313.

859. κτυπεῖ, more usually of the noise of the foot, but here of the sounds made by withdrawing the bar from withinside of the door. Probably this would be the side door, which usually represented the γυναικωνῖτις.

865. Menelaus and Helen have stepped aside while the inspired daughter of Proteus, attended by two or more maidens bearing torches and purificatory implements, come in procession on the stage. The scene, which must have been highly impressive and effective, closely resembles that in Troad. 308 seqq., where Cassandra appears with a torch-bearing troop, and foretells evil to Agamemnon and Ulysses. After giving some instructions to her attendants, Theonöe turns to Helen and

ΕΛΕΝΗ. 169

θείου δὲ σεμνὸν θεσμὸν αἰθέρος μυχὸν,
ὡς πνεῦμα καθαρὸν οὐρανοῦ δεξώμεθα·
σὺ δ᾽ αὖ κέλευθον, εἴ τις ἔβλαψεν ποδὶ
στείβων ἀνοσίῳ, δὸς καθαρσίῳ φλογὶ,
κροῦσον δὲ πεύκην, ἵνα διεξέλθω, πάρος.   870
νόμον δὲ τὸν ἐμὸν θεοῖσιν ἀποδοῦσαι, πάλιν
ἐφέστιον φλόγ᾽ ἐς δόμους κομίζετε.
Ἑλένη, τί τἀμὰ πῶς ἔχει θεσπίσματα;
ἥκει πόσις σοι Μενέλεως ὅδ᾽ ἐμφανὴς,
νεῶν στερηθεὶς τοῦ τε σοῦ μιμήματος.   875
ὦ τλῆμον, οἵους διαφυγὼν ἦλθες πόνους,
οὐδ᾽ οἶσθα νόστον οἴκαδ᾽, εἴτ᾽ αὐτοῦ μενεῖς·

Menelaus, and informs them of the divided opinion of the gods concerning their safe return to Sparta.—For σύ μοι Pflugk and Dindorf needlessly read σὺ μὲν after Elmsley.

866. θείου σεμνὸν θεσμόν. 'Fumigate with sulphur according to the solemn rite.' The old reading was θεῖον δὲ (or δὲ εἰς) σεμνοῦ θεσμὸν αἰθέρος μυχῶν. To Pflugk is due θείου (the imperative middle of θειοῦσθαι), to Hermann σεμνὸν θεσμὸν, which is much better than the improbable compound σεμνόθεσμον, proposed by Pflugk and adopted by Dindorf. Hermann compares, for the use of the accusative, Soph. Ajac. 1107, τὰ σέμν᾽ ἔπη κόλαζ᾽ ἐκείνους, as if the full construction had been σεμνὸν θεσμὸν σώζουσα, φυλάσσουσα. See below, v. 1126. With respect to the custom, Musgrave has quoted a passage from Plutarch, De Isid. et Osir. p. 383, B, where it is stated that the Egyptian priests fumigate the morning air to remove the oppressive effects of night vapours, by burning rue (ῥητίνη), and at mid-day with myrrh.

867. δεξώμεθα Schaefer for δεξαίμεθα.

870. κρούειν πεύκην is precisely what the Romans called *quatere facem*, viz. to knock the lighted torch against a wall or post, or perhaps merely to brandish it to and fro, for the same purpose that the neater process of snuffing candles was introduced. Compare Propert. i. 3, 9, 'Ebria cum multo traherem vestigia Baccho, Et quaterent sera nocte facem pueri.' Again, lib. iv. 16, 15, 'Luna ministrat iter, demonstrant astra salebras, Ipse Amor accensas percutit ante faces,' where *ante*

well illustrates the correction of Reiske, adopted by Hermann, πάρος for πυρός. It is clear that πῦρ πεύκης would be required rather than πεύκην πυρός, and the addition of the latter word after an intervening clause, when the mind is satisfied with πεύκην, is intolerable. For the sense of πάρος Hermann compares Soph. El. 1502, σοὶ βαδιστέον πάρος.—It is hardly necessary to add that ἵνα is 'in order that,' not 'wherever,' as Matthiae rather strangely explains it. Of course, her object was that the air should be purified by fire before she inhaled it.

871. νόμον τὸν ἐμὸν, *legem a me observari suetam*, Hermann.—"Bene vero delegit verbum ἀποδοῦσαι in re, quae est in parte officii et debiti instar," Pflugk.— ἐφέστιον φλόγα, the flame which has been, as it were, *borrowed* from the sacred hearth. It was thought essential to light a torch from a lucky or sacred fire. Propert. v. 3, 13, 'Quae mihi deductae fax omen praetulit, illa Traxit ab everso lumina nigra rogo.' All these notions about fire were derived from the Pelasgi, and therefore an illustration from a Roman author equally applies to Greek customs.

873. τί—πῶς; Cf. v. 1543. 'What now of my prophecy? How is it verified?' She had declared that Menelaus would return, v. 517, or, at least, that he was still alive.

874. ὅδε, because Menelaus is still standing by her.—μιμήματος, the εἴδωλον that had vanished, ἀρθεῖσ᾽ ἄφαντος, v. 606. The correction of H. Stephens for τιμήματος.

ἔρις γὰρ ἐν θεοῖς σύλλογός τε σοῦ πέρι
ἔσται πάρεδρος Ζηνὶ τῷδ' ἐν ἤματι.
Ἥρα μὲν, ἥ σοι δυσμενὴς πάροιθεν ἦν, 880
νῦν ἐστὶν εὔνους, κεἰς πάτραν σῶσαι θέλει
ξὺν τῇδ', ἵν' Ἑλλὰς τοὺς Ἀλεξάνδρου γάμους
δώρημα Κύπριδος ψευδονύμφευτον μάθῃ·
Κύπρις δὲ νόστον σὸν διαφθεῖραι θέλει,
ὡς μήτ' ἐλεγχθῇ μηδὲ πριαμένη φανῇ 885
τὸ κάλλος Ἑλένης οὕνεκ' ἀνονήτοις γάμοις.
τέλος δ' ἐφ' ἡμῖν, εἴθ', ἃ βούλεται Κύπρις,
λέξασ' ἀδελφῷ σ' ἐνθάδ' ὄντα διολέσω,
εἴτ' αὖ μεθ' Ἥρας στᾶσα σὸν σώσω βίον,
κρύψασ' ὁμαίμον', ὅς με προστάσσει τάδε 890
εἰπεῖν, ὅταν γῆν τήνδε νοστήσας τύχῃς.
τίς εἶσ' ἀδελφῷ τόνδε σημανῶν ἐμῷ
παρόνθ', ὅπως ἂν τοὐμὸν ἀσφαλῶς ἔχῃ;
ΕΛ. ὦ παρθέν', ἱκέτις ἀμφὶ σὸν πίτνω γόνυ,

883. ψευδονύμφευτον Herm. for -ους. He observes, first, that the editions of Hervagius give ψευδονυμφεύτου, secondly, that δώρημα Κύπριδος is alone a weak and useless ἐπεξήγησις of γάμους. Translate, 'that Hellas may at length know, that the marriage of Helen with Paris was a gift of Cypris that resulted in sham nuptials.'

886. ἀνονήτοις Pierson for ὠνητοῖς. The point to be avoided by Cypris was not so much that she gained the decision in her favour by a bribe, for each of the three goddesses had notoriously proposed their own terms, (see Tro. 925 seqq.), but that the bargain was unreal and therefore fraudulent. The verb ὄνασθαι was commonly used of a fortunate marriage. Alcest. 335, σοῦ γὰρ οὐκ ὠνήμεθα. Ibid. 412, ἀνόνατ' ἀνόνατ' ἐνύμφευσας. Hippol. 757, κακονυμφοτάταν ὄνασιν.—Ἑλένης οὕνεκ', i. e. Ἑλένην ὡς μισθὸν προϊσχομένη. For μήτ' ἐλεγχθῇ the Dindorfs read μὴ 'ξελεγχθῇ, which Hermann rightly rejects. We closely represent μήτε—μηδὲ by 'neither—nor yet.' If Menelaus did not return to Greece with his true bride, Cypris entertained the hope that the affair of the εἰδώλου, put upon her by her rival Hera, would never be known to the Greeks.

888. σ' for γ' is Reiske's.

890. κρύψασα, concealing it (your presence here) from my brother Theoclymenus. Cf. Hec. 570, κρύπτουσ' ἃ κρύπτειν ὄμματ' ἀρσένων χρεών.—προστάσσει—ὅταν, the praesens historicum for προσέταξε—ὁπότε νοστήσαις. 'He bids me tell him when you *have* returned' is not, in strict logic, applicable to one who now stands before her. But the Greeks were very fond of adapting the actual words of a speaker to indirect narrative. What Theoclymenus had charged her with was this, εἰπέ μοι ὅταν νοστήσῃ, while the event which has now happened was still pending.—After this verse we must suppose a short pause, as if of earnest deliberation as to which alternative she should adopt. At length, wishing perhaps to be entreated, she tells one of her attendants to carry the news, so adverse to Helen, to her brother. But the frantic action of Helen, who immediately throws herself at the feet of the prophetess, arrests a mission which, perhaps, as Barnes observed, was not really intended.—σημανῶν, Scaliger's correction for σημανῶ γ'. It is needless to read σημανοῦσ', τις being quite indefinitely used.

ΕΛΕΝΗ. 171

καὶ προσκαθίζω θᾶκον οὐκ εὐδαίμονα 895
ὑπέρ τ' ἐμαυτῆς τοῦδέ θ', ὃν μόλις ποτὲ
λαβοῦσ' ἐπ' ἀκμῆς εἰμὶ κατθανόντ' ἰδεῖν·
μή μου κατείπῃς σῷ κασιγνήτῳ πόσιν
τόνδ' εἰς ἐμὰς ἥκοντα φιλτάτας χέρας·
σῶσον δὲ, λίσσομαί σε· συγγόνῳ δὲ σῷ 900
τὴν εὐσέβειαν μὴ προδῷς τὴν σήν ποτε,
χάριτας πονηρὰς κἀδίκους ὠνουμένη.
μισεῖ γὰρ ὁ θεὸς τὴν βίαν, τὰ κτητὰ δὲ
κτᾶσθαι κελεύει πάντας, οὐκ ἐς ἁρπαγάς.
[ἐατέος δ' ὁ πλοῦτος, ἄδικός τις ὤν.] 905
κοινὸς γάρ ἐστιν οὐρανὸς πᾶσιν βροτοῖς
καὶ γαῖ', ἐν ᾗ χρὴ δώματ' ἀναπληρουμένους
τἀλλότρια μὴ 'χειν μηδ' ἀφαιρεῖσθαι βίᾳ.
ἡμᾶς δὲ μακαρίως μὲν, ἀθλίως δ' ἐμοὶ,

896. μόλις ποτὲ, 'at last.' The early edd. give σὺ μόλις ποτὲ, which Hermann supposes to be a corruption of another reading οὐ μόλις, non parum, (v. 334,) intended to be construed with ἐπ' ἀκμῆς εἰμί.
898. μή μου, ' do not inform against me (i. e. do not reveal my secret) to your brother, that' &c. Hermann approves, and Dindorf adopts, μή μοι from Seidler. If the genitive be right, it depends not on πόσιν, but on the κατά. This compound is nearly a synonym of μηνύειν, and is used either with or without a genitive of the person. So Ion 1215, ὤφθη δὲ καὶ κατεῖπ' ἀναγκασθεὶς μόγις Τόλμας Κρεούσης.
901. τὴν εὐσέβειαν. By this noun the Greeks meant righteous behaviour, arising primarily from reverence to the god, who punished the contrary conduct, though this idea is sometimes lost sight of, as in Antig. 731, οὐδ' ἂν κελεύσαιμ' εὐσεβεῖν ἐς τοὺς κακούς, ' to show any consideration for the bad.' Thus too Hippolytus complains that his εὐσεβία towards his fellow-men has been vain, v. 1368, and Admetus in the *Alcestis* is enjoined to continue his considerate conduct, εὐσεβεῖν τὸ λοιπόν, to strangers, though this indeed was a real religious obligation. Here then Theonöe is implored not to sell to her brother for unjust rewards (χάριτας) the duty she owes to a suppliant in distress. The explanation of εὐσέβεια, as far as it has reference to the gods, is introduced by the following γὰρ, ' for the god hates such violence as would be shown, if Theoclymenus were to murder Menelaus.'
904. οὐκ ἐς ἁρπαγάς. The sense is, κτᾶσθαι ἀλλὰ μὴ ἁρπάζειν, 'to gain fairly, but not to seize by violence,' as Theoclymenus would seize Helen. The meaning of ἐς is, ' not going so far as ' &c. Compare Tro. 1210, οὓς Φρύγες νόμους τιμῶσιν, οὐκ ἐς πλησμονὰς θηρώμενοι. Ibid. 1201, οὐ γὰρ ἐς κάλλος τύχας δαίμων δίδωσιν, and see on Bacch. 457. In the next verse ἄδικος (ὁ ἄδ.) is given for ἄδικος, and the same obvious correction occurred to Hermann. Thus ὁ πλοῦτος ὁ ἄδικος ὢν is a specification of the sort of wealth which should be let alone. But the addition of τις (and in a less degree, the fact that the next speech has only 49 verses) makes it probable that this line is an interpolation. Dindorf indeed thinks fit to inclose the whole of these interesting verses (903—908) within brackets as spurious, because "tota illa declamatio aliena ab hoc loco videtur." So far from being *aliena*, it is a reflexion which follows very naturally on the mention of Theoclymenus' intention towards Helen.
909. μακαρίως, ἀθλίως δέ. Fortunately, in so far as she had escaped the evils

Z 2

172 ΕΥΡΙΠΙΔΟΥ

Ἑρμῆς ἔδωκε πατρὶ σῷ σώζειν πόσει 910
τῷδ', ὃς πάρεστι κἀπολάζυσθαι θέλει.
πῶς οὖν θανὼν ἂν ἀπολάβοι; κεῖνος δὲ πῶς
τὰ ζῶντα τοῖς θανοῦσιν ἀποδοίη ποτέ;
ἤδη τὰ τοῦ θεοῦ καὶ τὰ τοῦ πατρὸς σκόπει,
πότερον ὁ δαίμων χὠ θανὼν τὰ τῶν πέλας 915
βούλοιντ' ἂν ἢ *οὐ βούλοιντ' ἂν ἀποδοῦναι πάλιν.
δοκῶ μέν. οὔκουν χρή σε συγγόνῳ πλέον
νέμειν ματαίῳ μᾶλλον ἢ χρηστῷ πατρί.
εἰ δ', οὖσα μάντις καὶ τὰ θεῖ' ἡγουμένη,
τὸ μὲν δίκαιον τοῦ πατρὸς διαφθερεῖς, 920
τῷ δ' οὐ δικαίῳ συγγόνῳ δώσεις χάριν,
αἰσχρὸν τὰ μέν σε θεῖα πάντ' ἐξειδέναι,
τά τ' ὄντα καὶ μή, τὰ δὲ δίκαια μὴ εἰδέναι.

which the other Helen had caused, but unhappily to herself, as far as personal trials and temptations were concerned.— σώζειν πόσει, cf. Suppl. 1203, σώζειν θεῷ δὸς ᾧ Δελφῶν μέλει. Alcest. 1020, γυναῖκα τήνδε μοι σῶσον λαβών. Inf. 964.

912. κεῖνος, Proteus, who is still, though dead, regarded as the keeper of Helen. In the next line the old reading was ἂν ἀποδοίη. Hermann is clearly right in ejecting ἂν, which was added by some one who did not see that the idiom was the same as that in v. 769. Pflugk and Dindorf give ἀποδοίη ποτ' ἂν after Porson.

916. οὐ was inserted before βούλοιντ' ἂν by Canter. So it has apparently been lost before βούλεται in Med. 708.

917. δοκῶ μέν, ' of course they would.' See on Suppl. 771.—πλέον νέμειν, Suppl. 241, δεινοὶ, νέμοντες τῷ φθόνῳ πλεῖον μέρος. The meaning of μάταιος is here the same as μῶρος, amorous. Aesch. Suppl. 194, τὸ μὴ μάταιον δ' ἐκ μετωποσωφρόνων ἴτω προσώπων. Ibid. 225, οὐδὲ μὴ 'ν Ἅιδου θανὼν φύγῃ μάταιος αἰτίαν.

919. τὰ θεῖ' ἡγουμένη. 'Believing in the reality of divine dispensations.' So Hec. 800, νόμῳ γὰρ τοὺς θεοὺς ἡγούμεθα. Suppl. 732, νῦν τήνδ' ἄελπτον ἡμέραν ἰδοῦσ' ἐγὼ θεοὺς νομίζω.—διαφθερεῖς, see on Hipp. 388. Here the sense is, 'if you shall alter and so thwart the just intentions of your father' Proteus; 'if you shall, by your conduct, degenerate from the example of justice,' set by him. So διαφθείρειν παροιμίαν μεταβάλλοντες, to change the purport of a proverb, Plat. Symp. p. 174, B.

922. τὰ μέν σε θεῖα. The interpolation of a word besides μέν between the article and its noun is of very unfrequent occurrence. Cf. Phoen. 512, ταῖς γὰρ ἂν Θήβαις τόδε γένοιτ' ὄνειδος. Aesch. Suppl. 1039, τὸ μὲν ἂν βέλτατον εἴη, for τὸ β. εἴη ἂν, like τὰ λῷστ' ἂν εἴη in Heracl. 1021.

923. τὰ ὄντα καὶ (τὰ) μή, i.e. things present and future. Mr. Clark would read τά τ' ὄντα καὶ μέλλοντα, τὰ δὲ δίκαια μή. See v. 14. There is a little irony in the passage, as if the μάντεις were not always δίκαιοι, disinterested. See v. 756. After this verse Hermann thinks a line has been lost, in which some petition for the safety of Menelaus was uttered. The τε which introduces the next verse somewhat confirms the supposition. Barnes gives τὴν δ', which, Hermann objects, should rather have been ἀλλά. Certainly, the passage would read less abruptly with the addition of some such verse as ἀλλ' ὦ φίλη μοι παρθέν', ἐκσῶσον πόσιν, κτλ. Not much weight, perhaps, is to be attributed to the circumstance that this ῥῆσις and the following one of Menelaus, contain each forty-nine verses. See however on Heracl. 221. In Hecuba v. 1132 seqq. both Polymestor and Hecuba speak exactly fifty-one lines apiece; as in Aesch. Theb. 563 seqq. the messenger and Eteocles each speak twenty-nine. There are many other instances; too

ΕΛΕΝΗ. 173

τήν τ' ἀθλίαν ἔμ', οἶσιν ἔγκειμαι κακοῖς,
ῥῦσαι, πάρεργον δοῦσα τοῦτο τῆς τύχης· 925
Ἑλένην γὰρ οὐδεὶς ὅστις οὐ στυγεῖ βροτῶν·
ἣ κλῄζομαι καθ' Ἑλλάδ' ὡς προδοῦσ' ἐμὸν
πόσιν Φρυγῶν ᾤκησα πολυχρύσους δόμους.
ἢν δ' Ἑλλάδ' ἔλθω κἀπιβῶ Σπάρτης πάλιν,
κλύοντες, εἰσιδόντες, ὡς τέχναις θεῶν 930
ὤλοντ', ἐγὼ δὲ προδότις οὐκ ἄρ' ἦν φίλων,
πάλιν μ' ἀνάξουσ' ἐς τὸ σῶφρον αὖθις αὖ,
ἑδνώσομαί τε θυγατέρ', ἣν οὐδεὶς γαμεῖ,
τὴν δ' ἐνθάδ' ἐκλιποῦσ' ἀλητείαν πικρὰν
ὄντων ἐν οἴκοις χρημάτων ὀνήσομαι. 935
κεἰ μὲν θανὼν ὅδ' εἰς πυρὰν κατεσφάγη,

many, indeed, to attribute the circumstance always to chance: compare Med. 465—519, with 522—575.

924. οἶσιν—κακοῖς. For ῥῦσαι κακῶν οἷς ἔγκειμαι. Hermann, who objects to supplying τούτων, might have remembered Alcest. 770, κακῶν γὰρ μυρίων ἐρρύετο.—πάρεργον κτλ., granting me this favour as a piece of extra good-fortune; because, as she says in the next line, it was hardly to be expected that one so universally detested could meet with mercy. Pflugk does not seem to have understood this rightly. He explains it ὑπουργήσασα τοῦτο τῇ τύχῃ, ἐκπληρώσασα τὰ τῆς τύχης. If he had meant 'helping or co-operating with fortune in our preservation,' the dative τῇ τύχῃ would have been required.

928. πολυχρύσους. It was alleged that Helen had been tempted by the wealth of Paris. See Androm. 169. Troad. 994—7. The Spartans, with all their affectation of simplicity, bore the character of being αἰσχροκερδεῖς,—a phenomenon not without examples in the history of human inconsistencies. Their warmest apologist, Xenophon, admits this, Resp. Lac. § 14, πρόσθεν μὲν οἶδα αὐτοὺς φοβουμένους χρυσίον ἔχοντας φαίνεσθαι· νῦν δ' ἔστιν οὓς καὶ καλλωπιζομένους ἐπὶ τῷ κεκτῆσθαι.

929. ἔλθω, see v. 846. ' Now, if I should have returned to Hellas, and have set foot once more in Sparta, (my countrymen,) not merely hearing, but seeing for themselves how through the stratagems of deities they had suffered by the war, and that I was not, after all, the betrayer of my friends, will restore me again to my character for chastity.' Hermann is quite right in defending οὐκ ἄρ' ἦν against the reading adopted by Dindorf and Pflugk from the Etymol. M. p. 430, 15, who quotes ἐγὼ δὲ προδότης οὐκ ἤμην τέκνον as if from the Ἑλένης ἀπαίτησις, which, in fact, was a play of Sophocles, though he adds παρ' Εὐριπίδῃ. There is no doubt that the grammarian referred to this passage; but he was misled either by his memory or by a false reading, as ἤμην is barbarous in the earlier Attic dialect. Indeed, he himself adds ζήτει to the end of his gloss, as if in doubt about the reading; just as we should append *quaere* to a doubtful statement. In point of sense, ἄρ' ἦν is obviously better than ἤμην.

933. ἑδνώσομαι Hermann, ἐκδώσομαι Elmsley and Dindorf, for ἑδνάσομαι, which Pflugk retains, apparently without suspicion. Bothe suggests ἑδνώσομεν. The forms ἑδνάω and ἑδνάζω are alike unknown; but ἑδνόω, or rather ἑδνοῦσθαι, is epic, (Od. ii. 56.)—ἣν οὐδεὶς γαμεῖ, perhaps from the ill-repute of the mother; whereas such an objection might be overcome by a large dower.

934. ἀλητείαν, see on Ion 576.

936. εἰς πυρὰν, viz. as a prisoner of war, sacrificed at the tomb of a Patroclus or an Achilles. Hermann's reading ἐν πέρα, ' on the opposite continent,' viz. in the Peloponnesus, is ingenious, but not very probable, from the rarity of the substantive, which occurs only in Aesch. Suppl. 258, Agam. 182, and as a variant for πέτρας, Pers. 392. Besides, κατεσφά-

πρόσω σφ' ἀπόντα δακρύοις ἂν ἠγάπων,
νῦν δ' ὄντα καὶ σωθέντ' ἀφαιρεθήσομαι;
μὴ δῆτα, παρθέν', ἀλλά σ' ἱκετεύω τόδε·
δὸς τὴν χάριν μοι τήνδε, καὶ μιμοῦ τρόπους   940
πατρὸς δικαίου· παισὶ γὰρ κλέος τόδε
κάλλιστον, ὅστις ἐκ πατρὸς χρηστοῦ γεγὼς
ἐς ταὐτὸν ἦλθε τοῖς τεκοῦσι τοὺς τρόπους.
ΧΟ. οἰκτρὸν μὲν οἱ παρόντες ἐν μέσῳ λόγοι,
οἰκτρὰ δὲ καὶ σύ. τοὺς δὲ Μενέλεω ποθῶ   945
λόγους ἀκοῦσαι τίνας ἐρεῖ ψυχῆς πέρι.
ΜΕ. ἐγὼ σὸν οὔτ' ἂν προσπεσεῖν τλαίην γόνυ
οὔτ' ἂν δακρῦσαι βλέφαρα· τὴν Τροίαν γὰρ ἂν
δειλοὶ γενόμενοι πλεῖστον αἰσχύνοιμεν ἄν.
καίτοι λέγουσιν ὡς πρὸς ἀνδρὸς εὐγενοῦς   950
ἐν ξυμφοραῖσι δάκρυ' ἀπ' ὀφθαλμῶν βαλεῖν.

γη is exactly the word which is suited to εἰς πυρὰν, whereas ἐν πέρᾳ διώλετο would have been a more appropriate expression. For no one will say that κατεσφάγη is rightly used in the same general way as the Romans say *interfectus esset*.—On the meaning of ἀγαπᾶν, properly 'to hug,' see on Suppl. 764. The primary sense is well shown by Od. xxiii. 214, where Penelope, having just embraced Ulysses, (v. 207, ἀμφὶ δὲ χεῖρας Δειρῇ βάλλ' Ὀδυσῆι,) says to him μή νῦν μοι τόδε χώεο μηδὲ νεμέσσα, Οὔνεκά σ' οὐ τὸ πρῶτον, ἐπεὶ ἴδον, ὧδ' ἀγάπησα. Cf. Hes. Opp. 57, τοῖς δ' ἐγὼ ἀντὶ πυρὸς δώσω κακόν, ᾧ κεν ἅπαντες τέρπωνται κατὰ θυμὸν, ἑὸν κακὸν ἀμφαγαπῶντες.

941. παισὶ has been restored by Porson and others from Stobaeus, for παιδί.

944—6. First assigned to the Chorus instead of to Theonoë by L. Dindorf.

945. τοὺς for τοῦ Hermann.—ψυχῆς πέρι, for his life. A common expression. See the note on Aesch. Eum. 114. Heracl. 984, μηδ' ἄλλο μηδὲν τῆς ἐμῆς ψυχῆς πέρι λέξοντα.

947. Menelaus adds his own entreaties to Theonoë, who is now the sole arbiter of his fate. He will not condescend to embrace her knees, nor to shed a tear for the sake of exciting compassion; that were unworthy of the hero of Troy. He will leave it to her own choice, whether or not she will save a stranger who is merely seeking to regain his own rights. He will appeal for justice to the spirit of her departed father; he will invoke Hades, who owes him a debt for the many victims he has sent to the abodes beneath; let him either restore them to life, or compel the daughter to perform a duty which the father refuses to satisfy. Both he and Helen are under an oath, if their request is refused, either to meet Theoclymenus, sword in hand, and slay him or be slain; or, if he declines the combat, and tries to starve them in the sanctuary, to die by their own hands on the grave where they have taken refuge. None other but Menelaus shall be called the husband of Helen.

948. " Rigandi potestatem hic habet δακρῦσαι: quem rariorem usum praeivit Homerus illis δεδάκρυνται δὲ παρειαί, et τίπτε δεδάκρυσαι;" Hermann. We may compare the double use of διαίνειν, primarily 'to moisten,' then 'to bewail,' as *sup.* v. 379.—τὴν Τροίαν, for τὸ Τρωϊκὸν κλέος. Compare v. 808. 845.

950. Most probably this idea arose from the doctrine of αἰδὼς being closely connected with εὐγένεια, on which see Alcest. 601. For the notion of *shame* is also connected with that of shedding tears, especially as the Greeks regarded the eyes as the seat of shame. Hence Aesch. Suppl. 572, δακρύων δ' ἀποστάζει πένθιμον αἰδῶ.

ἀλλ' οὐχὶ τοῦτο τὸ καλόν, εἰ καλὸν τόδε,
αἱρήσομαι τὸ πρόσθε τῆς εὐψυχίας.
ἀλλ' εἰ μὲν ἄνδρα σοι δοκεῖ σῶσαι ξένον,
ζητοῦντά γ' ὀρθῶς ἀπολαβεῖν δάμαρτ' ἐμήν, 955
ἀπόδος τε καὶ πρὸς σῶσον· εἰ δὲ μὴ δοκεῖ,
ἐγὼ μὲν οὐ νῦν πρῶτον, ἀλλὰ πολλάκις
ἄθλιος ἂν εἴην, σὺ δὲ γυνὴ κακὴ φανεῖ.
ἃ δ' ἄξι' ἡμῶν καὶ δίκαι' ἡγούμεθα,
καὶ σῆς μάλιστα καρδίας ἀνθάψεται, 960
λέξω τάδ' ἀμφὶ μνῆμα σοῦ πατρὸς πόθῳ·
ὦ γέρον, ὃς οἰκεῖς τόνδε λάϊνον τάφον,
ἀπόδος, ἀπαιτῶ τὴν ἐμὴν δάμαρτά σε,
ἣν Ζεὺς ἔπεμψε δεῦρό σοι σώζειν ἐμοί.
οἶδ' οὕνεχ' ἡμῖν οὔποτ' ἀποδώσεις θανών· 965
ἀλλ' ἥδε πατέρα νέρθεν ἀνακαλούμενον
οὐκ ἀξιώσει τὸν πρὶν εὐκλεέστατον
κακῶς ἀκοῦσαι· κυρία γάρ ἐστι νῦν.

953. τὸ πρόσθε, as that which is preferable to. The article perhaps combines with πρόσθε as in Suppl. 758, τοὐκεῖθεν ἢ τοὐνθένδε; Porson on Med. 722 proposes αἱρήσομαι 'γὼ, which Dindorf writes with a crasis, αἱρήσομἀγώ. Hermann adopts the emendation; but it is far from a convincing one. There is no necessary emphasis on the personal pronoun; and the elision, or crasis, is neither very elegant nor very common.—For εὐψυχίας the old reading was εὐδαιμονίας, which Tyrwhitt acutely perceived was a gloss on the corrupt reading εὐτυχίας, the ψ and the τ being confused (as in Suppl 623 ψυχὰς for τύχας). Hermann gives εὐανδρίας, but this presupposes that another gloss had still earlier crept into the text, εὐψυχίας, which in its turn was supplanted by εὐδαιμονίας.

955. ζητοῦντά γ'. Perhaps δ'. Dindorf gives μ' with Reiske. But the γε is not redundant; it is exegetical, and means εἰ μὴ πάντως, ἀλλὰ ὀρθῶς γε ζητοῦντα κτλ.

957. The meaning is, that by refusing the request, Theonoë will herself receive worse harm than Menelaus; for *he* is inured to misfortune, but she will be thought base, while hitherto she has been thought pious, θεοσεβής.

961. σοῦ πατρὸς πόθῳ, "quasi pater tuus superstes esset." Pflugk. This is rather a forced translation; but it seems safer than Hermann's transposition of the verses,

λέξω τόδ' ἀμφὶ μνῆμ'· ἃ σοῦ πατρὸς πόθῳ
καὶ σῆς μάλιστα καρδίας ἀνθάψεται,

where the καὶ involves some ellipse, as οὐ μόνον ἐκείνου ἀνθάψεται, ἀλλὰ καὶ σοῦ, διὰ τὸν πόθον τοῦ πατρός. The common reading is equivalent to σὸν πατέρα ποθῶν, 'regretting the absence of one who would have rendered effectual assistance.' We might even read ποθῶν, sc. αὐτὸν, *cum ipsum alloqui non possim*. There is little probability in πίτνων or πεσών.

965. ἀποδώσεις Brodaeus for ἀπολέσεις. 'I well know that you can never restore her, since you are now dead; yet (my request will not be altogether vain, for) your daughter will not allow her father who once was most renowned, to have an ill name when invoked from below; for she now has become the possessor,' viz. of the sacred deposit entrusted to you in life; and she owes it to her father's good name that that deposit should be safely returned. —This and what follows is very fine. It is seldom that Euripides displays the character of Menelaus to such advantage.

ὦ νέρτερ᾽ Ἅιδη, καὶ σὲ σύμμαχον καλῶ,
ὃς πόλλ᾽ ἐδέξω τῆσδ᾽ ἕκατι σώματα   970
πεσόντα τὠμῷ φασγάνῳ, μισθὸν δ᾽ ἔχεις·
ἢ νῦν ἐκείνους ἀπόδος ἐμψύχους πάλιν,
ἢ τήνδ᾽ ἀνάγκασόν γε *μὴ εὐσεβοῦς πατρὸς
ἥσσω φανεῖσαν τἀμά γ᾽ ἀποδοῦναι λέχη.
εἰ δέ με γυναῖκα τὴν ἐμὴν συλήσετε,   975
ἅ σοι παρέλιπεν ἥδε τῶν λόγων, φράσω.
ὅρκοις κεκλήμεθ᾽, ὡς μάθῃς, ὦ παρθένε,
πρῶτον μὲν ἐλθεῖν διὰ μάχης σῷ συγγόνῳ·
κἀκεῖνον ἢ ᾽μὲ δεῖ θανεῖν· ἁπλοῦς λόγος.
ἢν δ᾽ ἐς μὲν ἀλκὴν μὴ πόδ᾽ ἀντιθῇ ποδί,   980
λιμῷ δὲ θηρᾷ τύμβον ἱκετεύοντε νᾅ,
κτανεῖν δέδοκται τήνδ᾽ ἐμοί, κἄπειτ᾽ ἐμὸν
πρὸς ἧπαρ ὦσαι δίστομον ξίφος τόδε,
τύμβου ᾽πὶ νώτοις τοῦδ᾽, ἵν᾽ αἵματος ῥοαὶ
τάφου καταστάζωσι· κεισόμεσθα δὲ   985
νεκρὼ δύ᾽ ἑξῆς τῷδ᾽ ἐπὶ ξεστῷ τάφῳ,
ἀθάνατον ἄλγος σοι, ψόγος δὲ σῷ πατρί.
οὐ γὰρ γαμεῖ τήνδ᾽ οὔτε σύγγονος σέθεν
οὔτ᾽ ἄλλος οὐδείς· ἀλλ᾽ ἐγώ σφ᾽ ἀπάξομαι,
εἰ μὴ πρὸς οἴκους δυνάμεθ᾽, ἀλλὰ πρὸς νεκρούς.   990
τί ταῦτα; δακρύοις ἐς τὸ θῆλυ τρεπόμενος
ἐλεινὸς εἴην μᾶλλον ἢ δραστήριος.

973. μὴ εὐσεβοῦς πατρὸς ἥσσω is Hermann's admirable correction for γ᾽ εὐσεβοῦς πατρὸς κρείσσω, 'proving herself not inferior to a righteous father.' " Quum omissum esset μὴ colliquescens cum sequente diphthongo, quae saepe vel omissionis vel ut μ᾽ scriberetur caussa fuit, ἥσσω sententiae jam repugnans in κρείσσω ab librariis erat mutatum." So ἥσσω and κρείσσω are confused in Androm. 707. Dindorf acquiesces in Elmsley's reading δυσσεβοῦς, but further suggests νόμου for πατρός. Under no circumstances could Proteus be called δυσσεβής. Cf. v. 61. The γε properly belongs to τήνδε,—'if you do not do that, at least compel *her*,' &c. In English the difference is not apparent; but in Greek γε is not a particle commonly annexed to an imperative.— τἀμά γ᾽ Barnes for τἄμ᾽.

982. ἐμοί. Hermann gives τήνδε μοι, after L. Dindorf, but there is an antithesis in the persons, '*I* have resolved to kill *her*.'

985. καταστάζωσι. See the note on Heracl. 1041. Hermann would read τάφον. For the accusative cf. Hec. 241. —ξεστῷ τάφῳ, Alcest. 836.

989. Alcest. 47, κἀπάξομαί γε νερτέραν ὑπὸ χθόνα.

992. εἴην. So Barnes after Scaliger. The old reading was ἐλεεινὸς ἦν, but ἂν is added in one MS. (Par. E. Herm.), if not in others (Dind.). However, ἦν ἂν is not the meaning required, but εἴην ἄν. The omission of ἄν may be justified by Hippol. 867, ἐμοὶ μὲν οὖν ἀβίωτος βίου τύχα πρὸς τὸ κρανθὲν εἴη τυχεῖν. Ibid. 1186, καὶ θᾶσσον ἢ λέγοι

ΕΛΕΝΗ.

κτεῖν', εἰ δοκεῖ σοι· δυσκλεῶς γὰρ οὐ κτενεῖς·
μᾶλλόν γε μέντοι τοῖς ἐμοῖς πείθου λόγοις,
ἵν' ᾖς δικαία καὶ δάμαρτ' ἐγὼ λάβω. 995
ΧΟ. ἐν σοὶ βραβεύειν, ὦ νεᾶνι, τοὺς λόγους.
οὕτω δὲ κρῖνον ὡς ἅπασιν ἀνδάνῃς.
ΘΕΟΝ. ἐγὼ πέφυκά τ' εὐσεβεῖν καὶ βούλομαι·
φιλῶ τ' ἐμαυτήν, καὶ κλέος τοὐμοῦ πατρὸς
οὐκ ἂν μιάναιμ', οὐδὲ συγγόνῳ χάριν 1000
δοίην ἄν, ἐξ ἧς δυσκλεὴς φανήσομαι.
ἔνεστι δ' ἱρὸν τῆς δίκης ἐμοὶ μέγα
ἐν τῇ φύσει· καὶ τοῦτο Νηρέως πάρα
ἔχουσα σώζειν Μενέλεων πειράσομαι·
Ἥρα δ' ἐπείπερ βούλεταί σ' εὐεργετεῖν, 1005
ἐς ταὐτὸν οἴσω ψῆφον. ἡ Κύπρις δέ μοι
ἵλεως μὲν εἴη, συμβέβηκε δ' οὐδαμοῦ·
πειράσομαι δὲ παρθένος μένειν ἀεί.
ἃ δ' ἀμφὶ τύμβῳ τῷδ' ὀνειδίζεις πατρὶ
ἡμῖν ὅδ' αὑτὸς μῦθος· ἀδικοίημεν ἄν, 1010
εἰ μὴ 'ποδώσω· καὶ γὰρ ἂν κεῖνος βλέπων
ἀπέδωκεν ἄν σοι τήνδ' ἔχειν, ταύτῃ δὲ σέ.
καὶ γὰρ τίσις τῶνδ' ἐστὶ τοῖς τε νερτέροις

τις κτλ. On the Attic form ἐλεινὸς see Porson in the Preface to Hecuba (p. 3, ed. Scholefield). There is an allusion perhaps to the custom of culprits appealing to the δικασταὶ with tears and sighs.
998. Theonöe sums up the arguments. She is naturally disposed to act righteously, and such too was the disposition of her father, whom she is bound to prefer to her unrighteous brother. Since Hera has resolved on saving Menelaus, she will give her vote on the same side; and may Cypris pardon the opposition to her will! She admits that Helen has descended to her from her father, as a deposit to be restored to the owner. There is such a thing as punishment hereafter. The soul of man loses not its consciousness after it has departed to the celestial ether whence it was derived. It will be a favour done to her brother, if she prevents him from committing a wrong. Let them devise some means of escape, and she will aid them at least by her silence. And their first object must be, to propitiate Hera and Cypris.
1002. ἱρὸν δίκης. Similarly Aeschylus speaks of the altar of Justice, Agam. 375. Eum. 511.—Νηρέως, cf. v. 15.
1007. συμβέβηκε, she has never been near me, I have had nothing to do with her. Ar. Ran. 807, οὔτε γὰρ Ἀθηναίοισι συνέβαιν' Αἰσχύλος. Soph. Aj. 1281, ὃν οὐδαμοῦ φῂς οὐδὲ συμβῆναι ποδί.
1013. καὶ γάρ. ('And I would not knowingly commit any such wrong;) for there is a retribution for these actions to all men, both those below and those (yet) on earth.' This passage is very remarkable. Why it should be considered (1013—16) an interpolation by Dindorf, is by no means clear. The punishment due for sin in a future state, though perhaps not elsewhere alluded to by Euripides, was distinctly taught by Aeschylus; see Suppl. 225. The doctrine that the soul was derived from ether and returned to it, is laid down clearly in Eur.

VOL. II. A a

178   ΕΥΡΙΠΙΔΟΥ

καὶ τοῖς ἄνωθεν πᾶσιν ἀνθρώποις. ὁ νοῦς
τῶν κατθανόντων ζῇ μὲν οὔ, γνώμην δ' ἔχει   1015
ἀθάνατον, εἰς ἀθάνατον αἰθέρ' ἐμπεσών.
ὡς οὖν περαίνω μὴ μακράν, σιγήσομαι
ἅ μου καθικετεύσατ', οὐδὲ μωρίᾳ
ξύμβουλος ἔσομαι τοῦ κασιγνήτου ποτέ.
εὐεργετῶ γὰρ κεῖνον οὐ δοκοῦσ' ὅμως,   1020
ἐκ δυσσεβείας ὅσιον εἰ τίθημί νιν.
αὐτοὶ μὲν οὖν εὑρίσκετ' ἔξοδόν τινα,
ἐγὼ δ' ἀποστᾶσ' ἐκποδὼν σιγήσομαι.
ἐκ τῶν θεῶν δ' ἄρχεσθε, χἰκετεύετε
τὴν μέν σ' ἐᾶσαι πατρίδα νοστῆσαι Κύπριν,   1025
Ἥρας δὲ τὴν ἔννοιαν ἐν ταὐτῷ μένειν
ἣν ἐς σὲ καὶ σὸν πόσιν ἔχει σωτηρίας.
σὺ δ', ὦ θανών μοι πάτερ, ὅσον γ' ἐγὼ σθένω,
οὔποτε κεκλήσει δυσσεβὴς ἀντ' εὐσεβοῦς.

ΧΟ.   οὐδείς ποτ' ηὐτύχησεν ἔκδικος γεγώς,   1030
ἐν τῷ δικαίῳ δ' ἐλπίδες σωτηρίας.

ΕΛ.   Μενέλαε, πρὸς μὲν παρθένου σεσώσμεθα.
τοὐνθένδε δὴ σὲ τοὺς λόγους φέροντα χρὴ
κοινὴν ξυνάπτειν μηχανὴν σωτηρίας.

ΜΕ.   ἄκουε δή νυν· χρόνιος εἶ κατὰ στέγας,   1035
καὶ συντέθραψαι προσπόλοισι βασιλέως.

Suppl. 532. The poet appears here to mean, that the soul, after it has left the human body, still retains its consciousness even when dissolved into its kindred element. Thus the punishment in a future state is regarded as arising from memory and remorse. The doctrine was doubtless derived from Anaxagoras.

1017. περαίνω μὴ μακρὰν is an expression made up of two, ὡς περαίνω τὸν λόγον, and ὡς μὴ μακρὰν μηκύνω.

1019. τῇ for τοῦ Dind. after Dobree,— a very arbitrary alteration, for the article often represents the possessive pronoun. —μωρίᾳ, see on v. 918. Hippol. 161. Ion 545.

1022. εὑρίσκετ' ἔξοδόν τινα Hermann for τὴν ἔξοδόν γ' εὑρίσκετε. Both the γε and the article are wrong, to say nothing of the metre. The error arose from the accidental transposition of the words, τίν' ἔξοδον εὑρίσκετε.

1025. τὴν μὲν—Κύπριν. The Homeric use of the article, 'the one of them,— namely, Cypris.' Similarly Bacch. 1230, τὴν δ' εἰπέ μοί τις δεῦρο βακχείῳ ποδὶ στείχειν Ἀγαύην. Pflugk quotes El. 781, ὁ δ' εἶπ' Ὀρέστης. Sophocles has many instances of this usage, e.g. Phil. 371, ὁ δ' εἶπ' Ὀδυσσεύς. For the crasis of καὶ ἴ (ἵ) into χἰ (ἵ), see Suppl. 344, χὐπερορρωδοῦσα. Androm. 736, χὐποχείριον λαβεῖν.

1029. εὐσεβοῦς. See v. 973. Here Theonöe finally leaves the stage.

1032. πρὸς μὲν παρθένου, i. e. ἕκατι, as far as her concurrence is concerned.

1033. τοὺς λόγους. The meaning of the article is this, χρή σε τοὺς λόγους φέρειν ἐς τὸ κοινόν, ὥστε συνάπτειν κτλ.

ΕΛΕΝΗ.

ΕΛ. τί τοῦτ' ἔλεξας; εἰσφέρεις γὰρ ἐλπίδας,
ὡς δή τι δράσων χρηστὸν ἐς κοινόν γε νῷν.
ΜΕ. πείσειας ἄν τιν' οἵτινες τετραζύγων
ὄχων ἀνάσσουσ' ὥστε νῷν δοῦναι δίφρους; 1040
ΕΛ. πείσαιμ' ἄν· ἀλλὰ τίνα φυγὴν φευξούμεθα,
πεδίων ἄπειροι βαρβάρου τ' ὄντες χθονός;
ΜΕ. ἀδύνατον εἶπας. φέρε, τί δ', εἰ κρυφθεὶς δόμοις
κτάνοιμ' ἄνακτα τῷδε διστόμῳ ξίφει;
ΕΛ. οὔ τἂν ἀνάσχοιτ' οὐδὲ σιγήσειεν ἂν 1045
μέλλοντ' ἀδελφὴ σύγγονον κατακτανεῖν.
ΜΕ. ἀλλ' οὐδὲ μὴν ναῦς ἔστιν ᾗ σωθεῖμεν ἂν
φεύγοντες· ἣν γὰρ εἴχομεν θάλασσ' ἔχει.
ΕΛ. ἄκουσον, ἤν τι καὶ γυνὴ λέξῃ σοφόν.
βούλει λέγεσθαι μὴ θανὼν λόγῳ θανεῖν; 1050
ΜΕ. κακὸς μὲν ὄρνις· εἰ δὲ κερδανῶ λέγων,
ἕτοιμός εἰμι μὴ θανὼν λόγῳ θανεῖν.
ΕΛ. καὶ μὴν γυναικείοις ἂν οἰκτισαίμεθα

1040. ὄχων ἀνάσσειν is like κώπης ἄνακτες Cycl. 86, πέλτης ἄναξ Alcest. 498. See on Aesch. Pers. 380, and compare Alcest. 428, τέθριππά θ' οἳ ζεύγνυσθε καὶ μονάμπυκας πώλους. — In the next verse ἂν was first added by Canter. The common reading πείσαιμ' was a correction of πεισαίμαν wrongly taken for πεισαίμην, a barbarous word.

1043. At φέρε there is perhaps a slight pause, as if it were φέρε ἄλλο τι βουλεύωμεν. Τί δ' εἰ, κτλ.

1045. The old reading οὐκ ἂν is more probably a corruption of οὔ τοι ἂν than of οὐκ ἄν σε, which latter Dind. Pflugk, and Hermann have edited after Portus. The error is a very common one (see Med. 867), and the correction of it so easy that little reliance can be placed on W. Dindorf's theory, that ἂν was sometimes used as a long syllable.—κατακτενεῖν W. Dindorf.

1047. ἀλλ' οὐδὲ μήν. 'And besides, we have not even a ship,' &c. So Aesch. Cho. 181, ἀλλ' οὐδὲ μήν νιν ἡ κτανοῦσ' ἐκείρατο. Theb. 665. Orest. 1117. Androm. 256, ἀλλ' οὐδ' ἐγὼ μὴν πρόσθεν ἐκδώσω μέ σοι.

1048. θάλασσ' ἔχει. See v. 410.
1049. καὶ γυνή. See Med. 1082. Suppl. 294. Aesch. Ag. 339.
1050. λόγῳ θανεῖν. Hermann, objecting to λέγεσθαι λόγῳ, and still more to the repetition of the same words in the reply of Menelaus, v. 1052, reads, after Fritzsche, βούλει λέγεσθαι, μὴ θανὼν ἔργῳ, θανεῖν; The correction may be ingenious, but it is certainly not highly probable. The punctuation is too artificial for Euripides. The poet's mind, intent on the antithesis, λόγῳ θανεῖν, καίπερ ἔργῳ μὴ θανών, took no heed of the accident that λέγεσθαι had preceded.

1051. εἰ κερδανῶ. It would be a mistake to regard this as intended by the poet to disparage the character of Menelaus. On the contrary, such was the ordinary doctrine and practice of the Greeks. See on Alcest. 537.—λέγων for λέγειν Barnes. He means, by relating his own pretended death, v. 1077. 1518.

1053. καὶ μήν. 'Well, then, we (Helen and the chorus) will mourn for you with shorn hair and dirges after the manner of women, addressing ourselves to that impious man' (Theoclymenus). So θρηνεῖν ζῶσα πρὸς τύμβον, Aesch. Cho. 912. αὐτὴ θησόμεσθ' ἃ πάσχομεν. Hermann adds σ' after γυναικείοις. See on v. 802. For καὶ μὴν in this *confirmatory* sense (when it is not followed by γε) compare vv. 1071, 1079.

A a 2

180   ΕΥΡΙΠΙΔΟΥ

κουραῖσι καὶ θρήνοισι πρὸς τὸν ἀνόσιον.
ΜΕ. σωτηρίας δὲ τοῦτ᾽ ἔχει τί νῶν ἄκος;   1055
ἀπαιόλη γὰρ τῷ λόγῳ γ᾽ ἔνεστί τις.
ΕΛ. ὡς δὴ θανόντα σ᾽ ἐνάλιον κενῷ τάφῳ
θάψαι τύραννον τῆσδε γῆς αἰτήσομαι.
ΜΕ. καὶ δὴ παρεῖκεν· εἶτα πῶς ἄνευ νεὼς
σωθησόμεσθα κενοταφοῦντ᾽ ἐμὸν δέμας;   1060
ΕΛ. δοῦναι κελεύσω πορθμίδ᾽, ᾗ καθήσομεν
κόσμον τάφῳ σῷ πελαγίας εἰς ἀγκάλας.
ΜΕ. ὡς εὖ τόδ᾽ εἶπας, πλὴν ἕν· εἰ χέρσῳ ταφὰς
θεῖναι κελεύσει σ᾽, οὐδὲν ἡ σκῆψις φέρει.
ΕΛ. ἀλλ᾽ οὐ νομίζειν φήσομεν καθ᾽ Ἑλλάδα   1065
χέρσῳ καλύπτειν τοὺς θανόντας ἐναλίους.
ΜΕ. τοῦτ᾽ αὖ κατορθοῖς· εἶτ᾽ ἐγὼ συμπλεύσομαι
καὶ συγκαθήσω κόσμον ἐν ταὐτῷ σκάφει.
ΕΛ. σὲ καὶ παρεῖναι δεῖ μάλιστα τούς τε σοὺς
πλωτῆρας, οἵπερ ἔφυγον ἐκ ναυαγίας.   1070
ΜΕ. καὶ μὴν ἐάνπερ ναῦν ἐπ᾽ ἀγκύρας λάβω,
ἀνὴρ παρ᾽ ἄνδρα στήσεται ξιφηφόρος.
ΕΛ. σὲ χρὴ βραβεύειν πάντα· πόμπιμοι μόνον
λαίφει πνοαὶ γένοιντο καὶ νεὼς δρόμος.

1055. ἄκος σωτηρίας. Generally a remedy *against*, here a remedy preventing one thing and bringing the contrary. The next verse, which Tyrwhitt restored to Menelaus, was wrongly given to Helen. Hermann's emendation of the old reading παλαιότης is worthy of all praise. He quotes Hesychius, ἀπαιόλη, ἀπάτη, ἀποστέρησις. Αἰσχύλος Περραιβοῖς (Frag. 172 Dind.), Τέθνηκεν αἰσχρῶς χρημάτων ἀπαιόλῃ. Ar. Nub. 1150, εὖ γ᾽ ὦ παμβασίλει᾽ Ἀπαιόλη. Ion 549, τοῦτο κἄμ᾽ ἀπαιολᾷ. Nothing can be weaker than the interpretations given of παλαιότης, 'You talk of an event that had happened long ago,' or 'there is something of old-fashioned simplicity in your words,' or lastly, 'your proposal is folly.' In the emended reading, the force of γε is this; 'your proposal, at least, is well calculated for deception, if only it can be successfully carried out,'—λόγῳ γοῦν, εἰ μὴ ἔργῳ.

1059. καὶ δὴ παρεῖκεν. 'Suppose then that he grants it.' See Med. 386, καὶ δὴ τεθνᾶσι. The perfect active is so rare that we should perhaps restore the aorist παρῆκεν, even though the perfect is the more proper tense in the formula καὶ δή. Compare however τέθεικε in El. 7. Sophocles is said to have employed παρεῖκα (frag. 305).

1061. καθήσομεν for -μαι Musgrave. This is a common error. In Rhes. 949, ἐπάξομεν for ἐπάξομαι is highly probable.

1065. οὐ νομίζειν, scil. τοὺς Ἕλληνας. With καθ᾽ Ἑλλάδα we should have expected νομίζεσθαι.

1069. σὲ καί. The καί belongs to παρεῖναι μάλιστα, '*You* must be present even before all others.' Of course, no accurate scholar will take the meaning to be καὶ σὲ—τούς τε σοὺς, or σὲ καὶ for καὶ σὲ, 'you also.' There is a similar verse in Aesch. Cho. 878, σὲ καὶ ματεύω, 'I have been even looking for you.'

1071. ἐπ᾽ ἀγκύρας, scil. ὀχουμένην. Cf. v. 277.

ΕΛΕΝΗ. 181

ΜΕ. ἔσται· πόνους γὰρ δαίμονες παύσουσί μου. 1075
    ἀτὰρ θανόντα τοῦ μ' ἐρεῖς πεπυσμένη ;
ΕΛ. σοῦ· καὶ μόνος γε φάσκε διαφυγεῖν μόρον
    Ἀτρέως πλέων σὺν παιδὶ, καὶ θανόνθ' ὁρᾶν.
ΜΕ. καὶ μὴν τάδ' ἀμφίβληστρα σώματος ῥάκη
    ξυμμαρτυρήσει ναυτικῶν ἐρειπίων. 1080
ΕΛ. ἐς καιρὸν ἦλθε, τότε δ' ἄκαιρ' ἀπώλλυτο.
    τὸ δ' ἄθλιον κεῖν' εὐτυχὲς τάχ' ἂν πέσοι.
ΜΕ. πότερα δ' ἐς οἴκους σοὶ συνεισελθεῖν με χρὴ,
    ἢ πρὸς τάφῳ τῷδ' ἥσυχοι καθώμεθα ;
ΕΛ. αὐτοῦ μέν'· ἢν γὰρ καί τι πλημμελές σε δρᾷ, 1085
    τάφος σ' ὅδ' ἂν ῥύσαιτο φάσγανόν τε σόν.
    ἐγὼ δ' ἐς οἴκους βᾶσα βοστρύχους τεμῶ,
    πέπλων τε λευκῶν μέλανας ἀνταλλάξομαι,
    παρῇδί τ' ὄνυχα φόνιον ἐμβαλῶ χροός.
    μέγας γὰρ ἀγών, καὶ βλέπω δύο ῥοπάς· 1090
    ἢ γὰρ θανεῖν δεῖ μ', ἢν ἁλῶ τεχνωμένη,
    ἢ πατρίδα τ' ἐλθεῖν καὶ σὸν ἐκσῶσαι δέμας.
    ὦ πότνι', ἢ Δίοισιν ἐν λέκτροις πίτνεις,

1079. ἀμφίβληστρα σώματος, the garments which he had before described as ναὸς ἔκβολα v. 422. The construction, according to Hermann, is τάδ' ἀμφ. σώματος ξυμμ. ῥάκη ν. ἐρειπίων, ' will confirm my assertion that they are rags from the wreck.' One might suspect however that the poet wrote thus (cf. frag. 688),

καὶ μὴν τάδ' ἀμφίβλητα σώματος ῥάκη
ξυμμαρτυρήσει ναυτικοῖς ἐρειπίοις,

i. e. will bear joint attestation to the wreck. So ναυτικῶν ἐρειπίων means 'fragments of ships' in Ag. 643. In Tro. 1025, ἐν πέπλων ἐρειπίοις is adduced by Pflugk to justify the syntax ῥάκη ἐρειπίων. But according to this it should rather have been ἐρείπια ῥακέων.

1081. ἐς καιρὸν κτλ. 'They (your present tattered garments) now come appropriately ; but then (those which you wore) were lost when they were most needed.'—ἀπώλλυτο, scil. τὰ καλλίω καὶ βασιλικὰ ἀμφιβλήματα. J. Barnes.

1085. Photius, πλημμελεῖν, τὸ ἀτακτεῖν καὶ ὑβρίζειν καὶ ῥαθυμεῖν· καὶ πλημμελὲς, τὸ ἐκμελὲς καὶ ἀπαίδευτον.

1088. ἀνταλλάξομαι, ' I will *take* in exchange.' On this verb, active and middle, see Alcest. 462. In the next verse, Heath, Hermann, and others construe φόνιον χροὸς, *qui cutem cruentet*,—a syntax more artificial than is usual with Euripides. It seems obvious to read χερὸς, ' the bloody nail of my hand.'

1090. δύο ῥοπὰς, two turnings of the scale, two opposite results of our scheme, death or escape.

1093. ὦ πότνια. This is a very fine prayer, and a very impressive one too, from the action which accompanied it, and the energy of despair which inspired it. To Cypris her petition is addressed next after Hera, because these two goddesses, as rivals, had willed both the destruction of Troy and the misfortunes of Helen, whose marriage the latter had frustrated after it had been promised by the former to Paris as a bribe. The mythology by which she is represented as the daughter of Dione is less common. Theocritus invokes her as Κύπρι Διωναία, Id. xv. 106. Plato (Symp. p. 180. E.) and Apollodorus make Aphrodite the daughter of Zeus and Dione, who was

182   ΕΥΡΙΠΙΔΟΥ

Ἥρα, δύ᾽ οἰκτρὼ φῶτ᾽ ἀνάψυξον πόνων,
αἰτούμεθ᾽, ὀρθὰς ὠλένας πρὸς οὐρανὸν   1095
ῥιπτοῦνθ᾽, ἵν᾽ οἰκεῖς ἀστέρων ποικίλματα.
σύ θ᾽, ἣ 'πὶ τὠμῷ κάλλος ἐκτήσω γάμῳ,
κούρη Διώνης Κύπρι, μή μ᾽ ἐξεργάσῃ.
ἅλις δὲ λύμης, ἥν μ᾽ ἐλυμήνω πάρος,
τοὔνομα παρασχοῦσ᾽, οὐ τὸ σῶμ᾽, ἐν βαρβάροις.
θανεῖν δ᾽ ἔασόν μ᾽, εἰ κατακτεῖναι θέλεις,   1101
ἐν γῇ πατρῴᾳ. τί ποτ᾽ ἄπληστος εἶ κακῶν,
ἔρωτας ἀπάτας δόλιά τ᾽ ἐξευρήματα
ἀσκοῦσα φίλτρα θ᾽ αἱματηρὰ δωμάτων;
εἰ δ᾽ ἦσθα μετρία, τἄλλα γ᾽ ἡδίστη θεῶν   1105
πέφυκας ἀνθρώποισιν· οὐκ ἄλλως λέγω.
ΧΟ.   σὲ τὰν ἐναυλείοις ὑπὸ δενδροκόμοις   στρ. α'.
μουσεῖα καὶ θάκους ἐνίζουσαν ἀναβοάσω,
σὲ τὰν ἀοιδοτάταν ὄρνιθα μελῳδὸν

one of the Τιτανίδες, (lib. i. 1, 3, and 3, 1.) See likewise Ovid, Fast. ii. 461, and v. 309. Hom. Il. v. 370, ἡ δ᾽ ἐν γούνασι πῖπτε Διώνης δῖ᾽ Ἀφροδίτη, μητρὸς ἑῆς.— The Ionic form κούρη, if genuine, is deserving of notice.

1097. κάλλος ἐκτήσω, "pulchritudinis praemium adepta es," Pflugk. So Med. 218, δύσκλειαν ἐκτήσαντο καὶ ῥᾳθυμίαν. Hippol. 414, τόλμας οὐ καλὰς κεκτημένας. —ἐπὶ γάμῳ κτλ., by promising me to Paris.

1104. δωμάτων. Hermann gives σωμάτων after Musgrave. Those who retain the vulgate make it depend on αἱματηρά, which is at least needless, if not incorrect. It is sufficient to understand, that Cypris incites families to mutual murders.

1105. μετρία. Cf. Med. 630, εἰ δ᾽ ἅλις ἔλθοι Κύπρις, οὐκ ἄλλα θεὸς εὔχαρις οὕτω. Hippol. 443, Κύπρις γὰρ οὐ φορητὸν, ἢν πολλὴ ῥυῇ. Taken alone, such passages might be regarded as evidences that the poet was a sensualist, as some of his detractors have assumed. On this point the reader is referred to p. xliii of the Preface to Vol. i.—πέφυκας is rather irregular in construction; but the poet meant to say, 'It is your nature to be most pleasing to mankind, (and you would always be so,) if you did not come in excess.'

1107. The Chorus, while Menelaus remains alone and silent on the stage, within the asylum of the altar, (v. 1085—6,) invoke the aid of the nightingale to sing the woes of Helen and the calamities brought by Paris upon Troy. The Argive army too shared in the general disaster, for many were lost by shipwreck on their return. Menelaus himself was driven from the mountains of his native shore, when he approached it bringing back his supposed bride, the cloud-formed semblance of Helen. 'Tis impossible for man to understand the dealings of the god, seeing that these go according to the least expected way, and end in the strangest results. Here is Helen, a daughter of Zeus, as men say, and yet held up to infamy for the gravest crimes! Foolish are men who desire to gain glory and to end their disputes by war. If bloodshed is the only way of deciding them, there will never be wanting a cause of slaughter. The affair of Helen might have been settled by arbitration; but it is now too late to save those who have fallen from the grave, or the city from being a prey to the flames.

1108. μουσεῖα, a place of song; see above, v. 174.—ἐνίζειν with an accusative occurs also in Pers. 143, τόδ᾽ ἐνεζόμενοι στέγος ἀρχαῖον, and Cho. 786, οἵ τ᾽ ἔσω δωμάτων πλουτογαθῆ μυχὸν ἐνίζετε (according to Hermann's excellent emendation for νομίζετε).

ἀηδόνα δακρυόεσσαν, 1110
ἔλθ' ὦ διὰ ξουθᾶν γενύων ἐλελιζομένα,
θρήνοις ἐμοῖς ξυνεργὸς,
Ἑλένας μελέους πόνους
τὸν Ἰλιάδων τ' ἀει-
δούσᾳ δακρυόεντα †πόνον 1115
Ἀχαιῶν ὑπὸ λόγχαις,
ὅτ' ἔμολεν ἔμολε πεδία, βαρβάρῳ πλάτᾳ
ὃς ἔδραμε ῥόθια, μέλεα Πριαμίδαις ἄγων
Λακεδαίμονος ἄπο λέχεα
σέθεν, ὦ Ἑλένα, Πάρις αἰνόγαμος 1120
πομπαῖσιν Ἀφροδίτας.
πολλοὶ δ' Ἀχαιῶν ἐν δορὶ καὶ πετρίναις   ἀντ. α'.
ῥιπαῖσιν ἐκπνεύσαντες Ἄιδαν μέλεον ἔχουσιν,
τάλαιναν ὧν ἀλόχων κείραντες ἔθειραν·
ἄνυμφα μέλαθρα δὲ κεῖται· 1125

1111. ἔλθ' ὦ Musgrave for ἐλθέ.— ἐλελιζομένα, 'trilling through thy tawny throat.' The words ἐλελίζειν and ξουθὸς (which latter, as an epithet of bees and nightingales, seems to mean ' dark-brown,' though some referred it to the *sound* emitted,) were so familiarly applied to the bird of song, that we need not be surprised at the similarity of words in the *Aves*, which was brought out two years before the Helena, v. 213, ἐλελιζομένη διεροῖς μέλεσιν γενύος ξουθῆς. Pflugk, who says that Aristophanes copied Euripides, has failed in his preface to determine the date of the *Helena*. But his error was held in common with Valckenaer and others, as Hermann tells us.

1113. μελέους Herm. for μελέας. Thus in the next clause πόνον has a corresponding epithet δακρυόεντα. But the reading πόνον seems very improbable, on account of the awkward repetition. There is some probability that it is a gloss on ὕτλον (Aesch. Theb. 18), which the grammarians regularly explained by πόνον. In the antistrophic verse 1130 it is equally clear that we should read ἄκραις for ἀκταῖς, these words being commonly interchanged; see Heracl. 83, Hippol. 1208. (So Bothe has also corrected the vulgate.) Thus πόνον may be considered as metrically equivalent to the last syllable of ἄκραις, this being a glyconean and the next a pherecratean verse.—Ἰλιάδων, of the Trojan women, captives like the chorus themselves, v. 193.—ἀειδούσᾳ Herm. and Lachmann for ἀείδουσα.

1117. ὅτ' for ὃς Herm. after Hoffmann. They are clearly right; the sense being ὅτ' ἔμολεν ἐκεῖνος, ὃς ἔδραμε ῥόθια πλάτῃ, ἄγων Ἑλένην ἀπὸ Λακεδαίμονος, Πάρις κτλ. The comma, usually placed after πλάτᾳ, has been transferred by the present editor to πεδία, i. e. Τροίας. For the accusative ῥόθια see vv. 405. 532. 598.

1120. ὦ Ἑλένα is the clever restoration of Seidler for ὡς εἷλε.

1122. By πέτριναι ῥιπαὶ the whirling or whizzing of stones in battle is meant. Of the buzzing of the musquito in Agam. 866, λεπταῖς ὑπαὶ κώνωπος ἐξηγειρόμην ῥιπαῖσι θωΰσσοντος. In Oed. Col. 1245 seqq., cares are said to come from all quarters and at all times, ' both from the west and the east, at midday and *by night*,' νυχίαν ἀπὸ ῥιπᾶν, where the twinkling of the stars is apparently meant. Cf. Il. xii. 462, σανίδες δὲ διέτμαγεν ἄλλυδις ἄλλη, λᾶος ὑπὸ ῥιπῆς.

1124. ὧν for τῶν Matthiae. Hermann's remark on the former word is curious, " Unicus, quod sciam, hic Helenae locus apud tragicos est, in quo hoc pronomen, uti saepius apud poetas Alexandrinos, de eo quod plurium est dictum

πολλοὺς δὲ πυρσεύσας φλογερὸν σέλας ἀμφιρύταν
Εὔβοιαν εἷλ' Ἀχαιῶν
μονόκωπος ἀνὴρ, πέτραις
Καφηρίσιν ἐμβαλὼν
Αἰγαίαις τ' ἐνάλοις ἄκραις, 1130
δόλιον ἀστέρα λάμψας.
ἀλίμενα δ' ὄρεα †μέλεα βαρβάρου στολᾶς,
ὅτ' ἔσυτο πατρίδος ἀποπρὸ χειμάτων πνοᾷ
τέρας, οὐ τέρας, ἀλλ' ἔριν
Δαναῶν νεφέλαν ἐπὶ ναυσὶν ἄγων, 1135
εἴδωλον ἱρὸν Ἥρας.
ὅ τι θεὸς, ἢ μὴ θεὸς, ἢ τὸ μέσον,   στρ. β'.

invenitur."—κείραντες, causing them to cut their hair in mourning.

1126 seqq. A legend from the Cyclic Νόστοι is here mentioned, for which see v. 767, τὰ Ναυπλίου τ' Εὐβοικὰ πυρπολήματα. The story was that Nauplius had sailed from Troy in a fisherman's boat to intercept the Greeks at the s.e. extremity of Euboea. Hence he is called μονόκωπος.—πυρσεύειν Εὔβοιαν φλ. σέλας, 'to light up Euboea with a beacon-fire,' is the same construction as v. 866, θεῖον δὲ σεμνὸν θεσμὸν αἰθέρος μυχόν. Hence the reading of Matthiae, ἀμφιρύταν for ἀμφὶ ῥυτὰν, is unquestionably right. Photius, πυρσεύει, πῦρ ἐξάπτει. Cf. Electr. 694.

1130. ἄκραις for ἀκταῖς Bothe. See on v. 1113.—λάμψας, 'having lighted up.' For this active verb see Ion 83. Hermann's alteration of the text to δόλιον ἀκταῖς ἀστέρα λάμψας, 'and by lighting a deceitful beacon on the sea-shores,' does not fully satisfy the metre of the strophe, (v. 1115—6,) unless we there read Ἀργείων for Ἀχαιῶν. This (in one verse) would give a form of glyconean such as in Aesch. Suppl. 660, Ἄρτεμιν δ' Ἑκάταν γυναικῶν λόχους ἐφορεύειν, and Ag. 679, κελσάντων Σιμόεντος ἀκτὰς ἐπ' ἀκριτοφύλλους.—ἐνάλοις for ἐναλίοις was Musgrave's correction, as also Καφηρίσιν for Καφηρίαις.

1132. Μάλεα Herm. for μέλεα, and ἀποπρὸ χειμάτων Heath for ἄπο, προχευμάτων. The adjective Μάλεος from Μαλέα seems to follow no certain analogy. Possibly Μενέλεω may have been written; as ἀλίμενα δ' ὄρε' (so Aldus) ἀπέλασε Μενέλεω στολὰν, or ἐπέλασε βαρβάρῳ

στολᾷ (cf. Andr. 1167). After describing the fate of the other Greeks on the coast of Euboea, the poet went on to say, that Menelaus likewise was driven by adverse winds into Egypt, when he was returning home with his bride. Hermann compares Orest. 360, where Menelaus says of himself, Ἀγαμέμνονος μὲν γὰρ τύχας ἠπιστάμην, Μαλέᾳ προσίσχων πρῷραν, and the whole passage he explains as follows;—" *Maleae autem montes inhospitales fuere, quum longe a patria rejectus est ventis, qui barbaro vestitu pulcrum monstrum, inanem rixarum Danais caussam, secum ducebat.*" It seems, however, possible to follow the natural order of the words, and to construe ἀλίμενα βαρβάρου στολᾶς 'afforded no harbour to his Trojan ships,' i. e. the ships in which he brought back Helen and other Trojan spoils. So Aeschylus uses στολὴ for a naval armament, Suppl. 744, οὔτοι ταχεῖα ναυτικοῦ στρατοῦ στολή, or rather perhaps, as Photius explains it, ἡ ἀποστολὴ καὶ ἔκπεμψις. The genitive after ἀλίμενα is defended by παντὸς οἰωνοῦ λιμήν, Antig. 1000.

1134. τέρας, οὐ τέρας, a prodigy not recognised under the form of a beautiful woman. For ἀλλ' ἔριν Hermann reads ἔριν ἔριδι, which suits the metre of v. 1119, though we might there as easily read λέχη for λέχεα.

1137—43. The poet here insinuates the same doubts as to the personality of the supreme Being which he has in so many other places ventured to express. Cf. Troad. 885, ὅστις ποτ' εἶ σὺ, δυστόπαστος εἰδέναι, Ζεύς. Herc. F. 1263. Supra, 711 &c. To Hermann is due τίς φύσιν—εὗρεν, for τί φῂς—εὑρεῖν, for

ΕΛΕΝΗ.

τίς φύσιν ἐρευνήσας βροτῶν
μακρότατον πέρας ηὗρεν,
ὃς τὰ †θεῶν ἐσορᾷ   1140
δεῦρο καὶ αὖθις ἐκεῖσε
καὶ πάλιν ἀντιλόγοις
πηδῶντ᾽ ἀνελπίστοις τύχαις;
σὺ Διὸς ἔφυς, ὦ Ἑλένα, θυγάτηρ·
πτανὸς γὰρ ἐν κόλποις σε Λή-   1145
δας ἐτέκνωσε πατήρ.
κᾷτ᾽ ἰαχήθης καθ᾽ Ἑλλανίαν
ἄδικος, ἄπιστος, προδότις, ἄθεος· οὐδ᾽ ἔχω
τί τὸ σαφές, ὅ τι ποτ᾽ ἐν βροτοῖς.
τὸ θεῶν δ᾽ ἔπος ἀλαθὲς ηὗρον.   1150
ἄφρονες, ὅσοι τὰς ἀρετὰς πολέμῳ   ἀντ. β΄.

which Pflugk, after Matthiae, gives τίς φησὶν—εὑρεῖν, 'who can affirm that he has found out?' But φύσιν ἐρευνᾶν, to investigate nature, is a term altogether appropriate to the disciple of Anaxagoras. Translate, 'What is God, or what is not God, or what is intermediate, who of mortals that has searched furthest into Nature, has found out as a conclusion, who sees (i. e. when he sees) the various dispensations of the gods shifting first here and then there and back again with contrary and unlooked for results?' It seems better to take μακρότατον with ἐρευνήσας than with πέρας.—τὸ μέσον, midway between things visible and invisible, matter and spirit, human and divine. He appears to mean the δαίμονες, or perhaps Νοῦς or Φύσις. For the form of expression cf. Prom. 116, θεόσυτος, ἢ βρότειος, ἢ κεκραμένη. Theb. 184, ἀνήρ, γυνή τε, χὤτι τῶν μεταίχμιον.

1141. δεῦρο for δεινά Dobree, who likewise suggested ἀμφιλόγοις for ἀντιλόγοις. But the common reading is supported by πάλιν, implying contrariety. Literally, ἀντίλογοι τύχαι are casualties which, from their improbability, would admit of being reasoned against. But the chief force of the compound is in ἀντί, in the sense of ἀντιπάλοις, ἀντιστρόφοις.—πηδῶντα, cf. Tro. 1204, τοῖς τρόποις γὰρ αἱ τύχαι Ἔμπληκτος ὡς ἄνθρωπος ἄλλοτ᾽ ἄλλοσε Πηδῶσι.

1147. κᾷτ᾽ ἰαχήθης Hermann for καὶ ἰαχὴ σή. This correction is better than

W. Dindorf's νῦν δ᾽ ἰάχησαι, in as much as κᾷτ᾽ is very much nearer the MSS. than νῦν δ᾽. The initial ι is here long on account of the augment.—In the next verse the old reading was ἄδικος, προδότις, ἄπιστος κτλ. There is little to choose between Hermann's προδότις, ἄπιστος ἄδικος, and W. Dindorf's transposition as given in the text.

1148. οὐδ᾽ ἔχω κτλ. 'Nor know I what certainty is, whatever it be that is so considered among men.' This of course is in continuation of the sentiment at v. 1137 &c.

1150. τὸ θεῶν δ᾽. The δ᾽ was added by Barnes and Bothe. Hermann, who gives τό τοι θεῶν κτλ., alters the antistrophic verse to ἐν ἀθλίοις πάθεσιν Ἰλίοισιν. The last is unquestionably corrupt, according to the common reading, and therefore it is hardly safe, on such evidence, to tamper with the present verse. The poet appears to mean, that nothing is to be relied on but the plain declaration of the gods (by oracles or portents). Compare Electr. 399, Λοξίου γὰρ ἔμπεδοι χρησμοί, βροτῶν δὲ μαντικὴν χαίρειν ἐῶ.

1151. ἄφρονες, ὅσοι κτλ. This is one of several passages which seem to prove that Euripides was not, as has sometimes been alleged, attached to the war-party at Athens. The Helena was acted in the year after the failure of the Sicilian expedition, so that it is highly probable the passage contains an allusion to that event.

κτᾶσθε δορὸς ἀλκαίου τε λόγχαις, καταπαυόμενοι πο-
νους θνατῶν ἀμαθῶς·
εἰ γὰρ ἅμιλλα κρινεῖ νιν 1155
αἵματος, οὔποτ' ἔρις
λείψει κατ' ἀνθρώπων πόλεις·
†αἳ Πριαμίδος γᾶς ἔλιπον θαλάμους,
ἐξὸν διορθῶσαι λόγοις
σὰν ἔριν, ὦ Ἑλένα. 1160
νῦν δ' οἱ μὲν Ἅιδᾳ μέλονται κάτω,
τείχεα δὲ, φλογμὸς ὥστε Διὸς, ἐπέσυτο φλόξ,
ἐπὶ δὲ παθέα πάθεσι φέρεις
†ἀθλίοις ἐν συμφοραῖς Ἰλίοις.

ΘΕΟΚΛΥΜΕΝΟΣ.

ὦ χαῖρε, πατρὸς μνῆμ'· ἐπ' ἐξόδοισι γὰρ 1165

See the Preface to Vol. i. p. xix. A similar sentiment occurs in Suppl. 949, ὦ ταλαίπωροι βροτῶν, Τί κτᾶσθε λόγχας καὶ κατ' ἀλλήλων φόνους Τίθεσθε; παύσασθ', ἀλλὰ λήξαντες πόνων Ἄστη φυλάσσεθ' ἥσυχοι μεθ' ἡσύχων. As regards the reading, Hermann has slightly corrected v. 1152, κτᾶσθε, δορὸς ἀλκαίου λόγχαισι, while ἀμαθῶς for ἀπαθῶς is Musgrave's. The passage thus amended may be translated as follows:—' Senseless are ye, who win your reputations for valour by war and by the point of the martial spear, foolishly trying to have the troubles of men brought to an end in this way; for if bloody contest shall settle them, never will strife be wanting throughout the cities of men.' Hermann takes δορὸς ἀλκαίου to mean *auxiliatricis hastae*; but ἀλκὴ is commonly used simply for *fighting*. He also edits θανάτων for θνατῶν, and πόθους after Seidler. Probably in v. 1140 we should read τὰ θνήτ' ἐσορᾷ.—Pflugk, it is hardly necessary to add, is wrong in explaining λείψει κατὰ by καταλείψει.

1158. This line is corrupt. Hermann gives ἃ Π. γᾶς ἔπελεν θαλάμοις, but he admits that the imperfect of πέλω is not elsewhere found in the tragic writers. It seems likely that we should read ὃ Π. γᾶς ἔμολεν θαλάμοις 'which event came by the Trojan marriage, i. e. that of Helen and Paris, when they (the combatants) might have settled the quarrel about thee,

O Helen, by agreement.' Compare Suppl. 748, πόλεις τ' ἔχουσαι διὰ λόγου κάμψαι κακὰ, Φίλοις μὲν οὐ πείθεσθε, τοῖς δὲ πράγμασι.

1164. This verse also is corrupt. Dindorf suspects that it was inserted by some grammarian to fill up a *lacuna*. Hermann's πάθεσιν for συμφοραῖς has but little probability when πάθεσιν occurs in the preceding verse.

1165. Theoclymenus returns from hunting, (see v. 154,) and his first impulse, on revisiting his palace, is to pay his wonted regards to the spirit of his father, whose tomb stands in front of the entrance. He next dismisses his attendants, and is beginning to reproach himself for his remissness in not putting to death the guards who have allowed a strange Greek to have access, when he is startled by finding that Helen has left her sanctuary at the tomb. He is reassured however by seeing her and the stranger not far from the spot. She, according to the plan agreed upon (cf. v. 1087), is dressed in deep mourning. An opportunity is now offered of making their request with respect to the burial of Menelaus, said to be lost at sea. It is readily granted, and with a simplicity and liberality which is highly exciting to an audience who know that his gifts are all to be turned against himself.

ΕΛΕΝΗ.

ἔθαψα, Πρωτεῦ, σ᾽ ἕνεκ᾽ ἐμῆς προσρήσεως·
ἀεὶ δέ σ᾽ ἐξιών τε κεἰσιὼν δόμους
Θεοκλύμενος παῖς ὅδε προσεννέπει, πάτερ.
ὑμεῖς μὲν οὖν κύνας τε καὶ θηρῶν βρόχους,
δμῶες, κομίζετ᾽ ἐς δόμους τυραννικούς·   1170
ἐγὼ δ᾽ ἐμαυτὸν πόλλ᾽ ἐλοιδόρησα δή·
οὐ γάρ τι θανάτῳ τοὺς κακοὺς κολάζομεν.
καὶ νῦν πέπυσμαι φανερὸν Ἑλλήνων τινὰ
ἐς γῆν ἀφῖχθαι καὶ λεληθέναι σκοποὺς,
ἤτοι κατόπτην ἢ κλοπαῖς θηρώμενον   1175
Ἑλένην· θανεῖται δ᾽, ἤν γε δὴ ληφθῇ μόνον.
ἔα·
ἀλλ᾽, ὡς ἔοικε, πάντα διαπεπραγμένα
ηὕρηκα· τύμβου γὰρ κενὰς λιποῦσ᾽ ἕδρας
ἡ Τυνδαρὶς παῖς ἐκπεπόρθμευται χθονός.
ὠή, χαλᾶτε κλῇθρα, λύεθ᾽ ἱππικὰς   1180
φάτνας, ὀπαδοὶ, κἀκκομίζεθ᾽ ἅρματα,
ὡς ἂν πόνου γ᾽ ἕκατι μὴ λάθῃ με γῆς
τῆσδ᾽ ἐκκομισθεῖσ᾽ ἄλοχος, ἧς ἐφίεμαι.
ἐπίσχετ᾽· εἰσορῶ γὰρ οὓς διώκομεν
παρόντας ἐν δόμοισι κοὐ πεφευγότας.   1185
αὕτη, τί πέπλους μέλανας ἐξήψω χροὸς
λευκῶν ἀμείψασ᾽, ἔκ τε κρατὸς εὐγενοῦς
κόμας σίδηρον ἐμβαλοῦσ᾽ ἀπέθρισας,
χλωροῖς τε τέγγεις δάκρυσι σὴν παρηΐδα
κλαίουσα; πότερον ἐννύχοις πεπεισμένη   1190

1171. The δὴ here is separated from πολλὰ, to which it belongs, as in Oed. Col. 1215, ἐπεὶ πολλὰ μὲν αἱ μακραὶ ἁμέραι κατέθεντο δὴ λύπας ἐγγυτέρω.
1177. πάντα διαπ., 'all my schemes frustrated,' viz. his hopes of marrying Helen. Accustomed hitherto to find Helen at his father's tomb, he is now surprised to find it vacant, and concludes that she is gone.
1187. ἀμείψασα, ἀνταλλαξαμένη, having taken in exchange for. See Bach. 53.—ἀπέθρισας, the contracted aorist of ἀποθερίζω, which also occurs Agam. 519, αὐτόχθονον πατρῷον ἔθρισεν δόμον, and

Orest. 128.—χλωροῖς, fresh, abundant, like the Homeric θαλερὸν κατὰ δάκρυ χέουσα, compared by Hermann. Cf. Med. 922.
1190. πεπεισμένη, induced by, putting faith in, πιστεύουσα. There seems little cause for the objection which some critics have raised against the reading. So Aeschylus calls dreams ὀνείρων φάσματ᾽ εὐπειθῆ in Agam. 265.—φάτιν οἴκοθεν, see on v. 820. The words are indeed capable of another sense, 'hearing news from home.' But if we compare the passage just quoted from Aeschylus, where φάτις ἄπτερος, 'on omen not from birds,' is

στένεις ὀνείροις, ἢ φάτιν τιν' οἴκοθεν
κλύουσα λύπῃ σὰς διέφθαρσαι φρένας ;
ΕΛ. ὦ δέσποτ', ἤδη γὰρ τόδ' ὀνομάζω σ' ἔπος,
ὄλωλα· φροῦδα τἀμὰ κοὐδέν εἰμ' ἔτι.
ΘΕΟΚ. ἐν τῷ δὲ κεῖσαι συμφορᾶς ; τίς ἡ τύχη ;   1195
ΕΛ. Μενέλαος, οἴμοι, πῶς φράσω ; τέθνηκέ μοι.
ΘΕΟΚ. οὐδέν τι χαίρω σοῖς λόγοις, τὰ δ' εὐτυχῶ.
* * * *
ΘΕΟΚ. πῶς οἶσθα ; μῶν σοι Θεονόη λέγει τάδε ;
ΕΛ. κείνη τέ φησιν ὅ τε παρὼν, ὅτ' ὤλλυτο.
ΘΕΟΚ. ἥκει γὰρ ὅστις καὶ τάδ' ἀγγέλλει σαφῆ ;   1200
ΕΛ. ἥκει· μόλοι γὰρ, ὡς ἐγὼ χρῄζω μολεῖν.
ΘΕΟΚ. τίς ἐστί ; ποῦ 'στιν ; ἵνα σαφέστερον μάθω.
ΕΛ. ὅδ', ὃς κάθηται τῷδ' ὑποπτήξας τάφῳ.
ΘΕΟΚ. Ἄπολλον, ὡς ἐσθῆτι δυσμόρφῳ πρέπει.
ΕΛ. οἴμοι, δοκῶ μὲν κἀμὸν ὧδ' ἔχειν πόσιν.   1205
ΘΕΟΚ. ποδαπὸς δ' ὅδ' ἀνὴρ καὶ πόθεν κατέσχε γῆν ;
ΕΛ. Ἕλλην, Ἀχαιῶν εἷς, ἐμῷ σύμπλους πόσει.
ΘΕΟΚ. θανάτῳ δὲ ποίῳ φησὶ Μενέλεων θανεῖν ;
ΕΛ. οἰκτρόταθ' ὑγροῖσιν ἐν κλυδωνίοις ἁλός.

contrasted with dreams, we shall have good reason for preferring the other meaning, 'a warning voice from within.'

1197. τὰ δ' εὐτυχῶ, 'though in some respects I am fortunate.' Hermann remarks that a line must have been lost, both on account of the monostich dialogue, and because Theoclymenus replies πῶς (not πῶς δ') οἶσθα;

1199. For ὁ παρὼν, qui aderat, see Suppl. 649, and Soph. El. 927, τοῦ πλησίον παρόντος, ἡνίκ' ὤλλυτο.

1201. ὡς ἐγὼ χρῄζω, i. e. οὐχ ὡς σὺ χρῄζεις. Cf. Androm. 1170. Theoclymenus wished the supposed messenger to come in order that he might hear with his own ears the news of the death; for, as Aeschylus says, Cho. 834, οὐδὲν ἀγγέλων σθένος, ὡς αὐτὸν αὐτῶν ἄνδρα πεύθεσθαι πάρα. But Helena wished him to come in the person of her living husband, as he really had, though as a matter of course she disguises it. Thus μόλοι bears its simple and proper sense, utinam veniat. There is nothing very difficult in this verse, which has been altogether misunderstood by Pflugk; while Hermann, who does not seem to have noticed the emphatic personal pronoun, explains it in a somewhat unnatural sense, utinam venerit, sic ut ego venisse cupio; that is, (as Theoclymenus is to understand it,) 'I wish he could have come as I desire him (viz. the messenger) to have come,' viz. not come at all, but been lost at sea.— Menelaus, during this conversation, appears to be partly concealed behind the tomb of Proteus; cf. v. 1085. He comes forward again at v. 1250, but Helen points to him at v. 1203.

1206. κατέσχε, 'touched at.' Said of sailors κατέχοντες τὴν ναῦν, as Heracl. 83, κατέχετ' ἐκλιπόντες Εὐβοῖδ' ἄκραν.

1209. οἰκτρόταθ' Hermann and Tyrwhitt for οἰκτρότατον. The error arose from supposing the sense was οἰκτρότατον θάνατον, whereas the adverbial meaning is rather required.—ὑγροῖς ἐν κλ. has been restored by several critics for ὑγροῖσι κλ. —πελάγεσιν, see v. 375.

ΕΛΕΝΗ. 189

ΘΕΟΚ. ποῦ βαρβάροισι πελάγεσιν ναυσθλούμενον ; 1210
ΕΛ. Λιβύης ἀλιμένοις ἐκπεσόντα πρὸς πέτραις.
ΘΕΟΚ. καὶ πῶς ὅδ᾽ οὐκ ὄλωλε κοινωνῶν πλάτης ;
ΕΛ. ἐσθλῶν κακίους ἐνίοτ᾽ εὐτυχέστεροι.
ΘΕΟΚ. λιπὼν δὲ ναὸς ποῦ πάρεστιν ἔκβολα ;
ΕΛ. ὅπου κακῶς ὄλοιτο, Μενέλεως δὲ μή. 1215
ΘΕΟΚ. ὄλωλ᾽ ἐκεῖνος· ἦλθε δ᾽ ἐν ποίῳ σκάφει ;
ΕΛ. ναῦταί σφ᾽ ἀνεῖλον ἐντυχόντες, ὡς λέγει.
ΘΕΟΚ. ποῦ δὴ τὸ πεμφθὲν ἀντὶ σοῦ Τροίᾳ κακόν ;
ΕΛ. νεφέλης λέγεις ἄγαλμ᾽ ; ἐς αἰθέρ᾽ οἴχεται.
ΘΕΟΚ. ὦ Πρίαμε καὶ γῆ Τρῳὰς, *ὡς ἔρρεις μάτην. 1220
ΕΛ. κἀγὼ μετέσχον Πριαμίδαις δυσπραξίας.
ΘΕΟΚ. πόσιν δ᾽ ἄθαπτον ἔλιπεν ἢ κρύπτει χθονί ;
ΕΛ. ἄθαπτον· οἱ 'γὼ τῶν ἐμῶν τλήμων κακῶν.
ΘΕΟΚ. τῶνδ᾽ οὕνεκ᾽ ἔταμες βοστρύχους ξανθῆς κόμης ;
ΕΛ. φίλος γάρ ἐστιν, ὅς ποτ᾽ ἐστὶν, ἐνθάδ᾽ ὤν. 1225
ΘΕΟΚ. ὀρθῶς μὲν ἥδε συμφορὰ δακρύεται ;
ΕΛ. ἐν εὐμαρεῖ γοῦν σὴν κασιγνήτην θανεῖν.

1212. καὶ πῶς, as usual, marks surprise or incredulity. The sense is, 'Well but, if, as you say (v. 1207), he sailed with your husband, he would have been drowned together with him.'

1214. ναὸς ἔκβολα. Here, apparently, for ναυάγια, or the cast-up timbers on which he is supposed to have come ashore. Sup. 422. Ion 555. Barnes points out that the order is, ποῦ δὲ λιπὼν ναὸς ἔκβολα πάρεστιν; The question was one which Helen was especially concerned to avert, because the king would thus have discovered the survivors from the wreck, of whose existence she was aware, v. 1070. The answer of Helen seems generally to amount to this, 'I know not; the ship might perish unheeded, if only Menelaus had not perished with it.' Pflugk seems to be right in supplying with μὴ, ὤφελεν ὀλέσθαι.

1220. ὡς, omitted in the MSS. either on account of the similar termination of the preceding word, or because it was taken for a trisyllable, Τρωϊὰς, was added by Scaliger.

1224. ἔταμες. W. Dindorf gives ἔτεμες. Below, v. 1235, the old copies agree in the form τέμωμεν.

1225. ὅς ποτ᾽ ἐστίν. Helena means, 'whether he be a messenger (as you suppose) or my husband (as I know), he is dear to me, being here.' The verse is a mere quibble ; ἐνθάδ᾽ ὢν alluding to the pretended death of Menelaus, but his real presence, while ὅς ποτ᾽ ἐστὶν describes his ambiguous character. Hermann gives ὥσπερ ἐστὶν, which he thus explains; "Theoclymenum hoc ad inferos referre vult, ipsa sepulcrum, sub quo sedet Menelaus, in mente habet." It is clear that Theoclymenus himself is perplexed by the words ἐνθάδ᾽ ὤν, for he asks next, 'Are you sure that this calamity is rightly and reasonably lamented?'

1226. On the interrogative μὲν see Med. 676. Ion 520.

1227. ἐν εὐμαρεῖ. Compare ἐν εὐσεβεῖ inf. 1277. ἐν καλῷ Heracl. 971. ἐν εὐμαρεῖ Iph. A. 969. The γοῦν is ironical, the sense being, as Pflugk rightly explains it, 'Would you like your sister to die?' 'Would you think it a light thing?' &c. Hermann and Jacobs read λαθεῖν for θανεῖν, 'I could not deceive your sister, even if I could deceive you ;' and there are other instances of λαθεῖν and θανεῖν being confused. The reply of Helena amounting to

ΘΕΟΚ. οὐ δῆτα. πῶς οὖν ; τόνδ' ἔτ' οἰκήσεις τάφον ;
ΕΛ. τί κερτομεῖς με, τὸν θανόντα δ' οὐκ ἐᾷς ;
ΘΕΟΚ. πιστὴ γὰρ εἶ σὺ σῷ πόσει φεύγουσά με. 1230
ΕΛ. ἀλλ' οὐκέτ'· ἤδη δ' ἄρχε τῶν ἐμῶν γάμων.
ΘΕΟΚ. χρονία μὲν ἦλθες, ἀλλ' ὅμως αἰνῶ τάδε.
ΕΛ. οἶσθ' οὖν ὃ δρᾶσον ; τῶν πάρος λαθώμεθα.
ΘΕΟΚ. ἐπὶ τῷ ; χάρις γὰρ ἀντὶ χάριτος ἐλθέτω.
ΕΛ. σπονδὰς τέμωμεν καὶ διαλλάχθητί μοι. 1235
ΘΕΟΚ. μεθίημι νεῖκος τὸ σὸν, ἴτω δ' ὑπόπτερον.
ΕΛ. πρός νύν σε γονάτων τῶνδ', ἐπείπερ εἶ φίλος,
ΘΕΟΚ. τί χρῆμα θηρῶσ' ἱκέτις ὠρέχθης ἐμοῦ ;
ΕΛ. τὸν κατθανόντα πόσιν ἐμὸν θάψαι θέλω.
ΘΕΟΚ. τίς δ' ἔστ' ἀπόντων τύμβος ; ἢ θάψεις σκιάν ;
ΕΛ. Ἕλλησίν ἐστι νόμος, ὃς ἂν πόντῳ θάνῃ, 1241
ΘΕΟΚ. τί δρᾶν ; σοφοί τοι Πελοπίδαι τὰ τοιάδε.
ΕΛ. κενοῖσι θάπτειν ἐν πέπλων ὑφάσμασιν.
ΘΕΟΚ. κτέριζ'· ἀνίστη τύμβον οὗ χρῄζεις χθονός.
ΕΛ. οὐχ ὧδε ναύτας ὀλομένους τυμβεύομεν. 1245

this, 'I assure you the loss to me is as great as your sister's loss would be to you,' Theoclymenus, in accepting her evasive reply, consistently adds, 'Will you not then now marry me?'—ἔτ' οἰκήσεις, cf. 64—5.
1229. τί κερτομεῖς; 'why do you tease or distress me about this question of marriage, and why do you not forbear to speak of my departed husband ?'—' Because,' replies Theoclymenus, 'your fidelity to your husband makes you shun me.' The old reading πιστὴ γὰρ ἐσσὶ was corrected by Elmsley. But the σὺ is very questionable where no emphasis is conveyed. (See on v. 1201.) The true reading is probably, πιστὴ γὰρ οὖσα σῷ πόσει φεύγεις ἐμέ. Thus ἀλλ' οὐκέτ', scil. φεύξομαι, in the next verse, is no longer ambiguous. As the text stands, it might mean οὐκέτι πιστὴ ἔσομαι.
1234. ἐπὶ τῷ; 'On what terms ?' Cf. v. 838. Hipp. 459, and on Alcest. 375.— χάρις γὰρ κτλ., i. e. he is willing to do her a favour in return for her proffered reconciliation. That favour is not asked by Helen till v. 1239, the intermediate lines containing a mutual resolve to put themselves in amicable relations with each other.
1236. μεθίημι. The ι is here unusual; but perhaps the word was pronounced as if of three syllables. See on Hippol. 821.— νεῖκος τὸ σὸν, your jealousy of me, your quarrel with me for being your suitor. Compare νείκη μεθήσω in v. 1681, and λύω νεῖκος in Hippol. 1442. But Pflugk explains νεῖκος ὅ σοι εἶχον, and Barnes' marginal version gives *remitto indignationem adversus te susceptam*. In favour of this latter it is to be said, that μεθιέναι more naturally refers to his own feelings, than to his not retaining the remembrance of another's dislike. The metaphor here is the same as in Hippol. 827.
1238. ὠρέχθης, do you stretch out your arms to grasp me.
1241. ὃς ἄν. Hermann reads ὃς ἐν π. θάνῃ, with much probability, since the sense is not 'whoever shall have died,' but 'when a man shall have died at sea.' See on Ion 856. Med. 516.
1242. Πελοπίδαι, the Peloponnesians, i. e. the Doric people of Laconia in particular.
1243. πέπλων Scaliger for πέπλοις.

ΕΛΕΝΗ. 191

ΘΕΟΚ. πῶς δαί; λέλειμμαι τῶν ἐν Ἕλλησιν νόμων.
ΕΛ. ἐς πόντον ὅσα χρὴ νέκυσιν ἐξορμίζομεν.
ΘΕΟΚ. τί σοι παράσχω δῆτα τῷ τεθνηκότι;
ΕΛ. οὐκ οἶδ' ἔγωγ', ἄπειρος, εὐτυχοῦσα πρίν.
ΘΕΟΚ. ὦ ξένε, λόγων μὲν κληδόν' ἤνεγκας φίλην.   1250
ΜΕ. οὔκουν ἐμαυτῷ γ' οὐδὲ τῷ τεθνηκότι.
ΘΕΟΚ. πῶς τοὺς θανόντας θάπτετ' ἐν πόντῳ νεκρούς;
ΜΕ. ὡς ἂν παρούσης οὐσίας ἕκαστος ᾖ.
ΘΕΟΚ. πλούτου λέγ' οὕνεχ' ὅ τι θέλεις, ταύτης χάριν.
ΜΕ. προσφάζεται μὲν αἷμα πρῶτα νερτέροις.   1255
ΘΕΟΚ. τίνος; σύ μοι σήμαινε, πείσομαι δ' ἐγώ.
ΜΕ. αὐτὸς σὺ γίγνωσκ'· ἀρκέσει γὰρ ἂν διδῷς.
ΘΕΟΚ. ἐν βαρβάροις μὲν ἵππον ἢ ταῦρον νόμος.
ΜΕ. διδούς γε μὲν δή, δυσγενὲς μηδὲν δίδου.
ΘΕΟΚ. οὐ τῶνδ' ἐν ἀγέλαις ὀλβίαις σπανίζομεν.   1260

1246. λέλειμμαι, *non assequor*, 'I am deficient in the knowledge of Hellenic customs.'
1247. ἐξορμίζομεν. Literally, 'We send them out to sea and moor them there,' i. e. the ship, while the offerings are thrown in.
1249. The old reading, οὐκ οἶδ'. ἐγὼ δ' ἄπειρος κτλ., was corrected by Hermann. She means, that not having before lost a husband by sea, she has no exact knowledge, from her own experience, of the customary offerings. Hearing this, Theoclymenus turns to Menelaus, still seated at the tomb and requests from him the necessary information on the subject. And thus any suspicion that might arise, in consequence of the arrangements originating with herself, is shrewdly averted. Menelaus appears to give the required instructions as a disinterested and indifferent spectator.
1253. ὡς ἂν—οὐσίας. The genitive depends on ὡς as in the phrase ὡς τάχους, ὅπως ποδῶν &c. Cf. Electr. 751, πῶς ἀγώνος ἥκομεν; Sup. 313, πῶς δ' εὐμενείας τοισίδ' ἐν δόμοις ἔχεις;
1254. ταύτης χάριν. As if he had said δώσω instead of λέγε, 'specify what I must give, (and I will give it).' Dr. Donaldson, *New Cratylus*, p. 359, considers this verse to illustrate the distinction between ἕνεκα and χάριν, 'as far as wealth is concerned, say what you would have to please her.' To the present editor ταύτης χάριν seems rather to mean, 'for her sake,' i. e. that to show his affection for her, no request shall be refused.
1255. προσφάζεται. This passage seems to indicate the true sense of the rather obscure word πρόσφαγμα (Agam. 1249), which apparently meant 'the preliminary offering of blood,' as the first great propitiatory act, which placed the petitioner in amicable relations with the daemons or heroes to whom he was about to address any prayer. Hence it came to signify in general 'a victim,' as Hec. 41, Iph. Taur. 458, or 'the blood of a victim,' as Alcest. 845. Barnes rightly explains the word by προλείβεται τῶν σφαγίων αἷμα.
1257. ἀρκέσει and δίδῳς Barnes, for ἀρκέσειε and δίδως. The optative arose from the transcribers mistaking ἂν for ἄν. All the requests of Menelaus, it will be observed, have reference to supplying the ship with provisions &c. for a voyage. The mention of δυσγενὲς μηδὲν is a mere trick, that Theoclymenus may be kept in ignorance of the real motives. In all this scene the spirit of Greek deceit is strikingly shown. Every verse is a lie, in some form or other.
1258. ἵππον. It was the custom of the Persians to sacrifice a horse to the sun. Ovid, Fast. i. 385, 'Placat equo Persis radiis Hyperiona cinctum, Ne detur celeri victima tarda deo.'

ΜΕ. καὶ στρωτὰ φέρεται λέκτρα σώματος κενά.
ΘΕΟΚ. ἔσται· τί δ' ἄλλο προσφέρειν νομίζεται;
ΜΕ. χαλκήλαθ' ὅπλα· καὶ γὰρ ἦν φίλος δορί.
ΘΕΟΚ. ἄξια τάδ' ἔσται Πελοπιδῶν ἃ δώσομεν.
ΜΕ. καὶ τἆλλ' ὅσα χθὼν καλὰ φέρει βλαστήματα.   1265
ΘΕΟΚ. πῶς οὖν; ἐς οἶδμα τίνι τρόπῳ καθίετε;
ΜΕ. ναῦν δεῖ παρεῖναι κἀρετμῶν ἐπιστάτας.
ΘΕΟΚ. πόσον δ' ἀπείργει μῆκος ἐκ γαίας δόρυ;
ΜΕ. ὥστ' ἐξορᾶσθαι ῥόθια χερσόθεν μόλις.
ΘΕΟΚ. τί δή; τόδ' Ἑλλὰς νόμιμον ἐκ τίνος σέβει;   1270
ΜΕ. ὡς μὴ πάλιν γῇ λύματ' ἐκβάλλῃ κλύδων.
ΘΕΟΚ. Φοίνισσα κώπη ταχύπορος γενήσεται.
ΜΕ. καλῶς ἂν εἴη, Μενέλεῴ τε πρὸς χάριν.
ΘΕΟΚ. οὔκουν σὺ χωρὶς τῆσδε δρῶν ἀρκεῖς τάδε;
ΜΕ. μητρὸς τόδ' ἔργον ἢ γυναικὸς ἢ τέκνων.   1275
ΘΕΟΚ. ταύτης ὁ μόχθος, ὡς λέγεις, θάπτειν πόσιν.
ΜΕ. ἐν εὐσεβεῖ γοῦν νόμιμα μὴ κλέπτειν νεκρῶν.

1261. στρωτὰ λέκτρα. An empty bier represented the bodies of those who were absent. And hence perhaps it is, that in the Supplices, v. 1207, mention is made of *seven* pyres of the Argive chiefs, though Amphiaraus and Polynices were not included among the bodies brought on the stage. Their places may have been taken by similar empty litters. Pflugk well compares Thucyd. ii. 34, μία δὲ κλίνη κενὴ φέρεται ἐστρωμένη τῶν ἀφανῶν, οἳ ἂν μὴ εὑρεθῶσιν ἐς ἀναίρεσιν.

1268. πόσον μῆκος. 'What interval, what distance from the land is to keep the ship apart?' As ἐκ, not ἀπό, is used, we must construe πόσον μῆκος ἐκ γαίας, not ἀπείργει ἐκ γαίας. Perhaps we should read ἀπείργειν, viz. δεῖ.—ῥόθια, the foam caused by the waves dashing against the ship. Cf. Iph. T. 1387, λάβεσθε κώπης ῥόθιά τ' ἐκλευκαίνετε. It seems probable that our word *froth* is of common origin. But the Greeks meant by it *sound* rather than *appearance*. Photius, ῥόθιον καλεῖται παρὰ τὸν ῥόθον τὸν ἐκ τῶν κωπῶν ἀκουόμενον, ὅτ' ἂν σφοδρῶς ἐλαύνωσιν. Again, ῥόθιον, τὸ μετὰ ψόφου κῦμα, ἢ ῥεῦμα. Hence in Androm. ῥόθιον κακὸν is a murmur of discontent. Pers. 408, Περσίδος γλώσσης ῥόθος.

1270. τί δή; 'Why so? On what ground does Hellas hold this custom in regard?' Dindorf and Pflugk remove the stop at δή, making it a double interrogation, as in v. 873. But τί νόμιμον τόδε is a needless question when the nature of the νόμιμον had just been explained.

1272. Φοίνισσα κώπη. This does not mean, 'You shall have a swift Phoenician ship,' (for he would rather have said δοθήσεται than γενήσεται,) but, 'a Phoenician bark will soon perform the passage,' and bring you back again to the shore.

1273. τε for γε is Reiske's correction. The sense is, 'That will do very well, and will be agreeable to Menelaus,'—playing, of course, on the ambiguity between the living and the dead hero.—On δρῶν ἀρκεῖς see Alcest. 383, ἀρκοῦμεν ἡμεῖς οἱ προθνήσκοντες σέθεν, for ἀρκεῖ ἡμᾶς προθνήσκειν. 'Is it not enough,' asks Theoclymenus, 'that *you* should do these things without her?'

1277. ἐν εὐσεβεῖ. See v. 1227. 'It is not perhaps *necessary*,' replies Menelaus, 'that she should be present at the funeral; but it is a matter of piety not to deprive the dead of their rites.'—'Let her go,' is the reply; 'it is to our interest to train a wife to piety.'

ΕΛΕΝΗ.

ΘΕΟΚ. ἴτω· πρὸς ἡμῶν ἄλοχον εὐσεβῆ τρέφειν.
ἐλθὼν δ' ἐς οἴκους ἐξέλω κόσμον νεκρῷ.
καὶ σ' οὐ κεναῖσι χερσὶ γῆς ἀποστελῶ, 1280
δράσαντα τῇδε πρὸς χάριν. φήμας δέ μοι
ἐσθλὰς ἐνεγκὼν ἀντὶ τῆς ἀχλαινίας
ἐσθῆτα λήψει σῖτά θ', ὥστε σ' ἐς πάτραν
ἐλθεῖν, ἐπεὶ νῦν γ' ἀθλίως ἔχονθ' ὁρῶ.
σὺ δ', ὦ τάλαινα, μὴ 'πὶ τοῖς ἀνηνύτοις 1285
  *   *   *
τρύχουσα σαυτήν· Μενέλεως δ' ἔχει πότμον,
κοὐκ ἂν δύναιτο ζῆν ὁ κατθανὼν πόσις.
ΜΕ. σὸν ἔργον, ὦ νεᾶνι· τὸν παρόντα μὲν
στέργειν πόσιν χρὴ, τὸν δὲ μηκέτ' ὄντ' ἐᾶν·
ἄριστα γάρ σοι ταῦτα πρὸς τὸ τυγχάνον. 1290
ἢν δ' Ἑλλάδ' ἔλθω καὶ τύχω σωτηρίας,
παύσω ψόγου σε τοῦ πρὶν, ἢν γυνὴ γένῃ
οἵαν γενέσθαι χρή σε σῷ ξυνευνέτῃ.
ΕΛ. ἔσται τάδ'· οὐδὲ μέμψεται πόσις ποτὲ
ἡμῖν· σὺ δ' αὐτὸς ἐγγὺς ὢν εἴσει τάδε. 1295
ἀλλ', ὦ τάλας, εἴσελθε καὶ λουτρῶν τύχε

1279. ἐξέλω. Alcest. 160, ἐκ δ' ἑλοῦσα κεδρίνων δόμων ἐσθῆτα κόσμον τ' εὐπρεπῶς ἠσκήσατο. Hermann appears right in reading ἐξέλω, the aorist subjunctive, 'let me take,' for the future ἐξελῶ, for ἐξαιρήσω, does not occur in Attic Greek.—In the next verse καὶ σὲ is 'You too,' i. e. as well as providing gifts for the dead. The emphatic σὲ is not very unfrequently elided, as well as the enclitic.

1282. Hermann rightly ejects γ' after ἐνεγκών.

1285. After this verse Matthiae, Hermann, and Dindorf, place the mark of a *lacuna*. The old editions give τρύχου σὺ σαυτήν, but the two Florence MSS. have τρύχουσα σαυτήν. Pflugk supposes τρύχου to be the imperative of τρυχοῦν, and he quotes ἐκτρυχοῦν from Thucyd. iii. 93, vii. 48. Elmsley suggested τρύχου σεαυτῆς, from Ar. Pac. 989, οἵ σου τρυχόμεθ' ἤδη τρία καὶ δέκ' ἔτη. But this is a very different thing, 'who have been pining for, or about you, for thirteen years.' One might conceive the original to have stood thus:—

σὺ δ', ὦ τάλαινα, μὴ 'πὶ τοῖς ἀνηνύτοις
δάκρυε, μηδὲ σὸν διαφθείρῃς δέμας
τρύχουσα σαυτήν.

By τὰ ἀνήνυτα the impossibility of raising Menelaus from the dead is meant.—A more usual idiom would be Μενελέων δ' ἔχει πότμος.

1288. σὸν ἔργον. "Illud Theoclymeni ἴτω respicit, monens Helenam ut jam sacra funebria curet." *Herm.* By τὸν μηκέτ' ὄντα (πόσιν) he in fact means Theoclymenus, who has no longer any claim to the name.

1292. ψόγου. This word, as observed on Tro. 642, is especially used of blame attaching to the female sex. The right order of this distich (1292—3) was restored by Canter, the verses being transposed in the old copies.

1295. αὐτὸς εἴσει τάδε. She speaks, of course, of her real lord, Menelaus, being a witness to her promises of good behaviour, while Theoclymenus is to take πόσις as if said of himself, σὺ δ' αὐτὸς being addressed to the supposed messenger.

194   ΕΥΡΙΠΙΔΟΥ

ἐσθῆτά τ' ἐξάλλαξον.   οὐκ εἰς ἀμβολὰς
εὐεργετήσω σ'.   εὐμενέστερον γὰρ ἂν
τῷ φιλτάτῳ μοι Μενέλεῳ τὰ πρόσφορα
δρῴης ἄν, ἡμῶν τυγχάνων οἵων σε χρή.   1300
XO. ὀρεία ποτὲ δρομάδι κώλῳ   στρ. α'.
μάτηρ θεῶν ἐσύθη
ἀν' ὑλᾶντα νάπη
ποτάμιόν τε χεῦμ' ὑδάτων
βαρύβρομόν τε κῦμ' ἅλιον   1305

1297. Heracl. 270, κλάων ἄρ' ἄψει τῶνδε, κοὐκ ἐς ἀμβολάς.
1298. εὐμενέστερον κτλ. 'You will do what is right and proper for my dearest Menelaus (i. e. in the pretended burial) with the more hearty good will, if you find me such as you ought to find,' viz. liberal in rewarding you.—τυγχάνων ἡμῶν, as Alcest. 10, ὁσίου γὰρ ἀνδρὸς ὅσιος ἂν ἐτύγχανον.—χρή for χρῆν Matthiæ.
1301. The choral ode which here follows, though remarkably beautiful in itself, is liable to a charge which has often been brought against the lyric strains of the poet, of being wholly unconnected with the subject of the play. For what has the legend of Ceres and Proserpine, the wanderings of the disconsolate mother, the effects of her wrath on mankind, the persuasion of Zeus, and her reconciliation, —what has all this to do with Menelaus and Helen? Just thus much, it would seem, and no more, that the circumstances bear some resemblance to the restoration of Helen to her husband. Pflugk's explanation is far-fetched to the last degree; viz. that the supposed death of Menelaus is a judgment on Helena for having neglected the worship of Rhea or Cybele, a goddess peculiarly honoured by women. The chorus, so far from believing that Menelaus was dead, had heard the declaration of Theonöe (v. 515) that he was still alive. There is much more probability in Musgrave's suspicion, for which he assigns some reasons, that the *cultus* of Rhea had been translated to Athens (from Asia Minor) about this very time, and that the poet seized the occasion to delight his audience with her highly romantic history. There is an obscure allusion, at the beginning of antistr. β'., to Helen's neglect of Cybele, which has been compared with the similar case of Phaedra in Hippol. 141 seqq.; but Hermann contends that this forms no apology for the entire ode being on the subject of that goddess. "Vix credibile est," he writes, "ea caussa, ut paucis verbis adversi Helenae casus ex ira Idaeae matris repeterentur, cujus rei in tota tragoedia nullum vestigium est, raptum Proserpinae, luctum matris, gravem omnibus animantibus iram, singularem denique rationem, qua placata fuerit, esse descripta." And he adds this opinion (on v. 1376 of his edition), "Nisi fallor, histrionibus hoc debemus, qui pro eo carmine, quod Euripides posuerat, aliud inseruerunt, leviter mutatum, ut aliquo certe modo pertinere ad Helenae tragoediam videretur." By *leviter mutatum* he means that the last antistrophe was changed from an address to Cypris, who had inflamed Pluto with a love of Proserpina, to suit the supposed case of Helen herself. Whatever reason be assigned for the introduction of such an ode in this place, one point must be clearly understood by the student, that Rhea is confused or identified with Demeter. Nor is this difficult to explain; for both goddesses were supposed to symbolize Mother Earth.—The metre of the ode, which is both difficult and corrupt, consists of varieties of glyconean verse. Many of these are *polyschematistic*.
1301—8. ''Twas at full speed that the Mountain Mother once rushed over the woody dells and the streaming waters of rivers and the deep-roaring surge of the sea, through an eager longing for the mysterious maid who had gone from her.'—ὑλᾶντα for ὑλήεντα is L. Dindorf's metrical correction. Compare χρυσὸν τιμῆντα for τιμήεντα, Il. xviii. 475. The epithet ἄρρητος applied to Proserpine has reference to the secrecy of the Eleusinian Mysteries. Compare Oed. Col. 127—32 with v. 1051 *ibid*.

πόθῳ τὰς ἀποιχομένας
ἀρρήτου κούρας·
κρόταλα δὲ Βρόμια διαπρύσιον
ἱέντα κέλαδον ἀνεβόα,   1310
θηρῶν ὅτε ζυγίους
ζευξάσᾳ θεᾷ σατίνας
τὰν ἁρπασθεῖσαν κυκλίων
χορῶν ἔξω παρθενίων
μέτα κοῦραι ἀελλόποδες,
ἁ μὲν τόξοις Ἄρτεμις, ἁ δ'   1315
ἔγχει Γοργῶπα πάνοπλος
   *   *   *

αὐγάζων ἐξ οὐρανίων
ἄλλαν μοῖραν ἔκραινεν.
δρομαίων δ' ὅτε πολυπλανήτων   ἀντ. α'.

1309—17. 'And the Bacchic cymbals sending forth a piercing clang sounded aloud, when with the goddess, having fastened her car to her yoked lions in pursuit of her who had been carried off from without the ring of dancing maidens, the light-footed virgins Artemis with her bow and Pallas fully equipped with her spear, [went forth in company].' The difficulty of this passage, the true sense of which Hermann appears to have been the first to perceive, consists chiefly in the loss of the verb depending on ὅτε and governing θεᾷ. Hermann would supply προὐξωρμῶντο, but, as a whole verse has evidently dropped out, it is vain to guess at the exact word. Pflugk understands ἐσύθησαν, and a similar example has already been illustrated on v. 236. The dative, instead of ζεύξασα θεὰ, was restored by Hermann, and both sense and metre (θεᾷ being a monosyllable) require the change.—σατίνας for σατίναν is due to Musgrave. The word is not truly Greek, but borrowed from some oriental dialect.—For μέτα compare Alcest. 483, Θρῃκὸς τέτρωρον ἅρμα Διομήδους μέτα.—κοῦραι for κουρᾶν δ' Tyrwhitt, Pflugk, and others. That Pallas and Artemis, the two virgin goddesses, were often represented as the companions of Persephone at the time of her being carried off by Pluto, is observed by Hermann, after Welcker, to have been a common tradition.

1316. Γοργῶπα for Γοργὼ is Hermann's acute and satisfactory restoration. The final syllable πα was absorbed or lost in consequence of the πα in πάνοπλος. Matthiae's ἐν ἔγχει is not so good as Seidler's καὶ Γοργοῖ, viz., 'with spear and aegis.' But there is little force in Dindorf's criticism, "ineptum est ἔγχει πάνοπλος, nisi clipei mentio addatur." The dress of Pallas was that of a hoplite (Heracl. 695), which is easily implied by πάνοπλος, though the spear only is specified.

1317. Burges and L. Dindorf supply on conjecture Ζεὺς δ' ἑδράνων, which W. Dindorf has admitted into the text. In the old copies the δ' is added after αὐγάζων. By ἄλλαν μοῖραν he means that Zeus willed otherwise than that the pursuit should be successful.

1319—29. 'But when from the toil of her long and hurried wanderings the mother ceased, (and from) investigating the perplexing and crafty rape of her daughter, then it was that she crossed the snow-preserving heights of the Idean Nymphs, and rushed in her grief over the rocky thickets deep with snow; and for mortals not making the herbless plains of the earth to produce fruit in arable lands, she destroys the race of the inhabitants.' Expressed in a very few words, the sense is simply this: 'When Rhea gave up the pursuit in despair, she

ΕΥΡΙΠΙΔΟΥ

μάτηρ ἔπαυσε πόνων, 1320
ματεύουσ' ἀπόρους
θυγατρὸς ἁρπαγὰς δολίους,
χιονοθρέμμονας δ' ἐπέρασ'
Ἰδαιᾶν Νυμφᾶν σκοπιάς·
ῥίπτει δ' ἐν πένθει 1325
πέτρινα κατὰ δρία πολυνιφέα·
βροτοῖσι δ' ἄχλοα πεδία γᾶς
οὐ καρπίζουσ' ἀρότοις
λαῶν φθείρει γενεάν·
ποίμναις δ' οὐχ ἵει θαλερὰς 1330
βοσκὰς εὐφύλλων ἑλίκων·

threw herself into the solitudes of the mountains in profound grief, and caused a famine by neglecting to bless the year's crops.' In the above readings, ματεύουσ' ἀπόρους is Hermann's and Matthiae's correction of μαστεύουσα πόνους (πόρους H. Stephens), and Ἰδαιᾶν νυμφᾶν σκοπιὰς Elmsley's for Ἰδαίαν νυμφᾶν σκοπιᾶς. The reader will notice ἔπαυσε for ἐπαύσατο, and the exegetical use of the participle (= ἔπαυσε ματεύουσα), of which an exactly parallel instance occurs in Med. 420, Μοῦσαι δὲ παλαιγενέων λήξουσ' ἀοιδᾶν, τὰν ἐμὰν ὑμνεῦσαι ἀπιστοσύναν. We might also supply πόνων (οὓς εἶχε) ματεύουσα.—The δὲ in v. 1323 marks the apodosis, by a sufficiently common use. Hermann gives a strange interpretation of this passage. He reads διέπερσ', and says, "Prostravisse ac disjecisse Idaea cacumina dici debebat (?) dea, iisque obruisse saltus nivosos: ex quo sponte intelligitur reversam cogitari ad consuetas sedes." Dindorf follows him in this; but ῥίπτει (as the addition ἐν πένθει alone shows) means ῥίπτει ἑαυτήν. Compare Alcest. 897. Cycl. 166. Aesch. Suppl. 541, ἰάπτει κάσιδος δι' αἴας, which is precisely similar. The flight through the wild mountains was a mark of her grief for the ineffectual pursuit,—the λύπη ἀλάη in v. 1344.

1328. καρπίζειν is 'to fructify,' (Photius, εὔκαρπα ποιεῖν,) whence in the middle ἐκκαρπίζεσθαι is 'to have fruit produced from oneself,' Aesch. Theb. 597. See Bacch. 406.—ἀρότοις, 'crops.' Med. 1281. Suppl. 29. Diodorus Siculus, Lib. v. § 5, quotes ten lines of Carcinus the tragic writer, upon this subject. The famine she caused is described in similar words, πένθεσιν δὲ παρθένου σίτων ἄμοιρον διοτρεφὲς φθίνειν γένος. See also Ovid, Fast. iv. 1617.—δὲ after λαῶν was omitted by G. Dindorf, other critics having previously condemned it.

1330—7. 'And for the flocks she sent not forth the juicy food of leafy tendrils; therefore of many of them did the life fail, and there were no sacrifices to the gods; and on the altars the bread-offerings were not consumed; the dewy fountains of clear waters she stopped from springing, through inconsolable grief for her child.' For βοσκὰς Hermann chooses to read βοτὰς,—a change not metrically necessary, and one that introduces a word which he admits is "non aliunde notam," though βοτὸν and βοτὸς are cited as substantives by two or three obscure grammarians. The ἕλικες are any kind of young curling shoots. Both goats and other cattle in foreign countries are to this day fed on the clippings of vines mixed with other fodder of various kinds (συρφετὸς, Hes. Opp. 604).—Cf. Virg. Georg. iii. 531, who is speaking of a murrain among cattle: 'Tempore non alio dicunt regionibus istis Quaesitas ad sacra boves Junonis.' The last verse was restored by L. Dindorf from three MSS. It is omitted in the old editions. "In codicibus qui illum versum servarunt, adscriptum περισσόν. Redundare enim credebant metrici, quod non animadverterant excidisse unum ex strophicis versibus. Hinc factum, ut omitteretur in edd." Hermann.—ἀλάστῳ for ἀλάστωρ is the obvious correction suggested by L. Dindorf.

ΕΛΕΝΗ. 197

πολέων δ' ἀπέλειπε βίος,
οὐδ' ἦσαν θεῶν θυσίαι,
βωμοῖς τ' ἄφλεκτοι πέλανοι·
πηγάς τ' ἀμπαύει δροσερὰς   1335
λευκῶν ἐκβάλλειν ὑδάτων
πένθει παιδὸς ἀλάστῳ.
ἐπεὶ δ' ἔπαυσ' εἰλαπίνας   στρ. β'. 1337
θεοῖς βροτείῳ τε γένει,
Ζεὺς μειλίσσων στυγίους
ματρὸς ὀργὰς ἐνέπει,   1340
βᾶτε, σεμναὶ Χάριτες,
ἴτε, τὰν περὶ παρθένῳ
Δηοῖ θυμωσαμένᾳ
λύπαν ἐξαλλάξατ' ἀλᾶν,
Μοῦσαί θ' ὕμνοισι χορῶν.   1345
χαλκοῦ δ' αὐδὰν χθονίαν
τύπανά τ' ἔλαβε βυρσοτενῆ
καλλίστα τότε πρῶτα μακάρων
Κύπρις, γέλασέν τε θεά,

1338–1352. 'But after that she had put a stop to the banquets both for gods and men (i. e. the corn and the cattle), Zeus, by way of soothing the moody anger of the mother, said, Go, ye revered Graces, go, remove from Demeter who is wrathful the grief she has felt for her child in her wanderings; go, ye Muses too, with hymns of the dance. And then the rumbling noise of brass, and the skin-stretched tambourine, Cypris first seized, the fairest of the immortals; and the goddess (Rhea) smiled, and took into her hands the deep-toned flute, delighted with the din.'—τᾷ for τὰν is L. Dindorf's reading, adopted by W. Dindorf, but rightly rejected by Pflugk and Hermann, the construction being τὰν περὶ παρθένῳ λύπαν.—ἀλᾶν is Bothe's, ἅλας Hermann's independent conjecture for ἀλαᾷ. Matthiae and Pflugk give ἀλλάξαιτ' ἀλαᾷ after Musgrave. The sense and punctuation of the passage were determined by both Seidler and Hermann; but W. Dindorf has departed from it widely, reading λάβετε for τε λάβετε, and understanding this was the command of Zeus to the Muses, and πέλασεν, (perhaps by a misprint for γέλασεν,) instead of γέλασέ τε. Some minor and more obvious errors, as τύμπανα for τύπανα, and πυρσογενῆ for βυρσοτενῆ, were removed by Canter and others. The τύπανον was a circle of brass, probably like our tambourines, with moveable tinkling plates, (κρόταλα in v. 1309,) and stretched with skin. Its tone is called χθονία αὐδή, because, being deep like our drums, it was compared to earthquake rumblings. Musgrave most appositely quotes Aesch. frag. Edon. 54 Dind., τυπάνου δ' ἠχὼ ὥσθ' ὑπογείου βροντῆς φέρεται βαρυταρβής. There is no difficulty in taking αὐδὰν as the accusative after ἔλαβε, to which τύπανά τε is a sort of *epexegesis*. Hermann's summary of the general meaning is undoubtedly right; "Venerem fecit primam deorum tibias et tympana cepisse, ut eam exhilararet, quo facto risisse Idaeam matrem dicit, gavisamque isto concentu tibias manibus suis acceptasse. Neque id absurde invenit. Venus enim caussa doloris exstiterat, ut per quam amore incensus Pluto rapuisset Proserpinam."

198   ΕΥΡΙΠΙΔΟΥ

δέξατό τ' ἐς χέρα   1350
βαρύβρομον αὐλὸν
τερφθεῖσ' ἀλαλαγμῷ.
ὧν οὐ θέμις σ' οὔθ' ὁσία,   ἀντ. β'.
ἔκυρσας εὐνῶν θαλάμοις,
μῆνιν δ' ἔσχες μεγάλας   1355
ματρὸς, ὦ παῖ, θυσίας
οὐ σεβίζουσα θεᾶς.
μέγα τοι δύναται νεβρῶν
παμποίκιλοι στολίδες,
κισσοῦ τε στεφθεῖσα χλόα   1360
νάρθηκας εἰς ἱεροὺς,

1350. χέρα for χέρας Hermann, on account of the metre of v. 1366.
1353 seqq. The concluding antistrophe is exceedingly difficult; as much so, perhaps, as any passage in Euripides. The first two lines are thus given in the old copies; ὧν οὐ θέμις οὔθ' ὁσία ἐπύρωσας ἐν θαλάμοις. Canter and Hermann, guided by the metre, give ὃν οὐ θέμις σ', οὐδ' ὁσία, and the words so corrected are referred by some to Cypris, who inspired Pluto in Hades with love, by others to Helen, who did the same to Paris. Whether πυροῦν alone is ever used in this sense is justly doubted by Dindorf, who reads ἐπώρσας ἐν γᾶς θαλάμοις. Hermann, who takes the latter view, gives 'πύρωσας ἐν σοῖς θαλάμοις, but proposes also 'πύρωσας ἄνδρ' ἐν θαλάμοις. The present editor, venturing on some licence in a passage of more than usual perplexity, has given ἔκυρσας εὐνῶν (ἔκυρσας is also Heath's conjecture), on the supposition that the εὐν passed into ἐν, when the termination of the word had by some accident been lost, and the ὧν, added in the margin, was perhaps wrongly used to make up ἐκύρωσας (afterwards further corrupted to ἐπύρωσας) from ἔκυρσας. Thus the sense is made easy enough, and, in fact, is perfectly appropriate and natural, the allusion being to the amour of Helen and Paris, and the consequent anger of Cybele, who had already been incensed at Helen's neglect. For θαλάμοις, Helen's own house at Sparta, where Paris wooed her, see Androm. 593. The above emendation, it may be remarked, alone accounts for and retains the old reading ὧν οὐ θέμις. Adopting ἔσχες for ἔχεις from Seidler (εἶχες Musgrave and Hermann), and θεᾶς for θεοῖς from Heath, we may now translate as follows:—'A union which it was unlawful and unholy for you to have (κῦρσαι), you met with in your own marriage chamber; and so you incurred the anger of the great mother by not paying due respect to the sacrifices of the goddess.' Dindorf adopts the very improbable alteration of Seidler, συσσεβίζουσα, explaining μῆνιν ἔσχες iram cohibuisti.

1358. δύναται for δύνανται Musgrave. For this idiom (schema Pindaricum) see Ion 1146. Pers. 49. The meaning apparently is, that the cultus of Cybele, and the kindred orgiastic rites of Bacchus are of great power, are not to be slighted with impunity, as Helen has found to her cost.—στολίδες νεβρῶν, the νεβρίδες or fawn-skins worn by the Bacchantes. See Bacch. 696, and for στολίδες (tucks) ibid. 936.

1360. κισσοῦ for κισσῷ Matthiae. Hermann retains the dative, on the dubious ground that the fir-cone was called χλόη. Ancient drawings however (several of which have been published, among other sources, from the walls of Pompeii and Herculaneum,) sometimes represent the Bacchic wand (νάρθηξ as distinct from θύρσος) as a very long and slender reed surmounted simply with a tuft of ivy-leaves. Here therefore the κισσοῦ χλόα is said στεφθῆναι εἰς νάρθηκας, to be hung in tufts from the ferule. So στέφειν πρός τι in Aesch. Theb. 50.

ΕΛΕΝΗ.   199

ῥόμβων θ' ἑλισσομένα
κύκλιος ἔνοσις αἰθερία,
βακχεύουσά τ' ἔθειρα Βρομίῳ
καὶ παννυχίδες θεᾶς,   1365
εὖτέ νιν ὄμμασιν
ἔβαλε σελάνα.
[μορφᾷ μόνον ηὔχεις.]

ΕΛ. τὰ μὲν κατ' οἴκους εὐτυχοῦμεν, ὦ φίλαι·
ἡ γὰρ συνεκκλέπτουσα Πρωτέως κόρη,   1370
πόσιν παρόντα τὸν ἐμὸν ἱστορουμένη,
οὐκ εἶπ' ἀδελφῷ· κατθανόντα δ' ἐν χθονὶ
οὔ φησιν αὐγὰς εἰσορᾶν ἐμὴν χάριν.
κάλλιστα δῆτ' ἀνήρπασεν †ἐν τύχῃ πόσις·

1363. ἔνοσις, Tro. 1326. Bacch. 585, the brandishing of the drum, is called κύκλιος from its rotating and at the same time circular motion round the head. Similar antics may often be noticed among our modern street-players. Musgrave quotes the Schol. on Apoll. Rhod. i. 1139, 'Ρόμβος· τροχίσκος, ὃν στρέφουσιν ἱμᾶσι, τύπτοντες, καὶ οὕτως κτύπον ἀποτελοῦσι. Similarly Photius, 'Ρόμβος, ὃ ἔχουσιν οἱ ἐπιθειάζοντες ὡς τύμπανον· οὕτως Εὔπολις.

1364. ἔθειρα. Bacch. 864, δέραν εἰς αἰθέρα δροσερὸν ῥίπτουσα.

1366. The concluding three verses are very corrupt, and nothing can be made of them without admitting rather violent conjectures. Dindorf retains the vulgate, εὖ δέ νιν ἄμασιν ὑπέρβαλε σελάνα. μορφᾷ μόνον ηὔχεις, avowedly as being a hopeless farrago of words. There is some probability in Hermann's reading, as given in the text, 'when the (full) moon visits them with her light.' He quotes Troad. 1075, Φρυγῶν τε ζάθεοι σελᾶναι συνδώδεκα πλήθει, (literally, 'twelve together in fulness,') in proof that the nightly orgies of Cybele were celebrated on the day of the full moon every month. The last line he considers to be manifestly the patchwork of some grammarian, inserted to fill up the place of the genuine one which had been lost.—It remains only to give an English version of vv. 1358—1367: 'Great is the power which the speckled folds of the fawn-skin possess, and the verdure of ivy hanging in folds on the sacred wands, and the circular motion of the hoops whirled through the air, and the locks that revel for Bromius, the nightly vigils too of the goddess (Rhea), when the moon visits them with her full light.'

1369. Helen, who has been within the house to use her best endeavours to win Theonoë to her cause, now comes forward to announce her success. The daughter of Proteus, (with a readiness for falsehood not unworthy of a true Greek,) has consented to conceal the existence of Menelaus, and to assert that he is dead. Menelaus has himself taken charge of the arms which Helen had requested for offerings (v. 1263); and Theoclymenus is at this juncture seen with his attendants bringing such ornaments as had been bespoken for the funeral.

1371. ἱστορουμένη, 'informing herself about,' πυνθανομένη.—ἐν χθονὶ must be taken with εἰσορᾶν. Helen's own story had been, that he was lost at sea, v. 1209, and it is not likely that Theonoë should have spoken of him as κατθανόντα ἐν χέρσῳ. Translate therefore, ' But, to oblige me, she says that, being dead, he no longer sees the light of the sun on the earth.'

1374. This verse is corrupt. Hermann marks the loss of one line, supposing κάλλιστα to refer to the most available or beautiful of the arms in the palace which Menelaus could lay his hands upon. Both the want of caesura, if we omit ἐν, and the improper use of δῆτα show the

ΕΥΡΙΠΙΔΟΥ

ἃ γὰρ καθήσειν ὅπλ᾽ ἔμελλεν εἰς ἅλα, 1375
ταῦτ᾽ ἐμβαλὼν πόρπακι γενναίαν χέρα
αὐτὸς κομίζει, δόρυ τε δεξιᾷ λαβών,
ὡς τῷ θανόντι χάριτα δὴ συνεκπονῶν.
προὔργου δ᾽ ἐς ἀλκὴν σῶμ᾽ ὅπλοις ἠσκήσατο,
ὡς βαρβάρων τροπαῖα μυρίων χερὶ 1380
θήσων, ὅταν κωπῆρες εἰσβῶμεν σκάφος,
πέπλους ἀμείψας, ἀντὶ ναυφθόρου στολῆς,
ἀγώ νιν ἐξήσκησα, καὶ λουτροῖς χρόα
ἔδωκα, χρόνια νίπτρα ποταμίας δρόσου.
ἀλλ᾽ ἐκπερᾷ γὰρ δωμάτων ὁ τοὺς ἐμοὺς 1385
γάμους ἑτοίμους ἐν χεροῖν ἔχειν δοκῶν,
σιγητέον μοι· καὶ σὲ προσποιούμεθα
εὔνουν, κρατεῖν τε στόματος, ἢν δυνώμεθα
σωθέντες αὐτοὶ καὶ σὲ συσσῶσαί ποτε.

ΘΕΟΚ. χωρεῖτ᾽ ἐφεξῆς, ὡς ἔταξεν ὁ ξένος, 1390

passage to be faulty; and neither of these difficulties is removed by Barnes' conjecture τεύχη for ἐν τύχῃ. Possibly ἐν τύχῃ is a gloss on κάλλιστα, which has supplanted the genuine word. Thus, if the poet wrote κάλλιστα δὴ τήνδ᾽ ἀσπίδ᾽ ἥρπασεν πόσις, some grammarian may have explained it by ἐν τύχῃ, meaning that the taking of the shield on his arm was well done, was suitable to the occasion, as being an omen of the fight which, as a hoplite, he would soon have to engage in. A plausible correction has also been communicated, κάλλιστα δὴ τάδ᾽ ἥρπασεν τεύχη πόσις.

1375—8. 'For the arms which he intended to throw into the sea these he carries to the ship himself, having inserted his valiant arm within the handle, and taking the spear in his right hand.' The meaning is that, as it chanced, he held both shield and spear as a hoplite would do, though not as showing any hostile intention, but as if forsooth he were taking part in rites acceptable to the dead. By ὅπλα the ἀσπὶς is meant.

1379. προὔργου, opportunely, viz. because he would so soon have to use them. —ἠσκήσατο, cf. Alcest. 161.

1382. ἀμείψας. The old copies add δ᾽ after πέπλους. Hermann rightly omits it, so that the construction is continued from ἠσκήσατο, 'having taken as garments, in exchange for the dress of a shipwrecked sailor, what I dressed him out in,' &c. Bothe and Pflugk, apparently in ignorance of the old reading, give the alteration of Pierson, πέπλους δ᾽ ἀμείψασ᾽ ἀντὶ ναυφθόρου στολῆς Ἐγώ νιν ἐξήσκησα. But not only is ἀμείβειν incorrectly used of one who effects a change upon another, but, as Hermann remarks, this is to make him first put on the arms, and then to put off his clothes.

1387. καὶ σὲ κτλ. 'And you (the chorus) we claim as friends to our cause and (bid you) to control your tongue, if perchance we may be able, having ourselves got home safe, to bring you also home together at some future day.' Here again Pflugk and Bothe, following Matthiae, who was himself misled by the pretended MSS. of H. Stephens, give a corrupt reading κρατοῦντα στόματος, which should have been κρατοῦσαν, as referring to females. Hermann gives κρατεῖν γε, apparently regarding the infinitive as exegetical of εὔνουν.

1390. ἐφεξῆς, 'abreast,' i. e. in rank and file like a military λόχος. "Theoclymenus hic ingreditur in scenam, non modo corporis sui custodiis regiis septus, sed etiam longo famulitio comitatus, qui vestes, arma, et animalia ducebant ad navem Menelai exequiarum causa." *J. Barnes.*

ΕΛΕΝΗ. 201

δμῶες, φέροντες ἐνάλια κτερίσματα.
Ἑλένη, σὺ δ', ἤν σοι μὴ κακῶς δόξω λέγειν,
πείθου, μέν' αὐτοῦ· ταὐτὰ γὰρ παροῦσά τε
πράξεις τὸν ἄνδρα τὸν σὸν ἤν τε μὴ παρῇς.
δέδοικα γάρ σε μή τις ἐμπεσὼν πόθος   1395
πείσῃ μεθεῖναι σῶμ' ἐς οἶδμα πόντιον,
τοῦ πρόσθεν ἀνδρὸς χάρισιν ἐκπεπληγμένην·
ἄγαν γὰρ αὐτὸν οὐ παρόνθ' ὅμως στένεις.

ΕΛ. ὦ καινὸς ἡμῖν πόσις, ἀναγκαίως ἔχει
τὰ πρῶτα λέκτρα νυμφικάς θ' ὁμιλίας   1400
τιμᾶν· ἐγὼ δὲ διὰ τὸ μὲν στέργειν πόσιν
καὶ ξυνθάνοιμ' ἄν· ἀλλὰ τίς κείνῳ χάρις
ξὺν κατθανόντι κατθανεῖν; ἔα δέ με
αὐτὴν μολοῦσαν ἐντάφια δοῦναι νεκρῷ.
θεοὶ δὲ σοί τε δοῖεν οἷ' ἐγὼ θέλω   1405
καὶ τῷ ξένῳ τῷδ', ὅτι συνεκπονεῖ τάδε.
ἕξεις δέ μ' οἵαν χρή σ' ἔχειν ἐν δώμασι
γυναῖκ', ἐπειδὴ Μενέλεων εὐεργετεῖς
κἄμ'· ἔρχεται γὰρ δή τιν' ἐς τύχην τάδε·
ὅστις δὲ δώσει ναῦν, ἐν ᾗ τάδ' ἄξομεν,   1410
πρόσταξον, ὡς ἂν τὴν χάριν πλήρη λάβω.

ΘΕΟΚ. χώρει σὺ, καὶ ναῦν τοῖσδε πεντηκόντορον
Σιδωνίαν δὸς κἀρετμῶν ἐπιστάτας.

1392. Theoclymenus repeats his effort (cf. v. 1274) to induce Helen to stay on shore while the ceremonies are being performed. He is afraid lest through excess of grief she should throw herself into the sea. A plausible and clever answer suffices to allay his fears on that head, and he leaves her believing that he possesses her affection at least so far as that he will shortly become her husband.

1395. σε. So the MSS.; but the old edd. have σοι, which is equally good, if construed with ἐμπεσών.

1399. ὦ καινός. W. Dindorf gives ὁ καινὸς, which is quite needless. For we often find ὦ φίλος in direct address, and in Alcest. 569, ὦ πολύξεινος καὶ ἐλεύθερος ἀνδρὸς ἀεί ποτ' οἶκος. See on Androm. 1. The old reading κλεινὸς was corrected by Elmsley. The mention in the next verse of τὰ πρῶτα λέκτρα confirms this, which is of course spoken to Theoclymenus, now about to become her husband, as he supposes.

1405. οἷ' ἐγὼ θέλω. The emphatic ἐγὼ implies, οὐχ οἷα σὺ θέλεις, i. e. πάντα κακά. It is intended really as an imprecation on her persecutor. This is the meaning of a verse in the Acharnians which is often misunderstood, v. 446, εὐδαιμονοίης, Τηλέφῳ δ' ἀγὼ φρονῶ, sc. γένοιτο. See sup. v. 1201. Androm. 1170, οὐχ ὡς σὺ θέλεις.

1409. "Sententia haec est; nam haec ad aliquam bonam fortunam tendunt." Hermann. There is however, as Pflugk perceived, a latent meaning besides the apparent one,—'there is a certain fortune in this matter that you little suspect,' viz. that in assisting the dead, as you suppose, you are in fact assisting the living to escape from you.

VOL. II.   D d

ΕΛ. οὔκουν ὅδ' ἄρξει ναὸς ὃς κοσμεῖ τάφον;
ΘΕΟΚ. μάλιστ'· ἀκούειν τοῦδε χρὴ ναύτας ἐμούς.   1415
ΕΛ. αὖθις κέλευσον, ἵνα σαφῶς μάθωσί σου.
ΘΕΟΚ. αὖθις κελεύω, καὶ τρίτον γ', εἴ σοι φίλον.
ΕΛ. ὄναιο, κἀγὼ τῶν ἐμῶν βουλευμάτων.
ΘΕΟΚ. μή νῦν ἄγαν σὸν δάκρυσιν ἐκτήξῃς χρόα.
ΕΛ. ἥδ' ἡμέρα σοι τὴν ἐμὴν δείξει χάριν.   1420
ΘΕΟΚ. τὰ τῶν θανόντων οὐδέν, ἀλλ' ἄλλως πόνος.
ΕΛ. ἐστίν τι κἀκεῖ κἀνθάδ' ὧν ἐγὼ λέγω.
ΘΕΟΚ. οὐδὲν κακίω Μενέλεώ μ' ἕξεις πόσιν.
ΕΛ. οὐδὲν σὺ μεμπτός· τῆς τύχης με δεῖ μόνον.
ΘΕΟΚ. ἐν σοὶ τόδ', ἢν σὴν εἰς ἔμ' εὔνοιαν διδῷς.   1425
ΕΛ. οὐ νῦν διδαξόμεσθα τοὺς φίλους φιλεῖν.
ΘΕΟΚ. βούλει ξυνεργῶν αὐτὸς ἐκπέμψω στόλον;
ΕΛ. ἥκιστα· μὴ δούλευε σοῖς δούλοις, ἄναξ.
ΘΕΟΚ. ἀλλ' εἶα· τοὺς μὲν Πελοπιδῶν ἐῶ νόμους.

1416. αὖθις κέλευσον. The answer had been addressed to herself, but she wishes it to be explicitly given to the attendant who is conveying the king's orders.
1418. For ὄνασθαι with a genitive see Alcest. 335. Med. 1025. 'May I too be fortunate in *my* plans,' is to be understood by Theoclymenus as a hope that the funeral ceremonies will be safely and efficiently performed.
1420. τὴν ἐμὴν χάριν, 'the amount of my gratitude,'—i. e. how glad I shall be to escape from you.—ἄλλως in the next verse has been restored by Hermann and others from two MSS. for ἁπλῶς. Pflugk compares Tro. 1248, δοκῶ δὲ τοῖς θανοῦσι διαφέρειν βραχὺ, Εἰ πλουσίων τις τεύξεται κτερισμάτων· Κενὸν δὲ γαύρωμ' ἐστὶ τῶν ζώντων τόδε.
1422. καὶ ἐκεῖ καὶ ἐνθάδε, not only in Hades, but also here on earth. *She* means Menelaus, who is not ἐκεῖ but ἐνθάδε, while *he* supposes her to mean, that her affection is divided between her dead husband and her living suitor. Bothe's conjecture is both ingenious and probable, ὧν ἔχω λόγον, *quorum rationem habeo*. If ὧν ἐγὼ λέγω be right, she must mean τῶν θανόντων in the preceding verse:— 'What *I* mean by *the dead* are those who are in fact alive.'
1424. οὐδὲν σὺ μεμπτός. 'With you I have no reason to be dissatisfied; all I now require is to be fortunate (in my marriage).' So Theoclymenus is to understand it; but Helen of course means, luck in her enterprise. The old reading μέλει was corrected by Musgrave, whose emendation, adopted by Dind. and Herm., is rejected by Matth. and Pflugk.
1427. βούλει—ἐκπέμψω. The conjunctive is used because the question virtually is πότερον ἐκπέμψω; So Cycl. 149, βούλει σε γεύσω πρῶτον ἄκρατον μέθυ; Prom. v. 799, ἐλοῦ γὰρ ἢ πόνων τὰ λοιπά σοι φράσω σαφηνῶς, ἢ τὸν ἐκλύσοντ' ἐμέ.
1428. μὴ δούλευε. As the proposal of Theoclymenus is fatal to their chance of escape, and as at the same time the rejection of a courteous and well-meant offer might, by irritating the king, equally have frustrated the whole plan, some ready wit was required for framing a suitable answer. We may notice the truly Greek ingenuity with which inconvenient offers are evaded, ambiguous replies returned, and Theoclymenus is kept in the best humour with himself and his captives, while in fact he is being bantered by them. The poet was concerned to show that the βάρβαροι were no match in cunning for the Hellenes.
1429. ἀλλ' εἶα κτλ. The sense is 'Well! I have myself no further concern

καθαρὰ γὰρ ἡμῖν δώματ'· οὐ γὰρ ἐνθάδε 1430
ψυχὴν ἀφῆκε Μενέλεως· ἴτω δέ τις
φράσων ὑπάρχοις τοῖς ἐμοῖς φέρειν γάμων
ἀγάλματ' οἴκους εἰς ἐμούς· πᾶσαν δὲ χρὴ
γαῖαν βοᾶσθαι μακαρίαις ὑμνῳδίαις
ὑμέναιον Ἑλένης κἀμόν, ὡς ζηλωτὸς ᾖ. 1435
σὺ δ', ὦ ξέν' ἐλθὼν πελαγίους ἐς ἀγκάλας
τῷ τῆσδε πρίν ποτ' ὄντι δοὺς πόσει τάδε
πάλιν πρὸς οἴκους σπεῦδ', ἐμὴν δάμαρτ' ἔχων,
ὡς τοὺς γάμους τοὺς τῆσδε συνδαίσας ἐμοὶ
στέλλῃ πρὸς οἴκους, ἢ μένων εὐδαιμονῇς. 1440
ΜΕ. ὦ Ζεῦ, πατήρ τε καὶ σοφὸς κλῄζει θεός·
βλέψον πρὸς ἡμᾶς καὶ μετάστησον κακῶν.
ἕλκουσι δ' ἡμῖν πρὸς λέπας τὰς συμφορὰς
σπουδῇ σύναψαι· κἂν ἄκρᾳ θίγῃς χερί,
ἥξομεν ἵν' ἐλθεῖν βουλόμεσθα τῆς τύχης. 1445
ἅλις δὲ μόχθων οὓς ἐμοχθοῦμεν πάρος.
κέκλησθέ μοι, θεοὶ πολλά, χρήστ' ἐμοῦ κλύειν

with the customs of Greeks, for *my* house is free from the guilt of the stranger's death; let them go if they please then without me.' He thus dismisses the matter, and turns to give directions about his approaching marriage.

1432. γάμων ἀγάλματα, presents to increase the splendour of the royal nuptials. The Egyptian king is represented as supreme over divers petty sovereigns, like the king of the Persians.

1434. βοᾶσθαι. This might be regarded as the middle voice, with ὑμέναιον for its object, in the sense *canendum curare;* and indeed the only Attic future in use, βοήσομαι, seems to show that the present also once had a similar signification; and so indeed we may understand διὰ ταῦτα τὰ ἴδια ἐπιβοώμενος in Thucyd. vi. 16. It is however more probably passive, as Hermann explains it, the accusative ὑμέναιον depending on the meaning 'to resound.' So Iph. Aul. 437, κατὰ στέγας λωτὸς βοάσθω. Elmsley so far differed in his view, that he regarded ὑμέναιον as an accusative in apposition to the sentence, βοᾶσθαι being compared with αὐλεῖται πᾶν μέλαθρον Iph. T. 367, θνηπολεῖται ἄστυ Heracl. 402, to which

might be added El. 714, σελαγεῖτο δ' ἀν' ἄστυ | πῦρ ἐπιβώμιον Ἀργείων.

1436. It is needless to place commas, as even Hermann has done after other editors, before and after ἐλθών, for no one would construe ἐλθὼν ἐς ἀγκάλας rather than ἐλθὼν δοὺς τάδε ἐς ἀγκάλας. Pflugk's eulogy is certainly superfluous, " perite fecit, quisquis fuit, qui primus post hoc verbum interpunxit. Est enim hoc participium ex eo genere, quod abundare putatur."

1443. ἕλκουσι, the dative plural. The metaphor is from a yoke of oxen dragging a heavy load up a hill. Musgrave, who corrected λέπας for λύπας, happily compares Alcest. 499, καὶ τόνδε τοὐμοῦ δαίμονος πόνον λέγεις· σκληρὸς γὰρ αἰεὶ καὶ πρὸς αἶπος ἔρχεται. Of course σύναψαι is the imperative middle. 'Lend us a zealous hand as we drag our fortunes to the hilltop.' Compare Pers. 738, ἀλλ' ὅταν σπεύδῃ τις αὐτός, χὠ θεὸς ξυνάπτεται. Rhes. 318, ἕρπει κατάντης ξυμφορὰ πρὸς τἀγαθά.

1447. κέκλησθε κτλ. 'Ye have been invoked by me many times, ye gods, to hear both my joys and my sorrows,' or rather, perhaps, 'my probity and at the

καὶ λύπρ'· ὀφείλω δ' οὐκ ἀεὶ πράσσειν κακῶς,
ὀρθῷ δὲ βῆναι ποδί. μίαν δ' ἐμοὶ χάριν
δόντες τὸ λοιπὸν εὐτυχῆ με θήσετε.   1450
ΧΟ. Φοίνισσα Σιδωνιὰς ὦ   στρ. α΄.
ταχεῖα κώπα, ῥοθίοισι μάτηρ,
εἰρεσίᾳ φίλα,
χοραγὲ τῶν καλλιχόρων
δελφίνων, ὅταν αὔραις πέλαγος νήνεμον ᾖ,   1455
γλαυκὰ δὲ Πόντου θυγάτηρ
Γαλάνεια τάδ' εἴπῃ·
κατὰ μὲν ἱστία πετάσατ' αὔραις
λείποντες ἐναλίαις,   1460

same time (i. e. nevertheless) my misfortunes.' As he had acted towards them the part of a pious man, and had not only invoked them in his troubles, but also thanked them in his prosperity, he adds, as if upbraiding them for their present neglect, 'I ought not always to fare ill.' Such seems the sense of a passage which Porson (on Orest. 1662) pronounced corrupt, and Hermann has violently and improbably altered to χρῆστ' ἐμοὶ τυχεῖν κάλυπ'. In this he is followed by W. Dindorf, who more strangely still regards κέκλησθε as the imperative, and joins πολλὰ χρηστὰ κάλυπα. But πολλὰ is rightly taken for πολλάκις by Hermann, who compares Herc. F. 501, καίτοι κέκλησαι πολλάκις· μάτην πονῶ. Similarly we have κεκλημένους μὲν ἀνακαλούμεθ' αὖ θεούς. See Tro. 470. 1280.

1448. ὀφείλω δ' οὐκ. See the note on v. 835.

1449. ὀρθῷ βῆναι ποδὶ for μὴ χαμαὶ πεσόντα κεῖσθαι.

1450. "Discedunt Menelaus et Helena cum ministris a Theoclymeno datis ad portum, rex autem in domum se recipit." *Herm.*

1451. The Phoenician ship (1413), that is destined to carry Helen to her native shores, is addressed in a highly poetical strain, of the glyconean metre, in which a fair voyage is predicted, the festivals she will find in the course of celebration at Sparta are enumerated (as indicative of the season), and lastly, her brothers the Dioscuri are invoked, that they may send fair weather for the voyage.—The subject of this stasimon, it will at once be perceived, is closely connected with the plot of the play, and is not, like the preceding, a mere interpolatory ode to serve the purpose of a break or rest in the action. There are many difficulties, and some perplexing corruptions in the course of it; but the sagacity of Hermann has removed most of these in a satisfactory manner. The culpable carelessness of Pflugk in following the text of Matthiae, without troubling himself to inspect any of the early editions, has been justly exposed by the same accurate critic.

Ibid. The address to the ship does not at first appear to be followed by a request for any action on its part. But in fact λάβοις ἂν, v. 1467, refers to this vocative, as Bothe rightly perceived.—κώπῃ, as elsewhere πλάτῃ, is put for the ship generally; cf. v. 1272, but its attributes, εἰρεσίᾳ φίλα and ῥοθίοισι μήτηρ, (dear to the rowers and causing froth and foam in its movement,) are strictly applicable to the oar itself.

1454. χοραγὲ, leading the dances of the dolphins which sport round the ship. Electr. 435, ἵν' ὁ φίλαυλος ἔπαλλε δελφὶς πρῴραις κυανεμβόλοισιν εἱλισσόμενος.— αὔραις νήνεμον, Virg. Ecl. ii. 26, *quum placidum ventis staret mare*, compared by Pflugk. To the agent of a certain effect is sometimes, by a well-known poetical use, attributed the exactly contrary result.

1460. λείποντες for λιπόντες Seidler, who also gives εἰναλίαις. But this, though adopted by Hermann and Dindorf, does not suit the antistrophic verse, which imperatively requires the λ to be doubled in pronunciation. In proper names this licence is undisputed, as Τελλεύταντος Ajac.

ΕΛΕΝΗ. 205

λάβετε δ' εἰλατίνας πλάτας,
ἰὼ ναῦται, ἰὼ ναῦται,
πέμποντες εὐλιμένους
Περσείων οἴκων Ἑλέναν ἐπ' ἀκτάς·
ἦ που κόρας ἂν ποταμοῦ   ἀντ. α'. 1465
παρ' οἶδμα Λευκιππίδας, ἢ πρὸ ναοῦ
Παλλάδος ἂν λάβοις
χρόνῳ ξυνελθοῦσα χοροῖς
ἢ κώμοις Ὑακίνθου νυχίαν εὐφροσύναν,   1470
ὃν ἐξαμιλλησάμενος
τροχῷ τέρμονι δίσκου
ἔκανε Φοῖβος, ὅθεν Λακαίνᾳ
γᾷ βούθυτον ἁμέραν

210 (where Dindorf wrongly edits παῖ τοῦ Φρυγίοιο Τελεύταντος), and Αἰόλλου for Αἰόλου in Od. x. 36; probably also Ὀλλύμπου for Οὐλύμπου in Tro. 215. Herc. F. 872.—By λείποντες the poet means μεθιέντες, χαλῶντες, 'abandoning them to the breeze.'

1462. ἰὼ for ὦ at the beginning of the verse is Hermann's necessary correction. The metre is ⌣ _́ _́ ⌣ ⌣ _́ _ _.

1464. Περσείων. "Perseus condidisse Mycenas credebatur, de quo Pausanias ii. 15, 4. 16, 3. Memorat autem poeta Mycenas non, quod Menelaum infra (1586) precantem facit ut ad Naupliam feratur, sed antiquos auctores sequutus, qui eum priusquam Spartam veniret in portu Argivo navem appulisse tradiderant. Id illi autem collegerant ex Odysseae iii. 311 seqq., etsi nihil de ea re est in iv. 583 seqq." Hermann. The poet doubtless here follows the Cyclic poems.—Apollodor. ii. 4, 4, καὶ Μεγαπένθης μὲν ἐβασίλευσεν Ἀργείων, Περσεὺς δὲ Τίρυνθος, προστειχίσας Μίδειαν καὶ Μυκήνας.

1465. ἦ που κτλ. 'Methinks you may find by the waters of Eurotas the maiden priestesses of the daughters of Leucippus, or those of Pallas in front of her temple, having joined at length in the dances or in the revelries of Hyacinthus (the Hyacinthia).' The daughters of Leucippus, Hilaïra and Phoebe, were carried off by the Dioscuri (Theocr. xxii. 138. Apollodor. iii. 11, 2), but according to other accounts, for which Pausanias, iii. 16, 1, cites the authority of the Cyprian verses, they were deified as the daughters of Apollo, and had priestesses called Λευκιππίδες attached to their temple.—Παλλάδος, i. e. Χαλκιοίκου, sup. 228. 245.

1470. νυχίαν εὐφροσύναν Matthiae for νύχιον εἰς εὐφρόναν. Like convenire, ξυνελθεῖν seems to take an accusative in the sense of εἰσελθεῖν or κιγχάνειν, 'having joined the nightly sport in the dance,' &c. From not seeing this, the εἰς was added by some grammarian; and the verse being thus too long, εὐφροσύναν was cut down to εὐφρόναν.

1471. ὃν κτλ. 'Whom having driven from the contest (i. e. killed) by the far-thrown circle of the quoit, Phoebus slew, from which event the son of Zeus enjoined the Spartan land to keep a sacred day.' There is some difficulty here. Hermann seems right in regarding ὃν as the accusative after ἐξαμιλλησάμενος. We might compare the use of ἐξεχορεύσατο in v. 381. See Orest. 38. 431, sup. v. 387, where ἐξαμιλληθεὶς ἁμίλλας Οἰνομάῳ is, 'victorious in the contest with Oenomaus.'—τέρμονι he takes for τερμονίῳ, and this suits the sense, 'reaching its limit,' as well as the adjectival form of the word, better than to make τροχῷ mean τρέχοντι, with Dindorf. To Hermann also is due ὅθεν for τᾷ. The correction, bold as it seems, is quite necessary both to the sense and the metre. The needless addition of the article, which transcribers were very fond of inserting, probably caused the expulsion of ὅθεν on the principle noticed at v. 1470.

ὁ Διὸς εἶπε σέβειν γόνος, 1475
μόσχον θ', ἃν λιπέτην οἴκοις
* * *
ἃς οὔπω πεῦκαι πρὸ γάμων ἔλαμψαν.
δι' ἀέρος εἴθε ποτανοὶ στρ. β'.
γενοίμεθ' ὅθι στολάδες
οἰωνοὶ Λίβυες 1480
ὄμβρον λιποῦσαι χειμέριον
νίσσονται πρεσβυτάτᾳ
σύριγγι πειθόμεναι
ποιμένος, ὃς ἄβροχα πεδία καρποφόρα τε γᾶς 1485
ἐπιπετόμενος ἰακχεῖ.
ὦ πταναὶ δολιχαύχενες,

1476. μόσχον θ', i.e. καὶ λάβοις (καταλάβοις) ἂν, τὴν ὑπὸ Μενελάου καὶ Ἑλένης λειφθεῖσαν θυγατέρα Ἑρμιόνην. Again a rather violent correction of Hermann's, λιπέτην for λίποιτ', commends itself by its perfect and appropriate restoration of sense and metre. But Hermann, who appears to think λάβοις ἂν in v. 1467 is addressed to Helen, supposes λιπέτην to be the second person, though, if λάβοις ἂν is spoken to the ship, it follows that λιπέτην must be the third,—' you will find her whom her parents left,' &c. The following verse has been lost. Hermann supposes it may have been θάλλουσαν ἐν θαλάμοις.

1478. εἴθε for εἰ J. Barnes. 'Would that we could be borne on wings through the air, where the migratory Libyan cranes, having left the rains of the winter season, move along in obedience to the note of the oldest as their leader, who, as he flies over desert plains unmoistened by rain and fields fruitful in corn, utters a warning note.' The flight of cranes in orderly flocks (στολάδες) from the north into Libya is here beautifully and accurately described. Compare Hes. Opp. 446, φράζεσθαι δ' εὖτ' ἂν γεράνων φωνὴν ἐπακούσῃς ὑψόθεν ἐκ νεφέων ἐνιαύσια κεκληγυίης. Hermann thinks Euripides had in view the well-known lines of Homer, Il. iii. 3,

ἠΰτε περ κλαγγὴ γεράνων πέλει οὐρανόθι πρό,
αἵτ' ἐπεὶ οὖν χειμῶνα φύγον καὶ ἀθέσφατον ὄμβρον,
κλαγγῇ ταίγε πέτονται ἐπ' Ὠκεανοῖο ῥοάων.

Brodaeus well compares Ar. Av. 710, σπείρειν μὲν ὅταν γέρανος κρώζουσ' ἐς τὴν Λιβύην μεταχωρῇ.—ὅθι was inserted by Hermann, who also transposed the words στολάδες and Λίβυες, and again χειμέριον and λιποῦσαι. The two last however may stand according to the order in the old copies (as given in the text,) till the true reading of the antistrophic verse is ascertained.

1482. πρεσβυτάτᾳ. Perhaps we should read πρεσβυτάτου. It is known that cranes migrate in forked-shaped lines, at the vertex of which one takes its place as leader of the company. Aristotle (Hist. An. ix. 10,) observed that they are under the guidance of a leader, who, when they are resting, gives a warning note of approaching danger. He speaks also of the τοὺς ἐπισυρίπτοντας ἐν τοῖς ἐσχάτοις, but Euripides seems to have supposed, as perhaps Homer did, that the foremost bird kept up a continuous strain as it flew; and this strain, (not indeed, like that of the *cygnus musicus*, a harmonious one,) is compared to the pan-pipe of a shepherd.

1485. ἄβροχα. Not wetted by rain, like the Libyan desert; and so distinct from the καρποφόρα. It is not usual to couple mere epithets by the particle τε. Thus, unless δὲ be the true reading (ἄβροχα μὲν, καρποφόρα δὲ), it is better to repeat πεδία, or supply some other substantive implied in it. This verse makes a senarius, mostly of resolved feet.

1487. The old reading ὁπόταν was altered by H. Stephens to ὦ ποταναί, by Canter after him to ὦ πταναί.—σύννομοι,

ΕΛΕΝΗ. 207

σύννομοι νεφέων δρόμου,
βᾶτε Πλειάδας ὑπὸ μέσας
Ὠρίωνά τ᾽ ἐννύχιον, 1490
καρύξατ᾽ ἀγγελίαν,
Εὐρώταν ἐφεζόμεναι,
Μενέλεως ὅτι Δαρδάνου
πόλιν ἑλὼν δόμον ἥξει.
μόλοιτέ ποθ᾽ ἵππιον ἅρμα ἀντ. β'· 1495
δι᾽ αἰθέρος ἱέμενοι
παῖδες Τυνδαρίδαι,
λαμπρῶν †ἄστρων ὑπ᾽ ἀέλλαισιν
οἳ ναίετ᾽ οὐράνιοι,
σωτῆρες †τᾶς Ἑλένας 1500
γλαυκὸν ὑπὲρ οἶδμα κυανόχροά τε κυμάτων
ῥόθια πολιὰ θαλάσσας,
ναύταις εὐαεῖς ἀνέμων
πέμποντες Διόθεν πνοάς· 1505
δύσκλειαν δ᾽ ἀπὸ συγγόνου

companions (i.e. sharing) in the flight of the clouds, which are blown from the north. Pflugk's version, *nubium cursus sequaces*, is not very explicit. It is properly said, like σύγχορτος, of any animals which pasture together, as σύννομα μᾶλα Theocrit. vii. 56. 'Go, ye birds of flight,' say the chorus, 'and soaring under the highest heavens alight on the Eurotas, and tell Sparta that Menelaus is coming home, the conqueror of Troy.'—Μενέλεως for Μενέλαος, which is obviously required by the glyconean verse, was restored by Hermann, and timidly conjectured by Matthiae. So also Bothe.

1495. ἵππιον for ἵππειον Bothe and Elmsley. "Pind. Pyth. v. 11, legimus ἕκατι χρυσαρμάτου Κάστορος, ubi Castorem bigas invenisse narrant scholiastae." *Herm.* Probably ἅρμα is a cognate accusative rather than the direct object after ἱέμενοι, as if it were ὁδὸν ἱέμενοι. Whether ἵεσθαι ἅρμα is ever used in the sense of ἰέναι or ἐλαύνειν may be questioned. See below on v. 1665.

1498. It seems better to leave this verse, corrupt as it is, than to adopt an emendation of Hermann's which is far from satisfying the strophic verse, λαμπρῶν οἵτ᾽

ἄστρων ὑπ᾽ ἀέλλαισι ναίετ᾽ οὐράνιοι. The word ἀέλλαισι, which is interpreted to mean the apparent movement of the stars round the earth, is suspicious. See however on Bacch. 872. Probably the Tyndaridae were themselves called λαμπροὶ ἀστέρες, or at least were spoken of as numbered among the bright stars.

1500. τᾶς is undoubtedly corrupt. Hermann formerly proposed ἔσθ᾽, but afterwards edited εἴθ᾽, which he refers back to μόλοιτε. Neither reading seems to have any high probability. In the next verse he is perhaps more successful in restoring a senarius by giving ὑπὲρ οἶδμα for ἐπ᾽ οἶδμ᾽ ἅλιον.

1506—11. 'And remove from your sister the evil report of her marriage with a barbarian prince, which she has incurred in punishment for the decision of Paris on Mount Ida, though she never went to the land of Ilium, to the city built by Phoebus.' The reading of Scaliger, ποιναθεῖσ᾽ for πονηθεῖσ᾽ has been adopted by Hermann. The meaning is that Helen has been made to pay for the decision given against Hera by Paris, in that she has unjustly suffered in character, though only her εἴδωλον in fact went to Troy. Cf. v.

βάλετε βαρβάρων λεχέων,
ἃν Ἰδαίων ἐρίδων
ποιναθεῖσ' ἐκτήσατο, γᾶν
οὐκ ἐλθοῦσά ποτ' Ἰλίου 1510
Φοιβείους ἐπὶ πύργους.

ΑΓ. ἄναξ, †τὰ κάκιστ' ἐν δόμοις εὑρήκαμεν·
ὡς καίν' ἀκούσει πήματ' ἐξ ἐμοῦ τάχα.

ΘΕΟΚ. τί δ' ἔστιν;

ΑΓ. ἄλλης ἐκπόνει μνηστεύματα
γυναικός· Ἑλένη γὰρ βέβηκ' ἔξω χθονός. 1515

ΘΕΟΚ. πτεροῖσιν ἀρθεῖσ' ἢ πεδοστιβεῖ ποδί;

ΑΓ. Μενέλαος αὐτὴν ἐκπεπόρθμευται χθονός,
ὃς αὐτὸς αὑτὸν ἦλθεν ἀγγέλλων θανεῖν.

ΘΕΟΚ. ὦ δεινὰ λέξας· τίς δέ νιν ναυκληρία
ἐκ τῆσδ' ἀπῆρε χθονός; ἄπιστα γὰρ λέγεις. 1520

ΑΓ. ἥν γε ξένῳ δίδως σύ, τούς τε σοὺς ἔχων
ναύτας βέβηκεν, ὡς ἂν ἐν βραχεῖ μάθῃς.

31, where even the marriage of Helen with Paris (here alluded to in βαρβάρων λεχέων) is stated to have been a delusion. The phrase δύσκλειαν κτήσασθαι occurs also in Med. 218.—γᾶν for τὰν is Musgrave's correction, ἐλθοῦσά ποτ' for ἐλθοῦσαν Bothe's and Hermann's.—Φοιβείους, see Troad. 4.

1512. A messenger approaches in haste to inform Theoclymenus, whom he meets at the door of the palace, of the escape of Menelaus and Helen. The first verse is corruptly given in all the old copies, ἄναξ, τὰ κάκιστ' ἐν δόμοις εὑρήκαμεν, and it is not easy to divine the true reading. Matthiae gives κάκιστα τὰν δόμοις, "res domesticas tuas," viz. your intended marriage; but this is inappropriate in the mouth of one who had just arrived from the harbour, and indeed from the very scene of the successful enterprise. There is no doubt that the meaning ought to be, 'we have found you at home opportunely, since you shall forthwith hear bad news,' i.e. since we have bad tidings to communicate. Pierson's emendation, adopted by Bothe and not disapproved by Hermann, is τὰ κάλλιστ' ἐν δόμοις σ' εὑρήκαμεν. Hermann himself gives τὰ μάκιστ' &c., 'at last we have found you in the house.' Such a reading is very improbable in itself; and Dindorf further objects, that if the king had been at home all the time, the messenger would have found him at once, and without any search at all. One might suggest τάχιστά σ' ἐν δόμοις εὑρήκαμεν, i.e. τάχιστα, ὡς ἐν δόμοις ὄντα καὶ οὐκ ἔξω βεβηκότα. But then the repetition of τάχα at the end of the next line seems objectionable. The reading of the MSS. however would thus easily be accounted for, since κάκιστα having τά or τάχ written over it as a correction, would naturally pass into τὰ κάκιστα. Or perhaps, κάλλιστά σ', ἄναξ, κτλ. W. Dindorf leaves the verse in his text as the old copies exhibit it; and he conjectures with some probability that it is the clumsy insertion of a grammarian to fill up a *lacuna*.

1516. πτεροῖσιν. This is said in a bantering or incredulous tone perhaps, because he had been informed of the similar escape of the εἴδωλον, v. 1219. Compare Hec. 1264.—In the next line we have an example of the perfect passive used in a deponent sense. Cf. Heracl. 42, where ὑπηγκαλισμένη is for ὑπαγκαλισαμένη.

1519. ναυκληρία, as in Alcest. 112, seems here to mean the ship itself, on account of ἥν δίδως σύ following. But inf. 1589, δόλιος ἢ ναυκληρία, it must mean the στόλος or naval expedition.

ΕΛΕΝΗ.

ΘΕΟΚ. πῶς ; εἰδέναι πρόθυμος· οὐ γὰρ ἐλπίδων
εἴσω βέβηκα μίαν ὑπερδραμεῖν χέρα
τοσούσδε ναύτας, ὧν ἀπεστάλης μέτα. 1525
ΑΓ. ἐπεὶ λιποῦσα τούσδε βασιλείους δόμους
ἡ τοῦ Διὸς παῖς πρὸς θάλασσαν ἐστάλη,
σοφώταθ᾽ ἁβρὸν πόδα τιθεῖσ᾽ ἀνέστενε
πόσιν πέλας παρόντα κοὐ τεθνηκότα.
ὡς δ᾽ ἤλθομεν σῶν περίβολον νεωρίων, 1530
Σιδωνίαν ναῦν πρωτόπλουν καθείλκομεν,
ζυγῶν τε πεντήκοντα κἀρετμῶν μέτρα
ἔχουσαν· ἔργου δ᾽ ἔργον ἐξημείβετο·
ὁ μὲν γὰρ ἱστὸν, ὁ δὲ πλάτην καθίστατο
ταρσόν τε χειρὶ, λευκά θ᾽ ἱστί᾽ εἰς ἓν ἦν, 1535
πηδάλιά τε ζεύγλαισι παρακαθίετο.

1523. πρόθυμος, scil. εἰμὶ, according to a common ellipsis with such adjectives as ἄξιος, ἕτοιμος, &c.—οὐκ ἐλπίζω ὑπερδραμεῖν is equivalent to ἐλπίζω μὴ δυνήσεσθαι ὑπερδραμεῖν, and is the same idiom as οὐ δοκῶ, οὔ φημι &c.—ἀπεστάλης μέτα, in whose company you left the shore; the messenger himself having with difficulty escaped from the ship, v. 1615.

1528. σοφώτατα κτλ. 'Craftily setting her delicate foot,' as if it were the slow pace of grief, and not the lightsome step of one escaping from captivity. For ἁβρὸς πούς see Med. 1164. Troad. 506. 820. Possibly σοφώτατα ἀνέστενεν should be taken together; but the sense is not materially different.

1532. μέτρα, the size, proportions, of a first-rate sailing vessel; for this is πρωτόπλουν, rather than 'launched for her first voyage.' See *inf.* 1622. Androm. 865.—ἐξημείβετο, one work was succeeded by another; different hands were busied in the different operations.

1534. πλάτην ταρσόν τε. Though both words properly mean 'the blade of the oar,' (ταρροί: τὰ πλατύσματα τῶν κωπῶν, Photius,) the latter is also used, as Hermann remarks, of the *bank* of oars (*remigium*), which is here the meaning that best suits the context. 'One set up the mast, another placed the oar, and arranged the oarage to the rower's hand.' Cf. Thuc. vii. 40, ἔς τε τοὺς ταρσοὺς ὑποπίπτοντες τῶν πολεμίων νεῶν καὶ ἐς τὰ πλάγια παραπλέοντες [μεγάλα ἔβλαπτον].

Iph. T. 1345, ὁρῶμεν Ἑλλάδος νεὼς σκάφος ταρσῷ κατήρει πίτυλον ἐπτερωμένον, where the whole row or bank of oars, elsewhere called πτερὰ, is clearly meant. The fitting of the oars to the rowlocks is described, as Hermann has pointed out. He compares Pers. 377, ναυβάτης ἀνὴρ τροποῦτο κώπην σκαλμὸν ἀμφ᾽ εὐήρετμον. W. Dindorf thinks τε χειρὶ corrupt.

1535. The old reading, λευκὰ δ᾽ ἱστί᾽ εἰς ἓν ἦν, is allowed by all to be obscure, and by most critics to be corrupt: though, as εἰς ἓν was rather a favourite phrase with the poet (see Androm. 1172,) it is possible, with Hermann, to interpret, "*in unumque conjuncta cum his vela erant*: i. e. dum alii remos aptabant, idem fiebat velis." W. Dindorf reads εἱμέν᾽ ἦν, which seems very improbable. The present editor ventures to suggest ἐνετίθει or ἐνετέθη. This reading, with εἰς superscribed as a variant (i. e. εἰσετέθη) would have easily been mistaken by the next transcriber for εἰσενετέθη, and this again would as naturally have been cut down to εἰσενῆν. The sails and other tackle were commonly kept apart from the ship, Hes. Opp. 625. Od. xi. 3, ἐν δ᾽ ἱστὸν τιθέμεσθα καὶ ἱστία. As for the metre, a similar verse is 991, τί ταῦτα; δακρύοις εἰς τὸ θῆλυ τρεπόμενος, *inf.* 1546, ὃν Τυνδαρὶς παῖς ᾔδ᾽ ἀπόντα κενοταφεῖ, Hec. 1281, κτεῖν᾽, ὡς ἐν Ἄργει φόνια λουτρά σ᾽ ἀναμένει, besides many instances in other plays.

1536. πηδάλια, the rudders, or rather oars, one of which was inserted through

VOL. II. Ε e

κἂν τῷδε μόχθῳ τοῦτ' ἄρα σκοπούμενοι
Ἕλληνες ἄνδρες Μενέλεῳ ξυνέμποροι
προσῆλθον ἀκταῖς, ναυφθόροις ἠσθημένοι
πέπλοισιν, εὐειδεῖς μέν, αὐχμηροὶ δ' ὁρᾶν.   1540
ἰδὼν δέ νιν παρόντας Ἀτρέως γόνος
προσεῖπε, δόλιον οἶκτον ἐς μέσον φέρων,
ὦ τλήμονες, πῶς ἐκ τίνος νεώς ποτε
Ἀχαιΐδος θραύσαντες ἥκετε σκάφος;
ἆρ' Ἀτρέως παῖδ' ὀλόμενον συνθάπτετε,   1545
ὃν Τυνδαρὶς παῖς ἥδ' ἀπόντα κενοταφεῖ;
οἱ δ' ἐκβαλόντες δάκρυα ποιητῷ τρόπῳ
ἐς ναῦν ἐχώρουν, Μενέλεῳ ποντίσματα
φέροντες. ἡμῖν δ' ἦν μὲν ἥδ' ὑποψία
λόγος τ' ἐν ἀλλήλοισι, τῶν ἐπεισβατῶν   1550
ὡς πλῆθος εἴη· διεσιωπῶμεν δ' ὅμως,
τοὺς σοὺς λόγους σώζοντες· ἄρχειν γὰρ νεὼς

a hole on each side of the stern, and fastened there with a collar, ζεύγλη, (after the same metaphor by which ζυγὸν was used of a bench of rowers, Agam. 1596, because two sate ἐφεξῆς, like beasts under a yoke). These rudders are most clearly represented in paintings of Egyptian ships,—and that here described, though called a Sidonian galley, may fairly be referred to the same class,—and also in a perfect and important fresco-painting of two armed and manned ships of forty oars, discovered in the temple of Isis at Pompeii, and engraved in Plate 50 of "Raccolta de' più belli Dipinti" &c. from the Royal Museum at Naples. Wilkinson (Ancient Egyptians, Vol. ii. p. 125,) has a good account of these double rudders; and in p. 129 he observes, "sometimes the rudder, instead of traversing in a groove, merely rested on the taffrel, and was suspended and secured by a rope, or band." This is doubtless the ζεύγλη here described, and in the well-known, but not always well understood passage of the Acts, chap. xxvii. 40, τὰς ἀγκύρας περιελόντες εἴων εἰς τὴν θάλασσαν, ἅμα ἀνέντες τὰς ζευκτηρίας τῶν πηδαλίων. Musgrave compares Orph. Argon. 277, ἐπὶ δ' αὖτ' οἴηκας ἔδησαν, πρυμνόθεν ἀρτήσαντες, ἐπεσφίγξαντο δ' ἱμᾶσιν.

1537. τοῦτ' ἄρα κτλ., 'who, it seems,

had been on the look out for this,' viz. the τὸ ἑτοιμάζειν τὴν ναῦν. The common construction of ἄρα with the imperfect is here adapted to the present participle which represents that tense (οἱ τοῦτο ἐσκόπουν ἄρα). So Androm. 1088, καὶ τοῦθ' ὕποπτον ἦν ἄρ'.—ναυφθόροις πέπλοις, the dress of shipwrecked mariners, ναυτίλοι ἐφθαρμένοι, Iph. T. 276.

1543. πῶς ἐκ τίνος. See v. 873, and Ion 948.

1545. ἆρα συνθάπτετε; 'Can it be that you are for assisting at the funeral of Menelaus?' i. e. is that the purpose for which you are here present? Their answer is practically given in the affirmative, by their entering the ship with the presents they had brought for that very purpose. Pflugk therefore is wrong in explaining the present tense as a command or exhortation to the men to join the party. This would have been οὐκ— συνθάψετε;

1547. ποιητῷ τρόπῳ, in got-up style; in artificial manner.

1549. ἡμῖν δ' κτλ. 'Now to us this was indeed a matter of suspicion, and a subject of talk with one another, how that there was a large number of the supernumerary crew; nevertheless we maintained silence through the whole transaction in obedience to your commands.'—ἄρχειν νεώς, see v. 1415.

ΕΛΕΝΗ. 211

ξένον κελεύσας πάντα συνέχεας τάδε.
καὶ τἄλλα μὲν δὴ ῥᾳδίως εἴσω νεὼς
ἐθέμεθα κουφίζοντα· ταύρειος δὲ ποὺς   1555
οὐκ ἤθελ' ὀρθὸς σανίδα προσβῆναι κάτα,
ἀλλ' ἐξεβρυχᾶτ' ὄμμ' ἀναστρέφων κύκλῳ,
κυρτῶν τε νῶτα κεἰς κέρας παρεμβλέπων
μὴ θιγγάνειν ἀπεῖργεν. ὁ δ' Ἑλένης πόσις
ἐκάλεσεν, ὦ πέρσαντες Ἰλίου πόλιν,   1560
οὐκ εἶ' ἀναρπάσαντες Ἑλλήνων νόμῳ
νεανίαις ὤμοισι ταύρειον δέμας
ἐς πρῷραν ἐμβαλεῖτε, (φάσγανόν θ' ἅμα
πρόχειρον ὦθει) σφάγια τῷ τεθνηκότι;

1555. κουφίζοντα. From the mention of πούς in connexion with the next animal, it seems clear that the participle is not here truly intransitive, but, as in Rhes. 281, λόγον δὲ δὶς τόσου μ' ἐκούφισας, active, with πόδας supplied, 'stepping lightly.' It is needless therefore to compare ἐλαφρίζον γόνυ Frag. 531, 8, or Hes. Opp. 463, ἔτι κουφίζουσαν ἄρουραν.—κατὰ σανίδα, over the plank laid between the shore and the vessel : properly, according to its guidance or direction.

1558. παρεμβλέπων, looking askance towards his horn, i. e. taking sight along it, as bulls appear to do when meditating an attack. Cf. Bacch. 743, ταῦροι δ' ὑβρισταὶ κεἰς κέρας θυμούμενοι,—the irasci in cornua of Virgil, Georg. iii. 232.

1561. οὐκ εἶα—ἐμβαλεῖτε. A mixed construction of ἀλλ' εἶα, ἐμβάλλετε (cf. Med. 400, ἀλλ' εἶα, φείδου μηδὲν,) and οὐκ ἐμβαλεῖτε; which latter is virtually an imperative. Compare inf. 1597. Iph. T. 1423, οὐκ εἶα πώλοις ἐμβαλόντες ἡνίας παράκτιοι δραμεῖσθε;

1564. ὦθει for ὦσει, and the including the clause as a parenthesis, is due to Hermann, who in the former correction was preceded by Duport. But he further alters the vulgate text to φασγάνῳ θ' ἅμα πρόχειρος, 'with sword in hand he pushed the bull on to the deck.' The sword, he says, was ready, in fact to attack the Egyptian crew, but in pretence to defend himself against the bull. The point of the passage however seems to be this. Menelaus pretended to the crew that the animal was to be sacrificed immediately, and applied his drawn sword to its throat as if to slay it while held on the men's shoulders, for such was the Greek custom, Ἑλλήνων νόμος, as appears from Electr. 813, κἄσφαξ', ἐπ' ὤμων μόσχον ὡς ἦραν χεροῖν δμῶες. Agam. 226, where Agamemnon orders the attendants to hold Iphigenia δίκαν χιμαίρας ὕπερθε βωμοῦ ἀέρδην. On this Barnes correctly writes, "Mos erat Graecorum, ut bovem placide euntem (Od. iii. 439) duo juvenes cornibus ducerent; sin is restitaret, tum boni ominis gratia, ne taurus reluctando auspicia turbaret, ut robusti quidem et ad hoc parati juvenes uno impetu taurum adorti simul humeris abriperent ad aram." Hence Cassandra is asked, Agam. 1268, πῶς θεηλάτου βοὸς δίκην πρὸς βωμὸν εὐτόλμως πατεῖς; Of course, the action was only a feint; but it served at once as an excuse for disarming the suspicions of the crew, for holding his sword ready for action, and for getting the animal quickly on board. And this view is confirmed by the words ἐς πρῷραν ἐμβαλεῖτε, (for it was at the prow that the animal was sacrificed, v. 1582,) and the immediate mention of σφάγια τῷ τεθνηκότι. If it were possible, as Pflugk thinks, to construe ὦσει σφάγια victimam immolabit, the future would unquestionably be the best reading, 'Will you not take the bull and kill it?' But, though ὠθεῖν ξίφος διά τινος is common enough, it does not appear how the sword itself can be said ὠθεῖν τινὰ, unless it be one of those exceptional expressions like ἔκειρε πολύκερων φόνον, Ajac. 55. On the whole, it seems best to give the reading adopted by W. Dindorf.

οἱ δ' ἐς κέλευσμ' ἐλθόντες ἐξανήρπασαν 1565
ταῦρον φέροντές τ' εἰσέθεντο σέλματα.
μονάμπυκον δὲ Μενέλεως ψήχων δέρην
μέτωπά τ' ἐξέπεισεν εἰσβῆναι δόρυ.
τέλος δ' ἐπειδὴ ναῦς τὰ πάντ' ἐδέξατο,
πλήσασα κλιμακτῆρας εὐσφύρου ποδὸς 1570
Ἑλένη καθέζετ' ἐν μέσοις ἐδωλίοις,
ὅ τ' οὐκέτ' ὢν λόγοισι Μενέλεως πέλας·
ἄλλοι δὲ τοίχους δεξιοὺς λαιούς τ' ἴσοι
ἀνὴρ παρ' ἄνδρ' ἔζονθ', ὑφ' εἵμασι ξίφη
λαθραῖ' ἔχοντες, ῥόθιά τ' ἐξεπίμπλατο 1575
βοῆς, κελευστοῦ φθέγμαθ' ὡς ἠκούσαμεν.
ἐπεὶ δὲ γαίας ἦμεν οὔτ' ἄγαν πρόσω
οὔτ' ἐγγύς, οὕτως ἤρετ' οἰάκων φύλαξ·
ἔτ', ὦ ξέν', ἐς τὸ πρόσθεν, ἢ καλῶς ἔχει,
πλεύσωμεν; ἀρχαὶ γὰρ νεὼς μέλουσί σοι. 1580
ὁ δ' εἶφ', ἅλις μοι· δεξιᾷ δ' ἑλὼν ξίφος
ἐς πρῷραν εἶρπε, κἀπὶ ταυρείῳ σφαγῇ

1565. ἐς κέλευσμα ἐξανήρπασαν, 'caught up the bull at the word of command.' Hermann rightly understands this of the word given to all to lift together, for the simultaneous effort of several was necessary for hoisting so large a victim.
1566. εἰσέθεντο. Hermann reads εἰς ἔθεντο, but he seems to be wrong in saying the use of the accusative of *the place where* is confined to neuter verbs, as εἰσπίπτειν, εἰσθορεῖν, &c. Cf. Choeph. 68, θεοὶ—δούλιόν μ' ἐσᾶγον αἶσαν. Eur. Suppl. 876, χρυσὸν—οὐκ εἰσεδέξατ' οἶκον. Ion 1434, ἣν πρῶτ' Ἀθήνα σκόπελον εἰσηνέγκατο. By φέροντες εἰσέθεντο the antithesis is implied, φερόμενος ἀλλ' οὐ βαδίζων εἰσετέθη.
1567. μονάμπυκον, Alcest. 428, with a single rope round its horns in the manner of the halter or bridle of a riding-horse.—εἰσβῆναι δόρυ Pflugk rightly explains *ut in navi consisteret*, though he entirely misunderstands μονάμπυκον. The bull had been carried into the ship, and persuasion was only required that it should remain quiet. Mr. Clark thinks μονάμπυκος here stands for ἵππος, comparing v. 1258.—ψήχων, 'patting,' 'stroking.'
1570. πλήσασα. See Ion 1108. The meaning is, occupying successively all the steps of the ladder as she ascended the sides of the ship. — κλιμακτήρ is 'the round of a ladder,' as distinct from κλῖμαξ, the ladder itself.
1574. ἔζοντο τοίχους, took their seats at the sides of the ship ἐφεξῆς, two in a row, ἀνὴρ παρ' ἄνδρα. The usual accusative after verbs of sitting, and not, as Bothe supposes, that of *motion towards*. Musgrave understands 'singuli Graeci totidem Aegyptiis,' but this is hardly necessary. The fight seems to have been a general one, not a preconcerted scheme for each to stab his neighbour, v. 1594 seqq.
1575. ῥόθια for ὄρθρια Pierson.—βοῆς, the noise of the song, or perhaps the sounds extorted by the exertion. Cf. Iph. T. 1390, οἱ δὲ στεναγμὸν ἡδὺν ἐκβρυχώμενοι ἔπαισαν ἅλμην. The former however is more probably the meaning. Pflugk and others aptly cite Longus, iii. 21, εἷς μὲν αὐτοῖς κελευστὴς ναυτικὰς ᾖδεν ᾠδάς, οἱ δὲ λοιποὶ καθάπερ χορὸς ὁμοφώνως κατὰ καιρὸν τῆς ἐκείνου φωνῆς ἐβόων.
1580. σοι for μοι was acutely restored by Elmsley. Cf. 1415.

ΕΛΕΝΗ. 213

σταθεὶς νεκρῶν μὲν οὐδενὸς μνήμην ἔχων,
τέμνων δὲ λαιμὸν ηὔχετ', ὦ ναίων ἅλα
πόντιε Πόσειδον Νηρέως θ' ἁγναὶ κόραι, 1585
σώσατέ μ' ἐπ' ἀκτὰς Ναυπλίας δάμαρτά τε
ἄσυλον ἐκ γῆς. αἵματος δ' ἀπορροαὶ
εἰς οἶδμ' ἐσηκόντιζον οὔριαι ξένῳ.
καί τις τόδ' εἶπε, δόλιος ἡ ναυκληρία·
τί νῦν πλέωμεν Ναυπλίαν; κέλευε σύ· 1590
σὺ δὲ στρέφ' οἴακ'. ἐκ δὲ ταυρείου φόνου
Ἀτρέως σταθεὶς παῖς ἀνεβόησε συμμάχους,
τί μέλλετ', ὦ γῆς Ἑλλάδος λωτίσματα,
σφάζειν, φονεύειν βαρβάρους, νεώς τ' ἄπο
ῥίπτειν ἐς οἶδμα; ναυβάταις δὲ τοῖσι σοῖς 1595
βοᾷ κελευστὴς τὴν ἐναντίαν ὄπα,
οὐκ εἶ' ὁ μέν τις λοῖσθον ἀρεῖται δόρυ,
ὁ δὲ ζύγ' ἄξας, ὁ δ' ἀφελὼν σκαλμοῦ πλάτην,
καθαιματώσει κρᾶτα πολεμίων ξένων;
ὀρθοὶ δ' ἀνῇξαν πάντες, οἱ μὲν ἐν χεροῖν 1600

1583. μνήμην ἔχων, not, as was expected, making mention of a deceased person, but uttering quite a different prayer. Cf. Bacch. 46.
1588. οὔριαι Hermann, οὔριοι Elmsley, for οὔρια. He means that the ξένος himself deduced a favourable omen for his bold enterprise, from the manner in which the blood spurted into the sea. For, if it had not done so, it could not have been accepted by Poseidon to whom he prayed.
1590. The old reading πάλιν πλέωμεν Ναξίαν is allowed by all to be corrupt, if we except Pflugk, who seems scarcely conscious of any difficulty, but supposes Ναξία to be "locus omnibus ignotus." Hermann's correction is by no means probable, πάλιν πλέωμεν, ἀξιῶ 'γκέλευε σύ (a Paris MS. giving ἀξίαν). Mr. Clark suggests ἀντίαν κέλευε σύ. The words ought to convey the reason why the expedition was now discovered to be δόλιος. If we mistake not, the poet wrote τί νῦν πλέωμεν Ναυπλίαν; 'Why should we sail to Nauplia *now?*' i. e. when so different a purpose was alleged, viz. to sail scarcely out of sight of land, v. 1269. On Π corrupted to TI, see the note on Aesch. Suppl. 756. It is equally easy to perceive that N differs from the first part of ΑΛ only by a single stroke; and the V (i. e. Υ) would be mistaken for the other half of Λ and the following I. Thus when TI NVN had become ΠΑΛΙΝ, the reading Ναυπλίαν was altered, because it became a manifest absurdity. It does not seem likely that Ναξία could allude, as Barnes supposes, to the island of Pharos, where a light-house had been built before the poet's time by one Sostratus of Naxos. As plausible a conjecture might have been derived from Ar. Pac. 143, τὸ δὲ πλοῖον ἔσται Ναξιουργὴς κάνθαρος. Only, Naxos was so far out of their course from Egypt to Sparta.
1593. λωτίσματα, Hesych. λώτισμα· οἱ πρῶτοι καὶ ἐπίλεκτοι. So λωτίσασθαι is *carpere* in Aesch. Suppl. 940.
1595. τοῖσι σοῖς, the Egyptian crew of king Theoclymenus, who on their parts were exhorted by their boatswain to rise against the Greeks. This is said to assure the king that the ship was not surrendered to the Greeks without a struggle.
1597. οὐκ εἶα. See on v. 1561.— λοῖσθον δόρυ is interpreted by Hermann *ultĭmam, si quae forte relicta sit, hastam.* But perhaps nothing more is meant than 'any spare piece of wood.'

κορμοὺς ἔχοντες ναυτικούς, οἱ δὲ ξίφη.
φόνῳ δὲ ναῦς ἐρρεῖτο· παρακέλευσμα δ' ἦν
πρύμνηθεν Ἑλένης, ποῦ τὸ Τρωικὸν κλέος;
δείξατε πρὸς ἄνδρας βαρβάρους· σπουδῆς δ' ὕπο
ἔπιπτον, οἱ δ' ὠρθοῦντο, τοὺς δὲ κειμένους   1605
νεκροὺς ἂν εἶδες. Μενέλεως δ' ἔχων ὅπλα,
ὅπη νοσοῖεν ξύμμαχοι κατασκοπῶν,
ταύτῃ προσῆγε χειρὶ δεξιᾷ ξίφος,
ὥστ' ἐκκολυμβᾶν ναός· ἠρήμωσε δὲ
σῶν ναυβατῶν ἐρέτμ'. ἐπ' οἰάκων δὲ βὰς   1610
ἄναξ ἐς Ἑλλάδ' εἶπεν εὐθύνειν δόρυ.
οἱ δ' ἱστὸν ἦρον, οὔριαι δ' ἦκον πνοαί,
βεβᾶσι δ' ἐκ γῆς· διαφυγὼν δ' ἐγὼ φόνον
καθῆκ' ἐμαυτὸν εἰς ἅλ' ἄγκυραν πάρα.
ἤδη δὲ κάμνονθ' ὁρμιὰν τείνων μέ τις   1615
ἀνείλετ', ἐς δὲ γαῖαν ἐξέβησέ σοι
τάδ' ἀγγελοῦντα. σώφρονος δ' ἀπιστίας

1601. "Quos κορμοὺς ναυτικοὺς vocat, hi conti sunt: Homero ξυστὰ ναύμαχα Iliad. xv. 389. 677." *Herm.*
1602. ἐρρεῖτο, Pflugk adopts, and Shilleto on Dem. de Fals. Leg. p. 433, approves, Elmsley's inharmonious (and indeed, on account of the article, incorrect) alteration, φόνῳ δὲ ναῦς ἔρρει· τὸ παρακέλευσμα δ' ἦν κτλ. Hermann, who appears generally to have much deference for Elmsley as a critic, observes, that the article might mean '*the* exhortation that was given was from Helen standing at the stern.' It is clear however, that as no such exhortation had yet been alluded to, the article is at least wholly superfluous. Hermann defends the passive by ἱδρῶτι ῥεούμενον in an oracle ap. Herod. vii. 140, and by Phrynichus p. 220, who gives ἐρρεῖτο as an Attic form. Compare Lucian, Eunuch. p. 358, § 11, Βαγώας δὲ μᾶλλον ἐταράττετο καὶ παντοῖος ἦν ἐς μυρία τραπόμενος χρώματα καὶ ψυχρῷ τῷ ἱδρῶτι ῥεόμενος. That ῥεῖν had originally an active sense seems clear from Hec. 528, ἔρρει χειρὶ παῖς Ἀχιλλέως χοὰς θανόντι πατρί.
1605. οἱ δ' ὠρθοῦντο. 'And while some rose up again, others you might have seen lying dead.' It is singular enough that Hermann, generally so acute and so accurate, should have thought κειμένους "tam inutile et languidum, ut non dubitaverit νεκρούς τ' exhibere." The metaphor is a very common one, from a wrestler who, when unable to rise, was said κεῖσθαι πεσών. See Tro. 466. Agam. 1256, ὑπτίασμα κειμένου πατρός. Theocr. iii. 53, κεισεῦμαι δὲ πεσών, καὶ τοὶ λύκοι ὧδέ μ' ἔδονται. It is clear therefore, that so far from κειμένους being redundant, it contains a direct antithesis with ὠρθοῦντο.
1611. ἄναξ. Euripides, perhaps, used this word somewhat inadvertently; for though to *his* mind, in writing the narrative, Menelaus was κατ' ἐξοχὴν the ἄναξ, the messenger should have applied that title only to his own master, Theoclymenus. Mr. Clark proposes ἐπ' οἰάκων δὲ βὰς ἀρχάς, as in v. 1580. But ἄναξ (see on v. 1040) might fairly be explained thus: 'Taking his place on the steerage as master of it, he gave the order to sail for Hellas.' Hermann reads ἀλλάξ, from Hesych. ἀλλάξ· ἐνηλλαγμένως. Menelaus himself taking charge of the helm, shouted, as he turned the prow homewards, ιthe words ἐς Ἑλλάδα, 'For Greece!' at which inspiring sound his crew ἱστὸν ἦρον κτλ.
1617. σώφρονος ἀπιστίας. He means to hint, that Theoclymenus would have been wiser if he had not put such implicit trust in the strangers.

οὐκ ἔστιν οὐδὲν χρησιμώτερον βροτοῖς.
ΧΟ. οὐκ ἄν ποτ' ηὔχουν οὔτε σ' οὔθ' ἡμᾶς λαθεῖν
Μενέλαον, ὦναξ, ὡς ἐλάνθανεν παρών. 1620
ΘΕΟΚ. ὦ γυναικείαις τέχναισιν αἱρεθεὶς ἐγὼ τάλας.
ἐκπεφεύγασιν γάμοι με. κεἰ μὲν ἦν ἁλώσιμος
ναῦς διώγμασιν, πονήσας εἷλον ἂν τάχα ξένους·
νῦν δὲ τὴν προδοῦσαν ἡμᾶς τισόμεσθα σύγγονον,
ἥτις ἐν δόμοις ὁρῶσα Μενέλεων οὐκ εἶπέ μοι. 1625
τοιγὰρ οὔποτ' ἄλλον ἄνδρα ψεύσεται μαντεύμασιν.

ΠΡΟΣΠΟΛΟΣ.

οὗτος ὦ, ποῖ σὸν πόδ' αἴρεις, δέσποτ', ἐς ποῖον φόνον;
ΘΕΟΚ. οἷπερ ἡ δίκη κελεύει μ'. ἀλλ' ἀφίστασ' ἐκποδών.
ΠΡ. οὐκ ἀφήσομαι πέπλων σῶν, μεγάλα γὰρ σπεύδεις κακά.
ΘΕΟΚ. ἀλλὰ δεσποτῶν κρατήσεις δοῦλος ὤν; 1630
ΠΡ.   φρονῶ γὰρ εὖ.
ΘΕΟΚ. οὐκ ἔμοιγ', εἰ μή μ' ἐάσεις
ΠΡ.   οὐ μὲν οὖν σ' ἐάσομεν.
ΘΕΟΚ. σύγγονον κτανεῖν κακίστην.
ΠΡ.   εὐσεβεστάτην μὲν οὖν.
ΘΕΟΚ. ἥ με προὔδωκεν;
ΠΡ.   καλήν γε προδοσίαν δίκαια δρᾶν.
ΘΕΟΚ. τἀμὰ λέκτρ' ἄλλῳ διδοῦσα; ΠΡ. τοῖς γε κυριω-
τέροις.
ΘΕΟΚ. κύριος δὲ τῶν ἐμῶν τίς; 1635
ΠΡ.   ὃς ἔλαβεν πατρὸς πάρα.

1619. ηὔχουν. Either with or without ἄν, this word commonly means, 'I never thought that,'—properly, 'never said, or would have said that,' &c. See Agam. 489.—λαθεῖν, scil. παρόντα.
1622. εἰ μὲν ἦν κτλ. The ship could not be caught, because it was πρωτόπλους, a fast sailer, v. 1531. It could not yet have attained any great distance, for the Dioscuri afterwards address Helen, who therefore was at least still in sight.
1625. ἥτις οὐκ εἶπε, 'for not having told me.'
1628. ἀφίστασ' Porson for ἀφίστασθ'.
1630. κρατήσει, for κρατήσεις, is given by Hermann, because the chorus, being

women, could not, without great impropriety of language, be addressed in the singular masculine ὤν. Mr. Clark however is undoubtedly right in attributing the interference to an attendant, who now steps between the king and his sister, and ventures to argue with his master in her defence. He assigns this part in the dialogue as far as v. 1641 (including 1619—20) to the servant, instead of the chorus, as in the old copies.
1631. οὐ μὲν οὖν, 'nay, but we will *not* let you go.' Ar. Ach. 285, σὲ μὲν οὖν καταλεύσομεν, ὦ μιαρὰ κεφαλά. Cf. Hec. 1261.

ΘΕΟΚ. ἀλλ' ἔδωκεν ἡ τύχη μοι.   ΠΡ. τὸ δὲ χρεὼν
       ἀφείλετο.
ΘΕΟΚ. οὐ σὲ τἀμὰ χρὴ δικάζειν.   ΠΡ. ἤν γε βελτίω
       λέγω.
ΘΕΟΚ. ἀρχόμεσθ' ἄρ', οὐ κρατοῦμεν.
ΠΡ.   ὅσια δρᾶν, τὰ δ' ἔκδικ' οὔ.
ΘΕΟΚ. κατθανεῖν ἐρᾶν ἔοικας.
ΠΡ.   κτεῖνε· σύγγονον δὲ σὴν
   οὐ κτενεῖς ἡμῶν ἑκόντων, ἀλλ' ἔμ', *ὡς πρὸ δεσποτῶν
   τοῖσι γενναίοισι δούλοις εὐκλεέστατον θανεῖν.   1641

ΔΙΟΣΚΟΡΟΙ.

ἐπίσχες ὀργὰς, αἷσιν οὐκ ὀρθῶς φέρει,
Θεοκλύμενε, γῆς τῆσδ' ἄναξ· δισσοὶ δέ σε
Διόσκοροι καλοῦμεν, οὓς Λήδα ποτὲ
ἔτικτεν, Ἑλένην θ', ἣ πέφευγε σοὺς δόμους·   1645
οὐ γὰρ πεπρωμένοισιν ὀργίζει γάμοις,
οὐδ' ἡ θεᾶς Νηρῇδος ἔκγονος κόρη
ἀδικεῖ σ', ἀδελφὴ Θεονόη, τὰ τῶν θεῶν
τιμῶσα πατρός τ' ἐνδίκους ἐπιστολάς.
ἐς μὲν γὰρ ἀεὶ τὸν παρόντα νῦν χρόνον   1650
κείνην κατοικεῖν σοῖσιν ἐν δόμοις ἐχρῆν·
ἐπεὶ δὲ Τροίας ἐξανεστάθη βάθρα,
καὶ τοῖς θεοῖς παρέσχε τοὔνομ', οὐκέτι
ἐν τοῖσιν αὐτοῖς δεῖ νιν ἐζεῦχθαι γάμοις,
ἐλθεῖν δ' ἐς οἴκους καὶ συνοικῆσαι πόσει.   1655
ἀλλ' ἴσχε μὲν σῆς συγγόνου μέλαν ξίφος,

1638. Compare Med. 120, ὀλίγ' ἀρχόμενοι, πολλὰ κρατοῦντες.—τὰ δ' ἔκδικ' οὔ Porson for τἀνδ' ἐκδικῶ. The error in τἀνδε arose from a variant ἐκδικ'.

1640. ὡς before πρὸ was inserted by Porson and Hermann.

1642. For the idiom φέρεσθαι ἐλπίσιν &c. see Rhes. 15. Ion 1065.

1647. ἔκγονος Matthiae for ἐκγόνη.

1652. ἐπεὶ δὲ κτλ. 'But now that the very foundations of Troy have been rooted up, and Helen has lent her name to the gods, it is no longer destined for her to be united in the same marriage.' The same, i. e. as Theoclymenus has hitherto aspired to,—τοῖσιν αὐτοῖς οἷς πάρος ἔσπευδεν αὐτὴν ζευχθῆναι Θεοκλύμενος. Hermann follows Bothe in placing a stop at οὐκέτι, and reading ἐν τοῖσι δ' αὐτοῖς κτλ., i. e. her original marriage with Menelaus. Mr. Clark proposes ἐν δ' οἷσιν αὐτῆς, as in Oed. R. 1248. There is nothing however absurd in the text according to the reading given above. By παρέχειν ὄνομα it is meant that Helen *lent* her name to be borne by the εἴδωλον, or, according to our way of speaking, that a liberty was taken with her name by its being for a time appropriated to another.

ΕΛΕΝΗ. 217

νόμιζε δ' αὐτὴν σωφρόνως πράσσειν τάδε.
πάλαι δ' ἀδελφὴν καὶ πρὶν ἐξεσώσαμεν,
ἐπείπερ ἡμᾶς Ζεὺς ἐποίησεν θεούς·
ἀλλ' ἧσσον' ἦμεν τοῦ πεπρωμένου θ' ἅμα   1660
καὶ τῶν θεῶν, οἷς ταῦτ' ἔδοξεν ὧδ' ἔχειν.
σοὶ μὲν τάδ' αὐδῶ· συγγόνῳ δ' ἐμῇ λέγω
πλεῖν ξὺν πόσει σῷ. πνεῦμα δ' ἕξετ' οὔριον·
σωτῆρε δ' ἡμεῖς σὼ κασιγνήτω διπλῶ
πόντον παριππεύοντε πέμψομεν πάτραν.   1665
ὅταν δὲ κάμψῃς καὶ τελευτήσῃς βίον,
θεὸς κεκλήσει, καὶ Διοσκόρων μέτα
σπονδῶν μεθέξεις· ξένιά τ' ἀνθρώπων πάρα
ἕξεις μεθ' ἡμῶν· Ζεὺς γὰρ ὧδε βούλεται.
οὗ δ' ὥρισέν σε πρῶτα Μαιάδος τόκος   1670

1658. W. Dindorf, Matthiae, and Bothe, read κἂν πρὶν after Heath. Hermann thinks the omission of the ἂν justifiable, because the sentence, though virtually conditional, ἔσωσα μὲν ἂν, εἰ μὴ &c., is not put in the conditional form. So in English we say, 'We had saved her, but that' &c. Mr. Clark would read ἐξεσώζομεν. The dual ἥσσονε for ἥσσονες is Pierson's correction. For the doctrine of non-interference here implied, see Hipp. 1329, οὐδεὶς ἀπαντᾶν βούλεται προθυμίᾳ τῇ τῶν θελόντων, ἀλλ' ἀφιστάμεσθ' ἀεί.

1663. πλεῖν. With the infinitive we should have expected σὺν τῷ ἑαυτῆς πόσει. Pflugk compares the somewhat similar transition from the third to the second person, sup. v. 954—5. Here however we should probably restore the imperative πλεῖ, which occurs Troad. 103, πλεῖ κατὰ πορθμόν, πλεῖ κατὰ δαίμονα. Nor is it less likely because Lucian appears to reckon the monosyllabic imperative among the quaint and obsolete forms collected in his Lexiphanes, p. 342, οὐκοῦν, ᾗ δ' ὅς, σὺ μὲν, εἰ βούλει, πλεῖ καὶ νεῖ καὶ θεῖ κατὰ τοῦ κλύδωνος. The address to Helen herself, who must now have been far out at sea, is remarkable enough; but the Dioscuri, as speaking from the air, must be supposed to command a wide view. Hermann compares Iph. T. 1446, where Pallas says to Orestes, κλύεις γὰρ αὐδὴν, καίπερ οὐ παρὼν, θεᾶς.

1665. παριππεύοντε. As Castor was famed in life for his skill in the equestrian art, (Κάστωρ αἰολόπωλος, Theocr. xxii. 34,) so the two brothers when deified were represented as riding through the air, ἅρμα ἵππιον v. 1495, where the seat on steeds is perhaps merely meant, without reference to the appendage of a chariot. So in Rhes. 621, ὄχημα πωλικὸν is applied exclusively to the horses of Rhesus.

1666. κάμψῃς βίον. Hippol. 87, τέλος δὲ κάμψαιμ', ὥσπερ ἠρξάμην, βίου.

1668. ξένια. Musgrave quotes the Schol. on Pind. Ol. iii. 67, ἡ γινομένη θυσία τοῖς Διοσκούροις ξενισμὸς λέγεται. For the apotheosis of Helen is recorded not only by Isocrates and Lucian (quoted by Bothe from Brodaeus), but by Herod. vi. 61, where mention is made of τὸ τῆς Ἑλένης ἱρὸν, τὸ δ' ἔστι ἐν τῇ Θεράπνῃ καλευμένῃ ὕπερθε τοῦ Φοιβηΐου ἱροῦ.

1670—5. 'But the place to which Hermes first removed you from Sparta, after descending from his flight through the air, (having stolen you bodily away that Paris might not marry you,) I mean the guardian island that skirts the Attic coast, shall henceforth be called Helena among men, because it received you when you had been secretly conveyed from your home.' The meaning and right punctuation of this passage were first determined by Hermann, who quotes Philoct. 635, ὡς ἡμᾶς πολὺ πέλαγος ὁρίζῃ τῆς Ὀδυσσέως νεώς, in defence of ὥρισεν σε Σπάρτης. To him also is due φρουρὸν for φρουροῦ and τεταμένην for —η. He reads Ἀκτῇ, perhaps to avoid the concurrence

218   ΕΥΡΙΠΙΔΟΥ

Σπάρτης, ἀπάρας τῶν κατ᾽ οὐρανὸν δόμων,
κλέψας δέμας σὸν, μὴ Πάρις γήμειέ σε,
φρουρὸν παρ᾽ Ἀκτὴν τεταμένην νῆσον λέγω,
Ἑλένη τὸ λοιπὸν ἐν βροτοῖς κεκλήσεται,
ἐπεὶ κλοπὰς σὰς ἐκ δόμων ἐδέξατο.   1675
καὶ τῷ πλανήτῃ Μενέλεῳ θεῶν πάρα
μακάρων κατοικεῖν νῆσόν ἐστι μόρσιμον·
τοὺς εὐγενεῖς γὰρ οὐ στυγοῦσι δαίμονες,
τῶν δ᾽ ἀναριθμήτων μᾶλλόν εἰσιν οἱ πόνοι.

ΘΕΟΚ. ὦ παῖδε Λήδας καὶ Διὸς, τὰ μὲν πάρος   1680
νείκη μεθήσω σφῶν κασιγνήτης πέρι.
ἐγὼ δ᾽ ἀδελφὴν οὐκέτ᾽ ἂν κτάνοιμ᾽ ἐμήν.
κείνη δ᾽ ἴτω πρὸς οἶκον, εἰ θεοῖς δοκεῖ.
ἴστον δ᾽ ἀρίστης σωφρονεστάτης θ᾽ ἅμα
γεγῶτ᾽ ἀδελφῆς ὁμογενοῦς ἀφ᾽ αἵματος.   1685

of accusatives; but *extension along* is better expressed by the old reading Ἀκτήν. Strabo, lib. ix. 1, p. 399, πρόκειται δὲ τῆς παραλίας ταύτης, πρὸ μὲν τοῦ Θορίκου καὶ τοῦ Σουνίου, νῆσος Ἑλένη, τραχεῖα καὶ ἔρημος, παραμήκης ὅσον ἑξήκοντα σταδίους τὸ μῆκος. It is called φρουρὸς from its position like a sentinel in front of the Attic coast. Wordsworth (*Athens and Attica*, p. 211) says that the harbour of Thoricus (*Porto Mandri*) is completely sheltered by the long island of Macri, the ancient Helena, which is hence said to be 'stretched as a rampart by the shore.' The reading of most editions, after Stephens, is φρουρὰ, which Pflugk explains σκοπιά. The old copies however agree in φρουροῦ. W. Dindorf unreasonably objects to Hermann's interpretation, as against the natural order of the words; and he has recourse to his favourite theory, that v. 1671—2 are the interpolation of some grammarian.

1671. δόμων. Perhaps δρόμων. On μὴ for ἵνα μὴ see Hec. 344. The *fear* of an event implies the *purpose* of its prevention.

1676. θεῶν πάρα. As if δῶρον δέχεσθαι were to follow μόρσιμον.

1677. μακάρων νῆσον. This is taken from Homer, Od. iv. 562, Σοὶ δ᾽ οὐ θέσφατόν ἐστι, διοτρεφὲς ὦ Μενέλαε, Ἄργει ἐν ἱπποβότῳ θανέειν καὶ πότμον ἐπισπεῖν,

Ἀλλά σ᾽ ἐς Ἠλύσιον πεδίον καὶ πείρατα γαίης Ἀθάνατοι πέμψουσιν. Barnes cites a curious passage from Tzetzes on Lycophron, to show that the 'Happy lands' of the ancient Greeks were none other than England! Of course, it was a purely mythical country, though founded on early reports, doubtless of Phoenician navigators, of fertile lands in the far west.

1679. ἀναριθμήτων. Ion 837, ἄμητορ᾽, ἀναρίθμητον. Theocr. xiv. 48, ἄμμες δ᾽ οὔτε λόγω τινὸς ἄξιοι, οὔτ᾽ ἀριθματοὶ, Δύστανοι Μεγαρῆες, ἀτιμοτάτῃ ἐνὶ μοίρᾳ. Barnes compares Il. ii. 202, οὔτε ποτ᾽ ἐν πολέμῳ ἐναρίθμιος, οὔτ᾽ ἐνὶ βουλῇ. Obscure persons are elsewhere called, by an apparently contrary term, ἀριθμὸς, as we say, 'a mere cypher.' But this implies a number who are indiscriminately put together to be counted, without distinction of rank or eminence,—a mere ὄχλος.

1681. νείκη περὶ σφῶν κασιγνήτης, my former quarrel with your sister for rejecting my hand. See on v. 1236.

1685. ὁμογενοῦς Hermann, after Canter, for μονογενοῦς. "*Scitote vos optimae castissimaeque sororis communi genitore sanguine esse natos.*" Thus αἷμα ὁμογενὲς ἀδελφῆς is the blood of Zeus which produced Helen together with the Dioscuri. The connexion of the passage would be improved by reading κείνη τ᾽ ἴτω—, ἴστον τ᾽—, i. e. καὶ ὑμεῖς ἴστον.

καὶ χαίρεθ', Ἑλένης οὕνεκ' εὐγενεστάτης
γνώμης, ὃ πολλαῖς ἐν γυναιξὶν οὐκ ἔνι.
ΧΟ. πολλαὶ μορφαὶ τῶν δαιμονίων,
πολλὰ δ' ἀέλπτως κραίνουσι θεοί,
καὶ τὰ δοκηθέντ' οὐκ ἐτελέσθη, 1690
τῶν δ' ἀδοκήτων πόρον ηὗρε θεός.
τοιόνδ' ἀπέβη τόδε πρᾶγμα.

1686. καὶ χαίρεθ'. Cf. Hippol. 1437. As ὦ χαῖρε is used of greeting, so καὶ χαῖρε is the common conclusion of a farewell address.

1688. For these concluding anapaestics see Med. 1413, Andr. 1284, and the end of the Bacchae.

ΕΥΡΙΠΙΔΟΥ ΑΝΔΡΟΜΑΧΗ.

ΥΠΟΘΕΣΙΣ.

Νεοπτόλεμος ἐν Τροίᾳ γέρας λαβὼν Ἀνδρομάχην τὴν Ἕκτορος γυναῖκα, παῖδα ἔτεκεν ἐξ αὐτῆς τὸν Μολοττόν· ὕστερον δὲ ἐπέγημεν Ἑρμιόνην τὴν Μενελάου θυγατέρα. δίκας δὲ πρότερον ᾐτηκὼς τῆς Ἀχιλλέως ἀναιρέσεως τὸν ἐν Δελφοῖς Ἀπόλλωνα, πάλιν ἀπῆλθεν ἐπὶ τὸ χρηστήριον μετανοήσας, ἵνα τὸν θεὸν ἐξιλάσηται. ζηλοτύπως δ' ἔχουσα πρὸς τὴν Ἀνδρομάχην ἡ βασιλὶς ἐβουλεύετο κατ' αὐτῆς θάνατον, μεταπεμψαμένη τὸν Μενέλαον· ἡ δὲ τὸ παιδίον μὲν ὑπεξέθηκεν, αὐτὴ δὲ κατέφυγεν ἐπὶ τὸ ἱερὸν τῆς Θέτιδος. οἱ δὲ περὶ τὸν Μενέλαον καὶ τὸ παιδίον ἀνεῦρον, καὶ ἐκείνην ἀπατήσαντες ἀνήγειραν· καὶ σφάττειν μέλλοντες ἀμφοτέρους ἐκωλύθησαν, Πηλέως ἐπιφανέντος. Μενέλαος μὲν οὖν ἀπῆλθεν εἰς Σπάρτην· Ἑρμιόνη δὲ μετενόησεν, εὐλαβηθεῖσα τὴν παρουσίαν τοῦ Νεοπτολέμου. παραγενόμενος δὲ ὁ Ὀρέστης ταύτην μὲν ἀπήγαγε πείσας, Νεοπτολέμῳ δὲ ἐπεβούλευσεν· ὃν καὶ φονευθέντα παρῆσαν οἱ φέροντες. Πηλεῖ δὲ μέλλοντι τὸν νεκρὸν θρηνεῖν Θέτις ἐπιφανεῖσα τοῦτον μὲν ἐν Δελφοῖς ἐπέταξε θάψαι, τὴν δὲ Ἀνδρομάχην εἰς Μολοσσοὺς ἀποστεῖλαι μετὰ τοῦ παιδός, αὐτὸν δὲ ἀθανασίαν προσδέχεσθαι· τυχὼν δὲ ταύτης εἰς Μακάρων νήσους οἰκήσει.

Ἡ μὲν σκηνὴ τοῦ δράματος ἐν Φθίᾳ κεῖται· ὁ δὲ χορὸς συνέστηκεν ἐκ Φθιωτίδων γυναικῶν· προλογίζει δὲ Ἀνδρομάχη. τὸ δὲ δρᾶμα τῶν δευτέρων· ὁ πρόλογος σαφῶς καὶ εὐλόγως εἰρημένος. ἔστι δὲ καὶ τὰ ἐλεγεῖα τὰ ἐν τῷ θρήνῳ τῆς Ἀνδρομάχης ἐν τῷ δευτέρῳ μέρει· ῥῆσις Ἑρμιόνης τὸ βασιλικὸν ἐμφαίνουσα· καὶ ὁ πρὸς Ἀνδρομάχην λόγος καλῶς ἔχων· εὖ δὲ καὶ ὁ Πηλεύς, τὴν Ἀνδρομάχην ἀφελόμενος.

ANDROMACHE.

THE date of the *Andromache* has not been recorded, nor is there internal evidence which can enable us to assign it with anything like certainty. W. Dindorf, forming a conclusion from the plain and regular style of the metres, is inclined to place it as early as Ol. 87, or not much later than the *Medea* and the *Hippolytus*, while others have dated it as late as Ol. 92. Hermann, with much probability, considers it to belong to the end of Ol. 89, because in v. 733 there is an allusion to the enmity of Argos with Sparta, which may fairly be interpreted of the treaty ratified between Argos and Athens in Ol. 89. 4, (Thuc. v. 47,) B.C. 420. This is also the opinion of K. O. Müller, (Hist. Gr. Lit. p. 373,) who considers the severe language used against the Spartans to refer to their want of honour and sincerity in their transactions on that occasion. The object of the poet in writing it was clearly to set the customs and manners of the Spartans in an odious light before the eyes of his countrymen; for this he does not only by direct invective (v. 445—452), but by representing Hermione and Menelaus as cruel, false, and selfish characters.

The plot belongs to the same division of the Trojan affairs as the *Troades* and the *Hecuba*, viz. the fortunes of the captives after the destruction of their city. Neoptolemus, the son of Achilles, and grandson of the aged Peleus, who is still king of the Thessalian territory Pharsalia, conterminous to Phthiotis, has taken as his concubine, and held as a prize of honour, Andromache, the wife of Hector. By her he has had one son, Molossus. Afterwards having wedded Hermione as his lawful spouse, he transferred his affections to her; but on her proving childless, he returned to Andromache; and hence a jealousy arose on the part of Hermione, who conceived that secret drugs administered by her rival were the real cause of her barrenness. Neoptolemus, at the time of the action, is absent at Delphi, whither he has gone, anxious to propitiate Apollo for his former imprudence in demanding of him vengeance for the death of Achilles. Hermione, supported by Menelaus, seizes the occasion for oppressing Andromache. They obtain possession of the boy Molossus, who has been removed by his mother to conceal him from her enemies, and threaten to put him to death unless Andromache, who has taken sanctuary at the altar of Thetis, surrenders herself. Her maternal feelings prevail, and she gives herself up to death. Menelaus however basely deceives her, and declares that the life of the child must depend on his daughter's will. They are bound and led captive, but the old Peleus meets them, and chivalrously delivers them from the hands of Menelaus. Between the two kings, as before between Hermione and Andromache, a long altercation takes place, in which the pleadings on both sides of the case are given in the usual rhetorical style of Euripides on similar occasions; indeed, few of his plays are without this peculiar feature. Menelaus however has the worst of it both in argument and in action; he proves himself as cowardly as before he was base, and accordingly he departs with threats of what he will do when Neoptolemus shall have returned. Distracted at her failure, and stung with remorse, Hermione endeavours to commit suicide; but her intentions are changed by the sudden arrival of Orestes, who claims her as his long-promised bride, and explains that, having long ago conceived a hatred against Neoptolemus, he has laid a scheme for compassing his death by the hands of the exasperated populace at Delphi. Hermione makes no difficulty about transferring herself into the hands of her new husband. Peleus is informed of their departure, and of the imminent danger in which Neoptolemus is placed. He is about to dispatch a messenger to Delphi, when the news of his grandson's death arrives. Orestes has secretly instigated the Delphians against him as a thief in disguise intending to rob the temple of its treasures. He is attacked by the mob at the very altar, and after a brave and long-successful resistance, is slain. His body is finally brought on the stage with a Commos between Peleus and the chorus. Thetis then appears, and gives instructions that Neoptolemus shall be buried at Delphi, and there be worshipped as a hero; that Andromache shall marry Helenus, and Molossus, the sole surviving representative of the Aeacidae, shall be the founder of a long line of kings in Epirus. Peleus himself shall receive the reward of his cohabitation with a goddess, and shall be made an immortal among the gods of ocean.

This is by no means one of the best plays of Euripides, though it has had the good fortune to be preserved in many MSS., to be illustrated by Scholia, and to be one of the four printed in the valuable and accurate edition of Janus Lascaris in 1496. It was one of those plays which obtained the second prize, if this be the meaning of the words in the Greek Argument, τὸ δὲ δρᾶμα τῶν δευτέρων.

Hermann finds fault with what he calls its double action, viz. the chief interest centering first on Andromache, and then on Peleus; and he asserts that neither in the hero nor in the heroine is the course of events brought to a regular and natural conclusion. He maintains that the punishment of both Hermione and Menelaus ought to have appeared in the sequel; and complains that the death of Neoptolemus is a rather clumsy subterfuge to liberate Hermione for the claims of a new husband. "Ita tragoedia" (he writes[1]) " quam oportebat Menelai et Hermionae infortunio finiri, assuta parte aliena justam quidem magnitudinem adepta est, sed ita ut scelerati impuniti abirent, plecteretur autem is [Peleus], qui non solum ipse innocens erat, sed etiam innocentes liberaverat ab interitu." Be this as it may, (and it is very doubtful if such criticisms on ancient works of art are worthy of serious attention,) the play is by no means without its points of interest. The haughty pride of Hermione and the discreet humility of Andromache are well depicted; the speech of old Peleus against Menelaus is spirited and effective; the choral odes are short, but clearly expressed and tolerably pertinent to the action; and the account of the death of Neoptolemus, in the messenger's speech, is among the best specimens of the author's descriptive style.

The scene at v. 545 is remarkable, as Elmsley and Hermann have pointed out, for bringing four actors at once upon the stage; Andromache, Molossus, Peleus, and Menelaus. The introduction of children was a device rarely adopted; it is seen however in the *Alcestis*, as well as in the *Medea*; but when they are not mutes, as in the last play, it is Hermann's opinion that, though real boys were produced, (since the stature would otherwise have been unnatural,) the words were spoken for them by an actor behind a curtain; and thus the actor who, without being seen, spoke for Molossus, may immediately afterwards have personated Peleus.

The scene of the play is laid at Phthia in Thessaly, the dominion of Achilles. Here the aged Peleus had dwelt at the death of Achilles, Od. xi. 494,

εἰπὲ δέ μοι, Πηλῆος ἀμύμονος εἴ τι πέπυσσαι,
ἢ ἔτ᾽ ἔχει τιμὴν πολέσιν μετὰ Μυρμιδόνεσσιν,
ἦ μιν ἀτιμάζουσιν ἀν᾽ Ἑλλάδα τε Φθίην τε,
οὕνεκά μιν κατὰ γῆρας ἔχει χεῖράς τε πόδας τε.

In respect of time, this must have been ten or twelve years after the capture of Troy, since Menelaus is represented in the *Helena* as

---

[1] Praefat. p. xiv.

returning to Greece in the eighth year after the war (v. 776). In the *Troades* (v. 274), we find Andromache just allotted to Neoptolemus as a γέρας ἐξαίρετον, and that play follows next after the *Hecuba* in the historical order of events. In the *Orestes*, v. 1654, the marriage of Hermione with Orestes, and the death of Neoptolemus, are predicted by Apollo; so that it must be regarded as preceding the action of the *Andromache*.

The chorus consists of women of the country, whose affections appear to be enlisted in behalf of Andromache, though a γυνὴ βάρβαρος in their view.

ΤΑ ΤΟΥ ΔΡΑΜΑΤΟΣ ΠΡΟΣΩΠΑ.

ΑΝΔΡΟΜΑΧΗ.
ΘΕΡΑΠΑΙΝΑ.
ΧΟΡΟΣ.
ΕΡΜΙΟΝΗ.
ΜΕΝΕΛΑΟΣ.
ΜΟΛΟΣΣΟΣ.
ΠΗΛΕΥΣ.
ΤΡΟΦΟΣ.
ΟΡΕΣΤΗΣ.
ΑΓΓΕΛΟΣ.
ΘΕΤΙΣ.

ΕΥΡΙΠΙΔΟΥ ΑΝΔΡΟΜΑΧΗ.

ΑΝΔΡΟΜΑΧΗ.

Ἀσιάτιδος γῆς σχῆμα, Θηβαία πόλις,
ὅθεν ποθ' ἕδνων σὺν πολυχρύσῳ χλιδῇ
Πριάμου τύραννον ἑστίαν ἀφικόμην,
δάμαρ δοθεῖσα παιδοποιὸς Ἕκτορι,

1. In the prologue Andromache, formerly the wife of Hector, then the favourite concubine of Neoptolemus, the son of Achilles, (Troad. 274,) bewails the accumulated evils that have befallen her since the destruction of Troy. Besides the loss of her husband and her son Astyanax, (Troad. 720,) and her reluctant union, as a captive, with her present lord, she has now to endure the threats and insults of Hermione, the daughter of Menelaus, whom Neoptolemus has taken for his wedded wife, but who, being childless, accuses her of causing sterility by secret drugs. Her only son by Neoptolemus she has sent from home, in the absence of his father at Delphi. She herself has taken sanctuary at the shrine of Thetis; for Menelaus has arrived from Sparta, and is now co-operating with his daughter for her destruction.

Ibid. She addresses Thebes in Asia Minor, her birth-place, (Il. vi. 415,) not that she has anything to say in reference to it in what follows, beyond the above fact, but this is done, as in the beginning of the Alcestis and the Electra, by way of fixing the attention of the audience to the chief subject of the speaker's thoughts. Here the address to Thebes is the more remarkable, because it is not the scene of the play which is thus apostrophized.— For πόλις many copies give πόλι. Hermann defines the distinction to be this; —that the vocative *addresses*, the nominative *specifies*. So in Hel. 1399, ὦ καινὸς ἡμῖν πόσις means, 'O thou that hast appeared to me in the character of a new husband,' and in such phrases as ὦ φίλος, we are to understand ' O thou that standest in the light of a friend,' &c. This is plausible, though it does not so well apply to ὦ μῶρος, ὦ δύστηνος, and the like, which seem to have the true force of an exclamation, *me miserum!* &c., nor to such apostrophes as ὦ γάμος, ὦ γάμοι, *inf.* v. 1186. Whether therefore he is right in saying, that if πόλις be read, σχῆμα is the vocative, and conversely, if πόλι, it must be the nominative, does not seem certain. Whatever may be thought on this point, most certain it is that ἐστὶ is not here to be supplied.—σχῆμα, the ornament or glory of Asia. So ὦ σχήματ' οἴκων, Hec. 619. The exact force of the word can hardly be given in English. It implies anything which is presented to our eyes in its existing shape, either pleasing or the contrary.

4. παιδοποιὸς is by no means a mere epithet. It distinguishes the wife from the concubine, since the children of the former only were legitimate, and entitled to the name in a political point of view. For Hector's νόθοι see *inf.* 224. Schol.

230   ΕΥΡΙΠΙΔΟΥ

ζηλωτὸς ἔν γε τῷ πρὶν Ἀνδρομάχῃ χρόνῳ,   5
νῦν δ', εἴ τις ἄλλη, δυστυχεστάτη γυνή
[ἐμοῦ πέφυκεν ἢ γενήσεταί ποτε]·
ἥτις πόσιν μὲν Ἕκτορ' ἐξ Ἀχιλλέως
θανόντ' ἐσεῖδον, παῖδά θ' ὃν τίκτω πόσει
ῥιφθέντα πύργων Ἀστυάνακτ' ἀπ' ὀρθίων,   10
ἐπεὶ τὸ Τροίας εἷλον Ἕλληνες πέδον,
αὐτὴ δὲ δούλη, τῶν ἐλευθερωτάτων
οἴκων νομισθεῖσ', Ἑλλάδ' εἰσαφικόμην,
τῷ νησιώτῃ Νεοπτολέμῳ δορὸς γέρας
δοθεῖσα λείας Τρωικῆς ἐξαίρετον.   15
Φθίας δὲ τῆσδε καὶ πόλεως Φαρσαλίας

νομίμη, γνησία παιδοτρόφος· οἱ γὰρ σκότιοι παῖδες (see on Alcest. 990) ἐκρίπτονται.

7. The most probable account of this verse is, that it is the result of two ancient readings of the passage ; νῦν δ' οὔτις ἄλλη δυστυχεστέρα γυνὴ ἐμοῦ πέφυκεν κτλ., and νῦν δ', εἴ τις ἄλλη, δυστυχεστάτη γυνή. The common reading is νῦν δ' οὔτις ἄλλη δυστυχεστάτη κτλ., but several MSS. give εἴ τις for οὔτις. The edition of Lascaris (1496) has a reading which removes all difficulty, and which is adopted by Hermann, οὔτις —δυστυχεστέρα κτλ. Only, if this be genuine, it seems strange that no other MS. nor edition should support it. Examples of a text made up from two different readings (perhaps early revisions), precisely similar to the present instance, are Med. 777. Soph. Trach. 83—5. The latter passage stands thus :—

οὐκ εἶ ξυνέρξων, ἡνίκ' ἢ σεσώσμεθα
[ἢ πίπτομεν, σοῦ πατρὸς ἐξολωλότος]
κείνου βίου σώσαντος, ἢ οἰχόμεσθ' ἅμα;

8. πόσιν μέν. Answered by αὐτὴ δὲ below, παῖδα θ' &c. being intermediate.

10. ῥιφθέντα. For the death of the infant Astyanax, see Troad. 720 &c. The source of the story, on which the Cyclic poets probably enlarged, was, as Hermann points out, the prophecy of his mother in Il. xxiv. 735. Lascaris has ῥιφέντα, a form at least as rare as τυπείς, and apparently resting on much less authority. Cf. v. 1150.

14. That τῷ νησιώτῃ is said in contempt, or rather, in disparagement of the marriage, she herself being a queen and τῶν ἐλευθερωτάτων, it would be needless to remark, did not Pflugk think proper to deny it. See on Rhes. 701. Pyrrhus, otherwise called Neoptolemus, was born in the island Scyros. See Il. xix. 326, where Achilles, in grief for Patroclus, mentions his son as ὃς Σκύρῳ μοι ἔνι τρέφεται φίλος υἱός, and also Od. xi. 509. 15. Troad. 272, Ἀνδρομάχα τάλαινα, τίν' ἔχει τύχαν; ΤΑΛ. καὶ τήνδ' Ἀχιλλέως ἔλαβε παῖς ἐξαίρετον.

16. Φθίας. Achilles himself was from this part of Thessaly, otherwise called Achaea, whence Aeschylus addressed him as Φθιῶτ' Ἀχιλεῦ, Ar. Ran. 1264.— ξύγχορτα, 'neighbouring;' Aesch. Suppl. 5, δίαν χθόνα σύγχορτον Συρίᾳ. Eur. Frag. Antiop. 215. She means to describe her home as in a solitary spot on the confines of Phthia ; for if Peleus retained the sovereignty over Pharsalus, his grandson would be likely to retire to a sufficient distance during his life-time. The scene of the play therefore is properly near rather than at Phthia ; though she must point to it as represented not far off, on account of the demonstrative τῆσδε. It follows that the Thetideum was nearer to Phthia than to Pharsalus. There is however some uncertainty as to whether Θετίδειον was merely another name for the city Phthia, or a τέμενος sacred to Thetis, or lastly, a district or suburb so called. Hermann quotes both Strabo, p. 431, who says the Thetideum was close to old and new Pharsalus, and the Schol. on Pind. Nem. iv. 81, who mentioning this passage, calls it ἱερὸν, and places it at Phthia ; and also states from Pherecydes that Peleus lived both

ξύγχορτα ναίω πεδί', ἵν' ἡ θαλασσία
Πηλεῖ ξυνῴκει χωρὶς ἀνθρώπων Θέτις
φεύγουσ' ὅμιλον· Θεσσαλὸς δέ νιν λεὼς
Θετίδειον αὐδᾷ θεᾶς χάριν νυμφευμάτων.   20
ἔνθ' οἶκον ἔσχε τόνδε παῖς Ἀχιλλέως,
Πηλέα δ' ἀνάσσειν γῆς ἐᾷ Φαρσαλίας,
ζῶντος γέροντος σκῆπτρον οὐ θέλων λαβεῖν.
κἀγὼ δόμοις τοῖσδ' ἄρσεν' ἐντίκτω κόρον
πλαθεῖσ' Ἀχιλλέως παιδί, δεσπότῃ τ' ἐμῷ.   25
καὶ πρὶν μὲν ἐν κακοῖσι κειμένην ὅμως
ἐλπίς μ' ἀεὶ προσῆγε σωθέντος τέκνου
ἀλκήν τιν' εὑρεῖν κἀπικούρησιν κακῶν·
ἐπεὶ δὲ τὴν Λάκαιναν Ἑρμιόνην γαμεῖ
τοὐμὸν παρώσας δεσπότης δοῦλον λέχος,   30
κακοῖς πρὸς αὐτῆς σχετλίοις ἐλαύνομαι·
λέγει γὰρ ὥς νιν φαρμάκοις κεκρυμμένοις
τίθημ' ἄπαιδα καὶ πόσει μισουμένην,
αὐτὴ δὲ ναίειν οἶκον ἀντ' αὐτῆς θέλω
τόνδ', ἐκβαλοῦσα λέκτρα τἀκείνης βίᾳ·   35

ἐν Φαρσάλῳ καὶ ἐν Θετιδείῳ, meaning, apparently, by the latter the city of Phthia. That a temple of Thetis was on the spot appears from v. 43, Θέτιδος εἰς ἀνάκτορον θάσσω τόδ' ἐλθοῦσ'. The scholiast on the present verse says the Thetideum was between Pharsalus and Phthia.

24. As many good copies give τίκτω, and Euripides makes Andromache to have borne only one son to Neoptolemus, (viz. Molossus,) whereas others specify three, Lenting rather ingeniously reads ἕνα τίκτω κόρον. However, there are two objections to this; first, it is not consistent with the regular metre of this play; secondly, it implies, that what Euripides meant, was ἕνα μὲν ἄρσενα, ἄλλην δὲ θήλειαν παῖδα. Compare Hel. 9, Θεοκλύμενον μὲν ἄρσεν',—εὐγενῆ τε παρθένον Εἰδώ.—For δεσπότῃ τ' Hermann, after Brunck, gives δεσπότῃ γ', Dindorf, after Elmsley, δεσπότῃ δ'. Hermann's argument is, (if a quibble can be called an argument,) that 'the son of Achilles and my master' is illogical, though 'Neoptolemus and my master' would be logical, because " quae conjun-guntur, similia esse oportet." The question really is simply this; whether one and the same person, described under two attributes, did not appear to the Greek mind in much the same light as two distinct persons; for if it did, then τε is unquestionably right. See the notes on Agam. 1563, and Eur. Heracl. 827. Med. 970, where there is a similar verse, πατρὸς νέαν γυναῖκα, δεσπότιν τ' ἐμήν.

25. πλαθεῖσα, united in marriage; a sort of euphemism, for which this verb is often used, as Trach. 17, πρὶν τῆσδε κοίτης ἐμπελασθῆναί ποτε.

27. προσῆγε, kept leading me on, as it were, up to the very point of finding, πρὸς αὐτὸ τὸ εὑρεῖν. There seems little difficulty in the word, and certainly no occasion to alter it. Compare the use of ἄγειν in Electr. 1301. W. Dindorf gives προῆγε after Matthiae, comparing Hippol. 496. For ἐλπὶς εὑρεῖν = εὑρήσειν, see v. 311. Alcest. 146, ἐλπὶς μὲν οὐκέτ' ἐστὶ σώσασθαι βίον;

29. ἐπεὶ—γαμεῖ, ever since he has married her. For κακοῖς ἐλαύνειν see Alcest. 676.

ἀγὼ τὸ πρῶτον οὐχ ἑκοῦσ' ἐδεξάμην,
νῦν δ' ἐκλέλοιπα· Ζεὺς τάδ' εἰδείη μέγας,
ὡς οὐχ ἑκοῦσα τῷδ' ἐκοινώθην λέχει.
ἀλλ' οὔ σφε πείθω, βούλεται δέ με κτανεῖν,
πατήρ τε θυγατρὶ Μενέλεως συνδρᾷ τάδε.   40
καὶ νῦν κατ' οἴκους ἔστ', ἀπὸ Σπάρτης μολὼν
ἐπ' αὐτὸ τοῦτο· δειματουμένη δ' ἐγὼ
δόμων πάροικον Θέτιδος εἰς ἀνάκτορον
θάσσω τόδ' ἐλθοῦσ', ἤν με κωλύσῃ θανεῖν.
Πηλεύς τε γάρ νιν ἔκγονοί τε Πηλέως   45
σέβουσιν, ἑρμήνευμα Νηρῇδος γάμων.
ὃς δ' ἔστι παῖς μοι μόνος, ὑπεκπέμπω λάθρα
ἄλλους ἐς οἴκους, μὴ θάνῃ φοβουμένη.
ὁ γὰρ φυτεύσας αὐτὸν οὔτ' ἐμοὶ πάρα
προσωφελῆσαι παιδί τ' οὐδέν ἐστ', ἀπὼν   50
Δελφῶν κατ' αἶαν, ἔνθα Λοξίᾳ δίκην
δίδωσι μανίας, ἥν ποτ' ἐς Πυθὼ μολὼν
ᾔτησε Φοῖβον πατρὸς οὗ 'κτίνειν δίκην,

37. ἐκλέλοιπα. The assertion of Andromache, that she no longer cohabits with Neoptolemus, is an essential part of the story, since it at once shifts the blame wholly upon Hermione, who could not thus have been wronged by her rival.

46. ἑρμήνευμα, an evidence, a witness to the marriage of Peleus with Thetis. Schol. ὑπόμνησιν, σημεῖον, τεκμήριον. As the family of Peleus, viz. her lord and master Neoptolemus, pays religious reverence to this shrine, she expects that the goddess in return will afford her a safe refuge.

50. οὐδέν ἐστι, 'is as good as dead.'

52—3. This is a very obscure passage. What the poet means to say is clear enough; that Neoptolemus has gone to Delphi to ask pardon of the god for his former presumption, in demanding of him (Apollo) satisfaction for the death of his father Achilles. See *inf.* 1008. Hermann, followed by W. Dindorf, gives ὅς ποτ', which is just that sort of emendation that one may fairly distrust, because it makes all clear and easy, while it suggests no reason why grammarians should have altered it under such circumstances. Pflugk says the construction is, δίκην δίδωσι τῆς δίκης, ἥν ποτε ᾔτησε Φοῖβον πατρὸς οὗ ἐκτίνειν, and that the clause ἥν ποτε—δίκην is an *epexegesis* of μανίας. But what a strange phrase is δίκην διδόναι δίκης! Rather, the poet seems to have intended to say, ἥν (μανίαν) ἔχων, μολὼν ἐς Πυθὼ, ᾔτησε, κτλ., or, ἥν (μανίαν) ἔδειξε, μολὼν — αἰτήσας. The Scholiast explains, ἀπολογίαν δίδωσι τῆς τόλμης, ἥν ἐτόλμησε δίκας ὑπὲρ Ἀχιλλέως αἰτεῖν. An easier correction is Reiske's ᾗ for ἥν, adopted by Musgrave.—οὗ 'κτίνειν is Hermann's correction for οὗ τίνει or κτείνει, one MS. giving οὗ 'κτίνει. The confusion of these words is so common, that there can be little room for doubt that ἐκτίνειν is right. Matthiae places a colon at πατρὸς, and reads οὗ 'κτίνει, ' of which thing he is now offering satisfaction, if perchance, by begging off the consequences of his former errors, he may render the god propitious to himself for the future.' For the middle sense of παρασχέσθαι see Hippol. 619. The use of ἐξαιτεῖσθαι for παραιτεῖσθαι is remarkable. In Oed. Col. 1327, which Pflugk compares, it seems to have the ordinary sense of 'requesting,' but in Med. 971, ἱκετεύετ', ἐξαιτεῖσθε μὴ φεύγειν χθόνα, it may be taken for παραιτεῖσθε.

ΑΝΔΡΟΜΑΧΗ.

εἴ πως τὰ πρόσθε σφάλματ᾽ ἐξαιτούμενος
θεὸν παράσχοιτ᾽ ἐς τὸ λοιπὸν εὐμενῆ. 55

ΘΕΡΑΠΑΙΝΑ.

δέσποιν᾽, ἐγώ τοι τοὔνομ᾽ οὐ φεύγω τόδε
καλεῖν σ᾽, ἐπείπερ καὶ κατ᾽ οἶκον ἠξίουν
τὸν σόν, τὸ Τροίας ἡνίκ᾽ ᾠκοῦμεν πέδον·
εὔνους δὲ καὶ σοὶ ζῶντί τ᾽ ἦν τῷ σῷ πόσει,
καὶ νῦν φέρουσά σοι νέους ἥκω λόγους, 60
φόβῳ μέν, εἴ τις δεσποτῶν αἰσθήσεται,
οἴκτῳ δὲ τῷ σῷ· δεινὰ γὰρ βουλεύεται
Μενέλαος εἰς σὲ παῖς θ᾽, ἅ σοι φυλακτέα.

ΑΝ. ὦ φιλτάτη σύνδουλε, σύνδουλος γὰρ εἶ
τῇ πρόσθ᾽ ἀνάσσῃ τῇδε, νῦν δὲ δυστυχεῖ, 65
τί δρῶσι; ποίας μηχανὰς πλέκουσιν αὖ,
κτεῖναι θέλοντες τὴν παναθλίαν ἐμέ;

ΘΕΡ. τὸν παῖδά σου μέλλουσιν, ὦ δύστηνε σύ,
κτείνειν, ὃν ἔξω δωμάτων ὑπεξέθου.

ΑΝ. οἴμοι· πέπυσται τὸν ἐμὸν ἔκθετον γόνον; 70
πόθεν ποτ᾽; ὦ δύστηνος, ὡς ἀπωλόμην.

ΘΕΡ. οὐκ οἶδ᾽, ἐκείνων δ᾽ ᾐσθόμην ἐγὼ τάδε·
φροῦδος δ᾽ ἐπ᾽ αὐτὸν Μενέλεως δόμων ἄπο.

ΑΝ. ἀπωλόμην ἄρ᾽· ὦ τέκνον, κτενοῦσί σε
δισσοὶ λαβόντες γῦπες. ὁ δὲ κεκλημένος 75

---

56. A servant and fellow-captive enters to inform Andromache of a new alarm. Menelaus has just left the house, intending to get possession of her son Molossus in order to slay him. With a delicate consideration, and mindful of the time when she used to serve Hector and Andromache in Troy, she persists in still calling her *mistress*, though slavery reduces all to an equality. This is one of the many passages where Euripides shows his amiable sympathy for this unfortunate class.

62. οἴκτῳ τῷ σῷ, my feeling of compassion for you. Compare ὁ οἶκτος ὁ σὸς, Ion 1276. On φόβος εἰ, where we should rather expect μή, or μὴ οὐ, see Heracl. 791. Med. 184.

68. τὸν παῖδά σου. ''Tis not you, as you suppose, but your son whom they intend to kill.'

70. πέπυσται, viz. Hermione; for the servant adds Menelaus by name immediately afterwards. The correction of L. Dindorf, which W. Dindorf admits into the text, and Pflugk calls "elegans et ingeniosa," πέπυσθε — πόθεν ποτ᾽; — is rightly rejected by Hermann. The difficulties raised by L. Dindorf are imaginary. Andromache asks, πέπυσται Ἑρμιόνη τὸν ἐμὸν γόνον ἔκθετον ὄντα; πόθεν; 'who could have told her this?' To which the servant replies, 'I don't know who told her; but I know that they (she and her father) *have* learnt the secret, for I heard myself (ἐγώ) the matter from them.'

75. ὁ κεκλημένος πατήρ. This is said with something of reproach and bitterness, because she thinks her husband ought to

πατὴρ ἔτ' ἐν Δελφοῖσι τυγχάνει μένων.
ΘΕΡ. δοκῶ γὰρ οὐκ ἂν ὧδέ σ' ἂν πράσσειν κακῶς,
κείνου παρόντος· νῦν δ' ἔρημος εἶ φίλων.
ΑΝ. οὐδ' ἀμφὶ Πηλέως ἦλθεν, ὡς ἤξοι, φάτις ;
ΘΕΡ. γέρων ἐκεῖνος ὥστε σ' ὠφελεῖν παρών. 80
ΑΝ. καὶ μὴν ἔπεμψ' ἐπ' αὐτὸν οὐχ ἅπαξ μόνον.
ΘΕΡ. μῶν οὖν δοκεῖς σοῦ φροντίσαι τιν' ἀγγέλων ;
ΑΝ. πόθεν ; θέλεις οὖν ἄγγελος σύ μοι μολεῖν ;
ΘΕΡ. τί δῆτα φήσω χρόνιος οὖσ' ἐκ δωμάτων ;
ΑΝ. πολλὰς ἂν εὕροις μηχανάς· γυνὴ γὰρ εἶ. 85
ΘΕΡ. κίνδυνος· Ἑρμιόνη γὰρ οὐ σμικρὰ φύλαξ.
ΑΝ. ὁρᾷς ; ἀπαυδᾷς ἐν κακοῖς φίλοισι σοῖς.
ΘΕΡ. οὐ δῆτα· μηδὲν τοῦτ' ὀνειδίσῃς ἐμοί.
ἀλλ' εἶμ', ἐπεί τοι κοὺ περίβλεπτος βίος
δούλης γυναικός, ἤν τι καὶ πάθω κακόν. 90
ΑΝ. χώρει νυν· ἡμεῖς δ', οἷσπερ ἐγκείμεσθ' ἀεὶ

have returned before this to protect his family.

77. δοκῶ γάρ. 'Why, truly, I think you would not be faring as badly as you now are, were he present.' If οὐδ' for οὐκ be the true reading, (one MS. having δοκῶ γὰρ οὐδέν, and the double ἂν gives some strength to the suspicion,) the meaning would be very different, 'I think that, not even as matters are, you would be badly off, if' &c. The οὐ is used, by a not uncommon idiom, where μὴ might seem more regular, because the idea in the speaker's mind is, οἶμαι, οὐκ ἂν πράσσοις &c. See on Hel. 835.

80. γέρων. Matthiae and Pflugk add γ', with four MSS. Hermann's remark is a shrewd one, that the poet would rather have said γέρων ἐκεῖνός γ'.—παρών means, ' even if he were present.'

82. μῶν οὖ, the reading of Aldus and others, is clearly wrong in this place, though a legitimate combination elsewhere. See Aesch. Suppl. 411. Med. 733. The addition of οὖν to a particle already including that element (μῶν = μὴ οὖν, the Latin num,) is to be noticed. So Aesch. Cho. 169, μῶν οὖν Ὀρέστου κρύβδα δῶρον ἦν τόδε ;

83. σύ μοι μολεῖν is better than μολεῖν σύ μοι, Lascaris having the former order, Aldus the latter. The σὺ is of course emphatic, though its accent happens to be enclitic. The sense is, 'If others slight my requests, will you then go as a messenger?'

84. χρόνιος οὖσα. What excuse shall I give to Menelaus and Hermione, for so long an absence from home as this message will require ?

87. ἀπαυδᾷς φίλοις, you renounce, or disown your friends. See on Alcest. 487. Pflugk compares οὐκ ἀπειρηκὼς φίλοις, Med. 458.—ἐν κακοῖς, scil. οὖσιν, or ἐπεὶ πάρεστιν αὐτοῖς κακά.

88. μηδέν. Used for μὴ, as inf. 463. Aesch. Ag. 1438. Med. 153. The τοῦτο is emphatic, as well as the ἐμοί, ' that is not a fault with which I can be charged,' who have already avowed my firm attachment, v. 59.

89. On the particles ἐπεί τοι καὶ see Med. 677. Heracl. 507. 744. — περίβλεπτος, worth regarding, worth casting the eye around to look after it, &c. 'If I should suffer for it,' she says, 'I am but a slave, and of no value,'—δούλης θανούσης, εὐμαροῦς χειρώματος, as Aeschylus touchingly says, Agam. 1297. To the present passage Photius perhaps alludes ; —περίβλεπτος, ἔξοχος, μέγιστος. Generally it has the notion of honour or respect being paid, as περιβλέπεσθαι τίμιον, &c. Herc. 508. Iph. A. 429. Compare ἀπόβλεπτος, Hec. 355. Here the Schol. explains it by ἐπίσημος, ἔνδοξος.

θρήνοισι καὶ γόοισι καὶ δακρύμασιν,
πρὸς αἰθέρ' ἐκτενοῦμεν· ἐμπέφυκε γὰρ
γυναιξὶ τέρψις τῶν παρεστώτων κακῶν
ἀνὰ στόμ' ἀεὶ καὶ διὰ γλώσσης ἔχειν.   95
πάρεστι δ' οὐχ ἕν, ἀλλὰ πολλά μοι στένειν,
πόλιν πατρῷαν, τὸν θανόντα θ' Ἕκτορα,
στερρόν τε τὸν ἐμὸν δαίμον', ᾧ ξυνεζύγην,
δούλειον ἦμαρ εἰσπεσοῦσ' ἀναξίως.
χρὴ δ' οὔποτ' εἰπεῖν οὐδέν' ὄλβιον βροτῶν,   100
πρὶν ἂν θανόντος τὴν τελευταίαν ἴδῃς
ὅπως περάσας ἡμέραν ἥξει κάτω.

Ἰλίῳ αἰπεινᾷ Πάρις οὐ γάμον, ἀλλά τιν' ἄταν
ἀγάγετ' εὐναίαν ἐς θαλάμους Ἑλέναν.

93. πρὸς αἰθέρα. See Electr. 59. Med. 57.—γυναιξὶ κτλ. This natural softness (as the Greeks considered it) on the part of women is alluded to in Suppl. 83, τὸ γὰρ θανόντων τέκνων ἐπίπονόν τι κατὰ γυναῖκας ἐς γόους πέφυκε πάθος. There is a slight but obvious attraction of the genitive, 'pleasure in present evils, namely, to bewail them,' for 'pleasure in bewailing' &c. Compare ἡδονὰς τέκνων, Troad. 371, and see Frag. 578, ἀλλ' ἔστι γὰρ δὴ κἀν κακοῖσιν ἡδονὴ θνητοῖς ὀδυρμοὶ δακρύων τ' ἐπιρροαί.

98. στερρὸν τὸν ἐμὸν is a sort of hyperbaton, though strictly contrary to the laws of the Greek article, for τὸν ἐμὸν στερρὸν δαίμονα. See on μακαρίας τῆς σῆς χερὸς, Electr. 1006. At the same time, it is possible to regard στερρὸν as the predicate; στένειν τὸν ἐμὸν δαίμονα ὡς στερρὸν ὄντα.

100. χρὴ—οὔποτε. See on Hippol. 507, χρῆν μὲν οὔ σ' ἁμαρτάνειν. Ion 1314. Inf. 214. The sentiment is the same as in Troad. 510. Heracl. 866. Here again θανόντος depends by attraction on ἡμέραν, for ὅπως περάσας—ὁ θανὼν ἥξει κάτω, or it may be the genitive absolute, αὐτοῦ being supplied.

103. The insertion of an elegiac threnos in the speech of one of the actors is unique in Attic tragedy. It has been remarked on Suppl. 808, that choral hexameters are usually composed of pure dactyls; and it is evident that here, and likewise in the choral ode following, the same law has been applied. Indeed, as far as convenient, it has also been extended to the pentameters. In Tro. 590 seqq., we have not fewer than nine dactylic hexameters consecutively, with only one exceptional spondaic foot. Hence for αἰπεινᾷ it is by no means impossible that αἰπεινᾷ was, if not written, at least pronounced; compare the not unfrequent use of Ἀργεῖος for Ἀργεῖος. In v. 105, one can hardly hesitate to restore Τροΐα. See Rhes. 231. 262. So in Suppl. 274, οὓς ὑπὸ τείχεσι Καδμείοισιν ἀπώλεσα κούρους is answered antistrophically by γούνασιν ὧδε πίτνω, τέκνοις τάφον ἐξανύσασθαι. It is probable that in the one verse Καδμεΐοισιν, in the other τέκεσιν should be restored; though the occurrence of a spondee in the same foot in both is singular. (Compare Phoen. 787—9 with 804—6.) In v. 273 we have τέκνων τεθνεώτων κόμισαι δέμας, ὦ μελέα 'γώ, corresponding, (or rather not corresponding,) to βλέψον ἐμῶν βλεφάρων ἔπι δάκρυον, ἃ περὶ σοῖσι. Read τεθνηότων (τεθνεότων) τεκέων κτλ., on the analogy of τεθνᾶναι for τεθνηκέναι, Agam. 522. Here however there remains the spondee αὐτὰ δ' in v. 109. In Agam. 121, the metre of the strophic verse would be accurately restored by reading κεδνὸς ὅτε (vulg. δὲ) στρατόμαντις ἰδὼν δύο λήμασι δισσοὺς, κτλ. The form Ἴλιος for the more common Ἴλιον is to be noticed at the beginning of the elegy.

ἃς ἕνεκ', ὦ Τροία, δορὶ καὶ πυρὶ δηιάλωτον   105
εἷλέ σ' ὁ χιλιόναυς Ἑλλάδος ὠκὺς Ἄρης,
καὶ τὸν ἐμὸν μελέας πόσιν Ἕκτορα, τὸν περὶ τείχη
εἵλκυσε διφρεύων παῖς ἁλίας Θέτιδος·
αὐτὰ δ' ἐκ θαλάμων ἀγόμαν ἐπὶ θῖνα θαλάσσας,
δουλοσύναν στυγερὰν ἀμφιβαλοῦσα κάρᾳ.   110
πολλὰ δὲ δάκρυά μοι κατέβα χροὸς, ἁνίκ' ἔλειπον
ἄστυ τε καὶ θαλάμους καὶ πόσιν ἐν κονίαις·
ὤμοι ἐγὼ μελέα, τί μ' ἐχρῆν ἔτι φέγγος ὁρᾶσθαι,
Ἑρμιόνας δούλαν; ἃς ὕπο τειρομένα
πρὸς τόδ' ἄγαλμα θεᾶς ἱκέτις περὶ χεῖρε βαλοῦσα
τάκομαι ὡς πετρίνα πιδακόεσσα λιβάς.   116

ΧΟΡΟΣ.

ὦ γύναι, ἃ Θέτιδος δάπεδον καὶ ἀνάκτορα θάσ-
 σεις   στρ. α΄.
δαρὸν, οὐδὲ λείπεις,

106. "Mireris decenne bellum ὠκὺν Ἄρη dici. Videtur Euripides acrem dicere voluisse." *Herm.*
107. περὶ τείχη. Schol. παρ' ἱστορίαν· περὶ τὸ τεῖχος ἐδιώχθη ὑπὸ Ἀχιλλέως ὁ Ἕκτωρ· νεκρὸς γὰρ παρὰ τὸ Πατρόκλου σῆμα τρίτον ἐσύρη.
110. κάρᾳ L. Dindorf. for κάρα. The accusative, which Pflugk defends, would have been unexceptionable with ἀμφιβεβλημένη, as Hermann observes; but the Greeks do not appear to say ἀμφιβαλεῖν τινά τι. The idea in the speaker's mind seems to be that of putting on the yoke of slavery, ζυγῶν θιγεῖν, Agam. 1008.
112. Hermann and W. Dindorf follow Bothe in placing a comma after καὶ πόσιν, so that δάκρυα κατέβα χροὸς ἐν κονίαις is to be construed together. Nothing can be weaker than this. It is Hermann's own remark, in one of his notes on another play, that a sentence is always badly constructed, when, after all that is necessary to the sense has been said, and the mind rests satisfied, the reader unexpectedly finds afterwards that something was yet to have been added. This remark exactly applies to the present case. We have done with the tears down her cheeks, and have got to the cause of them, which was, that she had left home, house, and husband in the dust. The last, it is objected, was not left in the dust, but was given up to Priam to be buried. An absurd piece of hypercriticism. Even conceding, which we need not do, that ἐν κονίαις does not strictly apply to the dead Hector, it is quite enough that she can be said λιπεῖν ἄστυ ἐν κονίαις, i. e. κατασκαφῇ ἀϊστωθέν.
114. τειρομένα, 'hard-pressed.' Aesch. Suppl. 77, ἔστι δὲ κἀκ πολέμου τειρομένοις βωμὸς ἀρᾶς φυγάσιν ῥῦμα.—πρὸς τόδ' ἄγαλμα, supply from the context καταφεύγουσα.
116. τάκομαι κτλ. Niobe is clearly meant. See Antig. 823. The Schol. however does not notice the allusion.
117. The chorus, composed of native women, inhabitants of Phthia, but either slaves or subjects of Neoptolemus, (whom they call δεσπότης v. 142,) approach Andromache, seated as she is at the image of Thetis, to console and take counsel with her on her present distresses. They advise her not to contend with those more powerful than herself, a captive with her conquerors; but to leave the altar and submit to the will of her superiors. She should remember that a stranger on a foreign land is friendless. With further expressions of sympathy they retire, unsuccessful in inducing her to leave the sanctuary.

Φθιὰς ὅμως ἔμολον ποτὶ σὰν Ἀσιήτιδα γένναν,
εἴ τί σοι δυναίμαν   120
ἄκος τῶν δυσλύτων πόνων τεμεῖν,
οἳ σὲ καὶ Ἑρμιόναν ἔριδι στυγερᾷ συνέκλῃσαν
τλάμον' ἀμφὶ λέκτρων
διδύμων ἐπίκοινον ἐοῦσαν
ἀμφὶ παῖδ' Ἀχιλλέως·   125
γνῶθι τύχαν, λόγισαι τὸ παρὸν κακὸν, εἰς ὅπερ
    ἥκεις.   ἀντ. α'.
δεσπόταις ἁμιλλᾷ,
Ἰλιὰς οὖσα κόρα Λακεδαίμονος ἐκγενέταισι.
λεῖπε δεξίμηλον
δόμον τᾶς ποντίας θεοῦ. τί σοι   130
καιρὸς ἀτυζομένᾳ δέμας αἰκέλιον καταλείβειν
δεσποτῶν ἀνάγκαις ;
τὸ κρατοῦν δέ σ' ἔπεισι· τί μόχθον
οὐδὲν οὖσα μοχθεῖς ;
ἀλλ' ἴθι λεῖπε θεᾶς Νηρηΐδος ἀγλαὸν ἕδραν,   135
γνῶθι δ' οὖσ' ἐπὶ ξένας   [στρ. β'.
δμωῒς, ἐπ' ἀλλοτρίας πόλεος,
ἔνθ' οὐ φίλων τιν' εἰσορᾷς

119. Ἀσιήτιδα Herm. Pflugk, Bothe, with Aldus and most MSS. Ἀσιάτιδα Dindorf after Lascaris. But Ἀσιᾶτις is Attic rather than Doric ; see v. 1. Hence in a choral verse the epic form is to be preferred.— ποτὶ σὰν γένναν, πρὸς σὲ τὴν Ἀσιᾶτιν γένος.— ὅμως, i. e. καίπερ Ἑλληνὶς πρὸς βάρβαρον, which they appear to think was an act of condescension.

123. τλάμον'. Aldus has τλᾶμον, Lascaris τλάμων. Pflugk and others adopt the vocative. Hermann thinks the following clause exegetical of τλάμονα, miseram, quam communicare torum cum Hermiona oporteat. The construction is rather singular. The exact sense appears to be, 'they have involved you in an odious quarrel about a double bed, having to share it with another, in respect of the son of Achilles.' The ἐπὶ in composition implies interchange and reciprocity.

130. τί σοι καιρὸς κτλ. 'In what respect is it fitting for you, giving way to your grief, to disfigure your form by wasting it away in tears, through the compulsory service of a master?'—ἀνάγκαις, the causal dative, διὰ τὴν δουλείαν,— or perhaps 'through the cruel conduct of a mistress,' Hermione.— αἰκέλιον for ἀείκελιον Gaisford and Elmsley. Compare αἰκὲς πῆμα in Prom. 480. Inf. 828, σῶμα σὸν καταικιεῖ;

133. ἔπεισι has been restored by Hermann and Dindorf from the Schol., who explains ἀντὶ τοῦ καταλήψεται τὸ κράτος, and mentions as another reading, what is found in all the copies, δέ σε πείσει. This however is against the metre. Cf. Prom. 1036, οἷός σε χειμὼν καὶ κακῶν τρικυμία ἔπεισ' ἄφυκτος. The meaning is, 'the party in authority will come upon you,' will punish you. A few copies have τὸ κράτος, but the article would then be out of place.

137. πόλεος Herm. Dind. Bothe, for πόλεως, on account of the metre. For this use of ἐπὶ see Med. 134.

σῶν, ὦ δυστυχεστάτα,
ὦ παντάλαινα νύμφα.
οἰκτροτάτα γὰρ ἔμοιγ' ἔμολες, γύναι Ἰλιάς, οἴκους·
δεσποτῶν δ' ἐμῶν φόβῳ [ἀντ. β'.
ἡσυχίαν ἄγομεν, τὸ δὲ σὸν
οἴκτῳ φέρουσα τυγχάνω,
μὴ παῖς τᾶς Διὸς κόρας
σοί μ' εὖ φρονοῦσαν εὔρῃ.

ΕΡΜΙΟΝΗ.

κόσμον μὲν ἀμφὶ κρατὶ χρυσέας χλιδῆς
στολμόν τε χρωτὸς τόνδε ποικίλων πέπλων,
οὐ τῶν Ἀχιλλέως οὐδὲ Πηλέως ἄπο
δόμων ἀπαρχὰς δεῦρ' ἔχουσ' ἀφικόμην,
ἀλλ' ἐκ Λακαίνης Σπαρτιάτιδος χθονὸς

139. τῶν σῶν Hermann, and in the antistrophe (145) μὴ παῖς ἃ τᾶς Διὸς κόρας. Both are undoubtedly improvements, especially in a metrical point of view.
143. ἀσυχίαν Dindorf against all the copies. The clause τὸ δὲ σὸν—τυγχάνω is interposed, the construction being φόβῳ μὴ—εὔρῃ. 'I say nothing, though I pity your case, for fear lest the daughter of Helen should discover that I am your friend.'
146. εὔρῃ is Hermann's conjecture for ἴδῃ. Musgrave proposed εἰδῇ, which Pflugk and Dindorf adopt. This, as Hermann truly observes, can only have the subjunctive sense of οἶδα, for μὴ μάθῃ, μὴ γιγνώσκῃ. The Schol. has αἴσθηται, which suits εὔρῃ, the natural word in such a sentence, as well as ἴδῃ or εἰδῇ.
147. Enter *Hermione*, magnificently apparelled. She first addresses a few words to the chorus, intimating that her wealth and her position justify her in freely declaring her sentiments, and then turns to Andromache, and in an impassioned address, not without threats, charges her with having alienated the affections of her husband by detestable arts. She warns her, that in Hellas her eastern pride must give way; a slave she is, and to slavish offices she shall be kept. She even taunts her with flagrant indecency in cohabiting with her husband's murderer. The custom of bigamy she deprecates as unsuited to Hellas, however much it may be approved by eastern people.—The speech begins rather abruptly with the particle μέν. Compare the address of Theseus to the herald in Suppl. 381, τέχνην μὲν ἀεὶ τήνδ' ἔχων ὑπηρετεῖς πόλει τε κἀμοί, where no antithetical clause is expressed or even implied. So Soph. Electr. 516, ἀνειμένη μὲν, ὡς ἔοικας, αὖ στρέφει. No notice of Hermione's approach had been given, and she herself, though she talks of *replying* to the chorus in v. 154, had not been addressed by them. What she means to say, in her proud disdain, is this:—'I owe nothing, I am in no way beholden or indebted to, but on the contrary, I have conferred obligations on, you and yours; and therefore, if I speak out boldly, I shall not be thought ungrateful or uncourteous.' The meaning is, δεῦρ' ἀφικόμην ἔχουσα τόνδε κόσμον, οὐκ ἔλαβον ἀπαρχὰς παρὰ Πηλέως, &c. "Vultus intuebatur Hermione et ora chori, dum taceret, ipso tamen adventu et praesentia sua exprobrare visi nimiam crudelitatem." *Pflugk.*
150. ἀπαρχὰς is here improperly or metaphorically used of the best gifts and offerings which the house of Peleus could present to the bride on the occasion of her marriage.

ΑΝΔΡΟΜΑΧΗ. 239

Μενέλαος ἡμῖν ταῦτα δωρεῖται πατὴρ
πολλοῖς σὺν ἕδνοις, ὥστ' ἐλευθεροστομεῖν.
ὑμᾶς μὲν οὖν τοῖσδ' ἀνταμείβομαι λόγοις·
σὺ δ' οὖσα δούλη καὶ δορίκτητος γυνὴ   155
δόμους κατασχεῖν ἐκβαλοῦσ' ἡμᾶς θέλεις
τούσδε, στυγοῦμαι δ' ἀνδρὶ φαρμάκοισι σοῖς,
νηδὺς δ' ἀκύμων διὰ σέ μοι διόλλυται·
δεινὴ γὰρ Ἠπειρῶτις ἐς τὰ τοιάδε
ψυχὴ γυναικῶν· ὧν ἐπισχήσω σ' ἐγώ,   160
κοὐδέν σ' ὀνήσει δῶμα Νηρῇδος τόδε,
οὐ βωμὸς οὐδὲ ναὸς, ἀλλὰ κατθανεῖ.
ἢν δ' οὖν βροτῶν τίς σ' ἢ θεῶν σῶσαι θέλῃ,
δεῖ σ' ἀντὶ τῶν πρὶν ὀλβίων φρονημάτων
πτῆξαι ταπεινὴν, προσπεσεῖν τ' ἐμὸν γόνυ,   165
σαίρειν τε δῶμα τοὐμὸν, ἐκ χρυσηλάτων
τευχέων χερὶ σπείρουσαν Ἀχελῴου δρόσον,
γνῶναί θ' ἵν' εἶ γῆς. οὐ γάρ ἐσθ' Ἕκτωρ τάδε,

---

154. ὑμᾶς. To you then, the chorus, I reply thus to an anticipated objection, that being decked out with the wealth of my husband, I ought to speak with reserve of the members of his household. Musgrave fancies something must have been lost, to which the words of Hermione contained a pointed and definite reply; and W. Dindorf concurs in this opinion. See above on v. 147.

156. κατασχεῖν, 'to secure' (obtinere). See on Suppl. 15, Οἰδίπου παγκληρίας μέρος κατασχεῖν φυγάδι Πολυνείκει θέλων. Infra, v. 193.

157. φαρμάκοις, διὰ φάρμακα. See above, v. 132. Electr. 149. 376. Hel. 79, and on Heracl. 475.

158. ἀκύμων. Photius, κῦμα, τὸ κυούμενον. Aesch. Eum. 629, μήτηρ—τροφὸς κύματος νεοσπόρου. Translate, ' my barren womb continues fruitless through you.'

159. Ἠπειρῶτις, (agreeing with ψυχὴ instead of γυναικῶν by a common metathesis,) is here and inf. v. 652 used for Ἀσιᾶτις. Photius, on the authority of Isocrates, defines ἤπειρος to be ἡ ὑπὸ βασιλεῖ τῶν Περσῶν γῆ. Pflugk well illustrates the reputation of these people for baneful incantations and the use of potent drugs, from Aelian, de Nat. An. xv. 11, χρῶνται δὲ αὐτοῖς ἐς τὰ ὅμοια ἁλιεῖς, ὅσοι κατὰ τοὺς Ἠπειρώτας φαρμακεύουσι, πονηροὶ καὶ οὗτοι σοφισταὶ κακῶν. Hence Dionysus is styled γόης, ἐπῳδὸς Λυδίας ἀπὸ χθονὸς, in Bacch. 234.

163. ἢν δ' οὖν. ' But if any one of gods or men should care to save you,' &c. For the formula ἢν δ' οὖν in this peculiar sense see Alc. 850. Rhes. 572.—ὄλβιον φρόνημα means ' pride in prosperity,' τὸ δοκεῖν ὀλβίαν εἶναι, just as καρτερὸν φρόνημα is ' pride in strength,' Prom. 215 ; and so perhaps in that difficult passage Suppl. 907, πλούσιον φρόνημα κτλ. may mean, ' a pride in being thought rich, which was shown in his munificent actions rather than in merely boasting of it.'

167. Aldus and two MSS. give περισπείρουσαν.—Ἀχελῴου, see Bacch. 625.

168. οὐ—τάδε. ' You have not Hector here, nor Priam and his gold, but a Greek city.' For the use of τάδε see Med. 182. Troad. 100, οὐκέτι Τροία τάδε καὶ βασιλεῖς ἐσμὲν Τροίας. It is surprising that Hermann should be so dissatisfied with the common reading as to adopt Markland's violent conjecture (on Suppl. 109) οὐ Πρίαμος ὁ ζάχρυσος. ' Not Priam nor his gold' is however so clearly the same in sense as

240   ΕΥΡΙΠΙΔΟΥ

οὐ Πρίαμος, οὐδὲ χρυσὸς, ἀλλ' Ἑλλὰς πόλις.
ἐς τοῦτο δ' ἥκεις ἀμαθίας, δύστηνε σὺ,   170
ἣ παιδὶ πατρὸς, ὃς σὸν ὤλεσεν πόσιν,
τολμᾷς ξυνεύδειν καὶ τέκν' αὐθέντου πάρα
τίκτειν. τοιοῦτον πᾶν τὸ βάρβαρον γένος·
πατήρ τε θυγατρὶ παῖς τε μητρὶ μίγνυται
κόρη τ' ἀδελφῷ, διὰ φόνου δ' οἱ φίλτατοι   175
χωροῦσι, καὶ τῶνδ' οὐδὲν ἐξείργει νόμος.
ἃ μὴ παρ' ἡμᾶς εἴσφερ'· οὐδὲ γὰρ καλὸν
δυοῖν γυναικοῖν ἄνδρ' ἕν' ἡνίας ἔχειν,
ἀλλ' ἐς μίαν βλέποντες εὐναίαν Κύπριν
στέργουσιν, ὅστις μὴ κακῶς οἰκεῖν θέλει.   180
ΧΟ. ἐπίφθονόν τι χρῆμα θηλειῶν ἔφυ,
καὶ ξυγγάμοισι δυσμενὲς μάλιστ' ἀεί.
ΑΝ. φεῦ φεῦ.
κακόν γε θνητοῖς τὸ νέον, ἐν δὲ τῷ νέῳ

'not the rich Priam,' that it seems hardly worth altering the text even on much more probable grounds.

170. ἀμαθίας. Here a synonym of μωρίας, incontinency. See on Ion 545. Hel. 1018. Troad. 981, μὴ ἀμαθεῖς ποίει θεὰς τὸ σὸν κακὸν κοσμοῦσα.—ἢ τολμᾷς for ὥστε τολμᾶν.—αὐθέντου, see on Suppl. 442.—πάρα, for ἐξ, ἀπὸ, with the physical notion of receiving the child from the male.

176. τῶνδ' οὐδέν. This may either mean, 'and none of these things the law prohibits,' or, 'and from these things the law does not at all prohibit them.' Compare μηδὲν for μὴ in v. 88.

179. εὐναίαν Κύπριν. The epithet here, as before in v. 4, has peculiar force. It was not a wife and a mistress, but *two wives* which the Greek law prohibited. See below, v. 222. So in v. 182, it is the ξύγγαμοι, not the indulgence of a mistress beside a wife, which is said to excite the ire of women. Med. 265, ὅταν δ' ἐς εὐνὴν ἠδικημένη κυρῇ, οὐκ ἔστιν ἄλλη φρὴν μιαιφονωτέρα. Properly speaking, Andromache was only the concubine of Neoptolemus; but then she had borne him a son, while his true wife was childless. Hence not only her jealous fears made her look on the captive as a rival wife, but there was a probability of Neoptolemus legitimizing his child by declaring her so. With reference to this last point in particular Andromache argues in the following speech.

184. Andromache defends herself from the charge of having caused barrenness, by showing its extreme improbability. Her fear at the outset is, that, being a slave, she will not be allowed to speak freely; or that, if allowed, and having the better of the argument, she should on that account suffer harm, through the natural dislike of a superior to hear justice and reason from an inferior.—On what grounds, she asks, should she, a humble captive, seek to eject Hermione from her place as a wedded wife? Is Andromache possessed of more personal beauty or more national influence than Hermione? Why, should she hereafter bear children to Neoptolemus, they will be slaves like herself; so that at least rivalry and ambition are out of the question. Her children can never succeed to the throne of Phthia, for the Hellenes must ever detest one who has been a queen of their enemies the Trojans. No, 'tis not by *her* arts that Hermione appears to be held secondary in her husband's esteem. He does not like her as a wife. 'Your pride,' she says, 'and your disparaging references to your husband's obscurity, have made you odious to him.'

ΑΝΔΡΟΜΑΧΗ.

τὸ μὴ δίκαιον ὅστις ἀνθρώπων ἔχει. 185
ἐγὼ δὲ ταρβῶ μὴ τὸ δουλεύειν μέ σοι
λόγων ἀπώσῃ, πόλλ' ἔχουσαν ἔνδικα,
ἢν δ' αὖ κρατήσω, μὴ 'πὶ τῷδ' ὄφλω βλάβην·
οἱ γὰρ πνέοντες μεγάλα τοὺς κρείσσους λόγους
πικρῶς φέρουσι τῶν ἐλασσόνων ὕπο· 190
ὅμως δ' ἐμαυτὴν οὐ προδοῦσ' ἁλώσομαι.
εἴπ', ὦ νεᾶνι, τῷ σ' ἐχεγγύῳ λόγῳ
πεισθεῖσ' ἀπωθῶ γνησίων νυμφευμάτων;
ὡς ἡ Λάκαινα τῶν Φρυγῶν μείων πόλις,
τύχῃ θ' ὑπερθεῖ κἄμ' ἐλευθέραν ὁρᾷς; 195
ἢ τῷ νέῳ τε καὶ σφριγῶντι σώματι
πόλεώς τε μεγέθει καὶ φίλοις ἐπηρμένη
οἶκον κατασχεῖν τὸν σὸν ἀντὶ σοῦ θέλω;

Besides, her intolerance of a second favourite of his was displeasing. What is this in fact, but to be convicted of a discreditable sensualism? Hector himself was not always faithful; yet Andromache never loved him the less. It is not jealousy but a generous confidence that wins the affection of a husband. Let not Hermione imitate her infamous mother Helen. Wise children will ever shun the ways of bad mothers.

Ibid. ἐν δέ. So Stobaeus for ἔν τε. And his reading is justly preferred by Hermann and Dindorf. The sense is, 'Youth is bad, when, combined with youth, there is a principle of injustice.' Thus, τὸ μὲν νέον alone may be bad, but it is certainly so when injustice is added to it, because the natural energy of youth supplies the means of carrying out unjust intentions. 'Now *my* fear is,' continues Andromache, 'not that the unfairness of my cause, but that my inferior position, should prevent me from addressing you.' There is evidently a rhetorical antithesis between τὸ μὴ δίκαιον and πολλὰ ἔνδικα, the one on the side of Hermione, the other on that of Andromache.

190. ὕπο. Hermann reads ἄπο, with great probability. He observes that the Schol. explains it by παρὰ τῶν ἐλασσόνων δικαιοτέρους λόγους ἀκούειν. Though the whole phrase may indeed be resolved into πικρῶς φέρουσι νουθετούμενοι ὑπὸ τῶν ἐλασσόνων, still he correctly lays down the distinction, that this is rightly used when a person hears something said of himself, or against himself by another; whereas here the reference is chiefly to the source from which the words proceed.

193. πεισθεῖσα. 'In compliance with what trustworthy reason am I repelling you from your lawful marriage-rights?' So ἐννύχοις πεπεισμένη ὀνείροις, and other similar expressions, where the process of *persuasion* is transferred from another to the reasonings of the party who is himself convinced.

194. ὡς κτλ. It cannot be because Troy is a more powerful state than Sparta, and because my fortune is superior to yours, and I am free while you are a slave. The very contrary to all this is the case; and so the fallacy of your suspicions on other grounds, my wealth, beauty, friends, &c., may be demonstrated.

196. σφριγῶντι, plump, well-conditioned, *en bon point*. Suppl. 478, μὴ—σφριγῶντ' ἀμείψῃ μῦθον. Ar. Lysistr. 80, ὡς δ' εὐχροεῖς, ὡς δὲ σφριγᾷ τὸ σῶμά σου. Photius, σφριγῶν, νεάζων, αὔξων, σφύζων, βράζων, εὐσωματῶν, ἀκμάζων, ἀνθῶν.

197. The arguments by which Hermann defends Brunck's conjecture πλούτου for πόλεως are quite inconclusive. If the Schol. gives πλήθει, he evidently means to show, that by μέγεθος not so much the size of the city as the extent of the population is meant.—κατασχεῖν, see v. 156.

VOL. II. I i

ΕΥΡΙΠΙΔΟΥ

πότερον ἵν' αὐτὴ παῖδας ἀντὶ σοῦ τέκω
δούλους, ἐμαυτῇ γ' ἀθλίαν ἐφολκίδα ; 200
ἢ τοὺς ἐμούς τις παῖδας ἐξανέξεται
Φθίας τυράννους ὄντας, ἢν σὺ μὴ τέκῃς ;
φιλοῦσι γάρ μ' Ἕλληνες Ἕκτορός τ' ἄπο,
αὐτή τ' ἀμαυρὰ κοὐ τύραννος ἦν Φρυγῶν.
οὐκ ἐξ ἐμῶν σε φαρμάκων στυγεῖ πόσις, 205
ἀλλ' εἰ ξυνεῖναι μὴ 'πιτηδεία κυρεῖς.
φίλτρον δὲ καὶ τόδ'· οὐ τὸ κάλλος, ὦ γύναι,
ἀλλ' ἀρεταὶ τέρπουσι τοὺς ξυνευνέτας.
σὺ δ' ἤν τι κνισθῇς, ἡ Λάκαινα μὲν πόλις
μέγ' ἐστὶ, τὴν δὲ Σκῦρον οὐδαμοῦ τίθης, 210
πλουτεῖς δ' ἐν οὐ πλουτοῦσι, Μενέλεως δέ σοι
μείζων Ἀχιλλέως. ταῦτά τοί σ' ἔχθει πόσις.
χρὴ γὰρ γυναῖκα, κἂν κακῷ δοθῇ πόσει,
στέργειν, ἅμιλλάν τ' οὐκ ἔχειν φρονήματος.

199. αὐτὴ ἀντὶ σοῦ. The real fact being, that I am a slave, and that my children must be the same, it follows that I can hardly wish to supplant you, whose heirs would certainly succeed to the throne, in the desire for having offspring. —ἐμαυτῇ γ' (for τ') Hermann, which is better, because it implies that the statement is made in a tone of irony,—'to follow, forsooth, in my train, as wretched slaves as myself.' Photius, ἐφόλκια, καράβια μικρὰ, παρὰ τὸ ἕλκεσθαι ὑπὸ τῶν κωπηλατῶν ἢ τῶν μεγάλων πλοίων. Herc. F. 631, ἔξω λαβών γε τούσδ' ἐφολκίδας χεροῖν, ναῦς δ' ὡς ἐφέλξω.

201. ἐξανέξεται—ὄντας. Cf. Alcest. 304, τούτους ἀνάσχου δεσπότας ἐμῶν δόμων. Ion 1070, οὐ γὰρ δόμων γ' ἑτέρους ἄρχοντας—ἀνέχοιτ' ἄν.

203. φιλοῦσι κτλ. Ironically said. The real meaning is, 'the Greeks hate me, both as the wife of Hector and as the Queen presumptive of the Trojans.' The phrase ἀπὸ Ἕκτορος appears to be rightly explained by the Schol. διὰ τὸν Ἕκτορα. She means, τὸ εἰς ἐμὲ μῖσος Ἑλλήνων ἀπό τε Ἕκτορος προσγέγονε, καὶ διότι αὐτὴ τύραννος ἦν.

205. 'No! 'tis not through any drugs of mine that your husband dislikes you, but (he naturally does so) if you are not a wife congenial to his affections. For this also is a charm in wedded life; it is not merely their beauty, but the conjugal excellences in wives that afford satisfaction to their husbands.' Schol. ἀρετὴ δὲ γυναικὸς ἡ πρὸς τὸν ἄνδρα ὁμόνοια.

209. κνίζειν is used of the stings of jealousy, especially as applied to matrimonial disappointment. Cf. Med. 568, οὐδ' ἂν σὺ φαίης, εἴ σε μὴ κνίζοι λέχος. The sense is, If you (emphatic, for Andromache is contrasting her own conduct with Hermione's,) are in any respect nettled, you immediately taunt your husband with the superiority of your birth over his; with his comparative poverty, and the greater celebrity and power of your father. 'You reckon Scyros no where,' means, you call him in disparagement νησιώτης, v. 14. For this sort of irony, which states as a fact what is meant to be conceived as absurd or false, compare v. 204, and Suppl. 737, ἡμῖν γὰρ ἦν τό τ' Ἄργος οὐχ ὑπόστατον αὐτοί τε πολλοὶ καὶ νέοι βραχίοσιν. See also Herc. F. 467.—μέγ' ἐστὶ, not, of course, for μεγάλη, but κόμπος σοι ἐστὶ, μεγαλύνεται.

214. οὐκ ἔχειν. See on v. 100. 'Even if,' she says, 'which you are not, a woman is wedded to an obscure husband, she ought not to show her pride by invidiously contrasting their respective families,'

εἰ δ' ἀμφὶ Θρῄκην χιόνι τὴν κατάρρυτον 215
τύραννον ἔσχες ἄνδρ', ἵν' ἐν μέρει λέχος
δίδωσι πολλαῖς εἷς ἀνὴρ κοινούμενος,
ἔκτεινας ἂν τάσδ'; εἶτ' ἀπληστίαν λέχους
πάσαις γυναιξὶ προστιθεῖσ' ἂν ηὑρέθης.
αἰσχρόν γε. καίτοι χείρον' ἀρσένων νόσον 220
ταύτην νοσοῦμεν, ἀλλὰ προὔστημεν καλῶς.
ὦ φίλταθ' Ἕκτορ, ἀλλ' ἐγὼ τὴν σὴν χάριν
σοὶ καὶ ξυνήρων, εἴ τί σε σφάλλοι Κύπρις,
καὶ μαστὸν ἤδη πολλάκις νόθοισι σοῖς
ἐπέσχον, ἵνα σοι μηδὲν ἐνδοίην πικρόν. 225
καὶ ταῦτα δρῶσα τἀρετῇ προσηγόμην

215. Hermann's reading, Θρῃκῶν—γῆν, is unquestionably an improvement; for the article, by emphasizing what is a mere descriptive adjunct, draws the attention away from the real point of the argument, which is not the *climate* of Thrace, but its customs. Similarly in Hec. 8, ὃς τὴν ἀρίστην Χερσονησίαν πλάκα σπείρει is objectionable, because no *particular* reference is wanted to the fertility of the soil. Here Hermann rightly reads τήνδ'. 'Supposing,' she asks, 'you had been one of the many wives of a Thracian king; would you have put all of them to death, that you alone might have him for a husband? And yet, to be consistent in your present wish of making away with me as your rival, you would have done this, even though the consequence would have been, that all the sex would be reviled for sensuality through you.' The reading of Lascaris and some MSS., κοιμώμενος, is manifestly inferior to the Aldine κοινούμενος. For προστιθέναι τι, to fasten the charge of any thing on a person, see Heracl. 475. *Inf.* 360.

221. προὔστημεν. 'We manage it cleverly,' i.e. we conceal our feelings while they show theirs by violent emotions. She speaks, of course, and speaks truthfully too, of the sex in general. Hermann does not show good taste in reading προσταῖμεν. He says, "Non potest Andromache hic dicere quid soleant facere mulieres; non enim omnes temperantes sunt, et non est, quicum loquitur, Hermiona: sed quid optandum sit ut faciant, dicere eam oportet." Truly, a weak and impotent conclusion to this psychological comparison of the sexes, 'but may we women master it well!' When Andromache describes what women in general do, she alludes in fact to what Hermione in particular does *not* do; and hence the pointedness of the reproach. That προὔστημεν does not refer merely to Andromache is evident, because ἀλλ' ἐγὼ is distinctively added immediately afterwards. For the use of προστῆναι (whence προστάτης, a patron, a defender), Musgrave compares Ajac. 803, οἳ 'γὼ, φίλοι, πρόστητ' ἀναγκαίας τύχης. Schol. καλῶς περιστέλλομεν αὐτὰ καὶ οὐ φανεραὶ γιγνόμεθα, and ἀλλὰ προϊστάμεθα αὐτῆς καρτεροῦσαι. See Heracl. 306.

223. ξυνήρων, so far from hating my rival, I loved her because my husband loved her. A magnificent, though impossible concession to true affection. It has been elsewhere observed, that the παλλάκη or mistress was tolerated even by the wife, so long as both were not under the same roof. See on Med. 694, and compare Trach. 445, 460. For σφάλλειν, used peculiarly of the frailties of love, see Rhes. 917. Ion 1523. The commentators well compare Homer, Il. v. 69, Πήδαιον δ' ἄρ' ἔπεφνε Μέδης, Ἀντήνορος υἱόν, ὅς ῥα νόθος μὲν ἔην, πύκα δ' ἔτρεφε δῖα Θεανὼ, ἶσα φίλοισι τέκεσσι, χαριζομένη πόσεϊ ᾧ.

225. ἐνδοίην. The meaning is, ἵνα μηδὲν ἐνορῴης ἐν ἐμοὶ εἰς ὀργὴν καὶ πικρότητα τρέπον. This use of ἐνδιδόναι is rare. It is illustrated by Pflugk from Herod. vii. 52, οἱ δὲ δικαιοσύνην καὶ πικρότητα ἐνέδωκαν, ἄχαρι δὲ οὐδέν. Cf. Hec. 1239. *Inf.* 965.

226. καὶ ταῦτα κτλ. 'And by acting

πόσιν· σὺ δ' οὐδὲ ῥανίδ' ὑπαιθρίας δρόσου
τῷ σῷ προσίζειν ἀνδρὶ δειμαίνουσ' ἐᾷς.
μὴ τὴν τεκοῦσαν τῇ φιλανδρίᾳ, γύναι,
ζήτει παρελθεῖν· τῶν κακῶν γὰρ μητέρων   230
φεύγειν τρόπους χρὴ τέκν', ὅσοις ἔνεστι νοῦς.
ΧΟ. δέσποιν', ὅσον σοι ῥᾳδίως παρίσταται,
τοσόνδε πείθου τῇδε συμβῆναι λόγοις.
ΕΡ. τί σεμνομυθεῖς κεἰς ἀγῶν' ἔρχει λόγων,
ὡς δὴ σὺ σώφρων, τἀμὰ δ' οὐχὶ σώφρονα;   235
ΑΝ. οὔκουν ἐφ' οἷς γε νῦν καθέστηκας λόγοις.
ΕΡ. ὁ νοῦς ὁ σός μοι μὴ ξυνοικοίη, γύναι.
ΑΝ. νέα πέφυκας καὶ λέγεις αἰσχρῶν πέρι.
ΕΡ. σὺ δ' οὐ λέγεις γε, δρᾷς δέ μ' εἰς ὅσον δύνᾳ.
ΑΝ. οὐκ αὖ σιωπῇ Κύπριδος ἀλγήσεις πέρι;   240

thus, I won over my husband to myself (i.e. diverted him from others) by my worth; whereas you, in your fears for his fidelity, allow not so much as a drop of dew to settle on your husband from the open air.' The meaning is, that she watches him with such jealousy, that he can hardly leave the house and return in the early morning, without being suspected by her. Schol. βούλεται δὲ λέγειν, ὅτι οὐκ ὀφείλει γυνὴ ἀνδρὶ ἑτέρᾳ γυναικὶ συνομιλοῦντι οὕτω φανερῶς ἀγανακτεῖν, καὶ εἰς μέσον φέρειν αὐτῆς τὸ πάθος, ἀλλὰ μᾶλλον ἰδίᾳ τῷ ἀνδρὶ ἐπιτιμᾶν, πειθοῖ τε καὶ κολακείᾳ ἀφιστᾶν αὐτὸν τῆς πρὸς τὰς ἄλλας πτώσεως.

229. τὴν τεκοῦσαν. 'Do not make it your aim to surpass your mother Helen in fondness for the male sex. Wise children will avoid rather than imitate the ways of their mothers.' Helen was called πολυάνωρ from the number of suitors and even husbands she had had.

232. The chorus, impressed with the soundness of Andromache's reasoning, beseech Hermione to yield to her arguments so far as she can do so without violence to her feelings. But Hermione is offended with Andromache, as people often are offended with plain truth; she takes no notice of the proposal for peace, but flies at her opponent, who on her part is by no means slow to retort.—παρίσταται, so far as occurs to you, as occasion offers, &c.—συμβῆναι, like συγχωρεῖν λόγοις, Hippol. 299.

235. ὡς δή. Cf. Suppl. 477. Aesch. Agam. 1611. Herc. F. 1407. Hel. 1057.

236. οὔκουν—γε. For οὐ γοῦν. 'Certainly you are not over modest on the claims upon which you now rest,' viz. the desire to possess your husband exclusively. It is needless to say, that Andromache's argument cannot be judged by modern usages and modern morality. Perhaps it is enough to translate, according to the Schol. ἐν οἷς νῦν λέγεις, 'according to your present avowals.'

237. ξυνοικοίη. Cf. Aesch. Cho. 992, τοιάδ' ἐμοὶ ξύνοικος ἐν δόμοισι μὴ γένοιτ'. The meaning here is the same; 'may I never have to live with a person who thinks as you do,' not, 'may your principles never find an abode in my breast.'

238. This verse has no reference to the last, but to the charge of being οὐχὶ σώφρων ἐν τοῖς νῦν λόγοις. A young person speaking on so delicate a subject can scarcely, she thinks, practise σωφροσύνη.

239. σὺ δέ γε οὐ μόνον λέγεις, ἀλλὰ καὶ δρᾷς αἰσχρά, ὅσον δύνασαι, viz. in trying to cause barrenness in your rival, and so depriving her of the affections of her husband. Cf. v. 158. The old reading δύνῃ was corrected by W. Dindorf. The subjunctive is here out of place. Compare ἐπίστᾳ for ἐπίστασαι, Eumen. 86.

240. οὐκ αὖ κτλ. 'What, *Love* again? Go and bear your disappointment in it in silence.' The verse is briefly put, because the limits of the στιχομυθία necessitate such a compendious way of speaking. The

ΑΝΔΡΟΜΑΧΗ.   245

ΕΡ. τί δ'; οὐ γυναιξὶ ταῦτα πρῶτα πανταχοῦ;
ΑΝ. καλῶς γε χρωμέναισιν· εἰ δὲ μή, οὐ καλά.
ΕΡ. οὐ βαρβάρων νόμοισιν οἰκοῦμεν πόλιν.
ΑΝ. κἀκεῖ τά γ' αἰσχρὰ κἀνθάδ' αἰσχύνην ἔχει.
ΕΡ. σοφὴ σοφὴ σύ· κατθανεῖν δ' ὅμως σε δεῖ.   245
ΑΝ. ὁρᾷς ἄγαλμα Θέτιδος ἔς σ' ἀποβλέπον;
ΕΡ. μισοῦν γε πατρίδα σὴν Ἀχιλλέως φόνῳ.
ΑΝ. Ἑλένη νιν ὤλεσ', οὐκ ἐγώ, μήτηρ γε σή.
ΕΡ. ἦ καὶ πρόσω γὰρ τῶν ἐμῶν ψαύσεις κακῶν;
ΑΝ. ἰδοὺ σιωπῶ κἀπιλάζυμαι στόμα.   250
ΕΡ. ἐκεῖνο λέξον, οὗπερ οὕνεκ' ἐστάλην.
ΑΝ. λέγω σ' ἐγὼ νοῦν οὐκ ἔχειν ὅσον σε δεῖ.
ΕΡ. λείψεις τόδ' ἁγνὸν τέμενος ἐναλίας θεοῦ;
ΑΝ. εἰ μὴ θανοῦμαί γ'· εἰ δὲ μή, οὐ λείψω ποτέ.
ΕΡ. ὡς τοῦτ' ἄραρε, κοὐ μενῶ πόσιν μολεῖν.   255
ΑΝ. ἀλλ' οὐδ' ἐγὼ μὴν πρόσθεν ἐκδώσω μέ σοι.
ΕΡ. πῦρ σοι προσοίσω, κοὐ τὸ σὸν προσκέψομαι.
ΑΝ. σὺ δ' οὖν κάταιθε, θεοὶ γὰρ εἴσονται τάδε.
ΕΡ. καὶ χρωτὶ δεινῶν τραυμάτων ἀλγηδόνας.
ΑΝ. σφάζ', αἱμάτου θεᾶς βωμὸν, ἣ μέτεισί σε.   260

retort is founded on the preceding ὁρᾷς με αἰσχρά, which revealed the true cause of her vexation.

242. Before this verse some copies prefix ναί, but it is wanting in the editions of Lascaris and Aldus. Hermann and W. Dindorf appear to be right in condemning it. The same remark applies to v. 586.

243. βαρβάρων, the easterns generally. We do not, she says, take from them *our* standard of τὸ καλὸν and τὸ μὴ καλόν.

247. φόνῳ. The dative is the same as in v. 157.

248. μήτηρ γε σή, 'aye, your mother.' So Aldus; and Hermann justly prefers it to μήτηρ δὲ σή, which W. Dindorf has edited after Lascaris and the MSS.

249. πρόσω, further than you have yet done, by touching upon family topics. Schol. περαιτέρω μοι θέλεις ὀνειδίσειν;

251. ἐκεῖνο, κτλ. Tell me that matter which I came here to learn, viz. τί με ἀπωθεῖς γνησίων νυμφευμάτων; v. 193. She replies, 'That I will not tell you; but I will tell you that you show a want of sense.'

254. εἰ μὴ θανοῦμαί γε. 'I will on condition that my life shall be spared; but otherwise, I will never leave it.'

256. οὐδὲ μήν. See Hel. 1047. Hec. 401. The use of με for ἐμαυτὴν, as the *object* of a verb, is rather unusual. Hel. 842, τύμβου 'πὶ νώτοις σὲ κτανὼν ἐμὲ κτενῶ. Aesch. Suppl. 108, ζῶσα γόοις με τιμῶ. Hippol. 1409, στένω σε μᾶλλον ἢ 'μὲ τῆς ἁμαρτίας. Iph. A. 677, ζηλῶ σὲ μᾶλλον ἢ 'μὲ τοῦ μηδὲν φρονεῖν.

257. τὸ σὸν, i. e. σέ. I shall have no consideration for you, but only for the obligations of religion, which does not permit me to force you from the altar. Cf. Med. 459, τόσον γε προσκοπούμενος, γύναι, where some read τὸ σόν γε. Schol. οὐ τὸ σὸν συμφέρον προνοήσω.

258. σὺ δ' οὖν. For this combination see on Rhes. 336. Ion 408.—θεοὶ εἴσονται, the gods will take cognizance of this, will be ἵστορες, or witnesses of it.

260. Hermann cites Bekker's Anecdota, p. 362, αἱμάτου, ἀντὶ τοῦ ἐξαιμάτου. Εὐριπίδης· αἱμάτου θεᾶς βωμόν. We have

ΕΡ. ὦ βάρβαρον σὺ θρέμμα καὶ σκληρὸν θράσος,
ἐγκαρτερεῖς δὴ θάνατον; ἀλλ' ἐγώ σ' ἕδρας
ἐκ τῆσδ' ἑκοῦσαν ἐξαναστήσω τάχα·
τοιόνδ' ἔχω σου δέλεαρ. ἀλλὰ γὰρ λόγους
κρύψω, τὸ δ' ἔργον αὐτὸ σημανεῖ τάχα. 265
κάθησ' ἑδραία· καὶ γὰρ εἰ πέριξ σ' ἔχει
τηκτὸς μόλυβδος, ἐξαναστήσω σ' ἐγώ,
πρὶν ᾧ πέποιθας παῖδ' Ἀχιλλέως μολεῖν.

ΑΝ. πέποιθα· δεινὸν δ' ἑρπετῶν μὲν ἀγρίων
ἄκη βροτοῖσι θεῶν καταστῆσαί τινα, 270
ἃ δ' ἔστ' ἐχίδνης καὶ πυρὸς περαιτέρω,
οὐδεὶς γυναικὸς φάρμακ' ἐξηύρηκέ πω
κακῆς· τοσοῦτόν ἐσμεν ἀνθρώποις κακόν.

ΧΟ. ἦ μεγάλων ἀχέων ἄρ' ὑπῆρξεν, ὅτ' Ἰδαίαν στρ. α'.

the simple verb in Eur. Suppl. 77. Ar. Pac. 1019, οὐχ ᾕδεται δήπουθεν Εἰρήνη σφαγαῖς, οὐδ' αἱματοῦται βωμὸς, and the participle ᾑματωμένος in Ran. 476. Bacch. 1135.

262. ἐγκ. δὴ θάνατον; 'So you brave death, do you?' Cf. Alcest. 1071, χρὴ δ', ὅστις εἶσι, καρτερεῖν θεοῦ δόσιν. She says this, disappointed that her threats of torture do not make her leave the sanctuary.—ἑκοῦσαν, without using violence, and so committing sacrilege.

266. κάθησο, keep your seat there before the altar. Schol. ἰσχυρῶς καθιδρυμένη. Compare the use of δρομαῖος, 'at full speed.' In Rhes. 783, ἑδραία ῥάχις is the part of the horse's back where the rider sits. The mention of melted lead refers to the method of fixing statues on their pedestals.—At the end of her speech Hermione leaves the stage, and does not reappear till v. 825.

268. ᾧ πέποιθας. So Lascaris and others. Aldus has ὃν πέποιθας, scil. μολεῖν. The former seems rightly to be preferred by the recent editors.

270. θεῶν καταστῆσαι. This is the reading of Stobaeus, who quotes these fine verses (269—273), lxxiii. 19. The MSS. and editions of Euripides agree in ἐγκαταστῆσαι, but Aldus gives βροτοῖς θεῶν, and Lascaris βροτοῖσιν, without θεῶν. The reading originated probably in the ignorance of some transcriber that θεῶν might be a monosyllable; and so, omitting the word, as Lascaris has done, he filled up the verse by adding the useless preposition to the verb. Others recalled θεῶν, and adapted it to the metre as they best could. Hence Aldus has ἄκη βροτοῖς θεῶν καταστῆσαί τινα.

271. ἃ δ' ἔστι. Hermione was going to say ἐκείνων δὲ ἑρπετῶν (or rather, κνωδάλων,) to which γυναικῶν would have formed the epexegesis. Dobree would read ὃ δ' ἔστι, which W. Dindorf approves.

274. The subject of this ode is the Judgment of Paris. 'Twas a day of woe when the three fair rivals were led by Hermes to the homestead of the solitary herdsman. All that they could do, that they did, to enhance their natural charms, and so they appeared before the umpire. Cypris gained the victory by crafty and false promises, which proved the ruin of Troy. Would that Paris had been slain by his mother, who was warned in time by her daughter Cassandra what a firebrand he was destined to be! Then would none of the evils have occurred, which have now oppressed both Hellas and Troy.—The metres are of a simple kind, dactylic, cretic, iambic, anapaestic; but v. 280 is a glyconean, and v. 282 an antispastic verse.

Ibid. The subject to ὑπῆρξεν may be either ὁ Μαίας τόκος, or τὸ πρᾶγμα. Pflugk, perhaps rightly, prefers the latter. The word Ἰδαίαν, and οὐρειὰν in the antistrophe, should perhaps be pronounced as a cretic. So οὐρεία is to be scanned in Tro. 533.

ἐς νάπαν ἦλθ' ὁ Μαίας τε καὶ Διὸς τόκος, 275
τρίπωλον ἅρμα δαιμόνων
ἄγων τὸ καλλίζυγὲς,
ἔριδι στυγερᾷ κεκορυθμένον εὐμορφίας
σταθμοὺς ἐπὶ βούτα 280
βοτῆρά τ' ἀμφὶ μονότροπον νεανίαν
ἔρημόν θ' ἑστιοῦχον αὐλάν.
ταὶ δ' ἐπεὶ ὑλόκομον νάπος ἤλυθον, οὐρειᾶν ἀντ. ά.
πιδάκων νίψαν αἰγλᾶντα σώματ' ἐν ῥοαῖς· 285
ἔβαν δὲ Πριαμίδαν ὑπερ-
βολαῖς λόγων δυσφρόνων
παραβαλλόμεναι. Κύπρις εἷλε λόγοισι δολίοις, 290
τερπνοῖς μὲν ἀκοῦσαι,
πικρὰν δὲ σύγχυσιν βίου Φρυγῶν πόλει

277. τρίπωλον ἅρμα, which ought to mean 'a three-horsed chariot,' especially with the addition of καλλιζυγὲς, does in fact mean nothing more than 'three young and fair goddesses.' For πῶλος is often used for παρθένος, and ἅρμα or ὄχημα for a team of horses. Pflugk compares Troad. 924, ἔκρινε τρισσὸν ζεῦγος ὅδε τρισσῶν θεῶν.
279. κεκορυθμένον, ἐστεφανωμένον, ἐστολισμένον, a word difficult to translate, but implying that each was *armed* for a contest respecting her beauty. The Homeric κορύσσειν occurs also in Rhes. 933.
281. μονότροπον, μόνον, ἔρημον. This is one of those compounds, like μονόστολος in Alcest. 407, μονόψηφος in Aesch. Suppl. 367, where the first part of the word alone conveys the meaning, the latter being comparatively *otiose* or ornamental.—ἑστιοῦχον αὐλάν, like ἑστιοῦχον γαῖαν, Pers. 513, is the home which contains its hearth or domestic altar, as opposed to the mere shed or stall of oxen. The Scholiast observes that σταθμὸς is the shelter of herds, αὐλὴ the abode of men. Hence αὐλίζεσθαι is 'to live in a cottage,' Electr. 304.
285. The old copies vary between νίψαντο, ἐνίψαντο, ἔνιψαν. To Hermann νίψαν is due; to Musgrave αἰγλᾶντα for αἰγλάεντα. Compare the contracted form τιμῆντα in Il. ix. 605. Theocr. xxviii. 25. —ἐν ῥοαῖς Aldus. Lascaris and the MSS. omit ἐν, and so Dindorf. See, for this bath of the rival goddesses, Hel. 678.

286. ἔβαν δὲ κτλ. 'And they went to the son of Priam, comparing their respective charms in no measured terms of jealousy.' Hermann gives ἔβαν τε, with Aldus and others, and places a full stop at Πριαμίδαν. He then reads ὑπερβολαῖς λόγων δ' εὐφρόνων &c., and supposes the intended sense to have been Κύπρις μὲν εἷλε, Ἥρα δὲ καὶ Ἀθηνᾶ ἐνικήθησαν. Thus the εὔφρονες λόγοι would be winning, specious words, viz. designed to gain the favour of Paris by promises and flattery. The Schol. however paraphrases the vulgate thus, ἐπαγγελίαις λόγων αὐτὸν βλαπτόντων καὶ τὴν πόλιν, παραβάλλουσαι τὰ κάλλη ἀλλήλων καὶ συγκρίνουσαι ἐμφιλονεικῶς. The absence of a connecting particle, as the next clause now stands, is certainly a difficulty. In one MS. Κύπρις δ' is found, but this is against the metre. For λόγοισι (or λόγοις) δολίοις Hermann gives δόλοις with the marks of a lacuna, W. Dindorf λόγοις αἰόλοις after Musgrave. Were this last word as certain as Dindorf asserts, we might read λόγοις δ' αἰόλοις. But the vulgate satisfies both sense and metre, the first long syllable of the cretic being resolved, as it very often is, into two short.—εἷλε, 'gained the cause.'
292. σύγχυσιν. This is a remarkable example of an accusative in apposition to the sentence, (see Hel. 77,) but connected with a preceding dative by μὲν and δέ. It would, of course, be wrong to suppose there is an ellipse of ἔχουσιν, or, as the

ταλαίνᾳ περγάμοις τε Τροίας.
εἴθε δ' ὑπὲρ κεφαλᾶς ἔβαλεν κακὸν　　　　　στρ. β'.
ἁ τεκοῦσά νιν μόρον　　　　　　　　　　　　　　295
πρὶν Ἰδαῖον κατοικίσαι λέπας,
ὅτε νιν παρὰ θεσπεσίῳ δάφνᾳ
βόασε Κασσάνδρα κτανεῖν,
μεγάλαν Πριάμου πόλεως λώβαν.
τίν' οὐκ ἐπῆλθε, ποῖον οὐκ ἐλίσσετο　　　　　300
δαμογερόντων βρέφος φονεύειν;
οὔτ' ἂν ἐπ' Ἰλιάσι ζυγὸν ἤλυθε　　　　　　　ἀντ. β'.
δούλιον, σύ τ' ἂν, γύναι,
τυράννων ἔσχεθες δόμων ἔδρας·
παρέλυσε δ' ἂν Ἑλλάδος ἀλγεινοὺς　　　　　305
πόνους, ὅτ' ἀμφὶ Τρωίαν
δεκέτεις ἀλάληντο νέοι λόγχαις·

Schol. supposes, of κατασκενάζουσα. In Latin, *verbis auditu jucundis, sed quae esset misera Trojanis vitae perturbatio.*

295. μόρον has been acutely restored by Hermann from the Scholia, for Πάριν. Aldus gives an unmetrical and evidently altered reading, which is retained by Pflugk, ἅτις τέκεν ποτὲ Πάριν. The commentators generally follow Barnes in supposing ὑπὲρ κεφαλᾶς alludes to the well-known custom of tossing defilements or polluted things over the head without looking back; cf. Aesch. Cho. 91. But the Schol. is clearly right: εἴθε ὑπὲρ κεφαλῆς τοῦ Πάριδος ἔβαλε θάνατον ἡ τεκοῦσα τὸν Πάριν. Hence also it appears how Πάριν, an explanation of νιν, has crept into the text, some transcriber supposing that κακὸν, 'mischief,' was sufficient in itself. 'To put death over a person's head' is an unusual phrase, alluding probably to a blow unperceived by the victim.—κεφαλὰν Lascaris and the MSS. For the legend here alluded to, the portentous birth of Paris and the evil predicted therefrom, see Troad. 592, 922, &c.

297. παρὰ θ. δάφνᾳ—κτανεῖν. To slay him at the family altar, which, as Virgil tells us from the Cyclic poems, was overshadowed by a bay-tree, ii. 513, 'ingens ara fuit, juxtaque veterrima laurus Incumbens arae,' &c. This is much simpler than to suppose, with the Scholiast, that Cassandra's inspiration by Apollo is meant, as if the Greek could signify either δάφνην κατέχουσα or δάφνῃ κατεχομένη.

300. ποῖον (δημογ.) follows τίνα by a well-known use; Aesch. Suppl. 888. Theocr. ii. 90.

303. σύ τ' ἂν Pflugk for οὔτε σὺ or οὔτ' ἂν σύ. The οὐ was added by some one who fancied that δόμων τυράννων ἕδρας meant the house of Neoptolemus, whereas the palace of Priam is undoubted alluded to. "*Tuque nacta esses regiae domus sedes*, Hectore nimirum Priamo succedente." *Herm.*—ἔσχεθες for ἔσχες ἂν is W. Dindorf's correction. The repetition of ἂν, unless with an optative, or in some cases with the infinitive, is rare; and ἔσχες has elsewhere been written by mistake for ἔσχεθες.

306. ὅτ' for οὓς Hermann. The old reading violates the metre, and involves a very harsh construction, ἀλᾶσθαι πόνους for πάσχειν πόνους διὰ τὸ ἀλᾶσθαι. W. Dindorf approves Pflugk's conjecture ὅσ' ἀμφὶ κτλ., which is liable to the same grammatical objection as οὕς.—For παραλύειν, a metaphor from the yoke, see Alcest. 931, πολλοὺς ἤδη παρέλυσεν θάνατος δάμαρτος.

307. νέοι. The flower of the people, ἄνθος Ἀργείων, Aesch. Agam. 190. Hermann gives κενοὶ, a bold but not improbable conjecture. In the next verse the same critic prefers ἔρημ' ἂν οὐκ ἂν, with Aldus and several MSS. But see above, v. 303.

ΑΝΔΡΟΜΑΧΗ. 249

λέχη τ' ἔρημ' ἂν οὔποτ' ἐξελείπετο,
καὶ τεκέων ὀρφανοὶ γέροντες.

ΜΕΝΕΛΑΟΣ.

ἥκω λαβὼν σὸν παῖδ', ὃν εἰς ἄλλους δόμους
λάθρα θυγατρὸς τῆς ἐμῆς ὑπεξέθου. 310
σὲ μὲν γὰρ ηὔχεις θεᾶς βρέτας σῶσαι τόδε,
τοῦτον δὲ τοὺς κρύψαντας· ἀλλ' ἐφηυρέθης
ἧσσον φρονοῦσα τοῦδε Μενέλεω, γύναι.
κεἰ μὴ τόδ' ἐκλιποῦσ' ἐρημώσεις πέδον,
ὅδ' ἀντὶ τοῦ σοῦ σώματος σφαγήσεται. 315
ταῦτ' οὖν λογίζου, πότερα κατθανεῖν θέλεις,
ἢ τόνδ' ὀλέσθαι σῆς ἁμαρτίας ὕπερ,
ἣν εἰς ἔμ' ἔς τε παῖδ' ἐμὴν ἁμαρτάνεις.

ΑΝ. ὦ δόξα δόξα, μυρίοισι δὴ βροτῶν
οὐδὲν γεγῶσι βίοτον ὤγκωσας μέγαν. 320
εὔκλεια δ' οἷς μέν ἐστ' ἀληθείας ὕπο,
εὐδαιμονίζω· τοὺς δ' ὑπὸ ψευδῶν ἔχειν

309. Menelaus, who at v. 73 had been described as absent in quest of Andromache's son, now returns, bringing the boy as a hostage. If she does not leave the sanctuary, the child shall be slain in her sight. This was one of the miserable compromises between cruelty and superstition which the Greeks, (and not the Greeks only,) could persuade themselves was no violation of religion. To slay a suppliant at the altar was the deepest sacrilege; but to starve him, burn him out, let him die of cold or of his wounds, or to entice him away by fraud or cruelty to his feelings, was a right and regular proceeding.

311. σώσειν W. Dindorf after Dobree; but verbs of hoping &c. rightly take an aorist infinitive, as above v. 28.

315. σφαγήσεται. He holds a drawn sword at the throat of the boy.

319. Andromache replies by inveighing against the false notions of glory and honour which prevail in the world. Here is a man,—a hero it may be,—who conquered Troy at the head of his chosen Argives, and who is now bringing war against a woman. The boast of wisdom is senseless; if there is any thing that makes a man seem great, it is perhaps wealth,—an equally vain thing. She then proceeds to discuss the matter by argument. Suppose Hermione to succeed in compassing her death; in the opinion of the many, Menelaus will be regarded as an accomplice. If, however, she should be spared, and her child slain in her stead, let him look for a speedy vengeance from Neoptolemus. He will insist on the expulsion of Hermione from her home; and who will marry an ejected wife? None will believe that the fault is on the side of Neoptolemus. It were better to see Hermione wronged many times over, as she vainly fancies she has already been wronged, than to endure these calamities in his family. If women are bad, men need not imitate them in that respect. If she has really caused sterility to Hermione, she is willing to stand her trial for it before all the members of his family, who are equally aggrieved with himself.

322. The construction is, τοὺς δ' ὑπὸ ψευδῶν ἔχοντας εὔκλειαν, οὐκ ἀξιώσω ἔχειν αὐτήν, ἀλλὰ μόνον δοκεῖν κτλ., 'except so far as they are thought to be clever through mere luck.' The ὑπὸ is used, as if she had said ὑπὸ τῶν ἀληθῶς λεγόντων κεκλημένοι εὐκλεεῖς, &c. Cf. v. 190.

VOL. II. K k

ΕΥΡΙΠΙΔΟΥ

οὐκ ἀξιώσω πλὴν τύχῃ φρονεῖν δοκεῖν.
σὺ δὴ στρατηγῶν λογάσιν Ἑλλήνων ποτὲ
Τροίαν ἀφείλου Πρίαμον, ὧδε φαῦλος ὤν ; 325
ὅστις θυγατρὸς ἀντίπαιδος ἐκ λόγων
τοσόνδ᾽ ἔπνευσας, καὶ γυναικὶ δυστυχεῖ
δούλῃ κατέστης εἰς ἀγῶν· οὐκ ἀξιῶ
οὔτ᾽ οὖν σὲ Τροίας οὔτε σοῦ Τροίαν ἔτι.
ἔξωθέν εἰσιν οἱ δοκοῦντες εὖ φρονεῖν 330
λαμπροί, τὰ δ᾽ ἔνδον πᾶσιν ἀνθρώποις ἴσοι,
πλὴν εἴ τι πλούτῳ· τοῦτο δ᾽ ἰσχύει μέγα.
Μενέλαε, φέρε δὴ διαπεράνωμεν λόγους·
τέθνηκα δὴ σῇ θυγατρὶ καί μ᾽ ἀπώλεσε·
μιαιφόνον μὲν οὐκέτ᾽ ἂν φύγοι μύσος, 335
ἐν τοῖς δὲ πολλοῖς καὶ σὺ τόνδ᾽ ἀγωνιεῖ
φόνον· τὸ συνδρῶν γάρ σ᾽ ἀναγκάσει χρέος.
ἢν δ᾽ οὖν ἐγὼ μὲν μὴ θανεῖν ὑπεκδράμω,
τὸν παῖδά μου κτενεῖτε ; κᾆτα πῶς πατὴρ
τέκνου θανόντος ῥᾳδίως ἀνέξεται ; 340
οὐχ ὧδ᾽ ἄνανδρον αὐτὸν ἡ Τροία καλεῖ·

324. σὺ δὴ κτλ. 'What! you at the head of your chosen troops took Troy from Priam, poltroon that you are!' Similarly στρατηλατεῖν takes a dative, Electr. 321. Bacch. 52.
326. ἀντίπαις is used of either sex, and means one just emerged from childhood. See Aesch. Eum. 38.—ἔπνευσας. have blown such a gale. Cf. Troad. 1277, ὦ μεγάλα δήποτ᾽ ἐμπνέουσ᾽ ἐν βαρβάροις Τροία.
329. By saying 'neither are you worthy of Troy, nor Troy of you,' she means, that he was not the man who should have taken Troy, and that it was deserving of a better fate than to be taken by him.
330. ἔξωθεν—τὰ ἔνδον. For the explanation of this see the note on Med. 658. Soph. Antig. 709, οὗτοι διαπτυχθέντες ὤφθησαν κενοί. Plato, Sympos. p. 215, B, φημὶ γὰρ δὴ ὁμοιότατον αὐτὸν εἶναι τοῖς σειληνοῖς τούτοις τοῖς ἐν τοῖς ἑρμογλυφείοις καθημένοις, οὕς τινας ἐργάζονται οἱ δημιουργοὶ σύριγγας ἢ αὐλοὺς ἔχοντας, οἳ διχάδε διοιχθέντες φαίνονται ἐνδόθεν ἀγάλματα ἔχοντες θεῶν. Xenophon, Hiero, § ii. 4, ἡ τυραννὶς τὰ μὲν

δοκοῦντα πολλοῦ ἄξια κτήματα εἶναι ἀνεπτυγμένα θεᾶσθαι φανερὰ πᾶσι παρέχεται, τὰ δὲ χαλεπὰ ἐν ταῖς ψυχαῖς τῶν τυράννων κέκτηται ἀποκεκρυμμένα.
332. πλούτῳ. "Acerbe tangitur Menelaus, cujus opulentiam paullo ante jactaverat Hermione." Herm. See v. 147 seqq.
334. δὴ for τῇ is Reiske's correction, adopted by Hermann and W. Dindorf. It is like καὶ δὴ in Med. 386, Hel. 1059, &c., 'suppose now that I am slain.' The dative, for ὑπὸ σῆς θυγατρὸς, may be compared with that illustrated on Ion 455.
336. ἐν τοῖς πολλοῖς, at the tribunal of public opinion.—τὸ συνδρῶν χρέος, the fact, the circumstance, of being an accomplice. Schol. ἡ γὰρ χρεία τοῦ συνδράσαι τῇ θυγατρὶ ἀναγκάσει σε μὴ ἐκφυγεῖν τὸ μύσος.
338. On ἢν δ᾽ οὖν, 'if I should escape,' see above, v. 163. Here the usual emphasis conveyed by this idiom on the contingency of the event, is necessarily transferred to the person by the addition of ἐγώ, 'but even supposing that I should escape,' &c.

ἀλλ' εἰσὶν οἳ χρή· Πηλέως γὰρ ἄξια
πατρός τ' Ἀχιλλέως ἔργα δρῶν φανήσεται.
ὥσει δὲ σὴν παῖδ' ἐκ δόμων· σὺ δ' ἐκδιδοὺς
ἄλλῳ τί λέξεις ; πότερον ὡς κακὸν πόσιν   345
φεύγει τὸ ταύτης σῶφρον ; ἀλλ' ἐψεύσεται.
γαμεῖ δὲ τίς νιν ; ἢ σφ' ἄνανδρον ἐν δόμοις
χήραν καθέξεις πολιόν ; ὦ τλήμων ἄνερ,
κακῶν τοσούτων οὐχ ὁρᾷς ἐπιρροάς ;
πόσας ἂν εὐνὰς θυγατέρ' ἠδικημένην   350
βούλοι' ἂν εὑρεῖν ἢ παθεῖν ἁγὼ λέγω ;
οὐ χρὴ 'πὶ μικροῖς μεγάλα πορσύνειν κακά,
οὐδ', εἰ γυναικές ἐσμεν ἀτηρὸν κακὸν,
ἄνδρας γυναιξὶν ἐξομοιοῦσθαι φύσιν.
ἡμεῖς γὰρ εἰ σὴν παῖδα φαρμακεύομεν   355
καὶ νηδὺν ἐξαμβλοῦμεν, ὡς αὐτὴ λέγει,
ἑκόντες οὐκ ἄκοντες, οὐδὲ βώμιοι
πίτνοντες, αὐτοὶ τὴν δίκην ὑφέξομεν
ἐν σοῖσι γαμβροῖς, οἷσιν οὐκ ἐλάσσονα
βλάβην ὀφείλω, προστιθεῖσ' ἀπαιδίαν.   360
ἡμεῖς μὲν οὖν τοιοίδε· τῆς δὲ σῆς φρενὸς
ἕν σου δέδοικα· διὰ γυναικείαν ἔριν

346. τὸ ταύτης σῶφρον. This is a taunt on Hermione's alleged ἀπληστία λέχους, which Andromache had charged her with in v. 218, &c.—ἐψεύσεται, 'it will be a lie,' 'it will have been falsely said.' So Hermann, Dindorf, and others correct the common reading ψεύσεται. Porson objected to it on metrical grounds; but Hermann's grammatical reason has more weight, that ψεύσεται would have an active sense, and require some nominative like τὸ σὸν ῥῆμα to be supplied, as the Schol. perceived. In fact, the poet should then have said ψεύσει, 'you will speak falsely.' See Hec. v. 729.
348. πολιόν. More commonly πολιάν. On the idea conveyed by this word applied to women, see Hel. 283.—ἐπιρροὰς, cf. Suppl. 824.
350. πόσας Herm. and Dind. with two or three MSS., for πόσας δ'. Of the two explanations given by the Schol., the latter seems the best; βέλτιον ἐστὶν ἀν-

ἔχεσθαι πολλῶν εὐνῶν, ὅ ἐστι, φέρειν τὸν ἄνδρα εἰ καὶ πολλαῖς πολλάκι χρῷτο, ἢ ταῦτα ὑποστῆναι ἃ ἐγὼ λέγω.
351. βούλοι' ἂν—ή. From the sense of προαιρεῖσθαι, this verb, as occasionally ἐλέσθαι, takes the construction of a comparative. Barnes well compares Il. i. 117, βούλομ' ἐγὼ λαὸν σόον ἔμμεναι ἢ ἀπολέσθαι.
360. προστιθεῖσα. Here, as in v. 219, the word is used of attaching the charge or blame of a thing.
362. ἕν σου δέδοικα. "Tuae mentis unum (mulierositatem) a te metuo." Herm. The uxoriousness of Menelaus is very often alluded to. She means, that she fears Menelaus will not punish Hermione as he ought, if the charge should be proved untrue, but will ruin herself, as he ruined Troy, in slavish submission to a woman's will. W. Dindorf approves, while Hermann with better judgment rejects, Scaliger's conjecture ἕν που.

καὶ τὴν τάλαιναν ὤλεσας Φρυγῶν πόλιν.
ΧΟ. ἄγαν ἔλεξας, ὡς γυνὴ πρὸς ἄρσενας,
καί σου τὸ σῶφρον ἐξετόξευσεν φρενός. 365
ΜΕ. γύναι, τάδ' ἐστὶ σμικρὰ καὶ μοναρχίας
οὐκ ἄξι', ὡς φῄς, τῆς ἐμῆς, οὐδ' Ἑλλάδος.
εὖ δ' ἴσθ', ὅτου τις τυγχάνει χρείαν ἔχων,
τοῦτ' ἔσθ' ἑκάστῳ μεῖζον ἢ Τροίαν ἑλεῖν.
κἀγὼ θυγατρὶ, μεγάλα γὰρ κρίνω τάδε, 370
λέχους στέρεσθαι, σύμμαχος καθίσταμαι·
τὰ μὲν γὰρ ἄλλα δεύτερ', ἂν πάσχῃ γυνή·
ἀνδρὸς δ' ἁμαρτάνουσ' ἁμαρτάνει βίου.
δούλων δ' ἐκεῖνον τῶν ἐμῶν ἄρχειν χρεών,
καὶ τῶν ἐκείνου τοὺς ἐμοὺς ἡμᾶς τε πρός· 375
φίλων γὰρ οὐδὲν ἴδιον, οἵτινες φίλοι
ὀρθῶς πεφύκασ', ἀλλὰ κοινὰ χρήματα.
μένων δὲ τοὺς ἀπόντας, εἰ μὴ θήσομαι

364. The chorus, who take the part of Andromache, remark that she has spoken somewhat more freely than a woman usually does in reply to a man; and that the virtue of her mind has expended all its arrows, and left nothing more to be said on the subject. Ἐκτοξεύειν is 'to shoot away,' and πᾶν βέλος may be supplied from the parallel expression in Eum. 646, ἡμῖν μὲν ἤδη πᾶν τετόξευται βέλος. The Schol. explains, 'has over-shot the mark:' but ἐκτοξεύειν is very different from ἔξω τοξεύειν.

366. Menelaus says in reply, and in defence of his conduct from the charge of pusillanimity, that though she may think and say that he is acting unworthily of Troy, (cf. v. 329,) yet when a man has an object at heart, it requires and calls for all his energies to accomplish it. He has undertaken to support his daughter in her nuptial rights, and he is determined to do it. As Neoptolemus has a claim, on the score of relationship and friendship, to have power over the slaves of Menelaus, by the same principle Menelaus and his daughter shall deal with the slaves of Neoptolemus (i. e. with Andromache) as they think fit. As for the absent husband, it would be folly to wait for his return before setting his own affairs to rights.

367. Hermann places an interrogation at the end of this verse; 'Do you call this conduct of mine unworthy of Troy?' But the same meaning is conveyed without the question; 'You say it is unworthy; I tell you it is not.'

372. ἂν πάσχῃ Musgrave, Bothe, Hermann, for ἂν πάσχῃ or πάσχοι. Since Stobaeus quotes the two verses with πάσχῃ (lxxiv. 23,) and the sense is better than with the optative, their judgment seems to be sound. Matthiae however and W. Dindorf give πάσχοι. 'All other wrongs,' says Menelaus, 'whatsoever they may be, that a woman may have to endure, are secondary to matrimonial slights.' Compare Med. 265, ὅταν δ' ἐς εὐνὴν ἠδικημένη κυρῇ, οὐκ ἔστιν ἄλλη φρὴν μιαιφονωτέρα.

374—5. 'Now, as it is right that he should have control over my slaves, so my relations, (i. e. my daughter,) and myself too, ought to have power over his slaves.' The argument will appear from v. 580 seqq. Menelaus regards Andromache as his captive, and though nominally the slave of another, still as virtually his own, on the principle that the possessions of friends (and slaves were always regarded as κτήματα,) are common. Cf. Iph. A. 859. For the elision of ι in the third person plural, see Ion 1624.

378. τοὺς ἀπόντας, the absent Neoptolemus. Cf. v. 568. If, he says, he

τἄμ' ὡς ἄριστα, φαῦλός εἰμι κοὐ σοφός.
ἀλλ' ἐξανίστω τῶνδ' ἀνακτόρων θεᾶς· 380
ὡς, ἢν θάνῃς σύ, παῖς ὅδ' ἐκφεύγει μόρον,
σοῦ δ' οὐ θελούσης κατθανεῖν, τόνδε κτενῶ.
δυοῖν δ' ἀνάγκη θατέρῳ λιπεῖν βίον.

AN. οἴμοι, πικρὰν κλήρωσιν αἵρεσίν τέ μοι
βίου καθίστης, καὶ λαχοῦσά τ' ἀθλία, 385
καὶ μὴ λαχοῦσα δυστυχὴς καθίσταμαι.
ὦ μεγάλα πράσσων αἰτίας μικρᾶς πέρι,
πιθοῦ· τί καίνεις μ'; ἀντὶ τοῦ; ποίαν πόλιν
προὔδωκα; τίνα σῶν ἔκτανον παίδων ἐγώ;
ποῖον δ' ἔπρησα δῶμ'; ἐκοιμήθην βίᾳ 390
ξὺν δεσπόταισι· κᾆτ' ἔμ', οὐ κεῖνον, κτενεῖς,
τὸν αἴτιον τῶνδ', ἀλλὰ τὴν ἀρχὴν ἀφεὶς
πρὸς τὴν τελευτὴν ὑστέραν οὖσαν φέρει;
οἴμοι κακῶν τῶνδ'· ὦ τάλαιν' ἐμὴ πατρίς,
ὡς δεινὰ πάσχω· τί δέ με καὶ τεκεῖν ἐχρῆν, 395
ἄχθος τ' ἐπ' ἄχθει τῷδε προσθέσθαι διπλοῦν;
ἀτὰρ τί ταῦτ' ὀδύρομαι, τὰ δ' ἐν ποσὶν

---

shall neglect to see his own daughter righted, pending the return of her husband, he has but little sense of courage. He means, that he is not to be deterred by the hints of vengeance Andromache had dropped, v. 340—3.

382. οὐ θελούσης. 'Or, since you do not consent, I shall slay your son here.' This is a better explanation than to suppose οὐ θελούσης = ἀναινομένης, *si tu nevis*, with Hermann, which should properly have been expressed by μὴ θελούσης. After μόρον we may conceive a momentary pause, as if in expectation of her assent; but that being as yet withheld, he proceeds, 'well, then, since *you* do not choose,' &c.

385. λαχοῦσά τε καὶ μὴ λαχοῦσα, 'equally whether it falls to my lot to die, or not.' τ' for γ' is Hermann's correction. But perhaps εἰ λαχοῦσά γ' is the genuine reading; ''tis a sad choice this which you offer; since (εἴ γε) in either event I am unhappy.'

387. μεγάλα. If this is not ironically said, she means that he is proceeding to extremes which are not justified by trifling jealousies between two women.

390. βίᾳ. It was against my will that I cohabited with my present lord and master; and therefore I never sought to eject your daughter from the marriage bed.

392. 'Not noticing the beginning you proceed at once to the end,' means, 'Acquitting Neoptolemus, the real cause of the supposed wrong, you show your resentment against me, whose conduct was but the inevitable result of his will.' So we say in colloquial phrase, 'You begin at the wrong end.' The pleonastic use of ὑστέραν οὖσαν is illustrated by οὕτινος ἄνωθεν ἡμένου σέβει κάτω, Aesch. Suppl. 591. Schol. τὸ γὰρ τέλος τῆς ἀρχῆς δευτερεύει καὶ ὑστερεῖ.

397. ὀδύρομαι. Porson proposed δύρομαι, (cf. Hec. 740,) but he is not followed by the more recent critics. See on Bacch. 1125. 'Why,' she asks, 'should I look back, and lament my fallen country and the time when I was made a mother, and not rather bewail the pressure of present ills,—the being a widow, a slave, the partner of my own husband's murderer,

ΕΥΡΙΠΙΔΟΥ

οὐκ ἐξικμάζω καὶ λογίζομαι κακά;
ἥτις σφαγὰς μὲν Ἕκτορος τροχηλάτους
κατεῖδον οἰκτρῶς τ' Ἴλιον πυρούμενον, 400
αὐτὴ δὲ δούλη ναῦς ἐπ' Ἀργείων ἔβην,
κόμης ἀποσπασθεῖσ'· ἐπεὶ δ' ἀφικόμην
Φθίαν, φονεῦσιν Ἕκτορος νυμφεύομαι.
τί δῆτ' ἐμοὶ ζῆν ἡδύ; πρὸς τί χρὴ βλέπειν;
πρὸς τὰς παρούσας ἢ παρελθούσας τύχας; 405
εἷς παῖς ὅδ' ἦν μοι λοιπὸς ὀφθαλμὸς βίου·
τοῦτον κτανεῖν μέλλουσιν οἷς δοκεῖ τάδε.
οὐ δῆτα τοὐμοῦ γ' οὕνεκ' ἀθλίου βίου·
ἐν τῷδε μὲν γὰρ ἐλπὶς, εἰ σωθήσεται,
ἐμοὶ δ' ὄνειδος μὴ θανεῖν ὑπὲρ τέκνου. 410
ἰδοὺ προλείπω βωμὸν ἥδε χειρία
σφάζειν, φονεύειν, δεῖν, ἀπαρτῆσαι δέρην.
ὦ τέκνον, ἡ τεκοῦσά σ', ὡς σὺ μὴ θάνῃς,
στείχω πρὸς Ἅιδην· ἢν δ' ὑπεκδράμῃς μόρον,
μέμνησο μητρὸς, οἷα τλᾶσ' ἀπωλόμην, 415
καὶ πατρὶ τῷ σῷ, διὰ φιλημάτων ἰὼν
δάκρυά τε λείβων καὶ περιπτύσσων χέρας,
λέγ' οἷ' ἔπραξα. πᾶσι δ' ἀνθρώποις ἄρ' ἦν

and lastly, about to be deprived of my son, my sole remaining consolation?— ἐξικμάζω is a word depending for its authority on a gloss of Hesychius, ἐξικμάζεται, ἐξόλλυται, ἐξικνεῖται. Schol. δακρύω, ἀναζητῶ, ἐρευνῶ. Matthiae adds ἐξικμασαμένη χώρα from Suidas. Properly, the word meant to extract the moisture, and so cause the withering and decay of a thing. Hence, 'to shed tears at,' exactly as διαίνειν πῆμα is used in Hel. 379. W. Dindorf regards the word as corrupt, and made up of some reading like ἐξιχνεύω, with a superscribed gloss ἐξετάζω.

402. There seems no reason why ἀποσπασθεῖσ' should be altered to ἐπισπασθεῖσ', though several MSS. give the latter. Both expressions were in use. The vulgate is sufficiently defended by Aesch. Suppl. 882, ἕλξειν ἔοιχ' ὑμᾶς ἀποσπάσας κόμης.

405. παρελθούσας. For the article omitted see Ion 7.

407. κτενεῖν W. Dindorf, with Aldus. But μέλλω is rightly followed by an aorist.

408. οὐ δῆτα. 'Certainly they shall not do so, if my wretched life is the cost of his safety; for there is yet a hope for him, if he escapes, while to me it would be a discredit not to die for my child.' In other words, life is nothing to me, while to him it may yet end prosperously. The οὕνεκα (for which Aldus and two or three MSS. give εἵνεκα, perhaps rightly), is used much as in Med. μητρὸς οὕνεκ' εὐκλεεῖς, 'as far as that consideration is concerned,' &c. The μὲν and the δὲ seem so clearly to correspond in the next and the following verse, that the colon usually placed after σωθήσεται has been removed. Barnes has a comma in his text.

411. χειρία, ὑποχειρίαν ἐμαυτὴν διδοῦσα. Cf. inf. 628. Ion 1257.

417. π. χέρας. This expression occurs Alcest. 350.

418. The fondness of Euripides for

ΑΝΔΡΟΜΑΧΗ. 255

ψυχὴ τέκν'· ὅστις δ' αὔτ' ἄπειρος ὢν ψέγει,
ἧσσον μὲν ἀλγεῖ, δυστυχῶν δ' εὐδαιμονεῖ. 420
ΧΟ. ᾤκτειρ' ἀκούσασ'· οἰκτρὰ γὰρ τὰ δυστυχῆ
βροτοῖς ἅπασι, κἂν θυραῖος ὢν κυρῇ.
ἐς ξύμβασιν δὲ χρή σε σήν τε παῖδ' ἄγειν,
Μενέλαε, καὶ τήνδ', ὡς ἀπαλλαχθῇ πόνων.
ΜΕ. λάβεσθέ μοι τῆσδ', ἀμφελίξαντες χέρας, 425
δμῶες· λόγους γὰρ οὐ φίλους ἀκούσεται.
ἐγὼ δ', ἵν' ἁγνὸν βωμὸν ἐκλίποις θεᾶς,
προὔτεινα παιδὸς θάνατον, ᾧ σ' ὑπήγαγον
ἐς χεῖρας ἐλθεῖν τὰς ἐμὰς ἐπὶ σφαγήν.
καὶ τἀμφὶ σοῦ μὲν ὧδ' ἔχοντ' ἐπίστασο· 430
τὰ δ' ἀμφὶ παιδὸς τοῦδε παῖς ἐμὴ κρινεῖ,
ἤν τε κτανεῖν νιν ἤν τε μὴ κτανεῖν θέλῃ.
ἀλλ' ἕρπ' ἐς οἴκους τούσδ', ἵν' εἰς ἐλευθέρους

children is apparent from many passages. That he sometimes praises and sometimes blames a life of celibacy, is no inconsistency; for it is according as the blessing or the risk of children appears to him at the time to predominate. See Ion 489. 'I never fully felt it before,' Andromache says, 'but I now find that to myself as well as to all others, children are the very life and soul of a parent. It is easy for those, who have them not, to speak lightly of the tie; they are indeed spared from much pain and sorrow; but their supposed happiness is, after all, but wretchedness.' On the distinction between εὐτυχία and εὐδαιμονία see Med. 1230. For the use of ψυχὴ Pflugk well compares Hesiod, Opp. 688, χρήματα γὰρ ψυχὴ πέλεται δειλοῖσι βροτοῖσιν. For εὐτυχεῖν used of those who are blessed with offspring, see Ion 699, 772, 775. *Inf.* v. 713. Schol. ὁ τοιοῦτος κατὰ τὸ μὲν εἶναι ἄτεκνος δυστυχεῖ, κατὰ δὲ τὸ ἀπολελύσθαι τῆς τῶν παίδων φροντίδος, εὐδαιμονεῖ.

422. θυραῖος, unconnected by blood. See Alcest. 811. And this is perhaps the true meaning in a verse of the Agamemnon (1586), where Aegisthus, having called himself δίκαιος φόνου ῥαφεὺς, adds, καὶ τοῦδε τἀνδρὸς ἠψάμην θυραῖος ὤν, not as an immediate blood relation, (and therefore being exempt from the more heinous crime,) but in the position of a stranger coming from another country, where he had lived an exile.

423. σήν τε παῖδ' Elmsley for καὶ σὴν παῖδ' or σήν γε παῖδ'. Lascaris gives ἐχρῆν σε σὴν παῖδ' ἐξάγειν, but these are all so many attempts to complete the verse after the τε had dropped out. See on v. 548. Aldus has χρὴ for χρῆν or ἐχρῆν, and the present tense certainly suits the subjunctive following rather better. Besides, χρῆν would mean, 'you ought to have done so, but you have not;' whereas χρὴ allows that there is yet time for a reconciliation. And the reply of Menelaus to this is quite consistent; 'Seize her; she shall hear anything rather than terms of peace.' Matthiae's objection to χρὴ has little force, " Si monere voluisset chorus, quid nunc etiam faciendum esset Menelao, haud dubie plura addidisset, quibus magis etiam persuaderet Menelao." It is sufficient to reply, that the chorus rarely interposes more than three or four (generally two) verses in the dialogue of two actors; e. g. *inf.* 642, 691, 727, 954, &c. However, Pflugk, Hermann, Bothe, and Dindorf agree with him in preferring χρῆν.

427. ἐγὼ δ' Hermann for ἐγώ σ', one MS. having ἔγωγ'. The σε is only defensible on the ground that the poet was going to say ἐξηπάτησα παιδὸς θάνατον προτείνας.

δούλη γεγῶσα μήποθ' ὑβρίζειν μάθῃς.
ΑΝ. οἴμοι· δόλῳ μ' ὑπῆλθες, ἠπατήμεθα.   435
ΜΕ. κήρυσσ' ἅπασιν· οὐ γὰρ ἐξαρνούμεθα.
ΑΝ. ἦ ταῦτ' ἐν ὑμῖν τοῖς παρ' Εὐρώτᾳ σοφά;
ΜΕ. καὶ τοῖς γε Τροίᾳ, τοὺς παθόντας ἀντιδρᾶν.
ΑΝ. τὰ θεῖα δ' οὐ θεῖ', οὐδ' ἔχειν ἡγεῖ δίκην;
ΜΕ. ὅταν τάδ' ᾖ, τότ' οἴσομεν. σὲ δὲ κτενῶ.   440
ΑΝ. ἦ καὶ νεοσσὸν τόνδ', ὑπὸ πτερῶν σπάσας;
ΜΕ. οὐ δῆτα· θυγατρὶ δ', ἢν θέλῃ, δώσω κτανεῖν.
ΑΝ. οἴμοι· τί δῆτά σ' οὐ καταστένω, τέκνον;
ΜΕ. οὔκουν θρασεῖά γ' αὐτὸν ἐλπὶς ἀναμένει.
ΑΝ. ὦ πᾶσιν ἀνθρώποισιν ἔχθιστοι βροτῶν,   445
Σπάρτης ἔνοικοι, δόλια βουλευτήρια,
ψευδῶν ἄνακτες, μηχανορράφοι κακῶν,
ἑλικτὰ κοὐδὲν ὑγιὲς, ἀλλὰ πᾶν πέριξ
φρονοῦντες, ἀδίκως εὐτυχεῖτ' ἂν Ἑλλάδα.

434. μήποθ'. Perhaps μηκέθ'. Cf. v. 609.
439. ἔχειν δίκην. ' Do you imagine that God has no justice? Are you persuaded that there is no divine law of retribution for the guilty?' A lax use of ἔχειν δίκην, which is properly said of those who have got, or those who have given, satisfaction for a fault.
440. τάδ' ᾖ. When this divine retribution which you talk of arrives, I shall be prepared to bear it.
441. ὑπὸ πτερῶν. See Hec. 53. Electr. 495.
443. τί οὐ καταστένω; Why do I not at once commence the θρῆνος over you, as over a corpse, if you are to be given up to the tender mercies of Hermione? In the next verse οὔκουν—γε is for οὐ γοῦν, as is often the case.—θρασεῖα ἐλπὶς, like θάρσος ἐλπίδος Hec. 370.
445. This well-known speech against the Spartans must of course be taken to represent the poet's dislike of that people. This is clear also from the bad and deceitful character he generally attaches to Menelaus, and especially in the present play, where it has evidently been intentionally drawn so as to give a plausible ground for a political invective. See also Suppl. 187, and the exposure of Spartan customs, *inf.* 595. But why did Euripides so bitterly assail that people? His detractors are ever ready to reply, ' Because he wished to incite the Athenian people to prosecute the war against them with vigour.' No, that was not his reason; far from it. He disliked them just for those vices which to every good and honest and virtuous man are peculiarly odious; because they were deceitful, treacherous, fond of gain, lax in their public morals, unscrupulous in their political relations. He wished his own countrymen to have a better character through the nations of Hellas, and therefore he spoke plainly against the faults of their opponents. And he could do this in a time of war, though it might have been imprudent or impossible in a time of peace. Even Xenophon, that professed advocate and admirer of Spartan institutions, makes a curious admission at the close of his treatise on the Spartan polity, that the nation have sadly degenerated from what they were in the time of Lycurgus.
446. βουλευτήρια, the thing for the person, δόλια βουλευόμενοι. Aesch. Theb. 571, κακῶν Ἀδράστῳ τῶνδε βουλευτήριον.—ἄνακτες, σοφισταί, ἐπιστήμονες. Cf. Hel. 1267. Alcest. 498.
448. ἑλικτὰ—πέριξ. For σκολιά, οὐκ ὀρθῶς, φρονοῦντες,—as we say of an honest man that he is ' straight-forward.' Iph. A. 332, πλάγια φρονεῖν. Schol. ἡ μεταφορὰ ἀπὸ τῶν παρὰ γεωμέτραις γραμμάτων. For οὐδὲν ὑγιὲς see Bacch. 262.

τί δ' οὐκ ἐν ὑμῖν ἐστίν; οὐ πλεῖστοι φόνοι; 450
οὐκ αἰσχροκερδεῖς; οὐ λέγοντες ἄλλα μὲν
γλώσσῃ, φρονοῦντες δ' ἀλλ' ἐφευρίσκεσθ' ἀεί;
ὄλοισθ'· ἐμοὶ δὲ θάνατος οὐχ οὕτω βαρὺς
ὡς σοὶ δέδοκται. κεῖνα γάρ μ' ἀπώλεσεν,
ὅθ' ἡ τάλαινα πόλις ἀναλώθη Φρυγῶν 455
πόσις θ' ὁ κλεινὸς, ὅς σε πολλάκις δορὶ
ναύτην ἔθηκεν ἀντὶ χερσαίου κακόν.
νῦν δ' ἐς γυναῖκα γοργὸς ὁπλίτης φανεὶς
κτείνεις μ'. ἀπόκτειν'· ὡς ἀθώπευτόν γέ σε
γλώσσης ἀφήσω τῆς ἐμῆς καὶ παῖδα σήν. 460
ἐπεὶ σὺ μὲν πέφυκας ἐν Σπάρτῃ μέγας,
ἡμεῖς δὲ Τροίᾳ γ'. εἰ δ' ἐγὼ πράσσω κακῶς,
μηδὲν τόδ' αὔχει· καὶ σὺ γὰρ πράξειας ἄν.

XO. οὐδέποτε δίδυμα λέκτρ' ἐπαινέσω βροτῶν   στρ. α'.
οὐδ' ἀμφιμάτορας κόρους,

451. αἰσχροκερδεῖς. Cf. Ar. Pac. 622,
κἀνέπειθον τῶν Λακώνων τοὺς μεγίστους
χρήμασιν·
οἱ δ' ἆτ' ὄντες αἰσχροκερδεῖς καὶ διειρω-
νόξενοι
τήνδ' ἀπορρίψαντες αἰσχρῶς τὸν πόλεμον ἀνήρπασαν.

Pflugk, who also compares the above passage, adds, for what follows, Herod. ix. 54, ἐπιστάμενοι τὰ Λακεδαιμονίων φρονήματα ὡς ἄλλα φρονεόντων καὶ ἄλλα λεγόντων. This was, unfortunately, a characteristic of the Hellenic people generally, ἕτερον μὲν κεύθειν ἐνὶ φρεσὶν, ἄλλο δὲ βάζειν, as Homer expresses it.

454. ὡς. Hermann gives ὃς, after Lenting, because δέδοκται means 'has been determined upon' rather than 'appears to be.' However, the change does not seem necessary, since δέδοκται may mean, 'as has been concluded by you,' 'as you have determined to believe.' Schol. νενόμισται, δεδοκίμασται.

457. χερσαίου, 'a landsman,' χέρσος and πόντος being regularly opposed to each other. She means, of course, 'who often drove you back to your ships.'

463. μηδέν. See on v. 88. If the doctrine of *reverses* was a favourite one with the Greeks, who regarded unmixed happiness as next to an impossibility, so especially the gloomy temperament of Euripides was fond of dwelling upon it.— At the conclusion of the speech Andromache and her child are conducted within by the attendants who have held them in custody since v. 425. They appear to move slowly off the stage; for they are not yet out of sight of the spectators when Peleus arrives, v. 547.

464. The evils of a double marriage bed (i. e. of a wife and a concubine) are illustrated in the following ode by the comparison of two supreme rulers in a state, two musicians in a concert, and two pilots in a ship. The conduct of Hermione has shown this; for, intolerant of a rival, she would kill Andromache and her child, for the sake of her own nuptial rights. The time however will come, when she shall have cause to repent of her conduct.—The metres are, iambic trimeter and other varieties, antispastic (469 —70), and in the second strophe, besides three iambic trimeter verses, one wholly of resolved feet (484), v. 480 seems to be dactylic with an anacrusis, and v. 485 antispastic.

Ibid. ἀμφιμάτορας, with two mothers, i. e. several sons born from two or more women, but begotten by the same father. —For ἔριν μὲν Lascaris and several MSS. with the Scholiast give ἔριδας. Hermann suspects ἐρίσματ' οἴκων to be the true reading, as in Il. iv. 37, μὴ τοῦτό γε

ἔριν μὲν οἴκων, δυσμενεῖς τε λύπας.
μίαν μοι στεργέτω πόσις γάμοις
ἀκοινώνητον ἀνδρὸς εὐνάν.   470
οὐδέ γ' ἐνὶ πόλεσι δίπτυχοι τυραννίδες   ἀντ. α'.
μιᾶς ἀμείνονες φέρειν,
ἄχθος τ' ἐπ' ἄχθει καὶ στάσις πολίταις.   475
τόνων θ' ὕμνου συνεργάταιν δυοῖν
ἔριν Μοῦσαι φιλοῦσι κραίνειν·
πνοαὶ δ' ὅταν φέρωσι ναυτίλους θοαί,   στρ. β'.

νεῖκος ὀπίσσω σοὶ καὶ ἐμοὶ μέγ' ἔρισμα μετ' ἀμφοτέροισι γένηται. This is confirmed by the fact, that in more passages than one ὕβριν seems to have superseded ὕβρισμα. See Bacch. 1298. Yet ἔριδας may have been the ignorant correction of a grammarian offended by the singular between two plural nouns.

470. It seems best to construe γάμοις ἀκοινώνητον ἀνδρὸς, 'unshared by the man's marriage with another,' i. e. as Neoptolemus has a wife besides a concubine. See *sup.* v. 216. Pflugk would construe ἀκ. γάμοις, 'the marriage of a man not shared in by other alliances;' and lastly, the Scholiast explains εὐνὴν τὴν ἐμήν, καὶ αὐτὴν ἀκοινώνητον ἄλλου ἀνδρὸς, ἀντὶ τοῦ ἄμικτον.

471. The old reading οὐδὲ γὰρ ἐν πόλεσι was corrected by Lenting, whom Hermann follows. W. Dindorf transposes thus, οὐδ' ἐνὶ πόλεσι γάρ. The Spartan institution of having two kings at once may perhaps be alluded to. Some however have referred these words to the rivalry between Nicias and Alcibiades. The Schol. quotes the well-known verse of Homer, οὐκ ἀγαθὸν πολυκοιρανίη· εἷς κοίρανος ἔστω. These, says the poet, are not so good to bear as a single one. Of course, to an Athenian mind the idea of a βασιλεὺς was as of a thing οὐ φορητὸν under any circumstances. It was an ἄχθος at best, and one which, if doubled, became a crushing load.

476. τόνων Hermann for τεκτόνοιν or -ων. This is an acute emendation. The strophic verse indeed was commonly read τὴν μίαν μοι κτλ., but the same critic has rightly condemned the article as contrary to the usage of the language.—For ὕμνοισιν ἐργάται or ὕμνοιν ἐργάταιν Duport, with not less creditable sagacity (and it was not very often that this worthy Professor hit upon a really good emendation) restored ὕμνου συνεργάταιν. The meaning is, 'between two persons who together set the tones (or compose the music) of a hymn, the Muses are wont to create a quarrel.' The Schol. compares Hesiod, Opp. 26, καὶ πτωχὸς πτωχῷ φθονέει καὶ ἀοιδὸς ἀοιδῷ.

479—81. On this very difficult passage neither Pflugk, nor Dindorf, nor even Bothe, has a word of explanation. The Scholiast noticed the obscurity of the phrase κατὰ πηδαλίων, for he gives, besides another and less probable explanation, this comment, δύο κυβερνῆται ἐν μιᾷ νηὶ διχοστατοῦντες κατὰ τῶν πηδαλίων γίνονται, οὐχ ὑπὲρ τῶν πηδαλίων. Hermann thinks γνῶμα κατὰ πηδαλίων means 'an opinion against steering in this or that direction;' and he reads, chiefly on metrical grounds, κατὰ πηδαλίων διδύμα πραπίδων σοφᾶν γνώμα τὸ πλῆθος κτλ., i. e. in a dispute about sailing between two pilots, the many taken together are of less weight than the judgment of one who has the command. This, unfortunately, loses sight of the important antithesis between the πλῆθος σοφῶν and the εἷς φαυλότερος. Besides, only three or four copies give δίδυμαι γνῶμαι, the rest having διδύμα γνῶμα, except the edition of Brubach, διδύμᾳ γνώμᾳ. On the whole, it seems best to place a colon at γνώμα and to translate thus:—'When violent breezes carry sailors on their course, a double opinion of knowing minds (πραπίδων) is unfavourable to steering; and a plurality of wise persons at one and the same time, is of less avail than even the inferior mind of one who has the sole management; for this (ὁ) is real power both in the palace and in the state, when men choose to find the right time of exercising it.'

ΑΝΔΡΟΜΑΧΗ. 259

κατὰ πηδαλίων διδύμα πραπίδων γνώμα· 480
σοφῶν τε πλῆθος ἀθρόον ἀσθενέστερον
φαυλοτέρας φρενὸς αὐτοκρατοῦς
ἑνὸς, ὃ δύνασις ἀνά τε μέλαθρα κατά τε πόλιας
ὁπόταν εὑρεῖν θέλωσι καιρόν. 485
ἔδειξεν ἡ Λάκαινα τοῦ στρατηλάτα   ἀντ. β'.
Μενέλα· διὰ γὰρ πυρὸς ἦλθ' ἑτέρῳ λέχει,
κτείνει δὲ τὴν τάλαιναν Ἰλιάδα κόραν
παῖδά τε δύσφρονος ἔριδος ὕπερ. 490
ἄθεος, ἄνομος, ἄχαρις ὁ φόνος. ἔτι σε, πότνια,
μετατροπὰ τῶνδ' ἔπεισιν ἔργων.
καὶ μὴν ἐσορῶ τόδε σύγκρατον
ζεῦγος πρὸ δόμων, 495
ψήφῳ θανάτου κατακεκριμένον.
δύστηνε γύναι, τλῆμον δὲ σὺ, παῖ,
μητρὸς λεχέων ὃς ὑπερθνήσκεις,
οὐδὲν μετέχων, 500
οὐδ' αἴτιος ὢν βασιλεῦσιν.

ΑΝ. ἅδ' ἐγὼ χέρας αἱματη-   στρ.

484. ὃ for ἃ Hermann, who removed the full stop commonly placed after αὐτοκρατοῦς. The old reading, ἁ δύνασις, which is against the metre, obviously originated with those who did not perceive that the sense was continued. To take ἃ as the neuter plural is possible; but it is much less probable than ὃ, a short way of saying τοῦτο γὰρ δύναμιν ἔχει, scil. τὸ ἕνα αὐτοκρατῆ εἶναι.
487. διὰ πυρὸς ἦλθε, she has proceeded to violent measures against a rival. Compare Electr. 1182.—λέκτρῳ Lenting and W. Dindorf for λέχει.
490. ἀμφ' ἔριδος Hermann, a bold and scarcely necessary metrical correction.
491. πότνια for δέσποινα. 'Yet, O Lady, reverses will come upon you in consequence of these deeds.' Unless, with the Scholiast, we understand μετατροπὰ of her penitence. Hermann reads πότνια μετατροπὰ, 'divine retribution,' comparing Heracl. 104, πότνια γὰρ δίκα τάδ' οὐ πείσεται.
494. σύγκρατον, amicitiae vinculo conjunctum, Dindorf and Pflugk. And this seems better than to explain una morituros, or to take σύγκρατον θανάτῳ together, like οἴκτῳ τῷδε συγκεκραμένην, Ajac. 895. δειλαίᾳ συγκέκραμαι δύᾳ, Antig. 1311, compared by Hermann. See on φιλίας ἀνακίρνασθαι, Hippol. 254. Hermann thinks it possible that κατακεκριμένον is an interpolation; and in truth it is a prosaic rather than a poetical form. Euripides *might* have written thus: —καὶ μὴν ἐσορῶ ζεῦγος πρὸ δόμων | τόδε σύγκρατον ψήφῳ θανάτου. Schol. συγκεκροτημένον, συνεζευγμένον, δεδεμένον. The first word refers to a variant σύγκροτον, which is found in Lascaris, Aldus, and several MSS.
501. αἴτιος βασιλεῦσιν, guilty in the sight of Menelaus and Hermione.
502. The scene which follows is written in the glyconean measure, a rhythm peculiarly adapted for exciting pathos, and for this reason much more employed by Euripides than by Sophocles or Aeschylus. The introduction of a child on the stage is a licence rather sparingly adopted; see the note on Alcest. 393. Hermann's opinion on this point is given in the Introduction to this play.

ράς βρόχοισι κεκλημένα
πέμπομαι κατὰ γαίας.

ΜΟΛΟΣΣΟΣ.

μᾶτερ μᾶτερ, ἐγὼ δὲ σᾷ
πτέρυγι συγκαταβαίνω. 505

AN. θῦμα δάϊον, ὦ χθονὸς
Φθίας κράντορες.

ΜΟ. ὦ πάτερ,
μόλε φίλοις ἐπίκουρος.

AN. κείσει δή, τέκνον, ὦ φίλος, 510
μαστοῖς ματέρος ἀμφὶ σᾶς
νεκρὸς ὑπὸ χθονὶ σὺν νεκρῷ τ'.

ΜΟ. ὤμοι μοι, τί πάθω τάλας
δῆτ' ἐγὼ σύ τε, μᾶτερ;

ΜΕ. ἴθ' ὑποχθόνιοι· καὶ γὰρ ἀπ' ἐχθρῶν σύστ. 515
ἥκετε πύργων· δύο δ' ἐκ δισσαῖν
θνῄσκετ' ἀνάγκαιν· σὲ μὲν ἡμετέρα
ψῆφος ἀναιρεῖ, παῖδα δ' ἐμὴ παῖς
τόνδ' Ἑρμιόνη· καὶ γὰρ ἄνοια 520
μεγάλη λείπειν ἐχθροὺς ἐχθρῶν,
ἐξὸν κτείνειν
καὶ φόβον οἴκων ἀφελέσθαι.

506—7. Hermann first assigned the words θῦμα—κράντορες to Andromache. They were commonly continued to Molossus; an error readily detected by the arrangement of the persons in the antistrophe. The address is to Peleus and Neoptolemus, not, as Pflugk says, to the citizens of Phthia generally.

510. κείσῃ δή is said to be found in three or four MSS. Lascaris has κεῖσ' ἤδη, Aldus κεῖσο δ' ἤδη. These are evidently mere corruptions of κείσῃ for κείσει.

513. "τί πάθω est *quid faciam*," says Hermann; and this opinion seems widely prevalent, from the fancied analogy of κακῶς πράσσειν = κακῶς πάσχειν. Yet it is simply impossible that δρᾶν or πράσσειν, and its correlative πάσχειν, should ever have interchanged meanings. The true sense of τί πάθω is, 'What will become of me?' The subjunctive here represents the old epic usage in place of the future, and is wholly distinct from the *deliberative* subjunctive. The idiom is well illustrated by Od. v. 465, ὤμοι ἐγὼ τί πάθω; τί νύ μοι μήκιστα γένηται;

520. ἄνοια. This is one of the few instances which occur of the final α being made long in words of this kind, on which see the editor's note on Aesch. Theb. 397. So in Trach. 350, ἃ μὲν γὰρ ἐξείρηκας, ἀγνοίᾳ μ' ἔχει. The old copies give the usual accent, ἄνοια, and it is a question if in both places the α is not really made long by the following μ, as in Ἱππομέδοντος σχῆμα, Theb. 483.—ἐχθρῶν, supply παῖδας. For the principle here advocated, see the note on Heracl. 1005.

ΑΝ. ὦ πόσις πόσις, εἴθε σὰν   ἀντ.
     χεῖρα καὶ δόρυ σύμμαχον
     κτησαίμαν, Πριάμου παῖ.   525
ΜΟ. δύστανος, τί δ' ἐγὼ μόρου
     παράτροπον μέλος εὕρω;
ΑΝ. λίσσου, γούνασι δεσπότου
     χρίμπτων, ὦ τέκνον. ΜΟ: ὦ φίλος,   530
     φίλος, ἄνες θάνατόν μοι.
ΑΝ. λείβομαι δακρύοις κόρας,
     στάζω, λισσάδος ὡς πέτρας
     λιβὰς ἀνήλιος ἁ τάλαιν'.
ΜΟ. ὤμοι μοι.   τί δ' ἐγὼ κακῶν   535
     μῆχος ἐξανύσωμαι;
ΜΕ. τί με προσπίτνεις ἁλίαν πέτραν   ἀντισύστ.
     ἢ κῦμα λιταῖς ὣς ἱκετεύων;
     τοῖς γὰρ ἐμοῖσιν γέγον' ὠφελία,
     σοὶ δ' οὐδὲν ἔχω φίλτρον, ἐπεί τοι   540
     μέγ' ἀναλώσας ψυχῆς μόριον
     Τροίαν εἷλον καὶ μητέρα σήν·
     ἧς ἀπολαύων
     Ἅιδην χθόνιον καταβήσει.
ΧΟ. καὶ μὴν δέδορκα τόνδε Πηλέα πέλας,   545
     σπουδῇ τιθέντα δεῦρο γηραιὸν πόδα.

ΠΗΛΕΥΣ.

ὑμᾶς ἐρωτῶ τόν τ' ἐφεστῶτα σφαγῇ,

527. μέλος, the common reading, is clearly better than τέλος, adopted by W. Dindorf from two MSS. Molossus simply says, ' what strain shall *I* devise, to avert my fate?' i. e. what appeal to Menelaus for mercy.
530. χρίμπτων. Here, as in Ion 156, used intransitively.
533. Compare *sup.* v. 116.
536. ἐξανύσωμαι, *consequar*. Cf. Bacch. 131.
538. κῦμα. Med. 28, ὡς δὲ πέτρος ἢ θαλάσσιος κλύδων ἀκούει νουθετημένη φίλων. Prom. 1022, ὀχλεῖς μάτην με κῦμ' ὅπως παρηγορῶν.

539. τοῖς ἐμοῖσιν, to my daughter Hermione.
541. μέγα ψυχῆς μόριον, a large moiety of life, viz. the ten years of the siege, and the wear and tear accompanying it.—ἧς ἀπολαύων, either Τροίας or μητέρος, ' whose fault it will be (and not mine) that you (Molossus) shall descend to Hades.' Cf. Hel. 77.
547. The captives, followed by Menelaus, are on the point of leaving the stage, when Peleus, supported by an attendant, appears just in time to save them. Menelaus endeavours to sneak off, but is arrested by the firm and authoritative tone

τί ταῦτα ; πῶς τε κἀκ τίνος λόγου νοσεῖ
δόμος ; τί πράσσετ᾽ ἄκριτα μηχανώμενοι ;
Μενέλα᾽, ἐπίσχες· μὴ τάχυν᾽ ἄνευ δίκης. 550
ἡγοῦ σὺ θᾶσσον· οὐ γὰρ ὡς ἔοικέ μοι
σχολῆς τόδ᾽ ἔργον, ἀλλ᾽ ἀνηβητηρίαν
ῥώμην μ᾽ ἐπαινῶ λαμβάνειν, εἴπερ ποτέ.
πρῶτον μὲν οὖν κατ᾽ οὖρον, ὥσπερ ἱστίοις,
ἐμπνεύσομαι τῇδ᾽· εἰπὲ, τίνι δίκῃ χέρας 555
βρόχοισιν ἐκδήσαντες οἵδ᾽ ἄγουσί σε
καὶ παῖδ᾽· ὕπαρνος γάρ τις ὡς ἀπόλλυσαι,
ἡμῶν ἀπόντων τοῦ τε κυρίου σέθεν.

ΑΝ. οἶδ᾽, ὦ γεραιὲ, σὺν τέκνῳ θανουμένην
ἄγουσί μ᾽ οὕτως ὡς ὁρᾷς. τί σοι λέγω ; 560
οὐ γὰρ μιᾶς σε κληδόνος προθυμίᾳ
μετῆλθον, ἀλλὰ μυρίων ὑπ᾽ ἀγγέλων.
ἔριν δὲ τὴν κατ᾽ οἶκον οἶσθά που κλύων
τῆς τοῦδε θυγατρὸς, ὧν τ᾽ ἀπόλλυμαι χάριν.
καὶ νῦν με βωμοῦ Θέτιδος, ἣ τὸν εὐγενῆ 565
ἔτικτέ σοι παῖδ᾽ ἣν σὺ θαυμαστὴν σέβεις,
ἄγουσ᾽ ἀποσπάσαντες, οὔτε τῳ δίκῃ

of the old man. This was a scene in which the Athenians took particular delight, the chivalrous rescue of a suppliant from a tyrannical oppressor.

548. πῶς τε Hermann. The old reading was πῶς ταῦτ᾽ or καὶ πῶς. The attempts to restore the verse after τε had been lost are similar to those in v. 423.—ἄκριτα, before the matter has been brought to a fair trial, (ἄνευ δίκης, v. seq.,) for ἀκρίτως, in point of sense, though μηχανώμενοι requires an accusative after it.

553. ἐπαινῶ, I advise, exhort, recommend. The με seems rather the object to ἐπαινῶ, than the subject to λαμβάνειν. See on v. 256. The με however is only found in two MSS., and is not recognised in the Scholia. Matthiae compares Alcest. 641, καί μ᾽ οὐ νομίζω παῖδα σὸν πεφυκέναι. The sense is, 'now, if ever, there is need that I should feel young again.' It is nearly equivalent to the hortative conjunctive, φέρε ἀναλάβω κτλ. Cf. Aesch. Suppl. 600, ὥστ᾽ ἀνηβῆσαί με γηραιᾷ φρενί.

554. μὲν οὖν. Aldus has γε μὲν, and it is a question if γε μὴν is not the true reading. For it is more consistent to say, 'Now is the time for valour, *but* first I will console this captive,' than to proceed, '*therefore* I will console her,' as if the youthful valour were needed for that purpose.—ἐμπνεύσομαι, 'I will inspire her with courage;' properly, 'I will blow upon her as a gale blows on the sails of a ship to give it a favourable course,' οὐριοδραμεῖν, ὥστε κατ᾽ οὖρον φέρεσθαι.

556. ἐκδήσαντες, having tied your hands so as to drag you by the rope attached therefrom.—ὕπαρνος, like a sheep with its lamb led to the slaughter. The simile consists in this, that the lamb unconsciously follows its mother, to which alone compulsion is applied, just as Molossus followed Andromache, though not himself put in bonds. For, as Hermann remarks, he could not have been so, since he is invited to assist in untying his mother, v. 723.

566. θαυμαστήν. See Med. 1144. Elect. 84.

ΑΝΔΡΟΜΑΧΗ.

κρίναντες οὐδὲ τοὺς ἀπόντας ἐκ δόμων
μείναντες, ἀλλὰ τὴν ἐμὴν ἐρημίαν
γνόντες τέκνου τε τοῦδ', ὃν οὐδὲν αἴτιον 570
μέλλουσι σὺν ἐμοὶ τῇ ταλαιπώρῳ κτανεῖν.
ἀλλ' ἀντιάζω σ', ὦ γέρον, τῶν σῶν πάρος
πίτνουσα γονάτων, χειρὶ δ' οὐκ ἔξεστί μοι
τῆς σῆς λαβέσθαι φιλτάτης γενειάδος,
ῥῦσαί με πρὸς θεῶν· εἰ δὲ μή, θανούμεθα, 575
αἰσχρῶς μὲν ὑμῖν, δυστυχῶς δ' ἐμοί, γέρον.
ΠΗ. χαλᾶν κελεύω δεσμὰ πρὶν κλαίειν τινά,
καὶ τῆσδε χεῖρας διπτύχους ἀνιέναι.
ΜΕ. ἐγὼ δ' ἀπαυδῶ γ' ἄλλος οὐχ ἥσσων σέθεν,
καὶ τῆσδε πολλῷ κυριώτερος γεγώς. 580
ΠΗ. πῶς; ἦ τὸν ἀμὸν οἶκον οἰκήσεις μολὼν
δεῦρ'; οὐχ ἅλις σοι τῶν κατὰ Σπάρτην κρατεῖν;
ΜΕ. εἷλόν νιν αἰχμάλωτον ἐκ Τροίας ἐγώ.
ΠΗ. οὑμὸς δέ γ' αὐτὴν ἔλαβε παῖς παιδὸς γέρας.
ΜΕ. οὔκουν ἐκείνου τἀμὰ τἀκείνου τ' ἐμά; 585
ΠΗ. δρᾶν εὖ, κακῶς δ' οὔ, μηδ' ἀποκτείνειν βίᾳ.
ΜΕ. ὡς τήνδ' ἀπάξεις οὔποτ' ἐξ ἐμῆς χερός.
ΠΗ. σκήπτρῳ δὲ τῷδε σὸν καθαιμάξω κάρα.
ΜΕ. ψαῦσον δ', ἵν' εἰδῇς, καὶ πέλας πρόσελθέ μου.
ΠΗ. σὺ γὰρ μετ' ἀνδρῶν, ὦ κάκιστε κἀκ κακῶν; 590
σοί που μέτεστιν ὡς ἐν ἀνδράσιν λόγου;

568. οὔτε—οὐδέ. 'Neither—nor yet.' W. Dindorf, after Lenting, reads οὔτε in the latter place, against all the copies.—τοὺς ἀπόντας, Neoptolemus. Cf. 378.
571. κτενεῖν Dindorf, with Aldus. See v. 407.
573. χειρί. She extends towards him, as far as she can do, her fettered hands; a stroke of pathos very characteristic of Euripides.
577. κλαίειν, οἰμώζειν, 'or somebody shall suffer for it.' Cf. v. 634.—διπτύχους, not simply for δισσὰς, but 'folded one upon another and tied there.'
581. τὸν ἀμόν. Some copies give ἀμόν, others ἐμόν. There is some probability in Lenting's conjecture, ἦ σὺ τὸν ἐμὸν κτλ.
584. οὑμὸς παῖς παιδός, 'my grandson.'

See Bacch. 1329.—γέρας, see Tro. 274.
585. ἐκείνου τἀμά. See above, v. 374.
586. Before this verse some MSS. insert ναί. Cf. v. 242.
589. ψαῦσον δ'. So Lascaris and others. The readings γ' and θ' are also found; but Hermann supposes the δ' takes up the δὲ of the preceding speaker, and observes that "altercantes eadem dicendi forma, qua alter usus erat, respondent," quoting a remarkable example from Oed. R. 547 —52. The δὲ however in 588 is rather irregular. The conjecture of Pflugk has much to commend it, σκήπτρῳ γε τῷδε σὸν καθαιμάξας κάρα, scil. ἀπάξω.—ἵν' εἰδῇς, see on Heracl. 65.
591. ὡς ἐν ἀνδράσιν, scil. ὄντι. The enclitic που is not very common in interrogative sentences. Prom. 762, τί

ΕΥΡΙΠΙΔΟΥ

ὅστις πρὸς ἀνδρὸς Φρυγὸς ἀπηλλάγης λέχους,
ἄκληστ', ἄδουλα δώμαθ' ἑστίας λιπών,
ὡς δὴ γυναῖκα σώφρον' ἐν δόμοις ἔχων,
πασῶν κακίστην. οὐδ' ἂν εἰ βούλοιτό τις   595
σώφρων γένοιτο Σπαρτιατίδων κόρη,
αἳ ξὺν νέοισιν ἐξερημοῦσαι δόμους
γυμνοῖσι μηροῖς καὶ πέπλοις ἀνειμένοις
δρόμους παλαίστρας τ' οὐκ ἀνασχετοὺς ἐμοὶ

που δράσεις, ὅταν τὰ λοιπὰ πυνθάνῃ κακά;
593. ἄκληστ', ἄδουλα. 'Without a bolt to fasten it, and without a slave to keep it.' An hyperbole in speaking; but the taunt intended is, that Menelaus was so carelessly indolent as to leave his young wife unguarded in the company of the handsome Paris. Compare Troad. 944, ὃν, ὦ κάκιστε, σοῖσιν ἐν δόμοις λιπὼν Σπάρτης ἀπῆρας νηὶ Κρησίαν χθόνα. Hermann, who is offended at the idea of a queen being left in the charge of slaves, and also at the expression δώμαθ' ἑστίας, where ἑστίαν δόμων is the usual phrase, ventures to edit ἄβουλα, which he construes with ἑστίας, 'a house whose interior has no βουλὴ or management.' This is decidedly bad. It has been elsewhere remarked (see Med. 1137), that δῶμα and δόμος often mean 'a room.' Hence δώματα ἑστίας is nothing more than θαλάμους δόμων.
595 seqq. This is a very interesting passage. It was consistent in Euripides, to whom the immorality of women was a perpetual scandal, to inveigh against what seemed to him, as an Athenian, a very lax usage,—the free society of the sexes in the athletic national games. Possibly the details of this well-known concession on the part of Lycurgus have been exaggerated by writers against it; but Lycurgus certainly understood human nature well. His direct object was, not to promote but to check unlawful appetites, and to provide for as fine and healthy a race of children as could be produced for the service of the state. Xenophon, De Republ. Lac. i. 4, ταῖς δ' ἐλευθέραις μέγιστον νομίσας εἶναι τὴν τεκνοποιίαν πρῶτον μὲν σωμασκεῖν ἔταξεν οὐδὲν ἧττον τὸ θῆλυ τοῦ ἄρρενος φύλου· ἔπειτα δὲ δρόμου καὶ ἰσχύος, ὥσπερ καὶ τοῖς ἀνδράσιν, οὕτω καὶ ταῖς θηλείαις ἀγῶνας πρὸς ἀλλήλας ἐποίησε, νομίζων ἐξ ἀμφοτέρων ἰσχυρῶν καὶ τὰ ἔκγονα ἐρρωμενέστερα γίγνεσθαι. On this subject the following sensible remarks are from a late writer on India. "Nor can we doubt, while we reprobate the system of Lycurgus, which sought to destroy by familiarity the pruriency of the imagination, that it was so far a successful, though a most ungraceful expedient; and one that, by uprooting personal bashfulness, and with it all our dreams of female sacredness and reverence, and in rendering common what is chiefly desired as rare, had a fatal tendency to divert the passions from their natural course, and beget an indifference in particulars wherein the most delicate nicety should prevail." This is true; but the general fact cannot be questioned, that great familiarity in the daily intercourse of the sexes is consistent with a great degree of chastity; and the customs of many barbarous nations to this day prove it. Propertius, though he writes as a sensualist, and for sensual reasons, expresses no virtuous horror at these Spartan institutions. He says (Lib. iv. 14, 1),

"Multa tuae, Sparte, miramur jura palaestrae,
  Sed mage virginei tot bona gymnasii,
Cum non infames exercet corpore ludos
  Inter luctantes nuda puella viros."

Theocr. xviii. 23,
ἄμμες γὰρ πᾶσαι συνομάλικες, αἷς δρόμος αὑτὸς
χρισαμέναις ἀνδριστὶ παρ' Εὐρώταο ῥεέθροις.

598. The γυμνοὶ μηροὶ refer to the custom of leaving the lower part of the χιτὼν open at each side, whence Spartan maids were called φαινομηρίδες: the πέπλοι ἀνειμένοι to the looseness of the κόλπος. They wore only the tunic, or rather, perhaps, did not wear the πέπλος or shawl

κοινὰς ἔχουσι. κᾆτα θαυμάζειν χρεὼν
εἰ μὴ γυναῖκας σώφρονας παιδεύετε;
Ἑλένην ἐρέσθαι χρῆν τάδ', ἥτις ἐκ δόμων
τὸν σὸν λιποῦσα φίλιον ἐξεκώμασε
νεανίου μετ' ἀνδρὸς εἰς ἄλλην χθόνα.
κᾆπειτ' ἐκείνης οὕνεχ' Ἑλλήνων ὄχλον
τοσόνδ' ἀθροίσας ἤγαγες πρὸς Ἴλιον·
ἣν χρῆν σ' ἀποπτύσαντα μὴ κινεῖν δόρυ,
κακὴν ἐφευρόντ', ἀλλ' ἐᾶν αὐτοῦ μένειν,
μισθόν τε δόντα μήποτ' εἰς οἴκους λαβεῖν.
ἀλλ' οὔ τι ταύτῃ σὸν φρόνημ' ἐπούρισας·
ψυχὰς δὲ πολλὰς κἀγαθὰς ἀπώλεσας,
παίδων τ' ἄπαιδας γραῦς ἔθηκας ἐν δόμοις,
πολιούς τ' ἀφείλου πατέρας εὐγενῆ τέκνα.
ὧν εἷς ἐγὼ δύστηνος, αὐθέντην δὲ σὲ,
μιάστορ' ὥς τιν', εἰσδέδορκ' Ἀχιλλέως,

600

605

610

615

properly so called. Hence Hec. 933, λέχη δὲ φίλια μονόπεπλος λιποῦσα, Δωρὶς ὡς κόρα, means μονοχίτων ἄνευ πέπλου.

602. ἐρέσθαι τάδε, viz. whether Spartan women are chaste.—ἥτις, 'inasmuch as she,' &c.—τὸν σὸν φίλιον, scil. Δία, for τὸ σὸν λέκτρον,—a remarkable ellipse. Photius, Φίλιος Ζεύς, ὁ τὰ περὶ τὰς φιλίας ἐπισκοπῶν. He cites a passage from Pherecrates, in the glyconean metre,

τοῖς δὲ κριταῖς
τοῖς νυνὶ κρίνουσι λέγω,
μὴ 'πιορκεῖν μηδ' ἀδίκως
κρίνειν, ἤ, νὴ τὸν Φίλιον,
μῦθον εἰς ὑμᾶς ἕτερον
Φιλοκράτης λέξει πολὺ τούτου κακηγοριστότερον.

Musgrave compares Plat. Alcib. i. p. 109, D, μὰ τὸν Φίλιον τὸν ἐμόν τε καὶ σὸν, ὃν ἐγὼ ἥκιστ' ἂν ἐπιορκήσαιμι. Add Lucian, Toxaris, § 11, p. 518, ὀμούμεθα, εἴ τι καὶ ὅρκου δεῖν νομίζεις. τίς δέ σοι τῶν ἡμετέρων θεῶν; ἆρ' ἱκανὸς ὁ Φίλιος;— ἐξεκώμασε, (as we say,) 'ran off with another gallant,' the κῶμος and κωμάζειν being especially used of lover's visits, as in the familiar verse of Theocritus, κω-μάσδω ποτὶ τὰν Ἀμαρυλλίδα.

605. κἄπειτα. 'And yet, faithless as she was, you nevertheless raised an army to regain her.'

609. μήποτ'. Perhaps μηκέτ', as in v. 434. So far from wishing to regain her, he should have been glad to pay a sum of money to any one who would rid him of such a burden.

610. ἐπούρισας. 'It was not this way that you directed the gale of your thoughts;' or, as we say familiarly, 'it was not *that* way that the wind blew.' Hesych. ἐπουρίσας, ἐφορμήσας, and so the Scholiast on this verse. In Prom. 986, Hermann has well restored ἐς τάσδε σαυτὸν πημονὰς κατούρισας, for καθώρμισας, the Med. MS. giving καθώροσας. These two last readings arose from a gloss καθώρμησας. Cf. Eum. 132, σὺ δ' αἱματηρὸν πνεῦμ' ἐπουρίσασα τῷ.

615. The editors, by placing a full stop at Ἀχιλλέως (Bothe however having a colon), materially weaken the sense of the whole passage (614—18), which is this; ' I regard you as the murderer of Achilles, not by your own prowess (for you avoided coming into close conflict), but by the secret and malign agency of some evil demon.'—οὐδὲ τρωθείς, 'without even a sword-wound,' opposed to βεβλημένος, hit with a javelin, as the Schol. well explains it. "Exprobrat Menelao Peleus, quod non comminus sit cum hoste congressus." *Herm.*

ὃς οὐδὲ τρωθεὶς ἦλθες ἐκ Τροίας μόνος,
κάλλιστα τεύχη δ' ἐν καλοῖσι σάγμασιν
ὅμοι' ἐκεῖσε δεῦρό τ' ἤγαγες πάλιν·
κἀγὼ μὲν ηὔδων τῷ γαμοῦντι μήτε σοι
κῆδος ξυνάψαι μήτε δώμασιν λαβεῖν   620
κακῆς γυναικὸς πῶλον· ἐκφέρουσι γὰρ
μητρῷ ὀνείδη. τοῦτο καὶ σκοπεῖτέ μοι,
μνηστῆρες, ἐσθλῆς θυγατέρ' ἐκ μητρὸς λαβεῖν.
πρὸς τοῖσδε δ' εἰς ἀδελφὸν οἷ' ἐφύβρισας,
σφάξαι κελεύσας θυγατέρ' εὐηθέστατα.   625
οὕτως ἔδεισας μὴ οὐ κακὴν δάμαρτ' ἔχοις.
ἑλὼν δὲ Τροίαν, εἶμι γὰρ κἀνταῦθά σοι,
οὐκ ἔκτανες γυναῖκα χειρίαν λαβών·
ἀλλ' ὡς ἐσεῖδες μαστόν, ἐκβαλὼν ξίφος
φίλημ' ἐδέξω, προδότιν αἰκάλλων κύνα,   630
ἥσσων πεφυκὼς Κύπριδος, ὦ κάκιστε σύ.
κἄπειτ' ἐς οἴκους τῶν ἐμῶν ἐλθὼν τέκνων
πορθεῖς ἀπόντων, καὶ γυναῖκα δυστυχῆ
κτείνεις ἀτίμως παῖδά θ', ὃς κλαίοντά σε
καὶ τὴν ἐν οἴκοις σὴν καταστήσει κόρην,   635

617. κάλλιστα τεύχη. Your shield undimmed, unsoiled, and without that πυκνὸς κροτησμὸς which a warrior's shield should exhibit on his return from war, Aesch. Theb. 556.—Photius, σάγμα, τὸ τῆς ἀσπίδος ἔλυτρον. Schol. θήκαις τῶν ἀσπίδων.

619. ηὔδων. Pflugk and others adopt ᾖδον, an inferior reading, and of much less authority. Herm. and Dind. rightly give ηὔδων with Lasc. Ald. and most of the MSS. 'I for my part kept telling Neoptolemus neither to contract an affinity with you, nor to receive in his house the child of a bad woman; for,' said I, 'they bring into another home the discredit that belongs to their mothers.' Schol. ἀπομάττονταί τι, καὶ κομίζουσιν εἰς τοὺς γάμους. On a somewhat different sense of ἐκφέρειν, 'to divulge,' see Hipp. 649.

622. The καὶ appears to mean, 'Take care to get not only a wife in herself good, but the child of a good mother also.'

625. Hermann and Pflugk place an interrogation at εὐηθέστατα, as if ποῖα, not οἷα, had preceded. See on Hel. 461. The neuter plural belongs to σφάξαι, not to κελεύσας. The *request* was selfish, cruel, heartless; the *act* on the part of Agamemnon was weakly compliant, and argued a simple and unsuspecting character.

626. ἔχοις W. Dindorf for ἔχῃς, several copies giving ἔχεις. The sense is, ἔδεισας μὴ ἁμάρτοις κτλ.

630. αἰκάλλων, fawning upon, wheedling, using blandishments to, &c. Ar. Equit. 47, ὑποπεσὼν τὸν δεσπότην ἤκαλλ', ἐθώπευ'. The story, which Hermann observes, after the Schol. on Lysistr. 155, was borrowed from the Cyclic poem of Lesches called "The Little Iliad," is alluded to by Aristophanes himself in the latter passage, ὁ γῶν Μενέλαος τᾶς Ἑλένας τὰ μᾶλά πα γυμνᾶς παρενιδὼν ἐξέβαλ', οἴω, τὸ ξίφος. Cf. Orest. 1287. Again the uxorious character of Menelaus is spoken of to his reproach.

ΑΝΔΡΟΜΑΧΗ.

κεἰ τρὶς νόθος πέφυκε.   πολλάκις δέ τοι
ξηρὰ βαθεῖαν γῆν ἐνίκησε σπορᾷ,
νόθοι τε πολλοὶ γνησίων ἀμείνονες.
ἀλλ' ἐκκομίζου παῖδα.   κύδιον βροτοῖς
πένητα χρηστὸν ἢ κακὸν καὶ πλούσιον   640
γαμβρὸν πεπᾶσθαι καὶ φίλον· σὺ δ' οὐδὲν εἶ.
ΧΟ. σμικρᾶς ἀπ' ἀρχῆς νεῖκος ἀνθρώποις μέγα
γλῶσσ' ἐκπορίζει· τοῦτο δ' οἱ σοφοὶ βροτῶν
ἐξευλαβοῦνται, μὴ φίλοις τεύχειν ἔριν.
ΜΕ. τί δῆτ' ἂν εἴποις τοὺς γέροντας ὡς σοφοὶ   645
καὶ τοὺς φρονεῖν δοκοῦντας Ἕλλησίν ποτε;
ὅτ' ὢν σὺ Πηλεὺς, καὶ πατρὸς κλεινοῦ γεγὼς,
κῆδος ξυνάψας, αἰσχρὰ μὲν σαυτῷ λέγεις,
ἡμῖν δ' ὀνείδη διὰ γυναῖκα βάρβαρον,
ἣν χρῆν σ' ἐλαύνειν τὴν ὑπὲρ Νείλου ῥοὰς   650

636. τρὶς νόθος. Musgrave well compares Soph. Oed. R. 1081, οὐδ' ἂν ἐκ τρίτης ἐγὼ μητρὸς φανῶ τρίδουλος, and Pflugk Dem. p. 1327, 3, πονηρὸς ἐκ τριγονίας.—In the next verse σπορᾷ is the reading of Lascaris and two MSS., but the Schol. recognizes only the nominative. The dative might mean 'in its crop,' ξηρᾷ γῇ being understood; but, like *seges*, σπορὰ seems to have been both the crop and the place where it grows. The γῆ βαθεῖα is that sort of land which Virgil in the Georgics deprecates as too rich, 'ah nimium ne sit mihi fertilis illa,' &c., because the corn was thought to produce great stalks but small ears. The Schol. explains the text to mean, 'rough land if cultivated is better than rich land untilled.' The word ξηρὰ means not merely 'dry' but what we call 'poor land,' as the antithesis shows.

638. νόθοι—γνησίων. Euripides, who is fond of what to his audience would seem paradoxes, as, that humble birth may be better than nobility, poverty than riches, and so forth, has the present statement also in Hipp. 309, νόθον, φρονοῦντα γνήσι', οἶσθά νιν καλῶς, Ἱππόλυτον.

639. ἐκκομίζου, get your daughter removed from the house.—κύδιον. Hesych. κρεῖττον, αἱρετώτερον. We have κύδιστος for βέλτιστος in Aesch. Suppl. 13. The positive was originally κυδὺς, like ὀξὺς, ἡδὺς, &c. Hence κῦδος and κυδρὸς, as αἰσχὺς gave αἶσχος, αἰσχρὸς, αἰσχίων, αἴσχιστος.

641. γαμβρὸν καὶ φίλον, whether as a relative by marriage, or as a friend. Pflugk needlessly restricts γαμβρὸν here to the sense of 'father-in-law.'

644. τεύχειν ἔριν. So τεύχειν στάσιν Aesch. Pers. 191. κακὸν Cho. 717.

645—6. τί δῆτα κτλ. 'Why then should you say of old men that they are wise, and of those who once had the reputation of good sense with the Greeks, (that they really had it)?'—τοὺς γέροντας, old men generally, τοὺς γ. ὄντας. The allusion in the next verse is special, viz. to the seven so-called wise men of Greece, whose gnomes or wise saws are often quoted by the tragic writers. After the next line Matthiae and Dindorf mark the loss of one or more verses. There is no appearance, in the context, of any *lacuna*; but κῆδος ξυνάψας was thought too indefinite in itself to convey any clear meaning. Hermann, Lenting, and Pflugk seem to judge more correctly in supposing ἐμοὶ to be understood; 'You have contracted a relationship-by-marriage with me (by your grandson having wedded my daughter), and then you insult me, as well as disgrace yourself, in taking part with a foreign woman.' Hermann thinks κῆδος ξυνάψας sufficiently explained by its close connexion with ἡμῖν δ' ὀνείδη.

650. The common reading of this verse,

ὑπέρ τε Φᾶσιν, κἀμὲ παρακαλεῖν ἀεί,
οὖσαν μὲν Ἠπειρῶτιν, οὗ πεσήματα
πλεῖσθ᾽ Ἑλλάδος πέπτωκε δοριπετῆ νεκρῶν,
τοῦ σοῦ τε παιδὸς αἵματος κοινουμένην·
Πάρις γάρ, ὃς σὸν παῖδ᾽ ἔπεφν᾽ Ἀχιλλέα,   655
Ἕκτορος ἀδελφὸς ἦν, δάμαρ δ᾽ ἥδ᾽ Ἕκτορος.
καὶ τῇδέ γ᾽ εἰσέρχει σὺ ταὐτὸν ἐς στέγος,
καὶ ξυντράπεζον ἀξιοῖς ἔχειν βίον,
τίκτειν δ᾽ ἐν οἴκοις παῖδας ἐχθίστους ἐᾷς;
ἀγὼ προνοίᾳ τῇ τε σῇ κἀμῇ, γέρον,   660
κτανεῖν θέλων τήνδ᾽ ἐκ χερῶν ἁρπάζομαι.
καίτοι φέρ᾽, ἅψασθαι γὰρ οὐκ αἰσχρὸν λόγου,

ἣν χρῆν σ᾽ ἐλαύνειν τήνδ᾽ κτλ., is defended by Pflugk on the ground that τήνδε is a pleonasm (he should have said, a confused construction or asyndeton) after the relative, as *inf.* 1115, ὧν Κλυταιμνήστρας τόκος εἷς ἦν ἁπάντων τῶνδε μηχανορράφος. Hermann adds Philoct. 315, οἷς Ὀλύμπιοι θεοὶ δοῖέν ποτ᾽ αὐτοῖς ἀντίποιν᾽ ἐμοῦ παθεῖν, (though here αὐτοῖς is emphatic, *et ipsis pati.*) The Scholiast seems to have read ἣν χρῆν σ᾽ ἐλαύνειν τῆσδ᾽, for he explains it ἀπορρίψαι ταύτης τῆς γῆς. And this is defensible, without doubt; compare Aesch. Cho. 281, διώκεσθαι πόλεως. Soph. Phil. 613, ἄγοιτο νήσου τῆσδε. *Inf.* v. 1061, ἄγων χθονὸς, scil. ἔξω. However, it seems best to choose one of two equally plausible emendations; that of W. Dindorf, as given in the text above, where ὁδὸν is to be supplied; ' whereas you ought to have driven her away by the route to the furthest south or the furthest east' &c., and that of L. Dindorf, ὃν χρῆν ἐλαύνειν τήνδε, κτλ. Hermann reads κἂν ὑπὲρ κτλ., " ut nonnihil restringatur nimia exaggeratio." This is as bold, if not as needless, as his alteration of the next verse to κἀμὲ τοῦτο παρακαλεῖν. The ἀεί seems to mean, that he ought constantly to have been exhorting Menelaus to assist him, until the deed was done.

652. Ἠπειρῶτιν. See v. 159. Here the fact of her coming from a hostile country is alone meant.—πεσήματα νεκρῶν is said in conformity with a rule laid down by Phrynichus, p. 375, that πτῶμα was not used alone for ' a corpse,' but πτώματα νεκρῶν &c. However, there is an exception in Aesch. Suppl. 647.—οὗ, scil. ἐν Ἠπείρῳ. Cf. Hec. 711.

654. Dindorf gives δὲ for τε. This sort of criticism proceeds on the fallacious principle of laying down certain fixed grammatical rules, and then altering every passage to suit them. Euripides seems to have had in mind some such sentence as this, ἢ ἄλλους τε πολλοὺς ὤλεσε, καὶ τοῦ σοῦ παιδὸς φόνου μεταιτία ἦν.

655. Πάρις γὰρ κτλ. The reasoning of Menelaus reminds us of the fable of the wolf and the lamb; but it was not the object of the poet to represent him either as logical or as just; besides, the Greek notion of revenge was not very limited in its application.

657. σύ. 'And do *you* (Peleus), of all men in the world, dare to enter the same house with the murderess of your son?'

661. For κτανεῖν W. Dindorf reads παύειν with Brunck; an alteration which has not the slightest probability. The poet meant to say ἃ προνοούμενος ὑπὲρ σοῦ καὶ ὑπὲρ ἐμοῦ, but he left the ἃ to be governed by the general sense of the clause. And so the Scholiast has rightly explained it.

662. καίτοι. (You will say, that to put her to death is a needless cruelty.) Well then, let us view the matter thus:—Suppose she lives, and bears children, while Hermione remains childless. Will you, Peleus, place on the throne of Phthia the foreign children who have supplanted my daughter in her just claims? And shall I still be told that I am foolish, in hating what is wrong, while you are wise, for the contrary reason?

ἢν παῖς μὲν ἡμὴ μὴ τέκῃ, ταύτης δ' ἄπο
βλάστωσι παῖδες, τῆσδε γῆς Φθιώτιδος
στήσεις τυράννους, βάρβαροι δ' ὄντες γένος   665
Ἕλλησιν ἄρξουσ' ; εἶτ' ἐγὼ μὲν οὐ φρονῶ,
μισῶν τὰ μὴ δίκαια, σοὶ δ' ἔνεστι νοῦς ;
κἀκεῖνό νυν ἄθρησον· εἰ σὺ παῖδα σὴν
δούς τῳ πολιτῶν, εἶτ' ἔπασχε τοιάδε,
σιγῇ κάθησ' ἄν ; οὐ δοκῶ· ξένης δ' ὕπερ   670
τοιαῦτα λάσκεις τοὺς ἀναγκαίους φίλους ;
καὶ μὴν ἴσον γ' ἀνήρ τε καὶ γυνὴ σθένει
ἀδικουμένη πρὸς ἀνδρός· ὡς δ' αὔτως ἀνὴρ
γυναῖκα μωραίνουσαν ἐν δόμοις ἔχων.
καὶ τῷ μέν ἐστιν ἐν χεροῖν μέγα σθένος,   675
τῇ δ' ἐν γονεῦσι καὶ φίλοις τὰ πράγματα.
οὔκουν δίκαιον τοῖς γ' ἐμοῖς ἐπωφελεῖν ;
γέρων γέρων εἶ· τὴν δ' ἐμὴν στρατηγίαν
λέγων ἔμ' ὠφελοῖς ἂν ἢ σιγῶν πλέον.
Ἑλένη δ' ἐμόχθησ' οὐχ ἑκοῦσ', ἀλλ' ἐκ θεῶν,   680

668. εἰ σὺ κτλ. If you, Peleus, had been in my place, and known that your daughter had been wronged as the wife of one of the citizens; would *you* have been as quiet under the affront as you advise me to be? Compare Ar. Ach. 541, φέρ', εἰ Λακεδαιμονίων τις, ἐκπλεύσας σκάφει, ἀπέδοτο φήνας κυνίδιον Σεριφίων, καθῆσθ' ἂν ἐν δόμοισιν; ἢ πολλοῦ γε δεῖ. The *nominativus pendens* presents no difficulty. He should have said, εἰ σὺ ἔδωκας, κᾆτα ἔπασχε, or εἰ σὺ δοὺς, ἔπειτα τοιάδε πάσχουσαν εἶδες. A similar instance is cited by Pflugk from Herc. F. 185, Δίρφυν δ' ἐρωτῶν, ἥ σ' ἔθρεψ', Ἀβαντίδα, οὐκ ἄν σ' ἐπαινέσειεν. It is however a question whether we should not read εἴγ' for εἶτ', in this sense; ἄθρησον, εἰ σύ, δοὺς παῖδα σὴν πολιτῶν τινί, σιγῇ καθῆσο ἂν, εἴγε ἐκείνη τοιάδε ἔπασχε. Thus, of course, the sentence ceases to be interrogative; but εἴπερ rather than εἴγε would seem to be required.

671. Photius, λάσκε, λέγε. Aesch. Ag. 579, ἔλασκον εὐφημοῦντες ἐν θεῶν ἕδραις. Suppl. 854, ἄγρια γὰρ σὺ λάσκεις. The construction is the same as in v. 645. Hipp. 119, &c.

672. καὶ μὴν—γε. "Hoc dicit poeta;

par mulieri, si ei a marito injuria fit, jus est, ac viro: sed vir in se ipso praesidium habet, mulier in parentibus et cognatis." Hermann on Elmsley's Medea, v. 313. By ἴσον σθένει he means, that the claims for redress are equally strong, though the methods of obtaining it are different.— ὡς αὔτως, i. e. καὶ ἀνὴρ ἀδικούμενος πρὸς γυναικός. For μωραίνειν is to be unfaithful to her marriage vows. See on Ion 545. Schol. αἱ ζεύξεις τῶν ἀνδρῶν πρὸς τὰς γυναῖκας ἐπὶ ἰσότητι γίνονται, οὐχ ἵνα ὁ μὲν ἀνὴρ ἀδικῇ, ἡ δὲ γυνὴ ἀδικῆται· οἷον ἴσον τὸ γυναῖκα ἀδικεῖσθαι ὑπὸ ἀνδρός, καὶ ἄνδρα ὑπὸ γυναικός. Stobaeus, lxxiv. 24, quotes v. 672—7, with the variant τοῖς ἐμοῖς ἔμ' ὠφελεῖν. Hence Matthiae and Pflugk, after Reiske, insert μ' after ἐμοῖς. But this is needless; see on Hel. 802.

678. γέρων εἶ. The implied antithesis is, ἀλλ' οὐ σοφῶς ὀνειδίζεις ἐμοὶ τὰ ἐν Τροίᾳ πραχθέντα, v. 616 seqq.

680. ἐμόχθησε. He uses a mild word, as Matthiae observes, to conceal his wife's guilt. 'Poor Helen's troubles were not of her own seeking, but were sent by heaven for the ultimate benefit of Hellas.' See this specious argument maintained in Troad. 932 by Helen herself; τοσόνδ'

καὶ τοῦτο πλεῖστον ὠφέλησεν Ἑλλάδα·
ὅπλων γὰρ ὄντες καὶ μάχης ἀΐστορες
ἔβησαν ἐς τἀνδρεῖον· ἡ δ' ὁμιλία
πάντων βροτοῖσι γίγνεται διδάσκαλος.
εἰ δ' ἐς πρόσοψιν τῆς ἐμῆς ἐλθὼν ἐγὼ   685
γυναικὸς ἔσχον μὴ κτανεῖν, ἐσωφρόνουν.
οὐδ' ἂν σὲ Φῶκον ἤθελον κατακτανεῖν.
ταῦτ' εὖ φρονῶν σ' ἐπῆλθον, οὐκ ὀργῆς χάριν.
ἢν δ' ὀξυθυμῇς, σοὶ μὲν ἡ γλωσσαλγία
μείζων, ἐμοὶ δὲ κέρδος ἡ προμηθία.   690
ΧΟ. παύσασθον ἤδη, λῷστα γὰρ μακρῷ τάδε,
λόγων ματαίων, μὴ δύο σφαλῆθ' ἅμα.
ΠΗ. οἴμοι, καθ' Ἑλλάδ' ὡς κακῶς νομίζεται.
ὅταν τροπαῖα πολεμίων στήσῃ στρατός,
οὐ τῶν πονούντων τοὔργον ἡγοῦνται τόδε,   695
ἀλλ' ὁ στρατηγὸς τὴν δόκησιν ἄρνυται,
ὃς εἷς μετ' ἄλλων μυρίων πάλλων δόρυ
οὐδὲν πλέον δρῶν ἑνὸς ἔχει πλείω λόγον.
σεμνοὶ δ' ἐν ἀρχαῖς ἥμενοι κατὰ πτόλιν

οὑμοὶ γάμοι ὤνησαν Ἑλλάδ', οὐ κρατεῖσθ' ἐκ βαρβάρων, οὔτ' ἐς δόρυ σταθέντες, οὐ τυραννίδι.
682. ἀΐστορες. Thucyd. i. 3, πρὸ γὰρ τῶν Τρωικῶν οὐδὲν φαίνεται πρότερον κοινῇ ἐργασαμένη ἡ Ἑλλάς.
685. εἰ δὲ κτλ. He here answers the charge made in v. 627 seqq. 'I could have wished,' he adds in a sort of countercharge, 'that *you* had possessed as much self-control as I, and had not killed Phocus your brother,' who was slain by Peleus and Telamon at the instigation of their mother, or, according to others, through jealousy of his excelling them in the manly exercises. See Apollodor. iii. 12. 6. This Phocus was the son of Psamathe and Aeacus, mentioned in Hel. 7.
689. γλωσσαλγία. See on Med 525. The sense is, 'If you are angry at my view of the matter, you may talk yourself tired in opposing it; but the course I am taking with regard to Andromache is a wise one as concerning my own interests.'
693. Peleus replies to the sophistries of Menelaus by throwing discredit on the Greek custom of giving all the glory and honour of a successful military enterprise to the general alone, while the common soldier, who has borne all the toil and shared all the danger, gets neither praise nor reward. Compare Hec. 306 seqq. These verses, Plutarch tells us, were directed by Clitus against the exploits of Alexander the Great; and the quotation cost the former his life. Euripides, in taking this democratic, but really most just, view of military reputation, was expressing a sentiment which could hardly be palatable to the leaders of the war party. Why a man who has shown some military genius should therefore make a shrewd politician or a wise and temperate minister, is a question that has been more often asked than answered.
694. στῆσαι τροπαῖον is said of the army generally, στήσασθαι of the general, because the latter *gets* it erected by the agency of others. Hence *inf.* 763, τροπαῖον αὐτοῦ στήσομαι.
698. πλέον ἑνός. Though at most he can only do the work of one single man, yet he gets credit, as if he had done the work of thousands.

φρονοῦσι δήμου μεῖζον, ὄντες οὐδένες· 700
οἱ δ' εἰσὶν αὐτῶν μυρίῳ σοφώτεροι,
εἰ τόλμα προσγένοιτο βούλησίς θ' ἅμα.
ὡς καὶ σὺ σός τ' ἀδελφὸς ἐξωγκωμένοι
Τροίᾳ κάθησθε τῇ τ' ἐκεῖ στρατηγίᾳ,
μόχθοισιν ἄλλων καὶ πόνοις ἐπηρμένοι. 705
δείξω δ' ἐγώ σοι μὴ τὸν Ἰδαῖον Πάριν
κρείσσω νομίζειν Πηλέως ἐχθρόν ποτε,
εἰ μὴ φθερεῖ τῆσδ' ὡς τάχιστ' ἀπὸ στέγης
καὶ παῖς ἄτεκνος, ἣν ὅδ' οὐξ ἡμῶν γεγὼς
ἐλᾷ δι' οἴκων τῶνδ' ἐπισπάσας κόμης, 710
ἣ στεῖρος οὖσα μόσχος οὐκ ἀνέξεται
τίκτοντας ἄλλους, οὐκ ἔχουσ' αὐτὴ τέκνα.
ἀλλ' εἰ τὸ κείνης δυστυχεῖ παίδων πέρι,
ἄπαιδας ἡμᾶς δεῖ καταστῆναι τέκνων;
φθείρεσθε τῆσδε, δμῶες, ὡς ἂν ἐκμάθω 715
εἴ τίς με λύειν τῆσδε κωλύσει χέρας.

700. οὐδένες. The plural is used in Ion 594. Iph. A. 371, βαρβάρους τοὺς οὐδένας.—μυρίῳ, unusually put for πολλῷ.
702. A general may have τόλμα without βούλησις, or he may have βούλησις without τόλμα. Any common soldier who happens to combine both qualities, is a better man than his commander.
706. δείξω κτλ. 'I will give you good reasons for thinking that not even your Trojan opponent and rival Paris was a greater enemy than Peleus will some day prove to have been.' The reading of the best copies is ἥσσω, but Aldus and others have μείζω. The Schol. takes μὴ ἥσσονα for μὴ ἥσσον, not one more than the other. Hermann, who has successfully emended Hel. 974, by restoring μὴ εὐσεβοῦς πατρὸς ἥσσω for εὐσεβοῦς πατρὸς κρείσσω, here less happily edits μὴ οὐ τὸν Ἰδαῖον Πάριν ἥσσω νομίζειν. It is very doubtful if this is even good Greek; for this is not a place for the combination μὴ οὐ, and to transfer the οὐ to ἥσσω, so as to make it equivalent to κρείσσω, is extremely harsh. There can hardly be a doubt that κρείσσω is here the true reading. A misapprehension of the meaning would lead to the substitution of ἥσσω, while the variant μείζω is an evident attempt to restore the right meaning, though by the use of the wrong word.

708. φθερεῖ. The Greeks often use φθείρεσθαι in the sense of ἔρρειν, not only (as the cognate *errare*) for 'to lose one's way,' (El. 234. Hel. 774,) but in the way of an imprecation, as Heracl. 284, φθείρου, τὸ γὰρ σὸν Ἄργος οὐ δέδοικ' ἐγώ, 'get you gone, and a plague upon you!' Hence also φθείρεσθαι and προσφθείρεσθαι πρός τινα, 'to come when one is not wanted,' 'to *bother* a person.' Cf. *inf.* 715. But in the bad sense, the word rather belongs to comic than to tragic phraseology.

709. οὐξ the present editor for ἐξ. Either this change, or L. Dindorf's ὅ γ' for ὅδ', seems necessary. But the γ' gives rather too pointed a sense, 'my son, if he is truly my son in entertaining the same feelings as his father,' &c. Whereas ὅδε is very appropriate, for Peleus speaks of him as if he were close at hand to execute the vengeance he predicts.

711. ἥ. Hermann gives εἰ, "propter futurum;" but there is no reason why the relative, which stands for ἐπεὶ ἐκείνη, should not take the future equally well.
— ἄλλους, for ἄλλην τίκτουσαν. The sentiment is put generally, without distinction of sex, 'others having children.'

713. δυστυχεῖ. See on v. 420.

716. τήνδε Hermann, with Lascaris.

ΕΥΡΙΠΙΔΟΥ

ἔπαιρε σαυτήν· ὡς ἐγώ, καίπερ τρέμων,
πλεκτὰς ἱμάντων στροφίδας ἐξανήσομαι.
ὧδ᾽, ὦ κάκιστε, τῆσδ᾽ ἐλυμήνω χέρας;
βοῦν ἢ λέοντ᾽ ἤλπιζες ἐντείνειν βρόχοις; 720
ἢ μὴ ξίφος λαβοῦσ᾽ ἀμυνάθοιτό σε
ἔδεισας; ἕρπε δεῦρ᾽ ὑπ᾽ ἀγκάλας, βρέφος·
ξύλλυε μητρὸς δέσμ᾽· *ἔτ᾽ ἐν Φθίᾳ σ᾽ ἐγὼ
θρέψω μέγαν τοῖσδ᾽ ἐχθρόν. εἰ δ᾽ ἀπῆν δορὸς
τοῖς Σπαρτιάταις δόξα καὶ μάχης ἀγών, 725
τἄλλ᾽ ὄντες ἴστε μηδενὸς βελτίονες.
ΧΟ. ἀνειμένον τι χρῆμα πρεσβυτῶν γένος,
καὶ δυσφύλακτον ὀξυθυμίας ὕπο.
ΜΕ. ἄγαν προνωπὴς ἐς τὸ λοιδορεῖν φέρει·
ἐγὼ δὲ πρὸς βίαν μέν, ἐς Φθίαν μολών, 730
οὔτ᾽ οὖν τι δράσω φλαῦρον οὔτε πείσομαι.
καὶ νῦν μέν, οὐ γὰρ ἄφθονον σχολὴν ἔχω,
ἄπειμ᾽ ἐς οἴκους· ἔστι γάρ τις οὐ πρόσω
Σπάρτης πόλις τις, ἣ πρὸ τοῦ μὲν ἦν φίλη,
νῦν δ᾽ ἐχθρὰ ποιεῖ· τήνδ᾽ ἐπεξελθεῖν θέλω 735
στρατηλατήσας χὑποχείριον λαβεῖν.
ὅταν δὲ τἀκεῖ θῶ κατὰ γνώμην ἐμήν,

723. ἔτ᾽ was inserted by Hermann, who well observes that the particle is often used in threats of what is still to come. This is much better than to read δέσματ᾽ with Bothe, or to transpose δεσμὰ μητρὸς with Heath. There is a beautiful pathos in this passage; just such a pathos as characterizes Euripides, and proves him to have been a very humane man.
725. δόξα. "Anachronismus hic est. Nam illa Spartanorum fortitudo ab Heraclidis et Lycurgo duxit originem." *Herm.*
726. μηδενὸς βελτίονες for πάντων χείρους. See Ion 1383. 'Know that ye are better than nobody' might mean, 'Ye are not, as ye think, better than any other.'
727. For γένος some MSS. give ἔφυ. The other has more authority; and ἔφυ may have been suggested by v. 181, ἐπίφθονόν τι χρῆμα θηλειῶν ἔφυ.—ἀνειμένον, scil. εἰς ὀργήν. Schol. προπετὲς, but he tells us that others took it for πρᾷον, ἡσύχιον. The ellipse is certainly remarkable, but must be supplied from ὀξυθυμίας in the next verse. Cf. Heracl. 3, ὁ δ᾽ εἰς τὸ κέρδος λῆμ᾽ ἔχων ἀνειμένον.
731. οὖν. Since I am come to Phthia, therefore, as a stranger here, I will not incur the risk of suffering harm by doing it to others.
733. For the repetition of τις see the note on Aesch. Suppl. 58. Hec. 1178, εἴ τις γυναῖκας τῶν πρὶν εἴρηκεν κακῶς, ἢ νῦν λέγων τίς ἐστιν, κτλ. Hermann finds a political allusion in this mention of Argos, which about the time when the *Andromache* was acted (Ol. 89. 4,) had been induced by Alcibiades to make a treaty with Athens against Sparta. See Thuc. v. 43—7.—τήνδ᾽ for ταύτην is a rather lax usage, and perhaps Hermann is right in giving τήν, i. e. ἥν.—ὥστε χειρίαν Pflugk after Pierson, Aldus having ὥσθ᾽ ὑποχείριον, others καὶ λαβεῖν ὑποχείριον. The true reading is given in Lascaris and several MSS. For the crasis with the aspirate see Hel. 1024.

ἥξω. παρὼν δὲ πρὸς παρόντας ἐμφανῶς
γαμβροὺς διδάξω καὶ διδάξομαι λόγους.
κἂν μὲν κολάζῃ τήνδε, καὶ τὸ λοιπὸν ᾖ 740
σώφρων, καθ' ἡμᾶς σῶφρον' ἀντιλήψεται·
θυμούμενος δὲ τεύξεται θυμουμένων,
ἔργοισι δ' ἔργα διάδοχ' ἀντιλήψεται.
τοὺς σοὺς δὲ μύθους ῥᾳδίως ἐγὼ φέρω·
σκιᾷ γὰρ ἀντίστοιχος ὢν φωνὴν ἔχεις, 745
ἀδύνατος οὐδὲν ἄλλο πλὴν λέγειν μόνον.
ΠΗ. ἡγοῦ, τέκνον, μοι δεῦρ' ὑπ' ἀγκάλαις σταθείς,
σύ τ', ὦ τάλαινα· χείματος γὰρ ἀγρίου
τυχοῦσα λιμένας ἦλθες εἰς εὐηνέμους.
ΑΝ. ὦ πρέσβυ, θεοί σοι δοῖεν εὖ καὶ τοῖσι σοῖς, 750
σώσαντι παῖδα κἀμὲ τὴν δυσδαίμονα.
ὅρα δὲ μὴ νῷν εἰς ἐρημίαν ὁδοῦ
πτήξαντες οἵδε πρὸς βίαν ἄγωσί με,
γέροντα μὲν σ' ὁρῶντες, ἀσθενῆ δ' μεὲ,
καὶ παῖδα τόνδε νήπιον· σκόπει τάδε, 755
μὴ νῦν φυγόντες εἶθ' ἁλῶμεν ὕστερον.
ΠΗ. οὐ μὴ γυναικῶν δειλὸν εἰσοίσεις λόγον;
χώρει, τίς ὑμῶν ἅψεται; κλαίων ἄρα

739. γαμβροὺς, i. e. Neoptolemus, whence κολάζῃ and θυμούμενος in the singular. Any relation by marriage was called γαμβρὸς, i. e. γαμερὸς, as in this case Neoptolemus was the son-in-law of Menelaus.—διδάξομαι, the passive; I will tell him what my wishes are, and will hear what he has to say in reply.
741. Hermann rightly places the comma at σώφρων. In other editions σώφρον καθ' ἡμᾶς is given. The sense is, τὸ καθ' ἡμᾶς, or ἡμῶν ἕκατι, τὰ ὅμοια ἀντιλήψεται.—v. 743 is perhaps spurious.
745. Hermann and Dindorf edit this verse as given above. The MSS. and edd. however give ὡς, and for the Aldine σκιᾷ Lascaris and other MSS. have σκιά. The verse is quoted, though corruptly, in the Etymol. Mag. p. 114, ἀντίστοιχον, τὸ ἴσον· σκιᾶς γὰρ ἀντίστοιχον φωνὴν ἔχεις. According to this, the meaning is simply, 'being like a shadow (i. e. as an old man,) you can do nothing but talk,'— you have no substantial and material existence. Still, there is much to be said in favour of σκιᾷ ἀντίστοιχος ὡς, 'like a shadow on a sun-dial.' Photius, στοιχεῖον, ἡ σκιά, and στοιχεῖον ἐκάλουν τὴν ναυτῶν σκιὰν, ᾗ τὰς ὥρας ἐσκοποῦντο. The exact meaning of σκιᾷ ἀντίστοιχος would be, 'the shadow that progresses on the sundial exactly opposite to the sun,' i. e. "still creeping with the creeping hours" on the other side of the intervening gnomon. Pflugk, who gives this reading with Matthiae, wrongly supplies σώματι with ἀντίστοιχος, 'like the shadow that follows a man as he goes.' But he well compares Frag. Melanipp. 500, τί δ' ἄλλο; φωνὴ καὶ σκιὰ γέρων ἀνήρ. The reading ὢν for ὡς is due to Musgrave and Reiske.
752. νῷν, lying in wait for her son and herself. Aldus and others have νῦν.
757. οὐ μὴ εἰσοίσεις, for μὴ εἴσφερε. See Bacch. 852. El. 982. For εἰσφέρειν λόγους compare Bacch. 650.
758. κλαίων, 'at his peril.' Aesch.

ΕΥΡΙΠΙΔΟΥ

ψαύσει. θεῶν γὰρ οὕνεχ' ἱππικοῦ τ' ὄχλου
πολλῶν θ' ὁπλιτῶν ἄρχομεν Φθίαν κάτα·   760
ἡμεῖς δ' ἔτ' ὀρθοὶ, κοὐ γέροντες, ὡς δοκεῖς,
ἀλλ' ἔς γε τοιόνδ' ἄνδρ' ἀποβλέψας μόνον
τροπαῖον αὐτοῦ στήσομαι, πρέσβυς περ ὤν.
πολλῶν νέων γὰρ κἂν γέρων εὔψυχος ᾖ
κρείσσων· τί γὰρ δεῖ δειλὸν ὄντ' εὐσωματεῖν;   765

ΧΟ. ἢ μὴ γενοίμαν, ἢ πατέρων ἀγαθῶν   στρ.
εἴην πολυκτήτων τε δόμων μέτοχος·
εἴ τι γὰρ πάθοι τις ἀμήχανον, ἀλκᾶς   770
οὐ σπάνις εὐγενέταις·
κηρυσσομένοισι δ' ἀπ' ἐσθλῶν δωμάτων
τιμὰ καὶ κλέος· οὗτοι
λείψανα τῶν ἀγαθῶν
ἀνδρῶν ἀφαιρεῖται χρόνος· ἁ δ' ἀρετὰ   775
καὶ θανοῦσι λάμπει.
κρεῖσσον δὲ νίκαν μὴ κακόδοξον ἔχειν   ἀντ.

Suppl. 902, κλαίοις ἂν, εἰ ψαύσειας, οὐ μάλ' ἐς μακράν.—θεῶν οὕνεχ', διὰ χάριν θεῶν. Lascaris, Aldus, and several MSS. give θεοῦ, which seems as good a reading.

763. στήσομαι. See above, v. 694. 'I shall put such a man as *that* to flight by a mere look.' Cf. Rhes. 335, φόβος γένοιτ' ἂν πολεμίοις ὀφθεὶς μόνον.

764. κἂν γέρων. A slight *hyperbaton* for καὶ γέρων, ἐὰν εὔψυχος ᾖ. In εὐσωματεῖν the poet alludes to the fine persons of a certain class whom he heartily despised, the foppish and conceited young men who attended only to their external appearance. See Preface to Vol. i. p. xlix. —τί γὰρ δεῖ; 'what is the use of?' &c. Cf. Suppl. 450.

766 seqq. In this *stasimon* the chorus, alluding to Hermione, expatiate on the advantages which attend noble birth; for not only do such persons possess resources in trouble, but they are honoured in life and not forgotten when dead. They proceed however to say, apparently with reference to Menelaus, that it is better not to obtain a discreditable victory, than to subvert justice by an invidious use of power. They would not wish for influence either in the state or in married life, unless such as can fairly and justly be exercised. In the *epode*, the exploits of Peleus when a youth are celebrated.—The metres are simple, being for the most part combinations of iambics and trochees with dactyls.

770. πάθοι W. Dindorf for ἂν πάσχοι, where ἂν, if not a solecism (see on Aesch. Ag. 903. Hel. 825,) is at least injurious to both sense and metre, while πάθοι suits the latter better than πάσχοι. Hermann indeed suggests μέντἄρ' in the antistrophe, v. 779.—ἀλκᾶς σπάνις, cf. Ion 481, where children are spoken of as ἀλκὰ ἐν κακοῖς, σύν τ' εὐτυχίαις φίλον.

772. κηρυσσομένοισι Herm. and L. Dindorf for κηρυσσομένων, (one MS. giving —οις.) In the following line W. Dindorf gives τιμὰν καὶ κλέος οὗτοι κτλ., with Valckenaer. But οὗτοι seems more appropriate as commencing a sententious remark. By τιμὰ καὶ κλέος the poet means, that whether they deserve it or not, (and Hermione does not,) they are honoured in life; and if they combine ἀρετὴ with εὐγένεια, they are held in respectful memory even when dead. Pflugk seems to have missed the point of the remark, in explaining "*eorum et honos omnibus et gloria curae est.*"

777. The μὴ in this verse belongs to ἔχειν, not to κακόδοξον. Lascaris with one MS. omits ἔχειν. This arose from

ΑΝΔΡΟΜΑΧΗ. 275

ἢ ξὺν φθόνῳ σφάλλειν δυνάμει τε δίκαν· 778
ἁδὺ μὲν γὰρ αὐτίκα τοῦτο βροτοῖσιν,
ἐν δὲ χρόνῳ τελέθει
ξηρὸν καὶ ὀνείδεσιν ἔγκειται δόμων.
ταύταν ᾔνεσα, ταύταν 785
καὶ φέρομαι βιοτάν,
μηδὲν δίκας ἔξω κράτος ἐν θαλάμοις
καὶ πόλει δύνασθαι.
ὦ γέρον Αἰακίδα,   ἐπῳδ. 790
πείθομαι καὶ σὺν Λαπίθαισί σε Κενταύροις ὁμιλῆσαι
    δορὶ κλεινοτάτῳ,
καὶ ἐπ᾿ Ἀργῴου δορὸς ἄξενον ὑγρὰν
ἐκπερᾶσαι ποντιᾶν Συμπληγάδων κλεινὰν ἐπὶ ναυ-
    στολίαν, 795
Ἰλιάδα τε πόλιν ὅτε πάρος

mistaking νίκαν for νικᾶν. One of the Scholiasts has this gloss, which Hermann has misunderstood; βέλτιον δικαίως ἡττᾶσθαι, ἤπερ θαρροῦντας βασκανίᾳ καὶ δυνάμει παραλύειν τὸ δίκαιον. He probably wrote, βέλτιον δικαίως (i. e. μὴ κακοδόξως) νικᾶν, ἤπερ κτλ., but νικᾶν was altered to the contrary, ἡττᾶσθαι, by some who saw what the sense required.
779. ἁδὺ W. Dindorf for ἡδύ.
784. ξηρὸν, unproductive; a metaphor from poor land, *sup.* v. 637.—For καὶ Aldus has καὶ μὴν καὶ, an addition consistent neither with metre nor sense, though retained by Pflugk and others.— ἔγκειται, 'is closely connected with,' *jacet in probris familiarum*, i.e. *numeratur inter dedecora domorum*, Bothe. We should have expected ἔγκειται δόμοις ὡς ὄνειδος.
786. φέρομαι. ἐν ταύτῃ φέρεσθαι θέλω, Schol., where ἐν ταύτῃ is probably an error of transcribers for ταύτην. The sense is, 'this is the life I aspire to,' the diction being borrowed from winning a prize at a contest.—μηδὲν κράτος δύνασθαι, 'to have no influence,' may be compared with οὐδένα καιρὸν δύναται in Med. 128. Thus the phrase resolves itself here into a cognate accusative, μηδεμίαν δύνασιν δύνασθαι, unless, with Pflugk, we take κράτος for νίκην.
791. πείθομαι κτλ. 'I believe (what

men say of you) both that you engaged, in alliance with the Lapithae, in the battle against the Centaurs, with your most renowned spear, and also that on the ship Argo you crossed the inhospitable sea through the Symplegades leading into the Pontus, in the well-known expedition (of the Argonauts).' For Κενταύροις most of the old copies have καὶ Κενταύρων. One MS. only gives Κενταύροις without καί. And so Hermann has rightly edited. The κλεινότατον δόρυ was evidently the famous Πηλιὰς μελίη given by Chiron to Peleus, Il. xvi. 140, and not that of the Centaurs. Again, ὁμιλῆσαι Κενταύροις is better than ὁμιλῆσαι δορὶ Κενταύρων. Pflugk well compares Od. iv. 345, τοῖος ἐὼν μνηστῆρσιν ὁμιλήσειεν Ὀδυσσεύς, though at the same time he edits Κενταύρων, as does W. Dindorf. The Scholiast too seems to have found the same reading; πολεμῆσαι ἐπὶ τῷ Κενταύρων στρατεύματι.
794. ποντιᾶν Συμπληγάδων Hermann for ποντίαν Συμπληγάδα. Euripides, he observes, always uses the word in the plural. (Though γῆν κυανέαν Συμπληγάδα occurs, Iph. T. 241.) The construction is, περᾶσαι ἄξενον ὑγρὰν ἐκ Συμπλ., where ὑγρὰ (Od. v. 45) is used for θάλασσα as χέρσος is often put for χέρσος γῆ, and as ἡ ἀμίαντος 'the unsullied' is similarly used in Pers. 580.
796. τὸ πάρος Hermann, who in the

εὐδόκιμον ὁ Διὸς ἶνις ἀμφέβαλε φόνῳ,
κοινὰν τὰν εὔκλειαν ἔχοντ᾽ 800
Εὐρώπαν ἀφικέσθαι.

ΤΡΟΦΟΣ.

ὦ φίλταται γυναῖκες, ὡς κακὸν κακῷ
διάδοχον ἐν τῇδ᾽ ἡμέρᾳ πορσύνεται.
δέσποινα γὰρ κατ᾽ οἶκον, Ἑρμιόνην λέγω,
πατρός τ᾽ ἐρημωθεῖσα συννοίᾳ θ᾽ ἅμα 805
οἷον δέδρακεν ἔργον, Ἀνδρομάχην κτανεῖν
καὶ παῖδα βουλεύσασα, κατθανεῖν θέλει,
πόσιν τρέμουσα, μὴ ἀντὶ τῶν δεδραμένων
ἐκ τῶνδ᾽ ἀτίμως δωμάτων ἀποσταλῇ,
ἢ κατθάνῃ κτείνασα τοὺς οὐ χρὴ κτανεῖν. 810
μόλις δέ νιν θέλουσαν ἀρτῆσαι δέρην
εἴργουσι φύλακες δμῶες, ἔκ τε δεξιᾶς
ξίφη καθαρπάζουσιν ἐξαιρούμενοι.
οὕτω μέγ᾽ ἀλγεῖ, καὶ τὰ πρὶν δεδραμένα
ἔγνωκε πράξασ᾽ οὐ καλῶς. ἐγὼ μὲν οὖν 815
δέσποιναν εἴργουσ᾽ ἀγχόνης κάμνω, φίλαι·
ὑμεῖς δὲ βᾶσαι τῶνδε δωμάτων ἔσω
θανάτου νιν ἐκλύσασθέ· τῶν γὰρ ἠθάδων

next line edits εὐδόκιμον for -μος. Others had omitted the article; but the verse seems to be a senarius of resolved feet. The expedition against Troy by Hercules, in order to claim the steeds of Laomedon, is here referred to. See Suppl. 1199. Troad. 804.—ἀφικέσθαι κτλ., scil. πείθομαι, 'that you returned to Europe having your renown in common with him.' There is a variant Εὐρώταν, but the other has been rightly adopted by the later editors from Lascaris.

802. The speaker of the following ῥῆσις is clearly the nurse of Hermione; for she calls her ὦ παῖ and τέκνον, vv. 828, 832, and speaks of herself as one of the ἠθάδες φίλοι in v. 818. And so one Paris MS. is said rightly to give, and another has τροφὸς prefixed to some of the speeches below. All the recent editions have adopted this with Hermann. Commonly the name θεράπαινα was prefixed. The correction has also been made in the *dramatis personae* on the authority of two or three MSS.—For κακῷ one MS. has κακῶν. Either case is right: cf. Hec. 583.

805. συννοίᾳ. 'Through remorse at what a deed she has done in plotting to kill Andromache.' Heracl. 381, ὦ παῖ, τί μοι σύννοιαν ὄμμασιν φέρων ἥκεις;

810. Lascaris and many copies give κτείνουσα τοὺς οὐ χρὴ θανεῖν, and the one reading is just as good as the other. Dindorf and Pflugk give χρῆν with Elmsley; but very needlessly.

811—3. ἀρτῆσαι—ξίφη. These two methods of suicide are often mentioned together. Both were honourable, but the latter the more so. Troad. 1012, ποῦ δῆτ᾽ ἐλήφθης ἢ βρόχους ἀρτωμένη, ἢ φάσγανον θήγουσ᾽, ἃ γενναία γυνὴ δράσειεν ἄν; Hel. 299, ἀσχήμονες μὲν ἀγχόναι μετάρσιοι, σφαγαὶ δ᾽ ἔχουσιν εὐγενές τι καὶ καλόν.

ΑΝΔΡΟΜΑΧΗ. 277

φίλων νέοι μολόντες εὐπειθέστεροι.
XO. καὶ μὴν ἐν οἴκοις προσπόλων ἀκούομεν 820
βοὴν ἐφ' οἷσιν ἦλθες ἀγγέλλουσα σύ.
δείξειν δ' ἔοικεν ἡ τάλαιν' ὅσον στένει
πράξασα δεινά· δωμάτων γὰρ ἐκπερᾷ
φεύγουσα χεῖρας προσπόλων, πόθῳ θανεῖν.
EP. ἰώ μοί μοι. στρ. α'. 825
σπάραγμα κόμας ὀνύχων τε δάϊ' ἀ-
μύγματα θήσομαι.
TP. ὦ παῖ, τί δράσεις; σῶμα σὸν καταικιεῖ;
EP. αἰαῖ αἰαῖ. ἀντ. α'.
ἔρρ' αἰθέριον πλοκάμων ἐμῶν ἄπο, 830
λεπτόμιτον φάρος.
TP. τέκνον, κάλυπτε στέρνα, σύνδησαι πέπλους.
EP. τί δέ με δεῖ καλύπτειν πέπλοις στρ. β'.
στέρνα; δῆλα, *δῆλα καὶ ἀμφιφανῆ καὶ ἄκρυπτα δε-
δράκαμεν πόσιν. 835
TP. ἀλγεῖς, φόνον ῥάψασα συγγάμῳ σέθεν;
EP. κατὰ μὲν οὖν στένω δαΐαν ἀντ. β'.
τόλμαν ἂν ἐρέξαμεν, ὦ κατάρατος ἐγὼ κατάρ-
ατος ἀνδράσιν.
TP. συγγνώσεταί σοι τήνδ' ἁμαρτίαν πόσις. 840
EP. τί μοι ξίφος ἐκ χερὸς ἠγρεύσω;

821. ἐφ' οἷσιν κτλ. Cf. Hec. 727. 'On the very subject you came to tell us about,' viz. her wish to commit suicide and their wish to prevent it. Hermione is accordingly seen rushing out of the women's apartment, when she is met by the nurse, who vainly tries to soothe her. As usual in such scenes, the excited party speaks either in the dochmiac or some equally rapid measure, while the other replies in trimeter iambics. See on Hel. 631. There is probability in Hermann's view, (though Barnes had anticipated him in it,) that from v. 825 to 840 is antistrophic, what follows being, from increasing excitement, exempt from that restraint.
828. καταικιεῖ. Schol. ὑβρίσεις, ἀφανίσεις.
830. The gloss of Photius, which Matthiae without much reason refers to this verse, ἔρριον· εἰς φθορὰν, Εὐριπίδης, should doubtless be read ἔρρ' ἰὼν, κτλ. In Hesychius the same correction is to be made, not, as Lenting thought, ἔρρε, ἴθι εἰς φθοράν.—φάρος, Schol. τὸ κρήδεμνον λέγει. It is so used in Hipp. 132, λεπτὰ δὲ φάρη ξανθὰν κεφαλὰν σκιάζειν, where, as here, the α is made short.
832. πέπλους. So Hermann with two MSS. for πέπλοις.
834. δῆλα was repeated by Hermann on account of the metre. 'Why,' she asks, 'should I cover my bosom, when the guilty deeds within it cannot be concealed?' This verse is troch. dipod. + dactylic tetrameter; the preceding is a resolved cretic with a dochmius.
837. δαΐαν τόλμαν Herm. for δαΐας τόλμας, and ἐρέξαμεν for ἔρεξ'.

ἀπόδος, ἀπόδος, ὦ φίλος, ἵν' ἀνταίαν
ἐρείσω πλαγάν· τί με βρόχων εἴργεις ;   845
ΤΡ. ἀλλ' εἴ σ' ἀφείην μὴ φρονοῦσαν, ὡς θάνοις ;
ΕΡ. οἴμοι πότμου.
ποῦ μοι πυρὸς φίλα φλόξ ;
ποῦ δ' εἰς πέτρας ἀερθῶ
*ἢ κατὰ πόντον ἢ καθ' ὕλαν ὀρέων,
ἵνα θανοῦσα νερτέροισιν μέλω ;   850
ΤΡ. τί ταῦτα μοχθεῖς ; συμφοραὶ θεήλατοι
πᾶσιν βροτοῖσιν ἢ τότ' ἦλθον ἢ τότε.
ΕΡ. ἔλιπες ἔλιπες, ὦ πάτερ, ἐπακτίαν
μονάδ' ἔρημον οὖσαν ἐνάλου κώπας.   855
ὀλεῖ ὀλεῖ με· τᾷδ' οὐκέτ' ἐνοικήσω
νυμφιδίῳ στέγᾳ.
τίνος ἀγαλμάτων ἱκέτις ὁρμαθῶ,
ἢ δούλα δούλας γούνασι προσπέσω ;   860

844. ἀπόδος, ἀπόδος, ὦ φίλος Hermann with Theodore Bergk, for ἀπόδος, ὦ φίλος (or ὦ φίλη), ἀπόδος. W. Dindorf omits ἵν', with Elmsley, taking ἐρείσω for the hortative conjunctive (see Hipp. 567), and retaining the common order of the words. The masculine φίλος is rightly given by Lascaris and others, because, as the nurse had stated at v. 813, some of the slaves set to watch Hermione had disarmed her before she rushed on the stage.
847. οἴμοι πότμου forms one verse. The two next are in the metre commonly known as Anacreontic, by no means a common one in tragedy. See Cycl. 496 seqq.
849. ἢ was prefixed to the first κατὰ by Seidler. The sense is, 'where shall I soar to find rocks, either situated in the sea or in mountain forests, that dying (by falling from thence) I may be a care (no longer to the living, but) to the dead?' She intends to ask how she may best kill herself in some other way, now that the sword had been denied her. Cf. Troad. 505, ἄγετε με — πέτρινα κρήδεμν', ὡς πεσοῦσ' ἀποφθαρῶ.
851—2. These verses were commonly assigned to the chorus. But the Schol. observes, ἄμεινον τῆς τρόφου εἶναι τὸ πρόσωπον.

855. ὡσεὶ before μονάδ' was omitted by Seidler. It was doubtless added to explain the simile, 'You have left me destitute of help like a boat left on the shore without oars.' Schol. ὥσπερ ναῦν ἐν τῷ αἰγιαλῷ ἐστερημένην πηδαλίου.— ἐνάλου Hermann for ἐναλίου, which however might be pronounced as of three syllables.
856. τᾷδ' οὐκέτ' for οὐκέτι τᾷδ' Seidler.
859. τίνος κτλ. 'To which of the statues shall I betake myself as a suppliant?' As regards the form, Aldus has ὁρμάθω, which Barnes defends as an Atticism like διωκάθω, εἰκάθω, μινύθω, &c. But it is not necessary to the metre that the α should be short; and the reading of Lascaris, ὁρμαθῶ, for ὁρμηθῶ, is supported by several MSS. It does not seem necessary either with Jacobs to read τίνος ἄγαλμα θεῶν κτλ., or, with Hermann, to suppose that something has been lost, like τίς ἀλκά; θεοῦ τίνος ἀγαλμάτων κτλ. Still less is it satisfactory to transpose the next verse but one so as to follow this verse, and to construe ὁρμαθῶ Φθιάδος ἐκ γαίας, as Hermann has edited.
860. δούλας is the reading of the Schol. and several MSS., the old editions giving δούλοις. Hermione proudly asks, 'or

Φθιάδος ἐκ γᾶς κυανόπτερος ὄρνις ἀερθείην,
ἢ πευκᾶεν σκάφος, ἃ
διὰ Κυανέας ἐπέρασεν ἀκτὰς
πρωτόπλοος πλάτα. 865

ΤΡ. ὦ παῖ, τὸ λίαν οὔτ' ἐκεῖν' ἐπῄνεσα,
ὅτ' ἐς γυναῖκα Τρῳάδ' ἐξημάρτανες,
οὔτ' αὖ τὸ νῦν σου δεῖμ' ὃ δειμαίνεις ἄγαν.
οὐχ ὧδε κῆδος σὸν διώσεται πόσις,
φαύλοις γυναικὸς βαρβάρου πεισθεὶς λόγοις. 870
οὐ γάρ τί σ' αἰχμάλωτον ἐκ Τροίας ἔχει,
ἀλλ' ἀνδρὸς ἐσθλοῦ παῖδα, σὺν πολλοῖς λαβὼν
ἕδνοισι, πόλεώς τ' οὐ μέσως εὐδαίμονος.
πατὴρ δέ σ' οὐχ ὧδ', ὡς σὺ δειμαίνεις, τέκνον,
προδοὺς ἐάσει δωμάτων τῶνδ' ἐκπεσεῖν. 875
ἀλλ' εἴσιθ' εἴσω, μηδὲ φαντάζου δόμων
πάροιθε τῶνδε, μή τιν' αἰσχύνην λάβῃς
πρόσθεν μελάθρων τῶνδ' ὁρωμένη, τέκνον.

ΧΟ. καὶ μὴν ὅδ' ἀλλόχρως τις ἔκδημος ξένος
σπουδῇ πρὸς ἡμᾶς βημάτων πορεύεται. 880

would you have me, as a slave, fall before the knees of a slave (Andromache), and ask her pardon?' The words Φθιάδος ἐκ γᾶς present some difficulty. They do not make much sense in continuation of προσπέσω, which is the common punctuation, and therefore it seems better to adopt Seidler's conjecture ἀερθείην for εἴθ' εἴην, and translate, ' Would that as a bird with sable pinions I might be wafted from the Phthian land, or that I were out at sea, a pine-built skiff, that first-launched vessel which passed through the projecting Symplegades.' As a ship is said ἀερθῆναι as well as a bird (as in the familiar phrase αἴρειν στόλον), the optative will apply both to ὄρνις and to σκάφος, though in a slightly different sense. It is probable that εἴθ' εἴην was a gloss in explanation of σκάφος, added by some one who did not perceive this, and which afterwards, from its similarity, superseded ἀερθείην. As for the metre, it seems best to combine 861—2 into one verse, which may be called asynartete, choriamb. + 2 dactyls + choriamb. + spondee. The next seems a glyconean verse, and 864 is logaoedic with an anacrusis.

866. The nurse is anxiously assuring Hermione that her husband is not likely to resign her, a lady of wealth and of noble birth, for a mere slave, when the sudden arrival of Orestes gives a new turn to affairs. He is on his way to Dodona, and has bethought himself of his cousin residing at Phthia. Hearing from herself an account of her domestic afflictions, he at once proposes to take her as his lawful wife, asserting that she was long ago espoused to him by Menelaus himself.

878. Hermann adopts Brunck's superfluous conjecture ὧδ' for τῶνδ'. The mere fact of being seen outside the house was enough to give rise to scandal in a young woman. Cf. Phoen. 95. Electr. 344. Dindorf and Bothe think the verse spurious.

880. βημάτων Brunck for δωμάτων.—ἀλλόχρως, Schol. ἀλλόμορφος.

ΟΡΕΣΤΗΣ.

ξέναι γυναῖκες, ἦ τάδ' ἔστ' Ἀχιλλέως
παιδὸς μέλαθρα καὶ τυραννικαὶ στέγαι;
ΧΟ. ἔγνως· ἀτὰρ τίς ὢν *σὺ πυνθάνει τάδε;
ΟΡ. Ἀγαμέμνονός τε καὶ Κλυταιμνήστρας τόκος·
ὄνομα δ' Ὀρέστης· ἔρχομαι δὲ πρὸς Διὸς 885
μαντεῖα Δωδωναῖ'. ἐπεὶ δ' ἀφικόμην
Φθίαν, δοκεῖ μοι ξυγγενοῦς μαθεῖν πέρι
γυναικὸς, εἰ ζῇ κεὐτυχοῦσα τυγχάνει
ἡ Σπαρτιᾶτις Ἑρμιόνη· τηλουρὰ γὰρ
ναίουσ' ἀφ' ἡμῶν πεδί' ὅμως ἐστὶν φίλη. 890
ΕΡ. ὦ ναυτίλοισι χείματος λιμὴν φανεὶς,
Ἀγαμέμνονος παῖ, πρός σε τῶνδε γουνάτων,
οἴκτειρον ἡμᾶς, ὧν ἐπισκοπεῖς τύχας,
πράσσοντας οὐκ εὖ. στεμμάτων δ' οὐχ ἥσσονας
σοῖς προστίθημι γόνασιν ὠλένας ἐμάς. 895
ΟΡ. ἔα·
τί χρῆμα; μῶν ἐσφάλμεθ' ἢ σαφῶς ὁρῶ
δόμων ἄνασσαν τήνδε Μενέλεω κόρην;
ΕΡ. ἥνπερ μόνην γε Τυνδαρὶς τίκτει κόρη
Ἑλένη κατ' οἴκους πατρί· μηδὲν ἀγνόει.
ΟΡ. ὦ Φοῖβ' ἀκέστορ, πημάτων δοίης λύσιν. 900
τί χρῆμα; πρὸς θεῶν ἢ βροτῶν πάσχεις κακά;
ΕΡ. τὰ μὲν πρὸς ἡμῶν, τὰ δὲ πρὸς ἀνδρὸς, ὅς μ' ἔχει,
τὰ δ' ἐκ θεῶν του. πανταχῇ δ' ὀλώλαμεν.
ΟΡ. τίς οὖν ἂν εἴη μὴ πεφυκότων γέ πω
παίδων γυναικὶ συμφορὰ πλὴν ἐς λέχος; 905

883. τίς ὢν σὺ κτλ. Hermann. The edition of Lascaris has τίς ὤν γε, Aldus ἀτὰρ δὴ τίς ὢν κτλ. These are evident attempts at filling up the verse when σὺ had been lost. Nor is the reading of one MS., which Dindorf adopts, anything better, ἀτὰρ δὴ πυνθάνει τίς ὢν τάδε; The emphatic σὺ greatly improves the sense:— 'Who are *you* that ask this?' Barnes gives ἀτὰρ δὴ τίς σὺ κτλ.

886. ἐπεὶ ἀφικόμην, 'now that I have come to Phthia.' The doctrine, taught by some, that an aorist indicative can never be construed as a perfect, is, in the opinion of the present editor, likely to lead to many erroneous interpretations.

894. στεμμάτων. See on Heracl. 124. Schol. ἐπεὶ ἔθος ἦν τοὺς δεομένους ἐλαίας κλάδους καὶ ταῖς χερσὶ καὶ τῷ στόματι ἔχοντας δέεσθαι.

899. μηδὲν ἀγνόει, i. e. ἵνα πάντ' εἰδῇς. Cf. v. 463.

ΕΡ. τοῦτ' αὐτὸ καὶ νοσοῦμεν· εὖ μ' ὑπηγάγου.
ΟΡ. ἄλλην τίν' εὐνὴν ἀντὶ σοῦ στέργει πόσις;
ΕΡ. τὴν αἰχμάλωτον Ἕκτορος ξυνευνέτιν.
ΟΡ. κακόν γ' ἔλεξας, ἄνδρα δίσσ' ἔχειν λέχη.
ΕΡ. τοιαῦτα ταῦτα. κᾆτ' ἔγωγ' ἠμυνάμην. 910
ΟΡ. μῶν ἐς γυναῖκ' ἔρραψας οἷα δὴ γυνή;
ΕΡ. φόνον γ' ἐκείνῃ καὶ τέκνῳ νοθαγενεῖ.
ΟΡ. κἄκτεινας, ἤ τις συμφορά σ' ἀφείλετο;
ΕΡ. γέρων γε Πηλεὺς, τοὺς κακίονας σέβων.
ΟΡ. σοὶ δ' ἦν τις ὅστις τοῦδ' ἐκοινώνει φόνου; 915
ΕΡ. πατήρ γ' ἐπ' αὐτὸ τοῦτ' ἀπὸ Σπάρτης μολών.
ΟΡ. κἄπειτα τοῦ γέροντος ἡσσήθη χερί;
ΕΡ. αἰδοῖ γε· καί μ' ἔρημον οἴχεται λιπών.
ΟΡ. ξυνῆκα· ταρβεῖς τοῖς δεδραμένοις πόσιν.
ΕΡ. ἔγνως· ὀλεῖ γάρ μ' ἐνδίκως. τί δεῖ λέγειν; 920
ἀλλ' ἄντομαί σε Δία καλοῦσ' ὁμόγνιον
πέμψον με χώρας τῆσδ' ὅποι προσωτάτω,
ἢ πρὸς πατρῷον μέλαθρον· ὡς δοκοῦσί με
δόμοι τ' ἐλαύνειν φθέγμ' ἔχοντες οἵδε γε,
μισεῖ τε γαῖα Φθιάς· εἰ δ' ἥξει πάρος 925
Φοίβου λιπὼν μαντεῖον ἐς δόμους πόσις,

909. ἄνδρα. Aldus adds ἕνα before, Lascaris after, this word. Compare *sup.* v. 464. Hermione speaks with contempt of her rival, as now a slave, if once a queen. Cf. Ajac. 211, λέχος δουριάλωτον στέρξας ἀνέχει θούριος Αἴας.
910. ἠμυνάμην, 'resented it;' requited my rival for her conduct.
914. τοὺς κακίονας, the inferior side; the weaker party. See on Heracl. 176.
917. τοῦ γέροντος, 'of one who was an old man.' Hermann suspects we should read πῶς γέροντος κτλ.
918. αἰδοῖ γε. 'Yes, through respect for his age, (but not through fear).'
919. ξυνῆκα. 'I understand what you mean by ἔρημον,' viz. that you are in need of aid against some persecutor: you are afraid of your husband for what you have done, διὰ τὰ δεδραμένα.
920. On the formula τί δεῖ or καὶ τί δεῖ λέγειν, see Aesch. Eum. 790. It is used when an obvious truth is suggested by circumstances, but which the speaker does not wish to dwell upon. — Δία ὁμόγνιον, sc. ὅμαιμον, by the god who presides over the sacred ties of blood-relationship. Orestes and Hermione were, of course, first cousins. It is unnecessary, with the Scholiast, to refer the invocation of Zeus to their common descent from him through Leda by the mother's side.—πέμψον, 'escort me,' conduct me safe away, ἔκσωσον, ἐκκομίζου, v. 639.
923. δοκοῦσί με. Aldus has μοι, a good reading, but not confirmed by other copies, which give γε both here and after δόμοι, though some few MSS. have δόμοι μ'. All the copies have οἷδε με at the end of the next verse. Hermann has transposed γε and με, and if γε has any force at all, it emphasises οἵδε δόμοι, 'take me to some other house, for *this* seems to say, *depart*, ἔξιθι, and to chase me away.'

κτενεῖ μ' ἐπ' αἰσχίστοισιν, ἢ δουλεύσομεν
νόθοισι λέκτροις, ὧν ἐδέσποζον πρὸ τοῦ.
πῶς οὖν ἂν εἴποι τις τάδ' ἐξημάρτανες ;
κακῶν γυναικῶν εἴσοδοί μ' ἀπώλεσαν,   930
αἵ μοι λέγουσαι τούσδ' ἐχαύνωσαν λόγους·
Σὺ τὴν κακίστην αἰχμάλωτον ἐν δόμοις
δούλην ἀνέξει σοὶ λέχους κοινουμένην ;
μὰ τὴν ἄνασσαν, οὐκ ἂν ἔν γ' ἐμοῖς δόμοις
βλέπουσ' ἂν αὐγὰς τἄμ' ἐκαρποῦτ' ἂν λέχη.   935
κἀγὼ κλύουσα τούσδε Σειρήνων λόγους,
σοφῶν, πανούργων, ποικίλων λαλημάτων,
ἐξηνεμώθην μωρίᾳ. τί γάρ μ' ἐχρῆν
πόσιν φυλάσσειν, ᾗ παρῆν ὅσων ἔδει,
πολὺς μὲν ὄλβος, δωμάτων δ' ἠνάσσομεν,   940
παῖδας δ' ἐγὼ μὲν γνησίους ἔτικτον ἄν,
ἡ δ' ἡμιδούλους τοῖς ἐμοῖς νοθαγενεῖς.
ἀλλ' οὔποτ' οὔποτ', οὐ γὰρ εἰσάπαξ ἐρῶ,
χρὴ τούς γε νοῦν ἔχοντας, οἷς ἔστιν γυνή,
πρὸς τὴν ἐν οἴκοις ἄλοχον εἰσφοιτᾶν ἐᾶν   945
γυναῖκας· αὗται γὰρ διδάσκαλοι κακῶν·
ἡ μέν τι κερδαίνουσα συμφθείρει λέχος,
ἡ δ' ἀμπλακοῦσα συννοσεῖν αὐτῇ θέλει,

927. ἐπ' αἰσχίστοις, 'on a charge of most base actions.' So a person is said φεύγειν ἐφ' αἵματι, 'for murder,' &c.
929. This verse is given to Orestes in the old copies, and is thus read, πῶς οὖν τάδ', ὡς εἴποι τις, ἐξημάρτανες ; And so Matthiae, Pflugk, and Bothe, have edited. Lenting perceived that the line belonged to Hermione, and Hermann made her to speak in good Attic Greek. Hermione's endeavour to shift her fault on the shoulders of bad advisers is curious. It reminds one of Atossa's apology for her son Xerxes, Pers. 748 seqq. There is a very similar warning against the ingress of gossiping women in Hippol. 645 seqq.
931. ἐχαύνωσαν, puffed me up with vanity. Suppl. 412, ἐκχαυνῶν λόγοις, where see the note.—τὴν κακίστην κτλ., 'that worthless captive,' &c.
934. μὰ τὴν ἄνασσαν, μὰ τὴν Ἥραν,—

one of the formulas of a woman's oath.
938. ἐξηνεμώθην. Cf. Hel. 32.
943—53. This fine passage is quoted by Stobaeus, lxxiv. 4. By γυναῖκας the poet here means 'married women.' He suggests three distinct motives for such treacherous conduct ; (1) self-interest, either in the way of bribes for assisting the wife to dishonour the husband, or for her own wicked ends ; (2) the wish to make others as guilty as themselves ; (3) an immodesty which delights to dwell on such subjects. For this last is meant by μαργότης, not stultitia (Bothe). The Schol. rightly explains it by πορνείᾳ. All this Euripides makes an argument for increasing the strictness of female seclusion. He was wrong here ; seclusion itself was the source of half the evil. See Preface to Vol. i. p. xl.

πολλαὶ δὲ μαργότητι. κἀντεῦθεν δόμοι
νοσοῦσιν ἀνδρῶν. πρὸς τάδ᾽ εὖ φυλάσσετε 950
κλήθροισι καὶ μοχλοῖσι δωμάτων πύλας·
ὑγιὲς γὰρ οὐδὲν αἱ θύραθεν εἴσοδοι
δρῶσιν γυναικῶν, ἀλλὰ πολλὰ καὶ κακά.
ΧΟ. ἄγαν ἐφῆκας γλῶσσαν εἰς τὸ σύμφυτον.
ξυγγνωστὰ μὲν νῦν σοι τάδ᾽, ἀλλ᾽ ὅμως χρεὼν 955
κοσμεῖν γυναῖκας τὰς γυναικείους νόσους.
ΟΡ. σοφόν τι χρῆμα τοῦ διδάξαντος βροτοὺς
λόγους ἀκούειν τῶν ἐναντίων πάρα·
ἐγὼ γὰρ εἰδὼς τῶνδε σύγχυσιν δόμων
ἔριν τε τὴν σὴν καὶ γυναικὸς Ἕκτορος, 960
φυλακὰς ἔχων ἔμιμνον, εἴτ᾽ αὐτοῦ μενεῖς
εἴτ᾽ ἐκφοβηθεῖσ᾽ αἰχμαλωτίδος φόβῳ
γυναικὸς οἴκων τῶνδ᾽ ἀπηλλάχθαι θέλεις.
ἦλθον δὲ σὰς μὲν οὐ σέβων ἐπιστολάς,
εἰ δ᾽ ἐνδιδοίης, ὥσπερ ἐνδίδως, λόγον, 965
πέμψων σ᾽ ἀπ᾽ οἴκων τῶνδ᾽. ἐμὴ γὰρ οὖσα πρὶν
σὺν τῷδε ναίεις ἀνδρὶ σοῦ πατρὸς κάκῃ,

954. εἰς τὸ σύμφυτον, 'against your sex.' On ἐφιέναι, to give free course to, see Aesch. Theb. 783, τέκνοισιν δ᾽ ἀρὰς ἐφῆκεν ἐπικότους τροφᾶς.

955. μὲν νῦν Canter for μὲν οὖν. Matthiae and Pflugk wrongly give μέν νυν with Valckenaer. See on Electr. 408.

956. κοσμεῖν, to make the best of, to array in comely guise. Troad. 981, μὴ ἀμαθεῖς ποίει θεὰς τὸ σὸν κακὸν κοσμοῦσα. Aldus has φύσεις for νόσους, and so Matth. Dind. Pflugk. But the other has the authority of ed. Lasc. and all the MSS., and may easily have been altered by those who mistook the moral for the physical sense.

957. τοῦ διδάξαντος. The sentiment was referred to Phocylides, and is similarly expressed in Heracl. 179, τίς ἂν δίκην κρίνειεν ἢ γνοίη λόγον, πρὶν ἂν παρ᾽ ἀμφοῖν μῦθον ἐκμάθῃ σαφῶς; Ar. Vesp. 725, ἦ που σοφὸς ἦν ὅστις ἔφασκεν, πρὶν ἂν ἀμφοῖν μῦθον ἀκούσῃς, οὐκ ἂν δικάσαις. —ἐγὼ γὰρ κτλ. The argument proceeds thus:—'For it was on this principle, viz. resolving to hear the matter out, and so to decide on your real guilt or innocence,

that I determined to await the result of the dispute.'—ἐκφοβηθεῖσα, scil. οἴκων, φόβῳ being for διὰ φόβων.

964. σὰς μὲν οὐ σέβων. So ed. Lasc. and many MSS. Aldus gives τὰς σὰς οὐ μένων, and so Hermann has edited. The latter is the plainer reading, 'without waiting for your orders,' while οὐ σέβων more naturally means, 'paying no attention to your orders,' viz. orders that had been given to Orestes that he should not come to Phthia. It might however also mean, that he had indeed been urged to come, but that his motive was not that request, but his own independent desire to take her away. And so it seems indeed better to understand, than with the Schol., whom Pflugk and Matthiae follow, 'not in obedience to any commands of yours,' but voluntarily, οὐ διὰ τὰς σὰς ἐπιστολάς, οὐ γὰρ ἐπεστάλη μοί τι παρὰ σοῦ.

966. πέμψων Heath for πέμψω.—ἐνδιδόναι λόγους is 'to give any fair and specious pretence for acting,' as in the present case she had shown him good cause for wishing to leave her home. See v. 225.

ὃς πρὶν τὰ Τροίας εἰσβαλεῖν ὁρίσματα,
γυναῖκ' ἐμοὶ δούς, εἶθ' ὑπέσχεθ' ὕστερον
τῷ νῦν σ' ἔχοντι, Τρῳάδ' εἰ πέρσοι πόλιν.   970
ἐπεὶ δ' Ἀχιλλέως δεῦρ' ἐνόστησεν γόνος,
σῷ μὲν συνέγνων πατρί, τὸν δ' ἐλισσόμην
γάμους ἀφεῖναι σούς, ἐμὰς λέγων τύχας
καὶ τὸν παρόντα δαίμον', ὡς φίλων μὲν ἂν
γήμαιμ' ἀπ' ἀνδρῶν, ἔκτοθεν δ' οὐ ῥᾴδιον,   975
φεύγων ἀπ' οἴκων ἃς ἐγὼ φεύγω φυγάς.
ὁ δ' ἦν ὑβριστὴς εἴς τ' ἐμῆς μητρὸς φόνον
τάς θ' αἱματωποὺς θεὰς ὀνειδίζων ἐμοί.
κἀγὼ ταπεινὸς ὢν τύχαις ταῖς οἴκοθεν
ἤλγουν μὲν ἤλγουν, ξυμφοραῖς δ' ἠνειχόμην,   980
σῶν δὲ στερηθεὶς ᾠχόμην ἄκων γάμων.
νῦν οὖν, ἐπειδὴ περιπετεῖς ἔχεις τύχας,
καὶ ξυμφορὰν τήνδ' εἰσπεσοῦσ' ἀμηχανεῖς,
ἄξω σ' ἀπ' οἴκων καὶ πατρὸς δώσω χερί.
τὸ συγγενὲς γὰρ δεινόν, ἔν τε τοῖς κακοῖς   985

969. ἐμοὶ δούς, εἶθ' Aldus, and so Hermann has edited. Others follow Lascaris and the MSS. in reading γυναῖκ' ἐμοί σε δοὺς κτλ. One MS. gives γυναῖκ' ἐμοί σε δοὺς εἶθ' κτλ., whence Hermann attributes the variety of reading solely to the interpolation of σε.
970. εἰ πέρσοι, viz. by the aid of Neoptolemus and the bow of Hercules; a subject treated by the Cyclic poets, and familiar to most from the *Philoctetes* of Sophocles.
975. For γαμεῖν ἀπό τινων see Rhes. 168.— ῥᾴδιον Lasc. Ald. and several MSS., the rest giving ῥᾳδίως. It is easy to supply εἴη. The addition of the emphatic ἐγὼ makes it highly probable that we should read φεύγοντ' ἀπ' οἴκων, 'that it was not easy for a man to obtain a wife from strangers, if he had been banished from home as *I* had been.' In every way this reading would be an improvement. It explains also the insertion of ῥᾳδίως, viz. because οὐ ῥᾴδιον (ἐμοί) appeared to be a parenthetical clause, when the nominative φεύγων was reverted to.
977. ἦν ὑβριστής. This then was the origin of the enmity between Neoptolemus and Orestes, which ended in the death of the former as described in the next scene.
—εἰς is used as if he had said ὕβριζεν.
980. ξυμφοραῖς. 'Yet on account of my misfortunes, I bore it.' The dative, which is found in all the old copies, carries out the meaning of ταπεινὸς ὢν κτλ. W. Dindorf gives ξυμφορὰς with Scaliger. The sense is, ἀλλ' ὅμως διὰ τὰς ξυμφορὰς ἔστεργον.
982. περιπετεῖς τύχας. He means, ἐπειδὴ ταῦτα οὕτω περιπέπτωκε, οὕτω ξυνέβη. Photius, περιπετῆ γενέσθαι, περιπεπτωκέναι. περιπέτεια, σύμπτωμα, ἢ σύμβασις.
985. τὸ συγγενὲς γὰρ κτλ. 'For relationship has a strong claim upon me,' (i. e. that I should not marry you at once without his formal consent, as ὁ κύριος,) 'and besides, in one's troubles there is nothing so good as a friend who is also a relation.' This last is given as an additional reason why he should visit Menelaus in person. Hermann assigns these two lines to the chorus, reading τοι for γὰρ, and ἐν κακοῖσί τε for ἔν τε τοῖς κακοῖς. But, according to the explanation just given, Orestes himself makes known in this concluding distich the motives which actuate him. Compare Prom. 39. Tro. 51.

ΑΝΔΡΟΜΑΧΗ. 285

οὐκ ἔστιν οὐδὲν κρεῖσσον οἰκείου φίλου.
ΕΡ. νυμφευμάτων μὲν τῶν ἐμῶν πατὴρ ἐμὸς
μέριμναν ἕξει, κοὐκ ἐμὸν κρίνειν τάδε.
ἀλλ' ὡς τάχιστα τῶνδέ μ' ἔκπεμψον δόμων,
μὴ φθῇ με προσβὰς δῶμα καὶ μολὼν πόσις,   990
ἢ παιδὸς οἴκους μ' ἐξερημοῦσαν μαθὼν
Πηλεὺς μετέλθῃ πωλικοῖς διώγμασιν.
ΟΡ. θάρσει γέροντος χεῖρα· τὸν δ' Ἀχιλλέως
μηδὲν φοβηθῇς παῖδ', ὅσ' εἰς ἔμ' ὕβρισε.
τοία γὰρ αὐτῷ μηχανὴ πεπλεγμένη   995
βρόχοις ἀκινήτοισιν ἕστηκεν φόνου
πρὸς τῆσδε χειρός, ἣν πάρος μὲν οὐκ ἐρῶ,
τελουμένων δὲ Δελφὶς εἴσεται πέτρα.
ὁ μητροφόντης δ', ἢν δορυξένων ἐμῶν
μείνωσιν ὅρκοι Πυθικὴν ἀνὰ χθόνα,   1000
δείξει γαμεῖν σφε μηδέν' ὧν ἐχρῆν ἐμέ.
πικρῶς δὲ πατρὸς φόνιον αἰτήσει δίκην
ἄνακτα Φοῖβον· οὐδέ νιν μετάστασις
γνώμης ὀνήσει, θεῷ διδόντα νῦν δίκας.
ἀλλ' ἔκ τ' ἐκείνου διαβολαῖς τε ταῖς ἐμαῖς   1005
κακῶς ὀλεῖται· γνώσεται δ' ἔχθραν ἐμήν.

---

991. ἢ παιδὸς οἴκους is the reading of Aldus, and it is a good and probable one, though not certainly genuine. The beginning of the verse seems to have been lost, and it has been variously supplied, ἢ πρέσβυς οἴκους, and (in one MS. only, which W. Dindorf here too confidently follows) οἴκους τε τούσδε μ'. Hermann omits the μ', perhaps rightly.

993. θάρσει. On the accusative after this verb see Alcest. 1130. Aesch. Theb. 358. We might punctuate thus, (as indeed Scaliger proposed,) θάρσει· γέροντος χεῖρα τόν τ' Ἀχ. κτλ., but it is better to make a distinction between Peleus and Neoptolemus, the latter being much the more to be dreaded by her. Orestes seems to say, 'fear not but that I shall be a sufficient protector against an old man; and as for the other, I have sufficiently disposed of him already, for his insolent treatment of me.'

998. τελουμένων, ἐν τῷ τελεῖσθαι αὐτά, when they are being put into execution.

999. ὁ μητροφόντης. 'I whom he was pleased to taunt (v. 977) as *the matricide*, will show him that he must marry none of those whom I ought to have married before him.' He should have said μηδεμίαν, and the masculine is strangely used, though the sentiment is generalized. Lascaris and Aldus give μηδέν. Perhaps the true reading is δείξει γαμεῖν σε μηδέν', ἣν ἐχρῆν ἐμέ, i.e. 'shall show, that no man may marry you, whom I alone ought to have married.' The σφε is very suspicious; and it is not unfrequently interchanged with σε.

1002. πικρῶς, to his cost he shall demand of Phoebus satisfaction for his father's death. Cf. v. 51.

1006. γνώσεται, he shall be made to feel, he shall know by experience.—μοῖραν, the luck or advantage which enemies have had, is wont to be turned into disaster.

ἐχθρῶν γὰρ ἀνδρῶν μοῖραν εἰς ἀναστροφὴν
δαίμων δίδωσι, κοὐκ ἐᾷ φρονεῖν μέγα.
ΧΟ. ὦ Φοῖβ᾽ ὁ πυργώσας τὸν ἐν Ἰλίῳ εὐτειχῆ πάγον, καὶ
πόντιε κυανέαις   στρ. α´.   1010
ἵπποις διφρεύων ἅλιον πέλαγος,
τίνος οὕνεκ᾽ ἄτιμον ὀργάναν χέρα τεκτοσύνας Ἐ-
νυαλίῳ δοριμήστορι προσθέντες τάλαιναν   1015
τάλαιναν μεθεῖτε Τροίαν;
πλείστους δ᾽ ἐπ᾽ ἀκταῖσιν Σιμοεντίσιν εὐίππους ὄχους
ἐζεύξατε καὶ φονίους   ἀντ. α´.
ἀνδρῶν ἁμίλλας ἔθετ᾽ ἀστεφάνους·   1020
ἀπὸ δὲ φθίμενοι βεβᾶσιν Ἰλιάδαι βασιλῆες,
οὐδ᾽ ἔτι πῦρ ἐπιβώμιον ἐν Τροίᾳ θεοῖσιν

Pflugk compares Rhes. 322, πόλλ᾽ ἀναστρέφει θεὸς, and Suppl. 331, ὁ γὰρ θεὸς πάντ᾽ ἀναστρέφει πάλιν.

1009 seqq. In this ode the divine founders of Troy, Phoebus and Poseidon, are upbraided for having given up to Ares, i.e. to destruction, their once-loved city. Many war-chariots were yoked for the bloody stadium along the Simois, but the victory was not for them. The long line of native kings, descendants of Ilus, have come to an end, and sacrifices are no longer offered on the altars. Agamemnon has fallen by the hands of his wife, who herself has met with a righteous retribution from Orestes. It was against her that the oracle given to Orestes was directed. Hermione may take consolation from the thought that other wives beside herself have suffered, some in the loss of their sons, others in being forced to leave their homes for other husbands. Hellas has been afflicted, and the storm of war has passed over her from Troy, dropping gore upon her fertile fields.—The metres are simple, being for the most part combinations of dactyls with trochees. They are variously arranged in the editions. The above is according to the distribution of W. Dindorf.

Ibid. For the building of Troy by Phoebus and Poseidon, see Troad. 5.

1014. τίνος οὕνεκα κτλ. 'On what account have you made over to the god of war, the lord of the spear, the handicraft of your cunning workmanship, now no longer held in regard, and given up the unhappy Troy?' By ὀργάνη χεὶρ τεκτοσύνας, a mere periphrasis for ἔργον τεκτοσύνης, the city itself is of course meant. There were two forms of a word which is properly a substantive, ὀργάνη and ἐργάνη, both recognised by the grammarians, and used as attributes of Athena. Aeschylus has μνήμης ἐργάνην, Prom. 469, where the MSS. give μνήμην, and the variant ἐργάτιν or ἐργάτην. Matthiae gives βασιλῆς for βασιλῆες in the antistrophe, against the metre, though he is followed by recent editors, except Hermann; and W. Dindorf adopts Bothe's transposition χέρ᾽ Ἐνυαλίῳ τεκτοσύνας κτλ., by which, if there is any thing in the natural order of the words, Ἐνυάλιος would be called τεκτοσύνας δοριμήστωρ.

1016. προσθέντες. Hesychius, προσθεῖναι, τὸ παραδοῦναι τῷ ἐωνημένῳ ὑπὸ κήρυκι, addicere, Bothe. Pflugk compares Suppl. 948, ὅταν δὲ τούσδε προσθῶμεν πυρί. Hec. 368, Ἅιδῃ προστιθεῖσ᾽ ἐμὸν δέμας. See also on Bacch. 676.

1020. θεῖναι ἀστεφάνους is νίκης στερῆσαι. Schol. κακοστεφάνους, τὰς ἐχούσας στέφανον τὸν θάνατον. Pflugk also interprets it infaustos. The metaphor is obviously from the Athenian stadium on the bank of the Ilissus; and the order of the words indicates that ἀστεφάνους is the predicate, and not a mere epithet.

1024. οὐδ᾽ ἔτι πῦρ κτλ. Compare Troad. 1071, φροῦδαί σοι θυσίαι χορῶν τ᾽ εὔφημοι κέλαδοι κατ᾽ ὄρφναν τε παννυχίδες θεῶν.

λέλαμπεν καπνῷ θυώδει. 1024
βέβακε δ' Ἀτρείδας ἀλόχου παλάμαις· στρ. β'.
αὐτά τ' ἐναλλάξασα φόνον θανάτῳ
πρὸς τέκνων ἀπηύρα·
θεοῦ θεοῦ νιν κέλευσμ' ἐπεστράφη 1030
μαντόσυνον, ὅτε νιν
Ἀργόθεν πορευθεὶς
Ἀγαμεμνόνιος κέλωρ
ἀδύτων ἐπιβὰς κτάνεν, ματρὸς φονεύς, 1035
ὦ δαῖμον, ὦ Φοῖβε, πῶς πείθομαι;
πολλαὶ δ' ἂν Ἑλλάνων ἀγόρους στοναχὰς ἀντ. β'.
μέλποντο δυστάνων τεκέων ἄλοχοι·
ἐκ δ' ἔλειπον οἴκους 1040
πρὸς ἄλλον εὐνάτορ'· οὐχὶ σοὶ μόνᾳ
δύσφρονες ἐπέπεσον,
οὐ φίλοισι, λῦπαι·

1026. The connexion, as Hermann has pointed out, is βεβᾶσι μὲν βασιλῆες, βέβακε δὲ Ἀτρείδης. In the next verse ἐναλλάσσειν is used in the simple sense of 'to exchange,' with the implied notion of *retribution*. *Caedem morte luens et tanquam commutans*, Pflugk. —ἀπηύρα like ἀπολαύειν in v. 543, something being left to be supplied, 'suffered the penalty of her crime from her own children.' Cf. Hes. Opp. 238, πολλάκι καὶ ξύμπασα πόλις κακοῦ ἀνδρὸς ἀπηύρα.

1030. ἐπεστράφη νιν, was directed at her. Properly used of a person who becomes conversant with a place, as Med. 666. Hel. 82.

1031. ὅτε νιν κτλ. 'What time the son of Agamemnon having gone from Argos to (Delphi) and ascended to the prophetic recess, slew her, matricide that he was.' The MSS. and edd. give κτεάνων, which was most absurdly explained 'having laid claim to his interdicted possessions.' Heath proposed ἔκτανεν, and so Hermann edits, giving σφιν for καὶ in the antistrophe, v. 1046. W. Dindorf more plausibly omits the καὶ and here edits κτάνεν, which is also nearer to κτεάνων. The corruption probably arose from ε, added as the augment, being copied into the wrong place.—κέλωρ, 'a son,' is a word of the rarest occurrence. Trach.

852, οἷον ἀναρσίων οὔπω Ζηνὸς κέλωρ' ἀγακλειτὸν ἐπέμολε πάθος οἰκτίσαι. It seems like a term borrowed from some other dialect.

1036. πῶς πείθομαι; How am I to believe that Phoebus could have given such an oracle?

1037. πολλαὶ δ' κτλ. 'And many wives through all the public meeting-places of the Greeks (i.e. the squares and market-places) sang strains of woe for their unhappy sons.' Compare the use of πένθος τινός, on which see Alcest. 336. Most copies give ἂν Ἑλλάνων ἀγοραὶ, ἀχόρους κτλ., the Schol. with three MSS. ἀγόρους. The origin of the error is very easily seen: ἀγοραὶ was added as a note, implying that such was the ordinary form, and not ἄγοροι. The gloss having crept into the text, ἂν' became ἂν, and ἀγόρους was changed to ἀχόρους. Of course, πολλαὶ was thus regarded as agreeing with ἀγοραὶ, and not with ἄλοχοι. The captive Trojan women are doubtless meant, who were exposed for sale in the various Greek towns on the return of the victorious army.

1041. σοὶ μόνᾳ. 'You, Hermione, and your relations, the Atridae.' Bothe thinks the chorus are addressing each other, because no mention of Hermione has been elsewhere made in the ode. The Scholiast referred σοὶ to Troy.

νόσον Ἑλλὰς ἔτλα νόσον·
διέβα δὲ Φρυγῶν πρὸς εὐκάρπους γύας   1045
σκηπτὸς σταλάσσων *τὸν Ἅιδα φόνον.
ΠΗ. Φθιώτιδες γυναῖκες, ἱστοροῦντί μοι
σημήνατ'· ᾐσθόμην γὰρ οὐ σαφῆ λόγον
ὡς δώματ' ἐκλιποῦσα Μενέλεω κόρη
φρούδη τάδ'· ἥκω δ' ἐκμαθεῖν σπουδὴν ἔχων   1050
εἰ ταῦτ' ἀληθῆ· τῶν γὰρ ἐκδήμων φίλων
δεῖ τοὺς κατ' οἶκον ὄντας ἐκπονεῖν τύχας.
ΧΟ. Πηλεῦ, σαφῶς ἤκουσας· οὐδ' ἐμοὶ καλὸν
κρύπτειν ἐν οἷσπερ οὖσα τυγχάνω κακοῖς·
βασίλεια γὰρ τῶνδ' οἴχεται φυγὰς δόμων.   1055
ΠΗ. τίνος φόβου τυχοῦσα, διαπέραινέ μοι.
ΧΟ. πόσιν τρέμουσα, μὴ δόμων νιν ἐκβάλῃ.
ΠΗ. μῶν ἀντὶ παιδὸς θανασίμων βουλευμάτων;
ΧΟ. ναὶ, καὶ γυναικὸς αἰχμαλωτίδος φόβῳ.
ΠΗ. ξὺν πατρὶ δ' οἴκους, ἢ τίνος λείπει μέτα;   1060
ΧΟ. Ἀγαμέμνονός νιν παῖς βέβηκ' ἄγων χθονός.
ΠΗ. ποίαν περαίνων ἐλπίδ'; ἢ γῆμαι θέλων;
ΧΟ. καὶ σοῦ γε παιδὸς παιδὶ πορσύνων μόρον.

1045. The common reading is διέβα δὲ Φρυγῶν καὶ πρὸς κτλ., but two or three copies give καὶ Φρυγῶν, and one of these has διέβαλον. For καὶ, which the metre does not require (see v. 1035), Hermann improbably reads σφιν, referring it to the Greeks generally, implied in Ἑλλάς. That καὶ is an interpolation may easily be shown. When διέβα δὲ had been written διέβαλε, i.e. Λ for Δ, the copula was wanting; and this was supplied by καὶ, in a manner which shows that a clumsy attempt at a senarius was made, some taking the υ in Φρυγῶν to be short, others to be long. The notion in the poet's mind seems to have been, that the disease which afflicted Hellas passed over also to Troy, i.e. the mania for blood. This disease is described as the stroke of a pestilence, λοιμοῦ σκηπτὸς, Aesch. Pers. 711, passing from one land to another, and raining blood in its progress. Photius, σκηπτὸς, κεραυνὸς ἄνωθεν διάπυρος, and the primary sense is doubtless 'a lightning-stroke.'—τὸν before Ἅιδα was inserted by Hermann.

1047. Peleus, on behalf of the absent Neoptolemus, comes to inquire as to the truth of the rumour, that Hermione has left her home. He learns that she has gone off with Orestes, who has laid a plot for his rival's destruction. A messenger is on the point of departing to warn Neoptolemus of his danger, when the news arrives of his death at Delphi.

1054. τυγχάνω. Pflugk's suggestion, τυγχάνει, is not supported by the Scholiast, οὐ πρέπει τὸ συμβὰν ἡμῖν κακὸν τῆς Ἑρμιόνης κρύπτειν. The chorus is speaking merely as the representative of Neoptolemus' family, and without regard to private feelings in the matter.

1058. ἀντὶ κτλ. In return for her plot to kill the son of Neoptolemus and Andromache. Cf. v. 68.

1061. ἄγων χθονός. See v. 984; and for the genitive, on v. 650.

1063. παιδὸς παιδὶ, your grandson Neoptolemus. Cf. v. 1083.—κατ' ὄμμα, 'face to face,' see Electr. 910.

ΠΗ. κρυπτὸς καταστὰς, ἦ κατ' ὄμμ' ἐλθὼν μάχῃ;
ΧΟ. ἁγνοῖς ἐν ἱροῖς Λοξίου Δελφῶν μέτα. 1065
ΠΗ. οἴμοι· τόδ' ἤδη δεινόν. οὐχ ὅσον τάχος
χωρήσεταί τις Πυθικὴν πρὸς ἑστίαν,
καὶ τἀνθάδ' ὄντα τοῖς ἐκεῖ λέξει φίλοις,
πρὶν παῖδ' Ἀχιλλέως κατθανεῖν ἐχθρῶν ὕπο;

ΑΓΓΕΛΟΣ.

ἰώ μοί μοι.
οἵας ὁ τλήμων ἀγγελῶν ἥκω τύχας 1070
σοί τ', ὦ γεραιὲ, καὶ φίλοισι δεσπότου.
ΠΗ. αἰαῖ· πρόμαντις θυμὸς ὥς τι προσδοκᾷ.
ΑΓ. οὐκ ἔστι σοι παῖς παιδὸς, ὡς μάθῃς, γέρον
Πηλεῦ· τοιάσδε φασγάνων πληγὰς ἔχει
Δελφῶν ὑπ' ἀνδρῶν καὶ Μυκηναίου ξένου. 1075
ΧΟ. ἆ ἆ, τί δράσεις, ὦ γεραιέ; μὴ πέσῃς·
ἔπαιρε σαυτόν.
ΠΗ. οὐδέν εἰμ'· ἀπωλόμην.
φρούδη μὲν αὐδή, φροῦδα δ' ἄρθρα μου κάτω.
ΑΓ. ἄκουσον, εἰ καὶ σοῖς φίλοις ἀμυνάθειν
χρῄζεις, τὸ πραχθὲν, σὸν κατορθώσας δέμας. 1080
ΠΗ. ὦ μοῖρα, γήρως ἐσχάτοις πρὸς τέρμασιν
οἷα με τὸν δύστηνον ἀμφιβᾶσ' ἔχεις.
πῶς δ' οἴχεταί μοι παῖς μόνου παιδὸς μόνος;
σήμαιν'· ἀκοῦσαι δ' οὐκ ἀκούσθ' ὅμως θέλω.
ΑΓ. ἐπεὶ τὸ κλεινὸν ἤλθομεν Φοίβου πέδον, 1085
τρεῖς μὲν φαεννὰς ἡλίου διεξόδους

1072. τι, scil. νέον.—πρόμαντις, Soph. El. 475, ἁ πρόμαντις Δίκα. Ion 681, ὦ παῖ πρόμαντι Λατοῦς. Aesch. Cho. 745, τούτων πρόμαντις οὖσα, πολλὰ δ', οἴομαι, ψευσθεῖσα. Aldus and others have προσδοκῶν, which Hermann and Pflugk prefer, supplying ἔστι with πρόμαντις.
1075. Μ. ξένου, Orestes.
1077. ἀπωλόμην. Cf. Hec. 440. Alcest. 391.
1079. εἰ καί. Though this combination generally means 'even though you *do* wish,' &c., whence Hermann here reads εἴπερ, W. Dindorf εἴ τι, still the remark made on Heracl. 632 probably holds good in this case, that the καὶ belongs strictly to what follows, and therefore was not intended to affect the sense of εἰ. 'Hear what has been done, if you wish not merely to hear, but to assist also.' Hermann and others give ἀμυναθεῖν, against the MSS. That these verbs in -έθω, -ύθω, -άθω, are really present tenses is maintained by some scholars, against Elmsley on Med. 186.
1084. οὐκ ἀκούσθ' (i.e. ἀκουστὰ) was restored by Reiske, and was afterwards found in one Paris MS., for οὐκ ἀκοῦσ' or οὐ κακοῦσ'.

VOL. II. P p

θέᾳ διδόντες ὄμματ' ἐξεπίμπλαμεν.
καὶ τοῦθ' ὕποπτον ἦν ἄρ'· ἐς δὲ συστάσεις
κύκλους τ' ἐχώρει λαὸς οἰκήτωρ θεοῦ.
Ἀγαμέμνονος δὲ παῖς διαστείχων πόλιν   1090
εἰς οὓς ἑκάστῳ δυσμενεῖς ηὔδα λόγους,
ὁρᾶτε τοῦτον, ὃς διαστείχει θεοῦ
χρυσοῦ γέμοντα γύαλα, θησαυροὺς βροτῶν,
τὸ δεύτερον παρόντ' ἐφ' οἷσι καὶ πάρος
δεῦρ' ἦλθε, Φοίβου ναὸν ἐκπέρσαι θέλων;   1095
κἀκ τοῦδ' ἐχώρει ῥόθιον ἐν πόλει κακὸν,
ἀρχαί τ' ἐπληροῦντ' ἔς τε βουλευτήρια
ἰδίᾳ θ', ὅσοι θεοῦ χρημάτων ἐφέστασαν,
φρουρὰν ἐτάξαντ' ἐν περιστύλοις δόμοις.
ἡμεῖς δὲ μῆλα, φυλλάδος Παρνησσίας   1100
παιδεύματ', οὐδὲν τῶνδέ πω πεπυσμένοι,
λαβόντες ἦμεν, ἐσχάραις τ' ἐφέσταμεν,
ξὺν προξένοισι μάντεσίν τε Πυθικοῖς.
καί τις τόδ' εἶπεν· ὦ νεανία, τί σοι
θεῷ κατευξώμεσθα; τίνος ἥκεις χάριν;   1105
ὁ δ' εἶπε, Φοίβῳ τῆς πάροιθ' ἁμαρτίας
δίκας παρασχεῖν βουλόμεσθ'· ᾔτησα γὰρ
πατρός ποτ' αὐτὸν αἵματος δοῦναι δίκην.

1088. ἦν ἄρ'. See Hel. 1537. The natural curiosity of the guests to see the wonders of the place, (as in the case of the chorus in the *Ion*, 184 seqq.,) was interpreted by the people, who were instigated by the false representations of Orestes, as an intention of robbing the sacred treasure. Hence they formed knots and circles to talk the matter over.—οἰκήτωρ θεοῦ, colonists or settlers of the god, i. e. occupiers of his sacred land, the whole ground and mountain soil of Delphi being regarded as holy.
1093. γύαλα. Cf. Ion 76. 220. 245. May the word here be interpreted 'subterranean cells?' See on Hec. 1008. It may, however, signify the mountain valleys and ravines in the immediate neighbourhood of the Temple.
1094. καὶ πάρος. Cf. v. 52.
1096. ῥόθιον, as remarked on Aesch. Theb. 7, often has the sense of 'a murmur of dissatisfaction,' though ἐπιρροθεῖν is 'to applaud,' as in Hec. 553. On the proper meaning of the word see Hel. 1268.
1097. ἀρχαὶ ἐπληροῦντο. 'The magistrates assembled in full numbers in the council-house, and in private, those who presided over the riches belonging to the god, had guards duly placed in the colonnaded temple.' See Ion 54. Aesch. Eumen. 540, πληρουμένου γὰρ τοῦδε βουλευτηρίου σιγᾶν ἀρήγει.
1101. παιδεύματα, nurslings. So Hippolytus is called ἁγνοῦ Πιτθέως παίδευμα, Hippol. 11. They had procured sheep from the neighbouring mountain-pastures for the purpose of sacrifice.—ἦμεν, ἤειμεν. Cf. Electr. 775.
1103. ξὺν προξένοισι. See Ion 335. Hel. 146, where the present passage is explained, and also Suppl. 2.
1108. δοῦναι δίκην. See on v. 52.

ΑΝΔΡΟΜΑΧΗ.

κἀνταῦθ' Ὀρέστου μῦθος ἰσχύων μέγα
ἐφαίνεθ' ὡς ψεύδοιτο δεσπότης ἐμὸς, 1110
ἥκων ἐπ' αἰσχροῖς. ἔρχεται δ' ἀνακτόρων
κρηπῖδος ἐντὸς, ὡς πάρος χρηστηρίων
εὔξαιτο Φοίβῳ, τυγχάνει δ' ἐν ἐμπύροις·
τῷ δὲ ξιφήρης ἀνθυφειστήκει λόχος
δάφνῃ πυκασθείς· ὧν Κλυταιμνήστρας τόκος 1115
εἷς ἦν, ἁπάντων τῶνδε μηχανορράφος.
χὡ μὲν κατ' ὄμμα στὰς προσεύχεται θεῷ·
οἱ δ' ὀξυθήκτοις φασγάνοις ὡπλισμένοι
κεντοῦσ' ἀτευχῆ παῖδ' Ἀχιλλέως λάθρα.
χωρεῖ δὲ πρύμναν· οὐ γὰρ ἐς καιρὸν τυπεὶς 1120

1109. ἰσχύων μέγα ἐφαίνετο, was perceived to have great influence with the people. The question of the πρόξενος was no doubt put publicly; and the reply was cavilled at by Orestes, who pretended to show the absurdity of it to the people, and declared that he had come for a base purpose, viz. sacrilege. At this time, Orestes himself seems to have been present at Delphi. See below, v. 1116.

1112. κρηπῖδος. The θριγκὸς or low inclosure mentioned in Ion 1321.—πάρος χρηστηρίων, Schol. πρὸ τῶν θυσιῶν, i. e. before offering the victims. It might also mean 'in front of the oracle,' because none were allowed access to the adytum without previously offering a victim. Ion 228, ἐπὶ δ' ἀσφάκτοις μήλοισι δόμων μὴ πάριτ' ἐς μυχόν.

1113. τυγχάνει κτλ., scil. ὤν, 'he was at the moment engaged in the burning of the offerings.' The participle is omitted as in Soph. El. 313, νῦν δ' ἀγροῖσι τυγχάνει. Hec. 971, ἐν τῷδε πότμῳ τυγχάνουσ', ἵν' εἰμὶ νῦν.

1114. τῷ δὲ κτλ. 'But against him a company armed with swords had placed themselves in ambuscade; of whom the son of Clytemnestra was one, the sole plotter of all this mischief.' The common reading, ἄρ' ὑφειστήκει (ἄρ' Barnes and others, but either particle is wholly unmeaning) was corrected by Hermann; and the present editor had made the same emendation independently.—ξιφήρης, cf. Rhes. 713, ῥακοδύτῳ στολᾷ πυκασθεὶς, ξιφήρης κρύφιος ἐν πέπλοις. So ξ. Ὠρίων, Ion 1153. ensifer Orion, Ovid.—σκιασθεὶς Aldus and some copies for πυκασθείς.

1116. The comma usually placed after εἷς ἦν has been removed in the recent editions; for it is inferred from v. 997 that Orestes had left Delphi, and awaited at a distance the success of the plot against his rival Neoptolemus. Hence it is thought necessary to construe ὧν—τῶνδε, or rather, to regard τῶνδε as pleonastically added after ὧν. Still it must be confessed that the meaning of the words seems rather to be that given above. It is difficult too to interpret v. 1110 in any other way than of the actual presence of Orestes at the time, and only just before the murder; and in v. 1242 the murder itself is φόνος τῆς Ὀρεστείας χερός. The truth seems to be, that, when Orestes leaves the stage with Hermione at v. 1008, he departs for Delphi in order to be present at the death of Neoptolemus; and indeed this purpose is avowed by the chorus at v. 1063—5. Hence a considerable interval of time has elapsed during the song of the chorus.

1117. κατ' ὄμμα. 'He then, standing with his face to the statue of the god, was engaged in praying to him.' This explains λάθρα, because they rose on him from behind when his face was turned away.

1120. χωρεῖ κτλ. 'And he steps back (lit. 'backs water'), for it chanced that he was struck not in a fatal part.' Photius, πρύμναν ἀνακρούεσθαί ἐστι τὸ κατ' ὀλίγον ὑπαναχωρεῖν, μὴ στρέψαντας τὸ πλοῖον. ὁ γὰρ οὕτως ἀναχωρῶν ἐπὶ τὴν πρύμναν κωπηλατεῖ· τοῦτο δὲ ποιοῦσιν, ἵνα δόξωσι μὴ φανερῶς φεύγειν, κατ' ὀλίγον ὑπαπιόντες· ἢ ἵνα μὴ τὰ νῶτα τοῖς πολεμίοις δόντες τιτρώσκωνται. These words of the lexicographer form an admirable comment on the present passage.

292   ΕΥΡΙΠΙΔΟΥ

ἐτύγχαν', ἐξέλκει δὲ, καὶ παραστάδος
κρεμαστὰ τεύχη πασσάλων καθαρπάσας
ἔστη 'πὶ βωμοῦ, γοργὸς ὁπλίτης ἰδεῖν,
βοᾷ δὲ Δελφῶν παῖδας, ἱστορῶν τάδε·
τίνος μ' ἕκατι κτείνετ', εὐσεβεῖς ὁδοὺς   1125
ἥκοντα; ποίας ὄλλυμαι πρὸς αἰτίας;
τῶν δ' οὐδὲν οὐδεὶς μυρίων ὄντων πέλας
ἐφθέγξατ', ἀλλ' ἔβαλλον ἐκ χειρῶν πέτροις.
πυκνῇ δὲ νιφάδι πάντοθεν σποδούμενος
προὔτεινε τεύχη κἀφυλάσσετ' ἐμβολὰς,   1130
ἐκεῖσε κἀκεῖσ' ἀσπίδ' ἐκτείνων χερί.
ἀλλ' οὐδὲν ἦνεν· ἀλλὰ πόλλ' ὁμοῦ βέλη,
οἰστοὶ, μεσάγκυλ' ἔκλυτοί τ' ἀμφώβολοι,
σφαγῆς ἐχώρουν βουπόροι ποδῶν πάρος·
δεινὰς δ' ἂν εἶδες πυρρίχας φρουρουμένου   1135
βέλεμνα παιδός. ὡς δέ νιν περισταδὸν
κύκλῳ κατεῖχον, οὐ διδόντες ἀμπνοὰς,
βωμοῦ κενώσας δεξίμηλον ἐσχάραν,
τὸ Τρωικὸν πήδημα πηδήσας ποδοῖν

1121. ἐξέλκει, (as we say) 'he draws,' i. e. his sword. "Gladium semper gestabant antiqui Graeci,—ἀτευχὴς is est, qui nec scutum neque galeam habet. Haec arma Neoptolemus de postibus deripit, iisque se tegit." *Herm.* Others translate *extrahit se*, ἐξέλκει πόδα. But cf. Hec. 544.—παραστάδος κρεμαστὰ, 'suspended from the side-pilasters' (*antae*), or square projections at each front angle of the building, where armour taken in battle used to be fixed up by nails. See Heracl. 695. Having armed himself with a shield by snatching one of these dedicatory offerings, he leaps upon the low altar immediately in front of the pronaos, and thence addresses the multitude in assertion of his innocence.

1124. βοᾷ παῖδας, like Αἴαντα φωνῶ, Ajac. 73.

1125. εὐσεβεῖς, without any sacrilegious intent.

1129. νιφάδι, a shower of stones. Aesch. Theb. 200, νιφάδος ὅτ' ὀλοᾶς νιφομένας βρόμος ἐν πύλαις.—σποδούμενος, Hippol. 1238.—τεύχη, his shield. —ἐφυλάσσετο, 'guarded against (warded off) their striking him.'

1132. ἦνεν. Most copies have ἤνυεν. The verb ἄνειν and the substantive ἄνη are both used by Aeschylus.

1133. μεσάγκυλα. Phoen. 1148, καὶ πρῶτα μὲν τόξοισι καὶ μεσαγκύλοις ἐμαρνάμεσθα, σφενδόναις θ' ἑκηβόλοις, where the Schol. has this note, μεσαγκύλοις, τοῖς ἀκοντίοις, διὰ τὸ κατὰ μέσον τοῦ ξύλου τὰ ἀκόντια ἀγκύλον τι καὶ κοῖλον ἔχειν. They seem essentially the same as the ἀγκυλωτὰ explained on Bacch. 1205. By ἀμφώβολοι Hermann understands the sacrificial spits, sharpened at both ends, and with the meat drawn off them, ἔκλυτοι. These same spits might be called exegetically σφαγῆς βουπόροι, 'beef-piercing cutters,' but it is better to explain the latter as the sacrificial knives; and some of the post-Aldine editions give σφαγεῖς τ', as Barnes has edited.

1135. Photius, πυρρίχαις, ταῖς ἐνόπλοις ὀρχήσεσιν. Neoptolemus, otherwise called Pyrrhus, seems represented as the inventor of this peculiar war-step; though on this occasion it was a dance of death, to avoid the shower of missiles.

1139. τὸ Τρωικὸν πήδημα. The Schol,

χωρεῖ πρὸς αὐτούς· οἱ δ' ὅπως πελειάδες 1140
ἱέρακ' ἰδοῦσαι πρὸς φυγὴν ἐνώτισαν.
πολλοὶ δ' ἔπιπτον μιγάδες ἔκ τε τραυμάτων
αὐτοί θ' ὑπ' αὐτῶν στενοπόρους κατ' ἐξόδους,
κραυγὴ δ' ἐν εὐφήμοισι δύσφημος δόμοις
πέτραισιν ἀντέκλαγξ·' ἐν εὐδίᾳ δέ πως 1145
ἔστη φαεννοῖς δεσπότης στίλβων ὅπλοις,
πρὶν δή τις ἀδύτων ἐκ μέσων ἐφθέγξατο
δεινόν τε καὶ φρικῶδες, ὦρσε δὲ στρατὸν
στρέψας πρὸς ἀλκήν. ἔνθ' Ἀχιλλέως πίτνει
παῖς ὀξυθήκτῳ πλευρὰ φασγάνῳ τυπεὶς 1150
Δελφοῦ πρὸς ἀνδρός, ὅσπερ αὐτὸν ὤλεσε
πολλῶν μετ' ἄλλων· ὡς δὲ πρὸς γαῖαν πίτνει,
τίς οὐ σίδηρον προσφέρει; τίς οὐ πέτρον,
βάλλων, ἀράσσων; πᾶν δ' ἀνάλωται δέμας
τὸ καλλίμορφον τραυμάτων ὑπ' ἀγρίων. 1155
νεκρὸν δὲ δή νιν, κείμενον βωμοῦ πέλας,
ἐξέβαλον ἐκτὸς θυοδόκων ἀνακτόρων.
ἡμεῖς δ' ἀναρπάσαντες ὡς τάχος χεροῖν
κομίζομέν νίν σοι κατοιμῶξαι γόοις

refers this to a certain well-known leap from the ship to the shore, made by Achilles, the hero's father, at Troy; though Hermann suspects it may mean, 'that famous spring against the enemy at Troy,' presuming such a feat to have been celebrated by the Cyclic poets. Something like this is indeed recorded in Od. xi. 513, where Ulysses replies to the inquiries of Achilles in Hades respecting his son,

αὐτὰρ ὅτ' ἐν πεδίῳ Τρώων μαρναίμεθα χαλκῷ,
οὔ ποτ' ἐνὶ πληθυῖ μένεν ἀνδρῶν οὐδ' ἐν ὁμίλῳ,
ἀλλὰ πολὺ προθέεσκε, τὸ ὃν μένος οὐδενὶ εἴκων.

1143. αὐτοί θ' ὑπ' αὐτῶν, scil. καταπατούμενοι. The old copies appear to give αὐτοὶ δ', but Barnes has αὐτοί θ' ὑφ' αὐτῶν.

1145. ἐν εὐδίᾳ. The metaphor is continued from νιφάδι in 1129. The object of the poet is to represent Neoptolemus single-handed as completely victorious over his countless assailants, till they were rallied by a supernatural voice from the god himself, who was angry with the hero for the cause hinted at in v. 1163.

1151. ὅσπερ αὐτὸν κτλ. Hermann's reasons for altering this to ὧνπερ αὐτὸς ὤλεσεν, are far from being conclusive. The tradition was, (he says, referring to the Schol. on Orest. 1649,) that one particular Delphian called Machaereus killed Neoptolemus; and he thinks it quite absurd to add that he did so with the aid of many others. But, in the first place, it is well known that Euripides was fond of varying received legends, so that ὅσπερ, having reference to Machaereus, may easily have had some words added, which greatly enhanced the valour of Neoptolemus, by showing that he was no easy victim. And secondly, the very construction of Hermann's reading is much too artificial to be safely admitted into the text. It is more likely that the clause should be expunged as spurious, than that it requires alteration.

κλαῦσαί τε, πρέσβυ, γῆς τε κοσμῆσαι τάφῳ. 1160
τοιαῦθ' ὁ τοῖς ἄλλοισι θεσπίζων ἄναξ,
ὁ τῶν δικαίων πᾶσιν ἀνθρώποις κριτὴς,
δίκας διδόντα παῖδ' ἔδρασ' Ἀχιλλέως,
ἐμνημόνευσε δ', ὥσπερ ἄνθρωπος κακὸς,
παλαιὰ νείκη. πῶς ἂν οὖν εἴη σοφός; 1165
ΧΟ. καὶ μὴν ὅδ' ἄναξ ἤδη φοράδην
Δελφίδος ἐκ γῆς δῶμα πελάζει·
τλήμων ὁ παθὼν, τλήμων δὲ, γέρον,
καὶ σύ· δέχει γὰρ τὸν Ἀχίλλειον
σκύμνον ἐς οἴκους, οὐχ ὡς σὺ θέλεις. 1170
αὐτός τε κακοῖς πήμασι †κύρσας
εἰς ἓν μοίρας συνέκυρσας.
ΠΗ. ὤμοι ἐγώ, κακὸν οἷον ὁρῶ τόδε, στρ. α'.
καὶ δέχομαι χερὶ δώμασιν ἀμοῖς.
ἰὼ μοί μοι, 1175
ὦ πόλι Θεσσαλία, διολώλαμεν,
οὐκέτι μοι γένος, οὐκέτι μοι τέκνα
λείπετ' ἐν οἴκοις.
ὦ σχέτλιος παθέων ἄρ' ἐγώ, φίλον
ἐς τίνα βάλλων τέρψομαι αὐγάς; 1180
ὦ φίλιον στόμα καὶ γένυ καὶ χέρες.

1161—5. These lines, so freely reflecting on the alleged justice, impartiality, and wisdom of Apollo, are quite in the style of Euripides. Compare the reproaches of Ion, in v. 436 seqq. of that play. Of course, the poet's enemies of old were delighted with the handle which such passages afforded against him. So Aristophanes, Thesm. 450, νῦν δ' οὗτος ἐν ταῖσιν τραγῳδίαις ποιῶν, τοὺς ἄνδρας ἀναπέπεικεν οὐκ εἶναι θεούς.—For μνημονεύειν with an accusative, see Aesch. Pers. 779.

1166. The body of Neoptolemus is now borne on the stage by attendants.—φοράδην, see Rhes. 888.—δῶμα, the accusative of motion towards, though πελάζειν commonly takes the dative.

1170. οὐχ ὡς σὺ θέλεις, scil. ἀλλ' ὡς οἱ πολέμιοι. The student will notice the emphatic σύ. See the note on οἵ ἐγὼ θέλω, Hel. 1405, and ibid. 1201.

1171. κύρσας appears to be corrupt.

Hermann reads τοῖς τοῦδ', which certainly suits the sense perfectly. Perhaps the passage has been interpolated, and should stand thus; σκύμνον ἐς οἴκους, αὐτός τε κακοῖς | εἰς ἓν κτλ. The formula εἰς ἓν occurs (if the text be right) Hel. 1535, Troad. 1155, Heracl. 403, Ion 1016, and elsewhere. Here it means εἰς τὴν αὐτὴν μοῖραν, and the dative may either depend on the idea of 'similarity with,' or may signify διὰ τὰ τοῦδε πήματα.

1176. Θεσσαλίας Hermann from one MS., for Θεσσαλία. Lascaris and the MSS. have ὦ πόλις.

1179—80. These lines were restored by Hermann, who inserted ἄρ' and transposed some of the words to suit the dactylics of the antistrophe. The old reading was quite unmetrical, ὦ σχέτλια παθὼν ἐγὼ εἰς τίνα δὴ φίλον αὐγὰς βάλλων τέρψομαι. Two MSS. only have σχέτλιος παθέων. Hermann's emendation has been

ΑΝΔΡΟΜΑΧΗ.

εἴθε σ' ὑπ' Ἰλίῳ ἤναρε δαίμων
Σιμοεντίδα παρ' ἀκτάν.
ΧΟ. οὗτός τ' ἂν ὡς ἐκ τῶνδ' ἐτιμᾶτ' ἂν, γέρον,
θανὼν, τὸ σὸν δ' ἦν ὧδ' ἂν εὐτυχέστερον. 1185
ΠΗ. ὦ γάμος ὦ γάμος, ὃς τάδε δώματα   ἀντ. α'.
καὶ πόλιν ὤλεσας *ὤλεσας ἀμὰν,
αἰαῖ. ὦ παῖ,
μήποτε σῶν λεχέων τὸ δυσώνυμον
ὤφελ' ἐμὸν γένος ἐς τέκνα καὶ δόμον 1190
ἀμφιβαλέσθαι
Ἑρμιόνας Ἀίδαν ἐπὶ σοὶ, τέκνον,
ἀλλὰ κεραυνῷ πρόσθεν ὀλέσθαι,
μηδ' ἐπὶ τοξοσύνᾳ φονίῳ πατρὸς

admitted by W. Dindorf. It will be observed that the spondee in the next verse is accurately retained in the antistrophe.
1182. εἴθε—ἤναρε. A similar wish is expressed by Electra in Aesch. Cho. 337, εἰ γὰρ ὑπ' Ἰλίῳ πρός τινος Λυκίων, πάτερ, δορίτμητος κατηναρίσθης.
1183. This verse is dochmiac with a long syllable.
1184—5. This distich is remarkable for being composed chiefly of monosyllabic words. The reading in the text is that of Lascaris and most of the MSS. Aldus has οὗτος μὲν οὖν ἐκ τῶνδ' κτλ. Hermann gives οὕτως γ' ἂν, two or three MSS. having οὕτως. In the second verse the Dindorfs and Pflugk give τὸ σόν τ' ἦν, but this seems an instance where μὲν —δὲ and τε—τε are mixed together. For οὗτος is opposed to σὺ, and yet the two are viewed as in one category, from the similarity of their circumstances. The meaning is, 'Had he died at Troy, he would have been held in honour, according to the circumstances (i. e. as dead men are honoured), and your fate would thus have been more fortunate.' The sentiment was a common one; see Od. i. 239 seqq., imitated by Aeschylus, Cho. 337—345.
1187. The ὤλεσας was doubled by Hermann, and both transposed before ἀμάν. The antistrophic arrangement admits of no doubt, and is therefore a sure guide in these minor metrical adaptations.
1189. μὴ—ὤφελε. See on Med. 1413. Hec. 395. These words are difficult. Hermann gives ὤφελ' ἐμοὶ γέρας κτλ.,

'would that the honourable privilege of her couch ill-omined (Andromache, ἡ ἀνδρὶ μαχομένη), to my son and my family, had not brought with itself against you (Neoptolemus) the fate which Hermione designed against Andromache.' In fewer words, 'would that your union with the captive Andromache, which was a γέρας ἐξαίρετον, v. 14, had not involved you in the death intended for her.' Nothing indeed can be more harsh, than a marriage 'putting on death,' i. e. bringing a fatal end, to a person,—unless it be the construing Ἑρμιόνας γένος instead of Ἑρμιόνας Ἀίδαν, as Pflugk does, adopting ἐμὸν for ἐμοὶ from Musgrave. Matthiae gives quite a different sense, μήποτε ἐμὸν γένος σῶν λεχέων (Molossus, the child of Andromache by Neoptolemus) ὤφελεν κτλ. 'Would that my descendant had not caused (by Hermione's jealousy of Andromache's fruitfulness) Neoptolemus' death.' W. Dindorf appears to acquiesce in this; and it seems hopeless to extract any better sense out of the words.
1194. μηδ' ἐπὶ κτλ. 'Nor, on account of the archery (of Paris) fatal to your father (Achilles) ought you, a mortal, to have attributed to the god Phoebus the guilt of that Jove-born hero's death.' For this was the object of Neoptolemus' fatal mission to Delphi; cf. v. 1107.— ἀνάψαι, i. e. ἀναφέρειν. The old reading was Φοίβου, but the editors long ago perceived that εἰς θεὸν Φοῖβον, or rather, εἰς Φοῖβον θεὸν ὄντα, was to be taken together. With μηδὲ it is obviously necessary to supply ὤφελες.

αἷμα τὸ διογενὲς ποτε Φοῖβον 1195
βροτὸς εἰς θεὸν ἀνάψαι.
ΧΟ. ὀτοτοῖ ὀτοτοῖ. στρ. β'.
θανόντα δεσπόταν γόοις
νόμῳ τῷ νερτέρων κατάρξω.
ΠΗ. ὀτοτοῖ ὀτοτοῖ. ἀντ. β'. 1200
διάδοχα δ' ὦ τάλας ἐγὼ
γέρων καὶ δυστυχὴς δακρύω.
ΧΟ. θεοῦ γὰρ αἶσα, θεὸς ἔκρανε συμφοράν. στρ. γ'.
ΠΗ. ὦ φίλος, ἔλειπες ἐν δόμῳ μ' ἔρημον, 1205
γέροντ' ἄπαιδα νοσφίσας. [στρ. δ'.
ΧΟ. θανεῖν θανεῖν σε, πρέσβυ, χρῆν πάρος τέκνων.
ΠΗ. οὐ σπαράξομαι κόμαν,
οὐκ ἐπιθήσομαι δ' ἐμῷ 1210
κάρᾳ κτύπημα χειρὸς ὀλοόν; ὦ πόλι,
διπλῶν τέκνων μ' ἐστέρησε Φοῖβος.
ΧΟ. ὦ κακὰ παθὼν ἰδών τε δυστυχὲς γέρον, στρ. ε'.
τίν' αἰὼν' ἐς τὸ λοιπὸν ἕξεις; 1215
ΠΗ. ἄτεκνος, ἔρημος, οὐκ ἔχων πέρας κακῶν ἀντ. ε'.
διαντλήσω πόνους ἐς Ἅιδαν.
ΧΟ. μάτην δέ σ' ἐν γάμοισιν ὤλβισαν θεοί. ἀντ. γ'.
ΠΗ. ἀμπτάμενα φροῦδα τἀμὰ πάντα κεῖται
κόμπων μεταρσίων πρόσω. 1220
ΧΟ. μόνος μόνοισιν ἐν δόμοις ἀναστρέφει. ἀντ. δ'.
ΠΗ. οὐκέτ' ἐστί μοι πόλις·

1199. κατάρξω, as Elmsley had conjectured, is given in two MSS. for κατάρξομαι. The phrase κατάρχειν τινὰ γόοις, for κατάρχεσθαι γόους τινὸς, is singular enough. Cf. Orest. 960. Hec. 685.—νόμῳ τῷ νερτέρων, with a death-strain, or threnos, called νεκρῶν ἴακχον, Tro. 1230.
1208. πάρος τέκνων, in preference to, sooner than, your son, i. e. as the senior. Cf. Suppl. 174.
1212. διπλῶν τέκνων. Achilles and his son Neoptolemus.
1218. ἐν γάμοισιν. At the marriage of Peleus with Thetis.
1220. κόμπων πρόσω. Far from the lofty boast, that Phoebus would give satisfaction for the death of Achilles. Cf. Suppl. 127, τὸ δ' Ἄργος ὑμῖν ποῦ 'στιν; ἢ κόμποι μάτην; The word ἀμπτάμενα seems rather irregularly used, not in the sense of 'having flown away,' and so in connexion with φροῦδα, (for κεῖται is inconsistent with this figure,) but rather in respect of μεταρσίων, 'having taken a lofty flight, now lie low on the earth' (φροῦδα κεῖται). The old reading κόμπῳ μεταρσίῳ was corrected by Reiske.
1222. οὐκέτ' ἐστὶ Hermann for οὐκέτι. So in Rhes. 17, οὐκ ἔστι has been restored for οὐκέτι. In the next verse the same critic has given τάδ' ἐρρέτω 'πὶ γᾶν for τ' ἐρρέτω τάδ' ἐπὶ γαῖαν.

ΑΝΔΡΟΜΑΧΗ.

σκῆπτρα τάδ' ἐρρέτω 'πὶ γᾶν,
σύ τ', ὦ κατ' ἄντρα νύχια Νηρέως κόρη,
πανώλεθρον γᾷ πίτνοντά μ' ὄψει.   1225
ΧΟ. ἰὼ ἰώ.
τί κεκίνηται; τίνος αἰσθάνομαι
θείου; κοῦραι, λεύσσετ', ἀθρήσατε·
δαίμων ὅδε τις, λευκὴν αἰθέρα
πορθμευόμενος, τῶν ἱπποβότων
Φθίας πεδίων ἐπιβαίνει.   1230

ΘΕΤΙΣ.

Πηλεῦ, χάριν σῶν τῶν πάρος νυμφευμάτων
ἥκω Θέτις λιποῦσα Νηρέως δόμους.
καὶ πρῶτα μέν σοι τοῖς παρεστῶσιν κακοῖς
μηδέν τι λίαν δυσφορεῖν παρήνεσα·
κἀγὼ γάρ, ἢν ἄκλαυστ' ἐχρῆν τίκτειν τέκνα,   1235
ἀπώλεσ' ἐκ σοῦ παῖδα τὸν ταχὺν πόδας
Ἀχιλλέα τεκοῦσα, πρῶτον Ἑλλάδος.
ὧν δ' οὕνεκ' ἦλθον, σημανῶ, σὺ δ' ἐνδέχου.
τὸν μὲν θανόντα τόνδ' Ἀχιλλέως γόνον
θάψον, πορεύσας Πυθικὴν πρὸς ἐσχάραν,   1240
Δελφοῖς ὄνειδος, ὡς ἀπαγγέλλῃ τάφος
φόνον βίαιον τῆς Ὀρεστείας χερός.
γυναῖκα δ' αἰχμάλωτον, Ἀνδρομάχην λέγω,
Μολοσσίαν γῆν χρὴ κατοικῆσαι, γέρον,

1225. γᾷ πίτνοντα μ' ὄψει Hermann for μ' ὄψεαι πιτνοῦντα πρὸς γᾶν. Others simply omit πρὸς γᾶν, but the form ὄψεαι is questionable. The ἄντρα νύχια are the Νηρέως δόμοι of v. 1232, the submarine grottos where Thetis resided.
1231. σῶν τῶν πάρος ν., 'my former marriage with you (now no longer existing).' But τῶν σῶν πάρος ν., which Matthiae was disposed to prefer, has only reference to the time when it took place, without regard to present circumstances, i. e., as Hermann explains it, the common reading means, that she came because she was *formerly* his wife. The difference of meaning is perhaps rather fanciful; but the position of the article in the pause of the verse is certainly objectionable.

1238. ἐνδέχου, στέργων δέχου. Cf. Suppl. 977, ἀοιδαὶ ἃς χρυσοκόμας Ἀπόλλων οὐκ ἐνδέχεται.
1241. ἀπαγγέλλῃ. That the inscription on his tomb may show to all that he died by the violence of Orestes, from whose injustice the Delphians ought to have protected him. If Orestes himself was not present at the death, (see on v. 1116,) of course the words must not be taken too literally. Compare however v. 1075.
1244. κατοικίσαι Hermann, with Lascaris and others. The words are perpetually interchanged; but Andromache was rather to settle in the land than to colonise it.

VOL. II.   Q q

Ἑλένῳ ξυναλλαχθεῖσαν εὐναίοις γάμοις, 1245
καὶ παῖδα τόνδε, τῶν ἀπ' Αἰακοῦ μόνον
λελειμμένον δή· βασιλέα δ' ἐκ τοῦδε χρὴ
ἄλλον δι' ἄλλου διαπερᾶν Μολοσσίας
εὐδαιμονοῦντας· οὐ γὰρ ὧδ' ἀνάστατον
γένος γενέσθαι δεῖ τὸ σὸν κἀμὸν, γέρον, 1250
Τροίας τε· καὶ γὰρ θεοῖσι τἀκείνης μέλει,
καίπερ πεσούσης Παλλάδος προθυμίᾳ.
σὲ δ', ὡς ἂν εἰδῇς τῆς ἐμῆς εὐνῆς χάριν,
[θεὰ γεγῶσα καὶ θεοῦ πατρὸς τέκος,]
κακῶν ἀπαλλάξασα τῶν βροτησίων 1255
ἀθάνατον ἄφθιτόν τε ποιήσω θεόν.
κἄπειτα Νηρέως ἐν δόμοις ἐμοῦ μέτα
τὸ λοιπὸν ἤδη θεὸς συνοικήσεις θεῷ·
ἔνθεν κομίζων ξηρὸν ἐκ πόντου πόδα
τὸν φίλτατον σοὶ παῖδ' ἐμοί τ' Ἀχιλλέα 1260
ὄψει δόμους ναίοντα νησιωτικοὺς
Λευκὴν κατ' ἀκτὴν ἐντὸς Εὐξείνου πόρου.
ἀλλ' ἕρπε Δελφῶν ἐς θεόδμητον πόλιν
νεκρὸν κομίζων τόνδε, καὶ κρύψας χθονὶ

1248. ἄλλον δι' ἄλλου. A singular phrase for ἄλλον ἄλλου διάδοχον.—Μολοσσίας Hermann for Μολοσσίαν. He takes διαπερᾶν for διατελεῖν, διάγειν, and the genitive to depend on βασιλέα. But Pflugk explains the vulgate *per Molossorum fines regnare*. It is very doubtful if the words could bear this meaning, especially as βασιλέα stands remote from the verb. This prophecy, if such it be called, was fulfilled, in so far as the famed Pyrrhus, king of Epirus, was destined, more than a century later, to become not only king of his ancestral land, but one of the most powerful and successful monarchs of his age.

1251. τἀκείνης, her heroes, i. e. the descendants from a Trojan queen, Andromache. The old reading κἀκείνης was corrected by Lenting, and his emendation is adopted by Hermann and Dindorf, not only because the καὶ is awkwardly repeated, but because the affairs, i. e. the people of Troy, are meant rather than the city itself.

1254. This verse is placed by Hermann after v. 1256. Dindorf incloses it in brackets, and the Scholiast says it was wanting in the majority of the copies.—εἰδέναι χάριν τινὸς, to be conscious of gratitude for a thing, and thence to acknowledge it, is a common Attic phrase. 'That you may have reason to be grateful,' she says, ' for your marriage with me, I will make you a god, and renew in the regions of the blest our common relation upon earth.'

1255. βροτησίων, an epic form for βροτείων, used also in Bacch. 4. Orest. 271. It follows the analogy of ἡμερήσιος, νυκτερήσιος.

1259. ξηρὸν πόδα. An ordinary mortal would be drowned, a divine being would not even wet his feet in rising from the watery depths below.

1262. Λευκὴ ἀκτή. An island opposite to the strip of land called Ἀχίλλειος δρόμος (*Tendera*) near the mouth of the Borysthenes (*Dnieper*). See Iph. Taur. 436.—δόμους ναίοντα, i. e. being worshipped in a temple there as a hero.

ΑΝΔΡΟΜΑΧΗ. 299

ἐλθὼν παλαιᾶς χοιράδος κοῖλον μυχὸν 1265
Σηπιάδος ἵζου· μίμνε δ', ἔς τ' ἂν ἐξ ἁλὸς
λαβοῦσα πεντήκοντα Νηρῄδων χορὸν
ἔλθω κομιστήν σου· τὸ γὰρ πεπρωμένον
δεῖ σ' ἐκκομίζειν· Ζηνὶ γὰρ δοκεῖ τάδε.
παῦσαι δὲ λύπης τῶν τεθνηκότων ὕπερ· 1270
πᾶσιν γὰρ ἀνθρώποισιν ἥδε πρὸς θεῶν
ψῆφος κέκρανται, κατθανεῖν τ' ὀφείλεται.
ΠΗ. ὦ πότνι', ὦ γενναῖα συγκοιμήματα,
Νηρέως γένεθλον, χαῖρε· ταῦτα δ' ἀξίως
σαυτῆς τε ποιεῖς καὶ τέκνων τῶν ἐκ σέθεν. 1275
παύσω δὲ λύπην, σοῦ κελευούσης, θεά,
καὶ τόνδε θάψας εἶμι Πηλίου πτυχὰς,
οὗπερ σὸν εἶλον χερσὶ κάλλιστον δέμας.
κᾆτ' οὐ γαμεῖν δῆτ' ἔκ τε γενναίων χρεὼν
δοῦναί τ' ἐς ἐσθλοὺς, ὅστις εὖ βουλεύεται; 1280
κακῶν δὲ λέκτρων μὴ 'πιθυμίαν ἔχειν,
μηδ' εἰ ζαπλούτους οἴσεται φερνὰς δόμοις.
οὐ γάρ ποτ' ἂν πράξειαν ἐκ θεῶν κακῶς.
ΧΟ. πολλαὶ μορφαὶ τῶν δαιμονίων,
πολλὰ δ' ἀέλπτως κραίνουσι θεοί, 1285
καὶ τὰ δοκηθέντ' οὐκ ἐτελέσθη,
τῶν δ' ἀδοκήτων πόρον ηὗρε θεός.
τοιόνδ' ἀπέβη τόδε πρᾶγμα.

1266. Σηπιὰς χοιρὰς, a reef near Iolcos, so called, one may suppose, either from its resemblance to a cuttle-fish, or from its being frequented by that sea-monster. It is now called *St. George*. It was here that the fleet of Xerxes met with such a heavy loss, Herod. vii. 188.
1272. κέκρανται. See Hec. 219. Recent editors omit the τε after κατθανεῖν, though found in all the copies but one. But this leaves the clause very abrupt; and there is no reason why τε should not be taken exegetically.
1277. πτυχάς. MSS. πτύχας. See Suppl. 979, where the form πτὺξ is required by the metre. But πτυχὴ seems to be the form ordinarily preferred.
1279. For γαμεῖν ἐκ or ἀπὸ τινῶν see Rhes. 168. *sup.* 975.
1283. πράξειαν. Scil. οἱ ἐκ γενναίων γαμοῦντες, &c. The preceding four verses are quoted by Stobaeus, lxxii. 3.

ΕΥΡΙΠΙΔΟΥ ΗΛΕΚΤΡΑ.

ΥΠΟΘΕΣΙΣ.

* * * * *

ἡ μὲν σκηνὴ τοῦ δράματος ὑπόκειται ἐν ὁρίοις τῆς Ἀργείας γῆς· ὁ δὲ χορὸς συνέστηκεν ἐξ ἐπιχωρίων γυναικῶν.

ELECTRA.

It has been the fashion of recent critics to disparage the Electra of Euripides, as compared with the plays of Sophocles and Aeschylus on the same subject. Because it is less full of the supernatural, that is, of the doctrines of Destiny, the consequences of ancestral crime, and the spiritual agencies of the departed in Hades; and because Euripides has made his characters speak naturally, like human beings, therefore he has been unsparingly assailed by those to whom Greek mythology is a more interesting subject than the human passions. Augustus W. Von Schlegel, who devotes some pages of his "Lectures[1]" to a burlesque summary of the plot, in which he tries to throw ridicule upon every incident, is pleased to say, that "the Electra is perhaps of all Euripides' extant plays *the very vilest;*" and he adds, that "to expose all its absurdities and contradictions would be an endless undertaking." O. Müller is much less vindictive; though he awards not one word of praise to the play, he merely says, that "in this piece Euripides goes farther than in any other in his endeavour to reduce the old mythical stories to the level of every-day life[2]." A recent writer has not hesitated to state, and indeed, has gone out of his way purposely to avow, as his opinion in reference to classical learning generally[3], that "Such plays as the Electra of Euripides seem unworthy of encouragement." What other plays he considers to belong to this category, we are not told: and therefore we are left to infer, either that there must be some minds singulaly unable to appreciate the Attic drama, or some others singularly disposed to admire what is not really worthy of admiration; for at least, to the present editor, the Electra of Euripides has always appeared by no means the least interesting of his plays. The incidents are far from common-place, though the plot is so contrived as to introduce much of common life in the characters. The scenes are often vividly and romantically

---

[1] See Theatre of the Greeks, p. 232—243.   [2] Hist. Gr. Lit. p. 374.
[3] Preface to "Thirteen Satires of Juvenal," p. xiii.

depicted; the recognition-scene especially is much more natural than either of the other tragic writers have contrived to make it. Dr. Robinson truly says [4], that "haec Tragoedia, licet haud inter optimas enumeranda, multa tamen et praeclara continet." Considered merely in a poetical light, the play is certainly very well written; it has many brilliant passages, and besides, many wise, and shrewd, and humane sentiments. What then are its faults? One says, that the story of the continent husband is unnatural and ridiculous, and that the manifest allusion to the ἀναγνώρισις in the *Choephori* of Aeschylus is unbecoming, and alien from genuine poetry. To the former objection the poet himself very finely replies in v. 50—3. Another sees more of comedy than of tragedy in the play [5]; a third regards it as "an attempt to draw out the human interest yet further, not so much by developing character as by varying and amplifying the circumstances;" and thinks the result of that attempt is, that "all the dignity and glory of tragedy have vanished under the process [6]."

A natural consequence of the ill-repute in which the play has been so generally held, is, that it is very much less read than it deserves to be. And this circumstance again accounts in some measure for the comparatively little attention that has been bestowed on its critical revision, Seidler's edition being, as yet, the most careful and complete that has appeared. The *Electra* has, however, some considerable advantages over others much more popular in the schools. It is rather an easy play; it is not very corrupt; it best illustrates the style and mind of Euripides, because it happens to be rather strongly contrasted with the *Electra* of Sophocles, and the *Choephori* of Aeschylus. The literary history of our poet's *Electra* is somewhat curious. It is not found in the Aldine and following editions, antecedent to the year 1545, when it was first published at Rome by Pietro Vettori (Petrus Victorius) with a dedicatory epistle to Cardinal Ardinghelli, and again in the same year at Florence. Both editions are of extreme rarity; and besides them, it does not appear that the collation of more than four MSS. has been obtained, two Parisian and two Florentine, of which the various readings are given in Matthiae's and Dindorf's notes. From what MS. the play was first published, is not stated; Vettori merely says that it was "inter medias ejus Poetae fabulas in vetustissimo codice interjecta." Of the genuineness of the play, as a work of Euripides, not the slightest doubt can be entertained.

[4] Praefat. ed. Cant. 1822.
[5] Schlegel, Lectures, p. 243. P. Victorius, in the Latin Argument.
[6] Prof. Conington, Introduction to the Choephoroe of Aeschylus, p. xx.

The plot may be briefly sketched as follows. Electra has been given in marriage by Aegisthus to a poor but honest and well-born agriculturist, or what we should call a day-labourer,—a class of men whom Euripides elsewhere delights to praise,—lest, if wedded to a person of rank and influence, her offspring should some day exact vengeance for the murder of her father. The scene, consequently, is laid, not at Argos, but in a part of the Argolic territory remote from the palace and throne which Aegisthus has unworthily occupied. The kind consideration which the married but virgin pair (for the husband resolutely abstains from cohabiting with a wife so much above him in dignity,) show to each other, and their simple and frugal cottage life, are touchingly described. Electra, in a monody, which is not quite so ridiculous as some have been pleased to imagine, but, on the contrary, contains an artless and natural expression of her feelings, bewails her own lot and the cruel death of her father, and calls upon her brother to come and deliver her. She is joined by the chorus, consisting of country-women, who, wishing to cheer her grief, invite her to take part in a coming festival of the Argive Hera; but she declines, as having neither heart for gaiety nor fit attire for joining in it. Orestes and Pylades are now seen by her, lurking near the cottage. At first she takes them for thieves, but is induced to await their approach. Without recognizing her brother, she informs him of all the circumstances of her present position, and he engages to report them to Orestes, from whom he pretends to bring news. The husbandman returns, and believing the stranger's message to be a real one, invites him into the house; but its scanty supplies are insufficient for himself and his friend Pylades, and a request is conveyed to an old servant of the Atridae, who happens to dwell near, to contribute provisions for the occasion. He arrives, and in fine recognizes Orestes by the token of an old scar, and together they plot the murder of Aegisthus and Clytemnestra. The queen is invited from the city to the cottage, under pretence of her daughter's recent delivery of a first-born child: Aegisthus happens to be absent in the country sacrificing to the Nymphs. Orestes is conducted by the old man to the spot, and the tyrant's death is easily effected under the plea of joining in the sacrifice. Shortly afterwards, Clytemnestra pays a visit in great state to her daughter's cottage. Electra gains permission to speak her mind freely on the subject of her conduct towards her late lord, and, in fact, proves to her that she has deserved no mercy at the hands of her children. At length she enters the cottage, within which Orestes is concealed; and the bloody deed is quickly done. The body of Aegisthus, which had previously been conveyed within the cottage, is now exposed before Electra and her brother. No sooner are the two corpses seen lying dead before them, than they are seized with a remorse at the deed, and mutually blame each other with having been the instigator of the murder. (This, of course, is very true to nature; and Von Schlegel has not a shadow of reason for stigmatizing such emotions as "a most despicable repentance," "a mere animal revulsion," &c.) At the end of the play, the Dioscuri appear, and inform Orestes of the future which awaits him and his long oppressed sister. Although the play, in a sense, ends happily, it is a great mistake on that account to call it a tragi-comedy. It is a true tragedy; but the tragic action is centered in the death of the guilty pair, and in the sufferings, trials, and strong mental emotions of the just avengers of their father. Clytemnestra is represented as not wholly devoid of kindness towards her daughter; and her own defence of her conduct is so far specious, that it somewhat increases the commiseration for her end. But in this the art of the writer is undoubtedly shown. He was not bound to represent her as stern and tyrannical, merely because Aeschylus and Sophocles had done so.

Of the date of the play nothing certain is known. Inferences however have been drawn from political allusions, for which see the note on v. 1347. In the order of the tragedies relating to Troy, it is clear from v. 1280 that it must be considered as immediately following the *Helena*.

As Von Schlegel "cannot see for what end Euripides wrote the play at all," it may be well to add, that the moral of it is a very noble and exalted theme; that the criminal indulgence of the passions entails a misery which no external splendour can abate; that the highest virtue is often found in the humblest lot; that, bad as faithlessness is in a wife, and severely censured as it is by the world, it is too often the heartless husband who is the cause of it, although *his* aberrations are only indiscretions, while hers are called crimes.

ΤΑ ΤΟΥ ΔΡΑΜΑΤΟΣ ΠΡΟΣΩΠΑ.

ΑΥΤΟΥΡΓΟΣ ΜΥΚΗΝΑΙΟΣ.
ΗΛΕΚΤΡΑ.
ΟΡΕΣΤΗΣ.
ΠΥΛΑΔΗΣ κωφὸν πρόσωπον.
ΧΟΡΟΣ.
ΚΛΥΤΑΙΜΝΗΣΤΡΑ.
ΠΡΕΣΒΥΣ.
ΑΓΓΕΛΟΣ.
ΔΙΟΣΚΟΡΟΙ.

ΕΥΡΙΠΙΔΟΥ ΗΛΕΚΤΡΑ.

ΑΥΤΟΥΡΓΟΣ.

Ὦ γῆς παλαιὸν Ἄργος, Ἰνάχου ῥοαὶ,
ὅθεν ποτ᾽ ἄρας ναυσὶ χιλίαις Ἄρη
ἐς γῆν ἔπλευσε Τρῳάδ᾽ Ἀγαμέμνων ἄναξ,
κτείνας δὲ τὸν κρατοῦντ᾽ ἐν Ἰλίᾳ χθονὶ
Πρίαμον, ἑλών τε Δαρδάνου κλεινὴν πόλιν, 5
ἀφίκετ᾽ ἐς τόδ᾽ Ἄργος, ὑψηλῶν δ᾽ ἐπὶ
ναῶν τέθεικε σκῦλα πλεῖστα βαρβάρων.

1. The unhappy position of Electra is described by a countryman, an honest farmer who lives with her nominally as her husband, but through respect for her family has spared her the indignity of having children by him. The death of Agamemnon by his own wife's hand, the usurpation of Aegisthus, his fear of the surviving children and his scheme of marrying the daughter to one in low life, lest her descendants should inherit that noble spirit that would never rest unavenged, are successively explained; and then the speaker anticipates an objection that the sensual may raise against his self-denying virtue, by saying that such persons measure true wisdom by the false standard of their own inclinations.

Ibid. The address to Argos is not followed by any direct reference to it, precisely as the Andromache commences with an appeal to Thebes, and the Alcestis with the mention of Admetus' house, —the object in these cases being either to define the scene of the action, or to fix the hearer's attention on some circumstance in the mind of the speaker.—γῆς, i.e. τῆσδε, or Ἑλληνίδος. The Greek idea of γῆ was pretty nearly the limits of Greek civilization, all others being βάρβαροι, and hardly considered in cases like the present, where all the associations of both the speaker and the audience are centered upon one of the earliest settlements of their own soil.—Ἰνάχου ῥοαὶ seems added to show that the district rather than the city is meant; for the countryman (see v. 246,) dwelt at some little distance without the walls. The epithet παλαιὸν is applied to Argos by Sophocles, El. 4.

2. ἄρας Ἄρη, like the customary phrase αἴρειν στόλον. Cf. Pers. 791. Agam. 45, στόλον Ἀργείων χιλιοναύταν τῆσδ᾽ ἀπὸ χώρας ἦραν.

4. Ἰλίᾳ for Ἰλιάδι Bothe. This correction is the more probable, because, as remarked on Alcest. 116, the grammarians were in the habit of introducing adjectival forms in —ὰς, even against the metre, e.g. Ἀσιὰς for Ἀσίς. Elmsley proposed ἐν Ἰδαίᾳ χθονί. Cf. Hec. 325.

7. τέθεικε. 'He *has* placed,' for ἀνατέθεικε. The speaker may be supposed to point towards the city, as if to add, 'where they are now to be seen.' This

κἀκεῖ μὲν ηὐτύχησεν· ἐν δὲ δώμασι
θνῄσκει γυναικὸς πρὸς Κλυταιμνήστρας δόλῳ
καὶ τοῦ Θυέστου παιδὸς Αἰγίσθου χερί.   10
χὠ μὲν παλαιὰ σκῆπτρα Ταντάλου λιπὼν
ὄλωλεν, Αἴγισθος δὲ βασιλεύει χθονὸς,
ἄλοχον ἐκείνου Τυνδαρίδα κόρην ἔχων.
οὓς δ᾽ ἐν δόμοις ἔλειφ᾽, ὅτ᾽ ἐς Τροίαν ἔπλει,
ἄρσενά τ᾽ Ὀρέστην θῆλύ τ᾽ Ἠλέκτρας θάλος,   15
τὸν μὲν πατρὸς γεραιὸς ἐκκλέπτει τροφεὺς
μέλλοντ᾽ Ὀρέστην χερὸς ὑπ᾽ Αἰγίσθου θανεῖν,
Στροφίῳ τ᾽ ἔδωκε Φωκέων ἐς γῆν τρέφειν·
ἣ δ᾽ ἐν δόμοις ἔμεινεν Ἠλέκτρα πατρὸς,
ταύτην ἐπειδὴ θαλερὸς εἶχ᾽ ἥβης χρόνος,   20
μνηστῆρες ᾔτουν Ἑλλάδος πρῶτοι χθονός.
δείσας δὲ μή τῳ παῖδ᾽ ἀριστέων τέκοι
Ἀγαμέμνονος ποινάτορ᾽, εἶχεν ἐν δόμοις
Αἴγισθος, οὐδ᾽ ἥρμοζε νυμφίῳ τινί.
ἐπεὶ δὲ καὶ τοῦτ᾽ ἦν φόβου πολλοῦ πλέων,   25
μή τῳ λαθραίως τέκνα γενναίῳ τέκοι,

perfect tense is one of the later Attic forms. We may compare the equally rare παρεῖκεν in Hel. 1059.—σκῦλα, *inf.* 1000. Hec. 1014. τὰ ἀπὸ τῶν πολεμίων ἀνῃρημένα, Photius. — ἐπὶ ναῶν, cf. Androm. 1121.

11. παλαιὰ σκῆπτρα Ταντάλου. According to Homer, Il. ii. 104, the sceptre borne by Agamemnon was made by Hephaestus and given first to Pelops, not to his father Tantalus.

14. ἔλειφ᾽. The old reading was ἔλιπεν. Seidler and others give δόμοισιν ἔλιφ᾽, but the imperfect is here quite as appropriate as the aorist, especially when followed by ἔπλει. The verse in the Orestes (63), ἣν γὰρ κατ᾽ οἴκους ἔλιφ᾽, ὅτ᾽ ἐς Τροίαν ἔπλει, proves nothing, for there the metre requires the aorist.

16, 17. τὸν μὲν—Ὀρέστην. Compare Hel. 1025, τὴν μέν σ᾽ ἐᾶσαι πατρίδα νοστῆσαι Κύπριν.

22. Porson's conjecture (on Med. 5), παῖδ᾽ ἀριστέων for παῖδας Ἀργείων, and ποινάτορ᾽ for ποινάτορας, is ingenious; but unfortunately it is not convincing, though on the whole it is sufficiently probable to be adopted, where some altera-

tion is absolutely necessary. There is no real difficulty in Ἀργείων, as Bothe shows; for among the suitors there might be some Argive nobles; and it was naturally these of whom he had the greatest fear. And ἀριστεῖς is hardly the word we should expect Euripides here to have used for 'princes' or 'nobles,' besides that he adds τῷ γενναίῳ below, v. 26. Perhaps the poet wrote μή τῳ παῖδ᾽ ὑπ᾽ Ἀργείων τέκοι. Bothe conjectures ἀπ᾽ Ἀργείων, like οὖσ᾽ ἐλευθέρων ἄπο, Hel. 275. In favour however of Porson's emendation it may be said that Τ, Γ, and Ι are often interchanged, and that the σ in ἀριστέων might by accident have been transferred to the end of παῖδα. Such accidents did occasionally arise from corrections not very legibly made. The favourite Greek doctrine, that honour and chivalrous spirit are intimately connected with high birth, is here plainly set forth. See Alcest. 601.

24. ἥρμοζε. "Pater dicitur ἁρμόζειν, sc. despondere filiam; sponsus dicitur ἁρμόζεσθαι, ut Herod. v. 32." *Robinson.*

25. πλέων Matthiae (as from πλέως) for πλέον.

κτανεῖν σφε βουλεύσαντος ὠμόφρων ὅμως
μήτηρ νιν ἐξέσωσεν Αἰγίσθου χερός.
εἰς μὲν γὰρ ἄνδρα σκῆψιν εἶχ' ὀλωλότα,
παίδων δ' ἔδεισε μὴ φθονηθείη φόνῳ.   30
ἐκ τῶνδε δὴ τοιόνδ' ἐμηχανήσατο
Αἴγισθος· ὃς μὲν γῆς ἀπηλλάχθη φυγὰς
Ἀγαμέμνονος παῖς, χρυσὸν εἶφ' ὃς ἂν κτάνῃ,
ἡμῖν δὲ δὴ δίδωσιν Ἠλέκτραν ἔχειν
δάμαρτα, πατέρων μὲν Μυκηναίων ἄπο   35
γεγῶσιν, (οὐ δὴ τοῦτό γ' ἐξελέγχομαι·
λαμπροὶ γὰρ ἐς γένος γε, χρημάτων δὲ δὴ
πένητες, ἔνθεν ηὐγένει' ἀπόλλυται,)
ὡς ἀσθενεῖ δοὺς ἀσθενῆ λάβοι φόβον.
εἰ γάρ νιν ἔσχεν ἀξίωμ' ἔχων ἀνήρ,   40
εὕδοντ' ἂν ἐξήγειρε τὸν Ἀγαμέμνονος
φόνον, δίκη τ' ἂν ἦλθεν Αἰγίσθῳ τότε.
ἣν οὔποθ' ἁνὴρ ὅδε, σύνοιδέ μοι Κύπρις,
ᾔσχυνεν εὐνῇ· παρθένος δ' ἔτ' ἐστὶ δή.

27. σφε βουλεύσαντος Seidler for σφ' ἐβουλεύσατ' or —σαντ', and ὅμως for δ' ὅμως or ἡ δ' ὅμως. This is not the genitive absolute, but seems rather to agree with Αἰγίσθου.
29. εἰς μὲν γὰρ ἄνδρα. She had some sort of excuse for killing her husband, viz. his attachment to Cassandra, or his having sacrificed her child Iphigenia; but to slay her surviving children merely to place her own life in security would have been an invidious act. Compare *inf.* v. 1067.
31. ἐκ τῶνδε, in consequence of this. See Ion 843.
33. χρυσὸν εἶπε, he proclaimed a reward, τῷ ἀποκτείναντι τὸν Ὀρέστην. Robinson compares Herod. vi. 23, μισθὸς δέ οἱ ἦν εἰρημένος ὅδε. The subjunctive κτάνῃ is used, because the conditions of obtaining the reward are supposed to be still in force, though the proclamation of it was an event long ago passed.
36. ἐξελέγχομαι, 'in *this* respect, certainly, I am not found fault with,' for οὐ τοῦτό γε ὀνειδίζεταί ἐμοί.
38. ἡ εὐγένεια, good birth generally, when it has not means to keep up its reputation in men's eyes, falls into neglect

and oblivion. The plural πένητες, scil. ἡμεῖς ἐσμέν, is used on account of ἡμῖν above. Stobaeus, 97, 5, gives γε μὴν for δὲ δή,—a better reading in itself, but perhaps to be regarded as inferior in authority.— ἔνθεν is ἐξ οὗ, 'from which cause,' as Matthiae remarks. Robinson well compares Juv. Sat. iii. 164,

'Haud facile emergunt, quorum virtutibus obstat
Res angusta domi.'

39. ἀσθενῆ φόβον, a fear not strong enough to cause him any serious anxiety.
41. ἐξήγειρε. ' He (the well-born husband) would have aroused the dormant murder of Agamemnon, and *then* (i. e. as an event necessarily consequent) justice would have come to Aegisthus.' Cf. Agam. 337, ἐγρηγορὸς τὸ πῆμα τῶν ὀλωλότων γένοιτ' ἄν. Eur. Suppl. 1148, οὔπω κακὸν τόδ' εὕδει.—Αἰγίσθῳ may depend either on δίκη or on ἦλθεν. Cf. Prom. 366, ἀλλ' ἦλθεν αὐτῷ Ζηνὸς ἄγρυπνον βέλος.
44. αἰσχύνειν and καταισχύνειν are peculiarly used in speaking of adultery. Here there is a similar notion of *disgrace* on account of his inferior station. He

αἰσχύνομαι γὰρ ὀλβίων ἀνδρῶν τέκνα   45
λαβὼν ὑβρίζειν, οὐ κατάξιος γεγώς.
στένω δὲ τὸν λόγοισι κηδεύοντ᾽ ἐμοὶ
ἄθλιον Ὀρέστην, εἴ ποτ᾽ εἰς Ἄργος μολὼν
γάμους ἀδελφῆς δυστυχεῖς εἰσόψεται.
ὅστις δέ μ᾽ εἶναί φησι μῶρον, εἰ λαβὼν   50
νέαν ἐς οἴκους παρθένον μὴ θιγγάνω,
γνώμης πονηροῖς κανόσιν ἀναμετρούμενος
τὸ σῶφρον ἴστω, καὐτὸς αὖ τοιοῦτος ὤν.

ΗΛΕΚΤΡΑ.

ὦ νὺξ μέλαινα, χρυσέων ἄστρων τροφὲ,
ἐν ᾗ τόδ᾽ ἄγγος τῷδ᾽ ἐφεδρεῦον κάρᾳ   55
φέρουσα πηγὰς ποταμίας μετέρχομαι,
οὐ δή τι χρείας ἐς τοσόνδ᾽ ἀφιγμένη,
ἀλλ᾽ ὡς ὕβριν δείξωμεν Αἰγίσθου θεοῖς,
γόους τ᾽ ἀφείην αἰθέρ᾽ ἐς μέγαν πατρί.
ἡ γὰρ πανώλης Τυνδαρὶς, μήτηρ ἐμὴ,   60
ἐξέβαλέ μ᾽ οἴκων, χάριτα τιθεμένη πόσει·

---

regards conjugal rights, which he might legally claim, in the light of a ὕβρις, morally considered, v. 46.

47. κηδεύοντα, for κηδεστὴν ὄντα. This class of verbs is very commonly both active and neuter. Hec. 1202, κηδεύσων τινά, for κῆδος ξυνάψων τινί. So we have in Oed. Col. 750, ἀεί σε κηδεύουσα καὶ τὸ σὸν κάρα πτωχῷ διαίτῃ. Cf. Med. 888.

53. τοιοῦτος ὤν, i.e. μῶρος, not however in the above sense of *foolish*, but in that of *sensual*, on which see *inf.* 1035. Ion 545. So σωφρονεῖν is used in a double meaning, Hippol. 1034. It is clear that the poet is himself anticipating an objection that would be raised to the improbability of his story. 'Let not any suppose,' he says, 'that chastity is impossible, merely because the objector himself is unchaste.'—" Certe nos legimus etiam inter Christianos Reges, qui in summa Fortuna positi, ultro a concessa Conjugii voluptate abstinuerint." *J. Barnes.*

54. Electra, attired in coarse and squalid garments (v. 304), is seen slowly advancing. She carries on her head a water-jar, after the fashion of slaves;—not, as she says, and as her husband hastens to assure her, from the necessity of performing such menial work, but both to exhibit herself before the sight of the gods in her degraded position of life, and to take advantage of the opportunity of disemburdening her mind. The custom of outpouring grief to the elements is well known; cf. Soph. El. 86. Med. 57. The time is early morning, as is clear from the mention of νύξ. Compare Antig. 100.

59. ἀφείην. So Portus for ἀφίην. This is much better than to read ἀφίημ᾽ as a continuation of μετέρχομαι, making vv. 57—8 parenthetical. The change from the subjunctive to the optative is abrupt, but not without precedent. Hec. 1138,

ἔδεισα μή σοι πολέμιος λειφθεὶς ὁ παῖς
Τροίαν ἀθροίσῃ καὶ ξυνοικίσῃ πάλιν,
γνόντες δ᾽ Ἀχαιοὶ ζῶντα Πριαμιδῶν τινα
Φρυγῶν ἐς αἶαν αὖθις ἄρειαν στόλον.

Cf. Ran. 23, τοῦτον δ᾽ ὀχῶ ἵνα μὴ ταλαιπωροῖτο.—πατρί, *for* my father, i.e. in honour and remembrance of him.

61. χάριτα. A rare form for χάριν,

τεκοῦσα δ' ἄλλους παῖδας Αἰγίσθῳ πάρα
πάρεργ' Ὀρέστην κἀμὲ ποιεῖται δόμων.
ΑΥ. τί γὰρ τάδ᾽, ὦ δύστην᾽, ἐμὴν μοχθεῖς χάριν
πόνους ἔχουσα πρόσθεν εὖ τεθραμμένη, 65
καὶ ταῦτ᾽ ἐμοῦ λέγοντος οὐκ ἀφίστασαι ;
ΗΛ. ἐγώ σ᾽ ἴσον θεοῖσιν ἡγοῦμαι φίλον·
ἐν τοῖς ἐμοῖς γὰρ οὐκ ἐνύβρισας κακοῖς.
μεγάλη δὲ θνητοῖς μοῖρα συμφορᾶς κακῆς
ἰατρὸν εὑρεῖν, ὡς ἐγὼ σὲ λαμβάνω. 70
δεῖ δή με κἀκέλευστον εἰς ὅσον σθένω
μόχθου 'πικουφίζουσαν, ὡς ῥᾶον φέρῃς,
συνεκκομίζειν σοὶ πόνους. ἅλις δ᾽ ἔχεις
τἄξωθεν ἔργα· τἀν δόμοις δ᾽ ἡμᾶς χρεὼν
ἐξευτρεπίζειν. εἰσιόντι δ᾽ ἐργάτῃ 75
θύραθεν ἡδὺ τἄνδον εὑρίσκειν καλῶς.
ΑΥ. εἴ τοι δοκεῖ σοι, στεῖχε· καὶ γὰρ οὐ πρόσω
πηγαὶ μελάθρων τῶνδ᾽. ἐγὼ δ᾽ ἅμ᾽ ἡμέρᾳ
βοῦς εἰς ἀρούρας εἰσβαλὼν σπερῶ γύας.
ἀργὸς γὰρ οὐδεὶς θεοὺς ἔχων ἀνὰ στόμα 80

though χάριτας and χάριτες are not uncommon. For χάριν θέσθαι see Ion 1104. Hec. 1211. Iph. T. 602.

63. πάρεργα ποιεῖται, regards as of secondary importance in the family. She can hardly mean νόθους, as Seidler thinks, for not only would such treatment of her children be obviously false, but it would be proclaiming her own disgrace.

66. καὶ ταῦτα, 'and besides, do not desist from doing so, though I am always telling you.' Dr. Donaldson is perhaps right in classing καὶ ταῦτα ' and that too,' with the objective καίτοι. Certainly Seidler wrongly joins ἐμοῦ λέγοντος ταῦτα. We might paraphrase it thus, καὶ οὐκ ἀφίστασαι, καίπερ ἐμοῦ λέγοντος.

71. ἀκέλευστον, on the principle of οὔ φημι &c., perhaps here means, 'even though told not to do it.' For her speech manifestly is an apology for acting directly contrary to his friendly and considerate injunctions.—μόχθου is the genitive, not depending on μέρος τι, but directly on the verb, as in Rhes. 281, λόγου δὲ δὶς τόσον μ' ἐκούφισας. For συνεκκομίζειν see Hipp. 464, πόσους δὲ παισὶ πατέρας ἡμαρτηκόσι

ξυνεκκομίζειν Κύπριν; 'to assist in bringing to a favourable issue.'—ἅλις, here adverbially used, for ἅλις σοι ἐστὶ ἃ ἔξωθεν (sc. ἐν ἀγροῖς) ἔργα ἔχεις. Hermann on Hel. 608 supplies πόνων. There is the same antithesis between τὰ ἔξω and τὰ ἔνδον, in describing the respective duties of husband and wife inverted, in Oed. Col. 339, οἱ μὲν ἄρσενες κατὰ στέγας θακοῦσιν ἱστουργοῦντες, αἱ δὲ σύννομοι τἄξω βίου τροφεῖα πορσύνουσ᾽ ἀεί.

78. ἅμ᾽ ἡμέρᾳ, when the day has fairly broken; when the sun is up; see v. 54, and especially v. 102.

80. θεοὺς ἔχων κτλ., while he invokes the gods, without putting his own shoulder to the wheel. In the same wise spirit the poet says, Hel. 756, οὐδεὶς ἐπλούτησ᾽ ἐμπύροισιν, ἀργὸς ὤν.—βίον ξυλλέγειν, to collect for himself a subsistence, victum corradere. A similar sentiment was expressed in the Bellerophontes, (frag. 293. 13,) but the verse containing the apodosis is lost;—οἶμαι δ᾽ ἂν ὑμᾶς, εἴ τις ἀργὸς ὢν θεοῖς εὔχοιτο, καὶ μὴ χειρὶ συλλέγοι βίον, —. Virgil, Georg. iii. 456, ' meliora deos sedet omina poscens.'

ΕΥΡΙΠΙΔΟΥ

βίον δύναιτ' ἂν ξυλλέγειν ἄνευ πόνου.

ΟΡΕΣΤΗΣ.

Πυλάδη, σὲ γὰρ δὴ πρῶτον ἀνθρώπων ἐγὼ
πιστὸν νομίζω καὶ φίλον ξένον τ' ἐμοί·
μόνος δ' Ὀρέστην τόνδ' ἐθαύμαζες φίλων,
πράσσονθ' ἃ πράσσω δείν' ὑπ' Αἰγίσθου παθὼν, 85
ὅς μου κατέκτα πατέρα χἠ πανώλεθρος
μήτηρ. ἀφῖγμαι δ' ἐκ θεοῦ μυστηρίων
Ἀργεῖον οὖδας, οὐδενὸς ξυνειδότος,
φόνον φονεῦσι πατρὸς ἀλλάξων ἐμοῦ.
νυκτὸς δὲ τῆσδε πρὸς τάφον μολὼν πατρὸς 90
δάκρυά τ' ἔδωκα καὶ κόμης ἀπηρξάμην
πυρᾷ τ' ἐπέσφαξ' αἷμα μηλείου φόνου,
λαθὼν τυράννους οἳ κρατοῦσι τῆσδε γῆς.
καὶ τειχέων μὲν ἐντὸς οὐ βαίνω πόδα,
δυοῖν δ' ἅμιλλαν ξυντιθεὶς ἀφικόμην 95
πρὸς τέρμονας γῆς τῆσδ', ἵν' ἐκβάλω ποδὶ
ἄλλην ἐπ' αἶαν, εἴ μέ τις γνοίη σκοπῶν

---

82. Electra and her husband have left the stage, the one to fetch water (cf. v. 140), the other to look after his oxen. A wayfaring man accompanied by a friend now appears upon it. It is Orestes, who has arrived with Pylades on the preceding night at Argos. He has visited his father's tomb near Argos, but did not dare to enter the walls of the city, lest he should be discovered. They retire a little on one side. Electra is now seen returning from the spring. Her monody, followed by commatic verses between herself and the chorus, closely resembles the scene in Hel. 165 seqq. Pylades, as in the same plays of Aeschylus and Sophocles, is a κωφὸν πρόσωπον, or mute.

84. ἐθαύμαζες, respected, looked up to. Med. 1144, δέσποινα δ' ἦν νῦν ἀντὶ σοῦ θαυμάζομεν.

87. μυστηρίων. Barnes gives χρηστηρίων on conjecture. The poet seems purposely to have varied the expression for 'an oracle.' The former word is used, though in its more common sense, in Rhes. 943. Suppl. 173. 470.

89. ἀλλάξων, 'to give in return.' In Bacch. 53, 'to take in exchange,'—this latter being more properly confined to the middle voice.

91. The offering of the κόμης ἀπαρχαί is mentioned also in Soph. El. 900. Aesch. Cho. 7. The blood-offering was to propitiate the shade; see on Heracl. 1041. Hel. 547.

94. βαίνω πόδα. See on Hec. 53, περᾷ γὰρ ἥδ' ὑπὸ σκηνῆς πόδα. Inf. 1172, βαίνουσιν ἐξ οἴκου πόδα.

95. δυοῖν ἅμιλλαν κτλ., combining two objects in one journey, viz. to find out my sister and to avenge my father, and to have a means of escape ready in case of being detected. Both these objects he considered would be best gained by retiring to the confines of Argolis. Hence it seems clear that the abode of the αὐτουργὸς is at some distance from the city. —ἐκβαλεῖν is intransitively used, like ἐμβαλεῖν στρατιᾷ, 'to invade,' &c. The syntax is γνοίη ζητοῦντα, should find out by spying that I am in search of my sister; or it may simply mean 'recognise me,' as infra v. 283—5.

ΗΛΕΚΤΡΑ. 315

ζητοῦντ' ἀδελφὴν, φασὶ γάρ νιν ἐν γάμοις
ζευχθεῖσαν οἰκεῖν, οὐδὲ παρθένον μένειν,
ὡς συγγένωμαι καὶ φόνου συνεργάτιν 100
λαβὼν τά γ' εἴσω τειχέων σαφῶς μάθω.
νῦν οὖν, Ἕως γὰρ λευκὸν ὄμμ' ἀναίρεται,
ἔξω τρίβου τοῦδ' ἴχνος ἀλλαξώμεθα.
ἢ γάρ τις ἀροτὴρ ἤ τις οἰκέτις γυνὴ
φανήσεται νῷν, ἥντιν' ἱστορήσομεν 105
εἰ τούσδε ναίει σύγγονος τόπους ἐμή.
ἀλλ' εἰσορῶ γὰρ τήνδε προσπόλων τινὰ
πηγαῖον ἄχθος ἐν κεκαρμένῳ κάρᾳ
φέρουσαν· ἑζώμεσθα κἀκπυθώμεθα
δούλης γυναικὸς, ἤν τι δεξώμεσθ' ἔπος 110
ἐφ' οἷσι, Πυλάδη, τήνδ' ἀφίγμεθα χθόνα.
ΗΛ. σύντειν', ὥρα, ποδὸς ὁρμάν· στρ. α΄.
ὦ ἔμβα ἔμβα κατακλαίουσ',
ἰὼ ἰώ μοί μοι.
ἐγενόμαν Ἀγαμέμνονος 115
καί μ' ἔτικτε Κλυταιμνήστρα,

99. οὐδέ. We might have looked for μηδέ, but see on Hel. 835.

100. συγγένωμαι, have an interview or conference with her as to the best course of action.—τὰ εἴσω τειχέων, viz. the conduct of Clytemnestra and Aegisthus, and the probability of taking vengeance upon them. The γε means, that he does not pretend to gain information about the Argives generally.

103. ἔξω τρίβου. See v. 216—7.

107. πρόσπολόν τινα W. Dindorf after Seidler, for προσπόλων.—ἐν κεκαρμένῳ Dobree for ἐγκ., which it is surprising that editors should so long have allowed to remain, the compounded preposition being here entirely out of place.

110. ἔπος ἐφ' οἷσι κτλ., information on the object for which &c.

112 seqq. Electra, addressing herself, urges her foot to return speedily, for it is time for her to be at home. As she walks along she recounts her woes. She is conscious that the citizens compassionate her; but her father's wretched end ever renews her grief. Then she thinks of her brother, perhaps a slave in some family, far away from his sister. She prays him to return to her aid, and to avenge Agamemnon's death. She then deposits the water jar, and sings a dirge to the spirit of her father, probably at his tomb represented, as in the Choephori, on the stage.

Ibid. σύντεινε. A pace is properly σύντονος when applied to animals under the yoke, which pull together by stepping in time. Hence brisk, active, and without flagging. Thus the huntsman is said συντείνειν δρόμημα κυνῶν, Bacch. 872. Compare ibid. 1091, συντόνοις δρομήμασι. —ὥρα, scil. ἔστι γάρ. But the reading of Dobree συντείνειν ὥρα κτλ., is more probable. Electra seems to mean that the morning is advancing, and her presence at home is needed. Musgrave well compares Ar. Ran. 377 and Eccles. 478 for this use of ἔμβα in hastening a person. The first three lines seem to form a *proodos* of irregular anapaestics. The common reading, ὦ ἔμβα, ἔμβα κατακλαίουσα, ἰὼ μοί μοι, is quite unmetrical. The verses following, to v. 212, are for the most part varieties of glyconean, interspersed with occasional dactylics.

116. ἔτικτε Seidler for τέκε, a change

s s 2

στυγνὰ Τυνδάρεω κόρα·
κικλήσκουσι δέ μ' ἀθλίαν
Ἠλέκτραν πολιῆται.
φεῦ φεῦ τῶν σχετλίων πόνων   120
καὶ στυγερᾶς ζόας.
ὦ πάτερ, σὺ δ' ἐν Ἅιδᾳ δὴ
κεῖσαι, σᾶς ἀλόχου σφαγεὶς
Αἰγίσθου τ', Ἀγάμεμνον.
ἴθι τὸν αὐτὸν ἔγειρε γόον,   μεσῳδ. 125
ἄναγε πολύδακρυν ἀδονάν.
σύντειν', ὥρα, ποδὸς ὁρμάν·   ἀντ. α΄.
ὦ ἔμβα ἔμβα κατακλαίουσ',
ἰὼ ἰώ μοί μοι.
τίνα πόλιν, τίνα δ' οἶκον, ὦ   130
τλᾶμον σύγγονε, λατρεύεις
οἰκτρὰν ἐν θαλάμοις λιπὼν
πατρῴοις ἐπὶ συμφοραῖς
ἀλγίσταισιν ἀδελφάν;
ἔλθοις τῶνδε πόνων ἐμοὶ   135

demanded by the antistrophic verse. The same critic expunged the gloss κούρα after Ἀγαμέμνονος.

117. Τυνδάρεω W. Dind. for Τυνδαρέου, the nominative being Τυνδάρεως, not —εος.

118. ἀθλίαν 'H., 'Electra the wretched.' Of course ἀθλίαν is not merely an epithet, but stands for the predicate.

121. ζόας for ζωᾶς W. Dindorf. See on Med. 976. Hec. 1108.

123. σφαγείς. The ellipse of ὑπὸ is barely defended by Orest. 497, πληγεὶς θυγατρὸς τῆς ἐμῆς ὑπὲρ κάρα, where however Hermann reads ὑπαὶ, i. e. ὑπὸ θυγατρός, and Porson, but for the present passage, would have edited θυγατρὸς ἐξ ἐμῆς. It is probable that in both places we should restore the dative of the instrument, σφαγαῖς and πληγαῖς. A third example of this use (for such phrases as φίλων νικώμενος &c., obviously belong to a different idiom) is cited from Soph. Phil. 3, ὦ κρατίστου πατρὸς Ἑλλήνων τραφεὶς Ἀχιλλέως παῖ Νεοπτόλεμε. But there πατρὸς may be in apposition to Ἀχιλλέως, and τραφεὶς regarded as redundant, as in Aesch. Theb. 789, θαρσεῖτε, παῖδες μητέρων τεθραμμέναι. The present passage therefore in fact stands nearly alone as an example of the preposition of the agent being omitted.

125—6. These two verses form a μεσῳδὸς, a choral division, or interruption of the regular response, which occurs also at v. 150—156. Both are glyconean, with resolved syllables. Electra continues to speak to herself, and says that the same lamentations which she has just uttered for her own case, should be repeated for Agememnon. On δακρύων ἡδονή see Andrbm. 93.

131. λατρεύειν οἶκον may be aptly compared with οἰκετεύειν οἶκον in Alcest. 437. In Iph. T. 1115 we have παῖδ' Ἀγαμεμνονίαν λατρεύω, which Seidler well defends by the analogy of θεραπεύειν τινά. Dindorf approves Dobree's proposal, τίν' ἂν' οἶκον κτλ.

133. ἐπὶ συμφ. ἀλγ., to be construed with οἰκτρὰν, seems to mean 'after my father's death.' Seidler explains *ad acerbissimam fortunam*, Bothe, as if for συμφ. συνοῦσαν. There is no doubt that πατρῴοις θαλάμοις should be taken together.— ἀδελφὰν for the epic ἀδελφεὰν is Heath's.

τᾷ μελέᾳ λυτὴρ,
ὦ Ζεῦ Ζεῦ, πατρί θ' αἱμάτων
ἐχθίστων ἐπίκουρος, Ἄρ-
γει κέλσας πόδ' ἀλάταν.
θὲς τόδε τεῦχος, ἐμῆς ἀπὸ κρατὸς ἑ-   στρ. β'. 140
λοῦσ', ἵνα πατρὶ γόους νυχίους
ἐπορθρεύσω,
ἰακχὰν, μέλος Ἀΐδα
*Ἀΐδα, πάτερ,
σοὶ κατὰ γᾶς ἐνέπω γόους,
οἷς ἀεὶ τὸ κατ' ἦμαρ   145
διέπομαι, κατὰ μὲν φίλαν
ὄνυχι τεμνομένα δέραν,
χέρα τε κρᾶτ' ἐπὶ κούριμον
τιθεμένα θανάτῳ σῷ.
ἐὴ ἐὴ, δρύπτε κάρα·   μεσῳδ. 150

137. αἱμάτων, for φόνον. Like θάνατοι, this word is sometimes used in the plural for a violent death.
140. θές. Electra cannot say this to herself, because ἐμῆς and not σῆς follows. Dobree would read θῶ. But she probably has some female attendant with her, whom she now addresses. To the same attendant she gives the order δρύπτε κάρα in v. 150, and σὺ μὲν &c. in v. 218, for it is not likely that she should ask the chorus to fly from their accustomed post. This second strophe commences with dactylics, but reverts to glyconics as before. For the feminine κρατὸς Markland cites an epigram from Athen. i. 16, κρατὸς ἐπὶ σφετέρης.
142. ἐπορθρεύσω. W. Dindorf seems to be right in restoring this form for ἐπορθοβοάσω (ἐπορθρ. Reiske). The latter was doubtlessly a gloss, ὀρθρεύειν being here used not in its ordinary sense of 'being early up' (Suppl. 978. Tro. 182), but with an accusative, like πανημερεύειν θιάσους Rhes. 361, 'to pour out the griefs of the night to the early dawn.' Cf. Theocr. x. 57, τὸν δὲ τεὸν, βουκαῖε, πρέπει λιμηρὸν ἔρωτα μυθίσδεν τᾷ ματρὶ κατ' εὐνὰν ὀρθρευοίσᾳ.
143. The MSS. add ἀοιδὰν after ἰαχὰν (ἰακχὰν Seidler) and give Ἀΐδα but once. Hermann saw that the antistrophe required the word to be repeated here. Matthiae takes ἀοιδὰν for a gloss; but it is clearly a corruption of Ἀΐδα transposed before μέλος. The initial A is made long contrary to the usual custom.
145. τὸ κατ' ἦμαρ, which Bothe interprets 'daily duties,' taking διέπομαι for διέπω, is probably as inf. 182. Ion 123, for 'daily.' So Plat. Phaedr. p. 240, B, ἐπιτηδευμάτων, οἷς τό γε καθ' ἡμέραν ἡδίστοισιν εἶναι ὑπάρχει. W. Dindorf suspects διέπομαι as "verbum neque aliunde cognitum neque aptum huic loco." If the reading be correct (and the metre does not prove it to be wrong) it would seem to mean 'in which I am ever engaged,' or 'which I pursue to the end' (persequor). The active διέπειν, 'to manage,' occurs in Eum. 891, but the use of it is apparently quite distinct.
149. θανάτῳ σῷ, the dative of the cause. See on Heracl. 475.—ἐπὶ κούριμον for ἀποκ. J. Barnes.
150—6. The μεσῳδός. In the first verse for ἒ ἒ the present editor has given ἐὴ ἐὴ, by which the metre becomes glyconean polyschematistic. The following lines are composed with remarkable uniformity. They are glyconean with the first foot resolved.—On the supposed piety of swans, see Bacch. 1362.

οἷα δέ τις κύκνος ἀχέτας
ποταμίοις παρὰ χεύμασιν
πατέρα φίλτατον ἀγκαλεῖ,
ὀλόμενον δολίοις βρόχων
ἕρκεσιν, ὡς σὲ τὸν ἄθλιον   155
πατέρ' ἐγὼ κατακλαίομαι,
λουτρὰ πανύσταθ' ὑδρανάμενον χροΐ,   ἀντ. β'.
κοίτᾳ ἐν οἰκτροτάτᾳ θανάτου.
ἰώ μοί μοι
πικρᾶς μὲν πελέκεως τομᾶς   160
σᾶς, πάτερ, πικρᾶς δ'
ἐκ Τροΐας ὁδίου βουλᾶς.
οὐ μίτραισι γυνή σε
δέξατ' οὐδ' ἐπὶ στεφάνοις,
ξίφεσι δ' ἀμφιτόμοις λυγρὰν
Αἰγίσθου λώβαν θεμένα   165
δόλιον ἔσχεν ἀκοίταν.

ΧΟΡΟΣ.

Ἀγαμέμνονος ὦ κόρα,   στρ. γ'.

153. ἀγκαλεῖ Seidler for καλεῖ.
157. Here is an instance of that rare licence, the antistrophe commencing in the middle of a sentence. See Rhes. 351. —κοίτᾳ, cf. Agam. 1496, ὦ μοί μοι κοίταν τᾶνδ' ἀνελεύθερον, | δολίῳ μόρῳ δαμεὶς | ἐκ χερὸς ἀμφιτόμῳ βελέμνῳ.
162. ὁδίου Herm. for ὁδοῦ. ' Alas too for the intention of returning from Troy, which proved your destruction!' The adjective occurs in ὅδιον κράτος αἴσιον Agam. 104. Here ὅδιος βουλή is virtually a periphrasis for ἄνοδος. Bothe reads βουλαῖς, οὐ μίτραις, σὲ κτλ., quoting several examples of βουλή used like δόλος, for a plot or trick. The antithesis however is too far-fetched to be probable, to say nothing of the requirements of the metre. The use of μίτρα here for a victorious wreath or crown is very remarkable. It is a woman's head attire in Hec. 924, and a Bacchic dress in Bacch. 833.
163. μίτραισι γυνή σε is Seidler's slight metrical change for οὐ μίτραις σε γυνή. The meaning is, that his wife did not receive him as a conqueror with chaplets and ribbands, but with the sword of Aegisthus. The metre here and in v. 165 would more accurately correspond to the antistrophic verses by a slight transposition of words, δέξατ', οὐ στεφάνοις ἔπι, and Αἰγίσθου θεμένα λώβαν. But the place of the choriambus in a glyconean verse appears to admit of variation in antithetical verses.—For ἐπὶ, with, see Bacch. 151.
165. Αἰγίσθου λώβαν. The order of the words certainly confirms Seidler's interpretation, ' making you the sport of Aegisthus,' i. e. allowing him to insult over the corpse. But on the other hand, one account represented Clytemnestra as using the sword of Aegisthus, not an axe, as the weapon of destruction. Cf. Choeph. 998, μαρτυρεῖ δέ μοι φᾶρος τόδ', ὡς ἔβαψεν Αἰγίσθου ξίφος. And in Agam. 1506, his death is called ξιφοδήλητος θάνατος. Thus λώβαν θεμένα would stand for λωβησαμένη, and ξίφεσιν Αἰγίσθου must be taken together.—ἔσχεν, scil. αὐτὸν, δόλιον ὄντα ἀκ.
167. The chorus now first enters the

ἤλυθον, Ἠλέκτρα, ποτὶ σὰν ἀγρότειραν αὐλάν.
ἔμολέ τις ἔμολεν γαλακτοπότας ἀνὴρ
Μυκηναῖος οὐριβάτας·   170
ἀγγέλλει δ᾽, ὅτι νῦν τριται-
αν καρύσσουσιν θυσίαν
Ἀργεῖοι, πᾶσαι δὲ παρ᾽ Ἥ-
ραν μέλλουσι παρθενικαὶ στείχειν.

ΗΛ. οὐκ ἐπ᾽ ἀγλαΐαις, φίλαι,   175
θυμὸν, οὐδ᾽ ἐπὶ χρυσέοις
ὅρμοισιν πεπόταμαι
τάλαιν᾽, οὐδὲ στᾶσα χοροῖς
Ἀργείαις ἅμα νύμφαις
ἑλικτὸν κρούσω πόδ᾽ ἐμόν.   180
δάκρυσι χορεύω, δακρύων δέ μοι μέλει
δειλαίᾳ τὸ κατ᾽ ἆμαρ.
σκέψαι μου πιναρὰν κόμαν
καὶ τρύχη τάδ᾽ ἐμῶν πέπλων,
εἰ πρέποντ᾽ Ἀγαμέμνονος   185
κούρᾳ τᾷ βασιλείᾳ
Τροίᾳ θ᾽, ἃ τοὐμοῦ πατέρος

orchestra. They come to invite Electra to take part in a festival about to be celebrated in honour of the Argive goddess Hera. She declines on account of her grief, her poor attire, and her want of interest in the amusements of the city.— The metre of v. 168 is an unusual form of glyconean, the next a dochmiac with a glyconean termination. The antistrophic verses have a slight syllabic variation.— γαλακτοπότας, a herdsman, one who lives on the produce of his own cattle.

170. This verse is a pure glyconean polyschematistic, like Hec. 632. W. Dindorf is clearly right in οὐριβάτας for οὐρειβάτας. See *inf*. 210.

171. τριταίαν. The antithesis with νῦν, or rather perhaps, the combination of νῦν τριταίαν, shows the meaning to be that the festival is to be held three days hence, not that it will be of three days' duration. Commonly, τριταῖος is 'three days ago.'

177. ὅρμοισιν πεπ., for the reading of the ed. princeps ὅρμοις ἐκπ., has been restored by Seidler from two Florence MSS.

The compound is perhaps less apt; at least in Theocritus, ii. 19, πᾶ τὰς φρένας ἐκπεποτᾶσαι implies the flying away from one's senses. Seidler compares Nub. 319, ἡ ψυχή μου πεπότηται.

178. χοροῖς for χορούς Seidler, who cites Iph. Taur. 1142, χοροῖς δὲ σταίην.— ἑλικτὸν, cf. Tro. 3, κάλλιστον ἴχνος ἐξελίσσουσιν ποδός.—πόδ᾽ ἐμὸν Canter for πόλεμον.

181. χορεύω for χεύω Porson. The probable cause of the error has been pointed out on Ion 189.—τὸ κατ᾽ ἆμαρ, *sup*. v. 145.

185. εἰ πρέποντ᾽ Reiske for εἴ πέρ ποτ᾽, —an emendation worthy of all praise. The τρύχη or rags of Euripides' characters are well enough known from Ar. Ach. 418. See *inf*. 501.

187. The old reading, τᾷ Τροίᾳ θ᾽ ἅ μου πατέρος, which is faulty on account of the article, was corrected by L. Dindorf. Barnes gives ἁ Τροίᾳ θ᾽ ἁμοῦ πατέρος κτλ., commencing a new sentence.

μέμναταί ποθ' ἁλοῦσα.
ΧΟ. μεγάλα θεός· ἀλλ' ἴθι,   ἀντ. γ'.   190
καὶ παρ' ἐμοῦ χρῆσαι πολύπηνα φάρεα δῦναι,
χρύσεά τε χάρισαι προσθήματ' ἀγλαΐας.
δοκεῖς τοῖσι σοῖς δακρύοις,
μὴ τιμῶσα θεοὺς, κρατή-
σειν ἐχθρῶν; οὔτοι στοναχαῖς,   195
ἀλλ' εὐχαῖσι θεοὺς σεβί-
ζουσ' ἕξεις εὐαμερίαν, ὦ παῖ.

ΗΛ. οὐδεὶς θεῶν ἐνοπὰς κλύει
τᾶς δυσδαίμονος, οὐ παλαιῶν πατρὸς σφαγιασμῶν.   200
οἴμοι τοῦ τε καπφθιμένου
τοῦ τε ζῶντος ἀλάτα,
ὅς που γᾶν ἄλλαν κατέχει
μέλεος ἀλαίνων ποτὶ θῆσσαν ἑστίαν,
τοῦ κλεινοῦ πατρὸς ἐκφύς.   205
αὐτὰ δ' ἐν χέρνησι δόμοις

189. μεγάλα θεός. She (Hera) is a great goddess, and her worship is not lightly to be set aside. Go therefore and take as a loan (borrow) from me embroidered garments to wear. This was evidently the custom on great festivals. So in Theoc. ii. 74, Simaetha goes to the show ἀμφιστειλαμένα τὰν ξυστίδα τὰν Κλεαρίστας.

191. χάρισαι. 'Accept as a favour golden appendages to your dress.' *Gratis accipe*, as Barnes' marginal version rightly interprets it. It seems rash to read χάρισιν with Musgrave: the poet probably gave to χαρίσασθαι an unusual sense, but one sufficiently defined by χρῆσαι. Nor is χάρισιν ἀγλαΐας, 'the grace of beauty,' a very satisfactory combination. The chorus offer trinkets as an additional ornament to a fine dress, χλιδή, τρυφή, κόσμος &c., being similar in meaning to ἀγλαΐα. Cf. v. 175. We might also explain χάρισαι 'indulge in,' σεαυτῇ being supplied. The argument which they use is this, that by paying honour to the festivals of the gods Electra is more likely to gain their favour than by tears and sighs.

196. εὐχαῖσι θεοὺς Seidler, Matthiae, for εὐχαῖς τοὺς θεούς γε. W. Dindorf gives in his text εὐχαῖς θεοὺς σὺ σεβίζουσ', where the σὺ, being unemphatic, is untenable. On the correspondence of this verse with the strophe, see on 163.

199. παλαιῶν σφαγιασμῶν. The sacrifices formerly offered by Agamemnon. The genitive follows the accusative after κλύει, which is not surprising, since the former case always implies an ellipse of φθόγγον or φωνήν.

201. καπφθιμένου. On this Aeolicism see Suppl. 984. The old reading τοῦ καταφθιμένου was corrected by Elmsley. The necessity of the correction may however be questioned, since καταφθιμένου perfectly satisfies the metre. Agamemnon the murdered and Orestes the exile are of course meant.

204. ποτὶ θῆσσαν ἑστίαν. Whether she means 'as a servant at another's table,' or 'entertained only with the fare of a slave,' is not quite clear; but the latter is probable; compare θῆσσαν τράπεζαν αἰνέσαι, Alcest. 2, and πρὸς πλουσίαν τράπεζαν ἵζουσα, Hel. 295.

206. ἐν χ. δόμοις, in the house of a working man, an αὐτουργός, i. e. a poor house.—φυγὰς, perhaps φυγαῖς, the long syllable being better suited to the metre.

ΗΛΕΚΤΡΑ. 321

ναίω ψυχὰν τακομένα
δωμάτων πατρῴων φυγὰς,
οὐρείας ἀν' ἐρίπνας. 210
μάτηρ δ' ἐν λέκτροις φονίοις
ἄλλῳ σύγγαμος οἰκεῖ.
ΧΟ. πολλῶν κακῶν Ἕλλησιν αἰτίαν ἔχει
σῆς μητρὸς Ἑλένη σύγγονος δόμοις τε σοῖς.
ΗΛ. οἴμοι, γυναῖκες· ἐξέβην θρηνημάτων· 215
ξένοι τινὲς παρ' οἶκον οἵδ' ἐφεστίους
εὐνὰς ἔχοντες ἐξανίστανται λόχου·
φυγῇ, σὺ μὲν κατ' οἶμον, ἐς δόμους δ' ἐγὼ,
φῶτας κακούργους ἐξαλύξωμεν ποδί.
ΟΡ. μέν', ὦ τάλαινα· μὴ τρέσῃς ἐμὴν χέρα. 220
ΗΛ. ὦ Φοῖβ' Ἄπολλον, προσπίτνω σε μὴ θανεῖν.
ΟΡ. ἄλλους κτάνοιμι μᾶλλον ἐχθίους σέθεν.
ΗΛ. ἄπελθε, μὴ ψαῦ' ὧν σε μὴ ψαύειν χρεών.
ΟΡ. οὐκ ἔσθ' ὅτου θίγοιμ' ἂν ἐνδικώτερον.
ΗΛ. καὶ πῶς ξιφήρης πρὸς δόμοις λοχᾷς ἐμέ; 225

On the ᾦ in πατρῷος see Alcest. 249. Bothe gives πατρίων.
210. ἀν' Musgr. for ναίουσ', which is doubtless a gloss. Cf. v. 489. Photius, ἐρίπναι· αἱ ἀπερρωγυῖαι πέτραι. Translate, 'in the mountain fastnesses.' Like the *pagi* of the Romans, the settlements of the pastoral Greeks were often in the mountains for the sake of security. This explains γαλακτοπόταs ἀνὴρ οὐριβάτας in v. 170. Compare Ἀργείων ὀρέων inf. v. 700.
211. φονίοις Barnes for φόνιος.
215. Electra here perceives the two strangers (Orestes and Pylades) lurking by the side of the way (ἔξω τρίβον, v. 103). They have just risen, and having heard the preceding lamentations of Electra, are satisfied that she is the very person they are seeking. She however, believing them to be robbers, is about to fly into her house, but is arrested by the hand of her brother.—ἐφεστίους, close to the house, i. e. with evil intentions against it.
218. σὺ μέν. This can hardly be addressed to the chorus, whom just before she had collectively called γυναῖκες. It refers rather to the attendant; see on v.

140.—κατ' οἶμον, 'along the road,' ᾗ ὁδὸς φέρει.—For the tautology φυγῇ— ποδὶ, Dindorf refers to Orest. 1468, φυγᾷ δὲ ποδὶ τὸ χρυσοσάνδαλον | ἴχνος ἔφερεν ἔφερεν.
220. ἐμὴν χέρα, emphatic; '*mine* is not the hand to be feared.'
222. κτάνοιμι, i. e. κτανεῖν θέλω. Dindorf and others give κτάνοιμ' ἂν, the old copies having ἂν κτάνοιμι. But Bothe rightly judges the ἂν to be the interpolation of a grammarian.
223. μὴ ψαῦε. So complete was the retirement of a married woman, that even to take her hand in public was regarded as a liberty. Hence the surprise of Achilles, when requested by Clytemnestra to shake hands, in Iph. A. 833, τί φῇς; ἐγώ σοι δεξιάν; αἰδοίμεθ' ἂν Ἀγαμέμνον', εἰ ψαύοιμεν ὧν μή μοι θέμις. Cf. inf. 344.
225. ξιφήρης, sword-in-hand; Rhes. 713, ξ. κρύφιος ἐν πέπλοις.—ἐμὲ for ἐμοῖς is the reading of Dindorf and Matthiae from a var. lect. in one MS. Cf. Alcest. 846, κἄνπερ λοχήσας αὐτὸν ἐξ ἕδρας συθεὶς μάρψω. Photius, λοχῶντες· ἐνεδρεύοντες. The meaning of καὶ πῶς is, as usual, objective: 'Well but, if you were a friend, you would not,' &c.

ΕΥΡΙΠΙΔΟΥ

ΟΡ. μείνασ' ἄκουσον, καὶ τάχ' οὐκ ἄλλως ἐρεῖς.
ΗΛ. ἕστηκα· πάντως δ' εἰμὶ σή· κρείσσων γὰρ εἶ.
ΟΡ. ἥκω φέρων σοι σοῦ κασιγνήτου λόγους.
ΗΛ. ὦ φίλτατ', ἆρα ζῶντος, ἢ τεθνηκότος;
ΟΡ. ζῇ· πρῶτα γάρ σοι τἀγάθ' ἀγγέλλειν θέλω.   230
ΗΛ. εὐδαιμονοίης, μισθὸν ἡδίστων λόγων.
ΟΡ. κοινῇ δίδωμι τοῦτο νῷν ἀμφοῖν ἔχειν.
ΗΛ. ποῦ γῆς ὁ τλήμων τλήμονας φυγὰς ἔχων;
ΟΡ. οὐχ ἕνα νομίζων φθείρεται πόλεως νόμον.
ΗΛ. οὔ που σπανίζων τοῦ καθ' ἡμέραν βίου;   235
ΟΡ. ἔχει μὲν, ἀσθενὴς δὲ δὴ φεύγων ἀνήρ.
ΗΛ. λόγον δὲ δὴ τίν' ἦλθες ἐκ κείνου φέρων;
ΟΡ. εἰ ζῇς, ὅπως τε ζῶσα συμφορᾶς ἔχεις.
ΗΛ. οὐκοῦν ὁρᾷς μου πρῶτον ὡς ξηρὸν δέμας.
ΟΡ. λύπαις γε συντετηκὸς, ὥστε με στένειν.   240
ΗΛ. καὶ κρᾶτα πλόκαμόν τ' ἐσκυθισμένον ξυρῷ.
ΟΡ. δάκνει σ' ἀδελφὸς ὅ τε θανὼν ἴσως πατήρ;
ΗΛ. οἴμοι, τί γάρ μοι τῶνδέ γ' ἐστὶ φίλτερον;
ΟΡ. φεῦ φεῦ· τί δαὶ σὺ σῷ κασιγνήτῳ δοκεῖς;

226. οὐκ ἄλλως ἐρεῖς, ὁμολογήσεις ἐμὲ ἐνδίκως σοῦ ψαύειν.
227. πάντως, whether I fly or not.
228. κασιγνήτου. Not *from* your brother, but 'tidings *about* him.' This idiom is illustrated on Ion 929. *Inf.* 347.
231. μισθόν. The accusative in apposition to the sentence, which is peculiarly the case with words implying reward or punishment, &c. See on Alcest. 7. Hel. 77. Rhes. 948, καὶ τῶνδε μισθὸν παῖδ' ἔχουσ' ἐν ἀγκάλαις θρηνῶ.
232. δίδωμι, i. e. οὐ μόνος ἐμαυτῷ δέχομαι τὸ χαίρειν.
234. φθείρεται, he is a wanderer. See Hel. 766. For νόμον Dio Chrysost. p. 420, gives τόπον, and in the preceding v. ἔχει for ἔχων, as also σπανίζει for σπανίζων. If νόμον be right (and Bothe cites νόμους νομίζειν from Lucian), the sense seems to be νόμους οὐ μιᾶς πόλεως, taking up the customs and habits of different states as he visits them.
238. ὅπως—συμφορᾶς Elmsley for ὅπου —συμφορᾶς (so Bothe). The construction is the same as Hel. 313, πῶς δ' εὐμενείας τοισίδ' ἐν δόμοις ἔχεις; *Inf.*

751, πῶς ἀγῶνος ἥκομεν; Though we might join ὅπου ζῶσα, and regard the whole phrase as equivalent to ὅπου ἄθλιον τρίβεις βίον. Nevertheless, as ὅποι, ὅπου, ὅπως, &c., are frequently confused, and also the singular and plural cases of the word συμφορά (see on Rhes. 806), and as the sense is greatly improved by the above emendation, it seems advisable to admit it, especially as the reply of Electra strongly confirms it.
239. ξηρὸν, opposed to λιπαρὸν, *sleek*. The phrase originated in the custom of anointing, which however was perhaps confined to males, for Theocritus speaks of Spartan maids as χρισαμέναις ἀνδριστὶ, Id. xviii. 23. — συντετηκὸς Reiske for —ας.
241. ἐσκυθισμένον, ἠκισμένον. See on Tro. 1026, where κρᾶτ' ἀπεσκυθισμένην occurs.
244. τί δοκεῖς; i. e. οὐ καὶ σὺ φιλτάτη δοκεῖς τῷ ἀδελφῷ; The reply is, 'he shows his affection by his absence,' not, as he ought, by his presence in my troubles. Robinson gives τί δ' αὖ σὺ κτλ., which is not improbable.

ΗΛΕΚΤΡΑ. 323

ΗΛ. ἀπὼν ἐκεῖνος, οὐ παρὼν ἡμῖν φίλος. 245
ΟΡ. ἐκ τοῦ δὲ ναίεις ἐνθάδ' ἄστεως ἑκάς ;
ΗΛ. ἐγημάμεσθ', ὦ ξεῖνε, θανάσιμον γάμον.
ΟΡ. ὤμωξ' ἀδελφὸν σόν. Μυκηναίων τινί ;
ΗΛ. οὐχ ὡς πατήρ μ' ἤλπιζεν ἐκδώσειν ποτέ.
ΟΡ. εἴφ', ὡς ἀκούσας σῷ κασιγνήτῳ λέγω. 250
ΗΛ. ἐν τοῖσδ' ἐκείνου τηλορὸς ναίω δόμοις.
ΟΡ. σκαφεύς τις ἢ βουφορβὸς ἄξιος δόμων.
ΗΛ. πένης ἀνὴρ γενναῖος ἔς τέ μ' εὐσεβής.
ΟΡ. ἡ δ' εὐσέβεια τίς πρόσεστι σῷ πόσει ;
ΗΛ. οὐπώποτ' εὐνῆς τῆς ἐμῆς ἔτλη θιγεῖν. 255
ΟΡ. ἅγνευμ' ἔχων τι θεῖον, ἤ σ' ἀπαξιῶν ;
ΗΛ. γονέας ὑβρίζειν τοὺς ἐμοὺς οὐκ ἠξίου.
ΟΡ. καὶ πῶς γάμον τοιοῦτον οὐχ ἥσθη λαβών ;
ΗΛ. οὐ κύριον τὸν δόντα μ' ἡγεῖται, ξένε.
ΟΡ. ξυνῆκ'· Ὀρέστῃ μή ποτ' ἐκτίσῃ δίκην. 260
ΗΛ. τοῦτ' αὐτὸ ταρβῶν, πρὸς δὲ καὶ σώφρων ἔφυ.
ΟΡ. φεῦ·
    γενναῖον ἄνδρ' ἔλεξας, εὖ τε δραστέον.
ΗΛ. εἰ δή ποθ' ἥξει γ' ἐς δόμους ὁ νῦν ἀπών.
ΟΡ. μήτηρ δέ σ' ἡ τεκοῦσα ταῦτ' ἠνέσχετο ;
ΗΛ. γυναῖκες ἀνδρῶν, ὦ ξέν', οὐ παίδων, φίλαι. 265

246. ἐκ τοῦ. Compare the use of ἐκ τῶνδε, v. 31. Cf. Hel. 92.

247. θανάσιμον. She appears to mean, a marriage accepted only as an alternative for death. For in v. 27 she asserts that Aegisthus had wished to kill her.

249. οὐχ ὡς. There is another reading οὐχ ᾧ, which would mean Castor, *inf.* 312.

251. τηλορός. W. Dindorf approves the suggestion of Seidler, τῆλ' ὅρος ναίω, i. e. ναίω ὅρος τῆλε ἄστεως. The form of the adjective elsewhere is τηλουρός, Orest. 1325, Prom. 1; but Matthiae compares ὅμορος, so that analogy is in favour of the received reading.—ἐκείνου δόμοις, viz. the husband alluded to in v. 247.

252. ἄξιος δόμων. Some common labourer is the fit person to inhabit such a house as this. Hel. 69, Πλούτου γὰρ οἶκος ἄξιος προσεικάσαι.

256. ἅγνευμα κτλ. 'Is it because he is under a vow of virginity to the gods, or because he disdains you ?' The old reading ἀναξιῶν was corrected by Schaefer. So Eum. 345, Ζεὺς γὰρ αἱματοσταγὲς ἀξιόμισον ἔθνος τόδε λέσχας ἇς ἀπηξιώσατο. The other, in the sense of ἀνάξιον νομίζων, is contrary to analogy, though Robinson retains it without suspicion.

259. κύριον. He does not consider that Aegisthus (cf. v. 34) had a right to dispose of me in marriage. The father being dead, the right of bestowing her hand would legally have devolved on Orestes. Seidler compares Iph. A. 703, Ζεὺς ἠγγύησε, καὶ δίδωσ' ὁ κύριος. Barnes here well remarks, "Hic iterum prudentissimus poeta oeconomiae suae fabulae consulit, et rationes accumulat, quare probabile videatur, cur Colonus Regiae Virgini castitatem non eripuerit."

265. ἀνδρῶν. The inference is, that she listened to the persuasions of Aegisthus more than to those of Electra.

T t 2

ΟΡ. τίνος δέ σ' οὕνεχ' ὕβρισ' Αἴγισθος τάδε;
ΗΛ. τεκεῖν μ' ἐβούλετ' ἀσθενῆ, τοιῷδε δούς.
ΟΡ. ὡς δῆθε παῖδας μὴ τέκοις ποινάτορας;
ΗΛ. τοιαῦτ' ἐβούλευσ', ὧν ἐμοὶ δοίη δίκην.
ΟΡ. οἶδεν δέ σ' οὖσαν παρθένον μητρὸς πόσις; 270
ΗΛ. οὐκ οἶδε· σιγῇ τοῦθ' ὑφαιρούμεσθά νιν.
ΟΡ. αἵδ' οὖν φίλαι σοι τούσδ' ἀκούουσιν λόγους;
ΗΛ. ὥστε στέγειν γε τἀμὰ καὶ σ' ἔπη καλῶς.
ΟΡ. τί δῆτ' Ὀρέστης πρὸς τάδ', Ἄργος ἢν μόλῃ;
ΗΛ. ἤρου τόδ'; αἰσχρόν γ' εἶπας· οὐ γὰρ νῦν ἀκμή; 275
ΟΡ. ἐλθὼν δὲ δὴ πῶς φονέας ἂν κτάνοι πατρός;
ΗΛ. τολμῶν ὑπ' ἐχθρῶν οἷ' ἐτολμήθη πατήρ.
ΟΡ. ἦ καὶ μετ' αὐτοῦ μητέρ' ἂν τλαίης κτανεῖν;
ΗΛ. ταὐτῷ γε πελέκει τῷ πατὴρ ἀπώλετο.
ΟΡ. λέγω τάδ' αὐτῷ, καὶ βέβαια τἀπὸ σοῦ; 280
ΗΛ. θάνοιμι μητρὸς αἷμ' ἐπισφάξασ' ἐμῆς.
ΟΡ. φεῦ·

267. ἀσθενῆ. Compare v. 39.
268. δῆθε. Elmsley, doubting this as ἅπαξ λεγόμενον, proposed to read ὡς παῖδα δῆθεν. W. Dindorf thinks the correction probable, ποινάτορας for —ρα occurring in like manner v. 23. Like πρόσθε, πάροιθε, τηλόθε, &c., the double form seems to have been allowed for metrical convenience. " Εἰρωνικῶς haec Orestes, ut qui Aegisthi consilia irrita se facturum speret." *Bothe*.
272. φίλαι, scil. οὖσαι.
273. στέγειν. Not simply 'to conceal,' but 'to keep safe.' The word properly means 'to be water-tight.' Cf. Hec. 880. Trach. 596, μόνον παρ' ὑμῶν εὖ στεγοίμεθ', ὡς σκότῳ κἂν αἰσχρὰ πράσσῃς, οὔποτ' αἰσχύνῃ πεσεῖ.—καὶ σ' ἔπη for καὶ τὰ σὰ ἔπη. For the omission of the article see Hel. 14; for the elision Suppl. 456. Before Orestes converses on the possibility of slaying their enemies, he ascertains whether the chorus are faithful to his cause.
274. The common reading, τί δῆτ' Ὀρέστης, πρὸς τόδ' Ἄργος ἢν μόλῃ; appears to require correction. The meaning should be, τί ποιήσει πρὸς τάδε; 'What does he intend to do in reference to this business, should he return to Argos?'—'Do you ask?' replies Electra. 'I am ashamed of you. Is it not now or never the time for action?' i. e. 'he will slay them, of course.' The phrase πρὸς ταῦτα is often so used, e. g. Prom. 1013. 1051.
277. τολμῶν κτλ. 'By venturing the same that was ventured against his father by his enemies.' A similar use is Hipp. 794, μῶν Πιτθέως τι γῆρας εἴργασται νέον; 'Has the old Pittheus had any harm done to him?'
280. λέγω κτλ. 'Should I say this to him, and that you are staunch?' So Ar. Ran. 1, εἴπω τι τῶν εἰωθότων; Inf. v. 377, ἀλλ' εἰς ὅπλ' ἔλθω; Electra as yet regards the stranger as one who has brought a message from Orestes, and who will carry back her reply. Cf. v. 237.
281. θάνοιμι, i. e. θανεῖν θέλω, ἑτοίμη εἰμί. So Aesch. Cho. 430, ἔπειτ' ἐγὼ νοσφίσας ὀλοίμαν.—ἐπισφάζειν has its proper sense, as in v. 92, to sacrifice the mother over the body of the husband. The remark may seem superfluous; but such notes as the following (in Robinson's edition) only mislead;—" ἐπισφάξασα, i. e. θύσασα, quo sensu supra accipitur v. 92."

ΗΛΕΚΤΡΑ. 325

  εἴθ' ἦν Ὀρέστης πλησίον κλύων τάδε.
ΗΛ. ἀλλ', ὦ ξέν', οὐ γνοίην ἂν εἰσιδοῦσά νιν.
ΟΡ. νέα γάρ, οὐδὲν θαῦμ', ἀπεζεύχθης νέου.
ΗΛ. εἷς ἂν μόνος νιν τῶν ἐμῶν γνοίη φίλων. 285
ΟΡ. ἆρ' ὃν λέγουσιν αὐτὸν ἐκκλέψαι φόνου;
ΗΛ. πατρός γε παιδαγωγὸς ἀρχαῖος γέρων.
ΟΡ. ὁ κατθανὼν δὲ σὸς πατὴρ τύμβου κυρεῖ;
ΗΛ. ἔκυρσεν ὡς ἔκυρσεν, ἐκβληθεὶς δόμων.
ΟΡ. οἴμοι, τόδ' οἷον εἶπας. αἴσθησις γὰρ οὖν 290
  κἀκ τῶν θυραίων πημάτων δάκνει βροτούς.
  λέξον δ', ἵν' εἰδὼς σῷ κασιγνήτῳ φέρω
  λόγους ἀτερπεῖς, ἀλλ' ἀναγκαίους κλύειν.
  ἔνεστι δ' οἶκτος, ἀμαθίᾳ μὲν οὐδαμοῦ,
  σοφοῖσι δ' ἀνδρῶν· καὶ γὰρ οὐδ' ἀζήμιον 295
  γνώμην ἐνεῖναι τοῖς σοφοῖς λίαν σοφήν.
ΧΟ. κἀγὼ τὸν αὐτὸν τῷδ' ἔρον ψυχῆς ἔχω.
  πρόσω γὰρ ἄστεως οὖσα τἀν πόλει κακὰ
  οὐκ οἶδα, νῦν δὲ βούλομαι κἀγὼ μαθεῖν.
ΗΛ. λέγοιμ' ἄν, εἰ χρή. χρὴ δὲ πρὸς φίλον λέγειν 300

---

287. πατρός γε κτλ. 'Aye, the old man who in former days was my father's keeper,' i. e. the slave who took care of him as a boy, for ἀρχαῖος merely means ὁ πρὶν ὢν κτλ.

291. κἀκ τῶν θ., resulting from the misfortunes even of others than ourselves. Dobree reads καὶ for κἀκ. Cf. θυραῖον ὄλβον in Agam. 810.

294. οἶκτος. 'Relate,' says Orestes, 'the whole circumstances of your present position, and be assured that the narrative will meet with compassion from one who is not churlish and ignorant, but well instructed.' This idea, that the wise are more capable of pity, is also given in Heracl. 458, where see the note. Hence it was that εὐγνώμων came to mean 'good-natured,' and ἀγνώμων 'brutal.' Orestes seems to say this of himself, by way of soliloquy, not as wishing to represent either the supposed stranger, or the supposed brother, as peculiarly susceptible to pity.

295. καὶ γὰρ Bothe with Stobaeus, 3, 27. W. Dindorf gives οὐ γὰρ οὐδ' with the MSS., but this is not an Attic combination in the sense of οὐδὲ γὰρ, though conversely a few examples of οὐδὲ—οὐ (ne—quidem) occur, on which see Aesch. Pers. 431. There is an ellipse of this kind; ('Not that *too much* wisdom is an aid to sympathy,) for even the educated may be too clever.' Against ἡ λίαν σοφία the poet speaks in Med. 296. 305. Hipp. 640.

297. κἀγὼ κτλ. The chorus enforces the request of Orestes, to hear the narrative of her sufferings from herself, on the ground that they reside too far from the city to have heard much news about the royal household.

300. The following ῥῆσις of Electra is in the poet's very best style. It is at once natural, pathetic, and full of the energy of indignation. She contrasts her own squalid and neglected condition with the wealth and almost eastern grandeur of her guilty mother, and the proud and insolent security of the usurper Aegisthus with the dishonoured tomb of Agamemnon. That Euripides was fond of dwelling on mere personal discomfort, and not only on mental griefs, is not perhaps

τύχας βαρείας τὰς ἐμὰς κἀμοῦ πατρός.
ἐπεὶ δὲ κινεῖς μῦθον, ἱκετεύω, ξένε,
ἄγγελλ' Ὀρέστῃ τἀμὰ κἀκείνου κακά,
πρῶτον μὲν οἵοις ἐν πέπλοις αὐλίζομαι,
πίνῳ θ' ὅσῳ βέβριθ', ὑπὸ στέγαισί τε   305
οἵαισι ναίω βασιλικῶν ἐκ δωμάτων,
αὐτὴ μὲν ἐκμοχθοῦσα κερκίσιν πέπλους,
ἢ γυμνὸν ἔξω σῶμα καὶ στερήσομαι,
αὐτὴ δὲ πηγὰς ποταμίους φορουμένη,
ἀνέορτος ἱρῶν καὶ χορῶν τητωμένη,   310
ἀναίνομαι γυναῖκας, οὖσα παρθένος,
ἀναίνομαι δὲ Κάστορ', ᾧ, πρὶν ἐς θεοὺς
ἐλθεῖν, ἔμ' ἐμνήστευον, οὖσαν ἐγγενῆ.
μήτηρ δ' ἐμὴ Φρυγίοισιν ἐν σκυλεύμασι

fairly to be objected as a fault. It may be doubted if, on the whole, either of the rival plays on this subject contains a finer outburst of heart-felt eloquence than the present speech.

302. ἐπεὶ δὲ κτλ. 'Since then you *have* mooted the subject,' &c. There is always some notion of revealing a secret, or touching reluctantly on a sacred subject, in κινεῖν. Cf. Oed. Col. 624, ἀλλ' οὐ γὰρ αὐδᾶν ἡδὺ τἀκίνηθ' ἔπη, ἔα μ' ἐν οἷσιν ἠρξάμην. Ar. Nub. 1397, ὦ καινῶν ἐπῶν κινητὰ καὶ μοχλευτά.

304. αὐλίζομαι, Hesych. ἐνδιατρίβω. But the meaning is, 'to live in a cottage.' See on Androm. 281. Sup. v. 168.

307. αὐτὴ μέν. The weaving of garments was generally the work of slaves, (see Bacch. 514,) though for religious purposes ladies frequently employed themselves in this way.—γυμνὸν, 'half-clad,' the proper meaning of the word.—ἢ, 'or otherwise.' So in Alcest. 626, φημὶ τοιούτους γάμους λύειν βροτοῖσιν, ἢ γαμεῖν οὐκ ἄξιον.

311. ἀναίνομαι. I am neither a married woman nor a single maid, being at once a wife and a virgin. She speaks of her own consciousness of the matter, and does not say ἀναίνονταί με αἱ γυναῖκες, but merely that she feels reluctant to take her place in the dance or in processions along with other married women. The construction, as Matthiae observes, is slightly irregular, for αὐτὴ μέν—αὐτὴ δὲ appeared to be a continuation of the sentence from ναίω, but we come rather unexpectedly upon a new verb, ἀναίνομαι. There is a very similar instance in Alcest. 284—7. In the ed. princeps of this play ἀναίνομαι δὲ γυναῖκας is given, with an evident perception of the irregularity.

313. μνηστεύειν is usually 'to woo,' here 'to betroth.' As the brother of Helen, from the same egg of Leda, Castor was the uncle of Electra. She now is unwilling to think of the intended connexion, as being wholly unworthy of it.

314—5. The preposition ἐν shows that by σκυλεύματα the gorgeous eastern tapestries are meant, such as are still used by eastern nations generally to recline upon. It is probable that neither Φρυγίοισιν nor Ἀσιάτιδες is to be scanned as an anapaestic foot, but that the ι in both was pronounced as our *y*; so in λογίων Ion 602, ἀβίωτος Hipp. 821, αἰφνίδιος Prom. 698. (The α is long, Ἀσιᾶτις. Cf. Pers. 12. Here the MSS. give Ἀσιήτιδες, corrected by L. Dindorf.) See Androm. 1. 119. The conjecture of Hermann, πρὸς δ' ἕδραισιν Ἀσίδες, is very probable, because these forms were very often interchanged. — στατίζουσ', 'are stationed,' with the idea of a stately and motionless gait. Here again the modern practice of Indian and Persian princes coincides. The passive occurs Alcest. 90. So στηρίζω is intransitively used in Hipp. 1207 and elsewhere. Hesych. στατίζουσιν, στάσιν ἔχουσιν.

θρόνῳ κάθηται, πρὸς δ' ἕδρας Ἀσιάτιδες 315
δμωαὶ στατίζουσ', ἃς ἔπερσ' ἐμὸς πατὴρ,
Ἰδαῖα φάρη χρυσέαις ἐζευγμέναι
πόρπαισιν. αἷμα δ' ἔτι πατρὸς κατὰ στέγας
μέλαν σέσηπεν· ὃς δ' ἐκεῖνον ἔκτανεν,
ἐς ταὐτὰ βαίνων ἅρματ' ἐκφοιτᾷ πατρὶ, 320
καὶ σκῆπτρ', ἐν οἷς Ἕλλησιν ἐστρατηλάτει,
μιαιφόνοισι χερσὶ γαυροῦται λαβών.
Ἀγαμέμνονος δὲ τύμβος ἠτιμασμένος
οὔπω χοάς ποτ' οὐδὲ κλῶνα μυρσίνης
ἔλαβε, πυρὰ δὲ χέρσος ἀγλαϊσμάτων. 325
μέθῃ δὲ βρεχθεὶς τῆς ἐμῆς μητρὸς πόσις
ὁ κλεινὸς, ὡς λέγουσιν, ἐνθρώσκει τάφῳ,
πέτροις τε λεύει μνῆμα λάϊνον πατρὸς,
καὶ τοῦτο τολμᾷ τοὔπος εἰς ἡμᾶς λέγειν·
ποῦ παῖς Ὀρέστης; ἆρά σοι τύμβῳ καλῶς 330
παρὼν ἀμύνει; ταῦτ' ἀπὼν ὑβρίζεται.
ἀλλ', ὦ ξέν', ἱκετεύω σ', ἀπάγγειλον τάδε.
πολλοὶ δ' ἐπιστέλλουσιν, ἑρμηνεὺς δ' ἐγὼ,
αἱ χεῖρες, ἡ γλῶσσ' ἡ ταλαίπωρός τε φρὴν

317. φάρη. For the long α see Hipp. 126; for the passive participle in the medial sense, Heracl. 42. Hec. 801.
319. σέσηπεν κτλ. The blood of my father yet visible in the house has turned black as it lies festering on the surface. The old superstition was, that the earth would not drink in the blood of a murdered man, like that of a victim. Cf. Choeph. 59, τίτας φόνος πέπηγεν οὐ διαρρύδαν, 'not running through.'
321. στρατηλατεῖν with a dative occurs Bacch. 52.—ἐν οἷς, for ἃ ἔχων.
324. οὔπω χοάς ποτ' Seidler and Thiersch for οὐπώποτ' οὐ χοάς. But Hermann on Hecub. v. 41 thinks it not unlikely that Euripides wrote οὔπω χοὰς, οὐ κλῶνα μυρσίνης ποτέ.—χέρσος, barren, ἐνδεὴς, properly said of untilled and unproductive land.
327. ὡς λέγουσιν does not refer to ὁ κλεινὸς, the irony of which would only be weakened by such a needless addition; but it implies that, as report had reached her, who lived far from the city, Aegisthus actually had, in a drunken fit, pelted Agamemnon's tomb with stones, after leaping upon it.
331. ταῦτ' ἀπὼν κτλ. 'Such are the insults which are heaped upon him (Orestes) in his absence.' There is an antithesis of words rather than of sense in παρὼν and ἀπών. Cf. v. 245. Suppl. 649, παρὼν γὰρ τοὺς ἀπόντας εὐφρανεῖς.
333. πολλοὶ κτλ. Many *voiceless* parts of me join in the urgent petition, and I am the interpreter or speaker in their behalf. Cf. Hec. 836, εἴ μοι γένοιτο φθόγγος ἐν βραχίοσι, καὶ χερσὶ καὶ κόμαισι καὶ ποδῶν βάσει,—ὡς πάνθ' ὁμαρτῇ σῶν ἔχοιτο γουνάτων, κλαίοντ', ἐπισκήπτοντα παντοίους λόγους.—ὁ ἐκείνου τεκών, Agamemnon. This is added, because he also, as being dead, may be enumerated among the voiceless petitioners. Cf. Ion 308, ὥς σου τὴν τεκοῦσαν ὤλβισα. Alcest. 167, ὥσπερ αὐτῶν ἡ τεκοῦσ' ἀπόλλυται. Hence Robinson's reading ἐκεῖνον is quite unnecessary.

κάρα τ' ἐμὸν ξυρῆκες ὅ τ' ἐκείνου τεκών. 335
αἰσχρὸν γάρ, εἰ πατὴρ μὲν ἐξεῖλεν Φρύγας,
ὁ δ' ἄνδρ' ἕν' εἷς ὢν οὐ δυνήσεται κτανεῖν,
νέος πεφυκὼς κἀξ ἀμείνονος πατρός.
ΧΟ. καὶ μὴν δέδορκα τόνδε, σὸν λέγω πόσιν,
λήξαντα μόχθου πρὸς δόμους ὡρμημένον. 340
ΑΥ. ἔα· τίνας τούσδ' ἐν πύλαις ὁρῶ ξένους;
τίνος δ' ἕκατι τάσδ' ἐπ' ἀγραύλους πύλας
προσῆλθον; ἢ 'μοῦ δεόμενοι; γυναικί τοι
αἰσχρὸν μετ' ἀνδρῶν ἑστάναι νεανιῶν.
ΗΛ. ὦ φίλτατ', εἰς ὕποπτα μὴ μόλῃς ἐμοί. 345
τὸν ὄντα δ' εἴσει μῦθον· οἵδε γὰρ ξένοι
ἤκουσ' Ὀρέστου πρός με κήρυκες λόγων.
ἀλλ', ὦ ξένοι, σύγγνωτε τοῖς εἰρημένοις.
ΑΥ. τί φασίν; ἀνὴρ ἔστι καὶ λεύσσει φάος;
ΗΛ. ἔστιν λόγῳ γοῦν· φασὶ δ' οὐκ ἄπιστ' ἐμοί. 350
ΑΥ. ἦ καί τι πατρὸς σῶν τε μέμνηται κακῶν;
ΗΛ. ἐν ἐλπίσιν ταῦτ'· ἀσθενὴς φεύγων ἀνήρ.
ΑΥ. ἦλθον δ' Ὀρέστου τίν' ἀγορεύοντες λόγον;
ΗΛ. σκοποὺς ἔπεμψε τούσδε τῶν ἐμῶν κακῶν·
ΑΥ. οὐκοῦν τὰ μὲν λεύσσουσι, τὰ δὲ σύ που λέγεις. 355
ΗΛ. ἴσασιν, οὐδὲν τῶνδ' ἔχουσιν ἐνδεές.
ΑΥ. οὐκοῦν πάλαι χρῆν τοῖσδ' ἀνεπτύχθαι πύλας.
χωρεῖτ' ἐς οἴκους· ἀντὶ γὰρ χρηστῶν λόγων
ξενίων κυρήσεθ', οἷ' ἐμὸς κεύθει δόμος.
αἴρεσθ', ὀπαδοί, τῶνδ' ἔσω τεύχη δόμων· 360

340. ὡρμημένον. Perhaps ὁρμώμενον.
346. τὸν ὄντα μῦθον, i. e. τὸν ἀληθῆ λόγον, τὴν αἰτίαν τῆς παρουσίας.
347. Ὀρέστου—λόγων. 'Bringing me tidings about Orestes.' See on v. 228.— τοῖς εἰρημένοις, the suspicions of my husband regarding your conversation with me.
352. ἐν ἐλπίσιν. The prospect of vengeance is still distant, still held by him in reserve. Bothe wrongly explains, *spero haec ita esse.* For thus the next clause has no connexion, the sense being, ἀσθενὴς ὥστε τίσασθαι διανοεῖσθαι. "Hic repetit Electra quod dixerat Orestes supra v. 236." *Robinson.*

354. σκοπούς. Here for ἐπισκόπους, αὐτόπτας.
359. κεύθει, holds in reserve, keeps in store. See on Rhes. 621.
360. τῶνδε τεύχη is apparently to be taken together. There seems some reason to explain τεύχη by σκεύη, ' the baggage,' with Barnes. This is the οἰκεία σάγη of Orestes in Cho. 662. Photius, τεύχεα, ὅπλα, σκεύη. Again, τεῦχος, πᾶν ἀγγεῖον, (cf. Hel. 258.) In the next line ἀντείπητε is addressed to Orestes and Pylades, ' do not say *no* to the invitation.' But perhaps we should read ναί, μηδὲν ἀντείπητε. So in Alcest. 1119, ναί, σῷζέ νυν. Med. 1276, ναί, πρὸς θεῶν ἀρήξατ'.

ΗΛΕΚΤΡΑ.

καὶ μηδὲν ἀντείπητε, παρὰ φίλου φίλοι
μολόντες ἀνδρός· καὶ γὰρ εἰ πένης ἔφυν,
οὔτοι τό γ' ἦθος δυσγενὲς παρέξομαι.

ΟΡ. πρὸς θεῶν, ὅδ' ἀνὴρ, ὃς συνεκκλέπτει γάμους
τοὺς σοὺς, Ὀρέστην οὐ καταισχύνειν θέλων; 365
ΗΛ. οὗτος κέκληται πόσις ἐμὸς τῆς ἀθλίας.
ΟΡ. φεῦ·
οὐκ ἔστ' ἀκριβὲς οὐδὲν εἰς εὐανδρίαν·
ἔχουσι γὰρ ταραγμὸν αἱ φύσεις βροτῶν.
ἤδη γὰρ εἶδον ἄνδρα γενναίου πατρὸς
τὸ μηδὲν ὄντα, χρηστά τ' ἐκ κακῶν τέκνα, 370
λιμόν τ' ἐν ἀνδρὸς πλουσίου φρονήματι,
γνώμην τε μεγάλην ἐν πένητι σώματι.
πῶς οὖν τις αὐτὰ διαλαβὼν ὀρθῶς κρινεῖ;
πλούτῳ; πονηρῷ τἆρα χρήσεται κριτῇ·
ἢ τοῖς ἔχουσι μηδέν; ἀλλ' ἔχει νόσον 375
πενία, διδάσκει δ' ἄνδρα τῇ χρείᾳ κακόν.
ἀλλ' εἰς ὅπλ' ἔλθω; τίς δὲ πρὸς λόγχην βλέπων
μάρτυς γένοιτ' ἂν ὅστις ἐστὶν ἀγαθός;

---

363. δυσγενὲς Canter for δυσμενές.
364. συνεκκλέπτει, concurs with you in concealing the circumstances of your marriage, i. e. keeping you in reserve for a more worthy alliance in future. Cf. 257.
366. κέκληται. A false notion of Monk's on Hippol. 2, that κεκλῆσθαι is often a mere synonym of εἶναι, has led to many wrong interpretations, and among them, of this passage. Electra does not mean he *is* her husband, i. e. in reality, but that he is *called* so in name only. The context alone might have made Dr. Robinson see this. See below, v. 899. In v. 1286, the husbandman is called in the same manner ὁ λόγῳ πενθερὸς, the *nominal* relative of Orestes.
367. The speech of Orestes contains a clear exposition of the poet's view on the subject of *birth*. He very sensibly observes, in opposition to those who made it a practice to flatter the aristocracy, that true merit has no connexion whatever with the accident of high birth,—πολλοὶ γὰρ ὄντες εὐγενεῖς εἰσὶν κακοί (v. 551). Goodness, and cleverness, and magnanimity, seem to be found in certain individuals, according to no rule. Neither wealth, nor poverty, nor the profession of arms, nor influence in the state, will ensure the possession of real virtue. Men must be judged by their morals and by the company they keep. It is such persons as this poor agriculturist who are really most fitted to direct states; for they have true integrity, while your handsome young nobles are often no better than the statues that adorn the agora. And then, in allusion to the popular notion, that honour and chivalry are inseparable from high birth, he adds, that it is not a strong arm that withstands an enemy better in battle, but the courage that is born in a man, i. e. in the poor man as much as in the rich.
371. λιμὸν, a poverty, meagreness of spirit, opposed to μεγαλοψυχία implied in the next verse.
373. διαλαβὼν, discriminating them.
376. διδάσκει κακόν, teaches a man to be bad through necessity.
378. ἀγαθὸς is used exactly as in Suppl. 852, where the same sentiment occurs,—

ΕΥΡΙΠΙΔΟΥ

κράτιστον εἰκῆ ταῦτ' ἐᾶν ἀφειμένα.
οὗτος γὰρ ἀνὴρ οὔτ' ἐν Ἀργείοις μέγας 380
οὔτ' αὖ δοκήσει δωμάτων ὠγκωμένος,
ἐν τοῖς δὲ πολλοῖς ὤν, ἄριστος ηὑρέθη.
οὐ μὴ ἀφρονήσεθ', οἳ κενῶν δοξασμάτων
πλήρεις πλανᾶσθε, τῇ δ' ὁμιλίᾳ βροτοὺς
κρινεῖτε καὶ τοῖς ἤθεσιν τοὺς εὐγενεῖς; 385
οἱ γὰρ τοιοῦτοι τὰς πόλεις οἰκοῦσιν εὖ
καὶ δώμαθ', αἱ δὲ σάρκες αἱ κεναὶ φρενῶν
ἀγάλματ' ἀγορᾶς εἰσίν. οὐδὲ γὰρ δόρυ
μᾶλλον βραχίων σθεναρὸς ἀσθενοῦς μένει·
ἐν τῇ φύσει δὲ τοῦτο κἀν εὐψυχίᾳ. 390

κενοὶ γὰρ οὗτοι τῶν τ' ἀκουόντων λόγοι καὶ τοῦ λέγοντος, ὅστις ἐν μάχῃ βεβὼς λόγχης ἰούσης πρόσθεν ὀμμάτων πυκνῆς σαφῶς ἀπήγγειλ' ὅστις ἐστὶν ἀγαθός.

As one individual in the battle was honoured with the prize of valour, the article is necessary to express the idea, 'who *the* brave one is.'

379. κράτιστον κτλ. ''Tis best to dismiss the question, and to let matters go as they please' (εἰκῆ ἀφιέναι), i. e. not to attempt to find out any certain criterion. So ἔφυρον εἰκῆ πάντα Prom. 458.

382. τοῖς δὲ πολλοῖς. So the present editor for τοῖς τε π., since there is clearly an antithesis between οἱ πολλοὶ and οἱ ὠγκωμένοι.

383. οὐ μὴ ἀφρονήσεθ', 'be no longer foolish, ye who, filled with vain opinions about wealth, are deceiving yourselves; but judge men by the company they keep, and the noble by their morals.' The common reading, for which the present editor has ventured to introduce the emendation in the text, is οὐ μὴ φρονήσεθ', which is interpreted, 'be not proud.' But in the first place φρονεῖν is not 'to be proud,' but 'to be wise,' unless μέγα be added, or φρονεῖν ἐπί τινι &c., so that the natural and obvious meaning of the old reading is exactly contrary to what the poet intended. It is surprising that Barnes, who supplies καλῶς καὶ ὀρθῶς, should have failed to see that thus οὐ φρονήσετε, without the μὴ, would be required. Bothe quotes Herc. F. 774, ὁ χρυσὸς ἅ τ' εὐτυχία φρονεῖν βροτοὺς ἐξάγεται, where however L. Dindorf gives φρενῶν. Secondly, the sense is faulty; for people are told not to be so silly as to value mere birth, not to guard against *pride*, which is the fault of the well-born themselves. The synizesis is sufficiently common; compare μὴ ἀμαθὴς in Suppl. 421. Troad. 981. μὴ ἀδικουμένους Suppl. 304. Stobaeus quotes this passage with οὐ μὴ φρονήσηθ', the meaning of which would be, 'there is no chance of your being wise.' But this does not suit the future κρινεῖτε, i. e. οὐ κρινεῖτε; See Bacch. 343, οὐ μὴ προσοίσεις χεῖρα, βακχεύσεις δ' ἰών; It is an old saying, that a man may be judged by the company he keeps; τοιοῦτός ἐστιν οἷσπερ ἥδεται ξυνών, Frag. 803. Cf. Hippol. 997 seqq. Hence ὁμιλίᾳ is to be taken literally here as a test of a man's character, not, with Seidler, *ex vita et moribus judicabitis*.

385. This verse is remarkable, because the caesura falls on the article, which is very rarely the case.

386. οἱ τοιοῦτοι, scil. οἷος οὗτος ὁ αὐτουργός, or rather, (though this amounts to the same thing,) οἱ τὰ ἤθη εὐγενεῖς. The order of the words should be observed, as conveying the proper emphasis; —'It is *this* class of persons that manage well both states and houses; while your well-fed bodies that are destitute of sense, are so many statues of the market-place.'

390. τῇ φύσει—καὶ εὐψυχίᾳ may be compared with τὰς πόλεις καὶ δώματα just above, γυναῖκα, μὴ τὸν ἄνδρα, *inf.* 933. It would be a mistake in passages of this kind to assign a difference of meaning (though it is possible to do so) in the substantive to which the article is prefixed.

ἀλλ' ἄξιος γὰρ ὅ τε παρὼν ὅ τ' οὐ παρὼν
Ἀγαμέμνονος παῖς, οὗπερ οὕνεχ' ἥκομεν,
δεξώμεθ' οἴκων καταλύσεις· χωρεῖν χρεὼν,
δμῶες, δόμων τῶνδ' ἐντός. ὡς ἐμοὶ πένης
εἴη πρόθυμος πλουσίου μᾶλλον ξένος.   395
αἰνῶ μὲν οὖν τοῦδ' ἀνδρὸς εἰσδοχὰς δόμων·
ἐβουλόμην δ' ἄν, εἰ κασίγνητός με σὸς
εἰς εὐτυχοῦντας ἦγεν εὐτυχῶν δόμους.
ἴσως δ' ἂν ἔλθοι· Λοξίου γὰρ ἔμπεδοι
χρησμοὶ, βροτῶν δὲ μαντικὴν χαίρειν ἐῶ.   400
ΧΟ. νῦν ἢ πάροιθεν μᾶλλον, Ἠλέκτρα, χαρᾷ
θερμαινόμεσθα καρδίαν· ἴσως γὰρ ἂν
μόλις προβαίνουσ' ἡ τύχη σταίη καλῶς.
ΗΛ. ὦ τλῆμον, εἰδὼς δωμάτων χρείαν σέθεν
τί τούσδ' ἐδέξω μείζονας σαυτοῦ ξένους;   405
ΑΥ. τί δ'; εἴπερ εἰσὶν, ὡς δοκοῦσιν, εὐγενεῖς,
οὐκ ἔν τε μικροῖς ἔν τε μὴ στέρξουσ' ὅμως;

391. ὅ τε παρὼν ὅ τ' οὐ παρών. Though the article, applied to two characters or impersonations of the same individual, might be defended (see on Heracl. 826), so as to describe Orestes in his pretended absence but real presence, it seems better, with Bothe, to suppose the αὐτουργὸς to be meant by the first. Thus, the sense will be, 'Well! as both the host is a worthy man, and the absent Orestes, whose representatives we are, let us accept the offered hospitality.'

395. πλουσίου μᾶλλον. Poverty with good will gives a better welcome than mere wealth. The Greeks thought much of the *manner* in which they were received as guests. Hence such phrases as προθύμως μᾶλλον ἢ φίλως Agam. 1569, δικαίων ὀμμάτων παρουσία Cho. 658, δέχεσθαι στυγνῷ προσώπῳ Alcest. 777, φαιδροῖς ὄμμασιν Agam. 503, &c.

396. αἰνῶ μὲν οὖν κτλ. 'I accept therefore with thanks.' It is remarkable that ἐπαινεῖν more commonly means 'to decline,' as Ar. Ran. 508, κάλλιστ', ἐπαινῶ, 'You are very good, but I had rather not.' So Hesiod. Opp. 641, νῆ' ὀλίγην αἰνεῖν, imitated by Virgil, Georg. ii. 412, 'laudato ingentia rura, Exiguum colito,' 'have nothing to do with a large farm,' &c.

397. ἐβουλόμην ἄν. I should have preferred it, if your brother had been here to receive me himself.

400. If Apollo said so, it will come to pass; but in the mere predictions of seers no confidence is to be placed. For the dislike of the poet to this class of pretenders, see Hel. 755.—χαίρειν ἐῶ, like χαίρειν λέγω, 'I have nothing to say to it,' Hipp. 113. 1059.

403. μόλις. The order of the words seems to indicate that this must be taken with προβαίνουσα, which indeed otherwise stands alone and without definite meaning. 'Perhaps our fortune which has gradually been advancing to this point, may now rest favourably,' i. e. without a reverse to evil. Similarly προβαίνων appears to be used in a very obscure passage, Agam. 1488, ὅποι προβαίνων (Ἄρης) δίκαν πάχνᾳ κουροβόρῳ παρέξει. Generally, μόλις is to be rendered 'at last,' in which case, of course, it best suits σταίη καλῶς.

405. μείζονας σαυτοῦ, above your means.

407. ὅμως. Seidler, followed by Dindorf, gives ὁμῶς. The latter word is but little used in tragedy, and the alteration is needless, the sense being καίπερ ἐν σμικροῖς ὅμως. 'They will be content, though it be with small fare, and equally content with abundant provision.'—ἔν τε μὴ, for

ΗΛ. ἐπεί νυν ἐξήμαρτες ἐν σμικροῖσιν ὤν,
ἔλθ᾽ ὡς παλαιὸν τροφὸν ἐμοῦ φίλον πατρός·
ὃς ἀμφὶ ποταμὸν Ταναὸν Ἀργείας ὅρους 410
τέμνοντα γαίας Σπαρτιάτιδός τε γῆς
ποίμναις ὁμαρτεῖ, πόλεος ἐκβεβλημένος·
κέλευε δ᾽ αὐτὸν ἐς δόμους ἀφιγμένον
ἐλθεῖν ξένων τ᾽ ἐς δαῖτα πορσῦναί τινα.
ἡσθήσεταί τοι καὶ προσεύξεται θεοῖς 415
ζῶντ᾽ εἰσακούσας παῖδ᾽, ὃν ἐκσώζει ποτέ.
οὐ γὰρ πατρῴων ἐκ δόμων μητρὸς πάρα
λάβοιμεν ἄν τι· πικρὰ δ᾽ ἀγγείλαιμεν ἄν,
εἰ ζῶντ᾽ Ὀρέστην ἡ τάλαιν᾽ αἴσθοιτ᾽ ἔτι.
ΑΥ. ἀλλ᾽, εἰ δοκεῖ σοι, τούσδ᾽ ἀπαγγελῶ λόγους 420
γέροντι· χώρει δ᾽ ἐς δόμους ὅσον τάχος,
καὶ τἄνδον ἐξάρτυε. πολλά τοι γυνὴ
χρῄζουσ᾽ ἂν εὕροι δαιτὶ προσφορήματα.

ἔν τε τοῖς μή. Eur. Frag. 420, μὴ δίκαια καὶ δίκαι᾽ ὁμοῦ. Aesch. Cho. 69, δίκαια καὶ μὴ δίκαια—αἰνέσαι. Med. 661, μὴ φίλους τιμᾶν, 'to honour such as are not friends.'

408. ἐπεί νυν. It has been remarked on Med. 1365, that νῦν appears to have no place except with an imperative or an optative (i. e. in its true sense of *wishing*). This passage is only an apparent exception, for the νυν undoubtedly belongs to ἐλθέ. Cf. Hipp. 952, ἤδη νυν αὔχει. *Inf.* 567, βλέψον νυν ἐς τόνδ᾽. In Trach. 71, τοίνυν is short without an imperative, πᾶν τοίνυν, εἰ καὶ τοῦτ᾽ ἔτλη, κλύοι τις ἄν. In Hippol. v. 20, the best editions give τούτοισι μέν νυν οὐ φθονῶ, but it is a question whether νῦν is not the true reading, as in Heracl. 834, τὰ πρῶτα μὲν νῦν πίτυλος Ἀργείου δορὸς ἐρρήξαθ᾽ ἡμᾶς. The enclitic νυν, it is now well ascertained, has the υ common. Its intimate connexion with νῦν (like our particle *now*, and like *jam*, but not *nunc*, of the Romans), makes it difficult in all cases to decide between the two forms, which have nearly the same relation as μέν and μήν, δέ and δή.—Seidler here remarks, that Electra pays no attention to her husband's objection. But this is incorrect; she in fact accepts his excuse, and rejoins, 'well then, since you *have* made a mistake in receiving guests, being only a poor man, go,' &c.—φίλον for φίλου has been restored from one MS. by Matthiae.

410. Ταναόν. Pausanias, ii. 38, 7, writes the word Τάνος, though the one form is as likely to be a mistake as the other. Barnes however adopts this reading in his text. Perhaps the root is Ταν or Δαν (Tanais, Danubius, &c.) rather than from τείνειν, in allusion to the length of a river's course, as in Bacch. 455, πλόκαμός τε γάρ σοι ταναός.

412. ἐκβεβλημένος, by Aegisthus, on account of his fidelity to the Atridae.

413. ἐς δόμους κτλ. The man was in the fields with his flocks; he must therefore return to his own house for provisions, and then come to the cottage of the αὐτουργός.

416. ποτέ. This word is used with the *praesens historicum* in Bacch. 2, ὃν τίκτει ποθ᾽ ἡ Κάδμου κόρη Σεμέλη.

418. πικρά. Dobree appears rightly to explain this, 'We should bring the news to our cost.' He might well have compared Hel. 448, πικρῶς ἂν οἶμαί γ᾽ ἀγγελεῖν τοὺς σοὺς λόγους.

423. προσφορήματα, additions, like προσθήματ᾽ ἀγλαΐας, v. 191, or simply, τὰ προσφέρεσθαι δυνάμενα, ἐπιτήδεια, 'proper to be served up.' Those who consider such details beneath the dignity of tragedy, should at least give the poet some credit for his truthfulness to nature.

ἔστιν δὲ δὴ τοσαῦτά γ' ἐν δόμοις ἔτι,
ὥσθ' ἕν γ' ἐπ' ἦμαρ τούσδε πληρῶσαι βορᾶς.   425
ἐν τοῖς τοιούτοις δ' ἡνίκ' ἂν γνώμη πέσῃ,
σκοπῶ τὰ χρήμαθ' ὡς ἔχει μέγα σθένος,
ξένοις τε δοῦναι, σῶμά τ' ἐς νόσον πεσὸν
δαπάναισι σῶσαι· τῆς δ' ἐφ' ἡμέραν βορᾶς
ἐς σμικρὸν ἥκει. πᾶς γὰρ ἐμπλησθεὶς ἀνὴρ   430
ὁ πλούσιός τε χὠ πένης ἴσον φέρει.
XO. κλειναὶ νᾶες, αἵ ποτ' ἔμβατε Τροίαν   στρ. ά.

424. γ' ἐν MSS. τὰν Ed. princ., and so Dind. Matth. Bothe.
426. ἐν τοῖς τοιούτοις κτλ. 'It is in cases of this kind, when my thoughts are engaged upon the question, that I observe the great use that wealth has.' Such is the poet's meaning, though in point of construction ἐν τοιούτοις belongs to πέσῃ. He disparages wealth under ordinary circumstances, but cannot help feeling this to be a case in which it may fairly be desired; and in saying this, he makes a wise and admirable remark. The passage is quoted by Stobaeus, and referred to by St. Chrysostom, and more than once by Plutarch.—The old reading πέσοι was corrected by Schaefer. Stobaeus, xci. 6, has γνώμης πέσω, whence Seidler gives γνώμῃ πέσω.
429. ἐφ' ἡμέραν, 'for the present day.' See on Bacch. 485. The genitive here is rather anomalous. The poet seems to have had in mind some such word as φροντὶς, 'the care for one's daily bread amounts to a small matter,' or perhaps δαπάνη must be repeated from δαπάναισι. The doctrine that the genitive alone signifies "quod attinet ad," rests on but small evidence. There would seem here to have been some confusion of construction, e. g. τῆς ἐφ' ἡμέραν βορᾶς σμικρὰ ἐξαρκεῖ.
431. φέρει. Not for φέρεται, but literally, 'the rich man's stomach cannot hold more than a poor man's.' It is a metaphor from the cargo of a ship. Robinson well compares Hor. Sat. i. 1, 46, 'Non tuus hoc capiet venter plus quam meus.'—The countryman here departs on his message. Electra and the strangers enter the house.
432 seqq. This is one of the choral odes of Euripides which seem merely ἐμβόλιμα, inserted to mark the intervals in the action without any reference to the plot of the play. See on Hel. 1301. Here we have simply a description of the shield of Achilles, which the poet feigns to have been carried by the Nereids across the Aegean sea, and describes, after his favourite manner, differently from the Homeric account in Il. xviii. The metre is an irregular kind of glyconean verse. The first may be scanned as a double dochmiac hypercatalectic; the third is glyconean polyschematistic. The following four verses are differently arranged in this edition, the Aldine order, which has been hitherto retained, being very inharmonious. In the fourth verse (435) the long syllable of the anacrusis is resolved into two short, as in v. 441.—The address to the ships, as in Troad. 122, πρῷραι ναῶν ὠκεῖαι, compared by Seidler, has no direct sequence; see on v. 1 of the present play. We might indeed in both places supply ἦτε, as in Med. 824, Ἐρεχθεΐδαι τὸ παλαιὸν ὄλβιοι, scil. εἰσὶ or ἦσαν. But it is more probable that the vocative is meant.— ἔμβατε, ἐνέβητε, literally, 'set foot on the Trojan land,' i. e. came ashore there.—τοῖς ἀμ. ἐρ., 'with those numberless oars,' the expedition being χιλιόναυς. Ships were rated by their number of oars, as ours are by their tonnage; and μέτρον was the term to express the size. Hence in Hel. 1532, a Phoenician ship is described as ζυγῶν τε πεντήκοντα κἀρετμῶν μέτρα ἔχουσα.— χοροὺς κτλ., 'escorting the dances with the Nereids,' for 'escorting the Nereids in their dances.' Cf. Tro. 2, ἔνθα Νηρῄδων χοροὶ κάλλιστον ἴχνος ἐξελίσσουσιν ποδός. Seidler well compares Hel. 1454, where the Sidonian ship is called χοραγὸς δελφίνων, and Oed. Col. 719, πλάτα— Νηρῄδων ἀκόλουθος.

τοῖς ἀμετρήτοις ἐρετμοῖς,
πέμπουσαι χοροὺς μετὰ Νηρήδων,
ἵν' ὁ φίλαυλος ἔπαλλε δελφὶς   435
πρώραις κυανεμβόλοισιν
εἱλισσόμενος, πορεύων τὸν τᾶς Θέτιδος
κοῦφον ἅλμα ποδῶν Ἀχιλῆ
σὺν Ἀγαμέμνονι Τρωικὰς   440
ἐπὶ Σιμουντίδας ἀκτάς.
Νηρῆδες δ' Εὐβοΐδας ἀκτὰς λιποῦσαι   ἀντ. α'.
Ἡφαίστου χρυσέων ἀκμόνων
μόχθους ἀσπιστὰς ἔφερον τευχέων,
ἀνά τε Πήλιον ἀνά τε πρύμνας   445
Ὄσσας ἱερὰς νάπας Νυμ-
φαίας σκοπιὰς ἐμάστευον, ἔνθα πατὴρ

435. φίλαυλος, from the story of Arion. There is a popular notion still prevalent that porpoises will follow music in a boat. Aristophanes quotes these two verses, Ran. 1317, where Aeschylus is holding up to ridicule what he would have called the *twaddle* of Euripidean lyrics.—ἔπαλλε, for ἐπάλλετο, 'floundered,' ἐσκίρτα.—πρώραις is the dative of place.

438. πορεύων, like πέμπων, escorting, forwarding on his way, not, of course, in the sense of πορθμεύων.

440. Τρωικὰς Seidler for Τροίας. Or we might read Τρωΐας, as Robinson has edited.

444. ἔφερον. If the text be right, this can only mean that the Nereids carried the arms made by Vulcan from the shores of Greece to Troy. This they may be supposed to have done as sister nymphs of Thetis. But Dobree acutely observes, that the sense apparently was, that nymphs and Nereids left their haunts to gaze on the arms. He proposes ἔμολον for ἔφερον, but this is hardly probable. Possibly the poet wrote μόχθους ἐπ' ἀσπιστὰς ἔτρεχον, which however would require χοροὺς προπέμπουσαι in the strophe. It is however to be remembered, that Achilles is here spoken of as sailing to Troy σὺν Ἀγαμέμνονι, on the first expedition; whereas the arms of Hephaestus were wrought for that hero, according to Homer, not until after the death of Patroclus. Hence not a little difficulty would attach to Dobree's theory, even if the text could be plausibly restored to suit it.—ἀσπιστὰς is here an adjective, as Agam. 394, ἀσπίστορας κλόνους τε καὶ λογχίμους ναυβάτας ὁπλισμούς.

445. πρύμνας Ὄσσας (genitive), not the *heights* of Ossa, as Seidler explains, but the *roots* or foot of the mountain. Photius, πρύμνην· κάτωθεν, ἐκ ῥιζῶν. πρυμνώρειαν, τὸ κάτω μέρος τοῦ ὄρους.

448. ἐμάστευον. The common reading, κόρας μάτευσ', is acknowledged by all to be corrupt. The metre of the strophe, as well as the barbarous form ματέω, proves this. The conjecture now given restores sense and metre without a very violent change. The Nereids sought through Pelion and Ossa for the spot where Chiron (or Peleus) had reared Achilles, vainly expecting to find him there, and to give him the arms, (which, perhaps, they had brought from the Liparaean factory;) but finding him not, they pursued him to the coast of Troy. Seidler suggests, that the poet may have meant the first suit of arms which Achilles inherited from Peleus, and which were equally of divine workmanship. These had been despoiled from the body of Patroclus by Hector, Il. xviii. 83. However, the mention of Ἡφαίστου ἀκμόνων μόχθους decisively negatives this supposition. On the whole, the explanation offered above presents the fewest difficulties. The Nereids are said μαστεύειν

ΗΛΕΚΤΡΑ.

ἱππότας τρέφεν Ἑλλάδι φῶς,
Θέτιδος εἰνάλιον γόνον, 450
ταχύπορον πόδ' Ἀτρείδαις.
Ἰλιόθεν δ' ἔκλυόν τινος ἐν λιμέσιν στρ. β'.
Ναυπλίοισι βεβῶτος
τᾶς σᾶς, ὦ Θέτιδος παῖ,
κλεινᾶς ἀσπίδος ἐν κύκλῳ 455
τοιάδε σήματα, δείματα
Φρύγια τετύχθαι·
περιδρόμῳ μὲν ἴτυος ἕδρᾳ
Περσέα λαιμοτόμον ὑπὲρ
ἁλὸς ποτανοῖσι πεδίλοισι φυὰν 460
Γοργόνος ἴσχειν, Διὸς ἀγγέλῳ σὺν Ἑρμᾷ,
τῷ Μαίας ἀγροτῆρι κούρῳ·
ἐν δὲ μέσῳ κατέλαμπε σάκει φαέθων ἀντ. β'.
κύκλος ἀελίοιο 465

σκοπιὰς ἔνθα κτλ., because they ascended the mountain heights in their search for Achilles, at once looking out for him and making inquiry about him.

449. πατὴρ ἱππότας. This may mean either Peleus the father of Achilles, or the centaur Chiron. Barnes quotes from Il. vii. 125, the epithet ἱππηλάτα Πηλεύς.

451. ταχ. πόδ' Ἀ., 'swift in foot for the Atreidae,' i. e. a swift ally. But Ἀτρείδαις may also depend on τρέφεν, as well as Ἑλλάδι.—πόδα is the same accusative as ἅλμα in v. 439.

452. Ἰλιόθεν κτλ. 'Now I heard from one who had landed at the port of Nauplia from Troy; that on the circle of thy far-famed shield, O Achilles, the following devices were wrought, a terror to the Phrygians' (i. e. Trojans).

458. ἴτυος ἕδρᾳ, on the outer margin or border of the shield. Photius, ἴτυς, περιφέρεια ὅπλου. The order of the following words is Περσέα λαιμοτόμον, πεδίλοισιν ὑπὲρ ἁλὸς ποτανοῖς, ἴσχειν Γοργόνος φυάν,—' that Perseus, having cut off her head, was holding the monstrous form of the Gorgon (i. e. the terrible head) as he flew,' &c. It was by the aid of Hermes, who lent Perseus his winged sandals, that Perseus safely slew the Gorgon. Apollodorus however says that Hermes supplied him with a knife of adamant, but that the sandals were obtained from certain nymphs, lib. ii. 4, 2. Hermes is called ἀγροτὴρ as being the god of Arcadia, a pastoral country. His first exploit as an infant was accordingly said to be the theft of a herd of oxen. The metre of v. 459 seems faulty. Probably we should read λαιμοτομοῦνθ' or λαιμοτόμον θ', the σὺν Ἑρμᾷ following being equivalent to Ἑρμῆν τε, or perhaps τε was answered by δὲ in 464.

465. ἀελίοιο. Homer mentions the sun, moon, and stars, wrought on the shield of Achilles, but says nothing about Perseus, the Sphinx, or the Chimaera. Cf. Il. xviii. 483,

ἐν μὲν γαῖαν ἔτευξ', ἐν δ' οὐρανὸν, ἐν δὲ θάλασσαν,
ἠέλιόν τ' ἀκάμαντα σελήνην τε πλήθουσαν,
ἐν δὲ τὰ τείρεα πάντα, τά τ' οὐρανὸς ἐστεφάνωται,
Πληιάδας θ' Ὑάδας τε τό τε σθένος Ὠρίωνος.

The mention of the Sphinx was perhaps suggested by the description of Parthenopaeus' shield, Aesch. Theb. 536.—ἂμ πτ. ἵπποις, on winged steeds. Cf. Ion 1148, ἵππους μὲν ἤλαυν' ἐς τελευταίαν φλόγα Ἥλιος. We have ἂμ for ἀνὰ in Aesch. Suppl. 345, ἂμ πέτραις ἠλιβάτοις.

ἵπποις ἃμ πτεροέσσαις,
ἄστρων τ' αἰθέριοι χοροί,
Πλειάδες, Ὑάδες, Ἕκτορος
ὄμμασι τροπαῖοι·
ἐπὶ δὲ χρυσοτύπῳ κράνει 470
Σφίγγες ὄνυξιν ἀοίδιμον
ἄγραν φέρουσαι· περιπλεύρῳ δὲ κύτει
πύρπνοος ἔσπευδε δρόμῳ λέαινα χαλαῖς
Πειρηναῖον ὁρῶσα πῶλον. 475
ἐν δὲ δόρει φονίῳ τετραβάμονες ἵπποι ἔπαλλον, ἐπῳδ.
κελαινὰ δ' ἀμφὶ νώθ' ἵετο κόνις.
τοιῶνδ' ἄνακτα δοριπόνων
ἔκανεν ἀνδρῶν, Τυνδαρὶ 480

468. Ὑάδες. Dindorf remarks that the Υ is made long, as in Ion 1156, Ὑάδες τε ναυτίλοις σαφέστατον σημεῖον.
469. τροπαῖοι Barnes for τροπαίοις. He is clearly right: compare Φρύγια δείματα in v. 456. These emblems were τροπήν ἐμποιοῦντα to the eyes of Hector, partly from their splendour, partly from the terrific and portentous nature of the device.
470. κράνει κτλ. On the helmet the Sphinx was represented, according to the usual way of painting it, carrying off a man in its talons; cf. Aesch. Theb. *ut sup.*, Phoen. 810.—ἀοίδιμον, celebrated in song.—χρυσοτύπῳ, is Seidler's slight but necessary metrical correction for χρυσεοτύπῳ.
472. περιπλεύρῳ κύτει, the casing round his chest, i. e. on the θώραξ or coat of mail. For the Chimaera see on Ion 203.—Πειρηναῖον πῶλον, Pegasus, the Corinthian winged steed, on which Bellerophon rode to slay the fire-breathing monster, which is described as looking up, probably with upturned head, to the horse hovering over it. Bothe gives θηρῶσα, after a conjecture of Milton's, for the old reading θορῶσα. This would suit the metre, if we regard the first syllable of ἀγροτῆρι in v. 462 to be made long, and it would also give a participle well suited to χηλαῖς, which must now be taken with δρόμῳ, 'hastened on its course with its claws,' i. e. not with uncleft feet, τετραβάμοσι χηλαῖς, as is said of the Sphinx, Phoen. 808. But the verse thus ceases to be glyconic like the rest.

W. Dindorf attributes to Bothe the much more probable correction ὁρῶσα. The θ' was probably first added to connect the participle with πύρπνοος.
476. ἐν δόρει (so Herm. for δορὶ) φονίῳ appears from the context to mean 'on his gory spear,' because hitherto shield, helmet, and cuirass, have been enumerated. But, since no mention appears elsewhere to be made of either sculpture or painting on spear-shafts, Bothe explains 'in battle:' "in altera parte loricae praelium caelatum fuisse dicit Tragicus, in altera Bellerophontis cum Chimaera pugnam." Whether δόρει is the right reading may be doubted; but at all events ἐν δὲ appears to mean 'and besides,' as in Oed. R. 27, ἐν δ' ὁ πυρφόρος θεὸς σκήψας ἐλαύνει.—ἔπαλλον for ἐπάλλοντο, as in v. 435. Cf. Ion 1150, μελάμπεπλος δὲ Νὺξ ἀσείρωτον ζυγοῖς ὄχημ' ἔπαλλεν. Perhaps all that the poet intended was, that a warrior was depicted in a car drawn by four-footed (not four) steeds, brandishing his spear as in the act of throwing it. Compare τριβάμων, one who walks with a stick, Tro. 275.
480. The old reading was Τυνδαρὶς ἀλέχεα, corrected by Seidler, who however wrongly gives ἔκανες for ἔκανεν. Robinson has ἃ λέχεα, *ejus maritum*, agreeing with ἄνακτα, and follows Barnes in supposing that Agamemnon's death by Clytemnestra's hand is meant. This is probable from what follows; otherwise the sense might be, that Helen's marriage with Paris caused the death of

ΗΛΕΚΤΡΑ.

σὰ λέχεα, κακόφρων κόρα.
τοιγὰρ σέ ποτ' οὐρανίδαι
πέμψουσιν θανάτοισι· σὰν δ'
ἔτ' ἔτι φόνιον ὑπὸ δέραν   485
ὄψομαι αἷμα χυθὲν σιδάρῳ.

ΠΡΕΣΒΥΣ.

ποῦ ποῦ νεᾶνις πότνι' ἐμὴ δέσποινά τε,
Ἀγαμέμνονος παῖς, ἥν ποτ' ἐξέθρεψ' ἐγώ;
ὡς πρόσβασιν τῶνδ' ὀρθίαν οἴκων ἔχει
ῥυσῷ γέροντι τῷδε προσβῆναι ποδί.   490
ὅμως δὲ πρός γε τοὺς φίλους ἐξελκτέον
διπλῆν ἄκανθαν καὶ παλίρροπον γόνυ.
ὦ θύγατερ, ἄρτι γάρ σε πρὸς δόμοις ὁρῶ,
ἥκω φέρων σοι τῶν ἐμῶν βοσκημάτων
ποίμνης νεογνὸν θρέμμ' ὑποσπάσας τόδε,   495
στεφάνους τε, τευχέων τ' ἐξελὼν τυρεύματα,
παλαιόν τε θησαύρισμα Διονύσου τόδε

Achilles. 'The lord of such warlike men, O daughter of Tyndareus, has thy marriage caused to be slain, thou evil-minded woman; therefore thee some day shall the gods consign to a violent death; and yet under thy gory neck shall I see blood shed by the steel.'—σὰν δ' for κἂν is L. Dindorf's correction.—ὄψομαι αἷμα Seidler for ὄψομ' αἷμα. The verse is evidently logaoedic, that preceding being a dochmiac following an iambus.

487. The old man (409) has promptly obeyed the summons of the αὐτουργός. He is seen ascending the stairs leading from the orchestra to the stage, loaded with provisions. He is old and feeble, and has come a long way; but his zeal for the family in which he spent his youthful days makes him persevere in his efforts. He brings good cheer for the guests; a kid, cheeses, a little old and strong wine, and myrtle boughs for chaplets. The passage is a pleasing one. Schlegel cannot resist a hit at the old man's tears; " The old keeper, who finds it right hard work to climb up-hill to the house, brings Electra a lamb, a cheese, and a skin of wine; hereupon he falls a weeping, *not forgetting, of course, to wipe his eyes with his tattered gar-*ments." (Theatre of the Greeks, p. 239.)

489. ὀρθίαν—ποδί. 'Steep for an old man like me (τῷδε) to approach on foot,' i. e. without support.

491. ἐξελκτέον Barnes for ἐξελκτέον or ἐξελεικτέον.—διπλῆν ἄκανθαν, a spine curved with age. *Duplex spina*, Virgil, Georg. iii. 87, though in a different sense. —παλίρροπον is simply 'bent,' not παλίντονον, 'bending backwards,' i. e. arching inversely from the knee-joint; for the effect of old age is to stiffen the limb, and so to produce a contrary effect.

496. στεφάνους. Hence it may be inferred that in the humblest houses myrtle crowns were worn at a banquet. The old man shows that these were of myrtle by v. 512. Cf. Alcest. 759, στέφει δὲ κρᾶτα μυρσίνης κλάδοις, ἄμουσ' ὑλακτῶν.

497. παλεὸν is given by W. Dindorf for παλαιόν. This correction is certainly better than πολιὸν, which Bothe adopts from Scaliger. There is some direct evidence, and also undoubted analogy, in favour of the shortened form, though the orthography may perhaps be called in question. It is well known that δείλαιος, γεραιὸς, ἱκταῖος (Aesch. Suppl. 379) &c., sometimes shorten the diphthong; so in Ar. Lysist. 988, ὑπὸ τῆς ὁδοῦ· παλαιόρ γα

VOL. II.   X X

ΕΥΡΙΠΙΔΟΥ

ὀσμῇ κατῆρες, σμικρὸν, ἀλλ᾽ ἐπεισβαλεῖν
ἡδὺ σκύφον τοῦδ᾽ ἀσθενεστέρῳ ποτῷ.
ἴτω φέρων τις τοῖς ξένοις τάδ᾽ ἐς δόμους· 500
ἐγὼ δὲ τρύχει τῷδ᾽ ἐμῶν πέπλων κόρας
δακρύοισι τέγξας ἐξομόρξασθαι θέλω.

ΗΛ. τί δ᾽, ὦ γεραιὲ, διάβροχον τόδ᾽ ὄμμ᾽ ἔχεις;
μῶν τἀμὰ διὰ χρόνου σ᾽ ἀνέμνησεν κακά;
ἢ τὰς Ὀρέστου τλήμονας φυγὰς στένεις 505
καὶ πατέρα τὸν ἐμὸν, ὅν ποτ᾽ ἐν χεροῖν ἔχων
ἀνόνητ᾽ ἔθρεψας σοί τε καὶ τοῖς σοῖς φίλοις;

ΠΡ. ἀνόνηθ᾽· ὅμως δ᾽ οὖν τοῦτό γ᾽ οὐκ ἠνεσχόμην.
ἦλθον γὰρ αὐτοῦ πρὸς τάφον, πάρεργ᾽ ὁδοῦ,
καὶ προσπεσὼν ἔκλαυσ᾽, ἐρημίας τυχὼν, 510
σπονδάς τε, λύσας ἀσκὸν ὃν φέρω ξένοις,
ἔσπεισα, τύμβῳ δ᾽ ἀμφέθηκα μυρσίνας.
πυρᾶς δ᾽ ἐπ᾽ αὐτῆς οἶν μελάγχιμον πόκῳ
σφάγιον ἐσεῖδον αἷμά τ᾽ οὐ πάλαι χυθὲν

ναὶ τὸν Κάστορα. Here however the Doric pronunciation may be supposed to have differed from the Attic; and again in Soph. Frag. 655, νυκτός τε πηγὰς, οὐρανοῦ τ᾽ ἀναπτυχὰς, Φοίβου τε παλαιὸν κῆπον, the τε is more probably an interpolation, though Dindorf would read παλεδν κῆπον. He also cites a passage from Herodian (περὶ μον. λεξ. p. 4, 18,) where γαλεδς, ἀλεδς, παλεδς should apparently be read, though the MS. gives γαλαιὸς and παλαιός. However, he cites three senarii from late writers quoted by Galen, in all which, as in the present passage, παλαιδς or παλεδς forms an anapaest at the beginning.—ὀσμῇ κατῆρες, literally, 'furnished with aroma,' i. e. not wanting in that peculiar fragrance which is described by οἶνος ἀνθοσμίας, Ar. Ran. 1150. Theocr. xiv. 16, ἄνφξα δὲ Βύβλινον αὐτοῖς εὐώδη, τετόρων ἐτέων σχεδὸν, ὡς ἀπὸ λάνω. On κατήρης see Eur. Suppl. 110.

499. τοῦδ᾽ for τῷδ᾽ Reiske. ''Tis agreeable to add a cup of *this* to weaker drink,' i. e. to such wine as you already possess. Bothe supposes that the old man brought both commoner wine in a skin (v. 511,) and also a little of the better sort in a jar, κέραμος. This is a probable explanation, if we suppose him to have pointed to each at τόδε and τῷδε.

504. ἀνέμνησεν Dobree for -σαν. 'Can it be that my present misfortunes have reminded you after so long a time,' i. e. of past events, the murder of Agamemnon, &c. Bothe explains the plural of the messengers, or rather the messenger who had summoned him; and the double accusative may be defended by Oed. R. 1132, ἀλλ᾽ ἐγὼ σαφῶς ἀγνῶτ᾽ ἀναμνήσω νιν.

508. ὅμως δ᾽ οὖν Elmsley for γοῦν. See Alcest. 73.—τοῦτό γ᾽, τὸ μὴ τιμῆσαι αὐτὸν, for this is implied in ἦλθον ΓΑΡ.—πάρεργ᾽ ὁδοῦ, as a secondary object of my journey. The accusative in apposition to the sentence.

511. λύσας ἀσκόν. See on Med. 679.—μυρσίνας, cf. 324.

513. μελάγχιμον. This was the proper offering to the dead. Od. xi. 32, Τειρεσίῃ δ᾽ ἀπάνευθεν ὄϊν ἱερευσέμεν οἴῳ παμμέλαν'. On the practice of making blood offerings on tombs see Alcest. 845. Hel. 547.—πυρᾶς ἐπ᾽ αὐτῆς is, 'on the very spot where the pyre stood,' though πυρὰ, like *rogus*, was sometimes said of the tomb or monument, as Soph. El. 900, ἐσχάτης ὁρῶ πυρᾶς νεωρῆ βόστρυχον. Orestes had said above, v. 92, πυρᾷ τ᾽ ἐπέσφαξ᾽ αἷμα μηλείου φόνου.

ΗΛΕΚΤΡΑ. 339

ξανθῆς τε χαίτης βοστρύχους κεκαρμένους. 515
καθαύμασ', ὦ παῖ, τίς ποτ' ἀνθρώπων ἔτλη
πρὸς τύμβον ἐλθεῖν· οὐ γὰρ Ἀργείων γέ τις.
ἀλλ' ἦλθ' ἴσως που σὸς κασίγνητος λάθρα,
μολὼν δ' ἐθαύμασ' ἄθλιον τύμβον πατρός.
σκέψαι δὲ χαίτην, προστιθεῖσα σῇ κόμῃ, 520
εἰ χρῶμα ταὐτὸ κουρίμης ἔσται τριχός.
φιλεῖ γὰρ, αἷμα ταυτὸν οἷς ἂν ᾖ πατρὸς,
τὰ πόλλ' ὅμοια σώματος πεφυκέναι.
ΗΛ. οὐκ ἄξι' ἀνδρὸς, ὦ γέρον, σοφοῦ λέγεις,
εἰ κρυπτὸν ἐς γῆν τήνδ' ἂν Αἰγίσθου φόβῳ 525
δοκεῖς ἀδελφὸν τὸν ἐμὸν εὐθαρσῆ μολεῖν.
ἔπειτα χαίτης πῶς συνοίσεται πλόκος;
ὁ μὲν παλαίστραις ἀνδρὸς εὐγενοῦς τραφεὶς,
ὁ δὲ κτενισμοῖς θῆλυς· ἀλλ' ἀμήχανον.
πολλοῖς δ' ἂν εὕροις βοστρύχους ὁμοπτέρους 530

516. ἔτλη, 'had dared.' A use of the aorist not unfrequent in narration.
519. ἐθαύμασε, 'paid his respects to.' See *sup.* v. 84.
520. σκέψαι κτλ. Aesch. Cho. 221, σκέψαι τομῇ προσθεῖσα βόστρυχον τριχὸς σαυτῆς ἀδελφοῦ. In this case the sister is requested to compare Orestes' hair with her own; in the other play, to put the lock found on the tomb close to the place whence it was cut from Orestes' head, the object in the latter instance being merely to identify the donor of the hair.
522. φιλεῖ γάρ. This remark is *generally true*, (and the poet himself represents it as exceptional, v. 530—1,) as regards physical appearance, colour of hair &c. And it was perhaps more observable among the ancient Greeks than it now is with us, in whom there is a much greater admixture of nations, Norman, Saxon, Celtic, &c. There is no doubt that Euripides, in making the old man draw the above inference and Electra show the fallacy of it, had in view the ἀναγνώρισις or recognition-scene in the Choephori, v. 166 seqq. The somewhat unusual word ὁμόπτερος is used by both of the colour or texture of the hair, as well as σύμμετρος of the measure of the feet, though in Cho. 218 seqq. the order of the verses appears to have been disarranged, as pointed out in the note there. Similarly,

Euripides has ἐξύφασμα for the third token, the embroidered garment (v. 539), which Aeschylus calls ὕφασμα τοῦτο, σῆς ἔργον χερὸς, in Cho. 223.
525. Electra first replies to the suggestion in v. 518, ἦλθ' ἴσως λάθρα, then to the argument from the colour of the hair. 'You speak unworthily of a wise man, if you think that my brave brother would have come *stealthily* into this land through fear of Aegisthus. In the next place,' she proceeds, 'how shall the lock of his hair agree with mine? The one is that of a well-born man, nurtured in the wrestling schools, the other is that of a woman, delicately dressed (τραφεὶς) by the frequent use of the comb.' Matthiae prefers to join παλαίστραις ἀνδρὸς εὐγενοῦς, but the poet is not speaking generally, but of the particular hair of each. Compare Bacch. 455, πλόκαμός τε γάρ σου ταναὸς, οὐ πάλης ὕπο. Some construe κτενισμοῖς θῆλυς 'made soft by combing;' but cf. *inf.* 781. Hel. 1025.
530. Photius, ὁμόπτεροι, ὁμότριχες. On 532—3 see on v. 544.—ἐκείρατο is used in the middle as in Cho. 164, 181.— The old reading, σκοποὺς λαθὼν (or λαβὼν) was altered by Seidler to σκότος λαβὼν,—a bad emendation, though adopted by both Matthiae and Dindorf. The true reading is σκοπὸς, meaning one of those mentioned at v. 354.

x x 2

καὶ μὴ γεγῶσιν αἵματος ταὐτοῦ, γέρον.
ἀλλ' ἤ τις αὐτοῦ τάφον ἐποικτείρας ξένος [545]
ἐκείρατ', ἢ τῆσδε σκοπὸς λαθὼν χθονός. [546]

ΠΡ. σὺ δ' εἰς ἴχνος βᾶσ' ἀρβύλης σκέψαι βάσιν,
εἰ σύμμετρος σῷ ποδὶ γενήσεται, τέκνον.

ΗΛ. πῶς δ' ἂν γένοιτ' ἂν ἐν κραταιλέῳ πέδῳ
γαίας ποδῶν ἔκμακτρον; εἰ δ' ἔστιν τόδε, 535
δυοῖν ἀδελφοῖν ποὺς ἂν οὐ γένοιτ' ἴσος
ἀνδρός τε καὶ γυναικός, ἀλλ' ἄρσην κρατεῖ.

ΠΡ. οὐκ ἔστιν, εἰ καὶ γῆν κασίγνητος μολὼν
       *   *   *   *

κερκίδος ὅτῳ γνοίης ἂν ἐξύφασμα σῆς,
ἐν ᾧ ποτ' αὐτὸν ἐξέκλεψα μὴ θανεῖν; 540

ΗΛ. οὐκ οἶσθ', Ὀρέστης ἡνίκ' ἐκπίπτει χθονὸς,
νέαν μ' ἔτ' οὖσαν; εἰ δὲ κἄκρεκον πέπλους,
πῶς ἂν τότ' ὢν παῖς ταὐτὰ νῦν ἔχοι φάρη,

---

534. κραταίλεως, 'rocky,' occurs in Agam. 649. She does not mean the place where they are now standing (which is in front of her husband's house), but the stony soil of the Necropolis where her father's tomb was; for in the ancient Greek cities such tombs were commonly hewn in the side of a rock. Hence when the old man says ἀρβύλης σκέψαι βάσιν, he means, that if she is incredulous about the evidence of the hair, she had better repair to the tomb where he found it, and measure footsteps.—ἔκμακτρον, 'an impression.' Theocr. xvii. 121, κονία στειβομένα καθύπερθε ποδῶν ἐκμάσσεται ἴχνη.

537. ἄρσην κρατεῖ, 'a male foot exceeds in size.' Dindorf gives ἄρσην, a very improbable crasis.

538. μολών. Musgrave μόλοι, Barnes, after Canter, εἰ παρῆν,—but this does not restore the passage. A little consideration will show that something must have been lost. Whatever opinions may be entertained on the use of εἰ with a participle in place of a finite verb, (on which see Med. 1109, and compare Ar. Ran. 1437,) it is certain that neither μολὼν nor μόλοι will satisfy the context. For how can the old man argue as follows? 'Is there not, even if Orestes *should* come (or, 'even if he *has* come'), some means of recognising the garment which you worked for him, and in which I stole him away?' This is simply nonsense. Doubtless the old man, driven from his two previous proofs of identity, now alleges a third and last. He has picked up on the tomb (otherwise how could he here mention it? For Orestes does not appear till v. 549) a piece of embroidered garment, left by Orestes together with a lock of his hair, and as a memento of himself to his father. This piece he now produces, and asks Electra if she cannot identify the work of her own loom when a girl. (Compare the ἀναγνώρισις effected by the same means in Ion 1417.) Probably, he inquired whether she had not some of the same work still remaining, to set side by side with the fragment he has found. On these considerations, the following may be suggested as representing the meaning of the original;—

ΠΡ. οὐκ ἔστιν· εἰ καὶ γῆν κασίγνητος
    μολὼν
δεῦρ' ἦλθεν, οὐκ ἂν ῥᾳδίως ἐγνώ-
    ρισας,
εἰ μή τι πέπλων λείψανον δόμοις
    ἔχεις,
κερκίδος ὅτῳ γνοίης ἂν ἐξύφασμα
    σῆς, κτλ.

543. πῶς ἂν κτλ. The old reading, corrected by Barnes and Elmsley on Med. 326, was πῶς ἂν τότ' ὢν παῖς νῦν ταῦτ'

ΗΛΕΚΤΡΑ.

εἰ μὴ ξυναύξοινθ' οἱ πέπλοι τῷ σώματι;
ΠΡ. οἱ δὲ ξένοι ποῦ; βούλομαι γὰρ εἰσιδὼν
αὐτοὺς ἐρέσθαι σοῦ κασιγνήτου πέρι.
ΗΛ. οἵδ' ἐκ δόμων βαίνουσι λαιψηρῷ ποδί.
ΠΡ. ἀλλ' εὐγενεῖς μέν, ἐν δὲ κιβδήλῳ τόδε. 550
πολλοὶ γὰρ ὄντες εὐγενεῖς εἰσὶν κακοί·
ὅμως δὲ χαίρειν τοὺς ξένους προσεννέπω.
ΟΡ. χαῖρ', ὦ γεραιέ. τοῦ ποτ', Ἠλέκτρα, τόδε
παλαιὸν ἀνδρὸς λείψανον φίλων κυρεῖ;
ΗΛ. οὗτος τὸν ἀμὸν πατέρ' ἔθρεψεν, ὦ ξένε. 555
ΟΡ. τί φῄς; ὅδ' ὃς σὸν ἐξέκλεψε σύγγονον;
ΗΛ. ὅδ' ἔσθ' ὁ σώσας κεῖνον, εἴπερ ἔστ' ἔτι.
ΟΡ. ἔα·
τί μ' εἰσδέδορκεν, ὥσπερ ἀργύρου σκοπῶν
λαμπρὸν χαρακτῆρ'; ἢ προσεικάζει μέ τῳ·
ΗΛ. ἴσως Ὀρέστου σ' ἥλικ' ἥδεται βλέπων. 560
ΟΡ. φίλου γε φωτός· τί δὲ κυκλεῖ πέριξ πόδα;

ἂν ἔχῃ φάρη. Barnes indeed gives in his text νῦν ἔχῃ ταῦτ' ἂν φάρῃ (φάρῃ), which is of course a solecism; but two MSS. give ἔχοι. But Elmsley would further read ταῦτ' ἀνὴρ ἔχοι φάρῃ, which is very ingenious and probable. Bothe's reading is bad, νῦν τάδ' ἄρ' ἔχοι φάρῃ (ἔχοι being omitted in his text by a mistake of the printers).

544. After this verse all the edd. and MSS. place the two lines which are now transposed after v. 531. Their fitness in that place will at once be apparent to all; whereas here Electra suddenly reverts to the lock of hair, after discussing the question of the embroidery. But there is another argument of very considerable weight. By this transposition Electra's speech is of *four* lines, corresponding to that before the speech of the πρέσβυς, who himself speaks *two* lines *before*, and *two after* these replies of Electra. Thus the *five* lines of the πρέσβυς at 538 seqq. (supposing the ellipse of two, as suggested above,) form a sort of μεσῳδός, corresponding to Electra's *five* lines at 503 seqq. interposed between *sixteen* of the πρέσβυς at 487 and 508 respectively, after which Electra again speaks *twice five* verses (524 seqq.). These coincidences are too remarkable to be the result of mere accident. See on Hel. 894, and the Preface to the present volume.

548. αὐτοὺς ἐρέσθαι (not εἰσιδὼν αὐτοὺς) is, 'to question them in person.' Compare Cho. 834, οὐδὲν ἀγγέλων σθένος, ὡς αὐτὸν αὐτῶν ἄνδρα πεύθεσθαι πάρα.

554. τοῦ φίλων κυρεῖ; 'of which of your friends is he the slave?' Otherwise he should have said τίς ποτ', Ἠλέκτρα, φίλων π. ἀνδρ. λ. κυρεῖ τόδε; And the answer virtually is, 'he was a slave in the service of the Atridae.'—ἀνδρὸς λείψανον, 'relics of a man,' is to be closely taken together. Compare Oed. Col. 109, οἰκτείρατ' ἀνδρὸς Οἰδίπου τόδ' ἄθλιον εἴδωλον, οὐ γὰρ δὴ τό γ' ἀρχαῖον δέμας.

556. ἐξέκλεψε Pierson for ἐξέθρεψε. It was not Orestes, but Agamemnon whom the old man had reared: cf. 409. 540.

558. ὥσπερ κτλ. Like one who closely inspects the device on a new coin (λαμπρὸν) to see if it be genuine, ὀρθῶς κοπέν. This passage shows, as the adjective παράσημος also appears to do, that coiners of false money were not uncommon in the time of Euripides: and it is also confirmed by κωδωνίζειν, to *ring* a coin, Ran. 723.

ΗΛ. καὐτὴ τόδ᾽ εἰσορῶσα θαυμάζω, ξένε.
ΠΡ. ὦ πότνι᾽, εὔχου, θύγατερ Ἠλέκτρα, θεοῖς,
ΗΛ. τί τῶν ἀπόντων ἢ τί τῶν ὄντων πέρι;
ΠΡ. λαβεῖν φίλον θησαυρὸν, ὃν φαίνει θεός. 565
ΗΛ. ἰδοὺ, καλῶ θεούς. ἢ τί δὴ λέγεις, γέρον;
ΠΡ. βλέψον νυν ἐς τόνδ᾽, ὦ τέκνον, τὸν φίλτατον.
ΗΛ. πάλαι δέδοικα, μὴ σύ γ᾽ οὐκέτ᾽ εὖ φρονῇς.
ΠΡ. οὐκ εὖ φρονῶ 'γὼ σὸν κασίγνητον βλέπων;
ΗΛ. πῶς εἶπας, ὦ γεραί᾽, ἀνέλπιστον λόγον; 570
ΠΡ. ὁρᾶν Ὀρέστην τόνδε τὸν Ἀγαμέμνονος.
ΗΛ. ποῖον χαρακτῆρ᾽ εἰσιδὼν, ᾧ πείσομαι;
ΠΡ. οὐλὴν παρ᾽ ὀφρὺν, ἥν ποτ᾽ ἐν πατρὸς δόμοις
νεβρὸν διώκων σοῦ μέθ᾽ ἡμάχθη πεσών.
ΗΛ. πῶς φῄς; ὁρῶ μὲν πτώματος τεκμήριον. 575
ΠΡ. ἔπειτα μέλλεις προσπίτνειν τοῖς φιλτάτοις;
ΗΛ. ἀλλ᾽ οὐκέτ᾽, ὦ γεραιέ συμβόλοισι γὰρ
τοῖς σοῖς πέπεισμαι θυμόν. ὦ χρόνῳ φανεὶς,
ἔχω σ᾽ ἀέλπτως. ΟΡ. κἀξ ἐμοῦ γ᾽ ἔχει χρόνῳ.
ΗΛ. οὐδέποτ᾽ ἐδόξασ᾽. ΟΡ. οὐδ᾽ ἐγὼ γὰρ ἤλπισα. 580
ΗΛ. ἐκεῖνος εἶ σύ;
ΟΡ. σύμμαχός γέ σοι μόνος,
ἢν ἐκσπάσωμαί γ᾽ ὃν μετέρχομαι βόλον.
πέποιθα δ᾽. ἢ χρὴ μηκέθ᾽ ἡγεῖσθαι θεοὺς,

563—5. εὔχου λαβεῖν. 'Pray that you may receive.' There is nothing in the aorist which is at variance with this version; and ὃν φαίνει shows the meaning to be, that the god is as it were holding out, προτείνων, a gift or a prize which she has yet to make her own. Bothe renders this, in questionable Latinity, *precare deos, ut acceperis*, i. e. 'that you may have received.' And such appears to be the sense of v. 595. It might also here mean, 'acknowledge with thanksgivings that you *have* received;' but cf. v. 810. Compare Cho. 204, εὔχου τὰ λοιπὰ, τοῖς θεοῖς τελεσφόρους εὐχὰς ἐπαγγέλλουσα, τυγχάνειν καλῶς.

571. ὁρᾶν. The ed. princ. has ὁρῶν, which is as good a reading.

573. οὐλήν. Barnes remarks that a scar was the proof by which Ulysses was recognised by the Nurse in Od. xix. 392.

577. συμβόλοισι, marks, tokens. Cf. Ion 1386, τὰ μητρὸς σύμβολ᾽ ὃς σέσωκέ μοι.

580. ἐδόξασ᾽. The following ἤλπισα seems to confirm the reading of all the old copies. Dindorf adopts Musgrave's correction οὐδέποτε δόξασ᾽. Either, of course, is good in itself, both δοκεῖν and δοξάζειν being used for προσδοκᾶν.

582. βόλον. Cf. Bacch. 847, ἀνὴρ δ᾽ ἐς βόλον καθίσταται. Theocr. i. 40, μέγα δίκτυον ἐς βόλον ἕλκει ὁ πρέσβυς, where it seems to mean 'for a cast.' Here it implies both the net and the prey inclosed in it. The next two verses were rightly assigned to Orestes by Musgrave, instead of to Electra.—ἡγεῖσθαι θεοὺς, cf. Hec. 800.

ΗΛΕΚΤΡΑ. 343

εἰ τἄδικ' ἔσται τῆς δίκης ὑπέρτερα.
ΧΟ. ἔμολες ἔμολες, ὦ χρόνιος ἀμέρα, 585
†κατέλαμψας, ἔδειξας ἐμφανῆ
πόλει πυρσὸν, ὃς παλαιᾷ φυγᾷ
πατρῴων ἀπὸ δωμάτων
τάλας ἀλαίνων ἔβα.
θεὸς αὖ θεὸς ἀμετέραν τις ἄγει 590
νίκαν, ὦ φίλα.
ἄνεχε χέρας, ἄνεχε λόγον,
ἵει λιτὰς ἐς θεοὺς
τύχᾳ σοι τύχᾳ κασίγνητον ἐμβατεῦσαι πόλιν. 595
ΟΡ. εἶεν· φίλας μὲν ἡδονὰς ἀσπασμάτων
ἔχω, χρόνῳ δὲ καῦθις αὐτὰ δώσομεν.
σὺ δ', ὦ γεραιὲ, καίριος γὰρ ἤλυθες,
λέξον, τί δρῶν ἂν φονέα τισαίμην πατρὸς
μητέρα τε τὴν κοινωνὸν ἀνοσίων γάμων. 600
ἔστιν τί μοι κατ' Ἄργος εὐμενὲς φίλων;
ἢ πάντ' ἀνεσκευάσμεθ', ὥσπερ αἱ τύχαι;

585—94. This brief ode, consisting chiefly of dochmiacs, which are used to express any kind of excitement, either of joy or grief, may be compared with Rhes. 131, 195. Hipp. 362, 669. There are not many instances in Euripides, but Aeschylus has several such short systems interposed in the middle of a scene, as in the *Suppliants* and *Seven against Thebes*. They are commonly antistrophic.

586. κατέλαμψας, 'you have lighted up and displayed visibly to the city a beacon light (in Orestes), who after a long exile, a wretched wanderer from his father's home, has returned.' Cf. Ion 86, Παρνησιάδες δ' ἄβατοι κορυφαὶ καταλαμπόμεναι, and the note there. Rhes. 43, διϊπετῇ δὲ πυρσοῖς νεῶν σταθμά. Photius, πυρσοί, λαμπάδες, πυρκαϊαί, λαμπτῆρες, φρυκτωρίαι. It is more than probable that ἔδειξας ἐμφανῆ is a mere gloss. We should read thus, ἔλαμψας πόλει πυρσὸν ὃς παλαιᾷ φυγᾷ, two dochmii between a cretic; or, which is better, μέγαν πυρσὸν ὃς κτλ., like μέγαν πανὸν in Agam. 275. The verse as it is commonly given is quite unmetrical.

589. ἔβα Seidler for ἔβασε, and he adds σὲ at the beginning of the next verse, by which, and the omission of τις, a dochmiac verse is gained, at the expense of some difficulties as to the sense.

590. αὖ, a word constantly used when the idea of reverses or a change of fortune is meant. See on Aesch. Theb. 702. 'Now the god is bringing *us* victory in our turn,' as before Aegisthus and Clytemnestra were victorious. This verse is anapaestic; the following are dochmiac.— ἄνεχε χέρας κτλ., 'hold up your hands, raise your voice in prayer, send supplications to the gods, that your brother may have set foot in his native city with good fortune.' — χέρας, as ὑπτιάσματα χερῶν Prom. 1026. The old reading was τύχᾳ, with a full stop after θεοὺς, as if the sense were, τύχη νῦν ἐστὶ κτλ. The sense was restored by Tyrwhitt.—ἐμβατεῦσαι, see Rhes. 225, Λυκίας ναὸν ἐμβατεύων, scil. 'Απόλλων. The aorist is employed somewhat unusually: see on v. 565.

597. δώσομεν for ἀποδώσομεν. He means that he will return the endearments of his sister on a more fitting occasion, his present concern being to revenge himself on his father's murderers.

598. ἤλυθες. A rare form, used Rhes. 660, and Tro. 374.—φονέα, with short ᾰ, is also against the common usage. Cf. v. 763. Hec. 882.

602. ἀνασκευάζειν is 'to pack up for removal,' hence here 'to be ruined.' The word is said to be properly applied to

τῷ συγγένωμαι; νύχιος, ἢ καθ' ἡμέραν;
ποίαν ὁδὸν τραπώμεθ' εἰς ἐχθροὺς ἐμούς;

ΠΡ. ὦ τέκνον, οὐδεὶς δυστυχοῦντί σοι φίλος. 605
εὕρημα γὰρ τὸ χρῆμα γίγνεται τόδε,
κοινῇ μετασχεῖν τἀγαθοῦ καὶ τοῦ κακοῦ.
σὺ δ', ἐκ βάθρων γὰρ πᾶς ἀνῄρησαι φίλοις
οὐδ' ἐλλέλοιπας ἐλπίδ', ἴσθι μου κλύων,
ἐν χειρὶ τῇ σῇ πάντ' ἔχεις καὶ τῇ τύχῃ 610
πατρῷον οἶκον καὶ πόλιν λαβεῖν σέθεν.

ΟΡ. τί δῆτα δρῶντες τοῦδ' ἂν ἐξικοίμεθα;
ΠΡ. κτανὼν Θυέστου παῖδα σήν τε μητέρα.
ΟΡ. ἥκω 'πὶ τόνδε στέφανον, ἀλλὰ πῶς λάβω;
ΠΡ. τειχέων μὲν ἐλθὼν ἐντὸς οὐδ' ἂν εἰ θέλοις. 615
ΟΡ. φρουραῖς κέκασται δεξιαῖς τε δορυφόρων;
ΠΡ. ἔγνως· φοβεῖται γάρ σε κοὐχ εὕδει σαφῶς.
ΟΡ. εἶεν· σὺ δὴ τοὐνθένδε βούλευσον, γέρον.
ΠΡ. κἀμοῦ γ' ἄκουσον· ἄρτι γάρ μ' εἰσῆλθέ τι.
ΟΡ. ἐσθλόν τι μηνύσειας, αἰσθοίμην δ' ἐγώ. 620
ΠΡ. Αἴγισθον εἶδον, ἡνίχ' εἷρπον ἐνθάδε.
ΟΡ. προσηκάμην τὸ ῥηθέν. ἐν ποίοις τόποις;

---

money changers who have failed, and are forced to move their tables.—τῷ συγγένωμαι; 'whose aid should I seek? And should I seek it by night (as a treasonable enterprise) or in open day (as having the Argives in my interest)?' See on Bacch. 485.—Porson would read πῶς ξυγγένωμαι;

605—7. 'My son, no one is a friend to you while you are in misfortune; for truly this is a thing of rare occurrence, (for another) to share one's good and bad fortune in common.' This was a well-known saying; the Romans too were fond of it; *donec eris felix, multos numerabis amicos*, &c.—εὕρημα is, 'a discovery,' 'a piece of luck,' ἑρμαῖόν τι. The infinitive without the article, exegetical of τόδε, is a well-known use; e.g. Aesch. Ag. 585—7.

608. πᾶς ἀνῄρησαι. The meaning is, πάντως ἀνάστατος γέγονας τὸ ἐς τοὺς φίλους, οὐδὲ λοιπὴν ἔχεις ἐλπίδα ἐν τοῖς σαυτοῦ πράγμασιν.—φίλοις is the dative of reference, 'as far as friends are concerned.'—ἴσθι μου κλύων seems to refer to the preceding clause; 'be assured of this,' i.e. if you flatter yourself that, as son of the late king, you still have adherents among the subjects of Aegisthus. —λαβεῖν, for ἀναλαβεῖν, ἀνακομίσασθαι. Compare v. 810.

612. τοῦδε. The genitive is used from the idea of shooting at and hitting a mark, τυγχάνειν. See the notes on Ion 1411, Bacch. 1099. Aesch. Cho. 1022, τόξῳ γὰρ οὔτις πημάτων προσίξεται. Xen. Anab. iii. 3, 7, οἱ ἀκοντισταὶ βραχύτερα ἠκόντιζον ἢ ὡς ἐξικνεῖσθαι τῶν σφενδονητῶν. The meaning is, 'by doing what then can we attain this object?' viz. τοῦ λαβεῖν πόλιν.—Θυέστου παῖδα, Aegisthus: cf. Agam. 1562.

616. κέκασται. A word (from the obsolete κάζομαι, root καδ) rarely used by the Greek dramatists. It occurs in Aesch. Eum. 736, Ar. Equit. 685. Photius, κεκασμένον, κεκοσμημένον.

617. The meaning is, σαφῶς γὰρ φοβεῖταί σε Αἴγισθος, καὶ οὐχ εὕδει διὰ τὸν φόβον.

622. προσηκάμην κτλ., 'I am glad to hear you say so.' Hesychius and Photius,

ΠΡ. ἀγρῶν πέλας τῶνδ' ἱπποφορβίων ἔπι.
ΟΡ. τί δρῶνθ'; ὁρῶ γὰρ ἐλπίδ' ἐξ ἀμηχάνων.
ΠΡ. Νύμφαις ἐπόρσυν' ἔροτιν, ὡς ἔδοξέ μοι.   625
ΟΡ. τροφεῖα παίδων, ἢ πρὸ μέλλοντος τόκου;
ΠΡ. οὐκ οἶδα πλὴν ἕν, βουσφαγεῖν ὡπλίζετο.
ΟΡ. πόσων μετ' ἀνδρῶν; ἢ μόνος δμώων μέτα;
ΠΡ. οὐδεὶς παρῆν Ἀργεῖος, οἰκεία δὲ χείρ.
ΟΡ. οὔ πού τις ὅστις γνωριεῖ μ' ἰδὼν, γέρον;   630
ΠΡ. δμῶες μέν εἰσιν, οἳ σέ γ' οὐκ εἶδόν ποτε.
ΟΡ. ἡμῖν δ' ἂν εἶεν, εἰ κρατοῖμεν, εὐμενεῖς;
ΠΡ. ἄλλων γὰρ ἴδιον τοῦτο, σοὶ δὲ σύμφορον.
ΟΡ. πῶς οὖν ἂν αὐτῷ πλησιασθείην ποτέ;
ΠΡ. στείχων ὅθεν σε βουθυτῶν εἰσόψεται.   635
ΟΡ. ὁδὸν παρ' αὐτὴν, ὡς ἔοικ', ἀγροὺς ἔχει.

προσίεται, ἀρέσκεται, προσδέχεται. Like ἐφίεσθαί τινος, 'to desire,' the word properly means 'to go towards a thing or person,' 'to meet it half way,' 'to receive it with a welcome.'

623. ἱπποφορβίοις may have been the original reading, corrupted on account of τῶνδ', which belongs to ἀγρῶν. The genitive seems to mean, 'on the horse-pasture.' It is not easy to supply πορευόμενον, 'going towards,' &c. Cf. 1343.

625. ἔροτιν. A very rare word, said by Hesychius to be *Cyprian*, but by a gloss in one of the MSS. of this play, *Aeolic*. It appears to be the same word as ἑορτή, by transposition of the ορ. Compare ῥέζειν with ἔρδειν, which is perhaps the true derivation of ἑορτή (for ἑορδή), the aspirate resulting from the initial ῥ. The root seems to be ερδ or ρεδ indifferently.

626. τροφεῖα. Here and in Aesch. Theb. 472, Ion 852, this is for θρέπτρα or θρεπτήρια, elsewhere for τροφήν. The sacrifice to the Nymphs, for having brought up a child from the womb, appears to have been part of the ἀμφιδρόμια, or festival on the eighth day after birth.

628. μόνος δμώων μέτα. The true explanation of this phrase is not, as Markland quoted by Robinson supposes, that μόνος signifies *praecipuus*, but that slaves and servants were οὐδένες in a Greek point of view.

629. οἰκεία χείρ, a band or company of his own domestics. This indicated that he doubted the fidelity of the Argives, and therefore the answer is favourable to Orestes.

631. οἴ σέ γ' Pierson for οὓς ἐγ' (i. e. ἐγώ). The meaning of this verse is obscure. We should have expected δμῶες γάρ εἰσιν, giving a reason why they would not recognize Orestes; and in this case the γε will combine with οἵ in the usual sense of *quippe qui*;—' No, for they are only servants (and *they* will not know you), inasmuch as they never saw you.' As the verse stands, it appears to mean, 'There are indeed servants, but they have never seen *you*' (though they were in the service of Agamemnon in past times). The γε will thus emphasize σέ.

633. δμώων is Porson's conjecture for ἄλλων or δίλων. The *editio princeps* has λέξω γάρ, which Dindorf thinks a conjectural restoration of a corrupt reading. Matthiae and Bothe give δούλων. But ΛΛ is as nearly identical with Μ, as Α is with Δ. Hence Porson's reading is preferable to δούλων. The only doubt is, whether there is not an intentional antithesis between ἄλλων and σοι. Perhaps he wrote, ἄλλων γὰρ ἴδιον ταὐτὸ σοί τε σύμφορον, 'Yes, for that which is to your advantage is also the interest of others.' But the common reading may mean, 'Why, that is the private concern of others, so long as it is to your advantage.'

VOL. II.   Y y

ΠΡ.   ὅθεν γ' ἰδών σε δαιτὶ κοινωνὸν καλεῖ.
ΟΡ.   πικρόν γε συνθοινάτορ', ἢν θεὸς θέλῃ.
ΠΡ.   τοὐνθένδε πρὸς τὸ πίπτον αὐτὸς ἐννόει.
ΟΡ.   καλῶς ἔλεξας.   ἡ τεκοῦσα δ' ἐστὶ ποῦ ;   640
ΠΡ.   Ἄργει· παρέσται δ' †ἐν πόσει θοίνην ἔπι.
ΟΡ.   τί δ' οὐχ ἅμ' ἐξωρμᾶτ' ἐμὴ μήτηρ πόσει ;
ΠΡ.   ψόγον τρέμουσα δημοτῶν ἐλείπετο.
ΟΡ.   ξυνῆχ'· ὕποπτος οὖσα γιγνώσκει πόλει.
ΠΡ.   τοιαῦτα· μισεῖται γὰρ ἀνόσιος γυνή.   645
ΟΡ.   πῶς οὖν ἐκείνην τόνδε τ' ἐν ταὐτῷ κτενῶ ;
ΗΛ.   ἐγὼ φόνον γε μητρὸς ἐξαρτύσομαι.
ΟΡ.   καὶ μὴν ἐκεῖνά γ' ἡ τύχη θήσει καλῶς.
ΗΛ.   ὑπηρετείτω μὲν δυοῖν ὄντοιν ὅδε.
ΠΡ.   ἔσται τάδ'· εὑρίσκεις δὲ μητρὶ πῶς φόνον ;   650
ΗΛ.   [λέγ', ὦ γεραιέ, τάδε Κλυταιμνήστρᾳ μολών·]
        λεχώ μ' ἀπάγγελλ' οὖσαν ἄρσενος τόκῳ.
ΠΡ.   πότερα πάλαι τεκοῦσαν, ἢ νεωστὶ δή ;
ΗΛ.   δέχ' ἡλίους, ἐν οἷσιν ἁγνεύει λεχώ.
ΠΡ.   καὶ δὴ τί τοῦτο μητρὶ προσβάλλει φόνον ;   655

637. καλεῖ. Musgrave remarks that it was the custom to invite all who happened to be near or passing by, to partake in a sacrifice. Hence the old man reckons confidently on an event, which might otherwise have seemed a mere chance.— The γε after ὅθεν was added by Pierson. Barnes also suggested it, though he wrongly preferred ὅθεν ἄν.
639. πρὸς τὸ πίπτον, pro re nata, 'according to circumstances.'
641. ἐν πόσει. This is of course corrupt; and the choice is not easy between ἐν τάχει (so Dind. after Reiske) and ἔτι πόσει, as Bothe edits after Seidler. Perhaps ᾧ πόσει, as the ι ascriptum is known to have often been mistaken for ν, or αὐτίχ' ὡς, (π and τι, os and ως, being easily interchanged.) Barnes also suggested ᾧ, but fancied that ἐν πόσει might mean 'at the drinking.'
643. ψόγον. A term especially applied to reproach cast upon women. See on Tro. 642. Inf. 904. 1039.
647. The γε belongs strictly to μητρός. 'I will make preparation for my mother's death,' you for that of Aegisthus. The reply is, 'Well but that matter (Aegisthus' death) fortune will arrange for us favourably,' viz. if it be true that he is so opportunely preparing a sacrifice.
650. εὑρίσκεις, what plan do you propose? The next verse is rightly marked as spurious by Matthiae. It breaks the order of the monostich dialogue, and is by no means necessary to the context. It was enough to say, 'report to her that I have been delivered of a male child.' Where either τόκος must mean partus, or ἄρσενος τόκος, 'the child of a male,' refers to that doctrine (illustrated on Aesch. Eum. 629), that the male child was generated by the father alone. So Choeph. 493, οἴκτειρε θῆλυν ἄρσενός θ' ὁμοῦ γόνον. Compare inf. v. 934, ὅστις τοῦ μὲν ἄρσενος πατρὸς οὐκ ὠνόμασται, τῆς δὲ μητρὸς ἐν πόλει.
654. δέχ' Elmsley on Heracl. 602 for λέγ'. On this day the thank-offerings to Ἄρτεμις Εἰλείθυια were commonly offered. The Jewish law prescribed the same rite; and in modern society women scruple to appear in public till they have been "churched."
655. καὶ δὴ τί κτλ. 'Well but, sup-

ΗΛ. ἥξει κλύουσα λόχι' ἐμοῦ νοσήματα.
ΠΡ. πόθεν; τί δ' αὐτῇ σοῦ μέλειν δοκεῖς, τέκνον;
ΗΛ. ναί· καὶ δακρύσει γ' ἀξίωμ' ἐμῶν τόκων.
ΠΡ. ἴσως· πάλιν τοι μῦθον ἐς καμπὴν ἄγω.
ΗΛ. ἐλθοῦσα μέντοι δῆλον ὡς ἀπόλλυται. 660
ΠΡ. καὶ μὴν ἐπ' αὐτάς γ' εἰσίτω δόμων πύλας.
ΗΛ. οὐκοῦν τραπέσθαι σμικρὸν εἰς Ἅιδου τόδε.
ΠΡ. εἰ γὰρ θάνοιμι τοῦτ' ἰδὼν ἐγώ ποτε.
ΗΛ. πρώτιστα μέν νυν τῷδ' ὑφήγησαι, γέρον.
ΠΡ. Αἴγισθος ἔνθα νῦν θυηπολεῖ θεοῖς; 665
ΗΛ. ἔπειτ' ἀπαντῶν μητρὶ τἀπ' ἐμοῦ φράσον.
ΠΡ. ὥστ' αὐτά γ' ἐκ σοῦ στόματος εἰρῆσθαι δοκεῖν.
ΗΛ. σὸν ἔργον ἤδη· πρόσθεν εἴληχας φόνου.

posing this happens, how does it bring death to your mother?'

657. The τί belongs to μέλειν, not to δοκεῖς. The reply shows that the question is equivalent to δοκεῖς γὰρ αὐτῇ σοῦ μέλειν; The τί, as it stands first, must be the real point of the interrogation; but it is lost sight of because the purport of the remark is to ascertain Electra's opinion as to her mother's sympathy.

658. δακρύσει γ'. Ironical, as Bothe remarks. Electra knew that such tears could hardly be sincere.—ἀξίωμα is a word of middle signification, and not necessarily used in a good sense. Here it means their social position, in a disparaging sense, though perhaps it is ironical, ' a birth so worthy of my family.'

659. πάλιν—ἄγω. ' Again I bring the question round to the point, viz. how will that effect her death?' The metaphor is from the stadium. Electra's replies appeared vague, and wandering from the point, so he leads her back again to the βαλβὶς or goal. Seidler reads ἄγε, with Musgrave.

661. εἰσίτω Musgrave for εἰσίω. ' Well, then, if her death is as certain as you say, let her come up to the very door of the palace,' before the attack is made. This verse is a sort of stage-excuse for perpetrating the supposed deed out of sight of the spectators. Seidler reads εἰσίω, which he supposes to be the subjunctive of εἰσίημι, ' let me admit her within the gates.' He is followed by Robinson, who ought to have known better than to perpetuate such an error.

662. τόδε, scil. τὸ εἰσιέναι. ' Why that truly would be to take the road to Hades at once.' The full sense would be, οὐκοῦν εἰ τοῦτο δράσει, σμικρὸν ἐστὶ τὸ εἰς Ἅιδου τραπέσθαι. Compare Agam. 1262, where Cassandra, who foreknows that she will enter the palace only to be slain, says Ἅιδου πύλας δὲ τάσδ' ἐγὼ προσεννέπω. Seidler again errs in supposing τραπέσθαι to have a transitive sense, like ἀλλάξαι, ' it is easy to change δόμων πύλας into Ἅιδου πύλας.'

663. ἐγώ. ' If I see this, (servant as I am,) I am content to die.'

664. τῷδ'. First conduct my brother to the place agreed upon (v. 635), then carry the message to my mother (v. 651).

666—7. ἀπαντῶν for πάντων and ὥστ' αὐτὰ for ὡς ταῦτα are the slight but ingenious corrections of Pierson and Elmsley respectively.

668. πρόσθεν εἴληχας. ' The lot of the murder has fallen to you first,' i. e. you, Orestes, are to undertake the first part of the action, to kill Aegisthus; for she had said, v. 647, ἐγὼ φόνον γε μητρὸς ἐξαρτύσομαι. The expression however can best be understood by referring it to the custom of drawing lots as to which of several criminals should die first: see the notes on Agam. 1271. Heracl. 970. Ar. Pac. 364, ἀπόλωλας, ὦ κακόδαιμον. ΤΡ. οὐκοῦν, ἢν λάχω· Ἑρμῆς γὰρ ἂν κλήρῳ ποιήσεις, οἶδ' ὅτι. But in this case it appears to be transferred from the πάσχων to the δρῶν.

ΟΡ. στείχοιμ' ἄν, εἴ τις ἡγεμὼν γίγνοιθ' ὁδοῦ.
ΠΡ. καὶ μὴν ἐγὼ πέμποιμ' ἂν οὐκ ἀκουσίως.   670
ΟΡ. ὦ Ζεῦ πατρῷε καὶ τροπαῖ' ἐχθρῶν ἐμῶν,
     οἴκτειρέ θ' ἡμᾶς, οἰκτρὰ γὰρ πεπόνθαμεν,
ΗΛ. οἴκτειρε δῆτα σούς γε φύντας ἐκγόνους.
ΟΡ. Ἥρα τε, βωμῶν ἣ Μυκηναίων κρατεῖς,
     νίκην δὸς ἡμῖν, εἰ δίκαι' αἰτούμεθα.   675
ΗΛ. δὸς δῆτα πατρὸς τοῖσδε τιμωρὸν δίκην.
ΟΡ. σύ τ', ὦ κάτω γῆς ἀνοσίως οἰκῶν, πάτερ,
     [καὶ Γῆ τ' ἄνασσα, χεῖρας ᾗ δίδωμ' ἐμὰς,]
     ἄμυν' ἄμυνε τοῖσδε φιλτάτοις τέκνοις.
     [νῦν πάντα νεκρὸν ἐλθὲ σύμμαχον λαβών,   680
     οἵπερ γε σὺν σοὶ Φρύγας ἀνάλωσαν δορί,
     χὤσοι στυγοῦσιν ἀνοσίους μιάστορας.]
     ἤκουσας, ὦ δείν' ἐξ ἐμῆς μητρὸς παθῶν;

670. καὶ μὴν ἐγὼ κτλ. 'Why truly *I* would not be sorry to escort you myself;' or, 'well, then, I will conduct you, by no means unwillingly.'

671. Ζεῦ πατρῷε. See Porson's note on Med. 1314. Properly speaking, Ζεὺς πατρῷος was not worshipped at Athens; in allusion to which Aeschylus said in the *Niobe* (frag. 146), that the Phrygians had an altar of Ζεὺς πατρῷος in the air. Here, of course, he is invoked as the god who avenges the outraged name of *Father*, and τροπαῖος as the supreme power who can give victory to those who defend the just cause. The τε in the next verse appears to be answered by Ἥρα τε in 674,—σύ τε οἴκτειρε ἡμᾶς, Ἥρα τε νίκην δός. Others read οἴκτειρ' ἔθ' ἡμᾶς, but the ἔτι is at least as awkwardly added as the τε. The goddess who was the patroness of the Argive race, as well as the wife of Zeus, is not less appropriately invoked.

673. σοῦ Barnes for σούς, and ἐκ γένους L. Dindorf for ἐκγόνους. But the correction here can hardly be considered a necessary one, since φύντας may represent ὄντας or γενομένους.

676. This verse should perhaps be assigned to the πρέσβυς, as well as v. 673. Yet it is clear that there are three actors in this scene; and τοῖσδε may refer to Orestes and the old man.—τιμωρὸν δίκην is a combination which occurs Soph. frag. 94, v. 9. Aesch. Cho. 136.

678. This verse, Matthiae observes, is probably spurious: at all events καὶ Γῆ τε is not good Greek. Bothe reads καὶ Γαῖ' ἄνασσα, and transposes this verse to follow v. 675. But this is contrary to the rigid law of the στιχομυθία, by which Orestes speaks *two* verses there as in the speech next but one preceding, 671—2. Aeschylus, it may be remarked, makes Orestes to invoke Earth, Cho. 480, ὦ Γαῖ, ἄνες μοι πατέρ' ἐποπτεῦσαι μάχην, but in conformity with his peculiar views of Earth being itself a power which could either detain or send up the souls of heroes to assist their relations in life. But here the very un-Greek phrase, χεῖρας διδόναι for χεῖρας προτείνειν, is conclusive against the genuineness of the verse. The simple fact is, that the whole passage, v. 680 to 682, is also an interpolation; and the only wonder is, that it has not been condemned before. To those intimately acquainted with the style of Euripides it is unnecessary to point out in detail the many feeble and incorrect expressions, such as καὶ Γῆ τε, οἵπερ γε, χὤσοι, &c. If accumulated proof were wanting, it would be found in the fact that the genuine verse, 683, occurs in the old copies before v. 682. For the sense, compare Aesch. Cho. 486, ΟΡ. ἆρ' ἐξεγείρει τοῖσδ' ὀνείδεσιν, πάτερ; ΗΛ. ἆρ' ὀρθὸν αἴρεις φίλτατον τὸ σὸν κάρα;

ΗΛΕΚΤΡΑ. 349

ΗΛ. πάντ', οἶδ', ἀκούει τάδε πατήρ· στείχειν δ' ἀκμή·
καί σοι προφωνῶ πρὸς τάδ' Αἴγισθον θανεῖν, 685
ὡς, εἰ παλαισθεὶς πτῶμα θανάσιμον πεσεῖ,
τέθνηκα κἀγώ, μηδέ με ζῶσαν λέγε·
παίσω κάρα γὰρ τοὐμὸν ἀμφήκει ξίφει.
δόμων δ' ἔσω βᾶσ' εὐτρεπὲς ποιήσομαι·
ὡς, ἢν μὲν ἔλθῃ πύστις εὐτυχὴς σέθεν, 690
ὀλολύξεται πᾶν δῶμα, θνήσκοντος δέ σου
τἀναντί' ἔσται τῶνδε· ταῦτά σοι λέγω.
ΟΡ. πάντ' οἶδα.
ΗΛ.   πρὸς τάδ' ἄνδρα γίγνεσθαί σε χρή.
ὑμεῖς δέ μοι, γυναῖκες, εὖ πυρσεύετε
κραυγὴν ἀγῶνος τοῦδε· φρουρήσω δ' ἐγὼ 695
πρόχειρον ἔγχος χειρὶ βαστάζουσ' ἐμῇ·
οὐ γάρ ποτ' ἐχθροῖς τοῖς ἐμοῖς νικωμένη

685. πρὸς τάδε (sup. 274) is here used for διὰ τοῦτο, or τοῦδε ἔνεκα, and the following ὡς is to be closely connected with it. The phrase πρὸς τάδε (Theb. 301. Eum. 516), or πρὸς ταῦτα (Prom. 1051), is much more common at the beginning of a sentence, 'wherefore,' 'on this account,' &c. The commentators do not seem to have rightly apprehended the meaning, which is as if she had said σοι πρὸς τάδε βλέποντι, 'on this account too I declare to you that Aegisthus must die, namely, because if *you* shall fall a deathfall being defeated in the contest, I too am dead.' She urges the certainty of her own suicide, if he should fail, as an additional motive for ensuring success. Bothe thinks the sense is, καὶ προσέτι προφωνῶ σοι τάδε, *et praeterea hoc tibi edico*; but it seems impossible to separate πρὸς τάδε. Moreover, the same phrase is repeated by Electra, by way of enforcing it, in v. 693.— Properly, προφωνεῖν is to speak with the fore-warning voice of a god, as Aesch. Eum. 444. ἄλγη προφωνῶν ἀντίκεντρα καρδίᾳ, but it is applied to the prediction of a king to his people, *id.* Suppl. 610, Ἱκεσίου Διὸς κότον μέγαν προφωνῶν.
689. εὐτρ. ποιήσομαι. See on Bacch. 440. Barnes appears right in supplying ξίφος, for this is implied in v. 692.
691. ὀλολύξεται, 'shall resound with a joyful female cry' (the ὀλολυγή). Compare Iph. T. 367, αὐλεῖται δὲ πᾶν μέλαθρον. Bacch. 593, Βρόμιος ὃς ἀλαλάξεται στέγης ἔσω.—δέ σου Dindorf, with the *ed. princeps.* Barnes has δὲ σοῦ, which has as good a sense, 'if *you* die' instead of Aegisthus.—τἀναντία τῶνδε, a euphemism for θρῆνος γενήσεται.—πύστις, 'tidings,' an uncommon word in the singular. Theb. 54, καὶ τῶνδε πύστις οὐκ ὄκνῳ χρονίζεται.
694. εὖ πυρσεύετε. 'Send me accurate intelligence of the cry arising from this contest,' viz. whether it is the deathcry of Aegisthus and the triumph of Orestes, or the contrary. The metaphor is taken from communicating news by beacons. Dobree well renders it, (or rather, compares with it the modern expression,) 'send me intelligence by telegraph.' On πυρσεύειν see Hel. 1126. Seidler cites Suidas, πυρσεύω σοι τὴν σωτηρίαν, ἀντὶ τοῦ ἐκφαίνω. An easy correction, were correction necessary, would be πορεύσατε, which scarcely involves any change but the transposition of the σ. And it must be confessed, that πυρσεύετε is here both a harsh and a strange expression, as Barnes felt, when he freely avowed himself unable to explain it. The chief argument in its favour is, that momentary intelligence was required of a conflict at a considerable distance; cf. v. 754.
697. οὐ γάρ ποτ' κτλ. 'For I will

350   ΕΥΡΙΠΙΔΟΥ

δίκην ὑφέξω σῶμ' ἐμὸν καθυβρίσαι.
ΧΟ. ἀταλᾶς ὑπὸ ματέρος   στρ. α'.
     Ἀργείων ὀρέων ποτὲ κληδὼν   700
     ἐν πολιαῖσι μένει φήμαις
     εὐαρμόστοις ἐν καλάμοις
     Πᾶνα μοῦσαν ἡδύθροον

never, by being conquered, allow my enemies to take satisfaction so as to insult my person.' See v. 757.

699—746. Orestes has departed on his mission, escorted by the old servant. Electra has retired within the cottage. The chorus then sings a stasimon on the legend of the golden ram. This story is not mentioned by Apollodorus; Lucian alludes to it, περὶ τῆς ἀστρολογίης, Vol. ii. p. 365, and explains it to mean that Thyestes first pointed out to the Argives the constellation Aries, while Atreus taught them that the earth and the sun pursue contrary orbits, so that what seems to be the setting is really the rising. Robinson quotes the Latin version of the tale, as given by Cicero de Nat. Deorum, 'Addo huc, quod mihi portento caelestum pater Prodigium misit regnum stabilimen mei; Agnum inter pecudes aurea clarum coma Quondam Thyestem clepere ausum [est] e regia, Qua in re adjutricem conjugem cepit sibi.' The legend is given at length by the Scholiast on Orest. 810 :—" Atreus and Thyestes were sons of Pelops. Now Atreus, being jealous of his half-brother Chrysippus, who was greatly beloved by his father, drowned him in a well. Pelops, discovering this, banished Atreus; but he returned after his father's death, and both the brothers laid claim to the throne, Atreus, as the elder, and the legal successor, Thyestes, as an usurper in defiance of the laws. Accordingly they made an agreement, that whichever of them should be able to exhibit some portent, he should be put in possession of the kingdom. Now among the flocks of Atreus there was found a golden lamb; and just as Atreus was about to exhibit the prodigy to the judges, and so to assume the sovereignty, his wife Aerope, who was then living in adultery with Thyestes, stole it, and gave it to her paramour. Thyestes then, having got the lamb, and produced it before the umpires, became master of the empire.

Atreus however, indignant at being unjustly superseded, not only took summary vengeance on Aerope for her adultery and her theft, by throwing her into the sea; but also the three sons of Thyestes, Aglaus, Orchomenus, and Caleus, he slew and served up at dinner to their own father; after which he killed Thyestes himself. For which impious deeds the Sun, not being able to endure such a violation of all law, for one day turned his course back, from west to east; and with him the Pleiads pursued an opposite path."—The above is as nearly as possible a summary of the ensuing ode, which is highly elegant, and on the whole is less difficult and corrupt than are many others. The metres are rather various; but they partake generally of a glyconic character.

Ibid. ἀταλᾶς, an epic form of ἀπαλᾶς, used also in Pers. 539.—ματρὸς for ματέρος, and in the next verse Ἀργηΐων for Ἀργείων are W. Dindorf's metrical corrections. Neither is necessary; the middle syllable of Ἀργείων is perhaps short, as οὐρείᾳ is a cretic in Troad. 532, and elsewhere. The genitive of course depends on the sense of ὑπὲκ, as Hecub. 53, περᾷ γὰρ ἤδ' ὑπὸ σκηνῆς πόδα. Andr. 441, ὑπὸ πτερῶν σπάσας. With ὀρέων the preposition is omitted, as it often is, e. g. Suppl. 496, Καπανέως κεραύνιον δέμας καπνοῦται κλιμάκων. Both genitives directly follow πορεῦσαι in v. 705. Translate:—' The story yet prevails in ancient legends, that once on a time Pan, the guardian of the fields, breathing a sweetly-sounding strain on well-compacted reeds (the Pan-pipe), took from under its tender mother and brought from the hills of Argos a lamb beautiful with golden fleece.' —πολιαὶ φῆμαι, as πολιῷ νόμῳ, by long-established law, Aesch. Suppl. 657.— ὀρέων, the shepherds' strong-holds in the mountains. See on v. 210. Pan is here mentioned merely as the protector of herds and flocks.

ΗΛΕΚΤΡΑ. 351

πνέοντ', ἀγρῶν ταμίαν,
χρυσέαν ἄρνα καλλιπλόκαμον πορεῦσαι·   705
πετρίνοις τ' ἐπιστὰς
κᾶρυξ ἰάχει βάθροις,
ἀγορὰν ἀγορὰν, Μυκηναῖοι,
στείχετε μακαρίων ὀψόμενοι τυράννων   710
φάσματα, δείματα.
χοροὶ δ' Ἀτρειδᾶν ἐγέραιρον οἴκους·
θυμέλαι δ' ἐπίτναντο χρυσ-   ἀντ. α'.
ήλατοι, σελαγεῖτο δ' ἀν' ἄστυ
πῦρ ἐπιβώμιον Ἀργείων·   715
λωτὸς δὲ φθόγγον κελάδει
κάλλιστον, Μουσᾶν θεράπων·
μολπαὶ δ' ηὔξοντ' ἐραταὶ
χρυσέας ἀρνὸς, ὡς †ἐπίλογοι Θνέστου·
κρυφίαις γὰρ εὐναῖς   720

706—11. 'And standing on rocky steps the herald cried aloud, *To the Agora, the Agora go, ye people of Mycenae, to see the portents, the causes of alarm, of the fortunate rulers!*' The people were summoned because, as one may fairly infer from the words of the Scholiast already quoted, the trial was to be a public one. In πέτρινα βάθρα there is probably an allusion to the βῆμα or λίθος in the Athenian Pnyx. The portent of the golden lamb is called δείματα, because, as there were two claimants of the throne, what was the hope of the one was the terror of the other. Erfurdt would read κῶμοι for χοροί, and this correction might be defended by Alcest. 343, παύσω δὲ κώμους συμποτῶν θ' ὁμιλίας. As the text stands, v. 711 may be regarded as a dochmiac; but W. Dindorf is probably right in arranging φάσματα—οἴκους as one verse. The antistrophe seems to be quite free from corruption, so that either χοροί or δείματα is liable to suspicion.—The ι in ἰάχει is short, and therefore the augment must be regarded as omitted.

712—19. 'And then the companies of dancers did honour to the house of the Atridae, and the gold-wrought thymelae were carpet-spread, and there blazed throughout the city fires on the Argive altars; and the pipe sounded its sweetest notes, that servant of the Muses, and delightful songs were composed about the golden lamb, how that *the fortune of the day is to Thyestes.*' Matthiae seems wrong in supposing that χοροί alludes to supplicatory or expiatory ceremonies, " ad placandam iram deorum, quae agno aureo portendi videbatur." The triumph of Thyestes, in whose cause the decision was given, is manifestly described. He had defeated his brother Atreus by a fraud, and now he shows his joy by a great feast and a public sacrifice.—θυμέλαι, properly the altar steps, or rather the platform (κρηπὶς) on which the sacrificer stood, and which perhaps was covered over with embroidered tapestries on great occasions. Cf. Aesch. Suppl. 652, καὶ γεραροῖσι πρεσβυτοδόκοι γερόντων θυμέλαι φλεγόντων (where γεραροῖσι remarkably coincides with ἐγέραιρον in this place) — ἐπίτναντο, an imperfect from πετάννυμαι, through the bye-form πίτναμαι.

714. σελαγεῖτο. The passive form occurs (see Hel. 1434) in Ar. Nub. 285, ὄμμα γὰρ αἰθέρος ἀκάματον σελαγεῖται μαρμαρέαις ἐν αὐγαῖς. So κτυπεῖσθαι Plut. 758.

719. The word ἐπίλογοι is corrupt. W. Dindorf adopts Seidler's ὡς ἐστὶ λόγος Θνέστου, but the sense rather requires ὡς ἐστὶ λάχος or πάλος Θνέστου, 'that the luck is to Thyestes.' Compare Pers. 775, κἀγὼ πάλου τ' ἔκυρσα, τοῦπερ ἤθελον.

720—25. 'For by a secret intercourse

πείσας ἄλοχον φίλαν
Ἀτρέως, τέρας ἐκκομίζει πρὸς
δώματα· νεόμενος δ' εἰς ἀγόρους ἀΰτει
τὰν κερόεσσαν ἔ-
χειν χρυσόμαλλον κατὰ δῶμα ποίμναν. 725
τότε δὴ τότε φαεννὰς   στρ. β'.
ἄστρων μετέβασ' ὁδοὺς
Ζεὺς καὶ φέγγος ἀελίου
λευκόν τε πρόσωπον ἀοῦς, 730
τὰ δ' ἕσπερα νῶτ' ἐλαύνει
θερμᾷ φλογὶ θεοπύρῳ,
νεφέλαι δ' ἔνυδροι πρὸς ἄρκτον
ξηραί τ' Ἀμμωνίδες ἕδραι

having gained over the dear wife of Atreus (Aerope), he conveys away the portent to his own house; and coming before the public he called out, *That he has got the horned lamb with the golden fleece in his house.*'—ἄγορος is perhaps the same as ὄχλος. Hesychius explains it by ἄθροισμα, στρατός. It occurs Herc. F. 412, Andr. 1037, Iph. A. 1096, ποθοῦσ' Ἑλλάνων ἀγόρους.—ἀΰτει should possibly be given for ἀΰτει, on account of the preceding ἐκκομίζει.

726—36. 'Then truly, then it was that Zeus changed the bright courses of the stars, the light of the sun, and the grey countenance of the morning, and drove his car over the back of the western sky with hot and heaven-kindled flame: and (now) there are watery clouds in the north, and the dry seats of Ammon fail, not being accustomed to dew, now that they are deprived of the beautifying showers from Zeus.'— μετέβασ', i. e. μετέβησε, is Musgrave's correction for μεταβὰς or μεταβάλλει. On the use of the first aorist, which is not common, see Alcest. 1055. Bacch. 466. The metres of this concluding strophe and antistrophe, correctly given in the old editions, have been perversely changed, without any conceivable reason, by Seidler, who is followed in W. Dindorf's edition.—For the miracle here described, compare Ovid, Trist. ii. 391, 'Si non Aeropen frater sceleratus amasset, Aversos solis non legeremus equos.' Orest. 1001, ὅθεν ἔρις τό τε πτερωτὸν | ἁλίου μετέβαλεν ἅρμα, | τὰν πρὸς ἑσπέραν κέλευθον | οὐρανοῦ προσαρμόσασα | μονόπωλον ἐς ἀῶ, | ἑπταπόρου τε δρόμημα Πελειάδος | εἰς ὁδὸν ἄλλαν Ζεὺς μεταβαίνει.

731. νῶτα. The accusative of transition over. See Hel. 598.—θερμᾷ Dobree for θερμά. In the next verse the glyconic metre requires that θεοπύρῳ should be a word of three syllables, as θεομανὲς probably is in Aesch. Theb. 650.

733. ἔνυδροι. The poet evidently means, that a contrary state of things followed from the contrary course of the sun; the parts of the world hitherto dry were now wet, and those which were wet now became dry; and he regards these effects as permanent, and the phenomenon itself as accounting for the present state of certain parts of the world. Hence Libya is presumed to have had all its moisture dried up by this sudden change, while the north, hitherto bound in ice and snow, now became supplied with water. The temple of Jupiter Ammon, which is situated in the oasis, and only surrounded by waterless deserts, was early known to the Greeks, from the celebrity of its oracle. The same phrase, as here, occurs Alcest. 115. It is twice mentioned by Aristophanes, Av. 619 and 716, in both places in conjunction with Delphi, and three times by Herodotus, i. 46, ii. 32 and 55.—ἀπειρόδροσοι Hermann and Bothe for ἄπειροι δρόσου. A similar compound is ἀπειρόδακρυς, Aesch. Suppl. 68. The meaning appears to be, that *because* it had no dew, it was drained of all its moisture when it lost the rain.

ΗΛΕΚΤΡΑ. 353

φθίνουσ' ἀπειρόδροσοι,   735
καλλίστων ὄμβρων διόθεν στερεῖσαι.
λέγεται, τὰν δὲ πίστιν   ἀντ. β'.
σμικρὰν παρ' ἔμοιγ' ἔχει,
στρέψαι θερμὰν ἀέλιον
χρυσωπὸν ἕδραν ἀλλάξαν-   740
τα δυστυχίᾳ βροτείῳ
θνατᾶς ἕνεκεν δίκας.
φοβεροὶ δὲ βροτοῖσι μῦθοι
κέρδος πρὸς θεῶν θεραπείας·
ὧν οὐ μνασθεῖσα πόσιν   745
κτείνεις, κλεινῶν συγγενέτειρ' ἀδελφῶν.
ἔα ἔα·
φίλαι, βοῆς ἠκούσατ', ἢ δοκῶ κενὴ
ὑπῆλθέ μ', ὥστε νερτέρα βροντὴ Διός;
ἰδοὺ τάδ' οὐκ ἄσημα πνεύματ' αἴρεται·

737—46. ' 'Tis said, but the credence which it obtains with me is small, that the Sun turned in the opposite direction his hotly-glowing golden throne, having changed it to the discomfort of mankind on account of a dispute between mortal men. However, legends of fear are salutary to men for promoting the worship of the gods. Yet of those gods you have no remembrance in slaying your husband, O common mother of illustrious brethren' (Orestes and Electra).—For τὰν δὲ Porson would read τάδε δέ. Neither reading well suits a glyconean verse, which might be restored by λέγεται, τὸ δὲ πίστιν, and in the strophe, v. 726, τότε δὴ τότε φανὰς, or λαμπρὰς, κτλ.—ἀέλιον is Canter's reading for ἀελίου. W. Dindorf condemns as both unmetrical and unmeaning the words ἀλλάξαντα—βροτείῳ, and attributes them to the patchwork of a grammarian to fill up a lacuna. There is however little ground for the suspicion. The glyconean verse is not incapable of the spondee following the choriambus, and the dative δυστυχίᾳ, for εἰς δυστυχίαν, is not without precedent. Cf. Thucyd. iii. 82, ξυμμαχίας ἅμα ἑκατέροις τῇ τῶν ἐναντίων κακώσει.

743. μῦθοι, fables, false tales, as in Hipp. 198, μύθοις δ' ἄλλως φερόμεσθα. The sentiment is somewhat Pindaric. It contains a remarkable confession of a doctrine which has been variously received by thinking people, that stories calculated to inspire awe, though not true in themselves, tend to good in their influence over illiterate minds, when presented to them as if really true.

745. ὧν, scil. τῶν θεῶν.—συγγενέτειρα, a word perhaps used only here, for γενέτειρα συνδυοῖν ἀδελφοῖν. Clytemnestra is meant, who is the common mother of two worthy children. Musgrave takes the σὺν for σὺν τῷ πόσει.

747. δοκῶ, δόξα or δόκησις. Similar forms are ἠχὼ and μελλὼ for μέλλησις, Agam. 1327.—νερτέρα βροντὴ, the usual phrase for the subterranean rumbling that precedes or accompanies an earthquake. As timid ears were apt to refer every vague and indistinct sound to this cause, the fitness of the comparison is apparent. —The iambic lines, from ἔα ἔα, are spoken by the Hegemon alone, as is clear from ὑπῆλθέ με, and the address to the rest of the chorus as φίλαι.

749. τάδε. Emphatic: 'Hark! *this* gale (i. e. a voice rising and dying away at intervals) rises by no means indistinct.' By αἴρεται the chorus seems to mean μείζω γίγνεται. — ἄμειψον, ' leave the house.' See on Bacch. 65. Aesch. Cho. 562, εἰ δ' οὖν ἀμείψω βαλὸν ἕρκειον πυλῶν.

VOL. II.   Z Z

δέσποιν', ἄμειψον δώματ', Ἠλέκτρα, τάδε.   750
ΗΛ. φίλαι, τί χρῆμα ; πῶς ἀγῶνος ἥκομεν ;
ΧΟ. οὐκ οἶδα πλὴν ἕν, φόνιον οἰμωγὴν κλύω.
ΗΛ. ἤκουσα κἀγώ, τηλόθεν μὲν, ἀλλ' ὅμως.
ΧΟ. μακρὰν γὰρ ἕρπει γῆρυς, ἐμφανής γε μήν.
ΗΛ. Ἀργεῖος ὁ στεναγμὸς, ἢ φίλων ἐμῶν ;   755
ΧΟ. οὐκ οἶδα· πᾶν γὰρ μίγνυται μέλος βοῆς.
ΗΛ. σφαγὴν ἀϋτεῖς τήνδε μοι· τί μέλλομεν ;
ΧΟ. ἔπισχε, τρανῶς ὡς μάθῃς τύχας σέθεν.
ΗΛ. οὐκ ἔστι· νικώμεσθα· ποῦ γὰρ ἄγγελοι ;
ΧΟ. ἥξουσιν· οὔτοι βασιλέα φαῦλον κτανεῖν.   760

ΑΓΓΕΛΟΣ.

ὦ καλλίνικοι παρθένοι Μυκηνίδες,
νικῶντ' Ὀρέστην πᾶσιν ἀγγέλλω φίλοις,
Ἀγαμέμνονος δὲ φονέα κείμενον πέδῳ
Αἴγισθον· ἀλλὰ θεοῖσιν εὔχεσθαι χρεών.
ΗΛ. τίς δ' εἶ σύ ; πῶς μοι πιστὰ σημαίνεις τάδε ;   765
ΑΓ. οὐκ οἶσθ' ἀδελφοῦ μ' εἰσορῶσα πρόσπολον ;
ΗΛ. ὦ φίλτατ', ἔκ τοι δείματος δυσγνωσίαν
εἶχον προσώπου· νῦν δὲ γιγνώσκω σε δή.
τί φῄς ; τέθνηκε πατρὸς ἐμοῦ στυγνὸς φονεύς ;
ΑΓ. τέθνηκε· δίς σοι ταῦθ', ἃ γοῦν βούλει, λέγω.   770

751. πῶς ἀγῶνος; Compare Hel. 313, πῶς δ' εὐμενείας τοισίδ' ἐν δόμοις ἔχεις; 'How have we fared in the contest?' or, 'How have we come off from,' &c.
754. μακρὰν γάρ. 'For the voice proceeds from a distance; nevertheless it is plain.' Cf. Agam. 1348, ἐμοὶ δ' ἀγὼν ὅδ' οὐκ ἀφρόντιστος πάλαι νίκης παλαιᾶς ἦλθε, σὺν χρόνῳ γε μήν.—Ἀργεῖος, that of Aegisthus. It must be confessed that there is not much probability in making the conflict between Orestes and Aegisthus, which took place at some distance (ἀγρῶν πέλας τῶνδ', v. 623; cf. v. 777), audible to those on the stage. The chorus had before been requested to bring the earliest intimation conveyed by the sound (v. 694), but neither they nor Electra had any certainty that either cries or uproar would attend the death of the tyrant. The truth is, neither time nor space is accurately accounted for in tragedy. Hence in the Helena, v. 1662, the Dioscuri address Helen and Menelaus from the stage, though they are far out at sea.
757. σφαγὴν κτλ. 'In saying this (viz. that there is yet no distinct note of victory) you bid me kill myself.' She had threatened this in case of failure, at v. 696.—τί μέλλομεν; viz. παίειν, which is implied in her gesture.
760. οὔτοι κτλ. ''Tis no trifling matter to slay a king,' and besides, there are body-guards, servants, porters, &c., to pass, before clear tidings can be gained.
763. φονέα. For the ἅ see sup. v. 599.
770. ταῦθ' Portus for ταῦθ'. Seidler and Dindorf are wrong in rejecting this emendation, by which alone γοῦν (γ' οὖν Elmsley) has its proper meaning, 'I say

ΧΟ. ὦ θεοί, Δίκη τε πάνθ' ὁρῶσ', ἦλθές ποτε.
ΗΛ. ποίῳ τρόπῳ δὲ καὶ τίνι ῥυθμῷ φόνου
κτείνει Θυέστου παῖδα βούλομαι μαθεῖν.
ΑΓ. ἐπεὶ μελάθρων τῶνδ' ἀπήραμεν πόδα,
εἰσβάντες ἦμεν δίκροτον εἰς ἁμαξιτὸν 775
ἔνθ' ἦν ὁ κλεινὸς τῶν Μυκηναίων ἄναξ.
κυρεῖ δὲ κήποις ἐν καταρρύτοις βεβὼς,
δρέπων τερείνης μυρσίνης κάρα πλόκους·
ἰδών τ' αὔτεῖ, χαίρετ', ὦ ξένοι· τίνες;
πόθεν πορεύεσθ' ἔστε τ' ἐκ ποίας χθονός; 780
ὁ δ' εἶπ' Ὀρέστης, Θεσσαλοί· πρὸς δ' Ἀλφεὸν
θύσοντες ἐρχόμεσθ' Ὀλυμπίῳ Διΐ.
κλύων δὲ ταῦτ' Αἴγισθος ἐννέπει τάδε·
νῦν μὲν παρ' ἡμῖν χρὴ συνεστίους ἐμοὶ

twice over such news at least as you *wish* to hear,' i. e. because you wish it. The precision and brevity of Greek speech was such, that δὶς ταὐτὸ λέγειν was commonly thought a fault requiring some excuse. Compare Ar. Ran. 1154, δὶς ταὐτὸν ἡμῖν εἶπεν ὁ σοφὸς Αἰσχύλος. Ibid. 1178, κἂν που δὶς εἴπω ταὐτὸν,—κατάπτυσον.

774. πόδα. As this word is very often added after words of *going*, even though properly neuter, as ἐλθεῖν, βαίνειν πόδα, sup. v. 941, it seems probable that ἀπαίρειν here retains its usual intransitive sense of ἀπελθεῖν, as in Med. 938. Cf. Iph. T. 967, νικῶν δ' ἀπῇρα φόνια πειρατήρια, ' I came away victorious in the trial for murder.' —ἦμεν, for ᾔειμεν. Cf. Androm. 1102. So προσῇτε Xen. Anab. vii. 6, 24. ᾖσθ' for ᾔεις Agam. 494.—δίκροτος ἁμαξιτὸς appears to be a road with double wheel-tracks, i. e. wide enough for two chariots to run abreast.

777. κυρεῖ δὲ κτλ. ' Now he happened at the moment to be walking in an irrigated pleasure-ground, culling wreaths of tender myrtle for his head,' viz. to be worn during the ceremonies of the sacrifice. The construction of τυγχάνειν or κυρεῖν with a participle implies rather the coincidence of one event with another in respect of time, than mere *chance* in the occurrence. Cf. inf. 785.—κήποις, not ' gardens ' (in our sense of the word) so much as ornamental grounds, planted with shady trees, and watered by artificial channels from a neighbouring stream (παροχετεύειν, *derivare*). This latter feature was probably essential to a κῆπος, whence Hippol. 78, Αἰδὼς δὲ ποταμίαισι κηπεύει δρόσοις. The same idea is expressed in Frag. 452, in the description which he gave of Messenia in the *Cresphontes*, κατάρρυτον μυρίοισι νάμασι. Photius, κῆπος καὶ παράδεισος διαφόρως παρ' αὐτοῖς (read παρὰ τοῖς αὐτοῖς) λέγεται. It is rather a rare word, and so is the adjective τέρην. Aesch. Suppl. 975, τέρειν' ὀπώρα. Med. 905, ὄψιν τέρειναν.

780. The old reading πορεύεσθέ τ' was happily corrected by Musgrave. The error arose from a common confusion between ἔτι and ἐστὶ, and the ἔστε being absorbed by the previous termination εσθε. Barnes gives πόθεν πορεύεσθόν τε κἀκ ποίας χθονός; after Canter. Various corrections have been proposed; but the above must satisfy every reasonable critic. Robinson thinks the passage hopelessly corrupt. The position of the article in the next verse may be compared with Hel. 1025, τὴν μέν σ' ἐᾶσαι πατρίδα νοστῆσαι Κύπριν. The invitation of Aegisthus had happened just as the old man had predicted in v. 637.—The form Ἀλφεὸς, collaterally with Ἀλφειὸς, shows the tendency of the Greeks to pronounce such diphthongs as ει and αι short; thus we have Ἀκταίων and Ἀκτέων, Bacch. 337; and so παλεὸς for παλαιὸς, sup. v. 497, has some analogy in its favour.

θοίνη γενέσθαι· τυγχάνω δὲ βουθυτῶν 785
Νύμφαις· ἑῷοι δ' ἐξαναστάντες λέχους
ἐς ταὐτὸν ἥξετ'· ἀλλ' ἴωμεν ἐς δόμους.
καὶ ταῦθ' ἅμ' ἠγόρευε καὶ χερὸς λαβὼν
παρῆγεν ἡμᾶς, οὐδ' ἀπαρνεῖσθαι χρεών.
ἐπεὶ δ' ἐν οἴκοις ἦμεν, ἐννέπει τάδε· 790
λούτρ' ὡς τάχιστα τοῖς ξένοις τις αἱρέτω,
ὡς ἀμφὶ βωμὸν στῶσι χερνίβων πέλας.
ἀλλ' εἶπ' Ὀρέστης, ἀρτίως ἡγνίσμεθα
λουτροῖσι καθαροῖς ποταμίων ῥείθρων ἄπο.
εἰ δὲ ξένους ἀστοῖσι συνθύειν χρεών, 795
Αἴγισθ', ἕτοιμοι, κοὐκ ἀπαρνούμεσθ', ἄναξ.
τοῦτον μὲν οὖν μεθεῖσαν ἐκ μέσου λόγον·
λόγχας δὲ θέντες, δεσπότου φρουρήματα,
δμῶες, πρὸς ἔργον πάντες ἴεσαν χέρας.
οἱ μὲν σφαγεῖον ἔφερον, οἱ δ' ἦρον κανᾶ, 800
ἄλλοι δὲ πῦρ ἀνῆπτον ἀμφί τ' ἐσχάρας
λέβητας ὤρθουν· πᾶσα δ' ἐκτύπει στέγη.
λαβὼν δὲ προχύτας μητρὸς εὐνέτης σέθεν
ἔβαλλε βωμούς, τοιάδ' ἐννέπων ἔπη·

785. θοίνῃ Seidler for θοίνην. Barnes not very improbably edits θοίνην πένεσθαι, from the Homeric δαῖτ' ἐπένοντο, &c.
787. ἐς ταὐτόν. To the same place you would have arrived at if you had not been detained by me. With the next verse compare Bacch. 1082, and the proverb ἅμ' ἔπος καὶ ἔργον.
789. χρεών. This is part of Aegisthus' speech, ' and you must not refuse me;' unless, perhaps, on account of παρῆγεν, he purposely avoided the more natural word παρῆν.
791. λουτρά. For the preliminary purification, before the χέρνιψ or lustral water was sprinkled on the altar and the company present; cf. Ar. Pac. 956, 961. Aesch. Ag. 1004. It may be asked, Why did Orestes formally decline the offer of water? Probably because, if he once enlisted himself among the *worshippers* at the altar, he would have felt the murder he intended to commit to be a sacrilegious act. So conversely, those who had already committed any such crime were not permitted to share in the χέρνιψ.

796. ἕτοιμοι, scil. ἐσμέν, a frequent ellipse. Cf. Med. 612.—ἐκ μέσου, apart from the company; in private conference with the king.
800. σφαγεῖον, the vessel to receive the victim's blood; κανοῦν (κανεὸν) the circular basket or *canister* containing the sacred meal and the sacrificial knife. The old reading, σφάγι' ἐνέφερον, was corrected by Scaliger. Photius, σφαγεῖον, τὸ ἀγγεῖον εἰς ὃ τὸ αἷμα τῶν σφαζομένων ἱερείων δέχονται.
802. Robinson compares Med. 1179, ἅπασα δὲ στέγη πυκνοῖσιν ἐκτύπει δρομήμασιν.
803. προχύτας. These were the barley-grains (ὀλαί) out of the κανοῦν. Compare Ar. Pac. 962, καὶ τοῖς θεαταῖς ῥίπτε τῶν κριθῶν. It is clear from both these passages that the grain was tossed about; but the meaning of the ceremony is lost in remote antiquity. It indicates some union between the offering of bloody sacrifices and of the fruits of the earth.

Νύμφαι πετραῖαι, πολλάκις με βουθυτεῖν 805
καὶ τὴν κατ' οἴκους Τυνδαρίδα δάμαρτ' ἐμὴν,
πράσσοντας ὡς νῦν, τοὺς δ' ἐμοὺς ἐχθροὺς κακῶς·
λέγων Ὀρέστην καὶ σέ· δεσπότης δ' ἐμὸς
τἀναντί' ηὔχετ', οὐ γεγωνίσκων λόγους,
λαβεῖν πατρῷα δώματ'. ἐκ κανοῦ δ' ἑλὼν 810
Αἴγισθος ὀρθὴν σφαγίδα, μοσχίαν τρίχα
τεμὼν, ἐφ' ἁγνὸν πῦρ ἔθηκε δεξιᾷ,
κἄσφαξ', ἐπ' ὤμων μόσχον ὡς ἦραν χεροῖν
δμῶες· λέγει δὲ σῷ κασιγνήτῳ τάδε·
ἐκ τῶν καλῶν κομποῦσι τοῖσι Θεσσαλοῖς 815
εἶναι τόδ', ὅστις ταῦρον ἀρταμεῖ καλῶς
ἵππους τ' ὀχμάζει. λάβε σίδηρον, ὦ ξένε,
δεῖξόν τε φήμην ἔτυμον ἀμφὶ Θεσσαλῶν.
ὁ δ' εὐκρότητον Δωρίδ' ἁρπάσας χεροῖν,
ῥίψας ἀπ' ὤμων εὐπρεπῆ πορπάματα, 820
Πυλάδην μὲν εἵλετ' ἐν πόνοις ὑπηρέτην,
δμῶας δ' ἀπωθεῖ· καὶ λαβὼν μόσχου πόδα
λευκὰς ἐγύμνου σάρκας, ἐκτείνων χέρα·
θᾶσσον δὲ βύρσαν ἐξέδειρεν ἢ δρομεὺς

805. βουθυτεῖν, scil. δότε. Compare Suppl. 3.
809. γεγωνίσκων, 'speaking audibly.' See on Prom. 645, τί δῆτα μέλλεις μὴ οὐ γεγωνίσκειν τὸ πᾶν;
811. ὀρθὴν, straight in the blade, not curved like a sabre. The custom of cutting a tuft of hair from the victim is mentioned Alcest. 76; the raising the animal on the shoulders while the throat is cut, Hel. 1562.
816. ἀρταμεῖ, Alcest. 494, 'dismembers.' Connected, perhaps, with *artus*.—ὀχμάζει, 'breaks,' πωλοδαμνεῖ. Photius, ὀχμάζεται, συνέχεται, χειροῦται. Properly, to fasten or constrain in such a position as to prevent struggles, τὸ σφαδάζειν. Compare Orest. 265. Prom. 5. 636. Musgrave appositely cites a Doric treatise on καλὸν and αἰσχρὸν, in which it is stated Θεσσαλοῖσι δὲ καλὸν τὼς ἵππως ἐκ τᾶς ἀγέλας λαβόντι αὐτὼς σφάξαι, καὶ ἐκδεῖραι, καὶ κατακόψαι. So far from imposing any menial service, this was evidently designed as a privilege and a compliment. On the poet's part, it is of course a device for getting a convenient weapon into the hands of Orestes.

818. ἔτυμον, scil. οὖσαν.
819. εὐκρότητον Δωρίδα, 'a well-hammered Dorian *blade*.' The grammarians, Seidler remarks, seem to have thought the word was δορὶς, from δέρειν 'to flay.' But it is clearly only an adjective; compare v. 836. The substantive is omitted from familiar use, just as the chivalrous youth in more recent times called a sword "a Toledo." Compare the use of χαλυβδικὸν for ξίφος, in Heracl. 161.—Soph. Antig. 430, ἐξ εὐκροτήτου χαλκέας ἄρδην πρόχου.
820. πορπάματα. The 'gracefully-buckled scarf' (Rhes. 442) is the *chlamys*, which was commonly worn hanging down the back, and fastened on the breast by a clasp or brooch. It is well illustrated in the 'Dictionary of Antiquities,' art. *Chlamys*.
823. λευκάς. The foot and shin of the calf appear quite white when freshly skinned.

δισσοὺς διαύλους ἱππίους διήνυσε, 825
κἀνεῖτο λαγόνας. ἱρὰ δ' ἐς χεῖρας λαβὼν
Αἴγισθος ἤθρει. καὶ λοβὸς μὲν οὐ προσῆν
σπλάγχνοις, πύλαι δὲ καὶ δοχαὶ χολῆς πέλας
κακὰς ἔφαινον τῷ σκοποῦντι προσβολάς.
χὠ μὲν σκυθράζει, δεσπότης δ' ἀνιστορεῖ, 830
τί χρῆμ' ἀθυμεῖς, ὦ ξέν'; Ὀρρωδῶ τινα
δόλον θυραῖον. ἔστι δ' ἔχθιστος βροτῶν
Ἀγαμέμνονος παῖς πολέμιός τ' ἐμοῖς δόμοις.
ὁ δ' εἶπε, φυγάδος δῆτα δειμαίνεις δόλον,
πόλεως ἀνάσσων; οὐχ, ὅπως πευστηρίαν 835

825. ἱππίους. Dindorf, after Musgrave, gives ἵππιος, but the *runner* is not on a horse (κέλης), but on foot, though the length of the heat, twice up and twice down the course, was that commonly performed on horseback, as appears from both Pollux and Pausanias, quoted by Musgrave. See, for the δίαυλος, Aesch. Agam. 335: on the stadium as a measure of time, Med. 1181. Wordsworth remarks (*Athens and Attica*, p. 158, where he adduces the present passage), that it was in sight of the theatre, from which it lay eastward, across and on the bank of the Ilissus.

826. ἀνεῖτο. Musgrave quotes Hesychius, ἀνιέναι, δέρειν, and Od. ii. 300, μνηστῆρας—αἶγας ἀνιεμένους σιάλους θ' εὔοντας ἐν αὐλῇ. The idea is evidently derived from the notion of relaxing the tightness of the skin, which gapes in the place where an incision is made.

827. λοβός. The lobe or compartment of the liver (σπλάγχνον, any of the large organs) was wanting, which was a portentous omen. The feature here meant is the *lobus quadratus* (not *lobus Spigelii*), which is adjacent to the gall-bladder, and (in the human subject at least) is sometimes so slightly defined as to appear to be altogether wanting.—πύλαι, the large vein which conveys the chyle to the liver. Aristot. Hist. An. i. 17, διὰ γὰρ τοῦ ἥπατος διέχει ἡ ἀπὸ τῆς μεγάλης φλεβὸς φλέψ, ᾗ αἱ καλούμεναι Πύλαι εἰσὶ τοῦ ἥπατος. It is still called the *portal vein*, and is situated nearly in the centre of that organ, in a line with the gall-bladder, δοχαὶ χολῆς.—πέλας ἔφαινον, scil. οὔσας, 'showed that a hostile attack was at hand for him who was inspecting them.' Cf. Choeph. 275, ἄλλας τε φωνεῖν προσβολὰς Ἐρινύων, 'assaults of the Furies,' the word being properly used of the grasp of a wrestler.

830. σκυθράζει, 'frowns,' σκυθρωπάζει. It was Aegisthus who did this; the *master* is Orestes, whose servant the messenger had been (v. 766). He, therefore, addresses Aegisthus as ὦ ξένε, and Aegisthus replies, Ὀρρωδῶ κτλ.

835. πευστηρίαν, viz. θοίνην or θυσίαν. *Sacrificium exploratorium*, Seidler, who compares ἱλαστήρια, σωτήρια, and might have added χαριστήρια. The occurrence of the neuter plural in these words makes it doubtful whether we should not here read πευστήρια. Orestes intended evidently to arm himself with a heavier weapon; and therefore he asks for a chopper or cleaver (κοπίς) to cut open the ribs, in order to lay bare some other of the internal organs besides the liver, though the same general term σπλάγχνα is again employed, v. 838.—ἀπορρήξω is probably the hortative subjunctive, ἀπορρῆξαι θέλω. But Musgrave with some reason proposes ἀπορρῆξαι.—χέλυς, the arched hollow of the breast, so called from the resemblance to a tortoise-shell. Barnes quotes from Pollux, ii. 77, νώτων τοίνυν ὑπ' αὐχένι κειμένων, τὸ μὲν ἔγκυρτον χελώνιον ὀνομάζεται. To do this required a strong and very sharp knife. The κοπίς seems to have been curved, like a scimetar, and so is contrasted with ὀρθὴ σφαγίς, v. 811. Robinson quotes Q. Curtius, viii. 14, 29, '*Copidas* vocant (Thraces) gladios leviter curvatos falcibus similes, quibus appetebant belluarum manus.'—Φθιάδα, i. e. Thessalian,—the national knife of the pretended strangers, v. 781.

ΗΛΕΚΤΡΑ. 359

θοινασόμεσθα, Φθιάδ᾽ ἀντὶ Δωρικῆς
οἴσει τις ἡμῖν κοπίδ᾽; ἀπορρήξω χέλυν.
λαβὼν δὲ κόπτει. σπλάγχνα δ᾽ Αἴγισθος λαβὼν
ἤθρει διαιρῶν. τοῦ δὲ νεύοντος κάτω,
ὄνυχας ἐπ᾽ ἄκρους στὰς κασίγνητος σέθεν   840
ἐς σφονδύλους ἔπαισε, νωτιαῖα δὲ
ἔρρηξεν ἄρθρα. πᾶν δὲ σῶμ᾽ ἄνω κάτω
ἤσπαιρεν, ἠλάλαζε δυσθνήσκων φόνῳ.
δμῶες δ᾽ ἰδόντες εὐθὺς ᾖξαν ἐς δόρυ,
πολλοὶ μάχεσθαι πρὸς δύ᾽. ἀνδρείας δ᾽ ὕπο   845
ἔστησαν ἀντίπρωρα σείοντες βέλη
Πυλάδης Ὀρέστης τ᾽. εἶπε δ᾽, οὐχὶ δυσμενὴς
ἥκω πόλει τῇδ᾽, οὐδ᾽ ἐμοῖς ὀπάοσι,
φονέα δὲ πατρὸς ἀντετιμωρησάμην
τλήμων Ὀρέστης. ἀλλὰ μή με κτείνετε,   850
πατρὸς παλαιοὶ δμῶες. οἱ δ᾽, ἐπεὶ λόγων
ἤκουσαν, ἔσχον κάμακας· ἐγνώσθη δ᾽ ὑπὸ
γέροντος ἐν δόμοισιν ἀρχαίου τινός.
στέφουσι δ᾽ εὐθὺς σοῦ κασιγνήτου κάρα
χαίροντες, ἀλαλάζοντες. ἔρχεται δὲ σοὶ   855
κάρα ᾽πιδείξων, οὐχὶ Γοργόνος φέρων,
ἀλλ᾽ ὃν στυγεῖς Αἴγισθον· αἷμα δ᾽ αἵματος
πικρὸς δανεισμὸς ἦλθε τῷ θανόντι νῦν.
XO. θὲς ἐς χορὸν, ὦ φίλα, ἴχνος,   στρ.

841. σφονδύλους, the vertebrae, Phoen. 1413. The spinal marrow was cut, and so the body quivered with convulsive twitchings.

843. δυσθνήσκων. The old reading was δυσθνῇσκον, but this does not appear tenable, because the body could not be said ἀλαλάζειν, but the man himself. The alteration was made by those who took πᾶν σῶμα for the nominative, whereas the sense is, 'he quivered in his whole frame, and uttered a cry as he died hard from the slaughter.' This is better than the exceedingly bold alteration of Valckenaer, ἐσφάδαζε, which W. Dindorf adopts. It must be confessed that the word ἀλαλάζειν, meaning a *joyful cry* (*inf.* 855. Bacch. 593), is open to some suspicion. Compare however the similar use of ἀνολολύζειν in Soph. Electr. 750.—On the form δυσθνήσκω see Rhes. 791.

849. δὲ for τε is Porson's necessary correction.

852. ἔσχον κάμακας, i. e. κατέσχον λόγχας. Cf. Rhes. 60, οὐκ ἂν ἔσχον εὐτυχοῦν δόρυ.

857. αἷμα κτλ., 'blood has come as a bitter repayment for blood to him who has now been put to death.' A metaphor from the loans of usurers.

859. The chorus, overjoyed at the news of the death of Aegisthus, call upon Electra to join them in the dance and the song. But she, in a more solemn mood, merely expresses her fervent thanks for the victory, and proposes to crown the head of her brother, as that of a conqueror at the games. To this they assent, re-

ὡς νεβρὸς, οὐράνιον 860
πήδημα κουφίζουσα σὺν ἀγλαΐᾳ.
νικᾷ στεφαναφορίαν
κρείσσω παρ' Ἀλφειοῦ ῥεέθροις τελέσας
κασίγνητος σέθεν· ἀλλ' ἐπάειδε
καλλίνικον ᾠδὰν ἐμῷ χορῷ. 865

ΗΛ. ὦ φέγγος, ὦ τέθριππον ἡλίου σέλας,
ὦ γαῖα καὶ νύξ, ἣν ἐδερκόμην πάρος,
νῦν ὄμμα τοὐμὸν ἀμπτυχαί τ' ἐλεύθεροι,
ἐπεὶ πατρὸς πέπτωκεν Αἴγισθος φονεύς.
φέρ', οἷα δὴ 'χω καὶ δόμοι κεύθουσί μου 870
κόμης ἀγάλματ' ἐξενέγκωμαι, φίλαι,
στέψω τ' ἀδελφοῦ κρᾶτα τοῦ νικηφόρου.

ΧΟ. σὺ μέν νυν ἀγάλματ' ἄειρε ἀντ.
κρατί· τὸ δ' ἀμέτερον
χωρήσεται Μούσαισι χόρευμα φίλον. 875
νῦν οἱ πάρος ἀμέτεροι

serving for themselves the proper province of expressing joy by tone and step.

861. κουφίζουσα. Seidler well compares Suppl. 1047, δύστηνον αἰώρημα κουφίζω, πάτερ. Intransitively, of a light and nimble step, Hel. 1555.

862. νικᾷ Canter for νίκας. The Doric στεφαναφορίαν is adopted by W. Dindorf from two Florence MSS., the *ed. princeps* having στεφανοφορίαν, against the metre. Musgrave proposed στεφανηφορίαν. Theocritus has στεφανηφόροι, Id. xvi. 47.—For κρείσσω W. Dindorf, with incredible audacity, gives οἴαν, which, so far from improving the sense, only renders the passage more perplexing. The oldest edition, with the MSS., adds τοῖς, which Canter altered to τῆς. This would give a good and simple sense, 'Your brother is victorious in a prize-fight greater than that at Olympia, having accomplished (his purpose);' but it is not easy to supply a corresponding syllable in v. 878, besides that the metre appears to be the same as in v. 861, *iambelegus*. Hence the article must be considered as an intrusion. Bothe gives τελέτας, 'greater than the festival at Olympia,' quoting Pind. Ol. 10. 53, and Nem. 10. 33. This emendation is not without considerable probability; for the omission of the article (τῆς παρ' Ἀ. ῥ.) see on Ion 377. The poet evidently alludes to v. 781, where the strangers had pretended to be going to Olympia. If the text be right, the sense appears to be, 'Your brother is victorious in an Olympian contest, greater (than the real one).'—τελέσας, supply αὐτήν.

868. ἀμπτυχαὶ, the unfolding of the light, i. e. the sun of safety as opposed to the night of grief. Cf. Ion 1445, ἰὼ ἰὼ λαμπρᾶς αἰθέρος ἀμπτυχαί. Or ὄμμα ἀμπτυχαί τε may possibly be an instance of ἓν διὰ δυοῖν, for ὄμματος ἀναπτυχαί, the opening of my eye to behold the light. Reiske ingeniously conjectured ἀμπνοαί, 'now I can both see and breathe freely.'

870. δὴ 'χω for δὴ 'γὼ is Canter's emendation.—κεύθουσι, 'have in store.' See above, v. 359. Hec. 880.

875. χωρήσεται suits the metre better than Seidler's conjecture χορεύσεται, besides that the latter is decidedly tame. The meaning is, προβήσεται, ὁρμήσει, and Μούσαισι φίλον implies that it shall be a μολπή, dancing accompanied with music. The middle future of χωρεῖν occurs in Suppl. 588.

876. οἱ πάρος κτλ., for οἱ πρόσθεν ἡμέτεροι ὄντες.—βασιλῆς, the true Attic

ΗΛΕΚΤΡΑ. 361

γαίας τυραννεύσουσι φίλοι βασιλῆς,
δικαίως τοὺς ἀδίκους καθελόντες.
ἀλλ' ἴτω ξύναυλος βοὰ χαρᾷ.
ΗΛ. ὦ καλλίνικε, πατρὸς ἐκ νικηφόρου 880
γεγὼς, Ὀρέστα, τῆς ὑπ' Ἰλίῳ μάχης,
δέξαι κόμης σῆς βοστρύχων ἀνδήματα.
ἥκεις γὰρ οὐκ ἀχρεῖον ἔκπλεθρον δραμὼν
ἀγῶν' ἐς οἴκους, ἀλλὰ πολέμιον κτανὼν
Αἴγισθον, ὃς σὸν πατέρα κἀμὸν ὤλεσε. 885
σύ τ', ὦ παρασπίστ', ἀνδρὸς εὐσεβεστάτου
παίδευμα, Πυλάδη, στέφανον ἐξ ἐμῆς χερὸς
δέχου· φέρει γὰρ καὶ σὺ τῷδ' ἴσον μέρος
ἀγῶνος· ἀεὶ δ' εὐτυχεῖς φαίνοισθέ μοι.
ΟΡ. θεοὺς μὲν ἡγοῦ πρῶτον, Ἠλέκτρα, τύχης 890
ἀρχηγέτας τῆσδ', εἶτα κἄμ' ἐπαίνεσον
τὸν τῶν θεῶν τε τῆς τύχης θ' ὑπηρέτην.
ἥκω γὰρ οὐ λόγοισιν, ἀλλ' ἔργοις κτανὼν
Αἴγισθον· ὡς δὲ τῷ σάφ' εἰδέναι τάδε

form, is Seidler's reading for βασιλῆες.— τοὺς for τούσδ' is Matthiae's correction.— ἀλλ' ἴτω κτλ., 'proceed then the shout which is attuned to joy,' i. e. the female cry ὀλολυγή, properly used on the successful event of a sacrifice.
880. Orestes, whose near approach, with the gory head of Aegisthus, had been announced by the messenger at v. 855, is now present with Pylades on the stage, attended perhaps by servants bearing the body (v. 959). His sister advances to place a crown upon his brows.—νικηφόρου μάχης, i. e. μάχην νικήσαντος.
882. ἀνδήματα Blomfield on Theb. 740, for ἀναδήματα. This simple emendation is amply supported by such forms as ἀνδαίοντες Agam. 296, ἐπανδιπλοίζω Eum. 970 (Hermann's certain metrical correction for ἐπιδιπλοίζω). Probably in the similar passage, Hippol. 82, χρυσέας κόμης ἄνδημα δέξαι is to be restored for the vulg. ἀνάδημα, for in his earlier plays Euripides rarely adopts the licence of an initial anapaest. Bothe, in a long note, labours to show that the present verse is not a senarius, but an *asynartete* or irregular lyrical one, interposed to express her mental emotions. It is to be observed however that this ῥῆσις of Electra is strictly antithetical to the following one of Orestes, each containing ten verses.
883. ἔκπλεθρον ἀγῶνα, the race in the stadium of six plethra (about 600 feet). See the note on Med. 1181. Supra, v. 825. 'You have returned,' says Electra, 'not having run a race in vain, but victorious over our father's murderer.'
887. παίδευμα, not for παῖς, but for παιδευθεὶς ὑπὸ ἀνδρὸς, viz. by Strophius his father. It was at his house (Agam. 854) that Orestes contracted his enduring friendship with Pylades. Cf. Hipp. 11, Ἱππόλυτος, ἁγνοῦ Πιτθέως παιδεύματα. —μέρος ἀγῶνος, a share in the prize of the contest.
894. Dindorf, Seidler, and Bothe, adopt Barnes' reading, ὡς δέ τῳ σάφ' εἰδέναι τάδε προθῶμεν, *ut autem cuivis clare haec proponamus*. This is specious; but a little consideration will show that it is nothing more. In the first place, Euripides would hardly have said, 'that *one* may know it, I bring *you* the dead body,' but rather σοι σάφ' εἰδέναι and νῦν φέρω. Secondly, πρόθες is rather awkwardly repeated in a somewhat different sense in

VOL. II. 3 A

ΕΥΡΙΠΙΔΟΥ

προσθῶμεν, αὐτὸν τὸν θανόντα σοι φέρω, 895
ὅν, εἴτε χρῄζεις, θηρσὶν ἁρπαγὴν πρόθες,
ἢ σκῦλον οἰωνοῖσιν, αἰθέρος τέκνοις,
πήξασ᾽ ἔρεισον σκόλοπι· σὸς γάρ ἐστι νῦν
δοῦλος, πάροιθε δεσπότης κεκλημένος.

ΗΛ. αἰσχύνομαι μέν, βούλομαι δ᾽ εἰπεῖν ὅμως. 900
ΟΡ. τί χρῆμα, λέξον, ὡς φόβου γ᾽ ἔξωθεν εἶ.
ΗΛ. νεκροὺς ὑβρίζειν, μή μέ τις φθόνῳ βάλῃ.
ΟΡ. οὐκ ἔστιν οὐδεὶς ὅστις ἄν μέμψαιτό σοι.
ΗΛ. δυσάρεστος ἡμῶν καὶ φιλόψογος πόλις.
ΟΡ. λέγ᾽, εἴ τι χρῄζεις, σύγγον᾽· ἀσπόνδοισι γὰρ 905
νόμοισιν ἔχθραν τῷδε συμβεβλήκαμεν.
ΗΛ. εἶεν· τίν᾽ ἀρχὴν πρῶτά σ᾽ ἐξείπω κακῶν;

the very next verse. Bothe objects, that "incerta confirmanda sunt, non certa;" and he seems to think this fatal to the old reading, which means, 'but, that I may add this ocular proof (τάδε τεκμήρια) to the certain knowledge you already have from my words, I bring you this head of Aegisthus,' which he now perhaps holds out to her in the cloth in which it had been wrapped. He had said just above, οὐ λόγοισιν ἀλλ᾽ ἔργοις κτανών, and so he now intends to say, οὐ λόγῳ ἀλλ᾽ ἔργῳ δηλώμεν. In other words he might have said, οἶσθα μὲν σαφῶς, ὅμως δὲ τόδε τῷ λόγῳ τεκμήριον προσθήσω.

898. σκόλοπι. Cf. Rhes. 514, πυλῶν ἐπ᾽ ἐξόδοισιν ἀμπείρας ῥάχιν στήσω πετεινοῖς γυψὶ θοινατήριον.

899. κεκλημένος, whom you before spoke of by the odious name of *master*. Robinson repeats here the erroneous opinion already alluded to at v. 366.

901. τί χρῆμα, scil. αἰσχύνει, not εἰπεῖν βούλει, for these last words allude to her desire to make a speech over her dead enemy, as at v. 907.

902. φθόνῳ βάλῃ, 'strike me with an evil eye,' look on me with detestation. *Tanquam telo me petat*, Matthiae. That such is the literal sense is clear from Agam. 920, μή τις πρόσωθεν ὄμματος βάλοι φθόνος. *Ib.* v. 454, βάλλεται γὰρ ὄσσοις Διόθεν κεραυνός, 'an envious (i. e. angry) glance is darted from the eye of Zeus.' Photius, ὀφθαλμίσαι, φθονῆσαι. Seidler is hardly right in explaining the present phrase by μή μέ τις βάλῃ εἰς φθόνον, though this might apply to Trach.

940, ὥς νιν ματαίως αἰτίᾳ βάλοι κακῇ, which is more properly to be rendered, 'that he had groundlessly assailed her with an evil charge.'—The *invidiousness* she fears is not, as Barnes supposes, from the exposing Aegisthus' head to the birds and beasts, but the speaking ill of a dead enemy. It is clearly this last that she calls νεκροὺς ὑβρίζειν.

904. ἡμῶν. Perhaps ἡμῖν, scil. ταῖς γυναιξί, for ψόγος, as remarked on v. 643, is especially used of women's character. If the genitive is right, it must be taken with πόλις. *Morosa est nostra, et ad convicia proclivis civitas*, Barnes.

905. ἀσπόνδοις νόμοις, 'on terms which allow of no truce,' or which demand no consideration on the part of the victor towards his vanquished foe. So Agam. 1206, ἄσπονδον ἀρὰν (or Ἀρην).—συμβαλεῖν ἔχθραν, for συνάπτειν, Med. 44.

907. The speech of Electra over the corpse of Aegisthus (see below on v. 961) is perhaps open to the charge of vindictiveness. Neither Aeschylus nor Sophocles has introduced this scene, though the former makes Orestes address the spectators in defence of his conduct, in presence (as some think) of the corpses of Clytemnestra and Aegisthus, Choeph. 960 seqq. And there indeed he inveighs against his mother in terms of the strongest reprobation. It was natural for Electra, though perhaps it does not tend to exalt her character, to give vent to her long-concealed feelings against her persecutor. To do so was in fact to excuse her participation in the murder; for unless the

ποίας τελευτάς ; τίνα μέσον τάξω λόγον ;
καὶ μὴν δι' ὄρθρων γ' οὔποτ' ἐξελίμπανον
θρυλοῦσ', ἅ γ' εἰπεῖν ἤθελον κατ' ὄμμα σὸν,   910
εἰ δὴ γενοίμην δειμάτων ἐλευθέρα
τῶν πρόσθε· νῦν οὖν ἐσμέν· ἀποδώσω δέ σοι
ἐκεῖν' ἅ σε ζῶντ' ἤθελον λέξαι κακά.
ἀπώλεσάς με κὠρφανὴν φίλου πατρὸς
καὶ τόνδ' ἔθηκας, οὐδὲν ἠδικημένος,   915
κἄγημας αἰσχρῶς μητέρ', ἄνδρα τ' ἔκτανες
στρατηλατοῦνθ' Ἕλλησιν, οὐκ ἐλθὼν Φρύγας.
ἐς τοῦτο δ' ἦλθες ἀμαθίας ὥστ' ἤλπισας
ὡς ἐς σὲ μὲν δὴ μητέρ' οὐχ ἕξεις κακὴν
γήμας, ἐμοῦ δὲ πατρὸς ἠδίκεις λέχη.   920
ἴστω δ', ὅταν τις διολέσας δάμαρτά του
κρυπταῖσιν εὐναῖς εἶτ' ἀναγκασθῇ λαβεῖν,

audience knew what she had suffered from him, neither could they know the justice of her revenge. The Greeks had peculiar ideas on this subject, which cannot fairly be tested by the views of modern society. Electra had something to *pay*, and she could now only pay it in words. Nor do those words contain any unseemly violence. They are rather reflections of a general nature on the relative characters, as they ought to be developed, in man and woman. On the whole, this ῥῆσις is well conceived; Electra shows a high spirit and a sound judgment, without either mere spite or the affectation of pedantry. The occasion is one of those which Euripides delights to avail himself of, both for a display of rhetoric and for remarks on the female character. Consequently it is one of those which are well worthy of study as being especially indicative of the mind and feelings of the poet.

Ibid. Instead of the more usual, τί κακὸν λέγω σε; 'what evil shall I say of you?' the enlarged phrase is used, equivalent to τί πρῶτον εἴπω σε, τί δ' ὕστατον;—μέσον τάξω is to be taken together, ἐν μέσῳ θῶμαι. Barnes compares Od. ix. 14, τί πρῶτον, τί δ' ἔπειτα, τί δ' ὑστάτιον καταλέξω;

909. καὶ μὴν, 'yet truly.' There is little need, she says, for hesitation, for she had long practised and considered her speech in the early dawn of the mornings. See v. 86—91. Tro. 182. Suppl. 978. The form ἐκλιμπάνειν occurs also Med. 800.— θρυλοῦσα, μελετῶσα, ὑμνοῦσα. Photius, θρυλεῖ, λαλεῖ, κυκᾷ.—κατ' ὄμμα, to your face. See Rhes. 371. Androm. 1064.

915. οὐδὲν ἠδικημένος. The Greek considered τὸ ἄρξαι ἀδικίας the point upon which justice or injustice entirely turned, in estimating injury done to another.

917. στρατηλατοῦντα. Aeschylus makes Orestes dwell particularly on the captaincy of his father, as greatly aggravating the crime of Aegisthus, Eum. 434. 595. Compare Agam. 1605.

918. ἐς τοῦτο δ' κτλ. 'But at such an excess of folly did you arrive, that you expected that towards yourself indeed you would not find my mother to be base, while you wronged the bed of my father,' i. e. caused her to act basely towards her rightful lord. It would be easy to read ἕξοις, which would better suit the past tenses ἤλπισας and ἠδίκεις. The following is a fine and a just reflection. 'But let a man know, when, after seducing another's wife by a clandestine connexion, he is himself compelled to take her, (that) he is miserably deceived if he supposes her in the former case (alone) not to have chastity, but to have it in alliance with himself.'—παρ' οἷ, rather unusual for παρ' ἑαυτῷ.

δύστηνός ἐστιν, εἰ δοκεῖ τὸ σωφρονεῖν
ἐκεῖ μὲν αὐτὴν οὐκ ἔχειν, παρ' οἷ δ' ἔχειν.
ἄλγιστα δ' ᾤκεις, οὐ δοκῶν οἰκεῖν κακῶς· 925
ᾔδησθα γὰρ δῆτ' ἀνόσιον γήμας γάμον,
μήτηρ δὲ σ' ἄνδρα δυσσεβῆ κεκτημένη.
ἄμφω πονηρὼ δ' ὄντ' ἀφαιρεῖσθον τύχην,
κείνη τε τὴν σὴν καὶ σὺ τοὐκείνης κακόν.
πᾶσιν δ' ἐν Ἀργείοισιν ἤκουες τάδε· 930
ὁ τῆς γυναικὸς, οὐχὶ τἀνδρὸς ἡ γυνή.
καίτοι τόδ' αἰσχρὸν, προστατεῖν γε δωμάτων
γυναῖκα, μὴ τὸν ἄνδρα· κἀκείνους στυγῶ
τοὺς παῖδας, ὅστις τοῦ μὲν ἄρσενος πατρὸς
οὐκ ὠνόμασται, τῆς δὲ μητρὸς ἐν πόλει. 935
ἐπίσημα γὰρ γήμαντι καὶ μείζω λέχη

925. οὐ δοκῶν. 'Though you seemed to others not to be living amiss.' For this use of οὐ δοκεῖν = δοκεῖν μή, see Med. 67, and compare also Prom. 393, κέρδιστον εὖ φρονοῦντα μὴ δοκεῖν φρονεῖν, ''tis best to be really wise, but to seem not to be so.' The reason of this secret distress,—of all seeming fair without while it was unsound within,—was the consciousness, on his part of having unlawfully married her, on her part of possessing an impious man for a husband. Why he is called δυσσεβής, as an adulterer, is clear enough. Aeschylus attaches to him some share in the murder of Agamemnon; and the two crimes together certainly made up the character of δυσσέβεια, 'unrighteousness.'

928. ἄμφω κτλ. 'And being together bad, you take away from each other, she your fortune (i. e. all that you had worth sharing), and you her criminality.' You have therefore lost all by your marriage, and have gained nothing from her in return, except the being identified with her in her crime; and so you are πονηρὸς as much as she. She has deprived you of your ἀγαθὴ τύχη, and you have got her κακὴ τύχη. The sense therefore is, κείνη τε πονηρὰ οὖσα ἀφαιρεῖται τὴν σὴν τύχην, καὶ σὺ πονηρὸς ὢν ἀφαιρεῖ τὸ ἐκείνης κακόν. If the poet did not mean this, it is hard to say what he did mean; for Seidler's explanation, " infelices eratis ambo, alter ex alterius scelere," and Bothe's " auferebatis (he should at least have said aufertis) tanquam praemium vobis dignum," give to ἀφαιρεῖσθαι the sense of φέρεσθαι, which it will not bear. Robinson, whose notes are filled with scraps of schoolboy information borrowed from Porson, Blomfield, and Monk, seldom or never has a word to say on a really difficult passage like the present.

930—7. Another reason why Aegisthus must have been secretly unhappy. The Argive people did not speak of *Aegisthus and Clytemnestra*, but of *Clytemnestra and Aegisthus*. He was regarded as the inferior, as taking the second part in the management of domestic and political affairs. So Aeschylus attributes to him θήλεια φρήν, Cho. 297, and calls him λέων ἄναλκις, Agam. 1195. Sophocles, El. 301, describes him as πάντ' ἄναλκις, and as fighting only by the aid of women (σὺν γυναιξί. Cf. Agam. 1622).

933. μὴ τὸν ἄνδρα. By a similar idiom we should say, 'a woman and not the man,' or 'a wife and not the husband,' the definite article attaching to the superior κατ' ἐξοχήν. See however on v. 390.

934. τοῦ μὲν ἄρσενος. See the note on v. 650. Translate, 'who is called in the city not the son of his father, who is the male, but of his mother,' who, according to the idea expressed in Orest. 552, is merely the nurse or recipient of the male's offspring.

936—7. These verses contain a shrewd

τἀνδρὸς μὲν οὐδείς, τῶν δὲ θηλειῶν λόγος.
ὃ δ' ἠπάτα σε πλεῖστον οὐκ ἐγνωκότα,
ηὔχεις τις εἶναι, τοῖσι χρήμασι σθένων·
τὰ δ' οὐδὲν εἰ μὴ βραχὺν ὁμιλῆσαι χρόνον.   910
ἡ γὰρ φύσις βέβαιος, οὐ τὰ χρήματα.
ἡ μὲν γὰρ ἀεὶ παραμένουσ' αἴρει κάρα·
ὁ δ' ὄλβος ἄδικος καὶ μετὰ σκαιῶν ξυνὼν
ἐξέπτατ' οἴκων, σμικρὸν ἀνθήσας χρόνον.
ἃ δ' ἐς γυναῖκας, παρθένῳ γὰρ οὐ καλὸν   945
λέγειν, σιωπῶ, γνωρίμως δ' αἰνίξομαι.
ὕβριζες, ὡς δὴ βασιλικοὺς ἔχων δόμους
κάλλει τ' ἀραρώς. ἀλλ' ἔμοιγ' εἴη πόσις
μὴ παρθενωπός, ἀλλὰ τἀνδρείου τρόπου.
τὰ γὰρ τέκν' αὐτῶν Ἄρεος ἐκκρεμάννυται,   950
τὰ δ' εὐπρεπῆ δὴ κόσμος ἐν χοροῖς μόνον.
ἔρρ', οὐδὲν εἰδὼς ὧν ἐφευρεθεὶς χρόνῳ

remark, and one that is verified by almost daily experience in the upper classes of life. The saying τὸ κηδεῦσαι καθ' ἑαυτὸν is had in view.

938—44. A *third* reason of his unhappiness. He had flattered himself that he was somebody, because his wealth gave him a certain influence; that is, he said, in the words of Aeschylus, Agam. 1616, ἐκ τῶν δὲ τοῦδε χρημάτων πειράσομαι ἄρχειν πολιτῶν. But he had found that something beyond mere wealth was wanted by him who would gain secure power over true-hearted citizens.

941. ἡ γὰρ φύσις. 'For 'tis a man's disposition that is lasting, not his wealth; for the one, staying ever by him, keeps its head erect, while wealth, if unjustly acquired and keeping company with fools, flits out of the house, having been in its prime but for a short time.'—κάρα is the emendation of Tyrwhitt for κακά. Bothe, in a long note, endeavours to show that the true reading is αἱρεῖ κακά, *vincit miserias*; but this gives a poor sense, little suited to the context. What the poet meant was, that ἀρετὴ (for this is conveyed under the general term φύσις), can always face the slanders of the envious, and is not liable to the sudden fall which mere wealth may any day suffer, and irretrievably.

945. ἃ δ' ἐς γυναῖκας, scil. ἐποίεις.

Bothe would have it that the construction is, ἃ δ' ἐς γυναῖκας ὕβριζες, σιωπῶ &c., but Bothe has little taste or judgment where what we may call the *feeling* of a passage is concerned. What Electra means, and indeed scarcely disguises under the form of an αἴνιγμα, may be read in Suppl. 452—5. He trusted not only to his influence as a τύραννος, but to his effeminate comeliness, for the purpose of seducing women,—which is often the meaning of ὑβρίζειν. Whether Aegisthus is elsewhere spoken of as *handsome*, does not appear. Probably a story to that effect was current, and very likely in some of the Cyclic poems.

948. ἀραρώς. This is a difficult expression. Perhaps it means παρεσκευασμένος: see on Bacch. 457. Valckenaer proposed κάλλει τε χαίρων. Perhaps ἀρέσκων is the true reading; for this is exactly suited to what follows. Moreover, the old copies give ἀραρών.

950. ἐκκρεμάννυται, depend on war as a pursuit; make war their stay; or cling to it as the delight and object of their existence. Though Euripides was no lover of war, yet he insists on the necessity of manly youths being trained to arms, and he often ridicules the fops of his day. See on this subject the Preface to Vol. i. p. xlix. *Supra*, v. 388. Frag. 875.

ΕΥΡΙΠΙΔΟΥ

δίκην δέδωκας ὧδέ τις κακοῦργος ὤν.
μή μοι, τὸ πρῶτον βῆμ' ἐὰν δράμῃ καλῶς,
νικᾶν δοκείτω τὴν δίκην, πρὶν ἂν πέλας   955
γραμμῆς ἵκηται, καὶ τέλος κάμψῃ βίου.

ΧΟ. ἔπραξε δεινά· δεινὰ δ' ἀντέδωκε σοὶ
καὶ τῷδ'. ἔχει γὰρ ἡ Δίκη μέγα σθένος.

ΟΡ. εἶεν· κομίζειν τοῦδε σῶμ' ἔσω χρεών
σκότῳ τε δοῦναι, δμῶες, ὡς ὅταν μόλῃ   960
μήτηρ, σφαγῆς πάροιθε μὴ εἰσίδῃ νεκρόν.

ΗΛ. ἐπίσχες· ἐμβάλωμεν εἰς ἄλλον λόγον.

ΟΡ. τί δ'; ἐκ Μυκηνῶν μῶν βοηδρόμους ὁρᾷς;

ΗΛ. οὐκ, ἀλλὰ τὴν τεκοῦσαν, ἥ μ' ἐγείνατο.

ΟΡ. καλῶς ἄρ' ἄρκυν ἐς μέσην πορεύεται.   965

ΗΛ. καὶ μὴν ὄχοις τε καὶ στολῇ λαμπρύνεται.

ΟΡ. τί δῆτα δρῶμεν μητέρ'; ἦ φονεύσομεν;

953. It seems best to remove the comma usually placed after δέδωκας, for the construction is χρόνῳ ἐφευρεθεὶς ὧδε κακοῦργός τις ὤν. 'Perish, ignorant as you have been (i. e. pretend to be) of what you have at last been punished for, having been proved to be thus base by the test of time.' Matthiae considers the sense to be virtually this, οὐδὲν εἰδὼς ὅτι δίκην δώσειν ἔμελλες &c. Possibly therefore we should read ὧν ἐφηυρέθης χρόνῳ δίκην δεδωκώς. This idea Electra appears to enforce by the following metaphor; 'Let not a man fancy, if he shall have made a good start in the race of life, that he is getting the better of justice, till he shall have got near the goal, and have passed the turning point in the close of life.' The sentiment is only a modification of the very favourite Greek saying, 'Call no man lucky till after he is dead.' See Androm. 100. The terms are borrowed from the stadium. Cf. Hipp. 87, τέλος δὲ κάμψαιμ', ὥσπερ ἠρξάμην, βίον. Hel. 1666, ὅταν δὲ κάμψῃς καὶ τελευτήσῃς βίον. Properly, γραμμή was the line drawn across the stadium, equivalent to the *carceres* of the Romans, and serving at once for a starting-point, βαλβίς, and also for a goal, because the runners returned to it after passing the stone pillar at the further end of the stadium. Whether βῆμα means 'a step' (cf. Choeph. 785), or, as Bothe and Musgrave suppose, a certain division of the course stepped off and marked with a stone or some other indication, is uncertain,

961. μὴ εἰσίδῃ (so Schaefer and others for μ' εἰσίδῃ) is a crasis sufficiently defended by the common occurrence of μὴ εἰδέναι. Bothe, after Barnes, less correctly gives μὴ 'σίδῃ. The εἰ is not absorbed, but coalesces with μὴ, like the ἀ in μὴ ἀδικεῖν &c. Seidler's reading μή σφ' ἴδῃ is ingenious and probable.—The body of Aegisthus, as is clear from this verse, had been brought on the stage by the attendants, when Orestes brought the head, v. 855.

963. βοηδρόμους, persons coming to the rescue. See Heracl. 339.

966. καὶ μήν. 'And here she comes resplendent both in her chariot and her dress.' Here καὶ μὴν does not seem objective, so as to require γε after ὄχοις, which Schaefer and Seidler have edited for τε. See on Alcest. 653. That Clytemnestra entered the stage on a chariot drawn by mules, will not excite surprise in the reader, who remembers Cassandra's similar entrance in the Agamemnon, and Clytemnestra's again in the *Iphigenia at Aulis*, v. 610.

967. τί δῆτα κτλ. 'What then should we do to our mother? Shall we slay her?' The common punctuation, μητέρ' ἦ φονεύσομεν, is certainly inferior. Ores-

ΗΛ. μῶν σ' οἶκτος εἷλε, μητρὸς ὡς εἶδες δέμας ;
ΟΡ. φεῦ.
πῶς γὰρ κτάνω νιν, ἥ μ' ἔθρεψε κἄτεκεν ;
ΗΛ. ὥσπερ πατέρα σὸν ἥδε κἀμὸν ὤλεσεν. 970
ΟΡ. ὦ Φοῖβε, πολλήν γ' ἀμαθίαν ἐθέσπισας,
ΗΛ. ὅπου δ' Ἀπόλλων σκαιὸς ᾖ, τίνες σοφοί ;
ΟΡ. ὅστις μ' ἔχρησας μητέρ', ἣν οὐ χρῆν, κτανεῖν.
ΗΛ. βλάπτει δὲ δὴ τί πατρὶ τιμωρῶν σέθεν ;
ΟΡ. μητροκτόνος νῦν φεύξομαι, τόθ' ἁγνὸς ὤν. 975
ΗΛ. καὶ μή γ' ἀμύνων πατρὶ δυσσεβὴς ἔσει.
ΟΡ. ἐγὼ δὲ μητρὶ τοῦ φόνου δώσω δίκας.
ΗΛ. τῷ δ' αὖ πατρῴαν διαμεθεὶς τιμωρίαν ;
ΟΡ. ἆρ' αὔτ' ἀλάστωρ εἶπ' ἀπεικασθεὶς θεῷ ;
ΗΛ. ἱρὸν καθίζων τρίποδ' ; ἐγὼ μὲν οὐ δοκῶ. 980
ΟΡ. οὐδ' ἂν πιθοίμην εὖ μεμαντεῦσθαι τάδε.
ΗΛ. οὐ μὴ κακισθεὶς εἰς ἀνανδρίαν πεσεῖ ;
ΟΡ. ἀλλ' ἦ τὸν αὐτὸν τῇδ' ὑποστήσω δόλον ;
ΗΛ. ᾧ καὶ πόσιν καθεῖλες Αἴγισθον κτανών.

tes uses the plural, though he is the real agent in the matter, from a desire that his sister should share the responsibility with himself.
970. On the occurrence of a tribrach, composed of a single word, in the second foot of a senarius, see Bacch. 18. Med. 375.
972. ὅπου—ᾖ. This passage well shows the difference caused by omitting the ἄν. For no one would here think of saying ὅπου ἂν ᾖ σκαιὸς, '*wherever* he is foolish.' See on Ion 856. The meaning, as usual, is ἐάν ποτε or ὅταν.
975. φεύξομαι, in the judicial sense, 'I shall be accused.' Orestes is alleging the various arguments against the slaughter of his mother, even though it was ordered by the god ;—(1) he will be tried as a matricide, having been up to this time (τότε) guiltless. (2) He will have to make satisfaction to his mother for murdering her, i. e. he will be pursued by her avenging Furies. Electra meets these objections by two counter-arguments, first, that it is equal impiety not to avenge his father, secondly, that if he does not, he will have to give satisfaction to Phoebus for disobeying him. For this is the meaning of τῷ δ' αὖ, Reiske's emendation for τῷ δαὶ, v. 978, scil. τῷ δ' αὖ δώσεις δίκην, ἐὰν διαμεθῇς κτλ. To the same critic is due μητρὶ for μητρὸς, and διαμεθεὶς for διαμεθίης.
979. ἆρ' αὔτ' κτλ. 'Was it not an evil daemon who declared it,' viz. that I must do this deed. This verse is an allusion to 973. The reply is equivalent to εὔφημα φώνει. She is shocked at the notion that Apollo, the ἀψευδὴς θεὸς, could be any other than Apollo on his own oracular seat. Seidler well compares Orest. 1668, καίτοι μ' ἐσῄει δεῖμα μή τινος κλύων Ἀλαστόρων δόξαιμι σὴν κλύειν ὄπα.
982. οὐ μὴ, see Bacch. 852.—πεσεῖ for πέσῃς Elmsley on Med. 1120.—κακισθεὶς, Ion 984.
983. ἀλλ' ἦ, see Alcest. 816.—ὑποστήσω, 'shall I set the same trap for her (as I did for him)?' This seems the sense implied by Electra's answer. Otherwise, Orestes might mean, 'shall I set the same trap for her as she set for her husband?' Cf. Aesch. Cho. 547, ὡς ἂν δόλῳ κτείναντες ἄνδρα τίμιον, δόλῳ τε καὶ ληφθῶσιν ἐν ταὐτῷ βρόχῳ.—ὑποστήσω, Aesch. Suppl. 455, εἰ μή τι πιστὸν τῷδ' ὑποστήσεις στόλῳ.

368   ΕΥΡΙΠΙΔΟΥ

ΟΡ. εἴσειμι· δεινοῦ δ' ἄρχομαι προβλήματος.   985
     καὶ δεινὰ δράσω γ'· εἰ θεοῖς δοκεῖ τάδε,
     ἔστω· πικρὸν δὲ χἠδὺ τἀγώνισμά μοι.
ΧΟ. ἰώ,
     βασίλεια γύναι χθονὸς Ἀργείας,
     παῖ Τυνδάρεω,
     καὶ τοῖν ἀγαθοῖν ξύγγονε κούροιν   990
     Διὸς, οἳ φλογερὰν αἰθέρ' ἐν ἄστροις
     ναίουσι, βροτῶν ἐν ἁλὸς ῥοθίοις
     τιμὰς σωτῆρας ἔχοντες·
     χαῖρε, σεβίζω σ' ἴσα καὶ μάκαρας
     πλούτου μεγάλης τ' εὐδαιμονίας.   995
     τὰς σὰς δὲ τύχας θεραπεύεσθαι
     καιρὸς *, ὦ βασίλεια.

                    ΚΛΥΤΑΙΜΝΗΣΤΡΑ.

     ἔκβητ' ἀπήνης, Τρῳάδες, χειρὸς δ' ἐμῆς
     λάβεσθ', ἵν' ἔξω τοῦδ' ὄχου στήσω πόδα.
     σκύλοισι μὲν γὰρ θεῶν κεκόσμηνται δόμοι   1000
     Φρυγίοις, ἐγὼ δὲ τάσδε, Τρῳάδος χθονὸς
     ἐξαίρετ', ἀντὶ παιδὸς ἣν ἀπώλεσα,
     σμικρὸν γέρας, καλὸν δὲ κέκτημαι δόμοις.
ΗΛ. οὔκουν ἐγώ, δούλη γὰρ ἐκβεβλημένη
     δόμων πατρῴων δυστυχεῖς οἰκῶ δόμους,   1005

985. προβλήματος, 'a risk.' Some explain it, 'a proposed plan.' Cf. Rhes. 183, ψυχὴν προβάλλοντ' ἐν κύβοισι δαίμονος. The two following verses are perhaps spurious.
991. αἰθέρα—ναίουσι. Compare Hel. 1498, λαμπρῶν ἀέλλαις ἀστέρων οἳ ναίετ' οὐράνιοι (as we should probably there read).—τιμὰς σωτῆρας, i. e. τοῦ σωτῆρας εἶναι, the office or prerogative of saving mariners from shipwreck.
997. After καιρὸς some word seems to have dropped out, perhaps γέγον'. The chorus, with intentional irony, tell the queen that now is the time for her great fortunes to have proper court paid to them; by which she is to understand, the duty of humble and faithful slaves; but *they* mean, now is the crisis, when no amount of care will enable her to preserve her regal splendours long.
998. χειρὸς λάβεσθε. Compare Phoen. 846, λαβοῦ δ' αὐτοῦ, τέκνον· ὡς πᾶσ' ἀπήνη πούς τε πρεσβυτῶν φιλεῖ χειρὸς θυραίας ἀναμένειν κουφίσματα. Iph. Aul. 617, καί μοι χερός τις ἐνδόθω στηρίγματα, θάκους ἀπήνης ὡς ἂν ἐκλίπω καλῶς.
1001. τάσδε. The Trojan captives, doubtless of great beauty and in gorgeous attire, whom she has already addressed in v. 998, and these are described in v. 315. There is no doubt that ἐγὼ is emphatic; the sense is, that the gods have got the captured arms in their temples, but *she* has obtained for her attendants the daughters of the noblest Trojan families; and this as a sort of requital for her lost Iphigenia.

ΗΛΕΚΤΡΑ. 369

μῆτερ, λάβωμαι μακαρίας τῆς σῆς χερός;
ΚΛ. δοῦλαι πάρεισιν αἴδε, μὴ σύ μοι πόνει.
ΗΛ. τί δ'; αἰχμάλωτόν τοί μ' ἀπῴκισας δόμων,
ἠρημένων δὲ δωμάτων ἠρήμεθα
ὡς αἴδε, πατρὸς ὀρφαναὶ λελειμμέναι. 1010
ΚΛ. τοιαῦτα μέντοι σὸς πατὴρ βουλεύματα
εἰς οὓς ἐχρῆν ἥκιστ' ἐβούλευσεν φίλων.
λέξω δὲ, καίτοι δόξ' ὅταν λάβῃ κακὴ
γυναῖκα, γλώσσῃ πικρότης ἔνεστί τις,
ὡς μὲν παρ' ἡμῖν οὐ καλῶς, τὸ πρᾶγμα δὲ 1015
μαθόντας, ἢν μὲν ἀξίως μισεῖν ἔχῃ,
στυγεῖν δίκαιον· εἰ δὲ μή, τί δεῖ στυγεῖν;

1006. μακαρίας τῆς σῆς χερός: See on Androm. 98. This passage defends Aesch. Cho. 487, ἆρ' ὀρθὸν αἴρεις φίλτατον τὸ σὸν κάρα; It has been objected to by Dr. Donaldson as a solecism on account of the position of the article; and he would read φιλτάτοις. That reading is in itself probable on other grounds; but the old one is clearly capable of defence in a grammatical point of view. Cf. Orest. 86, σὺ δ' ἡ μακαρία μακάριός θ' ὁ σὸς πόσις.
1009. ἠρήμεθα ὡς αἴδε. We are as much *captives* as they are, who have been left orphans by their father. Thus she replies to her mother's rejection of her services on the ground that she is not a slave. A comma is wrongly placed in the ordinary editions after ἠρήμεθα. Her father has been slain as well as theirs, and therefore the comparison is regarded as complete.
1011. The speech of Clytemnestra, in defence of her conduct towards her husband, contains exactly the same number of verses (40) as the reply of Electra. See on Hel. 923, and Hec. 1132, compared with 1187. These coincidences are important, as supplying a good critical test whether verses have either been interpolated or dropped out in the address of either of two speakers. It is a subject to which the attention of editors has not hitherto, it is believed, been directed. —τοιαῦτα κτλ. '(That is true;) and yet such plans did your father devise against those of his relations (viz. his own daughter Iphigenia) whom he least ought to have so treated. And on this matter I will proceed to speak; albeit, when a bad reputation has befallen a woman, there is a certain dislike in (attaching to) her words; in my case indeed, not rightly; but people ought first to know the facts, and then, if she is deserving of hatred, to detest her, but if not, why should they detest her?' Clytemnestra admits the forlorn and orphan condition of Electra, but excuses it on the plea that Agamemnon brought his own fate upon him; and she takes the occasion of the remark to endeavour to justify herself. And, lest she should seem to speak bitterly of her slain husband, she puts in the plea, that people never give a fair hearing to those whom they dislike. Seidler seems rightly to explain πικρότης 'disagreeableness,' as πικρὸς means 'disliked' in Hel. 296, i. e. the effect produced in the mind of the hearers towards the speaker. If however the poet meant this, he might much more easily have said ἀκοῦσαι πικρότης ἔνεστί τις. Indeed, this very reading is not far from the vulgate, in which the α made short before γλ is said to be unique in Euripides at least. Aeschylus however (frag. 176, ed. Herm.) has κέντημα γλώσσης, σκορπίου βέλος λέγω.
1015. ὡς παρ' ἡμῖν is more commonly to be rendered, 'in our judgment.' Cf. Heracl. 881, παρ' ἡμῖν μὲν γὰρ οὐ σοφὸν τόδε. Here to explain it 'as with me,' or 'in my case,' suits the context rather better.
1016. μαθόντα σ' and ἔχεις or ἔχῃς are parts of the same corruption, corrected respectively by Reiske and Seidler.

370   ΕΥΡΙΠΙΔΟΥ

ἡμᾶς δ' ἔδωκε Τυνδάρεως τῷ σῷ πατρὶ,
οὐχ ὥστε θνήσκειν, οὐδ' ἃ γειναίμην ἐγώ.
κεῖνος δὲ παῖδα τὴν ἐμὴν, Ἀχιλλέως   1020
λέκτροισι πείσας, ᾤχετ' ἐκ δόμων ἄγων
πρυμνοῦχον Αὖλιν· ἔνθ' ὑπερτείνας πυρᾶς
λευκὴν διήμησ' Ἰφιγόνης παρηΐδα.
κεἰ μὲν πόλεως ἅλωσιν ἐξιώμενος,
ἢ δῶμ' ὀνήσων τἆλλα τ' ἐκσώζων τέκνα   1025
ἔκτεινε πολλῶν μίαν ὕπερ, συγγνώστ' ἂν ἦν·
νῦν δ', οὕνεχ' Ἑλένη μάργος ἦν, ὅ τ' αὖ λαβὼν
ἄλοχον κολάζειν προδότιν οὐκ ἠπίστατο,
τούτων ἕκατι παῖδ' ἐμὴν διώλεσεν.
ἐπὶ τοῖσδε τοίνυν, καίπερ ἠδικημένη,   1030
οὐκ ἠγριούμην, οὐδ' ἂν ἔκτανον πόσιν·
ἀλλ' ἦλθ' ἔχων μοι μαινάδ' ἔνθεον κόρην
λέκτροις τ' ἐπεισέφρησε, καὶ νύμφα δύο
ἐν τοῖσιν αὐτοῖς δώμασιν κατείχομεν.

1019. ἃ γειναίμην. An elegant use of the indefinite optative in past narration. In Latin *neque quos ego peperissem.* Aesch. Eum. 588, οὐπώποτ' εἶπον μαντικοῖσιν ἐν θρόνοις,—ὃ μὴ κελεῦσαι Ζεὺς Ὀλυμπίων πατήρ. The reading in the text is due to Dawes. The old copies give ἃ 'γεινάμην.
1021. πείσας. The pretence of bringing Iphigenia to Aulis, when the fleet were detained there, was, that she was to be betrothed to Achilles. See Iph. Aul. 835, &c.
1022. πυρᾶς for πύλας Tyrwhitt. See on Hel. 1563, and compare Iph. A. 26, Aesch. Ag. 226.
1024. πόλεως ἅλωσιν. The allusion is to Praxithea, the wife of Erechtheus, who sacrificed one of her daughters in obedience to the oracle when the city was in danger from a hostile invasion. See Ion 278. Frag. Erechth. 353.
1027. μάργος has the same sense as μῶρος (*inf.* 1035), viz. weakly indulgent to the natural passions. So ἐξεμαργώθης φρένας, Troad. 992. See on Hippol. 161.
1030. ἐπὶ τοῖσδε, 'at this,' the same as ἐκ τῶνδε, 'on account of these things.' Generally, 'on these terms,' as Hel. 838, but here the idiom is the same as in μέγα φρονεῖν ἐπί τινι &c.
1033. ἐπεισέφρησε. On the force of

ἐπὶ, peculiarly used of a second wife, see Alcest. 304. *ibid.* 1056, καὶ πῶς ἐπεισφρῶ τήνδε τῷ κείνης λέχει;—μαινάδα, viz. Cassandra, Tro. 307. 415.
1034. ἐν τοῖσιν αὐτοῖς δώμασιν, viz. θαλάμοις. See Med. 378. It was not the having a παλλάκη over and above the lawful wife that alone constituted the offence. That was not unusual, and, as is clear from Androm. 223, gave but little concern even to a devoted wife. But it was, of course, unbearable that the wife and the mistress should live together under the same roof. Hence Deianira, though she speaks very gently of Hercules' frailties in Trach. 445, still is indignant at Iole being brought to the house, v. 539, καὶ νῦν δύ' οὖσαι μίμνομεν μιᾶς ὕπο χλαίνης ὑπαγκάλισμα.—The conjecture of Dawes, κατεῖχ' ὁμοῦ, is entitled to all praise for its elegance and high probability. Thus, of course, νύμφα δύο becomes the object instead of the subject. But there can be no doubt about κατέχειν being used intransitively for καταλύειν, 'to lodge;' cf. Ion 551, προξένων δ' ἐν τῷ κατέσχες; Thus it is impossible to assert that κατείχομεν is wrong; and Bothe appears justified in retaining it, against Seidler and W. Dindorf, who adopt the emendation.

ΗΛΕΚΤΡΑ. 371

μῶρον μὲν οὖν γυναῖκες, οὐκ ἄλλως λέγω· 1035
ὅταν δ', ὑπόντος τοῦδ', ἁμαρτάνῃ πόσις
τἄνδον παρώσας λέκτρα, μιμεῖσθαι θέλει
γυνὴ τὸν ἄνδρα χἄτερον κτᾶσθαι φίλον.
κᾆπειτ' ἐν ἡμῖν ὁ ψόγος λαμπρύνεται,
οἱ δ' αἴτιοι τῶνδ' οὐ κλύουσ' ἄνδρες κακῶς. 1040
εἰ δ' ἐκ δόμων ἥρπαστο Μενέλεως λάθρα,
κτανεῖν μ' Ὀρέστην χρῆν, κασιγνήτης πόσιν
Μενέλαον ὡς σώσαιμι; σὸς δὲ πῶς πατὴρ
ἠνέσχετ' ἂν ταῦτ'; εἶτα τὸν μὲν οὐ θανεῖν
κτείνοντα χρῆν τἄμ', ἐμὲ δὲ πρὸς κείνου παθεῖν;
ἔκτειν', ἐτρέφθην ἥνπερ ἦν πορεύσιμον 1046
πρὸς τοὺς ἐκείνῳ πολεμίους. φίλων γὰρ ἂν
τίς ἂν πατρὸς σοῦ φόνον ἐκοινώνησέ μοι;
λέγ', εἴ τι χρῄζεις, κἀντίθες παρρησίᾳ,
ὅπως τέθνηκε σὸς πατὴρ οὐκ ἐνδίκως. 1050
ΗΛ. δίκαι' ἔλεξας· ἡ δίκη δ' αἰσχρῶς ἔχει·

1035. μῶρον, see above, v. 1027. The remark here made is one which, from its profound truth, is applicable alike to all states of society. Women, he says, have less power to resist temptation in the first instance than men have, whom τὸ ἄρσεν ὠφελεῖ προσκείμενον, Hipp. 970. And with this disadvantage to begin with (ὑπόντος τοῦδε), a bad example set by the husband is sure to be imitated by the wife. But how fine, we might almost say, how painfully grand, is the verse, κᾆπειτ' ἐν ἩΜΙΝ ὁ ψόγος λαμπρύνεται,— in *our* case the misconduct is held up to the eyes of all; but the *man's* frailties are lightly dealt with.—For the peculiar sense of ψόγος see on Troad. 643, *supra*, 643. For ἁμαρτάνειν, Suppl. 900.

1041—5. 'Supposing now that Menelaus had been stealthily taken away from his home (as Helen was from her's), ought I to have put Orestes to death that I might get my sister's (Helen's) husband safe home again? How, I should like to know, would your father have borne that? And then shall I be told, that *he* ought not to have been killed for slaying my child, but that *I* should die at his hands (for slaying his)?' The right understanding of this passage depends in great measure on the doctrine, that the son was physically the father's, the daughter the mother's child. Her argument then amounts to this:—Agamemnon would certainly have killed me, if I had sacrificed his son to save my sister's husband; why then should *I* not have killed *him*, for sacrificing *my* child to save his brother's wife? And the case is very ingeniously and rhetorically laid down, a hypothetical case being put, which exactly and in every particular answers to the real case on which her defence is founded.

1045. κτείνοντα. Matthiae gives κτείναντα, and so W. Dindorf. See on Ion 1286.

1046. ἥνπερ, scil. ὁδόν. Compare Med. 384, κράτιστα τὴν εὐθεῖαν, where ὁδὸν πορεύεσθαι must be supplied. ' I had recourse,' she says, ' to his enemies for assistance,' viz. to Aegisthus; ' for none of his friends would have been likely to assist me in slaying your father.'

1047. The ἂν, as observed on Hel. 291, is not often doubled with the past tense of the indicative mood.

1051. αἰσχρῶς ἔχει. You have alleged what you fairly could in your defence; but still it does not exonerate you from disgrace. And the reason why, is given in what follows: a wife who is discreet ought to yield in all things to her lord's behests.

3 B 2

ΕΥΡΙΠΙΔΟΥ

γυναῖκα γὰρ χρὴ πάντα συγχωρεῖν πόσει,
ἥτις φρενήρης. ᾗ δὲ μὴ δοκεῖ τάδε,
οὐδ' εἰς ἀριθμὸν τῶν ἐμῶν ἥκει λόγων.
μέμνησο, μῆτερ, οὓς ἔλεξας ὑστάτους   1055
λόγους, διδοῦσα πρός σέ μοι παρρησίαν.
ΚΛ. καὶ νῦν γέ φημι, κοὐκ ἀπαρνοῦμαι, τέκνον.
ΗΛ. ἆρ' *οὖν κλύουσα, μῆτερ, εἶτ' ἔρξεις κακῶς;
ΚΛ. οὐκ ἔστι, τῇ σῇ δ' ἡδὺ προσθήσω φρενί.
ΗΛ. λέγοιμ' ἄν· ἀρχὴ δ' ἥδε μοι προοιμίου.   1060
εἴθ' εἶχες, ὦ τεκοῦσα, βελτίους φρένας.
τὸ μὲν γὰρ εἶδος αἶνον ἄξιον φέρει
Ἑλένης τε καὶ σοῦ, δύο δ' ἔφυτε συγγόνω,

Cf. Med. 222, χρὴ δὲ ξένον μὲν κάρτα προσχωρεῖν πόλει. Hipp. 299, τοῖσιν εὖ λεχθεῖσι συγχωρεῖν λόγοις.—χρὴ for χρῆν is due to Matthiae.

1053. Reiske's correction, ᾗ for εἰ, seems necessary to the context. The sense indeed is, εἴ τινι μὴ δοκεῖ τάδε, ἐκείνη οὐδὲ ἥκει κτλ. But then a nominative is not very easily supplied to ἥκει, unless it be implied from the dative of the relative. It is true that, the above sentiment being general, αὐτῇ might be supplied after δοκεῖ from γυναῖκα above, v. 1052, and so αὕτη ἡ γυνὴ would be the subject to ἥκει. The construction however is much more elegant according to Reiske's emendation, which W. Dindorf has adopted. Bothe, retaining εἰ, puts a comma at τάδε, and explains thus:—" si vero haec (tibi) displicent, neque in numerum meorum sermonum veniunt, i. e. si non sunt ea, quae tibi me dicere decet, matri filiam." But he must have forgotten, that εἰ μὴ would have been followed by μηδὲ, not οὐδέ. Hence a full stop must be placed at λόγων, the sense being, 'she who does not think so, does not even come into the account of my words,' i. e. I have nothing to say to her, no desire to argue with her. The next lines depend on a clause left to be supplied;—'With you however I am willing to discuss this point at length, if you will not be offended; and remember' &c. Cf. 1049.

1058. ἆρ' οὖν Dobree for ἆρα. There is a verse in the Alcestis, 542, αἰσχρὸν παρὰ κλαίουσι θοινᾶσθαι φίλοις, and another in Aesch. Cho. 839, οὔτοι φρένα κλέψειαν ὠμματωμένην, which appear to defend the ᾱ before κλ. In the last verse however φρέν' ἂν seems to be the true reading. Here the οὖν certainly improves the sense, though it is not very easy to account for its omission, if genuine. Elmsley's reading, adopted by Robinson, ἆρ' εὖ λέγουσα, which gives a good antithesis between ἔργον and λόγος, is equally far from the MSS.

1059. οὐκ ἔστι, scil. ὅπως κακῶς ἔρξω σε.—ἡδὺ κτλ., " immo quod animo tuo gratum erit, insuper tibi retribuam," Heath. (I will not only hear your reproof, but thank you for it.) " Sed tuae sententiae libenter assentiar," Bothe; who takes ἡδὺ for ἡδέως, and supplies τὴν ψῆφον with προσθήσω. Neither of these appears to be the true interpretation of this obscure verse. It should rather mean, to judge by the context, 'I will indulge your humour,' viz. in hearing your sentiments, whatever they may be. Bothe well observes, " Minus impudens fingitur Clytaemnestra, pronaque ad poenitentiam, quo magis ejus caede commoveamur."

1062. αἶνον ἄξιον φέρει, 'brings you the credit it deserves.' Dindorf reads φέρειν with Porson. It is hard to see wherein the supposed improvement consists. She uses the word ἄξιον ironically, contrasting εἶδος with φρήν. To the latter word ἔφυτε συγγόνω ματαίω refers. 'You were both of you fair enough, but because you were not also chaste enough, you got the evil reputation you both now possess.'

ἄμφω ματαίω Κάστορός τ' οὐκ ἀξίω.
ἡ μὲν γὰρ ἁρπασθεῖσ' ἑκοῦσ' ἀπώλετο, 1065
σὺ δ' ἄνδρ' ἄριστον Ἑλλάδος διώλεσας,
σκῆψιν προτείνουσ' ὡς ὑπὲρ τέκνου πόσιν
ἔκτεινας· οὐ γὰρ, ὡς ἔγωγ', ἴσασιν εὖ,
ἥτις, θυγατρὸς πρὶν κεκυρῶσθαι σφαγὰς,
νέον τ' ἀπ' οἴκων ἀνδρὸς ἐξωρμημένου, 1070
ξανθὸν κατόπτρῳ πλόκαμον ἐξήσκεις κόμης.
γυνὴ δ' ἀπόντος ἀνδρὸς ἥτις ἐκ δόμων
ἐς κάλλος ἀσκεῖ, διάγραφ' ὡς οὖσαν κακήν.
οὐδὲν γὰρ αὐτὴν δεῖ θύρασιν εὐπρεπὲς
φαίνειν πρόσωπον, ἤν τι μὴ ζητῇ κακόν. 1075
μόνην δὲ πασῶν οἶδ' ἐγώ σ' Ἑλληνίδων,

1065. ἑκοῦσ' ἀπώλετο. It was a great error in Pierson to propose ἀπῴχετο, and a great want of judgment in Seidler and W. Dindorf to admit such a conjecture into the text. Electra, of course, speaks with bitter irony when she says that Helen was *purposely* lost; i. e. that what she, Helen, was pleased to call τὸ ἀπολέσθαι, the being undone by a perfidious seducer, was a voluntary and deliberate act on her part. If any change was required, the imperfect ἀπώλλυντο might be worth consideration. Compare μεσονύκτιος ὠλλύμαν, Hec. 914.
1067. σκῆψιν. Cf. v. 29, εἰς μὲν γὰρ ἄνδρα σκῆψιν εἶχ' ὀλωλότα.
1068. Though σε may be supplied from the preceding σὺ, either οὐ γάρ σ', ὡς &c., or ἴσασί σ' εὖ is perhaps the true reading. The former, proposed by Dobree, is approved by W. Dindorf; the latter, which is Porson's, is adopted by Robinson. In the next verse ἥτις is a good emendation of L. Dindorf's for ἢ τῆς. The article is not only not required, but is irregular, unless it were added also to σφαγάς. But ἥτις has an implied sense very well suited to the context: 'they do not know you (to be a giddy woman) as I do, when, long before your daughter's death had been determined, and your husband had but just left his home, you used to dress your auburn hair in the mirror.' A similar vanity of dress is objected by Hecuba to Helen, Troad. 1022. Compare Med. 1161.
1072. γυνὴ δ' κτλ. ' But when a wife, in the absence of her lord from home, dresses herself up to look beautiful, blot out her name as a bad one.' A fine sentiment, though happily not applicable to the habits of modern society, where the seclusion of wives is no part of the national virtue, such as it is. Propertius, in the very beautiful first elegy of his first book, says much on this subject; and he sums all up in one golden verse, *Uni si qua placet, culta puella sat est* (v. 26). —ἐς κάλλος is not so much *ad pulchritudinem sibi conciliandam* (Matthiae), as, 'to the extent of making herself look handsome,' *usque ad delicias*. See on Bacch. 457, λευκὴν δὲ χροιὰν ἐς παρασκευὴν ἔχεις. Troad. 1201, οὐ γὰρ ἐς κάλλος τύχας δαίμων δίδωσιν. Ibid. 1211, οὐκ ἐς πλησμονὴν θηρώμενοι.—For διαγράφειν, to draw the pen across a writing in order to cancel it, see Nub. 773, οἴμ' ὡς ἥδομαι, ὅτι πεντετάλαντος διαγέγραπταί μοι δίκη. Robinson incorrectly renders it, ' Set her down as a bad woman.' This is ἐγγράφειν, Aesch. Cho. 686.
1076. μόνην δὲ κτλ. ' You were the only one of the Greek women whom I remember to have rejoiced when you heard of successes against the Argive army on the part of the Trojans; and the reason was, that you wished your husband to be detained there longer by the war.'—κεχαρμένος probably follows the analogy of δεδακρυμένος, κεκλαυμένος, *gaudio suffusus*. It is well rendered by our participle ' overjoyed.'—τὰ Τρώων εὐτυχοῖ is Musgrave's elegant emendation for πατρῷ' ἦν εὐτυχῇ. Cf. Troad. 1004,

ΕΥΡΙΠΙΔΟΥ

εἰ μὲν τὰ Τρώων εὐτυχοῖ, κεχαρμένην,
εἰ δ' ἧσσον εἴη, συννεφοῦσαν ὄμματα,
Ἀγαμέμνον' οὐ χρήζουσαν ἐκ Τροίας μολεῖν.
καίτοι καλῶς γε σωφρονεῖν παρεῖχέ σοι· 1080
ἄνδρ' εἶχες οὐ κακίον' Αἰγίσθου πόσιν,
ὃν Ἑλλὰς αὑτῆς εἵλετο στρατηλάτην·
Ἑλένης δ' ἀδελφῆς τοιάδ' ἐξειργασμένης,
ἐξῆν κλέος σοι μέγα λαβεῖν· τὰ γὰρ κακὰ
παράδειγμα τοῖς ἐσθλοῖσιν εἴσοψίν τ' ἔχει. 1085
εἰ δ', ὡς λέγεις, σὴν θυγατέρ' ἔκτεινεν πατήρ,
ἐγὼ τί σ' ἠδίκησ' ἐμός τε σύγγονος;
πῶς οὐ πόσιν κτείνασα πατρῴους δόμους
ἡμῖν προσῆψας, ἀλλ' ἀπηνέγκω λέχη
τἀλλότρια, μισθοῦ τοὺς γάμους ὠνουμένη; 1090
κοὔτ' ἀντιφεύγει παιδὸς ἀντὶ σοῦ πόσις
οὔτ' ἀντ' ἐμοῦ τέθνηκε, δὶς τόσως ἐμὲ
κτείνας ἀδελφῆς ζῶσαν· εἰ δ' ἀμείψεται

εἰ μὲν τὰ τοῦδε κρεῖσσον' ἀγγέλλοιτό σοι, Μενέλαον ἧνεις, παῖς ὅπως λυποῖτ' ἐμὸς, —εἰ δ' εὐτυχοῖεν Τρῶες, οὐδὲν ἦν ὅδε.

1080. καίτοι—γε. 'Yet surely you had the best opportunity for proving yourself a discreet wife;' i. e. you had no reason to leave your husband from any inferiority of his position.—παρεῖχε for ἐξῆν, for it is rather harsh to make Agamemnon the subject, 'he gave you every opportunity of being virtuous.'—οὐ κακίονα, i.e. πολλῷ ἀμείνονα.

1085. παράδειγμα εἴσοψίν τε, 'induce comparison with and attention to the good.' She means that what is bad in one exhibits by the contrast more strongly what is good in the other.—ἔχει for παρέχει. It will be observed that παράδειγμα is a rhetorical rather than a poetical word; and perhaps the substantive εἴσοψις does not elsewhere occur. It is Scaliger's correction for εἰς ὄψιν.

1086 seqq. The argument is this:—If your husband wronged you in killing your daughter, *we*, myself and my brother, have done you no wrong. You ought therefore to have shown that your resentment was confined to *him*, by giving over to us, his lawful heirs, the property of his house. But, instead of this, you sold them to Aegisthus, thus paying him the price of adultery. Besides, Aegisthus, your present lord, may be said, in a moral sense, to have slain me in a far worse manner than Agamemnon slew Iphigenia. Why have you not killed him to avenge me, as you killed Agamemnon to avenge, as you pretend, Iphigenia? Why at least is he not ordered to quit the kingdom? But instead of that, it is your own son Orestes whom you have banished!—The old reading, πῶς οὖν—οὐ πατρῴους, was corrected by Canter.

1090. μισθοῦ. Compare Aesch. Cho. 902, where to the charge of Orestes, διχῶς ἐπράθην, ὧν ἐλευθέρου πατρὸς, Clytemnestra replies, ποῦ δῆθ' ὁ τῖμος ὄντιν' ἀντεδεξάμην;—δὶς τόσως, cf. Rhes. 160. Med. 1194. The genitive depends on the implied meaning πολλῷ μᾶλλον.

1093. εἰ δὲ κτλ. 'But, if slaughter shall requite slaughter as the avenger of it, then I and your son Orestes shall kill you to avenge our father: for, if that conduct was right on your part, so also is this on ours.' She says this as a sort of justification in reference to the fixed intention she now has of committing the act. Thus Clytemnestra has unconsciously been put on her trial during the speech of her daughter. She has been formally impeached, and is found guilty both by

ΗΛΕΚΤΡΑ. 375

φόνον δικάζων φόνος, ἀποκτενῶ σ' ἐγὼ
καὶ παῖς Ὀρέστης πατρὶ τιμωρούμενοι·   1095
εἰ γὰρ δίκαι' ἐκεῖνα, καὶ τάδ' ἔνδικα.
ὅστις δὲ πλοῦτον ἢ εὐγένειαν εἰσιδὼν
γαμεῖ πονηρὰν, μῶρός ἐστι· μικρὰ γὰρ
μεγάλων ἀμείνω σώφρον' ἐν δόμοις λέχη.
ΧΟ. τύχη γυναικῶν ἐς γάμους· τὰ μὲν γὰρ εὖ,   1100
τὰ δ' οὐ καλῶς πίπτοντα δέρκομαι βροτῶν.
ΚΛ. ὦ παῖ, πέφυκας πατέρα σὸν στέργειν ἀεί.
ἔστιν δὲ καὶ τόδ'· οἱ μέν εἰσιν ἀρσένων,
οἱ δ' αὖ φιλοῦσι μητέρας μᾶλλον πατρός.
συγγνώσομαί σοι· καὶ γὰρ οὐχ οὕτως ἄγαν   1105
χαίρω τι, τέκνον, τοῖς δεδραμένοις ἐμοί.
σὺ δ' ὧδ' ἄλουτος καὶ δυσείματος χρόα
λεχὼ νεογνῶν ἐκ τόκων πεπαυμένη;
οἴμοι τάλαινα τῶν ἐμῶν βουλευμάτων·
ὡς μᾶλλον ἢ χρῆν ἤλασ' εἰς ὀργὴν πόσιν.   1110
ΗΛ. ὀψὲ στενάζεις, ἡνίκ' οὐκ ἔχεις ἄκη·
πατὴρ μὲν οὖν τέθνηκε· τὸν δ' ἔξω χθονὸς

the laws of logic and the laws of vengeance. This is quite after the fashion of Euripides, whom Aristophanes wittily called ποιητὴς ῥηματίων δικανικῶν.

1099. μεγάλων, scil. μὴ σωφρόνων.

1100. τύχη γυναικῶν. It is a chance what sort of wife one gets in marriage. The metaphor, as πίπτοντα shows, is from dice. Cf. Orest. 603, οἷς δὲ μὴ πίπτουσιν εὖ (γάμοι).

1102. πέφυκας, scil. φύσιν ἔχεις. 'It is your nature to take the side of your father in all things; and there is this peculiarity likewise (on the part of males); some are devoted to the parent of the manly sex, while others love their mothers more than the father.' The meaning of this will appear from the note on v. 1041. As a daughter was considered physically as the mother's child, a greater degree of affection for the mother was regarded as a natural instinct. Clytemnestra means therefore, that Electra's devotion to her father is a peculiarity of temperament, an idiosyncrasy to which some sons afford a parallel in their greater attachment to the mother.

On this principle Pallas, who was born from a father without a mother, or to whom, in other words, the father was the mother, says κάρτα δ' εἰμὶ τοῦ πατρὸς, Aesch. Eum. 708.

1105. οὐχ οὕτως κτλ., 'I am not so well satisfied with the deeds that I have done (as to wish to blame you).' Clytemnestra's penitence, and returning kindness for her daughter, is well conceived. It heightens the commiseration for her death, it sets off by the contrast the stern resolution of Electra, and it thus makes the tragedy more tragic than it would have been by the simple account of just retribution overtaking an odious and implacable character.

1108. λεχώ. See v. 652.

1111. ὀψὲ—ἄκη. Aesch. Cho. 507, μεθύστερον τιμᾷς' ἀνήκεστον πάθος.

1112. The sense is this;—'Remedy indeed, for your greater offence, you have none, for your husband is dead. But for the other offence, the banishment of Orestes, there is yet a remedy. Why then do you not have recourse to it?'—ἀλητεύοντα, 'homeless.' See Hel. 934.

ΕΥΡΙΠΙΔΟΥ

πῶς οὐ κομίζει παῖδ' ἀλητεύοντα σόν;
ΚΛ. δέδοικα· τοὐμὸν δ', οὐχὶ τοὐκείνου, σκοπῶ.
πατρὸς γὰρ, ὡς λέγουσι, θυμοῦται φόνῳ. 1115
ΗΛ. τί δαὶ πόσιν σὸν ἄγριον εἰς ἡμᾶς ἔχεις;
ΚΛ. τρόποι τοιοῦτοι· καὶ σὺ δ' αὐθάδης ἔφυς.
ΗΛ. ἀλγῶ γάρ· ἀλλὰ παύσομαι θυμουμένη.
ΚΛ. καὶ μὴν ἐκεῖνος οὐκέτ' ἔσται σοι βαρύς.
ΗΛ. φρονεῖ μέγ'· ἐν γὰρ τοῖς ἐμοῖς ναίει δόμοις. 1120
ΚΛ. ὁρᾷς; ἂν' αὖ σὺ ζωπυρεῖς νείκη νέα.
ΗΛ. σιγῶ· δέδοικα γάρ νιν, ὡς δέδοικ', ἐγώ.
ΚΛ. παῦσαι λόγων τῶνδ'· ἀλλὰ τί μ' ἐκάλεις, τέκνον;
ΗΛ. ἤκουσας, οἶμαι, τῶν ἐμῶν λοχευμάτων·
τούτων ὕπερ μοι θῦσον, οὐ γὰρ οἶδ' ἐγώ, 1125
δεκάτῃ σελήνῃ παιδὸς ὡς νομίζεται·
τρίβων γὰρ οὐκ εἴμ', ἄτοκος οὖσ' ἐν τῷ πάρος.
ΚΛ. ἄλλης τόδ' ἔργον, ἥ σ' ἔλυσεν ἐκ τόκων.
ΗΛ. αὐτὴ 'λόχευον κἄτεκον μόνη βρέφος.
ΚΛ. οὕτως ἀγείτον' οἶκον ἵδρυσαι φίλων; 1130
ΗΛ. πένητας οὐδεὶς βούλεται κτᾶσθαι φίλους.
ΚΛ. ἀλλ' εἶμι, παιδὸς ἀριθμὸν ὡς τελεσφόρον

Ion 576.—κομίζει, ἀνακομίζει, ἀναλαμβάνεις, ἀποκαθίστης.

1116. ἄγριον ἔχεις; i. e. τί οὐκ ἐπρᾶυνας εἰς ἡμᾶς;

1119. καὶ μὴν, 'well then, he on his part shall no longer be harsh towards you.' On βαρὺς, often used to express a moody and brooding resentment, see Med. 38.

1120. φρονεῖ μέγ'. He is haughty, and the reverse of courteous towards me, because he knows that he is the usurper of my home.

1121. ὁρᾷς; κτλ. 'There now! You are rekindling (old) strifes so as to make them new again.' This is an instance of *tmesis* which has been rightly restored by Bothe and others, the old reading being ἂν αὖ. The σὺ, as usual, is emphatic: 'it is *you*, not I, who are stirring up old strifes.'

1122. ὡς δέδοικα. She means, of course, that she does not fear him at all, because in fact he is now dead.

1125. τούτων ὕπερ. 'For this (viz. for my safe delivery) offer a sacrifice for me, for I do not myself know how, on the tenth night after the birth of the child, as is the custom.' She might have said 'to-night,' for Clytemnestra had been told (v. 654) that her daughter had been delivered ten days ago. Bothe gives δεκάτῃ σελήνῃ—νομίζεται, Musgrave δεκάτην σελήνην, as *inf.* 1132, and Ar. Av. 922, οὐκ ἄρτι θύω τὴν δεκάτην ταύτης ἐγώ; Musgrave, with his usual learning, explains the mention of σελήνη in place of νυκτὶ, by a Greek custom, mentioned in Plut. Symposiac. 3, 10, § 3, διὸ τὰ μὲν νήπια παντάπασιν αἱ τίτθαι δεικνύναι πρὸς τὴν σελήνην φυλάττονται· πλήρη γὰρ ὑγρότητος ὄντα, καθάπερ τὰ χλωρὰ τῶν ξύλων, σπᾶται καὶ διαστρέφεται. According to some, it was on the tenth day that the child was named, though also occasionally on the seventh. See on Ion 1127.

1127. τρίβων, well versed, conversant. See Rhes. 625. Bacch. 717.

1130. ἵδρυσαι Musgrave for ἵδρυται.

1132. ἀριθμόν. For the accusative see on 1125. We must supply ἀριθμὸν ἡμε-

θύσω θεοῖσι· σοὶ δ' ὅταν πράξω χάριν
τήνδ', εἶμ' ἐπ' ἀγρὸν, οὗ πόσις θυηπολεῖ
Νύμφαισιν. ἀλλὰ τούσδ' ὄχους, ὀπάονες, 1135
φάτναις ἄγοντες πρόσθεθ'. ἡνίκ' ἂν δέ με
δοκῆτε θυσίας τῆσδ' ἀπηλλάχθαι θεοῖς,
πάρεστε· δεῖ γὰρ καὶ πόσει δοῦναι χάριν.

ΗΛ. χώρει πένητας ἐς δόμους· φρούρει δέ μοι
μή σ' αἰθαλώσῃ πολύκαπνον στέγος πέπλους· 1140
θύσεις γὰρ οἷα χρή σε δαίμοσιν θύειν.
κανοῦν δ' ἐνῆρκται, καὶ τεθηγμένη σφαγὶς,
ἥπερ καθεῖλε ταῦρον, οὗ πέλας πεσεῖ
πληγεῖσα· νυμφεύσει δὲ κἀν Ἅιδου δόμοις
ᾧπερ ξυνηῦδες ἐν φάει· τοσήνδ' ἐγὼ 1145
δώσω χάριν σοι, σὺ δέ γ' ἐμοὶ δίκην πατρός. [στρ.

ΧΟ. ἀμοιβαὶ κακῶν· μετάτροποι πνέουσιν αὖραι δόμων.
τότε μὲν ἐν λουτροῖς ἔπεσεν ἐμὸς ἐμὸς ἀρχέτας,
ἰάκχησε δὲ στέγα, λάϊνοί τε θριγκοὶ δόμων, 1150
τάδ' ἐνέποντος· ὦ
σχέτλια, τί με, γύναι, φονεύεις, φίλαν
πατρίδα δεκέτεσιν σποραῖσιν ἐλθόντ' ἐμάν;

ρῶν παιδὸς, 'the full number of days which the child has lived.' Probably the mystic number *nine* is meant. When that was safely past, a thank-offering for it was made on the tenth. Some peculiar risk was perhaps thought to attach to the child on this day. By a very similar superstition, the ninth day is now believed by many to be replete with danger to the mother after her confinement.—For πράσσειν χάριν, 'to do a favour,' see Ion 36. 895.—εἶμι κτλ., see v. 641.

1140. πολύκαπνον στέγος. Compare δυσκάπνοις δώμασιν Ag. 747.

1141. θύειν. The υ in θύω is properly long; and though verbs in ύω, as κωλύω, ἠπύω, ἀλύω do occasionally, in some dialects, shorten the υ, still we can hardly doubt that here we should read οἷα δαίμοσιν θύειν σε χρή. Aeschylus however uses φύειν, in Theb. 530. The rest of Electra's remarks, which are no longer ambiguous, are not heard by Clytemnestra, who has now entered the cottage.

1143. ταῦρον. She means Aegisthus,

as Barnes observes. Cf. Aesch. Agam. 1194, ἰδοὺ ἰδού· ἄπεχε τῆς βοὸς τὸν ταῦρον, i. e. keep Agamemnon away from his wife, who will murder him.

1145. ᾧπερ ξυνηῦδες. Aesch. Cho. 892, τούτῳ θανοῦσα ξυγκάθευδ', ἐπεὶ φιλεῖς τὸν ἄνδρα τοῦτον.

1147. While the queen-mother is within the humble habitation of her despised daughter, now, by a righteous retribution, about to become her murderer, the chorus, in a system of vigorous dochmiacs, announce that the time has arrived when their murdered king's cry shall bring the avenging fury upon her who slew her lord with her own hands on his return to Argos.

1148. ἐν was added by Seidler before λουτροῖς.—ἀρχέτας, Heracl. 753.

1152. σχέτλια Seidler for σχετλία, chiefly for the metre's sake.—δεκέτεσιν σποραῖσιν, on the tenth sowing-season, the tenth year, the siege of Troy having lasted so long. Cf. Troad. 20, ὡς δεκασπόρῳ χρόνῳ ἀλόχους τε καὶ τέκν' εἰσίδωσιν ἄσμενοι.

VOL. II. 3 C

παλίρρους δὲ τάνδ᾽ ὑπάγεται δίκα διαδρόμου λέ-
χους,   ἀντ. 1155
μέλεον ἃ πόσιν χρόνιον ἱκόμενον εἰς οἴκους
Κυκλώπειά τ᾽ οὐράνια τείχε᾽ ὀξυθήκτῳ βέλει
ἔκανεν αὐτόχειρ,
πέλεκυν ἐν χεροῖν λαβοῦσα.   †τλάμων   1160
πόσις, ὅ τι ποτὲ τὰν τάλαιναν ἔσχεν κακόν,
ὀρεία τις ὡς λέαιν᾽ ὀργάδων
δρύοχα νεμομένα, τάδε κατήνυσεν.

ΚΛ. ὦ τέκνα, πρὸς θεῶν μὴ κτάνητε μητέρα.   1165
ΧΟ. κλύεις ὑπώροφον βοάν;
ΚΛ. ἰώ μοί μοι.
ΧΟ. ᾤμωξα κἀγὼ πρὸς τέκνων χειρουμένης.
νέμει τοι δίκαν θεός, ὅταν τύχῃ·
σχέτλια μὲν ἔπαθες, ἀνόσια δ᾽ εἰργάσω,   1170
τάλαιν᾽, εὐνέταν.
ἀλλ᾽ οἵδε μητρὸς νεοφόνοις ἐν αἵμασι
πεφυρμένοι βαίνουσιν ἐξ οἴκων πόδα,
τροπαῖα δείγματ᾽ ἀθλίων †προσφθεγμάτων.

1155. παλίρρους, with a turned tide; redounding upon the aggressors.—δίκα δ. λέχους is an obscure phrase. Musgrave explains it *vulgivagae Veneris,* 'the penalty for transferring her affections to another is now bringing this woman to judgment.' Probably διατρέχειν was used of those who run from one to another, and so show the fickleness of their character. So οἱ διατρέχοντες ἀστέρες, 'falling stars,' Ar. Pac. 838. Theocr. xxix. 14, τῷδε μὲν ἄματος ἄλλον ἔχεις κλάδον, | ἄλλον δ᾽ αὔριον, ἐξ ἑτέρω δ᾽ ἕτερον ματῇς.

1158. Κυκλώπεια, the walls of Mycenae or Argos: see Troad. 1087, ἱππόβοτον Ἄργος, ἵνα τε τείχη λάϊνα Κυκλώπι᾽ οὐράνια νέμονται. Where οὐράνια, as in this place, is probably a trisyllable.

1159. ἔκανεν, the reading of the *editio princeps*, satisfies the metre. The MSS. give 'καν' or 'κἀν', for which Seidler, followed by Matthiae and Dindorf, reads κατέκαν'.

1160. For τλάμων we should read ὦ τλάμων for the sake of the metre, or perhaps λαβοῦσ᾽ ἃ τλάμων πόσιν κτλ., where τάδε κατήνυσεν πόσιν would stand for τάδε ἔδρασε πόσιν. As the text stands, we may translate, 'Hapless husband, whatever madness it was which possessed his wretched wife.' Such bad wives were called by many names, as λέαινα, ἔχιδνα, Σκύλλα &c., the first of which is selected as the subject of the following clause.

1162. ὀργάδων δρύοχα, the thickets of the mountain glades. Cf. Bacch. 340. 445.

1168. ᾤμωξα κἀγώ. *I* also cry οἴμοι, to think that a mother should be slain by her own children.—νέμει δίκαν, awards justice. Cf. Aesch. Suppl. 397, Ζεὺς—νέμων εἰκότως ἄδικα μὲν κακοῖς, ὅσια δ᾽ ἐννόμοις.

1170. Perhaps we should read ἀνόσι᾽ εἰργάσω. This is better suited to the metre. The δὲ in a similar manner should perhaps be omitted in Suppl. 466, σοὶ μὲν δοκείτω ταῦτ᾽, ἐμοὶ [δὲ] τἀναντία.

1172. ἐν αἵμασι, as Bacch. 1164, ἐν αἵματι στάζουσαν χέρα. For βαίνειν πόδα see above, v. 94.

1174. τροπαῖα is the accusative in apposition to the sentence preceding, as in Heracl. 401, θυηπολεῖται δ᾽ ἄστυ μαντέων

ΗΛΕΚΤΡΑ. 379

οὐκ ἔστιν οὐδεὶς οἶκος ἀθλιώτερος 1175
τῶν Τανταλείων οὐδ' ἔφυ ποτ' ἐκγόνων.

ΟΡ. ἰὼ Γᾶ καὶ Ζεῦ, πανδερκέτα   στρ. α'.
βροτῶν, ἴδετε τάδ' ἔργα φόνι-
α μυσαρὰ, δίγονα σώματα
ἐν χθονὶ κείμενα πλαγᾷ
χερὸς ὑπ' ἐμᾶς, ἄποιν' ἐμῶν πημάτων. 1180

       *   *   *
          *   *   *

ΗΛ. δακρύτ' ἄγαν, ὦ σύγγον', αἰτία δ' ἐγώ.
διὰ πυρὸς ἔμολον ἁ τάλαινα ματρὶ τᾷδ',
ἅ μ' ἔτικτε κούραν.

ΟΡ. ἰὼ τύχας, τᾶς σᾶς τύχας, μᾶτερ τεκοῦσ',
ἄλαστα, μέλεα καὶ πέρα 1185
παθοῦσα σῶν τέκνων ὑπαί·
πατρὸς δ' ἔτισας φόνον δικαίως.
ἰὼ Φοῖβ' ἀνύμνησας δίκαν,   ἀντ. α'. 1190
ἄφαντα φανερὰ δ' ἐξέπρα-
ξας ἄχεα, φόνια δ' ὤπασας

ὕπο, τροπαῖά τ' ἐχθρῶν καὶ πόλει σωτήρια. For προσφθεγμάτων Musgrave not inelegantly conjectures προσφαγμάτων. The common reading can only allude to the mother's cry ὦ τέκνα &c. in v. 1165,—'trophies which are proofs of her appeal to them in distress,' viz. that she spoke the truth when she cried that they were slaying her. This however is not nearly so satisfactory as προσφαγμάτων. Cf. Aesch. Ag. 1249, θερμῷ κοπείσης φοινίῳ προσφάγματι. Perhaps a verse has been lost, in which some participle like φέροντες occurred.

1177. Orestes is now seen (probably by the *eccyclema*) standing over the bodies of his enemies. Of Aegisthus the body had before been brought in; see v. 959, so that the victor is now able to speak of them as δίγονα σώματα. Seidler perceived that these following verses (τὰ ἀπὸ σκηνῆς, as they are technically called) were antistrophic, and consequently that two verses have been lost after 1180. In 1179, the α is made long before πλ, as in v. 1160 before τλ, the verse being choriambic.—For ἄποινα in apposition to the sentence, see Alcest. v. 7.

1182. Like δι' ὀργῆς ἐλθεῖν τινὶ, so διὰ πυρὸς μολεῖν μητρὶ is 'to enter upon a violent proceeding against a mother.' Compare Androm. 487, διὰ γὰρ πυρὸς ἦλθ' ἑτέρῳ λέκτρῳ.

1184 seqq. These verses are given to Electra in the old copies, and so also in Bothe's edition. Seidler assigned them to Orestes. Bothe however denies that these verses (from 1177) are antistrophic.

1189. τίνειν φόνον, ἀδικίαν, &c., is sometimes used of those who pay the penalty in their own persons for a former crime. So in Agam. v. 1506, ξιφοδηλήτῳ θανάτῳ τίσας ἅπερ ἦρξεν.

1190. ἀνύμνησας δίκαν. You repeatedly told me of justice; you gave oracles advising it over and over again. See on Ion v. 6.—ἄφαντα Elmsley for ἄφατα, i.e. ἠφάνισας ἄχεα τὰ πρὶν φανερὰ ὄντα.

1192. That ὀπάζειν here and elsewhere (Il. viii. 341. xvii. 462,) means διώκειν, is evident from the context, which here also shows the meaning to be κατέπαυσας, ἐξέβαλες. And Photius has ὀπάζει· θεωρεῖ

380   ΕΥΡΙΠΙΔΟΥ

  λέχε' ἀπὸ γᾶς Ἑλλανίδος.
  τίνα δ' ἑτέραν μόλω πόλιν ; τίς ξένος,
  τίς εὐσεβὴς ἐμὸν κάρα   1195
  προσόψεται ματέρα κτανόντος ;
ΗΛ. ἰὼ ἰώ μοι. ποῖ δ' ἐγώ, τίν' ἐς χορὸν,
  τίνα γάμον εἶμι ; τίς πόσις με δέξεται
  νυμφικὰς ἐς εὐνάς ;   1200
ΟΡ. πάλιν πάλιν φρόνημα σὸν μετεστάθη [πρὸς αὖραν],
  φρονεῖς γὰρ ὅσια νῦν, τότ' οὐ
  φρονοῦσα, δεινὰ δ' εἰργάσω,
  φίλα, κασίγνητον οὐ θέλοντα.   1205
  κατεῖδες, οἷον ἁ τάλαιν' ἑῶν πέπλων στρ. β'.
  ἔβαλεν, ἔδειξε μαστὸν ἐν φοναῖσιν,
  ἰώ μοι, πρὸς πέδῳ
  τιθεῖσα γόνιμα μέλεα ; τακόμαν δ' ἐγώ.
ΗΛ. σάφ' οἶδα, δι' ὀδύνας ἔβας, ἰήιον   1210
  κλύων γόον ματρὸς, ἅ σ' ἔτικτεν.
ΟΡ. βοὰν δ' ἔλασκε τάνδε, πρὸς γένυν ἐμὰν ἀντ. β'.
  τιθεῖσα χεῖρα· τέκος ἐμὸν, λιταίνω·   1215
  παρῄδων τ' ἐξ ἐμᾶν
  ἐκρήμναθ', ὥστε χέρας ἐμὰς λιπεῖν βέλος.

ἢ παρέχει ἢ διώκει. So also Hesychius and other lexicographers referred to by Seidler. The primary idea is, attendance at a person's back. The meaning is, that a terrible lesson has been taught, sufficient to deter the matrons of Hellas from murdering their lords for the future.

1194. This verse is dochmiac; but the δὲ should perhaps be omitted here, and ὑπ' in v. 1180. Cf. 1170.

1197. τίν' ἐς χορόν. Compare sup. v. 310.—γάμον, i. e. as a guest at the marriage of another.

1201. The words πρὸς αὖραν appear to be the gloss of some interpreter who wished to point out that the metaphor was from a changing wind, as above v. 1147. They are omitted by W. Dindorf, and the strophic verse shows that they are spurious. Orestes says this to his sister in a moment of extreme remorse, and taking her words as the expression of penitence. He avers that he was unwilling to do the deed, but that she urged him to it.

1206. ἑῶν πέπλων. There would be scarcely a doubt but that we should read ἔξω πέπλων (for the genitive requires some preposition), had not the antistrophic verse been composed of pure iambic feet ; and yet we may compare v. 1184 with v. 1201. Porson proposed ἄνω, Elmsley ἐμῶν πέπλων ἐλάβετ'. Bothe absurdly construes ἁ τάλαιν' ἑῶν, misera per suos (liberos). The Greeks considered the showing of the breast as the most pathetic appeal. See Androm. 629. So Clytemnestra in the Choephori, v. 882,

ἐπίσχες, ὦ παῖ, τόνδε δ' αἴδεσαι, τέκνον,
μαστὸν, πρὸς ᾧ σὺ πολλὰ δὴ βρίζων ἅμα
οὔλοισιν ἐξήμελξας εὐτραφὲς γάλα.

—φοναῖσιν Seidler for φοναῖς.

1209. γόνιμα μέλεα, 'the limbs that bore me.' Cf. 1227.

1210. ἰήιον γόον, the cry of ἰὴ ἰή. Similarly ἰηίων καμάτων οὐκ ἀνέχουσι γυναῖκες, Oed. R. 174.

ΗΛ. τάλαινα. πῶς ἔτλας φόνον δι' ὀμμάτων
 ἰδεῖν σέθεν ματρὸς ἐκπνεούσας ;   1220
ΟΡ. ἐγὼ μὲν ἐπιβαλὼν φάρη κόραις ἐμαῖ-   στρ. γ'.
 σι φασγάνῳ κατηρξάμαν
 ματέρος ἔσω δέρας μεθείς.
ΗΛ. ἐγὼ δέ γ' ἐπεκέλευσά σοι,
 ξίφους τ' ἐφηψάμην ἅμα.   1225
 δεινότατον παθέων ἔρεξα.
ΟΡ. λαβοῦ * λαβοῦ, κάλυπτε μέλεα ματέρος   ἀντ. γ'.
 πέπλοις, καθάρμοσον σφαγάς·
 φονέας ἔτικτες ἆρά σοι.
ΗΛ. ἰδοὺ, φίλα τε κοὐ φίλα·   1230
 φάρεα δέ γ' ἀμφιβάλλομεν,
 τέρμα κακῶν μεγάλων δόμοισιν.
ΧΟ. ἀλλ' οἴδε δόμων ὑπὲρ ἀκροτάτων
 φαίνουσι τινὲς δαίμονες, ἢ θεῶν

1222. κατηρξάμην, as if by cutting a lock of hair from the head, as in a sacrifice. See Alcest. 74—6.—ἔσω δέρας, see on Hel. 354—6.
1225. ἐφηψάμαν Seidler. Cf. 1209.
1222. Orest. 1235 (quoted by Barnes), ΟΡ. ἔκτεινα μητέρ'. ΠΥ. ἡψάμην δ' ἐγὼ ξίφους. He also reads ἔρεξα for ἔρεξας, and this suits both the sense and the metre better. It is clear that Electra is here laying the blame on herself. Others give the verse to the chorus or to Orestes. The absence of a copula seems an objection; perhaps we should read δεινότατον παθέων τ' ἔρεξα.
1227. λαβοῦ was repeated by W. Dindorf, who however approves Seidler's proposal to read κόραις ἐμαῖς in 1221, and here κάλυπτε μέλεα ματέρος πέπλοις, | καὶ καθάρμοσον σφαγὰς, i. e. 'and close the gaping wound in her throat.'
1230. Bothe retains the common reading, ἰδοὺ, φίλαι τε, κοὺ φίλαι· φάρεα δέ γ' ἀμφιβάλλομεν. But, if Electra is speaking of herself alone, she should have said φίλοι τε. The objection to Seidler's reading, φίλαν—σέ γ', is not only that the γε is useless, but that the epithet does not very well precede the personal pronoun. Probably we should read either φίλα τε (scil. εἶ), or φιλεῖ τε, 'you are loved.' Thus the γε has its proper sense,

'but still we throw this garment upon you, to close the scene of these fearful calamities to the house.' On the favourite formula, φίλα κοὐ φίλα, of Euripides, see Preface to Vol. i. p. xxx.
1234. φαίνουσι. For φαίνονται, or rather, ἑαυτοὺς is left to be supplied. So ἀγανὰ φαίνουσ' ἐλπὶς in Agam. 101. The θεοὶ οὐράνιοι (Agam. 90) are here opposed to δαίμονες, heroes or demigods, and Bothe seems wrong in saying they are used without a difference. The words ὑπὲρ ἀκροτάτων δόμων seem to show that, whatever contrivance it was that was adopted for introducing these θεοὶ ἀπὸ μηχανῆς, they at least were seen above the roof of the palace or house which was always represented on the proscenium. See the note on Med. 1317. The same two gods appear at the end of the Helena. In both places they are appropriately introduced; first, as the brothers of both Helen and Clytemnestra, secondly, as gods of the sea, who had a mission to perform in safely convoying ships: see inf. 1347. Their object here is to give especial instructions respecting the surviving family of the Atridae. Electra is to marry Pylades, and to live at Phocis, with his father Strophius (v. 1287). Orestes is to fly to Athens to secure the protection of Pallas against the persecuting

τῶν οὐρανίων· οὐ γὰρ θνητῶν γ'
ἥδε κέλευθος· τί ποτ' εἰς φανερὰν
ὄψιν βαίνουσι βροτοῖσιν;

ΔΙΟΣΚΟΡΟΙ.

Ἀγαμέμνονος παῖ, κλῦθι· δίπτυχοι δέ σε
καλοῦσι μητρὸς σύγγονοι Διόσκοροι,
Κάστωρ κασίγνητός τε Πολυδεύκης ὅδε.
δεινὸν δὲ ναὸς ἀρτίως πόντου σάλον
παύσαντ' ἀφίγμεθ' Ἄργος, ὡς εἰσείδομεν
σφαγὰς ἀδελφῆς τῆσδε, μητέρος δὲ σῆς.
δίκαια μὲν νῦν ἥδ' ἔχει· σὺ δ' οὐχὶ δρᾷς,
Φοῖβός τε Φοῖβος, ἀλλ' ἄναξ γάρ ἐστ' ἐμὸς,
σιγῶ· σοφὸς δ' ὢν οὐκ ἔχρησέ σοι σοφά.
αἰνεῖν δ' ἀνάγκη ταῦτα. τἀντεῦθεν δὲ χρὴ
πράσσειν ἃ μοῖρα Ζεύς τ' ἔκρανε σοῦ πέρι.
Πυλάδῃ μὲν Ἠλέκτραν δὸς ἄλοχον ἐς δόμους,
σὺ δ' Ἄργος ἔκλιπ'· οὐ γάρ ἐστι σοι πόλιν
τήνδ' ἐμβατεύειν μητέρα κτείναντα σήν.
δειναὶ δὲ Κῆρές σ' αἱ κυνώπιδες θεαὶ
τροχηλατήσουσ' ἐμμανῆ πλανώμενον.
ἐλθὼν δ' Ἀθήνας Παλλάδος σεμνὸν βρέτας

1235

1240

1245

1250

Erinyes; and there he is to be tried and acquitted by the court of Areopagus. After that, he will retire into Arcadia and found a city to be called after his name. Aegisthus will be buried by the Argives, Clytemnestra by Menelaus and Helen, who have just returned safe from the court of the Egyptian Proteus.

1241. ναός. Barnes edits ναυσὶν, on conjecture; and the dative is conveniently governed by δεινόν. If ναὺς be right, we must suppose some particular ship to be meant, and πόντου σάλον to be regarded as one word, as if he had said ναὸς κίνδυνον.

1245. This is a curious aposiopesis: Φοῖβος ἔστι μὲν Φοῖβος, ἀλλ' ὅμως οὐκ ἔχρησε σοφά, σοφὸς ὤν. Euripides himself is ready enough at all times to make his characters impeach both the wisdom and the morality of Apollo; see Ion 436 seqq. But it was a point in Attic theology, that one god never interfered with the counsels of another; see on Hippol. 1329. Robinson admits a very improbable conjecture of Porson's, Φοῖβός σε, Φοῖβος, where ἠνάγκασε is presumed to be understood. The fact is, the poet intended to say, σὺ δὲ οὐ δρᾷς δίκαια, Φοῖβός τε οὐκ ἔχρησέ σοι σοφά, ὦ Ὀρέστα.—αἰνεῖν, to bear with, acquiesce in, Alcest. 2.

1252. Κῆρες. In the Eumenides, the goddesses called themselves the sisters of the Μοῖραι, v. 920. In v. 395 of the same play, they state that they are called Ἀραὶ in the regions below. The πολυωνυμία of these dread goddesses is remarkable: Ἐρινύες, Σεμναί, Εὐμένιδες, Ἀραί, Κῆρες or Μοῖραι, and very frequently Κύνες with some distinctive epithet.

1254. σεμνὸν βρέτας. The ancient wooden statue of Athena Polias in the Parthenon. This word was peculiarly applied to that, the most sacred of her images. Cf. Eum. 79, μολὼν δὲ Παλ-

ΗΛΕΚΤΡΑ. 383

πρόσπτυξον· εἴρξει γάρ νιν ἐπτοημένας 1255
δεινοῖς δράκουσιν, ὥστε μὴ ψαύειν σέθεν,
γοργῶφ᾽ ὑπερτείνουσά σου κάρᾳ κύκλον.
ἔστιν δ᾽ Ἄρεώς τις ὄχθος, οὗ πρῶτον θεοὶ
ἕζοντ᾽ ἐπὶ ψήφοισιν αἵματος πέρι,
Ἁλιρρόθιον ὅτ᾽ ἔκταν᾽ ὠμόφρων Ἄρης, 1260
μῆνιν θυγατρὸς ἀνοσίων νυμφευμάτων,
πόντου κρέοντος παῖδ᾽, ἵν᾽ εὐσεβεστάτη
ψῆφος βεβαία τ᾽ ἐστὶν ἔκ γε τοῦ θεοῖς.
ἐνταῦθα καὶ σὲ δεῖ δραμεῖν φόνου πέρι.
ἴσαι δέ σ᾽ ἐκσώσουσι μὴ θανεῖν δίκῃ 1265
ψῆφοι τεθεῖσαι· Λοξίας γὰρ αἰτίαν
εἰς αὑτὸν οἴσει, μητέρος χρήσας φόνον.
καὶ τοῖσι λοιποῖς ὅδε νόμος τεθήσεται,
νικᾶν ἴσαις ψήφοισι τὸν φεύγοντ᾽ ἀεί.
δειναὶ μὲν οὖν θεαὶ τῷδ᾽ ἄχει πεπληγμέναι 1270

λάδος ποτὶ πτόλιν, ἵζου παλαιὸν ἄγκαθεν λαβὼν βρέτας.

1255. ἐπτοημένας, scared, driven on by the snakes in their hair. Cf. Bacch. 214. In Choeph. 1038, they are πεπλεκταν-ημέναι πυκνοῖς δρακοῦσιν.

1257. κύκλον, her aegis, which the goddess was technically said ὑπερέχειν and ὑπερτείνειν τινός.

1259. ἐπὶ ψήφοισιν, for the purpose of giving their votes. The details of this well-known story, the trial of Ares, (whence the name of Areopagus,) for slaying Halirrhothius, the son of Poseidon, are given in Iph. Taur. 945 seqq., which play follows next after the Electra and the Orestes in the tragic history.

1260. Ἁλιρρόθιον. Pronounced as if Ἁλιρρόθοιν. See on Ion 285.

1261. μῆνιν. The accusative in apposition to the sentence, as ἄποινα is so often used. He might have said χολωθείς: cf. Alcest. 5. Apollodor. iii. 14, 2, Ἀγραύλου μὲν οὖν καὶ Ἄρεος Ἀλκίππη γίνεται. Ταύτην βιαζόμενος Ἁλιρρόθιος, ὁ Ποσειδῶνος καὶ νύμφης Εὐρύτης, ὑπὸ Ἄρεος φωραθεὶς κτείνεται. Ποσειδῶν δὲ ἐν Ἀρείῳ πάγῳ κρίνεται, δικαζόντων τῶν δώδεκα θεῶν, Ἄρει καὶ ἀπολύεται.

1262. εὐσεβεστάτῃ, 'most righteous.' See Hel. 901. Orest. 1651, πάγοισιν ἐν Ἀρείοισιν εὐσεβεστάτην ψῆφον διοίσουσ᾽.

—ἔκ γε τοῦ Schaefer for ἔκ τε τοῦ. One cannot say that γε here improves the sense, if it has any force at all. Perhaps he wrote ἐκ τούτου, which the transcribers changed to the more ordinary form ἐκ τοῦ, and so inserted τε or γε.—ἐστίν, 'has been established ever since.'—θεοῖς, in the eyes of the gods, or perhaps, 'for the gods, should any similar case occur again.' Euripides (like a good citizen as he was, whatever his detractors may say) thought it his duty to uphold the authority of the Areopagus by hinting at its divine sanction. Aeschylus, it is hardly necessary to add, does the same. But *he* derives the name from the fact of the Amazons sacrificing to Ares when they stormed the Acropolis of Athens, his object being to represent the trial of Orestes as the first that had ever been held there, and as the direct cause of the institution of that court.

1264. δραμεῖν, scil. ἀγῶνα περὶ φόνου. On ἴσαι ψῆφοι see the note on Eum. 704. —ἐκσώσουσι Porson for —ζουσι.

1267. οἴσει, ἀνοίσει, will take upon himself. Compare Eum. 193, ΧΟ. ἔχρησας ὥστε τὸν ξένον μητροκτονεῖν. ΑΠ. ἔχρησα ποινὰς τοῦ πατρὸς πέμψαι· τί μήν; Where perhaps we should read πρᾶξαι for πέμψαι.

1270. τῷδ᾽ ἄχει. Smitten with grief

πάγον παρ' αὐτὸν χάσμα δύσονται χθονὸς,
σεμνὸν βροτοῖσιν εὐσεβὲς χρηστήριον.
σὲ δ' Ἀρκάδων χρὴ πόλιν ἐπ' Ἀλφειοῦ ῥοαῖς
οἰκεῖν Λυκαίου πλησίον σηκώματος·
ἐπώνυμος δὲ σοῦ πόλις κεκλήσεται. 1275
σοὶ μὲν τάδ' εἶπον· τόνδε δ' Αἰγίσθου νέκυν
Ἄργους πολῖται γῆς καλύψουσιν τάφῳ.
μητέρα δὲ τὴν σὴν ἄρτι Ναυπλίαν παρὼν
Μενέλαος, ἐξ οὗ Τρωικὴν εἷλε χθόνα,
Ἑλένη τε θάψει· Πρωτέως γὰρ ἐκ δόμων 1280
ἥκει λιποῦσ' Αἴγυπτον, οὐδ' ἦλθεν Φρύγας.
Ζεὺς δ', ὡς ἔρις γένοιτο καὶ φόνος βροτῶν,
εἴδωλον Ἑλένης ἐξέπεμψ' εἰς Ἴλιον.
Πυλάδης μὲν οὖν κόρην τε καὶ δάμαρτ' ἔχων
Ἀχαιΐδος γῆς οἴκαδ' εἰσπορευέτω, 1285
καὶ τὸν λόγῳ σὸν πενθερὸν κομιζέτω

on account of this acquittal. Compare Eum. 750 seqq.—χάσμα, "a long wide chasm at the N. E. angle of the Areopagus, formed by split rocks, where there is a fountain of dark water in a gloomy recess." Wordsworth, *Athens and Attica*, p. 79. Cf. Eum. 986, βᾶτε—γᾶς ὑπὸ κεύθεσιν ὠγυγίοισιν.

1272. βροτοῖσιν εὐσεβὲς, held in awe by mortals; ὃ σέβονται βροτοί. Compare the passive use of ἀμαθὴς, Ion 916. Matthiae approves Reiske's conjecture ἀστιβές.

1273. Ἀρκάδων πόλιν. The discovery of the relics of Orestes in Tegea of Arcadia is well known from Herod. i. 68. On the origin of the town called Ὀρέστειον, Mr. Blakesley has given a good note on Herod. ix. 11, where he quotes the present passage, and Orest. 1646, κεκλήσεται δὲ σῆς φυγῆς ἐπώνυμον Ἀζᾶσιν Ἀρκάσιν τ' Ὀρέστειον καλεῖν. By Λυκαίου σήκωμα the temple of Zeus Lycaeus in Tegea is meant, for which Bothe cites Strabo viii. cap. 8, Τεγέα δ' ἔτι μετρίως συμμένει, καὶ τὸ ἱερὸν τῆς Ἀλαίας Ἀθηνᾶς τιμᾶται δ' ἔτι μικρὸν καὶ τὸ τοῦ Λυκαίου Διὸς ἱερὸν κατὰ τὸ Λύκαιον ὄρος.

1278. Ναυπλίαν παρών. For the construction see Bacch. 5, πάρειμι Δίρκης νάματα. For the narrative, Hel. 1586, σώσατέ μ' ἐπ' ἀκτὰς Ναυπλίας δάμαρτά τε.

In point of time, therefore, this immediately follows the *Helena*, where the detention at the court of Proteus is the subject of the play.—ἄρτι—ἐξ οὗ, only lately, though so long a time (eight years) since he captured Troy has elapsed.

1283. εἴδωλον Ἑλένης. See Hel. 582.

1285. Ἀχαιΐδος. See Ion 64.—εἰσπορευέτω, let him introduce her from Achaea into Phocis, where Strophius his father lived. The genitive depends on the idea of motion from, unless, with Reiske, ἐκπορευέτω be read, or either οἶκον for οἴκαδε, or Ἀχαιΐδ' ἐς γῆν should be restored. Thus the meaning would be, 'let him take her into Achaea in his route homewards,' οἴκαδε νοστῶν. The student will avoid an error into which Robinson has fallen, of confusing εἰσπορευέτω with εἰσπορευέσθω.— κόρην τε καὶ δάμαρτα, her who is at once a virgin and a wife. So the αὐτουργὸς is below called λόγῳ πενθερὸς, the nominal brother-in-law of Orestes, on account of his σωφροσύνῃ, which had spared a young bride. The words γαμβρὸς and πενθερὸς are occasionally used as synonyms; indeed, both words take the rather vague sense of any relation by marriage. See Hippol. 635—6. According to Photius in v. πενθερά, both Euripides and Sophocles employed the one word to signify what is properly meant by the other.

ΗΛΕΚΤΡΑ.

Φωκέων ἐς αἶαν, καὶ δότω πλούτου βάρος.
σὺ δ' Ἰσθμίας γῆς αὐχέν' ἐμβαίνων ποδὶ
χώρει πρὸς οἶκον Κεκροπίας εὐδαίμονα.
πεπρωμένην γὰρ μοῖραν ἐκπλήσας φόνου   1290
εὐδαιμονήσεις τῶνδ' ἀπαλλαχθεὶς πόνων.
ΧΟ. ὦ παῖδε Διὸς, θέμις εἰς φθογγὰς
τὰς ὑμετέρας ἡμῖν πελάθειν;
ΔΙ. θέμις, οὐ μυσαροῖς τοῖσδε σφαγίοις.
ΟΡ. κἀμοὶ μύθου μέτα, Τυνδαρίδαι;   1295
ΔΙ. καὶ σοί· Φοίβῳ τήνδ' ἀναθήσω
πρᾶξιν φονίαν.
ΧΟ. πῶς ὄντε θεὼ τῆσδέ τ' ἀδελφὼ
τῆς καπφθιμένης
οὐκ ἠρκέσατον κῆρας μελάθροις;   1300
ΔΙ. μοῖραν ἀνάγκης ἦγεν τὸ χρεὼν,

1288. σὺ δὲ κτλ. Do you, Orestes, proceed by land to Athens through the Isthmus of Corinth. By οἶκον Κεκροπίας the metropolis of Attica appears to be meant, whither he had already been directed to go, v. 1255, and now the route which he is to take is specified.

1290. ἐκπλῆσαι is to fill up the full term, to perform any thing to the uttermost, as τερπνὸν ἐκπλῆσαι βίον, Alcest. 169.—μοῖραν φόνου, the destiny or consequences resulting from the murder you have committed.

1293. πελάθειν. An Aeschylean word, as quoted by Aristoph. Ran. 1265 seqq., formed on the analogy of διωκάθω, ἀμυνάθω, &c., from the root πλε or πελ, whence πλησίον, ἔπλητο, and Homer's προσπλάζον for προσπελάζον.

1294. μυσαροῖς, which Matthiae plausibly alters to μυσαρούς, does not agree with σφαγίοις, but with ἡμῖν (or rather ὑμῖν implied in it from the change of persons). It is probable that to an Attic audience, the pronunciation was enough to show the real meaning in many passages which, to a modern reader, appear to have an ambiguous construction. The meaning is, 'it is lawful for you, the chorus, who are not defiled with these murders.' Compare Ion 220, ΧΟ. Θέμις γυάλων ὑπερβῆναι; ΙΩΝ. οὐ θέμις, ὦ ξέναι.

1296. ἀναθήσω, ἀνοίσω. Seidler well compares Orest. 75, προσφθέγμασιν γὰρ οὐ μιαίνομαι σέθεν, εἰς Φοῖβον ἀναφέρουσα τὴν ἁμαρτίαν. Elsewhere, σφάγιον is 'a victim.' Barnes here raises an objection, that it was inconsistent in the Dioscuri to consent to converse with the chorus, on the ground that *they* were innocent of the murder, while, both before and after, they in fact did speak to Orestes and Electra. Now, as to the first address, v. 1238 seqq., that may be regarded as a message conveyed to Orestes directly from Zeus (v. 1248). For the dialogue which follows, it is to be observed that Orestes distinctly asks and obtains the permission to converse, v. 1295,—a permission which is granted on the ground, that Phoebus himself was really the author of the murder. It was an Attic law, of which the poet here is by no means forgetful, that no one should hold converse with a murderer till after his expiation, ἄφθογγον εἶναι τὸν παλαμναῖον νόμος, Aesch. Eum. 426.

1299. καπφθιμένης Elmsley for καταφθιμένης. For this Aeolic form see Suppl. 984. *Supra,* v. 200.

1301. This verse was elegantly emended by Seidler, for μοίρας ἀνάγκης ἡγεῖτο χρεών. He compares Hec. 43, ἡ πεπρωμένη δ' ἄγει θανεῖν ἀδελφήν. In Aesch. Prom. 524, the Μοῖραι are called the comptrollers of Destiny, οἰακοστρόφοι Ἀνάγκης. Here it is a mere periphrasis:

Φοίβου τ' ἄσοφοι γλώσσης ἐνοπαί.
ΗΛ. τίς δ' ἔμ' Ἀπόλλων, ποῖοι χρησμοὶ
φονίαν ἔδοσαν μητρὶ γενέσθαι;
ΔΙ. κοιναὶ πράξεις, κοινοὶ δὲ πότμοι, 1305
μία δ' ἀμφοτέρους
ἄτη πατέρων διέκναισεν.
ΟΡ. ὦ σύγγονέ μοι, χρονίαν σ' ἐσιδὼν
τῶν σῶν εὐθὺς φίλτρων στέρομαι,
καὶ σ' ἀπολείψω σοῦ λειπόμενος. 1310
ΔΙ. πόσις ἔστ' αὐτῇ καὶ δόμος· οὐχ ἥδ'
οἰκτρὰ πέπονθεν, πλὴν ὅτι λείπει
πόλιν Ἀργείων.
ΟΡ. καὶ τίνες ἄλλαι στοναχαὶ μείζους
ἢ γῆς πατρῴας ὅρον ἐκλείπειν; 1315
ἀλλ' ἐγὼ οἴκων ἔξειμι πατρός,
καὶ ἐπ' ἀλλοτρίαις ψήφοισι φόνον
μητρὸς ὑφέξω.
ΔΙ. θάρσει· Παλλάδος
ὁσίαν ἥξεις πόλιν· ἀλλ' ἀνέχου. 1320
ΗΛ. περί μοι στέρνοις στέρνα πρόσαψον,
σύγγονε φίλτατε·
διὰ γὰρ ζευγνῦσ' ἡμᾶς πατρῴων
μελάθρων μητρὸς φόνιοι κατάραι.

'that which was destined brought with it an inevitable obligation.'—ἄσοφοι, cf. v. 1246.

1303. So Seidler for τί δαί μ' Ἀπ.—ἐμὲ is emphatic: 'how was it that Apollo made *me* also, a woman, to become the murderess of (murderous to) my mother?'—ἄτη πατέρων, the consequences of an ancestral crime; what Aeschylus calls the πρώταρχος ἄτη of the family, Agam. 1163, viz. the Thyestean banquet. 'As your actions were in common,' replies Castor, 'so is your fate; one and the same infatuated act of your forefathers has ruined both.'

1309. τῶν σῶν φίλτρων, your love for me.—ἀπολείψω κτλ., I shall have to leave you and to be left by you,—σοῦ μονωθεὶς, ἁμαρτών, ἀποτυχών.

1311. αὐτῇ Barnes for αὐτός.

1315. πατρῴας. See on v. 209. W. Dindorf and Bothe give πατρίας after Schaefer, who also reads πατρίων in v. 1323. But we have ἐν γῇ πατρῴᾳ, Alcest. 169. For the sentiment compare Med. 35, οἷον πατρῴας μὴ ἀπολείπεσθαι χθονός.

1317. ἐπ' ἀλλοτρίαις ψήφοις, in another people's court, viz. the Areopagus.—φόνον, for φόνου δίκην.

1320. ὁσίαν ἥξεις. Seidler would transpose ἥξεις ὁσίαν, on account of the dactyl preceding. If the actor thought it worth while, he could undoubtedly have pronounced ὁσίαν as a spondee. See however on Tro. 177.

1323. The form ζευγνῦσι for ζευγνύασι (ζεύγνυντι) is deserving of attention, as belonging to the new rather than the old Attic.

ΗΛΕΚΤΡΑ.

ΟΡ. βάλε, πρόσπτυξον σῶμα· θανόντος δ' 1325
ὡς ἐπὶ τύμβῳ καταθρήνησον.
ΔΙ. φεῦ φεῦ· δεινὸν τόδ' ἐγηρύσω
καὶ θεοῖσι κλύειν.
ἔνι γὰρ κἀμοὶ τοῖς τ' οὐρανίδαις
οἶκτοι θνητῶν πολυμόχθων. 1330
ΟΡ. οὐκέτι σ' ὄψομαι.
ΗΛ. οὐδ' ἐγὼ εἰς σὸν βλέφαρον πελάσω.
ΟΡ. τάδε λοίσθιά μοι προσφθέγματά σου.
ΗΛ. ὦ χαῖρε, πόλις,
χαίρετε δ' ὑμεῖς πολλά, πολίτιδες. 1335
ΟΡ. ὦ πιστοτάτη, στείχεις ἤδη ;
ΗΛ. στείχω, βλέφαρον τέγγουσ' ἁπαλόν.
ΟΡ. Πυλάδη, χαίρων ἴθι, νυμφεύου 1340
δέμας Ἠλέκτρας.
ΔΙ. τοῖσδε μελήσει γάμος· ἀλλὰ κύνας
τάσδ' ὑποφεύγων στεῖχ' ἐπ' Ἀθηνῶν·
δεινὸν γὰρ ἴχνος βάλλουσ' ἐπὶ σοὶ
χειροδράκοντες, χρῶτα κελαιναί, 1345
δεινῶν ὀδυνῶν καρπὸν ἔχουσαι·
νὼ δ' ἐπὶ πόντον Σικελὸν σπουδῇ

1325. βάλε, scil. χεῖρας. Unless we should read λάβε.
1336. πιστοτάτη. So Electra says to her brother in Choeph. 235, πιστὸς δ' ἀδελφὸς ἦσθ', ἐμοὶ σέβας φέρων,—i. e. an object of reliance to me in all my troubles.
1344. Jacobs' conjecture, πάλλουσ', is ingenious. Seidler defends the old reading as "verbum fortius," but neither tells us what is the exact idea, nor quotes any instance of βάλλειν πόδα or ἴχνος.—The *black* garb of the Furies was also adopted by Aeschylus, who calls them φαιοχίτωνες Cho. 1038, μελανείμονες Eum. 353. They are here " snake-handed" rather than snake-haired, as they are commonly represented ; i. e. they hold forth snakes in each extended hand. It is evident, from the word τάσδε, that a glimpse of these dread pursuers was afforded here to the spectators.
1346. καρπὸν ὀδυνῶν. This is rather obscure. If the poet meant παρέχουσαι ἀνθρώποις καρποῦσθαι ὀδύνας, he certainly did not express himself very clearly. We strongly suspect he wrote ἔχουσιν, viz. to those who have to endure pains as a reward for their sins.
1347. πόντον Σικελόν. It is a fancy of Müller's, (Hist. of Greek Lit. p. 374,) that this passage " clearly refers to the fleet which sailed from Athens to Sicily ; and the following lines possibly refer to the charge of impiety under which Alcibiades then laboured." It has been shown on Hel. 1151, that Euripides was no advocate of this expedition ; and it is pretty certain that he was no admirer of the political views or conduct of Alcibiades, though he may have had reasons for personally sparing him. Of course, if the supposed allusion could be established as certain, it would fix the date of the play at B.C. 415, for the words could only apply to the sailing out of the expedition ; and however much Euripides himself might (and we believe did,) disapprove of

σώσοντε νεῶν πρῴρας ἐνάλους.
διὰ δ' αἰθερίας στείχοντε πλακὸς
τοῖς μὲν μυσαροῖς οὐκ ἐπαρήγομεν,   1350
οἷσιν δ' ὅσιον καὶ τὸ δίκαιον
φίλον ἐν βιότῳ, τούτους χαλεπῶν
ἐκλύοντες μόχθων σώζομεν.
οὕτως ἀδικεῖν μηδεὶς θελέτω,
μηδ' ἐπιόρκων μέτα συμπλείτω·   1355
θεὸς ὢν θνητοῖς ἀγορεύω.
ΧΟ. χαίρετε· χαίρειν δ' ὅστις δύναται
καὶ ξυντυχίᾳ μή τινι κάμνει
θνητῶν, εὐδαίμονα πράσσει.

it, he could hardly withhold the expression of a hope for its safety and success. Müller says, "the Electra must obviously be referred to the period of the Sicilian expedition;" and he regards the allusion in v. 1281 as "an alteration in the story of Helen which he worked out shortly after (B.C. 412) in a separate play, the *Helena*."

1355. For the sentiment compare Aesch. Theb. 598, ξυνεισβὰς πλοῖον εὐσεβὴς ἀνὴρ ναύταισι θερμοῖς—ὄλωλεν κτλ.

1359. εὐδαίμονα. For εὐδαιμόνως. So κεδνὰ πράσσειν Alc. 605, γέλωτος ἄξια *ibid.* 803, ὀνομαστὰ Herc. F. 509, ἄτιμα Aesch. Ag. 1418.

ΕΥΡΙΠΙΔΟΥ ΒΑΚΧΑΙ.

ΑΡΙΣΤΟΦΑΝΟΥΣ ΓΡΑΜΜΑΤΙΚΟΥ ΥΠΟΘΕΣΙΣ.

Διόνυσος ἀποθεωθεὶς, μὴ βουλομένου Πενθέως τὰ ὄργια αὐτοῦ ἀναλαμβάνειν, εἰς μανίαν ἀγαγὼν τὰς τῆς μητρὸς ἀδελφὰς ἠνάγκασε Πενθέα διασπάσαι. ἡ μυθοποιία κεῖται παρ᾽ Αἰσχύλῳ ἐν Πενθεῖ.

ΑΛΛΩΣ.

Διόνυσον οἱ προσήκοντες οὐκ ἔφασαν εἶναι θεόν. ὁ δὲ αὐτοῖς τιμωρίαν ἐπέστησε τὴν πρέπουσαν. ἐμμανεῖς γὰρ ἐποίησε τὰς τῶν Θηβαίων γυναῖκας. ὧν αἱ τοῦ Κάδμου θυγατέρες ἀφηγούμεναι τοὺς θιάσους εἰσῆγον ἐπὶ τὸν Κιθαιρῶνα. Πενθεὺς δὲ ὁ τῆς Ἀγαύης παῖς παραλαβὼν τὴν βασιλείαν ἐδυσφόρει τοῖς γενομένοις. καί τινας μὲν τῶν Βακχῶν συλλαβὼν ἔδησεν, ἐπ᾽ αὐτὸν δὲ τὸν θεὸν ἀγγέλους ἀπέστειλεν. οἱ δὲ ἑκόντος αὐτοῦ κυριεύσαντες ἦγον πρὸς τὸν Πενθέα, κἀκεῖνος ἐκέλευσε δήσαντας αὐτὸν ἔνδον φυλάττειν, οὐ λέγων μόνον ὅτι θεὸς οὐκ ἔστι Διόνυσος, ἀλλὰ καὶ πράττειν πάντα ὡς κατ᾽ ἀνθρώπου τολμῶν. ὁ δὲ σεισμὸν ποιήσας κατέστρεψε τὰ βασίλεια. ἀγαγὼν δὲ εἰς Κιθαιρῶνα ἔπεισε τὸν Πενθέα κατόπτην γενέσθαι τῶν γυναικῶν, λαμβάνοντα γυναικὸς ἐσθῆτα. αἱ δ᾽ αὐτὸν διέσπασαν, τῆς μητρὸς Ἀγαύης καταρξαμένης. Κάδμος δὲ τὸ γεγονὸς καταισθόμενος τὰ διασπασθέντα μέλη συναγαγὼν τελευταῖον τὸ πρόσωπον ἐν ταῖς τῆς τεκούσης ἐφώρασε χερσίν. Διόνυσος δὲ ἐπιφανεὶς μὲν πᾶσι παρήγγειλεν, ἑκάστῳ δὲ ἃ συμβήσεται διεσάφησεν [ἔργοις], ἵνα μὴ λόγοις[1] ὑπό τινος τῶν ἐκτὸς ὡς ἄνθρωπος καταφρονηθῇ.

---

[1] W. Dindorf adopts Elmsley's conjecture, τὰ μὲν πᾶσι παρήγγειλεν, ἑκάστῳ δὲ ἃ συμβήσεται διεσάφησεν, ἵνα μὴ ἔργοις ἢ λόγοις κτλ. More probably, τοῖς μὲν πᾶσι, opposed to ἑκάστῳ. Whatever is the meaning of these obscure and perhaps corrupt words, they evidently refer to the purport of the lost speech of Dionysus at the end of the play. The word ἔργοις seems to be an interpolation. Translate, " But Dionysus having manifested himself gave injunctions to all collectively, and explained to each individually what is to befal them, that he might not be despised as a mere mortal man by any of the barbaric nations in their stories respecting him."

BACCHAE.

In many respects this is the most remarkable, as on the whole it is unquestionably one of the most beautiful, of the plays of Euripides. It was brought out after the death of the author, by his namesake, (either son or nephew,) together with the *Alcmaeon at Corinth* and the *Iphigenia at Aulis*[1]. Written at the court of Archelaus in Macedonia, and probably designed primarily for exhibition there, (for the allusions to *Pieria* are evidently of a complimentary character, as in v. 565,) it treats with a fine and free enthusiasm of the wild scenery and still wilder Bacchic worship which prevailed especially in that district. There is little doubt that the play, as we now have it, is a finished work of the poet's own composition; while the Iphigenia at Aulis, left perhaps in an imperfect state, has been rather extensively interpolated by another hand. The Bacchae is especially remarkable for exhibiting clearly and prominently the theological opinions of the poet in his latter days. All his life he had been deeply perplexed on the subject of the Divine Nature. Human reason and philosophy had entirely failed him. Disbelieving, as he had long done, the popular theology, he had found no satisfaction in his unbelief. Something was yet wanting to his thoughtful and naturally devout mind; and he was, probably, struck with the joyous buoyancy of a worship, which in form at least was new to him. As Socrates so wisely replied in the *Phaedrus*, when asked if he did not disbelieve the common mythology, we must apparently conclude of his friend Euripides that he now ἔχαιρεν ἐάσας ταῦτα, πειθόμενος δὲ τῷ νομιζομένῳ περὶ αὐτῶν. "In this play," O. Müller remarks[2], "he appears, as it were, converted into a positive believer, or, in other words, convinced that religion should not be exposed to the subtleties of reasoning; that the understanding of man cannot subvert ancestral traditions which are as old as time; that the philosophy which attacks religion is but a poor philosophy, and so forth; doctrines which are sometimes set forth with peculiar impressiveness in the

---

[1] Schol. on Ar. Ran. 67.   [2] Hist. Gr. Lit. p. 379.

speeches of the old men, Cadmus and Teiresias, or, on the other hand, form the foundation of the whole piece: although it must be owned that Euripides, with the vacillation which he always displays in such matters, ventures, on the other hand, to explain the offensive story about the second birth of Bacchus from the thigh of Zeus, by a pun on the word which he assumes to have been misunderstood in the first instance."

For these reasons the present editor [3] has described this remarkable play as one which, although rationalistic in its tendency, is yet curiously interspersed with passages in praise of the old traditional belief. Lobeck's view is given in the following words [4]:—"Dithyrambi quam tragoediae similior, totaque ita comparata, ut contra illius temporis Rationalistas scripta videatur, qua et Bacchicarum religionum sanctimonia commendatur, et rerum divinarum disceptatio ab eruditorum judiciis ad populi transfertur suffragia, aliaque multa in eandem sententiam, quae sive poeta pro se ipse probavit sive alienis largitus est auriculis, certe magnam vim, magnam auctoritatem apud homines illius aetatis habuerunt, quae ab impia Sophistarum levitate modo ad fanaticas defluxerat superstitiones."

"Next to the Hippolytus," says Schlegel, "I would assign to this play the first rank among the extant works of Euripides;" and he justly adds, "when modern critics rank this piece very low, I cannot help thinking they do not rightly know what they are about." Unquestionably they do not; they are fettered by certain arbitrary laws as to what is and what is not good tragedy; and such men have neither the taste nor the genius requisite for the just appreciation of this play. The truth is, the Bacchae stands quite alone in the extant Attic dramas. No other play has any analogy to it, either in the singular licence of the metres, or the tumultuous and almost satyric enthusiasm of the chorus. It is possible therefore that its merits will be differently estimated; though all must agree that a romantic interest attaches to the plot, which can hardly be surpassed. In respect of metre and diction, no play displays a greater departure from established usage. The great prevalence of dactyls and tribrachs in the senarii, and of resolved feet in the choral parts, is indeed a feature common to some of the poet's latest productions; but perhaps no other of his plays exhibits so many words which he has not elsewhere employed, at least in the extant tragedies [5].

The outline of the *Bacchantes* is as follows. Pentheus, the grand-

---

[3] Preface to vol. i. p. xxv. [4] Aglaopham. p. 623.
[5] A long list of these is given by Vater in his Prolegomena to the *Rhesus*, p. cix.

son of the aged Cadmus, and his successor on the throne of Thebes, is highly offended at the progress which the new worship of Dionysus has made among the female part of his subjects. His own mother Agave, and her sisters, Ino and Autonoë, having presumptuously denied that Dionysus was born from Zeus and Semele, who was also a daughter of Cadmus, had been convinced of the god's divinity by being struck with the Bacchic enthusiasm; and had gone off to the mountains, taking with them all the adult female population. Pentheus is determined to suppress the new worship with a strong hand. Cadmus however, under the advice of the aged seer Teiresias, is wiser than to oppose the manifestly miraculous claims of the god; and they both become votaries of his orgies, while Pentheus remains obstinately bent on resistance. Dionysus himself, in human form, appears before Pentheus as a prisoner, to answer for his alleged misdeeds in corrupting the women and beguiling them from their homes. He answers fearlessly; will concede nothing, and is committed to prison. But gods laugh at bolts and bars; forthwith he shakes off his fetters, throws down his prison-house, and stands free among his faithful but anxious followers. A messenger next arrives, —a herdsman from the mountains,—who gives an account of the vain attempt to capture the parties of Bacchantes, who, immediately on being seen engaged in their revelries, flew to arms, and not only completely routed their pursuers, but ravaged all the villages and herds they came near in their course. Exasperated at all this, Pentheus resolves to go himself as a spy on their actions. He is persuaded by Dionysus to assume a female garb; and fully attired as a Bacchante, with thyrsus and fawn-skin, he is led to the mountains, and seated in the top-most branches of a lofty silver-fir. A word from Dionysus brings the hordes of Bacchantes upon their devoted prey. He is torn limb from limb; and Agave, unconscious of what she has done, in the frenzy of excitement, and made by the god to believe she has slain a lion, brings her son's gory head in her hands, to affix it, as spoils of the chase, to the wall of the temple. Cadmus however, who has been to the mountains to collect the mangled limbs of his grandson, now returns, and soon convinces Agave of her dreadful mistake. Dionysus finally appears, and informs Cadmus of his destiny. In this part of the play there is, unfortunately, the loss of many verses; the legend, however, is well enough known from other sources.

The worship of Bacchus, if one may hazard a conjecture, was of two kinds; an old Hellenic cultus, early established in Macedonia, and, like the primitive religion of the Dorian Apollo, not unconnected with the elemental and symbolic worship of Nature; and a

Pelasgic or Asiatic form, partaking of the rites of Cybele, and derived in later times, through Thrace and Phrygia, from the confines of India. There was a rustic Dionysus, a god of the country, he of the phallus and the vineyard, and a Dionysus who was intimately associated with Apollo in his prophetic attributes. But, in the primary idea, he was simply the god of excitement or enthusiasm, whether physical, mental, or religious. Of the progress of this latter religion through Asia into Greece, Dionysus himself gives what appears to be a generally correct historical sketch in the prologue. The legend of the conquest of India by Bacchus, his car drawn by tigers, and the generally eastern character of his orgies, point in the same direction. Both Homer and Hesiod were acquainted with the Theban seat of the Hellenic worship. Il. xiv. 323,

$$\text{οὐδ᾽ ὅτε περ Σεμέλης οὐδ᾽ Ἀλκμήνης ἐνὶ Θήβῃ,}$$

(scil. ἔρως εἶχε Ζῆνα,)

$$\text{ἥ ῥ᾽ Ἡρακλῆα κρατερόφρονα γείνατο παῖδα,}$$
$$\text{ἡ δὲ Διώνυσον Σεμέλη τέκε, χάρμα βροτοῖσιν.}$$

See also Il. vi. 132. Od. xi. 325. xxiv. 74, in all which passages Διόνυσος, not Βάκχος, is the name given. So also in Hesiod, Theog. 940,

$$\text{Καδμείη δ᾽ ἄρα οἱ Σεμέλη τέκε φαίδιμον υἱὸν}$$
$$\text{μιχθεῖσ᾽ ἐν φιλότητι Διώνυσον πολυγηθέα,}$$
$$\text{ἀθάνατον θνητή.}$$

Perhaps the earliest occurrence of the name *Bacchus* is in Herod. iv. 79, where the god is called Διόνυσος Βακχεῖος, the latter word, however, being in fact only an epithet, of uncertain meaning, but probably a digammated form of Ἴακχος (ἰαχή). Aeschylus, who treated of the same subject in several plays, and especially in the tetralogy of the Λυκουργεία[6], uses the word Βάκχαι in Eum. 25,

$$\text{ἐξ οὗ τε Βάκχαις ἐστρατήγησεν θεὸς,}$$
$$\text{λαγὼ δίκην Πενθεῖ καταρράψας μόρον.}$$

The *Bacchae* of Euripides appears also to have been known by the name of the *Pentheus*, under which title Stobaeus twice quotes it; but Elmsley thinks the latter was never the genuine name. The date of its exhibition at Athens is unknown, nor is it a matter of much importance. It is enough to be sure (in the words of Elmsley),

---

[6] Ἠδωνοὶ, Βασσαρίδες, Νεανίσκοι, Λυκουργός. Also in the Πενθεὺς and the Ξαντρίαι.

"Euripidem sub extremum vitae tempus Bacchas scripsisse, idque in Macedonia, cujus regionis bis eam mentionem facit, ut ostendat se populo Macedonico placere voluisse." It is to be regretted that, from the many corruptions and paucity of MSS., the present play is by no means one of the easiest. Still, it may safely be said, that it is eminently adapted for school reading, not only from its exciting interest, but from the circumstance that Elmsley published a most complete and elaborate edition of it, to which Hermann's forms a kind of supplement of scarcely less value.

TA TOY ΔΡΑΜΑΤΟΣ ΠΡΟΣΩΠΑ.

ΔΙΟΝΥΣΟΣ.
ΧΟΡΟΣ ΒΑΚΧΩΝ.
ΤΕΙΡΕΣΙΑΣ.
ΚΑΔΜΟΣ.
ΠΕΝΘΕΥΣ.
ΘΕΡΑΠΩΝ.
ΑΓΓΕΛΟΣ.
ΕΤΕΡΟΣ ΑΓΓΕΛΟΣ.
ΑΓΑΥΗ.

ΕΥΡΙΠΙΔΟΥ ΒΑΚΧΑΙ.

ΔΙΟΝΥΣΟΣ.

Ἥκω Διὸς παῖς τήνδε Θηβαίων χθόνα
Διόνυσος, ὃν τίκτει ποθ᾽ ἡ Κάδμου κόρη
Σεμέλη λοχευθεῖσ᾽ ἀστραπηφόρῳ πυρί·
μορφὴν δ᾽ ἀμείψας ἐκ θεοῦ βροτησίαν

In the prologue Dionysus himself, who has purposely assumed the human form in order that he may introduce his own rites from Asia into Greece, states the cause of his resentment against the people of Thebes and their king Pentheus. To that city he had first come from the opposite continent, because Semele his mother was the daughter of Cadmus its founder. And Cadmus indeed did well in paying due honour to the tomb of Semele. But Pentheus, his grandson and successor, together with the daughters of Cadmus, sisters of Semele, contumaciously reject the miraculous evidences that Dionysus is the son of Zeus. They insist that Semele was seduced by some mortal, and tried to hide her shame by attributing her pregnancy to Zeus; that Zeus was indignant at the falsehood, and slew Semele in revenge. Therefore the recusants are the first who have been made to feel the power which Dionysus can exercise. They were struck with a sudden frenzy, and have gone off to the mountains together with all the adult female population. The punishment of Pentheus must still be his care. When he has given an example of his power in Thebes, he will leave it, and resuming his divine form, will seek some other land where he may not thus proudly be rejected. He calls on his chorus of Bacchanals to approach the house of Pentheus and beat the timbrel to a wild strain. He will meanwhile rejoin his followers on Mount Cithaeron.

Ib. Θηβαίων. Elmsley approves, and Hermann adopts, a variant preserved by the Schol. on Hephaestion and by Priscian, Θηβαίαν. Matthiae, in a long note, shows that one phrase is as common as the other; the general rule however being, that the mere *place* is mostly Ἀργεία, Θηβαία χθών, πόλις, &c., while a more direct reference to the *people* is expressed by Ἀργείων &c. Of course, it is simply a question whether the writer contemplates the geographical position, or the ethnological relations of a settlement.

3. πυρί. The legend arose from the fact that grapes grow best on volcanic soil, whence they came to be regarded as the offspring of eruptions. (See the editor's note on Propertius, lib. iv. 17, 21.) For the dative Elmsley compares Ion 455. See also *inf.* 119.

4. ἀμείψας (more usually in this sense ἀμειψάμενος), 'having taken a human in exchange for a divine form.' So *inf.* 53, εἶδος θνητὸν ἀλλάξας ἔχω. v. 1332, ὄφεος ἀλλάξει φύσιν. Ar. Av. 117, ὀρνίθων μεταλλάξας φύσιν. See on Hel. 1187.—βροτησίαν for βροτείαν, cf. Androm. 1255. —πάρειμι, 'I am come to,' the idea of motion attaching to the preposition. Com-

πάρειμι Δίρκης νάματ' Ἰσμηνοῦ θ' ὕδωρ. 5
ὁρῶ δὲ μητρὸς μνῆμα τῆς κεραυνίας
τόδ' ἐγγὺς οἴκων, καὶ δόμων ἐρείπια
τυφόμενα, δίου πυρὸς ἔτι ζῶσαν φλόγα,
ἀθάνατον Ἥρας μητέρ' εἰς ἐμὴν ὕβριν.
αἰνῶ δὲ Κάδμον, ἄβατον ὃς πέδον τόδε 10
τίθησι, θυγατρὸς σηκόν· ἀμπέλου δέ νιν
πέριξ ἐγὼ 'κάλυψα βοτρυώδει χλόῃ.
λιπὼν δὲ Λυδῶν τοὺς πολυχρύσους γύας
Φρυγῶν τε, Περσῶν θ' ἡλιοβλήτους πλάκας
Βάκτριά τε τείχη τήν τε δύσχιμον χθόνα 15
Μήδων ἐπελθὼν Ἀραβίαν τ' εὐδαίμονα
Ἀσίαν τε πᾶσαν, ἣ παρ' ἁλμυρὰν ἅλα

pare Eum. 233, πρόσειμι δῶμα καὶ βρέτας τὸ σόν, θεά. Cycl. 95, πόθεν πάρεισι Σικελὸν Αἰτναῖον πάγον. Cf. Electr. 1278.
8. δίου πυρὸς, the lightning of Zeus. Cf. τέκτονας δίου πυρὸς Alcest. 5. The omission of τε before πυρὸς, first tacitly made by Barnes, is approved by Hermann, who however construes τυφόμενα φλόγα πυρὸς, *fumantia ignis flammam*. Porson transposed thus, δίου τ' ἔτι πυρὸς ζ. φ., but W. Dindorf seems rightly to judge that the τε is unnecessary, and that the clause is simply the accusative of apposition. There is a variant ἁδροῦ πυρὸς quoted by Plutarch, p. 79, A., on which see Suppl. 857.—The smoke and flame are represented as supernaturally permanent, because the jealousy of Hera had willed that the proofs of Semele's condign punishment should be lasting. The visible exhalations of some ancient *solfatara* possibly give rise to the legend. But the exact meaning of ἀθάνατον is not very clear. It may mean (1) ἀείμνηστον, never to be forgotten (as Barnes explains it), or (2) destined to remain visibly to all time, or (3) ὕβριν ἀθανάτου θεᾶς εἰς θνητὴν μητέρα. And the last appears the most probable. As the bolt itself was δῖον πῦρ, so the punishment inflicted by Hera on her rival Semele was supernatural, such as a goddess alone could inflict. Nor does this interpretation altogether exclude the second.
10. αἰνῶ Κάδμον. The τὸ θεοσεβὲς of Cadmus meets with the approbation of Dionysus the more readily, because his children had rejected the claims of the god.—ἄβατον, railed round, like the tomb of those who had died by lightning, cf. Suppl. 938. It was the Roman *bidental*. The ἐγὼ in v. 12 is of course emphatic: Cadmus inclosed the tomb, but it was I who planted the grape-vine there.
13—16. These verses are twice quoted by Strabo, p. 27, and p. 687, in both places with τὰς, which Elmsley rightly changed to τούς. See Heracl. 839, ὦ τὸν Ἀργείων γύην σπείροντες. The epithet, Hermann observes, refers to the auriferous sands of the Pactolus. Hence Elmsley's proposed correction, τῶν πολυχρύσων, is needless. — The countries here enumerated, though nearly in inverse order, point to the ancient Pelasgic settlements west of the Indus as the ultimate source of the Bacchic rites. Dionysus in fact is commonly represented as an Indian god, and hence his car is drawn by tigers. His conquest of India (viz. the use of strong drink first introduced into that country), was a favourite theme for poetry. Cf. Propertius, iv. 17, 21, 'Dicam ego maternos Aetnaeo fulmine partus, Indica Nysaeis arma fugata choris.' *Arabia* is added merely as one of the lands of the vaguely-known east; for the poet could hardly have meant to specify the Semitic, i. e. the Phoenician and Egyptian elements which entered into the varied worship of Dionysus. And yet, the wish of the chorus in v. 400—5, to fly to Cyprus and Egypt, as one of the resorts of Bacchus, looks like a confirmation of this view.

ΕΥΡΙΠΙΔΟΥ

κεῖται, μιγάσιν Ἕλλησι βαρβάροις θ' ὁμοῦ
πλήρεις ἔχουσα καλλιπυργώτους πόλεις,
ἐς τήνδε πρῶτον ἦλθον Ἑλλήνων πόλιν· 20
κἀκεῖ χορεύσας καὶ καταστήσας ἐμὰς
τελετάς, ἵν' εἴην ἐμφανὴς δαίμων βροτοῖς,
* * * *
πρώτας δὲ Θήβας τῆσδε γῆς Ἑλληνίδος
ἀνωλόλυξα, νεβρίδ' ἐξάψας χροὸς,
θύρσον τε δοὺς ἐς χεῖρα, κίσσινον βέλος, 25
ἐπεί μ' ἀδελφαὶ μητρὸς, ἃς ἥκιστ' ἐχρῆν,
Διόνυσον οὐκ ἔφασκον ἐκφῦναι Διὸς,
Σεμέλην δὲ νυμφευθεῖσαν ἐκ θνητοῦ τινὸς
ἐς Ζῆν' ἀναφέρειν τὴν ἁμαρτίαν λέχους,

By the word ἐπελθὼν a *hostile* attack upon, i. e. a conquest over, the easterns is expressed. It would be better, with Bothe, to omit the τε after Περσῶν, i. e. it would make the sense plainer to readers of Greek who are not Greeks; for the order is, λιπὼν Λυδοὺς καὶ Φρύγας, ἐπελθὼν Πέρσας, &c., Ἀραβίαν Ἀσίαν τε, 'having left Lydia and Phrygia (whither he had come) after conquering Persia, &c. and the whole of Asia.' Hermann, who seems to explain ἐπελθὼν 'having visited,' says "ad Medos tantum et Arabiam atque Asiam referendum est." Matthiae has no decided opinion. "Non dici potest ad quos accusativos λιπὼν referri debeat, et ad quos ἐπελθών: utrumque enim ad omnes pertinet."
18. μιγάσιν. For the tribrach of one word composing the second foot, compare 261, 662.
19. καλλιπυργώτους. See on Tro. 46, where it is shown that the πύργοι or fortified walls were a characteristic of the ancient cities of Asia Minor.—μιγάσιν κτλ., a mixed population of Ionian colonists and Persian tributaries. These are contrasted with the pure Hellenes of Thebes, v. 20. The anachronism was a matter of no concern to Euripides, who does not hesitate to make Teiresias also a contemporary of Cadmus, though in the Phoenissae he places him many generations later, with Creon and Polynices. Elmsley is at a loss for an example of a dative after πλήρης "et similia." He might have found one in Aesch. Theb. 459, μυκτηροκόμποις πνεύμασιν πληρούμενοι. In the Appendix however he adduces Herc. F. 369, πεύκαισιν χέρας πληροῦντες. So also in Pers. 134, λέκτρα δ' ἀνδρῶν πόθῳ πίμπλαται δακρύμασιν.
22. After this verse there can hardly be a doubt that a line has dropped out, e. g. πολλοὺς ἔπεισα τῶν ἐμῶν νόμων κλύειν. Elmsley's expedient, of transposing v. 20 to this place, after Pierson's suggestion, is improbable in itself, because the very next verse is thus a mere tautology. Nor is Hermann's method much better, of putting the full stop at the end of v. 22, "peragratis multis Asiae regionibus, nunc primum ad hanc Graecorum urbem accessi, illic quoque sacris meis introductis." By ἐκεῖ the poet undoubtedly means Asia; and the inference is, that Dionysus is about to do in Thebes what he has uniformly done elsewhere.
24. ἀνωλόλυξα, I filled with the ὀλολυγὴ or joyous female cry; a very bold use of this verb.—χροὸς, scil. αὐτῶν.
26. ἐπεί. The reason is given why Thebes is the *first* Grecian city that has been inspired with the enthusiasm of the Bacchic rites, viz. because there first they were derided as an imposture.
29. τὴν ἁμαρτίαν. For the use of ἁμαρτάνειν, as applied to amours, see Electr. 1036. Nub. 1076. The ordinary construction would be either τὴν τοῦ λέχους ἁμ., or simply λέχους ἁμ. The rule is not invariably observed in poetry; yet it is seldom violated. See on μόχθους τῆς εὐσεβίας, Hipp. 1368, and on Agam. 869, τῶν σταθμῶν κύνα. Here perhaps we should read τήνδ' ἁμαρτίαν. See a similar

Κάδμου σοφίσμαθ', ὧν νιν οὕνεκα κτανεῖν 30
Ζῆν' ἐξεκαυχῶνθ', ὅτι γάμους ἐψεύσατο.
τοιγάρ νιν αὐτὰς ἐκ δόμων ὤστρησ' ἐγὼ
μανίαις· ὄρος δ' οἰκοῦσι παράκοποι φρενῶν·
σκευήν τ' ἔχειν ἠνάγκασ' ὀργίων ἐμῶν,
καὶ πᾶν τὸ θῆλυ σπέρμα Καδμείων, ὅσαι 35
γυναῖκες ἦσαν, ἐξέμηνα δωμάτων·
ὁμοῦ δὲ Κάδμου παισὶν ἀναμεμιγμέναι
χλωραῖς ὑπ' ἐλάταις ἀνορόφοις ἧνται πέτραις.
δεῖ γὰρ πόλιν τήνδ' ἐκμαθεῖν, κεἰ μὴ θέλει,
ἀτέλεστον οὖσαν τῶν ἐμῶν βακχευμάτων, 40
Σεμέλης τε μητρὸς ἀπολογήσασθαί μ' ὕπερ,
φανέντα θνητοῖς δαίμον', ὃν τίκτει Διί.
Κάδμος μὲν οὖν γέρας τε καὶ τυραννίδα
Πενθεῖ δίδωσι θυγατρὸς ἐκπεφυκότι,

correction of Hermann's in Hec. 8. Apollodor. iii. 4, 3, Σεμέλης δὲ Ζεὺς ἐρασθεὶς, Ἥρας κρύφα συνευνάζεται. Ἡ δὲ, ἐξαπατηθεῖσα ὑπὸ Ἥρας, κατανεύσαντος αὐτῇ Διὸς πᾶν τὸ αἰτηθὲν ποιήσειν, αἰτεῖται τοιοῦτον αὐτὸν ἐλθεῖν, οἷος ἦλθε μνηστευόμενος Ἥραν. Ζεὺς δὲ, μὴ δυνάμενος ἀνανεῦσαι, παραγίνεται εἰς τὸν θάλαμον αὐτῆς ἐφ' ἅρματος, ἀστραπαῖς ὁμοῦ καὶ βρονταῖς, καὶ κεραυνὸν ἵησιν. Σεμέλης δὲ διὰ τὸν φόβον ἐκλιπούσης, ἐξαμηνιαῖον βρέφος ἐξαμβλωθὲν ἐκ τοῦ πυρὸς ἁρπάσας, ἐνέρραψε τῷ μηρῷ. Ἀποθανούσης δὲ Σεμέλης, αἱ λοιπαὶ Κάδμου θυγατέρες διήνεγκαν λόγον, συνευντῆσθαι θνητῷ τινὶ Σεμέλην, καὶ καταψεύσασθαι Διὸς, καὶ διὰ τοῦτο ἐκεραυνώθη. Κατὰ δὲ τὸν χρόνον τὸν καθήκοντα, Διόνυσον γεννᾷ Ζεὺς λύσας τὰ ῥάμματα, καὶ δίδωσιν Ἑρμῇ. Ὁ δὲ κομίζει πρὸς Ἰνὼ καὶ Ἀθάμαντα, καὶ πείθει τρέφειν ὡς κόρην.

30. Κάδμου σοφίσματα. They pretended that Semele had been instructed by her father to lay the blame on Zeus; and they presumptuously added, that Zeus had killed her on that account.

32. νιν αὐτὰς, eas ipsas, Elmsley ; who rightly explains the sense to be αὐτάς τε καὶ πᾶν τὸ θῆλυ σπέρμα, v. 35.—ὤστρησα, from οἰστρεῖν, οἰστρᾶν being intransitive, Prom. 855, Iph. Aul. 77. Photius, οἰστρᾷ, συντόνως καὶ μανικῶς κινεῖται. Οἰστρεῖ, ἐρεθίζει, ἐκμαίνει. Cf. Plat. Phaedr. p. 251, D., πᾶσα κεντουμένη κύκλῳ ἡ ψυχὴ οἰστρᾷ καὶ ὀδυνᾶται. Hermann gives οἶστρησ' with the old copies, but his rule is somewhat fanciful, " Graeci in verbis valde usitatis, quae ab οι diphthongo incipiunt, usurpavisse augmentum videntur ; in iis autem quae minus essent usu trita, abstinuisse eo."

35. ὅσαι γυναῖκες ἦσαν, all who were adult, not mere παρθένοι, though the term is not intended to exclude unmarried women; cf. v. 694, νέαι, παλαιαί, παρθένοι τ' ἔτ' ἄζυγες. For the active ἐκμαίνειν see Hipp. 1229. Ar. Eccl. 965, Κύπρι, τί μ' ἐκμαίνεις ἐπὶ ταύτῃ; Theocr. v. 91, κἠμὲ γὰρ ὁ Κρατίδας τὸν ποιμένα λεῖος ὑπαντῶν Ἐκμαίνει. Soph. Trach. 1142, τὸν σὸν ἐκμῆναι πόθον. In the two last passages it bears the proper sense of exciting the passion of love. Apollodor. iii. 5, 2, δείξας δὲ Θηβαίοις ὅτι θεός ἐστιν, ἧκεν εἰς Ἄργος· κἀκεῖ πάλιν οὐ τιμώντων αὐτὸν, ἐξέμηνε τὰς γυναῖκας.

38. πέτραις. A better reading would be ἀνορόφους ἧνται πέτρας, like ὄχλον θάσσοντ' ἄκραν Orest. 871. They are called ἀνόροφοι, because πέτρα is often used for ἄντρον. But these women did not dwell in grottoes, but amongst rocks that afforded no shelter.

39. ἐκμαθεῖν ἀτέλεστον οὖσαν, to learn to its cost that it has yet to be initiated in the Bacchic orgies.

42. φανέντα, by proving to them that I am really a god, though now I have assumed a human form. Cf. v. 50.

ΕΥΡΙΠΙΔΟΥ

ὃς θεομαχεῖ τὰ κατ' ἐμὲ καὶ σπονδῶν ἄπο 45
ὠθεῖ μ', ἐν εὐχαῖς τ' οὐδαμῶς μνείαν ἔχει.
ὧν οὕνεκ' αὐτῷ θεὸς γεγὼς ἐνδείξομαι
πᾶσίν τε Θηβαίοισιν. ἐς δ' ἄλλην χθόνα,
τἀνθένδε θέμενος εὖ, μεταστήσω πόδα,
δεικνὺς ἐμαυτόν· ἢν δὲ Θηβαίων πόλις 50
ὀργῇ σὺν ὅπλοις ἐξ ὄρους βάκχας ἄγειν
ζητῇ, ξυνάψω μαινάσι στρατηλατῶν.
ὧν οὕνεκ' εἶδος θνητὸν ἀλλάξας ἔχω,
μορφήν τ' ἐμὴν μετέβαλον εἰς ἀνδρὸς φύσιν.
ἀλλ' ὦ λιποῦσαι Τμῶλον, ἔρυμα Λυδίας, 55
θίασος ἐμὸς, γυναῖκες, ἃς ἐκ βαρβάρων
ἐκόμισα παρέδρους καὶ ξυνεμπόρους ἐμοὶ,
αἴρεσθε τἀπιχώρι' ἐν πόλει Φρυγῶν
τύμπανα, Ῥέας τε μητρὸς ἐμά θ' εὑρήματα,
βασίλειά τ' ἀμφὶ δώματ' ἐλθοῦσαι τάδε 60
κτυπεῖτε Πενθέως, ὡς ὁρᾷ Κάδμου πόλις.
ἐγὼ δὲ βάκχαις, ἐς Κιθαιρῶνος πτυχὰς
ἐλθὼν, ἵν' εἰσὶ, συμμετασχήσω χορῶν.

---

45. τὰ κατ' ἐμέ. Though willing enough to worship other gods, he is a rebel against *my* divinity, on the plea that I am not one of the gods of his country.—ἐν εὐχαῖς κτλ., in prayers and supplications to other gods, he makes no mention of me. Cf. Aesch. Suppl. 266, μνήμην ποτ' ἀντίμισθον ηὕρετ' ἐν λιταῖς.— Elmsley has οὐδαμοῦ μνήμην, Herm. οὐδαμοῦ μνείαν. W. Dindorf οὐδαμῶς from three MSS.

51. βάκχας, the female population who have gone off to the mountains, v. 33. If, says Dionysus, they should attempt to regain them by force of arms, I will engage with them, putting myself at the head of my Bacchanals, (i. e. my faithful followers, whether Asiatics or ἐπιχώριοι.) For the dative, depending on the sense of ἡγούμενος, compare Eum. 25, ἐξ οὗτε βάκχαις ἐστρατήγησεν θεός. Electr. 321, σκῆπτρ' ἐν οἷς Ἕλλησιν ἐστρατηλάτει. Hermann observes, that we may also construe συνάψω Μαινάσι, 'I will fight them with my Maenads,' in which case στρατηλατῶν is for στρατιὰν ἐλαύνων.

53. ἀλλάξας ἔχω, ἤλλαξα, ἔχω μετηλλαγμένον. Cf. v. 4. Hermann reads ἀλλάξας ἐγὼ Μορφὴν ἐμὴν μετέβαλον, on the ground that the old reading is a mere tautology. The truth perhaps is, that the ambiguous use of ἀλλάξας, which means either 'taking' or 'giving in exchange,' induced the poet to add the second verse as an epexegesis.

56. θίασος. Photius, τὸ ἀθροιζόμενον πλῆθος ἐπὶ τέλει καὶ τιμῇ θεοῦ. Cf. *inf.* 630, ὁρῶ δὲ θιάσους τρεῖς γυναικείων χορῶν. Probably the word is not truly Greek, but Asiatic, with many others that seem to have been imported with the rites of Dionysus and Cybele.

58. ἐν πόλει Φρυγῶν, apparently a periphrasis for ἐν Φρυξί. Some understand by it *Pessinus*, where the statue of Cybele was fabled to have fallen from heaven.— τάδε, the palace represented, as usual, at the back of the proscenium.—κτυπεῖτε, scil. αὐτοῖς, make a noise with your timbrels, that the city of Cadmus, i. e. the whole population, may come out to see you.

62. πτυχὰς Elmsley for πτύχας. As neither πτὺξ nor πτυχὴ seems to occur, there is some uncertainty as to the in-

ΧΟΡΟΣ.

Ἀσίας ἀπὸ γαίας   στρ. α΄.   64
ἱερὸν Τμῶλον ἀμείψασα θοάζω Βρομίῳ πόνον ἡδὺν
κάματόν τ᾽ εὐκάματον, Βάκχιον ἀζομένα θεόν.
τίς ὁδῷ τίς ὁδῷ ; τίς   ἀντ. α΄.
μελάθροις ; ἔκτοπος ἔστω, στόμα τ᾽ εὔφημον ἅπας
ὁσιούσθω·   70
τὰ νομισθέντα γὰρ ἀεὶ Διόνυσον ὑμνήσω.

flexion of this word. The dative πτυχαῖς proves the existence of the latter form, the accusative πτύχα in Suppl. 979, that of the former. An undoubted instance of the final ας made long before a vowel would be an evidence of some weight. Photius has πτυχαί· αἱ τῶν ὀρῶν ἀποκλίσεις. See on Androm. 1277.

64—169. The parode. Here the chorus, probably habited in Asiatic costume, and each carrying a vine-dressed or ivy-clad wand, chaplet of ivy, and dappled fawn-skin, come upon the orchestra with a wild dance and the noise of their peculiar drum or tambourine (τύπανον). They extol the delights of the sweet worship of Bacchus, associated with the kindred orgies of Rhea, the Great Mother. They particularly insist on the preternatural birth of Dionysus from Semele, on which doubts had been impiously cast by Pentheus. They implore Thebes, the birth-place of Semele, not to reject the holy rites; and predict, with the usual enthusiasm of religious votaries, that the whole earth will soon be converted to the new worship. The invention of the Bacchic costume is attributed to the Curetes and Corybantes of Crete, with whom originated the dances of Satyrs in honour of Rhea. The progress of Bacchus over the mountains, with torches and wild gestures, everywhere giving miraculous manifestations of his presence, is in conclusion described. The metre is generally the glyconean ; but the Ionic *a minore* predominates at first, and in the epode there is a great mixture of dactylic, dochmiac, and asynartete verses, expressive of quick transitions and varied tones and gestures.

64. γαίας Hermann for γᾶς. Elmsley and Bothe retain γᾶς, not recognising the antistrophic character of 64—72. On the use of ἀμείψασα see Alcest. 462. So ἀμείψας νασιῶτιν ἑστίαν in Trach. 659, is ' having left Euboea ;' ἄμειψον δώματα, ' leave the house,' Eur. El. 750. For θοάζω cf. Tro. 349, Aesch. Suppl. 589, and *New Cratylus*, § 472. Translate, ' Coming from Asia's land, having left behind me the sacred Tmolus, I perform with rapid gestures a sweet toil (i. e. the dance) in honour of Bromius, a labour that is no labour, revering the Bacchic god.' The correction of Hermann, ἀζομένα for εὐαζομένα, is ingenious, and it seems to be rightly admitted by W. Dindorf. The active εὐάζω occurs *inf*. 1035, but the middle is not elsewhere found. This however is a circumstance of little weight in a play remarkable for its uncommon words. The verse of the antistrophe, if correct, has a syllable wanting to a complete Ionic foot, as is frequently the case in this metre.—θεὸν, which is here a monosyllable, as in v. 84 and 100, is omitted in the Palatine MS., while Aldus adds τὸν before Βάκχιον. All these facts show that this, and not the antistrophic verse, has been tampered with.

69. τίς ὁδῷ κτλ. Who is in the public way ? Who is in the house ? Let (the former) make room for us, and let all (i. e. both one and the other) observe a religious silence. This is Hermann's explanation, and it is far better than Elmsley's, (μελάθροις ἔκτοπος ἔστω, without the preceding τις,) for ἐκ τῆς ὁδοῦ ἔκτοπος ἔστω ἐν τοῖς μελάθροις. In fact, the passage is plain enough. Compare Ion 99, στόμα τ᾽ εὔφημον φρουρεῖν ἀγαθὸν κτλ.

70. The Palatine MS. has ἐξοσιούσθω, apparently a metrical correction like εὐαζομένα above, to complete the deficient syllable of the Ionic verse. Here ὁσιούσθω is a synonym of ὅσιος ἔστω.

72. Hermann considers the correction of Jacobs, εὐοῖ for αἰεὶ, " haud dubie

ΕΥΡΙΠΙΔΟΥ

ὦ μάκαρ, ὅστις εὐδαί-   στρ. β'.
μων τελετὰς θεῶν
εἰδὼς βιοτὰν ἁγιστεύει   75
καὶ θιασεύεται ψυ-
χὰν ἐν ὄρεσσι βακχεύ-
ων ὁσίοις καθαρμοῖσιν·
τά τε ματρὸς μεγάλας ὄργια Κυβέλας θεμιτεύων,
ἀνὰ θύρσον τε τινάσσων *κρᾶτα κισσῷ στεφανωθεὶς   80
Διόνυσον θεραπεύει.
ἴτε βάκχαι, ἴτε βάκχαι, Βρόμιον παῖδα θεὸν θεοῦ
Διόνυσον κατάγουσαι Φρυγίων ἐξ ὀρέων   85
Ἑλλάδος εἰς εὐρυχόρους ἀγυιὰς τὸν Βρόμιον·
ὅν ποτ' ἔχουσ' ἐν ὠδί-   ἀντ. β'.
νων λοχίαις ἀνάγ-
καισι πταμένας Διὸς βροντᾶς   90
νηδύος ἔκβολον μά-

---

vera." He adds as a reason, " id ipsum est τὸ νομισθὲν, εὐοῖ clamari. Aiei quidem neque cum τὰ νομισθέντα neque cum ὑμνήσω apte conjungi potest." But, as the chorus goes on to speak of the happiness of those who are initiated in the Bacchic worship, they probably mean to say, that they will never relinquish it; hence ἀεὶ ὑμνήσω may very well be taken together. The ῠ in ὑμνήσω is here made short, as in ὑμνῳδεῖ Agam. 962.

75. ἁγιστεύει, "pro ἁγνεύει," says Elmsley; and the words are here pretty nearly identical. As ἁγνεύω is ἁγνός εἰμι, so ἁγιστεύω is ἁγιστός εἰμι, 'I am ἅγιος,' that is, 'I have been hallowed.' The supposed happiness in Hades of those who had been initiated, οἱ μεμυημένοι, is well known from the chorus in the *Frogs*. Elmsley quotes Herc. F. 613, τὰ μυστῶν ὄργι' ηὐτύχησ' ἰδών. Strabo, Lib. x. p. 469, cites, and perhaps from memory, the whole of στρ. β', (with the exception of v. 76—78, and the omission of τελετὰς θεῶν εἰδὼς,) and also the whole of ἀντ. γ'. No readings of value are obtained from his text, the varieties being for the most part manifest corruptions, or inaccuracies inadvertently made in quoting.—For θιασεύεται see Ion 552. 'Happy,' says the poet, 'is he who has his soul disciplined in the Bacchic rites by holy purifications, while he revels on the mountains.' In ψυχὴ reference is made to the future state of the devotee of Bacchus.

79. Κυβέλας. This word, answered by θαλάμοις in v. 94, is a rare instance of a resolved Ionic foot. Perhaps both were pronounced as if Κύβλας and θάλμοις. Compare v. 372 with 387. The phrase θεμιτεύειν ὄργια is a singular one. It is like νομίζειν, to sanction by use, to look upon as a law human or divine (νόμος or θέμις). The old reading θεμιστεύων was corrected by Musgrave.

80. The common reading κισσῷ τε στεφανωθεὶς does not satisfy the metre. Strabo in quoting the passage omits τε. Hermann gives κατὰ κισσῷ στ., but κρᾶτα seems more likely, although the υ in χρυσέαισιν may be made short, v. 97. Compare v. 341, δεῦρό σου στέψω κάρα κισσῷ, and v. 177.

88. ἔχουσα, scil. ἑαυτὴν, for οὖσα. Musgrave well compares Ran. 704, καὶ ταῦτ' ἔχοντες κυμάτων ἐν ἀγκάλαις.

91. ἔκβολον. Probably a substantive, as in Ion 555. Hel. 422. The proper arrangement of these glyconean verses is due to Hermann. In Elmsley's edition they are very incorrectly divided.

τηρ ἔτεκεν, λιποῦσ᾽ αἰ-
ῶνα κεραυνίῳ πλαγᾷ·
λοχίοις δ᾽ αὐτίκα νιν δέξατο θαλάμοις Κρονίδας Ζεύς·
κατὰ μηρῷ δὲ καλύψας χρυσέαισιν συνερείδει
περόναις κρυπτὸν ἀφ᾽ Ἥρας.
ἔτεκεν δ᾽, ἀνίκα Μοῖραι τέλεσαν ταυρόκερων θεὸν, 100
στεφάνωσέν τε δρακόντων στεφάνοις, ἔνθεν ἄγραν
θυρσοφόροι μαινάδες ἀμφιβάλλονται πλοκάμοις.
ὦ Σεμέλας τροφοὶ Θῆ-   στρ. γ´.   105
βαι στεφανοῦσθε κισσῷ·
βρύετε βρύετε χλοήρει
σμίλακι καλλικάρπῳ,
καὶ καταβακχιοῦσθε δρυὸς
ἢ ἐλάτας κλάδοισι,   110
στικτῶν τ᾽ ἐνδυτὰ νεβρίδων

100. τέλεσαν, had made τέλειον, had brought to maturity. Diod. Sic. iii. 64, 25, μετὰ δὲ ταῦτα τοῦ κατὰ φύσιν τῆς γενέσεως χρόνου τὴν τελείαν αὔξησιν ποιήσαντος, ἀπενεγκεῖν τὸ βρέφος εἰς Νῦσαν τῆς Ἀραβίας. Pind. Pyth. iii. 9, τὸν μὲν εὐίππου Φλεγύα θυγάτηρ, πρὶν τελέσσαι ματροπόλῳ σὺν Εἰλειθυίᾳ κτλ. The Μοῖραι are mentioned as the goddesses connected with childbirth.—ταυρόκερων, cf. v. 920.

102. δρακόντων στεφάνοις. See on Ion 24.—ἔνθεν ἄγραν seems to be put for ὧν ἄγραν, 'some taken from which the Maenads still put in their hair;' otherwise, if ἔνθεν be taken for οὗ ἕνεκα, the ellipse of δρακόντων after ἄγραν is very harsh. The poet seems to have meant ὅθεν τούτων ἄγραν κτλ., but he has expressed himself shortly. Hermann's view, that ἄγραν is not the object but the predicate, (as if it were δράκοντας ποιοῦνται ἄγραν,) seems to require that the sentence should be fully developed thus, ἔνθεν δράκοντας ποιούμεναι ἄγραν ἀμφιβάλλονται αὐτοὺς πλοκάμοις. This last verse is, according to the arrangement in the text, which is W. Dindorf's, logaoedic preceded and followed by a choriambus.

107. χλοήρει Herm. Dind. for χλοηρᾷ, which Elmsley prefers. It is a question of probability, since both readings are found in MSS. In v. 1048 we have ποιηρὸν νάπος, so that the distinction usually observed between the terminations of adjectives in —ήρης and —ηρὸς (see on Ion 1128,) is perhaps only a general one.

108. σμίλακι Aldus, and so Hermann, while Elmsley and W. Dindorf give μίλακι with the Palatine MS. The word occurs Nub. 1007, Av. 216, where the metre admits of either form.

109. καταβακχιοῦσθε. Lobeck on Ajac. p. 375, (quoted by W. Dindorf,) explains this word 'be crowned,' from Hesych. βακχᾶν ἐστεφανῶσθαι, and Etym. M. βάκχος, ὁ κλάδος ὁ ἐν ταῖς τελεταῖς, ἢ στέφανος. The same learned scholar shows that the practice alluded to in the following lines is that of sewing tufts or patches of skin or fur of a different colour to imitate natural spots or pyebald marks. He well compares Tac. Germ. § 27, *eligunt feras et detracta velamina spargunt maculis pellibusque ferarum, quas exterior pontus gignit.* A similar device is still adopted in the manufacture of furs into articles of female attire, muffs, tippets, &c., where ermine spots are thus imitated; and so also the furs called in ancient heraldry *ermine* and *vair* appear to have been made up. Here it is clear that tufts of *wool* are described, or at least white strips of goat's hair.

111. ἐνδυτὰ νεβρίδων, the ornamental garments of dappled fawn-skins. Compare σαρκὸς ἐνδυτὰ for the hides of oxen, v. 746.

406   ΕΥΡΙΠΙΔΟΥ

στέφετε λευκοτρίχων πλοκάμων
μαλλοῖς· ἀμφὶ δὲ νάρθηκας ὑβρι-
στὰς ὁσιοῦσθ'. αὐτίκα γᾶ πᾶσα χορεύσει,
Βρόμιος εὖτ' ἂν ἄγῃ θιάσους   115
εἰς ὄρος εἰς ὄρος, ἔνθα μένει
θηλυγενὴς ὄχλος
ἀφ' ἱστῶν παρὰ κερκίδων τ'
οἰστρηθεὶς Διονύσῳ.
ὦ θαλάμευμα Κουρή-   ἀντ. γ'. 120
των ζάθεοι τε Κρήτας
Διογενέτορες ἔναυλοι,
τρικόρυθες ἔνθ' ἐν ἄντροις

113. ἀμφὶ νάρθηκας, 'be consecrated by intercourse with the saucy Bacchic wands,' i. e. with those who bear them. Part of the wild sport of the Bacchants was to strike each other (cf. v. 308) with the wand or ferule, by which the spectators or new comers were perhaps claimed as belonging to the god, and were said ὁσιοῦσθαι. These two verses are choriambic, but they may also be arranged in Ionics.

114. αὐτίκα κτλ. Soon the whole land, i. e. all Greece, will join the dance, when Bacchus brings his companies to the mountain, where &c. See v. 62. Hermann and Elmsley place a full stop at χορεύσει, and then read Βρόμιος, ὅστις ἄγει κτλ., ''tis Bacchus who is leading his bands.' The Aldine has ὅστις, but the MSS. ὅτ' ἄγῃ, whence Elmsley, followed by W. Dindorf, εὖτ' ἂν ἄγῃ. The use of ὅστις for ὃς, according to Hermann's view of the passage, seems very questionable.—ἔνθα μένει, where the Theban women still remain, refusing to return to their homes; which, as v. 51 shows, was the anxious wish of the government. When, therefore, Bacchus brings new converts to join them, there is a prospect of all the country soon following.—For the dative Διονύσῳ see v. 3.—παρὰ κερκίδων, as 'Ιλιάδος παρ' ἀκτᾶς Rhes. 366. This preposition commonly takes a genitive only of the person.

120 seqq. The meaning of this antistrophe is, that the instruments used in the worship of Bacchus were first adopted in Crete for the service of Rhea; which is another way of expressing the intimate connexion that subsisted between the orgiastic rites of these two deities. The legend was, that when Zeus was born in Crete, the Curetes made a noise to prevent the infant's cries being heard by Kronus, who would have devoured him, Apollodor. i. 1, 5. There is much difficulty in the words ἀνὰ δὲ βάκχια κτλ., not only because the reading of the best copies is βακχεία, while Strabo gives βακχείῳ, but because the poet is thus made to say, that the Curetes mixed up Bacchic strains with the harmony of the Phrygian flute, and so gave to Rhea what in fact they had borrowed from Bacchus; whereas he ought to say, that the satyrs took the tympanum from Rhea, and introduced it into the festivals of Bacchus. Hence Hermann, who rightly regards ἀνὰ—κέρασαν as a tmesis, reads Βακχάδι, temperarunt tympana concordante Bacchico Phrygiarum tibiarum spiritu. W. Dindorf regards βάκχια as used adverbially like εὔια in v. 157. Perhaps however it merely means that they joined such sounds as those afterwards peculiarly called Bacchic. Elmsley cannot be right in construing ἀνὰ βάκχια as if ἐν βακχίοις.—κτύπον is the accusative in apposition to κύκλωμα, not to βάκχια. The editions wrongly put a colon at ηὗρον. The clause ἀνὰ δὲ—θῆκαν is parenthetical. The old copies give ἐν or ἐν τ' ἄσμασι, corrected by Canter. Strabo has καλλίκτυπον εὔασμα βακχᾶν. 'A noise for the shouts of the Bacchants,' means an instrument for beating time to their cries of εὐοῖ.

123. ἔνθα. Aldus omits, most copies, with Strabo, put this word before τρικόρυθες.

βυρσότονον κύκλωμα τόδε
μοι Κορύβαντες ηὗρον, 125
ἀνὰ δὲ βάκχια συντόνῳ
κέρασαν ἁδυβόᾳ Φρυγίων
αὐλῶν πνεύματι, ματρός τε 'Ρέας
ἐς χέρα θῆκαν, κτύπον εὐάσμασι βακχᾶν·
παρὰ δὲ μαινόμενοι σάτυροι 130
ματέρος ἐξανύσαντο θεᾶς,
ἐς δὲ χορεύματα
συνῆψαν τριετηρίδων,
οἷς χαίρει Διόνυσος.
ἡδὺς ἐν οὔρεσιν, ὅταν ἐπῳδ. 135
ἐκ θιάσων δρομαίων
πέσῃ πεδόσε, νεβρίδος ἔχων
ἱερὸν ἐνδυτὸν, ἀγρεύων
αἷμα τραγοκτόνον, ὠμοφάγον χάριν,
ἱέμενος εἰς ὄρεα Φρύγια, Λύδια. 140
ὁ δ' ἔξαρχος Βρόμιος, εὐοῖ.
ῥεῖ δὲ γάλακτι πέδον, ῥεῖ δ' οἴνῳ, ῥεῖ δὲ μελισσᾶν
νέκταρι, Συρίας δ' ὡς λιβάνου καπνός.

131. ἐξανύσαντο, 'obtained it,' i. e. the τύπανον. So ἀνύσασθαι means *consequi* in Prom. 719. Choeph. 843. Theocr. v. 144, xviii. 17, ὄλβιε γάμβρ', ἀγαθός τις ἐπέπταρεν ἐρχομένῳ τοι Ἐς Σπάρταν, ὅποι ἄλλοι ἀριστέες, ὡς ἀνύσαιο.—συνῆψαν, scil. ἑαυτοὺς, joined in the dance. The ancient festivals of Bacchus seem to have been celebrated every third year. Virg. Aen. iv. 302, 'Qualis commotis excita sacris Thyias, ubi audito stimulant trieterica Baccho Orgia.' Cic. de Nat. D. iii. 23, ' Dionysos multos habemus;— quintum Niso (Nyso?) natum et Thyone, a quo trieterides constitutae putantur.' Ovid, Fast. i. 393, 'Festa corymbiferi celebrabas Graecia Bacchi, Tertia quae solito tempore bruma refert.' Diodor. Sic. iii. 65, *fin*. τριετηροῦς δὲ διαγεγενημένου τοῦ σύμπαντος χρόνου, [sc. τῆς ἐπ' Ἰνδοὺς στρατείας,] φασὶ τοὺς Ἕλληνας ἀπὸ ταύτης τῆς αἰτίας ἄγειν τὰς τριετηρίδας.

135. ἡδύς. This, as Bothe and Hermann take it, is not said of Bacchus, (who is mentioned below as the exarch of the company,) but of the followers of the god. Hermann, who thinks πέσῃ πεδόσε, taken in connexion with ἀγρεύων, must refer to hunting in the plains, as contrasted with the mountains, reads ἡδὺς, ἐν οὔρεσιν, ὅς τ' ἂν κτλ., which he explains *laetitiae plenus est, in montes, quique ex velocibus thiasis in campos sese contulerit*. If this be the poet's meaning, why not read ὅταν τ' ἐκ θ. &c.? But πέσῃ means simply that the wearied Bacchant throws himself on the ground through fatigue, (as *inf.* 683,) and ἀγρεύων is exegetical of θ. δρομαίων, as if it were ἄγρᾳ κεκμηκώς. The chief force of the expression is in δρόμων implied in the adjective. That the Bacchants attacked herds of cattle is seen below, v. 737 *seqq*. Of this hunting company, θίασος, Dionysus is himself the leader or *exarch* (Theatre of the Greeks, p. 13], note 8).—εὐοῖ, i. e. he gives the hunting-cry to be taken up by the rest.

144. καπνός, i. e. ἐστι, 'there is *as it were* a fragrance of Assyrian incense.' Cf. Agam. 1283, οὐ Σύριον ἀγλάισμα δώμασιν λέγεις. Translate, 'And the

ὁ βακχεὺς δ' ἔχων   145
πυρσώδη φλόγα πεύκας
ἐκ νάρθηκος ἀΐσσει
δρόμῳ, χοροὺς ἐρεθίζων πλανάτας,
ἰαχαῖς τ' ἀναπάλλων,
τρυφερὸν πλόκαμον εἰς αἰθέρα ῥίπτων.   150
ἅμα δ' ἐπ' εὐάσμασιν ἐπιβρέμει
τοιάδ'· ὦ ἴτε βάκχαι,
ὦ ἴτε βάκχαι,
Τμώλου χρυσορόου χλιδά,
μέλπετε τὸν Διόνυσον   155
βαρυβρόμων ὑπὸ τυμπάνων,
εὔια τὸν εὔιον ἀγαλλόμεναι θεὸν
ἐν Φρυγίαισι βοαῖς ἐνοπαῖσί τε,
λωτὸς ὅταν εὐκέλαδος ἱερὸς ἱερὰ   160
παίγματα βρέμῃ σύνοχα φοιτάσιν
εἰς ὄρος εἰς ὄρος· ἡδομένα δ' ἄρα

follower of Bacchus, holding the ruddy blaze of pine-wood on his wand, waves it about in his course, rousing the scattered bands of dancers as he goes.' The torch seems to have been placed at the end of the wand, for the purpose both of holding it aloft, and of giving it a wider range in brandishing it about. In this passage ἀΐσσει is probably active, in the sense in which the passive is used of widely-tossed hair, Oed. Col. 1261, κόμη δι' αὔρας ἀκτένιστος ᾄσσεται. Others translate ἀΐσσει δρόμῳ 'rushes along at full speed.'— χοροὺς Hermann for καὶ χοροῖς, but in MS. Pal. there is a mark under the ι indicating a doubtful reading. Elmsley gives δρόμῳ τε χοροὺς, comparing πώλους ἐρεθίζων in Rhes. 373.

145. ὁ βακχεύς. Used like θιασώτης in v. 548. In Ion v. 218 we have ὁ Βακχεὺς in apposition to Βρόμιος, and the article there may be regarded as representing ὁ ὀνομασθεὶς καὶ Βακχεύς. Here it means 'the bacchant.' See on v. 548.

151. ἐπ' εὐάσμασιν, 'With cries of Evoe !' So Eumen. ult., ὀλολύξατε νῦν ἐπὶ μολπαῖς, unless the sense there is, 'after our song.'

154. χρυσορόου, from χρυσορόας, having gold-washing rivulets descending from it.

157. ἀγαλλόμεναι, ἀγάλλουσαι, Med.

1027.—εὔια is the accusative like τὰ νομισθέντα, v. 72. Bacchico more, Elmsley; who regards it as used adverbially. The metre of this verse and of 160—1 is paeonic, each foot being a regular first paeon, $-\cup\cup\cup$. The remainder are dactylic. We should however, both on account of sense and metre, read ἀγαλλόμεθα, 'We thus honour the god whenever the pipe sounds,' &c., and perhaps also ἡδόμεθα δ' ἄρα in v. 162. The preceding would then stand thus; παίγματα βρέμῃ σύνοχα φοιτάσιν ἐς ὄρος. Thus in four paeonic verses, (the last being a monometer, ἡδόμεθα δ' ἄρα, the repetition of εἰς ὄρος being rejected by Hermann also,) the concluding syllables ⏑ ⏑ are uniformly restored. Possibly βάκχου might be retained in v. 169, instead of βάκχα, the conjecture of Musgrave; for the φοιτάδες, or inspired women, might well be said ἤδεσθαι, to take pleasure in the movements of their leader Bacchus. As the text now stands,—and no reliance can be placed on it,—the sense will be, ἡδομένη δὲ βάκχῃ ἄγει κῶλον ταχύπουν σκιρτήμασι, ὅπως πῶλος (σκιρτᾷ) ἅμα μητέρι.—σύνοχα here, as in Hel. 172, appears to be the same as συνῳδά.

πῶλος ὅπως ἅμα ματέρι φορβάδι
κῶλον ἄγει ταχύπουν σκιρτήμασι βάκχα.

ΤΕΙΡΕΣΙΑΣ.

τίς ἐν πύλαισι Κάδμον ἐκκαλεῖ δόμων, 170
Ἀγήνορος παῖδ', ὃς πόλιν Σιδωνίαν
λιπὼν ἐπύργωσ' ἄστυ Θηβαίων τόδε;
ἴτω τις, εἰσάγγελλε Τειρεσίας ὅτι
ζητεῖ νιν· οἶδε δ' αὐτὸς ὧν ἥκω πέρι,
ἅ τε ξυνεθέμην πρέσβυς ὢν γεραιτέρῳ, 175
θύρσους ἀνάπτειν καὶ νεβρῶν δορὰς ἔχειν,
στεφανοῦν τε κρᾶτα κισσίνοις βλαστήμασιν.

ΚΑΔΜΟΣ.

ὦ φίλταθ', ὡς σὴν γῆρυν ᾐσθόμην κλύων,
σοφὴν σοφοῦ παρ' ἀνδρὸς, ἐν δόμοισιν ὤν.
ἥκω δ' ἕτοιμος, τήνδ' ἔχων σκευὴν θεοῦ. 180
δεῖ γάρ νιν ὄντα παῖδα θυγατρὸς ἐξ ἐμῆς,
Διόνυσον, ὃς πέφηνεν ἀνθρώποις θεὸς,
ὅσον καθ' ἡμᾶς δυνατὸν αὔξεσθαι μέγαν.
ποῖ δεῖ χορεύειν, ποῖ καθιστάναι πόδα
καὶ κρᾶτα σεῖσαι πολιόν; ἐξηγοῦ σύ μοι 185
γέρων γέροντι, Τειρεσία· σὺ γὰρ σοφός.
ὡς οὐ κάμοιμ' ἂν οὔτε νύκτ' οὔθ' ἡμέραν
θύρσῳ κροτῶν γῆν· ἐπιλελήσμεθ' ἡδέως

---

170. Teiresias is now seen knocking for admission at the door of the palace. He speaks, as usual, to the door-keeper within; compare Aesch. Cho. 641, τίς ἔνδον, ὦ παῖ, παῖ, μάλ' αὖθις, ἐν δόμοις; Elmsley conjectures τίς ἐν πύλαισι; Κάδμον ἐκκάλει δόμων.—ἐκκαλεῖ may be the present, for τίς ἐκκαλεῖν θέλει; Cadmus, who is more θεοσεβὴς than his son, has agreed with the great Theban seer to pay public honours to Bacchus; to fulfil which engagement is the object of the present visit.

176. ἀνάπτειν, to dress the thyrsus or narthex with ivy.

178. ὡς σὴν γῆρυν κτλ., for I recognised your voice even before I saw you, and while yet within. "Rationem reddit, cur carissimum appellaverit Tiresiam, priusquam viderit. Dicit enim haec, dum aperiuntur fores." *Herm.*

182. W. Dindorf incloses this verse as spurious, after the opinion of Dobree, who thinks it was made up from v. 860. But the specifying of the person is very emphatic, though of course the context is complete without it.

185. ἐξηγοῦ, be my ἐξηγητὴς or interpreter. So Aesch. Eum. 565, ὁ μάντις ἐξηγεῖτό σοι μητροκτονεῖν; Ibid. 579, ἐξηγοῦ δέ μοι, Ἄπολλον, εἴ σφε σὺν δίκῃ κατέκτανον.

188. ἡδέως J. Barnes, for ἡδέων. The terminations ων and ως are often confused. The sense simply is, 'We gladly forget that we are old.'

γέροντες ὄντες.
ΤΕ.   ταῦτ' ἐμοὶ πάσχεις ἄρα.
    κἀγὼ γὰρ ἡβῶ κἀπιχειρήσω χοροῖς.   190
ΚΑ. οὐκοῦν ὄχοισιν εἰς ὄρος περάσομεν.
ΤΕ. ἀλλ' οὐχ ὁμοίως ἂν ὁ θεὸς τιμὴν ἔχοι.
ΚΑ. γέρων γέροντα παιδαγωγήσω σ' ἐγώ.
ΤΕ. ὁ θεὸς ἀμοχθὶ κεῖσε νῷν ἡγήσεται.
ΚΑ. μόνοι δὲ πόλεως Βακχίῳ χορεύσομεν;   195
ΤΕ. μόνοι γὰρ εὖ φρονοῦμεν, οἱ δ' ἄλλοι κακῶς.
ΚΑ. μακρὸν τὸ μέλλειν· ἀλλ' ἐμῆς ἔχου χερός.
ΤΕ. ἰδού, ξύναπτε καὶ ξυνωρίζου χέρα.
ΚΑ. οὐ καταφρονῶ 'γὼ τῶν θεῶν, θνητὸς γεγώς.
ΤΕ. οὐδὲν σοφιζόμεσθα τοῖσι δαίμοσι.   200
    πατρίους παραδοχὰς, ἅς θ' ὁμήλικας χρόνῳ

192. Elmsley needlessly alters the vulgate to ἀλλ' οὐχ ὁμοίαν ὁ θεὸς ἂν τιμὴν ἔχοι. Hermann rightly observes that the position of θεὸς, with the ictus falling on it, marks the emphasis; as if Teiresias had objected, 'that may be all very well for us, but the *god* would not be equally honoured.'

193. Gellius, N. A. xiii. 18, 'Sed etiam ille versus non minus notus, γέρων γέροντα etc., et in tragoedia Sophocli scriptus est, cui titulus Φθιώτιδες, et in Bacchis Euripidi.' Hence W. Dindorf has added it to the fragments of Sophocles, 623.

199. ἐγὼ here, as it usually does, conveys a marked emphasis; '*I* am not the man to despise the gods, born as I was a mortal.'

200. οὐδὲν σοφιζόμεσθα. We do not apply sophistry to the gods, i. e. we do not rationalise about them, as if our reason were capable of dealing with the question. This passage is remarkable enough as coming from Euripides, who was so fond of the very speculation which he here deprecates. It looks like a *palinodia* of his former opinions. The dative perhaps depends on the notion οὐ θεομαχήσω. Σοφίζεσθαι is very nearly our word 'to rationalise.' Plato, Phaedr. p. 229, C., εἰ ἀπιστοίην, ὥσπερ οἱ σοφοί, οὐκ ἂν ἄτοπος εἴην· εἶτα σοφιζόμενος φαίην αὐτὴν πνεῦμα Βορέου κατὰ τῶν πλησίον πετρῶν σὺν Φαρμακείᾳ παίζουσαν ὦσαι.

201—3. 'The traditions of our fathers, and those which we possess coeval with time itself, no arguments can overthrow, not even if wisdom has been attained by consummate intellect.'—πατρίους for πατρὸς has been restored from Plutarch, Op. M. p. 756, B, quoted by Valckenaer. That author quotes v. 203, with the variant δι' ἄκρας—φρενὸς, and paraphrases the foregoing by ἡ πάτριος καὶ παλαιὰ πίστις. Elmsley would read λόγοις, 'by arguments,' thus taking ηὕρηται in a middle sense.—ἄκρος is here, as in Agam. 611, for 'first-rate.' It is differently used in οὐκ ἀπ' ἄκρας φρενὸς ibid. 778, 'not from the mere surface of the mind.' The διὰ implies the agency whereby such wisdom is attained. By ὁμήλικας χρόνῳ, quae nata nobiscum habemus, Hermann understands those instincts of religion which are born in and grow up with us. With Brunck too he regards εὕρηται as the subjunctive, with τις implied. The question here is difficult; εἰ with a subjunctive is, in certain shades of meaning, as legitimate as ὅς, ὅτε, &c., while the perfect, to say nothing of the unusual form, is not very appropriate in the indicative, because the case is put only in a theoretical point of view. Perhaps οὐδ' οἷς is the true reading; 'not even (the arguments of those) by whom wisdom has been attained,' &c. The MSS. give καταβάλλει, or —η, but the editors generally acquiesce in Scaliger's correction καταβαλεῖ. If we retain καταβάλλει, the perfect seems defensible enough; 'no argument overthrows them, even *though* wisdom has

κεκτήμεθ', οὐδεὶς αὐτὰ καταβάλλει λόγος,
οὐδ' εἰ δι' ἄκρων τὸ σοφὸν ηὕρηται φρενῶν.
ἐρεῖ τις ὡς τὸ γῆρας οὐκ αἰσχύνομαι,
μέλλων χορεύειν, κρᾶτα κισσώσας ἐμόν. 205
οὐ γὰρ διῄρηχ' ὁ θεὸς εἴτε τὸν νέον
ἐχρῆν χορεύειν εἴτε τὸν γεραίτερον,
ἀλλ' ἐξ ἁπάντων βούλεται τιμὰς ἔχειν
κοινάς, δι' ἀριθμῶν δ' οὐδὲν αὔξεσθαι θέλει.
ΚΑ. ἐπεὶ σὺ φέγγος, Τειρεσία, τόδ' οὐχ ὁρᾷς, 210
ἐγὼ προφήτης σοι λόγων γενήσομαι.
Πενθεὺς πρὸς οἴκους ὅδε διὰ σπουδῆς περᾷ,
Ἐχίονος παῖς, ᾧ κράτος δίδωμι γῆς.
ὡς ἐπτόηται· τί ποτ' ἐρεῖ νεώτερον;

ΠΕΝΘΕΥΣ.

ἔκδημος ὢν μὲν τῆσδ' ἐτύγχανον χθονός, 215

been gained by the greatest talent,' i. e. not even the acutest sophists can successfully impugn them.

204. οὐκ αἰσχύνομαι. 'That I do not pay proper respect to my old age in being about to dance.' Some editions put a mark of interrogation at ἐμόν, rightly perhaps, though it gives a very different turn to the sentence; ἐρεῖ τις ὡς, Τὸ γῆρας οὐκ κτλ., 'Some will ask me, Am I not ashamed of my old age in thus being about to dance?' Elmsley quite mistakes the point of the question in supposing it would mean dicetne aliquis. The question is limited to οὐκ αἰσχύνομαι, the ὡς being redundant.

206. διῄρηκε, διώρισε, has not defined, distinguished between old and young in enforcing his worship.

209. δι' ἀριθμῶν, in which Elmsley and the earlier interpreters found much difficulty, is sufficiently explained by its antithesis to ἐξ ἁπάντων. The god does not choose to be honoured by a portion only, but by all. We might translate it sufficiently well, 'by the few.' Compare a similar contrast in Theocr. xvi. 87, ἀριθματοὺς ἀπὸ πολλῶν. Bothe is certainly wrong, per homines nullius pretii. He thinks the idiom the same as in Tro. 476, οὐκ ἀριθμὸν ἄλλως, and Heracl. 997, where see the note. The meaning of διὰ is, by a few here and a few there, taken at intervals.

211. προφήτης λόγων, literally, 'I will become a speaker of words for you in your place.' On the true meaning of this word see Ion 413. Bothe again entirely misses the sense, " vates ero sermonum, i. e. praedicam tibi, habitum iri hic quosdam sermones." Teiresias being blind could not see the approach of Pentheus. If he had, he would have made some observation on it, such as Cadmus now makes.

215 seqq. Pentheus enters with angry and imperious mien. He has just learnt, on his return to Thebes, that the adult women have run off to the mountains, under pretence of worshipping some newfangled god called Dionysus. He has heard much of their lewd and intemperate conduct, and he is resolved to punish all whom he can catch, especially the three sisters of his mother, who are the ringleaders in this new amusement. Some Lydian stranger is reported to have first introduced it; an effeminate and amorous impostor, who shall forfeit his head for his pains in misleading the women. He avers, forsooth, that this Dionysus is a god, and adds the most extravagant assertions respecting his birth. But what is this? Teiresias and

κλύω δὲ νεοχμὰ τήνδ' ἀνὰ πτόλιν κακά,
γυναῖκας ἡμῖν δώματ' ἐκλελοιπέναι
πλασταῖσι βακχείαισιν, ἐν δὲ δασκίοις
ὄρεσι θοάζειν, τὸν νεωστὶ δαίμονα
Διόνυσον, ὅστις ἐστί, τιμώσας χοροῖς· 220
πλήρεις δὲ θιάσοις ἐν μέσοισιν ἑστάναι
κρατῆρας, ἄλλην δ' ἄλλοσ' εἰς ἐρημίαν
πτώσσουσαν εὐναῖς ἀρσένων ὑπηρετεῖν,
πρόφασιν μὲν ὡς δὴ μαινάδας θυοσκόους,
τὴν δ' Ἀφροδίτην πρόσθ' ἄγειν τοῦ Βακχίου. 225
ὅσας μὲν οὖν εἴληφα, δεσμίους χέρας
σώζουσι πανδήμοισι πρόσπολοι στέγαις·
ὅσαι δ' ἄπεισιν, ἐξ ὄρους θηράσομαι,
Ἰνώ τ' Ἀγαύην θ', ἥ μ' ἔτικτ' Ἐχίονι,
Ἀκταίονός τε μητέρ', Αὐτονόην λέγω. 230
καὶ σφᾶς σιδηραῖς ἁρμόσας ἐν ἄρκυσι
παύσω κακούργου τῆσδε βακχείας τάχα.
λέγουσι δ' ὥς τις εἰσελήλυθε ξένος
γόης, ἐπῳδὸς Λυδίας ἀπὸ χθονός,
ξανθοῖσι βοστρύχοισιν, εὔοσμος κόμην, 235

Cadmus, the old and the venerable, seized with the same infatuation! He is ashamed of them both. Cadmus is implored to return, and Teiresias is plainly told that his grey hairs alone have saved him from imprisonment.

216. κλύω δὲ κτλ. The full meaning is, 'I happened to be absent when I first was informed of these proceedings; but I returned immediately to stop them, and some of the women I have already arrested,' &c. (v. 226.)

218. πλασταῖσι β., with feigned or sham orgies of Bacchus. He is impressed with the idea that these are a mere πρόσχημα or pretext for dissipation.

223. πτώσσουσαν, slinking off in different directions to the wilderness. Photius, πτώσσοντες· δειλιῶντες. Cf. Hec. 1065.

224. ὡς δὴ, i. e. οὔσας. See Hel. 1057. Andr. 235.—θυοσκόους, priestesses. There is no reason to attach to it the sense of *furibundas*, with Elmsley. The derivation of the word is very uncertain. Hesychius explains it τὸν δι' ἐμπύρων ἱερῶν τὰ σημαινόμενα νοοῦντα. (Hence in Photius, who under θυοσκόποι has nearly the same words, οἱ διὰ τῶν ἐμπύρων σημαίνοντες τὸ μέλλον, it is clear that we should read θυοσκόοι, especially as the gloss immediately preceding is θυοσκόπος.)

227. π. στέγαις, in the public prison. Compare v. 444.

231. σφᾶς, for αὐτάς. In tragedy we more commonly find σφέ.

234. Λυδίας χθονός. The people of Asia Minor were regarded as skilled in enchantments; see Androm. 159.

235. εὔοσμος. Aldus and one of the MSS. Flor. give εὔοσμον. Matthiae and Elmsley read εὔκοσμος, after Stephens; and so W. Dindorf has edited. But κοσμεῖν, as applied to the head, seems to require the mention of some extraneous ornament, as a chaplet or μίτρα. Hermann punctuates as in the text given above, but suspects εὔοσμον to be genuine, and that a verse has been lost. There is however nothing objectionable in the sentence as it now stands. The

ΒΑΚΧΑΙ. 413

οἰνωπὸς, ὅσσοις χάριτας ’Αφροδίτης ἔχων,
ὃς ἡμέρας τε κεὐφρόνας συγγίγνεται,
τελετὰς προτείνων εὐίους νεάνισιν.
εἰ δ’ αὐτὸν εἴσω τῆσδε λήψομαι στέγης,
παύσω κτυποῦντα θύρσον ἀνασείοντά τε   240
κόμας, τράχηλον σώματος χωρὶς τεμών.
ἐκεῖνος εἶναί φησι Διόνυσον θεὸν,
ἐκεῖνος ἐν μηρῷ ποτ’ ἐρράφθαι Διὸς,
ὃς ἐκπυροῦται λαμπάσιν κεραυνίαις
σὺν μητρὶ, δίους ὅτι γάμους ἐψεύσατο.   245
ταῦτ’ οὐχὶ δεινῆς ἀγχόνης ἔστ’ ἄξια,
ὕβρεις ὑβρίζειν, ὅστις ἐστὶν ὁ ξένος;
ἀτὰρ τόδ’ ἄλλο θαῦμα, τὸν τερασκόπον
ἐν ποικίλαισι νεβρίσι Τειρεσίαν ὁρῶ,
πατέρα τε μητρὸς τῆς ἐμῆς, πολὺν γέλων,   250
νάρθηκι βακχεύοντ’· ἀναίνομαι, πάτερ,

use of μύρον in the hair is often alluded to. So Ar. Eccl. 524, εἰ τῆς κεφαλῆς ὄζω μύρου.
236. MSS. οἰνωπὰς, οἰνωπάς τ’ or —πά τ’. Elmsley οἰνωπὸς, with Barnes. Hermann and Bothe οἰνῶπας ὅσσοις χάριτας κτλ., with Scaliger. The word is naturally used in describing the appearance of the god of wine; but 'ruddy' is all that is meant.
237. There is an intentional ambiguity in συγγίγνεται, as in Eum. 69, παλαιαὶ παῖδες, αἷς οὐ μίγνυται θεῶν τις οὐδ’ ἄνθρωπος.—προτείνων, offering them as a lure, προϊσχόμενος.
242. ἐκεῖνος. So all the old copies. Elmsley reads ἐκεῖνον, and others, as Matthiae, give Διόνυσος θεὸς after Reiske; 'This is the man who says that he is the god Bacchus.' However, neither Pentheus nor the Bacchants themselves as yet knew the identity of the Lydian stranger with the god. What Pentheus here means to say, as Hermann has well pointed out, is, that the assertion of the divinity of Bacchus rests on the sole authority of this Lydian impostor. Hence for ἐρράφη he gives ἐρράφθαι, with Reiske, Brunck, and Musgrave; and so also Bothe has edited. Translate: 'This is the man who says that Dionysus is a god; this the man who pretends that he (D.) was sewn up in the thigh of Zeus,—that very Dio-

nysus who was burnt out by the lightning's blaze together with his mother, because she falsely asserted her marriage with Zeus.' Matthiae is strangely mistaken in objecting to the above emended reading, that "ita hoc quoque in laudem dei jactare hospes dicendus esset, tanquam id, quo divinus Bacchi ortus demonstraretur." The fact is, Pentheus means to show the absurdity of any story which rests on any such slender evidence as this stranger's testimony. The repetition of ἐκεῖνος, 'Yes, this fellow,' &c., is most appropriate. Cf. Orest. 595–6. But for ὃς in v. 244 we should read ὅτ’, by which the ambiguity of the antecedent would be removed. W. Dindorf, according to his favourite theory, marks v. 243 as spurious.—ἐκπυροῦται, taken out of the womb by the agency of fire.
246. ἐπάξια Elmsley both here and Orest. 615. Bothe has ἦν ἄξια with a Paris MS. The plural ὕβρεις occurs, but by emendation, in Suppl. 495. Hermann thinks it is here to be taken literally of the several acts of the stranger, his enticing away the women, instituting a new worship, and spreading false reports about the pretended god. Elmsley would read ὕβρισμ’, as in Heracl. 18.
251. ἀναίνομαι, 'I disown you,' 'I am ashamed of you.' Cf. Electr. 311. Porson proposed νάρθηκι βακχεύοντας· αἰδοῦ-

τὸ γῆρας ὑμῶν εἰσορῶν νοῦν οὐκ ἔχον.
οὐκ ἀποτινάξεις κισσόν; οὐκ ἐλευθέραν
θύρσου μεθήσεις χεῖρ᾽, ἐμῆς μητρὸς πάτερ;
σὺ ταῦτ᾽ ἔπεισας, Τειρεσία; τόνδ᾽ αὖ θέλεις   255
τὸν δαίμον᾽ ἀνθρώποισιν εἰσφέρων νέον
σκοπεῖν πτερωτοὺς κἀμπύρων μισθοὺς φέρειν;
εἰ μή σε γῆρας πολιὸν ἐξερρύετο,
καθῆσ᾽ ἂν ἐν βάκχαισι δέσμιος μέσαις,
τελετὰς πονηρὰς εἰσάγων· γυναιξὶ γὰρ   260
ὅπου βότρυος ἐν δαιτὶ γίγνεται γάνος,
οὐχ ὑγιὲς οὐδὲν ἔτι λέγω τῶν ὀργίων.
XO. τῆς δυσσεβείας. ὦ ξέν᾽, οὐκ αἰδεῖ θεοὺς

μαι, πάτερ, and in fact the plural is found in three MSS., while in another, according to Elmsley, the ἂν of the verb has been corrected, so that the original reading seems doubtful. Porson's ingenious emendation is further confirmed by Nonnus, xlv. 73, (quoted by Hermann,) who makes Pentheus say to Teiresias αἰδέομαι σέο γῆρας. The plural however might have been introduced by some one who thought the participle should include both Teiresias and Cadmus, and feared that βακχεύοντα rather than βακχεύοντε would be understood, as no doubt it should be.

255. αὖ θέλεις. Bothe, in proposing with considerable confidence οὐ θέλεις, "non vis auguria captare," quod adhuc fecisti," failed to notice the sarcasm in ἐμπύρων μισθοὺς φέρειν, 'to get pay for your auguries.' For the μάντεις were commonly accused of avarice; see on Hel. 756. It appears best, with Dindorf, to mark a question at φέρειν,—' is this another device of yours to get pay?' &c. For the service of a new god was pretty sure to bring with it some new profits from the credulous; and especially as Bacchus was an oracular god, Rhes. 972. —φέρειν for φέρεσθαι, as in Oed. Col. 6. 651.—πτερωτούς, i. e. οἰωνούς. Cf. Hel. 747.

260. γυναιξί. Both the Greeks and the Romans thought it discreditable in women to be drinkers of wine. Hence one of the charges brought against Euripides in Ar. Thesm. 390 seqq., is that of calling the women οἰνοπότιδες.—ὑγιὲς οὐδὲν, cf. Hel. 746. Androm. 448. The expression seems borrowed from comedy, and the same perhaps may be said of the genitive of admiration which occurs in the next verse. Placed alone, it is more like the τῶν ἀλαζονευμάτων of Ar. Ach. 87, than the ἀλλὰ τῆς ἐμῆς κάκης of Med. 1051. — βότρυος, forming a tribrach in the second foot, of one word, is a rare licence. Cf. v. 18 and v. 662. Electr. 970. In Aesch. Cho. 1, Ἑρμῆ χθόνιε κτλ., it is more than probable that the latter word was pronounced as an iambus, the ι having sometimes the power of j or y, one of the effects of which must have been to convert yĕ or yă into ēy or āy. See Electr. 314.

263. τῆς δυσσεβείας. The old reading, τῆς εὐσεβείας, was corrected by Reiske. Elmsley, who refers to Iph. A. 327, ὦ θεοί, σῆς ἀναισχύντου φρενός, adopts this, remarking that the words are occasionally interchanged, as in Hel. 1021 Aldus has ἐξ εὐσεβείας for ἐκ δυσσεβείας. Hermann and Bothe retain the vulgate: the latter understanding 'have you no respect for the gods of piety,' which, he says, is the same as 'the goddess of piety.' Less absurd, but more complicated, is Hermann's explanation, 'Are you not abashed in the sight of the gods to disgrace both Cadmus on account of his piety (i. e. his acceptance of the new rites), and also, as a descendant of Echion, your own family?' W. Dindorf however rightly adopts Reiske's emendation, which scarcely admits of a doubt. Cf. Orest. 1666, ὦ Λοξία μαντεῖε, σῶν θεσπισμάτων. The remedy suggested by Musgrave was to transpose 264 and 265; and this is certainly plausible. However, the δὲ in 265 will bear this sense;—' What! you a descendant of Echion, and thus disgrace your family!' It will be observed that

Κάδμον τε τὸν σπείραντα γηγενῆ στάχυν;
Ἐχίονος δ' ὢν παῖς καταισχύνεις γένος. 265
ΤΕ. ὅταν λάβῃ τις τῶν λόγων ἀνὴρ σοφὸς
καλὰς ἀφορμὰς, οὐ μέγ' ἔργον εὖ λέγειν·
σὺ δ' εὔτροχον μὲν γλῶσσαν ὡς φρονῶν ἔχεις,
ἐν τοῖς λόγοισι δ' οὐκ ἔνεισί σοι φρένες.
θρασὺς δὲ, δυνατὸς καὶ λέγειν οἷός τ' ἀνὴρ, 270
κακὸς πολίτης γίγνεται, νοῦν οὐκ ἔχων.
οὗτος δ' ὁ δαίμων ὁ νέος, ὃν σὺ διαγελᾷς,
οὐκ ἂν δυναίμην μέγεθος ἐξειπεῖν ὅσος
καθ' Ἑλλάδ' ἔσται· δύο γὰρ, ὦ νεανία,
τὰ πρῶτ' ἐν ἀνθρώποισι, Δημήτηρ θεὰ, 275
Γῆ δ' ἐστίν· ὄνομα δ' ὁπότερον βούλει κάλει·

the chorus address the king as ὦ ξένε, because they are themselves strangers who have followed Bacchus as his worshippers.

266 seqq. Teiresias, in a calm and dignified speech, refutes the erroneous opinions of Pentheus. It is not very difficult, he says, to speak well on a good subject; but Pentheus has a glib tongue with but little reason on his side. Such an orator, clever but unsound in his views, becomes a dangerous citizen. This new god, who is thus ignorantly despised, will eventually become one of the most honoured in Hellas. Demeter and Dionysus, as the givers of those inestimable blessings to man, bread and wine, the one the support of life, the other the solace of cares, cannot fail to be regarded as the greatest of benefactors. Wine too is the medium whereby men draw blessings from heaven, by the means of libations. As for the miraculous birth of the god, that admits of a reasonable explanation. Mortal men mistook the two words μηρὸς and ὅμηρος, and thus supposed that he who was, by a stratagem of Zeus, made a *hostage* or *substitute*, was sewed into his *thigh*. Dionysus is moreover a prophetic god; he is an aid in war, for he can strike panics into a hostile army. In fine, Pentheus is advised to retract his opposition to the new worship. Human wisdom is sometimes fallacious. There is no fear of his corrupting the women, if they are by nature chaste. If the king of Thebes delights in being honoured by his subjects, why should not Dionysus too? For himself therefore, he is resolved to become a bacchant, old as he is; and Cadmus, the object of Pentheus' ridicule, will join him in the bacchic dance.

267. καλὰς ἀφορμὰς, a good theme to start from, a good subject to talk about. Cf. Hec. 1239, φεῦ φεῦ, βροτοῖσιν ὡς τὰ χρηστὰ πράγματα χρηστῶν ἀφορμὰς ἐνδίδωσ' ἀεὶ λόγων.

270—1. θρασὺς δὲ κτλ. These lines are supposed to be aimed at the demagogue Cleophon (Ar. Ran. penult.), who is also attacked in similar terms Orest. 907, ὅταν γὰρ ἡδὺς τοῖς λόγοις, φρονῶν κακῶς, πείθῃ τὸ πλῆθος, τῇ πόλει κακὸν μέγα. They are quoted by Stobaeus, Anth. xlv. 2, and the two preceding *ibid.* xxxvi. 9, both as from the *Pentheus*. Translate, 'Now a bold man, when he possesses influence and is skilled in speaking, becomes a bad citizen, because he is destitute of sound sense.' (If the poet had meant, '*if* destitute of sense,' he must have said νοῦν μὴ ἔχων). By δυνατὸς we must understand simply 'influential.' Compare Orest. 897, ὃς ἂν δύνηται πόλεος, ἔν τ' ἀρχαῖσιν ᾖ. Ion 596, τῶν μὲν ἀδυνάτων ὕπο μισησόμεσθα.

275—9. There is a slight anacoluthon here. He should have said, Δημήτηρ θεὰ Διόνυσός τε. But the epexegetical sentence about Demeter led the poet away from the intended construction.—Γῆ δ' ἐστὶν κτλ., i.e. those who are less disposed to symbolical terms may say, if they please, that the giver of corn is simply Earth. Cf. Prom. 217, Θέμις καὶ Γαῖα, πολλῶν ὀνομάτων μορφὴ μία. Eur. Suppl. 205—7.

416 ΕΥΡΙΠΙΔΟΥ

αὕτη μὲν ἐν ξηροῖσιν ἐκτρέφει βροτούς·
ὁ δ᾽ ἦλθεν ἐπὶ τἀντίπαλον, ὁ Σεμέλης γόνος·
βότρυος ὑγρὸν πῶμ᾽ ηὗρε κεἰσηνέγκατο
θνητοῖς, ὃ παύει τοὺς ταλαιπώρους βροτοὺς   280
λύπης, ὅταν πλησθῶσιν ἀμπέλου ῥοῆς,
ὕπνον τε, λήθην τῶν καθ᾽ ἡμέραν κακῶν,
δίδωσιν, οὐδ᾽ ἔστ᾽ ἄλλο φάρμακον πόνων.
οὗτος θεοῖσι σπένδεται θεὸς γεγώς,
ὥστε διὰ τοῦτον τἀγάθ᾽ ἀνθρώπους ἔχειν.   285
καὶ καταγελᾷς νιν, ὡς ἐνερράφη Διὸς

278. ὁ δ᾽ ἦλθε κτλ. 'But he, the son of Semele, took the opposite course; he invented the liquid draught of the grape and introduced it to mortals,' &c. Hermann reads ὃ δ᾽, on the ground that ὃ is not merely the article, but the demonstrative pronoun. Elmsley wrongly refers ὃ δὲ to ὑγρὸν πῶμα. W. Dindorf has ὃς δ᾽ ἦλθεν, by which the apparent abruptness in the next verse is avoided.—εἰσηνέγκατο, for εἰσήνεγκε. The middle is occasionally used as a synonym for the active, though φέρειν and φέρεσθαι are distinguished in the present tense. See *inf.* v. 1281. Ion 1434. Suppl. 583. But in Soph. Trach. 462 the aorist retains the true middle sense, κοὔπω τις αὐτῶν ἔκ γ᾽ ἐμοῦ λόγον κακὸν ἠνέγκατ᾽ οὐδ᾽ ὄνειδος.— ὃ παύει κτλ., cf. Ar. Equit. 92, ὁρᾷς; ὅταν πίνωσιν ἄνθρωποι, τότε—εὐδαιμονοῦσιν. Bacchus was called by the Roman poets *vitis repertor.* For his joint worship with Demeter see Ion 1074.

283. οὐδ᾽ ἔστ᾽ ἄλλο. Hermann gives δίδωσ᾽, ἵν᾽ οὐκ κτλ., *ubi non est aliud eorum remedium.* He says, "necesse est versum excidisse, in quo, quod deest, scriptum fuerit, nullum malorum remedium fortius esse ac potentius, quam vinum:—aut, si nihil excidit, verba necesse est corrupta esse." The *necessity* of either alternative may fairly be questioned. It is a little obscure whether the poet meant ἄλλο φάρμακον ἢ οἶνος, or ἢ ὕπνος. Neither, of course, is strictly true; nor even if we include both, 'no other remedy besides wine and sleep,' is it fair to exclude the solace of philosophy &c. However, such objections are hypercritical; all that the poet meant was, that there is nothing like wine for making a man forget his cares,—one cause of such forgetfulness being the sleep caused by wine.

284—97. These verses are inclosed by W. Dindorf as spurious. "His versibus ineptissime interrumpuntur quae Teiresias de virtutibus dei ab se celebrati exponit. Ipsa autem fabulae explicatio, quae verbis illis continetur, ita est comparata ut Proclum aliquem aut Olympiodorum audire videamur, non Euripidem, ridiculumque est ab Teiresia, qui cavere vult ne ridiculus Pentheo videatur Dionysus, ea proferri quibus et Deum illum et se ipsum deridendum praebeat." To which we may fairly reply, that the fondness of Euripides for etymologies (see Preface to Vol. i. p. 31), and the rationalising tendencies of his mind, will amply account for this attempt to explain away the only absurdity that was objected against the story of Dionysus' birth. It was the aim of Teiresias to show that there was nothing really absurd in the matter; that the mistake of a letter had led to serious misapprehension. Dindorf's assertion, that the passage contains "dictio inepta, confusa omninoque non Euripidea," says little in favour of his critical judgment. Some difficulties however require to be singly considered.

Ibid. οὗτος θεοῖσι κτλ. The obvious meaning is, that Bacchus himself, being a god, is offered in libations to the other gods. This, of course, is to identify the thing itself with the giver or inventor of it. Probably there is a play on the double sense of σπένδομαι, and the real sense is, 'This god makes peace for us with the other gods,' i. e. by giving us the means of appeasing them by offerings.

286. Perhaps, καὶ καταγελᾷς νιν, ὡς κτλ., διδάξω κτλ., i.e. if you think *this* ridiculous, I will convince you that there is no absurdity in it.

ΒΑΚΧΑΙ.

μηρῷ.   διδάξω σ' ὡς καλῶς ἔχει τόδε.
ἐπεί νιν ἥρπασ' ἐκ πυρὸς κεραυνίου
Ζεὺς, ἐς δ' Ὄλυμπον βρέφος ἀνήγαγεν νέον,
Ἥρα νιν ἤθελ' ἐκβαλεῖν ἀπ' οὐρανοῦ· 290
Ζεὺς δ' ἀντεμηχανήσαθ', οἷα δὴ θεός.
ῥήξας μέρος τι τοῦ χθόν' ἐγκυκλουμένου
αἰθέρος, ἔθηκε τόνδ' ὅμηρον, ἐκδιδοὺς
Διόνυσον, Ἥρας νεικέων· χρόνῳ δέ νιν
βροτοὶ τραφῆναί φασιν ἐν μηρῷ Διὸς, 295
ὄνομα μεταστήσαντες, ὅτι θεᾷ θεὸς
Ἥρᾳ ποθ' ὡμήρευσε, συνθέντες λόγον.
μάντις δ' ὁ δαίμων ὅδε· τὸ γὰρ βακχεύσιμον
καὶ τὸ μανιῶδες μαντικὴν πολλὴν ἔχει·
ὅταν γὰρ ὁ θεὸς ἐς τὸ σῶμ' ἔλθῃ πολὺς, 300
λέγειν τὸ μέλλον τοὺς μεμηνότας ποιεῖ.
Ἄρεώς τε μοῖραν μεταλαβὼν ἔχει τινά·

292—4. The difficulty of these verses is undeniable. What the poet appears to mean is this; that Zeus, finding Hera unwilling that the infant son of her spouse by another woman should remain in heaven, made a false εἴδωλον of a portion of ether (like the εἴδωλον of Helen, Hel. 34), and placed it in the hands of Hera as a hostage for his future fidelity to her; for, if he offended again, she would, as she thought, have this divine infant in her power. Others understand, that he made a rent in the circumambient ether, and hid Dionysus therein safe from the jealousies of Hera: while others again construe ἔθηκε τόνδε Διόνυσον, 'made this portion of air Dionysus.' In this case ὅμηρον ἐκδιδοὺς νεικέων must be construed together, 'giving a hostage against' &c. This is Hermann's view; but it is hardly satisfactory. The punctuation given in the text above seems the best, and it leaves no further difficulty than the somewhat unusual phrase ἐκδιδόναι τινὰ, 'to put away a person into another's hands.' And yet, we find this very sense in a slightly different idiom, 'to give a daughter in marriage.' What Zeus did with the real Dionysus is not here mentioned; but there can be no doubt that his education by the hands of the Nymphs is alluded to. Apollodorus, iii. 4, 3, expressly says this: Διόνυσον δὲ Ζεὺς εἰς ἔριφον ἀλλάξας, τὸν Ἥρας θυμὸν ἔκλεψε. καὶ λαβὼν αὐτὸν Ἑρμῆς πρὸς Νύμφας ἐκόμισεν ἐν Νύσῃ τῆς Ἀσίας κατοικούσας, ἃς ὕστερον Ζεὺς καταστερίσας ὠνόμασεν Ὑάδας. But *inf.* v. 520, Zeus is said to have committed the young Dionysus to the fountain Dirce for concealment.—For νείκη, 'jealousies,' see Aesch. Suppl. 292.

295. τραφῆναι. Pierson's conjecture ῥαφῆναι is ingenious and probable.

297. ὡμήρευσε. 'Was made a pledge.' Actively in Rhes. 434, τῶνδ' ὁμηρεύσας τέκνα.—συνθέντες λόγον, i.e. ψευσάμενοι. Elmsley compares σύνθετοι λόγοι, 'lies,' in Prom. 704.

299. μαντικήν. Plato derives the word from μανία, either seriously or in irony, Phaedr. p. 244, C. It is not clear whether Euripides intended any allusion to the same fanciful etymology, though this is likely enough, from his usual fondness for resemblances in words. In what follows he confounds the effects of drunkenness with that of religious enthusiasm; for in the former sense we must understand ἐς τὸ σῶμ' ἔλθῃ πολὺς, because ψυχὴν, not σῶμα, would otherwise have been used. Similar in words, yet different in meaning, is Hippol. 443, Κύπρις γὰρ οὐ φορητὸν, ἢν πολλὴ ῥυῇ. See above, v. 284.

VOL. II. 3 H

ΕΥΡΙΠΙΔΟΥ

στρατὸν γὰρ ἐν ὅπλοις ὄντα κἀπὶ τάξεσι
φόβος διεπτόησε, πρὶν λόγχης θιγεῖν·
μανία δὲ καὶ τοῦτ᾽ ἐστὶ Διονύσου πάρα.   305
ἔτ᾽ αὐτὸν ὄψει κἀπὶ Δελφίσιν πέτραις
πηδῶντα σὺν πεύκαισι δικόρυφον πλάκα,
βάλλοντα καὶ σείοντα βακχεῖον κλάδον,
μέγαν τ᾽ ἀν᾽ Ἑλλάδ᾽. ἀλλ᾽ ἐμοί, Πενθεῦ, πιθοῦ·
μὴ τὸ κράτος αὔχει δύναμιν ἀνθρώποις ἔχειν,   310
μηδ᾽, ἢν δοκῇς μέν, ἡ δὲ δόξα σου νοσεῖ,
φρονεῖν δόκει τι· τὸν θεὸν δ᾽ ἐς γῆν δέχου,
καὶ σπένδε καὶ βάκχευε καὶ στέφου κάρα.
οὐχ ὁ Διόνυσος σωφρονεῖν ἀναγκάσει

304. διεπτόησε, 'is wont to disperse in alarm.' Od. xviii. 340, ὣς εἰπὼν ἐπέεσσι διεπτοίησε γυναῖκας. Panics, as the word itself implies, were commonly attributed to Pan. But Bacchus also, as pre-eminently the god who affected the mind and the reason, may have been by others regarded as the author of such alarms. Hermann proposes a slightly different explanation:— "Quum terrores Panicos Baccho tribuit auctori, videtur id propterea facere, quod Pan comes esse Bacchi solet."

305. Pierson thought this verse an interpolation, and Dindorf adds, "non injuria." The meaning however is simple enough; 'And this also is a sort of madness from (sent by) Dionysus.'

306. The cultus of the god will not long be confined to Thebes, where it first appeared in Greece, but will spread to the neighbouring cities and nations.—καὶ ἐπὶ Δ. πέτραις. 'Even on the Delphian rocks,' which have hitherto been regarded as sacred to Apollo alone. In fact there was so much in common in the worship of these two gods, that the later comer would naturally be regarded rather as an associate than a usurper. Thus Sophocles, Trach. 217 seqq., mentions both in connexion as inspiring wild joys and raptures. —πηδῶντα πλάκα, bounding over the double peak of Parnassus, i. e. the one of two especially dedicated to him, the other being sacred to Apollo. See Ion 1126. The accusative is that of transition over; see Hel. 598. Ajac. 30, πηδῶντα πεδία. Bothe and Hermann are clearly wrong in reading πηδῶντα σὺν πεύκαισι, δικόρυφον πλάκα βάλλοντα, thyrso ferientem. Barnes also and Musgrave construe βάλλοντα πλάκα. But the poet seems to mean βάλλοντα τοὺς θιασώτας, unless the correction of Matthiae, πάλλοντα, approved by W. Dindorf, be admitted as true. See on v. 113.

310. μὴ τὸ κράτος κτλ. 'Do not presume that it is mere power that has influence with men,' and that you can, by your authority as king, control their consciences.

311. νοσεῖ. Bothe gives νοσῇ, 'if you should think yourself wise, while your opinion is erroneous.' This however is unnecessary. The clause may be considered parenthetical in this sense, 'for I can tell you that your opinion is unsound.' The meaning is, μὴ δόκει φρονεῖν, μηδ᾽ ἐὰν δοκῇς, 'do not attach any weight to your own conceit that you are clever.' The μέν and the δέ do not form the regular antithesis, unless νοσῇ is the true reading; but μέν is so often independently used, with an *implied* antithesis, that δέ may here very well mean γάρ.

314. Aldus has μὴ σωφρονεῖν, and so Stobaeus twice, with the Palatine MS., but with μή superscribed. It is manifestly an addition by those who thought the sense should be, 'Dionysus will not force them to be lewd,' as he is accused by his enemies of doing. See v. 223. Hermann reads μὴ φρονεῖν, *intemperantes ad Venerem esse.* Elmsley proposes οὐχ ὁ Δ. μὴ φρονεῖν ἀναγκάσῃ, i. e. οὐ μὴ ἀναγκάσῃ. In the judgment of the present editor, no other change is required than εἰ for ἐν, and this is in great measure justified by the reading of Stobaeus (Flor. 74, 8. Vol. iii. p. 53, ed. Teubner), ἀλλ᾽ εἰς τὴν φύσιν | τοῦτο

ΒΑΚΧΑΙ.   419

γυναῖκας ἐς τὴν Κύπριν, ἀλλ' εἰ τῇ φύσει   315
τὸ σωφρονεῖν ἔνεστιν ἐς τὰ πάντ' ἀεί,
τοῦτο σκοπεῖν χρή· καὶ γὰρ ἐν βακχεύμασιν
οὖσ' ἥ γε σώφρων οὐ διαφθαρήσεται.
ὁρᾷς; σὺ χαίρεις, ὅταν ἐφεστῶσιν πύλαις
πολλοί, τὸ Πενθέως δ' ὄνομα μεγαλύνῃ πόλις·   320
κἀκεῖνος, οἶμαι, τέρπεται τιμώμενος.
ἐγὼ μὲν οὖν καὶ Κάδμος, ὃν σὺ διαγελᾷς,
κισσῷ τ' ἐρεψόμεσθα καὶ χορεύσομεν,
πολιὰ ξυνωρίς, ἀλλ' ὅμως χορευτέον,
κοὐ θεομαχήσω σῶν λόγων πεισθεὶς ὕπο.   325
μαίνει γὰρ ὡς ἄλγιστα, κοὔτε φαρμάκοις
ἄκη λάβοις ἂν οὔτ' ἄνευ τούτων νοσεῖς.
ΧΟ. ὦ πρέσβυ, Φοῖβόν τ' οὐ καταισχύνεις λόγοις
τιμῶν τε Βρόμιον σωφρονεῖς, μέγαν θεόν.
ΚΑ. ὦ παῖ, καλῶς σοι Τειρεσίας παρῄνεσεν·   330
οἴκει μεθ' ἡμῶν, μὴ θύραζε τῶν νόμων.
νῦν γὰρ πέτει τε καὶ φρονῶν οὐδὲν φρονεῖς.

σκοπεῖν χρή. The intermediate verse, omitted here, but quoted v. 15, by Stobaeus, occurs Hipp. 79, where εἴ τις φύσει τὸ σωφρονεῖν εἴληχεν, seems probable for ἐν τῇ φύσει. In the present passage it is necessary to the context. 'Not Dionysus (nor any one else) will force women to be discreet (i. e. if their inclinations be evil); but whether chastity is in their disposition always in all circumstances, *that* is the point to be considered; for not even amidst Bacchic revelries will your discreet woman be corrupted, whatever others may do' (γε). The argument is this:—'You complain that the women who are votaries of the god are unchaste; it may be so; but that is the fault of their own natures. It is not Dionysus who can compel them to be good; it is enough that he does not corrupt them.' Compare Hipp. 1008, δεῖ δή σε δεῖξαι τῷ τρόπῳ διεφθάρην.

321. Elmsley compares Hipp. 7, ἔνεστι γὰρ δὴ κἀν θεῶν γένει τόδε, Τιμώμενοι χαίρουσιν ἀνθρώπων ὕπο.

324. ἀλλ' ὅμως. As if he had said γέροντες μὲν, ἀλλ' ὅμως, old age being commonly regarded as unfit for the lyre and the dance, Oed. Col. 1222.

327. ἄνευ τούτων. These words, as spoken by Teiresias, are oracular and therefore purposely ambiguous. 'You cannot be cured by medicines, and yet you are sick to a degree that demands a medicine,' i. e. the cruel death that awaits you. This is Hermann's explanation, and it is the best of several that have been proposed.

328. Φοῖβον κτλ. You speak worthily of Phoebus, whose seer you are.

331. θύραζε τῶν νόμων, for ἔξω τῶν νενομισμένων, according to Elmsley. The idea of evading or escaping any thing was not unfrequently expressed in this way. So ἔξω πημάτων πόδα ἔχειν, ἔξω πηλοῦ πόδα κομίζειν, &c., and in Oed. Col. 1231, τίς πλάγχθη πολύμοχθος ἔξω; 'who that is born to much toil can get out of the range of it?'

332. πέτει, 'you are flighty.' Elmsley. —γὰρ ἔστιν for γὰρ ἐστιν in the next line is Hermann's reading, by which an antithesis between εἶναι and λέγεσθαι is obtained. 'Even though this god is not a god, as you assert, let him be called so by you; and tell an honourable falsehood that he is the son of Semele, that she may be thought to have given birth to a god; and that, for our parts, honour may

3 H 2

κεἰ μὴ γὰρ ἔστιν ὁ θεὸς οὗτος, ὡς σὺ φῂς,
παρὰ σοὶ λεγέσθω· καὶ καταψεύδου καλῶς
ὡς ἐστὶ Σεμέλης, ἵνα δοκῇ θεὸν τεκεῖν, 335
ἡμῖν τε τιμὴ παντὶ τῷ γένει προσῇ.
ὁρᾷς τὸν Ἀκταίωνος ἄθλιον μόρον;
ὃν ὠμόσιτοι σκύλακες ἃς ἐθρέψατο
διεσπάσαντο, κρεῖσσον᾽ ἐν κυναγίαις
Ἀρτέμιδος εἶναι κομπάσαντ᾽, ἐν ὀργάσιν. 340
ὃ μὴ πάθῃς σύ, δεῦρό σου στέψω κάρα
κισσῷ· μεθ᾽ ἡμῶν τῷ θεῷ τιμὴν δίδου.
ΠΕ. οὐ μὴ προσοίσεις χεῖρα, βακχεύσεις δ᾽ ἰών,
μηδ᾽ ἐξομόρξει μωρίαν τὴν σὴν ἐμοί;
τῆς σῆς δ᾽ ἀνοίας τόνδε τὸν διδάσκαλον 345

attach to the whole family.' The morality of this advice is of course to be estimated by the Greek ideas of falsehood and truth; for which see on Alcest. 537.

335. Σεμέλης. Elmsley and Dindorf adopt Tyrwhitt's correction, Σεμέλη θ᾽ ἵνα δοκῇ. Hermann defends the vulgate on the ground that Pentheus had denied that Bacchus was the son of Semele, v. 245.

337. Ἀκτέωνος W. Dindorf, which form Elmsley also approves. But it is only found in one MS., and that as a correction. In v. 230 the metre requires Ἀκταίωνος, and it might perhaps be argued, that, as the short form of the genitive takes the long syllable preceding, so the long form would conversely require the short ε. This principle holds good in Μενέλαος and Μενέλεως, and many similar forms. This case of divine retribution is cited, because it had occurred in the family of Cadmus. Apollodor. iii. 4, 4, Αὐτονόης δὲ καὶ Ἀρισταίου παῖς Ἀκταίων ἐγένετο, ὃς τραφεὶς παρὰ Χείρωνι κυνηγὸς ἐδιδάχθη, καὶ ὕστερον κατεβρώθη ἐν τῷ Κιθαιρῶνι ὑπὸ τῶν ἰδίων κυνῶν. Καὶ τοῦτον ἐτελεύτησε τὸν τρόπον, ὡς μὲν Ἀκουσίλαος λέγει, μηνίσαντος τοῦ Διός, ὅτι ἐμνηστεύσατο Σεμέλην· ὡς δὲ οἱ πλείονες, ὅτι τὴν Ἄρτεμιν λουομένην εἶδε. Euripides, as he frequently does, varies the common legend.—ἐν ὀργάσιν, in the meadows, i. e. the low and level hunting plains. See Rhes. 282, καὶ πῶς πρὸς Ἴδης ὀργάδας πορεύεται; Electr. 1163. Photius, ὀργάς, χωρίον οἷον ἄλσος μέγα. Again, ὀργάς, τὰ λοχμώδη καὶ ὀρεινὰ χωρία καὶ οὐκ ἐπεργαζόμενα οὕτως καλεῖται.

341. W. Dindorf regards μὴ πάθῃς as an imperative. Elmsley makes the clause δεῦρο—κισσῷ a parenthesis. Hermann gives the punctuation in the text, the sense of which is, ' Now, that *you* may not suffer this, come hither and let me crown you with ivy,' where μὴ is for ἵνα μή. See Hec. 344.

343. Pentheus starts back with horror as the aged Cadmus approaches to place the ivy crown on his head. He vents his rage on Teiresias, as the author of his grandfather's folly, and gives orders for the immediate destruction of his augural seat. Others are charged to bring the effeminate stranger before him in chains. Thus by a double act of presumptuous impiety he is earning the reward of an untimely death.

Ibid. οὐ μὴ κτλ. ' Don't lay your hand upon me, but go and act the bacchant by yourself, and do not wipe off (i. e. leave the impress of) your folly on me.' For οὐ μὴ compare Hel. 437. Hipp. 606, οὐ μὴ προσοίσεις χεῖρα μηδ᾽ ἄψει πέπλων; Ajac. 75, οὐ σῖγ᾽ ἀνέξει μηδὲ δειλίαν ἀρεῖς; For ἐξομόρξει Elmsley compares Ar. Ach. 843, οὐδ᾽ ἐξομόρξεται Πρέπις τὴν εὐρυπρωκτίαν σοι. The figure is borrowed from the outline of a dirty hand laid upon a clean garment.

345. The δ᾽, added by Matthiae, is rightly adopted by Hermann and W. Dindorf, though rejected by Elmsley. As Hermann observes, there is here a transition of persons, from Cadmus to Teiresias; consequently the adversative particle

δίκην μέτειμι. στειχέτω τις ώς τάχος,
ελθών δε θάκους τούσδ', ίν' οιωνοσκοπεί,
μοχλοίς τριαίνου κανάτρεψον έμπαλιν,
άνω κάτω τα πάντα συγχέας ομού,
και στέμματ' ανέμοις και θυέλλαισιν μέθες.   350
μάλιστα γάρ νιν δήξομαι δράσας τάδε.
οι δ' ανά πόλιν στείχοντες εξιχνεύσατε
τον θηλύμορφον ξένον, ος εισφέρει νόσον
καινήν γυναιξί και λέχη λυμαίνεται.
κάνπερ λάβητε, δέσμιον πορεύσατε   355
δεύρ' αυτόν, ως αν λευσίμου δίκης τυχών
θάνη, πικράν βάκχευσιν εν Θήβαις ιδών.
ΤΕ. ω σχέτλι', ως ουκ οίσθα πού ποτ' ει λόγων.
μέμηνας ήδη, και πριν εξέστης φρενών.
στείχωμεν ημείς, Κάδμε, καξαιτώμεθα   360
υπέρ τε τούτου, καίπερ όντος αγρίου,
υπέρ τε πόλεως, τον θεόν μηδέν νέον
δράν. αλλ' έπου μοι κισσίνου βάκτρου μέτα·
πειρώ δ' ανορθούν σώμ' εμόν, κάγώ το σόν·
γέροντε δ' αισχρόν δύο πεσείν· ίτω δ' όμως.   365
τω Βακχίω γαρ τω Διός δουλευτέον.
Πενθεύς δ' όπως μη πένθος εισοίσει δόμοις
τοις σοίσι, Κάδμε· μαντική μεν ου λέγω,

is required.—δίκην in the next verse is Elmsley's correction, in conformity with the usual idiom, (see Med. 261,) for δίκη. He compares Eum. 221, δίκας μέτειμι τόνδε φώτα.

347. τούσδε, 'his seat yonder,' δεικτικώς. Hermann, Elmsley, and Dindorf give τούδ' after Musgrave's conjecture. It is the less probable, because τόνδε had just preceded, which was sufficient for specifying the person meant. Cf. Androm. 16.

348. τριαινούν is 'to upheave,' an idea borrowed from the effects supposed to be produced on rocks and islands by the trident of Poseidon. Cf. Herc. F. 946, στρεπτώ σιδήρω συντριαινώσειν πόλιν.

354. λυμαίνεται. The primary meaning of this verb is 'to prey upon,' said of a wild beast which tears and disfigures a body. It is occasionally used, like υβρίζειν, of adulterous intercourse. So Aesch.

Ag. 1413, κείται γυναικός τήσδε λυμαντήριος. Cho. 751, στείχω δ' επ' άνδρα τώνδε λυμαντήριον οίκων, i. e. the adulterer Aegisthus.

359. μέμηνας ήδη. 'Now you are downright mad; and before you were out of your right mind.' "Verba μέμηνας ήδη ad posteriorem Penthei ρήσιν, και πριν εξ. φρ. ad priorem spectant." Elmsl.

364. κάγώ το σόν, 'as I do yours.' Compare Eum. 135, έγειρ' έγειρε και συ τήνδ', εγώ δε σέ.

365. ίτω δ' όμως. 'However, never mind.' If an accident at once ill-omened and unseemly should occur, it will be in a good cause, and therefore need not be regarded.

367. πένθος. The fondness of Euripides for playing on the meaning of proper names is illustrated in p. xxxi of the Preface to Vol. i.

τοῖς πράγμασιν δέ· μῶρα γὰρ μῶρος λέγει.
ΧΟ. Ὁσία, πότνα θεῶν,   στρ. α΄.   370
Ὁσία δ᾽, ἃ κατὰ γᾶν
χρυσέαν πτέρυγα φέρεις,
τάδε Πενθέως ἀΐεις,
ἀΐεις οὐχ ὁσίαν
ὕβριν ἐς τὸν Βρόμιον   375
τὸν Σεμέλας τὸν παρὰ καλλιστεφάνοις
εὐφροσύναις δαίμονα πρῶτον μακάρων ; ὃς τάδ᾽ ἔχει,
θιασεύειν τε χοροῖς,
μετά τ᾽ αὐλοῦ γελάσαι
ἀποπαῦσαί τε μερίμνας, ὁπόταν βότρυος ἔλθῃ γάνος
ἐν δαιτὶ θεῶν,   380

369. τοῖς πράγμασιν, 'by facts,' 'by circumstances.' See Hel. 286. It requires no prophet, he says, to foresee the consequences of such folly. Compare Suppl. 747, φίλοις μὲν οὐ πείθεσθε, τοῖς δὲ πράγμασι. Stobaeus cites the concluding words, Flor. v. 24.

370. All parties having now left the stage, the chorus, improving the occasion, and in direct reference to the obdurate incredulity and profanity of Pentheus, sing an ode to *Sanctity*, whom they personify as a goddess. She is called upon to hear (i. e. to avenge) this impiety against the author of all joy and festive delight to mankind. The end of idle words and lawless folly is wretchedness : wisdom alone is lasting and secure. The gods dwell afar off, but they can discern the actions of mortals. That wisdom which sets itself on a level with the gods is no wisdom; life is too short for such exalted speculations. Fain would they fly to Cyprus, the sacred island of Aphrodite ; to Pieria (Thessaly) the abode of the Muses; there would they extend the glorious worship of Bacchus, so congenial to Love and to Music. The god rejoices in feasting and in peace ; he is averse to gloominess ; he is the friend of those who follow the dictates of ordinary reason, not of such as think themselves superior to the rest.— The metre of the first strophe is Ionic a minore alternating with choriambics. The second is a glyconic system. Hermann arranges the first entirely in Ionics ; but this involves much division of the words at the ends of verses.

Ib. Ὁσία. For ὁσιότης. The worshippers of Bacchus were said ὁσιοῦσθαι, v. 114 ; hence the chorus extol that quality or tone of mind which prevails among the gods as their natural feeling and impulse, and likewise among good and religious men as partaking of the same reverential respect for Good in the abstract. To show this double character of Ὁσία, it is repeated with the antithetical δὲ, as if it were Ὁσία μὲν παρὰ θεοῖς, Ὁσία δὲ παρ᾽ ἀνθρώποις νομιζομένη, as Hermann well paraphrases it. On earth it is represented as having gilt wings, wherewith it flies hither and thither among men. Elmsley, who wrongly proposes κατὰ γᾶς, seems to have thought, with some of the older commentators, that Proserpine was meant. So far does he go in this erroneous view that he edits χρύσεα σκῆπτρα in v. 372, (the old copies having χρύσεα, corrected by Hermann.) On the resolved syllable in πτέρυγα ($\cup\cup$ at the beginning of the word being isochronous with —), and similarly in μεγάλα, v. 395, see on v. 79. On ῠ in χρύσεος see Med. 633.

377. θιασεύειν, to introduce, initiate into the dance. Elmsley well compares Ion 552, ὅς με Δελφίσιν κόραις — ἐθιάσευσ᾽.—μετ᾽ αὐλοῦ, to the music of the flute, which was used in banquets and therefore in the worship of Bacchus Cf. Trach. 216, ἀείρομ᾽ οὐδ᾽ ἀπώσομαι | τὸν αὐλόν, ὦ τύραννε τᾶς ἐμᾶς φρενός, i. e. ὦ Βάκχε.

ΒΑΚΧΑΙ. 423

κισσοφόροις δ' ἐν θαλίαις ἀνδράσι κρατὴρ ὕπνον
  ἀμφιβάλλῃ.
ἀχαλίνων στομάτων   ἀντ. α'. 385
ἀνόμου τ' ἀφροσύνας
τὸ τέλος δυστυχία·
ὁ δὲ τᾶς ἡσυχίας
βίοτος καὶ τὸ φρονεῖν
ἀσάλευτόν τε μένει   390
καὶ συνέχει δώματα· πόρσω γὰρ ὅμως
αἰθέρα ναίοντες ὁρῶσιν τὰ βροτῶν Οὐρανίδαι·
τὸ σοφὸν δ' οὐ σοφία,
τό τε μὴ θνητὰ φρονεῖν.
βραχὺς αἰών· ἐπὶ τούτῳ δέ τις ἂν μεγάλα διώκων
  τὰ παρόντ' οὐχὶ φέροι.   396

384. ἀμφιβάλλῃ Barnes for ἀμφιβάλῃ.
385. The meaning of ἀχάλινον στόμα, an unbridled tongue, can only be fully comprehended by referring it to the Greek doctrine of silence and reserve on certain religious subjects. All readers of Herodotus know how frequently this reserve checks him in speaking of religious things. It was peculiarly impious to speak unguardedly on such topics. *Vetabo, qui Cereris sacrum vulgarit arcanae*, &c., says Horace.—τέλη, ὧν καὶ χρυσέα κλῆς ἐπὶ γλώσσᾳ βέβακε προσπόλων Εὐμολπιδᾶν, Oed. Col. 1053. So the ἀκόλαστος γλῶσσα is αἰσχίστη νόσος, Orest. 10. Aesch. Prom. 337, γλώσσῃ ματαίᾳ ζημία προστρίβεται. The application here evidently is to the free speaking of Pentheus on the subject of Dionysus' birth. Stobaeus quotes 385—7 and 393—9, Flor. xxxvi. 13, and xxii. 17.
389. τὸ φρονεῖν, the being wise, not in the sense of that σοφία against which he is writing, but the being prudent and cautious not to offend the gods.—πόρσω for πόρρω Elmsley. The γὰρ implies that the τὸ μὴ φρονεῖν, in the above sense, will certainly incur punishment; for the gods, though far off, can see what passes among men.
393. σοφία, i. e. wisdom so called is not real wisdom. For the quibble on words see Preface to Vol. i. p. xxxi. The τε in the next line is exegetical, 'such wisdom, that is, as consists in too proud thoughts.' Cf. Pers. 816, ὡς οὐχ ὑπέρφευ θνητὸν

ὄντα χρὴ φρονεῖν.—θνητὰ is retained by Hermann against Elmsley's correction θνατά, but his distinction is perhaps fanciful, "aliud est, quum mortales θνατοὶ vocantur, aliud θνητὰ φρονεῖν, in qua formula non puto locum esse Dorismo, nisi in scriptore Dorico."
395. ἐπὶ τούτου, for ἐπὶ τούτῳ, appears necessary to the syntax; for the latter can hardly mean ἐν τούτῳ, while the Greeks often use ἐπὶ with a genitive for 'in the time of.' Hermann indeed (as also Bothe), gives a widely different meaning to the passage, by adopting the Aldine punctuation, τό τε μὴ θνητὰ φρονεῖν βραχὺς αἰών. This he regards as taken from Il. v. 407, ὅττι μάλ' οὐ δηναιός, ὃς ἀθανάτοισι μάχηται, and he renders it thus, *et non mortalia spirare, brevis vita est: hac conditione magna quis persequens, quae ante pedes sunt, amittit*. More strangely still, he retains φέρει (φέροι Brunck and Elmsley), which he compares with the Homeric τῷ καί κέ τις εὔχεται ἀνήρ, Il. ξ. 484, where εὔχεται is only the old form for εὔχηται, a common epic construction, but utterly inconsistent with Attic usage. The poet's meaning here can hardly be doubted; that life is too short for refined speculations, and that it is wiser to enjoy what is before us. We seem here to see a reflection of the writer's own mind. All his life he had been a speculator on the nature of God, and like all other speculators on the same subject, ancient and modern, he had

μαινομένων οἵδε τρόποι καὶ κακοβούλων παρ' ἔμοιγε
φωτῶν.
ἱκοίμαν ποτὶ Κύπρον, στρ. β'. 400
νᾶσον τᾶς Ἀφροδίτας,
ἵν' οἱ θελξίφρονες νέμον-
ται θνατοῖσιν Ἔρωτες,
Πάφον θ', ἃν ἑκατόστομοι
βαρβάρου ποταμοῦ ῥοαὶ 405
καρπίζουσιν ἄνομβροι.
ὅπου καλλιστευομένα
Πιερία μούσειος ἕδρα,
σεμνὰ κλιτὺς Ὀλύμπου,
ἐκεῖσ' ἄγε με, Βρόμιε Βρόμιε, 410
προβακχήιε δαῖμον.
ἐκεῖ χάριτες, ἐκεῖ δὲ πόθος·

found himself no nearer to the truth at the end than he was at the beginning. Some such feelings of disappointment seem to be indicated in Hipp. 261, βιότου δ' ἀτρεκεῖς ἐπιτηδεύσεις φασὶ σφάλλειν πλέον ἢ τέρπειν.—φέροι for φέροιτο. See v. 257.

399. παρ' ἔμοιγε, in my judgment. Cf. Med. 761, ἐπεὶ γενναῖος ἀνὴρ, Αἰγεῦ, παρ' ἐμοὶ δεδόκησαι. Electr. 1015.

400 seqq. Κύπρον — Πάφον — Πιερία. Because Love and the Muses are congenial to Bacchus. The worship of Aphrodite was anciently established in Cyprus (probably by the Phoenicians or Assyrians, who called her Astarte), and hence her Greek name Κύπρις appears to have been derived. Aeschylus, alluding in all probability to Cyprus, Suppl. 549, calls it τᾶς Ἀφροδίτας πολύπυρον αἶαν. The old copies have τὰν Κύπρον, but both Elmsley and Hermann perceived that the article is an interpolation. By a contrary error ἵνα for ἵν' οἱ was read in v. 402, till emended by Heath.

404. Πάφον θ'. " Quid in animo habuerit Euripides, quum Paphum et Aegyptum hoc modo conjunxit, ego conjicere nequeo," says Elmsley, who marks the passage as corrupt. See however the note on v. 13. Hermann, who omits the τε, and makes Πάφον depend on νέμονται, considers the sense to be, that Paphos, a city on the western coast of Cyprus, is enriched by merchandize from the east, brought up the Nile. But καρπίζειν seems rather used of the fertilising effects of the Nile-water, which is poetically supposed to be carried (for the poet may not have known its true distance) as far as the opposite island of Cyprus. Cf. Hel. 1327, βροτοῖσι δ' ἄχλοα πεδία γᾶς | οὐ καρπίζουσ' ἀρότοις | λαῶν φθείρει γενεάν. The Nile is called ἑκατόστομος, 'many-mouthed,' doubtless by a poetical expression, to be compared, perhaps, with ἑκατόμποδες Νηρῇδες, Oed. Col. 719.—βαρβάρου, as being Egyptian. This people is repeatedly called βάρβαρος in the Helena.—ἄνομβροι, supplied by melted snow, and not swollen by rain. See Hel. 2. Matthiae's reading, ἄνομβρον, adopted by Bothe, is worse than needless.

407. καλλιστευομένα. For the passive form see Med. 947. The mention of Pieria (see inf. 565), is doubtless owing to the poet's sojourn in Magnesia and afterwards in Macedonia, where the present drama is said to have been composed. Thessaly seems to have been regarded especially as the seat of the Muses, who were hence called Pierides. In Rhes. 921 we find them passing into Thrace, as a conterminous country.

411. προβακχήιε. A coined word, implying that he preceded his crew of revellers in their migratory course. Cf. v. 920, καὶ ταῦρος ἡμῖν πρόσθεν ἡγεῖσθαι δοκεῖς.

ΒΑΚΧΑΙ. 425

ἐκεῖ δὲ βάκχαισι θέμις ὀργιάζειν. 415
ὁ δαίμων ὁ Διὸς παῖς   ἀντ. β'.
χαίρει μὲν θαλίαισιν,
φιλεῖ δ' ὀλβοδότειραν Εἰ-
ρήναν, κουροτρόφον θεάν.   420
ἴσαν δ' ἔς τε τὸν ὄλβιον
τόν τε χείρονα δῶκ' ἔχειν
οἴνου τέρψιν ἄλυπον·
μισεῖ δ' ᾧ μὴ ταῦτα μέλει,
κατὰ φάος νύκτας τε φίλας   425
εὐαίωνα διαζῆν·
σοφὸν δ' ἀπέχειν πραπίδα φρένα τε
περισσῶν παρὰ φωτῶν.
τὸ πλῆθος ὅ τι τὸ φαυλότερον   *common herd*   430
ἐνόμισε χρῆταί τε, τόδε τοι λέγοιμ' ἄν.

ΘΕΡΑΠΩΝ.

Πενθεῦ, πάρεσμεν, τήνδ' ἄγραν ἠγρευκότες,

420. Εἰρήνην. Brodaeus compares Hesiod, Opp. 226, εἰρήνη δ' ἀνὰ γῆν κουροτρόφος. As war cuts off the youth, so peace rears them to their full age. Hence in Suppl. 490 she is said τέρπεσθαι εὐπαιδίᾳ. That Euripides was a steady advocate for peace has been shown in p. xvi of the Preface to Vol. i.
424. μισεῖ δ' κτλ. 'But he dislikes him who does not make it his care to pass his life in secure happiness.' The word εὐαίων, as remarked on Ion 125, is properly said of the blessed life of the gods, and it is therefore a stronger expression than εὐδαίμων.
427. The MSS. give σοφὰν, Aldus σοφόν. Hermann, followed by Elmsley, reads σοφὰν δ' ἄπεχε πραπίδα κτλ., to which Matthiae objects, that the imperative is unusual when spoken by the chorus to mankind in general. At all events the singular is inappropriate. The true reading seems to be σοφόν, ' 'Tis wise to keep away from oneself the intellect and the mind that proceeds from men of more than common genius.' The teaching of the Sophists in particular appears to be meant. Elmsley and W. Dindorf would read ἀπὸ for παρὰ, which is too bold an alteration to be probable. For πραπίδες

see Androm. 480. Together, πράπιδα φρένα τε seem equivalent to σοφὴν φρένα, 'a cunning mind.' The περισσοὶ φῶτες are contrasted with ordinary men, πλῆθος τὸ φαυλότερον. See Hippol. 437. The meaning of the concluding lines appears to be this; 'whatever the common multitude thinks right and practises, that truly will I affirm,' i. e. adopt as my maxim. Hermann's view of the passage is somewhat different, ὅτι τὸ πλῆθος τὸ φαυλότερον ἐνόμισε χρῆταί τε, τόδε τοι λεγοίμην νομίζειν καὶ χρῆσθαι, i. e. 'that may I be said to adopt.' The point of the whole ode is to show, that human wisdom is worthless, and that it is wiser to follow the convictions of men in general respecting the gods, than to strike out new theories about them in the pride and conceit of human reasonings. Whether the poet says this of his own conviction, or puts it into the mouth of his chorus as appropriate to their position, must remain a matter of uncertainty.
434. A messenger arrives in haste to announce that the orders of Pentheus (v. 352) have been executed. The handsome stranger (who, of course, proves to be none other than Dionysus himself,) has been arrested, and is now brought in

VOL. II.   3 I

ἐφ' ἣν ἔπεμψας, οὐδ' ἄκρανθ' ὡρμήσαμεν. 435
ὁ θὴρ δ' ὅδ' ἡμῖν πρᾷος, οὐδ' ὑπέσπασε
φυγῇ πόδ', ἀλλ' ἔδωκεν οὐκ ἄκων χέρας,
οὐδ' ὠχρός, οὐδ' ἤλλαξεν οἰνωπὸν γένυν,
γελῶν δὲ καὶ δεῖν κἀπάγειν ἐφίετο,
ἔμενέ τε τοὐμὸν εὐτρεπὲς ποιούμενος. 440
κἀγὼ δι' αἰδοῦς εἶπον, ὦ ξέν', οὐχ ἑκὼν
ἄγω σε, Πενθέως δ', ὅς μ' ἔπεμψ', ἐπιστολαῖς.
ἃς δ' αὖ σὺ βάκχας εἶρξας, ἃς συνήρπασας
κἄδησας ἐν δεσμοῖσι πανδήμου στέγης,
φροῦδαί γ' ἐκεῖναι λελυμέναι πρὸς ὀργάδας 445
σκιρτῶσι, Βρόμιον ἀνακαλούμεναι θεόν.
αὐτόματα δ' αὐταῖς δεσμὰ διελύθη ποδῶν,
κλῇδές τ' ἀνῆκαν θύρετρ' ἄνευ θνητῆς χερός.
πολλῶν δ' ὅδ' ἀνὴρ θαυμάτων ἥκει πλέως
ἐς τάσδε Θήβας· σοὶ δὲ τἆλλα χρὴ μέλειν. 450
ΠΕ. μέθεσθε χειρῶν τοῦδ'· ἐν ἄρκυσιν γὰρ ὢν

bonds before the king. As for the bacchants who had been previously in custody, they have been mysteriously released, and have gone off again to the mountains. But the stranger himself not only offered no resistance, but voluntarily and with a smile submitted himself to his captors to be bound and led away.

438. οἰνωπόν. See v. 236. His naturally ruddy and florid complexion was not changed for the paleness of fear.

439. ἐφίετο, he bade us do so if we pleased.—τὸ ἐμὸν, my ungracious duty of securing him. The MSS., as usual, give εὐπρεπὲς, corrected by Canter. For the phrase εὐτρεπὲς ποιεῖσθαι Elmsley refers to Iph. T. 245. Herc. F. 497. Electr. 689. In all these places however the idea is the getting something ready for one's own use. Here it is evident that the action was made easy for another. The commentators consequently give several explanations of the present passage, and Hermann even reads thus, ἔμενέ τε τοὐμὸν, εὐτρεπὲς ποιούμενος, exspectabat, ut ego officium meum facerem, paratum id mihi reddens. The truth appears to be, that the poet used a convenient metrical phrase in a slightly inaccurate sense. It is quite consistent with his practice to do this; as remarked on Suppl. 74. He might indeed have written εὐχερὲς or εὐμαρὲς, 'regarding my proceedings as a matter of indifference,' and this would the more easily have been corrupted, from the familiarity of the other combination.

441. δι' αἰδοῦς εἶπον. Elmsley interprets, 'modestly said.' The simpler sense is, *pudore tactus*, as Hermann has it, i. e. through a feeling of awe and respect for his mild conduct.

448. ἀνῆκαν. A more common tragic use is ἀνεῖσαν, as in v. 662. See however on Herc. F. 590.—θύρετρα, perhaps what we call 'the wicket.' Photius θύρετρα, θυρώματα ἢ ἀραιόθυρα.

450. χρὴ μέλειν. It is, perhaps, worthy of remark, that three expressions in this ῥῆσις of the Servant,—the other two being ἐφίεσθαι 'to enjoin,' and ἐπιστολὴ 'a mandate,'—all occur in vv. 3 and 4 of the *Prometheus*, where, as here, the subject is τὸ δεσμεύειν τινά. The coincidence did not escape Barnes.

451. μέθεσθε G. Burges for μαίνεσθε. Aldus has λάζυσθε, and this is superscribed as a variant in the Palatine MS. The context however clearly shows that the liberation of the stranger's hands is meant. Cf. 503. Bothe's reading is very ingenious, μαίνεσθε χείρον τοῦδ', 'ye are worse maniacs than he,' if you suppose

οὐκ ἔστιν οὕτως ὠκὺς ὥστε μ' ἐκφυγεῖν.
ἀτὰρ τὸ μὲν σῶμ' οὐκ ἄμορφος εἶ, ξένε,
ὡς ἐς γυναῖκας, ἐφ' ὅπερ ἐς Θήβας πάρει·
πλόκαμός τε γάρ σου ταναὸς οὐ πάλης ὕπο,   455
γένυν παρ' αὐτὴν κεχυμένος πόθου πλέως·
λευκὴν δὲ χροιὰν ἐς παρασκευὴν ἔχεις
οὐχ ἡλίου βολαῖσιν, ἀλλ' ὑπὸ σκιᾶς,
τὴν Ἀφροδίτην καλλονῇ θηρώμενος.
πρῶτον μὲν οὖν μοι λέξον ὅστις εἶ γένος.   460
ΔΙ. οὐ κόμπος οὐδείς· ῥᾴδιον δ' εἰπεῖν τόδε·
τὸν ἀνθεμώδη Τμῶλον οἶσθά που κλύων.
ΠΕ. οἶδ', ὃς τὸ Σάρδεων ἄστυ περιβάλλει κύκλῳ.
ΔΙ. ἐντεῦθέν εἰμι, Λυδία δέ μοι πατρίς.
ΠΕ. πόθεν δὲ τελετὰς τάσδ' ἄγεις εἰς Ἑλλάδα;   465
ΔΙ. Διόνυσος ἡμᾶς εἰσέβησ' ὁ τοῦ Διός.

he can escape as you say the bacchants have escaped. The expression however is much too strong for the occasion; while μέθεσθε satisfies every requirement of the sense and the context. It is clear from v. 437 that his hands were tied, as was the custom with captives. Cf. Andром. 555.

454. ἐφ' ὅπερ. See v. 354.

455. οὐ πάλης ὕπο. This is explained ὑπ' ἀγυμνασίας, as οὐκ ἀπόδειξιν is 'the non-revelation,' in Hipp. 197, where Monk gives this and other examples in the note. Perhaps however it is enough to understand 'not from the exercise of wrestling (but from sitting at home and living an easy and effeminate life).' Cf. El. 527, πλόκος ὁ μὲν παλαίστραις ἀνδρὸς εὐγενοῦς τραφείς, ὁ δὲ κτενισμοῖς θῆλυς.

457. τε for δὲ Elmsley, Matthiae, Dindorf. But δὲ often answers to τε, and such changes are wholly arbitrary. The poet perhaps reverted to his former construction with μέν, in v. 453.—ἐς παρασκευήν, scil. τοῦ ἔρωτος, that you may be ready to captivate the first victim you may meet. Elmsley seems wrong in taking it for ἐκ παρασκευῆς, for this reason if for no other, that the poet would have so written it had he intended such a sense. It is however possible that the poet meant, 'to a degree which shows artificial appliances,' i. e. cosmetics, as Tro. 1201. Hel. 904. Electr. 1073, ἐς κάλλος ἀσκεῖ. Lucian uses the word in this sense, Ἔρωτες, vol. ii. p. 443, τίς οὖν ὁ μετὰ τὴν τοσαύτην παρασκευὴν βίος; where he has just been enumerating the various arts of female adornment. To be exposed to the sun was to contract that olive-brown complexion with which the Greeks contrasted λευκότης and the Romans *candor*. In southern complexions what we call *paleness* (from fear &c.) is a bilious yellow look, which the Greeks expressed by ὠχρός (v. 438) and χλωρός. On these points very incorrect ideas are entertained by those who compare only Teutonic countenances. The custom of avoiding exposure to the sun's heat in order to ensure a fair complexion is alluded to by Plato, Phaedr. p. 239, C., μαλθακόν τινα καὶ οὐ στερεόν, οὐδ' ἐν ἡλίῳ καθαρῷ τεθραμμένον ἀλλ' ὑπὸ συμμιγεῖ σκιᾷ. Such persons were ridiculed as ἐσκιατροφηκότες.

461. οὐδείς. Elmsley supplies εἰρήσεται. The meaning merely is, 'There is no need to make a long story of it.' For κόμπος is a pretentious speech of any kind, either in respect of the matter or the manner. Cf. Rhes. 438.

466. εἰσέβησε, 'introduced,' is the certain emendation of Abresch for εὐσέβησ'. Compare the transitive ἐξέβησε Hel. 1616. It is surprising that Elmsley should be dissatisfied with such a conjecture. The importation of the new worship and its votaries from Asia into Greece is evidently alluded to.

ΠΕ. Ζεὺς δ' ἔστ' ἐκεῖ τις, ὃς νέους τίκτει θεούς;
ΔΙ. οὔκ, ἀλλ' ὁ Σεμέλην ἐνθάδε ζεύξας γάμοις.
ΠΕ. πότερα δὲ νύκτωρ σ' ἢ κατ' ὄμμ' ἠνάγκασεν;
ΔΙ. ὁρῶν ὁρῶντα, καὶ δίδωσιν ὄργια. 470
ΠΕ. τὰ δ' ὄργι' ἐστὶ τίν' ἰδέαν ἔχοντά σοι;
ΔΙ. ἄρρητ' ἀβακχεύτοισιν εἰδέναι βροτῶν.
ΠΕ. ἔχει δ' ὄνησιν τοῖσι θύουσιν τίνα;
ΔΙ. οὐ θέμις ἀκοῦσαί σ', ἔστι δ' ἄξι' εἰδέναι.
ΠΕ. εὖ τοῦτ' ἐκιβδήλευσας, ἵν' ἀκοῦσαι θέλω. 475
ΔΙ. ἀσέβειαν ἀσκοῦντ' ὄργι' ἐχθαίρει θεοῦ.
ΠΕ. τὸν θεὸν ὁρᾶν γὰρ φῂς σαφῶς, ποῖός τις ἦν;
ΔΙ. ὁποῖος ἤθελ'· οὐκ ἐγὼ 'τασσον τόδε.
ΠΕ. τοῦτ' αὖ παρωχέτευσας εὖ, κοὐδὲν λέγων.

468. The old reading ὃς or ὁ Σεμέλης ἐνθάδ' ἔζευξεν γάμοις was corrected by Musgrave. The antithesis is between ἐκεῖ and ἐνθάδε, 'it was no new Zeus in Asia, as you suppose, but the same Zeus that you worship, who married Semele here at Thebes.' Compare the similar irony about a double Zeus in Hel. 490. Hermann gives ὁ Σεμέλης—γάμους, one MS. having a doubtful reading, γάμους or γάμοις.

469. ἠνάγκασεν is ironically used, as if Pentheus supposed that nothing short of coercion could have induced the stranger to take up so extravagant a worship. Hence he asks, 'Was it by the terrors of a dream, or face to face (ἐναργὴς), that he forced you into his service?'—'Seeing me as I saw him; and (as a proof of his personal presence,) he gave me his rites.' Photius, ὄργια, μυστήρια, ἱερά. That some tangible and visible thing, some symbol of his worship was communicated, seems clear from ἰδέαν in the next verse. Photius, ἰδέας, μορφὰς,—ἀπὸ τοῦ ἰδέσθαι. So Trach. 765, ὅπως δὲ σεμνῶν ὀργίων ἐδαίετο φλὸξ αἱματηρὰ, where the actual offerings must be meant. Still more clear is this from Theocr. xxvi. 7, where Ino, Autonoë, and Agave are described as erecting altars to Semele and Bacchus:—

ἱερὰ δ' ἐκ κίστας πεπονάμενα χερσὶν ἑλοῖσαι
εὐφάμως κατέθεντο νεοδρέπτων ἐπὶ βωμῶν.

But an alarm being given that Pentheus is at hand,

Αὐτονόα πράτα νιν ἀνέκραγε δεινὸν ἰδοῖσα,
σὺν δ' ἐτάραξε ποσὶν μανιώδεος ὄργια Βάκχου
ἐξαπίνας ἐπιοῦσα, τὰ δ' οὐχ ὁρέοντι βέβαλοι.

Where the last line illustrates the reply of Dionysus in the present passage, v. 472.

474. ἄξι' εἰδέναι. The benefits of initiation to the μύσται in the other world are here alluded to, as in v. 73.

475. ἐκιβδήλευσας, you have cunningly given a tinselled appearance to this matter, that I may wish to hear it. The reply to this is, (ἀλλ' οὐ χρή σε ἀκούειν,) τὸν γὰρ ἀσεβῆ ἐχθαίρει, ἀποπτύει, ὁ θεός.

477. Hermann understands this verse thus (in reference to v. 470), 'Do you mean to say you saw the god plainly, what he was like?' But this involves a needless ellipse in the answer, ('He appeared to me) under the form that he chose,' &c.

479. παρωχέτευσας, 'This again you have cleverly turned aside, and here too you have given me no reply.' This appears to be the force of καὶ οὐδὲν λέγων, though σοφὰ λέγων in the next verse suggests the meaning here to be, 'even though you talk foolishly.' In this case we must understand, καὶ τοῦτο καλῶς ἔλεξας, καίπερ μῶρα λέγων. It is rather difficult to decide. Bothe, *quamvis nihil dixeris*, καίπερ λέγων οὐδέν. It is not unlikely that the poet wrote κοὐδὲν λέγεις. Hermann admits that the καὶ is somewhat superfluous, and translates, *hoc quoque*

ΒΑΚΧΑΙ. 429

ΔΙ. δόξει τις ἀμαθεῖ σοφὰ λέγων οὐκ εὖ φρονεῖν. 480
ΠΕ. ἦλθες δὲ πρῶτα δεῦρ' ἄγων τὸν δαίμονα;
ΔΙ. πᾶς ἀναχορεύει βαρβάρων τάδ' ὄργια.
ΠΕ. φρονοῦσι γὰρ κάκιον Ἑλλήνων πολύ.
ΔΙ. τάδ' εὖ γε μᾶλλον· οἱ νόμοι δὲ διάφοροι.
ΠΕ. τὰ δ' ἱρὰ νύκτωρ ἢ μεθ' ἡμέραν τελεῖς; 485
ΔΙ. νύκτωρ τὰ πολλά· σεμνότητ' ἔχει σκότος.
ΠΕ. τοῦτ' εἰς γυναῖκας δόλιόν ἐστι καὶ σαθρόν.
ΔΙ. κἀν ἡμέρᾳ τό γ' αἰσχρὸν ἐξεύροι τις ἄν.
ΠΕ. δίκην σε δοῦναι δεῖ σοφισμάτων κακῶν.
ΔΙ. σὲ δ' ἀμαθίας γε κἀσεβοῦντ' ἐς τὸν θεόν. 490
ΠΕ. ὡς θρασὺς ὁ βάκχος κοὐκ ἀγύμναστος λόγων.
ΔΙ. εἴφ' ὅ τι παθεῖν δεῖ· τί με τὸ δεινὸν ἐργάσει;
ΠΕ. πρῶτον μὲν ἁβρὸν βόστρυχον τεμῶ σέθεν.
ΔΙ. ἱερὸς ὁ πλόκαμος· τῷ θεῷ δ' αὐτὸν τρέφω.
ΠΕ. ἔπειτα θύρσον τόνδε παράδος ἐκ χεροῖν. 495
ΔΙ. αὐτός μ' ἀφαιροῦ· τόνδε Διονύσου φορῶ.
ΠΕ. εἱρκταῖσί τ' ἔνδον σῶμα σὸν φυλάξομεν.

declinasti scite, et ut nihil diceres.—Photius and Suidas, παροχετεύοντες, μεταφέροντες. In Agam. 840, we have ὡς πρὸς οἶκον ὠχετεύετο φάτις. The metaphor is from irrigation, Virg. Georg. i. 108.

480. φρονεῖν. Stobaeus, Flor. iv. 18, quotes this verse with a variant λέγειν. The meaning, according to Hermann, is, that Pentheus, being infatuated and ignorant of divine things, ἀμαθής, does not comprehend that the reply ὁποῖος ἤθελ' &c., really alludes to the form of the stranger now conversing with him, which it has pleased the god to assume. Of course, if this be right, the antithesis between οὐδὲν λέγειν and σοφὰ λέγειν is only apparent.

481. ἦλθες δὲ κτλ. 'And is Thebes the first place to which you have brought the god?'—'Already the whole of Asia celebrates him in the dance.'

484. οἱ νόμοι κτλ., i.e. what one nation thinks wise, others regard as foolish.

485. μεθ' ἡμέραν, in open day. Sometimes καθ' ἡμέραν is used in the same sense, as Electr. 603, νύχιος ἢ καθ' ἡμέραν. But younger students should carefully distinguish this from its more proper meaning, 'day by day.' So also ἐφ' ἡμέραν, 'for the present day,' as Trach. 1128, τῆς ἐφ' ἡμέραν βορᾶς Electr. 429, *in diem*, while καθ' ἡμέραν (Electr. 182. Hec. 317. Alcest. 788,) is *quotidie*, 'day by day.' The former has regard to the duration of a limited time, the latter to the indefinite succession of it. Again, ἐξ ἡμέρας (Rhes. 445), has regard to what did occur yesterday, and may occur again to-day. But παρ' ἡμέραν is 'on alternate days,' 'every other day.'

487. εἰς γυναῖκας. Compare Frag. Meleag. 526, ἡ γὰρ Κύπρις πέφυκε τῷ σκότῳ φίλη, τὸ φῶς δ' ἀνάγκην προστίθησι σωφρονεῖν. So also σκότον τὸν ξυνεργάτην, Hipp. 417.

488. κἀν ἡμέρᾳ. Where there is an inclination to be unchaste, the daylight will serve as well as the night.

490. κἀσεβοῦντ', i.e. καὶ ἀσεβείας. The Aldine reading ἀσεβοῦντ' has been corrected from several MSS.

491. ὁ βάκχος, 'our bacchant.' Perhaps however we should read βακχεὺς in this sense, as in v. 145, for it is likely that there was some one established term for a votary of the god, and another for the god himself. But cf. v. 623.

497—8. Elmsley refers to Hor. Epist. i. 16, 77, who manifestly copies this passage; 'In manicis et Compedibus saevo

ΔΙ. λύσει μ' ὁ δαίμων αὐτός, ὅταν ἐγὼ θέλω.
ΠΕ. ὅταν γε καλέσῃς αὐτὸν ἐν βάκχαις σταθείς.
ΔΙ. καὶ νῦν ἃ πάσχω πλησίον παρὼν ὁρᾷ. 500
ΠΕ. καὶ ποῦ 'στιν; οὐ γὰρ φανερὸς ὄμμασίν γ' ἐμοῖς.
ΔΙ. παρ' ἐμοί· σὺ δ' ἀσεβὴς αὐτὸς ὢν οὐκ εἰσορᾷς.
ΠΕ. λάζυσθε, καταφρονεῖ με καὶ Θήβας ὅδε.
ΔΙ. αὐδῶ με μὴ δεῖν σωφρονῶν οὐ σώφροσιν.
ΠΕ. ἐγὼ δὲ δεῖν γε κυριώτερος σέθεν. 505
ΔΙ. οὐκ οἶσθ' ὅ τι ζῇς, οὐδ' ὃ δρᾷς, οὐδ' ὅστις εἶ.
ΠΕ. Πενθεύς, Ἀγαύης παῖς, πατρὸς δ' Ἐχίονος.
ΔΙ. ἐνδυστυχῆσαι τοὔνομ' ἐπιτήδειος εἶ.
ΠΕ. χώρει· καθείρξατ' αὐτὸν ἱππικαῖς πέλας
φάτναισιν, ὡς ἂν σκότιον εἰσορᾷ κνέφας. 510
ἐκεῖ χόρευε· τάσδε δ' ἃς ἄγων πάρει
κακῶν ξυνεργοὺς ἢ διεμπολήσομεν
ἢ χεῖρα δούπου τοῦδε καὶ βύρσης κτύπου
παύσας ἐφ' ἱστοῖς δμωίδας κεκτήσομαι.
ΔΙ. στείχοιμ' ἄν· ὅ τι γὰρ μὴ χρεών, οὔτοι χρεών 515

te sub custode tenebo. Ipse deus, simul atque volam, me solvet.' But Horace, as will appear from v. 614 seqq., gives a fanciful interpretation to λύσει μ' ὁ δαίμων, 'opinor Hoc sentit; moriar.'—ἐγὼ θέλω, 'whenever *I* choose it,' without regard to your orders.

499. ὅταν γε κτλ. 'Perhaps so, when you invoke him in the midst of your bacchants,' which, he implies, I will take care that you shall not do. "Sensus horum verborum est *Nunquam*." Elmsley.

502. αὐτὸν Elmsley for αὑτός, which however may mean, 'because you yourself have no religion (as I have).' The accusative would be rather awkwardly interposed.

503. με. The unusual accusative depends on the sense of ὑβρίζει. Elmsley refers to the Schol. on Ar. Ran. 103, who quotes this clause with the name of the play to illustrate the Attic idiom ἀρέσκειν τινά.

506. ὃ δρᾷς Reiske for οὐδ' ὁρᾷς. Hermann reads οὐδ' ὅστις for οὔθ' ὅστις, and, removing the stops, elicits this meaning, 'You are not aware that you are living without so much as knowing your own identity.' To which the answer is suitable enough, 'I am Pentheus,' &c.

508. ἐνδυστυχῆσαι. This elegant compound occurs also in Phoen. 727. Compare ἐγκαθηβᾶν Hipp. 1096. Elmsley adds several others, in all which ἐπιτήδειος forms an essential part of the expression. The meaning is, 'Your name is a fit one to be unlucky in.' For the play on πένθος and Πενθεὺς see above, v. 367.

513. δούπου—κτύπου. The Greek language, especially the epic, is rich in words implying *sound* in every variety; and the meaning of each is generally accurately observed. It will be useful for the student to specify the following:— δοῦπος, the *thump* of a heavy body; κτύπος, loud, reverberating noise, as of hammering; ἦχος, shrill noise; κέλαδος, yell; ψόφος, *stridor*, creaking (as of doors, shoes, &c.); κλαγγὴ, clear ringing note; ἄραβος, ἀραγμὸς, rattle; κόναβος, the clinking sound of hollow metallic bodies; πάταγος, clatter; ὄτοβος, startling *prolonged* noise (κτύπος being at intervals), βρόμος, roar.

514. κεκτήσομαι. Slaves were called κτήματα and their masters οἱ κεκτημένοι, because they were a part of the family possessions (οἶκος).

515. μὴ χρεών. The meaning is, one

BAKXAI. 431

παθεῖν· ἀτάρ τοι τῶνδ' ἄποιν' ὑβρισμάτων
μέτεισι Διόνυσός σ', ὃν οὐκ εἶναι λέγεις·
ἡμᾶς γὰρ ἀδικῶν κεῖνον ἐς δεσμοὺς ἄγεις.

XO. Ἀχελῴου θύγατερ   στρ.
πότνι', εὐπάρθενε Δίρκα, σὺ γὰρ ἐν σαῖς   520
ποτὲ παγαῖς τὸ Διὸς βρέφος ἔλαβες,
ὅτε μηρῷ πυρὸς ἐξ ἀθανάτου Ζεὺς
ὁ τεκὼν ἥρπασέ νιν τάδ' ἀμβοάσας·   525
ἴθι, Διθύραμβ', ἐμὰν ἄρσενα τάνδε βᾶθι νηδύν·
ἀναφαίνω σε τόδ', ὦ Βάκχιε, Θήβαις ὀνομάζειν.
σὺ δέ μ', ὦ μάκαιρα Δίρκα, στεφανηφόρους ἀπω-
θεῖ   530

can only suffer what is appointed by fate. Aesch. Suppl. 1031, ὅτι τοι μόρσιμόν ἐστιν, τὸ γένοιτ' ἄν.—ἄποινα, used as δίκην in v. 345.—ἀτάρ τοι is, 'be assured however that,' &c.

519 seqq. The chorus, again using the Ionic metre, reproaches Thebes, as the nurse of Dionysus, for rejecting his worship, and foretells that it will yet be foremost in his service. Pentheus is proving his earth-born descent from a fell dragon, by opposing the gods as the giants did of old. He has imprisoned their leader and he is seeking to arrest his followers. Where is the god, that he does not appear in his might to confound the impious rebel? Happy is Pieria, where he is now absent conducting the dance; happy, in that he will soon extend his rites over the land where once Orpheus lived and sang.

Ibid. Elmsley and Dindorf follow Musgrave in marking the loss of some words at the beginning, corresponding to οἵαν οἵαν ὀργὰν in the antistrophe. The address however is manifestly complete in itself; and Bothe and Hermann are more probably right in regarding the antistrophic words as an interpolation. They are indeed marked as such by the marginal note περισσὸν in the Laurentian MS., and the fact that they violate the metre is all but conclusive against them. —The poet represents the fountain Dirce as the daughter of Achelous, either because there was some legend about their subterranean connexion, as the spring Arethusa at Syracuse was said to come from the Alpheus at Elis (Moschus, Id. vii.), or the Achelous is used as a general term for river water, as inf. 625.—σὺ γάρ. As you once received Dionysus in person, so now you ought to receive his worship; which is implied in τί μ' ἀναίνει κτλ.

521. βρέφος. The Laurentian MS. has a gloss on this word, ἀντὶ μιᾶς, which means that in scanning it is equivalent to one long syllable. See on v. 79. So in v. 525, where W. Dindorf has perhaps rightly given ἀμβοάσας for ἀναβόασας or —ησας.

526. Διθύραμβε. The poet means that Dionysus was so called from Διὸς θύρα, being shut up and inclosed in the thigh of Zeus (see Herod. i. 23), or rather perhaps from δὶς and θύρα, the θήλεια and the ἄρσην νηδὺς, v. 526. For the etymology of this word the student is referred to *New Cratylus*, p. 394 seqq., where it is alleged that it comes from Διῒ θρίαμβος or θύραμβος (clearly identical with *triumphus*). The question however is, whether many of the words connected with imported religious rites from the east are not rather to be referred to Asiatic dialects than to known Greek roots. The derivation of θύρσος, which the same learned philologer assigns to a root θυρ, θορ, θρο, θρι, is perhaps beyond our powers of investigation, for the same reason.

527. ἀναφαίνω Hermann for ἀναφανῶ. Dindorf retains the future, which he fancies can be made long, though this is contrary to the analogy of verbal inflexions. It is well known that these forms were often confused by transcribers. The sense is, ἀναφαίνω σε Θήβαις, ὀνομάζειν σε τόδε τὸ ὄνομα, 'I hereby exhibit you to Thebes, to be called *Dithyrambus* from the manner of your birth,' Διὸς θύρα.

529. σὺ δέ μ' κτλ. 'And yet you, O

θιάσους ἔχουσαν ἐν σοί. τί μ' ἀναίνει; τί με φεύγεις;
ἔτι ναὶ τὰν βοτρυώδη Διονύσου χάριν οἴνας ἔτι
σοι   535
τοῦ Βρομίου μελήσει.
[οἴαν οἴαν ὀργὰν] ἀναφαίνει χθόνιον   ἀντ.
γένος ἐκφύς τε δράκοντός ποτε Πενθεύς,
ὃν Ἐχίων ἐφύτευσε χθόνιος,   540
ἀγριωπὸν τέρας, οὐ φῶτα βρότειον,
φόνιον δ' ὥστε γίγαντ' ἀντίπαλον θεοῖς,
ὃς ἔμ' ἐν βρόχοισι τὰν τοῦ Βρομίου τάχα ξυν-
άψει,   545
τὸν ἐμὸν δ' ἐντὸς ἔχει δώματος ἤδη θιασώταν
σκοτίαις κρυπτὸν ἐν εἱρκταῖς. ἐσορᾷς τάδ', ὦ Διὸς
παῖ   550
Διόνυσε, σοὺς προφήτας ἐν ἀμίλλαισιν ἀνάγκας;
μόλε χρυσῶπα τινάσσων ἀνὰ θύρσον κατ' Ὄλυμπον·
φονίου δ'
ἀνδρὸς ὕβριν κατάσχες.   555

Thebes, (in direct contradiction to this command,) reject and repel me, holding in your territory companies of myrtle-crowned dancers.' — μάκαιρα Elmsley thinks corrupt, and he would read πότνια. Hermann gives σκοτίαισι κρυπτὸν εἱρκταῖς in v. 549. But no change seems necessary; a common variety of the Ionic dipodia, ⏑⏑−⏑ | ⏑−⏑− corresponds here to the regular ⏑⏑−− though in more accurate systems (e. g. Aesch. Pers. 86 compared with 94), such verses are carefully balanced in the antistrophe.

535. οἴνη is a synonym of ἄμπελος, but οἰνάνθη (Phoen. 231) is *palmes*, the vine shoot, (Photius, ἡ τῆς ἀμπέλου ἔκφυσις.)

538. ἀναφαίνει. 'Pentheus publickly shows his earth-born descent, and that he originally sprung from a serpent; for him the earth-born Echion begot.' The point is, to compare the descent of the king of Thebes from the serpent slain by Cadmus, (Echion being one of the Σπαρτοί, cf. v. 1275,) with the γηγενεῖς or Titans who rebelled against Zeus. On the words οἴαν—ὀργὰν see on v. 519. The construction is double, ἀναφαίνει γένος and ἀναφαίνει ἐκφὺς, the τε being rather exegetical than copulative.

545. ὃς ἔμ' ἐν W. Dindorf for ὅς με. That he is right is shown not only by the metre, but by the emphatic pronoun being required, ἐμὲ τὰν τοῦ Βρομίου.

548. θιασώταν, κωμαστὴν, fellow-reveller. So in v. 145, Dionysus is called ὁ βακχεὺς, the bacchant. The chorus are not yet aware that the captive was Dionysus himself.

554. τινάσσων ἀνὰ θύρσον. The tmesis, if such it be, is remarkable, because the preposition commonly precedes the verb, from which it is separated by one or (rarely) more words. Hermann here reads ἄνα, the vocative of ἄναξ, for which he compares Oed. Col. 1485, Ζεῦ ἄνα, σοὶ φωνῶ. There however, ἄνα is perhaps for ἀνάστηθι, and so the Homeric Ζεῦ ἄνα, Δωδωναῖε, Πελασγικὲ κτλ.— χρυσῶπα (unless it be taken for the vocative of χρυσώπης) belongs to θύρσον, not, as Elmsley conceives, to Ὄλυμπον, which is here the mountain in Thessaly. For the chorus invoke the god to come from whatever place now detains him, to liberate his votaries. The ivy appears to be called χρυσὼψ from the colour of its berries.

ΒΑΚΧΑΙ. 433

πόθι Νύσης ἄρα τᾶς θηροτρόφου θυρσοφορεῖς   ἐπῳδ.
θιάσους, ὦ Διόνυσ', ἢ κορυφαῖς Κωρυκίαις;
τάχα δ' ἐν τοῖς πολυδένδρεσσιν Ὀλύμπου   560
θαλάμοις, ἔνθα ποτ' Ὀρφεὺς κιθαρίζων
σύναγεν δένδρεα Μούσαις, σύναγεν θῆρας ἀγρώτας.
μάκαρ ὦ Πιερία,   565
σέβεταί σ' Εὔιος, ἥξει τε χορεύσων
ἅμα βακχεύμασι, τόν τ' ὠκυρόαν
διαβὰς Ἀξιὸν εἱλισσομένας μαινάδας ἄξει,   570
Λοιδίαν τε, τὸν εὐδαιμονίας
βροτοῖς ὀλβοδόταν,
πατέρα τε, τὸν ἔκλυον
εὔιππον χώραν ὕδασιν
καλλίστοισι λιπαίνειν.   575
ΔΙ. ἰώ,

556. Νύσης. So Hermann with the old copies. Elmsley and W. Dindorf give Νύσας.—θιάσους is the accusative, not, as Elmsley says, of transition over, like πηδῶντα δικόρυφον πλάκα, v. 307, which is quite a distinct idiom, but depending on the sense of θυρσοφορεῖν, 'to lead the bands of dancers by wielding the thyrsus.' Perhaps however θιάσοις, 'for the dancers,' is the true reading.—Κωρυκίαις, see on Eum. 22, ἔνθα Κωρυκὶς πέτρα κοίλη, φίλορνις, δαιμόνων ἀναστροφή. A grotto on Parnassus was so called, situated near the summit, as appears from the mention of it in Herod. viii. 36, αὐτέων δὲ (sc. τῶν Δελφῶν) οἱ πλεῖστοι ἀνέβησαν ἐς τοῦ Παρνησσοῦ τὰς κορυφὰς, καὶ ἐς τὸ Κωρύκιον ἄντρον ἀνηνείκαντο.

563. σύναγεν, brought the trees together from the glens by his songs.

565. Πιερία. Here as in v. 408, the dominion of Archelaus is doubtless described, though properly only the country between the Peneus and the Haliacmon, i. e. the south-eastern coast of Macedonia is meant. In compliment to his patron he calls it μάκαρ, though ostensibly on account of its receiving the Bacchic rites while Thebes was rejecting them. The feminine form μάκαρ is used, as Elmsley remarks, in Hel. 375, ὦ μάκαρ Ἀρκαδία ποτὲ παρθένε Καλλιστοῖ.

571. Λοιδίαν. So W. Dindorf with Hermann, who however in his edition of 1823 gives Λυδίαν, with the MSS. Elms-

ley proposes Λοιδίαν in his margin. Herodotus has the form Λυδιεὺς in lib. vii. cap. 127. But Photius writes Λοιδίας, ποταμὸς Μακεδονίας, οὗ Αἰσχίνης μέμνηται, and similarly Harpocration, Λοιδίας, Αἰσχίνης ἐν τῷ περὶ τῆς παραπρεσβείας. ὅτι τῆς Μακεδονίας ἐστὶ ποταμὸς, ἄλλοι τε ἱστοροῦσι, καὶ Ἑκαταῖος ἐν περιόδῳ Εὐρώπης.

Ibid. τᾶς was omitted by Hermann and Bothe before εὐδαιμονίας. The article is alike against sense and metre, which seems to be choriambic, and so perhaps the next. V. 573, according to Hermann, is iambic; the next is glyconean, and the last pherecratean.

573. πατέρα. The river Apidanus, of which the poet says in Hec. 451, ἢ Φθιάδος, ἔνθα καλλίστων ὑδάτων πατέρα φασὶν Ἀπιδανὸν γύας λιπαίνειν. Bothe reads Λυδίαν τε, τὸν εὐδαιμονίας βροτοῖς ὀλβοδόταν πατέρα, τὸν ἔκλυον κτλ. The epithet εὔιππος, as Bothe himself perceived, is more applicable to the plains of Thessaly, to which the Apidanus pertained; and the attribute of πατὴρ to the same river both here and in the *Hecuba* makes it probable that the τε is genuine, especially as in both places κάλλιστα ὕδατα are mentioned as a characteristic.

576. A voice is heard from within the palace. It is succeeded by a loud rumbling sound. It is Dionysus calling to his followers to witness his dealings with the impious Pentheus. He has shaken

VOL. II.   3 K

ΕΥΡΙΠΙΔΟΥ

      κλύετ' ἐμᾶς κλύετ' αὐδᾶς,
      ἰὼ βάκχαι, ἰὼ βάκχαι.
ΧΟ. α΄. τίς ὅδε, τίς πόθεν ὅδ' ὁ κέλαδος ἀνά μ' ἐκάλεσεν
      Εὐίου;
ΔΙ.   ἰὼ ἰὼ, πάλιν αὐδῶ,   580
      ὁ Σεμέλας, ὁ Διὸς παῖς.
ΧΟ. β΄. ἰὼ ἰὼ δέσποτα δέσποτα.
ΧΟ. γ΄. μόλε νυν ἁμέτερον ἐς θίασον,
      ὦ Βρόμιε Βρόμιε.
ΧΟ. δ΄. πέδον χθονὸς —
ΧΟ. ε΄. ἔνοσι πότνια.   585
ΧΟ. στ΄. ἆ ἆ· τάχα τὰ Πενθέως
      μέλαθρα διατινάξεται πεσήμασιν.
ΧΟ. ζ΄. ὁ Διόνυσος ἀνὰ μέλαθρα.
ΧΟ. η΄. σέβετέ νιν.
ΧΟ. θ΄. σέβομεν ὦ.   590
ΧΟ. ι΄. εἴδετε λάϊνα κίοσιν ἔμβολα
      διάδρομα τάδε;
ΧΟ. ια΄. Βρόμιος *ὃς ἀλαλάξεται

the house wherein he was confined, and overthrown it. At length (603) he appears amongst them; but they still think it is their leader who has brought them from Asia (ὁ βάκχος, v. 623,) and fail to recognise him as Dionysus himself. Perhaps we should read, in a double dochmiac, ἰὼ, κλύετ' ἐμᾶς κλύετε νῦν αὐδᾶς.

579. πόθεν ὅδ' ὁ Herm. for πόθεν ὁ. He regards the verse as a resolved trochaic tetrameter catalectic, introductory to the same kind of metre at v. 603. He is doubtless right in dividing the following dialogue into consecutive speeches of single choreutae, though he only assigns it to five speakers. It appears to the present editor far more probable that each short and rapidly uttered clause is the ejaculation of a different person. The whole scene is one of alarm, confusion, and broken ejaculatory sentences. The characteristic of all the verses is an assemblage of resolved syllables, which it is not easy to reduce to certain metrical laws, though some may be called dactylic, others dochmiac. The number of speakers seems to be fourteen, i. e. the whole chorus, the Hegemon exempted, who pronounces vv. 608—9, whence the singular ἐσεῖδον is used.

584. πέδον χθονός. If this be regarded as the broken speech of one of the Choreutae, who was going to say σαλεύει, there is no difficulty in it. Hermann's idea, that ἔνοσι governs the accusative πέδον, as if it were ὦ Βρόμιε, ὁ πέδον χθονὸς κινῶν, is unworthy of that generally judicious critic. Elmsley gives πέδον χθονὸς ἔνοσι πότνια. For the word ἔνοσις, implying an earthquake motion, see Troad. 1326.

591. εἴδετε Dobree for ἴδετε. 'Do ye see the stone imposts on the pillars tossed to and fro yonder?' The addition of τάδε clearly shows that this was a real stage effect; and it is precisely like the overturning of the Trojan citadel at the conclusion of the *Troades*.

593. Βρόμιος ὃς κτλ. ''Tis Bacchus himself who will be victorious over his enemies within the house.' The ὃς was inserted by Musgrave, and is adopted by Hermann and W. Dindorf.—ἀλαλάξεται, 'will be celebrated with songs of triumph,' i.e. by us his faithful followers. They recognise the *voice* of the god, but they

στέγης ἔσω.
ΔΙ.   ἅπτε κεραύνιον αἴθοπα λαμπάδα,
         σύμφλεγε σύμφλεγε δώματα Πενθέως.   595
ΧΟ. ιβ'. ἆ ἆ,
         πῦρ οὐ λεύσσεις οὐδ' αὐγάζει
         Σεμέλας ἱερὸν ἀμφὶ τάφον,
         ἅν ποτε κεραυνόβολος ἔλιπε φλόγα
         δίου βροντᾶς ;
ΧΟ. ιγ'. δίκετε πεδόσε τρομερὰ σώματα,
         δίκετε Μαινάδες.   600
ΧΟ. ιδ'. ὁ γὰρ ἄναξ ἄνω κάτω τιθεὶς
         ἔπεισι μέλαθρα τάδε Διὸς γόνος.
ΔΙ.   βάρβαροι γυναῖκες, οὕτως ἐκπεπληγμέναι φόβῳ
         πρὸς πέδῳ πεπτώκατ'; ᾔσθησθ', ὡς ἔοικε, Βακ-
         χίου   605
         διατινάξαντος τὰ Πενθέως δώματ'· ἀλλ' ἀνίστατε
         σῶμα καὶ θαρσεῖτε, σαρκὸς ἐξαμείψασαι τρόμον.
ΧΟ.   ὦ φάος μέγιστον ἡμῖν εὐίου βακχεύματος,
         ὡς ἐσεῖδον ἀσμένη σε μονάδ' ἔχουσ' ἐρημίαν.
ΔΙ.   εἰς ἀθυμίαν ἀφίκεσθ', ἡνίκ' εἰσεπεμπόμην,   610

do not identify his *person*, when he steps forth unscathed from the ruins, and describes his delivery as effected by the agency of another. Cf. Electr. 691, ὀλολύξεται πᾶν δῶμα.
594—5. This distich was first assigned to Dionysus by Tyrwhitt, instead of to the Hemichorium.
596. πῦρ. See v. 623, καὶ μητρὸς τάφῳ πῦρ ἀνῆψε. Pentheus himself mistook this for a fire in his palace (v. 624), but the Maenads appear to distinguish it as a supernatural lightning-glare proceeding from the ἄβατος σηκὸς of Semele, v. 10.—ἂν φλόγα βροντᾶς is exegetical of πῦρ. Cf. v. 3, and v. 8, where the light on the tomb is spoken of as permanent, ἔτι ζῶσαν. Hence ἔλιπε is here used, as if it were a light that Semele had left behind as an undying memorial and warning to the Thebans. Here perhaps it is sufficient to suppose that the light was suddenly increased to a mighty blaze.
599. Hermann and Dindorf give δίκετε πεδόσε δίκετε τρομερά σώματα, the order of the words preserved in the Etymol. M.

p. 279. Matthiae gives as a reason for preferring this, "nam ubi idem verbum repetitur, alio verbo interjecto hoc fieri solet."—τιθεὶς for στρέφων. Compare Troad. 287.
602. After γόνος the old copies, with the exception of the Palatine MS., add the manifest gloss Διόνυσος, which it is surprising that Elmsley should retain.
606. τὰ Πενθέως δώματ' for δῶμα Πενθέως Musgrave. The error probably arose from an idea that Πενθέως must be a trisyllable, and thus the unrhythmical δῶμα Πενθέως διατινάξαντος was adopted. In the next verse σαρκὸς is Reiske's correction for σάρκας. He also proposed τρόμου or τρόμων for τρόμον, and it is probable that σάρκας is owing to an ancient variant τρόμου. Hermann retains σάρκας, but his explanation, that ἐξαμείβειν τρόμον is equivalent to *obfirmare* is very far-fetched.
609. μονάδ'. They had not only been on the wild mountains, ἐρημία, but deprived of their leader, μονωθεῖσαι.
610. Elmsley's view of the construction, εἰσεπεμπόμην Πενθέως, for εἰς τὰ Π. δώ-

ΕΥΡΙΠΙΔΟΥ

Πενθέως ὡς ἐς σκοτεινὰς ὀρκάνας πεσούμενος ;
ΧΟ. πῶς γὰρ οὔ ; τίς μοι φύλαξ ἦν, εἰ σὺ συμφορᾶς
τύχοις ;
ἀλλὰ πῶς ἠλευθερώθης, ἀνδρὸς ἀνοσίου τυχών ;
ΔΙ. αὐτὸς ἐξέσωσ᾽ ἐμαυτὸν ῥᾳδίως ἄνευ πόνου.
ΧΟ. οὐδέ σου συνῆψε χεῖρα δεσμίοισιν ἐν βρόχοις ; 615
ΔΙ. ταῦτα καὶ καθύβρισ᾽ αὐτόν, ὅτι με δεσμεύειν δοκῶν
οὔτ᾽ ἔθιγεν οὔθ᾽ ἥψαθ᾽ ἡμῶν, ἐλπίσιν δ᾽ ἐβόσκετο.
πρὸς φάτναις δὲ ταῦρον εὑρών, οὗ καθεῖρξ᾽ ἡμᾶς
ἄγων,
τῷδε περὶ βρόχους ἔβαλλε γόνασι καὶ χηλαῖς ποδῶν,
θυμὸν ἐκπνέων, ἱδρῶτα σώματος στάζων ἄπο, 620
χείλεσιν διδοὺς ὀδόντας· πλησίον δ᾽ ἐγὼ παρὼν
ἥσυχος θάσσων ἔλευσσον. ἐν δὲ τῷδε τῷ χρόνῳ
ἀνετίναξ᾽ ἐλθὼν ὁ βάκχος δῶμα καὶ μητρὸς τάφῳ
πῦρ ἀνῆψ᾽· ὁ δ᾽, ὡς ἐσεῖδε, δώματ᾽ αἴθεσθαι δοκῶν,
ᾖσσ᾽ ἐκεῖσε κᾆτ᾽ ἐκεῖσε, δμωσὶν Ἀχελῷον φέρειν 625
ἐννέπων, ἅπας δ᾽ ἐν ἔργῳ δοῦλος ἦν μάτην πονῶν.

ματα, does not seem capable of defence. Photius and Hesychius explain ὀρκάνη by εἰρκτή. Cf. v. 550. But Photius gives also the meaning of a fence or inclosure of any kind. See on Aesch. Theb. 336. The meaning is, 'Were you dejected at the prospect of losing me, when Pentheus took me to his palace with the intention of putting me in a dark dungeon?'

612. ἦν—τύχοις; This is shortly put for τίς λοιπὸς ἦν ἐμοί, ὥστε φύλακα γίγνεσθαι, εἰ σὺ κτλ. *Quis mihi dux futurus erat, si tibi aliquid mali accidisset?* Elmsley; who adds that ἦν is here for ἔμελλεν ἔσεσθαι, and he compares Herc. F. 467, σὺ δ᾽ ἦσθα Θηβῶν τῶν φιλαρμάτων ἄναξ, where see the note.

613. ἀνδρὸς—τυχών; See Alcest. 10, ὁσίου γὰρ ἀνδρὸς ὅσιος ὢν ἐτύγχανον.

615. συνῆψε, 'tied together,' i.e. one hand to the other; hence, apparently, the singular is used.

617. ἐβόσκετο. Cf. Aesch. Agam. 1646, οἶδ᾽ ἐγὼ φεύγοντας ἄνδρας ἐλπίδας σιτουμένους.

618. ταῦρον εὑρών. The delusion consisted in the circumstance that Bacchus himself was reputed to be κερασφόρος. One explanation of this was, that it symbolised the ploughing of the land by bulls. Diodor. Sic. iii. 64, παράσημον δ᾽ αὐτῷ ποιῆσαι κέρατα τοὺς κατασκευάζοντας τὰς γραφὰς ἢ τοὺς ἀνδριάντας, ἅμα μὲν δηλοῦντας ἑτέραν Διονύσου φύσιν [scil. ἐκ γῆς], ἅμα δὲ ἀπὸ τῆς περὶ τὸ ἄροτρον εὑρέσεως ἐμφαίνοντας τὸ μέγεθος τῆς ἐπινοηθείσης τοῖς γεωργοῖς εὐχρηστίας. So Propert. iv. 17, 19, 'Quod superesset vitae, per te et tua cornua vivam, Virtutisque tuae, Bacche, poeta ferar.' Ovid, Fast. iii. 789, 'Mite caput, Pater, huc placataque cornua vertas, Et des ingenio vela secunda meo.' *Inf.* v. 920, καὶ ταῦρος ἡμῖν πρόσθεν ἡγεῖσθαι δοκεῖς, καὶ σῷ κέρατε κρατὶ προσπεφυκέναι. "Apud Nonnum xlv. 235 seqq., Bacchus statim, ut comprehendere eum satellites Penthei volunt, taurum pro se substituit." *Hermann.*

621. ὀδόντας. Cf. Trach. 976, ἴσχε δακὼν στόμα σόν.

624. πῦρ ἀνῆψε. See on v. 596.—ὁ βάκχος, see on v. 576, and on v. 145.

625. Ἀχελῷον, for water generally, as in Androm. 167, and the well-known verse of Virgil, 'Poculaque inventis Acheloïa miscuit uvis.' The root is said to be αχ, as in Ἀχέρων, *aqua, lacrima*, &c.

ΒΑΚΧΑΙ. 437

διαμεθεὶς δὲ τόνδε μόχθον, ὡς ἐμοῦ πεφευγότος,
ἵεται ξίφος κελαινὸν ἁρπάσας δόμων ἔσω.
κᾆθ' ὁ Βρόμιος, ὡς ἔμοιγε φαίνεται, δόξαν λέγω,
φάσμ' ἐποίησεν κατ' αὐλήν· ὁ δ' ἐπὶ τοῦθ' ὡρμη-
 μένος   630
ᾖσσε κἀκέντει φαεννὸν *αἰθέρ', ὡς σφάζων ἐμέ.
πρὸς δὲ τοῖσδ' αὐτῷ τάδ' ἄλλα Βάκχιος λυμαίνεται·
δώματ' ἔρρηξεν χαμᾶζε· συντεθράνωται δ' ἅπαν
πικροτάτους ἰδόντι δεσμοὺς τοὺς ἐμούς· κόπου δ'
 ὕπο   634
διαμεθεὶς ξίφος παρεῖται. πρὸς θεὸν γὰρ ὢν ἀνὴρ
ἐς μάχην ἐλθεῖν ἐτόλμησ'· ἥσυχος δ' ἐκβὰς ἐγὼ
δωμάτων ἥκω πρὸς ὑμᾶς, Πενθέως οὐ φροντίσας.
ὡς δέ μοι δοκεῖ, ψοφεῖ γοῦν ἀρβύλη δόμων ἔσω,
ἐς προνώπι' αὐτίχ' ἥξει. τί ποτ' ἄρ' ἐκ τούτων ἐρεῖ;
ῥᾳδίως γὰρ αὐτὸν οἴσω, κἂν πνέων ἔλθῃ μέγα·   640
πρὸς σοφοῦ γὰρ ἀνδρὸς ἀσκεῖν σώφρον' εὐοργησίαν.
ΠΕ. πέπονθα δεινά· διαπέφευγέ μ' ὁ ξένος,

627. διαμεθεὶς, 'having relaxed *for an interval*' &c. Cf. v. 635. El. 978.
630. φάσμα. Elmsley, Hermann, Dindorf, and Bothe, agree in adopting, with Matthiae, Jacob's reading for φῶς. There was *light* enough in the house (v. 624), for Pentheus thought it was all on fire. What the context manifestly requires, is, some phantom for the deluded Pentheus to attack. The alteration was probably made from φάσμ' to φῶς on account of φαεννὸν αἰθέρα in the next verse. But αἰθήρ is itself 'luminous ether,' wherefore the epithet does not of necessity allude to what precedes. Compare Hel. 583, καὶ τίς βλέποντα σώματ' ἐξεργάζεται; ΕΛ. αἰθήρ. But it is not a little singular that this very word αἰθέρ' was restored on the conjecture of Canter, all the old copies omitting it.
632. τάδ' ἄλλα is the direct object to λυμαίνεται, which governs an accusative, not a dative. Cf. 354. Elmsley reads with Scaliger τά τ' ἄλλα—δωμά τ' ἔρρηξεν, to which Hermann objects, that this necessarily implies something over and above both the preceding (πρὸς τοῖσδε) and the destruction of the house which follows; whereas it does not appear that he did more than this.
635. παρεῖται. See *inf*. 683. Alcest. 204.
636. ἐκβὰς ἐγὼ Bothe (who however retains the corrupt reading of the MSS. in his text) for ἐκ βάκχας ἄγων. Elmsley gives ἥσυχος δὲ βασιλικῶν δωμάτων, Hermann (by a very improbable conjecture) δ' ἐκ Βακχάδων δ., *ex aedibus furore et perturbatione plenis*.
639. προνώπια, the front of the house, the vestibule, προπύλαια. Cf. Hipp. 374, to which the explanation of Photius more particularly applies, προνώπιον, τὸ προεκκείμενον.—ἐκ τούτων, after all this.
641. εὐοργησίαν, easiness of temper. See Hipp. 1039. Photius, εὐόργητος, πρᾶος.
642. The prediction of Dionysus is fulfilled as soon as it is uttered. Pentheus does appear, and in a very violent humour. He is met by his captive, the supposed bacchant, with cool indifference. The time however has not yet come for the god to manifest himself. He yet describes

438 ΕΥΡΙΠΙΔΟΥ

ὃς ἄρτι δεσμοῖς ἦν κατηναγκασμένος.
ἔα ἔα.
ὅδ᾽ ἐστὶν ἀνήρ· τί τάδε; πῶς προνώπιος 645
φαίνει πρὸς οἴκοις τοῖς ἐμοῖς, ἔξω βεβώς;
ΔΙ. στῆσον πόδ᾽, ὀργῇ δ᾽ ὑπόθες ἥσυχον πόδα.
ΠΕ. πόθεν σὺ δεσμὰ διαφυγὼν ἔξω περᾷς;
ΔΙ. οὐκ εἶπον ἢ οὐκ ἤκουσας ὅτι λύσει μέ τις;
ΠΕ. τίς; τοὺς λόγους γὰρ εἰσφέρεις καινοὺς ἀεί. 650
ΔΙ. ὃς τὴν πολύβοτρυν ἄμπελον φύει βροτοῖς.
ΠΕ. ὠνείδισας δὴ τοῦτο Διονύσῳ καλόν.
ΔΙ.   *   *   *   *
ΠΕ. κλῄειν κελεύω πάντα πύργον ἐν κύκλῳ.
ΔΙ. τί δ᾽; οὐχ ὑπερβαίνουσι καὶ τείχη θεοί;
ΠΕ. σοφὸς σοφὸς σύ, πλὴν ἃ δεῖ σ᾽ εἶναι σοφόν. 655
ΔΙ. ἃ δεῖ μάλιστα, ταῦτ᾽ ἔγωγ᾽ ἔφυν σοφός.
κείνου δ᾽ ἀκούσας πρῶτα τοὺς λόγους μάθε,
ὃς ἐξ ὄρους πάρεστιν ἀγγελῶν τί σοι·
ἡμεῖς δέ σοι μενοῦμεν, οὐ φευξούμεθα.

ΑΓΓΕΛΟΣ.

Πενθεῦ, κρατύνων τῆσδε Θηβαίας χθονὸς, 660

his delivery as due to another, the god invisibly acting in his behalf.—προνώπιος, ἐν προνωπίοις, cf. v. 639. Compare ἐξώπιος. Bothe most strangely explains the word by ἑκών.—φαίνει, the second person, not for φαίνεται, as in Electr. 1234.

647. πόδα. Hermann thinks that 'to subject a quiet foot to anger,' means 'to restrain a hasty pace,' and probably he is right, though πόδα is suspicious on account of στῆσον πόδα immediately preceding. Perhaps τρόπον, or ἡσύχην φρένα. Of course, ἥσυχον must be taken in the usual sense, ὥστε γίγνεσθαι &c.

649. ἢ οὐκ ἤκουσας Herm. Bothe, Dind., with one MS., for οὐκ εἶπον; οὐκ ἤκουσας κτλ.

652. It had occurred to the present editor, that two lines had probably been lost after this, by which the speech of Pentheus would be of four verses, as above, and as those of Dionysus below, v. 656 seqq. On this theory the passage might have stood thus:

ὠνείδισας δὴ τοῦτο Διονύσῳ καλόν,

σοὶ δ᾽ αἰσχρὸν, οὐ γὰρ ἀξίαν τιμὴν νέμεις.
ὑμᾶς δὲ, δμῶες οἱ παρεστῶτες πύλαις,
κλῄειν κελεύω πάντα πύργον ἐν κύκλῳ.

However, it seems more probable, either that this verse should be assigned to Dionysus, in answer to a lost verse of Pentheus, or that the στιχομυθία has been broken by the loss of Dionysus' reply, which may have been to the effect that, as he had now escaped, so never should Pentheus get him into his power again, κοὺ μήποτ᾽ αὖθις ἔκ γε σοῦ χειρώσομαι. To which Pentheus replies by defying his attempt to escape a second time, κλῄειν κελεύω κτλ. As for the sense of the present verse, which Elmsley thinks "non valde perspicuus," and compares Med. 514, καλόν γ᾽ ὄνειδος, perhaps Pentheus meant to say, 'That, so far from being any discredit, was a praiseworthy deed,' i. e. well, there is something to be said in favour of your Dionysus, after all. Bothe refers τοῦτο to τὸ λύειν αὐτὸν, in which case καλὸν will be ironical.

ΒΑΚΧΑΙ. 439

ἥκω Κιθαιρῶν᾽ ἐκλιπὼν, ἵν᾽ οὔποτε
λευκῆς χιόνος ἀνεῖσαν εὐαγεῖς βολαί.
ΠΕ. ἥκεις δὲ ποίαν προστιθεὶς σπουδὴν λόγου;
ΑΓ. βάκχας ποτνιάδας εἰσιδὼν, αἳ τῆσδε γῆς
οἴστροισι λευκὸν κῶλον ἐξηκόντισαν, 665
ἥκω, φράσαι σοὶ καὶ πόλει χρῄζων, ἄναξ,
ὡς δεινὰ δρῶσι θαυμάτων τε κρείσσονα.
θέλω δ᾽ ἀκοῦσαι, πότερά σοι παρρησίᾳ
φράσω τὰ κεῖθεν, ἢ λόγον στειλώμεθα.
τὸ γὰρ τάχος σου τῶν φρενῶν δέδοικ᾽, ἄναξ, 670
καὶ τοὐξύθυμον καὶ τὸ βασιλικὸν λίαν.
ΠΕ. λέγ᾽, ὡς ἀθῷος ἐξ ἐμοῦ πάντως ἔσει·
τοῖς γὰρ δικαίοις οὐχὶ θυμοῦσθαι χρεών.
ὅσῳ δ᾽ ἂν εἴπῃς δεινότερα βακχῶν πέρι,
τοσῷδε μᾶλλον τὸν ὑποθέντα τὰς τέχνας 675
γυναιξὶ τόνδε τῇ δίκῃ προσθήσομεν.

662. εὐαγεῖς, 'bright,' ἁγναὶ, καθαραὶ, as Hesychius gives among other meanings. Photius, εὐαγές, ἁγνὸν, εὐσεβὲς, ὅσιον, θειότατον. See on Eur. Suppl. 652, θεατὴς πύργον εὐαγῆ λαβὼν, 'commanding a clear view,' and on Aesch. Pers. 468. It is probable that the α is really long, though some derive it from ἄγος, piaculum, and this is obviously the meaning in Antig. 521, τίς οἶδεν εἰ κάτωθεν εὐαγῆ τάδε; The meaning of οὔποτε ἀνεῖσαν is not, 'where the snow never melts' (which is not the case), but 'where snow-showers never (i. e. rarely) cease.' For the metre, see on v. 260.

664. Whether ποτνιάδες is to be regarded as a mere epithet or as a proper name, is rather uncertain. Hermann and Elmsley take the latter view. The word is said to be derived from Potniae in Boeotia, where the horses of Glaucus went mad, and from which the play of Aeschylus, Glaucus Potnieus, took its name. Photius, Ποτνιάδας, Βάκχας, Εὐριπίδης. He must allude to this passage; for in Orest. 318, δρομάδες ὦ πτεροφόροι ποτνιάδες θεαὶ, it is used of the Furies, and there ποτνιὰς looks very like another form of πότνα or πότνια. In Phoen. 1124, Ποτνιάδες πῶλοι, it is of course a proper name. Hesychius, Ποτνιάδες, αἱ Βάκχαι, ἀντὶ τοῦ Μαινάδες καὶ λυσσάδες.

665. γῆς—ἐξηκόντισαν, have rushed away from their homes to the mountains; cf. v. 32—3. Here γῆς is for πόλεως, as Bothe thinks; though, as Cithaeron was on the confines of Boeotia, they may have stepped beyond the real limits of the land. —λευκὸν κῶλον some take for 'naked feet,' and Elmsley compares Cycl. 72, Βάκχαις σὺν λευκόποσιν. See on Ion 221. It may, of course, be merely an ornamental epithet. However, as Blomfield has shown on Prom. 137, to go forth ἀπέδιλος and ἀσάνδαλος was a phrase for any hasty exit.

669. στειλώμεθα, for συστ., contract, abridge our narrative. See on Troad. 108. The deliberative subjunctives are used as in Prom. 799, ἑλοῦ γὰρ ἢ πόνων τὰ λοιπά σοι φράσω σαφηνῶς, ἢ τὸν ἐκλύσοντ᾽ ἐμέ. Bothe thinks it is a metaphor from furling a sail, which is usually στέλλειν λαῖφος, Hec. 1080, Aesch. Suppl. 703, but also στέλλεσθαι, Il. i. 432. Photius, στειλάμενοι, στείλαντες, and again (which is perhaps applicable to the present passage), στειλάμενος, εὐσταλῶς ἐπελθών.

672. ἀθῷος, unpunished; see Med. 1300.

676. προσθήσομεν, 'we will devote to punishment.' On προσθεῖναι, addicere, see Androm. 1016. Phoen. 964.

ΑΓ. ἀγελαῖα μὲν βοσκήματ' ἄρτι πρὸς λέπας
μόσχων ὑπεξήκριζον, ἡνίχ' ἥλιος
ἀκτῖνας ἐξίησι θερμαίνων χθόνα.
ὁρῶ δὲ θιάσους τρεῖς γυναικείων χορῶν, 680
ὧν ἦρχ' ἑνὸς μὲν Αὐτονόη, τοῦ δευτέρου
μήτηρ Ἀγαύη σή, τρίτου δ' Ἰνὼ χοροῦ.
ηὗδον δὲ πᾶσαι σώμασιν παρειμέναι,
αἱ μὲν πρὸς ἐλάτης νῶτ' ἐρείσασαι φόβην,
αἱ δ' ἐν δρυὸς φύλλοισι πρὸς πέδῳ κάρα 685
εἰκῇ βαλοῦσαι σωφρόνως, οὐχ ὡς σὺ φῄς

677. The account of the messenger, respecting the doings of the Maenads on the mountains, is one of the most brilliant and picturesque narratives that Attic tragedy contains. This is so essential a part of the tragic drama, that very few plays are without it in some form or other; though few, like the present (*inf.* 1043), have two distinct and equally lengthy narrations, because few plots admit of a double crisis of events in their περιπέτεια. There is an instance of this in the Phoenissae, and also in the Hecuba, where both the death of Polyxena and the punishment of Polymnestor are described; but the latter is the narration, not of a messenger, but of the sufferer himself. The present messenger, who is a herdsman, had chanced to witness the bacchants in the hills at the moment when, summoned by their leader, they had started up from sleep with all the wild gestures and strange supernatural powers that Dionysus had imparted to them. He had called others to witness the scene, and a plan was concerted with them to seize Agave the leader by an ambuscade. They had however been speedily put to flight by the frantic crew, who, disappointed of their revenge, had attacked and torn to pieces a herd of oxen. Thence they had spread through the neighbouring towns, and begun to plunder houses; nor could the inhabitants oppose the thyrsus with the javelin. The man declares himself a convert, and advises the king to admit the new worship into the city. The tenour of the whole narrative is to show (as the fate of Pentheus afterwards proves) that the notion of *mystery* so strongly attached to the proceedings of the Bacchants, that for the uninitiated to behold them was in the highest degree dangerous. In this instance the herdsmen had only been allowed to escape because they had no evil designs, no presumptuous contempt for the power of the god.

678. ὑπεξήκριζον, which some take for the first person of a transitive verb, is more probably the plural in a neuter sense, ἀγελαῖα βοσκήματα being virtually equivalent to μόσχων ἀγέλαι. Compare ἐπήκρισε Aesch. Cho. 918 (Schol. ἐς ἄκρον ἦλθε), ἐξακρίζετ' αἰθέρα πτεροῖς Orest. 274, ὑπερακρίζει, 'overhangs,' Eur. Suppl. 988. The Etymol. Mag. explains the word, quoting this passage, τὸ ἄκροις ποσὶ πορεύεσθαι, which is clearly wrong. The sense appears to be, 'The herds of oxen which we fed (ἀγέλαι ἃς ἐβόσκομεν) were just surmounting the steep to the ridge,' &c. It was on attaining the summit, and looking down upon the opposite side of the mountain, that he suddenly came in sight of the Maenads.

682. τρίτη δ' Ἰνὼ τρίτου Hermann, two MSS. giving τρίτη.

683. σώμασιν, 'tired *in* their bodies,' more usually σώματα, with a dative of the cause, but Matthiae in a good note gives several examples of the present construction, among others Orest. 706, ναῦς ἐνταθεῖσα πρὸς βίαν ποδί. Hermann's κώμασιν παρειμέναι must be numbered among those conjectures which occasionally fell from the great critic when he was inclined to display his ingenuity rather than his sound judgment.

686. οὐχ ὡς σὺ φῂς, κτλ. For οὐ θηρῶσαι Κύπριν, ὡς σὺ φῂς αὐτὰς, (*sup.* v. 222.) Compare Rhes. 438, οὐχ ὡς σὺ κομπεῖς τὰς ἐμὰς ἀμύστιδας, for οὐ πίνων ἀμύστιδας, ὡς σὺ κομπεῖς.—λωτοῦ ψόφῳ, the noise of the pipe. Here ψόφος is somewhat improperly used; see above, v. 513. We may supply κηλουμένας from the foregoing participle.

ΒΑΚΧΑΙ. 441

ὠνωμένας κρατῆρι καὶ λωτοῦ ψόφῳ
θηρᾶν καθ' ὕλην Κύπριν ἠρημωμένας.
ἡ σὴ δὲ μήτηρ ὠλόλυξεν ἐν μέσαις
σταθεῖσα βάκχαις, ἐξ ὕπνου κινεῖν δέμας,   690
μυκήμαθ' ὡς ἤκουσε κεροφόρων βοῶν.
αἱ δ' ἀποβαλοῦσαι θαλερὸν ὀμμάτων ὕπνον
ἀνῇξαν ὀρθαί, θαῦμ' ἰδεῖν εὐκοσμίας,
νέαι, παλαιαί, παρθένοι τ' ἔτ' ἄζυγες.
καὶ πρῶτα μὲν καθεῖσαν εἰς ὤμους κόμας,   695
νεβρίδας τ' ἀνεστείλανθ', ὅσαισιν ἁμμάτων
σύνδεσμ' ἐλέλυτο, καὶ καταστίκτους δορὰς
ὄφεσι κατεζώσαντο λιχμῶσιν γένυν.
αἱ δ' ἀγκάλαισι δορκάδ' ἢ σκύμνους λύκων
ἀγρίους ἔχουσαι λευκὸν ἐδίδοσαν γάλα,   700
ὅσαις νεοτόκοις μαστὸς ἦν σπαργῶν ἔτι

689. ὀλολύζειν, the student will remember, was the sacrificial shout of *women*, distinctively. The κεροφόροι βόες were the messenger's own oxen, which the bacchants were incited by their leader to pursue.

692. θαλερὸν ὕπνον, 'refreshing sleep,' Elmsley. "Somnus, qui est in ipso flore, i. e. altus sopor," Hermann. The same difficulty attends the similar epithets χλωρὸν and θαλερὸν δάκρυ, Med. 922. Iph. A. 39, which are very variously explained. Photius, θαλεροί, διυγροί, νέοι, ἀκμαῖοι, ἢ ταχεῖς. Both perhaps are derived from the effects produced on the countenance. In Theocr. xiv. 32, ἔκλαεν ἐξαπίνας θαλερώτερον ἢ παρὰ ματρὶ παρθένος ἑξαέτις κόλπῳ ἐπιθυμήσασα, the sense evidently is 'more copiously.'—εὐκοσμίας, i. e. ἕνεκα.

695. καθεῖσαν. To let the hair fly loose was a natural trick of those who affected inspiration; σείων ἅμα τὴν κόμην ἄνετον ὥσπερ οἱ τῇ μητρὶ ἀγείροντές τε καὶ ἐνθεαζόμενοι, Lucian, Alexandr. p. 221. The action too had a sense of freedom from restraint, to which Phaedra alludes, when she says to her nurse βαρύ μοι κεφαλᾶς ἐπίκρανον ἔχειν, ἄφελ', ἀμπέτασον βόστρυχον ὤμοις, Hipp. 201. In Ion 1200, the form καθῆκαν is preferred. Compare ἀνεῖσαν v. 662 with ἀνῆκαν v. 448.

696. ἀνεστείλαντο, 're-adjusted,' i. e. girded up for running. This is clear from the context, 'those to whom the tie of the girdle (ζώνη) had previously been loosened.' By undoing the zone, the folds of the χιτὼν fell to the ankles. Theocr. xv. 134, λύσασαι δὲ κόμην καὶ ἐπὶ σφυρὰ κόλπον ἀνεῖσαι, στήθεσι φαινομένοις λιγυρᾶς ἀρξώμεθ' ἀοιδᾶς (where the writer is speaking of a κομμὸς to Adonis). The sense of στέλλεσθαι is the same as that in v. 669, but the ἀνὰ implies a previous loosening of the attire.

698. λιχμῶσιν Heath for λιχμῶσαν. The custom of taming snakes, which is still kept up in India, was early known to the Greeks; for the point of λιχμῶσιν γένυν, 'licking their (the bacchants') chins,' is to show the harmlessness of the creatures, though, of course, they are here presumed to have been made innoxious by Dionysus in a miraculous manner. Compare *inf.* 767, σταγόνα δ' ἐκ παρηίδων γλώσσῃ δράκοντες ἐξεφαίδρυνον χροός. Barnes compares Hor. Carm. ii. 19, 19, 'tu separatis uvidus in jugis Nodo coerces viperino Bistonidum sine fraude crines;' and Hermann well adds Nonnus, xliv. 410, κεφαλὴν κυκλώσατο Κάδμου Πρηϋς ὄφις, καὶ γλῶσσα πέριξ λίχμαζεν ὑπήνην.

701. σπαργῶν, swelling with milk, Cycl. 55. Photius, σπαργῶσα, ἢ ἀνθοῦσα ἢ σπαραττομένη ὑπὸ θλίψεως καὶ δεομένη ἐκκρίσεώς τινος. Plato, Symp. p. 206, E., τῷ

VOL. II. 3 L

ΕΥΡΙΠΙΔΟΥ

βρέφη λιπούσαις· ἐπὶ δ' ἔθεντο κισσίνους
στεφάνους δρυός τε σμίλακός τ' ἀνθεσφόρου.
θύρσον δέ τις λαβοῦσ' ἔπαισεν ἐς πέτραν,
ὅθεν δροσώδης ὕδατος ἐκπηδᾷ νοτίς· 705
ἄλλη δὲ νάρθηκ' ἐς πέδον καθῆκε γῆς,
καὶ τῇδε κρήνην ἐξανῆκ' οἴνου θεός·
ὅσαις δὲ λευκοῦ πώματος πόθος παρῆν,
ἄκροισι δακτύλοισι διαμῶσαι χθόνα
γάλακτος ἑσμοὺς εἶχον· ἐκ δὲ κισσίνων 710

κυοῦντί τε καὶ ἤδη σπαργῶντι πολλὴ ἡ πτόησις γέγονε περὶ τὸ καλὸν, κτλ.

703. σμίλακος. So Hermann and others for μίλακος. See on v. 108.

704—6. θύρσον — νάρθηκα. Here, as in Hel. 1361, a distinction seems to be implied ; and the latter is doubtless merely a light wand or ferule (either a fennel-stalk or some kind of reed), while the thyrsus is said to have had a shaft made of a vine stem, and to have been tipped with a point, like a dart, for which it was evidently capable of being used ; see v. 762 and 1099. Musgrave quotes from Lucian, *Bacchus* (vol. iii. p. 127, ed. Teubner,) καὶ αἱ Μαινάδες σὺν ὁλολυγῇ ἐνεπήδησαν αὐτοῖς δράκοντας ὑπεζωσμέναι κἀκ τῶν θύρσων ἄκρων ἀπογυμνοῦσαι τὸν σίδηρον. So in v. 733, when the bacchants had used their thyrsi as lances against the enemy, they are laid aside, and they attack the cattle χειρὸς ἀσιδήρου μέτα. Cf. ἄθυρσοι Βάκχαι, *unarmed*, Orest. 1492. In Ion 217, Bacchus slays one of the rebel giants, not with the thyrsus, but with the νάρθηξ, which is called ἀπόλεμον κίσσινον βάκτρον, 'an *unwarlike* staff.' Therefore, the other was a *warlike* weapon. Diodorus Siculus, lib. iv. § 4, speaks of the armies of female Bacchants, καθωπλισμένων λόγχαις τεθυρσωμέναις. All these passages seem decisive on the subject. Both thyrsus and narthex were intwined with ivy ; the latter however, (to judge from the painting referred to on Hel. 1361,) was merely tufted at the top. The thyrsus moreover bore a fir-cone at the end. Some have considered this to refer to the use of pitch in lining the wine-jars, as Martial says, ' *et vinum nuce condimus picata*.' Others, observing that what appears to be a fir-cone is often borne in the hand of sculptured figures found at Nineveh, would assign a mystic, —some would even say, a phallic,—symbolism to this natural product. May we not rather infer that it was found to be a ready and convenient mask or cover for the sharp point of the thyrsus, which was required as much for sportive and festive uses as for a weapon of defence ? It is worthy of notice, that the scene of the Bacchic revels is described as among *pine trees* (πεῦκαι and ἐλάται, v. 684, 1052, the stone-pine and silver-fir, *pinus pinea* and *picea pectinata*), so that these cones would always be at hand when the thyrsi were to be muffled for the sports ; and the very large cones of the former tree are, when unripe, very easily pierced with a steel point. Elmsley (on v. 705) appears to doubt whether the narthex was distinct from the thyrsus ; but the above considerations make this probable.

709. διαμῶσαι, 'clearing away.' Thucyd. iv. 26, διαμώμενοι τὸν κάχληκα οἱ πλεῖστοι ἐπὶ τῇ θαλάσσῃ ἔπινον οἷον εἰκὸς ὕδωρ. Od. v. 482, ἄφαρ δ' εὐνὴν ἐπαμήσατο χερσὶ φίλῃσιν εὐρεῖαν. Xen. Oecon. xvii. 13, ἀντιπροσαμήσασθαι τὴν γῆν. It may be doubted if Elmsley is right in referring δακτύλοις to the toes rather than to the fingers.

710. ἑσμοὺς, stores of milk ; properly *swarms*, from ἕζεσθαι, because bees alight on trees &c. Hence it is said of any aggregate of things or beings. Aesch. Suppl. 29, ἀρσενοπληθῆ ἑσμὸν ὑβριστὴν Αἰγυπτογενῆ. Elmsley appears to be wrong in saying "nescio an ἐκβολὰς potius quam πλῆθος in animo habuerit. Idem enim significant ἱέναι et ἐκβάλλειν." He seems indeed wrongly to derive it from ἵεσθαι, and so Photius, ἑσμὸς, πληθὺς, ὄχλος· κυρίως τῶν μελισσῶν· παρὰ τὸ ἅμα πεπομένας ἵεσθαι, except that the grammarian does not recognise the aspirate, which however is established by

θύρσων γλυκεῖαι μέλιτος ἔσταζον ῥοαί.
ὥστ᾽, εἰ παρῆσθα, τὸν θεὸν, τὸν νῦν ψέγεις,
εὐχαῖσιν ἂν μετῆλθες εἰσιδὼν τάδε.
ξυνήλθομεν δὲ βουκόλοι καὶ ποιμένες,
κοινῶν λόγων δώσοντες ἀλλήλοις ἔριν,   715
ὡς δεινὰ δρῶσι θαυμάτων τ᾽ ἐπάξια·
καί τις πλάνης κατ᾽ ἄστυ καὶ τρίβων λόγων
ἔλεξεν εἰς ἅπαντας, Ὦ σεμνὰς πλάκας
ναίοντες ὀρέων, θέλετε θηρασώμεθα
Πενθέως Ἀγαύην μητέρ᾽ ἐκ βακχευμάτων,   720
χάριν τ᾽ ἄνακτι θῶμεν; εὖ δ᾽ ἡμῖν λέγειν
ἔδοξε, θάμνων δ᾽ ἐλλοχίζομεν φόβαις
κρύψαντες αὑτούς· αἱ δὲ τὴν τεταγμένην
ὥραν ἐκίνουν θύρσον ἐς βακχεύματα,
Ἴακχον ἀθρόῳ στόματι, τὸν Διὸς γόνον,   725
Βρόμιον καλοῦσαι· πᾶν δὲ συνεβάκχευσ᾽ ὄρος

the compound ἄφεσμος.—For the mention of the three Bacchic gifts, wine, milk, and honey, see v. 143, ῥεῖ δὲ γάλακτι πέδον, ῥεῖ δ᾽ οἴνῳ, ῥεῖ δὲ μελισσᾶν νέκταρι.
712. ψέγεις, ἀτίζεις, speak contemptuously of.
716. Dobree thinks this verse made up from v. 667.
717. πλάνης κατ᾽ ἄστυ, an occasional frequenter of the city, for the purpose of being present at the ecclesia, where he had picked up a smattering of rhetoric. Of course, the poet writes in reference to Athenian customs. Compare Orest. 919, where it is said to the praise of a countryman that he was one ὀλιγάκις ἄστυ κἀγορᾶς χραίνων κύκλον. Such men were apt to become ἀγοραῖοι ἄνθρωποι, idlers in the market-place, to talk about politics. Cf. Rhes. 625, τρίβων γὰρ εἶ τὰ κομψά. Med. 686, σοφὸς γὰρ ἀνὴρ καὶ τρίβων τὰ τοιάδε.
721. θῶμεν. Elmsley would read either δῶμεν or θώμεθ᾽, because δοῦναι χάριν and θέσθαι χάριν are common expressions, but not θεῖναι χάριν. Bothe adopts θώμεθ᾽, but no correction is needed: θεῖναι is here a synonym of πράσσειν, for which see Ion 36, Λοξίᾳ δ᾽ ἐγὼ χάριν πράσσων ἀδελφῷ. Ibid. 895. Electr. 1133.
722. Young students will not confound the present ἐλλοχίζομεν with ἐλοχίζομεν.

723. τὴν τεταγμένην ὥραν, 'at the appointed hour,' is a rare accusative. See Hel. 479. It is so used in Eum. 109, καὶ νυκτίσεμνα δεῖπν᾽ ἐπ᾽ ἐσχάρᾳ πυρὸς ἔθυον, ὥραν οὐδενὸς κοινὴν θεῶν. It is clear that some considerable interval has occurred between the first movement of the bacchants and this endeavour to seize them. A council had been held, the usual time of their sports had been ascertained, and a proper station had been chosen for an ambuscade. From the mention of fire in v. 758, and a comparison of v. 486, it is probable that the time was night; but the first movement had been seen at early dawn, v. 678. The phrase κινεῖν θύρσον, like the Latin castra movere, may allude to the thyrsi being piled or stuck in the ground while the bacchants were resting; or it may merely mean that they began their revels.
726. ὄρος καὶ θῆρες. The mountain re-echoed, and every bird and beast was aroused and joined in the outcry. This is very true to nature; for in any nightly alarm the denizens of the forest utter a confused cry, one after the other as they awake, till the whole place rings with the chorus. From the reading of Robortello's edition and a Paris MS., in Longinus § 15, Porson preferred συνεβάκχευ᾽, and so Elmsley, Bothe, and Hermann have edited. The aorist however would mean,

καὶ θῆρες, οὐδὲν δ' ἦν ἀκίνητον δρόμῳ.
κυρεῖ δ' Ἀγαύη πλησίον θρώσκουσά μου·
κἀγὼ 'ξεπήδησ', ὡς συναρπάσαι θέλων,
λόχμην κενώσας, ἔνθ' ἐκρυπτόμην δέμας. 730
ἡ δ' ἀνεβόησεν, ὦ δρομάδες ἐμαὶ κύνες,
θηρώμεθ' ἀνδρῶν τῶνδ' ὕπ'· ἀλλ' ἕπεσθέ μοι,
ἕπεσθε, θύρσοις διὰ χερῶν ὡπλισμέναι.
ἡμεῖς μὲν οὖν φεύγοντες ἐξηλύξαμεν
βακχῶν σπαραγμόν, αἱ δὲ νεμομέναις χλόην 735
μόσχοις ἐπῆλθον χειρὸς ἀσιδήρου μέτα.
καὶ τὴν μὲν ἂν προσεῖδες εὔθηλον πόριν
μυκωμένην ἔχουσαν ἐν χεροῖν δίκῃ,
ἄλλαι δὲ δαμάλας διεφόρουν σπαράγμασιν.
εἶδες δ' ἂν ἢ πλεύρ' ἢ δίχηλον ἔμβασιν 740
ῥιπτόμεν' ἄνω τε καὶ κάτω· κρεμαστὰ δὲ
ἔσταζ' ὑπ' ἐλάταις ἀναπεφυρμέν' αἵματι.
ταῦροι δ' ὑβρισταὶ κεἰς κέρας θυμούμενοι

that at each cry of Ἴακχε there was a momentary and oft-repeated response, not one continuous accompaniment.

728. μου. Perhaps ἐμοῦ, as the man is speaking of his own feat as distinct from the rest.

730. ἐκρυπτόμην Dind. Herm. Barnes, for ἐκρύπτομεν. The change is so slight that it seems rightly admitted, though neither in the transition from the singular to the plural nor in the use of the imperfect for the aorist is there any real difficulty.

733. ὡπλισμέναι. Armed with them as offensive weapons (see on v. 704). Compare Aesch. Theb. 428, φλέγει δὲ λαμπὰς διὰ χερῶν ὡπλισμένη. More usually, διὰ χερῶν ἔχουσαι θύρσους.

736. ἀσιδήρου. This also is explained on v. 704. Elmsley's note here furnishes a curious example of the errors which the best scholars will sometimes commit. "Omnes libri χειρὸς ἀσιδήρου, anapaestum in quarta sede exhibentes." And he gives χερὸς in the text, forgetting that the ι in σίδηρος is short.

737. πόριν (a form used also in Suppl. 628), for πόρτιν, 'a calf,' whence εὔθηλον, well fed on milk; while δαμάλη is 'a heifer,' perhaps from δαμάζω, because old enough for bearing young. Elmsley, though he fails to distinguish them, cites a verse of Theocritus which is conclusive as to their difference, i. 75, πολλαὶ δ' αὖ δαμάλαι καὶ πόρτιες ὡδύραντο.

738. ἐν χεροῖν δίκῃ, for ὑποχειρίαν. The old reading was δίκα, corrected by Brodaeus, who explains it by ἐν χειρῶν νόμῳ. Cf. Herod. viii. 89, ἐν χειρῶν νόμῳ ἀπολλύμενοι. Aesch. Eum. 250, ὑπόδικος θέλει γενέσθαι χερῶν. Hesiod. Opp. 187, where χειροδίκαι is 'taking the law into their own hands.' Hermann and Dindorf prefer Scaliger's reading δίχα, divisum tenere. But if this means 'torn asunder,' then μυκωμένην is absurd, as Bothe truly objects. If we are to understand it χωρίς, δίχα τῶν ἄλλων, the adverbial use is both unusual and ambiguous.

743. εἰς κέρας θ. τὸ πρόσθεν, 'which before showed their anger by glancing at their horn,' as if taking sight for the attack, εἰς κέρας παρεμβλέπων, Hel. 1558. It is from this peculiar look of a bull when he meditates mischief, that the nurse says in Med. 92, ἤδη γὰρ εἶδον ὄμμα νιν ταυρουμένην τοῖσδ'. Elmsley, though he quotes the passage of the Helena, which is the key to the right interpretation, and other examples of εἰς κέρας θυμοῦσθαι, in cornua irasci, professes not to be clear about the exact meaning. It has been rightly ex-

τὸ πρόσθεν ἐσφάλλοντο πρὸς γαῖαν δέμας,
μυριάσι χειρῶν ἀγόμενοι νεανίδων.   745
θᾶσσον δὲ διεφοροῦντο σαρκὸς ἐνδυτὰ
ἢ σὺ ξυνάψαις βλέφαρα βασιλείοις κόραις.
χωροῦσι δ' ὥστ' ὄρνιθες ἀρθεῖσαι δρόμῳ,
πεδίων ὑποτάσεις, αἳ παρ' Ἀσωποῦ ῥοαῖς
εὔκαρπον ἐκβάλλουσι Θηβαίων στάχυν,   750
Ὑσίας τ' Ἐρυθράς θ', αἳ Κιθαιρῶνος λέπας
νέρθεν κατῳκήκασιν, ὥστε πολέμιοι,
ἐπεισπεσοῦσαι πάντ' ἄνω τε καὶ κάτω
διέφερον· ἥρπαζον μὲν ἐκ δόμων τέκνα,
ὁπόσα δ' ἐπ' ὤμοις ἔθεσαν, οὐ δεσμῶν ὕπο   755
προσείχετ', οὐδ' ἔπιπτεν ἐς μέλαν πέδον,
οὐ χαλκὸς, οὐ σίδηρος· ἐπὶ δὲ βοστρύχοις

plained by the learned author of the *New Cratylus*. Musgrave had before quoted ὀξὺ κέρας δόχμωσεν from Nonnus.

746. διεφοροῦντο. In familiar phrase, this passage might be rendered, 'they had their hides pulled off them in the twinkling of an eye.' Elmsley interprets σαρκὸς ἐνδυτὰ as a periphrasis for σάρκες, "ipsa caro, quae ossium tegumentum est," like ἐνδυτὰ νεβρίδων in v. 111, where see the note. There is no doubt that the skin or hide is here meant, though διαφορεῖν is 'to carry hither and thither,' as in v. 739, 754, Suppl. 382, Herc. F. 571. The meaning seems to be, that the hides were tugged this way and that in the attempts to remove them.

747. ἢ σὺ ξυνάψαις is the reading of Aldus and the Palatine MS. (the final s being superscribed in the latter). The rest give ἤ σε ξυνάψαι. The reading given above is that of Hermann and Elmsley; Dindorf pefers ἤ σε ξυνάψαι, and both are doubtless defensible. Compare Hipp. 1186, θᾶσσον ἢ λέγοι τις. There is however this difference in sense, that the infinitive would mean, 'too quick for you to close your eyes (to avoid the sight),' while the messenger seems to assign a measure of time, 'before your majesty could have closed your royal eye-lids' by winking the eyes.

749. πεδίων ὑποτάσεις, for τὰ ὑποτεταμένα πεδία. The accusative is that of transition over, as πηδῶντα δικόρυφον πλάκα v. 307, "Looking eastward (from the citadel of Tanagra), the plain of the Asopus stretches beneath us, from east to west. To the south of it is a range of mountains; of which Mount Elaté (Cithaeron) is the western, and Mount Noziὰ, the ancient Parnes, is the eastern extremity." *Athens and Attica,* p. 17.

751. Ὑσίας τ' κτλ. Elmsley quotes Pausanias ix. 2, 1, Γῆς δὲ τῆς Πλαταιΐδος ἐν τῷ Κιθαιρῶνι ὀλίγον τῆς εὐθείας ἐντραπεῖσιν ἐς δεξιὰ, Ὑσιῶν καὶ Ἐρυθρῶν ἐρείπιά ἐστι. πόλεις ποτὲ τῶν Βοιωτῶν ἦσαν, καὶ νῦν ἔτι ἐν τοῖς ἐρειπίοις τῶν Ὑσιῶν ναός ἐστιν Ἀπόλλωνος ἡμίεργος, καὶ φρέαρ ἱερόν. These two towns are mentioned together in the preceding chapter, § 3, καὶ σφᾶς αὐτίκα—τὴν ἐπὶ Ὑσιῶν ἦγε πρὸς Ἐλευθερῶν τε καὶ τῆς Ἀττικῆς. Bothe adds Strabo, lib. ix. cap. 1.

752. ὥστε πολέμιοι. We are not to suppose that these were the *ordinary* doings of the bacchants. On the present occasion they had been exasperated by the attempts to arrest them; and the messenger means to convince Pentheus of the danger of interfering with them.

755. At this verse all the MSS. except the Palatine abruptly leave off.

757. οὐ χαλκὸς, οὐ σίδηρος. Bothe is evidently wrong here, "intelligas ἦν, παρὴν αὐταῖς: neque aere neque ferro armatae erant." The practice of balancing weights on the shoulders is meant; and these words specify the more difficult sorts of burdens, 'not even brass nor iron' which they had plundered from the houses and carried off.

ΕΥΡΙΠΙΔΟΥ

πῦρ ἔφερον, οὐδ' ἔκαιεν, οἱ δ' ὀργῆς ὕπο
εἰς ὅπλ' ἐχώρουν, φερόμενοι βακχῶν ὕπο·
οὗπερ τὸ δεινὸν ἦν θέαμ' ἰδεῖν, ἄναξ.   760
τὰς μὲν γὰρ οὐχ ἤμασσε λογχωτὸν βέλος,
κεῖναι δὲ θύρσους ἐξανιεῖσαι χερῶν
ἐτραυμάτιζον κἀπενώτιζον φυγῇ
γυναῖκες ἄνδρας, οὐκ ἄνευ θεῶν τινός.
πάλιν δ' ἐχώρουν ὅθεν ἐκίνησαν πόδα,   765
κρήνας ἐπ' αὐτὰς, ἃς ἀνῆκ' αὐταῖς θεός·
νίψαντο δ' αἷμα, σταγόνα δ' ἐκ παρηΐδων
γλώσσῃ δράκοντες ἐξεφαίδρυνον χροός.
τὸν δαίμον' οὖν τόνδ', ὅστις ἔστ', ὦ δέσποτα,

758. οὐδ' ἔκαιεν Elmsley for οὐδ' ἐκαίεθ'. The meaning is, 'nor did it (the fire) burn them;' but ἐκαίετο would naturally signify 'nor did it (the fire) blaze,' which is exactly the contrary of what the poet meant to say. It is uncertain what trick this was; but the messenger evidently takes it for a supernatural power.

759. φερόμενοι, 'being plundered.'

760. τὸ δεινὸν θέαμα, that terrible spectacle which we witnessed. Elmsley compares, for the use of the article, Iph. T. 320, οὗ δὴ τὸ δεινὸν παρακέλευσμ' ἠκούσαμεν. Ibid. 1366, ὅθεν τὰ δεινὰ πλήγματ' ἦν γενειάδων.—τὰς μὲν Hermann, τοῖς μὲν Elmsley and Dindorf, τῶν μὲν Matthiae and Bothe. The Aldine reading is τοὺς, the Palatine MS. has τᾶς. If we read τοῖς, the accusative αὐτὰς remains to be supplied as the object of the transitive verb αἱμάσσειν. But τὰς μὲν seems at once easier and to have better authority. If, as Hermann observes, instead of κεῖναι δὲ the poet had used αἱ δὲ, this would have been inadmissible, because αἱ μὲν and αἱ δὲ necessarily imply different parties. But now the antithesis is this, 'Them indeed the pointed javelin (of the villagers) did not wound, while they, using their thyrsi as darts (see on v. 704), both inflicted wounds, and though only women, put to flight men.'

767. νίψαντο. This is one of the very few instances (see on Ion 1205) where, supposing the reading to be genuine, the augment must have been altogether omitted, because it cannot have been absorbed by the preceding word. So below, v. 1084 and 1134. Hermann has recourse to an improbable alteration, which he supports by very insufficient arguments, νίψαι τόδ' αἷμα, as if the messenger had heard the bacchants say, 'let us go back to wash off this blood.' If any correction were necessary, it would be easy to read (as Porson proposed in part) κρήναις τ' ἐπ' αὐταῖς, ἃς ἀνῆκ' αὐταῖς θεὸς, ἔνιψαν αἷμα. Aldus has κρήναις ἐπ' αὐταῖς, and if this was by mistake connected with ἐχώρουν by the accidental omission of τε, it would follow that ἔνιψαν αἷμα would pass into ἔνιψάν τ' and νίψαντο δ' αἷμα. Elmsley marks the present passage as corrupt. Those who care to examine all the supposed instances of omitted augment in the tragic senarius, will do well to consult his elaborate note on v. 1132 of this play, and Hermann's Preface to his edition of the same (1823). These two scholars are at issue on the main question, whether such licence was ever allowed; and Hermann concludes in the affirmative. The present editor inclines to his opinion, since the passages which seem to establish it are sufficiently numerous, and the proposed alterations of them are far from satisfactory. Moreover, the epic character of messengers' narratives sufficiently accounts for the occasional use of an epic licence.

768. δράκοντες. See on v. 698. The old reading δράκοντος was corrected by Reiske. The construction certainly is not, as Elmsley tells us, ἐκ παρηΐδων χροός. The words stand in their natural order: 'the blood-drop from off their cheeks with their tongue snakes licked clean from the skin.'

δέχου πόλει τῇδ᾽, ὡς τά τ᾽ ἄλλ᾽ ἐστὶν μέγας 770
κἀκεῖνό φασιν αὐτὸν, ὡς ἐγὼ κλύω,
τὴν παυσίλυπον ἄμπελον δοῦναι βροτοῖς.
οἴνου δὲ μηκέτ᾽ ὄντος οὐκ ἔστιν Κύπρις,
οὐδ᾽ ἄλλο τερπνὸν οὐδὲν ἀνθρώποις ἔτι.

ΧΟ. ταρβῶ μὲν εἰπεῖν τοὺς λόγους ἐλευθέρους 775
ἐς τὸν τύραννον, ἀλλ᾽ ὅμως εἰρήσεται·
Διόνυσος ἥσσων οὐδενὸς θεῶν ἔφυ.

ΠΕ. ἤδη τόδ᾽ ἐγγύς, ὥστε πῦρ, ἐφάπτεται
ὕβρισμα βακχῶν, ψόγος ἐς Ἕλληνας μέγας.
ἀλλ᾽ οὐκ ὀκνεῖν δεῖ· στεῖχ᾽ ἐπ᾽ Ἠλέκτρας ἰὼν 780
πύλας· κέλευε πάντας ἀσπιδηφόρους
ἵππων τ᾽ ἀπαντᾶν ταχυπόδων ἐπεμβάτας,
πέλτας θ᾽ ὅσοι πάλλουσι, καὶ τόξων χερὶ
ψάλλουσι νευράς· ὡς ἐπιστρατεύσομεν
βάκχαισιν. οὐ γὰρ ἀλλ᾽ ὑπερβάλλει τάδε, 785
εἰ πρὸς γυναικῶν πεισόμεσθ᾽ ἃ πάσχομεν.

ΔΙ. πείθει μὲν οὐδὲν, τῶν ἐμῶν λόγων κλύων,
Πενθεῦ· κακῶς δὲ πρὸς σέθεν πάσχων ὅμως
οὔ φημι χρῆναί σ᾽ ὅπλ᾽ ἐπαίρεσθαι θεῷ,
ἀλλ᾽ ἡσυχάζειν· Βρόμιος οὐκ ἀνέξεται 790
κινοῦντα βάκχας εὐίων ὀρῶν ἄπο.

ΠΕ. οὐ μὴ φρενώσεις μ᾽, ἀλλὰ δέσμιος φυγὼν

771. κἀκεῖνο κτλ. 'This also they say of him, that he gave,' &c. See v. 280 and 651.
775. ἐλευθέρους. Equivalent to ἐλευθέρως, if this be not rather the true reading. But cf. v. 650, τοὺς λόγους γὰρ εἰσφέρεις καινούς ἀεί. Ar. Vesp. 554, ἐμβάλλει μοι τὴν χεῖρ᾽ ἀπαλὴν, τῶν δημοσίων κεκλοφυῖαν. The position of the predicate here is rather more involved; εἰ οἱ λόγοι οὓς εἰπεῖν ἔχω ἐς τὸν τύραννον ἐλεύθεροι ἔσονται, τοῦτο μὲν ταρβῶ.—τὸν τύραννον, to one who is a king.
778. ἤδη. When I am told to my face this, and by one who has witnessed their outrageous doings, the matter affects me closely and personally, besides being a reproach to the Hellenic race at large.
780. Ἠλέκτρας. For this led in the direction of Cithaeron. See Suppl. 663.
785. οὐ γὰρ ἀλλὰ, 'for truly.' Cf.

Suppl. 570, κλύοιμ᾽ ἄν· οὐ γὰρ ἀλλὰ δεῖ δοῦναι μέρος.—At the end of this speech the messenger departs. In the Aldine the person of the messenger is prefixed to the speeches of Dionysus as far as v. 843, an error detected by Tyrwhitt.
791. κινοῦντα. Aldus has κινοῦντι, which Hermann retains, but defends on doubtful principles, as if it could mean διὰ τὸ κινεῖν σε Βάκχας.
792. οὐ μὴ κτλ. 'Lecture me not, but, having escaped from prison, make the best of that; (or, 'remember that you have escaped;') or I will see that justice shall again take its course against you.' Compare v. 343, οὐ μὴ προσοίσεις χεῖρα. Electr. 383, οὐ μὴ ἀφρονήσει᾽. The notion in ἀναστρέψω is, that Justice having now passed by, and suffered him to go unscathed, shall be turned back and sent in pursuit of him.

448   ΕΥΡΙΠΙΔΟΥ

   σώσει τόδ'; ἢ σοί πάλιν ἀναστρέψω δίκην.
ΔΙ. θύοιμ' ἂν αὐτῷ μᾶλλον ἢ θυμούμενος
   πρὸς κέντρα λακτίζοιμι θνητὸς ὢν θεῷ.   795
ΠΕ. θύσω, φόνον γε θῆλυν, ὥσπερ ἄξιαι,
   πολὺν ταράξας ἐν Κιθαιρῶνος πτυχαῖς.
ΔΙ. φεύξεσθε πάντες, καὶ τόδ' αἰσχρόν, ἀσπίδας
   θύρσοισι βακχῶν ἐκτρέπειν χαλκηλάτους.
ΠΕ. ἀπόρῳ γε τῷδε συμπεπλέγμεθα ξένῳ·   800
   ὡς οὔτε πάσχων οὔτε δρῶν σιγήσεται.
ΔΙ. ὦ τᾶν, ἔτ' ἔστιν εὖ καταστῆσαι τάδε.
ΠΕ. τί δρῶντα; δουλεύοντα δουλείαις ἐμαῖς;
ΔΙ. ἐγὼ γυναῖκας δεῦρ' ὅπλων ἄξω δίχα.
ΠΕ. οἴμοι· τόδ' ἤδη δόλιον ἔς με μηχανᾷ.   805
ΔΙ. ποῖόν τι, σῶσαί σ' εἰ θέλω τέχναις ἐμαῖς;
ΠΕ. ξυνέθεσθε κοινῇ τάδ', ἵνα βακχεύητ' ἀεί.
ΔΙ. καὶ μὴν ξυνεθέμην τοῦτό γ', ἴσθι, τῷ θεῷ.

795. On πρὸς κέντρα λακτίζειν, said of an ox that kicks back against the goad, Elmsley has a note in which, as usual, he collects examples rather than offers an explanation of the meaning. The phrase occurs in Eur. frag. 601. Aesch. Prom. 331. Agam. 1602, and elsewhere.

796. θύσω. 'Yes, I will sacrifice, and by stirring up a great slaughter of women in the valleys of Cithaeron, as ye deserve.' For this sense of ταράσσειν see on Aesch. Cho. 323.

799. ἐκτρέπειν. 'For the army of Pentheus to turn away in flight their brass-plated shields for (i.e. before) the thyrsus.'

800. ἀπόρῳ κτλ. 'Truly, a troublesome stranger this, whom we are hampered with; for neither when he is being himself punished nor when he is punishing us will he be quiet.' Elmsley and Dindorf give ὅς, by a very needless alteration. By οὔτε δρῶν he appears to mean, that he is not content with having escaped from prison, but must threaten to act in a hostile manner if Pentheus should take vengeance on his followers. Hermann refers it simply to his escape from prison, as if it were οὔτε πάσχων οὔτε μή. The Greeks were so fond of the antithesis between δρᾶσαι and παθεῖν, that we cannot be surprised if it is occasionally used rather as a rhetorical figure. The general sense is, 'Nothing will make him hold his tongue; he is as insolent in adversity as in success.' Bothe regards it as a proverb signifying 'never,'—" siquidem agendo et patiendo constat vita." Barnes compares the character given in Livy of Marcellus by Hannibal:—'Cum eo nimirum hoste res est, qui nec bonam nec malam ferre fortunam potest. Seu vicit, ferociter instat victis; seu victus est, instaurat cum victoribus certamen.'

803. δουλείαις for δούλοις, res pro persona. He meant that he is not going to act on the suggestion of any of his subjects.

808. The reading in the text is that of Elmsley, though he expresses himself not altogether satisfied with it. W. Dindorf however adopts it; and the punctuation at least seems better than Matthiae's, who makes τοῦτό γ' ἴσθι a parenthetical clause. For ἴσθι the MSS. and edd. give ἐστί, corrected by Musgrave. The sense appears to be, 'Nay, I made *that* compact (viz. ἵνα ἀεὶ βακχεύωμεν) with the god,' meaning, of course, with himself and no others; which is the same as saying, he asked the advice and concurrence of no one. Hermann reads κεἰ μὴ ξυνεθέμην, τοῦτό γ' ἔστι τῷ θεῷ, "etiam si non pactus sum, hoc quidem deo est, i.e. hoc ille suum sibi habet, neque eripi sibi patietur, ut semper bacchemur." (The Pala-

ΠΕ. ἐκφέρετέ μοι δεῦρ' ὅπλα· σὺ δὲ παῦσαι λέγων.
ΔΙ. ἆ·
 βούλει σφ' ἐν ὄρεσι συγκαθημένας ἰδεῖν ; 810
ΠΕ. μάλιστα, μυρίον γε δοὺς χρυσοῦ σταθμόν.
ΔΙ. τί δ' εἰς ἔρωτα τοῦδε πέπτωκας μέγαν ;
ΠΕ. λυπρῶς νιν εἰσίδοιμ' ἂν ἐξῳνωμένας.
ΔΙ. ὅμως δ' ἴδοις ἂν ἡδέως ἅ σοι πικρά ; 815
ΠΕ. σάφ' ἴσθι, σιγῇ γ' ὑπ' ἐλάταις καθήμενος.
ΔΙ. ἀλλ' ἐξιχνεύσουσίν σε, κἂν ἔλθῃς λάθρα.
ΠΕ. ἀλλ' ἐμφανῶς· καλῶς γὰρ ἐξεῖπας τάδε.
ΔΙ. ἄγωμεν οὖν σε, κἀπιχειρήσεις ὁδῷ ;
ΠΕ. ἄγ' ὡς τάχιστα, τοῦ χρόνου δ' οὔ σοι φθονῶ. 820
ΔΙ. στεῖλαί νυν ἀμφὶ χρωτὶ βυσσίνους πέπλους.
ΠΕ. τί δὴ τόδ' ; εἰς γυναῖκας ἐξ ἀνδρὸς τελῶ ;

tine MS. gives καὶ μὴ with ν superscribed.) Bothe has καὶ μὴν ξυνεθέμην τοῦτό γ' εἴς τι τῷ θεῷ, 'for a certain purpose,' i.e. for the mysteries of religion not to be named before an impious persecutor. This is, at least, better than Hermann's interpretation.

814. There are several ways of explaining this obscure verse. Pentheus may be made to say λυπρῶς unconsciously, in reference to the penalty he will have to pay for the sight, just as πικρὰ, 'to your cost,' in the next verse ; while the obvious sense, i. e. his own simple meaning, is, '(I have no *desire* to see them, no ἔρως :) it would be painful to look at them inebriated.' To which the reply is, 'And would you nevertheless be glad to see what would be a sad spectacle to you ?' The fact is, that Pentheus' wish to see them was simply thirst for revenge, and as far as possible removed from any pleasure or satisfaction in the sight itself, which was that of his own subjects drunk and disorderly. He would at once like and dislike to see such a sight. Elmsley gives up the passage as hopeless. Matthiae, construing λυπρῶς with ἐξῳνωμένας, understands, 'They will be drunk to their own cost, if I should see them,' and Bothe follows him. Hermann says, "Nihil hic versus difficultatis habet, modo, quod feci, signum interrogandi apponatur. *Possimne dolere, ubi eas inebriatas videam ?*" This would be equivalent to, τί γὰρ οὐκ ἂν βουλοίμην ἰδεῖν ; and the reply is then consistent enough, εἰ δὲ πικρά ἐστι ταῦτα τὰ πράγματα, πῶς ἂν ἡδέως ἴδοις ;

817. ἔλθῃς for θέλῃς Pierson. The ellipse of ἰέναι, suggested by Matthiae, seems hardly according to tragic use. Perhaps, κἂν θέλῃς λαθεῖν.

819. Between ἄγωμεν, the old reading, and ἄγω μὲν, preferred by W. Dindorf after Portus and others, there is little to choose. On the one hand, the μὲν is somewhat superfluous ; on the other, the singular ἄγε in the next verse seems rather in favour of ἄγω.

820. δ' οὔ σοι for δέ σ' οὐ is Bothe's and Dobree's correction. Hermann thinks the crasis σοι ου defensible ; cf. Aesch. Cho. 913, where some take σουρίζει for σοι οὐρίζει. Perhaps however the true reading is γὰρ οὐ, for δὲ and γὰρ are perpetually confused. The sense is, ' My time is at your service.' For φθονεῖν τινί τινος see Prom. 644.

821. βυσσίνους, of fine linen, or, as some will have it, of cotton texture. Aeschylus twice uses this adjective, Theb. 1042, and Pers. 127, as an epithet of πέπλοι.

822. τί δὴ τόδ' ; Supply ἐστὶν or εἶπας, as Elmsley observes, comparing Ion 275.—τελῶ, ' would you have me enlist myself among women, from having been a man ?' So Oed. R. 222, νῦν δ', ὕστερος γὰρ ἀστὸς εἰς ἀστοὺς τελῶ, κτλ.

VOL. II. 3 M

450 ΕΥΡΙΠΙΔΟΥ

ΔΙ. μή σε κτάνωσιν, ἢν ἀνὴρ ὀφθῇς ἐκεῖ.
ΠΕ. εὖ γ' εἶπας αὐτὸ, καί τις εἶ πάλαι σοφός.
ΔΙ. Διόνυσος ἡμᾶς ἐξεμούσωσεν τάδε. 825
ΠΕ. πῶς οὖν γένοιτ' ἂν ἃ σύ με νουθετεῖς καλῶς ;
ΔΙ. ἐγὼ στελῶ σε δωμάτων ἔσω μολών.
ΠΕ. τίνα στολήν ; ἢ θῆλυν ; ἀλλ' αἰδώς μ' ἔχει.
ΔΙ. οὐκέτι θεατὴς μαινάδων πρόθυμος εἶ.
ΠΕ. στολὴν δὲ τίνα φῂς ἀμφὶ χρωτ' ἐμὸν βαλεῖν ; 830
ΔΙ. κόμην μὲν ἐπὶ σῷ κρατὶ ταναὸν ἐκτενῶ.
ΠΕ. τὸ δεύτερον δὲ σχῆμα τοῦ κόσμου τί μοι ;
ΔΙ. πέπλοι ποδήρεις· ἐπὶ κάρᾳ δ' ἔσται μίτρα.
ΠΕ. ἦ καί τι πρὸς τοῖσδ' ἄλλο προσθήσεις ἐμοί ;
ΔΙ. θύρσον γε χειρὶ καὶ νεβροῦ στικτὸν δέρας. 835
ΠΕ. οὐκ ἂν δυναίμην θῆλυν ἐνδῦναι στολήν.
ΔΙ. ἀλλ' αἷμα θήσεις ξυμβαλὼν βάκχαις μάχην.
ΠΕ. ὀρθῶς· μολεῖν χρὴ πρῶτον ἐς κατασκοπήν.
ΔΙ. σοφώτερον γοῦν ἢ κακοῖς θηρᾶν κακά.
ΠΕ. καὶ πῶς δι' ἄστεως εἶμι Καδμείους λαθών ; 840

824. τις—σοφός. For τις τῶν σοφῶν. The sentiment is exactly the same as in Alcest. 58, πῶς εἶπας ; ἀλλ' ἦ καὶ σοφὸς λέληθας ὤν ; implying that such shrewd remarks could only proceed from one long versed in the subtleties of sophistry. The evasive replies of Dionysus at his examination before Pentheus, v. 460 seqq., had shown that he was an adept at chicanery.

826. There is equal difficulty in retaining σὺ, which Elmsley thinks an interpolation, and in reading ἀμέ for ἃ ἐμὲ, because in either case we have an emphatic pronoun where no emphasis on the person is required. Perhaps, πῶς οὖν γένοιτ' ἄν ; ὥς με νουθετεῖς καλῶς.

828. The student will notice ὁ καὶ ἡ θῆλυς, as Homer also has θῆλυς ἐέρση. This verse seems to have been rather celebrated, if we may judge by the number of quotations from the late Greek writers cited in Elmsley's note.

833. μίτρα. This kind of cap was peculiarly a part of the Bacchic guise. Propert. iv. 17, 29, 'Candida laxatis onerato colla corymbis Cinget Bassaricas Lydia mitra comas.' Lucian, *Bacchus*, § 2, describes the god as κερασφόρον, βότρυσιν ἐστεφανωμένον, μίτρᾳ τὴν κόμην ἀναδεδεμένον.

835. γε for τε Hermann.

837. αἷμα θήσεις. If you do not go as a woman, but as a man, you will be taken for an enemy, and be compelled to engage with them in self-defence ; and thus you will be the cause of bloodshed to your own subjects. Cf. φόνον τιθέναι Ion 1225.

838. ὀρθῶς. 'That is very true : we must first go to reconnoitre.' He acquiesces in the truth of the objection, but thinks the evil may be averted in another way than by putting on a female dress. Dionysus replies, 'that is at least a wiser course than to provoke wrong by wrong,' i. e. than to cause slaughter by openly invading their mysteries, which the uninitiated were not allowed to see.

840. καὶ πῶς κτλ. As usual, these particles imply an objection. 'Well but, if I go through the city, I shall be seen by the Theban people.' He does not seem here to allude to the female dress, which as yet he has declined to put on, but to the being seen alone with Teiresias going in the direction of the Bacchants, which was sure to give rise to

ΒΑΚΧΑΙ. 451

ΔΙ. ὁδοὺς ἐρήμους ἴμεν. ἐγὼ δ' ἡγήσομαι.
ΠΕ. πᾶν κρεῖσσον ὥστε μὴ 'γγελᾶν βάκχας ἐμοί.
ΔΙ. ἐλθόντ' ἐς οἴκους ἂν δοκῇ βουλεύσομεν.
ΠΕ. ἔξεστι· πάντῃ τό γ' ἐμὸν εὐτρεπὲς πάρα.
στείχοιμ' ἄν· ἢ γὰρ ὅπλ' ἔχων πορεύσομαι, 845
ἢ τοῖσι σοῖσι πείσομαι βουλεύμασιν.
ΔΙ. γυναῖκες, ἁνὴρ ἐς βόλον καθίσταται·
ἥξει δὲ βάκχας, οὗ θανὼν δώσει δίκην.
Διόνυσε, νῦν σὸν ἔργον, οὐ γὰρ εἶ πρόσω·
τισώμεθ' αὐτόν. πρῶτα δ' ἔκστησον φρενῶν, 850
ἐνεὶς ἐλαφρὰν λύσσαν· ὡς φρονῶν μὲν εὖ
οὐ μὴ θελήσει θῆλυν ἐνδῦναι στολήν,
ἔξω δ' ἐλαύνων τοῦ φρονεῖν ἐνδύσεται.
χρῄζω δέ νιν γέλωτα Θηβαίοις ὀφλεῖν
γυναικόμορφον ἀγόμενον δι' ἄστεως 855
ἐκ τῶν ἀπειλῶν τῶν πρίν, αἷσι δεινὸς ἦν.
ἀλλ' εἶμι κόσμον ὅνπερ εἰς Ἅιδου λαβὼν
ἄπεισι, μητρὸς ἐκ χεροῖν κατασφαγείς,
Πενθεῖ προσάψων· γνώσεται δὲ τὸν Διὸς

various surmises; and if he went *incognito*, i. e. disguised as a spy, there was a chance of his being recognised. If this explanation be rejected, σοφώτερον γοῦν κτλ. must of necessity be ironical, and said in ridicule of the idea of going as a scout; 'I suppose you think *that* wiser than to pursue one evil by another,' i. e. to catch the Bacchants by an unworthy trick. So θηρᾶν τἀμήχανα in Antig. 92.

842. μὴ 'γγελᾶν Pierson for μὴ γελᾶν. Cf. Alcest. 724, οὐκ ἐγγελᾷς γέροντα βαστάζων νεκρόν.

843. To this verse, and to 845—6, the Aldine edition prefixes the character of the ἄγγελος. Elmsley and Bothe give 842—3 to Pentheus, the next to Dionysus, and 845—6 to Pentheus. Hermann and Dindorf arrange the persons as above. But Hermann makes v. 843 interrogative, which does not seem at all necessary to the context.

844. ἔξεστι. 'By all means.' This formula of assent occurs in Hel. 442. Elmsley gives ἔξεστι πάντῃ, 'do as you please;' but πάντῃ means, 'in whatever way you are disposed to act, I am ready for you.' The correct punctuation is due to Hermann.

845. ἢ γὰρ—ἤ. I must choose between going disguised as a woman, or openly as an enemy.

851. ἐνείς. Burges plausibly reads ἐνθείς. Elmsley quotes πῦρ ἐνιέναι from Troad. 1262.—οὐ μὴ θελήσει κτλ., 'there is little chance of his consenting; but if he is no longer guided by his reason, he will put it on.' On οὐ μὴ see Hel. 292.

854. Hermann retains, perhaps accidentally, the Aldine reading ὄφλειν. Scholars are pretty well agreed on the point, that ὀφλισκάνω and not ὄφλω was the present in use. Yet Photius has this remark; ὄφλειν καὶ ῥοφεῖν: (ῥόφειν, but the word seems corrupt,) τὰς πρώτας συλλαβὰς τῶν τοιούτων οἱ Ἀττικοὶ ὀξύνουσιν.

856. ἐκ τῶν ἀπειλῶν. This refers to χρῄζω, and assigns the reason of the desire.

859. γνώσεται, he shall know by experience. Cf. Heracl. 65, γνώσει σύ. Androm. 1006, γνώσεται δ' ἔχθραν ἐμήν.—ὅς is not for οἷος, but, ' he shall know

3 M 2

ΕΥΡΙΠΙΔΟΥ

Διόνυσον, ὃς πέφυκεν ἐν τέλει θεὸς 860
δεινότατος, ἀνθρώποισι δ' ἠπιώτατος.

XO. ἆρ' ἐν παννυχίοις χοροῖς στρ.
θήσω ποτὲ λευκὸν
πόδ' ἀναβακχεύουσα δέραν
εἰς αἰθέρα δροσερὸν 865
ῥίπτουσ', ὡς νεβρὸς χλοεραῖς
ἐμπαίζουσα λείμακος ἡδοναῖς
ἡνίκ' ἂν φοβερὸν φύγῃ
θήραμ' ἔξω φυλακᾶς
εὐπλέκτων ὑπὲρ ἀρκύων, 870
θωΰσσων δὲ κυναγέτας
συντείνῃ δρόμημα κυνῶν,
μόχθοις τ' ὠκυδρόμοις τ' ἀέλλαις θρώσκῃ πεδίον

Dionysus, who is by nature most to be dreaded.' What is meant by ἐν τέλει is very uncertain. Hermann regards it as an *hyperbaton* for γνώσεται ἐν τέλει, 'he shall find out at last.' Elmsley explains it for παντελῶς, *omnino*. But Matthiae is probably right; 'who is in the end (i. e. when provoked) a most dread god, though (ordinarily) most lenient to men.' Bothe well compares Ion 1615, χρόνια μὲν τὰ τῶν θεῶν πως, ἐς τέλος δ' οὐκ ἀσθενῆ.

862. Pentheus and Dionysus have now retired within the palace. The chorus, who, though they have not been themselves imprisoned with their master, regard the restraint that has been put upon them as a common calamity, compare themselves to a captured fawn, which has escaped from the hunters and bounds away in freedom to its favourite haunts by the river and in the wood. This simile is beautifully and happily expressed. They then pass into a strain of grave reflexions on the dealings of the gods with men. 'To be victorious over one's foes is the first and best gift of heaven: and being so, it is ever dearest to one's heart. The gods will not in the end overlook insolence and impiety in man; vengeance may be slow in coming, but it will come at last. It costs but little to believe in the power of the gods, and to acquiesce in what is sanctioned at once by antiquity and by one's natural instincts. Happy are they who have found rest after many toils. Not all are born to prosperity and happiness, nor are even the hopes of all realised. The most fortunate is he to whom the present day brings no woe.' The metre of this stasimon is glyconic throughout.

863. λευκὸν πόδα, see v. 665. Ion 221.—ἆρα ποτέ, Rhes. 360, ἀρά ποτ' αὖθις ἁ παλαιὰ Τροία τοὺς προπότας πανημερεύσει θιάσους; Ion 563, πότ' ἄρα καὶ σὸν ὄψομαι δέμας;

865. αἰθέρα. This word is metrically equivalent to a spondee. Musgrave would read αἰθέρ' εἰς δροσερόν.

870. ὑπὲρ ἀρκύων. Cf. Aesch. Agam. 1347, ὕψος κρεῖσσον ἐκπηδήματος. Pers. 100, ἀρκύστατα τόθεν οὐκ ἔστιν ὑπὲρ θνατὸν ἀλύξαντα φυγεῖν.

872. συντείνῃ, σύντονον ποιῇ. Cf. Electr. 112, σύντειν', ὥρα, ποδὸς ὁρμάν.

874. θρώσκῃ πεδίον. See on Hel. 598. Hermann and Elmsley read θρώσκει with the Palatine MS., the former commencing a new sentence at μόχθοις τ', the latter marking ἡνίκ' ἂν — ἀέλλαις as a parenthesis. Neither appears to improve the sense, which is simply this; 'as a fawn does (scil. τίθησι πόδα) when it has escaped from the net, when the hunter is urging on his dogs in pursuit, and when with swift pace it has reached the wild country;' i. e. a place of safety.—μόχθοις,

ΒΑΚΧΑΙ.   453

παραποτάμιον, ἡδομένα
βροτῶν ἐρημίαις,   875
σκιαροκόμου τ' ἐν ἔρνεσιν ὕλας.
τί τὸ σοφὸν ἢ τί τὸ κάλλιον
παρὰ θεῶν γέρας ἐν βροτοῖς
ἢ χεῖρ' ὑπὲρ κορυφᾶς
ἐχθρῶν κρείσσω κατέχειν;   880
ὅ τι καλὸν φίλον ἀεί.
ὁρμᾶται μόλις, ἀλλ' ὅμως   ἀντ.
πιστὸν τό γε θεῖον
σθένος· ἀπευθύνει δὲ βροτῶν
τούς τ' ἀγνωμοσύναν   885
τιμῶντας καὶ μὴ τὰ θεῶν
αὔξοντας σὺν μαινομένᾳ δόξᾳ.
κρυπτεύουσι δὲ ποικίλως
δαρὸν χρόνου πόδα καὶ
θηρῶσιν τὸν ἄσεπτον. οὐ   890

which Elmsley strangely takes for εἰς μόχθους, means 'with labouring step,' 'with laborious effort.'—ἀέλλαις he well compares with ἀελλάδων ἵππων in Oed. R. 466. Possibly in Hel. 1498 we should read λαμπρῶν ἀέλλαις ἀστέρων | οἳ ναίετ' οὐράνιοι, 'who dwell among the rapidly revolving stars of heaven.'

877. It is easy to say, with Elmsley, "articuli abundant;" but it is better to inquire whether there is not some way of explaining an undoubtedly unusual construction. As for τί ἐστὶ τὸ σοφόν, 'what is wisdom, if this be not,' it is clearly the same as τί ἐστὶ σοφία. But τί ἐστὶ τὸ κάλλιον γέρας seems to mean τί ἐστὶ γέρας, ὃ ἄνθρωποι ὀνομάζουσι τὸ κάλλιον, where the article with the predicate will fall under the same head as the passages given on Heracl. 978. A similar use is Suppl. 852, σαφῶς ἀπήγγειλ' ὅστις ἐστὶν ἀγαθός, i. e. τίς ὁ ἀριστεύων. It must however be admitted that the metre of the verse is suggestive of some error. Allowing that ∪ ∪ may stand at the beginning for a long syllable, the following would at once give a better construction with better glyconean rhythm, τί τὸ σοφὸν ἢ τί κάλλι|ον γέρας ἐν βροτοῖσιν, κτλ. The article before ἐχθρῶν appears to be rightly omitted by Hermann, both here and in v. 900. The allusion of course is to the victory of Dionysus over his enemy Pentheus.

881. ὅ τι καλὸν κτλ. There seems a reference to κάλλιον, 'and if it is also honourable, it is dear.' But Elmsley cites two passages which show that this was a proverb; Plato, Lysid. p. 216, C., κινδυνεύει, κατὰ τὴν ἀρχαίαν παροιμίαν, τὸ καλὸν φίλον εἶναι, and Theognis, 17, ὅττι καλόν, φίλον ἐστί, τὸ δ' οὐ καλὸν οὐ φίλον ἐστί.

885. ἀγνωμοσύναν, churlishness, perverseness, want of tact or judgment.—σὺν δόξᾳ, for δόξαν ἔχοντας. Cf. Oed. R. 17, οἱ δὲ σὺν γήρᾳ βαρεῖς. Aesch. Suppl. 183, ὠμῇ ξὺν ὀργῇ τόνδ' ἐπόρνυται στόλον.

888. κρυπτεύουσι, 'they lie in wait,' ἐνεδρεύουσι, δοκεύουσι. See Hel. 541, οὔτι που κρυπτεύομαι Πρωτέως ἀσέπτου παιδὸς ἐκ βουλευμάτων;—χρόνου πόδα is the accusative of duration of time, 'for a long period.' The phrase χρόνου πούς was also used in the *Alexandra*, frag. 66, and it is ridiculed by Aristophanes, Ran. 100.

890. οὐ γὰρ κτλ. 'For 'tis not right at any time to entertain views and dwell upon subjects above the established doc-

γὰρ κρεῖσσόν ποτε τῶν νόμων
γιγνώσκειν χρὴ καὶ μελετᾶν.
κοῦφα γὰρ δαπάνα νομί-
ζειν ἰσχὺν τόδ᾽ ἔχειν,
ὅ τι ποτ᾽ ἄρα τὸ δαιμόνιον,
τό τ᾽ ἐν χρόνῳ μακρῷ 895
νόμιμον ἀεὶ φύσει τε πεφυκός.
τί τὸ σοφὸν ἢ τί τὸ κάλλιον
παρὰ θεῶν γέρας ἐν βροτοῖς
ἢ χεῖρ᾽ ὑπὲρ κορυφᾶς
ἐχθρῶν κρείσσω κατέχειν; 900
ὅ τι καλὸν φίλον ἀεί.
εὐδαίμων μὲν ὃς ἐκ θαλάσσας ἐπῳδ.
ἔφυγε κῦμα, λιμένα δ᾽ ἔκιχεν·
εὐδαίμων δ᾽ ὃς ὕπερθε μόχθων
ἐγένεθ᾽· ἕτερα δ᾽ ἕτερος ἕτερον 905
ὄλβῳ καὶ δυνάμει παρῆλθεν.
μυρίαι *δὲ μυρίοισιν
ἔτ᾽ εἴσ᾽ ἐλπίδες· αἱ μὲν
τελευτῶσιν ἐν ὄλβῳ
βροτοῖς, αἱ δ᾽ ἀπέβησαν·
τὸ δὲ κατ᾽ ἦμαρ ὅτῳ βίοτος 910
εὐδαίμων, μακαρίζω.

ΔΙ.   σὲ τὸν πρόθυμον ὄνθ᾽ ἃ μὴ χρεὼν ὁρᾶν

trines.' The νόμοι here mentioned are the same as those in Hec. 800, 847, viz. the received customs and usages of mankind, to which Euripides is apt to attribute a weight little short of a divine sanction. Hence below he combines τὸ δαιμόνιον with τὸ ἐν χρόνῳ μακρῷ νόμιμον, just as in Hec. 800 he speaks of even ὁ θεῶν κρατῶν νόμος.

903. It is doubtful whether Elmsley is right in referring this passage to a mystical doctrine, which he thinks also enunciated in the language of the initiators, Dem. de Cor. p. 516, Α., ἔφυγον κακὸν, εὗρον ἄμεινον. The comparison may be simply this:—As the sailor is fortunate who has escaped the storm, so is he blest who has surmounted his troubles by the aid of religion; for, he proceeds to say, there are troubles, though some may have a less share of them than others.

907. The δὲ was added by Hermann. The metre however is scarcely by this addition assimilated to the other verses of the epode. Perhaps we should read μυρίαι δ᾽ ἔτι μυρίοις | εἰσὶν ἐλπίδες, κτλ.—ἔτι means, that though some are more fortunate than others, there are yet hopes left for thousands of mortals who would otherwise have a cheerless lot.—ἀπέβησαν, ἄλλως, παρὰ γνώμην, ἐτελεύτησαν.

910. τὸ κατ᾽ ἦμαρ. See Ion 123.

912. During the song of the chorus, both Dionysus and Pentheus had been changing their habits within the house. Dionysus comes first upon the stage (doubtless attired with horns, as he was symbolically represented), while Pentheus,

ΒΑΚΧΑΙ. 455

σπεύδοντά τ' ἀσπούδαστα Πενθέα λέγω,
ἔξιθι πάροιθε δωμάτων, ὄφθητί μοι,
σκευὴν γυναικὸς μαινάδος βάκχης ἔχων, 915
μητρός τε τῆς σῆς καὶ λόχου κατάσκοπος·
πρέπεις δὲ Κάδμου θυγατέρων μορφὴν μιᾷ.
ΠΕ. καὶ μὴν ὁρᾶν μοι δύο μὲν ἡλίους δοκῶ,
δισσὰς δὲ Θήβας καὶ πόλισμ' ἑπτάστομον·
καὶ ταῦρος ἡμῖν πρόσθεν ἡγεῖσθαι δοκεῖς, 920
καὶ σῷ κέρατε κρατὶ προσπεφυκέναι.
ἀλλ' ἦ ποτ' ἦσθα θήρ; τεταύρωσαι γὰρ οὖν.
ΔΙ. ὁ θεὸς ὁμαρτεῖ, πρόσθεν ὢν οὐκ εὐμενής,
ἔνσπονδος ἡμῖν· νῦν δ' ὁρᾷς ἃ χρή σ' ὁρᾶν.
ΠΕ. τί φαίνομαι δῆτ'; οὐχὶ τὴν Ἰνοῦς στάσιν, 925
ἢ τὴν Ἀγαύης ἑστάναι, μητρός γ' ἐμῆς;
ΔΙ. αὐτὰς ἐκείνας εἰσορᾶν δοκῶ σ' ὁρῶν.
ἀλλ' ἐξ ἕδρας σοι πλόκαμος ἐξέστηχ' ὅδε,

---

whom he summons from within to follow him, is dressed in female costume and bears a thyrsus in his hand. There is much of comedy in this scene, as indeed was unavoidable from the nature of it. But the poet has treated it admirably.

914. ὄφθητί μοι, let me see how you look in your new dress. For this is the point of the next verse.

916. καὶ λόχου. Hermann, without assigning any reason, gives ἐκ λόχου. But the Bacchanalian company is well compared to a military λόχος. See v. 681. —In the next verse Hermann approves, and Bothe and Dindorf admit, Musgrave's slight alteration μορφὴν for μορφῇ. The dative, though it is hardly ambiguous, is inelegant in close combination with μιᾷ. For πρέπειν with a dative = ὅμοιον εἶναι, Elmsley compares Alcest. 1121, Aesch. Suppl. 296. Add Agam. 1299, where it is transitive, σκιᾷ τις ἂν πρέψειεν.

918. This idea of 'seeing double,' so familiarly used by us in reference to drunkards, seems to have been celebrated by subsequent writers, references to whom are given by Elmsley in a learned note. Virgil alludes to this, Aen. iv. 468, 'Eumenidum veluti demens videt agmina Pentheus, Et solem geminum, et duplices se ostendere Thebas.'

921. κέρατε. For the long ᾱ see Ion 883.

922. Though the particles ἀλλ' ἦ often mean num, 'can it be that?' &c. (see Rhes. 36. Alcest. 816), Hermann appears right in thinking the combination here somewhat out of place; and he reads ἀλλ' ἦ ποτ' ἦσθα θήρ· τεταύρωσαι γὰρ οὖν. We should rather have looked for ἀλλ' ἦσθ' ἄρ' ἡμῖν θήρ, 'we did not before know that we had a bull-god among us.' However the sense may be, 'Can it be that you were once a bull (and have now resumed your ancient shape)? For certainly you have the form of a bull.' For the particles γὰρ οὖν see Heracl. 202. Electr. 290. Medea is said to be ὄμμα ταυρουμένη, Med. 92.

924. νῦν δ' ὁρᾷς. 'So now you see what you ought to see.' He pretends that the god had hitherto disguised his true form, as being offended with Pentheus, but that he now vouchsafes to appear to him as he is.

925. On στῆναι στάσιν see Suppl. 987. Her. 671. He means to ask, if he does not make as good a Bacchante, with regard to figure and mien, as Agave herself. —The exegetical γε, which Elmsley renders utpote, Hermann adeo, we may render, 'my mother, I mean.'

928. ἐξ ἕδρας, out of its proper place.

456 ΕΥΡΙΠΙΔΟΥ

οὐχ ὡς ἐγώ νιν ὑπὸ μίτρᾳ καθήρμοσα.
ΠΕ. ἔνδον προσείων αὐτὸν ἀνασείων τ' ἐγὼ 930
   καὶ βακχιάζων ἐξ ἕδρας μεθώρμισα.
ΔΙ. ἀλλ' αὐτὸν ἡμεῖς, οἷς σε θεραπεύειν μέλει,
   πάλιν καταστελοῦμεν· ἀλλ' ὀρθοῦ κάρα.
ΠΕ. ἰδού, σὺ κόσμει· σοὶ γὰρ ἀνακείμεσθα δή.
ΔΙ. ζῶναί τέ σοι χαλῶσι, κοὐχ ἑξῆς πέπλων 935
   στολίδες ὑπὸ σφυροῖσι τείνουσιν σέθεν.
ΠΕ. κἀμοὶ δοκοῦσι παρά γε δεξιὸν πόδα·
   τἀνθένδε δ' ὀρθῶς παρὰ τένοντ' ἔχει πέπλος.
ΔΙ. ἦ πού με τῶν σῶν πρῶτον ἡγήσει φίλων,
   ὅταν παράλογον σώφρονας βάκχας ἴδῃς. 940
ΠΕ. πότερα δὲ θύρσον δεξιᾷ λαβὼν χερὶ
   ἢ τῇδε, βάκχῃ μᾶλλον εἰκασθήσομαι;
ΔΙ. ἐν δεξιᾷ χρὴ χἄμα δεξιῷ ποδὶ
   αἴρειν νιν· αἰνῶ δ' ὅτι μεθέστηκας φρενῶν.
ΠΕ. ἆρ' ἂν δυναίμην τὰς Κιθαιρῶνος πτυχὰς 945
   αὐταῖσι βάκχαις τοῖς ἐμοῖς ὤμοις φέρειν;
ΔΙ. δύναι' ἄν, εἰ βούλοιο· τὰς δὲ πρὶν φρένας
   οὐκ εἶχες ὑγιεῖς, νῦν δ' ἔχεις οἵας σε δεῖ.
ΠΕ. μοχλοὺς φέρωμεν, ἢ χεροῖν ἀνασπάσω,
   κορυφαῖς ὑποβαλὼν ὦμον ἢ βραχίονα; 950
ΔΙ. μὴ σύ γε τὰ Νυμφῶν διολέσῃς ἱδρύματα

930. ἔνδον, while yet within the house.
934. σοὶ ἀνακείμεσθα, 'we depend on you;' or, as Elmsley renders it, 'I give myself up to you.' The word is used in reference to statues or offerings which are dedicated and surrendered absolutely to some god. So Theocr. x. 33, χρύσεοι ἀμφότεροί κ' ἀνεκείμεθα τᾷ 'Αφροδίτᾳ.
936. στολίδες ὑπὸ σφυροῖσι, 'the tucks below the ankle.' To a female in an erect position, the stola fell so low as to nearly conceal the feet. Or if (which is not necessary) we take πέπλος in the strict sense of the *shawl*, στολίδες will be the border hanging in folds at the *lower* part, the folds over the breast being στολμοί.
—All this was evidently said to banter him in presence of the spectators.
938. παρὰ τένοντα, 'by the foot.' Whether the *tendo Achillis* or the sole of the foot was properly meant by this word, is uncertain. See on Med. 1166. Photius has τένοντας, τραχήλους, τὰ διατεταμένα νεῦρα. In neither of these passages of Euripides can it signify 'the neck;' while τενόντων ὑπογραφαὶ in Aesch. Cho. 201, can only mean the impression of the sole of the foot from heel to toe.
943. ἅμα δεξιῷ ποδί. The meaning of this is rather obscure. It must refer to some peculiar way of carrying the thyrsus, probably after the fashion of a spear, for which it was sometimes used; see v. 704. The apparent sense is, that the end of the thyrsus was to rest on the right foot, and so to be propelled by its action in walking. The Greek however might mean, ἅμα δεξιῷ ποδὶ προβαίνοντα. So we may explain, ἐν δεξιᾷ λαβεῖν, καὶ ἅμα δεξιῷ ποδὶ αἴρειν, to use it as a walking-stick in keeping time with your step.
951. μὴ σύ γε. On γε in expostulation

καὶ Πανὸς ἕδρας, ἔνθ' ἔχει συρίγματα.
ΠΕ. καλῶς ἔλεξας. οὐ σθένει νικητέον
γυναῖκας, ἐλάταισιν δ' ἐμὸν κρύψω δέμας.
ΔΙ. κρύψει σὺ κρύψιν ἥν σε κρυφθῆναι χρεών, 955
ἐλθόντα δόλιον μαινάδων κατάσκοπον.
ΠΕ. καὶ μὴν δοκῶ σφᾶς, ἐν λόχμαις ὄρνιθας ὥς,
λέκτρων ἔχεσθαι φιλτάτοις ἐν ἕρκεσιν.
ΔΙ. οὐκοῦν ἐπ' αὐτὸ τοῦτ' ἀποστέλλει φύλαξ·
λήψει δ' ἴσως σφᾶς, ἢν σὺ μὴ ληφθῇς πάρος. 960
ΠΕ. κόμιζε διὰ μέσης με Θηβαίας χθονός·
μόνος γάρ εἰμ' αὐτῶν ἀνὴρ τολμῶν τόδε.
ΔΙ. μόνος σὺ πόλεως τῆσδ' ὑπερκάμνεις, μόνος·
τοιγάρ σ' ἀγῶνες ἀναμένουσιν, οὓς ἐχρῆν.
ἕπου δέ· πομπὸς δ' εἰμ' ἐγὼ σωτήριος, 965
κεῖθεν δ' ἀπάξει σ' ἄλλος. ΠΕ. ἡ τεκοῦσά γε.
ΔΙ. ἐπίσημον ὄντα πᾶσιν. ΠΕ. ἐπὶ τόδ' ἔρχομαι.
ΔΙ. φερόμενος ἥξεις. ΠΕ. ἁβρότητ' ἐμὴν λέγεις.

see Alcest. 308, Hipp. 503. Elmsley, in supposing γε emphasizes the σύ, 'do not *you* of all people in the world, a votary of Bacchus, injure those who are his associates,' forgot the formula of entreaty, μή μοι σύ, Med. 964.

955. Hermann has a good note here. " Totum hoc colloquium ita compositum est, ut iis, quae Bacchus ambigua dicit, metus potius et miseratio quam irrisio aliqua Penthei in animis spectatorum excitetur eorum quidem, qui satis eruditi sint. Nam vulgus ridebat, neque id nolente poeta." It is in passages of this kind that the art of Greek tragedy is peculiarly shown. The Attic mind was singularly adapted to appreciate irony, which implies not only deceit, but also the ready capability of detecting it. A passage that had two distinct meanings, which would deal a double blow like a two-edged sword, would appear highly clever to those with whom prevarication itself was cleverness.

957. ἐν λόχμαις. This is apparently to be taken with ὄρνιθας ὥς, and therefore it seems best to punctuate as in the text. Photius, λόχμη, πλαγία σύμφυτος καὶ λοχμώδης. The meaning is, 'I doubt not they are engaged in amorous toying, like birds in a thicket.'

962. αὐτῶν. Θηβαίων implied in Θηβαίας, though ἀστῶν would be an easy alteration. 'I am the only one of the citizens worthy of the name of a man, in daring thus.' As king, he was not properly an ἀστός, but it is the custom of the Greeks to speak inclusively. Hermann and Bothe retain the old reading εἰμ' αὐτῶν, which Elmsley, followed by Dindorf, transposes to αὐτῶν εἰμ'. Hermann doubts whether such verses as this and Suppl. 303, σφάλλει γὰρ ἐν τούτῳ μόνῳ, τἆλλ' εὖ φρονῶν, were not intentionally admitted on account of some peculiar emphasis.

963. On μόνος repeated at the end of the verse, see Alcest. 722.

968. ἁβρότητ' ἐμήν. He fancies that he will be borne on a litter to save him the trouble of walking. The words ἁβρότης, τρυφή, and χλιδή, which are all used together in Plato's *Symposium*, p. 197, D., seem properly to differ in this, that ἁβρότης is that personal ease and genteel sufficiency of every thing, which constitutes what we call *comfort*, while τρυφή is a superfluous kind of living, or an assumed elegance of manner, implying *affectation;* but χλιδή is the *luxuriousness* of ostentation or outward show. With the word κόσμος, in the sense of

458   ΕΥΡΙΠΙΔΟΥ

ΔΙ.   ἐν χερσὶ μητρός.   ΠΕ. καὶ τρυφᾶν μ' ἀναγκάσεις.
ΔΙ.   τρυφάς γε τοιάσδ'.   ΠΕ. ἀξίων μὲν ἅπτομαι.   970
ΔΙ.   δεινὸς σὺ δεινὸς κἀπὶ δείν' ἔρχει πάθη,
      ὥστ' οὐρανῷ στηρίζον εὑρήσεις κλέος.
      ἔκτειν', Ἀγαύη, χεῖρας, αἵ θ' ὁμόσποροι
      Κάδμου θυγατέρες· τὸν νεανίαν ἄγω
      τόνδ' εἰς ἀγῶνα μέγαν· ὁ νικήσων δ' ἐγὼ   975
      καὶ Βρόμιος ἔσται· τἆλλα δ' αὐτὸ σημανεῖ.
ΧΟ.   ἴτε θοαὶ λύσσης κύνες ἴτ' εἰς ὄρος,   στρ.
      θίασον ἔνθ' ἔχουσι Κάδμου κόραι,
      ἀνοιστρήσατέ νιν
      ἐπὶ τὸν ἐν γυναικομίμῳ στολᾷ   980
      μαινάδων * κατάσκοπον λυσσώδη.
      μάτηρ πρῶτα νιν λευρᾶς ἀπὸ πέτρας ἢ
      σκόλοπος ὄψεται
      δοκεύοντα· μαινάσιν δ' ἀπύσει,
      Τίς ὅδε Καδμείων   985
      μαστὴρ οὔριον δρόμον ἐς ὄρος ἐς ὄρος
      ἔμολεν, ὦ βάκχαι; τίς ἄρα νιν ἔτεκεν;
      οὐ γὰρ ἐξ αἵματος γυναικῶν ἔφυ,

ornament, the idea of modesty, propriety, and becomingness, is generally associated; with χλιδή, that of pride and arrogant pretension.

970. τοιάσδε, scil. οἶαι ἄξιαι ἔσονται, to which implied idea Pentheus rejoins, 'Truly, I am engaging in a work deserving of it.' Elmsley compares Rhes. 182, χρὴ δ' ἐπ' ἀξίοις πονεῖν. The μὲν, Hermann remarks, either implies some antithesis, as ἀξίων δὲ τεύξομαι, or should be altered to γάρ.

972. οὐρανῷ στηρίζον. So Hipp. 1207, κῦμ' οὐρανῷ στηρίζον.

976. αὐτὸ σημανεῖ, the event itself will show. With these words Pentheus and his leader retire from the stage on that side which was supposed to lead into the country. Summoned by the voice of Dionysus, which is raised to a loud tone at v. 973, the chorus recite a system of dochmiac verses, with the rapid utterance and excited mien which that metre always presupposes. They foretell the speedy destruction of Pentheus, invoke Justice to the pursuit, and deprecate the folly of impiously opposing the will of the gods.

979. ἀνοιστρήσατε. See v. 32. The chorus urge some of their number to incite the other companies of Bacchantes, now in the mountains, to take vengeance on the disguised stranger. After Μαινάδων a syllable seems wanting; but it is not easy to supply it by conjecture. The verse should be a dochmiac preceded by two cretics, as in v. 988, 1001.—ἐπὶ τὸν κτλ. 'Against him in woman's dress, a demented spy of the Maenads,' is so to be taken, that τὸν belongs to ὄντα understood, not to κατάσκοπον. It is possible that τὸν should be repeated before κατάσκοπον, in the sense τὸν ὄντα λ. κατ. μ.

986. οὔριον δρόμον Hermann for οὐριοδρόμων. In the Palatine MS. ἔμολεν is repeated, but this does not suit the antistrophe. 'Who of the Thebans has come here to the mountains with swift pace as a spy upon us?' From this verse to 990 is the supposed speech of Agave.

λεαίνας δέ γέ τινος ἢ Γοργόνων Λιβυσσᾶν γένος. 990
ἴτω δίκα φανερὸς, ἴτω ξιφηφόρος,
φονεύουσα λαιμῶν διαμπὰξ
τὸν ἄθεον, ἄνομον, ἄδικον Ἐχίονος   995
γόνον γηγενῆ.
ὃς ἀδίκῳ γνώμᾳ παρανόμῳ τ' ὀργᾷ   ἀντ.
περὶ σὰ, Βάκχι', ὄργια ματρός τε σᾶς
μανείσᾳ πραπίδι
παρακόπῳ τε λήματι στέλλεται,   1000
τὰν ἀνίκατον ὡς κρατήσων βίᾳ.
γνώμαν σώφρονα θνατοῖς ἀπροφασίστως
ἐς τὰ θεῶν ἔφυ
βροτείαν τ' ἔχειν ἄλυπος βίος.
τὸ σοφὸν οὐ φθόνῳ   1005

990. Hermann gives λεαίνας δέ τινος ὅδ', the Palatine MS. omitting γε, and adding ὅδ' ἔφυ.

998. σὰ, Βάκχι', for τὰ Βάκχι' is Scaliger's correction, rendered necessary by the σᾶς which follows. Hermann is probably right in saying that the Tragics occasionally made ἰᾰ a long syllable. See on v. 260. The same opinion has been advanced by the present editor on Aesch. Eum. 764. Hermann however here refers to read τὰ Βάκχι' ὄργι' ᾃς ματέρος, *sacra ab Agave Baccho celebrata*. Elmsley retains the vulgate reading, marked as corrupt. Dindorf has edited περὶ σὰ, Βάκχι', ἔργα, a conjecture of Elmsley's. The περὶ depends rather on γνώμᾳ than on ὀργᾷ, 'with unjust opinions about,' &c.

1001. τὰν ἀνίκατον, her who is unconquerable, viz. his mother Agave.

1002. "Tandem pervenimus," says Elmsley, "ad locum totius tragoediae difficillimum:" and difficult it certainly is, though the near correspondence of the metres does not indicate an extensive corruption in the Aldine reading, γνώμαν σώφρονα, θάνατος ἀπροφασίστος, | εἰ τά τε θεῶν ἔφυ, | βροτείῳ τ' ἔχειν ἄλυπος βίος. The Palatine MS. however rightly gives εἰς τὰ θεῶν. Hermann, who, with Aldus, continues this sentence from the preceding, and reads τὰν ἀνίκατον ὡς κρατήσων βίᾳ | γνώμαν σώφρον', ἃ θνατοῖς ἀπροφασίστος &c., elicits a forced meaning from the passage, which it is impossible to commend to the reader. Dindorf gives as in the text, according to Heath's correction; and this, involving but slight alteration, seems to afford a reasonable sense; 'To keep a mind discreet, without excuses in things relating to religion, and one that is human (i. e. not too proud) is to mortals a life free from care.' And this is also the reading of Bothe, who, remarking that the *hyperbaton* (he should have said, the confusion of the words, from metrical necessity, in a long clause) causes the real difficulty, gives the order thus, ἀπροφασίστως ἔχειν γνώμαν σώφρονα βροτείαν τε, εἰς τὰ θεῶν ἔφυ ἄλυπος βίος θνατοῖς, which is nearly that of the above translation.

1005 seqq. The sentence which here follows is scarcely less obscure than the preceding. There is no proof however that the common reading is corrupt. The poet seems to say, that philosophy (or what we call *rationalism*) is not to be pursued so far as to offend the gods; but the other course also (viz. religious reverence and obedience) is proved to be of great avail in whatever conduces to the happiness of life, namely, to pass one's time piously by night and by day, and to honour the gods, rejecting all unlawful practices. If Hermann rightly sums up the general sense, the sentiment is a sufficiently remarkable one in the mouth of a Greek poet: "praestare ad vitam sine timore agendam dicit simplicem illam pietatem, quae credere de rebus divinis, quam non credendo in poenas incidere

460 ΕΥΡΙΠΙΔΟΥ

χαίρω θηρεύουσα, τὰ δ' ἕτερα μεγάλα
φανερὰ τῶν ἀεὶ ἐπὶ τὰ καλὰ βίον
ἦμαρ εἰς νύκτα τ' εὐαγοῦντ' εὐσεβεῖν,
τὰ δ' ἔξω νόμιμα δίκας ἐκβαλόντα τιμᾶν θεούς.   1010
ἴτω δίκα φανερὸς, ἴτω ξιφηφόρος,
φονεύουσα λαιμῶν διαμπὰξ
τὸν ἄθεον, ἄνομον, ἄδικον Ἐχίονος   1015
τόκον γηγενῆ.
φάνηθι ταῦρος ἢ πολύκρανος ἰδεῖν   ἐπῳδ.
δράκων ἢ πυριφλέγων ὁρᾶσθαι λέων.
ἴθ', ὦ βάκχε, τὸν θηραγρέταν βακχᾶν   1020
†γελῶντι προσώπῳ περίβαλε βρόχον ἐπὶ θανάσιμον ἀγέλαν πεσόντα τὰν μαινάδων.

ΑΓΓ. ὦ δῶμ', ὃ πρίν ποτ' ηὐτύχεις ἂν' Ἑλλάδα,   1025
Σιδωνίου γέροντος, ὃς τὸ γηγενὲς
δράκοντος ἔσπειρ' ὄφεος ἐν γαίᾳ θέρος,
ὥς σε στενάζω, δοῦλος ὢν μὲν, ἀλλ' ὅμως
χρηστοῖσι δούλοις συμφορὰ τὰ δεσποτῶν.

malit." And he explains ἦμαρ εἰς νύκτα *per diem usque ad noctem*, the τε and the δὲ coupling the two infinitives. The chief obscurity lies in the words τῶν ἀεὶ ἐπὶ τὰ καλὰ, for βίον εὐσεβεῖν must be taken together. Perhaps however we should read βίου, and so interpret τὰ ἀεὶ ἐπὶ τὰ καλὰ βίου (φέροντα), 'whatever tends to the good of life;' and the genitive will be for ἐν τοῖς ἀεὶ &c., 'amongst the number of.' Hermann gives τῶν ἀεὶ ἐπὶ τὰ κατὰ βίον, *ad vitae statum*. For εὐαγοῦντ' he compares Theocr. xxvi. 30, αὐτὸς δ' εὐαγέοιμι καὶ εὐαγέεσσιν ἄδοιμι. The common reading is εὖ ἄγοντ', but the MS. Pal. gives εὖ ἄγουντ'.

1020. τὸν θηραγρέταν for θηραγρέτα, is Matthiae's correction, who supposes περίβαλλε βρόχον to govern an accusative as if it were αἴρει. Examples of this construction are given on Med. 205. Otherwise τῷ θηραγρέτᾳ, and πεσόντι for πεσόντα, are but slight alterations. Hermann indeed defends πεσόντα following θηραγρέτᾳ, of which a well-known instance is Soph. El. 480. Pentheus is obviously meant, round whom Dionysus is asked to throw a net with smiling face, so that he may fall into the hands of the Maenads. But the words γελῶντι προσώπῳ, which do not fall in with the dochmiac verse, are probably a gloss: γελῶν would satisfy the metre.

1025. ηὐτύχεις for εὐτυχεῖς is Heath's correction, adopted by Elmsley and Dindorf. Hermann and Bothe retain the present, which might be defended by v. 2, Διόνυσος ὃν τίκτει ποθ' ἡ Κάδμου κόρη.

1027. Elmsley marks this verse as corrupt, and says, "si vulgata sana est, hic est ordo verborum; ὃς ὄφεος ἐν γαίᾳ ἔσπειρε τὸ γηγενὲς δράκοντος θέρος. Sed malim Ἄρεος ἐν γαίᾳ." Hermann gives ὄφεον, i. e. ὄφειον, from Barnes; a form unknown, but in some degree supporting and supported by the conjectural παλεὸν for παλαιὸν, Electr. 497. However, δράκων ὄφις seems not more irregular than παρθένος πηγή, σῦς κάπρος, γέρων λέμβος, and many similar expressions. Moreover, δράκων is really a participle from an obsolete δράκειν = δέρκεσθαι, of which the aorist ἔδρακον long remained in use.

1029. This verse occurs in Med. 54. Dobree thinks it is here interpolated, and would place a full stop at ὅμως. This however leaves the sentence bare and unfinished; and we may add, that Euripides

ΒΑΚΧΑΙ. 461

ΧΟ. τί δ' ἔστιν; ἐκ βακχῶν τι μηνύεις νέον;   1030
ΑΓΓ. Πενθεὺς ὄλωλε, παῖς Ἐχίονος πατρός.
ΧΟ. ὦναξ Βρόμιε· θεὸς φαίνει *νῦν μέγας·
ΑΓΓ. πῶς φῄς; τί τοῦτ' ἔλεξας; ἢ 'πὶ τοῖς ἐμοῖς
χαίρεις κακῶς πράσσουσι δεσπόταις, γύναι;
ΧΟ. εὐάζω ξένα μέλεσι βαρβάροις·   1035
οὐκέτι γὰρ δεσμῶν ὑπὸ φόβῳ πτήσσω.
ΑΓΓ. Θήβας δ' ἀνάνδρους ὧδ' ἄγεις   *   *
   *   *   *   *
ΧΟ. ὁ Διόνυσος ὁ Διόνυσος, οὐ Θῆβαι
κράτος ἔχουσ' ἐμόν.
ΑΓΓ. ξυγγνωστὰ μέν σοι, πλὴν ἐπ' ἐξειργασμένοις
κακοῖσι χαίρειν, ὦ γυναῖκες, οὐ καλόν.   1040
ΧΟ. ἔνεπέ μοι, φράσον, τίνι μόρῳ θνήσκει
ἄδικος ἀδικά τ' ἐκπορίζων ἀνήρ.
ΑΓΓ. ἐπεὶ Θεράπνας τῆσδε Θηβαίας χθονὸς

never loses an occasion of speaking a good word for a faithful slave. The MS. Pal. has τῆς δεσποτῶν.

1032. This verse, like the others of the chorus which follow, should be dochmiac, and not iambic; and therefore καὶ γὰρ, which Aldus adds before θεός, is doubtless an interpolation. Hermann however says "non videtur dubitari posse, quin trimeter sit hic versus;" and he reads ὦναξ Βρόμιε, θεός, θεὸς φαίνῃ μέγας. No senarius could well be less like Euripides' style. A better venture might have been, ὦ Βρόμιε, Βρόμιε, νῦν ἄναξ φαίνει μέγας. If the dochmiac is to be restored, we might read φαίνει νῦν μέγας, θεός being a monosyllable. And this is probably what the poet wrote, for νῦν is as essential to the sense as to the metre.

1037. After ἄγεις Hermann places the mark of a lacuna. It seems probable, as Seidler perceived, that a whole senarius has also been lost. For the messenger speaks in distichs before and afterwards. And the answer of the chorus, 'Dionysus, not Thebes, has power over me,' shows that something had been said to call forth these words of defiance. The sense would be complete thus,

Θήβας δ' ἀνάνδρους ὧδ' ἄγεις, ὥστ' ἐκ κακῶν
τῶν νῦν παρόντων μή σε τίσασθαι δίκην;

1041. After θνήσκει Hermann places an interrogation. He thinks this necessary for defending the hiatus at the end of the verse, and that the following line gives the reason why the chorus are justly rejoiced at his death.

1043. The messenger now relates, in a narrative of breathless interest, the events terminating in the death of Pentheus. This ῥῆσις, like the preceding, v. 677 seqq., is one of the most beautiful descriptive pieces that we possess perhaps in the whole range of Greek poetry; for it is well known that the Greeks in general do not show a very keen sensitiveness for picturesque scenery. The messenger who now arrives is a different person from the last. He was a herdsman (v. 714), and had been sent off by the king to summon the troops to go out against the Maenads (v. 780; though this order indeed may have been given to one of the king's body-guards). But this messenger was a slave (v. 1028), who had attended his master to the place, and probably never left his side from the first. The former messenger was not required as a guide, for Dionysus had said ἐγὼ ἡγήσομαι, v. 841. Elmsley thinks the speaker of the present ῥῆσις was the πρωταγωνιστὴς who also acted Agave's part.

Ibid. It is difficult to decide whether,

ΕΥΡΙΠΙΔΟΥ

λιπόντες ἐξέβημεν Ἀσωποῦ ῥοὰς,
λέπας Κιθαιρώνειον εἰσεβάλλομεν 1045
Πενθεύς τε κἀγὼ, δεσπότῃ γὰρ εἱπόμην,
ξένος θ᾽, ὃς ἡμῖν πομπὸς ἦν θεωρίας.
πρῶτον μὲν οὖν ποιηρὸν ἵζομεν νάπος,
τά τ᾽ ἐκ ποδῶν σιγηλὰ καὶ γλώσσης ἄπο
σώζοντες, ὡς ὁρῶμεν οὐχ ὁρώμενοι. 1050
ἦν δ᾽ ἄγκος ἀμφίκρημνον, ὕδασι διάβροχον,
πεύκαισι συσκιάζον, ἔνθα μαινάδες
καθῆντ᾽ ἔχουσαι χεῖρας ἐν τερπνοῖς πόνοις.
αἱ μὲν γὰρ αὐτῶν θύρσον ἐκλελοιπότα
κισσῷ κομήτην αὖθις ἐξανέστεφον, 1055
αἱ δ᾽ ἐκλιποῦσαι ποικίλ᾽ ὡς πῶλοι ζυγὰ
βακχεῖον ἀντέκλαζον ἀλλήλαις μέλος.
Πενθεὺς δ᾽ ὁ τλήμων, θῆλυν οὐχ ὁρῶν ὄχλον,
ἔλεξε τοιάδ᾽· ὦ ξέν᾽, οὗ μὲν ἕσταμεν,
οὐκ ἐξικνοῦμαι μαινάδων ὅποι μόθων· 1060

after Dindorf, Bothe, and Matthiae, Θεράπνας is to be interpreted αὐλῶνας, σταθμοὺς, (according to Hesychius; see on Troad. 211, Hec. 482,) or whether it is a proper name, Therapnae being a town of Boeotia, (Strabo, p. 409, A,) and lying pretty nearly in the direction between Thebes and Cithaeron. The rarity of the word in the sense of σταθμοὶ seems the chief objection to its use in the ῥῆσις of a messenger.

1044. ῥοὰς MS. Pal. But the Greeks are not averse to a construction which was common to the Romans also, as *egredi flumen, evadere silvas*, &c.

1049. τὰ ἐκ ποδῶν. Avoiding both noise from our footsteps and conversation with each other. He should have said, καὶ τὰ ἀπὸ γλώσσης. See Ion 7.

1051. ἀμφίκρημνον. A ravine between lofty rocks, over-arched with stone-pines, and watered by a stream along the bottom of the vale, is the romantic scene chosen by the poet for the sports of the Maenads. This affords a convenient situation for Pentheus to view from above their proceedings. It was upon a silver-fir close to the edge of the glen that they first assailed him from the opposite cliff, ἀντίπυργον ἐπιβᾶσαι πέτραν, v. 1097. Afterwards they seem to have crossed over to reach the foot of the tree itself, v. 1106.

1052. συσκιάζον. See Suppl. 1219. As κατασκιάζειν is also active in Ion 1142, so here we may interpret, with Hermann, *umbram faciens*. It is easy to supply some such accusative as τὸν ἔνερθε τόπον. The stone-pine (πεύκη) grows like our Scotch fir, with spreading boughs forming a wide and dense crown, totally unlike the spiry pyramidal outline of the silver-fir.

1054. ἐκλελοιπότα, '*worn out*,' Elmsley; who adds that κισσῷ κομήτην is used like διδάσκειν τινὰ σοφόν.

1056. αἱ δὲ, (ἀνειμέναι, or ἐκ πόνων πεπαυμέναι,) ὡς πῶλοι ἐκλιποῦσαι ζυγὰ, κτλ.

1060. ὅποι μόθων. For ἐκεῖσε ὅπου μόθων ἐστί. This is the conjecture of Musgrave for ὅσοι νόθων, and W. Dindorf and Matthiae seem to be right in adopting it, as the best correction that has been proposed. Stephens had alleged that μύθων was read in one of his MSS. Scaliger's conjecture, approved by Barnes, was ὅσαι μαθεῖν, ' so as to ascertain their number.' Hermann gives ὅσσοις ὅσον, *quantum oculis, non assequor Maenadas*. The word μόθων occurs in Ar. Equit. 697, where the Schol. has μόθων, φορτικὸν ὀρχήσεως εἶδος, and in Plut. 279, ὡς μόθων εἶ καὶ φύσει κόβαλος. Photius,

ΒΑΚΧΑΙ. 463

ὄχθον δ' ἐπεμβὰς ἢ 'λάτην ὑψαύχενα
ἴδοιμ' ἂν ὀρθῶς μαινάδων αἰσχρουργίαν.
τοὐντεῦθεν ἤδη τοῦ ξένου τι θαῦμ' ὁρῶ·
λαβὼν γὰρ ἐλάτης οὐράνιον ἄκρον κλάδον
κατῆγεν, ἦγεν, ἦγεν ἐς μέλαν πέδον· 1065
κυκλοῦτο δ' ὥστε τόξον ἢ κυρτὸς τροχός,
τόρνῳ γραφόμενος περιφορὰν, ἕλκει δρόμον·
ὣς κλῶν' ὄρειον ὁ ξένος χεροῖν ἄγων
ἔκαμπτεν ἐς γῆν, ἔργματ' οὐχὶ θνητὰ δρῶν.
Πενθέα δ' ἱδρύσας ἐλατίνων ὄζων ἔπι 1070
ὀρθὸν μεθίει διὰ χερῶν βλάστημ' ἄνω
ἀτρέμα, φυλάσσων μὴ ἀναχαιτίσειέ νιν.
ὀρθὴ δ' ἐς ὀρθὸν αἰθέρ' ἐστηρίζετο,

having both these passages of comedy in view, gives μόθων· ὄρχημα φορτικὸν καὶ κορδακῶδες· ἀπὸ δὲ τούτου καὶ ἀνάγωγος καὶ ὁ ἀκόλαστος ἄνθρωπος. It is not a very strong objection against the restoration of this word in the present passage, that it does not again occur in tragedy. It was probably one familiar enough to the hearers of satyric farces; and no word perhaps better expressed the unseemly rout or riot that the Maenads were carrying on. Elmsley, who marks the verse as corrupt, suggests ὅσον ποθῶ. In the Appendix to his notes, he tells us that Porson approved ὅποι μόθων.

1061. ἢ 'λάτην for εἰς ἐλάτην Tyrwhitt. Hermann gives ἐς ἐλάτην after Heath, 'mounting a bank (and climbing) into a silver-fir.' But ἐς is scarcely used for εἰς before a short vowel, unless in lyric verses (inf. 986. Rhes. 51). Elmsley well compares v. 982–3.—The silver-pine, which has a tall, straight, and flexible stem like the spruce-fir, was well adapted for bending downwards. It was from the same use of the same tree that Sinis the robber obtained the name of πιτυοκάμπτης.

1065. κατῆγεν, ἦγεν. It was somewhere remarked by Porson, that when a verb is repeated, it is generally used first in its compound, then in its simple form. This remarkable verse admirably expresses the successive efforts to bend the tree to the earth: 'he tugged it down, down, down, to the black ground.'

1067. ἕλκει for ἕλκη Brunck. The latter is found both in the Aldine edition and in the Palatine MS.; but there Elmsley says that the original reading seems to have been ἕλκει. He puts the comma after γραφόμενος, as does Aldus; but Hermann's punctuation seems better, 'when it has its periphery (outer circle) described in a lathe,' i. e. is being accurately rounded therein. Perhaps δρόμῳ would be better than δρόμον, 'as a wheel, when rounded in a lathe, trails its periphery in running.' Dindorf adopts Reiske's unsatisfactory emendation, περιφορὰν ἑλικόδρομον. Scaliger proposed ἑλκέδρομον, which is nearer to the old reading, and has the Homeric ἑλκεχίτωνες in its favour. Compare ἀρχέχορος, Tro. 151. Elmsley edits περιφορὰν ἕλκει δρόμον. But it is clear that a wheel on the lathe may be said ἕλκειν δρόμον just as a man is said ἕλκειν κῶλον, for no poet hesitates to attribute agency to inanimate objects. Hermann retains the subjunctive, ἕλκῃ,—an epic usage after ὥστε, which it seems somewhat rash unnecessarily to introduce into Attic Greek. See on Hec. 1026.

1072. ἀναχαιτίζειν is said of a horse who tries to dislodge a rider by throwing him over the neck; or rather, perhaps, of the attempt of the animal to shake off the collar, ζεύγλη, from the neck itself. Cf. Hipp. 1232. Rhes. 786, αἱ δ' ἔρεγκον ἐξ ἀντηρίδων θυμὸν πνέουσαι κἀνεχαίτιζον φόβῳ. Thus a sudden jerk of the fir-tree would have shaken Pentheus from his seat; for the metaphor taken from a rider is apparent, v. 1074.

1073. What is the exact sense of ὀρθὸς αἰθὴρ might well be questioned, if the

464　　　　　ΕΥΡΙΠΙΔΟΥ

ἔχουσα νώτοις δεσπότην ἐφήμενον.
ὤφθη δὲ μᾶλλον ἢ κατεῖδε μαινάδας·　　　　　1075
ὅσον γὰρ οὔπω δῆλος ἦν θάσσων ἄνω,
καὶ τὸν ξένον μὲν οὐκέτ' εἰσορᾶν παρῆν,
ἐκ δ' αἰθέρος φωνή τις, ὡς μὲν εἰκάσαι,
Διόνυσος ἀνεβόησεν, Ὦ νεάνιδες,
ἄγω τὸν ὑμᾶς κἀμὲ τἀμά τ' ὄργια　　　　　1080
γέλων τιθέμενον· ἀλλὰ τιμωρεῖσθέ νιν.
καὶ ταῦθ' ἅμ' ἠγόρευε, καὶ πρὸς οὐρανὸν
καὶ γαῖαν ἐστήριζε φῶς σεμνοῦ πυρός.
σίγησε δ' αἰθήρ, σῖγα δ' εὔλειμος νάπη
φύλλ' εἶχε, θηρῶν δ' οὐκ ἂν ἤκουσας βοήν.　　　　　1085
αἱ δ' ὠσὶν ἠχὴν οὐ σαφῶς δεδεγμέναι
ἔστησαν ὀρθαὶ καὶ διήνεγκαν κόρας.
ὁ δ' αὖθις ἐπεκέλευσεν· ὡς δ' ἐγνώρισαν
σαφῆ κελευσμὸν Βακχίου Κάδμου κόραι,
ᾖξαν πελείας ὠκύτητ' οὐχ ἥσσονες　　　　　1090
ποδῶν ἔχουσαι συντόνοις δρομήμασι
μήτηρ Ἀγαύη ξύγγονοί θ' ὁμόσποροι
πᾶσαί τε βάκχαι· διὰ δὲ χειμάρρου νάπης
ἀγμῶν τ' ἐπήδων θεοῦ πνοαῖσιν ἐμμανεῖς.
ὡς δ' εἶδον ἐλάτῃ δεσπότην ἐφήμενον,　　　　　1095

phrase occurred alone, and not as an amplification of ὀρθή. It would be no very violent change to read ὀρθῇ δ' ἐσαῦθις αἰθέρι στηρίζετο, where the dative would be as in v. 972, οὐρανῷ στηρίζον.

1076. ὅσον οὔπω, i. e. he would have been seen by the Maenads in a moment or two more. So Hecub. 143, ἥξει δ' Ὀδυσεὺς ὅσον οὐκ ἤδη. Thucyd. vi. 34, οἱ δὲ ἄνδρες καὶ ἐπέρχονται καὶ ἐν πλῷ εὖ οἶδ' ὅτι ἤδη εἰσὶ καὶ ὅσον οὔπω πάρεισι. In the next line καὶ is, 'when the stranger indeed vanished out of sight, but a voice from the sky' was heard.

1083. ἐστήριξε Hermann with Aldus. It is not very easy to say whether the aorist or the imperfect is here the more appropriate. In what follows, the former tense prevails; but on the other hand, the form in ξ is not lightly to be admitted in a senarius.

1084. σίγησε. Elmsley, unable to accept the doctrine, that the augment is occasionally omitted in the narratives of messengers, marks this verse as corrupt, but at the same time proposes the tamer reading, αἰθὴρ δ' ἐσίγα.

1089. σαφῆ. In reference to οὐ σαφῶς, v. 1086.

1090. If the reading οὐχ ἥσσονες, supported as it is by the quotation of these two verses in Christus Patiens, be true, it is better to regard it, with Matthiae, as a confused construction between οὐχ ἥσσονες πελείας ὠκύτητα, and ὠκύτητα ποδῶν οὐχ ἥσσονα πελείας ἔχουσαι, than to adopt Hermann's strange idea, that the meaning is οὐχ ἥσσονες οὖσαι ἔχουσαι (like σιγῶν ἔχω &c.) It is easy, with Heath, to read ἥσσονα, yet it does not seem a safe alteration. Accordingly, Matthiae, Herm., Dind., and Bothe, retain the vulgate. It is possible that v. 1091 is a mere interpolation, in connexion with an altered reading ἥσσονα.

ΒΑΚΧΑΙ. 465

πρῶτον μὲν αὐτοῦ χερμάδας κραταιβόλους
ἔρριπτον ἀντίπυργον ἐπιβᾶσαι πέτραν,
ὄζοισί τ' ἐλατίνοισιν ἠκοντίζετο·
ἄλλαι δὲ θύρσους ἵεσαν δι' αἰθέρος
Πενθέως, στόχον δύστηνον· ἀλλ' οὐκ ἤνυτον.   1100
κρεῖσσον γὰρ ὕψος τῆς προθυμίας ἔχων
καθῆστο τλήμων ἀπορίᾳ λελημμένος.
τέλος δὲ δρυΐνους συγκεραυνοῦσαι κλάδους
ῥίζας ἀνεσπάρασσον ἀσιδήροις μοχλοῖς.
ἐπεὶ δὲ μόχθων τέρματ' οὐκ ἐξήνυτον,   1105
ἔλεξ' Ἀγαύη, φέρε περιστᾶσαι κύκλῳ
πτόρθου λάβεσθε, μαινάδες, τὸν ἀμβάτην
θῆρ' ὡς ἕλωμεν, μηδ' ἀπαγγείλῃ θεοῦ
χοροὺς κρυφαίους. αἱ δὲ μυρίαν χέρα
προσέθεσαν ἐλάτῃ κἀξανέσπασαν χθονός·   1110
ὑψοῦ δὲ θάσσων ὑψόθεν χαμαιπετὴς
πίπτει πρὸς οὖδας μυρίοις οἰμώγμασι
Πενθεύς· κακοῦ γὰρ ἐγγὺς ὢν ἐμάνθανε.
πρώτη δὲ μήτηρ ἦρξεν ἱερία φόνου,
καὶ προσπίτνει νιν· ὁ δὲ μίτραν κόμης ἄπο   1115
ἔρριψεν, ὥς νιν γνωρίσασα μὴ κτάνοι
τλήμων Ἀγαύη, καὶ λέγει, παρηίδος
ψαύων, Ἐγώ τοι, μῆτερ, εἰμὶ παῖς σέθεν
Πενθεύς, ὃν ἔτεκες ἐν δόμοις Ἐχίονος·

1096. αὐτοῦ is the same genitive as τοῦδε τοξεύω Ion 1411, and Πενθέως inf. 1099, where στόχον is the accusative in apposition to the sentence, and follows the genitive as in Herc. F. 57, δυσπραξία, ἧς μήποθ', ὅστις καὶ μέσως εὔνους ἐμοί, τύχοι, φίλων ἔλεγχον ἀψευδέστατον.—κραταίβολος is formed like κραταίλεως, Electr. 534.—ἀντίπυργον πέτραν, an opposite height; compare the use of ἀντιπυργοῦν in Eum. 658, and see above on v. 1051.
1098. Hermann appears right in reading τ' for δ' in this verse. For the πρῶτον μὲν is answered by ἄλλαι δὲ in 1099.
1099. θύρσους ἵεσαν. On the use of the thyrsus as a warlike weapon, see on v. 704.—στόχον is Reiske's certain conjecture for τ' ὄχον.
1101. κρεῖσσον τῆς προθυμίας, too great for their eagerness, i. e. for them though eager, to reach him. For the Ionic form λελημμένος see Rhes. 74. Ion 1113.
1103. συγκεραυνοῦν is 'to rend,' 'to tear in pieces,' 'to shiver to atoms,' like a lightning-stroke. What the Maenads next did was this,—they used stakes to scratch and tear up the roots of the pine, which, in this species, lie close to the surface of the ground. Failing in this, they closed round the tree and forcibly pulled it up. Of course, the messenger regards this not merely as a feat of strength, but as the work of supernaturally assisted followers of the god. Cf. v. 1128.

VOL. II.   3 o

ΕΥΡΙΠΙΔΟΥ

οἴκτειρε δ' ὦ μῆτέρ με, μηδὲ ταῖς ἐμαῖς 1120
ἁμαρτίαισι παῖδα σὸν κατακτάνῃς·
ἡ δ' ἀφρὸν ἐξιεῖσα καὶ διαστρόφους
κόρας ἑλίσσουσ', οὐ φρονοῦσ' ἃ χρῆν φρονεῖν,
ἐκ Βακχίου κατείχετ', οὐδ' ἔπειθέ νιν.
λαβοῦσα δ' ὠλέναις ἀριστερὰν χέρα, 1125
πλευραῖσιν ἀντιβᾶσα τοῦ δυσδαίμονος,
ἀπεσπάραξεν ὦμον, οὐχ ὑπὸ σθένους,
ἀλλ' ὁ θεὸς εὐμάρειαν ἐπεδίδου χεροῖν.
Ἰνὼ δὲ τἀπὶ θάτερ' ἐξειργάζετο,
ῥηγνῦσα σάρκας, Αὐτονόη τ' ὄχλος τε πᾶς 1130
ἐπεῖχε βακχῶν· ἦν δὲ πᾶσ' ὁμοῦ βοή,
ὁ μὲν στενάζων, ὅσον ἐτύγχανεν πνέων,
αἱ δ' ἠλάλαζον. ἔφερε δ' ἡ μὲν ὠλένην,
ἡ δ' ἴχνος αὐταῖς ἀρβύλαις· γυμνοῦντο δὲ
πλευραὶ σπαραγμοῖς· πᾶσα δ' ἡματωμένη 1135
χεῖρας διεσφαίριζε σάρκα Πενθέως.

1121. ἁμαρτίαισι. This dative, equivalent to διὰ τὰς ἁμαρτίας, has frequently been noticed, and is a favourite idiom with Euripides.

1125. The metre of this verse, in which the fourth and fifth foot are formed by one word, is very rare in Euripides. It would be easy to read λαβοῦσα δ' ὠλέναισι χεῖρ' ἀριστερὰν, but similar instances of the want of caesura occur in Iph. Taur. 943, ἐς γῆν Ἀθηναίων ἔπεμπε Λοξίας. Frag. Dan. 317, 4, Ἀκρίσιος εἴληχεν, τύραννος τῆσδε γῆς. Hec. 355, γυναιξί, παρθένοις ἀπόβλεπτος μέτα. Andr. 397, ἀτὰρ τί ταῦτ' ὀδύρομαι, τὰ δ' ἐν ποσίν, κτλ. In Suppl. 699, the old reading καὶ ξυμπατάξαντες μέσον πάντα στρατὸν, has been altered to ξυμπατάξαντ' ἐς μέσον. Hec. 1159, γένοιτο διαδοχαῖς ἀμείβουσαι χεροῖν.

1131. βοή—ὁ μέν. Compare Prom. 208, στάσις τ' ἐν ἀλλήλοισιν ὠροθύνετο, οἱ μὲν θέλοντες ἐκβαλεῖν ἕδρας Κρόνου. Antig. 259, λόγοι δ' ἐν ἀλλήλοισιν ἐρρόθουν κακοί, φύλαξ ἐλέγχων φύλακα.

1134. ἴχνος κτλ., 'a foot, shoes and all.' Elmsley. For ἀρβύλη see Hipp. 1189. For γυμνοῦντο Elmsley would read γυμνοῦσι after Pierson, and πλευρὰ for πλευραί. He discusses in a long note, (referred to above, v. 767,) the various passages of the Tragic writers where the augment appears to be omitted; and the question seems to stand on the same footing with some other grammatical and metrical irregularities, viz. that they are *licences*, but not *violations* of any such rules, or absolute restrictions, as fastidious critics have attempted to impose. In the preceding verse, Aldus and the MS. Pal. give ἀνέφερε, for which Elmsley and others adopt the correction of Duport, ἔφερε. Hermann edits the passage thus:

αἱ δ' ἠλάλαζον· ἄγε, φέρ' ἡ μὲν ὠλένην,
ἡ δ' ἴχνος αὐταῖς ἀρβύλαις· γυμνοῦτε δὲ
πλευρὰς σπαραγμοῖς.

There is something plausible in this; though he writes a long note rather needlessly on the anatomical question, whether pulling off an arm and a foot could be said to *lay bare* the side; and answering this in the negative, he concludes that some third and independent process must be meant by γυμνοῦν πλευράς. It is pretty clear however that the poet speaks of the effects of rending away the arm, which may fairly be supposed to lacerate extensively the muscles under the armpit.

1136. διεσφαίριζε, tossed to and fro like a ball.—πᾶσα, here for ἑκάστη.

ΒΑΚΧΑΙ. 467

κεῖται δὲ χωρὶς σῶμα, τὸ μὲν ὑπὸ στύφλοις
πέτραις, τὸ δ' ὕλης ἐν βαθυξύλῳ φόβῃ,
οὐ ῥᾴδιον ζήτημα· κρᾶτα δ' ἄθλιον,
ὅπερ λαβοῦσα τυγχάνει μήτηρ χεροῖν, 1140
πήξασ' ἐπ' ἄκρον θύρσον ὡς ὀρεστέρου
φέρει λέοντος διὰ Κιθαιρῶνος μέσου,
λιποῦσ' ἀδελφὰς ἐν χοροῖσι μαινάδων.
χωρεῖ δὲ θήρᾳ δυσπότμῳ γαυρουμένη
τειχέων ἔσω τῶνδ', ἀνακαλοῦσα Βάκχιον 1145
τὸν ξυγκύναγον, τὸν ξυνεργάτην ἄγρας
τὸν καλλίνικον, ᾗ δάκρυα νικηφορεῖ.
ἐγὼ μὲν οὖν τῇδ' ἐκποδὼν τῇ ξυμφορᾷ
ἄπειμ', Ἀγαύην πρὶν μολεῖν πρὸς δώματα.
τὸ σωφρονεῖν δὲ καὶ σέβειν τὰ τῶν θεῶν 1150
κάλλιστον οἶμαι ταὐτὸ καὶ σοφώτατον
θνητοῖσιν εἶναι χρῆμα τοῖσι χρωμένοις.

ΧΟ. ἀναχορεύσωμεν Βάκχιον,
ἀναβοάσωμεν ξυμφορὰν
τὰν τοῦ δράκοντος ἐκγενέτα Πενθέως, 1155
ὃς τὰν θηλυγενῆ στολὰν
νάρθηκά τε, πιστὸν Ἅιδαν,
ἔλαβεν εὔθυρσον,
ταῦρον προηγητῆρα συμφορᾶς ἔχων.
βάκχαι Καδμεῖαι, 1160
τὸν καλλίνικον κλεινὸν ἐξεπράξατο

1140. ὅπερ. So ἐς τὸ κείνου κρᾶτα, Oed. R. 263.
1147. ᾗ, ἐν ᾗ ἄγρᾳ, δάκρυα φέρεται ἀντὶ νίκης. Hermann approves Reiske's conjecture ᾧ, 'in honour of whom she is carrying a mournful prize,' the head of her son. In this case καλλίνικον will be a distinct attribute; according to the common reading, an adjective agreeing with ξυνεργάτην. Barnes explains, 'to whom (viz. to Agave) Bacchus gives a victory of tears.'
1151. ταὐτὸ Reiske for γ' αὐτό. Hermann prefers οἶμαι δ' αὐτὸ, the reading in *Christus Patiens*, with a colon at κάλλιστον. These concluding lines appear to represent the poet's real opinion on the subject; see the introductory note.
1153. Βάκχιον Hermann for βακχεῖον or —ων. This and the next verse are dochmiac preceded by a resolved cretic.
1157. πιστὸν Ἅιδαν, 'a sure cause of his destruction.' Properly the thyrsus itself was πιστὸς, because he trusted to it and to his female dress for protection. But it is here ironically called 'a certain death' instead of 'a certain protection.' So Matthiae; and this is much simpler than Hermann's Ἅιδᾳ, to which he attaches a complex and improbable sense, referring it to ταῦρον, *fretum Orco thyrsigerum taurum.* Compare v. 922.
1161. As τὸν καλλίνικον here represents a substantive, ὕμνον being under-

3 O 2

εἰς γόον, εἰς δάκρυα.
καλὸς ἀγών, ἐν αἵματι στάζουσαν
χέρα περιβαλεῖν τέκνου.   1165
ἀλλ' εἰσορῶ γὰρ ἐς δόμους ὁρμωμένην
Πενθέως Ἀγαύην μητέρ' ἐν διαστρόφοις
ὄσσοις, δέχεσθε κῶμον εὐίου θεοῦ.

ΑΓΑΥΗ.

Ἀσιάδες βάκχαι.   ΧΟ. τί μ' ὀροθύνεις ὦ;   στρ.
ΑΓΑ. φέρομεν ἐξ ὀρέων   1170
ἕλικα νεότομον ἐπὶ μέλαθρα,
μακαρίαν θήραν.
ΧΟ. ὁρῶ γε καί σε δέξομαι σύγκωμον ὦ.
ΑΓΑ. ἔμαρψα τόνδ' ἄνευ βρόχων *
   * * νέον λῖν,
ὡς ὁρᾶν πάρα.
ΧΟ. πόθεν ἐρημίας;   1175

stood, it seems that κλεινὸν is the predicate, in the sense of ὥστε κλεινὸν εἶναι. 'She hath achieved a victory which is an illustrious one, (ending as it has) in groans and tears.'—γόον for γόνον is Canter's correction. For ἐκπράσσειν 'to effect,' compare Hel. 20, ὃς δόλιον εὐνὴν ἐξέπραξ' ὑπ' αἰετοῦ δίωγμα φεύγων. The old reading ἐξεπράξατο, which Scaliger altered to ἐξεπράξατε, is perhaps capable of defence, sibi consecuta est (Agave). For the following words refer to her, not to the Maenads in general; and thus καλὸς ἀγὼν is a fit epexegesis of καλλίνικον κλεινόν.—The ἐν is added, as if he had said ἐν αἵματι βεβαμμένην. Compare Electr. 1172, νεοφόνοις ἐν αἵμασι πεφυρμένοι. Elmsley says it is redundant here and in v. 1167. In the latter verse it means 'with,' as a person is often said, with reference to things external to him, to be ἐν ὅπλοις, ἐν πέπλοις &c. So Electr. 321, σκῆπτρ', ἐν οἷς Ἕλλησιν ἐστρατηλάτει.

1169. Agave now comes on the stage. She presents an awful spectacle; ecstatic madness has made her voice, her gestures, her looks, unlike to human. Panting with excitement, with starting eye-balls, dishevelled hair, and garments besprinkled with blood, she holds aloft in triumph the head of her own child. She asks if they see that. But she is unconscious as yet of the atrocity she has committed.—ὀροθύνεις is Hermann's excellent correction for τί με δή (or τί με) ὀρθεῖς ὤ.

1170. ὀρέων. Hermann prefers ὄρεος, a reading given by Plutarch in quoting the passage (Vit. Crass. c. 33), and θήραν for θήραμα. Agave, as a follower of Bacchus, not inaptly calls the newly-rended prey ἕλιξ, a fresh-cut vine tendril.

1173. Hermann gives ὁρῶ τε and σύγκωμος. The MS. Pal. omits γε, but there seems no reason why it should not be used here, as we should say, 'aye, I see it.' He thinks that the κῶμος of Agave, v. 1168, is alluded to, to which the chorus say they will be associates. The reading in the text however, by which σύγκωμον becomes the predicate, is much more natural.

Ibid. Something has been lost here. The word λῖν rests on the slender evidence of Stephens' boasted MSS. (which no one now believes to have existed), Aldus having νέον νιν. It is quite as probable that we should restore the passage in some such way as the following:—

ἔμαρψα τόνδ' ἄνευ βρόχων, νέον δέ νιν
ἐκράτησα, νέον αἷμα
ὡς ὁρᾶν πάρα.

1175. πόθεν. For ποῦ.' See on Rhes. 612.

ΒΑΚΧΑΙ. 469

ΑΓΑ. Κιθαιρὼν   ΧΟ. τί Κιθαιρών;
ΑΓΑ. κατεφόνευσέ νιν.
ΧΟ. τίς ἁ βαλοῦσα πρῶτα;
ΑΓΑ.   ἐμὸν τὸ γέρας.
μάκαιρ' Ἀγαύη κληζόμεθ' ἐν θιάσοις.   1180
ΧΟ. τίς ἄλλα;   ΑΓΑ. τὰ Κάδμου   ΧΟ. τί Κάδμου;
ΑΓΑ.   γένεθλα
μετ' ἐμὲ μετ' ἐμὲ τοῦδ'
ἔθιγε θηρός.   ΧΟ. εὐτυχεῖς τᾷδ' ἄγρᾳ.
ΑΓΑ. μέτεχέ νυν θοίνας.   ΧΟ. τί μετέχω τλάμων;   ἀντ.
ΑΓΑ. νέος ὁ μόσχος ἄρ-
τι γένυν ὑπὸ κόρυθ' ἁπαλότριχα   1185
κατάκομον βάλλει.
ΧΟ. πρέπει γὰρ ὥστε θηρὸς ἀγραύλου φόβῃ.
ΑΓΑ. ὁ Βάκχιος κυναγέτας σοφὸς σοφῶς
ἀνέπηλεν ἐπὶ θῆρα   1190
τόνδε μαινάδας.
ΧΟ. ὁ γὰρ ἄναξ ἀγρεύς.
ΑΓΑ. ἐπαινεῖς;   ΧΟ. τί δ'; ἐπαινῶ.
ΑΓΑ. τάχα δὲ Καδμεῖοι
ΧΟ. καὶ παῖς γε Πενθεὺς ματέρ'   1195

1179. πρῶτα Hermann for πρῶτα or πρωτά γε. This and the next verse are of the metre called *iambelegus*.

1180. The words κληζόμεθ' ἐν θιάσοις are given by Aldus to the messenger. This does not suit the arrangement of the antistrophic verse; and it is clear that Agave says of herself, 'we are spoken of in all the bacchic companies as *the fortunate Agave*.'

1181. τί Κάδμου; Scil. τί λέξεις περὶ τῶν Κάδμου; See Ion 286.—μετ' ἐμὲ, 'next after me.' The proper reply to τίς πρῶτα above.—γένεθλα occurs twice according to the old reading, but Heath rightly expunged the superfluous word. The metre is bacchiac.

1185. The sense seems to be, 'the whelp, being yet young, is just putting forth a hairy chin beneath its finely-haired crest.' She thinks it is a lion's head she has got, and calls the long tangled mane of that animal its κόρυς. At the same time the words are so selected, that they suit the physical aspect of her son's face. Thus βάλλει is for φύει. There does not seem any material difficulty in the passage, though it has been variously altered and interpreted. W. Dindorf follows Hermann in reading ἄπο for ὑπὸ, "*vitulus hic, juvenis adhuc genas, comatum molli crine amisit capitis ornamentum.*" Though the position of the article is rather in favour of construing νέος γένυν, still ἀποβάλλει for ἀπέβαλε, ἀπώλεσε, would be obscure; and besides, it is evident that the reply of the chorus better suits the interpretation given above.

1189. κυναγέτας, supply ὤν, as ὁ Βάκχιος is the proper name, not the adjective.

1190. Aldus has θῆρα. Hermann, followed by Dindorf, reads ἐπὶ θήρᾳ τοῦδε.

1192. ἀγρεύς. This, as well as Ζαγρεὺς, was a title of Bacchus.

1193. τί δ'; Compare El. 1008. *sup.* 654.

470   ΕΥΡΙΠΙΔΟΥ

ΑΓΑ.   ἐπαινέσεται,
    λαβοῦσαν ἄγραν τάνδε λεοντοφυῆ
ΧΟ. περισσὰν   ΑΓΑ. περισσῶς.   ΧΟ. ἀγάλλει ;
ΑΓΑ.   γέγηθα
    μεγάλα μεγάλα καὶ
    φανερὰ τᾷδε γᾷ κατειργασμένα.
ΧΟ. δεῖξόν νυν, ὦ τάλαινα, σὴν νικηφόρον   1200
    ἀστοῖσιν ἄγραν, ἣν φέρουσ᾽ ἐλήλυθας.
ΑΓΑ. ὦ καλλίπυργον ἄστυ Θηβαίας χθονὸς
    ναίοντες, ἔλθεθ᾽, ὡς ἴδητε τήνδ᾽ ἄγραν,
    Κάδμου θυγατέρες θηρὸς ἣν ἠγρεύσαμεν,
    οὐκ ἀγκυλωτοῖς Θεσσαλῶν στοχάσμασιν,   1205
    οὐ δικτύοισιν, ἀλλὰ λευκοπήχεσιν
    χειρῶν ἀκμαῖσι. κᾆτα κομπάζειν χρεὼν
    καὶ λογχοποιῶν ὄργανα κτᾶσθαι μάτην ;
    ἡμεῖς δὲ ταύτῃ χειρὶ τόνδε θ᾽ εἵλομεν
    χωρίς τε θηρὸς ἄρθρα διεφορήσαμεν.   1210
    ποῦ μοι πατὴρ ὁ πρέσβυς ; ἐλθέτω πέλας.
    Πενθεύς τ᾽ ἐμὸς παῖς ποῦ 'στιν ; αἱρέσθω λαβὼν
    πηκτῶν πρὸς οἴκους κλιμάκων προσαμβάσεις,

1196. ἐπαινέσεται. Though according to the old reading, which Elmsley has followed, the whole speech from τάχα δὲ to περισσῶς is given to Agave, it is clear that the antistrophic verses require to be distributed, like the strophic, between Agave and the chorus, as Hermann perceived. The words are taken out of the mouth of the chorus by Agave anticipating them. There is a similar example in Suppl. 1141, 1153.

1197. περισσὰν, 'extraordinary.' See Hippol. 437. supra, 429.

1199. τᾷδε γᾷ L. Dindorf for τάδ᾽ ἔργα. Hermann gives φανερὰ τἄργ᾽ ἐγώ. Elmsley says, "In τάδε ἔργα latet mendum, quod corrigere nequeo." The accusative after verbs of rejoicing, it is hardly necessary to add, is the usual construction. See on Hippol. 1340.

1207. The Thessalian javelins used in hunting (Hippol. 221) were called ἀγκυλωτὰ from the thong or loop in the middle, in which the forefinger was inserted in the act of hurling the weapon, Andr. 1133.

Aeschylus twice uses the form ἀγκυλητὸς, frag. 16 and 189, ed. Herm. Lucian, Ζεὺς Ἔλεγχ. Vol. ii. p. 637, makes the god to say, κεραυνὸν, ὡς ὁρᾷς, διηγκυλωμένος ἀνέχομαί σε, i. e. 'with my finger on the loop, in the act of poising the dart.' Xen. Anab. v. 2. 12, ὁ δὲ τοῖς πελτασταῖς πᾶσι παρήγγελλε διηγκυλωμένους ἰέναι.

Ibid. κομπάζειν, understand ἐπὶ εὐστοχίᾳ. The next line seems better read with a question than ironically understood, as Hermann prefers. Cf. Alcest. 831, κᾆτα κωμάζω κάρα στεφάνοις πυκασθείς ;

1210. χωρίς is to be construed with the verb. Cf. v. 1137, κεῖται δὲ χωρὶς σῶμα.

1213. πηκτῶν for πλεκτῶν Barnes, who compares Phoen. 491, προσφέρειν πύργοισι πηκτῶν κλιμάκων προσαμβάσεις. On this passage Dr. Wordsworth remarks (Athens and Attica, p. 118), "The marble *lion-head* antefixa, which still terminate the northern angles of the western pediments of the Parthenon, indicate that Euripides has not neglected in the delineation of her character one of the most natural and

ΒΑΚΧΑΙ. 471

ὡς πασσαλεύσῃ κρᾶτα τριγλύφοις τόδε
λέοντος, ὃν πάρειμι θηράσασ' ἐγώ. 1215
ΚΑ. ἕπεσθέ μοι φέροντες ἄθλιον βάρος
Πενθέως, ἕπεσθε, πρόσπολοι, δόμων πάρος,
οὗ σῶμα μοχθῶν μυρίοις ζητήμασι
φέρω τόδ' εὑρὼν ἐν Κιθαιρῶνος πτυχαῖς
διασπάρακτον, κοὐδὲν ἐν ταὐτῷ πέδῳ 1220
λαβὼν, ἐν ὕλῃ κείμενον δυσευρέτῳ.
ἤκουσα γάρ του θυγατέρων τολμήματα,
ἤδη κατ' ἄστυ τειχέων ἔσω βεβὼς
σὺν τῷ γέροντι Τειρεσίᾳ βακχῶν πάρα·
πάλιν δὲ κάμψας εἰς ὄρος κομίζομαι 1225
τὸν κατθανόντα παῖδα μαινάδων ὕπο.
καὶ τὴν μὲν Ἀκταίων' Ἀρισταίᾳ ποτὲ
τεκοῦσαν εἶδον Αὐτονόην Ἰνώ θ' ἅμα
ἔτ' ἀμφὶ δρυμοῖς οἰστροπλῆγας ἀθλίας,
τὴν δ' εἶπέ τίς μοι δεῦρο βακχείῳ ποδὶ 1230
στείχειν Ἀγαύην, οὐδ' ἄκραντ' ἠκούσαμεν·
λεύσσω γὰρ αὐτὴν, ὄψιν οὐκ εὐδαίμονα.

pathetic elements of madness, viz. its partial saneness and sense of propriety."

1216. Cadmus, the unhappy grandfather of the slain Pentheus, is now seen advancing before the palace with attendants, who are bearing on a covered bier the mangled limbs which have been with difficulty collected through the wood. Agave, still unconscious what she has done, runs to meet him with a smiling countenance, and exhibits the spoils she has brought away from the hunt.

1221. δυσευρέτῳ, if the reading be right, must mean δι' ἧς εὑρεῖν τὴν ἀτραπὸν οὐ ῥᾴδιόν ἐστι. Hermann gives δυσευρέτως. So long as the right word occurred in the clause, the poets were not always scrupulously careful to construe it with the noun to which in logical strictness it belonged. Here the epithet seems rather intended to apply to σῶμα. Accordingly, Reiske proposed to read δυσεύρετον.

1224. βακχῶν πάρα, scil. βεβὼς, a Bacchis redux, is Musgrave's correction for β. πέρι, and is admitted by Elmsley, Hermann, and Dindorf. Cadmus had accompanied Teiresias in the earlier part of the play, to the Bacchic orgies, of which both had professed themselves converts. Matthiae defends πέρι, on his favourite theory of mixed constructions, ἤκουσα θυγατέρων τολμήματα and ἤκουσα βακχῶν πέρι.

1227. Ἀκταίων'. Dindorf chooses to read Ἀκτέων'. See v. 337. The dative Ἀρισταίᾳ may be defended by Ion v. 3, ᾗ μ' ἐγείνατο Ἑρμῆν μεγίστῳ Ζηνί. Aldus has ἀριστέα, for which others give Ἀρισταίῳ, after Heath. There was probably a double form, Ἀριστέας and Ἀρίσταιος, so that L. Dindorf may be right in restoring Ἀριστέᾳ. Hesiod. Theog. 975, Κάδμῳ δ' Ἁρμονίη, θυγάτηρ χρυσέης Ἀφροδίτης, Ἰνὼ καὶ Σεμέλην καὶ Ἀγαύην καλλιπάρῃον, Αὐτονόην θ', ἣν γῆμεν Ἀρισταῖος βαθυχαίτης, γείνατο.

1230. τὴν δὲ—Ἀγαύην. Compare Hel. 1025, τὴν μέν σ' ἐᾶσαι πατρίδα νοστῆσαι Κύπριν.

1232. αὐτὴν for αὐτῆς Hermann after Scaliger, and this is undoubtedly an improvement; for, as he says, "non enim infelicem adspectum filiae, sed ipsam vi-

472 ΕΥΡΙΠΙΔΟΥ

ΑΓΑ. πάτερ, μέγιστον κομπάσαι πάρεστί σοι,
πάντων ἀρίστας θυγατέρας σπεῖραι μακρῷ
θνητῶν· ἁπάσας εἶπον, ἐξόχως δ' ἐμέ,   1235
ἣ τὰς παρ' ἱστοῖς ἐκλιποῦσα κερκίδας
εἰς μεῖζον ἥκω, θῆρας ἀγρεύειν χεροῖν.
φέρω δ' ἐν ὠλέναισιν, ὡς ὁρᾷς, τάδε
λαβοῦσα τἀριστεῖα, σοῖσι πρὸς δόμοις
ὡς ἂν κρεμασθῇ· σὺ δέ, πάτερ, δέξαι χεροῖν·   1240
γαυρούμενος δὲ τοῖς ἐμοῖς ἀγρεύμασι
κάλει φίλους ἐς δαῖτα· μακάριος γὰρ εἶ,
μακάριος, ἡμῶν τοιάδ' ἐξειργασμένων.

ΚΑ. ὦ πένθος οὐ μετρητὸν, οὐδ' οἷόν τ' ἰδεῖν,
φόνον ταλαίναις χερσὶν ἐξειργασμένων.   1245
καλὸν τὸ θῦμα καταβαλοῦσα δαίμοσιν
ἐπὶ δαῖτα Θήβας τάσδε κἀμὲ παρακαλεῖς.
οἴμοι κακῶν μὲν πρῶτα σῶν, ἔπειτ' ἐμῶν.
ὡς ὁ θεὸς ἡμᾶς ἐνδίκως μέν, ἀλλ' ἄγαν,
Βρόμιος ἄναξ ἀπώλεσ' οἰκεῖος γεγώς.   1250

ΑΓΑ. ὡς δύσκολον τὸ γῆρας ἀνθρώποις ἔφυ
ἔν τ' ὄμμασι σκυθρωπόν. εἴθε παῖς ἐμὸς

---

dere vult, quae praebet infelicem adspectum." W. Dindorf calls the emendation "valde probabilis," without admitting it into the text.

1236. κερκίδας. See Ion 197. 1419. Greek women, who sate at home, (οἰκουρεῖν, ἔνδον καθῆσθαι,) were wont so to employ their time. She here speaks contemptuously of such tame and monotonous occupations.—εἰς μεῖζον Herm. with MS. Pal.

1240. Hermann, who contends that ἂν is used after particles of purpose only when the subjunctive expresses possible contingency, here gives ὡς ἀγκρεμασθῇ. He compares ὡς πασσαλεύσῃ in v. 1214. Even supposing this doctrine could be established as a positive rule, (for it is undoubtedly *generally* true that ὡς is 'in order that it may,' ὡς ἂν 'so as that it may,' &c.,) we cannot rely on the poets, who have metre as well as sense to consult, invariably observing with rigid accuracy distinctions so subtle and minute.

1245. ἐξειργασμένων. The genitive after πένθος, perhaps, as Elmsley thinks, rather than the genitive absolute. He explains πένθος *facinus luctuosum*. That it nearly always signifies *mourning for a death* has been elsewhere observed. 'O woe immense and not to be looked upon, (the deed of women) who' &c.

1246. καλὸν τὸ θῦμα. 'A glorious victim is this which you have laid low for the gods, and now invite the Thebans here and me to the banquet!'

1249. ἄγαν. Either ἄγαν ἐνδίκως means ὑπερδίκως, or some word like ἀναιδῶς, νηλεῶς, must be supplied from the context. Similarly in Prom. 1051, ὡς ὅδ' οὐ πεπλασμένος ὁ κόμπος, ἀλλὰ καὶ λίαν εἰρημένος, it is necessary to understand λίαν ἀληθῶς. — οἰκεῖος γεγὼς means, 'having been born from our family,' viz. his own daughter Semele.

1252. σκυθρωπὸς MS. Pal., which is defensible on the ground that the speaker is thinking of a particular γέρων rather than of γῆρας generally. She cannot yet see why Cadmus should have said ὦ

ΒΑΚΧΑΙ. 473

εὔθηρος εἴη, μητρὸς εἰκασθεὶς τρόποις,
ὅτ' ἐν νεανίαισι Θηβαίοις ἅμα
θηρῶν ὀριγνῷτ'· ἀλλὰ θεομαχεῖν μόνον   1255
οἷός τ' ἐκεῖνος. νουθετητέος, πάτερ,
σοί τ' ἐστὶ κἀμοὶ μὴ σοφοῖς χαίρειν κακοῖς.
ποῦ 'στιν; τίς αὐτὸν δεῦρ' ἂν ὄψιν εἰς ἐμὴν
καλέσειεν, ὡς ἴδῃ με τὴν εὐδαίμονα;
ΚΑ. φεῦ φεῦ· φρονήσασαι μὲν οἷ' ἐδράσατε   1260
ἀλγήσετ' ἄλγος δεινόν· εἰ δὲ διὰ τέλους
ἐν τῷδ' ἀεὶ μενεῖτ', ἐν ᾧ καθέστατε,
οὐκ εὐτυχοῦσαι δόξετ' οὐχὶ δυστυχεῖν.
ΑΓΑ. τί δ' οὐ καλῶς τῶνδ', ἢ τί λυπηρῶς ἔχει;
ΚΑ. πρῶτον μὲν ἐς τόνδ' αἰθέρ' ὄμμα σὸν μέθες. 1265
ΑΓΑ. ἰδού· τί μοι τόνδ' ἐξυπεῖπας εἰσορᾶν;
ΚΑ. ἔθ' αὑτὸς, ἤ σοι μεταβολὰς ἔχειν δοκεῖ;
ΑΓΑ. λαμπρότερος ἢ πρὶν καὶ διιπετέστερος.

πένθος οὐ μετρητὸν κτλ., and she attributes it to the natural moroseness of old age.

1255. ὅτε ὀριγνῷτο is εἴ ποτε, one optative following another by a common kind of attraction. 'I wish my son may be as lucky as his mother, when he goes a-hunting in company with Theban youths.' The optative, even without ἄν, may be used of future time as well as of past, representing, as it properly does, a hypothetical contingency. See on Aesch. Eum. 695, οὐκοῦν δίκαιον τὸν σέβοντ' εὐεργετεῖν, ἄλλως τε πάντως χὤτε δεόμενος τύχοι; where ὅταν τύχῃ would be more usual. Soph. Antig. 666, ὃν πόλις στήσειε, τοῦδε χρὴ κλύειν, i. e. εἴ τινα στήσειε, or ὃν ἂν στήσῃ,—though here we should perhaps read χρῆν κλύειν, in this sense; 'No! rather than ordering others, he ought himself to have shown obedience to whomsoever the city *had set over* him.' That Pentheus' hunting at all is a mere hypothesis, is implied by the optative as well as by the context, ἀλλὰ &c. Photius, ὀριγνηθῆναι, ἀντὶ τοῦ ἐπιθυμῆσαι. Ὀριγνώμεθα, ὀρεγόμεθα. Hesiod, Scut. 190, ἔγχεσιν ἠδ' ἐλάτῃς αὐτοσχεδὸν ὠριγνῶντο. Theocr. xxiv. 44, ἤτοι ὅγ' ὠριγνᾶτο νεοκλώστου τελαμῶνος.—For ἅμα Dindorf admits a useless, and indeed bad, alteration, θαμά. With ἐν νεανίαις

ἅμα compare Ion 717, νυκτιπόλοις ἅμα σὺν νύμφαις.

1257. μὴ σοφοῖς κτλ. 'Not to take pleasure in sophistry which is bad in its results.' This, as before remarked, seems the real moral of the play. Cf. v. 200, οὐδὲν σοφιζόμεσθα τοῖσι δαίμοσι.

1260—1. μὲν—δέ. 'If you become conscious of what you have done, you will be deeply grieved; but, if you remain in your present state of insanity, though not being happy you will seem to be the reverse of unhappy,' because you will be incapable of feeling remorse, and live in a visionary enjoyment. By οὐ δυστυχεῖν the Greeks generally mean μεγάλως εὐτυχεῖν. Here we should rather have looked for μὴ δυστυχεῖν. See *inf.* v. 1348. Andr. 77, and on Hel. 835.

1268. διιπετέστερος, 'brighter.' On this word see Rhes. 43. Why Agave, on coming to her senses, should think the air looked *brighter*, does not appear. It is evident that Cadmus puts the question as a test of her sanity. See Herc. F. 1090. Surely the reply is indicative rather of continued phrenzy. It was one of the peculiar powers of Bacchus to create a sudden supernatural light; see vv. 624. 1083. Hence it seems not improbable, that in v. 1269, (which Aldus gives without an interrogation,) should be read τὸ γὰρ

VOL. II.   3 P

ΚΑ. τὸ δὲ πτοηθὲν τόδ' ἔτι σῇ ψυχῇ πάρα;
ΑΓΑ. οὐκ οἶδα τοὔπος τοῦτο, γίγνομαι δέ πως   1270
    ἔννους, μετασταθεῖσα τῶν πάρος φρενῶν.
ΚΑ. κλύοις ἂν οὖν τι, κἀποκρίναι' ἂν σαφῶς;
ΑΓΑ. ὡς ἐκλέλησμαί γ' ἃ πάρος εἴπομεν, πάτερ.
ΚΑ. ἐς ποῖον ἦλθες οἶκον ὑμεναίων μέτα;
ΑΓΑ. σπαρτῷ μ' ἔδωκας, ὡς λέγουσ', Ἐχίονι.   1275
ΚΑ. τίς οὖν ἐν οἴκοις παῖς ἐγένετο σῷ πόσει;
ΑΓΑ. Πενθεύς, ἐμῇ τε καὶ πατρὸς κοινωνίᾳ.
ΚΑ. τίνος πρόσωπον δῆτ' ἐν ἀγκάλαις ἔχεις;
ΑΓΑ. λέοντος, ὥς γ' ἔφασκον αἱ θηρώμεναι.
ΚΑ. σκέψαι νυν ὀρθῶς, βραχὺς ὁ μόχθος εἰσιδεῖν. 1280
ΑΓΑ. ἔα, τί λεύσσω; τί φέρομαι τόδ' ἐν χεροῖν;
ΚΑ. ἄθρησον αὐτὸ καὶ σαφέστερον μάθε.
ΑΓΑ. ὁρῶ μέγιστον ἄλγος ἡ τάλαιν' ἐγώ.
ΚΑ. μῶν σοι λέοντι φαίνεται προσεικέναι;
ΑΓΑ. οὔκ, ἀλλὰ Πενθέως ἡ τάλαιν' ἔχω κάρα.   1285
ΚΑ. ᾠμωγμένον γε πρόσθεν ἢ σὲ γνωρίσαι.
ΑΓΑ. τίς ἔκτανέν νιν; πῶς ἐμὰς ἦλθ' ἐς χέρας;
ΚΑ. δύστην' ἀλήθει', ὡς ἐν οὐ καιρῷ πάρει.
ΑΓΑ. λέγ', ὡς τὸ μέλλον καρδία πήδημ' ἔχει.

πτοηθὲν τόδ' ἔτι σῇ ψυχῇ πάρα, 'You think so, because you are yet flighty.' To which the answer is very apt: 'I don't know what you mean by *flighty*; but I am becoming conscious,' &c.

1270—1. This distich is remarkable, as occurring in a monostich dialogue, and where there seems no ground to suspect the integrity of the text.

1272. σαφῶς Reiske for σοφῶς. The latter would stand, if it could signify ἐμφρόνως.

1281. φέρομαι. Elmsley proposes φέρομεν. Hermann and Matthiae give the only explanation which the middle will properly bear, *quid hoc reporto?* See however above, v. 279.

1286. ᾠμωγμένον. 'Bewailed (by me) long before *you* recognized it as such.' What Hermann can mean in saying that ᾠμωγμένον can only stand if we read οὐ πρόσθεν, and consequently, in admitting Musgrave's conjecture ᾑμαγμένον, and also in denying that the emphatic σὲ is not here admissible on account of the sense, it appears difficult to divine. Without doubt, the enclitic σε is objectionable on metrical grounds, because, being an enclitic, and therefore virtually part of the preceding word, it forms a spondee before γν. See however Hec. 729.

1287. ἦλθεν χέρας Hermann, on Elmsley's suggestion.

1288. ἐν οὐ καιρῷ. This is more forcible than οὐκ ἐν καιρῷ, which Elmsley thinks would probably have been written had the metre allowed it. With us, 'in an unfit time' is a better phrase than 'not in a fit time.' See on οὐκ ἀπόδειξιν Hipp. 197, and above, v. 455. Cadmus' reluctance to tell her that she is herself the murderess is happily expressed by this verse. He wishes Truth had come at any moment rather than the present, when the shock may retard her recovery from madness.

1289. τὸ μέλλον is the accusative depending on the implied sense of δέδοικα.

ΚΑ. σύ νιν κατέκτας καὶ κασίγνηται σέθεν.   1290
ΑΓΑ. ποῦ δ᾽ ὤλετ᾽ ; ἢ κατ᾽ οἶκον, ἢ ποίοις τόποις ;
ΚΑ. οὗπερ πρὶν Ἀκταίωνα διέλαχον κύνες.
ΑΓΑ. τί δ᾽ ἐς Κιθαιρῶν᾽ ἦλθε δυσδαίμων ὅδε ;
ΚΑ. ἐκερτόμει θεὸν σάς τε βακχείας μολών.
ΑΓΑ. ἡμεῖς δ᾽ ἐκεῖσε τίνι τρόπῳ κατήραμεν ;   1295
ΚΑ. ἐμάνητε, πᾶσά τ᾽ ἐξεβακχεύθη πόλις.
ΑΓΑ. Διόνυσος ἡμᾶς ὤλεσ᾽· ἄρτι μανθάνω.
ΚΑ. ὕβριν γ᾽ ὑβρισθείς. θεὸν γὰρ οὐχ ἡγεῖσθέ νιν.
ΑΓΑ. τὸ φίλτατον δὲ σῶμα ποῦ παιδὸς, πάτερ ;
ΚΑ. ἐγὼ μόλις τόδ᾽ ἐξερευνήσας φέρω.   1300
ΑΓΑ. ἦ πᾶν ἐν ἄρθροις συγκεκλημένον καλῶς ;
ΚΑ.   *   *   *   *
ΑΓΑ. Πενθεῖ δὲ τί μέρος ἀφροσύνης προσῆκ᾽ ἐμῆς ;
ΚΑ. ὑμῖν ἐγένεθ᾽ ὅμοιος, οὐ σέβων θεόν.
     τοιγὰρ ξυνῆψε πάντας ἐς μίαν βλάβην,
     ὑμᾶς τε τόνδε θ᾽, ὥστε διολέσαι δόμους   1305
     κἄμ᾽, ὅστις ἄτεκνος ἀρσένων παίδων γεγὼς
     τῆς σῆς τόδ᾽ ἔρνος, ὦ τάλαινα, νηδύος
     αἴσχιστα καὶ κάκιστα κατθανόνθ᾽ ὁρῶ,
     ᾧ δῶμ᾽ ἀνέβλεφ᾽, ὃς συνεῖχες, ὦ τέκνον,

There is a very similar passage in Aesch. Suppl. 560, χλωρῷ δείματι θυμὸν πάλλοντ᾽ ὄψιν ἀήθη, 'were agitated with fear at the unwonted sight.'

1295. καταίρειν, like ἀπαίρειν, is intransitively used for ἰέναι, with the usual idea of going *down* into the country from the city.

1298. ὕβριν γ᾽ Matthiae for ὕβριν. Hermann thinks ὑμῖν may have been the true reading. Perhaps also ὕβρισμ᾽. In Suppl. 495, for οὓς ὕβρις ἀπώλεσεν, Porson proposes ὕβρισμ᾽. The γε however here is called for by the sense.

1301. After this verse Matthiae first pointed out, what seems self-evident, that at least one verse has been lost. Elmsley however says, "mihi non liquet," and prints the passage as if entire. But in fact the two distinct questions, 'Are the mangled limbs decently put together ?'— 'What share had Pentheus in *my* folly ?' manifestly imply some intervening answer. Indeed, it is probable that several lines are here lost : for the second question, as it now stands, is neither clear in itself, nor in any way connected with what precedes, unless it be referred to θεὸν γὰρ οὐχ ἡγεῖσθέ νιν, v. 1298. Compare v. 26, ἐπεί μ᾽ ἀδελφαὶ μητρὸς, ἃς ἥκιστ᾽ ἐχρῆν, Διόνυσον οὐκ ἔφασκον ἐκφῦναι Διός. Matthiae gives reasons for supposing that this passage was originally considerably longer. Elmsley refers the several references to verses not now found in the play, to the lacuna after v. 1330.

1307. ἔρνος. Compare ἕλικα νεότομον, v. 1171. Aesch. Eum. 635, οὐδ᾽ ἐν σκότοισι νηδύος τεθραμμένη, ἀλλ᾽ οἷον ἔρνος οὔτις ἂν τέκοι θεός. For the masculine participle in the next verse Elmsley well compares Troad. 735, ὦ περισσὰ τιμηθεὶς τέκνον. The ὅστις gives the reason why he may be said διολωλέναι, though yet alive.

1309. ᾧ δῶμ᾽ ἀνέβλεφ᾽, though the dative appears somewhat anomalous, is closely like our idiom, 'to whom the

476   ΕΥΡΙΠΙΔΟΥ

τοὐμὸν μέλαθρον, παιδὸς ἐξ ἐμῆς γεγώς,   1310
πόλει τε τάρβος ἦσθα· τὸν γέροντα δὲ
οὐδεὶς ὑβρίζειν ἤθελ᾽, εἰσορῶν τὸ σὸν
κάρα· δίκην γὰρ ἀξίαν ἐλάμβανεν.
νῦν δ᾽ ἐκ δόμων ἄτιμος ἐκβεβλήσομαι
ὁ Κάδμος ὁ μέγας, ὃς τὸ Θηβαίων γένος   1315
ἔσπειρα, κἀξήμησα κάλλιστον θέρος.
ὦ φίλτατ᾽ ἀνδρῶν, καὶ γὰρ οὐκέτ᾽ ὢν ὅμως
τῶν φιλτάτων ἔμοιγ᾽ ἀριθμήσει τέκνων,
οὐκέτι γενείου τοῦδε θιγγάνων χερὶ
τὸν μητρὸς αὐδῶν πατέρα προσπτύξει, τέκνον,   1320
λέγων, τίς ἀδικεῖ, τίς σ᾽ ἀτιμάζει, γέρον,
τίς σὴν ταράσσει καρδίαν λυπηρὸς ὤν;
λέγ᾽, ὡς κολάζω τὸν ἀδικοῦντά σ᾽, ὦ πάτερ.
νῦν δ᾽ ἄθλιος μέν εἰμ᾽ ἐγώ, τλήμων δὲ σύ,
οἰκτρὰ δὲ μήτηρ, τλήμονες δὲ σύγγονοι.   1325
εἰ δ᾽ ἔστιν ὅστις δαιμόνων ὑπερφρονεῖ,
ἐς τοῦδ᾽ ἀθρήσας θάνατον ἡγείσθω θεούς.

ΧΟ. τὸ σὸν μὲν ἀλγῶ, Κάδμε· σὸς δ᾽ ἔχει δίκην

house looked up.' The Palatine MS. has ὃν superscribed as a variant. In Suppl. 322, whatever Hermann may object, τοῖς κερτομοῦσι γοργὸν ἀναβλέπει seems to mean 'looks up sternly in the face of her accusers.' In Ion 1467, ἀελίου ἀναβλέπειν λαμπάσιν also is best explained 'looks up to the light of the sun.' The old reading ἀνέβλεπεν is retained by Matthiae and Hermann, on the ground that a vowel is occasionally made short before βλ. Elmsley reads ἀνέβλεπ᾽, but he should have adopted the aspirate. Dindorf compares ἔλιφ᾽ in Orest. 63.—συνεῖχες, continebas, 'kept up,' 'supported.' Cf. v. 391. Iph. T. 57, στῦλοι γὰρ οἴκων εἰσὶ παῖδες ἄρσενες.

1313. ἐλάμβανεν. "Formula rhetorica, sumens fieri, vel factum esse, quod certa conditione futurum esse dicendum erat." Hermann. See on Troad. 397. Closely resembling this is Plat. Symp. p. 190, C., οὔτε ὅπως ἀποκτείναιεν εἶχον καὶ ὥσπερ τοὺς γίγαντας κεραυνώσαντες τὸ γένος ἀφανίσαιεν—αἱ τιμαὶ γὰρ αὐτοῖς καὶ ἱερὰ τὰ παρὰ τῶν ἀνθρώπων ἠφανίζετο,—οὔθ᾽ ὅπως ἐῶεν ἀσελγαίνειν. It is not, perhaps, necessary here to understand either ἐλάμβανεν ἂν or λαβεῖν ἔμελλεν, since the actual results of a former experience may be meant; 'no one cared to insult Cadmus; for (whenever he did so) he used to get his deserts.' Elmsley remarks, both here and on Heracl. 852, on the interchange of δίκην δοῦναι and δίκην λαβεῖν.

1320. τὸν μητρὸς πατέρα. Cf. v. 43, Κάδμος μὲν οὖν γέρας τε καὶ τυραννίδα Πενθεῖ δίδωσι, θυγατρὸς ἐκπεφυκότι. Inf. 1328, σὸς παῖς παιδός, where Elmsley defends σὸς against the obvious correction σῆς, on the ground that παῖς παιδὸς is generally used by Euripides as one word. Cf. Androm. 584. 1073. 1083. In these two verses the true office of a chorus, to assuage, alleviate, and console, is well shown. It was their natural impulse to exult at the death of Pentheus; and exult they did, v. 1154 seqq. Now however, when they see the grief of Cadmus and the penitence of Agave, they hesitate not to express their sympathy, and to say, that though Pentheus deserved his fate, they are sorry for it on Cadmus' account.

ΒΑΚΧΑΙ. 477

παῖς παιδὸς ἀξίαν μὲν, ἀλγεινὴν δὲ σοί.
ΑΓΑ. ὦ πάτερ, ὁρᾷς γὰρ τἄμ' ὅσῳ μετεστράφη, 1330
*
ΔΙ. *
δράκων γενήσει μεταβαλὼν, δάμαρ τε σὴ
ἐκθηριωθεῖσ' ὄφεος ἀλλάξει τύπον,
ἣν Ἄρεος ἔσχες Ἁρμονίαν, θνητὸς γεγώς.
ὄχον δὲ μόσχων, χρησμὸς ὡς λέγει Διὸς,
ἐλᾷς μετ' ἀλόχου, βαρβάρων ἡγούμενος.
πολλὰς δὲ πέρσεις ἀναρίθμῳ στρατεύματι 1325
πόλεις· ὅταν δὲ Λοξίου χρηστήριον
διαρπάσωσι, νόστον ἄθλιον πάλιν
σχήσουσι· σὲ δ' Ἄρης Ἁρμονίαν τε ῥύσεται,

1330. There can be no doubt that a number of verses have been lost. One is quoted as from the *Bacchae* by the schol. on Ar. Plut. 908; and two others are supposed by Porson to have been borrowed from this part of the play by the author of *Christus Patiens*, 1309—10. Agave must here have spoken a θρῆνος of some length over the remains of her son; and indeed, it is expressly recorded that she did so by the rhetorician Apsines (circ. A.D. 235), whose words are cited by Elmsley; τοῦτον τὸν τρόπον κεκίνηκεν Εὐριπίδης οἶκτον ἐπὶ τῷ Πένθει κινῆσαι βουλόμενος. ἕκαστον γὰρ αὐτοῦ τῶν μελῶν ἡ μήτηρ ἐν ταῖς χερσὶ κρατοῦσα, καθ' ἕκαστον αὐτῶν οἰκτίζεται. It was therefore like the fine address of Hecuba over the mangled body of Astyanax in Troad. 1156. If we compare the speech of the θεὸς ἀπὸ μηχανῆς at the conclusion of the *Ion*, the *Helena*, the *Electra*, and the *Andromache*, (not to mention other plays,) we shall form a fair judgment of the length to which the speech of Dionysus probably extended, i. e. to from forty to fifty verses, of which fourteen only now remain; and of these the first was recovered by Matthiae from an inedited Scholium on Dionysius Periegetes, v. 391, where it is cited in connexion with the two following; Ἰστέον δὲ, ὅτι Κάδμος καὶ Ἁρμονία ἡ γαμετὴ μετεμορφώθησαν εἰς θηρία, ἐπειδὴ τοῦ Ἄρεος ὄφιν ἐφόνευσεν ὁ Κάδμος, ὃς τοὺς ἑταίρους αὐτοῦ ἀνεῖλεν, Ἔριφον καὶ Δηϊλέοντα, ὡς καὶ Εὐριπίδης ἐν Βάκχαις φησὶ περὶ Κάδμου, Δράκων γενήσῃ μεταβαλὼν, δάμαρ τε σὴ κτλ.

1332. ἀλλάξει. See on v. 4.

1333. Ἁρμονίαν. Apollodor. iii. 4, 2, Κάδμος δὲ, ἀνθ' ὧν ἔκτεινεν (viz. the armed men who sprung from the sown teeth of the dragon), ἀΐδιον ἐνιαυτὸν ἐθήτευσεν Ἄρει,— μετὰ δὲ τὴν θητείαν Ἀθηνᾶ αὐτῷ βασιλείαν κατεσκεύασε, Ζεὺς ἔδωκεν αὐτῷ γυναῖκα Ἁρμονίαν, Ἀφροδίτης καὶ Ἄρεος θυγατέρα, καὶ πάντες θεοὶ, καταλιπόντες τὸν οὐρανὸν, ἐν τῇ Καδμείᾳ τὸν γάμον εὐωχούμενοι ἀνύμνησαν. Ibid. iii. 5, 4, Ὁ δὲ Κάδμος μετὰ Ἁρμονίας Θήβας ἐκλιπὼν, πρὸς Ἐγχελέας παραγίνεται. Τούτοις δὲ ὑπὸ Ἰλλυριῶν πολεμουμένοις ὁ θεὸς ἔχρησεν Ἰλλυριῶν κρατήσειν, ἐὰν ἡγεμόνα Κάδμον καὶ Ἁρμονίαν ἔχωσιν. Οἱ δὲ πεισθέντες ποιοῦνται κατὰ Ἰλλυριῶν ἡγεμόνας τούτους, καὶ κρατοῦσι. Καὶ βασιλεύει Κάδμος Ἰλλυριῶν, καὶ παῖς Ἰλλύριος αὐτῷ γίνεται. Αὖθις δὲ μετὰ Ἁρμονίας εἰς δράκοντα μεταβαλὼν, εἰς Ἠλύσιον πεδίον ὑπὸ Διὸς ἐξεπέμφθησαν. Compare with this statement v. 1339, and the use of μεταβαλὼν intransitively in both writers. It is therefore probable that Apollodorus had this passage in view; and if so, the expedition of Cadmus against the Illyrians was part of the prediction of Dionysus. And this, in fact, is doubtless the meaning of βαρβάρων ἡγούμενος, leading the Ἐγχελεῖς against the Illyrians, v. 1334.

1338. σχήσουσι. Scil. οἱ Ἐγχελεῖς. The common belief was, that a disastrous return was the inevitable penalty of sacrilege committed by a victorious army in a conquered land. Hence it was that the Grecian fleet met with so many mishaps in their return from Troy. Compare Troad. 69—86. Aesch. Ag. 329 seqq. εἰ δ' εὐ-

μακάρων τ' ἐς αἶαν σὸν καθιδρύσει βίον.
ταῦτ' οὐχὶ θνητοῦ πατρὸς ἐκγεγὼς λέγω   1340
Διόνυσος, ἀλλὰ Ζηνός· εἰ δὲ σωφρονεῖν
ἔγνωθ', ὅτ' οὐκ ἠθέλετε, τὸν Διὸς γόνον
εὐδαιμονεῖτ' ἂν σύμμαχον κεκτημένοι.
ΑΓΑ. Διόνυσε, λισσόμεσθά σ', ἠδικήκαμεν.
ΔΙ. ὄψ' ἐμάθεθ' ἡμᾶς, ὅτε δ' ἐχρῆν, οὐκ ᾔδετε.   1345
ΑΓΑ. ἐγνώκαμεν ταῦτ'· ἀλλ' ἐπεξέρχει λίαν.
ΔΙ. καὶ γὰρ πρὸς ὑμῶν, θεὸς γεγώς, ὑβριζόμην.
ΑΓΑ. ὀργὰς πρέπει θεοὺς οὐχ ὁμοιοῦσθαι βροτοῖς.
ΔΙ. πάλαι τάδε Ζεὺς οὑμὸς ἐπένευσεν πατήρ.
ΑΓΑ. αἰαῖ, δέδοκται, πρέσβυ, τλήμονες φυγαί.   1350
ΔΙ. τί δῆτα μέλλεθ' ἅπερ ἀναγκαίως ἔχει;
ΚΑ. ὦ τέκνον, ὡς ἐς δεινὸν ἤλθομεν κακόν,
[σύ θ' ἡ τάλαινα σύγγονοί τε σαὶ *]

σεβοῦσι τοὺς πολισσούχους θεοὺς τοὺς τῆς ἀλούσης γῆς, θεῶν θ' ἱδρύματα, οὐτἂν ἑλόντες αὖθις ἀνθαλοῖεν ἄν. Musgrave quotes an important passage from Herod. ix. 42, ἔστι λόγιον (Mardonius is speaking), ὡς χρεών ἐστι Πέρσας ἀπικομένους ἐς τὴν Ἑλλάδα διαρπάσαι τὸ ἱρὸν τὸ ἐν Δελφοῖσι, μετὰ δὲ τὴν διαρπαγὴν ἀπολέσθαι πάντας.—τοῦτον δ' ἔγωγε τὸν χρησμὸν (adds the Historian), τὸν Μαρδόνιος εἶπε ἐς Πέρσας ἔχειν, ἐς Ἰλλυριούς τε καὶ τὸν Ἐγχελέων στρατὸν οἶδα πεποιημένον, καὶ οὐκ ἐς Πέρσας.

1343. εὐδαιμονεῖτ' ἄν, 'you would be happy (which now you are not).' Hermann is clearly right in adopting this emendation of Musgrave's. It had also been made many years ago by the present editor; and it is necessary to the sense; for, as Hermann remarks, εὐδαιμονοῖτ' ἄν, which is the old reading, retained by Matthiae, Elmsley, Dindorf, and Bothe, would mean, 'you may possibly be happy even yet.' But Dionysus speaks in reference to the death of Pentheus.

1345. ᾔδετε for the more usual ᾔδειτε seems recognised in Bekker's Anecdota, p. 98, (quoted by Elmsley,) ᾔδεται· Εὐριπίδης Βάκχαις, (αι and ε are constantly confused.) The Palatine MS. has εἴδετε, which does not seem a bad reading. In Oed. R. 1232, W. Dindorf edits λείπει μὲν οὐδ' ἃ πρόσθεν ᾔδεμεν τὸ μὴ οὐ βαρύστον' εἶναι.

1348. πρέπει—οὐκ is a common Greek hyperbaton for οὐ πρέπει. See on Hel.

835. Otherwise, if the οὐ directly negatived the infinitive, it should be μή. Compare χρῆν μὲν οὔ σ' ἁμαρτάνειν, Hipp. 507. δόξει· οὐχὶ δυστυχεῖν sup. v. 1263. This verse, with v. 1346 and 1344, were assigned by Elmsley to Agave instead of to Cadmus.

1350. φυγαί. Elmsley thinks this an *aposiopesis*, and supplies μένουσιν ἡμᾶς. Rather it appears to be an instance of the *schema Pindaricum*, for which see Ion 1146, ἐνῆν δ' ὑφανταὶ γράμμασιν τοιαίδ' ὑφαί. The next verse was restored by Elmsley from the Palatine MS., where it alone occurs.—μέλλετε, scil. δρᾶν.

1353. Elmsley, while he observes that the passage as it now stands is ἀνακόλουθος, adds, "nulla tamen mendi suspicio." The loss of a word in this verse is supplied in the Aldine edition by φίλαι at the end. Hermann thinks σύ θ' ἡ τάλαινα παῖς τε κτλ., is nearer the original. We might also read ἐγὼ σύ θ' ἡ τάλαινα, κτλ.; but perhaps the verse is spurious, and there has been a loss of several lines. Otherwise ἐγὼ δ', not ἐγώ θ', should come next. What follows is so difficult, that one cannot help thinking the interpretation must have depended in great measure on something preceding. It is clear that he should have either said ἔτι δέ μοι θέσφατόν ἐστι, or ἔτι δέ μοι τὸ θέσφατον λέγει, viz. the oracle or prediction in v. 1331 seqq. But, even if this were right, or supposing the poet to have written ὡς τὸ θέσφατον λέγει, εἰς Ἑλλάδ' ἀγαγών κτλ., (for Her-

ἐγώ θ' ὁ τλήμων βαρβάρους ἀφίξομαι
γέρων μέτοικος· ἔτι δέ μοι τὸ θέσφατον
εἰς Ἑλλάδ' ἀγαγεῖν μιγάδα βάρβαρον στρατόν.   1355
καὶ τὴν Ἄρεως παῖδ' Ἁρμονίαν, δάμαρτ' ἐμὴν,
δράκων δρακαίνης φύσιν ἔχουσαν ἀγρίαν,
ἄξω 'πὶ βωμοὺς καὶ τάφους Ἑλληνικοὺς
ἡγούμενος λόγχαισιν, οὐδὲ παύσομαι
κακῶν ὁ τλήμων, οὐδὲ τὸν καταιβάτην   1360
Ἀχέροντα πλεύσας ἥσυχος γενήσομαι.
ΑΓΑ. ὦ πάτερ, ἐγὼ δὲ σοῦ στερεῖσα φεύξομαι.
ΚΑ. τί μ' ἀμφιβάλλεις χερσὶν, ὦ τάλαινα παῖ,
ὄρνιν ὅπως κηφῆνα πολιόχρως κύκνος;
ΑΓΑ. ποῖ γὰρ τράπωμαι, πατρίδος ἐκβεβλημένη;   1365
ΚΑ. οὐκ οἶδα, τέκνον· σμικρὸς ἐπίκουρος πατήρ.
ΑΓΑ. χαῖρ', ὦ μέλαθρον, χαῖρ', ὦ πατρῷα   στρ.
πόλις· ἐκλείπω σ' ἐπὶ δυστυχίᾳ
φυγὰς ἐκ θαλάμων.
ΚΑ. στεῖχέ νυν, ὦ παῖ, τὸν Ἀρισταίου   1370
    *   *   *

mann's ὅτι δέ μοι τὸ θέσφατον, *qualecunque hoc mihi datum est oraculum,* cannot for a moment be maintained,) how are we to account for Cadmus repeating the very same prediction, that he should lead an army against the Illyrians, and that he and his wife should be changed into serpents? Still more, how shall we reconcile v. 1360 with v. 1339? The one sends him to the isles of the blest, the other makes him an unquiet daemon in Hades. And what are we to understand by his conducting his serpent-wife to the altars and tombs of the Hellenes? On all these points the commentators are silent. To point out the difficulty may be of service, even where no explanation is offered.

1364. ὄρνιν κηφῆνα, the decrepit bird, its parent. The old reading ὄρνις is altered to ὄρνιν on the suggestion of Elmsley. This removes every difficulty; for κηφῆν occurs in Troad. 191 in the same sense, γραῦς, ὡς κηφήν, δειλαία νεκροῦ μορφά. Hes. Opp. 302, κηφήνεσσι κοθούροις εἴκελος ὀργήν, οἵ τε μελισσάων κάματον τρύχουσιν ἀεργοὶ ἔσθοντες. Hermann, who objects to πολιόχρως unless applied to an *aged* bird, thinks that we should further read πολιόχρων κύκνον. Still the sentiment is rather bare, 'why do you embrace me like an aged swan?' It is much less feeble to ask, 'Why do you embrace me as a swan embraces his aged sire?' The solution of the difficulty which he adopts involves an awkward *hyperbaton* of the words, τί με ἀμφιβάλλεις, κηφῆνα ὄντα, ὡς κύκνος, ὄρνις πολιόχρως. On the supposed piety of the swan (perhaps confounded with that of the stork, from the similarity of its habits and appearance), Musgrave compares Soph. El. 1058, τί τοὺς ἄνωθεν φρονιμωτάτους οἰωνοὺς ἐσορώμενοι τροφᾶς κηδομένους ἀφ' ὧν τε βλάστωσιν ἀφ' ὧν τ' ὄνασιν εὕρωσι, κτλ., though it does not appear certain that the swan is there specifically meant. See also Eur. El. 151—5.

1366. Compare Iph. A. 1241.
1367. On the short ῳ in πατρῷος see Alcest. 249. Elmsley reads χαῖρε πατρῴα or χαῖρ' ὦ πατρία.
1368. ἐπὶ δυστυχίᾳ, in a time of trouble; on an occasion of misfortune. See Rhes. 649. Heracl. 291.
1370. A verse has been lost after this, as Hermann has pointed out, not only from the antithetical character of these lines, but because the ellipse of δόμον or

ΑΓΑ. στένομαί σε, πάτερ.
ΚΑ. κἀγὼ σὲ, τέκνον,
καὶ σὰς ἐδάκρυσα κασιγνήτας.
ΑΓΑ. δεινῶς γάρτοι τάνδ᾽ αἰκίαν   ἀντ.
Διόνυσος ἄναξ τοὺς σοὺς * εἰς
οἴκους ἔφερεν.   1375
ΚΑ. καὶ γὰρ ἔπασχεν δεινὰ πρὸς ὑμῶν,
ἀγέραστον ἔχων ὄνομ᾽ ἐν Θήβαις.
ΑΓΑ. χαῖρε, πάτερ, μοι.
ΚΑ. χαῖρ᾽, ὦ μελέα
θύγατερ. χαλεπῶς δ᾽ εἰς τόδ᾽ ἂν ἥκοις. 1380
ΑΓΑ. ἄγετ᾽ ὦ πομποί με, κασιγνήτας
ἵνα συμφυγάδας ληψόμεθ᾽ οἰκτράς.
ἔλθοιμι δ᾽ ὅπου
μήτε Κιθαιρὼν μιαρός *μ᾽ ἐσίδοι
μήτε Κιθαιρῶν᾽ ὄσσοισιν ἐγώ,   1385
μήθ᾽ ὅθι θύρσου μνῆμ᾽ ἀνάκειται·
βάκχαις δ᾽ ἄλλαισι μέλοιεν.
ΧΟ. πολλαὶ μορφαὶ τῶν δαιμονίων,
πολλὰ δ᾽ ἀέλπτως κραίνουσι θεοί,
καὶ τὰ δοκηθέντ᾽ οὐκ ἐτελέσθη,   1390
τῶν δ᾽ ἀδοκήτων πόρον ηὗρε θεός.
τοιόνδ᾽ ἀπέβη τόδε πρᾶγμα.

οἶκον, where the masculine article is added, seems without example. Aristeas or Aristaeus had married Autonoë the daughter of Cadmus, *sup.* v. 1227.

1373. γάρτοι Hermann for γάρ. Aldus has δεινῶς γὰρ δεινῶς κτλ., whence Elmsley gives δεινῶς, δεινῶς τάνδ᾽ αἴκειαν. In the latter word he appears to be wrong, as the ι in αἰκία is unquestionably long. In the next verse a syllable is wanting. Perhaps, ἤδη τοὺς σοὺς οἴκους ἔφερεν, or εἰς ἡμετέρους οἴκους κτλ.

1376. ἔπασχεν. So Hermann, who gives the verse to Cadmus instead of to Dionysus, for ἔπασχον. The god, he truly observes, has long ago performed his part, and left the stage.

1380. The δέ was inserted by Reiske. Aldus has καὶ σύ γε θύγατερ, which may indicate a var. lect. καὶ σύ γε χαῖρ᾽, ὦ θύγατερ.—εἰς τόδε, scil. εἰς τὸ χαίρειν.

1384. μ᾽ ἐσίδοι was inserted by Brunck from conjecture, and is admitted by Herm. Elmsl. Dind. and Matth. Here is another instance, and a very idiomatic one, of the Attic attraction of optatives: ἔλθοιμι ὅπου μὴ ἐσίδοιμι κτλ., *eam, ubi non videam,* or *videre contingat.* In fact, the clause with ὅπου is an integral part of the wish.

1388. Hermann's note on these concluding anapaestics is deserving of attention:—" Qui factum sit, ut Euripides quinque fabulas iisdem versibus finierit, non memini me a quoquam interpretum indicatum legisse. Scilicet, ut fit in theatris, ubi actorum partes ad finem deductae essent, tantus erat surgentium atque abeuntium strepitus, ut quae chorus in exitu fabulae recitare solebat, vix exaudiri possent. Eo factum, ut illis chori versibus parum curae impenderetur."

ΕΥΡΙΠΙΔΟΥ ΕΚΑΒΗ.

ΥΠΟΘΕΣΙΣ.

Μετὰ τὴν Τροίας ἅλωσιν ἄραντες οἱ Ἕλληνες καθωρμίσθησαν ἐν τῇ ἀντιπέραν Χερρονήσῳ τῆς Θρᾴκης, ἧς Πολυμήστωρ ἦρχεν· οὗ δὴ καὶ κενοτάφιον ἔχωσαν Ἀχιλλεῖ, ἐν Τροίᾳ ταφέντι. διατρίψαντες δὲ ἐκεῖ ἡμέρας δή τινας, ἐφ᾽ ᾧ τὰ αὐτῶν εὖ διαθήσονται, ἐπεὶ ἀναχθήσεσθαι ἔμελλον, φανὲν τὸ τοῦ Ἀχιλλέως εἴδωλον ἐπὶ τοῦ τάφου ἐπέσχε τοὺς Ἀχαιοὺς τῆς ἀναγωγῆς, αἰτοῦν γέρας αὐτῷ δοθῆναι τὴν παῖδα Πριάμου Πολυξένην, τὴν καὶ πρότερον κατεγγυηθεῖσαν αὐτῷ ὑπὸ τοῦ πατρός, δι᾽ ἣν καὶ ὑπὸ Πάριδος καὶ Δηιφόβου τοξευθεὶς ὅλωλεν, ὅτε τὰς ἐγγύας πρὸς τοῦτον πληροῦν ἔμελλε Πρίαμος. Ἕλληνες μὲν οὖν, ὧν εὖ ἔπαθον ὑπ᾽ αὐτοῦ μεμνημένοι καὶ τιμῶντες τὴν ἀρετὴν τοῦ ἀνδρός, ἐψηφίσαντο σφάξαι τὴν Πολυξένην ἐπὶ τῷ τάφῳ τοῦ ἥρωος. ἔπεμψαν δὲ τὸν Λαέρτου Ὀδυσσέα πρὸς τὴν μητέρα αὐτῆς Ἑκάβην, ὡς ἂν τήν τε παρθένον λάβῃ καὶ τῷ ποικίλῳ τῶν λόγων, τοιοῦτος γὰρ ἦν ὁ ἀνήρ, πείσῃ Ἑκάβην μὴ δυσχερῶς σχεῖν ἐπὶ τῇ τῆς παιδὸς ἀφαιρέσει. ἐλθὼν οὖν Ὀδυσσεὺς τήν τε κόρην συναιρομένην εὗρεν αὐτῷ τῆς σπουδῆς καὶ πείθουσαν τὴν μητέρα, ὡς τεθνήξεσθαι μᾶλλον αὐτῇ προσῆκον ἢ τὸ ζῆν παρ᾽ ἀξίαν. σφαγείσης δὲ τῆς παρθένου, Ἑκάβη θεράπαιναν αὐτῆς ἔπεμψε παρὰ τὰς ἀκτάς, ἐφ᾽ ᾧ ὕδωρ ἐκεῖθεν κομίσαι πρὸς λουτρὸν Πολυξένης. εὗρε δὲ Πολύδωρον ἐκεῖ κείμενον· ἁλοῦσαν γὰρ ὡς ἔγνω τὴν Τροίαν Πολυμήστωρ, σφάξας αὐτὸν ἔρριψεν εἰς τὴν θάλασσαν, ὡς ἂν αὐτὸς ἔχῃ τὸν χρυσὸν ὃν πρὸς αὐτὸν μετὰ τοῦ παιδὸς Πολυδώρου πρῴην Πρίαμος ἔπεμψε λάθρα, ἐπειδὴ ἑώρα τὸ Ἴλιον πρὸς κίνδυνον ἤδη χωροῦν. ἦν δὲ ὁ χρυσὸς οὗτος πολὺς ἄγαν καὶ ἱκανὸς ὀρθῶσαι καὶ αὖθις τὸ γένος τοῦ Πριάμου. ὡς οὖν τοῦτον εὗρεν ἡ δούλη κείμενον ἐπ᾽ ἀκταῖς, ἀνελομένη καὶ τῷ πέπλῳ εἰλίξασα κομίζει πρὸς τὴν Ἑκάβην. καὶ ἣ τὸν τῆς Πολυξένης νεκρόν, πρὶν ἐκκεκαλύφθαι τοῦτον, εἶναι νομίσασα, ἐπειδὴ ἔγνω Πολύδωρον, ἀθλίως τε ἔσχε καὶ ὅπως ἀμυνεῖται Πολυμήστορα μηχανᾶται τοιόνδε· κοινωσαμένη πρότερον τὴν περὶ τούτου γνώμην Ἀγαμέμνονι, πέμπει τὴν αὐτῆς δούλην ὡς Πολυμήστορα, αὐτόν τε καὶ τὰ τέκνα πρὸς ἑαυτὴν μετακαλουμένη περί τινος ἀναγκαίου πρὸς αὐτὸν κοινώσασθαι. οὗτος μὲν οὖν ἀγνοῶν ὅτι Πολύδωρος εὕρηται παρὰ τὰς ἀκτὰς, καὶ ἅμα καί τισιν ὑποκλαπεὶς μετὰ τῶν παίδων πρὸς αὐτὴν ἀφικνεῖται. Ἑκάβη δὲ πρὸς αὐτὸν τούτου χάριν ἔφη κεκληκέναι, ἵνα χρυσοῦ θησαυροὺς κεκρυμμένους ὑπ' αὐτῆς ἐν Ἰλίῳ μηνύσῃ. εἰσάγει δὲ καὶ τῆς σκηνῆς ἔνδον εἰποῦσα ὡς ἂν καὶ ἕτερ' ἄττα αὐτῷ δώσει χρήματα, μεθ' ὧν ἐξῆλθε τῆς Τροίας. ἐκέκρυπτο δὲ εἴσω πλεῖστος γυναικῶν ὄχλος· σὺν αἷς τοῦτον εἰσελθόντα Ἑκάβη ὀφθαλμῶν τε στερεῖ καὶ τὰ τέκνα αὐτοῦ ἀποσφάττει. δικάσαντος δὲ αὐτοὺς τοῦ Ἀγαμέμνονος ὕστερον, καὶ τοῦ Πολυμήστορος πολλὰ περὶ τῆς σφαγῆς Πολυδώρου διαπλασαμένου, Ἑκάβη περιεγένετο ἐλέγξασα αὐτὸν ὡς τοῦ χρυσοῦ χάριν καὶ οὐχ ὧν προύτεινε τὸν παῖδα ἀνεῖλε, σύμψηφον σχοῦσα καὶ Ἀγαμέμνονα.

Ἡ μὲν σκηνὴ τοῦ δράματος ὑπόκειται ἐν τῇ ἀντιπέραν τῆς Θράκης Χερρονήσῳ· ὁ δὲ χορὸς συνέστηκεν ἐκ γυναικῶν αἰχμαλωτίδων Τρῳάδων συμμαχησουσῶν τῇ Ἑκάβῃ.

HECUBA.

THAT the *Hecuba* is one of the most popular of the Greek tragedies, cannot be doubted; but that it is also one of the best, cannot perhaps justly be conceded. It has been objected by Hermann [1] and others, as a fault in the composition, that the play really has a double plot, that is, it involves two distinct tragic incidents, the self-devotion and sacrifice of Polyxena, and the crime and punishment of the Thracian king Polymestor, each of which is wholly unconnected with the other. The former part of the drama he admits to be, on the whole, well and touchingly told; of the latter he remarks, "Si verum dicendum est, hanc quae est tragoedia, inseruit alii, quae vocaretur tragoedia, sed praeter nomen et versus admodum nihil habet tragoediae." Nor does A. Von Schlegel [2] give a more flattering estimate of this concluding part, which he describes as "filled up with the vindictive cunning of Hecuba, the stupid avarice of Polymestor, and the miserable policy of Agamemnon, who dares not himself call the Thracian king to account, but plays him into the hands of the captive women."

The motive, however, in the poet's mind, is evident enough; and that, in fact, is all that we really have to do with. He wished to throw an overwhelming load of grief and suffering on Hecuba, the captive queen of Troy; and for this end, he represents the death of two of her children as occurring at nearly the same time, though by different causes and in different places. Both events are announced, according to the usual custom of Euripides, in the prologue; and Hecuba herself, in the opening monody, adds that she has been warned by a vision and an ominous dream that some misfortune is impending over both her children; which vision, as distinct from the other, is the ghost of the murdered Polydorus himself. So far therefore Euripides made a fair use of a complex or double plot, (somewhat after the method he has adopted in the *Andromache*,) because his leading idea was not the sufferings either of this or that child of Hecuba, but the weight of accumulated woe which fell on Hecuba herself.

[1] Praefat. ad Hec. p. xv. (ed. 1831.)   [2] Theatre of the Greeks, p. 246.

In respect of historical sequence, the plot of the *Hecuba* immediately precedes the *Troades;* for in the prologue of the latter play, Poseidon, speaking of Hecuba, says (v. 39),

$$ἣ παῖς μὲν ἀμφὶ μνῆμ' Ἀχιλλείου τάφου$$
$$λάθρα τέθνηκε τλημόνως Πολυξένη,$$

while that very event is the subject of the present drama. The Grecian army, having razed Troy, and divided the spoils, are on their homeward voyage, when contrary winds detain them at the Thracian Chersonese. Having been warned by the ghost of Achilles, (who, it will be remembered, was buried at Sigeum, and was also worshipped as a $δαίμων \ ἐπιχώριος$ in the neighbouring shore of Leuce Acte [3], which will account for his supernatural appearance in the vicinity of Troy,) that his shade must, ere they depart hence, be appeased by the blood of one of the Trojan captives, a dispute arises in the council of the Greeks, in which, contrary to the wish of Agamemnon, it is resolved to offer Polyxena, as the fittest victim to honour the noblest of the Achaean host. Of this decision Hecuba is first informed by the chorus, who urge her to petition the commander-in-chief for a remission of the cruel decree. Polyxena herself, being apprised of her imminent danger by her mother, gives vent to lamentations for her own and her mother's fate; and Ulysses, who has persuaded the army to sacrifice her, arrives to claim the victim. Hecuba endeavours to soften his heart by reminding him of the former favours she had conferred upon him; and points out that Helen is a much more fitting person to be chosen. Ulysses however has pledged his word, and dwells on the importance of showing all possible honour to the wishes of departed heroes, as the highest incentive to the pursuit of military renown. Polyxena then voluntarily surrenders herself, like Macaria the daughter of Hercules in the *Heraclidae;* the chorus sing a stasimon, the theme of which is their own captive state, and the Argive herald Talthybius forthwith arrives to inform Hecuba, which he does with much feeling, of the terrible details of the maiden's death. This part of the play is harrowing, and has a pathos such as none but Euripides knew how to impart. Hecuba, who, in this as in the *Troades,* appears in great measure to reflect the character and doctrines of the poet himself, moralizes on the advantage of noble birth, and then prepares to bury her child with such honours as she and her fellow-captives can pay. A servant, sent by her for water to wash the corpse, returns from the shore with the news of a fresh grief: the corpse of Polydorus, Hecuba's youngest son, who had

---

[3] Androm. 1262.

been sent by his father, with a considerable sum of money, to be taken care of by Polymestor, king of Thrace, has been found lying on the beach. Hecuba at once perceives that he has been murdered for his gold. The arrival of Agamemnon, to hasten the funeral of Polyxena, prior to the departure of the fleet, affords her an opportunity of requesting his aid in avenging herself on the treacherous Polymestor. Agamemnon hesitates, because the Thracians are regarded as allies of the Greeks, and the army will say that he is acting partially through his affection for Cassandra, the sister of Polyxena. He consents however, at length, at least not to offer any opposition to her plans of vengeance, which are these:—Polymestor and his children are to be invited into the tent of the captive ladies, under pretence that Hecuba has a secret to reveal to him, respecting a hidden treasure belonging to the family of Priam. Suspecting no harm, he dismisses his attendants, and enters the tent. There he is suddenly seized by a number of the captives; his children are slain, and he is himself deprived of sight. Madly rushing from the scene of the slaughter, he describes what he has endured; upon which Hecuba justifies her conduct before Agamemnon, who decides the cause in her favour. Polymestor, as a last act of his vengeance, fortells to Hecuba that she shall die by a fall from a mast, having first been changed into the canine form, and to Agamemnon that he will die by the hand of his wife.

The brutality of Hecuba's revenge is objected to by critics; but, although the civilized Greeks themselves seem to have regarded such tortures with dislike [4], we must remember, first, that Hecuba is a γυνὴ βάρβαρος, a character which they delighted to contrast with a γυνὴ Ἑλληνὶς, and secondly, that the Greek doctrine of revenge was in itself carried to a very great extent by the best Greek moralists. Hecuba indeed is not intended to be drawn as an amiable character: she is a rationalist professedly, and by no means patient or resigned under the trials sent her by the gods. Severe as her trials have been, she is not utterly prostrated by them, but rouses herself to a vengeance which is accomplished by the united aid of craft, persuasion, and daring. The object of tragedy, so far as the just punishment of crime is concerned, is fulfilled; and there, perhaps, we may be content to leave the matter, without any such unreasonable disparagement of the poet for his development of the plot, as Hermann has expressed, in calling the play as a whole " fabula plane monstruosa [5]."

---

[4] Aeschylus seems to speak of the ὀφθαλμωρύχοι δίκαι as un-Greek, Eum. 177.
[5] Praefat. p. xviii.

The scene is laid entirely in the Thracian Chersonese; for, although Achilles was said to be buried at Sigeum, it is only necessary to suppose that the immolation of Polyxena over his tomb was performed there by the army who had returned for that purpose, (ὄχλος πᾶς, v. 521.) The author of the Greek Argument assumes that there was a cenotaph in the Chersonese as well as a tomb in the Troad; and that the former was the place of the sacrifice.

The date of the play is not known. But v. 174 is quoted or rather parodied in v. 1165 of the "Clouds," which was brought out Ol. 89. 1; and it is believed to have been exhibited but a few years earlier, or in Ol. 88. Müller (Hist. Gr. Lit. p. 369) thinks that v. 650 refers to the misfortunes of the Spartans at Pylos, B.C. 425; and an allusion has been also found in v. 462 to the then recent restoration of the ancient religious Ionic rites in Delos by the Athenians, in the year 426. (Thuc. iii. 104.) As regards the style and metres, it is to be classed with the *Ion* and the *Helena*, as intermediate between the earlier and severer, and the latest and more floridly written plays of Euripides.

The chorus consists of Trojan captives, like that in the *Troades*. The stage represented, as the principal object, the tent of Agamemnon, in a compartment of which Hecuba was lodged (v. 53), while others of the captives resided perhaps in adjacent quarters (v. 616, 1016). Above this tent the ghost of Polydorus is seen to hover, and probably in front of the entrance, so as to be visible to Hecuba within. As the latter comes forth on the stage, the spectre retires from her view. In the same tent, and of course out of sight of the spectators, the punishment of Polymestor is supposed to be inflicted. The scene was also supposed to represent the station of the Grecian fleet. This is clear from v. 1015, where Polymestor says,

ποῦ δ'; αἵδ' Ἀχαιῶν ναύλοχοι περιπτυχαί.

ΤΑ ΤΟΥ ΔΡΑΜΑΤΟΣ ΠΡΟΣΩΠΑ.

ΠΟΛΥΔΩΡΟΥ ΕΙΔΩΛΟΝ.
ΕΚΑΒΗ.
ΧΟΡΟΣ ΑΙΧΜΑΛΩΤΙΔΩΝ ΓΥΝΑΙΚΩΝ.
ΠΟΛΥΞΕΝΗ.
ΟΔΥΣΣΕΥΣ.
ΤΑΛΘΥΒΙΟΣ.
ΘΕΡΑΠΑΙΝΑ.
ΑΓΑΜΕΜΝΩΝ.
ΠΟΛΥΜΗΣΤΩΡ ΚΑΙ ΟΙ ΠΑΙΔΕΣ ΑΥΤΟΥ.

ΕΥΡΙΠΙΔΟΥ ΕΚΑΒΗ.

ΠΟΛΥΔΩΡΟΥ ΕΙΔΩΛΟΝ.

Ἥκω, νεκρῶν κευθμῶνα καὶ σκότου πύλας
λιπών, ἵν᾽ Ἅιδης χωρὶς ᾤκισται θεῶν,
Πολύδωρος, Ἑκάβης παῖς γεγὼς τῆς Κισσέως

1. If it was a bold conception on the part of the poet to put the Prologue into the mouth of a ghost, we must remember that Aeschylus had exhibited both Darius in the *Persae* and Clytemnestra in the *Eumenides*, as spectral forms on the stage. These three however are the only examples in Attic tragedy. It must be admitted that such harrowing sights were more appropriate in the middle of the action, when expectation had been sufficiently raised to receive them, than at the commencement. — Polydorus, the youngest son of Hecuba, who had been sent away from Troy at the beginning of the war into Thrace, has been murdered by his treacherous host Polymestor, and thrown into the sea. So long as there seemed a chance of success for the unhappy Trojans, he had been well cared for, because vengeance would certainly have overtaken the perfidy of his host. But Hector and Priam are gone, and none are now left whom he need fear. While the Grecian fleet is detained in its homeward course by the unquiet daemon of Achilles, Hecuba, now a captive and a slave, shall be made acquainted with the death of this her youngest son, and shall also have to bewail the sacrifice of her daughter Polyxena over the tomb of Achilles. The corpse of Polydorus shall be found on the beach by a slave, and brought to his mother. For so it has been permitted by the powers below, that the honour of a tomb shall not be denied him.

2. χωρὶς θεῶν. One of the primeval and universal instincts of man is the notion of a *supernal* and an *infernal*, the one full of light and glory, the other of gloom and despair. According to a doctrine strongly held by the Greeks (Ion 1017) that the bad should ever be kept distinct from the good, this isolation of the abodes of gods and daemons was inculcated even by Homer, Il. xx. 65 (quoted by Pflugk), who calls the abode of Hades σμερδαλέ᾽ εὐρώεντα, τά τε στυγέουσι θεοί περ. It was the same feeling, somewhat differently developed in the mind of Aeschylus, which made him regard the Chthonian powers as hostile, and in a manner antagonistic to the Olympian gods, who were benevolently disposed to the human race.

3. Κισσέως. In Il. xvi. 718, Asius is called the own-brother of Hecuba, and the son of Dymas. Virgil calls her *Cisseis*, Aen. x. 705, and vii. 320, doubtless from the Cyclic poems. Apollodor. iii. 11, 5, Πρίαμος δὲ Ἀρίσβην ἐκδοὺς Ὑρτάκῳ, δευτέραν ἔγημεν Ἑκάβην τὴν Δύμαντος, ἢ ὥς τινές φασι, Κισσέως, ἢ ὡς ἕτεροι λέγουσιν, Σαγγαρίου ποταμοῦ καὶ Μετώπης. It is clear that there were different accounts, and there is no reason to suppose that Euripides himself invented the parentage of Cisseus. Homer, Il. xxi. 88, says that Priam had many wives; but he

Πριάμου τε πατρὸς, ὅς μ', ἐπεὶ Φρυγῶν πόλιν
κίνδυνος ἔσχε δορὶ πεσεῖν Ἑλληνικῷ, 5
δείσας ὑπεξέπεμψε Τρωικῆς χθονὸς
Πολυμήστορος πρὸς δῶμα, Θρηκίου ξένου,
ὃς τήνδ' ἀρίστην Χερσονησίαν πλάκα
σπείρει, φίλιππον λαὸν εὐθύνων δορί.
πολὺν δὲ σὺν ἐμοὶ χρυσὸν ἐκπέμπει λάθρα 10
πατὴρ, ἵν', εἴ ποτ' Ἰλίου τείχη πέσοι,
τοῖς ζῶσιν εἴη παισὶ μὴ σπάνις βίου.
νεώτατος δ' ἦν Πριαμιδῶν· ὃ καί με γῆς
ὑπεξέπεμψεν· οὔτε γὰρ φέρειν ὅπλα
οὔτ' ἔγχος οἷός τ' ἦν νέῳ βραχίονι. 15
ἕως μὲν οὖν γῆς ὄρθ' ἔκειθ' ὁρίσματα,
πύργοι τ' ἄθραυστοι Τρωικῆς ἦσαν χθονὸς,
Ἕκτωρ τ' ἀδελφὸς οὑμὸς ηὐτύχει δορὶ,
καλῶς παρ' ἀνδρὶ Θρηκὶ, πατρῴῳ ξένῳ,

makes Polydorus and Lycaon the sons of Laothoë the daughter of Altes, and states that Polydorus had been killed by Achilles, Il. xx. 407,

αὐτὰρ ὁ βῆ σὺν δουρὶ μετ' ἀντίθεον
Πολύδωρον
Πριαμίδην. τὸν δ' οὔ τι πατὴρ εἴασκε
μάχεσθαι,
οὕνεκά οἱ μετὰ παισὶ νεώτατος ἔσκε
γόνοιο,
καί οἱ φίλτατος ἔσκε, πόδεσσι δὲ πάντας ἐνίκα.

Now it was the object of Euripides to represent Hecuba as overwhelmed with an accumulation of grief for the loss of all that was dear to her. Hence Polydorus as well as Polyxena is represented as *her* child. (This remark, with the above references to Homer, is due to Hermann.)

8. Hermann seems right in restoring τήνδ' for τήν. The words are perpetually confused in MSS.; and the reason why the article is here faulty will be found in the note on Androm. 215. The reason too why transcribers preferred τὴν is obvious. They had fancied that Euripides lays the scene partly in the Thracian Chersonese, and partly in the Troad; and they thought that the difficulty might be removed by altering the demonstrative τήνδε.—φίλιππον, because the Thracian

steeds were admired for their superior race, as, for instance, the horses of Rhesus. Cf. Hes. Opp. 505, διὰ Θρήκης ἱπποτρόφου εὐρέϊ πόντῳ ἐμπνεύσας (Βορέας).

12. εἴη μὴ σπάνις. Probably μὴ is merely placed out of its true order, so that it is needless to regard μὴ σπάνις as = εὐπορία. See Hippol. 197. Bacch. 1288.

13. ὅ. Porson explains this as the subject to the verb, τὸ εἶναι νεώτατον. In this opinion he is not followed by the later editors, who more correctly take ὃ for δι' ὅ, this clause being in fact but a repetition of that in v. 6. So ταῦτα for διὰ ταῦτα, Andr. 212. Ion 346. Scholefield cites three instances of the phrase ὃ καὶ δέδοικα (or rather, we might say, of ὃ καὶ for δι' ὅ) from Phoen. 155, 263, Ar. Eccl. 338.

14—15. ὅπλα οὔτ' ἔγχος. The accoutrements of a ὁπλίτης, which, as a more creditable rank than the ψιλοὶ, a younger son of a king would have been, had he attained sufficient bodily strength. It is the τευχέων βάρος of this kind that the aged Iolaus is unable to cope with, Heracl. 723.

16. ὁρίσματα, the flanking walls, by which the circuit of a city is defined. Cf. Hipp. 1459. Schol. τῆς γῆς ὁρίσματα καὶ τὸ πύργοι Τρωϊκῆς χθονὸς, ταὐτόν ἐστιν.

τροφαῖσιν, ὥς τις πτόρθος, ηὐξόμην τάλας.   20
ἐπεὶ δὲ Τροία θ' Ἕκτορός τ' ἀπόλλυται
ψυχὴ, πατρῷα θ' ἑστία κατεσκάφη,
αὐτὸς δὲ βωμῷ πρὸς θεοδμήτῳ πίτνει
σφαγεὶς Ἀχιλλέως παιδὸς ἐκ μιαιφόνου,
κτείνει με χρυσοῦ τὸν ταλαίπωρον χάριν   25
ξένος πατρῷος, καὶ κτανὼν ἐς οἶδμ' ἁλὸς
μεθῆχ', ἵν' αὐτὸς χρυσὸν ἐν δόμοις ἔχῃ.
κεῖμαι δ' ἐπ' ἀκταῖς, ἄλλοτ' ἐν πόντου σάλῳ,
πολλοῖς διαύλοις κυμάτων φορούμενος,
ἄκλαυστος, ἄταφος· νῦν δ' ὑπὲρ μητρὸς φίλης   30
Ἑκάβης ἀΐσσω, σῶμ' ἐρημώσας ἐμὸν,
τριταῖον ἤδη φέγγος αἰωρούμενος,
ὅσονπερ ἐν γῇ τῇδε Χερσονησίᾳ
μήτηρ ἐμὴ δύστηνος ἐκ Τροίας πάρα.
πάντες δ' Ἀχαιοὶ ναῦς ἔχοντες ἥσυχοι   35
θάσσουσ' ἐπ' ἀκταῖς τῆσδε Θρῃκίας χθονός·
ὁ Πηλέως γὰρ παῖς ὑπὲρ τύμβου φανεὶς

21. ἀπόλλυται is rightly preferred by all the recent editors to the Aldine ἀπώλετο.
23. θεοδμήτῳ, simply *divine, sacred*, as βωμὸν καὶ θεηλάτους ἕδρας, Ion 1306.
26. κτείνει—καὶ κτανών. Pflugk cites the same expression from Herc. F. 33, and ἔσπειρεν—καὶ σπείρας from Phoen.
22. All these instances occur in prologues, where explicitness and clearness are especially appropriate.
27. ἔχῃ. "Conjunctivus non tam consilium Polymestoris indicat, quam possideri nunc ab eo aurum." *Herm.*
28. ἐπ' ἀκταῖς. Supply ἄλλοτε from the next clause. Of course, Polydorus speaks of his corpse, as he does *inf.* v. 47, not of his spirit or spectre, when he says φανήσομαι. This is clear from v. 778. But it is a singular confusion of ideas between the material and the immaterial, to speak of the ghost as identical with, and yet having power (v. 31) even to leave, the insensate body, ἀφεὶς τὸ σῶμα ἑαυτοῦ, καὶ μόνη ψυχὴ ὤν, in the words of the Schol. on v. 1. This was an error the Roman poets were perpetually committing.—διαύλοις κυμάτων, the movements backwards and forwards of the waves, as the wind or currents affected them. To explain the term of the *tide*, which is scarcely perceptible on the open shores of the Mediterranean, would be obviously wrong. He merely means ἄνω κάτω φορούμενος, the metaphor being from the double course, up and down, of the stadium, Aesch. Agam. 335.
30. ὑπὲρ μητρός. " Proprie intelligendum, quia in somnis umbra Polydori adstitit matri, ut Somnium apud Homerum, στῇ δ' ἄρ' ὑπὲρ κεφαλῆς." *Herm.* The scene is supposed to be night. Hecuba has just been scared by the vision seen from her couch ; see v. 54 and 69. On ἀΐσσω see Troad. 156. Bacch. 147.
32. αἰωρούμενος, having now been hovering, i. e. occasionally appearing suspended in mid-air, for the three days (and nights) during which my mother has been detained here. He should have said τριταῖος, but φέγγος is added as if it had been τρίτον. So Hippol. 275, τριταίαν οὖσ' ἄσιτος ἡμέραν.
37. ὑπὲρ τύμβου. There is some difficulty in this. It is not said where the tomb of Achilles was, though history placed it on the promontory of Sigeum; and it is not stated how the ghost, either

ΕΚΑΒΗ.   493

κατέσχ' Ἀχιλλεὺς πᾶν στράτευμ' Ἑλληνικὸν,
πρὸς οἶκον εὐθύνοντας ἐναλίαν πλάτην·
αἰτεῖ δ' ἀδελφὴν τὴν ἐμὴν Πολυξένην   40
τύμβῳ φίλον πρόσφαγμα καὶ γέρας λαβεῖν.
καὶ τεύξεται τοῦδ', οὐδ' ἀδώρητος φίλων
ἔσται πρὸς ἀνδρῶν· ἡ πεπρωμένη δ' ἄγει
θανεῖν ἀδελφὴν τῷδ' ἐμὴν ἐν ἤματι.
δυοῖν δὲ παίδοιν δύο νεκρὼ κατόψεται   45
μήτηρ, ἐμοῦ τε τῆς τε δυστήνου κόρης.
φανήσομαι γὰρ, ὡς τάφου τλήμων τύχω,
δούλης ποδῶν πάροιθεν ἐν κλυδωνίῳ.
τοὺς γὰρ κάτω σθένοντας ἐξῃτησάμην
τύμβου κυρῆσαι, κεἰς χέρας μητρὸς πεσεῖν·   50
τοὐμὸν μὲν οὖν ὅσονπερ ἤθελον τυχεῖν
ἔσται· γεραιᾷ δ' ἐκποδὼν χωρήσομαι
Ἑκάβῃ· περᾷ γὰρ ἥδ' ὑπὸ σκηνῆς πόδα
Ἀγαμέμνονος, φάντασμα δειμαίνουσ' ἐμόν.
φεῦ·
ὦ μῆτερ, ἥτις ἐκ τυραννικῶν δόμων   55

there or in the Chersonese, caused the detention of the ships. We are left to this, as the most probable supposition:—The ghost had warned the army on their departure (τύμβου ἐπιβὰς, v. 111), that a propitiatory offering must be made to his tomb, under certain penalties. This having been disregarded, they are now kept by contrary winds at the Chersonese, till the request is complied with. Cf. v. 900, νῦν δ', οὐ γὰρ Ἴησ' οὐρίους πνοὰς θεὸς, μένειν ἀνάγκη πλοῦν ὁρῶντας ἥσυχον. The case is thus exactly parallel to the sacrifice of Iphigenia at Aulis.

40. Here Polydorus distinctly specifies Polyxena as the victim. But the actual demand of Achilles seems indefinite, τῶν πολυμόχθων τινὰ Τρωιάδων, v. 97. In v. 390, Ulysses says that Achilles did not ask for Hecuba, but for Polyxena; and this shows that Hecuba had not been informed who was the person specified. In the Greek Argument, Polyxena is said to have been betrothed to Achilles; and this is given as a reason why she was demanded.

41. πρόσφαγμα. See on Hel. 1255. The propitiation of heroes and daemons by blood-offerings was an essential part of the Greek creed. See Heracl. 1041.

47. φανήσομαι, i. e. νεκρὸς οὑμὸς φανήσεται. Cf. 778.

53. περᾷ πόδα. Though περᾶν, like βαίνειν, is properly transitive, and βαίνω πόδα occurs Electr. 94, yet the addition of πόδα is so common in Euripides, even after neuter verbs, as ἐκβὰς πόδα Heracl. 802, προβὰς κῶλον δεξιὸν Phoen. 1412, ἐλθεῖν νόστιμον πόδα Alcest. 1153, πεζεύειν πόδα ibid. 869, that one may doubt if it be not more correctly explained in all these places alike as a cognate accusative.— ὑπὸ σκηνῆς, 'from under the tent.' That Porson should read ὑπὲρ σκηνὴν on the mere conjecture of Musgrave, may excite surprise. Not to cite the many instances of ὑπὸ with a genitive in this sense, collected by Hermann from Homer and Pindar, one in the Andromache, v. 441, νεοσσὸν τόνδ' ὑπὸ πτερῶν σπάσας, is conclusive.

55. ἥτις is not for ᾗ, but the construction is, ὡς πράσσεις κακῶς, ἥτις εἶδες κτλ., 'how unfortunate you are, in that you have seen slavery.'

δούλειον ἦμαρ εἶδες, ὡς πράσσεις κακῶς,
ὅσονπερ εὖ ποτ'. ἀντισηκώσας δέ σε
φθείρει θεῶν τις τῆς πάροιθ' εὐπραξίας.

ΕΚΑΒΗ.

ἄγετ', ὦ παῖδες, τὴν γραῦν πρὸ δόμων,
ἄγετ', ὀρθοῦσαι τὴν ὁμόδουλον,   60
Τρῳάδες, ὑμῖν, πρόσθε δ' ἄνασσαν.
λάβετε, φέρετε, πέμπετ', ἀείρετέ μου
γεραιᾶς χειρὸς προσλαζύμεναι·
κἀγὼ σκολιῷ σκίπωνι χερὸς   65
διερειδομένα σπεύσω βραδύπουν
ἤλυσιν ἄρθρων προτιθεῖσα.
ὦ στεροπὰ Διὸς, ὦ σκοτία νὺξ,

57. ἀντισηκώσας τῆς π. εὐπραξίας is, 'giving you a balance (of evil) against your former prosperity.' So Pers. 439, ὡς τοῖσδε καὶ δὶς ἀντισηκῶσαι ῥοπῇ.
59. Hecuba now appears, led by her handmaids, and supporting herself by their aid. She has been driven from within her tent in alarm at the apparition of her son, whom she believes to be safe and well in Thrace. She has had dreams too about Polyxena. Her mind is uneasy; she cannot shake off her apprehensions, and would fain consult her prophetic children, Cassandra and Helenus, as to the purport of these nightly visions. The previous appearance moreover of Achilles' shade over his tomb, in connexion with these more recent alarms, is a subject of dread.—The metre of this monody is the same kind of spondaic anapaestic, of which the principles have been explained on Troad. 99, where the same speaker utters a similar monody immediately after the prologue. The chorus follow in a system of regular anapaestics.
60. τὴν is the reading of all the later editors. Porson preferred νῦν, judging the article to be useless. The sense however is, τὴν νῦν μὲν ὁμόδουλον, πρόσθε δ' ἄνασσαν. The νῦν, which most copies add after ὁμόδουλον, is clearly an unnecessary interpolation.
62. Porson who, though a master of the trimeter senarius, was not very conversant with choral metres, (the laws of which, in fact, had been little investigated in his day,) reads thus, λάβετε, φέρετε, πέμπετε, | ἀείρετέ μου δέμας, which is simply no metre at all. The word δέμας is omitted in some copies, and was probably added by those who did not perceive the construction, προσλαζύμεναι, i.e. προσλαμβανόμεναι, μου γεραιᾶς χειρός, 'taking me by the hand,' as φάσγανον κώπης λαβὼν inf.
543. The first foot of the anapaestic verse, a spondee, is resolved into four short syllables. So in Troad. 124, δι' ἄλα τε πορφυροειδέα λιμένας θ'. ibid. 136, Πρίαμον ἐμέ τε τὰν μελέαν Ἑκάβαν. Ion 889, κρόκεα πέταλα φάρεσιν ἔδρεπον.— The middle syllable of γεραιᾶς is short, a usage which is now well ascertained. Porson thought γραίας would be more harmonious; but it appears Euripides thought otherwise.
65. σκίπων χερὸς, 'the staff of a hand,' (i.e. no real staff but a substitute for it,) is qualified, as Musgrave observes, by the epithet σκολιῷ, which is applicable to a bent arm, but not to a stick by nature straight. Cf. χερὸς στήριγμα, Iph. A. 617. In Troad. 150 however, Hecuba speaks of herself as σκῆπτρῳ Πριάμου διερειδομένα.—σπεύσω, κτλ., "festinabo, quantum licet per pedes senio graves." Pflugk.
68. στεροπὰ Διὸς is interpreted 'light of day' by Hermann, Pflugk, and Dindorf, after the Scholiast, ὦ ἡμέρα ἡ δίκην ἀστραπῆς λάμπουσα. Porson, who thinks this absurd, does not tell us what meaning he attaches to it. But Hermann well

ΕΚΑΒΗ. 495

τί ποτ' αἴρομαι ἔννυχος οὕτω
δείμασι, φάσμασιν; ὦ πότνια χθὼν,   70
μελανοπτερύγων μᾶτερ ὀνείρων,
ἀποπέμπομαι ἔννυχον ὄψιν,
ἃν περὶ παιδὸς ἐμοῦ τοῦ σωζομένου κατὰ Θρῄκην
ἀμφὶ Πολυξείνης τε φίλης θυγατρὸς δι' ὀνείρων   75
φοβερὰν ὄψιν ἔμαθον, ἐδάην.
ὦ χθόνιοι θεοὶ, σώσατε παῖδ' ἐμὸν,
ὃς μόνος οἴκων ἄγκυρ' ἔτ' ἐμῶν   80
τὴν χιονώδη Θρῄκην κατέχει,
ξείνου πατρῴου φυλακαῖσιν.
ἔσται τι νέον,
ἥξει τι μέλος γοερὸν γοεραῖς.
οὔποτ' ἐμὰ φρὴν ὧδ' ἀλίαστος   85

compares Trach. 99, where the sun is addressed as ὦ λαμπρᾷ στεροπᾷ φλεγέθων. Porson also objects to the *Earth* being called *Mother of Dreams*, and would transpose the clauses ὦ σκοτία νὺξ and ὦ πότνια χθών. He defends however the vulgate by Iph. T. 1262, νύχια χθὼν ἐτεκνώσατο φάσματ' ὀνείρων. Doubtless, the poet regarded dreams as sent up from the recesses of the earth, i.e. from Hades; and hence they are 'black-winged,' i.e. gloomy and of evil portent. This is what Homer had done before and what Virgil did after him, Od. xxiv. 12. Aen. vi. 283 &c. *Inf.* v. 704, οὐδὲ παρέβα με φάσμα μελανόπτερον.

72. ἀποπέμπομαι, *abominor*, ἀποδιώκω, I pray the gods to avert it. Cf. v. 99.

76. The reading of this verse is given according to the text of Pflugk, Matthiae, and Dindorf; and it had occurred also to the present editor independently. The common reading was ἃν—δι' ὀνείρων εἶδον. εἶδον γὰρ φοβερὰν κτλ. But some MSS. omit εἶδον, others εἶδον γὰρ, and there can be little doubt that both were added by grammarians who required a verb to govern ἃν, and regarded ὄψιν, which had already occurred, as the accusative of a new clause. Porson again departs from the anapaestic measure, in which the whole of this monody is undoubtedly composed, and edits εἶδον φοβερὰν ὄψιν, | ἔμαθον ἐδάην. Hermann gives εἶδον, εἶδον, | φοβερὰν κτλ., thinking it possible that εἶδον εἶδον may have formed a spondaic monometer. The verse as it now stands is a paroemiac, the spondee preceding the final long syllable being resolved into ᴗ ᴗ ᴗ ᴗ, as above, v. 62.

79. χθόνιοι θεοί. Schol. οἱ ἐγχώριοι, οἱ ἐντόπιοι. And so Dindorf and Hermann understand it. The latter quotes Oed. Col. 948, where the council of Areopagus is called χθόνιος, national and indigenous. —ἄγκυρ' ἔτ' ἐμῶν is given by W. Dindorf from one MS., another having ἔστ' ἐμῶν. The common reading is ἄγκυρά τ' ἐμῶν, which Hermann and Pflugk retain, but with a far-fetched explanation, 'the sole survivor and anchor of my house.' This sounds well enough in English; but μόνος ἄγκυρά τε does not read like Greek at all. The scholia recognise the τε, (μόνος ὑπάρχων ἐμοὶ, καὶ ἄγκυρα τῶν ἐμῶν οἴκων.) But another explanation suits the reading ἔτι much better; τελευταία ἄγκυρα, ἀπὸ μεταφορᾶς τῶν ναυτιλλομένων, οἳ τὰς ἄλλας ῥίψαντες ἀγκύρας—ἐπὶ τῇ τελευταίᾳ τὰς ἐλπίδας ἔχουσιν. Porson gives ἄγκυρ' ἅτ' ἐμῶν, after Reiske.

85. ἀλίαστος, unceasing, unalterable. An Homeric word, on which see Buttmann's Lexilogus. Photius explains λιάζειν by λίαν ἐσπουδακέναι (like ἀγάζειν from ἄγαν, Aesch. Suppl. 1046). But this λιάζειν is quite distinct from the ancient word, of uncertain etymology, λιάζεσθαι, 'to move away,' *inf.* 100. Compare Orest. 1479.

φρίσσει, ταρβεῖ.
ποῦ ποτε θείαν Ἑλένου ψυχὰν
ἢ Κασσάνδραν ἐσίδω, Τρῳάδες,
ὥς μοι κρίνωσιν ὀνείρους;
εἶδον γὰρ βαλιὰν ἔλαφον λύκου αἵμονι χαλᾷ   90
σφαζομέναν, ἀπ' ἐμῶν γονάτων σπασθεῖσαν ἀνάγκᾳ
οἰκτρῶς. καὶ τόδε δεῖμά μοι·
ἦλθ' ὑπὲρ ἄκρας τύμβου κορυφᾶς
φάντασμ' Ἀχιλέως·   95
ᾔτει δὲ γέρας τῶν πολυμόχθων
τινὰ Τρωιάδων.
ἀπ' ἐμᾶς οὖν, ἀπ' ἐμᾶς τόδε παιδὸς
πέμψατε, δαίμονες, ἱκετεύω.

ΧΟΡΟΣ.

Ἑκάβη, σπουδῇ πρός σ' ἐλιάσθην,   100

87. θείαν, inspired, prophetic. Schol. εἶπε δὲ ψυχὴν Ἑλένου, ἐπειδὴ τεθνηκὼς ἦν, Κασσάνδραν δὲ, καὶ οὐ Κασσάνδρας, ἐπειδὴ ζῶσα ἦν. That Helenus at least is represented as dead, and therefore that he could only be consulted διὰ νεκυομαντείας, is to be inferred, because Polydorus has just been called the only stay (i. e. the only male son, cf. Iph. T. 57) now left to the family. Most copies give Κασάνδρας.
90. βαλιὰν, dappled; see Alcest. 579. Rhes. 356. — αἵμονι, αἱματηρᾷ. Aesch. Suppl. 826, αἶμον' ἔσω σέ γ' ἐπ' ἄμαλα, a very doubtful passage, but having the scholium attached, ᾑμαγμένον σε καθίζω. Hermann suspects the word means 'greedy,' as in αἵμονα θήρης, Il. v. 49. His idea, that both this word and αἷμα are to be referred to ἀΐσσειν, (from the rapid movement or pulsation of the blood,) is ingenious. From ἀΐσσειν would come ἄϊγμα, like αἴνιγμα, κίνυγμα, from αἰνίσσειν, κινύσσειν. Pronounced αἴγμα, it would naturally pass into αἷμα, and the aspirate would be a compensation for the loss of the γ, or for the contraction of the word. Compare Ἄϊδης, ἐέρση, ἠέλιος, with Ἅιδης, ἕρση, ἥλιος.
93. οἰκτρῶς. Hermann places a lacuna after this word, and suspects that it should be repeated to complete the dimeter verse. Porson thinks ἀνοίκτως may have been supplanted by ἀνάγκᾳ, and he would read καὶ τόδε δεῖμά μοι· ἦλθ' ὑπὲρ ἄκρας |

τύμβου κορυφᾶς κτλ. In this case, οἰκτρῶς must be regarded as a gloss; and two MSS. have a very similar gloss, ἀνηλεῶς. Added to all this, one MS. gives ἀνάγκος for ἀνάγκᾳ, so that Porson's conjecture is highly plausible. — καὶ τόδε δεῖμα, this too, viz. the following circumstance, besides the apparition and the dream, is a third source of alarm; Achilles appeared some time ago to the army while yet in the Troad, and asked for the immolation of a female captive. Who shall say, (she reasons, in connexion with the dream about the deer and the wolf,) that the lot may not fall on my Polyxena?
97. Τρωιάδων. See above, v. 40. Why did he ask for the blood of a maiden, rather than one of those who had borne arms against him? The question is not very easily answered; but the romantic and sentimental Greeks doubtless exaggerated the pathos naturally incident to such an event as a human sacrifice, by preferring to make the softer sex the subject of these sanguinary legends. Hence Iphigenia dies at Aulis; hence Macaria devotes herself in the Heraclidae, and it is the daughter of Erechtheus who saves her country by her death, Ion 278.
99. On the anapaest following the dactyl in irregular anapaestic systems, see Troad. 177. Compare inf. v. 147.
100. The chorus, consisting of fellow-captives, approach Hecuba, and inform

ΕΚΑΒΗ. 497

τὰς δεσποσύνους σκηνὰς προλιποῦσ',
ἵν' ἐκληρώθην καὶ προσετάχθην
δούλη, πόλεως ἀπελαυννομένη
τῆς Ἰλιάδος, λόγχης αἰχμῇ
δοριθήρατος πρὸς Ἀχαιῶν, 105
οὐδὲν παθέων ἀποκουφίζουσ',
ἀλλ' ἀγγελίας βάρος ἀραμένη
μέγα, σοί τε, γύναι, κῆρυξ ἀχέων.
ἐν γὰρ Ἀχαιῶν πλήρει ξυνόδῳ
λέγεται δόξαι σὴν παῖδ' Ἀχιλεῖ 110
σφάγιον θέσθαι· τύμβου δ' ἐπιβὰς
οἶσθ' ὅτε χρυσέοις ἐφάνη σὺν ὅπλοις,
τὰς ποντοπόρους δ' ἔσχε σχεδίας
λαίφη προτόνοις ἐπερειδομένας,
τάδε θωΰσσων, 115
ποῖ δή, Δαναοί, τὸν ἐμὸν τύμβον
στέλλεσθ' ἀγέραστον ἀφέντες;
πολλῆς δ' ἔριδος ξυνέπαισε κλύδων,
δόξα δ' ἐχώρει δίχ' ἂν' Ἑλλήνων

her that her worst fears have been realized by the resolution of the Greeks to offer her daughter Polyxena to the angry shade of Achilles. They describe how various opinions were held on the subject in a full council of the Greeks, and how Ulysses at length prevailed on them to adopt the cruel decree. They apprize her that he will forthwith appear in person to demand the victim; and they counsel her to supplicate Agamemnon, who has been her friend in the dispute, to avert the calamity by his influence.—ἐλιάσθην, see v. 85.

107. ἄρασθαι is more properly said of one who takes up the burden of his own griefs, than of him who carries a load to be laid on another. The sense seems to be, 'having imposed on myself the heavy task of bearing bad tidings to you.' Hence it is equivalent to φέρουσα, προστιθεῖσα, as opposed to ἀποκουφίζουσα.

112. οἶσθ' ὅτε. 'You remember when' &c. Three commentators at least write at considerable length in explanation of a phrase which does not seem by any means obscure. Hermann is no doubt right in saying, that the full expression would be,

'you remember what took place when,' &c. So εἰδέναι ἡνίκα is used inf. v. 239. Troad. 70. Canter's conjecture οἶσθ' ὅτι would be objectionable on the ground that it is a mere colloquial formula. The appearance of Achilles' shade is evidently regarded as a not very recent event.

114. λαίφη κτλ. 'having their sails supported by the stays,' i. e. with all sail on. The πρότονοι, as the word implies, were fastened at or near the prow, the πόδες at the other end. Lucian, Ζεὺς Τραγῳδὸς, p. 695, reverses the order to describe confusion and chance position, ὁ μὲν πρότονος, εἰ τύχοι, ἐς τὴν πρύμναν ἀποτέταται, οἱ πόδες δὲ ἐς τὴν πρῷραν ἀμφότεροι. The πρότονος was the rope which secured the mast; the πόδες regulated the position of the sail according to the direction of the wind. For the detention of the ships see on v. 37. Either a dead calm or adverse winds had set in, when they had gone forward as far as the Chersonese, after leaving the spot where Achilles appeared.

119. ἐχώρει δίχα, made progress in two different directions, i. e. two different motions, to kill or to spare, gained their

VOL. II. 3 s

στρατὸν αἰχμητὴν, τοῖς μὲν διδόναι 120
τύμβῳ σφάγιον, τοῖς δ' οὐχὶ δοκοῦν.
ἦν δὲ τὸ μὲν σὸν σπεύδων ἀγαθὸν
τῆς μαντιπόλου βάκχης ἀνέχων
λέκτρ' Ἀγαμέμνων·
τὼ Θησείδα δ', ὄζω Ἀθηνῶν, 125
δισσῶν μύθων ῥήτορες ἦσαν·
γνώμῃ δὲ μιᾷ ξυνεχωρείτην,
τὸν Ἀχίλλειον τύμβον στεφανοῦν
αἵματι χλωρῷ, τὰ δὲ Κασσάνδρας
λέκτρ' οὐκ ἐφάτην τῆς Ἀχιλείας 130
πρόσθεν θήσειν ποτὲ λόγχης.
σπουδαὶ δὲ λόγων κατατεινομένων
ἦσαν ἴσαι πως, πρὶν ὁ ποικιλόφρων
κόπις, ἡδυλόγος, δημοχαριστὴς
Λαερτιάδης πείθει στρατιὰν 135
μὴ τὸν ἄριστον Δαναῶν πάντων
δούλων σφαγίων οὕνεκ' ἀπωθεῖν,
μηδέ τιν' εἰπεῖν παρὰ Περσεφόνῃ

respective adherents in the course of the discussion. Pflugk thinks it simply means ἐγίνοντο δίχα αἱ γνῶμαι.—δοκοῦν, see *inf.* 506.

123. ἀνέχων, *sustinens*, στέργων, 'liking,' 'having in regard.' Schol. τιμῶν καὶ περιποιούμενος. This is given as a reason why he spoke in behalf of the mother of Cassandra. Pflugk compares Ajac. 211, ἐπεί σε λέχος δουριάλωτον στέρξας ἀνέχει θούριος Αἴας. So also Oed. Col. 674, τὸν οἰνῶπ' ἀνέχουσα κισσὸν, where W. Dindorf needlessly edits νέμουσα.

126. δισσῶν μύθων. The meaning is, as the Scholiast and Hermann explain it, that they both voted that a sacrifice should be offered, but one of them was in favour of slaying Polyxena, the other, a different captive. Their names, Acamas and Demophon, will be remembered by readers of the *Heraclidae*; see v. 35. They are styled, in Homeric phrase, 'offshoots of an Athenian stock,' like πτόρθος, v. 20. Homer does not mention either Theseus or his sons among the warriors against Troy, if the verse in Il. i. 265 is rightly rejected as spurious.

129. χλωρῷ, fresh, living blood. Trach. 1055, ἐκ δὲ χλωρὸν αἷμά μου πέπωκεν ἤδη.

132. Photius, κατατείνας, συντείνας. He also cites κατατείνας ἐρῶ from Plato, Polit. ii. (p. 592, A), a passage which Musgrave had adduced in illustration of the present verse. The κατὰ implies the contention of one speaker against the other. The sense is, the partisans of the arguments that were bandied on both sides were about equal, till Ulysses turned the scale in favour of those who were for slaying Polyxena. Achilles had asked τινὰ Τρωϊάδων, v. 97; and when Polyxena was named as the most fitting, Agamemnon opposed it on family grounds, viz. her relationship to Cassandra. It was jealousy of his interference on private interests that induced one of the sons of Theseus and Ulysses to insist on Polyxena's death in particular; for so we must understand δούλων σφαγίων in v. 137, as is clear from the context.

134. κόπις, in the sense of 'an orator,' seems only to be used in this passage and twice in Lycophron.

ΕΚΑΒΗ.

στάντα φθιμένων
ὡς ἀχάριστοι Δαναοὶ Δαναοῖς 140
τοῖς οἰχομένοις ὑπὲρ Ἑλλήνων
Τροίας πεδίων ἀπέβησαν.
ἥξει δ' Ὀδυσσεὺς ὅσον οὐκ ἤδη,
πῶλον ἀφέλξων σῶν ἀπὸ μαστῶν,
ἔκ τε γεραιᾶς χερὸς ὁρμήσων. 145
ἀλλ' ἴθι ναοὺς, ἴθι πρὸς βωμοὺς,
ἵζ' Ἀγαμέμνονος ἱκέτις γονάτων·
κήρυσσε θεοὺς τούς τ' οὐρανίδας
τούς θ' ὑπὸ γαῖαν.
ἢ γάρ σε λιταὶ διακωλύσουσ' 150
ὀρφανὸν εἶναι παιδὸς μελέας,
ἢ δεῖ σ' ἐπιδεῖν τύμβου προπετῆ
φοινισσομένην αἵματι παρθένον
ἐκ χρυσοφόρου
δειρῆς νασμῷ μελαναυγεῖ.

ΕΚ. οἲ 'γὼ μελέα, τί ποτ' ἀπύσω ; 155

143. ὅσον οὐκ ἤδη. See on Bacch. 1076.
147. On the metre see v. 99. For κηρύσσειν τινὰ compare Ar. Ach. 748, ἐγὼ δὲ καρύξω Δικαιόπολιν ὅπα. Aesch. Cho. 117, κηρύξας ἐμοὶ τοὺς γῆς ἔνερθε δαίμονας. Here the sense is merely κάλει. So βοᾶν and φωνεῖν τινὰ are used in much the same sense.—οὐρανίδας, cf. Electr. 1234.
149. γαῖαν Herm. and Pflugk with all the copies,—" contra metrum," says Porson, who gives γαίας. The last syllable however (according to a better arrangement of the verses) is common, on account of the full stop in the sentence; as in v. 72 and 83 ; and Pflugk cites τῶν ὑπὸ γαῖαν from Alcest. 896, and Aesch. Eum. 912, παρά τ' ἀθανάτοις τοῖς θ' ὑπὸ γαῖαν. Dindorf not unreasonably thinks γαίας more probable, because the corruption is easy, and the short syllable could have been avoided at the option of the poet. Similarly κατὰ γαῖαν, ' on the earth,' and κατὰ γαίας, ' below the earth,' are occasionally confused, at least in MSS., though the two phrases are properly distinct.
152. τύμβου προπετῆ. A somewhat singular expression for πρὸ τύμβου πε-σοῦσαν. The Schol. has προκειμένην.
154. χρυσοφόρου. Porson, remarking that among the ancients, meaning the Greeks, it was the custom for maidens to wear many golden trinkets, and quoting Il. ii. 872, ὃς καὶ χρυσὸν ἔχων πολεμόνδ' ἴεν, ἠΰτε κούρη, might have added, that in every age and every country, barbarous and civilized, the same usage has prevailed: for the love of that precious metal knows no limits of time or place.
155. The reply of Hecuba is given, like that of Polyxena in v. 198 seqq., in the same irregular spondeo-anapaestic system as above, v. 59. Hermann considers the two speeches as antistrophic ; and the coincidence of 166 seqq., Τρῳάδες ὢ κάκ' ἐνεγκοῦσαι, with 207 seqq., σᾶς ἄπο, λαιμότομόν θ' Ἅιδᾳ, both being followed by a dactylic verse, is remarkable. But it is a question not easily decided, whether irregular anapaestics (and indeed regular systems) were not often exempted from antistrophic laws ; and when to this consideration is added the necessity of making some alterations to establish the coincidence, and that v. 175—7 is made by Hermann the strophe to v. 195—7, it seems on the whole better with W. Din-

ΕΥΡΙΠΙΔΟΥ

ποίαν ἀχώ ; ποῖον ὀδυρμόν ;
δειλαία δειλαίου γήρως,
δουλείας τᾶς οὐ τλατᾶς,
τᾶς οὐ φερτᾶς· ὤμοι μοι.
τίς ἀμύνει μοι ; ποία γενεά, 160
ποία δὲ πόλις ;
φροῦδος πρέσβυς, φροῦδοι παῖδες.
ποίαν, ἢ ταύταν ἢ κείναν,
στείχω ; ποῖ δ' ἥσω ; ποῦ τις
θεῶν ἢ δαίμων ἐπαρωγός ; 165
ὦ κάκ' ἐνεγκοῦσαι Τρῳάδες, ὦ
κάκ' ἐνεγκοῦσαι
πήματ', ἀπωλέσατ', ὠλέσατ'· οὐκέτι μοι βίος
ἀγαστὸς ἐν φάει.
ὦ τλάμων, ἄγησαί μοι, 170
πούς, ἄγησαι τᾷ γραίᾳ
πρὸς τάνδ' αὐλάν· ὦ τέκνον, ὦ παῖ
δυστανοτάτας ματέρος, ἔξελθ'
ἔξελθ' οἴκων· ἄϊε ματέρος

---

dorf and Pflugk, not to regard the following dialogue as antithetical.

160. γενεά, proposed by Porson instead of γέννα, has been admitted by Pflugk. Hermann defends γέννα by comparing v. 72 and 83, (where the short syllable is justified by the pause in speaking,) W. Dindorf by supposing that here and in Iph. T. 154, γέννᾶ is Doric for γέννη, as the Attics used occasionally the Ionic forms τόλμη and πρύμνη. In Ion v. 1416 the reading ἣ γε τόλμα for ἡ τόλμα γέ σου is as easy as γενεά in this place ; and the change seems safer than the dependence on such questionable theories.

164—5. In the old copies these two verses appear to have undergone some interpolations. For δαιμόνων there can be no doubt that Musgrave rightly gave δαίμων, which is also found in four MSS. Porson, from a late and worthless MS., reads ἢ δαίμων ἔστ' ἐπαρωγός ; But Hermann remarks that Euripides would doubtless have preferred ἐστὶν ἀρωγός. He considers ποῖ δ' ἥσω spurious, and arranges the verses thus,

στείχω ; ποῦ τις θεῶν ἢ δαίμων
ἐπαρωγός ; ἰὼ κάκ' ἐνεγκοῦσαι
Τρῳάδες, ὦ κάκ' ἐνεγκοῦσαι κτλ.

which involves no other change than ἰὼ for ὦ. This is probable; but W. Dindorf's text is given above; for it is certain that in anapaestics of this kind the most irregular verses are allowable. As for ἰέναι used intransitively, it occurs in Pers. 472, but only as a variant of ἤϊξε, and in a passage of very doubtful genuineness.

166. κάκ' ἐνεγκοῦσαι, who have brought me tidings of evil.

171. γηραιᾷ Herm. for γραίᾳ (γηραιᾷ Dind.). The reading given above is after Porson and Pflugk.

174. Arist. Nub. 1165, (pointed out by Porson, on the authority of a MS. Scholium in loc., as referring to this passage,) ὦ τέκνον, ὦ παῖ, ἔξελθ' οἴκων, ἄϊε σοῦ πατρός. This is the only evidence known respecting the date of the Hecuba, viz. that it must be anterior to B.C. 423. For φήμη, 'bad news,' see Hipp. 157. 572.

αὐδὰν, ὦ τέκνον, ὡς εἰδῇς 175
οἴαν οἴαν ἀΐω φάμαν
περὶ σᾶς ψυχᾶς.

ΠΟΛΥΞΕΝΗ.

ἰώ,
μᾶτερ μᾶτερ, τί βοᾷς ; τί νέον
καρύξασ' οἴκων μ', ὥστ' ὄρνιν,
θάμβει τῷδ' ἐξέπταξας ; 180
ΕΚ. ἰώ μοι, τέκνον.
ΠΟΛΥΞ. τί με δυσφημεῖς ; φροίμιά μοι κακά.
ΕΚ. αἰαῖ, σᾶς ψυχᾶς.
ΠΟΛΥΞ. ἐξαύδα, μὴ κρύψῃς δαρόν.
δειμαίνω δειμαίνω, μᾶτερ, 185
τί ποτ' ἀναστένεις.
ΕΚ. τέκνον, τέκνον μελέας ματρός.
ΠΟΛΥΞ. τί τόδ' ἀγγέλλεις ;
ΕΚ. σφάξαι σ' Ἀργείων κοινὰ
ξυντείνει πρὸς τύμβον γνώμα 190
Πηλείδα γέννᾳ.
ΠΟΛΥΞ. οἴμοι, μᾶτερ, πῶς φθέγγει
ἀμέγαρτα κακῶν ; μάνυσόν μοι
μάνυσον, μᾶτερ.
ΕΚ. αὐδῶ, παῖ, δυσφήμους φάμας· 195
ἀγγέλλουσ' Ἀργείων δόξαι
ψήφῳ τᾶς σᾶς περί μοι ψυχᾶς.

180. The transitive use of ἐκπτήσσειν is rather remarkable. The Greek paraphrast has πετασθῆναί με ἐποίησας.
182. τί με δυσφημεῖς; i. e. τί με δυσφήμως ἐκκαλεῖς; Cf. Heracl. 600, δυσφημεῖν γὰρ ἄζομαι θεάν. Soph. El. 1182, οὔτοι ποτ' ἄλλην ἢ 'μὲ δυσφημεῖς, ξένε.
187. Porson gives the MSS. reading, which is wholly unmetrical, ὦ τέκνον, τέκνον, | μελέας ματρός, (though by reading ματέρος he might have made a dochmiac, as in v. 186.) Hermann omits ὦ, comparing μᾶτερ, μᾶτερ, in v. 178. W. Dindorf has τέκνον ὦ, τέκνον.
191. γέννᾳ is unquestionably right, though most copies (and so Hermann and Porson) give γέννα, i. e. ὦ θυγάτερ. This is weak to the last degree; although, on the other hand, Πηλείδης for Πηλεὺς is so unusual, that Πηλείᾳ γέννᾳ should probably be restored, like τᾶς Τηρείας μήτιδος for Τηρέως, in Aesch. Suppl. 58, and Νηληΐῳ υἷι in Homer, &c. One of the old readings was κοινᾷ γνώμᾳ, which the Schol. thus attempts to explain; ὁ υἱὸς τοῦ Ἀχιλλέως ὁ Νεοπτόλεμος, κοινῇ γνώμῃ τῶν Ἀργείων, συντείνει καὶ σπεύδει σφάξαι σε πρὸς τὸν τάφον, τοῦ πατρὸς αὐτοῦ δηλονότι. Cf. v. 224.
196. ἀγγέλλουσι κτλ. 'They tell me that a resolution concerning your life has been passed by a vote of the Argives.'

ΠΟΛΥΞ. ὦ δεινὰ παθοῦσ', ὦ παντλάμων,
ὦ δυστάνου μᾶτερ βιοτᾶς,
οἵαν οἵαν αὖ σοι λώβαν 200
ἐχθίσταν ἀρρήταν τ'
ὦρσέν τις δαίμων.
οὐκέτι σοι παῖς ἅδ' οὐκέτι δὴ
γήρᾳ δειλαία δειλαίῳ
ξυνδουλεύσω.
σκύμνον γάρ μ' ὥστ' οὐριθρέπταν
μόσχον δειλαία δειλαίαν 205
εἰσόψει χειρὸς ἀναρπαστὰν
σᾶς ἄπο, λαιμότομόν θ' Ἅιδᾳ
γᾶς ὑποπεμπομέναν σκότον, ἔνθα νεκρῶν μέτα
τάλαινα κείσομαι. 210
σὲ μέν, ὦ μᾶτερ δύστανε βίου,
κλαίω πανδύρτοις θρήνοις·
τὸν ἐμὸν δὲ βίον, λώβαν λύμαν τ',
οὐ μετακλαίομαι, ἀλλὰ θανεῖν μοι
ξυντυχία κρείσσων ἐκύρησεν. 215

202. W. Dindorf regards this verse as dochmiac, like v. 186. Perhaps it is rather an anapaestic monometer hypercatalectic; cf. v. 183, 194, and Ion 115, 178. Hermann, guided by his antistrophic theory, thinks something has been lost from the foregoing verse, which he supposes to have been οἴμοι, λώβαν ἐχθίσταν, and in the next he reads ἀρρήταν τ' ὦρσεν δαίμων. The MSS. give ὦρσε. It is quite as likely that one of the two epithets is an interpolation, though the Scholiast recognizes both; or we might read οἵαν λώβαν ἐχθίσταν | ἀρρήταν τ' ὦρσεν δαίμων.
204. οὐρειθρέπταν Porson, from one MS., who calls οὐριθρέπταν " gravissimus error." But this is a hasty remark. Euripides never hesitates to make a vowel long in such words as μελάθρα, ὀλέθριος, &c.; and though both ὁριβάτης (Ar. Av. 276,) and ὀρειβάτης are right, and likewise οὐριβάτης, Electr. 170, the *two* syllables cannot be lengthened in the same word.
206. For the rhythm of this verse compare v. 166, 215. It is needless to say that such could only occur in irregular systems.
210. The old copies give ἁ τάλαινα. Seidler omitted the article, comparing v. 169.
211. So Porson (in ed. 2), Pflugk, Dind., Herm., for the old reading καὶ σὲ μέν, μᾶτερ δύστανε, κλαίω, some copies giving δυστάνου βίον. " Matrem, quod maneat in vita, deflendam; se quod relinquet vitam, non deflendam esse dicit Polyxena." *Herm.*
212. πανδύρτοις Dind. after Blomfield for πανοδύρτοις, the spondaic verse being the more probable form in a matter where MSS. have no real authority, since the transcribers did not know the existence of δύρεσθαι along with ὀδύρεσθαι.
214. μετακλαίομαι. Similar compounds are μεταλγεῖν in Aesch. Suppl. 400, and μεταστένεσθαι in Med. 996. The notion of all seems to be *sero ingemiscere*, ' to weep when it is too late.' Thus Polyxena here knows that her fate is sealed, and that if she did bewail her lot, it would be useless to do so. The Scholiast has μεταβαλλομένη κλαίω, but this has no adequate meaning.

ΕΚΑΒΗ. 503

ΧΟ. καὶ μὴν Ὀδυσσεὺς ἔρχεται σπουδῇ ποδός,
Ἑκάβη, νέον τι πρὸς σὲ σημανῶν ἔπος.

ΟΔΥΣΣΕΥΣ.

γύναι, δοκῶ μέν σ' εἰδέναι γνώμην στρατοῦ
ψῆφόν τε τὴν κρανθεῖσαν, ἀλλ' ὅμως φράσω.
ἔδοξ' Ἀχαιοῖς παῖδα σὴν Πολυξένην   220
σφάξαι πρὸς ὀρθὸν χῶμ' Ἀχιλλείου τάφου.
ἡμᾶς δὲ πομποὺς καὶ κομιστῆρας κόρης
τάσσουσιν εἶναι· θύματος δ' ἐπιστάτης
ἱερεύς τ' ἐπέστη τοῦδε παῖς Ἀχιλλέως.
οἶσθ' οὖν ὃ δρᾶσον; μήτ' ἀποσπασθῇς βίᾳ   225
μήτ' ἐς χερῶν ἅμιλλαν ἐξέλθῃς ἐμοί·
γίγνωσκε δ' ἀλκὴν καὶ παρουσίαν κακῶν
τῶν σῶν. σοφόν τοι κἀν κακοῖς ἃ δεῖ φρονεῖν.

ΕΚ. αἰαῖ· παρέστηχ', ὡς ἔοικ', ἀγὼν μέγας,
πλήρης στεναγμῶν οὐδὲ δακρύων κενός.   230
κἀγὼ γὰρ οὐκ ἔθνησκον οὗ μ' ἐχρῆν θανεῖν,
οὐδ' ὤλεσέν με Ζεύς, τρέφει δ', ὅπως ὁρῶ
κακῶν κάκ' ἄλλα μείζον' ἢ τάλαιν' ἐγώ.
εἰ δ' ἔστι τοῖς δούλοισι τοὺς ἐλευθέρους
μὴ λυπρὰ μηδὲ καρδίας δηκτήρια   235
ἐξιστορῆσαι, σοὶ μὲν εἰρῆσθαι χρεών,

---

219. κραίνειν ψῆφον is a phrase that occurs in several places. To the passages quoted by Pflugk, Troad. 780, Androm. 1272, add Aesch. Suppl. 919, τοιάδε δημόπρακτος ἐκ πόλεως μία ψῆφος κέκρανται.
223. It may be doubted whether the close occurrence of ἐπιστάτης and ἐπέστη was not an oversight on the part of the poet. At all events the genitive depends on the substantive. In Hel. 1267, ἐρετμῶν ἐπιστάτας means 'managers of the oar,' and in Tro. 436, the Cyclops is called ὠμόφρων ἐπιστάτης, where the omission of ποιμνίων is remarkable.
229. ἀγὼν μέγας. Not, as Pflugk says, because she cannot, through her own wretchedness, assist Polyxena; but because she has been spared but to hear of her cruel fate; and it is the bearing this which is her trial, her ἀγών. The γάρ as well as the καί in 231 has caused difficulty to some; and W. Dindorf admits a very unsatisfactory alteration of his brother's, κἄγωγ' ἄρ'. The meaning of γάρ is clear enough according to the explanation above; and καί means that she too, as well as others, seems to have been specially reserved for misery, when death would have ended her troubles. Hermann compares v. 284.
236. σοὶ μὲν κτλ. 'Tis fit that an end should be made of your speech, and that you should attend to my questions.' So Hermann. Nevertheless, ἀκούειν τινὰ is very unusual Greek: and the poet might have said, σοὶ μὲν εἰρήσθω λόγος, ἡμῶν δ' ἄκουε τῶν ἐρωτώντων τάδε. The words in the text would also mean, (and, in the opinion of the present editor, they do mean,) 'it is to you (ἐλευθέρῳ) that our words must be spoken, and it is for us who ask (δούλους) to hear your reply.'

ἡμᾶς δ' ἀκοῦσαι τοὺς ἐρωτῶντας τάδε.
ΟΔ. ἔξεστ', ἐρώτα· τοῦ χρόνου γὰρ οὐ φθονῶ.
ΕΚ. οἶσθ' ἡνίκ' ἦλθες Ἰλίου κατάσκοπος,
δυσχλαινίᾳ τ' ἄμορφος, ὀμμάτων τ' ἄπο   240
φόνου σταλαγμοὶ σὴν κατέσταζον γένυν;
ΟΔ. οἶδ'· οὐ γὰρ ἄκρας καρδίας ἔψαυσέ μου.
ΕΚ. ἔγνω δέ σ' Ἑλένη, καὶ μόνῃ κατεῖπ' ἐμοί;
ΟΔ. μεμνήμεθ' ἐς κίνδυνον ἐλθόντες μέγαν.
ΕΚ. ἦψω δὲ γονάτων τῶν ἐμῶν ταπεινὸς ὤν;   245
ΟΔ. ὥστ' ἐνθανεῖν γε σοῖς πέπλοισι χεῖρ' ἐμήν.
ΕΚ. τί δῆτ' ἔλεξας, δοῦλος ὢν ἐμὸς τότε;
ΟΔ. πολλῶν λόγων εὑρήμαθ', ὥστε μὴ θανεῖν.
ΕΚ. ἔσωσα δῆτά σ', ἐξέπεμψά τε χθονός;
ΟΔ. ὥστ' εἰσορᾶν γε φέγγος ἡλίου τόδε.   250
ΕΚ. οὔκουν κακύνει τοῖσδε τοῖς βουλεύμασιν,

Schol. πρὸς σὲ χρεὼν καὶ πρέπον ἐστὶν εἰρῆσθαι, ὑπ' ἐμοῦ δηλονότι, ἡμᾶς δὲ τοὺς ἐρωτῶντας ἀκοῦσαι ταῦτα.

238. χρόνου. Similar expressions are, σχολῆς τόδ' ἔργον,—καὶ γὰρ οὐ κάμνω σχολῇ,—σχολῇ πλείων ἢ θέλω πάρεστι, &c.—For οἶσθ' ἡνίκα see above, v. 112.

240. ὀμμάτων ἄπο. In Rhes. 711, where the same adventure is described (either from Od. iv. 244 &c., or from the Cyclic poems), he is spoken of as ὕπαφρον ὄμμ' ἔχων, an obscure phrase, but perhaps meaning 'moistened with blood,' or rheum. He feigned to have received bruises, αὐτόν μιν πληγῇσιν ἀεικελίῃσι δαμάσσας, doubtless on the face; and the effect of these is to produce bloodshot eyes. Poetically, he is described as having blood trickling from his eyes to his chin; and indeed, there is nothing impossible in the literal acceptation. Pflugk has very happily quoted Iph. T. 1373, οἱ μὲν ἐν κάρᾳ κάθαιμ' ἔχοντες τραύμαθ', οἱ δ' ἐν ὄμμασιν, and Hermann, not less so, Frag. Thes. 388, ὀμμάτων δ' ἄπο αἱμοσταγῆ πρηστῆρε ῥεύσονται κάτω. Porson, who gives δυσχλαινίαις, (the word is used in the plural in Hel. 416,) and thinks φόβου the true reading for φόνου, appears to have felt a difficulty about the meaning which, without much reason, other commentators have shared in.

242. οἶδ' κτλ. 'I well remember it; for the circumstance took no light hold of my heart,' i. e. it was too serious a business, too dangerous an adventure, easily to be forgotten. On ἄκρα καρδία see Bacch. 203.

243. ἐμοὶ Brunck for μοι. The emphatic pronoun is obviously required by the sense. Homer makes Helen alone to have recognised Ulysses in his disguise. The making Hecuba a confidant is probably an invention of Euripides. For κατειπεῖν see Ion 1215. Hel. 898.

245. ταπεινὸς, in a suppliant posture. Pflugk compares Androm. 165, πτῆξαι ταπεινὴν, προσπεσεῖν τ' ἐμὸν γόνυ.

246. ἐνθανεῖν πέπλοις, a singular but elegant phrase, to express that the hand was clasped with a mental and bodily emotion so intense, that it became fixed like that of a statue.

247. δοῦλος ὢν ἐμός. Scil. ὥσπερ ἐγὼ νῦν σὸς δοῦλός εἰμι, when I had you in my power as completely as you now have me. This and the following verse are placed after the next couplet in all the MSS. but three. Porson in his first edition retained the old order, but in his second edited as above,—in which Hermann, Pflugk, and others have followed him. The reason is plain; what Hecuba is all along leading him to admit, is the fact that she saved his life in a time of danger; and therefore this should evidently be placed last, as the crowning point of the whole dialogue.

ΕΚΑΒΗ. 505

ὃς ἐξ ἐμοῦ μὲν ἔπαθες οἷα φῂς παθεῖν,
δρᾷς δ' οὐδὲν ἡμᾶς εὖ, κακῶς δ' ὅσον δύνᾳ;
ἀχάριστον ὑμῶν σπέρμ', ὅσοι δημηγόρους
ζηλοῦτε τιμάς· μηδὲ γιγνώσκοισθέ μοι, 255
οἳ τοὺς φίλους βλάπτοντες οὐ φροντίζετε,
ἢν τοῖσι πολλοῖς πρὸς χάριν λέγητέ τι.
ἀτὰρ τί δὴ σόφισμα τοῦθ' ἡγούμενοι
ἐς τήνδε παῖδα ψῆφον ὥρισαν φόνου;
πότερα τὸ χρῆν σφ' ἐπήγαγ' ἀνθρωποσφαγεῖν 260
πρὸς τύμβον, ἔνθα βουθυτεῖν μᾶλλον πρέπει;
ἢ τοὺς κτανόντας ἀνταποκτεῖναι θέλων
ἐς τήνδ' Ἀχιλλεὺς ἐνδίκως τείνει φόνον;
ἀλλ' οὐδὲν αὐτὸν ἥδε γ' εἴργασται κακόν.
Ἑλένην νιν αἰτεῖν χρῆν τάφῳ προσφάγματα· 265
κείνη γὰρ ὤλεσέν νιν ἐς Τροίαν τ' ἄγει.
εἰ δ' αἰχμάλωτον χρή τιν' ἔκκριτον θανεῖν
κάλλει θ' ὑπερφέρουσαν, οὐχ ἡμῶν τόδε·

253. δύνᾳ Porson for δύνῃ. See Androm. 239. Hermann has a fancy that δύνῃ is to be retained here and elsewhere, and that δύνᾳ is a Doricism; but he gives no reason for his opinion (unless it be an obscure scholiast on Il. Ξ. 199, quoted in W. Dindorf's note).
254—7. A fine and striking passage against the mischievous and selfish ambition of the demagogues, to whom (as has been shown in the Preface to Vol. i. p. xviii) Euripides was ever consistently opposed. Whether any particular statesman is here alluded to, is uncertain; at least, the poet speaks very generally and comprehensively.
258. ἀτὰρ κτλ. '(It is indeed a natural ambition in a man to be thought σοφὸς,) yet what plausible reasoning did they consider this to be, when they gave the decisive vote (decided a vote) of death against this child of mine? Was it an inevitable necessity that induced them to slay a human victim at a tomb, where to sacrifice oxen is more proper? Or was it from a wish to kill in return those who had killed him, that Achilles justly threatens death against her?'—τὸ χρῆν, for χρῆναι, is confirmed by the authority of Eustathius (quoted by Porson), who says καὶ τὸ χρῆναι—καὶ χρῆν μονοσυλ-

λάβως λέγεται παρά τε Εὐριπίδῃ καὶ Σοφοκλεῖ. It is the same form as ζῆν from ζάω or ζῆμι. In Herc. F. 828, τὸ χρῆν νιν ἐξέσωζεν seems a more correct reading than τὸ χρεών, which is found in all the MSS. in Iph. T. 1486, though there also Dindorf has edited τὸ γὰρ χρῆν σοῦ τε καὶ θεῶν κρατεῖ. It remains however a question if χρῆν is not really the imperfect, whether τὸ be taken for ὃ (quod decebat), or the impersonal verb be regarded as a neuter noun. Compare τὸ μὴ θέμις, Aesch. Suppl. 330. Cho. 630.
263. τείνειν φόνον is necem intentare, probably a metaphor from directing a javelin.
265. χρῆν for χρῆ, conjectured by Elmsley (Heracl. 959), has been recovered from two MSS. It is rather surprising that Porson's accurate and intuitive knowledge of Greek did not lead him to the same suggestion. Not indeed that χρὴ is wrong ('he ought to ask, which it is not yet too late to do'), but that χρῆν is better ('he ought to have asked, which he has not done'), since he merely requested τινὰ Τρωιάδων, v. 97.
268. οὐχ ἡμῶν τόδε, this does not belong to our side, but to the Greeks, who possess Helen, the most beautiful of women.

VOL. II. 3 T

ΕΥΡΙΠΙΔΟΥ

ἡ Τυνδαρὶς γὰρ εἶδος εὐπρεπεστάτη,
ἀδικοῦσά θ' ἡμῶν οὐδὲν ἧσσον ηὑρέθη.   270
τῷ μὲν δικαίῳ τόνδ' ἁμιλλῶμαι λόγον·
ἃ δ' ἀντιδοῦναι δεῖ σ', ἀπαιτούσης ἐμοῦ,
ἄκουσον. ἤψω τῆς ἐμῆς, ὡς φῄς, χερὸς
καὶ τῆς γεραιᾶς προσπίτνων παρηΐδος·
ἀνθάπτομαί σου τῶνδε τῶν αὐτῶν ἐγώ,   275
χάριν τ' ἀπαιτῶ τὴν τόθ', ἱκετεύω τέ σε,
μή μου τὸ τέκνον ἐκ χερῶν ἀποσπάσῃς,
μηδὲ κτάνητε. τῶν τεθνηκότων ἅλις·
ταύτῃ γέγηθα κἀπιλήθομαι κακῶν·
ἥδ' ἀντὶ πολλῶν ἐστί μοι παραψυχή,   280
πόλις, τιθήνη, βάκτρον, ἡγεμὼν ὁδοῦ.
οὐ τοὺς κρατοῦντας χρὴ κρατεῖν ἃ μὴ χρεών,
οὐδ' εὐτυχοῦντας εὖ δοκεῖν πράξειν ἀεί.
κἀγὼ γὰρ ἦν ποτ', ἀλλὰ νῦν οὐκ εἴμ' ἔτι,
τὸν πάντα δ' ὄλβον ἦμαρ ἕν μ' ἀφείλετο.   285
ἀλλ', ὦ φίλον γένειον, αἰδέσθητί με,
οἴκτειρον· ἐλθὼν δ' εἰς Ἀχαιϊκὸν στρατὸν
παρηγόρησον, ὡς ἀποκτείνειν φθόνος

269. ἐκπρεπεστάτη Dind. after Brunck.
271. τῷ μὲν δικαίῳ, τῇ δίκῃ. 'Against his (Achilles') claims on the score of *justice* I press this (the above) argument; and now hear what I demand from you on the law of requital,' &c. The former has regard to ἐνδίκως, v. 263, viz. to the right of Achilles in demanding Polyxena rather than another; the latter to the question of gratitude for former favours conferred on Ulysses, whom she regards (cf. 135) as the author of the present misfortune.
274. τῆσδε γραίας Porson and Hermann. The common reading is τῆσδε γεραιᾶς, where, of course, as in v. 64, the middle syllable must be regarded as short. But τῆς γεραιᾶς, which Hermann says " valde languet," is rightly given by Dind. Matth. and Pflugk from one MS. It is obvious that τῆς ἐμῆς γεραιᾶς must be understood from the preceding verse.
282. οὐ—χρεών. The first negative might seem to belong strictly to χρὴ, but the sense probably is this, 'it is not because people have power, that they should exercise it amiss.' The reading of Stobaeus, Ecl. cv. 20, οὔ τοι κρατοῦντα, seems highly probable.
283. Hermann, Matthiae, and Pflugk, prefer πράσσειν, most MSS. giving πράττειν. The present tense is defensible; see the note on Troad. 1203.
284. ἦν ποτε. Contrasted with οὐκ εἴμ' ἔτι, this clearly means 'I was once somebody' (as we say), i. e. was happy and prosperous: nor is it necessary to supply εὐτυχὴς, or ὀλβία from the next verse, since εἶναι alone meant that sort of life which deserves the name of life. Cf. Alcest. 802, οὐ βίος ἀληθῶς ὁ βίος, ἀλλὰ συμφορά.
288. παρηγόρησον, 'talk them over.' Cf. πατρῴας μόγις παρειποῦσα φρένας, Prom. 132. And παρηγορεῖν is so used *ibid.* 664, 1022. Photius, παρηγορίας, συμβουλῆς ἢ παρακλήσεως. It may be doubted if Hermann is right in explaining ὡς nam (ἐπεὶ), as if the following sentence was Hecuba's remark to Ulysses,

γυναῖκας, ἃς τὸ πρῶτον οὐκ ἐκτείνατε
βωμῶν ἀποσπάσαντες, ἀλλ' ᾠκτείρατε. 290
νόμος δ' ἐν ὑμῖν τοῖς τ' ἐλευθέροις ἴσος
καὶ τοῖσι δούλοις αἵματος κεῖται πέρι.
τὸ δ' ἀξίωμα, κἂν κακῶς λέγῃς, τὸ σὸν
πείσει· λόγος γὰρ ἔκ τ' ἀδοξούντων ἰὼν
κἀκ τῶν δοκούντων αὑτὸς οὐ ταὐτὸν σθένει. 295
ΧΟ. οὐκ ἔστιν οὕτω στερρὸς ἀνθρώπου φύσις,
ἥτις γόων σῶν καὶ μακρῶν ὀδυρμάτων
κλύουσα θρήνους οὐκ ἂν ἐκβάλοι δάκρυ.
ΟΔ. Ἑκάβη, διδάσκου, μηδὲ τῷ θυμουμένῳ
τὸν εὖ λέγοντα δυσμενῆ ποιοῦ φρενί. 300

not his to be made for the instruction of the army. The meaning is, πεῖθε αὐτοὺς ὡς οὐ χρὴ κτείνειν γυναῖκας, ἃς πρόσθεν οὐκ ἔκτειναν.
291. νόμος—ἴσος. The Athenian law made no distinction between slave and freeman in the matter of ὕβρις and φόνος. Xenophon, De Rep. Ath. i. § 10, τῶν δούλων δ' αὖ καὶ τῶν μετοίκων πλείστη ἐστὶν Ἀθήνησιν ἀκολασία, καὶ οὔτε πατάξαι ἔξεστιν αὐτόθι οὔτε ὑπεκστήσεταί σοι ὁ δοῦλος (cf. Ion 637). Demosth. p. 529 (referred to by Hermann), καὶ τοσαύτῃ γ' ἐχρήσατο ὑπερβολῇ (ὁ νομοθέτης), ὥστε κἂν εἰς δοῦλον ὑβρίζῃ τις, ὁμοίως ἔδωκεν ὑπὲρ τούτου γραφήν. οὐ γὰρ ὅστις ὁ πάσχων ᾤετο δεῖν σκοπεῖν, ἀλλὰ τὸ πρᾶγμα ὁποῖόν τι τὸ γιγνόμενον· ἐπειδὴ δ' εὗρεν οὐκ ἐπιτήδειον, μήτε πρὸς δοῦλον μηθ' ὅλως ἐξεῖναι πράττειν ἐπέτρεψεν.
293. λέγῃς Porson and Dindorf, after Muretus and others. λέγῃ all the copies of Euripides, and so Aulus Gellius xi. 4, and Stobaeus, Flor. 45, 6. Hermann and Pflugk defend λέγῃ, in this sense, *tua auctoritas, etiam si deteriora suadet, vincit.* 'Your influence, even if it should speak on the wrong side, or urge a wrong cause (which now it will not), will prevail.' Ennius, whose version of this passage is given by Gellius, seems to have read λέγῃς, *haec tu etsi pervorse dices, facile Achivos flexeris*. The sense in either case is the same, so that the question is not very important. By κακῶς λέγειν is meant, not bad or ineffective oratory, but oratory in a cause which the majority consider a bad one. For πείσει Gellius has νικᾷ, which would apply to the general results of his eloquence, as proved by experience, and gives a much tamer sense.
295. τῶν δοκούντων, scil. εἶναί τι, 'those held in repute.' So Troad. 609, τὰ δὲ δοκοῦντ' ἀπώλεσαν, scil. οἱ θεοί.
296. οὐκ ἔστιν. Porson gives τίς ἔστιν from Gregory of Corinth, p. 26, but there also Hermann says that one MS. has οὐκ ἔστιν. There is no difficulty in ἥτις οὐκ = ὥστε μή. Cf. Hel. 501—2.
299. Ulysses justifies his conduct by arguments on the score of expediency. He freely admits his obligation to Hecuba, and would return it if it were possible; but he has passed his word to the army that Polyxena shall be given up for a victim, and he cannot retract it. He lays it down as a doctrine, that public honours should be paid after death to those who have been conspicuously brave; for this is the only incitement to the living, to witness the glory of the dead. For himself, he would prefer an honoured tomb to riches in life. Besides, Hecuba is not worse off than others: there are many Greek mothers who have to bewail their sons slain at Troy, many widows their husbands. The very course which Hellas would desire their eastern enemies to pursue is this, so fatal to rising valour, namely, to neglect and contemn the memory of those who have died for their country.
300. μὴ ποιοῦ. Do not in your anger regard in your mind one that speaks rightly as if he were your enemy. The causal dative stands for διὰ τὴν ὀργήν.

ἐγὼ τὸ μὲν σὸν σῶμ', ὑφ' οὗπερ ηὐτύχουν,
σώζειν ἕτοιμός εἰμι, κοὐκ ἄλλως λέγω·
ἃ δ' εἶπον εἰς ἅπαντας, οὐκ ἀρνήσομαι,
Τροίας ἁλούσης ἀνδρὶ τῷ πρώτῳ στρατοῦ
σὴν παῖδα δοῦναι σφάγιον ἐξαιτουμένῳ.   305
ἐν τῷδε γὰρ κάμνουσιν αἱ πολλαὶ πόλεις,
ὅταν τις ἐσθλὸς καὶ πρόθυμος ὢν ἀνὴρ
μηδὲν φέρηται τῶν κακιόνων πλέον.
ἡμῖν δ' Ἀχιλλεὺς ἄξιος τιμῆς, γύναι,
θανὼν ὑπὲρ γῆς Ἑλλάδος κάλλιστ' ἀνήρ.   310
οὔκουν τόδ' αἰσχρόν, εἰ βλέποντι μὲν φίλῳ
χρώμεσθ', ἐπεὶ δ' ἄπεστι, μὴ χρώμεσθ' ἔτι;
εἶεν· τί δῆτ' ἐρεῖ τις, ἤν τις αὖ φανῇ
στρατοῦ τ' ἄθροισις πολεμίων τ' ἀγωνία;
πότερα μαχούμεθ', ἢ φιλοψυχήσομεν,   315
τὸν κατθανόνθ' ὁρῶντες οὐ τιμώμενον;
καὶ μὴν ἔμοιγε ζῶντι μέν, καθ' ἡμέραν,

301. τὸ μὲν σὸν σῶμα is opposed to τὴν σὴν δὲ παῖδα in v. 305, where the aorist δοῦναι (for δώσειν) is used as it not unfrequently is, with verbs of promising, hoping, intending, &c. Pflugk compares Orest. 269, οἷς μ' εἶπ' Ἀπόλλων ἐξαμύνασθαι θεάς. See also Andromach. 27. 311.
304. Τροίας ἁλούσης. This is not to be taken as a vow made before the event, but as a reason why he now voted for the measure, viz. because Troy had been captured by the aid of Achilles.
306—8. Quoted by Stobaeus, Flor. 43, 19. 'This is the weak point in most states, that your brave man gains nothing more than your coward.' Euripides perhaps intended to reproach his countrymen for the same fault which they are charged with in Andromach. 693, viz. the neglect of the truly brave and deserving soldier if he did not happen to hold a high rank.
309. ἄξιος τιμῆς ἡμῖν, 'deserving of honour at our hands,' as Alcest. 434, ἀξία δέ μοι τιμῆς (τιμᾶν). The dative may be explained either as 'in our judgment,' or 'from (at) us,' like the epic δέξατό οἱ σκῆπτρον, &c.
310. κάλλιστ' ἀνήρ, for εἷς ἀνήρ, 'as nobly as a man could.' See Rhes. 500, καὶ πλεῖστα χώραν τήνδ' ἀνὴρ καθυβρίσας.
312. ἄπεστι. So the recent editors on the authority of one MS. Porson gives the common reading ὄλωλε, which is believed to be a gloss. Hermann well observes, that the *absence* of a man is a much more significant reason why he should be forgotten; but at the same time, one would have thought Euripides would have adopted a favourite antithesis by using παρόντι in place of βλέποντι.
317—20. καὶ μὴν κτλ. The particles which introduce this passage seem to refer to some suppressed idea; and that idea has been finely developed in Troad. 1248. (' Some perhaps will say, Honours to the dead are vain tributes;) and yet for myself indeed, while in life, even if I possessed little, any thing would be enough for daily subsistence; but for my *tomb*, I should wish all to see it that it is held in honour; for the gratification is for a long time.' On καθ' ἡμέραν see Bacch. 485. Dindorf wrongly punctuates ζῶντι μὲν καθ' ἡμέραν, for the latter words belong to ἀρκούντως ἔχοι, ζῶντι μὲν being opposed to θανὼν δὲ implied in the next clause. There is some emphasis in τὸν ἐμόν, which it is difficult to convey in English ; ' my own tomb, at least, though others may be forgotten or dishonoured.' To show any insult to a man's monument, was to insult his memory and his shade

ΕΚΑΒΗ. 509

κεἰ σμίκρ' ἔχοιμι, πάντ' ἂν ἀρκούντως ἔχοι·
τύμβον δὲ βουλοίμην ἂν ἀξιούμενον
τὸν ἐμὸν ὁρᾶσθαι· διὰ μακροῦ γὰρ ἡ χάρις.   320
εἰ δ' οἰκτρὰ πάσχειν φῂς, τάδ' ἀντάκουέ μου·
εἰσὶν παρ' ἡμῖν οὐδὲν ἧσσον ἄθλιαι
γραῖαι γυναῖκες ἠδὲ πρεσβῦται σέθεν,
νύμφαι τ' ἀρίστων νυμφίων τητώμεναι,
ὧν ἥδε κεύθει σώματ' Ἰδαία κόνις.   325
τόλμα τάδ'· ἡμεῖς δ', εἰ κακῶς νομίζομεν
τιμᾶν τὸν ἐσθλόν, ἀμαθίαν ὀφλήσομεν·
οἱ βάρβαροι δὲ μήτε τοὺς φίλους φίλους
ἡγεῖσθε μήτε τοὺς καλῶς τεθνηκότας
θαυμάζεθ', ὡς ἂν ἡ μὲν Ἑλλὰς εὐτυχῇ,   330
ὑμεῖς δ' ἔχηθ' ὅμοια τοῖς βουλεύμασιν.
ΧΟ. αἰαῖ· τὸ δοῦλον ὡς κακὸν πέφυκ' ἀεί,
τολμᾷ θ' ἃ μὴ χρὴ τῇ βίᾳ νικώμενον.
ΕΚ. ὦ θύγατερ, οὑμοὶ μὲν λόγοι πρὸς αἰθέρα
φροῦδοι μάτην ῥιφθέντες ἀμφὶ σοῦ φόνου·   335

---

below. Hence it is said of Aegisthus that he used to pelt the tomb of Agamemnon, Electr. 328, πέτροις τε λεύει μνῆμα λάϊνον πατρός.
326. ἡμεῖς δὲ κτλ. A prose writer would probably have said ἡμεῖς μὲν γάρ, for the usual antithesis between βάρβαροι and Ἕλληνες is meant. 'We Greeks, of course, if we wrongly adopt the practice of honouring the brave, shall incur the charge of folly for it; but, for you barbarians, we can only wish that you may never regard your friends as friends, or pay any respect to those who have nobly died; so as that Hellas may be prosperous, and you may have fortunes corresponding to your counsels,' i. e. bad fortunes.—μήτε κτλ., the imperative; they are told to go on doing that which it is to the interest of their foes that they should do.
330. ὡς ἂν κτλ. Hermann says this means dummodo, si modo. It would be more correct to say, that it expresses the result rather than the intention, 'so as that' rather than 'in order that.'
332—3. There are two readings of this passage, between which it is very difficult to choose; πεφυκέναι (the edd. and MSS.) and πέφυκ' ἀεί, Stobaeus, Flor. lxii. 25, who likewise gives κρατούμενον for νικώμενον. Porson, followed by Pflugk, gives πεφυκέναι and τολμᾶν θ', Hermann πεφυκέναι and τολμᾷ θ', but the latter attaches to it a sense which few will approve, though it is given by one of the scholiasts, 'how bad is slavery, to be born to it, and (how) it has to bear what it ought not, coerced by force.' Pflugk too ventures something out of the natural and obvious sense, (which is, ὡς κακόν ἐστι τὸ πεφυκέναι τινὰ δοῦλον,) and suspects the poet meant, 'how bad slavery always is, and (how its nature is) to have to bear,' &c. Dindorf edits as given above; and it is at least as good as the other; 'Alas! how sad is slavery in all circumstances, and how it endures what it should not, being overcome by the necessity imposed on it.'
335. ῥιφέντες Porson and Hermann, with the great majority of copies. If any passage can be adduced where the metre requires ῥιφεὶς, there is an end of the question; but meanwhile, both here and in Androm. 10, the other form seems the safest. The phrase ῥίπτειν λόγους is

σὺ δ' εἴ τι μείζω δύναμιν ἢ μήτηρ ἔχεις,
σπούδαζε, πάσας ὥστ' ἀηδόνος στόμα
φθογγὰς ἱεῖσα, μὴ στερηθῆναι βίου.
πρόσπιπτε δ' οἰκτρῶς τοῦδ' Ὀδυσσέως γόνυ,
καὶ πεῖθ'. ἔχεις δὲ πρόφασιν· ἔστι γὰρ τέκνα 340
καὶ τῷδε, τὴν σὴν ὥστ' ἐποικτεῖραι τύχην.
ΠΟΛΥΞ. ὁρῶ σ', Ὀδυσσεῦ, δεξιὰν ὑφ' εἵματος
κρύπτοντα χεῖρα, καὶ πρόσωπον ἔμπαλιν
στρέφοντα, μή σου προσθίγω γενειάδος.
θάρσει· πέφευγας τὸν ἐμὸν ἱκέσιον Δία· 345
ὡς ἕψομαί γε τοῦ τ' ἀναγκαίου χάριν
θανεῖν τε χρῄζουσ'· εἰ δὲ μὴ βουλήσομαι,
κακὴ φανοῦμαι καὶ φιλόψυχος γυνή.
τί γάρ με δεῖ ζῆν; ᾗ πατὴρ μὲν ἦν ἄναξ
Φρυγῶν ἁπάντων· τοῦτό μοι πρῶτον βίου· 350
ἔπειτ' ἐθρέφθην ἐλπίδων καλῶν ὕπο,
βασιλεῦσι νύμφη, ζῆλον οὐ σμικρὸν γάμων

common, and often means, 'to speak earnestly,' 'hastily,' &c., without μάτην. See Aesch. Prom. 319. Suppl. 478. But Med. 1404, μάτην ἔπος ἔρριπται.

337. ἀηδόνος. Because the notes of this bird are at once varied (πάσας φθογγὰς) and melancholy. The short ἰ in ἱημι is also used in Aesch. Theb. 488. It is long inf. v. 367. 900.

340. ἔχεις πρόφασιν. You have a fair plea for doing so, because being a parent as well as your mother, he will not be insensible to the appeal. She adds τὴν σὴν τύχην where we might have looked rather for τὴν ἐμήν, but the meaning is, that he can realise the position of a child of his own under the like circumstances.

342. Polyxena, instead of asking for her life, resigns it without a murmur; not indeed in a chivalrous spirit, like Macaria in the Heraclidae, but because it is not worth contending for. She had seen prosperity, and she has seen misery; and this is the fate of all others which the Greeks thought the most truly pitiable. (See Troad. 634.) She enumerates the various ignominies that are certain to befal her in captivity, and concludes that it is better to die. And she entreats her mother not to oppose her determination by a word or a deed.

343. χεῖρα. Here we have, what is not very often the case, an exact description of the position occupied by a Greek actor during an address. It is a fine conception, and one that might be finely transferred either to canvas or marble.— μὴ, for ἵνα μὴ, is a more usual Latin than Greek idiom, ne te tangam &c. When the Greeks use μὴ alone, it usually refers to some action or emotion on the part of the person concerned, as δέδοικα μὴ &c. Here, in fact, δεδοικότα is implied by the context; and though προσθίγω is the act of another person, the effect upon himself is virtually regarded, δεδοικότα μὴ ὑπ' ἐμοῦ πεισθῇς.

345. τὸν ἐμὸν ἱκ. Δία, the consequences of my curse; the μίασμα or crime which will result to you if you spurn a suppliant's prayer. Aesch. Suppl. 379, μένει τοι Ζηνὸς Ἱκταίου κότος | δυσπαράθελκτος παθόντος οἴκτοις.

350. πρῶτον βίου. Not for ἡ ἀρχὴ, but, as the Schol. explains, and Hermann and Dindorf think, κατὰ τὸ ἀξίωμα, 'in respect of estimation,' i. e. 'this was the first and highest part of my lot in life.'

352. ζῆλον—ἀφίξομαι. 'Having had the honour of being much sought for in marriage, as to whose home and hearth I should come.' Such purely Greek idioms

ἔχουσ', ὅτου δῶμ' ἑστίαν τ' ἀφίξομαι·
δέσποινα δ' ἡ δύστηνος Ἰδαίαισιν ἦν
γυναιξὶ, παρθένοις ἀπόβλεπτος μέτα, 355
ἴση θεοῖσι, πλὴν τὸ κατθανεῖν μόνον·
νῦν δ' εἰμὶ δούλη. πρῶτα μέν με τοὔνομα
θανεῖν ἐρᾶν τίθησιν, οὐκ εἰωθὸς ὄν·
ἔπειτ' ἴσως ἂν δεσποτῶν ὠμῶν φρένας
τύχοιμ' ἄν, ὅστις ἀργύρου μ' ὠνήσεται, 360
τὴν Ἕκτορός τε χἀτέρων πολλῶν κάσιν,
προσθεὶς δ' ἀνάγκην σιτοποιὸν ἐν δόμοις,
σαίρειν τε δῶμα κερκίσιν τ' ἐφεστάναι
λυπρὰν ἄγουσαν ἡμέραν μ' ἀναγκάσει·
λέχη δὲ τἀμὰ δοῦλος ὠνητός ποθεν 365
χρανεῖ, τυράννων πρόσθεν ἠξιωμένα.
οὐ δῆτ'· ἀφίημ' ὀμμάτων ἐλεύθερον
φέγγος τόδ', Ἅιδῃ προστιθεῖσ' ἐμὸν δέμας.
ἄγ' οὖν μ', Ὀδυσσεῦ, καὶ διέργασαί μ' ἄγων·
οὔτ' ἐλπίδος γὰρ οὔτε του δόξης ὁρῶ 370
θάρσος παρ' ἡμῖν ὥς ποτ' εὖ πρᾶξαί με χρή.
μῆτερ, σὺ δ' ἡμῖν μηδὲν ἐμποδὼν γένῃ

it is very difficult exactly to translate. By ζῆλος γάμων she means the jealous contests of rivals for her hand; and this ζῆλος she is said ἔχειν, because she herself is the object of it, and the consequences of her own natural gifts fall upon herself.

355. παρθένοις τ' Porson with some copies. For the metre however see the note on Bacch. 1125, λαβοῦσα δ' ὠλέναις ἀριστερὰν χέρα. As ἀποβλέπειν τινὰ is 'to look *off* from one object to some greater point of attraction,' so ἀπόβλεπτος is θαυμαστὸς, ἀποσκοπούμενος. — μετὰ, 'amongst;' a use of the dative rare in Attic Greek. Compare Pers. 615, λιβάσιν ὑδρηλαῖς παρθένου πηγῆς μέτα. Hermann inclines to Canter's conjecture μέγα, though it is slighted by Porson. In the next line it is singular that Porson should prefer the Aldine θεῇσι, with the brief comment "Alii θεοῖσι." The feminine, as Dindorf after Hermann remarks, would have been 'equal to the goddesses in beauty,' whereas she means, 'equal to the gods in prosperity, εὐδαιμονία, except only in being mortal.'

358. εἰωθὸς, εἰθισμένον. The addition of ὄν is unusual. Porson well compares Ar. Ran. 721, τούτοισιν, οὖσιν εὖ κεκιβδηλευμένοις,—χρώμεθ' οὐδέν.

359. ὠμῶν φρένας. Aesch. Agam. 1011, οἳ δ' οὔποτ' ἐλπίσαντες ἤμησαν καλῶς, ὠμοί τε δούλοις πάντα καὶ παρὰ στάθμην. —ἀργύρου κτλ., cf. Alcest. 675, Λυδὸν ἢ Φρύγα κακοῖς ἐλαύνειν ἀργυρώνητον σέθεν.

366. χραίνειν, 'to touch,' with the notion of pollution attending the act, occurs Hippol. 1266, τὸν τἀμ' ἀπαρνηθέντα μὴ χρᾶναι λέχη.

368. προςτιθεῖσα, 'dedicating,' 'giving up to.' See Androm. 1016.

369. ἄγ' οὖν Porson, omitting the μ', with Thomas Magister in v. διαχρῶμαι.

371. ἐλπὶς—εὖ πρᾶξαι. See above, v. 305.

372. μηδὲν for μὴ or μηδαμῶς, as Androm. 88. Before λέγουσα μὴ is to be supplied. It should properly have been μήτε λ. μήτε δ. Porson gives μήτε δρῶσα, but it is well known that μὴ is rather followed by μηδέ.

λέγουσα μηδέ δρῶσα· συμβούλου δέ μοι
θανεῖν, πρὶν αἰσχρῶν μὴ κατ' ἀξίαν τυχεῖν.
ὅστις γὰρ οὐκ εἴωθε γεύεσθαι κακῶν, 375
φέρει μέν, ἀλγεῖ δ' αὐχέν' ἐντιθεὶς ζυγῷ·
θανὼν δ' ἂν εἴη μᾶλλον εὐτυχέστερος
ἢ ζῶν· τὸ γὰρ ζῆν μὴ καλῶς μέγας πόνος.

ΧΟ. δεινὸς χαρακτὴρ κἀπίσημος ἐν βροτοῖς
ἐσθλῶν γενέσθαι, κἀπὶ μεῖζον ἔρχεται 380
τῆς εὐγενείας ὄνομα τοῖσιν ἀξίοις.

ΕΚ. καλῶς μὲν εἶπας, θύγατερ· ἀλλὰ τῷ καλῷ
λύπη πρόσεστιν. εἰ δὲ δεῖ τῷ Πηλέως
χάριν γενέσθαι παιδί, καὶ ψόγον φυγεῖν
ὑμᾶς, Ὀδυσσεῦ, τήνδε μὲν μὴ κτείνετε, 385
ἡμᾶς δ' ἄγοντες πρὸς πυρὰν Ἀχιλλέως
κεντεῖτε, μὴ φείδεσθ'· ἐγὼ 'τεκον Πάριν,
ὃς παῖδα Θέτιδος ὤλεσεν τόξοις βαλών.

ΟΔ. οὐ σ', ὦ γεραιά, κατθανεῖν Ἀχιλλέως
φάντασμ' Ἀχαιούς, ἀλλὰ τήνδ', ᾐτήσατο. 390

ΕΚ. ὑμεῖς δέ μ' ἀλλὰ θυγατρὶ συμφονεύσατε,
καὶ δὶς τόσον πῶμ' αἵματος γενήσεται
γαίᾳ νεκρῷ τε τῷ τάδ' ἐξαιτουμένῳ.

ΟΔ. ἅλις κόρης σῆς θάνατος· οὐ προσοιστέος
ἄλλος πρὸς ἄλλῳ· μηδὲ τόνδ' ὠφείλομεν. 395

373. συμβούλου, i. e. σὺν ἐμοὶ βούλου ἐμὲ θανεῖν.
377. We should not regard μᾶλλον here as redundant, but rather that εὐτυχέστερος is in a manner attracted to it, when εὐτυχὴς was sufficient. Thus, θανὼν μᾶλλον ἢ ζῶν γένοιτο ἂν αὐτὸς ἑαυτοῦ (or ἢ τὸ πρὶν) εὐτυχέστερος. Stobaeus gives v. 375—8, Flor. xxx. 3 (with πόνων for κακῶν), and the three next in lxxxviii. 6.
379. χαρακτὴρ ἐπίσημος, a deeply marked or conspicuous impression, ἐπίσημα εὖ κεχαραγμένον. Milton, Comus, " Reason's mintage Charactered in the face." Cf. Med. 516—9.—δεινὸς, ' of deep import,' as δεινὸν τὸ τίκτειν, τὸ ξυγγενές τοι δεινόν, &c. The advantages of εὐγένεια are often extolled by Euripides, but always conditionally upon

the possessor being himself a good man. Hence he here takes care to add τοῖσιν ἀξίοις. See Electr. 369 seqq. By ἐπὶ μεῖζον ἔρχεται he means, that the truly noble man advances from the mere name to the reality, from the ὄνομα or λόγος to the ἔργα εὐγενείας.
384. ψόγον. The blame of neglecting the memory of the brave.
390. ἀλλὰ τήνδ'. See on v. 40.
393. γαίᾳ. This is according to the older Aeschylean mythology, by which not only the δαίμων but Earth herself was regarded as a sentient power, and one of those naturally hostile to man, and therefore requiring propitiation.—δὶς τόσον, for διπλάσιον, Rhes. 281. Med. 1134. El. 1092.
395. On μὴ preceding ὤφελον see Med. 1413. Alcest. 880, μήποτε γήμας ὤφελον

ΕΚ. πολλή γ' ἀνάγκη θυγατρὶ συνθανεῖν ἐμέ.
ΟΔ. πῶς; οὐ γὰρ οἶδα δεσπότας κεκτημένος.
ΕΚ. ὁποῖα κισσὸς δρυὸς ὅπως τῆσδ' ἕξομαι.
ΟΔ. οὐκ, ἤν γε πείθῃ τοῖσι σοῦ σοφωτέροις.
ΕΚ. ὡς τῆσδ' ἑκοῦσα παιδὸς οὐ μεθήσομαι. 400
ΟΔ. ἀλλ' οὐδ' ἐγὼ μὴν τήνδ' ἄπειμ' αὐτοῦ λιπών.
ΠΟΛΥΞ. μῆτερ, πιθοῦ μοι· καὶ σύ, παῖ Λαερτίου,
χάλα τοκεῦσιν εἰκότως θυμουμένοις.
σύ τ', ὦ τάλαινα, τοῖς κρατοῦσι μὴ μάχου.
βούλει πεσεῖν πρὸς οὖδας, ἑλκῶσαί τε σὸν 405
γέροντα χρῶτα πρὸς βίαν ὠθουμένῃ,
ἀσχημονῆσαί τ' ἐκ νέου βραχίονος
σπασθεῖσ'; ἃ πείσει· μὴ σύ γ'· οὐ γὰρ ἄξιον.
ἀλλ', ὦ φίλη μοι μῆτερ, ἡδίστην χέρα
δὸς καὶ παρειὰν προσβαλεῖν παρηίδι· 410
ὡς οὔποτ' αὖθις, ἀλλὰ νῦν πανύστατον
ἀκτῖνα κύκλον θ' ἡλίου προσόψομαι.
τέλος δέχει δὴ τῶν ἐμῶν προσφθεγμάτων.
ὦ μῆτερ, ὦ τεκοῦσ', ἄπειμι δὴ κάτω.
ΕΚ. ὦ θύγατερ, ἡμεῖς δ' ἐν φάει δουλεύσομεν. 415
ΠΟΛΥΞ. ἄνυμφος, ἀνυμέναιος, ὧν μ' ἐχρῆν τυχεῖν.

οἰκεῖν μετὰ τῆσδε δόμους. Androm. 1189, μήποτε σῶν λεχέων τὸ δυσώνυμον ὄφελ' ἐμὸν γένος—ἀμφιβαλέσθαι ''Αιδαν. The sense is, εἴθε μηδὲ τόνδε θάνατον ἀνάγκη ἦν γενέσθαι, or φέρειν ὠφείλομεν.
396. The γε here seems to add force to the entreaty, as in the common formula of expostulation μὴ—γε, inf. 403; see on Bacch. 951. Hermann, thinking the particle out of place, gives πολλὴ δ', but suspects πολλή 'στ' ἀνάγκη to be the genuine reading.
398. Ego ut hedera huic ut quercui adhaerebo. Hermann; who compares Troad. 147, μάτηρ δ' ὥς τις πτανοῖς κλαγγὰν ὄρνισιν ὅπως ἐξάρξω 'γώ. Porson's view, that ὅπως ἕξομαι is to be construed 'I will take care to cling,' &c., is hardly tenable. That idiom (ὅρα ὅπως &c.), rare as it is with the first person, (and doubly rare with the first person singular, for obvious reasons,) is confined to exhortation, as Orest. 1060, ἀλλ' εἶ', ὅπως γενναῖα κἀγαμέμνονος δράσαντε κατθανούμεθ' ἀξιώ-

τατα.
400. ὡς, for ἴσθι ὡς. Cf. Andr. 587. Med. 609.
401. ἀλλ' οὐδὲ μήν. See Hel. 1047. Andr. 256.
407. ἀσχημονῆσαι. This is explained by εὐσχήμως in v. 569.—ἃ πείσει, 'and yet this is what you will suffer,' unless you yield.—οὐ γὰρ ἄξιον, scil. σοι, for ἀναξία γὰρ εἶ ταῦτα παθεῖν.
411—12. This distich occurs also in Alcest. 207—8.
413. δή, 'thus then.' Aldus has δέχου, which is not inferior as a reading, but it has much less MSS. authority. In the next verse the δή may be compared with Med. 1067, ἀλλ' εἶμι γὰρ δὴ τλημονεστάτην ὁδόν.
415. ἐν φάει κτλ. And I your mother shall live on to be a slave. Porson prints this verse as a question.
416. ὧν, scil. ὑμεναίων. So Suppl. 174, ἀλλ' ὡς νεκροὺς θάψωσιν, ὧν αὐτὰς ἐχρῆν. —τυχεῖν, i.e. ταφῶν.

VOL. II. 3 U

ΕΚ. οἰκτρὰ σὺ, τέκνον, ἀθλία δ' ἐγὼ γυνή.
ΠΟΛΥΞ. ἐκεῖ δ' ἐν Ἅιδου κείσομαι χωρὶς σέθεν.
ΕΚ. οἴμοι τί δράσω; ποῖ τελευτήσω βίον;
ΠΟΛΥΞ. δούλη θανοῦμαι, πατρὸς οὖσ' ἐλευθέρου.   420
ΕΚ. ἡμεῖς δὲ πεντήκοντά γ' ἄμμοροι τέκνων.
ΠΟΛΥΞ. τί σοι πρὸς Ἕκτορ' ἢ γέροντ' εἴπω πόσιν;
ΕΚ. ἄγγελλε πασῶν ἀθλιωτάτην ἐμέ.
ΠΟΛΥΞ. ὦ στέρνα μαστοί θ' οἵ μ' ἐθρέψαθ' ἡδέως.
ΕΚ. ὦ τῆς ἀώρου θύγατερ ἀθλία τύχης.   425
ΠΟΛΥΞ. χαῖρ', ὦ τεκοῦσα, χαῖρε Κασσάνδρα τέ μοι.
ΕΚ. χαίρουσιν ἄλλοι, μητρὶ δ' οὐκ ἔστιν τόδε.
ΠΟΛΥΞ. ὅ τ' ἐν φιλίπποις Θρῃξὶ Πολύδωρος κάσις.
ΕΚ. εἰ ζῇ γ'· ἀπιστῶ δ'· ὧδε πάντα δυστυχῶ.
ΠΟΛΥΞ. ζῇ καὶ θανούσης ὄμμα συγκλείσει τὸ σόν.   430
ΕΚ. τέθνηκ' ἔγωγε πρὶν θανεῖν κακῶν ὕπο.
ΠΟΛΥΞ. κόμιζ', Ὀδυσσεῦ, μ' ἀμφιθεὶς κάρα πέπλοις·
ὡς πρὶν σφαγῆναί γ' ἐκτέτηκα καρδίαν
θρήνοισι μητρὸς, τήνδε τ' ἐκτήκω γόοις.
ὦ φῶς· προσειπεῖν γὰρ σὸν ὄνομ' ἔξεστί μοι,   435

421. The restoration of this verse, which is correctly quoted by Eustathius on Il. vi. p. 639, is due to the sagacity of Porson. The old copies give πεντήκοντ' ἄμοιροι δὴ, some having γ' ἄμοιροι. Dindorf says the genuine verse is also given in two Florence MSS.
423. That ἐμὲ is emphatic will not escape the reader's notice. The injunction might have been ἄγγελλέ με κτλ., 'say that I am most wretched;' but the sense is, 'say that of all women *I* am the most wretched.'
425. ἀθλία Porson for ἀθλίας. Either this correction, or Hermann's σῆς for τῆς, seems required; for the application of the remark to Polyxena in particular is secured by either change.
426. Κασάνδρα τ' ἐμὴ Porson after Aldus and several MSS. But though 'my Cassandra' sounds well enough in English, the Greeks, as Hermann shrewdly remarks, do not use it. On the contrary, χαῖρέ μοι is a common phrase; and so Matthiae and others have edited, many MSS. giving Κασάνδρα τ' ἐμοί. Schol. τὸ ἐμοὶ οὐ πρὸς τὸ Κασάνδρα ἐστὶν, εἰ γὰρ ἦν οὕτω, διὰ τοῦ τ ὤφειλε γράφεσθαι· ἀλλὰ πρὸς τὸ χαῖρε σύναπτε ἢ καὶ πρὸς ἀμφότερα, χαῖρέ μοι τεκοῦσα, καὶ χαῖρέ μοι ὦ Κασάνδρα.
427. χαίρουσιν ἄλλοι. The meaning is, ἄλλων τὸ χαίρειν, or εἰ καὶ ἄλλοι χαίρουσιν, ἀλλὰ μήτηρ οὐ χαίρει. Cf. Phoen. 618, μῆτερ, ἀλλά μοι σὺ χαῖρε. ΙΟ. χαρτὰ γοῦν πάσχω, τέκνον. Hermann's view of this verse is, "Graecos dicit, qui immolatione Polyxenae laetentur." But this seems somewhat far-fetched; at least, it is unnecessary to the context.—For τόδε there is another reading χαρά, but the schol. explains τὸ χαίρειν δηλονότι.
428. φιλίπποις, cf. v. 9.—Θρῃξὶ Hermann and Matth. for Θρᾳξί.
432. It would be easy to read κάρα πέπλους, but verbs of this kind, both in Latin and Greek writers, take either the person or the thing as the immediate object. Hermann well compares Phoen. 306, ἀμφιβαλλέ μαστὸν ὠλέναισι ματέρος.
433. The force of the γε will be best understood by supplying some suppressed clause, as μετὰ δὲ τὸ σφαγῆναι λύπης ἀποπαύσομαι.
435. ὄνομα. That this, the common

ΕΚΑΒΗ. 515

μέτεστι δ' οὐδὲν πλὴν ὅσον χρόνον ξίφους
βαίνω μεταξὺ καὶ πυρᾶς Ἀχιλλέως.
ΕΚ. οἲ 'γώ· προλείπω· λύεται δέ μου μέλη.
ὦ θύγατερ, ἅψαι μητρὸς, ἔκτεινον χέρα,
δός· μὴ λίπῃς μ' ἄπαιδ', ἀπωλόμην, φίλαι. 440
[ὡς τὴν Λάκαιναν ξύγγονον Διοσκόροιν
Ἑλένην ἴδοιμι· διὰ καλῶν γὰρ ὀμμάτων
αἴσχιστα Τροίαν εἷλε τὴν εὐδαίμονα.]
ΧΟ. αὔρα, ποντιὰς αὔρα, στρ. α'.
ἅτε ποντοπόρους κομίζεις 445
θοὰς ἀκάτους ἐπ' οἶδμα λίμνας,
ποῖ με τὰν μελέαν πορεύσεις;
τῷ δουλόσυνος πρὸς οἶκον

reading, and not ὄμμα, the conjecture of Jacobs, is right, may be inferred from the theological notion which this invocation of the sun by a dying person involved. See the note on Alcest. 207. A Greek would probably have said either προσειπεῖν σὸν ὄνομα, or προσβλέπειν σὸν ὄμμα. Besides, there is a sort of antithesis, 'I can call you by name, though I shall no longer feel your benign influence.'
437. The words καὶ πυρᾶς κτλ. are a mere *exegesis* of ξίφους, and there cannot be a doubt that μεταξὺ ξίφους is shortly put for μεταξὺ τοῦδε τοῦ τόπου καὶ ξίφους. Thus βαίνω is by no means for βέβηκα, *adsto*, as Pflugk explains it, but the sense is, 'I can only feel the sun's blessed rays during the short time that I spend in walking from this place to that.' *Quantum mihi spatii reliquum est ad ferrum, quo in tumulo Achillis jugulabor.* Hermann.
440. ἀπωλόμην, φίλαι. At these words, addressed to the chorus, Hecuba falls fainting into their arms. Compare Androm. 1077, and Alcest. 391, where the same words ἀπωλόμην and προλείπειν are used in a very similar scene. Was this latter word technically used for ' to faint,' λιποψυχεῖν? It is clear, that if Hecuba, as the words imply, falls senseless through grief, the following three verses cannot have been spoken by her. Either Hermann is right in assigning them to the chorus, or W. Dindorf is right in regarding them as spurious. To the latter opinion the present editor inclines; for (to say nothing of a unique instance in Euripides of the choral ode being introduced by senarii, as in Agam. 342, Cho. 917), the verses themselves are not very Euripidean, and the pun on the name (Ἑλένη from ἑλεῖν), which the commentators do not seem to have noticed, occurs also in Troad. 891, ὁρῶν δὲ τήνδε, φεῦγε, μή σ' ἕλῃ πόθῳ. αἱρεῖ γὰρ ἀνδρῶν ὄμματ', ἐξαιρεῖ πόλεις. The most suspicious point in these verses is ὡς ἴδοιμι for οὕτως ἔχουσαν, since ὡς is very rarely used by Attic writers. Cf. Bacch. 1068.
444. Polyxena has been removed from the stage by Ulysses, and Hecuba is lying on the ground insensible (cf. 486). The chorus now sing the first stasimon in the glyconean metre, in which they dolefully anticipate the fate which awaits them as captives in the various states of Greece. The theme of their song closely resembles that in Troad. 197 seqq. A more appropriate subject, one would have thought, might have been furnished by the immediate prospect of Polyxena's fate.
445. ἅτε. The metre allows a trochee in the first foot, or even an iambus, to stand in place of a spondee. Porson, observing that the conjecture ἅτις is not metrically necessary, might have added, that neither is it good Greek.
449. δουλόσυνος κτηθεῖσα. As slaves were regarded as κτήματα, so their masters were called οἱ κεκτημένοι, Bacch. 514. The phrase therefore means, ἐς δουλοσύνην ὑπὸ δεσποτῶν ἀπαγομένη.

κτηθεῖσ' ἀφίξομαι;
ἢ Δωρίδος ὅρμον αἴας,   450
ἢ Φθιάδος, ἔνθα καλλίστων ὑδάτων πατέρα
φασὶν Ἀπιδανὸν γύας λιπαίνειν;
ἢ νάσων, ἁλιήρει   ἀντ. α΄.   455
κώπᾳ πεμπομέναν τάλαιναν,
οἰκτρὰν βιοτὰν ἔχουσαν οἴκοις,
ἔνθα πρωτόγονός τε φοῖνιξ
δάφνα θ' ἱεροὺς ἀνέσχε
πτόρθους Λατοῖ φίλᾳ   460
ὠδῖνος ἄγαλμα δίας;
σὺν Δηλιάσιν τε κούραις Ἀρτέμιδός τε θεᾶς
χρυσέαν ἄμπυκα τόξα τ' εὐλογήσω;   464, 5
ἢ Παλλάδος ἐν πόλει   στρ. β΄.
τᾶς καλλιδίφρου τ' Ἀθαναίας ἐν κροκέῳ πέπλῳ
ζεύξομαι ἅρματι πώλους,   469

450. Δωρίδος αἴας, the Peloponnese.—Φθιάδος, Θετταλικῆς, Photius.—Apidanus, Bacch. 573, πατέρα τε, τὸν ἔκλυον εὔιππον χώραν ὕδασιν καλλίστοισι λιπαίνειν. This river was a branch of the Peneus, and celebrated by the poets for the fertility of its valley as well as for the purity of its waters. The article τὸν or τῶν before καλλίστων was omitted by Porson, and τὰς which occurs in some copies before γύας.

455. νάσων, scil. ἐς τίνα, implied in the preceding ποῖ. Pflugk adopts a less obvious construction νάσων—ἔνθα, for εἰς ἐκείνην τὴν νῆσον κτλ. Any of the Aegean islands, not excluding Sicily (Troad. 220) are meant. But they specify Delos in particular, as Hermann remarks after Matthiae, because after Ol. lxxxviii. 3, the Athenians claimed Delos as an ancestral possession, and the present play is believed to have been acted shortly before Ol. lxxxix. The date-palm and the bay-tree, which were held sacred in connexion with the birth of Apollo, are mentioned Ion 919, Iph. T. 1100 &c. The palm is called πρωτόγονος because it was first created on the occasion of Latona's labour. Schol. εἰς Δῆλον ἡ Λητὼ ἀφικομένη ἔτεκεν Ἀπόλλωνα καὶ Ἄρτεμιν, δύο φυτῶν ὑπὸ Διὸς τότε ἀναφυέντων, φοίνικος καὶ δάφνης.

464. Professor Scholefield, in allowing, with Porson, that χρυσέαν is here a dissyllable, is wrong in questioning the fact, pointed out by Elmsley, that the first υ is frequently short. In this instance it may be either one or the other, though it is probably long, the ε having the virtue of y or j. See however Med. 633. Tro. 520. 856. The ἄμπυξ, or golden frontal, seems mentioned as a characteristic ornament of Artemis. See Aesch. Suppl. 425. The τε after Ἀρτέμιδος belongs properly to ἄμπυκα.

466. ἢ Παλλάδος κτλ. Or shall I be conveyed to Athens, to work as a slave at the loom in embroidering the peplus of Athena? See Ion 197. Iph. T. 222. For the insertion of τ' after καλλιδίφρου the present editor is responsible. It is answered by ἢ in v. 472, of which usage not a few examples exist. The metre requires that καλλιδίφρου should be a choriambus; and the hiatus does not seem more defensible than W. Dindorf's καλλιδιφροῦς, or Porson's καλλιδίφροι', where the elision of the final o is without example. Hermann, who scans τᾶς καλλιδίφρου Ἀθα|ναίας, alters the antistrophic verse to ὤμοι χθονὸς πατρῴας.—The epithet refers to a traditional representation of Athena as seated in her war-chariot in the battle against the Giants. Ion 1528, μὰ τὴν παρασπίζουσαν ἅρμασίν ποτε Νίκην Ἀθάναν Ζηνὶ γηγενεῖς ἔπι.

ἐν δαιδαλέαισι ποικίλλουσ' ἀνθοκρόκοισι πήναις,
ἢ Τιτάνων γενεὰν,
τὰν Ζεὺς ἀμφιπύρῳ
κοιμίζει φλογμῷ Κρονίδας ;
ὤμοι τεκέων ἐμῶν, ἀντ. β'. 475
ὤμοι πατέρων, χθονός θ', ἃ καπνῷ κατερείπεται
τυφομένα, δορίληπτος
ὑπ' Ἀργείων· ἐγὼ δ' ἐν ξείνᾳ χθονὶ δὴ κέκλημαι
δούλα, λιποῦσ' Ἀσίαν 481
Εὐρώπας θεράπναν,
ἀλλάξασ' Ἅιδα θαλάμους.

ΤΑΛΘΥΒΙΟΣ.

ποῦ τὴν ἄνασσαν δήποτ' οὖσαν Ἰλίου
Ἑκάβην ἂν ἐξεύροιμι, Τρῳάδες κόραι ; 485
ΧΟ. αὕτη πέλας σου, νῶτ' ἔχουσ' ἐπὶ χθονὶ,
Ταλθύβιε, κεῖται, συγκεκλημένη πέπλοις.
ΤΑ. ὦ Ζεῦ, τί λέξω ; πότερά σ' ἀνθρώπους ὁρᾶν ;

470. ἐν δαιδαλέαισι. Hermann omits ἐν, and also ὑπ' in v. 480, where Porson gives πρὸς on conjecture, but the MSS. generally omit the preposition. W. Dindorf here edits δαιδαλταῖσι, but all these are but corruptions of a common and legitimate form of glyconean verse, consisting of a choriambus with an anacrusis, followed by an iambus with or without a long syllable. Hermann is clearly right in giving the resolved form Ἀργείων.— Τιτάνων κτλ., cf. Ion 207 seqq.
482. θεράπναν, for which most of the old copies give θεράπαιναν, here, as in Herc. F. 370, Troad. 1070, seems to mean σταθμὸν, 'the neighbouring settlement or colony of Europe;' see on Bacch. 1043. Otherwise we must punctuate the passage thus, λιποῦσ' Ἀσίαν, Εὐρώπας θεράπναν ἀλλάξασ', Ἅιδα θαλάμους, ' having left Asia and got in exchange a home in Europe, an abode of death.' So ἀλλάσσειν is 'to take in exchange,' Bacch. 53. There is however no difficulty in supplying ἀντὶ τῶν νῦν θαλάμων. Cf. v. 914 seqq. Pflugk's explanation, adopted by W. Dindorf, and also given in nearly the same terms by Hermann, is this, ' having got slavery instead of death,'

i. e. which would have been the better fate of the two. Both compare Antig. 944, ἔτλα καὶ Δανάας οὐράνιον φῶς ἀλλάξαι δέμας. See also Iph. T. 135.
484. δήποτε, 'so lately.' Cf. Tro. 506. 1277. inf. 891.
486. νῶτ' ἔχουσα. The poet perhaps merely meant ' lying on the ground,' this being a token of extreme grief, as in Suppl. 21, Ἄδραστος ὅδε κεῖται. But those who take the words very literally, and are offended at an untragic posture, seek for an excuse in the supposition that Hecuba, who had fainted at v. 440, had been laid on her back by the attendants. —συγκεκλημένη Herm. Dind. for ξυγ- or συγκεκλεισμένη, one MS. giving συγκεκλιμένη. The form in σ is not Attic; indeed, the σ is contrary to analogy, unless where euphony demands it (as in πεπεισμένος), or in a participle from a verb in —ζω. Nevertheless, the transcriber who gave συγκεκλιμένη doubtless deduced it from συγκλίνειν.
488. Talthybius, who shows much consideration as a herald (a class of men whom Euripides much disliked), and who in the Troades also is represented as performing his ungracious duty with reluc-

ἢ δόξαν ἄλλως τήνδε κεκτῆσθαι μάτην
ψευδῆ, δοκοῦντας δαιμόνων εἶναι γένος,   490
τύχην δὲ πάντα τἀν βροτοῖς ἐπισκοπεῖν ;
οὐχ ἥδ' ἄνασσα τῶν πολυχρύσων Φρυγῶν ;
οὐχ ἥδε Πριάμου τοῦ μέγ' ὀλβίου δάμαρ ;
καὶ νῦν πόλις μὲν πᾶσ' ἀνέστηκεν δορί,
αὕτη δὲ δούλη, γραῦς, ἄπαις, ἐπὶ χθονὶ   495
κεῖται, κόνει φύρουσα δύστηνον κάρα.
φεῦ φεῦ. γέρων μέν εἰμ'· ὅμως δέ μοι θανεῖν
εἴη, πρὶν αἰσχρᾷ περιπεσεῖν τύχῃ τινί.
ἀνίστασ', ὦ δύστηνε, καὶ μετάρσιον
πλευρὰν ἔπαιρε καὶ τὸ πάλλευκον κάρα.   500
ΕΚ. ἔα· τίς οὗτος σῶμα τοὐμὸν οὐκ ἐᾷς
κεῖσθαι ; τί κινεῖς μ', ὅστις εἶ, λυπουμένην ;
ΤΑ. Ταλθύβιος ἥκω, Δαναϊδῶν ὑπηρέτης,
Ἀγαμέμνονος πέμψαντος, ὦ γύναι, μέτα.

tance, approaches Hecuba, who by this time is returning to her senses; and, after moralising on the strange dispensations of heaven and the caprices of fortune, relates the death of her daughter Polyxena in presence of the Greeks at the tomb of Achilles on Sigeum.—ὁρᾶν, ἐπιδεῖν, ἐποπτεύειν, ἐπισκοπεῖν. In the next verse it is by no means necessary to supply ἀνθρώπους before κεκτῆσθαι, from the preceding line, i. e. to convert the object of one verb into the subject of another ; nor is it more necessary to remove the comma after ψευδῆ and take δοκοῦντας for the direct subject, as Hermann does, regardless of the order of the words. Talthybius is thinking of himself and his fellow-men, and has ἡμᾶς in mind, which Porson thinks should perhaps be restored for ἄλλως, since ἄλλως μάτην is a pleonasm. Translate, 'Shall I say that thou hast regard to man, or that we have wrongly acquired to no purpose this false opinion, in supposing the race of gods to exist?' On the poet's views respecting Chance, see Preface to Vol. i. p. xxiv.

495. αὐτὴ Elmsley, Dind., Pflugk ; a probable, but by no means necessary alteration. There is no difficulty in αὕτη and ἥδε used together in the same sense. Soph. Antig. 673, αὕτη πόλεις ὄλλυσιν, ἥδ' ἀναστάτους οἴκους τίθησιν. Compare Hipp. 195. Hel. 709—10. Electr. 1311.

—On φύρουσα see v. 958.

497. Ennius, who was no great Grecian, and who often turns a Greek verse in a very lax manner (see on v. 592), seems in some way to have misunderstood the meaning of this distich ; ' senex sum, utinam mortem oppetam priusquam evenat, Quod in pauperie mea senex graviter gemam.' (Nonius in v. *evenat*, quoted by Porson.) For he seems to have construed πρὶν περιπεσεῖν (κακῷ) τινὶ ἐν αἰσχρᾷ τύχῃ, i. e. ἐν πενίᾳ. A most curious example of mistranslation has been pointed out by a distinguished scholar in Virgil's *omnia vel medium fiant mare*, from Theocr. i. 134, πάντα δ' ἔναλλα γένοιτο, as if it had been ἐνάλια. —By γέρων μέν εἰμι κτλ., he means, that *though* he is an old man (and so, if he came to misfortune, he would not, in the course of nature, have to endure it long), still he would rather die outright than incur the chance of it.

501. ἐᾷς. So Pors. Dind. Pflugk from two MSS. ἐᾷ Hermann. It is clear that Hecuba does not see the man. Cf. v. 487.

503. ὑπηρέτης. This was a term applied to heralds. See on Suppl. 381.

504. μέτα, i. e. μετά σε. Hermann regards it as a *tmesis*, comparing Ἀμυρταίου μεταπέμποντος (τὰς ναῦς) in Thuc. i. 112. Scholefield compares Aesch. Ag.

ΕΚΑΒΗ. 519

ΕΚ. ὦ φίλτατ᾽, ἆρα κἄμ᾽ ἐπισφάξαι τάφῳ 505
δοκοῦν Ἀχαιοῖς ἦλθες; ὡς φίλ᾽ ἂν λέγοις.
σπεύδωμεν, ἐγκονῶμεν, ἡγοῦ μοι, γέρον.
ΤΑ. σὴν παῖδα κατθανοῦσαν ὡς θάψῃς, γύναι,
ἥκω μεταστείχων σε· πέμπουσιν δέ με
δισσοί τ᾽ Ἀτρεῖδαι καὶ λεὼς Ἀχαϊκός. 510
ΕΚ. οἴμοι, τί λέξεις; οὐκ ἄρ᾽ ὡς θανουμένους
μετῆλθες ἡμᾶς, ἀλλὰ σημανῶν κακά;
ὄλωλας, ὦ παῖ, μητρὸς ἁρπασθεῖσ᾽ ἄπο·
ἡμεῖς δ᾽ ἄτεκνοι τοὐπὶ σ᾽· ὦ τάλαιν᾽ ἐγώ.
πῶς καί νιν ἐξεπράξατ᾽; ἆρ᾽ αἰδούμενοι; 515
ἢ πρὸς τὸ δεινὸν ἤλθεθ᾽, ὡς ἐχθρὰν, γέρον,
κτείνοντες; εἰπὲ, καίπερ οὐ λέξων φίλα.
ΤΑ. διπλᾶ με χρῄζεις δάκρυα κερδᾶναι, γύναι,
σῆς παιδὸς οἴκτῳ· νῦν τε γὰρ λέγων κακὰ
τέγξω τόδ᾽ ὄμμα, πρὸς τάφῳ θ᾽, ὅτ᾽ ὤλλυτο. 520
παρῆν μὲν ὄχλος πᾶς Ἀχαϊκοῦ στρατοῦ
πλήρης πρὸ τύμβου σῆς κόρης ἐπὶ σφαγάς·
λαβὼν δ᾽ Ἀχιλλέως παῖς Πολυξένην χερὸς
ἔστησ᾽ ἐπ᾽ ἄκρου χώματος, πέλας δ᾽ ἐγώ·
λεκτοί τ᾽ Ἀχαιῶν ἔκκριτοι νεανίαι, 525
σκίρτημα μόσχου σῆς καθέξοντες χεροῖν,
ἕσποντο· πλῆρες δ᾽ ἐν χεροῖν λαβὼν δέπας
πάγχρυσον ἔρρει χειρὶ παῖς Ἀχιλλέως

1330, τοῦ δρῶντός ἐστι καὶ τὸ βουλεῦσαι πέρι, scil. περὶ τοῦ δρωμένου.
506. δοκοῦν, for δόξαν, as in v. 121, where however the present participle is accurately used, as the question was not then settled.
515. πῶς καί. She does not say καὶ πῶς, which would have implied incredulity, ' You don't mean to say you slew her?' See Alcest. 482.—ἆρ᾽ αἰδούμενοι; ' Was it with all due respect, and mercifully?'—πρὸς τὸ δεινὸν, to dreadful extremes, to wanton and malicious cruelty. Cf. Med. 393, τόλμης εἶμι πρὸς τὸ καρτερόν.
519. νῦν τε γὰρ κτλ. He means, καὶ νῦν λέγων, καὶ τότε ὁρῶν. Cf. Hel. 770, λέγων τ᾽ ἄν σοι κάκ᾽ ἀλγοίην ἔτι, πάσχων

τ᾽ ἔκαμνον. Oed. Col. 363, δὶς γὰρ οὐχὶ βούλομαι πονοῦσά τ᾽ ἀλγεῖν καὶ λέγουσ᾽ αὖθις πάλιν. With πρὸς τάφῳ supply ἔτεγξα.
526. σκίρτημα, viz. in case she should struggle to escape. Prom. 611, σκιρτημάτων δὲ νήστισιν αἰκίαις λαβρόσυτος ἦλθον.
528. ἔρρει. Pflugk, in comparing the phrase ῥεῖν γάλα, 'to flow milk,' &c., said of a river, did not perceive that the latter is a cognate accusative, while ῥεῖν χοὰς is really a remarkable if not unique expression for ἐκχεῖν. That ῥεῖν originally had an active sense is probable from the passive and middle forms that remain; and perhaps this explains φόνῳ ναῦς ἐρρεῖτο in Hel. 1602.

520   ΕΥΡΙΠΙΔΟΥ

χοὰς θανόντι πατρί· σημαίνει δέ μοι
σιγὴν Ἀχαιῶν παντὶ κηρῦξαι στρατῷ.   530
κἀγὼ παραστὰς εἶπον ἐν μέσοις τάδε·
σιγᾶτ᾽, Ἀχαιοί, σῖγα πᾶς ἔστω λεώς·
σίγα, σιώπα· νήνεμον δ᾽ ἔστησ᾽ ὄχλον.
ὁ δ᾽ εἶπεν, ὦ παῖ Πηλέως, πατὴρ δ᾽ ἐμὸς,
δέξαι χοάς μοι τάσδε κηλητηρίους,   535
νεκρῶν ἀγωγούς· ἐλθὲ δ᾽, ὡς πίῃς μέλαν
κόρης ἀκραιφνὲς αἷμ᾽, ὅ σοι δωρούμεθα
στρατός τε κἀγώ· πρευμενὴς δ᾽ ἡμῖν γενοῦ,
λῦσαί τε πρύμνας καὶ χαλινωτήρια
νεῶν δὸς ἡμῖν, πρευμενοῦς τ᾽ ἀπ᾽ Ἰλίου   540
νόστου τυχόντας πάντας ἐς πάτραν μολεῖν.
τοσαῦτ᾽ ἔλεξε, πᾶς δ᾽ ἐπηύξατο στρατός.
εἶτ᾽ ἀμφίχρυσον φάσγανον κώπης λαβὼν
ἐξεῖλκε κολεοῦ, λογάσι δ᾽ Ἀργείων στρατοῦ
νεανίαις ἔνευσε παρθένον λαβεῖν.   545
ἡ δ᾽, ὡς ἐφράσθη, τόνδ᾽ ἐσήμηνεν λόγον·
ὦ τὴν ἐμὴν πέρσαντες Ἀργεῖοι πόλιν,
ἑκοῦσα θνῄσκω· μή τις ἅψηται χροὸς
τοὐμοῦ· παρέξω γὰρ δέρην εὐκαρδίως.
ἐλευθέραν δέ μ᾽, ὡς ἐλευθέρα θάνω,   550

529. Photius, σημαίνει, ἐπιτάττει. Cf. Oed. Col. 703.
536. ὡς πίῃς. See Od. xi. 96. 153. The spirit was not merely propitiated by the sacrifice, but was thought actually to taste it.—ἀκραιφνὲς, " proprie id est, quod modo ab ipso fonte exiit, eoque nondum adulteratum est." *Hermann*. The word may either be contracted from ἀκεραιοφανὴς, or may signify τὸ ἐπ᾽ ἄκρας φανὲν, and if so, it should rather mean that which rises to the surface, and is separable from sedimentary remains. It seems an epithet traditionally attached to αἷμα. Here it means ' virgin.'
546. ἐφράσθη, συνῆκεν, ἔγνω, ἐνόησεν, Hesychius. Pflugk, who cites instances of φράζεσθαι in a sense which every body knows, does not notice the peculiarity of the passive aorist for ἐφράσατο. This idiom is rare. We have ὑποδεχθεὶς in Heracl. 757, μὴ ἐπιλεχθῇς = μὴ νομίσῃς

in Agam. 1475, διελέχθη Herod. iii. 51. Bekk. Anecd. p. 82, ἀπολογηθῆναι· ἀντὶ τοῦ ἀπολογήσασθαι. Hermann adds φρασθεὶς from Herod. vii. 46.
548. ἅψηται. As the Greeks say μὴ ποιήσῃς rather than μὴ ποίησον, so in the third person of the aorist they prefer μὴ ἅψηται to μὴ ἁψάσθω. The meaning in both cases is rather a *warning* than a command, ὅρα ὅπως, or σκεπτέον μὴ &c., and here the schol. rightly éxplains it by ὅρα ἵνα μή τις ἅψηται. Only, the student will remember (1), That such phrases as μὴ δοκησάτω τινὶ (Aesch. Theb. 1030), though rare, are good Greek ; and (2) that the present subjunctive may be so used in the *third*, though it cannot be in the *second* person. Thus Agam. 332, ἔρως δὲ μή τις πρότερον ἐμπίπτῃ στρατῷ πορθεῖν ἃ μὴ χρή.
550. ἐλευθέρα. Elmsley on Heracl. 559, reads ἐλευθέρως. But the idea is,

πρὸς θεῶν μεθέντες κτείνατ'· ἐν νεκροῖσι γὰρ
δούλη κεκλῆσθαι βασιλὶς οὖσ' αἰσχύνομαι.
λαοὶ δ' ἐπερρόθησαν, Ἀγαμέμνων τ' ἄναξ
εἶπεν μεθεῖναι παρθένον νεανίαις.
[οἱ δ', ὡς τάχιστ' ἤκουσαν ὑστάτην ὄπα,   555
μεθῆκαν, οὗπερ καὶ μέγιστον ἦν κράτος.]
κἀπεὶ τόδ' εἰσήκουσε δεσποτῶν ἔπος,
λαβοῦσα πέπλους ἐξ ἄκρας ἐπωμίδος
ἔρρηξε λαγόνος εἰς μέσον παρ' ὀμφαλὸν,
μαστούς τ' ἔδειξε στέρνα θ', ὡς ἀγάλματος,   560
κάλλιστα· καὶ καθεῖσα πρὸς γαῖαν γόνυ
ἔλεξε πάντων τλημονέστατον λόγον·
ἰδοὺ τόδ', εἰ μὲν στέρνον, ὦ νεανία,

that she will hold in Hades the same position, servile or free, that she held at the moment of her death. But the adverb would mean, 'in a manner becoming one who is free-born.'

553. The τε is used in this verse, because the command of Agamemnon was the immediate consequence of the applause expressed by the shouts of the people. Had it been an independent action, and, as it were, the next step in the narration, the poet would have said Ἀγαμέμνων δ' ἄναξ.

555—6. This distich, on which Porson makes no remark, has been rejected by Jacobs and others (Herm. Matth. Dind.) as an interpolation. The objections (independently of considerations arising from the context), are, the strange expression ὑστάτην ὄπα, the awkward interposition of μεθῆκαν, in the middle of a clause, the epic character of the designation of the commander-in-chief, ὅου κράτος ἐστὶ μέγιστον, in the words of Homer; and the incorrect use of οὗπερ for οὗ. Pflugk, according to his custom, defends the verses at length; but he shows more ingenuity in these matters, i. e. in special pleading, than sound judgment as a critic. He explains ὑστάτην ὄπα on the supposition that the words were scarcely out of the speaker's mouth before a ready obedience was shown to his commands; and he might have quoted the Greek proverb for a speedy performance, ἅμ' ἔπος τε καὶ ἔργον. And the addition of οὗπερ μέγιστον ἦν κράτος he regards as indicating the motive of so prompt an obedience. When, however, all has been said that can be said, there remains the evident connexion of τόδε ἔπος in 557 with εἶπεν in 554, and the fact, that her own free action sufficiently implies that she was no longer held in control.

558. ἐπωμίδος. The scholiast observes that this word has two meanings, the top part of the arm, which is here meant, and a sort of garment, εἶδος ἐνδύματος.

559. λαγόνος εἰς μέσον, to the waist. The modesty of the description is unimpeachable; to its beauty and touching pathos the most apathetic by nature can hardly be insensible. The comparison of a living form to a statue is a curious proof of the Greek feeling for fine art. Greek statues were often draped from the zone downwards, and left nude above. Wordsworth (*Athens and Attica*, p. 221), heard it said of a young Albanian bride, " She is so lovely that you would take her picture," and he well adds, that " the expression has probably remained in the language from the deep-felt influence of ancient art." In the very fine verses of Chaeremon, quoted by Hermann on this verse, a maiden *in dishabille* is said to 'expose a living picture to the gaze of ether,' γυμνὴν δ' αἰθέρος θεάμασιν ζῶσαν γραφὴν ἔφαινε. In Aesch. Ag. 233, compared by Jacobs, πρέπουσα ὡς ἐν γραφαῖς refers rather to the *silence* than to the *beauty* of Iphigenia at the altar.

562. τλημονέστατον, 'most courageous.' See Heracl. 570. The schol. wrongly paraphrases it by ἀθλιώτατον.

563. ἰδοὺ τόδ', i. e. σώματος μέρος, as

VOL. II.   3 x

ΕΥΡΙΠΙΔΟΥ

παίειν προθυμεῖ, παῖσον, εἰ δ' ὑπ' αὐχένα
χρῄζεις, πάρεστι λαιμὸς εὐτρεπὴς ὅδε.   565
ὁ δ' οὐ θέλων τε καὶ θέλων, οἴκτῳ κόρης,
τέμνει σιδήρῳ πνεύματος διαρροάς·
κρουνοὶ δ' ἐχώρουν· ἡ δὲ καὶ θνήσκουσ' ὅμως
πολλὴν πρόνοιαν εἶχεν εὐσχήμως πεσεῖν,
κρύπτουσ' ἃ κρύπτειν ὄμματ' ἀρσένων χρεών.   570
ἐπεὶ δ' ἀφῆκε πνεῦμα θανασίμῳ σφαγῇ,
οὐδεὶς τὸν αὐτὸν εἶχεν Ἀργείων πόνον,
ἀλλ' οἱ μὲν αὐτῶν τὴν θανοῦσαν ἐκ χερῶν
φύλλοις ἔβαλλον, οἱ δὲ πληροῦσιν πυρὰν,
κορμοὺς φέροντες πευκίνους, ὁ δ' οὐ φέρων   575
πρὸς τοῦ φέροντος τοιάδ' ἤκουεν κακά·
ἕστηκας, ὦ κάκιστε, τῇ νεάνιδι
οὐ πέπλον, οὐδὲ κόσμον ἐν χεροῖν ἔχων;
οὐκ εἶ τι δώσων τῇ περίσσ' εὐκαρδίῳ
ψυχήν τ' ἀρίστῃ; τοιάδ' ἀμφὶ σῆς λέγω   580
παιδὸς θανούσης· εὐτεκνωτάτην δέ σε
πασῶν γυναικῶν δυστυχεστάτην θ' ὁρῶ.
ΧΟ. δεινόν τι πῆμα Πριαμίδαις ἐπέζεσε
πόλει τε τῇμῇ· θεῶν ἀναγκαῖον τόδε.

she points to her chest. The common punctuation, ἰδοὺ, τόδ' εἰ μὲν στέρνον &c., was well altered by Hermann. Perhaps, when ἰδοὺ ceases to be a mere exclamation, we should write ἰδοῦ, as Porson has here edited.
566. οὐ θέλων τε καὶ θέλων. See on Electr. 1230. The sense is, καίπερ θέλων, ὅμως οὐ θέλων δι' οἶκτον κόρης.
569. εὐσχήμως. Ovid appears to imitate this striking passage in describing the suicide of Lucretia, Fast. ii. 833, 'Tum quoque jam moriens ne non procumbat honeste Respicit: haec etiam cura cadentis erat.' See also Met. xiii. 479 seqq. In the next verse the common reading κρύπτειν θ' ἃ κρύπτειν was corrected by Brunck and Porson from MSS. and the quotations of the passage by Clement of Alexandria and Eustathius.
573. ἐκ χερῶν ἔβαλλον, scil. ἱέντες. The act was that of crowning one who had been victorious in death. It was called φυλλοβολία, and a form of this ancient custom is still retained in the throwing of flowers on the stage in honour of a favourite actor.
574. πληροῦσιν. So πυρᾶς πλήρωμα in Trach. 1213.
580. λέγω. The old reading was λέγον, but two or three copies give λέγων. Hermann retains this latter, and reads εὐτεκνωτάτην τε κτλ., thus making λέγων—ὁρῶ one clause. But W. Dindorf more correctly judges that λέγω was ignorantly changed to λέγον, i. e. ἔλεγον, by those who thought he meant to recapitulate what the men had said to each other in praise of Polyxena.
584. Hermann, who removes the stop at τῇμῇ, construes θεῶν ἀναγκαῖον πῆμα, 'an evil necessitated by the gods.' It is perhaps enough to say that θεῶν is the genitive of the cause or origin, as if it had been ἐκ θεῶν. The schol. also joined πῆμα τόδε ἀναγκαῖον, which he explains by χαλεπὴ βλάβη τῶν θεῶν, ἥγουν ἧς αἴτιοι οἱ θεοί, ἀπαραίτητος. It would be

ΕΚΑΒΗ. 523

ΕΚ. ὦ θύγατερ, οὐκ οἶδ᾽ εἰς ὅ τι βλέψω κακῶν, 585
πολλῶν παρόντων· ἢν γὰρ ἄψωμαί τινος,
τόδ᾽ οὐκ ἐᾷ με, παρακαλεῖ δ᾽ ἐκεῖθεν αὖ
λύπη τις ἄλλη διάδοχος κακῶν κακοῖς.
καὶ νῦν τὸ μὲν σὸν ὥστε μὴ στένειν πάθος
οὐκ ἂν δυναίμην ἐξαλείψασθαι φρενός· 590
τὸ δ᾽ αὖ λίαν παρεῖλες, ἀγγελθεῖσά μοι
γενναῖος. οὔκουν δεινόν, εἰ γῆ μὲν κακὴ
τυχοῦσα καιροῦ θεόθεν εὖ στάχυν φέρει,
χρηστὴ δ᾽ ἁμαρτοῦσ᾽ ὧν χρεὼν αὐτὴν τυχεῖν
κακὸν δίδωσι καρπόν, ἀνθρώποις δ᾽ ἀεὶ 595

better in this case to regard πῆμα ἀναγκαῖον as a synonym of δουλεία, as ἀνάγκη ἀμφίπτολις in Aesch. Cho. 66. Inf. v. 639.

585 seqq. The speech of Hecuba, on receiving the thrilling details of her daughter's death, is not unworthy of a mother who regarded bravery in her children as the first and noblest quality. It is true that she seems to moralise more coldly than the occasion would have suggested to others to do; but she shows her collected and resigned mind, her perfect self-possession and composure, not only in this, but in the commands she gives respecting her child's obsequies. Of course, those who can see in Euripides nothing but overstrained pathos and pedantic sophistry, regard this fine ῥῆσις as confirmatory of their views. Such critics would have Hecuba to have broken out into a paroxysm of grief; but Euripides did not waste the opportunity on profitless common-places.

586—8. ἢν κτλ. 'For, if I take in hand (i. e. deal exclusively with) one, another does not let me rest; and from that in its turn another grief calls me away, taking up new in succession to old evils.' "Idem est ac si dixisset, ἡ κακὰ κακοῖς διαδέχεται." Porson.

589. The μὲν properly belongs to μὴ στένειν.—παρεῖλες, see Hippol. 1315. 'And yet on the other hand you have taken away the excess of sorrow by being reported to me as noble.'

592—8. 'Is it not then strange, that land indeed (even) when bad, if it gets a favourable season from the god, bears corn well, while good land, failing in what it ought to obtain, gives meagre crops;

while among men invariably he of an evil nature is nothing else but base, while the good is good, and does not even under the pressure of calamity alter his disposition for the worse, but remains excellent always?' Of the unchangeable and inherent influence of good birth in producing ἀρετὴ and καλοκἀγαθία, the Greeks had the highest opinion. The poet meant to say, that when a person is truly γενναῖος, his conduct is less acted upon by external circumstances than the analogies of nature would lead us to expect. If the verses of Ennius (as they are believed to be) quoted by Hermann from Cic. Tusc. Q. ii. 4, really were taken from this passage, it is probable that the old Italian missed the point of the Greek. (See above on v. 497.) They are as follows:—'probae etsi in segetem sunt deteriorem datae | fruges, tamen ipsae suapte natura enitent.' But W. Dindorf thinks they are not paraphrased from Euripides.

595. Hermann, followed by W. Dindorf, gives ἄνθρωποι, "not," as he says, "because he thinks it genuine, but because ἀνθρώποις is false." His very words are these; "nego enim ac pernego, ἀνθρώποις hic dici potuisse." To the emphatic assertion of so consummate a grammarian the greatest deference is due. Nevertheless, the Greek writers occasionally use the dative of reference to a thing or person, even when no distinct idea of advantage or disadvantage is entertained. There is a decided instance in Aesch. Ag. 215, βροτοῖς θρασύνει γὰρ αἰσχρόμητις τάλαινα παρακοπὰ πρωτοπήμων, and Thuc. v. 111 (quoted in the note there) πολλοῖς γὰρ τὸ αἰσχρὸν ἐπεσπάσατο, scil. αὐτούς. The schol. therefore does not seem far

ΕΥΡΙΠΙΔΟΥ

ὁ μὲν πονηρὸς οὐδὲν ἄλλο πλὴν κακὸς,
ὁ δ' ἐσθλὸς ἐσθλὸς, οὐδὲ συμφορᾶς ὕπο
φύσιν διέφθειρ', ἀλλὰ χρηστός ἐστ' ἀεί.
ἆρ' οἱ τεκόντες διαφέρουσιν, ἢ τροφαί;
ἔχει γε μέντοι καὶ τὸ θρεφθῆναι καλῶς   600
δίδαξιν ἐσθλοῦ· τοῦτο δ' ἤν τις εὖ μάθῃ,
οἶδεν τό γ' αἰσχρὸν κανόνι τοῦ καλοῦ μαθών.
καὶ ταῦτα μὲν δὴ νοῦς ἐτόξευσεν μάτην·
σὺ δ' ἐλθὲ καὶ σήμηνον Ἀργείοις τάδε,
μὴ θιγγάνειν μοῦ μηδέν', ἀλλ' εἴργειν ὄχλον   605
τῆς παιδός. ἔν τοι μυρίῳ στρατεύματι
ἀκόλαστος ὄχλος ναυτική τ' ἀναρχία
κρείσσων πυρὸς, κακὸς δ' ὁ μή τι δρῶν κακόν.
σὺ δ' αὖ λαβοῦσα τεῦχος, ἀρχαία λάτρι,
βάψασ' ἔνεγκε δεῦρο ποντίας ἁλὸς,   610

wrong in explaining ἐν δὲ τοῖς ἀνθρώποις. Hermann's suspicion is, that the poet wrote ἐν βροτοῖς δ' ἀεί.
598. On διαφθείρειν, to spoil, alter, enfeeble a moral principle, &c., see Hippol. 388.
599—600. ἆρα κτλ. 'Is it the parents who differ, or the ways of bringing up (the bad and the good respectively)?' Hermann remarks on the omission of the article with the latter substantive, and compares Ajac. 1250, οὐ γὰρ οἱ πλατεῖς οὐδ' εὐρύνωτοι φῶτες ἀσφαλέστατοι. We might however say, that οἱ τεκόντες may be taken to represent γονεῖς without the article.—γε μέντοι, 'not but that even the being brought up well is a way of teaching good.' He adds this, lest, if the whole blame should be thought to rest with a man's parentage, education should appear useless.—ἐσθλοῦ, used substantively, like κακόν, for ἀρετῆς. Euripides held that there were some qualities which must be spontaneous to be genuinely useful, but that, in default of these, a good training, or well-formed habits, will teach what is good. He goes on to say, that if a man has no innate or moral sense of τὸ αἰσχρὸν (and this is a question still speculated on by casuists), it is enough if he learns by education τὸ καλὸν, since he will thus have gained a standard or criterion by which the contrary may readily be known.
603. μάτην, i. e. ἀκαίρως, ἀνωφελῆ ἔρ-ριψεν, because such speculations are of little avail in her present troubles. The poet appears to anticipate an objection that might be raised against the ἀτοπία τοῦ φιλοσοφεῖν. For τοξεύειν see Ion 256.
605. μοῦ. Pflugk and Dindorf give μοι from one MS., but the enclitic stands for ἐμῆς, and παιδὸς is the genitive after εἴργειν as well as after θιγγάνειν.
606. ἔν τοι. Aldus and others have ἐν γάρ.
607. ναυτική. The sailors, who had been detained on their voyage home till the sacrifice to Achilles had been made, might have offered some indignity to the corpse of a Trojan captive.— πυρὸς, the symbol of all that is violent and irresistibly aggressive. Cf. Androm. 271.— κακὸς κτλ., i. e. a man may be bad as the associate of others, though he has not yet proved it by his actions. Or, as the scholiast explains it, κακὸς ὀνομάζεται παρὰ τοῖς ναύταις ὁ μὴ σὺν αὐτοῖς δρῶν τι κακόν, ἢ ὡς οὐχ ἑπόμενος αὐτοῖς, καὶ τὰ αὐτῶν πράττων αἴσχιστα. In this sense, perhaps, κακὸς means one who is morally a coward, or afraid of doing wrong.
609. σὺ δ' αὖ. The αὖ refers to this command being given to a different person from that in v. 604. That was addressed to Talthybius; cf. v. 727.—ἔνεγκε ἁλὸς, 'bring some sea-water,' as we say by a corresponding idiom, and as the French say apporter de l'eau.

ΕΚΑΒΗ.

ὡς παῖδα λουτροῖς τοῖς παννυστάτοις ἐμὴν
νύμφην τ' ἄνυμφον παρθένον τ' ἀπάρθενον
λούσω προθῶμαί θ'· ὡς μὲν ἀξία, πόθεν;
οὐκ ἂν δυναίμην· ὡς δ' ἔχω· τί γὰρ πάθω;
κόσμον τ' ἀγείρασ' αἰχμαλωτίδων πάρα,   615
αἵ μοι πάρεδροι τῶνδ' ἔσω σκηνωμάτων
ναίουσιν, εἴ τις τοὺς νεωστὶ δεσπότας
λαθοῦσ' ἔχει τι κλέμμα τῶν αὑτῆς δόμων.
ὦ σχήματ' οἴκων, ὦ ποτ' εὐτυχεῖς δόμοι,
ὦ πλεῖστ' ἔχων κάλλιστά τ', εὐτεκνώτατε   620
Πρίαμε, γεραιά θ' ἥδ' ἐγὼ μήτηρ τέκνων,
ὡς ἐς τὸ μηδὲν ἥκομεν, φρονήματος
τοῦ πρὶν στερέντες. εἶτα δῆτ' ὀγκούμεθα
ὁ μέν τις ἡμῶν πλουσίοις ἐν δώμασιν,
ὁ δ' ἐν πολίταις τίμιος κεκλημένος.   625
τὰ δ' οὐδέν· ἄλλως φροντίδων βουλεύματα,
γλώσσης τε κόμποι. κεῖνος ὀλβιώτατος,
ὅτῳ κατ' ἦμαρ τυγχάνει μηδὲν κακόν.

ΧΟ. ἐμοὶ χρῆν συμφορὰν,   στρ.

612. ἀπάρθενον. The α here has the force of δυς. It is needless to suppose any reference to her having been betrothed to Achilles, and so being virtually a νύμφη rather than a παρθένος. — προθέσθαι, to lay out a corpse, Alcest. 664. Suppl. 53. Phoen. 1319, ὅπως λούσῃ προθῆταί τ' οὐκέτ' ὄντα παῖδ' ἐμόν.
614. τί πάθω; See on Androm. 513.
615. κόσμον τ'. Hermann approves, and W. Dindorf admits, Wakefield's reading κόσμον γ'. But γε, though it might here be called exegetical, reads very unlike the style of Euripides. Porson connects βάψασα ἀγείρασά τε, by supposing a long parenthesis. But what sort of sense is this? — 'Do you bring hither some water, having dipped your pitcher and collected ornaments from the captives.' The real meaning is, αὐτή τε ἐξ ὧν ἔχω, καὶ παρ' ἄλλων ἀγείρασα. The κόσμος for the dead, as suggested on Alcest. 160, probably comprised golden trinkets, which are here perhaps meant, because they would be more easily concealed from the Greeks than costly garments.

619. σχήματ' οἴκων. See on Andr. 1.
620. Hermann, though he does not object to Porson's punctuation after ἔχων, by which κάλλιστα εὐτεκνώτατε is taken together like μέγιστον ἐχθίστη in Med. 1323, nevertheless prefers the simpler sense ὦ πλεῖστα κάλλιστά | τε ἔχων, i. e. both wealth and happiness in the highest degree. And so Pflugk also edits, comparing the phrase πολλὰ καὶ κακὰ &c., though that is somewhat different in principle.
623. ὀγκούμεθα. Cf. Electr. 381.
626. τὰ δ' οὐδέν. So Reiske. Porson has the old reading τάδ' οὐδὲν, without remark.
628. τυγχάνει, συμβαίνει. Cf. Heracl. 930. So κυρεῖ inf. 690.
629. Hecuba appears to have left the stage for a brief interval in order to collect the required ornaments. During her absence the chorus sings a short strain, indicating a break or pause in the action. They declare that calamity was destined to befal them ever since the time when Paris launched his ship to fetch away the fairest of women, Helen. Toils and

ἐμοὶ χρῆν πημονὰν γενέσθαι,　　　　　　630
Ἰδαίαν ὅτε πρῶτον ὕλαν
Ἀλέξανδρος εἰλατίναν
ἐτάμεθ᾽, ἅλιον ἐπ᾽ οἶδμα ναυστολήσων
Ἑλένας ἐπὶ λέκτρα, τὰν
καλλίσταν ὁ χρυσοφαὴς　　　　　　　635
Ἅλιος αὐγάζει.
πόνοι γὰρ καὶ πόνων　　　　　　　　ἀντ.
ἀνάγκαι κρείσσονες κυκλοῦνται.
κοινὸν δ᾽ ἐξ ἰδίας ἀνοίας　　　　　　640
κακὸν τᾷ Σιμουντίδι γᾷ
ὀλέθριον ἔμολε, συμφορά τ᾽ ἀπ᾽ ἄλλων.
ἐκρίθη δ᾽ ἔρις, ἂν ἐν Ἴ-
δᾳ κρίνει τρισσὰς μακάρων　　　　　645
παῖδας ἀνὴρ βούτας,
ἐπὶ δορὶ καὶ φόνῳ καὶ ἐμῶν μελάθρων λώβᾳ·　ἐπῳδ.
στένει δὲ καί τις ἀμφὶ τὸν εὔροον Εὐρώταν　650
Λάκαινα πολυδάκρυτος ἐν δόμοις κόρα,
πολιόν τ᾽ ἐπὶ κρᾶτα μάτηρ
τέκνων θανόντων τίθεται

slavery worse than toils have quickly succeeded ; the infatuated act of one brought sufferings to many. The source of it all was the decision that Paris gave to the rival goddesses. Now not only Trojan, but Spartan women too have cause to weep for those they have lost.— The verses are for the most part varieties of the glyconean measure.

639. ἀνάγκαι seems rightly explained by Pflugk *mala servitutis.* See v. 584. This slavery is called ' worse than troubles,' i. e. those general troubles and inconveniences which are inseparable from war.

640—3. The sense is, that though the folly was that of one only, viz. Paris, yet the misfortune came to the people in general both from him and from the Greeks who invaded the land. " Κοινὸν patet sic dictum esse, ut sensu etiam ad συμφορὰν referatur." *Herm.*

645. ἂν κρίνει—παῖδας. For the double accusative, one of which is the cognate, κρίνει κρίσιν, compare Aesch. Suppl. 226, Ζεὺς—δικάζει τἀπλακήματα ὑστάτας δί-

κας.—ἐπὶ δορί, which was to result in war &c. Generally, ἐπὶ so used has direct reference to the *intention* of the actor.

650. Euripides was so fond of bringing in etymologies of proper names, that Pflugk may be right in supposing εὔροον Εὐρώταν a designed combination. The old reading εὔρουν or εὔρρουν was corrected by Hermann for metrical reasons. This and the preceding verse consist of an iambic penthemimeris followed by two dactyls, a long syllable, and a spondee. They may be called iambelegus + spondaic base. Some have fancied that this reference to the Spartan women alludes to the capture of Pylos, B.C. 425. Such opinions however are little better than vague surmises. There was reason enough to mention Sparta, as feeling the consequences of the Trojan war, since both Helen and Menelaus belonged to it.

653. πολιόν. Hermann gives πολιὰν from four MSS., but the epithet is thus too far removed from its substantive χέρα.

χέρα, δρύπτεταί τε παρειάν, 655
δίαιμον ὄνυχα τιθεμένα σπαραγμοῖς.

ΘΕΡΑΠΑΙΝΑ.

γυναῖκες, Ἑκάβη ποῦ ποθ᾽ ἡ παναθλία,
ἡ πάντα νικῶσ᾽ ἄνδρα καὶ θῆλυν σπορὰν
κακοῖσιν; οὐδεὶς στέφανον ἀνθαιρήσεται. 660
ΧΟ. τί δ᾽, ὦ τάλαινα σῆς κακογλώσσου βοῆς;
ὡς οὔποθ᾽ εὕδει λυπρά σου κηρύγματα.
ΘΕ. Ἑκάβῃ φέρω τόδ᾽ ἄλγος· ἐν κακοῖσι δὲ
οὐ ῥᾴδιον βροτοῖσιν εὐφημεῖν στόμα.
ΧΟ. καὶ μὴν περῶσα τυγχάνει δόμων ὕπο 665
ἥδ᾽, ἐς δὲ καιρὸν σοῖσι φαίνεται λόγοις.
ΘΕ. ὦ παντάλαινα, κἄτι μᾶλλον ἢ λέγω,
δέσποιν᾽, ὄλωλας, οὐκέτ᾽ εἶ βλέπουσα φῶς,
ἄπαις, ἄνανδρος, ἄπολις ἐξεφθαρμένη.
ΕΚ. οὐ καινὸν εἶπας, εἰδόσιν δ᾽ ὠνείδισας. 670
ἀτὰρ τί νεκρὸν τόνδε μοι Πολυξένης
ἥκεις κομίζουσ᾽, ἧς ἀπηγγέλθη τάφος
πάντων Ἀχαιῶν διὰ χερὸς σπουδὴν ἔχειν;
ΘΕ. ἥδ᾽ οὐδὲν οἶδεν, ἀλλά μοι Πολυξένην

658. The servant, who had been sent to the shore to fetch water (at v. 609), now returns, doubtless accompanied by one or more assistants, bearing the covered body of Polydorus, whom she has found washed up on the sea-strand.
660. κακοῖσιν. Hermann, offended (though very needlessly) at the want of connexion in the next clause, reads κακοῖς, ἵν᾽ οὐδεὶς κτλ., " in certamine, ubi ei nemo palmam praeripiet."
662. οὔποθ᾽ εὕδει. Not that she had brought evil tidings on former occasions, but that the loud voice and alarmed manner of the speaker made the chorus feel sure that some further evil was at hand, of which she was the bearer. Hermann thinks that some emphasis is to be laid on σῆς, to which σου corresponds; 'I say, *your* evil-boding clamour, for these doleful announcements of yours know no rest, coming as they do so quickly after the bad tidings brought by Talthybius.' The apology of the servant, who says it is hard to use good words in trouble, shows that the chorus had v. 659 more particularly in view.
665. ὕπο. It is difficult to choose between this (cf. v. 53) and ὕπερ, which Porson and Hermann prefer. Most of the copies give ἄπο, several ὕπερ, one only ὕπο, as a variant. Certainly, περᾶν ὑπὲρ δόμων, 'to pass beyond the limits of the house,' is an unusual expression.
668. βλέπουσα. Hermann takes this for καίπερ βλέπουσα, as one of the scholiasts appears also to have done, οὐκέτι βλέπεις φάος, καὶ ζῶσα οὐ ζῇς.
671. τί—ἥκεις; ' Why have you come and brought the body of my Polyxena which I supposed was now being buried?' i. e. how has it happened, what is the meaning of this?
674. ἥδ᾽. It would be better, perhaps, to give ἡ δ᾽, as τὰ δ᾽ οὐδὲν in v. 626. For, as this distich is said aside, the less direct reference to Hecuba seems the more appropriate.—οὐχ ἅπτεται, she does not grasp, does not comprehend, οὐ ξυναρπάζει φρενί.

θρηνεῖ, νέων δὲ πημάτων οὐχ ἅπτεται. 675
ΕΚ. οἳ 'γὼ τάλαινα, μῶν τὸ βακχεῖον κάρα
τῆς θεσπιῳδοῦ δεῦρο Κασσάνδρας φέρεις;
ΘΕ. ζῶσαν λέλακας, τὸν θανόντα δ' οὐ στένεις
τόνδ'. ἀλλ' ἄθρησον σῶμα γυμνωθὲν νεκροῦ,
εἴ σοι φανεῖται θαῦμα καὶ παρ' ἐλπίδας. 680
ΕΚ. οἴμοι, βλέπω δὴ παῖδ' ἐμὸν τεθνηκότα
Πολύδωρον, ὅν μοι Θρῇξ ἔσῳζ' οἴκοις ἀνήρ.
ἀπωλόμην δύστηνος, οὐκέτ' εἰμὶ δή.
ὦ τέκνον, τέκνον,
αἰαῖ, κατάρχομαι νόμον 685
βακχεῖον, ἐξ ἀλάστορος
ἀρτιμαθὴς κακῶν.
ΘΕ. ἔγνως γὰρ ἄτην παιδὸς, ὦ δύστηνε σύ;
ΕΚ. ἄπιστ' ἄπιστα, καινὰ καινὰ δέρκομαι.
ἕτερα δ' ἀφ' ἑτέρων κακὰ κακῶν κυρεῖ· 690
οὐδέποτ' ἀστένακτος, ἀδάκρυτος ἀμέρα ἐπισχήσει.
ΧΟ. δείν', ὦ τάλαινα, δεινὰ πάσχομεν κακά.
ΕΚ. ὦ τέκνον, τέκνον ταλαίνας ματρὸς, 695
τίνι μόρῳ θνήσκεις, τίνι πότμῳ κεῖσαι; πρὸς τίνος
ἀνθρώπων;
ΘΕ. οὐκ οἶδ'. ἐπ' ἀκταῖς νιν κυρῶ θαλασσίαις.
ΕΚ. ἔκβλητον, ἢ πέσημα φοινίου δορός,

679. γυμνωθὲν, uncovered. The corpse had been brought to her enveloped in a cloth.
685. κατάρχομαι. Cf. Orest. 960, κατάρχομαι στεναγμὸν, ὦ Πελασγία. Andr. 1199, θανόντα δεσπόταν γόοις νόμῳ τῷ νερτέρων κατάρξω. In the preceding verse W. Dindorf omits the second τέκνον, with many MSS. It is better however to regard this as the first of a series of dochmiacs, uttered by Hecuba in the usual rapid and excited tone, interposed with iambic verses from the more composed messenger. Compare Iph. T. 830, Hel. 646 seqq. That the following lines are not antistrophic appears to be rightly concluded by both Pflugk and Hermann, though the former expresses himself diffidently on the question. In truth, the regularity of antithetical verses is little suited to the vehement outbursts of passion and grief.

691. The common reading, retained by Porson and Pflugk, οὐδέποτ' ἀδάκρυτος, ἀστένακτος | ἀμέρα μ' ἐπισχήσει, is wholly unmetrical. Pflugk indeed gives ἀδάκρυτον &c., with some copies; and the schol. recognises both readings. The dochmiac measure was restored by Hermann, who transposes the two adjectives, but needlessly gives ἀμέρα 'πισχήσει. For the final α may be made short in this metre before the ἐ. The accusative seems to have resulted from the interpolation of μ', and the latter, perhaps, from a dislike of the hiatus. It is as easy to explain ἀδάκρυτον by παύσει με ὥστε μὴ δακρύειν, as ἀδάκρυτος by ὀλβία, 'never more will a tearless day stop me (from my present woes).'
693. κυρῶ. Here and v. 690 for τυγχάνω.

ἐν ψαμάθῳ λευρᾷ ; 700
ΘΕ. πόντου νιν ἐξήνεγκε πελάγιος κλύδων.
ΕΚ. ὤμοι, αἰαῖ, ἔμαθον ἔνυπνον ὀμμάτων
ἐμῶν ὄψιν, οὐδὲ παρέβα με φάσμα μελανόπτερον, 705
ἂν εἰσεῖδον ἀμφὶ τέκνον, οὐκέτ᾽ ὄντα Διὸς ἐν φάει.
ΧΟ. τίς γάρ νιν ἔκτειν᾽ ; οἶσθ᾽ ὀνειρόφρων φράσαι ;
ΕΚ. ἐμὸς ἐμὸς ξένος, Θρήκιος ἱππότας, 710
ἵν᾽ ὁ γέρων πατὴρ ἔθετό νιν κρύψας.
ΧΟ. ὤμοι, τί λέξεις ; χρυσὸν ὡς ἔχῃ κτανών ;
ΕΚ. ἄρρητ᾽, ἀνωνόμαστα, θαυμάτων πέρα,
οὐχ ὅσι᾽, οὐδ᾽ ἀνεκτά. ποῦ δίκα ξένων ; 715
ὦ κατάρατ᾽ ἀνδρῶν, ὡς διεμοιράσω
χρόα, σιδαρέῳ τεμὼν φασγάνῳ
μέλεα τοῦδε παιδὸς, οὐδ᾽ ᾤκτισας. 720
ΧΟ. ὦ τλῆμον, ὥς σε πολυπονωτάτην βροτῶν
δαίμων ἔθηκεν, ὅστις ἐστί σοι βαρύς.
ἀλλ᾽ εἰσορῶ γὰρ τοῦδε δεσπότου δέμας
Ἀγαμέμνονος, τοὐνθένδε σιγῶμεν, φίλαι. 725

ΑΓΑΜΕΜΝΩΝ.

Ἑκάβη, τί μέλλεις παῖδα σὴν κρύπτειν τάφῳ
ἐλθοῦσ᾽ ἐφ᾽ οἷσπερ Ταλθύβιος ἤγγειλέ μοι

700. Porson, who, with the old copies, assigns ἐν ψαμάθῳ λευρᾷ to the following speech of the servant, does not seem to have noticed that the one party speaks chiefly in dochmiacs, the other solely in iambics. Hence it is clear that Hermann rightly gives these words to Hecuba.

702. ἔνυπνον Hermann for ἐνύπνιον, on account of the metre, and also in the next verse οὐδὲ παρέβα με for οὔ με παρέβα.

706—7. No attempts of the editors have succeeded in making this verse scan. In Porson's edition the whole passage is quite unmetrical; ὤμοι, αἶ αἶ, | ἔμαθον ἐνύπνιον, ὀμμάτων ἐμῶν | ὄψιν, οὔ με παρέβα φάσμα | μελανόπτερον, ἂν ἐσεῖδον | ἀμφί σ᾽, ὦ τέκνον, οὐκέτ᾽ | ὄντα Διὸς ἐν φάει. It seems surprising, at the present day, that any one with an ear for choral metres should tolerate such a farrago as this. The present editor has ventured to restore a trimeter dochmiac by giving εἰσεῖδον with several of the MSS., and

ἀμφὶ τέκνον for ἀμφί σ᾽, ὦ τέκνον, on conjecture. The reading was probably altered, and so the metre was destroyed, by some scribe who thought that ὄντα could not agree with τέκνον. But cf. Troad. 735, ὦ περισσὰ τιμηθεὶς τέκνον. Bacch. 1307, ἔρνος—κατθανόντα.

708. ὀνειρόφρων. Porson gives ὀνειρόφρον, with Aldus and some MSS. But the sense is, 'Can you tell us by the information of your dreams who killed him?' There is a slight irony, because, as v. 713 shows, the chorus are yet incredible that he could have been murdered.—ἔχοι Porson, with Aldus.

715. οὐχ ὅσιά τ᾽, οὐδ᾽ ἀνεκτὰ Porson, with Aldus. But, as the MSS. generally omit τ᾽, the probability is that it was inserted to make up a senarius.

724. δέμας. Pflugk compares θυγατρὸς Ἑρμιόνης δέμας Orest. 107, ἀδελφῆς δέμας Iph. T. 1440.

727. ἐφ᾽ οἷσπερ κτλ. On the ground of (or after) the request conveyed to me

μὴ θιγγάνειν σῆς μηδέν' Ἀργείων κόρης ;
ἡμεῖς μὲν οὖν ἐῶμεν, οὐδὲ ψαύομεν·
σὺ δὲ σχολάζεις, ὥστε θαυμάζειν ἐμέ.   730
ἥκω δ' ἀποστελῶν σε· τἀκεῖθεν γὰρ εὖ
πεπραγμέν' ἐστίν, εἴ τι τῶνδ' ἐστὶν καλῶς.
ἔα· τίν' ἄνδρα τόνδ' ἐπὶ σκηναῖς ὁρῶ
θανόντα Τρώων ; οὐ γὰρ Ἀργείων, πέπλοι
δέμας περιπτύσσοντες ἀγγέλλουσί μοι.   735
ΕΚ. δύστην', ἐμαυτὴν γὰρ λέγω λέγουσα σὲ,
Ἑκάβη, τί δράσω ; πότερα προσπέσω γόνυ
Ἀγαμέμνονος τοῦδ', ἢ φέρω σιγῇ κακά ;
ΑΓ. τί μοι προσώπῳ νῶτον ἐγκλίνασα σὸν
δύρει, τὸ πραχθὲν δ' οὐ λέγεις, τίς ἔσθ' ὅδε.   740
ΕΚ. ἀλλ' εἴ με δούλην πολεμίαν θ' ἡγούμενος
γονάτων ἀπώσαιτ', ἄλγος ἂν προσθείμεθα.

from yourself, (v. 604,) that none of the Greeks should touch Polyxena. Cf. Androm. 821, ἀκούομεν βοὴν ἐφ' οἷσιν ἦλθες ἀγγέλλουσα σύ. He goes on to say, that that request had been at once granted, and that up to the present time the body had been kept for her. Hermann remarks on this entrance of Agamemnon, " Parum scite Euripides regem ipsum venientem, ut arcessat Hecubam, fecit." If however it had been managed otherwise, the interview between these two principal persons of the drama, which the poet, as usual, made an occasion of displaying his rhetorical and philosophical powers, must have been brought about in some way, perhaps less direct and natural. Though Hecuba was a captive, she was still a person of consideration; and as such, she had a lodging in Agamemnon's own tent, v. 53. Above all, she was the mother of his favourite Cassandra.

729. οὐδὲ ψαύομεν. To avoid the supposed violation of the pause, ἐψαύομεν and ἐψαύσαμεν have been proposed. See Androm. 346. Ion 1.

731. ἥκω δ'. 'So I have come to fetch you away; for matters there (i. e. the preparations for the pyre) have been well accomplished, if aught of these things is well.' — ἐκεῖθεν for ἐκεῖ, perhaps with the idea of ὑπ' ἐκείνων. But cf. Bacch. 1175.

734. Ἀργείων, scil. αὐτὸν εἶναι. Hermann gives οὐ γὰρ Ἀργεῖοι πέπλοι κτλ., with two or three MSS., ' his ungreek dress tells me that he is no Greek.'

736. δύστηνε. Hermann thinks this is addressed to Polydorus, but then applied to herself, as being in fact the more unhappy of the two. And so some of the ancient grammarians, quoted in the scholia, explained the passage. Dindorf says, " inepte," and regards δύστηνε Ἑκάβη as to be taken together, the intermediate words being an apology for addressing herself in the vocative, as if another person. In the opinion of the present editor, this is correct. Otherwise she would have gone on to ask τί δράσεις; But, for the convenience of the construction, since the deliberative is only applicable to the first person, she says τί δράσω, as if ἡ δύστηνος in the nominative had preceded.

739. προσώπῳ κτλ., ' turning your back upon my face.' Hecuba takes no notice of the king, but continues to soliloquize till v. 752, when she rather abruptly addresses him.

742. ἄλγος ἂν προσθείμεθα Aldus. Most MSS. repeat ἂν at the end, and so Porson and Hermann have edited. W. Dindorf gives ἄλγος αὖ, after Brunck. But αὖ does not seem very appropriate, in the sense of νέον ἄλγος. The repetition of ἂν is not in place, unless some additional idea is conveyed beside the simple proposition. This is hardly at-

ΑΓ. οὔτοι πέφυκα μάντις, ὥστε μὴ κλύων
ἐξιστορῆσαι σῶν ὁδὸν βουλευμάτων.
ΕΚ. ἆρ' ἐκλογίζομαί γε πρὸς τὸ δυσμενὲς   745
μᾶλλον φρένας τοῦδ', ὄντος οὐχὶ δυσμενοῦς ;
ΑΓ. εἴ τοί με βούλει τῶνδε μηδὲν εἰδέναι,
ἐς ταυτὸν ἥκεις· καὶ γὰρ οὐδ' ἐγὼ κλύειν.
ΕΚ. οὐκ ἂν δυναίμην τοῦδε τιμωρεῖν ἄτερ
τέκνοισι τοῖς ἐμοῖσι. τί στρέφω τάδε ;   750
τολμᾶν ἀνάγκη, κἂν τύχω κἂν μὴ τύχω.
Ἀγάμεμνον, ἱκετεύω σε τῶνδε γουνάτων
καὶ σοῦ γενείου δεξιᾶς τ' εὐδαίμονος.
ΑΓ. τί χρῆμα μαστεύουσα ; μῶν ἐλεύθερον
αἰῶνα θέσθαι ; ῥᾴδιον γάρ ἐστί σοι.   755
ΕΚ. οὐ δῆτα· τοὺς κακοὺς δὲ τιμωρουμένη,
αἰῶνα τὸν ξύμπαντα δουλεῦσαι θέλω.
ΑΓ. καὶ δὴ τίν' ἡμᾶς εἰς ἐπάρκεσιν καλεῖς ;
ΕΚ. οὐδέν τι τούτων ὧν σὺ δοξάζεις, ἄναξ.
ὁρᾷς νεκρὸν τόνδ', οὗ καταστάζω δάκρυ ;   760
ΑΓ. ὁρῶ· τὸ μέντοι μέλλον οὐκ ἔχω μαθεῖν.
ΕΚ. τοῦτόν ποτ' ἔτεκον κἄφερον ζώνης ὕπο.
ΑΓ. ἔστιν δὲ τίς σῶν οὗτος, ὦ τλῆμον, τέκνων ;
ΕΚ. οὐ τῶν θανόντων Πριαμιδῶν ὑπ' Ἰλίῳ.
ΑΓ. ἦ γάρ τιν' ἄλλον ἔτεκες ἢ κείνους, γύναι ;   765
ΕΚ. ἀνόνητά γ', ὡς ἔοικε, τόνδ' ὃν εἰσορᾷς.
ΑΓ. ποῦ δ' ὢν ἐτύγχαν', ἡνίκ' ὤλλυτο πτόλις ;
ΕΚ. πατήρ νιν ἐξέπεμψεν, ὀρρωδῶν θανεῖν.
ΑΓ. ποῖ τῶν τότ' ὄντων χωρίσας τέκνων μόνον ;

tained by Hermann's explanation, καὶ πρὸς ἂν ἀλγήσαιμεν ἄν.—In this and the next distich but one, Hecuba considers the arguments for the plan she had suggested to herself, προσπεσεῖν γόνυ, v. 737. On the one hand, if he should spurn her, she would be worse off than before ; on the other hand, perhaps she is mistaken in supposing he has hostile feelings towards her. The γε in v. 745, which Hermann says "intendit atque auget vim verborum," seems rather to be an adjunct to ἄρα. So Theocr. vii. 149, ἆρά γέ πα

τοιόνδε Φόλω κατὰ λάϊνον ἄντρον κρατῆρ' Ἡρακλῆι γέρων ἐστάσατο Χείρων ;
748. ἐς ταυτὸν, scil. ἐμοί. The same phrase is used Orest. 1280.
755. ῥᾴδιον, viz. ἐμοὶ τοῦτο χαρίσασθαί σοι.
760. Hermann's opinion is probable, that a verse has been lost before this, in which some question was asked that introduced the otherwise abrupt ὁρᾷς κτλ. The order of the *stichomythia* is of course an additional argument in his favour.

ΕΚ. ἐς τήνδε χώραν, οὗπερ ηὑρέθη θανών. 770
ΑΓ. πρὸς ἄνδρ', ὃς ἄρχει τῆσδε Πολυμήστωρ χθονός;
ΕΚ. ἐνταῦθ' ἐπέμφθη πικροτάτου χρυσοῦ φύλαξ.
ΑΓ. θνήσκει δὲ πρὸς τοῦ καὶ τίνος πότμου τυχών;
ΕΚ. τίνος δ' ὑπ' ἄλλου; Θρῂξ νιν ὤλεσε ξένος.
ΑΓ. ὦ τλῆμον, ἦ που χρυσὸν ἠράσθη λαβεῖν; 775
ΕΚ. τοιαῦτ', ἐπειδὴ ξυμφορὰν ἔγνω Φρυγῶν.
ΑΓ. ηὗρες δὲ ποῦ νιν, ἢ τίς ἤνεγκεν νεκρόν;
ΕΚ. ἥδ', ἐντυχοῦσα ποντίας ἀκτῆς ἔπι.
ΑΓ. τοῦτον ματεύουσ', ἢ πονοῦσ' ἄλλον πόνον;
ΕΚ. λούτρ' ᾤχετ' οἴσουσ' ἐξ ἁλὸς Πολυξένῃ. 780
ΑΓ. κτανών νιν, ὡς ἔοικεν, ἐκβάλλει ξένος.
ΕΚ. θαλασσόπλαγκτόν γ', ὧδε διατεμὼν χρόα.
ΑΓ. ὦ σχετλία σὺ τῶν ἀμετρήτων πόνων.
ΕΚ. ὄλωλα, κοὐδὲν λοιπόν, Ἀγάμεμνον, κακῶν.
ΑΓ. φεῦ φεῦ· τίς οὕτω δυστυχὴς ἔφυ γυνή; 785
ΕΚ. οὐκ ἔστιν, εἰ μὴ τὴν τύχην αὐτὴν λέγοις.
ἀλλ' ὧνπερ οὕνεκ' ἀμφὶ σὸν πίπτω γόνυ,
ἄκουσον· εἰ μὲν ὅσιά σοι παθεῖν δοκῶ,
στέργοιμ' ἄν· εἰ δὲ τοὔμπαλιν, σύ μοι γενοῦ
τιμωρὸς ἀνδρὸς ἀνοσιωτάτου ξένου, 790
ὃς οὔτε τοὺς γῆς νέρθεν οὔτε τοὺς ἄνω
δείσας δέδρακεν ἔργον ἀνοσιώτατον·
κοινῆς τραπέζης πολλάκις τυχὼν ἐμοί,
[ξενίας τ' ἀριθμῷ πρῶτα τῶν ἐμῶν ξένων,
τυχὼν δ' ὅσων δεῖ καὶ λαβὼν προμηθίαν,] 795

774. τίνος δ' Herm. Dind. with three or four MSS. The old reading was τίνος γ' ὑπ' ἄλλου. Porson in his second edition gave τίνος πρὸς ἄλλου, as some copies omit γ', and these two prepositions are occasionally interchanged. It is easier to construe the γ' with Scholefield, 'why, by whom else?' than to defend its use by similar examples.
776. ἐπειδὴ ἔγνω. See above, v. 21 seqq.
786. τύχην. As Fortune is either good or bad, and the context shows that the latter is meant, it was unnecessary to say δυστυχίαν.

794—5. These two verses are regarded by Matthiae as spurious. Not only is the repetition of τυχὼν inharmonious and clumsy, but πρῶτα for τὰ πρῶτα (i. e. πρῶτος) is without example. Porson gives πρῶτος ὤν, supposing πρῶτα to have been a metrical correction after πρῶτος ὢν τῶν ἐμῶν or πρῶτος τῶν ἐμῶν had been wrongly written. Still, it does not seem likely that so obvious a reading as πρῶτος ὤν should have been tampered with; and besides, the use of ξενίας for ξένων, depending on ἀριθμῷ, is scarcely good Greek. W. Dindorf goes further than Matthiae, and condemns 794—7, but on insufficient

ἔκτεινε, τύμβου δ', εἰ κτανεῖν ἐβούλετο,
οὐκ ἠξίωσεν, ἀλλ' ἀφῆκε πόντιον.
ἡμεῖς μὲν οὖν δοῦλοί τε κἀσθενεῖς ἴσως·
ἀλλ' οἱ θεοὶ σθένουσι χὠ κείνων κρατῶν
νόμος· νόμῳ γὰρ τοὺς θεοὺς ἡγούμεθα,   800
καὶ ζῶμεν ἄδικα καὶ δίκαι' ὡρισμένοι·
ὃς εἰς σ' ἀνελθὼν εἰ διαφθαρήσεται,
καὶ μὴ δίκην δώσουσιν οἵτινες ξένους
κτείνουσιν ἢ θεῶν ἱερὰ τολμῶσιν φέρειν,
οὐκ ἔστιν οὐδὲν τῶν ἐν ἀνθρώποις ἴσον.   805
ταῦτ' οὖν ἐν αἰσχρῷ θέμενος αἰδέσθητί με,
οἴκτειρον ἡμᾶς, ὡς γραφεύς τ' ἀποσταθεὶς

grounds, as it seems to the present editor. He appears however to be right in referring λαβὼν προμηθίαν to v. 1137. Hermann, who undertakes the defence of the received text, but not very successfully, gives πρῶτα τῶν ἐμῶν φίλων τυχὼν ὅσων δεῖ καὶ λαβὼν προθυμίαν, where πρῶτα is adverbial, πρὸ τῶν ἄλλων φίλων.

796. εἰ κτανεῖν κτλ. He should have said, ὥσπερ ἔδει, εἰ κτλ. And that this is not said, W. Dindorf regards as one of the evidences that the passage is spurious. If the poet had written εἰ καὶ ἐβούλετο κτλ., this objection would hardly have been raised.

800. νόμος. By this word she does not mean the law of nature or of fate (as Pflugk explains), so much as the established custom of mankind, which is a stronger feeling in us, or at least, a stronger motive in all our actions, than the belief in the gods; for it is because it is the custom, rather than from any innate convictions, that ordinary men adopt some religious opinions, and act on certain principles of justice and injustice. In this sense, and no other, it is said that νόμος κρατεῖ θεῶν, and Pflugk wrongly compares Prom. 525, where Zeus is said to be weaker than Destiny. The scholiast, it should be added, takes a very different view of the sense. He construes ὁ κείνων νόμος, κρατῶν (πάντων), and supposes the meaning to be, that the very existence of a divine law implies, and causes us to believe in, a divine author of it. For the use of the article in τοὺς θεοὺς, i. e. such of the gods as we do believe in, Hermann compares Antig. 189, ταύτης ἔπι πλέοντες ὀρθῶς τοὺς φίλους ποιούμεθα.—ὡρισμένοι

for ὁρισάμενοι, ὡρισμένα ἔχοντες. Cf. Heracl. 42. Electr. 317, Ἰδαῖα φάρη χρυσέαις ἐξευγμέναι πόρπαισιν. Thuc. vi. 36, τὸν ἐκεῖ πόλεμον μήπω βεβαίως καταλελυμένους.

802. ὃς εἰς σ' κτλ. 'Now if this law, devolving upon you (i. e. for its execution) shall lose its force, then is there nothing in human affairs that is impartial.' If Agamemnon does not punish Polymestor for his treachery, any criminal may expect to go unpunished.

804. "Quod dicit, ἢ θεῶν ἱερὰ τολμῶσιν φέρειν, quum non quadret in Polymestoris facinus, haud dubie ad aliquid refertur, quod eo tempore, quo haec fabula scripta est, indignationem commoverat Atheniensium." *Hermann.* The supposition is not improbable; but it is to be observed that the Greeks, in describing a complicated wickedness that is sure to meet with its reward here or hereafter, are fond of uniting in one category *injury to strangers, impiety to the gods, undutifulness to parents.* Under the second head the present allusion to sacrilege manifestly comes. Compare Aesch. Eum. 516 (where the first and last are enumerated), and Ar. Ran. 150, where the second is placed under the specific head of perjury. Lucian Ζεὺς Ἔλεγχ. p. 640, § 18, τίνας κολάζει μάλιστα (Μίνως); Ζ. τοὺς πονηροὺς δηλαδὴ, οἷον ἀνδροφόνους καὶ ἱεροσύλους.

806. ἐν αἰσχρῷ θέμενος. Schol. αἰσχρὸν καὶ ἄδικον ἡγησάμενος. The idiom is the same as ἐν καλῷ, ἐν ἀσφαλεῖ, ἐν εὐμαρεῖ &c. See Hel. 1227.

807. ἀποσταθείς. Standing at a little distance, as a painter does to command

ἰδού με κἀνάθρησον οἷ᾽ ἔχω κακά.
τύραννος ἦν ποτ᾽, ἀλλὰ νῦν δούλη σέθεν,
εὔπαις ποτ᾽ οὖσα, νῦν δὲ γραῦς ἄπαις θ᾽ ἅμα,   810
ἄπολις, ἔρημος, ἀθλιωτάτη βροτῶν.
οἴμοι τάλαινα, ποῖ μ᾽ ὑπεξάγεις πόδα;
ἔοικα πράξειν οὐδέν· ὦ τάλαιν᾽ ἐγώ.
τί δῆτα θνητοὶ τἄλλα μὲν μαθήματα
μοχθοῦμεν ὡς χρὴ πάντα καὶ μαστεύομεν,   815
πειθὼ δὲ τὴν τύραννον ἀνθρώποις μόνην
οὐδέν τι μᾶλλον ἐς τέλος σπουδάζομεν
μισθοὺς διδόντες μανθάνειν, ἵν᾽ ἦν ποτε
πείθειν ἅ τις βούλοιτο, τυγχάνειν θ᾽ ἅμα;
πῶς οὖν ἔτ᾽ ἄν τις ἐλπίσαι πράξειν καλῶς;   820
οἱ μὲν τοσοῦτοι παῖδες οὐκέτ᾽ εἰσί μοι,
αὐτὴ δ᾽ ἐπ᾽ αἰσχροῖς αἰχμάλωτος οἴχομαι·
καπνὸν δὲ πόλεως τόνδ᾽ ὑπερθρώσκονθ᾽ ὁρῶ.
καὶ μὴν ἴσως μὲν τοῦ λόγου κενὸν τόδε,
Κύπριν προβάλλειν· ἀλλ᾽ ὅμως εἰρήσεται·   825
πρὸς σοῖσι πλευροῖς παῖς ἐμὴ κοιμίζεται
ἡ φοιβὰς ἣν καλοῦσι Κασσάνδρα Φρύγες.

the best view of his object. See on Hipp. 1005.

812. ὑπεξάγεις. 'Whither are you withdrawing your foot away from me?' The με depends on the idea of φεύγεις contained in the more complex phrase. See the notes on Med. 205. Electr. 774. It is generally admitted that Porson's explanation is wrong, *quo meum pedem subducis?* i. e. *quo me cogis te sequi?* Prof. Scholefield, though he rightly disapproves this, wrongly states the construction to be, ποῖ ὑπεξάγεις πόδα σὸν (κατά) με;

816. τὴν τύραννον κτλ., i. e. τὴν μόνην οὖσαν τύραννον. The expensive instructions of the Sophists, as Protagoras and Prodicus, of whom Euripides himself had been a hearer, are clearly alluded to, and even pointedly, in the words μισθοὺς διδόντες.—ἵν᾽ ἦν is Elmsley's certain emendation for ἵν᾽ ᾖ. Pflugk defends ἵν᾽ ᾖ, and distinguishes between the two readings thus; ἣν δεῖ μανθάνειν, ἵν᾽ ᾖ κτλ., but ἣν ἔδει μανθάνειν, ἵν᾽ ἦν ποτέ. The subjunctive is retained by Porson without suspicion; but, especially as combined with βούλοιτο, it is rather doubtful Greek. For the use of ἵνα with an imperfect, compare Hipp. 647, ἵν᾽ εἶχον μήτε προσφωνεῖν τινά. Oed. R. 1389. Translate, 'In which case it would have been possible on occasions to convince others in whatever one wished, and to gain one's end at the same time.' With τυγχάνειν we may supply either ὧν βουλόμεθα or τῶν ἀκουόντων. See Hipp. 328, μεῖζον γὰρ ἢ σοῦ μὴ τυχεῖν τί μοι κακόν;

822. ἐπ᾽ αἰσχροῖς, for servile offices beneath my rank. She details these indignities in Tro. 490 seqq.

823. καπνὸν τόνδε. She points to the cloud of smoke hanging over the city, as if it were close at hand; for the scene is laid in the Chersonese. So τῆσδε is used, Andr. 16. Cf. Tro. 8, ἡ νῦν καπνοῦται, καὶ πρὸς Ἀργείου δορὸς ὄλωλε πορθηθεῖσα.

825. προβάλλειν, προτείνειν, προφέρειν, to put forth as a plea or defence.

827. Κασσάνδρα Hermann for Κασσάν-

ποῦ τὰς φίλας δῆτ' εὐφρόνας δείξεις, ἄναξ,
ἢ τῶν ἐν εὐνῇ φιλτάτων ἀσπασμάτων
χάριν τίν' ἕξει παῖς ἐμή, κείνης δ' ἐγώ ;   830
[ἐκ τοῦ σκότου γὰρ τῶν τε νυκτέρων πάνυ
φίλτρων μεγίστη γίγνεται βροτοῖς χάρις.]
ἄκουε δή νυν· τὸν θανόντα τόνδ' ὁρᾷς ;
τοῦτον καλῶς δρῶν ὄντα κηδεστὴν σέθεν
δράσεις. ἑνός μοι μῦθος ἐνδεὴς ἔτι.   835
εἴ μοι γένοιτο φθόγγος ἐν βραχίοσι
καὶ χερσὶ καὶ κόμαισι καὶ ποδῶν βάσει,
ἢ Δαιδάλου τέχναισιν ἢ θεῶν τινὸς,
ὡς πάνθ' ὁμαρτῇ σῶν ἔχοιτο γουνάτων
κλαίοντ', ἐπισκήπτοντα παντοίους λόγους·   840
Ὦ δέσποτ', ὦ μέγιστον Ἕλλησιν φάος,
πιθοῦ, παράσχες χεῖρα τῇ πρεσβύτιδι
τιμωρὸν, εἰ καὶ μηδέν ἐστιν, ἀλλ' ὅμως.
ἐσθλοῦ γὰρ ἀνδρὸς τῇ δίκῃ θ' ὑπηρετεῖν

δρᾶν, on his own conjecture subsequently confirmed by one MS. For he rightly remarks, the poet did not mean, 'whom the Trojans call Cassandra,' but 'whom the Trojans call *the inspired one*,' φοιβάδα. The two clauses are so mixed together that the words are slightly out of their logical order.—It has been objected, that Hecuba basely and indelicately uses this argument, that gratitude is due to herself in consequence of Agamemnon having shared her child's affections. This is one of those points in judging of which we apply modern feelings somewhat too rigidly. Thus much at least is to be said for Hecuba, that the emergency of her case was such, that she was hardly likely to reject any appeal that might influence the king: and that this of all others was the most likely, who will deny ?

830. τίν' Scholef. and others for τιν'. 'What return for the many nightly endearments shall my daughter Cassandra have, and I for her ?'

831—2. This distich is rightly condemned by Matthiae, whom the recent editors follow. The feebleness of πάνυ is at once apparent, not to mention that there is a various reading νυκτέρων τ' ἀσπασμάτων φίλτρων ὁμοῦ τε, which alone throws discredit on the genuineness of the verses, though Porson does not seem to have been offended at them.

834. ὄντα, for τὸν ὄντα. The omission of the article is deserving of notice. Compare Aesch. Cho. 353. Pers. 247.—κηδεστὴν, the brother of your wife Cassandra. One might suppose that the poet had intended to say τοῦτον καλῶς δρῶν, ἅτε κηδεστήν σου ὄντα, οὐχ ἁμαρτήσει, but that he slightly altered the construction by repeating (καλῶς) δράσεις. Hermann makes a similar remark on ἑνὸς μῦθος ἐνδεὴς, which means, 'my speech has only one thing yet left to be urged.'

839. ὡς—ἔχοιτο. More regularly, ὥστε ἔχεσθαι, or ὡς ἂν ἔχοιτο. But one optative is often attracted to another ; and the sense is, 'I wish that I had a voice in each single member, that all *might* together cling to your knees,' &c. Some copies give ἔχοιντο.

842. Hermann retains πάρασχε, the reading of all the copies ; and Porson, though he adopts παράσχες from Brunck, considers the other "analogiae regulis consentaneum." Though ἔσχον might take an imperative in ε, like βάλε, ἐλθὲ, &c., it seems that the stronger form σχὲς (Hipp. 1354) was preferred to the weak monosyllable σχέ.

536   ΕΥΡΙΠΙΔΟΥ

καὶ τοὺς κακοὺς δρᾶν πανταχοῦ κακῶς ἀεί.   845
ΧΟ. δεινόν γε, θνητοῖς ὡς ἅπαντα συμπίτνει·
καὶ τὰς ἀνάγκας οἱ νόμοι διώρισαν,
φίλους τιθέντες τούς γε πολεμιωτάτους,
ἐχθρούς τε τοὺς πρὶν εὐμενεῖς ποιούμενοι.
ΑΓ. ἐγὼ σὲ καὶ σὸν παῖδα καὶ τύχας σέθεν,   850
Ἑκάβη, δι' οἴκτου χεῖρά θ' ἱκεσίαν ἔχω,
καὶ βούλομαι θεῶν θ' οὕνεκ' ἀνόσιον ξένον
καὶ τοῦ δικαίου τήνδε σοι δοῦναι δίκην,
εἴ πως φανείη γ' ὥστε σοί τ' ἔχειν καλῶς,
στρατῷ τε μὴ δόξαιμι Κασσάνδρας χάριν   855
Θρῄκης ἄνακτι τόνδε βουλεῦσαι φόνον.
ἔστιν γὰρ ᾗ ταραγμὸς ἐμπέπτωκέ μοι·
τὸν ἄνδρα τοῦτον φίλιον ἡγεῖται στρατός,
τὸν κατθανόντα δ' ἐχθρόν· εἰ δὲ σοὶ φίλος

845. πανταχοῦ—ἀεί, in all places and at all times. It was a boast with Theseus, ἀεὶ κολαστὴς τῶν κακῶν καθεστάναι, Suppl. 342. This couplet is quoted by Stobaeus, Flor. ix. 6.

846—9. δεινόν γε κτλ. ' 'Tis strange, how among mortals all things clash confusedly together: even their social ties (of friends and relations) it is *custom* that has defined, making friends those who were most hostile, and regarding as enemies those who were before kindly disposed.' The same νόμος is meant as in v. 800. The plural is used, and with the article, because different customs prevail in different parts of the world. It is not surprising that those who took τὰς ἀνάγκας for τὴν εἱμαρμένην, should find great difficulty in this passage. All that the chorus means is, that mankind are wont to bend to circumstances, and not to act on any one rigid notion of right and wrong. Thus, Agamemnon, who would naturally be an enemy to Hecuba, is inclined to become her friend, and Polymestor conversely has changed from a confidential guest to a base and avaricious traitor. Hermann's explanation is slightly different:—' Hecuba ought to have hated Agamemnon for slaying Polyxena, but the law of vengeance due to Polymestor compels her to make a friend of him.' Pflugk, ' The authority and majesty of the laws (which Polymestor has violated) have determined the sort of relations or bonds that shall exist between Agamemnon and Hecuba, i. e. not those of enmity, but those of co-operation in a common cause.' Schol. ἐάν τις ἀνάγκη συμβῇ, ὥσπερ καὶ νῦν, ὁ μὲν φίλος ἐχθρὸς, ὁ δὲ ἐχθρὸς φίλος καθίσταται.

850. Agamemnon temporises, as great people often do. He would gladly assist her, of course; but there is an *if* in the case. Unfortunately, the army regards Polymestor and Polydorus in exactly the opposite light to what she does: the one is a friend, the other was an enemy. But *if* he can avoid a collision with the army in general, he will be prompt enough to assist her.

854. φανείη γ' Porson, Pflugk, W.Dindorf; φανείην γ' Hermann. Both readings are found in the MSS. If we prefer φανείην, it is not difficult to supply βουλόμενος τοῦτο γενέσθαι. But to make δόξαιμι depend on ὥστε rather than on εἰ, as Scholefield and Hermann do, seems unnecessarily awkward. Schol. δέον δόξαι εἰπεῖν, πρὸς τὸ σοί τ' ἔχειν, (ὁ γὰρ τὲ σύνδεσμος τοῦτο ἀπῄτει,) δόξαιμι εἶπε, πρὸς τὸ φανείην. There is a little change in the sentence at the next verse, which should have been ἐμέ τε μὴ δόξαι κτλ.

859. σοὶ φίλος. ' If this man, Polydorus, is dear to you, that is a private matter, and one which the army has nothing to do with.' Elmsley proposed εἰ

ΕΚΑΒΗ. 537

ὅδ' ἐστὶ, χωρὶς τοῦτο κοὐ κοινὸν στρατῷ. 860
πρὸς ταῦτα φρόντιζ'· ὡς θέλοντα μέν μ' ἔχεις
σοὶ ξυμπονῆσαι καὶ ταχὺν προσαρκέσαι,
βραδὺν δ', Ἀχαιοῖς εἰ διαβληθήσομαι.

ΕΚ. φεῦ·
οὐκ ἔστι θνητῶν ὅστις ἔστ' ἐλεύθερος·
ἢ χρημάτων γὰρ δοῦλός ἐστιν ἢ τύχης, 865
ἢ πλῆθος αὐτὸν πόλεος ἢ νόμων γραφαὶ
εἴργουσι χρῆσθαι μὴ κατὰ γνώμην τρόποις.
ἐπεὶ δὲ ταρβεῖς τῷ τ' ὄχλῳ πλέον νέμεις,
ἐγώ σε θήσω τοῦδ' ἐλεύθερον φόβου.
ξύνισθι μὲν γὰρ, ἤν τι βουλεύσω κακὸν 870
τῷ τόνδ' ἀποκτείναντι, συνδράσῃς δὲ μή.
ἢν δ' ἐξ Ἀχαιῶν θόρυβος ἢ 'πικουρία
πάσχοντος ἀνδρὸς Θρῃκὸς οἷα πείσεται
φανῇ τις, εἶργε μὴ δοκῶν ἐμὴν χάριν.
τὰ δ' ἄλλα, θάρσει, πάντ' ἐγὼ θήσω καλῶς. 875

ΑΓ. πῶς οὖν; τί δράσεις; πότερα φάσγανον χερὶ
λαβοῦσα γραίᾳ φῶτα βάρβαρον κτενεῖς,
ἢ φαρμάκοισιν, ἢ 'πικουρίᾳ τίνι;
τίς σοι ξυνέσται χείρ; πόθεν κτήσει φίλους;

ΕΚ. στέγαι κεκεύθασ' αἵδε Τρῳάδων ὄχλον. 880
ΑΓ. τὰς αἰχμαλώτους εἶπας, Ἑλλήνων ἄγραν;

δ' ἐμοὶ φίλος. But Pflugk and Hermann rightly object, that this would be virtually admitting that his advocacy was really due to his love for Cassandra. He does not indeed mean to deny that he has an interest in Polydorus for his family's sake; but χωρὶς is used much as the French say *c'est entre nous*.
867. μὴ κατὰ γνώμην, as μὴ παρὰ γνώμην Aesch. Ag. 904. It seems better to take the words in their natural order, and construe εἴργουσιν (ὥστε) χρῆσθαι, 'constrain him to employ his natural bent not according to his convictions,' (or, 'to adopt a manner not after his judgment,') than to regard μὴ as belonging to χρῆσθαι, for which Pflugk compares Thuc. iii. 6, καὶ τῆς μὲν θαλάσσης εἴργον μὴ χρῆσθαι τοὺς Μυτιληναίους. The remark is a very wise one, that public men are often unable to act according to their consciences, because such action would be either unpopular, or illegal, or would damage them in their fortunes or their high position (τύχη).
868. πλέον νέμεις. See Suppl. 241.
874. μὴ δοκῶν, 'pretending not to do so on my account.' See on Med. 67. Electr. 925. The μὴ is dependent on the preceding imperative; εἴργων μὴ δόκει εἴργειν.
875. θάρσει. After this word a colon is commonly placed. The punctuation suggested by Reiske and Elmsley seems to be better.
876—8. φάσγανον — φαρμάκοις. On these two instruments of female vengeance see Med. 379—85. Ion 616.—τίνι, for τινί, Porson and the editors after Barnes.

VOL. II. 3 z

ΕΚ. ξὺν ταῖσδε τὸν ἐμὸν φονέα τιμωρήσομαι.
ΑΓ. καὶ πῶς γυναιξὶν ἀρσένων ἔσται κράτος;
ΕΚ. δεινὸν τὸ πλῆθος, ξὺν δόλῳ τε δύσμαχον.
ΑΓ. δεινόν· τὸ μέντοι θῆλυ μέμφομαι γένος. 885
ΕΚ. τί δ'; οὐ γυναῖκες εἷλον Αἰγύπτου τέκνα,
καὶ Λῆμνον ἄρδην ἀρσένων ἐξῴκισαν;
ἀλλ' ὡς γενέσθω· τόνδε μὲν μέθες λόγον,
πέμψον δέ μοι τήνδ' ἀσφαλῶς διὰ στρατοῦ
γυναῖκα. καὶ σὺ Θρῃκὶ πλαθεῖσα ξένῳ 890
λέξον, Καλεῖ σ' ἄνασσα δήποτ' Ἰλίου
Ἑκάβη, σὸν οὐκ ἔλασσον ἢ κείνης χρέος,
καὶ παῖδας· ὡς δεῖ καὶ τέκν' εἰδέναι λόγους
τοὺς ἐξ ἐκείνης. τὸν δὲ τῆς νεοσφαγοῦς
Πολυξένης ἐπίσχες, Ἀγάμεμνον, τάφον, 895
ὡς τώδ' ἀδελφὼ πλησίον μιᾷ φλογὶ,
δισσὴ μέριμνα μητρὶ, κρυφθῆτον χθονί.
ΑΓ. ἔσται τάδ' οὕτως· καὶ γὰρ εἰ μὲν ἦν στρατῷ
πλοῦς, οὐκ ἂν εἶχον τήνδε σοι δοῦναι χάριν·
νῦν δ', οὐ γὰρ ἵησ' οὐρίους πνοὰς θεὸς, 900
μένειν ἀνάγκη πλοῦν ὁρῶντας ἥσυχον.
γένοιτο δ' εὖ πως· πᾶσι γὰρ κοινὸν τόδε,

882. φονέα. The final α is made short, as Porson remarks, only here and in Electr. 599. 763. The common rule does not strictly apply to the comic writers.
885. μέμφομαι, I distrust, have no opinion of. See Hel. 31.
886. Αἰγύπτου τέκνα. See Aesch. Prom. 881. Apollodor. ii. 1, 5.—Λῆμνον, Aesch. Cho. 620. Apollodor. i. 9, 17.
888. ὡς γενέσθω. This formula occurs also Tro. 721. Iph. T. 603, in the former case, as here, with the variant γενέσθαι. It is one of the few instances where ὡς for οὕτως is used by the Attic poets. See on v. 441.
891. δήποτ'. See v. 484.
892. χρέος. Used like χάριν in v. 874, a sort of accusative absolute, 'on your own business not less than on hers.'
901. ὁρῶντας. The ships are supposed to be in sight of the stage; cf. v. 1015. Elmsley on Heracl. 7, and Hermann on this passage, independently arrive at the same conjecture, ὁρῶντά μ' for ὁρῶντας, on the ground that πλοῦς ἥσυχος is an improbable expression for 'a calm voyage,' and that the people themselves are said θάσσειν ἥσυχοι in v. 35. One MS. gives ὁρῶντα, and many instances of the like error might be cited, e. g. πράσσοντας for πράσσοντα in Prom. 273. Still it is more in accordance with modern use than with ancient Greek custom, for a general to say, 'I am waiting for a fair wind.' Pflugk takes ἥσυχον for ἡσύχως. It would be easy indeed to read ἡσύχους. Still, there is no valid reason for denying that Euripides may have used πλοῦς ἥσυχος for εὔπλοια, or even for ἄπλοια. To Hermann's alteration it may be objected, that πλοῦν ὁρῶντά μ' ἥσυχον would be ambiguous, and that if πλοῦν ἥσυχον was wrong, it would hardly have been left open to the audience to construe it so if they pleased.

ἰδίᾳ θ' ἑκάστῳ καὶ πόλει, τὸν μὲν κακὸν
κακόν τι πάσχειν, τὸν δὲ χρηστὸν εὐτυχεῖν.
ΧΟ. σὺ μὲν, ὦ πατρὶς Ἰλιὰς,   στρ. α'. 905
τῶν ἀπορθήτων πόλις οὐκέτι λέξει·
τοῖον Ἑλλάνων νέφος ἀμφί σε κρύπτει
δορὶ δὴ δορὶ πέρσαν.
ἀπὸ δὲ στεφάναν κέκαρσαι   910
πύργων, κατὰ δ' αἰθάλου
κηλῖδ' οἰκτροτάταν κέχρωσαι,
τάλαιν', οὐκέτι σ' ἐμβατεύσω.
μεσονύκτιος ὠλλύμαν,   ἀντ. α'.
ἦμος ἐκ δείπνων ὕπνος ἡδὺς ἐπ' ὄσσοις   915
κίδναται, μολπᾶν δ' ἄπο καὶ χοροποιῶν
θυσιᾶν καταπαύσας
πόσις ἐν θαλάμοις ἔκειτο,
ξυστὸν δ' ἐπὶ πασσάλῳ,   920

905. The beautiful ode here following describes a subject by no means new, the capture of Troy; and for this very reason perhaps no ordinary poet could have so successfully handled the theme. The chorus of captives describe what they saw and felt and did on that eventful night, when in the midst of security and repose the Argive troops first broke in upon the unconscious populace. It was midnight, and there had been a festival in the city. Wearied with the dance, the warrior had hung his idle spear, and thinking of anything rather than of the Grecian host, had flung himself on the couch. The wife was at her toilet, binding her hair before the mirror, when the war-cry of Argos reached her ears. The enemy are upon her; she delays not, but flings herself half-clad out of the chamber, and betakes herself to the sanctuary of the temples. In vain; she sees her husband lying in his blood, and is carried away a captive, giving a last sad look to her native city as the ship stood out to sea. Could she refrain from muttering an imprecation on Helen and Paris, the cause of all her woes? May that faithless wife never again know a father's home.—The metre is glyconic, interspersed with some iambic versicles in the latter half.

906. τῶν ἀπορθήτων — λέξει. 'You shall no longer be called one of the cities that have never been ravaged.' This is said in reference to the boasted title of Athens, for which see Aesch. Pers. 350. Med. 827. Oed. Col. 702.

910—12. The student will not confound the idiom ἀποκέκαρσαι στεφάναν, 'you have been shorn of your crowning towers,' which is like δίκαια ὡρισμένοι in v. 801, with κέχρωσαι κηλῖδα, where it is a cognate accusative. For χρῴζειν see Med. 497. Phoen. 1625. Some copies with Aldus give κηλῖδ' οἰκτροτάτα, where however the elision of the ι would be inadmissible. A similar error formerly existed in Aesch. Suppl. 6, οὔτιν' ἐφ' αἵματι δημηλασίᾳ—γνωσθεῖσαι.

914. ὠλλύμαν, a common use of the imperfect for εἰς δουλείαν ἀπηγόμην, cf. v. 937.

920. ξυστὸν, properly *hastile*, a spear-shaft. Photius, δορύλλιον, ἀκόντιον, καὶ τὸ τέλειον δόρυ. In the last sense it is here used, viz. a shaft with the λόγχη or iron point. This line is parenthetical, since ὁρῶν refers back to πόσις, as if he had said ξυστὸν κρεμασάμενος. It was the custom to hang arms on a peg near the bed for the sake of protection. So Amphitryo, in Theocr. xxiv. 42, when summoned by Alcmena to assist in the dead of night, took down his sword, δαιδάλεον

ναύταν οὐκέθ᾽ ὁρῶν ὅμιλον
Τροίαν Ἰλιάδ᾽ ἐμβεβῶτα.
ἐγὼ δὲ πλόκαμον ἀναδέτοις   στρ. β΄.
μίτραισιν ἐρρυθμιζόμαν
χρυσέων ἐνόπτρων   925
λεύσσουσ᾽ ἀτέρμονας εἰς αὐγὰς,
ἐπιδέμνιος ὡς πέσοιμ᾽ ἐς εὐνάν.
ἀνὰ δὲ κέλαδος ἔμολε πόλιν·
κέλευσμα δ᾽ ἦν κατ᾽ ἄστυ Τροίας τόδ᾽· ὦ
παῖδες Ἑλλάνων, πότε δὴ πότε τὰν   930
Ἰλιάδα σκοπιὰν πέρσαντες ἥξετ᾽ οἴκους;
λέχη δὲ φίλια μονόπεπλος   ἀντ. β΄.
λιποῦσα, Δωρὶς ὡς κόρα,
σεμνὰν προσίζουσ᾽   935
οὐκ ἤνυσ᾽ Ἄρτεμιν ἀ τλάμων·
ἄγομαι δὲ θανόντ᾽ ἰδοῦσ᾽ ἀκοίταν
τὸν ἐμὸν ἅλιον ἐπὶ πέλαγος,
πόλιν τ᾽ ἀποσκοποῦσ᾽, ἐπεὶ νόστιμον

ὥρμησε μετὰ ξίφος, ὃ ῥ᾽ οἱ ὕπερθεν κλιντῆρος κεδρίνῳ περὶ πασσάλῳ αἰὲν ἄωρτο. —οὐκέθ᾽ ὁρῶν, i. e. οὐ φρονίζων, οὐκ ὀσσόμενος.

924. ῥυθμίζεσθαι κόμην, like σχηματίζεσθαι Med. 1161, is used in the middle with reference to the services of the κομμώτρια. The μίτρα was a close cap tied under the chin, whence ἀναδέτοις.— ἀτέρμονας αὐγὰς, the light which, proceeding from a fixed point, viz. the mirror itself, is flashed back without any definite limit. The scholiast's explanation, κυκλοτερεῖς, is deserving of no credit.

927. ἐπιδέμνιος, needlessly altered by Porson to ἐπιδέμνιον, merely means ἐπὶ δέμνιον εὐνῆς, on the bed-stead supporting the bedding; for δέμνιον differs from εὐνή as *lectus* from *torus*.

931. Ἰλιάδα σκοπιὰν, the Pergamus or citadel of Troy.

933. μονόπεπλος. See on Androm. 598. The words of the scholiast here are well worthy of being quoted:—αἱ Λακεδαιμόνιαι κόραι διημερεύουσιν ἄζωστοι καὶ ἀχίτωνες, ἱμάτιδιον ἔχουσαι πεπορπημένον ἐφ᾽ ἑκατέρου τῶν ὤμων· καὶ Καλλίμαχος, Ἔσκεν ὅτ᾽ ἄζωστος χἀτερόπορπος ἔτι· καὶ ἐν ταῖς ἀρχαίαις γραφαῖς οὐκ ὀλίγα ὧδε ἔσταλται· καὶ Δωριάζειν τὸ γυμνὰς φαίνεσθαι τὰς γυναῖκας.

936. οὐκ ἤνυσα, I failed in my object. Cf. Bacch. 1100, ἀλλ᾽ οὐκ ἤνυτον, scil. Πενθέως ἱέντες. Why Artemis is particularly named is not clear, except that she appears to have some tutelary relations to married women. In Aesch. Theb. 134, her aid against the enemy is sought on the ground of her being armed with a bow. Some think there is an allusion to the special cultus of Artemis by Doric maidens; but it is certain that Δωρὶς ὡς κόρα refers only to the epithet μονόπεπλος.

939. ἀποσκοποῦσα. There appears to be some little confusion arising from the several participles not exactly suiting the verbs. Thus, some take ἄγομαι—ἰδοῦσα —ἀποσκοποῦσά τε, while others put a colon at πέλαγος, and connect ἀποσκοποῦσα with ἀπεῖπον, while some again, with Hermann and Matthiae, regard τάλαιν᾽ ἀπεῖπον ἄλγει as a parenthesis. The schol. says that τινὲς τῶν ψυχρῶν took κατάρα διδοῦσα with ἀπεῖπον. All things considered, it seems best to put up with the charge of ψυχρότης, and translate thus:—'And looking back on my

ναῦς ἐκίνησεν πόδα καί μ' ἀπὸ γᾶς 940
ὥρισεν Ἰλιάδος, τάλαιν', ἀπεῖπον ἄλγει,
τὰν τοῖν Διοσκόροιν Ἑλέναν κάσιν, Ἰδαῖόν τε βού-
ταν ἐπῳδ.
αἰνόπαριν κατάρᾳ διδοῦσ', ἐπεί με γᾶς 946
ἐκ πατρῴας ἀπώλεσεν
ἐξῴκισέν τ' οἴκων γάμος, οὐ γάμος, ἀλλ' ἀλάστορός
τις οἰζύς· 950
ἂν μήτε πέλαγος ἅλιον ἀπαγάγοι πάλιν,
μήτε πατρῷον ἵκοιτ' ἐς οἶκον.

ΠΟΛΥΜΗΣΤΩΡ.

ὦ φίλτατ' ἀνδρῶν Πρίαμε, φιλτάτη δὲ σὺ,
Ἑκάβη, δακρύω σ' εἰσορῶν πόλιν τε σὴν,
τήν τ' ἀρτίως θανοῦσαν ἔκγονον σέθεν. 955
φεῦ·
οὐκ ἔστιν οὐδὲν πιστὸν οὔτ' εὐδοξία
οὔτ' αὖ καλῶς πράσσοντα μὴ πράξειν κακῶς.
φύρουσι δ' αὐτὰ θεοὶ πάλιν τε καὶ πρόσω,
ταραγμὸν ἐντιθέντες, ὡς ἀγνωσίᾳ

city, when the ship had commenced its homeward voyage, and had separated me from the Trojan land, unhappy that I was, I felt my heart sink within me for grief, as I consigned to curses Helen the sister of the Dioscuri, and the herdsman of Ida, that ill-starred Paris.' The ship is said κινεῖν πόδα either with regard to the nautical use of πούς, or by a metaphor from setting out to walk. Perhaps both ideas are combined.

950. γάμος, οὐ γάμος. Pflugk compares Androm. 103, Ἰλίῳ αἰπεινᾷ Πάρις οὐ γάμον, ἀλλά τιν' ἄταν, ἠγάγετ' εὐναίαν εἰς θαλάμους Ἑλέναν.

953. Polymestor, king of Thrace, who to his villainous treachery has added consummate hypocrisy, has obeyed the summons sent by Hecuba at v. 890, and fallen into the snare laid for wreaking a woman's vengeance on him. He pretends to condole with Hecuba's sorrows, and is at first answered by fair words. It is craft against craft; Greek characters both, though numbered geographically among the βάρβαροι. There is perhaps

truth in the remark of the scholiast, that σὺ is added in direct address to Hecuba, as being present, while ὦ φίλτατε Πρίαμε merely apostrophises one whom he knew to be dead.

956. οὔτ' εὐδοξία. He appears to mean, οὔτε τὸ εὖ ἀκούειν οὔτε τὸ καλῶς πράσσειν βέβαιόν ἐστιν ἀνθρώποις.

958. οἱ θεοὶ MSS. θεοὶ Herm.—πάλιν καὶ πρόσω, scil. στρέφοντες. Properly, as remarked on Suppl. 201, φύρειν and φυρᾶν mean to mix flour, earth, or other solid ingredients, with any liquid, so as to form paste. Hence γῆν φυράσειν φόνῳ, Aesch. Theb. 48. Supra, v. 496, κόνει φύρουσα δύστηνον κάρα. Hes. Opp. 61, "Ηφαιστον δ' ἐκέλευσε περικλυτὸν ὅττι τάχιστα γαῖαν ὕδει φύρειν. The working of the mass up and down is expressed by πάλιν καὶ πρόσω.

959. ἀγνωσίᾳ, τῶν ἡμετέρων πραγμάτων. For, if men knew certainly what awaited them, they would fall into a fatalism which would ignore the very existence of the gods as agents in human affairs.

σέβωμεν αὐτούς· ἀλλὰ ταῦτα μὲν τί δεῖ 960
θρηνεῖν, προκόπτοντ' οὐδὲν ἐς πρόσθεν κακῶν;
σὺ δ' εἴ τι μέμφει τῆς ἐμῆς ἀπουσίας,
σχές· τυγχάνω γὰρ ἐν μέσοις Θρῄκης ὅροις
ἀπών, ὅτ' ἦλθες δεῦρ'· ἐπεὶ δ' ἀφικόμην,
ἤδη πόδ' ἔξω δωμάτων αἴροντί μοι 965
ἐς ταυτὸν ἥδε συμπίτνει δμωῒς σέθεν,
λέγουσα μύθους ὧν κλύων ἀφικόμην.
ΕΚ. αἰσχύνομαί σε προσβλέπειν ἐναντίον,
Πολυμῆστορ, ἐν τοιοῖσδε κειμένη κακοῖς.
ὅτῳ γὰρ ὤφθην εὐτυχοῦσ', αἰδώς μ' ἔχει 970
ἐν τῷδε πότμῳ τυγχάνουσ', ἵν' εἰμὶ νῦν,
κοὐκ ἂν δυναίμην προσβλέπειν σ' ὀρθαῖς κόραις.
ἀλλ' αὐτὸ μὴ δύσνοιαν ἡγήσῃ σέθεν,
Πολυμῆστορ· ἄλλως δ' αἴτιόν τι καὶ νόμος,
γυναῖκας ἀνδρῶν μὴ βλέπειν ἐναντίον. 975
ΠΟΛΥΜ. καὶ θαυμά γ' οὐδέν. ἀλλὰ τίς χρεία σ' ἐμοῦ;
τί χρῆμ' ἐπέμψω τὸν ἐμὸν ἐκ δόμων πόδα;
ΕΚ. ἴδιον ἐμαυτῆς δή τι πρὸς σὲ βούλομαι
καὶ παῖδας εἰπεῖν σούς· ὀπάονας δέ μοι
χωρὶς κέλευσον τῶνδ' ἀποστῆναι δόμων. 980
ΠΟΛΥΜ. χωρεῖτ'. ἐν ἀσφαλεῖ γὰρ ἥδ' ἐρημία.
φίλη μὲν εἶ σύ, προσφιλὲς δέ μοι τόδε
στράτευμ' Ἀχαιῶν. ἀλλὰ σημαίνειν σε χρὴ
τί χρὴ τὸν εὖ πράσσοντα μὴ πράσσουσιν εὖ
φίλοις ἐπαρκεῖν· ὡς ἕτοιμός εἰμ' ἐγώ. 985

961. προκόπτοντα οὐδέν, making no advance, οὐδὲν προχωροῦντα. See on this word Hipp. 23.
970. αἰδώς μ' ἔχει, being equivalent to αἰδοῦμαι ὀφθῆναι, takes the nominative participle after it. So in the passage just quoted, Hipp. 23, τὰ πολλὰ δὲ πάλαι προκόψασ', οὐ πόνου πολλοῦ με δεῖ. We might easily read κἂν τῷδε πότμῳ—οὐκ ἂν δυναίμην. Porson thought v. 971 spurious; but this seems very doubtful. The mere fact, that the passage would stand equally well without it, is quite inconclusive.— ὀρθαῖς κόραις, opposed to λοξὰ βλέπειν, to look one in the face without flinching.

Theocr. v. 35, μέγα δ' ἄχθομαι, εἰ σύ με τολμᾷς ὄμμασι τοῖς ὀρθοῖσι ποτιβλέπεν. Iph. Aul. 851, χαῖρ', οὐ γὰρ ὀρθοῖς ὄμμασίν σ' ἔτ' εἰσορῶ ψευδὴς γενομένη. Hermann takes προσβλέπειν to depend also on αἰδώς μ' ἔχει.
976. τίς χρεία σ' ἐμοῦ; scil. ἔχει. An Homeric idiom, χρεὼ βουλῆς ἐμὲ καὶ σέ, &c.—ἐπέμψω, μετεπέμψω, though the μετὰ would be rather an adjunct, than necessary to the sense, since πέμπεσθαί τινα is 'to get a person conducted to you.'
981. ἐν ἀσφαλεῖ. See on Hel. 1227. Supra, v. 806.

ΕΚΑΒΗ. 543

ΕΚ. πρῶτον μὲν εἰπὲ παῖδ' ὃν ἐξ ἐμῆς χερὸς
   Πολύδωρον ἔκ τε πατρὸς ἐν δόμοις ἔχεις,
   εἰ ζῇ· τὰ δ' ἄλλα δεύτερόν σ' ἐρήσομαι.
ΠΟΛΥΜ. μάλιστα· τοὐκείνου μὲν εὐτυχεῖς μέρος.
ΕΚ. ὦ φίλταθ', ὡς εὖ κἀξίως σέθεν λέγεις.   990
ΠΟΛΥΜ. τί δῆτα βούλει δεύτερον μαθεῖν ἐμοῦ ;
ΕΚ. εἰ τῆς τεκούσης τῆσδε μέμνηταί τί μου.
ΠΟΛΥΜ. καὶ δεῦρό γ' ὡς σὲ κρύφιος ἐζήτει μολεῖν.
ΕΚ. χρυσὸς δὲ σῶς, ὃν ἦλθεν ἐκ Τροίας ἔχων ;
ΠΟΛΥΜ. σῶς, ἐν δόμοις γε τοῖς ἐμοῖς φρουρούμενος.   995
ΕΚ. σῶσόν νυν αὐτὸν, μηδ' ἔρα τῶν πλησίον.
ΠΟΛΥΜ. ἥκιστ'· ὀναίμην τοῦ παρόντος, ὦ γύναι.
ΕΚ. οἶσθ' οὖν ἃ λέξαι σοί τε καὶ παισὶν θέλω ;
ΠΟΛΥΜ. οὐκ οἶδα· τῷ σῷ τοῦτο σημανεῖς λόγῳ.
ΕΚ. ἔστω φιληθεὶς ὡς σὺ νῦν ἐμοὶ φιλεῖ.   1000
ΠΟΛΥΜ. τί χρῆμ', ὃ κἀμὲ καὶ τέκν' εἰδέναι χρεών ;
ΕΚ. χρυσοῦ παλαιαὶ Πριαμιδῶν κατώρυχες.
ΠΟΛΥΜ. ταῦτ' ἔσθ' ἃ βούλει παιδὶ σημῆναι σέθεν ;
ΕΚ. μάλιστα, διὰ σοῦ γ'· εἰ γὰρ εὐσεβὴς ἀνήρ.

989. εὐτυχεῖς, for οὐκ ἄπαις εἶ. Cf. Androm. 420. Ion 699.
997. ὀναίμην τοῦ παρόντος. See Alcest. 335. Med. 1025. Hel. 1418.
1000. Neither Porson nor Pflugk have a single word to say on the very difficult verse, ἔστω φιληθεὶς κτλ. To refer the first words to Polydorus would be absurd, because *her* love to Polymestor was no love at all, but hate. The scholiast has the following commentary ;—ἀγαπηθήτω ὁ παῖς μου ὑπὸ σοῦ, ὡς νῦν σὺ ἀγαπᾷ ὑπ' ἐμοῦ. κατὰ μὲν τὸ φαινόμενον λέγει, ἀγαπάσθω ὁ Πολύδωρος ὑπὸ σοῦ οὕτως, καθὰ σὺ νῦν φιλεῖ ὑπ' ἐμοῦ· κατὰ δὲ τὸ νοούμενον, ὡς σὺ φιλεῖ ἀρτίως παρ' ἐμοῦ, οὕτως ἐφιλεῖτο καὶ ὁ Πολύδωρος παρὰ σοῦ. But the last part of his explanation, regarding Hecuba's hidden meaning, does not seem to be tenable. If, with Schaefer, we take λόγος as the subject of ἔστω, the double sense is sufficiently well maintained, viz. the meaning *he* is to receive, 'pay all regard and attention to my instructions, in proportion to my present love for you,' and *her* real meaning,

'Take it, and much good may it do you.' Hermann's objection, that v. 1002 will not stand for want of a verb, is groundless. In fact, Polymestor reverts to the object of his anxiety, what he has been sent for to learn ; and he says, ' What is it, that I and my children are to be informed of ?' And she replies, ' Certain ancient deposits of gold belonging to the family of Priam.' Hermann, whom W. Dindorf follows, reads ἔστ', ὦ φιληθεὶς κτλ., and takes the whole sentence as if it were εἰσὶ, ὦ ἔχθιστε Πολυμῆστορ, παλαιαὶ χρυσοῦ κατώρυχες κτλ. The address ἔστ', ὦ φιληθεὶς, strikes the ear rather harshly ; though ἀλλ', ὦ φιληθεῖσ', occurs Iph. T. 983 ; besides which, the emphatic σὺ ceases to have any meaning unless φιληθεὶς refers to some contrasted thing or person. Cf. v. 1006. To take the lowest grounds, there can be no necessity of altering the text. The participle with εἰμὶ, for the imperative φιληθήτω, may be compared with ἀντιδοὺς ἔσει, Antig. 1067, γηρυθεῖσ' ἔσει Aesch. Suppl. 454.
1004. εὐσεβὴς, righteous, upright. She

ΠΟΛΥΜ. τί δῆτα τέκνων τῶνδε δεῖ παρουσίας ; 1005
ΕΚ. ἄμεινον, ἢν σὺ κατθάνῃς, τούσδ' εἰδέναι.
ΠΟΛΥΜ. καλῶς ἔλεξας· τῇδε καὶ σοφώτερον.
ΕΚ. οἶσθ' οὖν Ἀθάνας Ἰλίας ἵνα στέγαι ;
ΠΟΛΥΜ. ἐνταῦθ' ὁ χρυσός ἐστι ; σημεῖον δέ τι ;
ΕΚ. μέλαινα πέτρα γῆς ὑπερτέλλουσ' ἄνω. 1010
ΠΟΛΥΜ. ἔτ' οὖν τι βούλει τῶν ἐκεῖ φράζειν ἐμοί ;
ΕΚ. σῶσαί σε χρήμαθ' οἷς συνεξῆλθον θέλω.
ΠΟΛΥΜ. ποῦ δῆτα, πέπλων ἐντὸς, ἢ κρύψασ' ἔχεις ;
ΕΚ. σκύλων ἐν ὄχλῳ ταῖσδε σώζεται στέγαις.
ΠΟΛΥΜ. ποῦ δ' ; αἵδ' Ἀχαιῶν ναύλοχοι περιπτυχαί.
ΕΚ. ἴδιαι γυναικῶν αἰχμαλωτίδων στέγαι. 1016
ΠΟΛΥΜ. τἄνδον δὲ πιστὰ, κἀρσένων ἐρημία ;
ΕΚ. οὐδεὶς Ἀχαιῶν ἔνδον, ἀλλ' ἡμεῖς μόναι.
ἀλλ' ἕρπ' ἐς οἴκους· καὶ γὰρ Ἀργεῖοι νεῶν
λῦσαι ποθοῦσιν οἴκαδ' ἐκ Τροίας πόδα· 1020
ὡς πάντα πράξας ὧν σε δεῖ στείχῃς πάλιν

speaks ironically, alluding to his ἀσέβεια περὶ ξένους. On the meaning of the word see Hel. 901.
1007. Hermann, with Boissonade, places the colon after ἔλεξας instead of the comma after τῇδε.
1008. στέγαι, the cells or subterranean treasure-vaults of Athena the patroness of Troy. The exact spot she describes as marked by a black, i. e. a basaltic or trap rock, jutting out above the surface of the ground. Cf. Orest. 6, κορυφῆς ὑπερτέλλοντα δειμαίνων πέτρον, which makes it probable that γῆς here depends on the participle rather than on ἄνω, and so the Greek paraphrast, ὑπερκειμένη τῆς γῆς. Such treasure-houses seem really to have existed; and it is well known that one of the principal causes of the demolition of ancient ruins in Greece and Asia Minor has been the search after such treasure, which in a few instances has been really found.
1013. ἦ Porson after Valckenaer, calling the vulgate ἢ "leve vitium." But Hermann seems to be right in retaining it :—' Where then is it ? Have you got it in the folds of your garments, or have you concealed it (elsewhere) ?'
1015. The scholiast tells us that the true punctuation is ποῦ δ' αἵδ'; Ἀχαιῶν ναύλοχοι περιπτυχαί; 'Where are these apartments (στέγαι)? Do you mean the Argive ships ?' i. e. that your money is there. But, as observed on v. 901, it is clear that the station of the ships was supposed,—perhaps represented,—to be close at hand. Thus Polymestor means to throw distrust on her statement that she has money concealed from the Greeks, because he cannot understand where she could hide it in sight of the very fleet. It is possible to take ναύλοχοι περιπτυχαὶ of the semicircular row of tents occupied by the crew and their generals, and which presupposed the ships to be riding in some adjacent bay. It is possible too, as the theatre commanded a view of the sea (*Athens and Attica*, p. 98), that the speaker pointed in that direction, so as to give an apparent reality to the action.
1021. ὧν σε δεῖ. We should expect ἅ σε δεῖ, scil. πράσσειν, but the construction is like δεῖ σε Προμηθέως, Aesch. P. 86. Of course the words are ambiguous; for Hecuba means ὧν δεῖ σε δοῦναι δίκην, and οὗπερ ᾤκισας is εἰς Ἅιδου. With these words she conducts Polymestor within the tent, and the chorus, knowing the plot, anticipates a speedy vengeance.

ΕΚΑΒΗ. 545

ξὺν παισὶν οὔπερ τὸν ἐμὸν ᾤκισας γόνον.
ΧΟ. οὔπω δέδωκας, ἀλλ᾽ ἴσως δώσεις δίκην,
ἀλίμενόν τις ὡς εἰς ἄντλον πεσὼν 1025
λέχριος ἐκπέσῃ φίλας καρδίας,
ἀμέρσας βίον. τὸ γὰρ ὑπέγγυον
δίκᾳ καὶ θεοῖσιν οὗ ξυμπίτνει, 1030
ὀλέθριον, ὀλέθριον κακόν.
ψεύσει σ᾽ ὁδοῦ τῆσδ᾽ ἐλπὶς, ἥ σ᾽ ἐπήγαγε
θανάσιμον πρὸς Ἅιδαν, ἰὼ ἰὼ τάλας·
ἀπολέμῳ δὲ χειρὶ λείψεις βίον.
ΠΟΛΥΜ. ὤμοι, τυφλοῦμαι φέγγος ὀμμάτων τάλας. 1035
ΧΟ. ἠκούσατ᾽ ἀνδρὸς Θρηκὸς οἰμωγὴν, φίλαι;
ΠΟΛΥΜ. ὤμοι μάλ᾽ αὖθις, τέκνα, δυστήνου σφαγῆς.
ΧΟ. φίλαι, πέπρακται καίν᾽ ἔσω δόμων κακά.
ΠΟΛΥΜ. ἀλλ᾽ οὔτι μὴ φύγητε λαιψηρῷ ποδί·

1025 seqq. There is nothing particularly difficult in these verses, which are regular dochmiacs, unless it be the epic construction ὡς—ἐκπέσῃ, of which perhaps this is a unique instance in Attic Greek. See on Bacch. 1067. So however Homer frequently uses it; e. g. ὡς δὲ λέων ἐν βουσὶ θορὼν ἐξ αὐχένα ἄξῃ &c. Prof. Scholefiel dwishes Porson had edited ἐκπεσεῖ, and such is the reading of W. Dindorf, and perhaps the schol. (στερηθήσῃς), i. e. you, Polymestor, shall lose your life as suddenly and unexpectedly as a man who breaks his neck by falling sideways into a ship's hold. The words ἀμέρσας βίον, i.e. ἀφανίσας, which Pflugk thinks so obscure, and which some refer to Polymestor's slaughter of Polydorus, merely means 'having extinguished his life by the fall.' There is no truth at all in Pflugk's notion, that ἀμέρδειν βίον is "non simpliciter mori, sed pessimo mortis genere affici." As for λέχριος, it either means, when the ship is inclined on one side, or, as in Med. 1168, that the man has deviated a little from the straight course, and so slipped into the aperture he should have avoided. The bilge-water is ἀλίμενος simply because it offers no means of getting out of it. See on Heracl. 168.
1030. οὗ Musgrave and others for οὐ. "Hoc dicit: diis et justitiae obnoxia in quem expetunt, pestiferum malum est,

i. e. qui se adversus deos et justitiam impiavit, magno id suo cum malo luit." Hermann. Pflugk follows the scholiast in the utterly untenable translation of οὐ ξυμπίτνει, for οὐκ ἀπόλλυται, οὐκ ἀφανίζεται, 'a grievous crime which is under the ban of heaven, is not lost sight of.' The sense is rather, ὃς ξυμπίτνει τῷ ἐκ δίκης καὶ τῷ ἐκ θεῶν ὑπεγγύῳ, like Aesch. Eum. 322, τοῖσιν αὐτουργίαι ξυμπέσωσιν μάταιοι, where see the note. Compare also θεόθεν ὑπέγγυοι in Cho. 35, which the scholiast there, as in the present passage, interprets ἠσφαλισμένοι. Translate, 'For where the obligation to justice and to the gods (i. e. to human and divine law) is coincident, there is some fatal mischief.'"
1032. Porson and Hermann give πρὸς Ἀΐδαν, ὦ τάλας. But it seems safer to give ἰὼ ἰὼ (pronounced yo yo) to complete the dochmiac, with two or three copies, than to make Ἀΐδης a cretic on the authority of a verse given by Lucian to Euripides, but probably in joke, οὐκ, ἀλλ᾽ ἔτ᾽ ἔμπνουν Ἀΐδης μ᾽ ἐδέξατο.
1036. ὤμοι. The groan proceeds, of course, from within the tent. Compare Aesch. Ag. 1314, ὤμοι πέπληγμαι καιρίαν πληγὴν ἔσω, where ἔσω might mean ἐντὸς δόμων, as inf. 1038.
1039. οὐ μὴ κτλ. 'There is no chance of your escape, nimble-footed as you are.' See on Hel. 292.

VOL. II. 4 A

546   ΕΥΡΙΠΙΔΟΥ

βάλλων γὰρ οἴκων τῶνδ' ἀναρρήξω μυχούς.   1040
ἰδού, βαρείας χειρὸς ὁρμᾶται βέλος.
ΧΟ. βούλεσθ' ἐπεισπέσωμεν; ὡς ἀκμὴ καλεῖ
Ἑκάβῃ παρεῖναι Τρῳάσιν τε συμμάχους.
ΕΚ. ἄρασσε, φείδου μηδέν, ἐκβάλλων πύλας·
οὐ γάρ ποτ' ὄμμα λαμπρὸν ἐνθήσεις κόραις,   1045
οὐ παῖδας ὄψει ζῶντας, οὓς ἔκτειν' ἐγώ.
ΧΟ. ἦ γὰρ καθεῖλες Θρῆκα καὶ κρατεῖς ξένου,
δέσποινα, καὶ δέδρακας οἷάπερ λέγεις;
ΕΚ. ὄψει νιν αὐτίκ' ὄντα δωμάτων πάρος
τυφλόν, τυφλῷ στείχοντα παραφόρῳ ποδί,   1050
παίδων τε δισσῶν σώμαθ', οὓς ἔκτειν' ἐγὼ
ξὺν ταῖς ἀρίσταις Τρῳάσιν· δίκην δέ μοι
δέδωκε· χωρεῖ δ', ὡς ὁρᾷς, ὅδ' ἐκ δόμων.
ἀλλ' ἐκποδὼν ἄπειμι κἀποστήσομαι
θυμῷ ζέοντι Θρῃκὶ δυσμαχωτάτῳ.   1055
ΠΟΛΥΜ. ὤμοι ἐγώ, πᾶ βῶ, πᾶ στῶ, πᾶ κέλσω;

1041. The hand itself seems called βέλος, on account of the epithet βαρείας. He shakes and pushes the door from within. There is much probability in Hermann's view, supported by the scholiast, that this verse should be assigned to Polymestor instead of the chorus. For thus both he and Hecuba speak *three* verses, while the speech of each is followed by *two* of the chorus. W. Dindorf is wrong in his remark, that ἰδού suits the chorus better than Polymestor. In familiar terms, he would say, 'here goes my heavy fist.' If βέλος meant stones pelted by the hand, as the schol. thinks, the epithet βαρείας would be worse than useless.
1044. ἐκβάλλων, schol. ἐκριζῶν, knocking them down by pulling up the doorposts.
1047. This verse is rather awkwardly expressed. He should have said, ἦ γὰρ κρατεῖς (κεκράτηκας) Θρῃκὸς ξένου, καὶ καθεῖλες αὐτόν; As it is, there is not only a case of ὕστερον πρότερον, but Θρῆκα and ξένου, which ought to agree, take different constructions. Hermann plausibly suggests ξένον.
1052. ταῖς ἀρίσταις. 'Those brave Trojan ladies.' Hermann's ταῖσδ' is quite unnecessary.

1055. ζέοντι for ῥέοντι Porson and others, with two or three copies. So Oed. Col. 434, ὁπηνίκ' ἔζει θυμός. The two datives appear to stand in apposition.
1056. Polymestor rushes upon the stage. In a system of irregular anapaestics with interposed dochmiacs, he denounces vengeance against the women, if only he can succeed in grasping them. While speaking, he moves about with hands extended, fancying that his persecutors are still close to him.
Ibid. πᾶ βῶ, πᾶ στῶ; 'Which way should I go, and which way having gone, should I stand still?' Cf. Alcest. 864, ποῖ βῶ; πᾶ στῶ; τί λέγω; Hermann compares στῆναι τρίβον, Orest. 1251, to show that the verb has the notion of going somewhere and then stopping.—τίθεσθαι βάσιν θηρὸς ἐπὶ χεῖρα is 'to walk like a beast on all-fours,' and κατ' ἴχνος has the usual sense of 'in the track of the object pursued.' There is however some difficulty in the accusative χεῖρα, for which χειρὶ would be a more usual construction. Aristophanes (Ran. 681) has a similar use, Θρῃκία χελιδὼν ἐπὶ βάρβαρον ἑζομένη πέταλον, only there it is easier to explain it by ἐλθοῦσα ἐπὶ πέταλον καὶ ἑζομένη αὐτοῦ. Hermann construes πᾶ κέλσω βάσιν θηρός, τιθέμενος

τετράποδος βάσιν θηρὸς ὀρεστέρου
τιθέμενος ἐπὶ χεῖρα κατ' ἴχνος ; ποίαν,
ταύταν ἢ τάνδ', ἐξαλλάξω   1060
τὰς ἀνδροφόνους μάρψαι χρῄζων
Ἰλιάδας, αἵ με διώλεσαν ;
τάλαιναι κόραι τάλαιναι Φρυγῶν,
ὦ κατάρατοι, ποῖ καί με φυγᾷ
πτώσσουσι μυχῶν ;   1065
εἴθε μοι ὀμμάτων αἱματόεν βλέφαρον
ἀκέσαι' ἀκέσαιο, τυφλὸν, Ἅλιε,
φέγγος ἀπαλλάξας.
ἆ ἆ.
σίγα, κρυπτὰν βάσιν αἰσθάνομαι
τάνδε γυναικῶν. πᾶ πόδ' ἐπᾴξας   1070
σαρκῶν ὀστέων τ' ἐμπλησθῶ,
θοίναν ἀγρίων θηρῶν τιθέμενος
ἀρνύμενος λώβαν,
λύμας ἀντίποιν' ἐμᾶς ; ἰὼ τάλας
ποῖ, πᾶ φέρομαι τέκν' ἔρημα λιπὼν   1075
βάκχας Ἅιδου διαμοιρᾶσαι,
σφακτὰν κυσί τε φοινίαν δαῖτ' ἀνήμερόν τ' οὐρείαν
ἐκβολάν ;

ἔπι χεῖρα, *quo applicem quadrupedis montanae ferae gressum, imponens* (solo) *manum?* But it may be doubted if this is any improvement, the omission of χθονὸς after ἔπι being extremely harsh. This verse may be scanned either as dochmiac or anapaestic, in the latter case ⏑ ⏑ ⏑ ⏑ standing for — —, as in v. 1072.

1060. ταύταν Hermann with two or three MSS., for ἢ ταύταν. Properly, ὁδὸν ἐξαλλάσσειν is to take one path after another, to go from this to that, and from that to this.

1062. This verse is dochmiac, preceded by a resolved cretic. In the next, Seidler and Hermann have transposed the words which were commonly read τάλαιναι τάλαιναι κόραι Φρυγῶν. Porson, in whose time the dochmiac rhythm was very little understood, retains this without remark.

1064. As φυγᾷ πτώσσουσι is the same in sense as φεύγουσι πτώσσουσαι, the accusative of the person is added, just as in v. 812, ποῖ μ' ὑπεξάγεις πόδα;

1067. This verse should be anapaestic ; perhaps, τυφλόν θ'—ἀπαλλάξαις. W. Dindorf badly edits ἀκέσσαι' ἀκέσσαι', Ἅλιε, τυφλὸν φέγγος ἀπαλλάξας, in order to make a dochmiac trimeter.—τυφλὸν φέγγος, for τυφλότητα ὀμμάτων. Cf. v. 1035.

1070. τάνδε Seidler for τᾶνδε or τῶνδε.

1072. θοίναν κτλ., making for myself a feast on flesh, as wild beasts do. For the metre see v. 1059.

1074. ὦ τάλας Hermann ; but ἰὼ is a monosyllable ; see v. 1032.

1077—8. There is some difficulty in reducing this passage to the dochmiac metre. Hermann suggests, and W. Dindorf adopts, σφακτὰ κυσίν τε, but the latter goes much further, and, as before, gives an unmetrical verse after violent

πᾶ στῶ, πᾶ βῶ, πᾶ κάμψω,
ναῦς ὅπως ποντίοις πείσμασι λινόκροκον 1080
φᾶρος στέλλων, ἐπὶ τάνδε συθεὶς
τέκνων ἐμῶν φύλαξ ὀλέθριον κοίταν.
ΧΟ. ὦ τλῆμον, ὥς σοι δύσφορ' εἴργασται κακά· 1085
δράσαντι δ' αἰσχρὰ δεινὰ τἀπιτίμια
[δαίμων ἔδωκεν, ὅστις ἐστί σοι βαρύς].
ΠΟΛΥΜ. αἰαῖ, ἰὼ Θρῄκης λογχοφόρον, ἔνοπλον,
εὔιππόν τ' Ἄρει τε κάτοχον γένος. 1090
ἰὼ Ἀχαιοί, ἰὼ Ἀτρεῖδαι,

and needless alterations, σφακτὰ κυσίν τε δαῖτ' ὀρείαν τ' ἐκβολάν. The reading in the text, approved by Hermann and adopted by Pflugk, after Matthiae, involves no change but the transposition of τε, which in the MSS. follows οὐρείαν τ'. Thus v. 1078 is a dochmius followed by a cretic. For οὐρεῖος see Troad. 533, Androm. 284.

1079. The common reading πᾶ στῶ; πᾶ κάμψω; πᾶ βῶ; is retained by Porson, who inclines to think πᾶ βῶ, πᾶ στῶ, πᾶ κάμψω, the true reading, as in v. 1056. Hermann does not disapprove, and W. Dindorf admits this, one MS. placing πᾶ κάμψω last.—κάμψω is, ' where shall I rest ?' Cf. inf. 1150, κάμπτειν γόνυ Prom. 32. Hence στέλλων φᾶρος literally means, ' tucking up my mantle,' and metaphorically, ' furling my sail,' or coming into haven. Compare Aesch. Suppl. 703, and see the note on Hel. 147.—πείσμασι, not to be taken with στέλλων, but depending on some word like δεθεῖσα, ' where must I rest, furling my sail, as a ship (rests) on its cables.'

1084. τέκνων ἐμῶν. Perhaps τέκνων μου or μοι, which would give a dochmiac dimeter. As it stands, the dochmius is preceded by three iambic feet. Schol. ἐπὶ τήνδε τὴν ὀλέθριον κοίτην πορευθεὶς τῶν ἐμῶν τέκνων φύλαξ. As he calls the spot where they lay dead ὀλεθρία, φύλαξ must mean τῶν σωμάτων, to watch the bodies.

1085. σοι εἴργασται, ' have been done to you.' The more obvious sense would be, ' by you;' but the allusion is to his blindness, not to the murder he has committed. In the next verse the well-known Greek law, δράσαντι παθεῖν, is expressed. —ἐπιτίμιον, which Aeschylus uses in the singular, Theb. 1024, occurs in the plural

Soph. El. 1382. Properly, it meant ' a fine imposed.' Hermann omits v. 1087, as repeated from v. 722, and the opinion is confirmed not only by the variant δέδωκεν in this place, but by the evident propriety of the utmost brevity in enuntiating a sententious proposition. Moreover, the chorus speaks only two lines below, v. 1106—7.

1088 seqq. The metres in this speech of Polymestor are for the most part obscure. It may indeed be plausibly conjectured that the frantic ravings of a man beside himself with pain and rage were purposely exempted from metrical, still more from antistrophic laws. Hermann, who regards the next verse as identical with 1100, viz. paeonic, reads λογχοφόρον, εὔοπλον, ἔφιππον, Ἄρεός τε κάτοχον γένος. Porson also gives εὔοπλον from Eustathius, who cites the words εὔοπλον—γένος, in place of the vulg. ἔνοπλον. Hermann defends the τε after Ἄρεος by the comment of one of the scholiasts, who has λογχοφόρους αὐτοὺς ὀνομάσας Ἄρει τε κατόχους, whereas the grammarian would probably have said καὶ κατόχους, were the copula added by himself. The present editor has ventured to restore two dochmiac verses by also adding τε to εὔιππον.—By κάτοχον he means κατεχόμενον, ' possessed by Ares,' i. e. with a warlike spirit. The adjective is used in Pers. 225, τἄμπαλιν δὲ τῶνδε γαίᾳ κάτοχα μαυροῦσθαι σκότῳ.

1091. This verse is made up of two iambic penthemimers; the next, if we omit βοάν, (which the MSS. place twice at the beginning, one copy excepted,) will give a dochmius preceded by an iambus or an iambic dipodia with a cretic; but the former is the more probable, from the similarity of the next verse, which Her-

βοᾶν αὑτῶ, βοάν·
ἴτ' ἴτε, μόλετε πρὸς θεῶν.
κλύει τις, ἢ οὐδεὶς ἀρκέσει; τί μέλλετε;
γυναῖκες ὤλεσάν με, 1095
γυναῖκες αἰχμαλώτιδες.
δεινὰ δεινὰ πεπόνθαμεν· ὤμοι ἐμᾶς λώβας.
ποῖ τράπωμαι, ποῖ πορευθῶ; 1099
ἀμπτάμενος οὐράνιον ὑψιπετὲς ἐς μέλαθρον, Ὠρίων
ἢ Σείριος ἔνθα πυρὸς φλογέας
ἀφίησιν ὄσσων αὐγάς, ἢ τὸν Ἅιδα
μελανόχρωτα πορθμὸν ἄξω τάλας; 1105

XO. ξυγγνώσθ', ὅταν τις κρείσσον' ἢ φέρειν κακὰ
πάθῃ, ταλαίνης ἐξαπαλλάξαι ζόης.

ΑΓ. κραυγῆς ἀκούσας ἦλθον· οὐ γὰρ ἥσυχος
πέτρας ὀρείας παῖς λέλακ' ἀνὰ στρατὸν 1110
Ἠχώ, διδοῦσα θόρυβον. εἰ δὲ μὴ Φρυγῶν
πύργους πεσόντας ᾖσμεν Ἑλλήνων δορί,
φόβον παρέσχεν οὐ μέσως ὅδε κτύπος.

mann edits ἴτ', ὦ, ἴτ', ὦ, μόλετε, πρὸς θεῶν, some copies giving ὦ ἴτε.

1100. Hermann and W. Dindorf omit αἰθέρ' before ἀμπτάμενος on the authority of one of the scholiasts, ἔν τισι τὸ αἰθέρα περισσὸν, καὶ οὐ φέρεται. The verse may either be called paeonic, or is composed of resolved cretics.—On the two common alternatives of escape, flight above or sinking below, see Med. 1296. Ion 1237. Herc. F. 1158, πτερωτὸς ἢ κατὰ χθονὸς μολών.

1102—3. According to W. Dindorf's distribution, which seems at least as good as any other, the first of these is dactylic with the anacrusis, the latter bacchiac. But this involves the correction τὸν Ἅιδα for τὸν ἐς Ἀΐδα. The last verse is a regular dochmiac. Dindorf gives μελαγχρῶτα, which is supported by one copy, but is not metrically a better reading.

1108. ζόης. This example of the word, as ending a senarius, should have been added to those from lyric passages given in the note on Med. 976. The MSS., as usual, give ζωῆς. The omission of ἑαυτὸν is to be remarked after the infinitive; though ἀπαλλάσσειν is not unfrequently intransitive, e. g. Aesch. Ag. 1260. Hermann's remark on the sentiment, which he calls frigid, is this:—" Multo rectius Euripides dixisset, hunc esse fructum impii facinoris, ut quis punito sibi vitam non vitalem esse censeat." The chorus sarcastically says, that the best thing he can now do is, to kill himself. On the poet's real views with respect to suicide, see Preface to Vol. i. p. xlviii.

1113. παρέσχεν. Porson gives παρέσχ' ἂν, with Heath, and so also Pflugk; but it is now well known that the Attic writers objected to this elision. See the note on a similar idiom in Tro. 397. The meaning is; 'The noise was alarming enough, only we knew that Troy was razed, and therefore it could not be a sudden attack from the city.'—ᾖσμεν for ᾔδειμεν, like ᾖσαν for ᾔδεσαν &c.—Agamemnon, in the present and concluding scene, assumes the character of judge or umpire between the disputants, who plead the cause before him, in the usual forensic manner of which the poet is so fond, although he has been previously biassed in favour of Hecuba. Polymestor, as Pflugk observes, naturally expects that Agamemnon will take *his* side, and for that reason

ΠΟΛΥΜ. ὦ φίλτατ', ἠσθόμην γὰρ, Ἀγάμεμνον, σέθεν
φωνῆς ἀκούσας, εἰσορᾷς ἃ πάσχομεν; 1115
ΑΓ. ἔα·
Πολυμῆστορ ὦ δύστηνε, τίς σ' ἀπώλεσε;
τίς ὄμμ' ἔθηκε τυφλὸν, αἱμάξας κόρας,
παῖδάς τε τούσδ' ἔκτεινεν; ἦ μέγαν χόλον
σοὶ καὶ τέκνοισιν εἶχεν, ὅστις ἦν ἄρα.
ΠΟΛΥΜ. Ἑκάβη με σὺν γυναιξὶν αἰχμαλωτίσιν 1120
ἀπώλεσ', οὐκ ἀπώλεσ', ἀλλὰ μειζόνως.
ΑΓ. τί φής; σὺ τοὔργον εἴργασαι τόδ', ὡς λέγει;
σὺ τόλμαν, Ἑκάβη, τήνδ' ἔτλης ἀμήχανον;
ΠΟΛΥΜ. ὤμοι, τί λέξεις; ἦ γὰρ ἐγγύς ἐστί που;
σήμηνον, εἰπὲ ποῦ 'σθ', ἵν' ἁρπάσας χεροῖν 1125
διασπάσωμαι καὶ καθαιμάξω χρόα.
ΑΓ. οὗτος, τί πάσχεις;
ΠΟΛΥΜ.   πρὸς θεῶν σε λίσσομαι,
μέθες μ' ἐφεῖναι τῇδε μαργῶσαν χέρα.
ΑΓ. ἴσχ'. ἐκβαλὼν δὲ καρδίας τὸ βάρβαρον
λέγ', ὡς ἀκούσας σοῦ τε τῆσδέ τ' ἐν μέρει 1130
κρίνω δικαίως, ἀνθ' ὅτου πάσχεις τάδε.
ΠΟΛΥΜ. λέγοιμ' ἄν. ἦν τις Πριαμιδῶν νεώτατος

---

he speaks more calmly in his first appeal for justice.

1119. Hermann says, "Distinxi post ἦν. Nam ἄρα ad χόλον εἶχεν pertinet."

1126. τί πάσχεις; 'what is coming over you?' 'What is the matter with you?'

1128. μαργῶσαν, eager, not under the restraint of reason. Photius, evidently with this passage in view, has μαργῶσαν, χέρα (MS. χεῖρα)· μαινομένην χεῖρα. Pflugk compares Phoen. 1156, ἀλλ' ἔσχε μαργῶντ' αὐτὸν ἐναλίου θεοῦ Περικλύμενος παῖς, and ibid. 1247.

1129. τὸ βάρβαρον. Ferocity and giving way to anger. For the Greeks regarded their μουσικὴ as a remedy against such ἀκράτεια. Compare the use of βάρβαρος in Hel. 501.

1132. The speech of Polymestor (which exactly coincides, in the number of lines, to that of Hecuba in reply, like Electra's and Clytemnestra's in El. 1011, 1060, and Helen's and Menelaus' in Hel. 894 seqq.), contains a brief excuse, and of course a false one, for his making away with Polydorus; and a more lengthy account of the vengeance taken upon him; while Hecuba, after a somewhat sophistical exordium, meets his defence by a direct denial of its truth. He slew Polydorus simply as a measure of precaution, because, while he was alive, the Greeks might any time return to Troy, and so damage his Thracian kingdom by hostile incursions. He craftily represents himself (v. 1176) as having been a benefactor to Agamemnon by this deed, and so as a sufferer in his cause. To which Hecuba replies (1202) that neither was his pretended regard for Agamemnon likely in itself, nor his fear of the hostility of the Greeks real; for the one is incompatible with the other. If his friendship for Agamemnon had been sincere, and avarice not the real motive, he would have

ΕΚΑΒΗ.

Πολύδωρος, Έκάβης παῖς, ὃν ἐκ Τροίας ἐμοὶ
πατὴρ δίδωσι Πρίαμος ἐν δόμοις τρέφειν,
ὕποπτος ὢν δὴ Τρωικῆς ἁλώσεως.   1135
τοῦτον κατέκτειν'· ἀνθ' ὅτου δ' ἔκτεινά νιν,
ἄκουσον, ὡς εὖ καὶ σοφῇ προμηθίᾳ.
ἔδεισα μὴ σοὶ πολέμιος λειφθεὶς ὁ παῖς
Τροίαν ἀθροίσῃ καὶ ξυνοικίσῃ πάλιν,
γνόντες δ' Ἀχαιοὶ ζῶντα Πριαμιδῶν τινα   1140
Φρυγῶν ἐς αἶαν αὖθις ἄρειαν στόλον,
κἄπειτα Θρῄκης πεδία τρίβοιεν τάδε
λεηλατοῦντες, γείτοσιν δ' εἴη κακὸν
Τρώων, ἐν ᾧπερ νῦν, ἄναξ, ἐκάμνομεν.
Ἑκάβη δὲ παιδὸς γνοῦσα θανάσιμον μόρον   1145
λόγῳ με τοιῷδ' ἤγαγ', ὡς κεκρυμμένας
θήκας φράσουσα Πριαμιδῶν ἐν Ἰλίῳ
χρυσοῦ· μόνον δὲ σὺν τέκνοισί μ' εἰσάγει
δόμους, ἵν' ἄλλος μή τις εἰδείη τάδε.
ἵζω δὲ κλίνης ἐν μέσῳ κάμψας γόνυ·   1150
πολλαὶ δὲ χειρὸς αἱ μὲν ἐξ ἀριστερᾶς,

slain her son, or at least brought him a captive, long before Troy fell. Moreover, he should have proved his sincerity by bringing the gold to them, when they so much wanted it. He might have gained credit by showing that test of all true friendship, adhesion in misfortune; he might also have found a resource, in case of his own poverty, in the wealth of his ward. But all these opportunities he has thrown away, and he has proved himself altogether unworthy of Agamemnon's support.

1135. ὢν δή. 'Being, it seems (or as the event showed), suspicious of,' &c. He cunningly adds σοὶ πολέμιος λειφθεὶς, as if his forethought took into due consideration the interests of Agamemnon.

1141. ἄρειαν Herm. Dind. Pflugk, αἴροιεν Porson. The majority of copies are in favour of the latter; but as αἴρειν στόλον, to set sail, is scarcely to be conceived as a continuous action, like the ravaging of the country, πεδία τρίβειν, the aorist suits the sense better. And the Scholiast gives κινήσειαν ναυτικὸν—καὶ ἀφανίζοιεν τὰ χωρία. Whether the poet really intended the difference of meaning which Pflugk and Hermann find in the subjunctive and the optative, may perhaps be questioned, viz. that the subjunctive expresses *apprehension*, the optative *conjecture* as to the consequences. Others have held, that the former mood expresses the action nearer in time, the latter one more remotely future. A similar change of moods occurs Electr. 58—9.

1144. ἐν ᾧπερ κτλ., 'the very evil by which we have lately been oppressed.' In Homer, and in the *Rhesus*, the Thracians are spoken of as allies of the Trojans, as indeed their contiguity and common Pelasgic affinities would suggest. Pflugk rather shrewdly remarks, that ἄναξ is added in a sort of deprecatory or apologetic tone, because it was not complimentary to Agamemnon to tell him that his presence was unwelcome to the neighbouring people.

1150. κάμψας γόνυ, 'resting myself.' See above, v. 1079. Oed. Col. 19, οὗ κῶλα κάμψον τοῦδ' ἐπ' ἀξέστου πέτρου.

1151. χειρός. So J. Milton for χεῖρες, an error which obviously arose from the

αἱ δ' ἔνθεν, ὡς δὴ παρὰ φίλῳ, Τρώων κόραι
θάκους ἔχουσαι, κερκίδ' Ἡδονῆς χερὸς
ᾔνουν, ὑπ' αὐγὰς τούσδε λεύσσουσαι πέπλους·
ἄλλαι δὲ κάμακα Θρηκίαν θεώμεναι   1155
γυμνόν μ' ἔθηκαν διπτύχου στολίσματος.
ὅσαι δὲ τοκάδες ἦσαν, ἐκπαγλούμεναι
τέκν' ἐν χεροῖν ἔπαλλον, ὡς πρόσω πατρὸς
γένοιντο διαδοχαῖς ἀμείβουσαι χερῶν.
κᾆτ' ἐκ γαληνῶν πῶς δοκεῖς προσφθεγμάτων   1160
εὐθὺς λαβοῦσαι φάσγαν' ἐκ πέπλων ποθὲν
κεντοῦσι παῖδας, αἱ δὲ πολεμίων δίκην
ξυναρπάσασαι τὰς ἐμὰς εἶχον χέρας
καὶ κῶλα· παισὶ δ' ἀρκέσαι χρῄζων ἐμοῖς,

assimilation of case to πολλαί. Schol. πολλαὶ χεῖρες, ἤγουν γυναῖκες. Cf. λαιᾶς χειρὸς in Prom. 733.

1153. θάκους ἔχουσαι for θάκουν, ἔχουσαι κερκίδ' κτλ., and the omission of θ' after ᾔνουν, is Hermann's highly ingenious emendation of a passage which was formerly regarded as one of the most conclusive respecting the occasional omission of the augment. The error arose from mistaking θάκους for θάκουσ', in consequence of wrongly construing ἔχουσαι with κερκίδα, and then altering it to θάκουν to suit ᾔνουν, and so of necessity adding the copula after the latter. It is an interesting confirmation of Hermann's view, though he has not himself noticed it, that the scholiast, who had θάκουν in his copy, also found ᾔνουν, and not ᾔνουν θ'. His comment is this:—πολλαὶ δὲ κόραι Τρῴων παρθένοι ἐκάθηντο, κρατοῦσαι τὸ ὕφασμα τῆς Μακεδονικῆς χειρὸς ἐπ-ῄνουν. The principal objection to the vulgate is not so much the omission or absorption of the augment, as the absurd meaning which must thus be given to κερκίδ' ἔχουσαι, 'holding in their hands embroidery.' Clearly, ᾔνουν κερκίδα is 'they praised the shuttle,' i. e. the skilful use of it by the Thracians. Sitting by him on each side, they took hold of his garments in feigned admiration, but in fact to detain him on his seat.

1154. ὑπ' αὐγὰς, 'to the light.' The phrase may be accounted for by the general absence of windows in Greek houses, and the practice of regarding objects by light admitted from above.

Plato, Phaedr. p. 268, A., ἐῶμεν δὴ τά γε σμικρά· ταῦτα δὲ ὑπ' αὐγὰς μᾶλλον ἴδωμεν, τίνα καί ποτ' ἔχει τὴν τῆς τέχνης δύναμιν. Photius, ὑπ' αὐγὰς, ὑπὸ τὸν ὄρθρον, ἢ ὑπὸ τὸν πεφωτισμένον ἀέρα. In Ar. Thesm. 500, ὡς ἡ γυνὴ δεικνῦσα τἀνδρὶ τοὔγκυκλον ὑπαυγὰς οἷόν ἐστιν, W. Dindorf perhaps rightly gives ὑπ' ὄρθρον. Musgrave cites ὑπ' αὐγὰς from two passages of Plutarch.

1156. διπτύχου στολίσματος, the spear and cloak (or perhaps scarf, χλαμύς). Hermann compares Suppl. 659, λαιὸν δὲ Πάραλον, ἐστολισμένον δορί.—ἐκπαγλούμεναι, θαυμάζουσαι. Aesch. Cho. 211, ξύνοιδ' Ὀρέστην πολλά σ' ἐκπαγλουμένην. Cf. Orest. 890.

1159. γένοιτο Porson, with two or three copies; but τέκνα takes a plural, as it occasionally takes even a masculine gender in agreement (Tro. 735), as a synonym of παῖδες. On the metre of this verse see Bacch. 1125. Porson proposed to introduce a quasi-cæsura, διαδοχαῖς τ' ἀμείβουσιν χεροῖν. This however is untenable, for this reason; the clause ὡς—γένοιντο is explanatory of ἀμείβουσαι, not of ἔπαλλον, 'passing them from hand to hand that they might be far from their father;' and consequently, as commencing a new proposition, the copulative, if any, must have been placed in it, and could not have occurred after ἀμείβουσαι.

1160. πῶς δοκεῖς, a mere expletive, like κάρτα. Cf. Hipp. 445, τοῦτον λαβοῦσα πῶς δοκεῖς καθύβρισεν. Perhaps the meaning would be better represented by ἀέλπτως than by any other adverb.

ΕΚΑΒΗ.   553

εἰ μὲν πρόσωπον ἐξανισταίην ἐμὸν, 1165
κόμης κατεῖχον, εἰ δὲ κινοίην χέρας,
πλήθει γυναικῶν οὐδὲν ἤνυον τάλας.
τὸ λοίσθιον δὲ, πῆμα πήματος πλέον,
ἐξειργάσαντο δείν· ἐμῶν γὰρ ὀμμάτων,
πόρπας λαβοῦσαι, τὰς ταλαιπώρους κόρας 1170
κεντοῦσιν, αἱμάσσουσιν· εἶτ' ἀνὰ στέγας
φυγάδες ἔβησαν· ἐκ δὲ πηδήσας ἐγὼ
θὴρ ὣς διώκω τὰς μιαιφόνους κύνας,
ἅπαντ' ἐρευνῶν τοῖχον, ὡς κυνηγέτης,
βάλλων, ἀράσσων. τοιάδε σπεύδων χάριν 1175
πέπονθα τὴν σὴν, πολέμιόν τε σὸν κτανὼν,
Ἀγάμεμνον. ὡς δὲ μὴ μακροὺς τείνω λόγους,
εἴ τις γυναῖκας τῶν πρὶν εἴρηκεν κακῶς,
ἢ νῦν λέγων τίς ἐστιν, ἢ μέλλει λέγειν,
ἅπαντα ταῦτα συντεμὼν ἐγὼ φράσω· 1180
γένος γὰρ οὔτε πόντος οὔτε γῆ τρέφει
τοιόνδ'· ὁ δ' ἀεὶ ξυντυχὼν ἐπίσταται.

ΧΟ. μηδὲν θρασύνου, μηδὲ τοῖς σαυτοῦ κακοῖς
τὸ θῆλυ συνθεὶς ὧδε πᾶν μέμψῃ γένος·
[πολλαὶ γὰρ ἡμῶν αἱ μὲν εἴσ' ἐπίφθονοι, 1185
αἱ δ' εἰς ἀριθμὸν τῶν κακῶν πεφύκαμεν.]

1165. εἰ μέν, i. e. ὁπότε μέν. For the genitive κόμης cf. Androm. 402.
1168. πῆμα κτλ. Cf. Agam. 837, κακοῦ κάκιον ἄλλο πῆμα. For οὐδὲν ἤνυον, cf. Bacch. 1100.
1179. λέγων τίς ἐστιν is given by Dindorf from one MS., the other copies having λέγων ἔστι τις. Porson gives the verse as it is quoted by Stobaeus, Flor. lxxiii. 9, ἢ νῦν λέγει τις, ἢ πάλιν μέλλει λέγειν. Wakefield's conjecture is probable, ἢ νῦν λέγων ἔστ', ἢ πάλιν κτλ. On the repetition of τις see Androm. 733. Hermann gives λέγων ἐστίν τις, "in qua," he adds, "nihil est quod reprehendi possit." Yet it may safely be asserted, that the Attics rarely use ν ἐφελκυστικὸν in order to lengthen a syllable before a consonant.
1182. ὁ δ' ἀεὶ κτλ. 'Whoever has had to do with them, knows it to his cost.' More commonly γιγνώσκει is used in this sense. With equal bitterness Euripides makes Hippolytus declaim against women, v. 664 &c.
1185—6. These two lines are inclosed as spurious by W. Dindorf, and there can be little doubt that he is right; for the chorus afterwards (1238) speak only *two* verses; and the sense is both obscure and feeble, 'some of us are exposed to blame, while others are numbered among the (downright) bad.' The expression πεφυκέναι εἰς ἀριθμὸν τινῶν does not sound Euripidean; and Hermann's ἀντάριθμοι, e contraria parte aequamus numerum malarum, is extremely far-fetched and improbable. The fact that Stobaeus, Flor. lxix. 16, quotes this distich, together with the preceding, only shows, as W. Dindorf remarks, that the interpolation is older than his time (5th cent. A.D.). The interpolator doubtless wished to make some reservation in favour of good women, as the poet himself has done in Ion 399,

VOL. II.   4 B

ΕΚ. Ἀγάμεμνον, ἀνθρώποισιν οὐκ ἐχρῆν ποτὲ
τῶν πραγμάτων τὴν γλῶσσαν ἰσχύειν πλέον.
ἀλλ' εἴτε χρήστ' ἔδρασε, χρήστ' ἔδει λέγειν,
εἴτ' αὖ πονηρά, τοὺς λόγους εἶναι σαθροὺς, 1190
καὶ μὴ δύνασθαι τἄδικ' εὖ λέγειν ποτέ.
σοφοὶ μὲν οὖν εἰσ' οἱ τάδ' ἠκριβωκότες,
ἀλλ' οὐ δύνανται διὰ τέλους εἶναι σοφοί,
κακῶς δ' ἀπώλοντ'· οὔτις ἐξήλυξέ πω.
καί μοι τὸ μὲν σὸν ὧδε φροιμίοις ἔχει· 1195
πρὸς τόνδε δ' εἶμι, καὶ λόγοις ἀμείψομαι,
ὃς φῂς Ἀχαιῶν πόνον ἀπαλλάσσων διπλοῦν
Ἀγαμέμνονός θ' ἕκατι παῖδ' ἐμὸν κτανεῖν.
ἀλλ', ὦ κάκιστε, πρῶτα ποῦ ποτ' ἂν φίλον
τὸ βάρβαρον γένοιτ' ἂν Ἕλλησιν γένος; 1200
οὐτἂν δύναιτο. τίνα δὲ καὶ σπεύδων χάριν
πρόθυμος ἦσθα; πότερα κηδεύσων τινά,

κἂν ταῖς κακαῖσιν ἀγαθαὶ μεμιγμέναι μισούμεθ'.

1187. Hecuba commences by lamenting that the art of rhetoric should ever have been carried so far, that the bad cause may be made by special pleading to seem the just one. Words ought to have been the index of facts, so that the truth in right or wrong might at once be known.

1192. οἱ τάδ' ἠκριβωκότες are not, certainly, the Sophists, of whom Euripides was not likely to say anything evil, but those unprincipled speakers, demagogues perhaps, who have attained perfection in the detestable art of making wrong seem right by the mere force of eloquence. These men, he says, are commonly called σοφοί, but in the end public opinion is sure to turn against them. There is some uncertainty in the reading of the next verse, all the copies but one of no great authority giving κοὔτις. One other also has δύναιντ' ἂν for δύνανται. The aorist indicative must refer to the general result in such cases; but it does not very well accord with δύναιντ' ἂν (the reading of W. Dindorf), implying a particular contingency. Hermann gives κακῶς δ' ὄλοιντο, supplying ἂν from the preceding verse. But this is liable to the decided objection, that the formula is one of imprecation, and could hardly have been taken in any other sense. The καὶ, so far from being wanted, really seems to weaken the strong emphasis intended.

1195. τὸ μὲν σόν. What I have to say to *you* by way of prelude, stands thus.

1197. διπλοῦν πόνον, the trouble of taking Troy twice, v. 1141. See also v. 1175. Aldus with many copies has πῶς φῄς.

1199. πρῶτα ποῦ ποτ' for πρῶτον οὔποτ', and οὐτἂν for οὔτ' ἂν, are Hermann's emendations. The first is confirmed both by the reading of two or three MSS. πρῶτον μὲν, which point to the common combination of πρῶτα μὲν followed by τε, and also by the comment of the Scholiast, ὁ Ἀγαμέμνων Ἕλλην, σὺ βάρβαρος, πῶς μέλλετε φιλιωθῆναι; Which perhaps should be read thus; σὺ, ὦ Ἀγαμέμνων, Ἕλλην, καὶ σὺ βάρβαρος, πῶς κτλ. There are other objections to the vulgate, viz. οὔτ' following οὐ, and the poor antithesis οὔτε γένοιτο ἂν οὔτε δύναιτο γενέσθαι. Dindorf gives οὐδ' ἂν, but οὔτοι ἂν is obviously a great improvement to the sense. For the use of the interrogative ποῦ, see on Heracl. 369, ποῦ ταῦτα καλῶς ἂν εἴη παρά γ' εὖ φρονοῦσι; 'These things can never be right in the sight of the wise.'

1202. κηδεύσων τινά; 'Was it (which is utterly improbable) that you wished to contract a relationship by marriage with one of the Hellenes?'

ΕΚΑΒΗ.

ἢ ξυγγενὴς ὤν, ἢ τίν' αἰτίαν ἔχων;
ἢ σῆς ἔμελλον γῆς τεμεῖν βλαστήματα
πλεύσαντες αὖθις; τίνα δοκεῖς πείσειν τάδε; 1205
ὁ χρυσὸς, εἰ βούλοιο τἀληθῆ λέγειν,
ἔκτεινε τὸν ἐμὸν παῖδα καὶ κέρδη τὰ σά.
ἐπεὶ δίδαξον τοῦτο· πῶς, ὅτ' ηὐτύχει
Τροία, πέριξ δὲ πύργος εἶχ' ἔτι πτόλιν,
ἔζη τε Πρίαμος, Ἕκτορός τ' ἤνθει δόρυ, 1210
τί δ' οὐ τότ', εἴπερ τῷδ' ἐβουλήθης χάριν
θέσθαι, τρέφων τὸν παῖδα κἀν δόμοις ἔχων
ἔκτεινας, ἢ ζῶντ' ἦλθες Ἀργείοις ἄγων;
ἀλλ' ἡνίχ' ἡμεῖς οὐκέτ' ἦμεν ἐν φάει,
καπνῷ δ' ἐσήμην' ἄστυ πολεμίων ὕπο, 1215
ξένον κατέκτας σὴν μολόντ' ἐφ' ἑστίαν.
πρὸς τοῖσδέ νυν ἄκουσον ὡς φανεῖ κακός.
χρῆν σ', εἴπερ ἦσθα τοῖς Ἀχαιοῖσιν φίλος,
τὸν χρυσὸν ὃν φῂς οὐ σὸν, ἀλλὰ τοῦδ' ἔχειν,
δοῦναι φέροντα πενομένοις τε καὶ χρόνον 1220
πολὺν πατρῴας γῆς ἀπεξενωμένοις·
σὺ δ' οὐδὲ νῦν πω σῆς ἀπαλλάξαι χερὸς
τολμᾷς, ἔχων δὲ καρτερεῖς ἔτ' ἐν δόμοις.
καὶ μὴν τρέφων μὲν ὥς σε παῖδ' ἐχρῆν τρέφειν
σώσας τε τὸν ἐμὸν εἶχες ἂν καλὸν κλέος· 1225

1204. ἔμελλον κτλ. See v. 1142.
1210. Ἕκτορος δόρυ. Cf. Troad. 1162, ὅθ' Ἕκτορος μὲν εὐτυχοῦντος ἐς δόρυ διωλλύμεσθα, κτλ. Supra, v. 18.
1211. τί δ' οὐ τότ'. The poet varies the πῶς which he should have repeated from v. 1208. 'How was it, I say, that you did not then, if you really wished to confer a favour on Agamemnon here, having the boy in your care and keeping him in your house, kill him, or at least take him alive as a captive to the Argives?'
1215. ἐσήμηνε is here singularly elliptical, whether we supply with the Scholiast τὸ ἡμᾶς μηκέτι εἶναι ἐν φάει, or, what is more obvious to the sense, though more remarkable as left to be suggested by the context, ἐσήμηνε ἀΐστωθέν. The latter is defended by the very similar verse in

Agam. 791, καπνῷ δ' ἁλοῦσα νῦν ἔτ' εὔσημος πόλις. As σημαίνειν is often used absolutely, without indeed either subject or object being expressed, the meaning is here, 'the city showed by the smoking ruins (that all had perished) by the enemy's hand,' i. e. and therefore that none were left to avenge the murder of Polydorus.—Porson edits ἐσήμαιν' after Aldus.
1218. τοῖς Ἀχαιοῖσιν is suspicious on account of the article. There may be some irony in it, 'those Argives of yours.' Hermann thinks either ὀρθῶς or ὄντως ἦσθ' Ἀχαιοῖσιν is the true reading.
1220. " Non videtur poeta satis circumspecte πενομένους dixisse eos, qui capta urbe praeda onusti reverterentur." Herm. But she is speaking of the sufferings of the Greeks during the siege.

4 B 2

ἐν τοῖς κακοῖς γὰρ ἀγαθοὶ σαφέστατοι
φίλοι· τὰ χρηστὰ δ' αὔθ' ἕκαστ' ἔχει φίλους.
εἰ δ' ἐσπάνιζες χρημάτων, ὁ δ' ηὐτύχει,
θησαυρὸς ἄν σοι παῖς ὑπῆρχ' οὑμὸς μέγας·
νῦν δ' οὔτ' ἐκεῖνον ἄνδρ' ἔχεις σαυτῷ φίλον, 1230
χρυσοῦ τ' ὄνησις οἴχεται παῖδές τέ σοι,
αὐτός τε πράσσεις ὧδε. σοὶ δ' ἐγὼ λέγω,
Ἀγάμεμνον, εἰ τῷδ' ἀρκέσεις, κακὸς φανεῖ·
οὔτ' εὐσεβῆ γὰρ οὔτε πιστὸν οἷς ἐχρῆν,
οὐχ ὅσιον, οὐ δίκαιον εὖ δράσεις ξένον· 1235
αὐτὸν δὲ χαίρειν τοῖς κακοῖς σε φήσομεν
τοιοῦτον ὄντα· δεσπότας δ' οὐ λοιδορῶ.
XO. φεῦ φεῦ· βροτοῖσιν ὡς τὰ χρηστὰ πράγματα
χρηστῶν ἀφορμὰς ἐνδίδωσ' ἀεὶ λόγων.
ΑΓ. ἀχθεινὰ μέν μοι τἀλλότρια κρίνειν κακά· 1240
ὅμως δ' ἀνάγκη· καὶ γὰρ αἰσχύνην φέρει
πρᾶγμ' ἐς χέρας λαβόντ' ἀπώσασθαι τόδε.
ἐμοὶ δ', ἵν' εἰδῇς, οὔτ' ἐμὴν δοκεῖς χάριν
οὔτ' οὖν Ἀχαιῶν ἄνδρ' ἀποκτεῖναι ξένον,
ἀλλ' ὡς ἔχῃς τὸν χρυσὸν ἐν δόμοισι σοῖς. 1245
λέγεις δὲ σαυτῷ πρόσφορ', ἐν κακοῖσιν ὤν.
τάχ' οὖν παρ' ὑμῖν ῥᾴδιον ξενοκτονεῖν·
ἡμῖν δέ γ' αἰσχρὸν τοῖσιν Ἕλλησιν τόδε.
πῶς οὖν σε κρίνας μὴ ἀδικεῖν φύγω ψόγον;

1227. τὰ χρηστὰ κτλ. Goodness wherever it is, or in every instance, finds friends; and therefore you, had you been in distress, and yet acted honourably by Polydorus, would certainly have secured his assistance. This idea is more explicitly stated in the following verses.
1237. τοιοῦτον ὄντα. She does not directly say κακὸν ὄντα for the reason she proceeds to give, δεσπότας οὐ λοιδορῶ. This therefore may be regarded as a formula of indirect reproof. The passage in Electr. 50—4 is exactly similar, where καὐτὸς αὖ τοιοῦτος ὢν stands for οὐχ ἧσσον μῶρος.
1239. ἀφορμάς. Cf. Bacch. 266, ὅταν λάβῃ τις τῶν λόγων ἀνὴρ σοφὸς καλὰς ἀφορμὰς, οὐ μέγ' ἔργον εὖ λέγειν.—ἐνδίδωσι, cf. Andr. v. 965. Hermann says this sentiment is "satis frigida." The comment on it is v. 1189, that a good cause is always a topic suggestive of a sound and really good speech, while all other speeches have but the plausible appearance of being so. Stobaeus quotes this couplet, Flor. xiii. 12.
1245. τὸν χρυσόν. 'That gold,' or, 'his gold,' will sufficiently express the force of the article. Compare v. 1206 with 1231. One MS. gives ἔχεις, which points to a reading ἔχοις. The subjunctive however expresses not merely the intention at the time, but the resolution even now persisted in.—πρόσφορα, Schol. συμφέροντα.
1248. τοῖσιν Ἕλλησιν, scil. οὖσιν.

ΕΚΑΒΗ. 557

οὐκ ἂν δυναίμην. ἀλλ' ἐπεὶ τὰ μὴ καλὰ 1250
πράσσειν ἐτόλμας, τλῆθι καὶ τὰ μὴ φίλα.
ΠΟΛΥΜ. οἴμοι, γυναικὸς, ὡς ἔοιχ', ἡσσώμενος
δούλης ὑφέξω τοῖς κακίοσιν δίκην.
ΕΚ. οὔκουν δικαίως, εἴπερ εἰργάσω κακά; 1254
ΠΟΛΥΜ. οἴμοι τέκνων τῶνδ' ὀμμάτων τ' ἐμῶν, τάλας.
ΕΚ. ἀλγεῖς; τί δ' ἡμᾶς; παιδὸς οὐκ ἀλγεῖν δοκεῖς;
ΠΟΛΥΜ. χαίρεις ὑβρίζουσ' εἰς ἔμ', ὦ πανοῦργε σύ.
ΕΚ. οὐ γάρ με χαίρειν χρή σε τιμωρουμένην;
ΠΟΛΥΜ. ἀλλ' οὐ τάχ', ἡνίκ' ἄν σε ποντία νοτὶς
ΕΚ. μῶν ναυστολήσῃ γῆς ὅρους Ἑλληνίδος; 1260
ΠΟΛΥΜ. κρύψῃ μὲν οὖν πεσοῦσαν ἐκ καρχησίων.
ΕΚ. πρὸς τοῦ βιαίων τυγχάνουσαν ἁλμάτων;
ΠΟΛΥΜ. αὐτὴ πρὸς ἱστὸν ναὸς ἀμβήσει ποδί.
ΕΚ. ὑποπτέροις νώτοισιν, ἢ ποίῳ τρόπῳ;
ΠΟΛΥΜ. κύων γενήσει πύρσ' ἔχουσα δέργματα. 1265
ΕΚ. πῶς δ' οἶσθα μορφῆς τῆς ἐμῆς μετάστασιν;
ΠΟΛΥΜ. ὁ Θρῃξὶ μάντις εἶπε Διόνυσος τάδε.
ΕΚ. σοὶ δ' οὐκ ἔχρησεν οὐδὲν ὧν ἔχεις κακῶν;
ΠΟΛΥΜ. οὐ γάρ ποτ' ἂν σύ μ' εἷλες ὧδε σὺν δόλῳ.
ΕΚ. θανοῦσα δ' ἢ ζῶσ' ἐνθάδ' ἐκπλήσω βίον; 1270

1254. This verse is commonly assigned to Agamemnon, but Hermann's reasons for giving it, with the Latin version in some of the earlier editions, to Hecuba, have great weight. "Regem semel dixisse sententiam satis est. Hecuba autem ut responderet ista, satis excitabatur gravi reprehensione Polymestoris, servilem conditionem, contemptu dignam, ei exprobrantis." Porson quotes εἴπερ εἴργασται τάδε from the Schol. on Il. xiii. 154, observing that this indicates an ancient variant εἴργασαι. Some two or three MSS. of Euripides give τάδε for κακά.
1256. τί δ' ἡμᾶς (scil. παθεῖν) Porson for τί δέ με or τί δαί με.
1261. καρχησίων, the top-mast. Photius, καρχήσιον, τὸ ἄκρον τοῦ ἱστοῦ.
1263. πρὸς ἱστὸν, 'by the mast,' i. e. clinging to it. " Auxit portenta portentis, quum canem dixit per malum in carchesia adscensuram." Hermann; who thinks the minute details become tame, when Hecuba says at the end that she

does not care. She could not however have said so much as that, unless she had first heard her fate.
1265. πυρσὰ δέργματα, fiery-red eyes. The change of Hecuba into one of the canine species was, as Hermann shows in a learned note, much celebrated by antiquity. It seems to have been invented to account for the name of Κυνὸς Σῆμα, a station near Abydos. Juvenal, among others, attributes the metamorphosis to her snappish and snarling disposition, Sat. x. 271, 'sed torva canino Latravit rictu quae post hunc vixerat uxor.' Pflugk adds Cicero, Tusc. Disp. iii. 26, 'Hecubam autem putant propter animi acerbitatem quandam et rabiem fingi in canem esse conversam.'
1267. Διόνυσος. Herod. vii. 111, where see Mr. Blakesley's excellent note. Rhes. 972, Βάκχου προφήτης ὥστε Παγγαίου πέτραν ᾤκησε σεμνὸς τοῖσιν εἰδόσιν θεός.
1270. ἐκπλήσω βίον. W. Dindorf gives πότμον, after Musgrave; but both Her-

ΠΟΛΥΜ. θανοῦσα· τύμβῳ δ' ὄνομα σῷ κεκλήσεται
ΕΚ. μορφῆς ἐπῳδόν, ἢ τί, τῆς ἐμῆς ἐρεῖς ;
ΠΟΛΥΜ. κυνὸς ταλαίνης σῆμα, ναυτίλοις τέκμαρ.
ΕΚ. οὐδὲν μέλει μοι, σοῦ γέ μοι δόντος δίκην.
ΠΟΛΥΜ. καὶ σήν γ' ἀνάγκη παῖδα Κασσάνδραν θανεῖν.
ΕΚ. ἀπέπτυσ'· αὐτῷ ταῦτά σοι δίδωμ' ἔχειν.   1276
ΠΟΛΥΜ. κτενεῖ νιν ἡ τοῦδ' ἄλοχος, οἰκουρὸς πικρά.
ΕΚ. μήπω μανείη Τυνδαρὶς τοσόνδε παῖς.
ΠΟΛΥΜ. καὐτόν γε τοῦτον, πέλεκυν ἐξάρασ' ἄνω.
ΑΓ. οὗτος σύ, μαίνει, καὶ κακῶν ἐρᾷς τυχεῖν ;   1280
ΠΟΛΥΜ. κτεῖν', ὡς ἐν Ἄργει φόνια λουτρά σ' ἀναμένει.
ΑΓ. οὐχ ἕλξετ' αὐτόν, δμῶες, ἐκποδὼν βίᾳ ;
ΠΟΛΥΜ. ἀλγεῖς ἀκούων ;   ΑΓ. οὐκ ἐφέξετε στόμα ;
ΠΟΛΥΜ. ἐγκλείετ'· εἴρηται γάρ.
ΑΓ.   οὐχ ὅσον τάχος
νήσων ἐρήμων αὐτὸν ἐκβαλεῖτέ ποι,   1285

mann and Pflugk have observed, that ἐνθάδε is to be construed with θανοῦσα ἢ ζῶσα, not with ἐκπλήσω βίον (on which phrase see Alcest. 169. Electr. 1290). The meaning is therefore, 'Am I to die there (viz. where I shall leap into the sea) or to live on, and so fill the allotted term of my existence?' Porson calls βίον "manifesto mendosum," and inclines to Musgrave's πότμον. Perhaps we might elicit the poet's meaning more fully thus, θανοῦσα ἐκεῖ, ἢ ζῶσα ἐνθάδε, ἐς βίου τέλος ἀφίξομαι ;
1272. ἐπῳδόν. To charm, i. e. to console me, for the change of form. Or possibly ἐπῳδὸν may here mean ἐπώνυμον. Porson gives ἢ τι without any stop, but Hermann and others have restored the old reading, as given above.
1278. μήπω. Pflugk has a good note, showing that in wishes this word is used where we should expect μήποτε, and he cites, among other instances, Heracl. 358, μήπω ταῖς μεγάλαισιν οὕτω καὶ καλλιχόροις Ἀθάναις εἴη. In fact, instead of extending the deprecatory wish to all future time (μήποτε), the speaker confines himself to a hope, that matters have not yet come to such a pitch as to justify any apprehensions respecting a person's conduct. Probably some degree of incredulity, or at least of irony, attaches in all cases to this expression.
1279. καὐτόν σε τοῦτον (for γε, τε, or δὲ) is given by Brunck, Pflugk, and W. Dindorf from several MSS. Porson and Hermann have καὐτόν γε τοῦτον, which is much better, not only because σε τοῦτον is not easily defensible for σε τόνδε, although the appellative οὗτος σὺ is used; but also because, as Porson acutely observed, the preceding verse should have been spoken by Agamemnon, to account for Polymestor turning so suddenly and so fiercely upon him.
1281. ἀμμένει W. Dindorf; but this is at least needless. Cf. Hel. 1535. The same critic gives ἐγκλῄετ' against all the copies, in v. 1284.
1285. Hermann's criticism on this exercise of Agamemnon's authority is scarcely fair. He says, ' Euripides cannot have thought much about what he was writing, in making Agamemnon banish a Thracian king, as if he had been a common soldier of his own army.' Agamemnon had sate as judge on Polymestor as a culprit; and he is therefore, if entitled to judge him at all, also entitled to award him a fitting sentence. Besides, the βάρβαροι were altogether disregarded when put in comparison with an Hellenic monarch. A Thracian sovereign was a nonentity when set against the "King of Men." But in

ΕΚΑΒΗ.

ἐπείπερ οὕτω καὶ λίαν θρασυστομεῖ ;
Ἑκάβη, σὺ δ', ὦ τάλαινα, διπτύχους νεκροὺς
στείχουσα θάπτε· δεσποτῶν δ' ὑμᾶς χρεὼν
σκηναῖς πελάζειν, Τρῳάδες· καὶ γὰρ πνοὰς
πρὸς οἶκον ἤδη τάσδε πομπίμους ὁρῶ.   1290
εὖ δ' ἐς πάτραν πλεύσαιμεν, εὖ δὲ τὰν δόμοις
ἔχοντ' ἴδοιμεν, τῶνδ' ἀφειμένοι πόνων.
ΧΟ. ἴτε πρὸς λιμένας σκηνάς τε, φίλαι,
τῶν δεσποσύνων πειρασόμεναι
μόχθων· στερρὰ γὰρ ἀνάγκη.   1295

truth, Agamemnon's pride is wounded by the prophecy, and he hastily says, 'away with this brawler.'
1286. καὶ λίαν. Pflugk appears to be wrong in taking these words together. The καί is the usual adjunct to ἐπεί, as in the well-known combination ἐπεί τοι καί.
1288. δεσποτῶν, of your respective masters, as enumerated in the *Troades*. The tents, as is clear from v. 1015, were close to the ships, and hence this order was given as a preparation for embarking. That event now only awaits Hecuba's return from the funeral of her children; as in Troad. 1148 it had similarly awaited her performance of the funeral rites over Astyanax.
1291. τὰ ἐν δόμοις. In saying this, he is of course unconscious that all was going on wrongly in his own house.

INDICES.

INDEX I.

OF WORDS AND PROPER NAMES.

A.

ἀβάκχευτος B. 472
ἄβατος I. 86. B. 10
ἁβροκόμας I. 920
ἁβρότης B. 968
'Αγαμέμνων A. 884. 1061. E. 3. 1078. Hec. 124. 738. 1114. 1176
ἀγαπᾶν H. 937
ἀγαστὸς Hec. 169
'Αγαύη B. 229. 682. 728. 926
ἀγγέλλειν, ἤγγελον, H. 448
'Αγήνωρ B. 171
ἀγιστεύειν B. 74
ἀγκυλωτὸς B. 1205
ἄγκυρα H. 277. 1071. 1614. Hec. 80
ἀγλαΐα E. 175. 191. 861
ἀγλάϊσμα H. 11. 282. E. 325
ἁγνεύειν E. 654
ἄγνευμα E. 256
ἁγνίζειν E. 793
ἀγνῦναι H. 410. 1598
ἀγνωμοσύνη B. 885
ἀγνωσία Hec. 959
'Αγραυλίδες I. 23. 496
ἀγρεύειν B. 1237
ἀγρεὺς B. 1192
ἀγριοῦσθαι E. 1031
ἀγρότειρα E. 168
ἀγροτὴρ E. 462
ἀγρώτης B. 564
ἀγυιᾶτις I. 186
ἀγχόνη H. 299. B. 246
ἀγχόνιος βρόχος H. 686
ἀγωνία Hec. 314
ἀγωνίζεσθαι ἀγῶνα I. 939. H. 843
ἀδοξεῖν Hec. 294
ἀδύνατοι I. 596. B. 270

'Αερόπη H. 391
ἀηδόνιος πέτρα I. 1482
ἀηδὼν H. 1110. Hec. 337
'Αθάνα 'Ιλία Hec. 1008
ἀθύρειν I. 53
ἀθώπευτος A. 459
Αἰακίδης A. 790
Αἰακὸς H. 7. A. 1246
Αἴας H. 94. 848
Αἰγαῖον πέλαγος H. 766. 1130
Αἰγικορῆς I. 1581
αἰγὶς I. 996. 1423
Αἴγισθος E. 10. 764. 885. 1276
Αἴγυπτος H. 461. Hec. 886
αἰδὼς, ἀργὸς θεὸς, I. 337
αἴθαλος Hec. 911
αἰθαλοῦν E. 1140
αἰκάλλειν A. 630
αἱματοῦν A. 260. B. 1135
αἴμων Hec. 90
αἰνίσσεσθαι I. 430. E. 946
αἰνόπαρις Hec. 945
Αἴολος I. 63. 292. 842. 1297
αἰσχρουργία B. 1062
αἰώρημα H. 353
ἀκεῖσθαι Hec. 1067
ἀκέστωρ A. 900
ἀκραιφνὴς Hec. 537
ἀκεσφόρος I. 1005
ἀκριβοῦν Hec. 1192
'Ακταίων B. 230. 337. 1227. 1292
'Ακτὴ H. 1673
ἀκύμων, barren, A. 158
ἀκύρωτος I. 801
ἀλάστωρ E. 979. Hec. 686. 950
'Αλέξανδρος H. 24—8. 882. Hec. 632
ἀλεξητήριος Herc. 470
ἀλητεία I. 576. H. 934. E. 1113

ἀλίαστος Hec. 85
Ἁλιρρόθιος E. 1260
ἀλλάσσειν E. 89. 103. 740. B. 53. Hec. 483
ἀλλ᾽ οὐδὲ μὴν H. 1047. A. 256. Hec. 401
Ἀλφειὸς I. 175. E. 781. 863. 1273
ἁμαξιτὸς E. 775
Ἀμαζόνες I. 1145
ἀμέρδειν Hec. 1028
ἁμιλλᾶσθαι H. 165. Hec. 271
Ἀμμωνίδες ἕδραι E. 734
ἀμφήρης I. 1128
ἀμφίβλημα H. 70. 423
ἀμφίβληστρον H. 1079
ἀμφίπυρος I. 716. Hec. 473
ἀμφώβολος A. 1133
ἀναβλέπειν B. 1309. I. 1467
ἀναλαβεῖν, to retract, I. 426
ἀναμετρεῖσθαι I. 250. 1271
ἀνανεοῦσθαι H. 722
ἀναπτεροῦν H. 633
ἀναπτυχὴ I. 1445. E. 868
ἀναρίθμητος I. 837
ἀνασκευάζειν E. 602
ἀναστροφὴ A. 1007
ἀναχαιτίζειν B. 1072
ἀναψύχειν H. 1094
ἀναψυχὴ I. 1604
Ἀνδρομάχη A. 5. 806. 1243
ἀνειλείθυια I. 453
ἀνέορτος E. 310
ἀνέχειν Hec. 123
ἀνηβᾶν I. 1465
ἀνηβητήριος A. 552
ἀνθάμιλλος I. 606
ἀνθρωποσφαγεῖν Hec. 260
ἀνιέναι = δέρειν E. 826
ἄνοια (ᾱ) A. 520
ἀνοιστρᾶν τινα B. 979
ἀνομία I. 443
ἀνοτοτύζειν H. 371
ἀντέχεσθαι τινὸς I. 970. 1404
ἀντήλιος I. 1550
ἀντίπαις A. 326
ἀντίπηξ I. 19. 40. 1338. 1380
ἀντισηκοῦν Hec. 57
ἀντίστοιχος A. 745
Ἀξιὸς B. 570
ἀξιοῦσθαι (passive) H. 403
ἀπαιόλη H. 1056
ἀπαιολᾶν I. 549
ἀπαξιοῦν E. 256
ἀπάρχεσθαι E. 91
ἀπαυδᾶν τινὶ A. 87
ἀπασπαίρειν I. 1207

ἀπεμπολᾶν I. 1371
Ἀπιδανὸς Hec. 453
ἀπόβλεπτος Hec. 355
ἀποθερίζειν H. 1188
ἀπολαύειν τινὸς H. 77. A. 543
ἀπονήσασθαι I. 875
ἀποξενοῦν Hec. 1221
ἀπονωτίζειν B. 763
ἀποπέμπεσθαι, abominari, Hec. 72
ἀπορραντήριον I. 435
ἀποτίνεσθαί τινα I. 972
ἀρά γε Hec. 745
Ἀραβία B. 16
ἀράσσειν Hec. 1044. 1175
ἀρβύλη E. 532. B. 638. 1134
Ἀργαδῆς I. 1580
Ἀρισταῖος B. 1370
Ἀριστέας B. 1227
Ἄρκτος I. 1154
ἁρμόζειν νύμφην E. 24
Ἁρμονία B. 1333—8. 1356
ἀροτὴρ E. 104
ἀρταμεῖν E. 816
Ἄρτεμις B. 340. Hec. 463. 936
ἀρχέτας E. 1149
ἀρτιμαθὴς Hec. 687
ἀσείρωτος I. 1150
Ἀσία Hec. 481
Ἀσιὰς B. 1169. I. 1356. 1586
Ἀσιᾶτις E. 315. A. 1. 119
Ἀστυάναξ A. 10
ἀσχημονεῖν Hec. 407
Ἀσωπὸς B. 749. 1044
ἀταλὸς E. 699
Ἀτθὶς γῆ I. 13
Ἄτλας I. 1
Ἀτρείδαι Hec. 510
Ἀτρεὺς H. 390. 1078. 1541—5
ἀτύζεσθαι A. 131
αὐγάζειν H. 1318. B. 596
αὐθέντης A. 614
αὐλίζεσθαι E. 304
Αὖλις E. 1022
αὐτεῖν E. 757. 779
Αὐτονόη B. 230. 681
ἀφασία H. 549
ἄφετος I. 822
ἀφορμὴ I. 474. Hec. 1239. B. 267
Ἀφροδίτη B. 225. 236. 459
ἀφυδραίνεσθαι I. 97
Ἀχαιὸς I. 1592
Ἀχελῷος A. 167. B. 519. 625
Ἀχέρων B. 1361
Ἀχιλλεὺς H. 847. A. 8. 149. 343. Hec. 24. 38. 386—9
ἀχλαινία H. 1282

INDEX I.

ἄχρωστος H. 831
ἀψὶς I. 88

B.

βάθρον H. 1652. E. 608
βαίνειν (active) H. 1616. E. 727. 1173. B. 466
βαλιὸς Hec. 90
Βάκτριος B. 15
βακχεῖος Hec. 676. B. 1057
βακχεύειν I. 1204
Βακχεὺς I. 218. B. 145
βακχεύσιμος B. 298
βάκχευσις B. 357
βάκχη Hec. 123. 1076
βακχιάζειν B. 931
Βάκχιος I. 550—3. 716. B. 67. 195. 225. 1089
βάκχος B. 491. 623
βλάβος I. 998
βλασφημία I. 1189
βοᾶσθαι H. 1434
βολὴ B. 662
βόλος E. 582. B. 847
βοσκὴ H. 1331
βουθυτεῖν I. 1031. E. 635. 785. 805. Hec. 261
βούθυτος ἡδονὴ I. 664.—ἡμέρα H. 1474
βουλευτήριον A. 446. 1097
βουπόρος A. 1134
βουσφαγεῖν E. 627
βουφορβὸς E. 252
βραβεύειν H. 996. 1073
βραβεὺς H. 703
βρέχειν E. 326
Βρόμιος I. 216. H. 1309. 1364. B. 84. 584. 726. 1250
βροτήσιος A. 1255. B. 4
Βύβλινος οἶνος I. 1195

Γ.

γαλακτοπότης E. 169
Γαλήνεια H. 1458
γαμφηλαὶ I. 1495
γὰρ οὖν B. 922. E. 290
γαυροῦσθαι E. 322. B. 1144. 1241
γεγωνεῖν I. 696
γεγωνίσκειν E. 809
γενέθλια θῦσαι I. 653. προθῦσαι I. 805
γενέται θεοὶ I. 1130
γενέτης, a son, I. 916

γεραίρειν E. 712
γεύεσθαι Hec. 375
Γίγαντες I. 207. 988
γλωσσαλγία A. 689
γόης B. 234
Γοργόνες B. 990. I. 224. 989. E. 461. 856
γοργὸς A. 458. 1123
Γοργοφόνη I. 1478
Γοργὼ I. 1003. 1053. 1265. 1421
γραμμὴ E. 956
γραφεὺς Hec. 807
γραφὴ I. 271. Hec. 866
γύαλα I. 76. 220. 245. H. 189. A. 1093
γύης H. 3. 89. A. 1046. E. 79
γὺψ A. 75

Δ.

δαὶ E. 244. 1116
Δαίδαλος Hec. 838
δανεισμὸς E. 858
Δάρδανος H. 1493. E. 5
δειματοῦσθαι A. 42
δέλεαρ H. 755. A. 264
δελφὶς E. 435
Δελφὶς πέτρα A. 998. B. 306
Δελφοὶ A. 1065. I. 54 94
δεξίμηλος A. 129. 1138
δέραια I. 1431
δεῦρ' ἀεὶ I. 56. H. 761
Δηλιάδες Hec. 462
Δηλιὰς λίμνη I. 167
Δῆλος I. 919
Δημήτηρ B. 275
δημογέροντες A. 301
δημοχαριστὴς Hec. 134
Δηὼ H. 1343
διαβάλλεσθαι Hec. 863
διαγράφειν E. 1073
δίαιμος Hec. 656
διάλλαγμα H. 586
διαμᾶν B. 709. E. 1023
διαμεθιέναι E. 978. B. 627. 635
διαμοιρᾶσθαι Hec. 717
διανταῖος I. 767
διαντλεῖν A. 1217
διαπρύσιος H. 1309
διὰ πυρὸς ἐλθεῖν τινὶ A. 487. E. 1182
διαπτοεῖν A. 304
διασφαιρίζειν B. 1136
διαφθείρειν H. 920
διαφορεῖν B. 746. 739
Διθύραμβος B. 526
διϊπετὴς B. 1268

Διόνυσος I. 1232. E. 497. B. 2. 652.
777. 825. 1079. 1374. Hec. 1267
διορίζειν I. 46. H. 394. 828
Διοσκόρω H. 284. 720. 1644. E. 990.
1239. Hec. 441. 943
δίπτυχος A. 578. Hec. 1287. I. 1010.
E. 1238
Δίρκη B. 5. 520. 530
δὶς τόσος E. 1092. Hec. 392
δισκεύειν I. 1268
δίσκος H. 1472
Διώνη H. 1098
δοκεύειν B. 984
δοκῶ E. 747
δοκῶ μὲν H. 917
δοκῶ οὐ πράξειν &c. A. 77. B. 1261
δόρυ = ναῦς H. 1268
δορύξενος A. 999
δοῦπος B. 513
δοχὴ E. 828
δράσαντα παθεῖν I. 1247. A. 438
δρίον H. 1326
δρύοχα E. 1164
δύρεσθαι Hec. 740
δυσγνωσία E. 767
δυσείματος E. 1107
δυσθνήσκων E. 843
δυσθυμεῖσθαι I. 255
δύσνοια Hec. 973
δυστέκμαρτος H. 712
δυσφημεῖν τινα Hec. 182
δυσφορεῖν A. 1234
δυσχλαινία H. 416. Hec. 240
Δωδώνη A. 886
Δωρική (κοπὶς) E. 836
Δωρὶς E. 819. Hec. 450
Δῶρος I. 1590

E.

ἐγκαρτερεῖν A. 262
Ἐγκέλαδος I. 209
ἐδνοῦσθαι H. 933
Εἰδὼ H. 11
εἰκάδες I. 1076
εἰκὼ H. 73. 77
Εἰνοδία I. 1048. H. 570
εἰσφέρειν λόγους B. 650. A. 757
Ἑκάβη ἡ Κισσέως Hec. 3. 53. 485.
1043. 1133
Ἑκάτη H. 569
ἐκβαίνειν τόπον B. 1044
ἐκβακχεύειν B. 1296
ἔκβολον, τὸ, I. 555. H. 422. B. 91
ἐκβρυχᾶσθαι H. 1557

ἐκδίδαγμα I. 1419
ἐκθηριοῦν B. 1333
ἐκθυμιᾶν I. 1174
ἐκκαρποῦσθαι I. 815
ἐκκολυμβᾶν H. 1609
ἐκκρεμάννυσθαι E. 950
ἐκκρήμνασθαι I. 1613
ἐκκυνηγετεῖν I. 1422
ἐκκωμάζειν A. 603
ἐκλιμπάνειν E. 909
ἔκμακτρον E. 535
ἐκμουσοῦν B. 825
ἐκπαγλεῖσθαι Hec. 1157
ἐκπιμπλάναι I. 1107
ἐκπονεῖν I. 375. 1040
ἐκπορθμεύειν H. 1517
ἐκπτήσσειν Hec. 180
ἐκτεκνοῦσθαι I. 438
ἐκτελὴς I. 780
ἐκτοξεύειν A. 365
ἐκτρίβειν I. 2   E.
ἐκ τῶνδε = τούτων ἕνεκα I. 843.
   31
ἐκφαιδρύνειν B. 768
ἐκχορεύσασθαί τινα H. 381
ἐλαύνειν ἔξω φρενῶν B. 853
Ἑλένη E. 1027. H. 22. 75. Hec. 265.
   442. A. 899. 943
Ἕλενος H. 751. A. 1245. Hec. 87
Ἑλλὰς γυνὴ I. 1367
ἑλκοῦν Hec. 405
ἐλπὶς (with aorist) A. 27. 311. Hec.
   305. 371
ἐμβατεύειν E. 595. 1251. Hec. 913
ἐναύλεια H. 1107
ἐνδιδόναι τι Hec. 1239. A. 225. 965
ἐνδυστυχεῖν B. 508
ἐνθύμιος I. 1347
ἔνοπτρον Hec. 925
ἔνοσις H. 1363. B. 585
ἐνστρέφεσθαι I. 300
Ἐννάλιος A. 1015
ἐντάφια H. 1404
ἐξαλείφειν H. 262
ἐξαμιλλᾶσθαι ἄμιλλαν H. 387
ἐξαμβλοῦν A. 356
ἐξανεμοῦν H. 32. A. 938
ἐξανύσασθαι, to acquire from, A. 536.
   B. 131
ἔξαρχος B. 141
ἐξελίσσειν I. 397
ἐξευλαβεῖσθαι A. 644
ἐξευτρεπίζειν E. 75
ἐξιᾶσθαι E. 1024
ἐξικμάζειν A. 398
ἐξιχνεύειν B. 352

INDEX I.

ἐξογκοῦσθαι A. 703
ἐξομοιοῦσθαι A. 354
ἐξομόρξασθαι B. 344
ἐξορμίζειν H. 1247
ἐξυπειπεῖν B. 1266
ἐπαυρίσκεσθαι H. 469
ἐπερείδεσθαι Hec. 114
ἐπ' αὐτοφώρῳ I. 1214
ἐπείσακτος I. 590
ἐπεισφρεῖν E. 1033
ἐπὶ, with, I. 228
ἐπιδρομαὶ H. 404
ἐπὶ τοῖσδε H. 838. E. 1030
ἐπιρροαὶ κακῶν A. 349
ἐπιρροθεῖν Hec. 553
ἐπισημαίνεσθαι I. 1593
ἐπιστρέφεσθαι H. 83
ἐπιστροφὴ H. 440
ἐπισφάζειν E. 92. 281
ἐπιτίμια Hec. 1086
ἐπορθρεύειν E. 142
ἑρμήνευμα A. 46
ἑρμηνεὺς E. 333
ἐπουρίζειν A. 610
ἐπῳδὸς B. 234
ἐπωμὶς Hec. 558
Ἐρεχθεὺς I. 277. 725. 1465. 1573
Ἐρεχθεῖδαι I. 1057. 1060
Ἐριχθόνιος I. 21. 268. 999
ἐρίπναι E. 210
Ἑρμιόνη A. 29. 114. 520. 804
ἔροτις E. 625
Ἐρυθραὶ B. 751
ἑσμὸς B. 710
εὐαγεῖν B. 1009
εὐαγὴς B. 662
εὐάζειν B. 1035
εὐαὴς H. 1504
εὐαίων I. 125. B. 426
εὔασμα B. 151
Εὔβοια I. 294. H. 1127
Εὐβοιῖς I. 60. E. 442
Εὐβοικὸς H. 767
εὐγώνιος I. 1136
εὐδαιμονία, εὐτυχία A. 420
εὐημερία E. 196
Εὔιος B. 566. 579
Εὔξεινος A. 1262
εὐοργησία B. 641
εὔοχθος I. 1169
Εὐρώπη A. 801. I. 1356. Hec. 482
Εὐρωπία I. 1587
εὔρως I. 1393
Εὐρώτας H. 124. 162. 209. 350. A. 437. Hec. 650
εὐσέβεια H. 901. I. 1045

εὐσωματεῖν A. 765
εὐτυχεῖν opposed to ἄπαιδα εἶναι, I. 775. Hec. 699. 989
εὖ φρονεῖν = εὐφραίνεσθαι I. 517
ἐφιέναι A. 954
ἔφοδος I. 1049
ἐφολκὶς A. 200
ἐχέγγυος A. 192
Ἐχίων B. 213. 265. 507. 995
Ἕως E. 102. I. 1158

Z.

ζάπλουτος A. 1282
ζεῖν Hec. 1055
ζεῦγλαι (νεὼς) H. 1536
ζεῦγος, a pair, A. 495
Ζεὺς ὁμόγνιος A. 921
—— Ὀλύμπιος E. 782
ζηλοῦν, to aspire to, Hec. 255
ζόη Hec. 1108. E. 121
ζυγὸν πόλεως I. 595
—— δουλείας Hec. 376
—— βασίλεων H. 392
ζώνη B. 935
ζωπυρεῖν E. 1121

H.

η and οι confused, I. 253. 1351. 1396
Ἠδωνοὶ Hec. 1153
ἠθὰς A. 818
Ἤλεκτραι πύλαι B. 780
Ἠλέκτρα E. 15. 19. 119. 1249
ἤμην H. 931
ἦν (first person) I. 280
ἠπειρῶτις A. 159. 652
Ἡρακλῆς I. 1144
-ηρὸς, -ήρης, terminating adjectives, B. 107
ἤτριον I. 1421
Ἥφαιστος E. 443
Ἠχὼ Hec. 1111

Θ.

θαλερὸς ὕπνος B. 692
θεήλατος I. 1306. A. 851
θειοῦσθαι H. 866
θεμιστεύειν H. 371
Θεοκλύμενος H. 9. 1168. 1643
θεομαχεῖν B. 45. 325. 1255
Θεονόη H. 13. 145. 319. 529. 821. 859

Θεράπναι B. 1043
θεράπνη Hec. 482
θέραψ I. 94
θερμαίνειν E. 402
Θεσσαλία A. 1176
Θεσσαλὸς A. 19. E. 781. 818
Θεστιὰς H. 133
Θετίδειον A. 20
Θέτις H. 847. A. 18. 43. 108. 565. 1232. Hec. 388
θεωρία B. 1047
Θήβη A. 1
Θῆβαι B. 23. 919. 1247
θηλύμορφος B. 353
θηροκτόνος H. 154
θησαύρισμα I. 1394. E. 497
Θησείδα Hec. 125
θιασεύειν I. 552. B. 75. 378
θιασώτης B. 548
θοάζειν B. 65. 219
θοινᾶν τινα I. 982
θοινάτωρ I. 1206. 1217
Θρῇκες Hec. 428. 682. 873. 1267
Θρῄκη Hec. 81. 963
θριγκοὶ I. 156. 172. 1321. H. 430. E. 1151
θρυλεῖν E. 910
θύειν (ὔ) E. 1141
Θυέστης E. 10. 613. 719. 773
θνηπολεῖν E. 665. 1134
θυμέλαι I 46. 228. E. 713
θυραῖος for ὄθνειος A. 422
θυμοῦσθαι ἐς κέρας B. 743
θυοσκόος B. 224
θυρσοφορεῖν B. 556
θύρσος B. 704
θωΰσσειν B. 871. Hec. 115

I.

Ἴακχος B. 725
Ἴδα H. 358
Ἰδαῖος H. 1508. A. 275. Hec. 325. 943
ἱέραξ A. 1141
ἰήϊος E. 1210
Ἰλιὰς A. 128. 140. Hec. 905. 1062
Ἴλιος A. 103
ἱμὰς A. 718
Ἰνὼ B. 229. 682. 925
Ἴναχος E. 1
Ἰόλαος I. 198
ἰὸς I. 1015
Ἴσθμιον νάπος I. 176

Ἰσθμὸς E. 1288
Ἰσμηνὸς B. 5
ἴτυς E. 458
Ἰφιγόνη E. 1023
Ἴων I. 74. 81. 661. 802. 831
Ἴωνες I. 1588

K.

Κάδμος B. 2. 10 et passim
καθιγνίζειν I. 709
καὶ δὴ H. 1059
καίνειν A. 388
καιρὸς (vital part) A. 1120
κακίζεσθαι I. 984. E. 982
Κάλλιστὼ H. 375
καλλίφλοξ I. 706
Καλλίχοροι πηγαὶ I. 1075
Κάλχας H. 749
κάμαξ Hec. 1155
καμπὴ E. 659
κανοῦν E. 800. 810. 1142
κανὼν E. 52. Hec. 602
καπφθίμενος E. 1299
καραδοκεῖν H. 739
καρπίζειν H. 1328
καρπὸς, offspring, I. 922.—wrist, I. 891 1009
καρτερεῖν Hec. 1223
καρχήσια Hec. 1261
Κασσάνδρα A. 298. Hec. 88. 677. 827. 855
Κασταλία I. 95. 148
Κάστωρ H. 205. E. 312. 1064. 1240
καταβακχιοῦσθαι B. 109
καταιβάτης B. 1360
καταιδεῖσθαι H. 805
καταιθαλοῦν I. 215
καταικίζειν A. 828
κατάλυσις, a lodging, E. 393
καταμπίσχειν H. 853
κατάρχειν τινὰ (θρηνεῖν) A. 1199
κατάρχεσθαι E. 1222. Hec. 685
κατειπεῖν I. 1215. H. 898. Hec. 243
κατέχειν, to lodge, I. 551. E. 1034
———, to occupy, Hec. 81. E. 201
——— ναῦν H. 1206
———, to secure, A. 156. 198
κατήρης E. 498
κατομνύναι τινὰ H. 348
κατώρυξ Hec. 1002
Καφηρίδες πέτραι H. 1129
κείρειν, κέκαρσαι, -μένος, E. 108. 515. Hec. 910
κεῖσθαι πέσων H. 1605

κέκασμαι E. 616
Κεκροπία πέτρα I. 936
Κεκροπία, Attica, E. 1289
Κεκροπίδαι I. 296
Κέκροψ I. 272. 1163. 1400
κέλευσμα H. 1565. A. 1030
κελευστής H. 1576. 1596
κέλωρ A. 1034
κενοταφείν H. 1060. 1546
Κένταυροι A. 792
κεντείν Hec. 387
κηδεστής Hec. 834
κηδεύειν E. 47. Hec. 1202
Κήρες E. 1252
κηφήν B. 1364
Κηφισός I. 1261
κίβδηλος E. 550
κιβδηλεύειν B. 475
Κιθαιρών B. 62. 661. 751. 797. 945. 1142. 1384
κινείν μύθον E. 302
κληρούν, κληρούσθαι I. 909
κλιμακτήρ H. 1570
κλίμαξ B. 1213
Κλυταιμνήστρα A. 884. 1115. E. 9
κομίζειν, νομίζειν, confused, I. 1362
κομιστήρ Hec. 222
κοπίς E. 837
κόπις Hec. 134
κορμός H. 1601. Hec. 575
Κορύβαντες B. 125
κορύσσειν A. 279
Κουρήτες B. 120
κουφίζειν (intrans.) H. 1555
――― (trans.) E. 861
κράντωρ A. 507
κρασπεδούν I. 1423
κραταίβολος B. 1096
κραταίλεως E. 534
κρέκειν E. 542
κρήμνασθαι E. 1217
κρηπίς I. 38. 510. H. 547. A. 1112
Κρήτη H. 768. B. 121
Κρονίδης Hec. 474
κρούειν πεύκην H. 870
κρυπτεύειν H. 541. B. 888
κρωσσός I. 1173
κτενισμός E. 529
κτερίζειν H. 1244
κτερίσματα H. 1391
κτίστωρ I. 74
Κυάνεαι A. 864
Κυβέλη B. 78
κύδιον A. 639
Κυκλάδες E. 1583
κυκλούσθαι Hec. 639. B. 1066

VOL. II.

Κυκλώπειος E. 1158
Κύπρις, origin of name, B. 401
Κύπρος H. 148. B. 401
κυρούν E. 1069
Κωρυκία κορυφή B. 559

Λ.

Λαερτιάδης Hec. 135
Λαέρτιος Hec. 402
Λάκαινα Hec. 441. 651. A. 29. 151
Λακεδαίμων H. 474. A. 128
λακείν Hec. 678
λακτίζειν πρός κέντρα B. 795
λάμπειν (active) I. 83. H. 1131
λαμπρύνεσθαι E. 1039
Λάπιθαι A. 792
λάσκειν A. 671
λατρεύειν τινά E. 131
λαχνόγυιος H. 378
λεηλατείν Hec. 1143
λείμαξ B. 867
Λερναίος ύδρα I. 191
λεύειν E. 328
Λευκή ακτή A. 1262
Λευκιππίδες H. 1466
λεχώ E. 652—4. 1108
Λήδα H. 19. 134. 200. 1145. 1644
λήζεσθαι H. 475
Λήμνος Hec. 887
Λητώ I. 126. 922. 1619. Hec. 460
λιάζεσθαι Hec. 100
λιβάς A. 116. 534
Λιβύη H. 768. 1211
Λίβυσσα B. 990
Λίβυς λωτός H. 170
――― οιωνός H. 1480
λινόκροκος Hec. 1080
λιπαίνειν B. 575
λίς B. 1173
λοβός E. 827
λογάδες Hec. 544
λόγος τινός (talk about a person) I. 929. E. 228. 347
Λοιδίας B. 571
Λοξίας E. 1266. I. 67
λοχάν τινα E. 225
λοχεύειν τινά I. 948. B. 3. E. 1129
Λυδία B. 234. 464
λύειν πόδα Hec. 1020
Λύκαιος E. 1274
λυμαίνεσθαι H. 1099. A. 719. B. 354. 632
λύματα H. 1271
λύσσα B. 851. 977

4 D

M.

λώτισμα H. 1593
λωτός B. 160

Μαῖα I. 3. A. 276. E. 462
Μαιὰς H. 243. 1670
Μακραὶ (πέτραι) I. 13. 283. 494. 937. 1400
μαντευτὸς I. 1211
μεγαλύνειν B. 320
με = ἐμαυτὴν A. 256
μέθη E. 326
μεθ' ἡμέραν &c. B. 485
μειλίσσειν H. 1339
μεμηχανημένως I. 809
μέμφεσθαι, to be dissatisfied, Hec. 885. 962. Hel. 31
μὲν (interrogative) I. 520. H. 1226
Μενέλαος H. 116. 123. 504. 1215. A. 152
Μέροψ H. 382
μεσάγκυλα A. 1133
μετὰ with dative, Hec. 355
μετακλαίεσθαι Hec. 214
μεταπεσεῖν I. 412
μὴ, whether, I. 1523. H. 119
μηχανορράφος A. 447. 1116
μιάστωρ A. 615. E. 682
μιγάδες B. 18. 1355. A. 1142
μίλαξ B. 108. 703
Μίμας I. 215
μιξόθηρ I. 1161
μίτρα E. 163. Hec. 924. B. 833. 929
μόθων B. 1060
Μολοσσία γῆ A. 1244—8
μόλυβδος A. 267
μουσεῖον H. 174. 1108
μουσεῖος B. 408
μυθεύεσθαι I. 197. 265
Μυκηναῖος A. 1075
Μυκηνίδες E. 761
μυστήρια E. 87
μῶν οὖν A. 82
μωραίνειν A. 674
μωρία I. 545. H. 1018
μῶρος E. 50. 53

N.

Ναῖς H. 187
νάρθηξ H. 1361. B. 113. 251. 1157
Ναυπλία E. 1278. H. 1586. 1590
Ναύπλιος H. 767. 1586. E. 453
ναυσθλοῦσθαι H. 1210
ναυστολεῖν Hec. 634. 1260
ναυστολία A. 795
ναυφθόρος H. 1382. 1539
Νεῖλος H. 1. 462. 491. 671. A. 650
Νεοπτόλεμος A. 14
νεοσφαγὴς Hec. 894
νεώρια H. 1530
Νηλεὺς H. 849
Νηρεὺς H. 15. 1003. 1585. 1224. A. 1224—32
Νηρηῒς H. 318. 1647. A. 46. 135. 1267. E. 442
νησιωτικὸς H. 149. A. 1261
Νίκη 'Αθάνα I. 1529
νικηφορεῖν τι B. 1147
νῦν E. 408
νοτὶς Hec. 1259
νουθετητέος I. 436. B. 1256
Νῦσα B. 556
νωτίζειν A. 1141

Ξ.

ξένια H. 480. 1668. E. 359
ξενοκτονεῖν Hec. 1247
ξενοῦν I. 820
ξεστὸς τάφος H. 986
ξηρὸς B. 277. A. 637. 784. 1259. E. 239
ξιφήρης E. 225. I. 1153. 1258
ξόανα I. 1403
Ξοῦθος I. 58. 292. 393. 513. 1125. 1533. 1602
ξουθὸς H. 1111
ξυρήκης E. 335
ξυρὸν E. 241
ξυστὸν Hec. 920

O.

ὀγκοῦν I. 388. A. 320. E. 381. Hec. 623
ὀδοῦν I. 1050
ὀδουρὸς I. 1617
'Οδυσσεὺς Hec. 143. 216. 385
οἰκήτωρ I. 1299. A. 1089
οἰκτίζεσθαί τινα H. 1053
οἴνη B. 535
οἰνηρὸς I. 1179
Οἰνόμαος H. 386
οἰστρᾶν, -εῖν, B. 32. 119
οἰστροπλὴξ B. 1229
οἶτος H. 164

οἰωνοσκοπεῖν B. 347
Ὄλυμπος B. 409. 560
ὁμηρεύειν B. 297
ὅμηρος B. 293
ὀξυθυμεῖν A. 689
ὀπάζειν = διώκειν E. 1192
Ὅπλητες I. 1580
ὀπτήρια I. 1127
ὀργάδες E. 1163. B. 340. 445
ὄργανα B. 1208
ὀργάνη A. 1015
ὄργια B. 470
ὀργιάζειν B. 415
ὀρέγεσθαί τινος I. 842. H. 1238
Ὀρέστης A. 885. E. 15. 17. 505
ὀρθοστάται I. 1133. H. 547
ὀριγνᾶσθαι B. 1255
ὁρμιά H. 1615
ὀρρωδεῖν Hec. 768
Ὀρφεὺς B. 561
Ὁσία B. 370
Ὄσσα E. 446
ὅτε μὴ = εἰ μὴ I. 1243
οὐκ εἴα with fut. interrog., H. 1561
οὐλὴ E. 573
οὐ for μὴ with infin. E. 99
οὐ μὴ with subj. H. 292. Hec. 1039
―― future, B. 852. E. 982. A. 757
οὐραῖα, τὰ, I. 1154
οὐριβάτης E. 170
οὐριθρέπτης Hec. 204
οὐχ ὅσον H. 481
οὔτε―οὐδὲ A. 567―8
ὀχμάζειν E. 817

Π.

Παιὰν I. 124. 938
παιδαγωγεῖν B. 193
παιδαγωγὸς E 287
παίδευμα A. 1101. E. 887
παῖς παιδὸς A. 1063. 1083
παλαιότης H. 1056
παλεὸς, παλαιὸς, E. 497
παλίμφημος I. 1096
παλίρροπος E. 492
παμπησία I. 1305
Παλλὰς χρυσόλογχος I. 9
καλλίδιφρος Hec. 468
Πὰν I. 492. 938. H. 190. E. 703.
B. 952
παρὰ = ἐξ, A. 172
παραβλέπειν I. 624
παράδειγμα E. 1085
παραλύειν A. 305
παρὰ σταθμὴν I. 1514

παραστὰς (-άδος) A. 1121
παρεμβλέπειν εἰς κέρας H. 1558
παράφορος Hec. 1050
παραψυχὴ Hec. 280
παρηγορεῖν = πείθειν, Hec. 288
παρθενεύεσθαι H. 283
παρθένευμα I. 1425. 1474
παρθενωπὸς E. 949
παριέναι, to relax, I. 1208. B. 635. 683
――, to enter, H. 451
παριππεύειν H. 1665
Πάρις H. 29. 586. 1672. A. 103. 706. Hec. 387
Παρνησιὰς I. 86. 714
Παρνησὸς I. 155. 1267
παροχετεύειν B. 479
παρρησία I. 672. E. 1049
πατρικὴ I. 1304
Πάφος B. 404
Πειρηναῖος E. 475
πελάθειν E. 1293
Πέλοψ H. 387
Πελοπία I. 1591
Πελοπίδαι H. 1242. 1264
πέμπεσθαί τινα Hec. 957
Πενθεὺς B. 44. 212. 320. 367. 507
πένεσθαι Hec. 1220
πέπαται I. 675. A. 641
περίβλεπτος A. 89
περιπετὴς A. 982
περίπτυγμα I. 1391
περιπτυχὴ I. 1516. Hec. 1015
περισσὸς B. 429
Πέρσαι B. 14
Περσεὺς H. 769. E. 459
Πέρσειος H. 1464
Περσεφόνη I. 1442. Hec. 138
πευστήριος E. 835
Πηλείδης Hec. 191
Πηλεὺς H. 98. A. 18. 45. 149. 342. 545. 914. Hec. 37. 383
Πήλιον A. 1277. E. 445
Πιερία B. 408. 565
πίνος E. 305
Πῖσα H. 386
πλέθρον I. 1136
Πλειὰς I. 1152. H. 1489. E. 468
πλέκειν τέχνην I. 1279
πλέκειν πλοκὰς I. 826. 1410
πλημμελὴς H. 1085
Πλούτου οἶκος H. 69
ποικίλλειν Hec. 470
ποικίλματα ἀστέρων H. 1096
ποινᾶσθαι H. 1509
ποινάτωρ E. 23. 268

πόλος I. 1154
Πολυδεύκης E. 1240
Πολύδωρος Hec. 3. 428. 682. 987
πόνος = τὸ ἐκπονηθὲν I. 1088
Πολυμήστωρ Hec. 7. 771. 969
Πολυξένη Hec. 40. 523. 895. 674. 780
πόντισμα H. 1548
πόρπαξ H. 1376
πόρπη Hec. 1170
Ποσειδῶν H. 1585
ποτνιὰς B. 664
ποῦ = πῶς I. 528
πράπιδες A. 480. B. 427. 999
Πριαμίδαι Hec. 13. 583. 764. 1002. 1147. A. 287
Πρίαμος H. 35. E. 5. A. 3. 299. Hec. 4. 493. 1210
προβακχήϊος B. 411
πρόβλημα = τόλμα, E. 985
προθέσθαι νεκρὸν Hec. 613
προκόπτειν Hec. 961
προλάζυσθαι I. 1027
Προμηθεὺς I. 455
προνώπια B. 639
προξενεῖν I. 335. H. 146
πρόξενος A. 1103
προοίμιον E. 1060
προπόλευμα I. 113
προσαιτεῖν H. 791
προσειλεῖν H. 445
προσήκειν οὐδὲν I. 434
προσλάζυσθαί τινος Hec. 63
προσποιεῖσθαι H. 1387
προστιθέναι τι = αἰτίαν τινὸς, A. 219. 360
προστιθέναι, addicere, A. 1016. Hec. 368. B. 676
πρόσρησις H. 1166
πρὸς τάδε = διὰ τοῦτο E. 685
προστρόπαιος I. 1260
πρόσφαγμα Hec. 41. 265
προσφάζειν H. 1255
προσφορήματα E. 423
πρόσφορος τινὸς H. 508
προσῳδὸς I. 359
πρότονοι Hec. 114
προὔργου H. 1379
προφητεύειν I. 369. 413
προφήτης B. 211
πρόχοος I. 435
προχύται E. 803
πρυμνοῦχος E. 1022
Πρωτεὺς H. 4. 46. 460. 787. E. 1280
πρωτόπλοος H. 1531. A. 865
πτερὰ, arrows, H. 76

πτερὰ, omens, I. 377
————, sails, H. 147
πτέρυξ πέπλων I. 1143
πτερωτοὶ H. 747. B. 257
πτήσσειν I. 1280. B. 1036. A. 165. 753
πτοεῖσθαι B. 214. E. 1255
πτώσσειν B. 223. Hec. 1065
Πύθιος I. 285
Πυθόχρηστος I. 1218
Πυθὼ A. 52
Πυλάδης E. 847. 887. 1249
πυρπόλημα H. 767
πυρριχὴ A. 1135
πυρσεύειν H. 1126. E. 694
πύστις E. 690
πῶς (with genitive) E. 751. H. 313
πῶς καὶ Hec. 515

P.

ῥανὶς A. 227
ῥάπτειν φόνον A. 836. 911
'Ρέα B. 59. 128
'Ρίον I. 1592
ῥιπὴ H. 1123
ῥίπτειν (ἑαυτὸν) H. 1325
ῥόθιον H. 1268. 1452. A. 1096. E. 992
ῥόμβος H. 1362
ῥοπὴ H. 1090
ῥόπτρα I. 1612
ῥυθμίζεσθαι κόμην Hec. 924
ῥυθμὸς E. 772
ῥυσιάζειν I. 523. 1406
ῥυσὸς E. 490

Σ.

σάγμα A. 617
σαθρὸς B. 487. Hec. 1190
σαίνειν I. 685
σαίρειν I. 115. 121. A. 166. Hec. 363
Σαλαμὶς H. 88. 150
σανὶς H. 1556
Σάρδεις B. 463
σατίνη H. 1312
σάτυροι B. 130
σαφής, true, H. 21. 309
σεβίζειν = ἀγαπᾶν, H. 358
Σειρῆνες H. 169. A. 936
Σείριος Hec. 1102
σελαγεῖσθαι E. 714

Σεμέλη B. 3. 28. 335
σεμνὸς, fine, H. 431
σηκὸς I. 300. B. 11
σήκωμα E. 1274
σήπειν E. 319
Σηπιὰς χοιρὰς A. 1266
Σιδώνιος H. 1413. 1531. B. 171. 1026. H. 1451
Σικελὸς E. 1347
Σιμοέντιος H. 250
Σιμοεντὶς A. 1018. 1183. E. 441. Hec. 641
σιτοποιὸς ἀνάγκη Hec. 362
σκαλμὸς H. 1598
Σκάμανδρος H. 52. 368. 609
σκαφεὺς E. 252
σκήπτειν, to pretend, H. 834
σκηπτὸς A. 1047
σκίπων Hec. 65
σκιρτᾶν B. 446
σκίρτημα B. 169
σκόλοψ E. 898
σκυθίζειν E. 241
σκυθράζειν E. 830
σκῦλα Hec. 1014. E. 7. 897. 1000
σκύλευμα E. 314
Σκῦρος A. 210
σμύρνη I. 89. 1175
σοφίζεσθαι B. 200
σπαργᾶν B. 701
σπαργανοῦν I. 955
Σπάρτη H. 17. 30. 58. 472. 1671. A. 446
Σπαρτιᾶτις H. 115. A. 151. 596. 889. E. 411
σπαρτὸς B. 1275
σποδεῖσθαι A. 1129
στάθμη I. 1514
σταλάσσειν A. 1047
στατίζειν E. 316
στέγειν E. 273. I. 1412. Hec. 880
στεῖρος A. 711
στέλλειν ναῦν, λαῖφος &c. H. 147. Hec. 1081
στῆναι στάσιν B. 925
στηρίζειν B. 972. 1073. 1083
στιβάδες H. 798
στολάδες H. 1479
στολίδες H. 1359. B. 936
στρατηλατεῖν τινι E. 321. B. 52. A. 324
στροφὶς A. 718
Στρόφιος E. 18
σὺ for σὺ αὐτὸς I. 847
συγγενέτειρα E. 746
συγκεραυνοῦν B. 1103

σύγχορτος A. 17
σύμβολα I. 1386. H. 291. E. 577
συμβόλαια I. 411
Συμπληγάδες A. 795
συμπυθέσθαι H. 328
συμφέρεσθαι I. 694
συνδαίειν H. 1439
συνεκκομίζειν E. 73
συνεργάτις E. 100
συνθοινάτωρ E. 638
συνθρανοῦν B. 633
συννεφοῦν E. 1078
σύννοια A. 805
σύνοχος H. 172. B. 161
συντείνειν δρόμον &c. E. 112. B. 872
συνωδίνειν H. 727
συνῳδὸς H. 174
συνωρίζεσθαι B. 198
συσσίτιον I. 1165
σύστασις A. 1088
σφαγεῖον E. 800
σφαγεὺς A. 1134
σφαγιασμὸς E. 199
σφάγιον E. 514. Hec. 137. 305
σφαγὶς E. 811. 1142
σφαλῆναι (of love) I. 1523. A. 223
Σφὶγξ E. 471
σφόνδυλος E. 841
σφριγᾶν A. 196
σωφρονεῖν = εὖ φρονεῖν I. 521. H. 97

T.

Ταλθύβιος Hec. 487. 503. 727
Ταναὸς ποταμὸς E. 410
Τάνταλος E. 11
ταυροῦσθαι B. 922
τε—ἢ Hec. 468
Τειρεσίας B. 173. 210. 249. 1224
Τελαμὼν H. 88. 92
Τελέων I. 1579
τετράπους Hec. 1058
Τεῦκρος H. 87
τεῦχος νεοσσῶν, an egg, H. 258
―――, baggage, E. 360
τηκτὸς A. 267
τηλορὸς E. 251
τηλουρὸς A. 889
τητᾶσθαι H. 274. E. 310. Hec. 324
τιθήνη Hec. 281
τίκτειν, τίκτεσθαι, H. 214
Τιτανὶς H. 382
Τιτὰν I. 455. Hec. 472
Τμῶλος B. 55. 154. 462
τοκὰς Hec. 1157

τοξεύειν τινὸς I. 1411. Β. 1099
───── μάτην Hec. 603
τοξοσύνη Α. 1194
τόρνος Β. 1067
τριαινοῦν Β. 348
τρίβων Β. 717. Ε. 11. 27
τρίγλυφοι Β. 1214
τριετηρίδες Β. 133
Τριτωνιὰς λίμνη I. 872
τρόπις Η. 411
τροφεῖα I. 852. 1493. Ε. 626
Τροφώνιος I. 300. 393
τροχηλατεῖν Ε. 1253
τρυφᾶν I. 1376. Β. 969
τρῦχος Ε. 184. 501
τυγχάνειν, to befal, Hec. 628
τυμβεύειν Η. 1245
τύμβευμα I. 933
Τυνδαρίδαι Η. 1497. Ε. 1295
Τυνδαρὶς Η. 472. 614. 1546. Α. 898.
  Ε. 13. Hec. 269. 1278
Τυνδάρεως Η. 17. 494. 568. Ε. 1018
τύρευμα Ε. 496
τύφεσθαι Hec. 478. Β. 8
τυφλὸν φέγγος = τυφλότης Hec. 1067
τυφλοῦσθαι Hec. 1035

Υ.

Ὑάδες I. 1156. Ε. 468
Ὑάκινθος Η. 1469
ὑγιὲς οὐδὲν Β. 262. Α. 448. Η. 746
Ὕδρα Λερναῖος I. 191
ὑδραίνειν Ε. 157
ὑμνῳδία I. 681. Η. 1434
ὑπάγειν Α. 428
ὑπάγεσθαι Ε. 1155. Α. 906
ὑπαγκάλισμα Η. 242
ὕπαρνος Α. 557
ὕπαρχος Η. 1432
ὑπέγγυος Hec. 1029
ὑπεξακρίζειν Β. 678
ὑπεξαντλεῖν I. 927
ὑπερθεῖν Α. 195
ὑπερθρώσκειν Hec. 823
ὑπερτελὴς I. 1549
ὑπερτέλλειν Hec. 1010
ὑπιδέσθαι I. 1023
ὑπόπτερος Η. 618. 1236. Hec. 1264
ὑποπτήσσειν Η. 1203
ὕποπτος Hec. 1135.
ὑφαιρεῖσθαί τί τινα Ε. 271
ὑφὴ I. 1146
Ὕσιαι Β. 751

Φ.

φαιδρύνειν Η. 678
φαναὶ I. 550
φαντάζεσθαι Α. 876
φαρμακεύειν Α. 355
φᾶρος Ε. 317
φᾶρος Ε. 543. 1221. Α. 831
Φάρος Η. 5
Φαρσαλία Α. 16. 22
Φᾶσις Α. 651
φέρεσθαι ἔς τι Η. 311
───── τινὶ Η. 1642
───── τι Α. 786
φερνὴ Α. 1282
Φερσέφασσα Η. 175
φῆμαι I. 99. 180. Η. 614. 1281. Ε.
  701
φθείρεσθαι, to lose oneself, Ε. 234.
  Η. 774
───── = ἕρρειν Α. 708. 715
Φθία Α. 16. 202. 403
Φθιὰς Α. 119. Hec. 451
Φθιῶτις Α. 664. 1048
φιάλη I. 1182
φίλιος Ζεὺς Α. 603
φιλοψυχεῖν Hec. 315
φιλόψυχος Hec. 348
Φλέγρα I. 988
φλέψ I. 1011
φοιβὰς Hec. 827
Φοῖβος ἀκέστωρ Α. 900
φοινικοσκελὴς I. 1207
φοινικοφαὴς I. 163
φοῖνιξ Δηλία I. 920. Hec. 458
───── πέπλος Η. 181
Φοίνισσα κώπη Η. 1272. 1451
φοινίσσεσθαι Hec. 152
φονεύς, φονεᾶ Ε. 599. 763. Hec. 882
φοράδην Α. 1166
φορβὰς Β. 168
φρενήρης Ε 1053
φρικώδης Α. 1148
φρίσσειν Hec. 86
φύρειν Hec. 496. 958
Φωκεῖς Ε. 18. 1287
Φῶκος Α. 687

Χ.

χαλᾶν Hec. 403. I. 637
χαλινωτήρια νεῶν Hec. 539
χαλκίοικος Η. 228. 245
Χαλκωδοντίδαι I. 59

INDEX I.

χαρακτήρ E. 559. 572. Hec. 379
χάριν πράσσειν I. 36. 895. E. 1133
— θέσθαι I. 1104. E. 61. Hec. 1211
— θεῖναι B. 721
Χάριτες H. 1341
χάσμα E. 1271
χαυνοῦν A. 931
χειμάζεσθαι I. 966
χείριος A. 411. 628. I. 1257
χειροδράκων E. 1345
χειροῦσθαι E. 1168
χέλυς E. 837
χερμὰς B. 1096
χέρνης E. 206
χερσαῖος A. 457
Χερσόνησος Hec. 8. 33
χέρσος I. 1584. H. 1063—6. E. 325
χηλαὶ I. 1208. 1241. E. 474. B. 619. Hec. 90
χῃδὺ E. 987
χἰκετεύειν (καὶ ἱκ.) H. 1024
χιονοθρέμμων H. 1323
χιονόχρως H. 216
χοιρὰς A. 1265
χολὴ E. 828
χρῆν = χρῆναι Hec. 260
χρηστήριον, a victim, I. 419.—oracle, I. 1611. E. 1272
χρηστήριος, oracular, H. 822. I. 1320
χρίμπτειν (intrans.) A. 530. I. 156
χρυσαυγὴς I. 890
χρυσοφύλαξ I. 54
χρύσωμα I. 1030. 1430
χρῴζειν Hec. 912

χὐποχείριον A. 736
χωρεῖν πρύμναν A. 1120

Ψ.

Ψ and Τ confused, H. 953
ψακὰς H. 2
ψάλλειν B. 784
ψαλμὸς I. 173
Ψαμάθη H. 7
ψέγειν A. 419
ψευδονύμφευτος H. 883
ψεύδειν τινά τινος Hec. 1032
ψήχειν H. 1567
ψόγος (of women) E. 643. 1039. Hec. 1249
ψυχῆς πέρι H. 946

Ω.

ὠμόσιτος B. 338
ὠμότης I. 47
ᾠμωγμένος B. 1286
ὠνεῖσθαι H. 902
ὠνητὸς H. 816. Hec. 365
ᾠνωμένος B. 687
Ὠρίων I. 1153. H. 1490. Hec. 1101
ὡς (sic) E. 155. Hec. 441. B. 1068
ὡς = ἴσθι ὡς A. 587. Hec. 400
ὡς δὴ H. 1057. A. 235. 594. E. 947. B. 224
ὡς τί δὴ I. 525
ὠχρὸς B. 438

INDEX II.

GRAMMATICAL, PHILOLOGICAL, &c.

A.

a long in γέννα, τόλμα, 500
a short in φονέα, 'Ατρέα, &c. 143. 538
―――― before γλ, 369
a long in ἀνοιᾶ, &c. 260
―――― before κλ, 372
Achaea, same as Phthiotis, 14
Achilles, shield of, described, 333—5
―――― slain by Paris, 295
――――, arms of, carried by Nereids, 334
――――, tomb of at Sigeum, 492
――――, worshipped at Λευκὴ ἀκτὴ, 298
Acropolis, why Μακραὶ, 10. 66—7
―――― impress of trident in, 27
―――― producing olives, 97
Actaeon, devoured by his dogs, 420
Accusative, in apposition to sentence, 122. 247. 322. 378. 383. 465
―――― cognate, 275. 493. 526. 539
―――― of exclamation, 96
―――― depending on sense, 474. 534
―――― of route taken, ὁδὸν understood, 268
―――― of transition over, 150. 154. 418. 445
―――― *pendens*, 542
―――― of point of time, 147. 443
―――― of duration of time, 124. 453
Achelous, for water generally, 239. 436

Adjectives in -ήρης, -ηρὸς, 78, 405
Adverbs describe modes of action, not states of things, 135
Aeacus, his descendants to be kings of Epirus, 298
―――― his marriage with Psamathe, 118
Aegis, description of, 69
Aegisthus, personal comeliness of, 365
Aërope, story of, 350
Aether (see *Ether*)
Aglauros, Agraulos, 11
―――― grotto of, in Acropolis, 39, 95
αι pronounced short, 337, 355
Alcibiades, supposed allusion to, 258, 387
Amazons, spoils from, dedicated by Hercules, 79
Ammon, temple of Jupiter, 352
ἀν with imperfect in conditions fulfilled, 153
— seldom repeated with indicative, 136. 248. 371
— when repeated with optative, 530
— omitted with subjunctive, 367.—with optative, 445.—with imperfect, 476
— ε of third person elided before, 31. 549
— with future infinitive, 146
Anapaestics, spondaic, 18. 494. 499
―――― resolved syllables in irregular systems, 18. 63. 494—5. 547
―――― not antistrophic, 499
Anchor, metaphor from, 134. 495
Antilochus son of Nestor, 167

INDEX II.

Antistrophe beginning in middle of a sentence, 318
Aorist, infinitive after verbs of *praying*, 342.—after verbs of *hoping*, 231. 249. 508. 511
——— both first and second active very rare, 147
——— passive in middle sense, 520
———participle expressing *attempt*, 101
——— indicative in sense of perfect, 280
Aphrodite, daughter of Dione, 181—2
——— why called Κύπρις, 424
Apidanus, the, 433. 516
Apollo, god of justice, 31. 294.—of joy, 25. 49
——— worship of, connected with Bacchus, 37. 418
——— charged with immorality, 36
——— accused of injustice, 282. 294
——— why ἀγυιεὺς, 21.—αἰγλήτης, 27
Areopagus, why called, 383
Argos, alliance with Athens against Sparta, 272
Arms suspended in temples, 292
Article, used with both or neither of two nouns, 400
——— in demonstrative sense, 40
——— separated by two words from its noun, 172
——— Homeric use of, 178. 310. 471
——— omitted with the latter of two nouns, 10. 254. 324. 330. 524
——— omitted with a participle specifying the person, 535
——— with proper names, 37. 45
——— caesura rarely falls on, 330
——— used twice in specifying same person, 331
——— irregular position of, 235. 369.
——— with predicate, 452
——— wrongly used with otiose epithets, 243
——— proper with distinctive epithets, 128
Asia, why καλλίπυργος, 400
——— infamous for enchanter's arts, 239. 412
——— Ionic colonies of, 92. 105
Astronomy, poet's love of, 80
Asylum, abuse of, 90. 249
——— sanctity of, 88

VOL. II.

Athenians, boast of being indigenous, 46
——— jealous in admitting strangers to state offices, 46
——— called ἀπόρθητοι, 539
Athena *Chalcioecus*, 131. 205
——— Nikè, 103
Atlas, bearer of heaven, 9
Attica, ancient tribes of, 105
Attic, forms of the new dialect, 310. 386
Augment of verbs in οι, 401
——— omitted in messengers' speeches, 83. 446. 464—6.
——— omitted in choral trochaics, 139

B.

Bacchantes, fantastic dress of, 403
——— why called *Potniades*, 439
Bacchus, twofold worship of, Hellenic and Pelasgic, 395
——— giver of wine, 416
——— later name than *Dionysus*, 395
——— worshipped together with Demeter, 74
——— his Indian conquests, 399
——— a Semitic god, 399
——— festivals every third year, 407
——— oracular deity, 414
——— reared by Nymphs, 417
——— sewn in thigh of Zeus, 405, 413. 417
——— slayer of giants, 23
——— why tauriform, 436. 455
Bay-tree used for brooms, 14
——— in palace of Priam, 248
——— in Delos, 65. 516
Beacons, news conveyed by, 349
Birds, driven from temples and statues, 20
Birth, associated with honour, 310
——— overlooked in poverty, 311
——— no certain criterion of valour, 329
——— advantages of good, 274. 523
——— conspicuous in worthy men, 512
Birth-day, sacrifice on tenth day after, 376
——— feast in celebration of, 50
——— presents at (ὀπτήρια), 78

4 E

Blood-offerings, 314. 338. 493. 512
—————— why προσφάγματα, 191
—————— of maidens preferred, 496
—————— poured into graves by a pipe, 151
—————— drunk by ghost, 520
Blood of murdered person indelible, 327
Boughs, use of suppliant, 35. 89
Bow, metaphors from, 26. 252. 524
—— worn by Apollo, 41.—by Teucer, 122.
Bravery, difficult to discern in heat of battle, 329
—————— to be rewarded in especial manner, 508
Breast, uncovering of, in appeal for mercy, 380
Bulls, how said θυμοῦσθαι ἐς κέρας, 211. 444

C.

Caesura, want of in senarii, 457. 466. 511. 552
Calchodon, king of Euboea, 13
Callichorus, well of, 74
Callisto, legend of, 141
Cecrops, daughters of, 11
—————— meaning of name, 11
—————— serpentine form of, 11. 81
Ceilings, hypaethral or covered with awning, 79
Centaurs, battle of, with Lapithae, 275
Chance rules human affairs, 518
Chariots, brought upon the stage, 366
Chastity, possibility of, 312
—————— not compulsory but spontaneous, 418—9
Childlessness (τὸ δυστυχεῖν), 53. 57. 255
Children, poet's love of, 13. 255
—————— how represented on the stage, 226
Chimaera, 22. 336
Chorus, number of fifteen, 20
—————— speak singly in turn, 434
—————— accomplices in crime by promising secrecy, 54
—————— office of in consoling, 476
—————— speak only three or four verses between long ῥήσεις, 553

Chorus, odes of, unconnected with subject of play, 194. 333
Coin, test of spurious, 341
—————— impress on, for "character," 512
Commatic verses, 127
Corybantes, inventors of Bacchic music, 403, 407
Cranes, migration of, 206
Curetes, connected with Bacchus, 406
Custom (νόμος), force of, 533
Cybele, confounded with Demeter, 194
—————— worship of, connected with Bacchic orgies, 406
Cyclades, colonisation of, 105
Cyclic poems, reference to, 163. 184. 205. 266
Cyclopian walls, 378

D.

Dactyl, followed by anapaest, 23. 386. 496. 499
—————— following anapaest, 16
—————— preferred to spondees in choral hexameters, 235
Dative, causal, 237. 239. 466. 507
—————— of part affected, 440
—————— of place where, 141
—————— of agent, 37
—————— of reference to, 523
Dead, cast unburied on hard rock, 168
—————— to be held in honour and grateful memory, 508
Death, order of, determined by lots, 347
Delos, claimed by Athenians, 516
Delphi, sculptures on temple of, 21
—————— supposed centre of earth, 23
—————— portico at, dedicated by Athenians, 21
Demagogues, a selfish race, 505
—————— their real worth found out at last, 554
Demeter, giver of corn, 415
—————— and Cora, Eleusinian cultus of, 75
—————— grief of, for lost daughter, 194—6
Dice, metaphor from, 34
Dionysus, earlier name than Bacchus, 395

Dionysus, a Thracian prophet, 557
Dioscuri, as θεοὶ ἀπὸ μηχανῆς, 381
Dirce, receiver of infant Bacchus, 431
———- why daughter of Achelous, 431
Dithyrambus, meaning of the name, 431
Dochmiacs, alternating with iambics, express different feelings, 156. 277. 528—9
————- caesura in, 57
————— hiatus allowable in, 528
Dolphins, fond of music, 334
Drunkenness, prophetic, 417
————————— seeing double in, 455

E.

ε rarely elided before ἂν, 31
Earth, mother of Dreams, 495
————— propitiated by blood, 512
Ecclesia, attendance of countrymen at, 443
Eccyclema, use of, 379
εἰ with subjunctive, 410
Electra, unfair criticisms on the, 304—5
Elegiacs, unique instance of in tragedy, 235
Ennius, his erroneous translations, 518. 523
Epodus, often wrongly applied to antithetical verses, 131
Erechtheus, slays his own daughters, 27
Erichthonius, birth of, 11. 26
Eros, winged god, 158
Ether (αἰθήρ), source of life, 120
———- soul returns to, 177
———- εἴδωλον formed out of, 120. 417
———- luminous fluid, 437
Etymologies, poet's fondness for, 416—7. 421. 526
Eye, organ of envy, 362
Euripides, fond of rationalising, 294. 410
——————— opposed to the Sicilian expedition, 185. 387
——————— a humane man, 272
——————— speculator on nature of gods, 184. 423
——————— change of views in old age, 392

Euripides, his sojourn in Magnesia, 424
——————— an advocate of peace, 425
——————— fond of children, 13. 254 —5
——————— opposed to Spartans, 256

F.

Fawn, simile from captured, 452
Fawn-skins in Bacchic dress, 405. 450
Fables, adopted in the service of religion, 353
Fates, comptrollers of Destiny, 385
Father, political use of name, 103
Feet, relative size in male and female, 340
Festivals, use of borrowed garments at, 320
Fir-cones, use of on thyrsus, 442
Flute, in worship of Bacchus, 422.
—of Cybele or Demeter, 197
Fops, poet's dislike of, 274. 330. 365
Friends, rare in misfortune, 344
Froth, etymology of, 192
Furies, snake-handed, dark-skinned, 387
———— many names of, 383
———— subterranean abode of, 384
Future active, following aorist subjunctive, 57
———— with οὐ μή in imperative sense, 145. 330. 420

G.

Gardens, Greek notion of, 359
Genitive of agent, ὑπό implied, 316
——————— after verbs of aiming at, 344
——————— after words of motion from, 268
——————— of part taken hold of, 494. 553
——————— of exclamation, 414
——————— of point of time, 124
Ghosts, rarely employed in tragedy, 490
Giants, battle of the, 22. 103. 517
Glyconean verse, varieties of sometimes antithetical, 318
Glory, emptiness of false, 249
——— wrongly given to generals alone, 270

INDEX II.

Gods, alleged lawlessness of, 36
—— doubts about nature of, 184
Gold, worn by Greek maidens, 499
—— buried in the earth, 544
Gorgon, slain by Perseus, 335
—————- born in Phlegraean plains, 69
—————- poison from blood of, 70—1
—————- wrought in embroidery, 96
Grief, disemburdening of to the elements, 63. 312
Guests, how to be received, 331

H.

Hades, why distinct from celestial abodes, 490
Halirrhothius, trial for murder of, 383
Hair, offering of on tombs, 314
—— same colour in brother and sister, 339
—— made manly by wrestling school, 339. 427
—— letting loose in frenzied action, 441
—— tuft cut from victim's head, 357
—— bound up before the mirror, 540
Harmonia, wife of Cadmus, 477
Hecate, presides over poisons, 73
———— daughter of Demeter, 73
———— sends up spectres, 152
Hecuba, daughter of Cisseus, 490
———— her transformation, 557
Helene, island of (*Macri*), 218
Hercules, allusion to labours of, 81
———— his expedition against Troy, 276
Herdsmen, strongholds of in mountains, 321. 350
Hermes, parentage of, 10
Honour, connected with high birth, 174
Horace, his translation from the *Bacchae*, 429
Horses, sacrifice of, 191
Hyacinthia, celebration of at Sparta, 205

I.

ἴ in ἰέναι, 510
i pronounced as *y* or *j*, 326. 414
—— elided in 3d plural of perfect, 108. 252. 537

ῐᾱ = a long syllable, 459
Idleness, vain to invoke gods in, 313
————- folly of trusting to seers in, 162
Imperfect, with ἄν rhetorically omitted, 476
————— with ἵνα, 'in which case,' 534
Initiated, future happiness of the, 404
Interpolated verses, 72. 79. 171. 348. 515. 521. 532. 535. 553
Ionic *a minore*, resolved feet in, 404. 422
———————— variations in, 432
Ionicisms, 104. 127. 150. 182. 465
Irony, Attic love of, 457
—— affirmative form of, 242
Islanders, name of contempt, 230

J.

Javelins, metaphors from, 505
———— sent by the loop (ἀγκύλη), 292. 470
Joy, to be kept separate from grief, 25
Justice, attribute of Apollo, 31. 294
———— impiously demanded of Apollo, 232

L.

Lamb, legend of golden, 350
Land, simile from rich and barren, 267. 523
Laomedon, horses of, 276
Lathe (τόρνος) in rounding chariot-wheels, 463
Latona, her delivery at Delos, 65. 516
Lead, used for fixing statues, 246
Leda, egg of, 133
Leucippides (priestesses), 205
Libations, at banquets, 82
Litters, representing absent bodies, 192
Liver, anatomy of, 358
Lycurgus, his institutions respecting women, 264

M.

Madness, test of, by looking at the sky, 473

Male, sons the offspring of the, 364. 371. 375
Marriage, evils of unequal, 365
——— better than single life, 38
——— danger of with daughter of bad mother, 266
Menelaus, uxoriousness of, 251. 266
——— charged with cowardice, 265—6
——— apotheosis of, 218
——— seven years wandering of, 124. 164
Merops, daughter of, 142
Metoeci, Athenian jealousy of, 45
Mistress, tolerated along with a lawful wife, 240. 370
——— evils of beside a wife, 257
Mitra, various meaning of, 318. 540
——— Bacchic dress, 450
Moon, supposed influence on infants, 376
Murderers, excluded from converse, 385.—from sacrifices, 356
Musicians, simile from rival, 258
Myrtle, crowns of, 337. 355
——— broom of, 17
——— offered at tombs, 338

N.

ν (ἐφελκυστικὸν), seldom used before a consonant, 553
Narthex, distinct from thyrsus, 198. 442
Nauplius, his device against the Greek fleet, 184
Necropolis, rocky ground of, 340
Neoptolemus, death of at Delphi, 293
——— why νησιώτης, 230
Nereids, companion of ships, 333
——— convey arms of Achilles, 334
Net, metaphors from, 94. 342. 460
Nicias, supposed allusion to, 258
Nightingale, invoked in grief, 183
——— suppliant voice compared to, 510
Nile, why καλλιπάρθενος, 117
——— ἑκατόστομος, 424
Nominative, when used in addressing, 229
——— pendens, 269
Nymphs, sacrifice to, for children, 345

O.

οι and η confused, 25. 92
Olive, wreath of, placed on infants, 97
——— brought to Acropolis by Pallas, 97
Olympia, games at, 360
Omens from sounds, 166. — from birds, 32.—from bad words, 82
Optative, by Attic attraction, 145. 473. 480. 535
——— form of in -οιν, 134
——— without ἂν, 176. 445
——— use of in indefinite past action, 370
——— in future contingencies without ἂν, 473
Oracle, return from, to be met with joy, 34
Oracles, regular days for delivering, 16. 35
Oratory, dangerous unless guided by sense, 414
Orestes, why hostile to Neoptolemus, 284
Oresteum, 384
οὐ, added or omitted by transcribers, 87. 172
— used apparently for μὴ, 124. 167. 234. 473. 478

P.

Paeans, for dirges, 128
Paeonic verses, probable arrangement of, 408
Painting, terms from, 134. 533
Palamedes, legend of, 163
Pallas, ancient statue of (βρέτας), 382
——— Promachus, 10
——— miraculous birth of, 37
——— aegis of, 69
——— peplus of, 516
Paneum in Acropolis, 10. 39. 95
Panics, attributed to Bacchus, 418
Paphos, fertilized by Nile, 424
Participle, masculine agreeing with neuter noun, 475
——— singular with plural verb, 43. 85
——— of perfect passive in middle sense, 533
——— meaning of with τυγχάνειν, 355

Paris, judgment of, 158. 246. 526
Parthenon, supposed allusion to proportions of, 79
Parnassus, double peak of, 77. 418
Pause, violation of in senarius, 9. 474. 530
Peace, how κουροτρόφος, 425
Pelasgi, Bacchic worship introduced by, 399
—— fire-worshippers, 161
Phocus, slain by Peleus, 270
Phormio, victory of at Rhium, 21. 106
Phocylides, saying of, 283
Pieria, limits of, 433
Pity, inherent in the wise, 325
Pnyx, allusion to Athenian, 351
Poison, double nature of Gorgon's, 70
Poverty, teacher of vice through need, 329
Praesens historicum, 332
Prologue, the poet's peculiar use of, 9
Pronouns, personal, emphatic in the nominative, 61. 89.—ἐμὲ for ἐμαυτὸν used as object of a verb, 245
Prophet, proper meaning of the word, 34
Proteus, king of Egypt, 118—9
Pylos, allusion to capture of, 526
Pyrrhic dance, 292

R.

Relative, used in exclamations, but not in direct questions, 146
Revenge inculcated as a duty, 91. 268. 487
Reverses, doctrine of, often inculcated, 257
Rhea, worship of, connected with Bacchus, 395. 406
—— identified with Demeter, 194
Rhium, victory at, 106
Rings on Greek doors, 107
River-gods, tauriform, 86
Rudders, Egyptian, 210
—— management of in a storm, 258

S.

Sacrifices, ceremonies at, 356—7
—— custom of inviting bystanders to, 346

Sacrifices, offered before entering Delphic temple, 24. 291
—— unlucky words at, 82
Sacrilege, Greek ideas respecting, 533
Sailors, simile from storm-tossed, 454
—— difficult to control, 524
Sails, simile from, 262
Salamis, allusion to battle of, 79. 81
—— in Cyprus, 126
Sanctity (Ὁσία), invocation of, 422
Schema Pindaricum, 79. 198. 478
Sea-purple, effect of sun-light on, 129
Seers, poet's dislike of, 331
—— accused of avarice, 162. 414
—— mischievous influence of, 162
Semele, tomb of, 399
—— her delivery by fire, 398
Serpents, in Bacchic worship, 405
—— use of tame, by Bacchants, 441
—— golden, affixed to infants, 11
Shrines, domestic, 166
Ships, metaphors from, 258. 333
—— equipment of for sea, 209. 497
Silence enjoined on religious subjects, 423
Sicilian expedition, allusion to, 387
Sin, future punishment of, 177
Sirens, address to in grief, 128
Skins, artificially spotted (στικτὰ), 405
Slaves, employed at the loom, 21. 430. 516
—— poet's kind feeling for, 55. 161. 233
—— regarded as common property of friends, 252. 263
—— selling offspring of, 93
—— miserable lot of, 509
—— law of ὕβρις respecting, 507
—— regarded as κτήματα, 252. 430. 515
Snakes (see *serpents*).
Society, men tested by their, 330
Sophists, allusion to teaching of, 425. 450
—— expensive instructions of, 534
Sounds, epic words expressive of different, 430
Sparta, poet's invectives against, 256
—— called αἰσχροκερδὴς, 173. 256
—— institutions respecting women, 264

Spartan maidens, dress of, 264. 540
Spear, hung up in time of truce, 539
Spondees, rarely used in choric hexameters, 235
Stadium, metaphors from, 286. 361. 366
—— as a measure of time, 358
—— visible from the theatre, 358
Stage, stairs from orchestra to, 54
Statues, beautiful persons compared to, 521
—— fixed on bases by lead, 246
—— made to open, 250
—— dedication of, 456
—— a refuge in distress, 278
Stesichorus, his *palinodia*, 112
Subjunctive followed by optative, 312. 551
—————— with $\mu\dot{\eta}$ for $\ddot{\iota}\nu a$ $\mu\dot{\eta}$, 510
—————— with $\dot{\omega}s$ and $\dot{\omega}s$ $\ddot{a}\nu$, 472. 509
—————— after relative words without $\ddot{a}\nu$, 61
—————— epic use for future, 260
—————— after $\ddot{\omega}\sigma\tau\epsilon$, 463. — $\dot{\omega}s$ (*as*), 545
—————— in imperative sense with $\mu\dot{\eta}$, 520
Suicide thought noble, 276
—— by the sword, 136. 276
Sulphur, in purificatory rites, 169
Sun, a device in embroidery, 80
—— changes his course, 352
—— appealed to by dying persons, 515
—— effect of on complexion, 427
—— chariot of the, 15. 80
Sun-dial, simile from, 273
Suppliants, vengeance due to neglect of, 510
Swans, alleged piety of, 317. 479
Syllables dropped by transcribers in long words, 21
Synizesis, 27, 47

T.

Tambourines in worship of Cybele, 197.—of Bacchus, 406
Teiresias, anachronism respecting, 400
Tent, construction of at Delphi, 78
Theatres, aspect of Greek, 78. 104
Theseus, sons of at Troy, 498
Thessalians, darts of ($\dot{a}\gamma\kappa\upsilon\lambda\omega\tau\dot{a}$), 470

Thetideum, 230
Thrace, horses of, 491
—— ally of Troy, 551
Thyrsus, how different from narthex, 198. 442
—— how carried, 456
—— a warlike weapon, 442. 465
Tmesis, 432
Tokens, given to friends, $\sigma\dot{\upsilon}\mu\beta o\lambda a$, 135
Tombs, used as altars for burning victims, 151
—— honoured after death, 509
—— cut in rocks, 340
—— human victims offered at, 173. 505
Torches, precede entry of sacred persons, 169
Traditions, not to be overthrown by sophistry, 410
Tribrach, of one word in second foot of senarius, 68. 367. 400. 414
—————— in fifth foot of senarius, 209
Trochaics rarely conclude plays, 108
Trophonius, oracle of, 34
Troy, building of by Poseidon and Phoebus, 286
—— account of capture of, 539
Tyrants, constant terror of, 48
—— rival in a state, 258

U.

Ulysses, his adventure as a spy at Troy, 504

V.

Verbs in $\epsilon\dot{\upsilon}\omega$ or $\dot{\epsilon}\omega$ active and neuter, 312. 316. 417. 422
—————— active and passive, 151. 351. 424
—— in $\dot{a}\theta\omega$, $\dot{\epsilon}\theta\omega$, 289
—— law of compound in $\dot{\epsilon}\omega$, 63
—— singular preceding plural nouns masculine or feminine, 79. 198. 478
Verses, equal number of in speeches of two persons, 72. 172. 341. 369. 550
Victim, sacrificed on men's shoulders, 211. 357
Victory (Nίκη), temple of at Athens, 37

Victory, her part in Gigantomachia, 103
Virtue, voluntary and forced, 49
Vocative, nominative when used for, 229
Voices, supernatural (φῆμαι), 166

W.

Weaving, the work of slaves, 326
Wealth, not lasting in the hands of the unjust, 365
—— true use of in hospitality, 333
Wine, the solace of cares, 416
Wisdom, folly of too refined, 325. 423. 425
Wise Men, the Seven, 267
Wives, faithlessness of towards a paramour, 363
—— dressing to please another, 373
—— prone to poison husbands, 48
—— when pleasing to husbands, 242
Women, judged more severely than men, 371
—— vicious customs of Spartan, 264
—— early maturity of Greek, 53
—— strong to avenge themselves, 538
—— naturally disposed to indulge grief, 235

Women conceal their real affection, 243
—— danger of bad advisers to, 282
—— compared to vipers, 246
—— wine-drinkers, 414
—— not inferior in virtue to men, 75
—— retirement of, 321. 542
—— poet's invectives against, 553
Words, ill-omined, at religious ceremony, 16. 82
—— repetition of in the later choral odes, 130
Wrestling, metaphors from, 95. 214
—— hair made manly by, 339. 427

X.

Xuthus, son of Aeolus or Hellen, 13

Y.

Yoke, metaphor from, 463. 512
—— of slavery, 236
Youth, evils of in the unscrupulous, 241

Z.

Zeus, not worshipped as πατρῷος at Athens, 348
Zone, loosening of in female dress, 441

END OF VOL. II.

A SELECTION OF WORKS,

PUBLISHED BY

WHITTAKER AND CO., AVE MARIA LANE.

	£ s. d.
ANTHON'S VIRGIL. Adapted for the Use of English Schools, by the Rev. F. METCALFE. With Notes at the end. 12mo. cloth	0 7 6
BAIRD'S Classical Manual. 12mo. cloth	0 4 0
BEATSON'S Progressive Exercises on the Composition of Greek Iambic Verse. 12mo. cloth	0 3 0
BELLENGER'S French Conversations. New edition. 12mo. cloth	0 2 6
BELL'S Life of Mary, Queen of Scots. 8vo. sewed	0 3 6
BIBLIOTHECA CLASSICA.	
ÆSCHYLUS. With a Commentary, by F. A. PALEY, M.A.	0 18 0
CICERO'S ORATIONS. With a Commentary, by G. LONG, M.A. 4 vols. 8vo. cloth	3 4 0
₊ The volumes are sold separately.	
DEMOSTHENES. With a Commentary, by the Rev. R. WHISTON. Vol. I. 8vo. cloth	0 16 0
EURIPIDES. With a Commentary, by F. A. PALEY, M.A. 3 vols., sold separately. 8vo. cloth, each	0 16 0
HERODOTUS. With English Notes, &c., by the Rev. J. W. BLAKESLEY, B.D. 2 vols. 8vo. cloth	1 12 0
HESIOD. With English Notes, by F. A. PALEY, M.A. 8vo. cloth	0 10 6
HORACE. With a Commentary, by the Rev. A. J. MACLEANE. 8vo. cloth	0 18 0
JUVENAL and PERSIUS. With a Commentary, by the Rev. A. J. MACLEANE. 8vo. cloth	0 14 0
SOPHOCLES. With a Commentary, by the Rev. F. H. M. BLAYDES, M.A. Vol. I. 8vo. cloth	0 18 0
TERENCE. With a Commentary, by the Rev. ST. JOHN PARRY. 8vo. cloth	0 18 0
VIRGIL. With a Commentary, by JOHN CONINGTON, M.A. Vol. I., containing the Eclogues and Georgics. 8vo. cloth	0 12 0
₊ Other volumes will shortly be published.	
BOYES'S (Rev. J. F.) English Repetitions in Prose and Verse. 12mo. cloth	0 3 6
BROWNING'S History of the Huguenots. 8vo. sewed	0 6 0
BUTTMANN'S (Dr. P.) Intermediate, or Larger Greek Grammar. New edit., by Dr. CHARLES SUPF. 8vo. cloth	0 12 0
BYTHNER'S Lyre of David. By the Rev. T. DEE, A.B. New edition, by N. L. BENMOHEL, A.M. 8vo. cloth	1 4 0
CÆSAR de Bello Gallico. With English Notes, &c., by GEORGE LONG, M.A. 12mo. cloth	0 5 6
CAMPAN'S (Madame) Conversations in *French and English.* New edition. 12mo. cloth	0 3 6
———————————————————— in *German and English.* 12mo. cloth	0 4 0

	£	s.	d.
CARRICK'S Life of Sir William Wallace. 8vo. sewed	0	3	0
CHEPMELL'S (Rev. Dr. H. Le M.) Course of History. First Series. New edition. 12mo. cloth	0	5	0
———— Second Series. 2 vols. 12mo. cloth	0	12	0
———— Questions on the First Series. 12mo. sewed	0	1	0
CICERO'S Minor Works. De Officiis, &c. &c. With English Notes, by W. C. Taylor, LL.D. New edit. 12mo. cloth	0	4	6
CICERO de Amicitia, de Senectute, &c. With Notes, &c., by G. Long, Esq., M.A., Trin. Coll., Camb. 12mo. cloth	0	4	6
COMSTOCK'S System of Natural Philosophy. New edition, by Lees. 18mo. bound	0	3	6
DAWSON'S Greek-English Lexicon to the New Testament. New edition, by Dr. Taylor. 8vo. cloth	0	9	0
DRAKENBORCH'S LIVY. With Crevier's Notes, &c. 3 vols. 8vo. cloth	1	11	6
EURIPIDES (Porson's). New edition, with Notes from Schaefer and others. 8vo. cloth	0	10	6
⁎ The four Plays separate. 8vo. sewed . each	0	2	6
FLUGEL'S German and English, and English and German Dictionary. With numerous alterations and corrections. New edition. 2 vols. 8vo. cloth	1	4	0
———— Abridged. New and revised edition. 12mo. bound	0	7	6
FOREIGN CLASSICS. 12mo. cloth :—			
CHARLES XIIth. By Direy	0	3	6
FONTAINE'S FABLES. By Gasc	0	3	0
PICCIOLA, SAINTINE. By Dubuc	0	3	0
SCHILLER'S WALLENSTEIN. By Buchheim	0	6	6
TELEMAQUE, FENELON. By Delille	0	4	6
GRADUS ad PARNASSUM. Pyper. New and improved edition. 12mo. cloth	0	7	0
GREEK TESTAMENT (The). With Notes, &c., by the Rev. J. F. Macmichael, B.A. 12mo. cloth	0	7	6
HAMEL'S New Universal French Grammar. New edition. 12mo. bound	0	4	0
———— French Exercises. New edition. 12mo. bound	0	4	0
———— Key to ditto. New edition. 12mo. bound	0	3	0
———— French Grammar and Exercises. By Lambert. 12mo. bound	0	5	6
———— Key to ditto, by Lambert. 12mo. bound	0	4	0
HEALE'S (Rev. E. M.) Manual of Geography, for the Use of Military Students. New edition. 12mo. cloth	0	4	6
HINCKS' Greek and English School Lexicon. square, bound	0	7	6
———— Summary of Ancient and Modern History. New edition. 18mo. cloth	0	3	0
HOBLYN'S Dictionary of Medical Terms. New edition, much enlarged. sm. 8vo. cloth	0	12	6
HORACE. With English Notes, by the Rev. A. J. Macleane, M.A. Abridged from the edition in the Bibliotheca Classica. 12mo. cloth	0	6	6
HOSE'S Elements of Euclid. With New and Improved Diagrams. 12mo. cloth	0	4	6
JUVENALIS SATIRÆ XVI. With English Notes, by H. Prior, M.A. 12mo. cloth	0	4	6

OF STANDARD WORKS.

	£	s.	d.
KEIGHTLEY'S History of India. 8vo. cloth	0	8	0
KOCH'S History of Europe. 8vo. cloth	0	6	0
LARCHER'S Notes to Herodotus. By COOLEY. 2 vols. 8vo. cloth	1	8	0
LEBAHN'S Practice in German. 12mo. cloth	0	6	0
LEVIZAC'S French Dictionary. New edition. 12mo. bound	0	6	6
LE BRETON'S French Scholar's First Book. 12mo. cloth	0	3	0
LIBRARY OF MEDICINE. Edited by Dr. TWEEDIE:—			
Practical Medicine. 5 vols. 8vo. cloth . . each	0	10	6
Dr. Rigby's Midwifery. 8vo. cloth	0	10	6
Cruvelhier's Anatomy. 2 vols. 8vo. cloth . each	0	18	0
LIVY. With English Notes, by Dr. STOCKER. 4 vols. 8vo. boards	2	8	0
LONG'S (George, M.A.) Atlas of Classical Geography. With copious Index, &c. New edition. 8vo. half-bound	0	12	6
———————— Grammar School Atlas of Classical Geography. 8vo. cloth	0	5	0
MOORE'S Dictionary of Quotations. 8vo. cloth	0	12	0
MORRISON'S (C.) System of Practical Book-keeping by Single and Double Entry. New edition. 8vo. half-bound	0	8	0
NIBLOCK'S Latin-English and English-Latin Dictionary. square 12mo. bound	0	9	0
OLLENDORFF'S (Dr. H. G.) French Method. New edition. 8vo. cloth	0	12	0
Key to ditto, by Dr. OLLENDORFF. 8vo. cloth	0	7	0
———————— German Method. Part I. New edition. 8vo. cloth	0	12	0
———————— Part II. New edition. 8vo. cloth	0	12	0
Key to ditto (*both parts*). 8vo. cloth	0	7	0
———————— Introductory Book to his German Method. 12mo. cloth	0	3	6
———————— Italian Method. New edition. 8vo. cloth	0	12	0
Key to ditto, by Dr. OLLENDORFF. 8vo. cloth	0	7	0
———————— Spanish Method. 8vo. cloth	0	12	0
Key to ditto, by Dr. OLLENDORFF. 8vo. cloth	0	7	0
———————— Introductory Book to Latin. 12mo. cloth	0	2	6
OVID'S FASTI. With English Notes, &c., by F. A. PALEY, M.A. 12mo. cloth	0	5	0
WHITTAKER'S IMPROVED EDITIONS OF			
PINNOCK'S HISTORY OF ENGLAND. New and revised edition. 12mo. bound roan	0	6	0
———————— ROME. New edition. 12mo. bound roan	0	5	6
———————— GREECE. New edition. 12mo. bound roan	0	5	6
———————— Explanatory English Reader. 12mo. bound	0	4	6
———————— Introduction to ditto. 12mo. cloth	0	3	0
———————— English Spelling Book. 12mo. cloth	0	1	6
———————— Exercises in False Spelling. 18mo. cloth	0	1	6
———————— First Spelling Book. 18mo. cloth	0	1	0
———————— Juvenile Reader. 12mo. cloth	0	1	6
———————— (W. H.) First Latin Grammar. Ollendorff's system. 12mo. cloth	0	3	0
———————— Catechisms of the Arts and Sciences. 12 vols. 18mo. cloth	3	12	0
⁎ Separately, 18mo. sewed . . . each	0	0	9

WHITTAKER'S STANDARD WORKS.

£ s. d.

PENROSE'S (Rev. John) Easy Exercises in Latin Elegiac Verse. New edition. 12mo. cloth 0 2 0
PLATO'S APOLOGY. With Latin Version, by STANFORD. 8vo. cloth 0 10 6
PLATT'S Literary and Scientific Class Book. New and revised edition. 12mo. bound 0 5 0

SALLUST. With English Notes, by GEORGE LONG, M.A. 12mo. cloth 0 5 0
SHAKESPEARE'S Plays and Poems. A Library Edition. Edited by J. PAYNE COLLIER, F.S.A. 6 vols. 8vo. cloth 4 0 0
———————— Edited by J. PAYNE COLLIER, Esq. With Portrait and Vignette. Super-royal 8vo. cloth . 1 1 0
———————— Notes and Emendations on the Text of. By J. PAYNE COLLIER, Esq. 8vo. cloth . . . 0 14 0
SOPHOCLES (Mitchell's). With English Notes, Critical and Explanatory. 2 vols. 8vo. cloth 1 8 0
*** The Plays can be had separately. 8vo. cloth . each 0 5 0

TACITUS. Germania and Agricola. With English Notes, by the Rev. P. FROST. 12mo. cloth 0 3 6
TAYLOR'S (Dr. W. C.) History of France and Normandy. 12mo. bound 0 6 0
———————— History of the Overthrow of the Roman Empire. 12mo. cloth 0 6 6
THEATRE of the GREEKS. By DONALDSON. New edition. 8vo. cloth 0 14 0
TYTLER'S Elements of Universal History, with Continuation. 8vo. cloth 0 4 6

VALPY'S GRADUS, Latin and English. New edition. royal 12mo. bound 0 7 6
———————— Greek Testament, for Schools. New edition. 12mo. bound 0 5 0
———————— SALLUST. New edition. 12mo. cloth . 0 2 6
———————— With English Notes, by HICKIE. 12mo. cloth 0 4 6
———————— Cornelius NEPOS. New edition. 12mo. cloth . 0 2 6
———————— With English Notes, by HICKIE. 12mo. cloth 0 3 6
———————— Schrevelius's Greek and English Lexicon. New edition, by Dr. MAJOR. 8vo. cloth 0 10 6
VENERONI'S Italian Grammar. New edition. 12mo. bound. 0 6 0

WALKER'S DICTIONARY. Remodelled by SMART. New edition. 8vo. cloth 0 12 0
———————— Epitomized by ditto. 12mo. cl. 0 6 0
WALKINGAME'S Tutor's Assistant. By FRASER. New edition. 12mo. cloth 0 2 0
Key to ditto. New edition. 12mo. cloth 0 3 0
WEBER'S Outlines of Universal History. Translated by Dr. M. BEHR. 8vo. cloth 0 9 0
WHITTAKER'S (Rev. G.) Florilegium Poeticum. 18mo. cloth 0 3 0
———————— Latin Exercises; or, Exempla Propria. 12mo. cl. 0 3 0

XENOPHON'S Anabasis. With Notes, &c., by the Rev. J. F. MACMICHAEL, B.A. New edition. 12mo. cloth . . 0 5 0
———————— Cyropædia. With English Notes, by the Rev. G. M. GORHAM, M.A. 12mo. cloth . . 0 6 0